Frommer's®
Germany

Our Germany

by Darwin Porter & Danforth Prince

GERMANY IS AS TRADITIONAL AS HEIDELBERG CASTLE, AND AS MODERN as a Frank Gehry high-rise along the Düsseldorf waterfront. Recurring contrasts like these draw the two of us, year after year, to this powerful, ever-changing land.

You can still find Germans in *lederhosen* hefting beer steins, but the modern, sophisticated Germany is best experienced in Berlin, where cutting-edge blueprints are in constant transition. "If men suddenly start wearing chartreuse lipstick and magenta eye shadow, this new style will first appear on the streets of Berlin," young designer Ernst Mielke told us. "We're *that* cutting edge."

The pictures in this photo essay capture some of our favorite moments in Germany: climbing the solar cone of Berlin's daringly contemporary Reichstag (Germany's seat of government); walking the *Alte Brücke* (old bridge), which spans the Neckar River into the *Altstadt* (old town) of Heidelberg; biking along the lush vineyards of the Mosel valley, where tender vines produce one of the world's most memorable white wines; skiing in the Bavarian Alps; wandering the time-warped streets of Quedlinburg, or strolling the garishly neon-lit Reeperbahn in Hamburg's red-light district. It's the new Germany. Soon it will be yours.

© J.D. Heaton/AGE Fotostock

The prototype of the "castle in the sky" that Walt Disney built and named Cinderella's castle came from the dreamy—some say mad—mind of the ill-fated King Ludwig II. Before his enemies had him declared insane, he built his fairytale castle, **NEUSCHWANSTEIN (left)**, in Bavaria. Inspired by the settings of such Wagnerian operas as *Tannhäuser* and *Lohengrin,* Ludwig situated the castle over a gorge of the River Pöllat. He designed towers, gables, courtyards, and spiral staircases—an orgy of opulence that bankrupted the Bavarian treasury between 1868 and 1892.

The university town of **HEIDELBERG (above)** is Germany's most romantic city. Bisected by the Neckar River, the city is set against a backdrop of lush mountains, forests, and vineyards. Since 1786, scores of poets, writers, and composers, from Goethe to Schumann, have trod the *Alte Brücke* (old bridge), including the tough-to-impress American author Mark Twain, who fell in love with Heidelberg. In the background looms the celebrated 15th-century Heidelberg Castle.

From Düsseldorf's **RHINE TOWER (above right)**, you'll have a panoramic view at 172 meters (564ft) of the increasingly fashionable MedienHafen district, where 1800s warehouses stand side by side with avant-garde architecture. Gehry, best known for his construction of the Guggenheim Museum in Bilbao, Spain, has transformed Düsseldorf with his **NEUER ZOLLHOF (above)**—the curvy buildings on the left. His architecture is like a mammoth public sculpture with the interior hollowed out for office and living space.

The Rhine's most famous tributary, the **MOSEL RIVER (right)**, flows from Trier to Koblenz. We love biking along this river in the Mosel valley, full of storied castles and rich vineyards whose grapes are turned into one of Germany's most celebrated and famous white wines, the dry white Riesling, a refreshingly light but slightly pungent wine with an extremely delicate bouquet.

It's hardly the heart-healthy menu a doctor would prescribe, but **A TYPICAL GERMAN MEAL (right)**, consists of *Wurst* (sausage), *Sauerkraut, Brötchen* (bread rolls), and beer. "We're a pig-and-potato land," one Munich gourmand informed us.

In Dresden, the ***FRAUENKIRCHE (below)*** was reduced to a burnt shell on the night of February 13, 1945, as Allied bombs rained down on the city. Left in evocative ruins by the East German government during the Cold War, the church has been reconstructed in all its baroque glory. The dark-colored bits that pepper the new façade are original pieces culled from the rubble.

Berlin's neo-Renaissance style *Reichstag* (Parliment) building is crowned by a **MODERN GLASS DOME (above).** Designed by British architect Sir Norman Foster, it was constructed around an upside-down "solar cone" that provides power to the Reichstag.

The Pergamon Museum, in Berlin, displays Germany's 19th-century plunder from ancient lands to the east. No remnant generates more interest than the colossal **ISHTAR GATE (right)** of Babylon. The gate, erected during the reign of Nebuchadnezzar II (604-562 B.C.), depicts sacred animals, including dragons and bulls.

The most famous **CHRISTKINDLMARKT (CHRISTMAS MARKET)** in Germany takes place each year at the Hauptmarkt in Nürnberg. We love to explore the market on a cold day with a glass of *Glühwein* (mulled red wine), surveying the Vendors hawking locally made crafts and ornaments. However, the *Christkindlmarkt* is not just for shopping; devour small but delectable *Rostbratwurst* (a regional sausage), homemade cheese, and a slice of *Lebkuchen* (candied gingerbread) from the food stalls.

Framed by a modern sculpture called "Berlin," unveiled on the occasion of the 750th anniversary of the city, Old and New Berlin stand side by side at the **KAISER-WILHELM CHURCH (left)**. The old church was partially destroyed in a 1945 Allied bombing raid. West Berliners didn't rebuild it, but left the church as a reminder of war's devastation. A modern church, designed by Egon Eierman, was built directly adjacent to the old church.

The Bavarian Alps are filled with ski resorts. Pictured here is a gondola rising above the slopes of one of the best: **GARMISCH-PARTENKIRCHEN (below)**, site of the 1936 Winter Olympics. Towering over Garmisch is the 9,720-foot (2,650m) Zugspitze—the tallest mountain in Germany.

CRUISING THE RIVER SPREE (above) for three hours is a fun and relaxing way to see Berlin. You are treated to panoramic views and can indulge in a beer or a coffee as you float downstream. In the background is the *Nikolaiviertel* (St. Nicholas' Quarter) —a neighborhood of medieval and baroque buildings. Some are original, restored buildings, but most were reconstructed after World War II in an attempt to recreate a medieval village.

Berlin's trendy *HACKESCHE HÖFE* (right), a series of nine interconnecting courtyards set against a backdrop of buildings with geometric designs (often in a Moorish-mosaic pattern), has risen to become a symbol of the new Eastern Berlin. These old warehouses, built at the turn of the 20th century, are prime examples of Art Nouveau industrial architecture. We love to stroll through the courtyards, which overflow with restaurants, bars, boutiques, art galleries, and theaters.

On **RUGEN ISLAND, OFF THE BALTIC COAST (above)**, the climate is mild in the summer, but sun-worshipers still use protective wicker baskets to guard against the blustery winds that sweep across these beaches. A dip in these cold Baltic waters gives a body a jolt of electricity, but thousands of visitors still flock here as they did during the Cold War era. Ugly Stalinist buildings open onto these beaches—evocative reminders of the Communist era. This eerily beautiful coast remains virtually undiscovered by foreigners; it is one of our favorite escapes.

The best way to discover the time-warped beauty of UNESCO World Heritage city **QUEDLINBURG (right)**, which remained relatively untouched by massive Allied bombing raids during World War II, is to wander its narrow cobblestone streets on foot. Spend a few hours pondering its endless pastel-colored antique homes, its historic squares, and its perfectly-restored half-timbered houses.

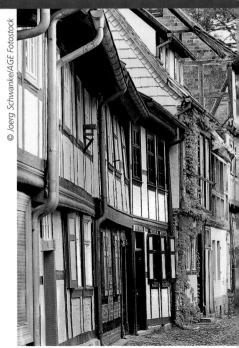

The garish, neon-lit **REEPERBAHN (right)**—"the world's most sinful mile"—cuts through Hamburg's famously notorious St. Pauli district. At night, this hyper-sexed street scene bursts with strip joints, peep shows, and bordellos. Surprisingly, there is a broad menu of other diversions, including excellent restaurants, taverns, and (non-pornographic) theater.

Bavaria's Romantic Road connects 180 miles (290 km) of medieval villages between Würzburg and Füssen. Rothenburg-ob-der-Tauber's most picturesque corner, **PHÖNLEIN (below)**, is formed by the junction of two cobblestoned streets—one level, one descending.

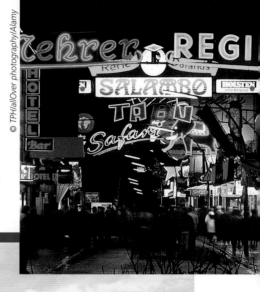

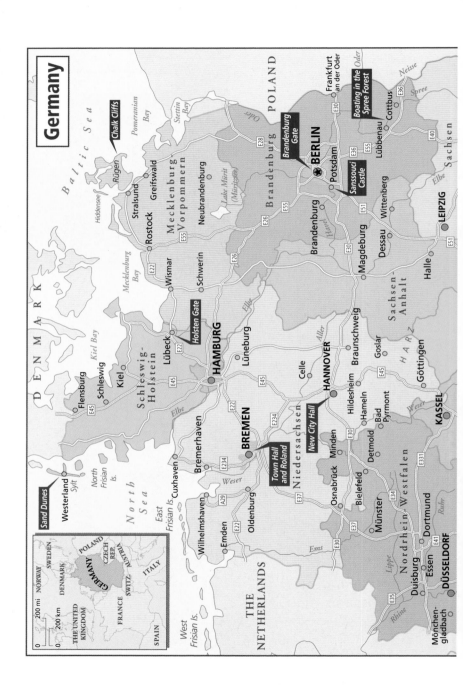

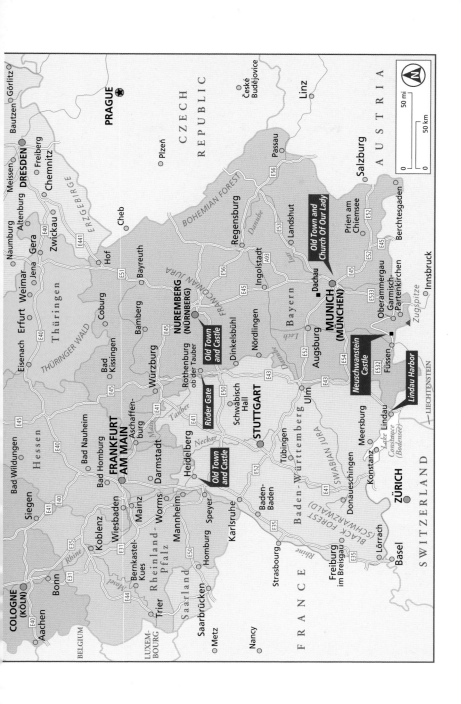

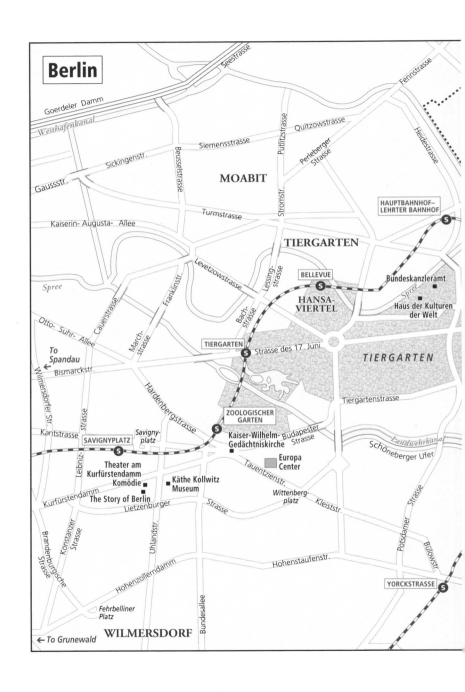

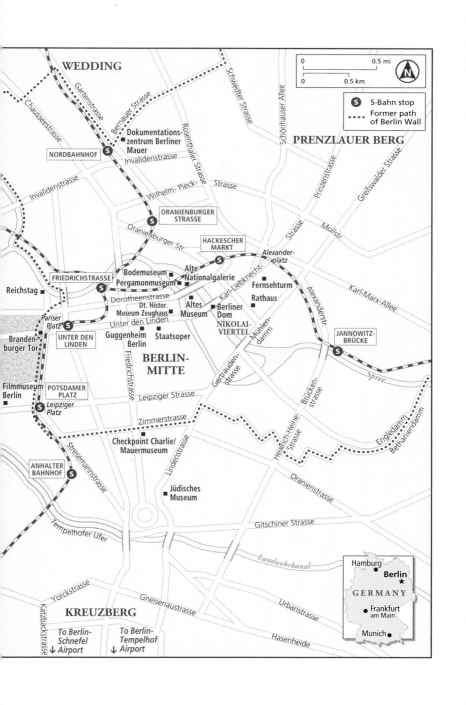

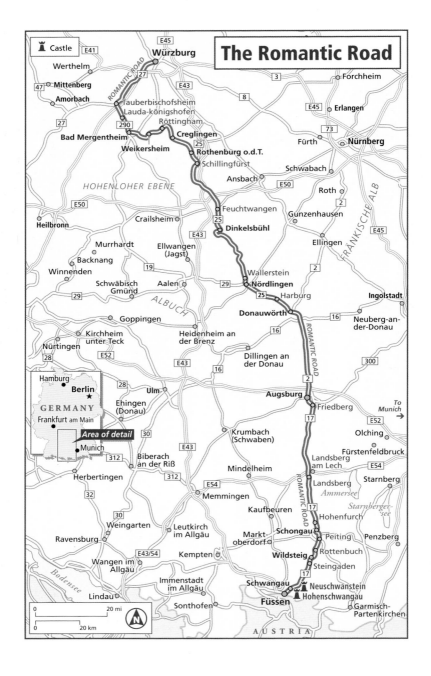

The Romantic Road

⌖ Castle

Werthelm
Mittenberg
Amorbach
Tauberbischofsheim
Lauda-königshofen
Röttingham
Bad Mergentheim
Creglingen
Weikersheim
Rothenburg o.d.T.
Schillingfürst
Ansbach
Schwabach
Roth
Feuchtwangen
Günzenhausen
Crailsheim
Dinkelsbühl
Ellingen
Murrhardt
Ellwangen (Jagst)
Backnang
Wallerstein
Winnenden
Schwäbisch Gmünd
Aalen
Nördlingen
Harburg
Ingolstadt
Heilbronn
Goppingen
Heidenheim an der Brenz
Donauwörth
Neuberg-an-der-Donau
Kirchheim unter Teck
Nürtingen
Dillingen an der Donau
Augsburg
Friedberg
Ehingen (Donau)
Ulm
Krumbach (Schwaben)
Olching
Fürstenfeldbruck
Landsberg am Lech
Biberach an der Riß
Mindelheim
Landsberg
Starnberg
Herbertingen
Memmingen
Kaufbeuren
Hohenfurch
Weingarten
Leutkirch im Allgäu
Markt-oberdorf
Schongau
Peiting
Penzberg
Ravensburg
Wildsteig
Rottenbuch
Wangen im Allgäu
Kempten
Steingaden
Schwangau
Neuschwanstein
Immenstadt im Allgäu
Hohenschwangau
Lindau
Sonthofen
Füssen
Garmisch-Partenkirchen

Würzburg
Forchheim
Erlangen
Nürnberg
Fürth

HOHENLOHER EBENE

FRANKISCHE ALB

ALBUCH

Bodensee

Ammersee
Starnberger-See

To Munich →

GERMANY
Hamburg
Berlin ★
Frankfurt am Main
Munich
Area of detail

ROMANTIC ROAD

0   20 mi
0   20 km

N

AUSTRIA

Frommer's®

Germany

2009

by Darwin Porter & Danforth Prince

Here's what the critics say about Frommer's:

"Amazingly easy to use. Very portable, very complete."

—*Booklist*

"Detailed, accurate, and easy-to-read information for all price ranges."
—*Glamour Magazine*

"Hotel information is close to encyclopedic."
—*Des Moines Sunday Register*

"Frommer's Guides have a way of giving you a real feel for a place."
—*Knight Ridder Newspapers*

WILEY
Wiley Publishing, Inc.

Published by:

Wiley Publishing, Inc.

111 River St.
Hoboken, NJ 07030-5774

ISBN 978-0-470-28784-2
Editor: Ian Skinnari
Production Editor: Eric T. Schroeder
Cartographer: Tim Lohnes
Photo Editor: Richard Fox
Production by Wiley Indianapolis Composition Services

Front cover photo: Rothenburg, Bavaria: Detail of a half timbered house
Back cover photo: Munich, Bavaria: People sitting at the trendy Nektar restaurant

For information on our other products and services or to obtain technical support, please contact our Customer Care Department within the U.S. at 800/762-2974, outside the U.S. at 317/572-3993 or fax 317/572-4002.

Wiley also publishes its books in a variety of electronic formats. Some content that appears in print may not be available in electronic formats.

Manufactured in the United States of America

5   4   3   2   1

Contents

17 The Fairy-Tale Road 573

18 Hamburg 622

19 Schleswig-Holstein 652

Appendix: Fast Facts, Toll-Free Numbers & Websites 669

Index 676

List of Maps

An Invitation to the Reader

In researching this book, we discovered many wonderful places—hotels, restaurants, shops, and more. We're sure you'll find others. Please tell us about them, so we can share the information with your fellow travelers in upcoming editions. If you were disappointed with a recommendation, we'd love to know that, too. Please write to:

Frommer's Germany 2009
Wiley Publishing, Inc. • 111 River St. • Hoboken, NJ 07030-5774

An Additional Note

Please be advised that travel information is subject to change at any time—and this is especially true of prices. We therefore suggest that you write or call ahead for confirmation when making your travel plans. The authors, editors, and publisher cannot be held responsible for the experiences of readers while traveling. Your safety is important to us, however, so we encourage you to stay alert and be aware of your surroundings. Keep a close eye on cameras, purses, and wallets, all favorite targets of thieves and pickpockets.

About the Authors

As a team of veteran travel writers, **Darwin Porter** and **Danforth Prince** have produced dozens of previous titles for Frommer's, including many of their guides to Europe, the Caribbean, Bermuda, The Bahamas, and parts of America's Deep South. A film critic, columnist, and radio broadcaster, Porter is also a noted biographer of Hollywood celebrities, garnering critical acclaim for overviews of the life and times of, among others, Marlon Brando, Katharine Hepburn, Howard Hughes, and Michael Jackson. Prince was formerly employed by the Paris bureau of *The New York Times*, and is today the president of www.BloodMoonProductions.com and other media-related firms. In 2008, Porter and Prince collaborated on the release of their newest book about Hollywood, sexuality, and sin as filtered through 85 years of celebrity excess, *Hollywood Babylon—It's Back!*

Other Great Guides for Your Trip:

Berlin Day by Day
Frommer's Europe
Frommer's Munich & the Bavarian Alps
Frommer's Germany's Best-Loved Driving Tours
Germany For Dummies

Frommer's Star Ratings, Icons & Abbreviations

Every hotel, restaurant, and attraction listing in this guide has been ranked for quality, value, service, amenities, and special features using a **star-rating system.** In country, state, and regional guides, we also rate towns and regions to help you narrow down your choices and budget your time accordingly. Hotels and restaurants are rated on a scale of zero (recommended) to three stars (exceptional). Attractions, shopping, nightlife, and towns, and regions are rated according to the following scale: zero stars (recommended), one star (highly recommended), two stars (very highly recommended), and three stars (must-see).

In addition to the star-rating system, we also use **seven feature icons** that point you to the great deals, in-the-know advice, and unique experiences that separate travelers from tourists. Throughout the book, look for:

Finds	Special finds—those places only insiders know about
Fun Fact	Fun facts—details that make travelers more informed and their trips more fun
Kids	Best bets for kids and advice for the whole family
Moments	Special moments—those experiences that memories are made of
Overrated	Places or experiences not worth your time or money
Tips	Insider tips—great ways to save time and money
Value	Great values—where to get the best deals

The following **abbreviations** are used for credit cards:

AE	American Express	DISC	Discover	V	Visa
DC	Diners Club	MC	MasterCard		

Frommers.com

Now that you have this guidebook to help you plan a great trip, visit our website at **www. frommers.com** for additional travel information on more than 4,000 destinations. We update features regularly to give you instant access to the most current trip-planning information available. At Frommers.com, you'll find scoops on the best airfares, lodging rates, and car rental bargains. You can even book your travel online through our reliable travel booking partners. Other popular features include:

- Online updates of our most popular guidebooks
- Vacation sweepstakes and contest giveaways
- Newsletters highlighting the hottest travel trends
- Podcasts, interactive maps, and up-to-the-minute events listings
- Opinionated blog entries by Arthur Frommer himself
- Online travel message boards with featured travel discussions

What's New in Germany

BERLIN Accommodations: Rising 17 floors, the limestone exterior of **Concorde Berlin** (✆ **030/8009990**) is a new entry on the skyline of western Berlin. With its understated elegance and minimalist decor, the new chain-run hotel is a major player among the first-class hotels of the city. It's located near the Kurfürstendamm, which was the city's main street in the Cold War days. See p. 103.

Restaurants: Emerging as one of Berlin's best trattorie, **Arlecchino** (✆ **030/8812563**) is gaining more and more favorable press. It's also affordable in high-price Berlin, drawing both Berliners, homesick Italian expats, and visitors to its take on Mediterranean cuisine. See p. 118.

Attractions: At long last, the **Bode Museum** (✆ **030/266-3666**), one of Europe's greatest museums, reopened on Museumsinel. Long closed for a major restoration, it has been greatly enlarged and better arranged. It's actually an array of many museums, the most celebrated of which is its Egyptian collections, including the huge sphinx of Hatsheput (1490 B.C.). Of eternal fascination is the Egyptian Burial Cult Room with its coffins and mummies. The Museum of Late Ancient and Byzantine Art alone is worth the trip here. See p. 132.

In a new location, the **Berlinische Galerie** (✆ **030/7890-2600**) is more alluring than ever, with its exhibitions devoted to modern art, photography, and architectural models from 1870 to the present day. The collection of fine art alone comprises some 5,000 works, mostly paintings. Those grotesque portraits of Georg Grosz are only a small part of the vast array of exhibitions, including some 15,000 works of graphic art. See p. 138.

Also in a new location, **Martin-Gropius-Bau** (✆ **030/254860**) is devoted to the architect Martin Gropius, uncle of the more famous Walter Gropius. This museum displays everything from Aztec sculptures to set designs from Stanley Kubrick's *A Clockwork Orange*. See p. 140.

After Dark: One of the most famous of the old eastern Berlin nightclubs, **Clärchens Ballhaus** (✆ **030/282-9295**), which opened in 1913, has come back to life. Miraculously, its building survived the massive Allied bombings of 1945. Today it's a venue for everything from live bands to tango dancers. See p. 163.

POTSDAM This city, a virtual suburb of Berlin, now has a grand Michelin-starred restaurant: **Friedrich-Wilhelm** (✆ **0331/55050**) in the Hotel Bayrisches Haus. Its German and international cuisine is served in a romantic setting, and is cooked to precision with market-fresh ingredients. See p. 172.

DRESDEN The Steigenberger hotel chain has moved into Dresden with the opening of **Hotel de Saxe** (✆ **0351/43860**), which has risen on the site of a famous hotel that stood here in the 18th century. The deluxe bastion of luxury stands directly opposite the fabled Frauenkirche. Despite its old-fashioned architecture, its spacious bedrooms are among the most luxurious in town. See p. 207.

In other developments, **Lesage** (✆ **0351/4202-250**) has opened in a Volkswagen factory. Serving a deluxe German and international cuisine, it dresses waiters in white lab jackets. The cuisine is wonderfully rich and inventive, and, if you wish, you can drive off after lunch or dinner in a new Phaeton. See p. 209.

FRANKFURT   Accommodations: The latest bastion of luxury to open is **Fleming's Deluxe Hotel** (✆ **069/4272320**), whose dramatic rooftop terrace is the most panoramic in the city. Top-quality materials and warm earth colors create a cozy nest with one of the best hotel health clubs in Frankfurt. On another front, **Gubermühle** (✆ **069/965-2290**) has opened in a former romantic villa where Goethe pursued his first love. Bedrooms are individually decorated in a country-house style. See p. 469 and 470.

In the Eastend, **Goldman 25hours Frankfurt** (✆ **069/40586890**) attracts artists and media. Filled with whimsy, it's also comfortable. Rooms are individually decorated and stylishly avant-garde. See p. 473.

Restaurants: King Kamehameha Suite (✆ **069/71035277**) is the most sought after address among chic young people of Frankfurt. In a historic building across from the opera house, it's a lounge, bar, cafe, restaurant, and night club. Its international cuisine, prepared with market-fresh ingredients, is among the finest in the city. See p. 475.

In the courtyard of the Städel, **Holbein's** (✆ **069/66056666**) is an elegant choice for carefully crafted international cuisine. Its dining room has been likened to a jewel box. The food is a Lucullan treat and often quite delicate. See p. 479.

A pocket of Little Italy has come to Frankfurt, **Das Leben ist Schön** (✆ **069/430570**), lying in the once-unfashionable Eastend. Guests share wooden tables and select the day's special from a

blackboard. Prices are reasonable, and the chefs turn out the best pizzas in Frankfurt, each one on a paper-thin crust. See p. 479.

GARMISH-PARTENKIRCHEN   After media publicity, **Waxenstein** (✆ **08821/9840**) is luring guests away from the center of the resort to the satellite village of Grainau, lying 2km (1½ miles) away. Spacious and elegant bedrooms open onto panoramic sweeps of the Zugspitze, and the hotel is known for its hospitality and the excellent regional cookery of its Toedt's Restaurant. See p. 369.

HAMBURG   A "city within a city" is growing up in the former docklands that extend for 3km (2 miles) along the Elbe River. Known as HafenCity, this district is expected to double the population of Hamburg. Tours are available for those wishing a sneak preview of coming attractions.

In the St. Pauli district a monument to the Beatles is being constructed where they first sang "Love Me Do" in 1962, launching their career some 45 years ago.

Accommodations: Between the harbor and the Hamburg city hall, the deluxe **Sofitel Hamburg Alter Wall** (✆ **040/369500**) has opened overlooking the Alster Canal. It was created from a 19th-century building that originally housed a postal bank. The chain-run hotel is imbued with all the modern technology, creating extreme comfort. See p. 630.

Lying behind an evocative red-brick Hanseatic facade, **Lindner Hotel Am Michel** (✆ **040/3070670**) offers elegantly furnished rooms and suites. In St. Pauli, the nightlife district, the hotel bedrooms are soundproof. Guests receive a free pass to a top-rated health club on the seventh floor. See p. 631.

The best budget deal is found at the new **Superbude** (✆ **040/3808780**), in the up-and-coming St. Georg district. Rated only two stars by the government, it is simplicity itself, although well maintained and comfortable. The cheapest way to go is to book a bed in a dormitory-style room housing four guests. See p. 631.

Restaurants: *Fashionistas* and the media elite are flocking to **Tarantella** (© 040/65067790) to sample its German and international cuisine. The chefs are superb at grandmotherly old-fashioned cooking as well as imaginative and creative postmillennium style dishes. See p. 637.

MUNICH   Accommodations: In hotel news, Munich witnessed the opening of **Charles Hotel** (© 089/5445550), a luxurious hotel that's linked to the famous Rocco Forte chain of establishments. Rated five stars by the government, Charles stands in its own gardens. Its spacious and beautifully furnished bedrooms, which use natural materials and tasteful fabrics, open onto the Alps in the distance. Near the Hauptbahnhof, **Sofitel Munich Bayerpost** (© 089/599380) now graces the Munich skyline. It combines a state-of-the-art modernity with a lot of architectural overtures to yesterday, including Wilhelminian architecture. See p. 301 and 304.

Close to the grounds where Oktoberfest is celebrated, **Brack** (© 089/747255) is a restored hotel offering excellent, tastefully decorated, and affordable bedrooms. Its architecture is traditional, but its amenities are modern. It even offers the free use of bikes. See p. 307.

If you're not too demanding, one of the best values in Munich is found at **Creatif Hotel Elephant** (© 089/555-785) in the area of the main railway station. Its bedrooms are small, and to some it evokes a college dormitory, but it's fairly comfortable. Management also makes a deal for you to have half-price meals at a restaurant nearby. See p. 307.

Media exposure has led to the discovery of a gem of a hotel in the suburb of Nymphenburg, near the famous palace. It's the **TOP Hotel Erzgiesserei Europe** (© 089/126-820), a 5-minute U-Bahn ride from the center. It's a first-class hotel with sleekly modern and comfortable bedrooms, plus an on-site first-class restaurant where tables overflow into a garden courtyard in summer. See p. 310.

Restaurants: Seven Fish (© 089/2300-0219) has emerged as one of the best seafood restaurants of Munich, lying near the open-air market, Viktualienmarkt. Its menu is based on the best catches of the day. Two Greek brothers even offer sushi. See p. 313.

Bier- und Oktoberfest Museum (© 089/2423-1607) has opened as an offbeat choice for dining. You're given a tour, a Bavarian snack, and a glass of beer for only 4€ ($6.40). Or else you can stick around and enjoy one of the most authentic Bavarian dinners in town. The staff even serves *Schmalz* (chicken fat) to spread over your rye bread. See p. 317.

STUTTGART   Vincent Klink, operating **Wielandshöhe** (© 0711/6408848), is now acclaimed as one of the leading chefs of Germany. He runs the greenest restaurant in Stuttgart, focusing on food raised without pesticides or chemical additives. He's committed to changing the menu monthly, posting each new *carte* like a work of art. See p. 452.

TRIER   A wine estate in a suburb of Trier (Olewig) has been turned into the **Becker's Hotel** (© 0651/938080). Individually decorated bedrooms overlooking the vineyards are available, but most guests drop in to drink the wine and enjoy the food. There's an expensive gourmet restaurant on-site, but you can also enjoy affordable food at an informal restaurant or in a wine cellar. See p. 568.

1

The Best of Germany

In this chapter, you'll find our carefully compiled lists of the best that Germany has to offer, from castles and cathedrals to spas, restaurants, and sightseeing—and nearly everything else you'll want to see and do.

1 The Best Travel

- **Exploring the New Berlin:** Anyone who lived through the fear of the Cold War can't help but shudder at the memory of the Berlin Wall. Since reunification, civic planners, with almost manic enthusiasm, have demolished large sections of what once stood as a scar across the face of a defeated nation. The architectural changes and urban developments that constantly update the cityscape around Berlin's Friedrichstrasse and Potsdamer Platz can be confusing. But regardless of which renewal program is churning up rubble at the time of your visit, a pilgrimage through what used to be the most bitterly contested urban turf in Europe can't help but provoke powerful emotions. See chapter 5.

- **Spending a Midsummer's Night in a Biergarten:** When the temperature rises, head for the unpretentious cheer of the nearest biergarten (everybody in Germany seems to have a favorite, so we're not even going to try to name the "best"). These watering holes, which often feature trellises, climbing vines, Chinese lanterns, and arbors, offer low-cost fun on soft summer nights. You can order platters of hearty food with your beer or bring your own picnic.

- **Cruising the Elbe, the Danube, and the Rhine:** This trio of rivers, along with their tributaries, dominated German commerce for hundreds of years. Today, an armada of tugboats, barges, and cruise ships still plies the muddy waters beside riverbanks lined with the historic majesty (and sometimes the industrial might) of central Europe. Cruises begin and end at large cities of historic interest and last anywhere from 6 hours to 7 days. See "A Cruise on the Elbe" in chapter 6, "Cruising the Danube" in chapter 7, and "Cruising the Mythically Rich Rivers of Germany" in chapter 15.

- **Boating on the Königssee:** A romantic poet would praise this lake, near Berchtesgaden in Bavaria, for the forest-covered mountains that surround its cold, deep, dark waters. The baroque chapels and fairy-tale hamlets on its shores supplement its natural grandeur. The boat you ride will be powered by very quiet electric motors, so you can hear the extraordinary echoes that bounce off the rock faces. See p. 356.

- **Hiking in the Bavarian Alps:** In summer, alpine hiking is a major attraction in Germany. Hikers can observe a variety of wildlife, often including endangered species. Two of the best areas are the 1,240m (4,070-ft.) **Eckbauer** peak, on the southern fringe of Partenkirchen, and the **Berchtesgaden National Park,** bordering the Austrian province of Salzburg. See chapter 10.

- **Ascending the Zugspitze:** If the gentle inclines of the Harz Mountains or the Thuringian forests aren't dramatic enough for you, ride the cable car from Garmisch-Partenkirchen to the top of Germany's tallest mountain, 2,960m (9,709 ft.) above sea level. The view from the top is suitably panoramic, and you'll find an appealing aura of German-ness that comes from the many climbers and trekkers who fan out across the hiking trails. See p. 374.

- **Experiencing a German Spa:** In Germany, the question isn't whether to visit a spa, but rather which spa to visit. Each resort has its own virtues and historical associations and can supply a list of the health benefits associated with its awful-tasting waters. Regardless of your choice, you'll emerge from your treatment with a more relaxed attitude and a greater appreciation of German efficiency and sensuality. The most famous spas are in Baden-Baden. See p. 425.

- **Motoring along the Neckar:** The Neckar River meanders through about 80km (50 miles) of some of Germany's most famous vineyards. But the real appeal of the winding road along the water is the medieval castles scattered along the way. Highlights en route include Heidelberg, Neckarsteinach, Hirschhorn, Eberbach, Zwingenberg, and Burg Hornberg. Don't forget to stop en route for samplings of the local wines. See chapter 13.

- **Spending Harvest Time in the German Vineyards:** Springtime in Germany brings the promise of bounty to the legendary vineyards of the Rhine and Mosel valleys, but the autumn harvest is truly the time to visit. Between late August and mid-October, the banks of the rivers turn gold and russet, and armies of workers gather buckets of grapes from rows of carefully pruned vines. Most of the medieval villages and historic castles scattered between Koblenz and Trier are associated with estates where you can sample the wines. See chapters 15 and 16.

- **Touring the Fairy-Tale Road (Märchenstrasse):** This is one of the newer marketing ideas of the German tourist authorities, but considering its appeal, you'll wonder why they didn't think of it earlier. From the town of Hanau (a 30-min. drive northeast of Frankfurt), the route zigzags northward along the Weser River for about 600km (370 miles), through some of Germany's most evocative folkloric architecture, ending in Bremen. Scores of well-marked detours pepper the way. Required reading for the trip is a collection of the fairy tales of the Brothers Grimm and the Nibelungen legends. Don't overlook the psychological implications of Goldilocks, the Big Bad Wolf, and the Pied Piper of Hamelin. See chapters 4 and 17.

- **Lounging on the Island of Sylt:** Don't expect a lush or verdant island—the climate is temperamental, the setting is savage, the winds blow cold from the north even in summer, and the grasses that manage to survive in the sandy dunes are as weathered and sturdy as the soldiers in a Prussian regiment. Why is it wonderful? Here, the no-nonsense residents of north Germany can preen, flutter, and show off to each other, far from the strictures of their workplaces and the hardworking grind of their everyday lives. See p. 664.

2 The Best Museums

Financial prosperity, artistic flair, and academic curiosity have helped the Germans develop some of the finest museums anywhere.

- **Bode Museum,** Berlin: One of the greatest museums of Germany, the Bode reopened in 2008 to great acclaim. Its Egyptian Museum remains among the greatest, along with its collection of late ancient and Byzantine art and its Burial Cult Room stuffed with prehistoric coffins, mummies, and funereal objects, some showing great craftsmanship. See p. 132.

- **Gemäldegalerie,** Berlin: This is one of Europe's leading art museums, with a celebrated collection of works from the 13th to the 18th centuries. The cavalcade of major European masters ranges from Botticelli and Brueghel to Vermeer and Velázquez. Divided during the Cold War, the collection has been reunited in one home since 1998. The lighting and displays are better than ever. See p. 134.

- **Pergamon Museum,** Berlin: Built in 1930 on an island in the Spree, this museum contains entirely reconstructed temples from ancient Assyria, Greece, Rome, and Sumer. Don't miss the sprawling exhibitions devoted to the ancient art of the Islamic world and the Far East. See p. 132.

- **Zwinger,** Dresden: A vast rectangular esplanade flanked with pavilions, heroic statues, formal gardens, and galleries, this museum was designed for Augustus the Strong (elector of Saxony and king of Poland), by his favorite architect, Pöppelmann (1662–1736). The destruction of the Zwinger (in the final days of World War II), one of Dresden's most beautiful buildings, was a great loss, though its postwar reconstruction was a triumph for the East German government. Among the treasures amassed inside are paintings, 18th-century Dresden porcelain, and an ornamental collection of antique weapons. See p. 213.

- **Deutsches Museum,** Munich: Since 1925, this museum has been one of the most important showcases of science and technology in the world. Occupying an island in the Isar River, it features many hands-on and historical exhibits. See p. 326.

- **Alte Pinakothek,** Munich: This massive and symmetrical building is one of the most visible in Munich, with a wraparound garden where urbanites like to walk during lunch hour. Inside is a staggering assortment of important paintings from every era, scattered over two sprawling floors of dignified splendor. See p. 323.

- **Dachau Concentration Camp Memorial Site,** Dachau, near Munich: Heinrich Himmler first organized Dachau as a concentration camp for enemies of the Reich in 1933. An escaped inmate, Joseph Rovan, described it as "implacable, perverted, an organization that was totally murderous, a marvelous machine for the debasement and dehumanizing of man." Today, it's one of the most poignant museums in the world. See p. 347.

- **Lenbachhaus,** Munich: Housed in the former villa of portrait painter Franz von Lenbach, this museum has a stunning and internationally renowned collection of modern art, including the Blaue Reiter (Blue Rider) period, best represented by Kandinsky. It also has a rich collection of Gothic artwork. See p. 327.

- **Gutenberg Museum,** Mainz: This museum is one of the most comprehensive tributes to printing and publishing anywhere in the world. The bulky presses, on which Johannes Gutenberg used movable type (42 lines per page), and two of the earliest Bibles ever printed are the primary displays here. There's also a historical rundown on the science and technologies that have dominated the printing industry ever since. See p. 514.

- **Museum Ludwig,** Cologne: This is the home of one of the world's largest collections of the works of Pablo Picasso, equaled only by the Picasso museums of Barcelona and Paris. The museum's collection was beefed up when Irene Ludwig, widow of the late German art patron Peter Ludwig, donated 774 works of Picasso to the museum. See p. 541.
- **Wallraf-Richartz Museum/Foundation Corboud,** Cologne: The oldest museum in Cologne presents one of Germany's grandest collections of art,

covering the 14th to the 19th centuries. The collection of Gothic works alone is one of the finest in Europe, and the galleries are a virtual encyclopedia of art, from Flemish old masters to the French Impressionists. See p. 542.

- **Kunsthalle,** Hamburg: The leading art museum in northern Germany, the Kunsthalle is one of the most important in Europe, with some 3,000 paintings in its treasure trove, along with some 400 sculptures. Some of its rare treasures date from the 14th century, including works by Bertram, the leading German master of the time. One section of the gallery also displays modern works, including pieces by such artists as Andy Warhol, Joseph Beuys, and Picasso. See p. 640.

3 The Best Castles & Palaces

During the Middle Ages, Germany was divided into many intensely competitive feudal states and principalities. This unstable atmosphere encouraged the construction of fortified castles. As hostilities died down, architects began to design for comfort, style, and prestige, adding large windows, gilded stucco and plaster, frescoes, and formal gardens. As a result, Germany is full of all kinds and styles of *Burg* (castles) and *Schloss* (palaces).

- **Sans Souci Palace,** Potsdam: Frederick the Great's retreat, where he came to read, listen to music, and generally renew his allegiance to the principles of the Enlightenment, is Germany's most successful blend of landscape and architecture. The more than 120 hectares (296 acres) of intricately landscaped gardens have enough pavilions, fountains, orangeries, and heroic statues to keep a visitor intrigued for days. The palace itself is an architectural highlight, approached

by a terraced staircase of sublime beauty. See p. 173.

- **Schloss Wartburg,** Eisenach: Built between the 11th and 16th centuries, this was the headquarters of the Landgraves of Thuringia, a center of patronage for the *Minnesinger* (troubadours) of Germany, and a place of refuge for Martin Luther, who completed his translation of the Bible within its massive walls. Wagner used it as inspiration for the setting of *Tannhäuser,* and Johann Sebastian Bach and Goethe both visited. Today, from its position on a rocky hilltop, it's a regional museum. See p. 189.
- **Residenz,** Würzburg: Built between 1720 and 1744 as the official residence of the powerful bishops of Würzburg, this is one of the most massive baroque palaces in Germany. It combines a *Hofkirche* (chapel) with gardens, a gallery of paintings, frescoes by Tiepolo, and enough decoration to

satisfy the most demanding taste for ornamentation. Also within its showrooms are a worthy collection of ancient Greek and Roman artifacts and valuable paintings from the 14th to the 19th centuries. See p. 262.

- **Neuschwanstein,** near Füssen: When the creators of California's Disneyland needed an inspiration for their fairy-tale castle, this is the model they picked. Neuschwanstein is the most lavishly romantic (and impractical) castle in the German-speaking world. A 19th-century theatrical set designer drew it up in a neofeudal style. The man who ordered its construction was (who else?) "Mad" King Ludwig II of Bavaria. See p. 291.

- **Hohenschwangau Castle,** near Füssen: It was completed in 1836 and built on the ruins of a 12th-century fortress. Its patron was the youthful prince regent, Maximilian II of Bavaria, who used it to indulge his taste for "troubadour romanticism" and the life of the English country manor. See p. 291.

- **Schloss Nymphenburg,** Munich: It was originally conceived and constructed between 1664 and 1674 as an Italian-inspired summer home for the Bavarian monarchs. Subsequent Bavarian kings added on to its structure until around 1780, by which time the building and its lavish park bore a close resemblance to the French palace at Versailles. A highlight of the interior is the green, gold, and white banqueting hall, with frescoes and ornate stucco that are among the most memorable in Bavaria. See p. 329.

- **Schloss Linderhof,** near Oberammergau: This palace was built in the 1870s as a teenage indulgence by Ludwig II. Its architects created a whimsically eclectic fantasy, inspired by Italian baroque architecture. In the surrounding park, Moorish pavilions and Mediterranean cascades appear against alpine vistas in combinations that are as startling as they are charming. See p. 378.

- **Altes Schloss,** Meersburg: Legend has it that this palace's cornerstone was laid in 628 by Dagobert, king of the Franks. The palace remained a Catholic stronghold even during the Protestant Reformation, housing bishops who appreciated its 3m-thick (10-ft.) walls as a bulwark against the rising tempest around them. In the early 1800s, when its owners threatened to tear the palace down, a German Romantic, Baron Joseph von Lassberg, bought it and transformed it into a refuge for writers, poets, and painters. Although it remains mostly a private residence, you can visit many parts of the palace. See p. 391.

- **Heidelberg Castle,** Heidelberg: This castle originated as a Gothic-Renaissance masterpiece in the 1500s and was massively expanded as rival rulers competed for control of the Rhineland. After the French sacked and burned the town and the castle in 1689, it never regained its original glory. Today, the ruins brood in dignified severity from a position on a rocky hilltop high above the student revelry and taverns of the folkloric city below. See p. 441.

- **Burg Eltz,** Moselkern, near Cochem: Its multiple turrets and towers, which rise amid a thick forest near the Mosel River, evoke the chivalry and poetry of the Middle Ages. This is one of the best-preserved medieval castles in Germany. See p. 560.

4 The Best Cathedrals

- **Kaiserdom (Imperial Cathedral),** Speyer: Partly because of their age, Romanesque churches are the most impressive symbols of early medieval Germany. This massive church, from 1030, has four bell towers, a cornerstone laid by one of Germany's earliest kings, Konrad II, and an undeniable sense of the (anonymous) architect's aesthetic links with the traditions of ancient Rome. See p. 505.
- **Dom St. Peter,** Worms: This church is a grand example of High Romanesque style, its oldest section dating from 1132. The Diet of Worms, held here in 1521, condemned the beliefs of the young Martin Luther and banished him to the far boundaries of the Holy Roman Empire. See p. 508.
- **Cologne Cathedral,** Cologne: Based on French Gothic models in Paris and Amiens, this cathedral was envisioned as one of the largest religious buildings

in Christendom. It required 600 years to finish—work stopped for about 300 years (1560–1842), until the neo-Gothic fervor of the Romantic age fueled its completion. In 1880, it was inaugurated with appropriate pomp and circumstance in the presence of the German kaiser. Today, its vast russet-colored bulk towers, above Cologne, are instantly recognizable from miles away. See p. 539.
- **Dom (Cathedral),** Aachen: Its size and the stonework dating from 1414 are deeply impressive, but even more so is the cathedral's association with the earliest of German emperors, Charlemagne. He was crowned in an older building on this site in A.D. 800. The cathedral's treasury contains gem-encrusted Christian artifacts from the 10th century, with heft and barbaric glitter that evoke pre-Christian Germania. See p. 531.

5 The Most Charming Small Villages

- **Quedlinburg:** Spared in part from the ravages of World War II, this town in the Harz mountains still evokes the Middle Ages with its 1,600 half-timbered buildings, more than any other town in the country. Named a UNESCO World Heritage Site, Quedlinburg is a gem of yesterday and was an imperial residence for 2 centuries. Wander the cobblestone streets of the Altstadt (old town) for a journey back in time. See p. 201.
- **Meissen:** Some 25km (16 miles) north of Dresden, this is a romantic little town built along the banks of the River Elbe. It's celebrated for its porcelain, which carries a trademark of two crossed blue swords and is valued by collectors the world over. Even without its porcelain factory, the town merits a visit for its quiet

charm, its old buildings, and its 15th-century castle. See p. 219.
- **Rothenburg:** If you have time for only one stop along the Romantic Road, make it Rothenburg ob der Tauber (on the Tauber River), which may be your only chance in life to see a still-intact medieval walled city. Rothenburg exists in a time capsule, though 40% of the town was destroyed during World War II. Luckily, locals quickly rebuilt their Altstadt in its former style to reclaim their glorious architectural past. See p. 270.
- If you have time for a second stop along the Romantic Road, try **Dinkelsbühl.** Though not as grand as the more celebrated Rothenburg, it has far fewer tourists and therefore retains more old-time charm. See p. 276.

- **Mittenwald:** This town has long been celebrated as the most beautiful in the Bavarian Alps. Its magnificently decorated houses have painted facades and ornately carved gables. In the mid–17th century, it was known as "the Village of a Thousand Violins" because of the stringed instruments made here. See p. 366.

- **Lindau:** Dating from the 9th century, this former free imperial town of the Holy Roman Empire is like a fantasy of what a charming Bavarian lakeside village should look like, if only in the movies. But this garden "city," under landmark protection, is for real. Lindau is enveloped by aquamarine waters, and one part of it is known as the Gartenstadt because of its luxuriant flowers and shrubs. See p. 381.

- **Rüdesheim:** The Rhine Valley's most popular wine town is set along the edge of the mighty river. Rüdesheim is known for its half-timbered buildings and its Drosselgasse, or "Thrush Lane," a narrow cobblestone lane stretching for 180m (600 ft.) and lined with wine taverns and cozy restaurants. See p. 516.

- **Cochem:** If you're seeking an idyllic medieval riverside town during your "grape tour" of the Mosel River valley, make it Cochem, famous for its towering castle, dating from 1027. On the left bank of the Mosel, Cochem lies in a picture-postcard setting of vineyards. Little inns serving a regional cuisine along with plenty of Mosel wine make Cochem a highly desirable overnight stop and a nice alternative to the more commercial centers found along the nearby Rhine. See p. 557.

6 The Best Driving Tours

The appeal of the open road is a prominent part of German culture. Some of the best drives include:

- **The Romantic Road:** This well-traveled route, which stretches between the Main River and the beginning of the Bavarian Alps, is dotted with lovely medieval towns. See chapter 8.

- **The Fairy-Tale Road:** The colorful characters of the Brothers Grimm live again along this 595km (369 mile) stretch, beginning in the little town of Hanau and stretching all the way north to Bremen. This is one of the great motor trips of Germany for those who thrilled to those nursery room favorites. See "Suggested Itineraries" in chapter 4 for an abbreviated route. For the complete route, refer to chapter 17.

- **Alpine Road:** Scenic majesty and architectural charm combine for an unforgettable experience on this 480km (300-mile) road through the foothills of the Bavarian Alps. See "Exploring the Region by Car" in chapter 10.

- **Upper Black Forest:** Fairy tales always seem more believable when you're in the Black Forest, and the twisting secondary roads that connect Freiburg with Lake Titisee pass through lots of charming scenery and architecture. See the box "An Excursion to the Upper Black Forest," on p. 409.

- **Mosel Valley:** The road along this Rhine tributary passes by some of the country's most famous vineyards. At least a half-dozen of the cities en route are worth visiting as well. See chapter 16.

7 The Best Walks

- **The Royal Castle Walk:** For one of the grandest panoramas in all of the Alps (in any country), hike up to the Marienbrücke, the bridge that spans the Pöllat Gorge behind Neuschwanstein Castle. From there, if you're up to it, you can continue uphill for about an hour for an amazing view of "Mad" King Ludwig's fantasy castle. See "Neuschwanstein & Hohenschwangau" in chapter 8.

- **Partnachklamm:** One of the most dramatic walks in all of the Bavarian Alps starts from the great winter sports resort of Garmisch-Partenkirchen. A signposted trail leads to the dramatic Partnachklamm Gorge. Carved from solid rock, the route passes two panoramic bottlenecks amid the thunder of falling water and clouds of spray. See "Hiking in the Bavarian Alps" in chapter 10.

- **Mainau Island:** A walk across the footbridge to Mainau, in Lake Constance, is like a visit to a tropical country. Mainau is filled with exotic plants collected by the Baden princes and members of the Royal House of Sweden. Tropical brushwood and other botanical wonders still thrive in this mild climate. You'll hardly believe you're in Germany. See p. 395.

- **Cochem:** Reichsburg Cochem (Cochem Castle), which towers over the little town of Cochem, can be reached on foot in about 15 minutes from the town's Marktplatz, or market square. Although hardly an alpine climb, this walk is one of the most rewarding you'll find in Germany, with panoramas in all directions. See p. 557.

8 The Best Biking

- **Munich by Bike:** You see so many locals riding bikes that you might think Munich is the biking capital of Germany. If you'd like to join the fun, pick up a copy of the pamphlet *Rad-Touren für unsere Gäste (Bike-Riding for Our Guests)* at the tourist office. It outlines itineraries for touring Munich by bike. See p. 299.

- **Lake Constance:** Rent a bike at the train station in the former imperial town of Lindau and set out in any direction to enjoy the views of this beautiful lake. The Lindau tourist office will provide a map and suggestions for the best routes to follow. See p. 381.

- **The Neckar Valley Cycle Path:** This signposted path allows you to follow the source of the Neckar, beginning in Villingen-Schwenningen and going all the way to the confluence of the Rhine at Mannheim. Instead of going the entire way, many visitors prefer to pick up a bicycle in Heidelberg and cycle along the riverbanks until they find a good spot for a picnic. See "Exploring on Two Wheels" in chapter 13.

- **Lüneburg Heath:** This wild heath in northern Germany is one of the country's major natural attractions. (Some of Germany's greatest poets have waxed rhapsodic about this shrub-covered land.) Rent a bike, pick up a map at the Lüneburg tourist office, and set out on your adventure. See p. 611.

9 The Best Spas

- **Bad Reichenhall:** Many spa lovers head for this remote corner of Bavaria to "take the waters." Europe's largest saline source was first tapped in pre-Christian times and the place has a definite 19th-century aura. And though some of the hotels in the town are better than others, all have equal access to the spa and lie about a 5-minute walk away. See "Bad Reichenhall" in chapter 10.

- **Baden-Baden:** There's no better spa in all of Germany, and certainly none more fashionable or famous. Baden-Baden is also the site of the country's most celebrated casino. The spa's been going strong since the leisure class of the 19th century discovered its healing waters, although the Roman legions of Emperor Caracalla had discovered the springs long before that. As at Bad Reichenhall, all hotels, no matter the price range, have equal access to the spa. See "Baden-Baden" in chapter 12.

- **Wiesbaden:** One of Germany's oldest cities, Wiesbaden attracted Roman legions to its hot springs, and lures today's fashionable traveler as well. It's not as chic as Baden-Baden, but Wiesbaden has one of Germany's most elegant casinos and concert halls, along with two gourmet restaurants. In summer, the beer garden at the Kurhaus is one of the liveliest along the Rhine. See "Side Trips from Frankfurt" in chapter 14.

- **Bad Homburg:** Bad Homburg lies at the foot of the Taunus Hills in a setting of medieval castles and luxuriant forests. There are more than 31 fountains in the town's Kurpark. The Bad Homburg Palace was once the summer residence of Prussian kings. See "Side Trips from Frankfurt" in chapter 14.

- **Bad Nauheim:** What do William Randolph Hearst and Elvis Presley have in common? Both stayed at Bad Nauheim—the newspaper czar by choice and Elvis on orders from the U.S. Army. The warm carbonic-acid springs are used in the treatment of heart and circulatory ailments and rheumatic diseases. See "Side Trips from Frankfurt" in chapter 14.

10 The Best Luxury Hotels

German efficiency and cleanliness are legendary, so it's not surprising that you can choose from a great number of well-managed hotels.

- **Grand Hotel Esplanade,** Berlin (© 413/2412541; www.esplanade.de): This strikingly contemporary hotel near several foreign embassies is one of the most prestigious in the German capital. With its collection of modern art, its spacious, cheerfully decorated rooms, and its first-class service, it is a prime address for the luxury-minded. See p. 103.

- **The Regent,** Berlin (© 888/201-1806 in the U.S., or 030/20338; www.regenthotels.com): One of Germany's great luxury hotels, the Regent is all about opulence, superb service, and comfort. It's discreet, tasteful, reliable, and a brilliant addition to the roster of luxury leaders in Germany's capital. See p. 114.

- **Hotel Elephant,** Weimar (© 03643/8020; www.starwoodhotels.com): This is one of Germany's most interesting hotels because of its age (over 300 years), its name, its 50-year survival in Germany's eastern zone, and its associations with such luminaries as Schiller, Liszt, and Goethe. Today, it's a cost-conscious treasure chest of German history. See p. 178.

- **Eisenhut (Iron Helmut),** Rothenburg ob der Tauber (✆ **09861/7050;** www.eisenhut.com): This hotel's 16th-century walls and valuable collection of antiques enhance the appeal of the most authentic Renaissance town in Germany. See p. 272.

- **Kempinski Hotel Vier Jahreszeiten München,** Munich (✆ **800/426-3135** in the U.S., or 089/21250; www.kempinski-vierjahreszeiten.de): Munich's most prestigious choice offers elegance and luxury. The wealthy and titled have checked in here for more than a century, enjoying the ambience, the antiques, the style, and the grace. See p. 304.

- **Bayerischer Hof & Palais Montgelas,** Munich (✆ **089/21200;** www.bayerischerhof.de): This deluxe hotel and 17th-century Bavarian palace together form Munich's answer to New York's Waldorf-Astoria. This is the only hotel in Munich to provide serious competition for the Kempinski Hotel. See p. 301.

- **Der Kleine Prinz,** Baden-Baden (✆ **07221/346600;** www.derkleineprinz.de): This hotel's director once helped manage the New York Hilton and the Waldorf-Astoria. Today, he and his wife run a century-old pair of neo-baroque houses in the heart of Germany's most elegant resort,

Baden-Baden. Der Kleine Prinz is among the most romantic of Germany's many romantic hotels. See p. 426.

- **Krone Assmannshausen,** Rüdesheim-Assmannshausen (✆ **06722/4030;** www.hotel-krone.com): Sprawling along the banks of the Rhine in an oversize, grangelike, gingerbread-laden fantasy, this hotel has witnessed the arrival of many important Germans (including Goethe) in its 400 years. It also contains one of the best traditional restaurants in town. See p. 518.

- **Fürstenhof Celle,** Celle (✆ **05141/2010;** www.fuerstenhof.de): This 17th-century manor, enlarged with half-timbered wings, stands out even in a town legendary for its medieval and Renaissance buildings. There's a cozy bar in the medieval cellar and one of the best dining rooms in Lower Saxony. See p. 613.

- **Raffles Vier Jahreszeiten,** Hamburg (✆ **800/223-6800** in the U.S. and Canada, or 040/34943151; www.hvj.de): Its dignified interior is as opulent as its 19th-century facade. This hotel's appeal is correctly aristocratic, but it has a touch of the saltwater zestiness that makes Hamburg a great city. See p. 632.

11 The Best Small Inns & Hotels

- **Art'otel,** Berlin (✆ **030/884470;** www.artotels.com): This hotel in the heart of Berlin is chic, discreet, and unique. The swirling action of the Ku'damm lies right outside the door, but inside, the decor is soothing and serene, the work of some of the Continent's top designers. See p. 110.

- **Altstadt-Hotel,** Passau (✆ **0851/3370;** www.altstadt-hotel.de): This inexpensive hotel stands at the convergence of three rivers—the Danube,

the Ilz, and the Inn. But the hotel offers more than river views—it's comfortably and traditionally furnished, and its regional cuisine and convivial pub attract the locals. See p. 249.

- **Gästehaus Englischer Garten,** Munich (✆ **089/3839410;** www.hotelenglischergarten.de): This is an oasis of charm and tranquillity, close to the Englischer Garten, where buffed Munich lies out nude in the sun. The furnishings are in an old-fashioned Bavarian style, but the comfort level is first-rate. See p. 309.

- **Parkhotel Atlantic Schlosshotel,** Heidelberg (℗ **06221/60420;** www.parkhotel-atlantic.de): This 24-room inn is on the wooded outskirts of Heidelberg, near the famous castle. Every room is comfortable and convenient, and in the afternoon you can go for long walks along the woodland trails surrounding the property. See p. 438.
- **Antik-Hotel Bristol,** Cologne (℗ **0221/120195;** www.antik-hotel-bristol.de): In the heart of this cathedral city along the Rhine, this unique hotel is filled with antiques, both country rustic and town-house elegant, making the atmosphere both authentic and inviting. See p. 536.
- **Hanseatic Hotel,** Hamburg (℗ **040/485772;** www.hanseatic-hamburg.de): This little hotel evokes a prim and proper English gentleman's club. Rooms are one of a kind, often containing antiques. In summer, the owner may be out front tending his flower garden, getting ready to welcome you. See p. 634.

12 The Best Restaurants

- **Die Quadriga,** Berlin (℗ **030/214050**): Critics hail this gastronomic wonder in the Hotel Brandenburger Hof as Berlin's finest dining choice. Celebrated for its modern Continental cuisine, it's where the president of Germany takes his favorite guests when he wants to "show off." While seated in a 1904 chair designed by Frank Lloyd Wright, you can enjoy food that is, in a word, sublime. See p. 117.
- **Essigbrätlein,** Nürnberg (℗ **0911/225131**): Food critics single this out as the best dining spot in Nürnberg, and we heartily agree. Its upscale Franconian and Continental cuisine is reason enough to visit the city. See p. 236.
- **Weinhaus Zum Stachel,** Würzburg (℗ **0931/52770**): This is the oldest (ca. 1413) wine house in a town loaded with them. Food is good, portions are copious, the wine flows, and everyone has a wonderful time. This is old-time Deutschland at its most appealing. See p. 261.
- **Tantris,** Munich (℗ **089/3619590**): Savvy German food critics have honored Tantris's Hans Haas as the country's top chef. He definitely serves some of the finest and most innovative food in Bavaria. See p. 319.
- **Hanse Stube,** Cologne (℗ **0221/2701**): Located in a landmark hotel, this restaurant lies on the same square as the fabled Rhineland cathedral. French cuisine in Cologne doesn't get any better than this—the chefs have a prodigious talent for preparing food using only the finest and freshest ingredients. See p. 538.
- **Victorian Restaurant,** Düsseldorf (℗ **0211/8655020**): Regulars know what a treasure they have in this restaurant: Market-fresh ingredients and a steady hand in the kitchen produce award-winning traditional and modern food. See p. 550.
- **Waldhotel Sonnora,** outside Bernkastel-Kues (℗ **06578/406;** www.hotel-sonnora.de): In the Mosel Valley, the Waldhotel Sonnora is one of the most justifiably acclaimed restaurants in the country. Be sure to make a reservation as far in advance as possible and prepare yourself for a gastronomic adventure in Continental cuisine. Herr Thieltges, the chef,

told us, "We don't just serve dishes—rather, culinary masterpieces." We agree. See p. 565.

- **Fischereihafen Restaurant,** Altona, near Hamburg (© **040/381816**): Patrons from Tina Turner to Helmut Kohl have pronounced the food here delightful. From a window seat, you can overlook the boats that might have hauled in your sole, eel, turbot, herring, or flounder from the seas that day. See p. 637.

13 The Best Beer Halls & Taverns

- **Auerbachs Keller,** Leipzig (© **0341/216100**): The most famous tavern in eastern Germany, this is where Goethe staged the debate between Faust and Mephistopheles. The tavern dates from 1530 and has a series of murals evoking the Faust legend. See p. 193.
- **Hofbräuhaus am Platzl,** Munich (© **089/221676**): The Hofbräuhaus is the world's most famous beer hall and can accommodate some 4,500 beer drinkers on any given night. Music from live bands and huge mugs of beer served at wooden tables combine to produce the best of Bavarian nighttime fun. See p. 342.
- **Zum Roten Ochsen,** Heidelberg (© **06221/20977**): Over the years, "The Red Ox" has drawn beer drinkers from Mark Twain to Bismarck. Students have been getting plastered here since 1703, and the tradition continues to this day. See p. 444.
- **Ratskeller,** Bremen (© **0421/321676**): This is one of the most celebrated Ratskellers in Germany. A tradition for decades, it serves topnotch German and international food and some of the best suds along the Rhineland, as well as one of the longest lists of vintage wines from the country's vineyards. See p. 605.

14 The Best Shopping

The best way to approach shopping here is to make it a part of your overall experience and not an end unto itself. Though Berlin and Munich are the major shopping centers in Germany, the rest of the country is okay—neither a shopper's mecca nor the bargain basement of Europe. Still, you can find some good buys here, such as:

- **Porcelain:** For centuries, Germany has been known for the quality of its porcelain. Names such as KPM, Rosenthal, and Meissen are household words. KPM, for example, has been a Berlin tradition for more than 2 centuries.
- **Handicrafts:** In the Bavarian Alps, woodcarvers still carry on their time-honored tradition. The best place to purchase woodcarvings is in the alpine village of Oberammergau. See "Shopping for Woodcarvings" in chapter 10.
- **Timepieces:** Corny though they may be, carved Black Forest cuckoo clocks remain an enduring favorite. See chapter 12.
- **Cutlery:** WMF (Württembergische-Metalwaren-Fabrik) and J. A. Henckels are two of the country's premier producers of fine cutlery. Their knives are expensive, but longtime users say they last forever. Both WMF and Henckels stores are found all over Germany.

2

Germany in Depth

A unified, wealthy, industrial yet beautiful Germany awaits you and promises some of the most intriguing travel experiences in Europe.

Many of its treasures were lost in World War II, but much remains and much has been restored. Natural scenery, particularly in the Black Forest, the Mosel Valley, the Harz Mountains, and the Bavarian Alps, is a potent lure.

For those who want to see history in the making, we'd recommend visiting Potsdam, Leipzig, Dresden, Meissen, and Weimar, all centers of East Germany before German unification in October 1990. Keep in mind, however, that although political developments have been fast paced, the infrastructure of the five new states cannot change overnight, and living standards here are still different from those in (the former) West Germany.

Germany is one of the most modern and, at the same time, the most traditional of countries. Its advanced technology and industry are the envy of the rest of the world. Here you'll likely meet people of learning and sophistication, boasting a long cultural heritage and devotion to music and the arts.

This guide is meant to help you decide where to go in Germany and how best to enjoy its charms, but ultimately the most gratifying rewards will be your own serendipitous discoveries—drinking beer in a yard shaded by chestnut trees, picnicking in a Bavarian meadow, or spending time chatting with a wine maker in the Mosel Valley. You will surely remember experiences like these for years to come.

1 Germany Today

The new chancellor of Germany, Angela Merkel, is giving the Germans what they seem to want—the status quo. Her popularity is at an all-time high—at least for now. For the moment she is shying away from the deep economic restructuring she advocated during her campaign in 2005.

Instead she lets the other government leaders focus on economics, and even terrorism, while she goes green. She even visited Greenland to see how the glaciers are doing during their meltdown. As writer Nicholas Kulish proclaimed, "It is as if Ronald Reagan has turned into Al Gore after being elected."

Before she turned politician, Merkel was a physicist, and she was the minister of the environment in Germany from 1994 to 1998. She still takes her former job seriously.

Under her new government, any radical change in the health system, government pensions, and employment laws have been dead on arrival. Kulish also said that the "German people don't really want aggressive reforms. They are more than content to let the state care for them, from kindergarten all the way to retirement."

So far, Merkel has been governing from the center. She prefers to leave well enough alone now that the German economy is on the rise in contrast to the United States. When she took office the unemployment rate was 12%. It has now dropped to 9%.

Problems may be in store for her, and her popularity may inevitably fall, but right now she's telling Parliament she wants "to do what is doable."

How does one define the values and ethics that permeate Merkel's Germany of today?

Despite record-breaking prosperity that began in the '80s, with the inevitable slumps, many Germans live with a pervasive sense of being both envied and censored within the European community. The friends you're likely to meet in Germany (and you're likely to meet many) will probably be well educated and will possess linguistic skills (almost certainly including English) that, by the standards of the rest of the world, particularly the United States, are astonishing. Many younger Germans are likely to be guided by a sense of idealism, even zeal, for ecological and other causes.

Germans, like Americans, are worried about job security. The greatest fear sweeping across Germany today is of "job hemorrhage." German companies are finding that more and more of their manufacturing plants and jobs can be farmed out to other locations, including, ironically enough, Alabama and South Carolina, where wages and benefits for workers at a BMW plant are about 30% less than in Germany. In the Czech Republic, just across the border, wages are equivalent to 10% of those paid in Germany, for workers nearly as well qualified.

Nevertheless, as a result of its citizens' intelligence, talents, education, and drive, Germany will probably prosper and certainly retain its unique identity. You can be sure the country will continue to welcome its visitors with its customary warmth and verve.

2 Looking Back at Germany

EARLY DAYS

"A large build, very strong in the attack, but not suitable to the same extent for heavy work" was how Tacitus, the Roman historian, described the Teutons in A.D. 60. The Romans had been trying to push the borders of their empire up to the Rhineland, with mixed success, since 9 B.C., but the Teutonic tribes fought back ferociously. The first recognized German national hero was Arminius, who led his tribe (the Cherusci) in defeating three Roman legions near modern-day Bielefeld in A.D. 9.

After the deterioration of the Roman Empire, the Franks ruled much of what we now know as Germany. In 800, a Frankish king, Charlemagne, extended the Carolingian Empire from the Pyrenees to Saxony and Bavaria. His rule marks the high point of cultural and political development of that period. He divided the empire into counties, each with an administrator directly responsible to him, and promoted education, scholarship, and the revival of Greek and Roman culture.

THE HOLY ROMAN EMPIRE

After Charlemagne's death, the Carolingian Empire fell apart. In 843, the Treaty of Verdun granted the empire's eastern territory to Louis the German, marking the beginning of German history.

In 962, the pope recognized Otto I as emperor of what was later called the Holy Roman Empire. This new political entity was formed both to impose unity on the European political world and to create a bulwark against the invasion of non-Christian tribes. It claimed direct links to the grandeur of ancient Rome and to the more contemporary might of the church.

Unity, however, did not prevail. The empire splintered into a bickering alliance of dukedoms, bishoprics, and principalities. The emperor's authority was often dependent on German nobles and the pope. A capital city that could have served as a center of power was never established—the monarch simply moved from one city to another, mustering an army and collecting revenue wherever he could—so the possibilities for dynastic intrigues were endless. In subsequent jockeying, the church itself was a voracious competitor for power. This power struggle broke out into open conflict in 1076, when Pope Gregory VII excommunicated the emperor, Henry IV, who was forced to stand barefoot in the snow outside Canossa, humiliated, awaiting a repeal.

To strengthen their position as the Holy Roman Empire declined, the emperors turned to alliances with the wealthy, independent trading ports to the north and east, under the federation of the Hanseatic League. Such German cities as Hamburg, Lübeck, and Bremen grew in both economic and political power. Eventually the league controlled trade as far as Novgorod in Russia.

THE REFORMATION & THE RELIGIOUS WARS

When an Augustinian monk, Martin Luther, nailed his theological and political complaints to a church door in Wittenberg in 1517, he set off a political and religious wildfire that spread across the landscape of Europe. The fragmented political situation in Germany played into Luther's hands: For every prince who condemned him, he found one to protect him. Luther's Reformation fanned the flames of Germany's political factions. A new conflict between Catholics and Protestants set the stage for the devastation of the Thirty Years' War (1618–48),

which entrenched the divided sensibilities of the splintered nation.

The only powerful German state to emerge from these conflicts was Prussia, a tiny northeast kingdom on the Baltic Sea. The rise of Prussian power continued through the 18th century until, led by soldier and patron of the Enlightenment, Frederick the Great, Prussia became a major kingdom, with Berlin as its capital.

NAPOLEON ARRIVES

After the French Revolution, Napoleon and his new political ideas swept across Europe. The left bank of the Rhine came under French control. Under these pressures, the Holy Roman Empire officially came to an end in 1806. Around the same time, Napoleon's armies invaded Prussia, making it, for a brief time, a part of the French Empire. But Napoleon was defeated at Leipzig in 1813; 2 years later, Britain and Prussia crushed him at the Battle of Waterloo.

BISMARCK & PRUSSIA

The Congress of Vienna (1814–15) redrew the map of Germany after Napoleon's defeat, giving more territory to Prussia but making Austria the leader in a German Confederation. During this time, there was a rising spirit of nationalism, exploited to good effect by Prince Otto von Bismarck when he became Prussia's prime minister in 1862. Prussia triumphed in the Austro-Prussian War of 1866, and after the subsequent Franco-Prussian War (1870–71), when Prussia laid siege to Paris, Bismarck succeeded in his goal of unification. Wilhelm I was made emperor of all Germany in 1871, and a strong, unified Germany at last took shape. Under Bismarck's leadership, Germany adopted an advanced social welfare system and brought its military and industrial production, as well as technical and scientific achievements, to new heights.

Impressions

Take, for instance, the Prussians: they are saints when compared with the French. They have every sort of excellence; they are honest, sober, hardworking, well instructed, brave, good sons, husbands, and fathers and yet . . . all with whom I have been thrown were proud as Scotchmen, cold as New Englanders, and touchy as only Prussians can be.

—Henry Labouchere, 1871

WORLD WAR I

By 1907, Europe was divided into two camps: the Triple Alliance (Germany, Austria-Hungary, and Italy) and the Triple Entente (France, Great Britain, and Russia). The match that ignited the powder keg was struck at Sarajevo in 1914, with the assassination of Archduke Franz Ferdinand, heir to the Austro-Hungarian Empire. The subsequent German invasion of France launched the bloodiest war the world had ever seen. A new and particularly demoralizing form of battle, "trench warfare," produced staggering casualties. On August 8, 1918, the Allies penetrated German lines, and the German high command realized the situation was hopeless.

To get more favorable treatment from the Allies, the Germans voluntarily declared a parliamentary democracy, ending the reign of the kaiser. Despite that concession, in 1918 Germany was forced to sign the humiliating Treaty of Versailles, which demanded the surrender of strategic territories including Alsace-Lorraine, just west of the Rhine. The Allies—especially the French—also demanded huge monetary reparations.

WEIMAR REPUBLIC

In 1919, the National Assembly met in Weimar to draw up a new constitution, hailed at the time as the most progressive in the world. But in defeated and humiliated postwar Germany, extremists from both the left and the right launched savage attacks against the inexperienced and idealistic government. Enormous payments demanded by the Allies crippled the German economy. When Germany couldn't make reparations, France retaliated by occupying the Ruhr, one of Germany's most valuable industrial resources. Inflation destroyed what was left of the German economy.

THE RISE OF NAZISM

This was just the right climate for the rise of Adolf Hitler and the Nazi Party. The Nazis believed in the superiority of the Aryan race and blamed non-Aryans, particularly Jews, for Germany's woes. At first Hitler's anti-Semitic, nationalist ideas failed to gain popular support, even with right-wingers. Nazi membership in the Reichstag (parliament) dropped from 25 in 1925 to only a dozen following the elections of 1928.

In 1932, Hitler lost the electoral race for president against the compromise candidate of the democratic parties, war hero Paul von Hindenburg. Nevertheless, Hitler's power increased, and on January 30, 1933, Hindenburg submitted to right-wing pressure and appointed Hitler chancellor. Upon Hindenburg's death in 1934, Hitler declared himself *Führer* (leader) of the Third Reich, a new German empire. Protected by hastily drafted laws and regulations, he made his power absolute.

On June 30, 1934, Hitler disposed of any opposing elements in his own party in the "Night of Long Knives," when hundreds were massacred, including Ernst Röhm, chief of his notorious Brownshirts.

Heinrich Himmler's black-shirted *Schutz-staffel* (SS) became a powerful political force. Surrounded by adoring fans (or, at best, passive witnesses), Hitler now viewed his empire as a worthy successor to those of Charlemagne and Bismarck.

In 1936, Hitler remilitarized the Rhineland and signed agreements with Japan and fascist Italy, forming the Axis alliance. In 1938, he enforced the *Anschluss* (annexation) of Austria and marched triumphantly into the country of his birth, and he occupied the German-speaking Sudetenland in Czechoslovakia, an act that other western powers could not summon the will to oppose.

The horrors of unchecked Nazi rule lasted until 1945. The Gestapo, or secret police, launched one of the most notorious reigns of terror in history. Anyone whom the Nazis considered enemies or simply undesirables—which included Communists, Social Democrats, homosexuals, political dissidents, Gypsies, and many others—were persecuted. Jews were disenfranchised, terrorized, and forced into ghettos and concentration camps.

WORLD WAR II

In late August 1939, Hitler signed a nonaggression pact with the Soviet Union that gave him free reign to launch an invasion of Poland, which he did on September 1. France and Britain, honoring their agreements with Poland, declared war on Germany. Germany scored early victories, and in one of the most stunning campaigns of the 20th century, invaded and occupied France in June 1940. In 1941, Hitler turned on the Soviet Union.

Meeting in the Berlin suburb of Wannsee in 1942, the Nazi leadership formulated the implementation of the "final solution" to the "Jewish question," the systematic extermination of millions of Jews. The mass murders of homosexuals,

Gypsies, Communists, Slavs, and other "undesirables" were less systematic but also numbered in the millions.

Following Japan's attack on Pearl Harbor, Germany declared war on the United States on December 11, 1941. But after defeats in north Africa in 1942 and at Stalingrad in 1943, the recurrent theme became one of Nazi retreat. The D-day landings along the coast of Normandy on June 6, 1944, began the steady advance of the Allied armies from the west, while Soviet armies relentlessly marched toward Berlin from the east. Hitler committed suicide in Berlin in April 1945. His country, along with much of Europe, lay in ruins.

DIVISION OF GERMANY

At war's end, Germany and its capital were divided. The nation shrank in size, losing long-held territories (among them East Prussia and Upper Silesia). The United States, Great Britain, France, and the Soviet Union divided the country into four zones of occupation. Berlin, in the heart of the Soviet district, was also divided among the four powers. In the late 1940s, the Soviet Union tried to cut off Allied access to Berlin, but a massive U.S.-sponsored airlift into the city thwarted the effort. In 1949, the Soviets established the German Democratic Republic (GDR). In response, the Federal Republic of Germany was established in the American, British, and French zones. In 1961, the GDR sealed off its borders and erected the Berlin Wall, a stark symbol of the Cold War.

Throughout the 1960s, the financial world buzzed with the talk of an economic miracle in Germany. Led by Ludwig Erhard, the economist, this miracle was called *Wirtschaftswunder,* and it saw West Germany rise to become the fourth-largest economy in the world.

This era of prosperity also saw the rise of a young German leader, Willy Brandt. Along with his Social-Liberal Coalition, Brandt, as chancellor, brought about long-overdue reform, an overhaul of education, and much improvement in industrial relations. His controversial Eastern policy *(Ostpolitik)* improved relations with Soviet-dominated East Germany and other Communist countries to the east of Germany. His efforts in normalizing relations with the GDR brought Brandt the Nobel Prize of 1971.

The 1972 Summer Olympic Games were meant to show the entire world the bold new face of a radically rebuilt Munich. However, the terrorist attack on and murder of 11 Israeli athletes revived memories of the recent past.

Helmut Schmidt became chancellor in 1974, as West Germany continued to amaze the world with its economic muscle. Problems such as mounting unemployment remained, however, and in 1982, Helmut Kohl became the new German leader, pursuing welfare cuts, a tight-fisted money policy, and military cooperation with the U.S. The Kohl era saw the Green Party rise as a political force, with its goals of disarmament and protecting a fragile environment.

FALL OF THE WALL & UNIFICATION

The year 1989 was one of change and turmoil. In the wake of the collapse of Communist power across eastern Europe, the Berlin Wall also fell. The following year was perhaps the most significant in postwar German history. The two German nations announced economic unification in July, followed by total unification—with its thousands of inherent problems and headaches—on October 3, 1990. In 1991, Parliament voted to quit Bonn, seat of the West German government, and reestablish the once-mighty capital of Berlin.

After the first heady period of reunification, disillusionment set in, especially in eastern Germany, which was riddled with unemployment and unrealized expectations. Resentment against immigrant workers led to some violent neo-Nazi marches, bombings, and physical assaults. However, most Germans rose up to condemn the ultra-rightists and the sporadic violence.

Psychological and emotional differences between the two zones were almost overwhelming, as were the vast disparities in industrial development. As the influential newspaper *Frankfurter Rundschau* editorialized, "The terms of east and west are not so much geographical expressions as they are descriptions of states of mind."

MODERN GERMANY

As the 21st century began, Germany, despite the enormous costs of reunification, remained an economic powerhouse in Europe. As a member of the European Union (E.U.), NATO, and the G8 group of the world's industrial powers, Germany's influence extends throughout Europe and across the globe.

Moving deeper into the 21st century, Berlin has become the center of the Continent. Of the three major European powers, including France and Great Britain, Germany appears to be the most dynamic. In fact, of all E.U. members, Germany most actively pursued the abandonment of national currencies, such as its own historic deutsche mark, and the adoption of the euro as the standard unit of currency for all E.U. countries. Other countries, such as Great Britain, though a member of the E.U., still hold back. German economists continue to hope that the adoption of a single currency for Europe will lead to prosperity for all in a future "United States of Europe."

Homosexuals, once persecuted by the Nazis and sent to death camps along with Jews and Gypsies, moved significantly forward in postmillennium Germany. In 2001, in spite of fierce opposition from some conservatives, same-sex partners won legal status in Germany. The law, announced in Germany's unofficial gay capital of Berlin, allows gay couples to register their unions at government offices and requires a court decision for divorce. Same-sex couples also receive the inheritance and health-insurance rights given married spouses.

In the aftermath of World War II, Germany had become an economic giant but remained a military midget. Because of its aggression in Hitler's war, Germany appeared reluctant to make a strong show of military force anywhere in the world. But in 2001, Chancellor Gerhard Schröder announced a major change in military policy in which Germany would pursue a "more muscular policy." He pronounced as "irrevocably passed" the day when Germany would be economically powerful but militarily passive. Schröder stated that now that Germany was reunited, it had to take on more responsibilities in the international community. As proof of his stated goal, Germany sent troops to aid the United States in its military strikes against terrorist bases in Taliban-controlled Afghanistan following the terrorist attacks against the United States on September 11, 2001.

But support for U.S. policies abruptly ended in 2003, when Chancellor Schröder took a stance against America's war with Iraq. While this course proved politically rewarding in Germany, where most voters opposed U.S. involvement, it created a sharp rift with Washington, D.C., and irritated President George W. Bush. Schröder's opposition to the war led to the lowest point in German-American relations since World War II. Since then, relations have been more cordial. In 2004 Schröder and Bush issued a joint statement on "The German-American Alliance for the 21st Century." Schröder also attended the funeral of President Reagan as well as the 60th anniversary of the commemoration of the Allied D-day invasion of Normandy.

In a surprise development in 2005, conservative Angela Merkel became the first woman to govern modern Germany and the country's first leader to grow up under communism in the Soviet-occupied East. Her conservatives finished just 1 percentage point ahead of Chancellor Gerhard Schröder's center-left Social Democrats, with neither party getting a majority.

Merkel campaigned on pledges to shake up Germany's highly regulated labor market and get the stagnant economy going again. She also promised to reinvigorate relations with the U.S. Merkel faced massive problems, including unemployment. Like the United States, the German economy remained strong but there were horrendous problems, including an economic slowdown. The financial burden of reunification has exerted a terrible price on Germany.

The new "First Man" of Germany, Merkel's husband is mild-mannered chemistry professor, Joachim Sauer, who likes to cook for friends and watch old Dustin Hoffman movies.

Although Germany in 2006 and early 2007 didn't do anything earthshaking enough to discuss here, a significant historical event occurred in Luxembourg. An agreement was reached by the summer of 2006 to open up millions of Nazi secret archives locked away since World War II. The vast archive has been hidden for decades in the German town of Bad Arolsen, but will in time become available to researchers.

An 11-nation International Commission has overseen the archives since the war. The files will also be available to Holocaust survivors and families of victims whose fate may not be clear. The files contain most of what the Nazis recorded on their death camps, including the prisoners held there, not only Jews but Gypsies and gay people, including "patients" subjected to cruel medical experiments.

By 2008 Merkel's popularity had ballooned with the resurgence of the German economy, which has grown nearly

3% as unemployment dropped to 9% after hitting a high of 12% when she took office in 2005.

As Germany went into the uncertainties of 2008, it still boasted the third-largest economy in the world and continued to be a European Union power player.

3 Art & Architecture

Germany's art ranges from medieval carved wood statues to Dürer prints to expressionist paintings, its architecture from Gothic cathedrals and riotous baroque chapels to neoclassical temples and Bauhaus buildings. This overview should help you make sense of it all.

GERMAN ART
ROMANESQUE (11TH–12TH C.)

Artistic expression in early medieval Germany was largely church-related. Because Mass was said in Latin, the illiterate masses had to learn Bible lessons via **bas reliefs** (sculptures that project slightly from a flat surface) and **wall paintings,** which told key tales to inspire faith in God and fear of sin.

The best examples of this period include scraps of surviving Romanesque sculpture on the 11th-century, carved wood doors at **Cologne's St. Maria im Kapitol** (p. 543), **Augsburg's Dom St. Maria** (p. 285), and the intricate *The Shrine of the Magi* reliquary (1182–1220) in **Kölner Dom** (**Cologne Cathedral;** p. 539).

GOTHIC (13TH–15TH C.)

Late medieval German art continued to be largely ecclesiastical, including **stained glass, church facades,** and massive **wooden altarpieces** festooned with **statues** and **carvings.** In Gothic **painting** and **sculpture,** figures tended to be more natural looking than in the Romanesque, but remained highly stylized.

The best examples and artists include **stained glass** in **Ulm Münster, Rothenburg's St. Jakobskirche,** and **Cologne's St. Gereon's Sacristy** (p. 225, 276, and 543). **Stephan Lochner** (active 1400–51) was the premier artist of the School of Cologne, where he painted the **Cologne Cathedral**'s *Altar of the City Patrons* (ca. 1440; p. 541) and the **Wallraf-Richartz Museum**'s *Madonna in the Rose Garden* (1450; p. 542). **Bamberger Reiter** is an anonymous equestrian statue in Bamberg's Kaiserdom, a masterpiece of 13th-century sculpture (p. 231). **Tilman Riemenschneider** (1460–1531) was Germany's genius Gothic woodcarver of languid figures draped in flowing, folded robes. Some of his best works remain in **Würzburg,** including statues in the **Mainfränkisches Museum** (p. 262).

RENAISSANCE (LATE 15TH THROUGH 16TH C.)

The German Renaissance masters, striving for greater naturalism, included the greatest of them all, Albrecht Dürer (1471–1528). A genius painter, superb illustrator, and one of the greatest draughtsman ever, Dürer was the most important Renaissance artist outside Italy. His art matched the scientific and geometric precepts of the Florentine Renaissance with a command of color learned in Venice, a Flemish eye for meticulous detail, and the emotional sensibility of the German Gothic. He was the first to paint stand-alone self-portraits (including one in **Munich's Alte Pinakothek;** p. 323), as well as watercolors and gouaches for their own sake rather than merely as sketches. His paintings grace **Berlin's Gemäldegalerie** (p. 134) and the **Germanisches Nationalmuseum** (p. 239) in his native **Nürnberg.** Also see the box on p. 239.

    Lucas Cranach the Elder (1472–1553) melded Renaissance sensibilities with a still somewhat primitive, medieval look. As a young artist in Vienna, he helped popularize landscape painting as a member of the Danube School (*Rest on the Flight into Egypt* [1504] in **Berlin's Gemäldegalerie;** p. 134), and invented the full-length portrait (*Duke of Saxony* [1514] and *The Duchess* [1514] in **Dresden's Gemäldegalerie Alte Meister,** in the Zwinger complex; p. 213). **Hans Holbein the Younger** (1497–1543) was second only to Dürer in the German Renaissance, and one of the greatest portraitists ever. Germany preserves precious little of his work, but you can see the *Portrait of Georg Gisze* (1532) in **Berlin's Gemäldegalerie** (p. 134) and a Nativity in the **Freiburg Cathedral** (p. 408).

BAROQUE & ROCOCO (16TH–18TH C.)

The **baroque** is more theatrical and decorative than the Renaissance, mixing a kind of super-realism based on the use of peasant models and the exaggerated *chiaroscuro* ("light and dark") of Italy's Caravaggio with compositional complexity and explosions of dynamic fury, movement, color, and figures. **Rococo** is this later baroque art gone awry, frothy and chaotic. Artists from this period include **Andreas Schlüter** (1660–1714), whose sculptures can now be found at Berlin's **Schloss Charlottenburg** (p. 130). **Balthazar Permoser** (1651–1732) was court sculptor at Dresden. His stone pulpit stands in **Katholische Hofkirche** (p. 212), his sculptures in the **Zwinger** (p. 213).

ROMANTIC (19TH C.)

The paintings of the Romantics were heroic, historic, dramatic, and beautiful in contrast to the classically minded Renaissance artists or the overly exuberant baroque artists. **Adam Elsheimer** (1578–1610) created tiny paintings that bridged the gap from late Renaissance Mannerism (a style characterized by twisting figures in exaggerated positions), through baroque, to proto-Romantic. His *Flight into Egypt* (1609) resides in **Munich's Alte Pinakothek** (p. 323). **Caspar David Friedrich** (1774–1840) was the greatest of the German Romantics. **Dresden's Gemäldegalerie Alte Meister** in the Zwinger complex (p. 213) houses his famous *Cross in the Mountains* (1808).

EARLY 20TH CENTURY

Until Hitler, Germany was one of Europe's hotbeds of artistic activity. But the Nazis outlawed and confiscated what they called "degenerate" modern art. Almost all the artists listed below are represented at **Cologne's Museum Ludwig** (p. 541), save Höch and Grosz, who you can find at **Berlin's Neue Nationalgalerie** (p. 137). At least one artist from every movement is at **Stuttgart's Staatsgalerie** (p. 455), and there are also good modern collections at **Düsseldorf's Kunstsammlung Nordrhein-Westfalen** (p. 553) and **Dresden's Albertinum** (p. 213). **Munich's Pinakothek der Moderne** (p. 327) is strong on expressionist artists.

The major artists and movements of the early 20th century include **expressionism,** which abandoned realism and embraced, to varying degrees, exaggeration, visible artistry (thick paint, obvious brushstrokes, and strong colors) and, most importantly, abstraction—all to try to "express" the emotions or philosophy of the artist himself. Pure expressionism fell into two main groups, especially **Die Brücke,** founded in 1905 Dresden, which sought inspiration in folk art, medieval examples, and "unspoiled" landscapes. Its greatest members were **Ernst Kirchner** (1880–1938) and **Karl Schmidt-Rottluff** (1884–1976), though Impressionist **Emil Nolde** (1867–1956) also later joined for a while. They have their own **Brücke Museum** in Berlin (p. 139). The second movement was **Der Blaue Reiter group** set up in Munich in 1911 by Russian-born **Wassily Kandinsky** (1866–1944), **Franz Marc** (1880–1916), and **August Macke** (1887–1914) to oppose the cultural insularity and antimodern stance of Die Brücke. The "Blue Riders" embraced international elements, modern abstraction techniques, and bright, vibrant color schemes to seek an emotional, visceral intensity in their work. **Dadaists** were by turns abstract, nihilistic (inviting gallery visitors to help destroy the art), and just generally anti-art (many made random collages of found materials). Its proponents included **Hannah Höch** (1889–1978), who collaged photographs and magazine cut-outs to make social statements; **George Grosz** (1893–1959), who was more strictly a painter, and later moved on to the Neue Sachlichkeit movement (below); and **Kurt Schwitters** (1887–1948), who eventually started his own splinter group called "Merz" which experimented with abstract and Russian constructivist elements.

Both **Max Ernst** (1891–1976) and Alsatian **Jean "Hans" Arp** (1887–1966) started as Blaue Reiter expressionists and, after their Dada collage period, ended up in Paris as surrealists (Ernst as a painter, Arp as a sculptor and painter of amorphous shapes).

Neue Sachlichkeit (New Objectivity) was a 1920s Berlin movement opposed to the abstraction of the expressionists. Their caricature-filled art was painted in harsh colors and focused on even harsher subjects such as sex and violence. Proponents included **Otto Dix** (1891-1969), who started as an expressionist but quickly became one of the most scathing and disturbing New Objectivity painters; **George Grosz** (see above); and **Max Beckmann** (1884–1950), who also was originally an expressionist.

POST–WORLD WAR II ART

Germany hasn't had any one style or school to define its art since World War II, though terms such as neo-expressionism (an anti-abstract, antiminimalist, anticonceptual trend that grounds itself more in tradition and figurative art) are often bandied about. There have been, however, several important artists. All three listed below are represented in **Stuttgart's Staatsgalerie** (p. 455) and **Bonn's Kunstmuseum** (p. 526). Notable Post–World War II artists include **Josef Beuys** (1921–86), an iconoclast and nonconformist who made constructivist sculpture from trash; **Anselm Kiefer** (b. 1945), who made a return to huge, mixed-media figurative art often with a strong historical bent; and **Georg Baselitz** (b. 1938), a figurative painter—and a sculptor, since the 1980s—a neo-expressionist with a penchant for portraying people upside down.

ARCHITECTURE

Romanesque architects concentrated on building large churches with wide aisles to accommodate the masses. Identifiable features include rounded arches, thick walls, small windows, huge piers, tall towers, dual chancels, and blind arcades.

Dom, Mainz

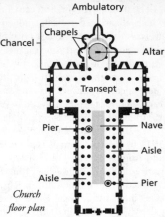
Church floor plan

The best examples include **Mainz's Dom** (p. 514), which looks more like a castle fortress than a church; **Worms's Dom St. Peter** (p. 508), with a dual-chancel arrangement and two imposing facades; and **Speyer's Kaiserdom** (p. 505), the largest cathedral in Germany, a four-towered Romanesque basilica with dwarf galleries and blind arcades.

GOTHIC (13TH–16TH C.)

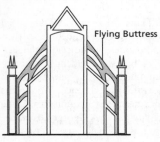
Cross section of a Gothic church

Ceilings began to soar with Gothic architects; walls became thinner, and windows—often stained glass—proliferated. On the exterior, graceful buttresses and soaring spires rose over a town. Pointed arches, it was discovered, carried more weight than rounded ones. Other features included cross vaulting, a facade flanked by two towers, flying buttresses, spires, gargoyles, and delicate, lacy spider tracery.

The best examples of Gothic include **Cologne Cathedral** (p. 539), Germany's finest, at once massive and graceful; **Freiburg Cathedral** (p. 408), built almost entirely during the Middle Ages; and **Ulm Münster** (p. 255), second in size only to Cologne's cathedral, Ulm's Münster sports the world's tallest spire—though it did take 500 years to complete. The best-preserved town centers with Gothic-style houses and buildings include **Rothenburg ob der Tauber, Goslar, Regensburg,** and **Tübingen** (p. 270, 615, 243, and 456).

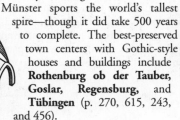
Cross vault

Cologne Cathedral

RENAISSANCE (LATE 15TH THROUGH MID–17TH C.)

Germany was so busy with the Reformation that the country had little time for the Renaissance, which really only had an effect in southern Germany (transalpine influences from Italy) and a few isolated examples in the far north (influences from Flemish and Dutch neighbors). Other than a close eye to the Renaissance ideals of proportion, symmetry, and the Classical orders (distinguished by the use of three column capitals: Corinthian, Ionic, and Doric), little specifically identifies Italianate Renaissance buildings.

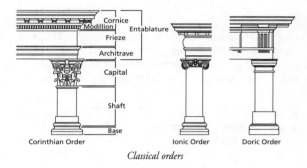

Classical orders

Weser Renaissance was a late-16th- and early-17th-century style prevalent in Lower Saxony, distinguishable on houses by pinnacled gables (the triangular upper portion of a wall at the end of a pitched roof), heavy scrollwork, elaborate dormers (an upright window projecting from a sloping roof), rounded pediments (a low-pitched feature above a window, door, or pavilion), and decorative stone bands.

Celle is the best preserved town center in the Weser Renaissance style, including its moated **Herzogschloss** (p. 615). The Pied Pier town of **Hameln** has several fine Weser Renaissance houses, including the **Rattenfängerhaus, Hochzeitshaus,** and **Dempterscheshaus** (p. 594). The only solidly Renaissance church in Germany is **Michaelskirche** in Munich, built 1583 to 1597 by Jesuits to resemble their church in Rome (p. 332).

BAROQUE & ROCOCO (17TH–18TH C.)

With a seamless meshing of architecture and art, the German baroque flourished in the south and in Lower Saxony. Germany's brand of over-the-top, baroque chaos worked better perhaps than in any other country. Whereas **rococo** is usually used as a derogatory term for the baroque gone awry into the grotesque, in Germany the rococo actually succeeds (sometimes). Baroque lines follow a complex geometry and interplay of concave and convex surfaces. The overall effect is to lighten the appearance of structures and add movement of line and vibrancy to the static look of the Renaissance.

The best example of a baroque palace is the **Residenz** in **Würzburg** (1720–44; p. 262), designed by Balthasar Neumann, including a monumental staircase under the world's largest ceiling fresco by the Italian master Tiepolo. Frederik the Great's **Sans Souci Palace** at **Potsdam** (1744–1860) is one of Europe's best examples of the rococo (p. 173).

Jean François de Cuvilliés (1698–1767), a French dwarf, was originally the elector of Bavaria's court jester until his talent for architecture was recognized. After schooling

Amalienburg, Schloss Nymphenburg

in France, he returned to **Munich** to craft its greatest rococo monuments, including the jewel box of the **Residenz's Altes Residenztheater** (p. 341), which now bears his name, and the facade of the baroque **Theatinerkirche** (p. 332). His masterpiece is **Schloss Nymphenburg's Amalienburg** hunting lodge (p. 330), which became a model for palaces across Europe.

NEOCLASSICISM & ROMANTIC (MID–18TH THROUGH 19TH C.)

As a backlash against the excesses of the baroque and rococo, by the middle of the 18th century architects began turning to the austere simplicity and grandeur of the Classical Age and inaugurated the **neoclassical** style. Their work was inspired by the rediscovery of Pompeii and other ancient sites. However, many of their interiors continued to be rococo, though more muted than before. The sterility of German neoclassicism didn't last long, however, and the 19th century left the increasing nationalist German society looking into its own past for inspiration, kicking off the neo-Gothic **Romantic Movement.**

Neuschwanstein

The Prussians remade Berlin in a neoclassical image, starting with the **Brandenburger Tor** (p. 143) and moving on to the buildings of Karl Friedrich Schinkel (1781–1841), among which **Altes Museum, Schloss Charlottenhof,** and **Nikolaikirche** are his best (p. 131, 130, and 146). There's a museum devoted to him called the **Friedrichswerdersche Kirche–Schinkelmuseum** (p. 144). In Munich, Ludwig I had Leo von Klenze lay out neoclassical structures across his "new Athens," including those surrounding **Königsplatz** (p. 323) and the nearby **Alte and Neue pinakotheks** (p. 323 and 331). Caught up in Wagner's dramatic operas set in the heroic Middle Ages, "Mad" King Ludwig II was the ultimate Romantic, building for himself a series of faux medieval fairy-tale castles, including **Herrenchiemsee's Neues Schloss** (p. 363) and the incomparable fantasy of **Neuschwanstein Castle** (p. 291), a festival of banner-fluttering towers and battlements right out of a Brothers Grimm folk tale, its entire setting chosen solely for its picture-postcard perfection.

20TH-CENTURY GERMAN ARCHITECTURE

Germany's take on the early-20th-century Art Nouveau movement was called **Jugendstil.** The **Bauhaus** was a 1920s avant-garde school of architecture led by **Walter Gropius** (1883–1969) that combined industrial-age architecture with art and craft to create functional buildings and furnishings. Among its chief designers and institute teachers were Marcel Breuer, Wassily Kandinsky, Oskar Schlemmer, and Paul Klee. The Nazis closed the school down in 1933, though it was reborn in Chicago. Jugendstil houses and hotels exist across Germany, but the movement took its name from *Jugend* magazine published in the **Schwabing district of Munich,** where many buildings in the style survive. Munich is also home to the **Jugendstil Museum** in the Stuck-Villa, a hybrid neoclassical/Jugendstil (Art Nouveau) structure. Bauhaus structures, too, pepper Germany in unobtrusive ways, often in city outskirts. One fine example includes Berlin's **Die Siemensstadt,** the first modern housing complex, built with long "slab" blocks by Walter Gropius (the founder of the Bauhaus movement). Berlin also has the **Bauhaus-Archiv Museum für Gestaltung** (p. 133), devoted to Bauhaus drawings, photographs, and some design examples.

Siemensstadt

4 Germany in Popular Culture: Books, Film & Music

BOOKS
BIOGRAPHY

Taylor, A. J. P. *Bismarck: The Man and the Statesman.* Random House, 1967. This is the story of the "Iron Chancellor," who was instrumental in unifying the German states into the German Empire.

Trevor-Roper, Hugh. *The Last Days of Hitler.* Macmillan, 1986. This is an insightful reconstruction of the twilight of the Third Reich.

FICTION

Goethe, Johann Wolfgang von. *The Sorrows of Young Werther.* Random House, 1990. This is required reading for every German schoolchild. Goethe explored the theme of suicide in this early epistolary novella.

Grass, Günter. *Dog Years* (Harcourt Brace Jovanovich, 1989), *The Tin Drum* (Random House, 1990), and *The Flounder* (Harcourt Brace Jovanovich, 1989). Grass's works deal with the German psyche coming to terms with the dreadful legacy of Nazism and World War II.

Isherwood, Christopher. *The Berlin Stories.* New Directions, 1954. Isherwood lived in Berlin from 1929 to 1933. His most famous story was "Good-Bye to Berlin," which became the source of the stage and film versions of *Cabaret.*

Mann, Thomas. *The Magic Mountain.* Random House, 1969. This is Mann's most celebrated masterpiece.

Remarque, Erich Maria. *All Quiet on the Western Front.* Fawcett, 1987. This is a classic novel of World War I.

German Literature: From Gutenberg to Grass

Even before Gutenberg invented the first printing press in the Western world in the 15th century, German literature—both oral and written—was being produced. The first written literary work known is *The Lay of Hildebrand,* a narrative poem handed down by ancient storytellers and copied by monks at the Benedictine Abbey at Fulda. Such tales of valor, love, sorrow, and death were strong in oral tradition, with the Rhine valley giving rise to many legends and songs through the centuries, Lohengrin, Roland, the Lorelei, and the Nibelungen being among the subjects.

The age of chivalry gave birth to lyric poetry in Germany. Like the troubadours in France, *Minnesingers* of the Holy Roman Empire roamed the land singing songs of love and derring-do inspired by the Crusades. One of these, **Walter von der Vogelweide,** a knight of the late 12th and early 13th centuries, is seen as the father of lyric poetry in Germany. Another early-13th-century poet of note was **Wolfram von Eschenbach,** whose epic, *Parsifal,* glorifies chivalry and religious devotion. By the 16th century, another "hero" had joined German folklore and literature, Til Eulenspiegel, a clownish fellow whose life around 1300 became the subject of story and song.

From the time of the Reformation (16th century), **Martin Luther**'s influence can be traced in many fields of the German life of the mind and spirit. His translation of the Bible into modern German was hailed as the first great literary work in the language. A Luther contemporary, **Hans Sachs,** a *Meistersinger* (a "master singer" who carried on the traditions of the earlier Minnesingers), was a prolific author of stories, poems, plays, and songs.

Publications of a picaresque novel, *Simplicissimus,* by **Grimmelshausen** (17th century), marked the start of production of long prose narratives in the country. The Age of Enlightenment in German literature dawned in the late 17th century, inaugurated by **Klopstock** in his epic, *Der Messias,* and his *Odes,* and it continued into the 18th century. Rationalization was the watchword in this Enlightenment period, or *Aufklärung.* Much writing was in the form of philosophical treatises, for example, the works of **Leibniz** and **Kant.** Also in this era, the principles of German drama were laid out by **Lessing.**

As a reaction to rationalization, a literary movement known as *Sturm und Drang* was born in the 18th century, marked especially by poetry and drama extolling both sentiment and grand passions and rejecting previous social, political, moral, and literary authority.

In this time, when ideas of storm and stress dominated the literati, **Johann Wolfgang von Goethe** arrived on the scene, a giant of letters. Dramatist, novelist, philosopher, and Germany's greatest poet, Goethe followed the pattern of the times in youth and early manhood (the *Urfaust* or *Early Faust, Egmont,* and *The Sorrows of Young Werther*). However, he soon became disenchanted with *Sturm und Drang,* turning in midlife after a stay in Italy to a classical mode *(Nausikaa).* During this period, he reworked *Faust,* so that the final product begins with storm and stress and then levels off into tranquil classicism. It was after his sojourn in Italy that he also produced *Wilhelm Meisters Lehrjahre,* a novel that served for decades as the prototype of the best German fiction.

Another literary immortal, **Johann Friedrich Schiller,** playwright and poet, a contemporary and friend of Goethe, also turned away from Sturm und Drang after presentation of *Don Carlos,* a powerful historic drama honoring liberty. Similar dramas were *Wallenstein* and *William Tell.* Schiller's outlook placed his interests in the fields of history and philosophy.

Besides these two masters of the literary world, which soon moved on from classicism to romanticism to historical romanticism, such names of world note as the brothers **Jakob and Wilhelm Grimm,** famous for their collection of fairy tales, folk tales, and myths, and **Heinrich Heine,** appeared. Many of the works of Heine, second only to Goethe as Germany's greatest poet, have become folk songs.

A poet who became known for his work in the first quarter of the 20th century was **Rainer Maria Rilke.** Another German, the novelist **Erich Maria Remarque** *(All Quiet on the Western Front),* moved to the United States to escape the political conditions of his homeland. **Franz Kafka** became known for his novels of the absurd. **Bertolt Brecht** *(The Threepenny Opera* and *Mother Courage)* chose to live in East Germany after World War II.

In 1959 **Gunther Grass** burst on to the scene with his extraordinary first novel, *Blechtrommel (The Tin Drum).* He became a spokesman for the German generation that grew up in the Nazi era and received the Nobel Prize for literature in 1999 as a poet, novelist, and playwright.

Other Germans who won the Nobel Prize for literature have been:

- **Theodor Mommsen,** 1902, philosopher
- **Paul J. L. Heyse,** 1910, novelist, dramatist, and poet
- **Gerhart J. R. Hauptmann,** 1912, dramatist
- **Thomas Mann,** 1929, novelist
- **Hermann Hesse,** 1946, novelist
- **Heinrich Böll,** 1972, novelist

The influence of German thought on the Western mind has been powerful, from as far back as the 13th century when **Albertus Magnus** became known as a scholastic philosopher, naturalist, and theologian. Through the centuries, other notable philosophers have been **Kant, Moses, Mendelssohn, Schopenhauer, Hegel, Marx, Engels,** and **Nietzsche** *(Thus Spake Zarathustra).*

FOLKLORE & LEGENDS

Grimm, Jacob, and Wilhelm Grimm. *Complete Grimm Tales.* Pantheon, 1974. This is the world's most famous collection of folktales, with a cast of characters that includes everybody from Little Red Riding Hood to Tom Thumb.

The Nibelungenlied. Penguin, 1965. Every school kid in Germany reads this great epic poem, which details the exploits of Siegfried and Kriemhild and the fall of the Burgundians. The Nibelungenlied is characterized by the violence of its emotions and its uncompromising emphasis on vengeance.

HISTORY

Beevor, Antony. *The Fall of Berlin 1945.* Viking, 2002. This is one of the most vivid accounts of the Red Army's assault on Berlin ever written.

Large, David Clay. *Berlin.* Basic Books, 2000. In this controversial and caustic survey of Berlin since 1871, the author claims that "no other place has so dramatically encapsulated the highs and lows of our modern human experience" as Berlin.

Schneider, Peter. *The German Comedy: Scenes of Life after the Wall,* translated by Leigh Hafrey and Philip Boehm. Farrar, Straus & Giroux, 1992. Comic absurdities surrounding the collapse of the Wall fill this book, but Schneider (author of *The Wall Jumper*) also explores resurgent anti-Semitism and how West Germans are coping with the flood of refugees from the former East Germany.

Shirer, William L. *The Rise and Fall of the Third Reich: A History of Nazi Germany.* Simon & Schuster, 1959–60. This story has never been told better—the complete saga of Hitler's empire from beginning to end.

Taylor, Frederick. *Dresden: Tuesday, February 12, 1945.* This book takes a new look at the destruction of Dresden by allied bombings, which was more famously brought home in Kurt Vonnegut's 1969 novel, *Slaughterhouse Five.* A British historian, Taylor debunks the theory that Dresden contributed little toward the Nazi war effort, but was "one of the foremost industrial locations of the Reich."

TRAVEL

Twain, Mark. *A Triumph Abroad.* Hippocrene Books, 1989. The American humorist's travels through Germany are comically detailed here. Read also his comments on "The Awful German Language."

MUSIC

Music is an important and pervasive facet of German life. German disunity over the centuries actually helped foster German music. The many small principalities and bishoprics that split up the German-speaking world meant that there were many courts to offer opportunities to musicians, both composers and instrumentalists. As a result, the German-speaking nations produced more composers of indisputable greatness than any other.

Today, the musical scene in Germany is as vibrant as ever. Every major city has an opera house and an orchestra, many of them world renowned. New composers are encouraged, and productions are often at the cutting edge.

A HISTORY OF GERMAN MUSIC

BAROQUE MUSIC The greatest composer of the baroque era was **Johann Sebastian Bach** (1685–1750), who was a supreme master of all musical forms of his time. Bach produced many church cantatas, especially for St. Thomas Church in

Leipzig (see chapter 6), where he served as cantor. His compositions were technically outstanding, vigorous, and profound. Little of his music was published during his lifetime, but after his death, his influence steadily grew, especially that of his organ works. The musical tradition in his large family was maintained by two of his talented sons, Carl Philipp Emanuel Bach (1714–88) and Johann Christian Bach (1735–82). The Brandenburg Concertos are highly recommended.

Bach's contemporary, **George Frideric Handel** (1685–1759), was another great composer. He first rose to prominence as musician of the court of Hannover, a post that he left to become composer at the court of St. James of England. He was a leading composer of operas and instrumental music for the court. Listen to his oratorio, *Messiah.*

THE CLASSICAL PERIOD **Wolfgang Amadeus Mozart** (1756–91), although an Austrian, cannot be omitted from any discussion of German music. His operas, with their contemporary themes and lively musical characterizations, paved the way for later composers. **Franz Joseph Haydn** (1732–1809), another Austrian, also exerted great influence on German music, especially instrumental music. Listen to Mozart's *The Marriage of Figaro* and *Don Giovanni* and Haydn's "Drum Roll" Symphony no. 103.

THE 19TH CENTURY & ROMANTICISM The 19th century was rich in musical genius. **Ludwig van Beethoven** (1770–1827) ushered in romanticism. His works included symphonies, piano concertos, piano sonatas, quartets, and many others. He greatly expanded and developed the orchestra. Tragically, he completely lost his hearing in 1819. However, the chamber music he wrote after this event shows an even greater depth and complexity than his previous compositions. Listen to symphonies no. 5 and no. 9.

Other great composers of the era include **Franz Schubert** (1797–1828), **Felix Mendelssohn** (1809–47), **Robert Schumann** (1810–56), and **Johannes Brahms** (1833–97). Listen to Schubert's *Lieder,* Mendelssohn's "Overture" to *A Midsummer Night's Dream,* Schumann's "Scenes from Childhood," and Brahms's *German Requiem.*

The giant of the 19th-century opera world was **Richard Wagner** (1813–83). His theories of musical drama exerted a tremendous influence on everyone who followed him, even his detractors. His influence can best be heard in the music of the later Romantic composer **Richard Strauss** (1864–1949), whose operas carry Wagner's ideas of character development to greater psychological depth. Listen to Wagner's *The Ring of the Nibelungs* and Strauss's *Salome.*

THE 20TH CENTURY Musical experimentation flourished in early-20th-century Germany. Austrian-born **Arnold Schoenberg** (1874–1951) developed the 12-tone system of musical structure. **Kurt Weill** (1900–50) and **Paul Hindemith** (1895–1963) tried to reach a more popular audience. During the Nazi era, many composers fled Germany. Others, like **Hans Pfitzner** (1869–1949) and Strauss, remained in an uneasy relationship with the Nazis. Listen to Schoenberg's *Five Pieces for Orchestra,* Weill's *Threepenny Opera,* and Hindemith's *Mathis der Maler.* The music of Pfitzner is still heard in such operas as *Palestrina* from 1917 and *Das Herz* from 1931. The compositions of Strauss are among the most frequently played around the globe, especially his operas such as *Salome* (1905) and *Elektra* (1909).

More recently, major composers such as **Karlheinz Stockhausen** (1928–2007) and **Hans Werner Henze** (b. 1926) have

Beyond Baroque: the Modern German Music Scene

Modern German music tastes are heavily influenced by the American or British pop worlds, but many German musicians have created their own Teutonic sounds, notably the amusingly named "Krautrock." Kraut, of course, was originally an ethnic slur used by American GIs to refer to Nazi soldiers. One critic defined Krautrock "as a mix of Anglo-American post-psychedelic jamming and moody progressive rock." Its stars were the band **Can,** often compared to the Velvet Underground, and the band **Faust,** which became one of the first acts to sign with Richard Branson's Virgin Records.

Crossing international boundaries is the German industrial metal band, **Rammstein,** which nonetheless performs almost exclusively in German. The group is known for its rock hit, "Du Hast." Rammstein is also controversial—a liquid-ejecting dildo earned them a night in the Massachusetts jail. Rammstein band members much admire the music of **Nina Hagen,** who often leads protests concerning issues such as the war in Iraq. She headlined the Drop Dead Festival in New York City in 2005.

Germany reaches its peak of electronic-techno/trance music at Berlin's annual **Love Parade,** a popular festival that originated in Berlin in 1989 and has now spread about the world. Concerts at the parade are mainly trance, house, techno, and schranz, the latter the name given to hard techno.

New German wave (Neue Deutsche Welle) was a form of punk rock and new wave music that rose in the mid-'70s. Out of this movement came a German band from Berlin, **Wir Sind Helden (We Are Heroes),** who have achieved great success, including sold-out concerts in London, with non-English lyrics.

Punk music became popular in the 1970s in the wake of the success of British bands like the Sex Pistols, who developed a devoted following in West Germany. After reunification, many punk bands such as **Slime** rose to rant against politicians who ignore the dangers of neo-Nazis in Germany. The late '70s also saw the rise of goth rock, with strong ties to the English punk rock scene. Since the turn of the millennium, goth rock has declined in popularity but still flourishes in pockets.

German hip-hop entered the main stream only in the early '90s, bringing with it graffiti and break dancing. The controversial and mysterious Berlin rapper **Sido** released *Maske,* a debut album in 2004, which was hailed as the first real German hip-hop music. His most recent release is the 2008 album *Ich und meine Maske (Me and My Mask).*

brought the traditions of Germany's musical past into the present. Listen to Stockhausen's *Gesang der Jünglinge (Song of the Youths).* Henze has won cultural awards around the world for such compositions as *The English Cat* in 1980 and *La Cubana* in 1973.

FILM

German cinema came into its own in the aftermath of World War I, although it actually began in 1895, when the brothers Skladanowsky presented their Bioscop in the Wintergarten at Berlin. Early German film has not only earned a place in cinema history, but also has been enormously influential in both Europe and the United States. *Das Cabinet des Dr. Caligari (The Cabinet of Dr. Caligari),* directed by Dr. Robert Wiene and released in Berlin in 1920, was hailed "as the first work of art on the screen." After viewing the film, the French coined the term *Caligarisme* to describe the "all upside-down" postwar world.

The 1920s saw the production of many notable German films, such as Fritz Lang's *Dr. Mabuse, the Gambler* (1922), a screen version of a novel by Norbert Jacques. In 1924, Lang achieved great popular success with his two *Nibelungen* films, which became classics. The influence of Lang's science fiction film *Metropolis* (1927) can still be seen today, and his *The Spy* (1928) became the forerunner of the Hitchcock thrillers. Carl Mayer achieved renown for his scripts, which were called "screen poems." These include the expressionist film *Genuine* (1920) and *The Last Laugh* (1924). Mayer is said to have "unchained" the camera.

In the late 1920s, Hollywood began drawing away Germany's brightest stars, including directors Ernst Lubitsch and F. W. Murnau (*Faust,* 1926) and stars such as Conrad Veidt and Emil Jannings. As the worldwide recession hit Germany, film production suffered further. The most notable film to come out of this troubled period was *Der Blaue Engel (The Blue Angel),* released in 1930. It starred Emil Jannings and brought world acclaim to its female lead, Marlene Dietrich, who later found even greater glory in Hollywood.

When the Nazis came to power, German films became propaganda tools. Nazi films reached the zenith of their power in Leni Riefenstahl's 1934 *Triumph of the Will,* acclaimed for its cinematic techniques in spite of its glorification of Nazism. She went on to make *Olympia,* her classic account of the 1936 Berlin Olympics. Her innovative camera angles and close-ups of the athletes in action were brilliant, but the films won her both praise and condemnation.

In the first decades after World War II, the German film industry was not very creative. By the 1970s, however, a group of talented directors was emerging, including Rainer Werner Fassbinder, Werner Herzog, Wim Wenders, and Volker Schlöndorff.

Currently, there are few screen giants in Germany. The Berlin Film Festival often honors golden oldies, such as *Pandora's Box,* by G. W. Pabst, starring American Louise Brooks. Many Pabst films have been restored and reconstructed. Pabst's critical treatment of social issues earned him the sobriquet "The Red Pabst" during the Weimar Republic. Franz Seitz is often honored for producing some 80 films during his career, including 1979's *The Tin Drum.*

The story of a doomed Nazi submarine, *Das Boot* (1981) still holds the record for the most Academy Award nominations for a German film, a total of six. In 2006, *Das leben der Anderen (The Lives of Others)* won an Academy Award as best foreign-language film. The film documented how Stasi (the East German secret police) spied on the lives of its citizens. In 2007, *Die Fälscher (The Counterfeiters)* also won an Oscar as best foreign-language film. Shot in Berlin, this Austro-German production told the story of how forgers were assigned the job of producing massive amounts of fake U.S. dollars and British pounds in an effort by the Nazi regime to weaken the Allied economy.

Modern films continue to offer us a glimpse of contemporary German life and culture, as well. Most of these are available in the U.S. either dubbed or translated into English. Tom Tykwer's *Lola Rennt* (1998) remains one of our favorites. It was called *Run Lola Run* in its

English release. Starring Franka Potenta as Lola, the film has been called iconic of a reunified Germany. The plot involves a young woman who has 20 minutes to find and bring 100,000 German marks to her boyfriend before he robs a supermarket. The action is riveting, the soundtrack dynamic.

In *Der Krieger und die Kaiserin (The Princess and the Warrior),* director Tykwer is reunited with Potenta. First released in 2000, the film follows the travails of Sissi, who works in a psychiatric hospital. She becomes involved with a tormented ex-soldier who stages a bank robbery. A near-death experience throws Sissi's life into chaos.

One of the freshest post-reunification films is Wolfgang Becker's 2003 comedy *Goodbye, Lenin!,* set in East Germany in 1989. A young man, to protect his fragile mother from a fatal shock after a long coma, tries to prevent her from learning that her beloved East Germany has disappeared.

5 Eating & Drinking in Germany

Though traditional dishes like dumplings, *Wurst* (sausages), pastries, and beer may make Germany seem the worst possible place to eat healthily, in reality, restaurants are offering foreign foods and neue Küche (modern cuisine). Chefs trained in Switzerland, France, or Italy return to Germany to open Continental restaurants, and Italians and Turks, many of whom originally came to Germany as "guest workers," own restaurants featuring their own culinary traditions.

REGIONAL SPECIALTIES

* **Bavaria & Franconia:** In southern Germany, you can feast on such hearty fare as *Leberkäs* (a chilled mold of minced pork, beef, and liver), *Knödel* (dumplings or soaked bread), *Haxen* (pork or veal trotters, most often consumed with sauerkraut), *Rostbratwürste* (small finger sausages), and *Leberknödel* (large liver dumplings in a clear broth). *Schweinwurst mit Kraut* (pork sausages with sauerkraut) is another unforgettable local dish.
* **Lower Saxony & Schleswig-Holstein:** Here in northwest Germany, with its maritime tradition, a typical local dish is *Aalsuppe*—sweet-and-sour eel soup flavored with bacon, vegetables, and sometimes even pears and prunes (or perhaps other fruits).

The sailor's favorite is *Labskaus,* a ground-together medley of pork, salt herring, and beef, along with potatoes and beets. The traditional topping is a fried egg and a side dish of cucumbers. *Bruntes Huhn* is salt beef on a bed of diced vegetables, a robust winter favorite. *Rollmops,* pickled herring rolled in sour cream, is another local specialty, as is *Finkenwerder Scholle* (plaice) and oysters, raw or baked with cheese.

* **Berlin:** During those cold nights in old Prussia, Berliners took comfort in their soups, notably *Kohlsuppe* (cabbage soup) and *Erbsensuppe* (pea soup), along with dark bread, especially Westphalia pumpernickel. *Hase im Topf* is a delicious rabbit pâté. Other favorites are bratwurst, a pork sausage, and *Regensburger,* a spicy pork sausage. For dessert, Berliners like *Kugelhupf,* a marvelous coffeecake, and *Käsekuchen,* or cheesecake. But probably the most typical Berlin delicacy is *Eisbein,* pigs' knuckles.
* **Hessen & Westphalia:** Famed for its hams, this region eats food guaranteed to put hair on your chest. Sample their *Sulperknochen,* made from the pigs' trotters (feet), ears, and tail,

The Best of the Wurst

The German love affair with *Wurst* (sausage) dates from the dawn of history. Every region of Germany has its own specialty, but the overall favorite seems to be bratwurst from Nürnberg, made of seasoned and spiced pork. Germans often take their *Wurst* with a bun and a dab of mustard. *Weisswurst* (white sausage) is a medley of veal, calves' brains, and spleen. *Bauernwurst* (farmer's sausage) and *Knockwurst* are variations of the frankfurter, which originated (naturally) in Frankfurt. (Oddly enough, small frankfurters, which are called wieners or Vienna sausages in the United States and *Wienerwurst* in Germany, are known as frankfurters in Austria.) *Leberwurst* (made from liver) is a specialty of Hesse. *Rinderwurst* and *Blutwurst* (beef sausage and blood sausage) are Westphalian specialties and are often eaten with *Steinhager* (corn brandy).

and served traditionally with pea pudding and pickled cabbage. Try *Tüttchen,* a ragout of herb-flavored calves' heads and calves' brains, or settle for *Pickert,* sweet-potato cakes flavored with raisins.

- **Baden-Württemberg:** In the southern region around Stuttgart, begin with such dishes as *Schneckensuppe* (snail soup), *Spätzle* (egg-based pasta), or perhaps *Maultaschen* (ravioli stuffed with ground meat, spinach, and calves' brains). A dish beloved in the area and widely consumed is *Geschnetzeltes* (slices of veal in a cream sauce). The favorite local dish in Stuttgart itself is *Gaisburger Marsch,* a beef stew. Another commonly served dish is *Rostbraten,* braised beef, invariably accompanied by sauerkraut or *Linsen mit Saiten,* lentil stew cooked with sausages.

- **Saxony & Thuringia:** In eastern Germany, you can feast on everything from *Linsensuppe mit Thüringer Rotwurst* (lentil soup with Thuringian sausages) to *Rinderzunge in Rosinen-Sauce* (calves' tongues in grape sauce). *Kartoffelsuppe* (potato soup) remains a favorite of the district, as does a baked appetizer, *Quarkkeulchen,* made from

curd, boiled potatoes, flour, sugar, and raisins, topped with cinnamon and served with applesauce. Each city in the district also has its own popular local dishes. Leipzig, for example, has its *Leipziger Allerlei,* a blend of carrots, peas, asparagus, cauliflower, mushrooms, crayfish, ox tails, bits of veal, and dumplings.

- **Rhineland:** The Rhineland features dishes that have made Germans the subject of good-natured ridicule, especially in neighboring France. For example, there's *Saumagen,* stuffed pork belly with pickled cabbage. Also beloved is *Schweinepfeffer,* a highly seasoned and spicy pork ragout that's thickened with pig blood. After that feast, it's on to *Hämchen,* pork trotters with pickled cabbage and potatoes, or else *Sauerbraten,* beef marinated in wine vinegar and spices. Postwar Chancellor Konrad Adenauer was a Rhinelander, and one of his favorite foods was *Reibekukchen,* small potato pancakes with a blueberry or applesauce. Taverns along the Rhine fill up when *Federweisser,* partially fermented new wine, comes in. They drink it while devouring onion tarts.

Fun Fact *O' Zapfstisl* ("The Barrel Is Tapped")

The oldest brewery in the world is at Weihenstephan, a former Benedictine monastery 30km (19 miles) northeast of Munich in Old Bavaria. It dates from the year 1040, although there is evidence that a hop garden already existed near the grounds of the monastery in A.D. 768. The monks here brought beer to the masses in Europe. Even today, the oldest brewery within Munich itself, **Augustiner,** reflects brewing's monastic heritage.

Over the centuries, monks brewed a strong beer for consumption during the fasting period of Lent, during which they were technically supposed to drink only water. The story goes that the pope heard about this custom and ordered that the beer be transported to Rome for him to sample. When the pope finally tasted the beer after its long journey (it didn't have preservatives back then), he decided it tasted foul and decreed that the beer was strong enough punishment for the Bavarian monks to drink it during Lent. Today, all Munich breweries brew this strong beer during Lent: *Salvator* and *Triumphator* are the best-known brands. *Ator* in German means a strong beer. By long-standing tradition, the names of German Doppelbock beers (strong beers) end with an "-ator" suffix.

BEER & WINE

BEER For variety and quality, German beer is unequaled. The world's oldest brewery is in Bavaria, but other regions in Germany have proud beer-making traditions. **Export beers** and the rather more bitter *Pils,* the most popular type of beer, are also produced in Berlin, Hamburg, the Ruhr, Hesse, and Stuttgart. *Altbier,* a very early product of the brewer's art, can be found today all over Germany.

In Germany, if you go into a beer hall and ask the bartender for *ein Bier,* you'll probably get the standard stock beer, *Vollbier,* which is 4% alcohol. More potent is *Export* at 5% or *Bockbier* at 6%. Connoisseurs specify the type of beer they want and often the brewery. The following is a bit of beer vocabulary. When the malt has been darkly roasted and fermented for much longer, it becomes *dunkles Bier,* or dark beer. *Doppelbock* is an extra dark beer with a 6% alcoholic content. *Helles Bier* is light and brewed from

malt dried and baked by the local brewery, or *Brauerei.* Many Germans, especially the citizens of Bamberg, like their beer "smoked." If that appeals to you, request *Rauchbier.* In nearby Bayreuth, Richard Wagner's old hometown, locals prefer a "steam beer" known as *Dampfbier.* The denizens of Düsseldorf and Frankfurt can often be heard requesting *Alt,* a brown, barley-malt brew. *Kölsch* is a light beer drunk mainly in Cologne in tall fluted glasses. *Hefeweizen* is a yeasty wheat beer consumed often with a squeeze of lemon. *Berliner Weisse* is made from wheat, like a Bavarian white beer, but with a dash of raspberry or woodruff syrup. Dark and sweet, **malt beer** has hardly any alcohol, whereas *Starkbierzeit* is a powerful beer served when the barrels are opened after the post-Lenten celebrations in March. It has the highest alcohol content of them all. Finally, *Pils,* or pilsner, beers are light and contain more hops. Dortmund has earned a reputation in this field.

WINE Germany has produced delightful wines for centuries, but sometime in the 1970s, German wine became the butt of jokes. The postwar German economic miracle had led to a boom in wine production. Many new vineyards sprung up suddenly, and quality was not always their first priority. Cheap, cloyingly sweet table wines flooded the market. One label in particular, Liebfraumilch, began to sully the reputation of the entire industry; the mere mention of its name to anyone in the know met with a knowing titter or contemptuous sneer. Today, however, German viticulture has many smaller producers producing excellent wines.

Good German wine is renowned for its natural lightness and its delicate balance of sweetness and acidity. Most vineyards flourish on steep hillsides, protected from harsh winds by wooded neighboring hills, especially on the banks of the Rhine and the Mosel rivers and their tributaries. The vineyards profit from the warmth reflected off the sunlit water. The slow maturing of the grapes gives German wines their typical fresh, fruity acidity.

Germany does produce red wine, but as a rule it's better to stick to white or perhaps a rosé. *Trocken* (dry) or *halbtrocken* (semidry) are often given on the labels; look for them if you want to escape anything sweet. This avoidance, however, should not extend to the dessert wines, which resemble nectar.

The overload of information on a German wine label is often puzzling to foreigners, but it's not really that hard to decipher. First of all, the grape variety should be indicated. Legally, German wines are only required to contain 85% of the declared variety. The classic is *Riesling,* which can range widely in taste from fruity to spicy. Other grapes include *Weisburgunder,* used to make dry wines, often with an aroma of melon or pear, and *Scheurebe,* which produces delicious, high-quality wine with the aroma

of red currant. No grape reference on the label often means a poorly blended, inferior quality wine.

"Vintage" refers to when the grapes were grown (not harvested). The question of origin is also something to keep an eye on. It's best if the label gives a single vineyard, but these can only be distinguished from the less specific vineyard zones if you are in the know or can consult a pocket guide, such as Johnson's.

Next, check for the level of ripeness. German law distinguishes between *Tafelwein* (**table wine**) and *Qualitätswein* (**quality wine**). QbA (*Qualitätswein bestimmter Anbaugebiete*) on a bottle means the wine is made from the approved grape varieties, which will give it the particular and traditional taste of its region. **QmP** refers to *Qualitätswein mit Prädikat* (wine with distinction) and carries one of six special attributes. These, in order of ascending price, are *Kabinett, Spätlese, Auslese, Beerenauslese* (BA), *Eiswein,* and the exclusive *Trockenbeerenauslese* (TBA).

As a classification, *Kabinett* was first used by Eberbach Abbey in 1712 to denote quality. This wine is especially good as an aperitif with light snacks or veal. The mildly sweet and fruity *Auslese* from the Mosel-Saar-Ruwer region and the rich *Spätlese* are well suited to richer dishes such as duck, smoked fowl, and oysters. Those *trocken* and *halbtrocken* Rieslings from the Rheingau and Mosel-Saar-Ruwer are perfect with pork, sausages, and sauerkraut as well as with mild cheeses. A fuller-bodied Riesling *Spätlese* and *Auslese Trocken* from Rheingau or Pfalz goes excellently with wild boar and lobster. The rarest vintages, those sweet wines carrying the BA and TBA designations, are best left for anything oily or pungent in flavor, such as gooseliver pâté or rich cheeses. They are also wonderful with desserts.

Many foreign visitors tour one of the wine-growing districts. Since reunification, a number of wine districts have emerged in eastern Germany; however, the traditional German wine country, stretching from the middle Rhine at Bonn down to Lake Constance on the Swiss border, is still the most charming, with its classic scenery of imposing castle ruins, elegant spas, and Brothers Grimm villages replete with spires and black-and-white gabled houses.

3

Planning Your Trip to Germany

This chapter covers everything you need to know to make trip planning a snap, from when to go to how to shop for the best airfare. Browse through it to get started and make sure you've covered all the bases.

1 Visitor Information

All cities and nearly all larger towns in Germany have tourist offices. The **German National Tourist Board** headquarters is at Beethovenstrasse 69, 60325 Frankfurt am Main (② **069/75-19-03**; www.visits-to-germany.com, www.germany-tourism.de, or www.cometo germany.com).

IN THE U.S. 122 E. 42nd St., Suite 2000, New York, NY 10168-0072 (② **800/651-7010** or 212/661-7174).

IN CANADA 480 University Ave., Suite 1500, Toronto, ON M5G 1V2 (② **877/315-6237** or 416/968-1685).

IN THE U.K. P.O. Box 2695, London W1A 3TN (② **020/7317-0908**).

MAPS The tourist offices of every major German town or city will give you a map of their town. Most of these are adequate unless you're seeking the most obscure streets or lanes. If you're going on a road tour of Germany, you can purchase road maps at all gasoline stations and most major bookstores. In our experiences the most detailed and reliable of German road maps are published by either *Falk Verlag* or else the auto club, *ADAC,* by Shell.

2 Entry Requirements

PASSPORTS & VISAS

Visas are not needed by citizens of the U.S., Canada, Ireland, Australia, New Zealand, or the U.K. for visits of less than 3 months. You do need a valid passport, unless you're a citizen of another E.U. country (in which case you need only an

Tips Passport

Allow plenty of time before your trip to apply for a passport; processing normally takes 3 weeks but can take longer during busy periods (especially spring). And keep in mind that if you need a passport in a hurry, you'll pay a higher processing fee. When traveling, safeguard your passport in an inconspicuous, inaccessible place, such as a money belt, and keep a copy of the critical pages containing your passport number in a separate place. If you lose your passport, visit the nearest consulate of your native country as soon as possible for a replacement.

Traveling with Minors

It's always wise to have plenty of documentation when traveling in today's world with children. For changing details on entry requirements for children traveling abroad, keep up-to-date by going to the U.S. Department of State website: http://travel.state.gov/foreignentryreqs.html.

To prevent international child abduction, E.U. governments have initiated procedures at entry and exit points. These often (but not always) include requiring documentary evidence of relationship and permission for the child's travel from the parent or legal guardian not present. Having such documentation on hand, even if not required, facilitates entries and exits. All children must have their own passport. To obtain a passport, the child *must* be present—that is, in person—at the center issuing the passport. Both parents must be present as well. If not, then a notarized statement from the parents is required.

Any questions parents or guardians might have can be answered by calling the **National Passport Information Center** at ℂ **877/487-6868** Monday to Friday 8am to 8pm Eastern Standard Time.

identity card, though we recommend you always carry a passport anyway).

For information on how to get a passport, go to "Passports" in the "Fast Facts: Germany" section in the appendix—the websites listed provide downloadable passport applications as well as the current fees for processing passport applications. For an up-to-date country-by-country listing of passport requirements around the world, go to the "Foreign Entry Requirement" Web page of the U.S. Department of State at **http://travel.state.gov**.

MEDICAL REQUIREMENTS

For information on medical requirements and recommendations, see "Health," p. 57.

CUSTOMS

You can take into Germany most personal effects and the following items duty-free: one video camera or two still cameras with 10 rolls of film each; a portable radio, a tape recorder, and a laptop PC, provided they show signs of use; 400 cigarettes, 50 cigars, or 250 grams of tobacco; 2 liters of wine or 1 liter of liquor per person over 17 years old; fishing gear; one bicycle; skis; tennis or squash racquets; and golf clubs.

Returning **U.S. citizens** who have been away for at least 48 hours can bring back, once every 30 days, US$800 worth of merchandise duty-free. You'll be charged a flat rate of 4% duty on the next US$1,000 worth of purchases. Be sure to have your receipts handy. On mailed gifts, the duty-free limit is US$200. With some exceptions, you cannot bring fresh fruits and vegetables into the United States. For specifics on what you can bring back, download the invaluable free pamphlet *Know Before You Go*, online at **www.cbp.gov**. Or contact the **U.S. Customs & Border Protection (CBP)**, 1300 Pennsylvania Ave. NW, Washington, DC 20229 (ℂ **877/287-8667**) and request the pamphlet.

For a clear summary of **Canadian** rules, write for the booklet *I Declare*, issued by the **Canada Border Services Agency** (ℂ **800/461-9999** in Canada or 204/983-3500; www.cbsa-asfc.gc.ca). Canada allows a C$750 exemption, which can be used only once a year and only after an absence of 7 days. You're allowed to bring back duty-free one carton of cigarettes, one can of tobacco, 40 imperial ounces of liquor, and 50 cigars.

Cut to the Front of the Airport Security Line as a Registered Traveler

In 2003, the **Transportation Security Administration (TSA;** www.tsa.gov) approved a pilot program to help ease the time spent in line for airport security screenings. In exchange for information and a fee, persons can be prescreened as registered travelers, granting them a front-of-the-line position when they fly. The program is run through private firms—the largest and most well known is Steven Brill's **Clear** (www.flyclear.com), and it works like this: Travelers complete an online application providing specific points of personal information including name, addresses for the previous 5 years, birth date, Social Security number, driver's license number, and a valid credit card (you're not charged the **$99 fee** until your application is approved). Print out the completed form and take it, along with proper ID, with you to an "enrollment station" (this can be found in more than 20 participating airports and in a growing number of American Express offices around the country, for example). It's at this point where it gets seemingly sci-fi. At the enrollment station, a Clear representative will record your biometrics necessary for clearance; in this case, your fingerprints and your irises will be digitally recorded.

Once your application has been screened against no-fly lists, outstanding warrants, and other security measures, you'll be issued a clear plastic card that holds a chip containing your information. Each time you fly through participating airports (and the numbers are steadily growing), go to the Clear Pass station located next to the standard TSA screening line. Here you'll insert your card into a slot and place your finger on a scanner to read your print—when the information matches up, you're cleared to cut to the front of the security line. You'll still have to follow all the procedures of the day like removing your shoes and walking through the x-ray machine, but Clear promises to cut 30 minutes off your wait time at the airport.

On a personal note: Each time I've used my Clear Pass, my travel companions are still waiting to go through security while I'm already sitting down, reading the paper, and sipping my overpriced smoothie. Granted, registered traveler programs are not for the infrequent traveler, but for those of us who fly on a regular basis, it's a perk I'm willing to pay for.

—David A. Lytle

In addition, you're allowed to mail gifts to Canada valued at less than C$60 a day, provided they're unsolicited and don't contain alcohol or tobacco (write on the package "Unsolicited gift, under C$60 value"). You should declare all valuables on the Y-38 form before departing Canada, including serial numbers of valuables you already own, such as expensive foreign cameras.

Citizens of the U.K. who are **returning from an E.U. country** will go through a separate Customs exit (called the "Blue Exit"). In essence, there is no limit on what you can bring back from an E.U. country, as long as the items are for personal use (including gifts) and you have already paid the necessary duty and tax. However, Customs law sets out guidance levels. If you bring in more than these levels, you may be asked to prove that the goods are for your use. Guidance levels on goods bought in the E.U. for your own use are 3,200 cigarettes, 200 cigars, 400 cigarillos, 3 kilograms of smoking tobacco, 10 liters of spirits, 90 liters of wine, 20 liters of fortified wine (such as port or sherry), and 110 liters of beer. For information, contact **HM Revenue Customs** at *©* **0845/010-9000** (*©* 02920/501-261 from outside the U.K.), or consult their website at **www.hmrc.gov.uk**.

The duty-free allowance in **Australia** is A$900 or, for those 17 and under, A$450. Citizens can bring in 250 cigarettes or 250 grams of loose tobacco, and 2.25 liters of alcohol. If you're returning with valuables you already own, such as foreign-made cameras, you should file form B263. A helpful brochure available from Australian consulates or Customs offices is *Know Before You Go*. For more

information, call the **Australian Customs Service** at *©* **1300/363-263,** or log on to www.customs.gov.au.

The duty-free allowance for **New Zealand** is NZ$700. Citizens over age 17 can bring in 200 cigarettes, 50 cigars, or 250 grams of tobacco (or a mixture of all three if their combined weight doesn't exceed 250g); plus 4.5 liters of wine and beer, or 1.125 milliliters of liquor. New Zealand currency does not carry import or export restrictions. Fill out a certificate of export, listing the valuables you are taking out of the country, so you can bring them back without paying duty. Most questions are answered in a free pamphlet available at New Zealand consulates and Customs offices: *New Zealand Customs Guide for Travellers, Notice no. 4.* For more information, contact **New Zealand Customs Service,** The Customhouse, 17–21 Whitmore St., Box 2218, Wellington (*©* **0800/428-786** or 04/473-6099 in New Zealand, or 04/473-6099; www.customs.govt.nz).

3 When to Go

The most popular tourist months are May to October, although winter travel to Germany is becoming increasingly popular, especially to the ski areas in the Bavarian Alps. Germany's climate varies widely. In the north, winters tend to be cold and rainy; summers are most agreeable. In the south and in the Alps, it can

be very cold in the winter, especially in January, and very warm in summer, but with cool, rainy days even in July and August. Spring and fall are often stretched out—in fact, we've enjoyed many a Bavarian-style "Indian summer" until late in October.

Berlin's Average Daytime Temperature & Rainfall (in.)

	Jan	Feb	Mar	Apr	May	June	July	Aug	Sept	Oct	Nov	Dec
°F	30	32	40	48	53	60	64	62	56	49	40	34
°C	–1	0	4	9	12	16	18	17	13	9	4	1
Rainfall	2.2	1.6	1.2	1.6	2.3	2.9	3.2	2.7	2.2	1.6	2.4	1.9

Frankfurt's Average Daytime Temperature & Rainfall (in.)

	Jan	Feb	Mar	Apr	May	June	July	Aug	Sept	Oct	Nov	Dec
°F	34	36	42	49	57	63	66	66	58	50	41	35
°C	1	2	6	9	14	17	19	19	14	10	5	2
Rainfall	6.5	5.1	5.6	5.7	5.9	5.5	5	5.1	4.2	4.8	6.5	6

CALENDAR OF EVENTS

All dates and events are subject to change. Contact the German National Tourist Board (see "Visitor Information," earlier in this chapter) for more information. The board publishes a free calendar of forthcoming events three times a year, in April, October, and January; the first two are biannual calendars and the last is a yearly preview. They give the dates of trade fairs and exhibitions, theatrical and musical performances, local folk festivals, sporting events, conferences, and congresses throughout Germany.

For an exhaustive list of events beyond those listed here, check http://events.frommers.com, where you'll find a searchable, up-to-the-minute roster of what's happening in cities all over the world.

January

New Year's Day International Ski Jumping, Garmisch-Partenkirchen. This is one of Europe's major winter sporting events. For more information, contact the tourist bureau on Richard-Strauss-Platz (✆ **08821/180700;** www.garmisch-partenkirchen.de). January 1.

February

International Film Festival, Berlin (at various theaters; announced in local newspapers). Stars, would-be stars, directors, and almost anyone with a film to peddle show up at this well-attended festival. It lasts for 10 days and is a showcase for the work of international film directors as well as the latest German films. Tickets can be purchased at any box office. Contact the **Berlin International Film Festival** (✆ **030/259200;** www.berlinale.de) for more information. Early February.

Ambiente. This is one of the principal consumer-goods trade fairs of Europe. Its origins go back centuries. For information, call ✆ **069/75-75-0;** www.ambiente.messefrankfurt.com). Mid-February.

Fasching. Carnival festivals take place throughout Germany, reaching their peak on the Tuesday (Mardi Gras) before Ash Wednesday. Particularly famous Carnivals take place in Bonn, Cologne, Düsseldorf, and especially Munich.

March

Spring Fairs. Highlights throughout Germany, especially in Augsburg, Münster, Nürnberg, Hamburg, and Stuttgart. Dates vary from year to year.

April

Walpurgis Festivals. Celebrated in the Harz Mountains. Festivities occur on the night of April 30.

May

Hamburg Summer. An entire series of cultural events, including concerts, plays, festivals, and special exhibitions throughout May, June, and July. For information, contact the **Hamburg Tourist Bureau,** in Hauptbahnhof (✆ **040/30051300;** www.hamburg-tourism.de).

International May Theatre Festival, Wiesbaden. This city near Frankfurt hosts a premier cultural event—a series of artistic celebrations lasting 1 month. For information, contact the **Wiesbaden Tourist Office,** Marktstrasse 6 (✆ **0611/17-29-780;** www.wiesbaden.de).

June

Floodlighting of the Castle, Heidelberg. Fireworks enliven the display in this storied university city. For more information, contact the **Heidelberg Tourist Bureau,** Ziegelhäuser Landstrasse 3 (✆ **06221/14220;** www.cvb-heidelberg.de). June, July, and September.

Mozart Festival, Würzburg. Mozart fans flock to this major cultural event in the baroque city of Würzburg. For more information, contact **Tourismus Zentrale,** Falkenhaus am Markt Centrum (✆ **0931/372336;** www.wuerzburg.de or www.mozartfest-wuerzburg.de). Early June to early July.

July

See **Floodlighting of the Castle,** Heidelberg, under June, above.

Freiburg Wine Tasting. Local residents and visitors enjoy the first vintages from grapes grown in the Black Forest district. For more information, contact the **Freiburg Tourist Bureau,** Rotteckring 14 (© **0761/3881-880;** www.freiburg.de). Early July.

Richard Wagner Festival, Bayreuth. One of Europe's two or three major opera events, this festival takes place in the composer's Festspielhaus in the capital of upper Franconia. Note that opera tickets often must be booked years in advance. For information, contact Festival Administration, **Bayreuther Festspiele,** Kartenbüro, Postfach 100262 (© **0921/78780;** www.festspiele.de). Late July to late August.

August

Red Wine Festival, Rüdesheim/Assmannshausen. This is held in Assmannshausen, the Rhine village most famous for red wines. For exact dates, contact the **Rüdesheim Tourist Bureau,** Geisenheimer Strasse 22 (© **06722/19433;** www.ruedesheim.de). Late August.

Musikfest Berlin, Schaperstrasse 24 (© **030/254-89-244;** www.berliner festspiele.de) takes place for a little more than 2 weeks. During the festival, Berlin plays host to orchestras, ensembles, conductors, and soloists from around the world. The festival is organized in conjunction with the Stiftung Berliner Philharmoniker. Late August to mid-September.

September

See **Floodlighting of the Castle,** Heidelberg, under June, above.

Oktoberfest, Munich. Much of Germany's most famous festival takes place in September, not October. Millions show up, and hotels are packed. Most activities are at Theresienwiese, where local breweries sponsor gigantic tents that can hold up to 6,000 beer drinkers. Contact the **Munich Tourist Bureau** (© **089/230018-0;** www.muenchen-tourist.de) for particulars or just show up. Reserve hotel rooms well in advance. Mid-September to mid-October.

October

Frankfurt Book Fair. A major international event for publishers, book dealers, agents, and authors. For more information call © **069/2102-0;** www.frankfurt-book-fair.com or contact the **Frankfurt Tourist Office** (© **069/21-23-88-00;** www.frankfurt-tourismus.de). Mid-October.

Spielzeit'europa. Schaperstrasse 24, Berlin (© **030/254-89-0;** www.berliner festspiele.de) is a 4-month season of theater and dance performances at Festspiele. October to January.

November

Jazz-Fest Berlin. This annual festival, staged at the Philharmonie, attracts some of the world's finest jazz artists, ranging from traditional to experimental. Contact the **Berlin Festspiele Ticket Office** (© **030/254-89-0;** www.berlinerfestspiele.de) for more information. Early November.

Winter Dom, Hamburg. An annual amusement fair (sometimes called Hamburg Dom) at the Heiligengeistfeld. For more information, contact the **Hamburg Tourist Bureau,** in Hauptbahnhof (© **040/30051300;** www.hamburg-tourism.de). Early November to early December.

December

Christmas Fair, Mainz. Mainz stages its Christmas fair on the Rhine for the 4 weeks preceding Christmas. For more information, contact the **Mainz Tourist Bureau,** Brueckenturm am Rathaus (© **06131/286210;** www.mainz.de). December. (Other German towns hold Christmas fairs in Nov.)

4 Getting There & Getting Around

BY PLANE

Lufthansa (© **800/645-3880** in the U.S., 800/563-5954 in Canada, or 01/805-83-84-26 in Germany; www.luft hansa.com) operates the most frequent service and flies to the greatest number of Germany's airports. From North America, Lufthansa serves 23 gateway cities. In any season, there are more than 100 weekly flights from these cities to Germany. The largest of the gateways is the New York City area, where flights depart from both JFK and Newark airports. Lufthansa has an alliance with **United Airlines** and **Air Canada** to provide seamless air service to Germany and other parts of the globe from North America. Dubbed "Star Alliance," the union allows cross-airline benefits, including travel on one or all of these airlines on one ticket and frequent-flier credit to the participating airline of your choice.

American Airlines (© **800/443-7300;** www.aa.com) flies nonstop from Chicago and Dallas to Frankfurt daily, and American's flights connect easily with ongoing flights to many other German cities on Lufthansa or British Airways. **Continental Airlines** (© **800/525-0280;** www.continental.com) offers daily nonstop service from Newark to Frankfurt. **Delta Airlines** (© **800/241-4141;** www.delta.com) offers daily connecting service to Hamburg (via Paris) and nonstop to Frankfurt from Atlanta, Cincinnati, and New York's JFK; nonstop to Munich from Atlanta; and nonstop to Berlin from JFK. **United Airlines** (© **800/538-2929;** www.ual.com) offers daily nonstops from Los Angeles, New York, and Chicago to Frankfurt and Munich, and because of the Star Alliance, discussed above, all German flights by Lufthansa or Air Canada will also be honored as a part of a United ticket. **US Airways** (© **800/428-4322;** www.us airways.com) also flies to Frankfurt and Munich daily (with nonstops from Charlotte and Philadelphia).

From London, **British Airways** (© **0870/850-9850;** www.britishairways. com) and **Lufthansa** (© **0871/945-9124;** www.lufthansa.com) are the most convenient carriers to the major German cities, including Düsseldorf, Cologne, Frankfurt, Munich, and Berlin. **British Midland** (© **0870/607-0555;** www.fly bmi.com) has daily flights to Cologne, Düsseldorf, Frankfurt, Hamburg, and Munich.

FLYING FOR LESS: TIPS FOR GETTING THE BEST AIRFARE

- Passengers who can book their ticket either **long in advance or at the last minute,** or who **fly midweek** or **at less trafficked hours** may pay a fraction of the full fare. If your schedule is flexible, say so, and ask if you can secure a cheaper fare by changing your flight plans.

- Search **the Internet** for cheap fares. The most popular online travel agencies are **Travelocity** (www.travelocity. co.uk); **Expedia** (www.expedia.co.uk and www.expedia.ca); and **Orbitz.** In the U.K., go to **Travelsupermarket** (© **0845/345-5708;** www.travel supermarket.com), a flight search engine that offers flight comparisons for the budget airlines whose seats often end up in bucket-shop sales. Other websites for booking airline tickets online include **Cheapflights. com, SmarterTravel.com, Priceline** (www.priceline.com), and **Opodo** (www.opodo.co.uk). Meta-search sites (which find and then direct you to airline and hotel websites for booking) include **Sidestep.com** and **Kayak.com**—the latter includes fares for budget carriers such as JetBlue and Spirit as well as the major airlines. **Lastminute.com** is a great

Tips Getting Through the Airport

- Arrive at the airport at least 2 hours before an international flight to Germany. You can check the average wait times at your airport by going to the TSA **Security Checkpoint Wait Times** site (http://waittime.tsa.dhs.gov).
- Know what you can carry on and what you can't. For the latest updates on items you are prohibited to bring in carry-on luggage, go to **www.tsa.gov/travelers/airtravel**.
- Beat the ticket-counter lines by using the self-service electronic ticket kiosks at the airport or even printing out your boarding pass at home from the airline website. Using curbside check-in is also a smart way to avoid lines.
- Help speed up security before you're screened. Remove jackets, shoes, belt buckles, heavy jewelry, and watches and place them either in your carry-on luggage or the security bins provided. Place keys, coins, cellphones, and pagers in a security bin. If you have metallic body parts, carry a note from your doctor. When possible, keep packing liquids in checked baggage.
- Use a TSA-approved lock for your checked luggage. Look for Travel Sentry certified locks at luggage or travel shops and Brookstone stores (or online at www.brookstone.com).

source for last-minute flights and getaways. In addition, most **airlines** offer online-only fares that even their phone agents know nothing about.

- Keep an eye on local newspapers for **promotional specials** or **fare wars,** when airlines lower prices on their most popular routes.
- **Consolidators,** also known as bucket shops, are wholesale brokers in the airline-ticket game. Consolidators buy deeply discounted tickets ("distressed" inventories of unsold seats) from airlines and sell them to online ticket agencies, travel agents, tour operators, corporations, and, to a lesser degree, the general public. Consolidators advertise in Sunday newspaper travel sections (often in small ads with tiny type), both in the U.S. and the U.K. They can be great sources for cheap international tickets. On the down

side, bucket-shop tickets are often rigged with restrictions, such as stiff cancellation penalties (as high as 50% to 75% of the ticket price). And keep in mind that most of what you see advertised is of limited availability. Several reliable consolidators are worldwide and available online. **STA Travel** (www.statravel.com) has been the world's leading consolidator for students since purchasing Council Travel, but their fares are competitive for travelers of all ages. **Flights.com** ((© 201/541-3826) has excellent fares worldwide, particularly to Europe. They also have "local" websites in 12 countries. **FlyCheap** ((© 800/FLY-CHEAP** [359-2432]; www.1800flycheap.com) has especially good fares to sunny destinations. **Air Tickets Direct** ((© 888/858-8884; www.air

Tips **Don't Stow It—Ship It**

Though pricey, it's sometimes worthwhile to travel luggage-free, particularly if you're toting sports equipment, meetings materials, or baby equipment. Specialists in door-to-door luggage delivery include **Virtual Bellhop** (www.virtual bellhop.com), **SkyCap International** (www.skycapinternational.com), **Luggage Express** (www.usxpluggageexpress.com), and **Sports Express** (www.sports express.com).

ticketsdirect.com) is based in Montreal and will book trips to places that U.S. travel agents won't touch, such as Cuba.

- Join **frequent-flier clubs.** Frequent-flier membership doesn't cost a cent, but it does entitle you to free tickets or upgrades when you amass the airline's required number of frequent-flier points. You don't even have to fly to earn points; **frequent-flier credit cards** can earn you thousands of miles for doing your everyday shopping. But keep in mind that award seats are limited, seats on popular routes are hard to snag, and more and more major airlines are cutting their expiration periods for mileage points—so check your airline's frequent-flier program so you don't lose your miles before you use them. *Inside tip:* Award seats are offered almost a year in advance, but seats also open up at the last minute, so if your travel plans are flexible, you may strike gold. To play the frequent-flier game to your best advantage, consult the community bulletin boards on **FlyerTalk** (www.flyertalk.com) or go to Randy Petersen's **Inside Flyer** (www.insideflyer.com). Petersen and friends review all the programs in detail and post regular updates on changes in policies and trends.

BY TRAIN

Many passengers, especially holders of the **Eurailpass,** travel to Germany by train from other European cities. (See "Getting Around Germany," later in this chapter, for information on purchasing rail passes.)

British Rail runs four trains a day to Germany from Victoria Station in **London,** going by way of the Ramsgate-Ostend ferry or jetfoil. Two trains depart from London's Liverpool Street Station, via Harwich-Hook of Holland. Most trains change at Cologne for destinations elsewhere in Germany. You can purchase tickets through British Rail travel centers in London (© **866/BRITRAIL** [274-8724]; www.britrail.com). See "Via the Chunnel," below, for information about the Eurostar service running between London and Brussels via the Channel Tunnel.

Train journeys can be lengthy. If you go by jetfoil, Cologne is 9½ hours away from London; by Dover-Ostend ferry, it's 12½ hours; and via the Ramsgate-Ostend ferry, it's 13 hours. Berlin can be reached in about 20 hours. Travel from London to Munich, depending on the connection, can take from 18 to 22 hours; it's often cheaper to fly than to take the train.

BY CAR & FERRY

To bring a car over from England, you face a choice of ports from which you'll continue on driving to Germany. **P & O Ferries** (© **08716/645-645** in the U.K.; www.poferries.com) has 30 to 35 ferry-boat crossings a day, depending on the season, between Dover and Calais. The crossing can take as little as 1 hour and 15 minutes. Once in Calais, the drive to Cologne takes about 3 hours. Other options involve passage from Harwich to the Hook of Holland, a sea crossing of about 8 hours. You can also take your car via the Chunnel (see below).

VIA THE CHUNNEL

The $15-billion **Channel Tunnel** (or "Chunnel"), one of the great engineering feats of all time, is the first link between Britain and the Continent since the Ice Age. The tunnel was built beneath the seabed through a layer of impermeable chalk marl and sealed with a reinforced concrete lining. The 50km (30-mile) journey between Britain and France takes 35 minutes, although actual time in the Chunnel is only 19 minutes. Once on the Continent, you can connect to Germany fairly easily.

Rail Europe sells tickets on the **Eurostar** direct train service between London and Paris or Brussels (© **800/ EUROSTAR** [387-6782]; www.eurostar. com). In the U.K., make reservations for **Eurostar** at © **0870/5186186.** The train operates 24 hours a day, 365 days a year, running every 15 minutes during peak travel times and at least once an hour at night.

The tunnel also accommodates passenger cars, charter buses, taxis, and motorcycles from Folkestone to Calais. Tickets may be purchased at the tollbooth.

GETTING AROUND GERMANY BY PLANE

From Frankfurt, most **Lufthansa** (© **800/ 645-3880** in U.S. or 800/563-5954 in Canada; www.lufthansa.com) destinations in Germany can be reached in an average of 50 minutes, with at least four flights daily.

All German cities with commercial airports have an airport shuttle service, offering reduced fares and fast connections between the city center and the airport. Departure points are usually the airlines' town offices and the city's main rail terminal. Luggage can be checked at

the DB (Deutsche Bahn/GermanRail) baggage counter at the airport for delivery to the railroad station at your ultimate destination.

BY TRAIN

Whether you travel first or second class, you'll find that the trains of **GermanRail** (**DB Rail;** © **0800/1507090;** www. bahn.de) deserve their good reputation for comfort, cleanliness, and punctuality. All are modern and fast. Both first- and second-class trains carry smoker and nonsmoker compartments. A snack bar or a dining car, serving German and international cuisine as well as good wine and beer, can usually be found on all trains except locals.

For city sightseeing, you can leave your baggage in a locker or check it at the station's baggage counter. In many cities, GermanRail provides door-to-door baggage service, allowing passengers to have luggage picked up at or delivered to their hotels. Accompanying baggage can be checked for a nominal fee. Suitcases, baby carriages, skis, bicycles, and steamer trunks are permitted as baggage. Insurance policies of various kinds, including a travel medical plan, are also available.

About 20,000 **InterCity (IC;** www. bahn.de) passenger trains offer express service every hour between most large and medium-size German cities. IC trains have adjustable cushioned seats and individual reading lights, and often offer telephone and secretarial services. Bars, lounges, and dining rooms are available, too. A network of **EuroCity (EC)** trains connecting Germany with 13 other countries offers the same high standards of service as those of IC.

Germany's high-speed rail network, known as **InterCity Express (ICE),** is among the fastest in Europe, their trains reaching speeds of 280kmph (174 mph). One of these trains runs from Hamburg, via Würzburg and Nürnberg, to Munich; another from Frankfurt, via Stuttgart to

Munich; and yet another from Berlin, via Frankfurt to Munich. Each train makes stops along the way. ICE significantly reduces travel time, making transits north to south across the country easily possible in the course of a single day. Some 200 east-west connections have been added to the GermanRail timetable to link the Deutsche Bundesbahn (west) and the Deutsche Reichsbahn (east). Additional connections make Leipzig and Dresden more accessible.

InterCity Night (ICN)—one of the most comfortable night trains in Europe—operates between Berlin and Bonn, and Berlin and Munich. Even though the train doesn't depart until 10 or 11pm, you may board as early as 8 or 8:30pm. Arrival the next morning is between 6:55 and 7:55am, and you have the option of remaining aboard until 9 or 9:30am.

The ICN offers first and tourist class. Sleeping accommodations in first class include single or double compartments with shower and toilet, and they are equipped with key cards, phones for wake-up service, luggage storage, and other amenities. Tourist class offers open seating with sleeperettes (reclining seats). The ICN is equipped with a restaurant and bistro car, and a breakfast buffet is included in the first-class fare. For an extra cost, a limited menu for dinner is offered. Advance reservations are mandatory for all sleeping accommodations.

GermanRail issues tickets for the ICN and also makes reservations. Eurail and GermanRail pass holders are accepted on this train but have to pay for the seat or sleeper reservation and also for meals. Youth-pass holders are only accepted in tourist class. Children under the age of 4 travel free, provided they do not require a separate seat; those between 4 and 12 are charged half fare.

Before leaving for Germany, you can get complete details about **GermanRail** and the many plans it offers, as well as information about Eurailpasses, at Rail Europe (© **877/272-RAIL** [272-7245]; www.raileurope.com).

GERMANRAIL TOURIST PASSES
You can buy a **GermanRail Pass** from a travel agent before you leave home. The pass allows 4 days of travel in 1 month and costs $358 first class or $277 second class. Additional days cost $48 first class and $32 second class.

A youth version of the same pass, valid only for persons 25 years of age or under and available only in second class, costs $229 for 4 days in 1 month, $245 for 5 days in 1 month, $261 for 6 days in 1 month, $277 for 7 days in 1 month, $293 for 8 days in 1 month, $309 for 9 days in 1 month, and $325 for 10 days in 1 month. Another bargain is a **Twinpass,** for two adults traveling together. This pass costs $558 for 4 days in 1 month for first class or $412 for second class. You can purchase up to 6 more days for an additional $66 first class and $50 second class.

The passes also entitle the bearer to additional benefits, such as free or discounted travel on selected bus routes operated by **Deutsche Touring/Europabus,** including destinations not serviced by trains, or excursions along particularly scenic highways such as the Romantic Road and the Castle Road. The pass also includes free travel on **KD German Line steamers** (day trips only) along the Rhine, Main, and Mosel rivers.

These passes are most conveniently available from **Rail Europe** (© **877/272-RAIL** [272-7245]). Rail Europe can also arrange cost-effective "Rail and Drive" packages that combine a certain number of days on the train with a certain number of days in a rental car. Here's an example of how it might work: Ride the train from Frankfurt to Munich, spend 3 days exploring the city, and then rent a car for a 2-day excursion to Berchtesgaden and the Bavarian Alps. The GermanRail

Flexipass is also sold by **DER Inc.** (© 800/721-2882 in the U.S. and Canada; www.der.com).

WHERE TO BUY RAIL PASSES Travel agents in all towns and railway agents in major North American cities sell all these tickets, but the biggest supplier is **Rail Europe** (© 877/272-RAIL [272-7245]; www.raileurope.com), which can also give you informational brochures.

Many different rail passes are available in the U.K. for travel in Britain and continental Europe. Stop in at the **International Rail Centre,** Victoria Station, London SW1V 1JY (© 0870/5848-848 in the U.K.). Some of the most popular passes, including Inter-Rail and Euro Youth, are offered only to travelers 25 years of age or under; these allow unlimited second-class travel through most European countries.

BY CAR

British travelers who want to bring their own cars over should see "By Car & Ferry" under "Getting There & Getting Around," earlier in this chapter.

Competition in the European car-rental industry is fierce, so make sure you comparison shop. You can make reservations by calling these toll-free numbers: **Avis** (© 800/331-1212; www.avis.com), **Budget** (© 800/472-3325; www.budget.com), **Hertz** (© 800/654-3001; www.hertz.com), **Kemwel Drive Group** (© 877/820-0668; www.kemwel.com), and **Auto Europe** (© 800/223-5555; www.autoeurope.com). You can often rent a car in one German city and return it to another for no additional charge.

There are some advantages to **prepaying rentals** in dollars before leaving the United States. You get an easy-to-understand net price, the rental process is more streamlined, and you can avoid unpleasant surprises caused by sudden unfavorable changes in currency exchange rates. Remember, however, that if you opt to prepay and your plans change, you'll have to go through some rather complicated paperwork for changing or canceling a prepaid contract.

DRIVING RULES In Germany, you drive on the right side of the road. Both front- and back-seat passengers must wear safety belts. Children 5 and younger cannot ride in the front seat.

Easy-to-understand international road signs are posted, but U.S. travelers should remember that road signs are in kilometers, not miles. In congested areas, the speed limit is about 50kmph (about 30 mph). On all other roads except the autobahns, the speed limit is 100kmph (about 60 mph).

In theory, there is no speed limit on the autobahns (in the left, fast lane), but many drivers going too fast report that they have been stopped by the police and fined, and the government recommends a speed limit of 130kmph (81 mph). Reasonable caution is recommended, for safety if nothing else. A German driver on the autobahn can be a ferocious creature, and you may prefer the slow lane.

Note: Drinking while driving is a very serious offense in Germany. Be sure to keep any alcoholic beverages in the trunk or other storage area.

BREAKDOWNS/ASSISTANCE The major automobile club in Germany is **Automobilclub von Deutschland (AvD),** Lyoner Strasse 16, 60528 Frankfurt (© 069/6606-00; www.avd.de). If you have a breakdown on the autobahn, you can call from one of many emergency phones, spaced about a mile apart. On secondary roads, go to the nearest phone. If you don't belong to an auto club, call © 01802/222222. In English, ask for "road service assistance." Emergency assistance is free, but you pay for parts and materials.

DRIVER'S LICENSES American drivers, and those from E.U. countries, need only a domestic license to drive. However, in Germany and throughout the rest of Europe, you must also have an international insurance certificate, known as a *carte verte* (green card). Any car-rental agency will automatically provide one of these as a standard part of the rental contract, but it's a good idea to double-check all documents at the time of rental, just to be sure that you can identify the card if asked by border patrol or the police.

BY BUS

An excellent, efficient bus network services Germany. Many buses are operated by **Bahnbus,** which is owned by the railway. These are integrated to complement the rail service. Bus service in Germany is particularly convenient during slow periods of rail service, normally around midday and on Saturday and Sunday. German post offices often operate local bus services (contact local post offices for schedules and prices).

The most popular bus ride is along the Romantic Road (see chapter 8), where special green-and-white buses carry tourists regularly from town to town. For more information, ask a travel agent or call **Deutsche Touring GmbH,** Am Römerhof 17, Frankfurt (© **069/ 790351;** www.deutsche-touring.com).

BY BOAT

Perhaps Germany's most beautiful features are its lakes and rivers. The mighty Rhine is the country's most traveled waterway. German cruise ships also run on the Main River between Mainz and Frankfurt; on the Danube from Nürnberg to Linz (Austria), going on to Vienna and Budapest; and on the Mosel between Cochem and Trier.

To cruise the mythically rich rivers of Germany, especially the legendary Rhine, you can book cruises on the principal carrier, **Viking River Cruises** (© **800/ 304-9616;** www.vikingrivers.com). See chapter 15 for more details.

5 Money & Costs

The major cities of Germany are some of the world's most expensive. So if you want to see the country without breaking the bank, you may want to cut short your time in Frankfurt, Munich, or Berlin and concentrate on interesting regional capitals such as Freiburg in the Black Forest, where you can cut your travel cost by anywhere from 20% to 40%. You may also want to consider a rail pass.

Although prices in Germany are high, you generally get good value for your money. The inflation rate has remained low. Hotels are usually clean and comfortable, and restaurants generally offer good cuisine and ample portions made with quality ingredients. Trains are fast and on time, and most service personnel treat you with respect.

Many people come to Germany just for winter sports. The most expensive resorts are places like Garmisch-Partenkirchen. However, if you avoid the chic places, you can enjoy winter fun at a moderate cost.

Foreign Currencies vs. the U.S. Dollar

Conversion ratios between the U.S. dollar and other currencies fluctuate, and their differences could affect the relative costs of your trip. The figures reflected in the currency chart below were valid at the time of this writing, but they might not be valid by the time of your departure. This chart is useful for conversions of relatively small amounts of money; but if you're planning on any major transactions, check for updated rates prior to making any serious commitments.

The Euro, the U.S. Dollar, the British Pound & the Canadian Dollar

The U.S. Dollar & the Euro: At the time of this writing, US$1 was worth approximately .625 eurocents. Inversely stated, 1€ was worth approximately US$1.60.

The British Pound, the U.S. Dollar, & the Euro: At press time, £1 equaled approximately US$2, and approximately 1.25€.

The Canadian Dollar, the U.S. Dollar, & the Euro: At press time, CD$1 equaled approximately US$1 and approximately 1.60€.

The chart inserted below reflects the figures in the paragraphs above, but because international currency ratios can and almost certainly will change prior to your arrival in Europe, you should confirm up-to-date currency rates shortly before you go.

Euro	US$	UK£	CD$	Euro	US$	UK£	CD$
1	1.60	0.80	1.60	75	120.00	60.00	120.00
2	3.20	1.60	3.20	100	160.00	80.00	160.00
3	4.80	2.40	4.80	125	200.00	100.00	200.00
4	6.40	3.20	6.40	150	240.00	120.00	240.00
5	8.00	4.00	8.00	175	280.00	140.00	280.00
6	9.60	4.80	9.60	200	320.00	160.00	320.00
7	11.20	5.60	11.20	225	360.00	180.00	360.00
8	12.80	6.40	12.80	250	400.00	200.00	400.00
9	14.40	7.20	14.40	275	440.00	220.00	440.00
10	16.00	8.00	16.00	300	480.00	240.00	480.00
15	24.00	12.00	24.00	350	560.00	280.00	560.00
20	32.00	16.00	32.00	400	640.00	320.00	640.00
25	40.00	20.00	40.00	500	800.00	400.00	800.00
50	80.00	40.00	80.00	1000	1,600.00	800.00	1,600.00

Some of the winter spots in the Bavarian Alps that haven't been overrun by the beautiful people give you great value for your money. And prices in a village next to a resort are often 30% lower than at the resort itself.

In Germany, many prices for children (generally defined as ages 6–17) are considerably lower than for adults. And fees for children 5 and younger are often waived entirely.

CURRENCY

The **euro** (€) is the single European currency of Germany and other participating countries. Exchange rates of participating countries are locked into a common currency fluctuating against the dollar.

For more details on the euro, check out **www.europa.eu.int/euro**.

You can exchange money at your local **American Express** (© **800/528-4800;** www.americanexpress.com) or **Thomas Cook** (© **800/223-7373;** www.thomas cook.com) office or your bank. If you're far away from a bank with currency-exchange services, American Express offers travelers checks and foreign currency, though with a $15 order fee and additional shipping costs.

Tips **Easy Money**

You'll avoid lines at airport ATMs by exchanging at least some money—just enough to cover airport incidentals and transportation to your hotel—before you leave home. When you change money, ask for some small bills or loose change. Petty cash will come in handy for tipping and public transportation. Consider keeping the change separate from your larger bills, so that it's readily accessible and you'll be less of a target for theft.

ATMs

The easiest way to get cash away from home is from an ATM (automated teller machine), sometimes referred to as a *geldautomat*. The **Cirrus** (© 800/424-7787; www.mastercard.com) and **PLUS** (© 800/843-7587; www.visa.com) networks span the globe; look at the back of your bank card to see which network you're on, then call or check online for ATM locations at your destination. Be sure you know your personal identification number (PIN) and daily withdrawal limit before you depart. *Note:* Remember that many banks impose a fee every time you use a card at another bank's ATM, and that fee can be higher for international transactions (up to $5 or more) than for domestic ones (where they're rarely more than $2). In addition, the bank from which you withdraw cash may charge its own fee. For international withdrawal fees, ask your bank.

Note: Banks that are members of the **Global ATM Alliance** charge no transaction fees for cash withdrawals at other Alliance member ATMs; these include Bank of America, Scotiabank (Canada, Caribbean, and Mexico), Barclays (U.K. and parts of Africa), Deutsche Bank (Germany, Poland, Spain, and Italy), and BNP Paribas (France).

CREDIT CARDS

Credit cards are another safe way to carry money. They also provide a convenient record of all your expenses, and they generally offer relatively good exchange rates. You can withdraw cash advances from your credit cards at banks or ATMs, but high fees make credit card cash advances a pricey way to get cash. Keep in mind that you'll pay interest from the moment of your withdrawal, even if you pay your monthly bills on time. Also, note that many banks now assess a 1% to 3% "transaction fee" on *all* charges you incur abroad (whether you're using the local currency or your native currency).

In Germany, American Express, Diners Club, MasterCard, and Visa are commonly accepted, with the latter two cards predominating.

For tips and telephone numbers to call if your wallet is stolen or lost, go to "Lost & Found" in the "Fast Facts: Germany" section in the appendix.

TRAVELER'S CHECKS

You can buy traveler's checks at most banks. They are offered in denominations of $20, $50, $100, $500, and sometimes $1,000. Generally, you'll pay a service charge ranging from 1% to 4%.

The most popular traveler's checks are offered by **American Express** (© 800/528-4800 or 800/221-7282 for cardholders—this latter number accepts collect calls, offers service in several foreign languages, and exempts AmEx gold and platinum cardholders from the 1% fee); **Visa** (© 800/732-1322—AAA members can obtain **Visa** checks for a $9.95 fee for checks up to $1,500 at most AAA offices or by calling © 866/339-3378); and **MasterCard** (© 800/223-9920).

American Express, Thomas Cook, Visa, and **MasterCard** offer **foreign**

What Things Cost in Berlin	US$	UK£
Taxi from Tegel Airport to Europa-Center	38.00	19.00
Average ride on the Underground (U-Bahn)	2.10	1.05
Double room at the Brandenburger Hof (very expensive)	384.00	192.00
Double room at the Savoy (expensive)	234.00	117.00
Double room at Askanischer Hof (moderate)	189.00	94.50
Double room at Alexandra Hotel Pension (inexpensive)	102.00	51.00
Lunch for one at Malatesta (moderate)	29.00	14.50
Lunch for one at Keller-Restaurant im Brecht-Haus-Berlin (inexpensive)	20.00	10.00
Dinner for one, without wine, at Alt-Luxemburg (very expensive)	102.00	51.00
Dinner for one, without wine, at Funkturm Restaurant (moderate)	40.00	20.00
Dinner for one, without wine, at Dressler (inexpensive)	24.00	12.00
Half a liter of beer	4.00–8.80	2.00–4.40
Coca-Cola in a restaurant	3.20–5.60	1.60–2.80
Cup of coffee	3.20–5.60	1.60–2.80
Glass of wine	5.60–12.80	2.80–6.40
Admission to New National Gallery	13.00	6.50
Movie ticket	16.00–17.60	8.00–8.80
Ticket to Berlin Philharmonic Orchestra	32.00	16.00

currency traveler's checks, which are useful if you're traveling to one country, or to the euro zone; they're accepted at locations where dollar checks may not be.

If you carry traveler's checks, keep a record of the serial numbers separate from your checks, in the event that they are stolen or lost. You'll get a refund faster if you know the numbers.

Tips **Dear Visa: I'm Off to Schleswig-Holstein!**

Some credit card companies recommend that you notify them of any impending trip abroad so that they don't become suspicious when the card is used numerous times in a foreign destination and block your charges. Even if you don't call your credit card company in advance, you can always call the card's toll-free emergency number (see "Lost & Found" in the "Fast Facts: Germany" section of the appendix) if a charge is refused—a good reason to carry the phone number with you. But perhaps the most important lesson here is to carry more than one card with you on your trip; a card may not work for any number of reasons, so having a backup is the smart way to go.

---

6 Health

Germany should not pose any major health hazards. The heavy cuisine may give some travelers mild diarrhea, so take along some antidiarrhea medicine and moderate your eating habits. The water is safe to drink throughout Germany; however, don't drink from mountain streams, no matter how clear and pure the water looks.

WHAT TO DO IF YOU GET SICK AWAY FROM HOME

German medical facilities are among the best in the world. If a medical emergency arises, your hotel staff can usually put you in touch with a reliable doctor. If not, contact the American embassy or a consulate; each one maintains a list of English-speaking doctors. Medical and hospital services aren't free, so be sure that you have appropriate insurance coverage before you travel.

For travel abroad, you may have to pay all medical costs upfront and be reimbursed later. Medicare and Medicaid do not provide coverage for medical costs outside the U.S. Before leaving home, find out what medical services your health insurance covers. To protect yourself, consider buying medical travel insurance (see "Insurance" under "Fast Facts: Germany" in the appendix).

U.K. nationals will need a **European Health Insurance Card (EHIC;** (C) **0845/606-2030;** www.ehic.org.uk) to receive free or reduced-costs health benefits during a visit to a European Economic Area (EEA) country (European Union countries plus Iceland, Liechtenstein, and Norway) or Switzerland.

If you suffer from a chronic illness, consult your doctor before your departure. Pack **prescription medications** in your carry-on luggage and carry them in their original containers, with pharmacy labels—otherwise they won't make it through airport security. Carry the generic name of prescription medicines, in case a local pharmacist is unfamiliar with the brand name.

If you worry about getting sick away from home, consider purchasing **medical travel insurance** and carry your ID card in your purse or wallet. In most cases, your existing health plan will provide the coverage you need. See "Insurance," under "Fast Facts: Germany," in the appendix for more information.

If you suffer from a chronic illness, consult your doctor before you depart. For conditions such as epilepsy, diabetes, or heart problems, wear a **MedicAlert Identification Tag** ((C) **888/633-4298;** www.medicalert.org), which will immediately alert doctors to your condition and give them access to your records through MedicAlert's 24-hour hot line.

Contact the **International Association for Medical Assistance to Travelers (IAMAT;** (C) **716/754-4883** or 416/652-0137; www.iamat.org) for tips on travel and health concerns in the countries you're visiting and lists of local, English-speaking doctors. The U.S. **Centers for Disease Control and Prevention**

Healthy Travels to You

The following government websites offer up-to-date health-related travel advice.

- **Australia:** www.smartraveller.gov.au
- **Canada:** www.hc-sc.gc.ca/index_e.html
- **U.K.:** www.nhs.uk/Healthcareabroad
- **U.S.:** www.cdc.gov/travel

(© **800/311-3435** or 404/498-1515; www.cdc.gov) provides up-to-date information on necessary vaccines and health hazards by region or country.

Travel Health Online (www.trip prep.com), sponsored by a consortium of travel medicine practitioners, may also offer helpful advice on traveling abroad. You can find listings of reliable medical clinics overseas at the **International Society of Travel Medicine** (www.istm.org).

7 Safety

Overall, the security risk to travelers in Germany is low. However, Germany experiences a number of demonstrations every year on a variety of political and economic themes. These demonstrations have a tendency to spread and turn violent, and anyone in the general area can become the victim of a random attack. Prior police approval is required for public demonstrations in Germany, and police oversight is routinely provided to ensure adequate security for participants and passersby. Nonetheless, situations may develop that could pose a threat to public safety. All foreign visitors are cautioned to avoid the area around protests and demonstrations and to check local media for updates on the situation.

In addition, hooligans, most often young and intoxicated "skinheads," have been known to harass or even attack people whom they believe to be foreigners or members of rival youth groups. While U.S. citizens have not been specific targets, several Americans have reported that they were assaulted for racial reasons or because they appeared "foreign."

Violent crime is rare in Germany, but it can occur, especially in larger cities or high-risk areas such as train stations. Most incidents of street crime consist of theft of unattended items and pickpocketing.

There have been a few reports of aggravated assault against U.S. citizens in higher-risk areas. You should take the same precautions against becoming a crime victim as you would in any city.

Report the loss or theft abroad of your passport immediately to the local police and the nearest embassy or consulate. If you are the victim of a crime while overseas, in addition to reporting to local police, contact the nearest embassy or consulate for assistance. The embassy/consulate staff, for example, can assist you in finding appropriate medical care, contacting family members or friends, and explaining how funds could be transferred. Although the investigation and prosecution of the crime is solely the responsibility of local authorities, consular officers can help you understand the local criminal justice process and find an attorney, if needed.

U.S. citizens may refer to the Department of State's pamphlet, *A Safe Trip Abroad*, for ways to promote a trouble-free journey. The pamphlet is available by mail from the Superintendent of Documents, U.S. Government Printing Office, Washington, DC 20402, or via the U.S. Department of State website at http://travel.state.gov/travel/tips/safety/safety_1747.html.

8 Specialized Travel Resources

TRAVELERS WITH DISABILITIES

Germany is one of the better countries for travelers with disabilities. All the large cities have excellent facilities. The local tourist offices can issue permits for drivers to allow them access to disabled parking areas. Newer hotels are more sensitive to the needs of those with disabilities, and the more expensive restaurants, in general, are wheelchair accessible.

Older, smaller towns may pose more of a problem, however, especially where the streets are cobblestone. Also, because of Germany's many hills and endless flights of stairs, visitors with disabilities may have difficulty getting around outside of major cities, but conditions are slowly improving. If the areas you wish to visit seem inaccessible or you are not certain, you may want to consider taking an organized tour specifically designed to accommodate travelers with disabilities.

Organizations that offer assistance to travelers with disabilities include **Moss-Rehab** (© **800/CALL-MOSS** [225-5667]; www.mossresourcenet.org), which provides a library of accessible-travel resources online; **SATH (Society for Accessible Travel and Hospitality;** © **212/447-7284;** www.sath.org), which offers a wealth of travel resources for all types of disabilities and informed recommendations on destinations, access guides, travel agents, tour operators, vehicle rentals, and companion services; and the **American Foundation for the Blind (AFB;** © **800/232-5463** or 212/502-7600; www.afb.org), a referral resource for the blind or visually impaired that provides information on traveling with Seeing Eye dogs.

AirAmbulanceCard.com (© **877/424-7633**) is now partnered with SATH and allows you to preselect top-notch hospitals in case of an emergency.

Access-Able Travel Source (© **303/232-2979;** www.access-able.com) offers a comprehensive database on travel agents from around the world with experience in accessible travel; destination-specific access information; and links to such resources as service animals, equipment rentals, and access guides.

Many travel agencies offer customized tours and itineraries for travelers with disabilities. Among them are **Flying Wheels Travel** (© **507/451-5005;** www.flying wheelstravel.com) and **Accessible Journeys** (© **800/846-4537** or 610/521-0339; www.disabilitytravel.com).

Flying with Disability (www.flying-with-disability.org) is a comprehensive information source on airplane travel.

Also check out the quarterly magazine *Emerging Horizons* (www.emerging horizons.com), available by subscription ($17/year U.S.; $22 outside U.S).

The "Accessible Travel" link at **Mobility-Advisor.com** (www.mobility-advisor. com) offers a variety of travel resources to persons with disabilities.

British travelers should contact **Holiday Care** (© **0845/124-9971** in the U.K. only; www.holidaycare.org.uk) to access a wide range of travel information and resources for disabled and elderly people.

For more on organizations that offer resources to travelers with disabilities, go to Frommers.com.

GAY & LESBIAN TRAVELERS

Although Germany is one of the "gayest" countries of Europe, there is also prejudice and hostility here. Violence against gays and foreigners (especially nonwhite) is not unknown. On the other hand, homosexuality is widely accepted by a vast number of the country's millions, especially young people. All major cities have a wide and varied gay and lesbian nightlife. Keep in mind that western Germany is far more gay-friendly than the more isolated outposts of the former East Germany. The legal minimum age for consensual homosexual sex is 18.

The **International Gay and Lesbian Travel Association (IGLTA;** © **954/630-1637;** www.iglta.org) is the trade association for the gay and lesbian travel industry and offers an online directory of gay- and lesbian-friendly travel businesses; go to its website and click on "Members."

Frommers.com: The Complete Travel Resource

It should go without saying, but we highly recommend **Frommers.com,** voted Best Travel Site by *PC Magazine.* We think you'll find our expert advice and tips; independent reviews of hotels, restaurants, attractions, and preferred shopping and nightlife venues; vacation giveaways; and an online booking tool indispensable before, during, and after your travels. We publish the complete contents of over 128 travel guides in our **Destinations** section covering nearly 3,800 places worldwide to help you plan your trip. Each weekday, we publish original articles reporting on **Deals and News** via our free **Frommers.com Newsletter** to help you save time and money and travel smarter. We're betting you'll find our new **Events** listings (http://events. frommers.com) an invaluable resource; it's an up-to-the-minute roster of what's happening in cities everywhere—including concerts, festivals, lectures, and more. We've also added weekly **podcasts, interactive maps,** and hundreds of new images across the site. Check out our **Travel Talk** area featuring **Message Boards** where you can join in conversations with thousands of fellow Frommer's travelers and post your trip report once you return.

Many agencies offer tours and travel itineraries designed specifically for gay and lesbian travelers. **Above and Beyond Tours** (© 800/397-2681; www.above beyondtours.com) is a gay Australian tour specialist. **Now, Voyager** (© 800/255-6951; www.nowvoyager.com) is a well-known San Francisco–based gay-owned and -operated travel service. **Olivia Cruises & Resorts** (© 800/631-6277; www.olivia.com) charters entire resorts and ships for exclusive lesbian vacations and offers smaller group experiences for both gay and lesbian travelers. **Gay.com Travel** (© 415/834-6500; www.gay.com/travel or www.outandabout.com) is an excellent online successor to the popular *Out & About* print magazine. It provides regularly updated information about gay-owned, gay-oriented, and gay-friendly lodging, dining, sightseeing, nightlife, and shopping establishments in every important destination worldwide. British travelers should click on the "Travel" link at **www.uk.gay.com** for advice and gay-friendly trip ideas.

The Canadian website **GayTraveler** (www.gaytraveler.ca) offers ideas and advice for gay travel all over the world.

The following travel guides are available at many bookstores, or you can order them from any online bookseller: *Spartacus International Gay Guide,* 35th edition (Bruno Gmünder Verlag; www.spartacusworld.com/gayguide); *Odysseus: The International Gay Travel Planner,* 17th edition (www.odyusa.com); and the *Damron* guides (www.damron.com), with separate annual books for gay men and lesbians.

For more gay and lesbian travel resources, visit Frommers.com.

SENIOR TRAVELERS

Mention that you're a senior when you make your travel reservations. Although all major U.S. airlines have canceled their senior discount and coupon book programs, many hotels still offer discounts for seniors. In most cities, people over the age of 60 qualify for reduced admission to theaters, museums, and other attractions, as well as discounted fares on public transportation.

Members of **AARP,** 601 E St. NW, Washington, DC 20049 (© **888/687-2277;** www.aarp.org), get discounts on hotels, airfares, and car rentals. AARP offers members a wide range of benefits, including *AARP: The Magazine* and a monthly newsletter. Anyone older than 50 can join.

Many reliable agencies and organizations target the 50-plus market. **Elderhostel** (© **800/454-5768;** www.elder hostel.org) arranges study programs for those ages 55 and over (and a spouse or companion of any age) in the U.S. and in more than 80 countries around the world. Most courses last 5 to 7 days in the U.S. (2–4 weeks abroad), and many include airfare, accommodations in university dormitories or modest inns, meals, and tuition.

Recommended publications offering travel resources and discounts for seniors include the quarterly magazine *Travel 50 & Beyond* (www.travel50andbeyond. com) and the bestselling paperback *Unbelievably Good Deals and Great Adventures That You Absolutely Can't Get Unless You're Over 50 2005–2006,* 16th edition (McGraw-Hill), by Joann Rattner Heilman.

Frommers.com offers more information and resources on travel for seniors.

9 Sustainable Tourism

Sustainable tourism is conscientious travel. It means being careful with the environments you explore, and respecting the communities you visit. Two overlapping components of sustainable travel are **ecotourism** and **ethical tourism. The International Ecotourism Society (TIES)** defines ecotourism as responsible travel to natural areas that conserves the environment and improves the well-being of local people. TIES suggests that ecotourists follow these principles:

- Minimize environmental impact.
- Build environmental and cultural awareness and respect.
- Provide positive experiences for both visitors and hosts.
- Provide direct financial benefits for conservation and for local people.
- Raise sensitivity to host countries' political, environmental, and social climates.
- Support international human rights and labor agreements.

You can find some eco-friendly travel tips and statistics, as well as touring companies and associations—listed by destination under "Travel Choice"—at the **TIES** website, www.ecotourism.org. Also check out **Ecotravel.com,** which lets you search for sustainable touring companies in several categories (water-based, land-based, spiritually oriented, and so on).

While much of the focus of ecotourism is about reducing impacts on the natural environment, ethical tourism concentrates on ways to preserve and enhance local economies and communities, regardless of location. You can embrace ethical tourism by staying at a locally owned hotel or shopping at a store that employs local workers and sells locally produced goods.

Responsible Travel (www.responsible travel.com) is a great source of sustainable travel ideas; the site is run by a spokesperson for ethical tourism in the travel industry. **Sustainable Travel International** (www.sustainabletravelinternational.org) promotes ethical tourism practices, and manages an extensive directory of sustainable properties and tour operators around the world.

In the U.K., **Tourism Concern** (www. tourismconcern.org.uk) works to reduce social and environmental problems connected to tourism. The **Association of Independent Tour Operators (AITO;** www.aito.co.uk) is a group of specialist

Tips   It's Easy Being Green

Here are a few simple ways you can help conserve fuel and energy when you travel:

- Each time you take a flight or drive a car, greenhouse gases release into the atmosphere. You can help neutralize this danger to the planet through "carbon offsetting"—paying someone to invest your money in programs that reduce your greenhouse gas emissions by the same amount you've added. Before buying carbon offset credits, just make sure that you're using a reputable company, one with a proven program that invests in renewable energy. Reliable carbon offset companies include **Carbonfund** (www.carbonfund.org), **TerraPass** (www.terrapass.org), and **Carbon Neutral** (www.carbonneutral.org).

- Whenever possible, choose nonstop flights; they generally require less fuel than indirect flights that stop and take off again. Try to fly during the day—some scientists estimate that nighttime flights are twice as harmful to the environment. And pack light—each 15 pounds of luggage on a 5,000-mile flight adds up to 50 pounds of carbon dioxide emitted.

- Where you stay during your travels can have a major environmental impact. To determine the green credentials of a property, ask about trash disposal and recycling, water conservation, and energy use; also question if sustainable materials were used in the construction of the property. The website **www.greenhotels.com** recommends green-rated member hotels around the world that fulfill the company's stringent environmental requirements. Also consult **www.environmentallyfriendlyhotels.com** for more green accommodation ratings.

- At hotels, request that your sheets and towels not be changed daily. (Many hotels already have programs like this in place.) Turn off the lights and air-conditioner (or heater) when you leave your room.

- Use public transport where possible—trains, buses, and even taxis are more energy-efficient forms of transport than driving. Even better is to walk or cycle; you'll produce zero emissions and stay fit and healthy on your travels.

- If renting a car is necessary, ask the rental agent for a hybrid, or rent the most fuel-efficient car available. You'll use less gas and save money at the tank.

- Eat at locally owned and operated restaurants that use produce grown in the area. This contributes to the local economy and cuts down on greenhouse gas emissions by supporting restaurants where the food is not flown or trucked in across long distances.

operators leading the field in making holidays sustainable.

Volunteer travel has become popular among those who want to venture beyond the standard group-tour experience to learn languages, interact with locals, and make a positive difference while on vacation. Volunteer travel usually doesn't require special skills—just a willingness to work hard—and programs vary in length from a few days to a number of weeks. Some programs provide free housing and food, but many require volunteers to pay for travel expenses, which can add up quickly.

For general info on volunteer travel, visit **www.volunteerabroad.org** and **www.idealist.org**.

Before you commit to a volunteer program, it's important to make sure any money you're giving is truly going back to the local community, and that the work you'll be doing will be a good fit for you. **Volunteer International** (www.volunteer international.org) has a helpful list of questions to ask to determine the intentions and the nature of a volunteer program.

10 Packages for the Independent Traveler

Before you start your search for the lowest airfare, you may want to consider booking your flight as part of a travel package. Package tours are not the same thing as escorted tours. Package tours are simply a way to buy the airfare, accommodations, and other elements of your trip (such as car rentals, airport transfers, and sometimes even activities) at the same time and often at discounted prices—kind of like one-stop shopping. Packages are sold in bulk to tour operators—who resell them to the public at a cost that usually undercuts standard rates.

The airlines are good sources of package deals. Most major airlines offer air/land packages, but among airline packagers, **Lufthansa Airlines** (© **800/399-5838** in the U.S., or 01/805-83-84-26 in Germany; www.lufthansa.com) leads the way. You may also wish to try **American Airlines Vacations** (© 800/321-2121; www.aavacations.com), **Delta Vacations** (© **800/654-6559;** www.deltavacations.com), **Continental Airlines Vacations** (© **800/301-3800;** www.covacations.com), and **United Vacations** (© **888/854-3899;** www.unitedvacations.com).

Several big **online travel agencies**—Expedia, Travelocity, Orbitz, and Lastminute.com—also do a brisk business in packages. If you're unsure about the pedigree of a smaller packager, check with the Better Business Bureau in the city where the company is based, or go online to

---

Tips Ask Before You Go

Before you invest in a package deal or an escorted tour:

- Always ask about the **cancellation policy.** Can you get your money back? Is there a deposit required?
- Ask about the **accommodations choices and prices** for each. Then look up the hotels' reviews in a Frommer's guide and check their rates online for your specific dates of travel. Also find out what types of rooms are offered.
- Request a complete **schedule** (escorted tours only).
- Ask about the **size** and demographics of the group (escorted tours only).
- Discuss what is included in the **price** (transportation, meals, tips, airport transfers, and so on; escorted tours only).
- Finally, look for **hidden expenses.** Ask whether airport departure fees and taxes, for example, are included in the total cost—they rarely are.

www.bbb.org. If a packager won't tell you where it's based, don't fly with it.

Travel packages are also listed in the travel section of your local Sunday newspaper. Or check ads in national travel magazines such as *Arthur Frommer's Budget Travel Magazine, Travel + Leisure, National Geographic Traveler,* and *Condé Nast Traveler.*

11 Escorted General-Interest Tours

Escorted tours are structured group tours with a group leader. The price usually includes everything from airfare to hotels, meals, admission costs, and local transportation.

Many people derive a sense of ease and security from escorted trips. Escorted tours—whether by bus, motorcoach, train, or boat—let travelers sit back and enjoy the trip without having to spend lots of time behind the wheel or worrying about details. You know your costs upfront, and there are few surprises. Escorted tours can take you to the maximum number of sights in the minimum amount of time with the least amount of hassle—you don't have to sweat over the plotting and planning of a vacation schedule. Escorted tours are particularly convenient for people with limited mobility. They can also be a great way to meet people.

On the downside, an escorted tour often requires a big deposit upfront, and lodging and dining choices are predetermined. You'll have few opportunities for serendipitous interactions with locals. The tours can be jam-packed with activities, leaving little room for individual sightseeing, whim, or adventure—plus they also often focus only on the heavily touristed sites, so you miss out on lesser known gems.

American Express Vacations (© 800/335-3342; www.americanexpressvacations.com) is one of the biggest tour operators in the world. Its offerings are comprehensive, and unescorted customized package tours are available, too.

Brendan Vacations (© 800/421-8446; www.brendanvacations.com) has a selection of 8- to 15-day tours. Accommodations are at the better hotels, and rates include everything except airfare. **Collette Vacations** (© 800/340-5158; www.collettevacations.com) has an Alpine Countries tour that covers southern Germany, Austria, and Switzerland. **Globus & Cosmos Tours** (© 800/338-7092; www.globusandcosmos.com) offers 9- to 16-day escorted tours of various parts of Germany. It also has a budget branch that offers tours at lower rates. **Maupintour** (© 800/255-4266; www.maupintour.com) has a selection of upscale tours, such as a Rhine River tour of Berlin, Dresden, Meissen, Nürnberg, and Heidelberg. Its most popular tour is a 14-day trip that takes in such cities as Dresden, Berlin, Rothenburg, Munich, Meissen, Baden-Baden, Potsdam, and a Rhine River cruise past the Lorelei Rock.

Abercrombie & Kent (© 800/554-7016; www.abercrombiekent.com) provides customized group tours to various areas of Germany.

CRUISES

The most popular cruises in Germany are along the Rhine. For more details, refer to chapter 15.

Jody Lexow Yacht Charters rents hotel barges (including crew, food, and beverages) and smaller self-drive craft for touring the canals and rivers of Germany. For additional information, contact 26 Coddington Wharf, Newport, RI 02840 (© 800/662-2628; www.jodylexowyachtcharters.com).

Canal barge cruises are the way to see a rarely viewed part of Germany. The best such packages are available through

European Barging, 25132 Oakhurst Dr., No. 130, Spring, TX 77386 (© 888/869-7907; www.european barging.com). German itineraries focus on Berlin and the Mecklenberg lakes, and the Mosel Cruise, from Trier to Koblenz.

12 Special-Interest Trips

Germany is one of the great outdoor destinations of Europe. From its mountains to its beaches, from its rivers to its castles, there is much to see and explore. It has summer attractions galore, plus skiing on its alpine slopes in winter. Here is but a sampling of the offerings that await you.

OUTDOOR ACTIVITY TOURS

E.E.I. Travel, 19021 120th Ave. NE, Suite 102, Bothell, WA 98011 (© 800/927-3876; www.eeitravel.com), offers a variety of self-guided walking and biking tours as well as cross-country skiing trips throughout Germany. It covers such areas as the Black Forest and King Ludwig's Trail, and can customize your trip.

BIKING

In Germany you can bike through green valleys and past rivers while enjoying rural landscapes and villages. **Allgemeiner Deutscher Fahrrad-Club,** P.O. Box 107747, 28077 Bremen (© 0421/346290; www.adfc.de), offers complete information on biking in Germany.

For over 20 years, **Classic Adventures,** P.O. Box 143, Hamlin, NY 14464 (© 800/777-8090; fax 585/964-7297; www.classicadventures.com), has offered bike tours of such areas as the Romantic Road. **Euro-Bike and Walking Tours,** P.O. Box 990, DeKalb, IL 60115 (© 800/321-6060 or 815/758-8851 outside the U.S.; www.eurobike.com), has a full range of bicycling and walking tours of Bavaria, as well as a 9-day biking tour of Germany, Switzerland, and France.

Dozens of companies in Britain offer guided cycling tours. One of the best is the **Cyclists Touring Club,** Parklands, Railton Road, Guildford, Surrey GUZ 9JX

(© 0870/873-0060; www.ctc.org.uk). It charges £35 a year for membership.

GOLF

Most German golf courses welcome visiting players who are members of courses at home. Weekday greens fees are usually around 48€ ($77), rising to as much as 90€ ($144) on Saturday and Sunday. For information about the various golf courses, write to the **Deutscher Golf/Verband,** Viktoriastrasse 16, 65189 Wiesbaden (© 0611/990200; www.golf.de/dgv).

The Swabian region of Allgäu has several good courses. **Golf Club Oberstaufen und Steibis** (© 08386/8529; www.golf-oberstaufen.de), at Oberstaufen, is an 18-hole course close to a forest and nature park. Ofterschwang, a small, peaceful resort on the scenically beautiful Tiefenberger Moor, has **Golf Club Sonnenalp** (© 08321/272-76; www.golfresort-sonnenalp.de). A good 18-hole course is found at **Golf Bodensee** (© 08389/89190; www.gcbw.de) on Lake Constance in southern Germany. Farther north, the city of Augsburg has an 18-hole course at **Golf Augsburg** (© 08234/5621; www.golfclub-augsburg.de).

HIKING & MOUNTAIN CLIMBING

These sports are popular in the German uplands. It's estimated that Germany has more than 80,000 marked hiking and mountain-walking tracks. The **Deutschen Wanderverband,** Wilhelmshöher Alle 157–159, 34121 Kassel (© 0561/938730; www.wanderverband.de), services the trails and offers details about trails, shelters, huts, and addresses

Germany for Jewish Visitors

Jews in eastern Europe have decreased in population because of emigration; the Jewish populations in some western countries have also decreased because of intermarriage. Germany's Jewish population, on the other hand, is slowly increasing, mostly through immigration. It's estimated that between 40,000 and 80,000 Jews now live in Germany, a figure that's nowhere near the prewar high of 500,000, but that still represents significant growth. The most prominent of the new arrivals are from the former Soviet Union. Some 70% of Jews in such cities as Bremen and Hamburg are native Russian speakers.

Berlin's Jewish community is the largest. Its 10,000 to 20,000 members are well served by several kosher restaurants, a Jewish high school, the new Mendelssohn Center at nearby Potsdam University, and a weekly and a monthly paper. Other important Jewish communities are located in Frankfurt (7,000), Munich (3,000), Düsseldorf (2,000), Stuttgart (1,600), Cologne (1,500), and Hamburg (1,500). Another 75 smaller communities are scattered throughout the country.

While anti-Semitism has not disappeared completely, in general, postwar Germany has worked hard to confront its past—far more so than Austria, for example. Some 30 museums today deal with Jewish issues, and former concentration camp sites display grisly reminders to visitors. German high schools include Holocaust studies in their curriculum. In politics, there are about 80 extreme-right groups; 20 or so are classified as neo-Nazi, with maybe 65,000 members, a small minority in a country of more than 80 million people.

Berlin has the country's highest concentration of places of interest to Jewish visitors. The **Jüdischer Friedhof at Weisensee,** a suburb of Berlin, was Europe's largest Jewish cemetery and today contains around 110,000 graves and a memorial to Jews murdered in the Nazi era. A darker sight is the chillingly elegant **Wannsee Villa,** overlooking the Wannsee (lake), where the "Final Solution" was formally proposed in January 1942. The most hopeful landmark is the newly renovated **Oranienburger Strasse Synagogue.** Unlike the other five Berlin synagogues, this glorious and immense Moorish-style structure operates only as a memorial and museum. Berlin also has two museums dedicated to the city's Jews and many monuments, such as the **Wives of Jewish Husbands Memorial,** dedicated to the hundreds of non-Jewish women who demonstrated outside Gestapo headquarters, in February 1943, after their husbands had been arrested.

of hiking associations in various regions. The **Deutscher Alpenverein (DAV),** Von-Kahr-Strasse 2–4, 80997 Munich (© **089/140030;** www.alpenverein.de), owns and operates 50 huts in and around the Alps that are open to all mountaineers.

This association also maintains a 15,000km (9,300-mile) network of alpine trails.

The best **alpine hiking** is in the Bavarian Alps, especially the 1,240m (4,070-ft.) Eckbauer, on the southern fringe of

Partenkirchen. The tourist office will supply hiking maps and details (see chapter 10). Another great place for hiking is **Berchtesgaden National Park,** Kurgarten, Maximilianstrasse 1, Berchtesgaden (© **08652/64343;** www.national park-berchtesgaden.bayern.de), bordering the Austrian province of Salzburg (p. 349). This park offers the best-organized hikes and will hook you up with various groups offering hikes.

WINTER SPORTS

More than 300 winter-sports resorts operate in the German Alps and wooded hill country such as the Harz Mountains and the Black Forest. In addition to outstanding ski slopes, trails, lifts, jumps, toboggan slides, and skating rinks, many larger resorts also offer ice hockey, ice boating, and bobsledding. Curling is very popular as well, especially in upper Bavaria. The Olympic sports facilities at Garmisch-Partenkirchen enjoy international renown, as do the ski jumps of Oberstdorf and the artificial-ice speed-skating rink at Inzell. More than 250 ski lifts are found in the German Alps, the Black Forest, and the Harz Mountains. Information on winter-sports facilities is available from local tourist bureaus and the offices of the German National Tourist Board (see "Visitor Information," earlier in this chapter).

Garmisch-Partenkirchen (see chapter 10) is Germany's most famous winter-sports center. Set in beautiful alpine scenery, this picturesque resort is close to Zugspitze, Germany's highest mountain. A mountain railway and a cable car can take you to the peak. In the town is the Olympic Ice Stadium, built in 1936, and the Ski Stadium, which has two jumps and a slalom course. Skiers of every level will be satisfied with the slopes on the mountain above the town. For information, contact the **Tourist Office** on Richard-Strauss-Platz (© **08821/180700**).

---

13 Staying Connected

TELEPHONE

The country code for Germany is 49. To call Germany from the United States, dial the international access code 011, then 49, then the city code, then the regular phone number. *Note:* The phone numbers listed in this book are to be used within Germany; when calling from abroad, omit the initial 0 in the city code.

For directory assistance: Dial © **11837** if you're looking for a number inside Germany, and dial © **11834** for numbers to all other countries.

For operator assistance: If you need operator assistance in making a call, dial © **0180/200-1033.**

Local and long-distance calls may be placed from all post offices and from most public telephone booths, about half of which operate with phone cards, the others with coins. Phone cards are sold at post offices and newsstands in denominations of 6€ to 25€ ($9.60–$40). Rates are measured in units rather than minutes. The farther the distance, the more units are consumed. Telephone calls made through hotel switchboards can double, triple, or even quadruple the base charges at the post office, so be alert to this before you dial. In some instances, post offices can send faxes for you, and many hotels offer Internet access—for free or for a small charge—to their guests.

German phone numbers are not standard. In some places, numbers have as few as three digits. In cities, one number may have five digits, whereas the phone next door might have nine. Germans also often hyphenate their numbers differently. But since all the area codes are the same, these various configurations should have little effect on your phone usage once you get used to the fact that numbers vary from place to place.

Be careful dialing **toll-free numbers.** Many companies maintain a service line beginning with 0180. However, these lines might appear to be toll-free but really aren't, costing .12€ (19¢) per minute. Other numbers that begin with 0190 carry a surcharge of 1.85€ ($3) per minute—or even more. Don't be misled by calling a 1-800 number in the United States from Germany. This is not a toll-free call but costs about the same as an overseas call.

To call the U.S. or Canada from Germany, dial 01, followed by the country code (1), then the area code, and then the number. Alternatively, you can dial the various telecommunication companies in the States for cheaper rates. From Germany, the access number for **AT&T** is 🕾 **0800/8880010,** and for **MCI,** 🕾 **0800/8888000. USA Direct** can be used with all telephone cards and for collect calls. The number from Germany is 🕾 **013/00010. Canada Direct** can be used with Bell Telephone Cards and for collect calls. This number from Germany is 🕾 **013/00014.**

If you're calling from a public pay phone in Germany, you must deposit the basic local rate.

Toll-free numbers: Numbers beginning with 08 and followed by 00 are toll-free. But be careful. Numbers that begin with 08 followed by 36 carry a .35€ (55¢) surcharge per minute.

CELLPHONES

The three letters that define much of the world's wireless capabilities are GSM (Global System for Mobiles), a big, seamless network that makes for easy cross-border cellphone use. In general, reception is good. But you'll need a Subscriber Identity Module card (SIM). This is a small chip that gives you a local phone number and plugs you into a regional network. In the U.S., T-Mobile, AT&T Wireless, and

Cingular use this quasi-universal system; in Canada, Microcell and some Rogers customers are GSM, and all Europeans and most Australians use GSM. Unfortunately, per-minute charges can be high—usually $1 to $1.50 in western Europe.

For many, **renting** a phone is a good idea. While you can rent a phone from any number of overseas sites, including kiosks at airports and at car-rental agencies, we suggest renting the phone before you leave home. North Americans can rent one before leaving home from **InTouch USA** (🕾 **800/872-7626** or 703/222-7161; www.intouchglobal.com) or **RoadPost** (🕾 **888/290-1616** or 905/272-5665; www.roadpost.com). InTouch will also, for free, advise you on whether your existing phone will work overseas.

Buying a phone can be economically attractive, as many nations have cheap prepaid phone systems. Once you arrive at your destination, stop by a local cellphone shop and get the cheapest package; you'll probably pay less than $100 for a phone and a starter calling card. Local calls may be as low as 10¢ per minute, and in many countries incoming calls are free.

INTERNET & EMAIL
WITH YOUR OWN COMPUTER

More and more hotels, cafes, and retailers are signing on as Wi-Fi (wireless fidelity) "hot spots." **T-Mobile Hotspot** (www.t-mobile.com/hotspot or www.t-mobile.co.uk) serves up wireless connections at coffee shops nationwide. **Boingo** (www.boingo.com) and **Wayport** (www.wayport.com) have set up networks in airports and high-class hotel lobbies. IPass providers (see below) also give you access to a few hundred wireless hotel lobby setups. To locate other hot spots that provide **free wireless networks** in cities in Germany, go to **www.jiwire.com**.

For dial-up access, most business-class hotels offer dataports for laptop modems, and a few thousand hotels in Germany

Online Traveler's Toolbox

Veteran travelers usually carry some essential items to make their trips easier. Following is a selection of handy online tools to bookmark and use.

- **Airplane Food** (www.airlinemeals.net)
- **Airplane Seating** (www.seatguru.com and www.airlinequality.com)
- **Foreign Languages for Travelers** (www.travlang.com)
- **Maps** (www.mapquest.com)
- **Subway Navigator** (www.subwaynavigator.com)
- **Time and Date** (www.timeanddate.com)
- **Travel Warnings** (http://travel.state.gov, www.fco.gov.uk/travel, www.voyage.gc.ca, or www.smartraveller.gov.au)
- **Universal Currency Converter** (www.xe.com/ucc)
- **Visa ATM Locator** (www.visa.com), **MasterCard ATM Locator** (www.mastercard.com)
- **Weather** (www.intellicast.com and www.weather.com)

now offer free high-speed Internet access. In addition, major Internet service providers (ISPs) have **local access numbers** around the world, allowing you to go online by placing a local call. The **iPass** network also has dial-up numbers around the world. You'll have to sign up with an iPass provider, who will then tell you how to set up your computer for your destination(s). For a list of iPass providers, go to www.ipass.com and click on "Individuals Buy Now." One solid provider is **i2roam** (© **866/811-6209** or 920/233-5863; www.i2roam.com).

Wherever you go, bring a **connection kit** of the right power and phone adapters, a spare phone cord, and a spare Ethernet network cable—or find out whether your hotel supplies them to guests.

WITHOUT YOUR OWN COMPUTER

To find cybercafes check **www.cyber captive.com** and **www.cybercafe.com**. Cybercafes are found in large cities, especially Berlin and Frankfurt. But they do not tend to cluster in any particular neighborhoods because of competition. They are spread out, but can be found on almost every business street in large cities.

Aside from formal cybercafes, most **youth hostels** and **public libraries** have Internet access. Avoid **hotel business centers** unless you're willing to pay exorbitant rates.

Most major airports now have **Internet kiosks** scattered throughout their gates. These give you basic Web access for a per-minute fee that's usually higher than cybercafe prices.

14 Tips on Accommodations

In general, Germany has one of the highest standards of innkeeping in the world. Hotels range from five-star palaces of luxury and comfort to plain country inns and simple guest houses *(Gasthäuser),* with a huge variation in rates. The cheapest accommodation is in pensions *(Fremdenheime)* or rooms in private homes (look for a sign saying ZIMMER FREI, meaning there's room for rent). Hotels listed as *garni* provide no meals other than breakfast.

Also, tourist offices will often book you into a room for a small charge. Obviously, the earlier you arrive in these offices, the more likely you are to get a good room at the price you want.

SURFING FOR HOTELS

In addition to the online travel booking sites **Travelocity, Expedia, Orbitz, Priceline,** and **Hotwire,** you can book hotels through **Hotels.com, Quikbook** (www.quikbook.com), and **Travelaxe** (www.travelaxe.net).

HotelChatter.com is a daily webzine offering smart coverage and critiques of hotels worldwide. Go to **TripAdvisor. com** or **HotelShark.com** for helpful independent consumer reviews of hotels and resort properties.

It's a good idea to **get a confirmation number** and **make a printout** of any online booking transaction.

Throughout Germany, as in many tourist centers worldwide, hotels routinely overbook, so booking by credit card doesn't automatically hold your room if you arrive later than expected or after 6pm. The hotel clerk always asks when you expect to arrive, and the hotel usually holds the room until that time. Always pad your expected arrival by a few hours to be safe. However, all bets are off after 7pm., and the hotel is likely to give your room away unless you call and specifically ask them to hold it. If you've made a reservation very far in advance, confirm within 24 hours of your expected arrival. If you're experiencing a major delay, alert the hotel as soon as you can.

Beware of billing. Readers report that sometimes in Germany they booked a room online (say, $100/£50 a night), but were charged $125 (£63) when they checked out. Keep your online confirmation in case of a dispute.

SAVING ON YOUR HOTEL ROOM

The **rack rate** is the maximum rate that a hotel charges for a room. Hardly anybody pays this price, however, except in high season or on holidays. To lower the cost of your room:

- **Ask about special rates or other discounts.** You may qualify for corporate, student, military, senior, frequent flier, trade union, or other discounts.
- **Dial direct.** When booking a room in a chain hotel, you'll often get a better deal by calling the individual hotel's reservation desk rather than the chain's main number.
- **Book online.** Many hotels offer Internet-only discounts, or supply rooms to Priceline, Hotwire, or Expedia at rates much lower than the ones you can get through the hotel itself.
- **Remember the law of supply and demand.** You can save big on hotel rooms by traveling in a destination's off season or shoulder seasons, when rates typically drop, even at luxury properties.
- **Look into group or long-stay discounts.** If you come as part of a large group, you should be able to negotiate a bargain rate. Likewise, if you're planning a long stay (at least 5 days), you might qualify for a discount. As a general rule, expect 1 night free after a 7-night stay.
- **Sidestep excess surcharges and hidden costs.** Many hotels have adopted the unpleasant practice of nickel-and-diming its guests with opaque surcharges. When you book a room, ask what is included in the room rate, and what is extra. Avoid dialing direct from hotel phones, which can have exorbitant rates. And don't be

tempted by the room's minibar offerings: Most hotels charge through the nose for water, soda, and snacks. Finally, ask about local taxes and service charges, which can increase the cost of a room by 15% or more.

- Carefully consider your hotel's meal plan. If you enjoy eating out and sampling the local cuisine, it makes sense to choose a **Continental Plan (CP),** which includes breakfast only, or a **European Plan (EP),** which doesn't include any meals and allows you maximum flexibility. If you're more interested in saving money, opt for a **Modified American Plan (MAP),** which includes breakfast and one meal, or the **American Plan (AP),** which includes three meals. If you must choose a MAP, see if you can get a free lunch at your hotel if you decide to do dinner out.
- **Book an efficiency.** A room with a kitchenette allows you to shop for groceries and cook your own meals. This is a big money saver, especially for families on long stays.
- **Consider enrolling in hotel chains' "frequent-stay" programs,** which are upping the ante lately to win the loyalty of repeat customers. Frequent guests can now accumulate points or credits to earn free hotel nights, airline miles, in-room amenities, merchandise, tickets to concerts and events, discounts on sporting facilities—and even credit toward stock in the participating hotel, in the case of the Jameson Inn hotel group. Perks are awarded not only by many chain hotels and motels (Hilton HHonors, Marriott Rewards, Wyndham ByRequest, to name a few), but individual inns and B&Bs. Many chain hotels partner with other hotel chains, car-rental firms, airlines, and credit card

companies to give consumers additional incentive to do repeat business.

For more tips on surfing for hotel deals online, visit www.frommers.com.

LANDING THE BEST ROOM

Somebody has to get the best room in the house. It might as well be you. You can start by joining the hotel's frequent-guest program, which may make you eligible for upgrades. A hotel-branded credit card usually gives its owner "silver" or "gold" status in frequent-guest programs for free. Always ask about a corner room. They're often larger and quieter, with more windows and light, and they often cost the same as standard rooms. When you make your reservation, ask if the hotel is renovating; if it is, request a room away from the construction. Ask about nonsmoking rooms and rooms with views. Be sure to request your choice of twin, queen- or king-size beds. If you're a light sleeper, ask for a quiet room away from vending or ice machines, elevators, restaurants, bars, and discos. Ask for a room that has been recently renovated or refurbished.

If you aren't happy with your room when you arrive, ask for another one. Most lodgings will be willing to accommodate you.

In resort areas, ask the following questions before you book a room:

- What's the view like? Cost-conscious travelers may be willing to pay less for a back room facing the parking lot, especially if they don't plan to spend much time in their room.
- Does the room have air-conditioning or ceiling fans? Do the windows open? If they do, and the nighttime entertainment takes place alfresco, you may want to find out when showtime is over.
- What's included in the price? Your room may be moderately priced, but

if you're charged for beach chairs, towels, sports equipment, and other amenities, you could end up spending more than you bargained for.

- How far is the room from the beach and other amenities? If it's far, is there transportation to and from the beach, and is it free?

B&B STAYS

Many travelers prefer to go the B&B route when touring Germany. This can be an inexpensive alternative to all those pricey hotels. However, some B&Bs, just like in America, are more luxurious than even a first-class hotel. Naturally, these come with a higher price tag. Breakfast, as promised in the name, is served, and often the staff at a B&B will pack you a picnic lunch if you're staying over in the area and want to go hiking. In some cases, and only if arranged in advance, a home-cooked German dinner might be served.

For reservations, contact **Bed & Breakfast Inns Online** (© **800/215-7365** or 615/868-1945; www.bbonline.com), or **BnB Finder.com** (© **888/547-8226** or 212/432-7693; www.bnbfinder.com).

BUNGALOW, VILLA & APARTMENT RENTALS

Dozens of agencies handle such rentals, the best of which include **At Home Abroad, Inc.** (© 212/421-9165; www.athomeabroadinc.com). **Drawbridge to Europe** (© **888/268-1148;** www.drawbridgetoeurope.com), offers vacation rentals in Mittel Europa, including not only Germany but Switzerland and Austria. The staff will event rent you a private castle. **Interhome** (© **800/882-6864** or 954/791-8282; www.interhome.us) offers properties in 21 countries, including Germany.

CASTLE HOTELS

There are more *Schloss,* or castle hotels, in Germany than anywhere else in Europe.

After unification, many castles in the old East Germany were restored and opened to the public. Some are rather basic, having more character than comfort, but others are luxurious with antiques such as four-poster beds and a baronial atmosphere, often harking back 3 centuries or more. Most of them have installed modern plumbing. Some visitors with a sense of the romantic book castle hotel packages throughout Germany. The best source for such vacations is **Euro-Connections** (© **800/645-3876** in the U.S.; www.euro-connection.com).

FARM VACATIONS

Growing in its appeal to tourists, a vacation down on the farm—*Urlaub auf dem Bauernhof* in German—cuts costs and is an adventure as well. Nearly every local tourist office has a list of farmhouses in its area that take in paying guests. Sometimes only bed and breakfast is offered; at other places a farm-style home-cooked dinner can be included if you wish it. For more information, you can contact **DLG (German Agricultural Association)** at © **069/247-880;** www.landtourismus.de.

HOUSE SWAPPING

House swapping is becoming a more popular and viable means of travel; you stay in their place, they stay in yours, and you both get a more authentic and personal view of a destination, the opposite of the escapist retreat many hotels offer. Try **HomeLink International** (www.homelink.org), the largest and oldest home-swapping organization, founded in 1952, with more than 11,000 listings worldwide ($75/£38 yearly membership). **HomeExchange.com** ($50/£25 for 6,000 listings) and **InterVac.com** ($69/£35 for more than 10,000 listings) are also reliable.

ROMANTIK HOTELS

Throughout Germany you'll encounter hotels with a "Romantik" in their names.

This is not a chain, but a voluntary association of small inns and guesthouses that have only one theme in common: They are usually old and charming, and romantic in architecture. If you like a traditional ambience as opposed to bandbox modern, then a Romantik hotel might be for you. The requirement is that the hotel be in a historic building (or at least one of vintage date) and personally managed by the owner. Usually you get a regional cuisine and good, personal service, along with an old-fashioned setting and cozy charm. Sometimes the plumbing could be better, and standards of comfort vary widely, but all of them have been inspected.

For more information, contact **Romantik Hotels and Restaurants** (© **800/650-8018** in the U.S. or 069/661-2340 in Germany; www.romantik hotels.com).

SPA HOTELS

More than any other country in Europe, Germany has developed the spa process to a high art. The heyday of German spa construction coincided with the rise of the bourgeoisie in the 19th century, when a lavish series of resorts was built around the dozens of mineral springs bubbling from the soil. Many of these springs had been known since the Middle Ages, or even Roman times, and to each was attributed specific cures for arthritis, gout, infertility, hypertension, and gynecological problems. (The German word *Kur—Kurort* means "spa"—is derived from the Latin *cura,* meaning "care.") Going to a spa became an intensely ritualized social experience.

In our view, no spa in Germany tops **Baden-Baden** in the Black Forest. Baden-Baden has everything—not only the waters at its opulent Kurhaus, but also Germany's best casino. And Baden-Baden has more sightseeing attractions than any other spa in Germany, more

deluxe hotels (plenty of stars and political figures come here), and better food.

Another fabled spa, though somewhat less grand than Baden-Baden, is **Wiesbaden,** which is located outside Frankfurt, in the shelter of the Rhine and the Taunus Mountains. It has one of the finest open-air thermal pools in the country, and its thermal baths include both indoor and outdoor pools, along with endless massage rooms and solariums.

After Wiesbaden and Baden-Baden, the other leading spas fall off a bit, attracting mostly those interested in specific cures. For example, **Bad Reichenhall** in the Bavarian Alps is known for its saline waters, and has a good reputation for the treatment of respiratory problems, skin ailments, and rheumatism. **Bad Kissingen** is known for mud baths, seawater Jacuzzis, and saunas—but it's a bit dull when stacked up against its more glamorous siblings. **Bad Homburg,** in the foothills of the Taunus Mountains, is long past its 19th-century heyday, but it still enjoys a reputation for the treatment of heart and circulatory diseases.

Regardless of the various medical claims made at the spas of Germany, the real reason to go to any spa, in our view, is to momentarily escape the stress of everyday life.

For more information, contact **Deutschen Heilbaderverbandes**, Schumannstrasse 111, 53113 Bonn (© **0228/201200;** fax 0228/2012040; www.deutscher-heilbaederverband.de).

YOUTH HOSTELS

Called *Jugendherbergen,* Germany has some of the best and most modern youth hostels in the world—some 550 of them are scattered throughout the country. Reservations are imperative in all cases, but especially in July and August. Venues range from rather bleak modern buildings to old castles in bucolic settings.

For more information and requirements, contact **DJH Service GmbH,** Bismarckstrasse 8, 32756 Detmold (© **05231/74010;** www.jugendherberge. de). Most hostels in Germany are affiliated with **Hostelling International USA** (© **301/495-1240;** www.hiusa.org).

Suggested Germany Itineraries

4

Germany has so much enchantment off the beaten path that it's easy to get lost here. In fact, one of the joys of travel is wandering about at leisure, making new discoveries of your own.

If you're a time-pressed traveler, you may find these two itineraries most helpful: **Germany in 1 Week** or **Germany in 2 Weeks.** If you've been to Germany before, you might want to focus on less visited parts of the country—perhaps a drive along the **Fairy-Tale Road.**

Germany is so vast and so filled with treasures that you can't even skim the surface in 1 or 2 weeks—so relax, don't even try. Instead, we recommend you enjoy only the nuggets on a first visit, including Berlin, Munich, Heidelberg, Ludwig's castles, and highlights of the Romantic Road, saving the best of the rest for another trip.

Germany ranks with France and England in offering Europe's fastest and best-maintained highway systems (autobahns), and it has one of the most efficient public transportation systems in the world, especially in its national train system.

The itineraries that follow take you to major attractions and charming towns. The pace may be a bit breathless for some visitors, so skip a town or sight occasionally to have some chill-out time—after all, you're on vacation.

1 The Regions in Brief

Germany lies in the heart of Europe, bordered by Switzerland and Austria to the south; France, Luxembourg, Belgium, and the Netherlands to the west; Denmark to the north; and Poland and the Czech Republic to the east. The country encompasses 356,216 sq. km (138,924 sq. miles) and has a population of about 80 million.

BERLIN & POTSDAM

Berlin has once again taken its place as Germany's capital and cultural center. It beckons visitors with glorious museums, wonderful cultural offerings, and cutting-edge nightlife. Southwest of Berlin is Potsdam, with its famous palace and elegant gardens and parks, set in an idyllic landscape along the Havel River. See chapter 5.

THURINGIA

Long a tourist mecca for workers from the Eastern Bloc countries, Thuringia, with its untouched villages, churches, and medieval fortress ruins, is now being discovered by westerners. If your idea of East Germany is grim industrial cities and cheap housing projects, be prepared for a surprise. Here you can still see the small towns once known to Luther, Bach, and Wagner. The region's densely forested mountains are prime hiking country. The cultural center, with many attractions, is the city of Weimar, once the bastion of such greats as Walter Gropius, Mies van der Rohe, Liszt, Goethe, and Schiller. See chapter 6.

SAXONY: LEIPZIG & DRESDEN

Known for its annual trade fair that draws participants from around the world, Leipzig is the most important industrial center in the east after Berlin. But this city, once the home of Bach, is also a cultural treasure, with museums, old churches, and Thomanerchor (the famous boys' choir). For those who find Berlin too overwhelming, Leipzig offers an excellent alternative. See chapter 6.

But if it's a choice between Leipzig and Dresden, make it Dresden, still one of the most beautiful cities in Germany, though 80% of its center was destroyed in an infamous 1945 Allied air raid. Today, Dresden is bouncing back fast, particularly in light of the reopening of the Frauenkirche in 2005. See chapter 6.

FRANCONIA & THE GERMAN DANUBE

Some of Germany's greatest medieval and Renaissance treasures came from this region, which gave the world such artists as Albrecht Dürer and Lucas Cranach the Elder. Come here to visit some of the most beautiful and historical towns in Germany, notably Regensburg, Bamberg, Nürnberg, and Bayreuth, where Wagner built his theater and created Festspiele, the famous opera festival. Though tourists often pass it by, Regensburg, about 100km (60 miles) southeast of Nürnberg, is well worth a visit. It suffered no major bombings in World War II and so remains one of the best-preserved cities in Germany. Nürnberg, although it holds much interest today with its many preserved art treasures, was heavily bombed and had to be virtually rebuilt. The Danube, which flows through this region, isn't blue and doesn't have the allure, dramatic scenery, or castles of the Rhine, but it's worth exploring for its own quiet charm. See chapter 7.

THE ROMANTIC ROAD

One of the most scenically beautiful (but overrun) attractions in Germany, the Romantische Strasse winds south from Würzburg to the little town of Füssen at the foot of the Bavarian Alps. Don't miss Würzburg, Germany's baroque city on the banks of the Main River. This glorious old city is overlooked by a fortified castle. Along the way, Rothenburg ob der Tauber is one of the most splendidly preserved medieval towns in Europe. The road comes to an end at "Mad" King Ludwig's most fantastic creation: Neuschwanstein Castle. The Romantic Road, originally a bit of PR hype to promote the area, was launched in 1950. It was such a success that the road is now clogged with traffic in summer, so the trip is best made in spring or autumn, before the tour buses arrive. (For an admittedly less scenic, but still charming, "romantic road," try the Fairy-Tale Road in Lower Saxony and North Hesse; see below.) The region of the Romantic Road is known for its folk traditions, old-world charm, and unspoiled medieval towns still surrounded by their original walls. Despite its drawbacks, the road remains one of the most beautiful and interesting trails in Europe. See chapter 8.

MUNICH & THE BAVARIAN ALPS

Rebuilt from the rubble of World War II, Munich is one of the most visited cities of Europe and probably the best place in Germany for old-fashioned fun. It should be included even on the briefest of itineraries. As chic and cosmopolitan as Frankfurt or Berlin, Munich is also kitschy in the best sense of Bavarian tradition. A night at the Hofbräuhaus, Germany's most fabled beer hall, with its liter mugs and oom-pah bands, will get you into the spirit of Munich life. After strolling through the Englischer Garten and having a glass of

Bavarian wine in Schwabing (the legendary artists' district), you can tackle Munich's vast array of museums and palaces. Save time for the Deutsches Museum, the largest technological museum in the world. Munich also lies at the gateway to the Bavarian Alps. Shimmering alpine lakes, half-timbered houses frescoed with paintings, and picture-postcard towns like Mittenwald and Oberammergau are all here, plus hiking, nature, wildlife, and alpine-ski trails in winter. See chapters 9 and 10.

LAKE CONSTANCE (BODENSEE)

The 260km (162-mile) coastline of the Bodensee is shared with Austria and Switzerland, but Germany got the best part, the lake's beautiful northern rim. A boat trip on the Bodensee, while not comparable to a Rhine cruise, is a major attraction. The tour takes in castles and towns built on islands near the shoreline. The best place to be based is Lindau, at the southeastern part, near the Austrian border. Reached by a causeway, this island town has the most luxuriant flowers and shrubs of any resort along the lake. But Konstanz, the largest city on the lake, also merits a visit because it's one of the best-preserved major medieval cities in Germany. See chapter 11.

THE BLACK FOREST (SCHWARZWALD)

This dense fir forest, filled with beauty, charm, and myth, actually receives more sunshine than most other forests in Germany. The major center of the region is Freiburg, but the most visited city is the elegant Baden-Baden resort. Black Forest cake and smoked ham may be reason enough to visit the area, but other draws include casino gambling, great spas, hiking, bicycling, and cross-country skiing. Freiburg im Breisgau remains one of the most beautiful and historic towns in Germany and makes the best center for exploring the region. If you want a Black

Forest cuckoo clock—just as good as those sold in Switzerland—head for Triberg. See chapter 12.

HEIDELBERG & THE NECKAR VALLEY

Except for the Bavarian Alps, there is no more tranquil and scenic part of Germany than the Neckar Valley. The area's Burgenstrasse (Castle Rd.) has more castles than any comparable stretch along the mighty Rhine, and the Neckar River Valley is just as romantically charming as the more overrun Romantic Road. Allow time to take detours into hidden side valleys to see sleepy little towns, most often with a protective castle hovering over them. Heidelberg, the apotheosis of romantic Germany, needs no selling. This famous medieval university town, with its historic castle, perfectly captures the spirit of south Germany and has attracted poets and composers over the decades. Goethe and hard-to-impress Mark Twain both fell in love here—Goethe with a woman of striking beauty and the more cynical Twain with Heidelberg itself. Unfortunately, Heidelberg suffers from overcrowding, especially in July and August, when tourists descend by the busload. See chapter 13.

STUTTGART & TUBINGEN

The capital of the state of Baden-Württemberg, Stuttgart is an industrial giant, headquarters of both Mercedes and Porsche. It's also a city of world-class museums and home to the acclaimed Stuttgart Ballet and Stuttgart State Opera. Its setting, surrounded by green hills with vineyards and orchards, is attractive, but the town isn't a serious contender for visitors when compared to Berlin or Munich. If you can give Stuttgart a day, fine. If not, head at once to nearby Tübingen, the ancient university city on the upper Neckar that has been compared favorably to Heidelberg.

It doesn't have Heidelberg's grandeur (or its hordes of visitors), but we prefer its youthful air, its tranquillity, and the quiet beauty of its half-timbered houses and alleyways. Don't worry about rushing around to see a lot of attractions—just soak up the old-time atmosphere. See chapter 13.

FRANKFURT

Called "the Manhattan of Germany" because of its location on the Main River, Frankfurt is vibrant, dynamic, and flashy, earning it the dubious distinction of the most Americanized city in Germany, maybe in Europe. Come here for the glitz and excitement of a major world player on the financial scene, the thriving, modern, and international metropolis, not for "Romantic Road" architecture. Our recommendation is to treat it as a center worthy of at least 2 days of your time (it has any number of attractions), rather than as a transit hub. For many visitors, Frankfurt is their introduction to Germany, in the way that New York is the entry to America for thousands. Like New York, Frankfurt is hardly typical of the country in which it sits, but that doesn't mean you can't have a good time here. It's very civilized and filled with artistic treasures—in fact, the metropolis spends more per year on the arts than any other city in Europe. When not attending the ballet, a Frankfurter may be found slugging down a few jugs of apple wine in the open-air taverns of Sachsenhausen on the city's Left Bank. See chapter 14.

THE RHINELAND

After the Rhine's beginnings, in the mountains of Switzerland, as a narrow stream, this mighty river of legend flows for some 1,370km (850 miles) through one of the most picturesque and industrialized regions of Europe. For 2,000 years, it has been a major trade route. Bonn, Cologne, Düsseldorf, and Koblenz all lie on its banks. For most visitors, the number-one attraction is a romantic cruise down the Rhine, through gorges and past ancient castles, vineyards, and the fabled Lorelei. The most panoramic stretch is between Rüdesheim and Koblenz. Start your Rhine cruise at Rüdesheim, Germany's favorite wine village, about 72km (45 miles) west of Frankfurt. If you have time for only one Rhineland city, make it Cologne rather than the more commercialized Düsseldorf. Cologne is dominated by its famous cathedral, the largest in Germany, but this ancient city is also filled with dozens of other attractions, including restored Romanesque churches, striking Roman ruins, and the best modern-art galleries in the country. See chapter 15.

THE MOSEL VALLEY

Known as La Moselle in nearby France, the Mosel River weaves a snakelike path through the mountains west of the Rhineland. It doesn't have the Rhine's dramatic scenery, but we somehow prefer it, with its vineyards, castles, and fortresses that attract far fewer visitors. The swift-moving Rhine is filled with commercial traffic, but the Mosel is slow moving, tranquil, and inviting, dotted with sleepy wine towns where you can sample some of the world's greatest vintages. Trains rumble all night along the Rhine, but not on the Mosel. (The inevitable tour buses do get through, however.) The best time to visit is during the annual fall grape harvest, centering in Cochem or Bernkastel-Kues. We've saved the best of this area for last: Near the Luxembourg border lies Trier, one of Europe's most fascinating antiques and the oldest city in Germany; it existed 1,300 years before Rome. Trier is a virtual theme park of Roman culture and architecture. See chapter 16.

LOWER SAXONY & NORTH HESSE: THE FAIRY-TALE ROAD

Hansel and Gretel, Rumpelstiltskin, the Pied Piper, and even Cinderella list their addresses as "the Fairy-Tale Road." Frankly, the Fairy-Tale Road isn't as architecturally splendid as the Romantic Road, but it's also not as crowded, and it does have a wealth of treasures for visitors interested in German lore and legend or lovers of the tales of the Brothers Grimm, who lived and worked here. The road begins at Hanau, just east of Frankfurt, and stretches for 600km (370 miles) north, coming to an end in Bremen. The trail passes through colorful towns with half-timbered buildings and past plenty of castles. Naturally, it's haunted by witches, goblins, and memories of the Pied Piper of Hameln. See chapter 17.

HAMBURG

The port city of Hamburg is exhilarating. The Germans often go to Frankfurt "for the banking," but to Hamburg "to have a good time." This Hanseatic city along the Elbe River has been beautifully rebuilt after the devastation caused by bombers in World War II, especially the night of July 28, 1943. A city of lakes, parks, and tree-lined canals, it is more famous for the tall tales of its red-light district. But these steamy after-dark diversions are only a small part of what Hamburg is. Restored architectural masterpieces and historic churches give this industrial city of two million prestige and allure. The world press may still call Hamburg Germany's "capital of lust" because of its sex clubs, but the city is also concerned with its environment, historical preservation, and art and intellectual pursuits. If you can, spend at least 2 days here. See chapter 18.

SCHLESWIG-HOLSTEIN

This northwestern corridor of Germany, sandwiched between the North Sea and the Baltic, evokes bucolic Denmark, to which it was linked before Bismarck's defeat of that Scandinavian country in 1867.

Germany's northernmost province is one of our favorites because of its offshore vacation islands and the chance it offers to escape from the industrialization of northern Germany into acres upon acres of rolling green fields used for agriculture. Large areas are still forested, and there is enough moorland to delight a native of Yorkshire, England. Most interesting historically is the ancient merchant city of Lübeck, former capital of the Hanseatic League and the hometown of Thomas Mann, the great German writer. Although heavily restored after World War II, Lübeck is loaded with attractions, and its Altstadt (old town) has been designated a UNESCO World Heritage Site. The province is also home to Germany's most sophisticated seaside resort and its northernmost point, the island of Sylt, famed for its cosmopolitan atmosphere, its celebrities, and its climate of iodine-rich air and lots of rain. The port city of Kiel is short on charm because it was severely bombed in World War II, but the ancient stronghold of Schleswig invites wandering, exploring, and dreaming of the golden age of the Vikings. See chapter 19.

2 Germany in 1 Week

The very title of this tour is a misnomer. There is no way you can see Germany in 1 week. But you can have a memorable vacation in Berlin and Munich and see some highlights of Germany in 1 week, if you budget your time carefully.

Days ❶ & ❷: Arrive in Berlin ⟨★★★⟩

Take a flight that arrives in Berlin as early as possible on **Day 1.** After unpacking at your hotel, set out to visit the **Brandenburg Gate** (p. 143), symbol of Berlin, and then walk down **Unter den Linden** (the main drag of Berlin), stopping for a German pastry and a coffee at one of the cafes that line the edges of this boulevard.

Spend the rest of the morning at the **Gemäldegalerie** (p. 134) museum, viewing some of the great masterpieces of early German artists as well as an array of international painters (especially rich in the Italian department). If the weather's fair, take a boat tour of the Spree (the main river of Berlin) and have lunch in a typical tavern. In the afternoon, climb the dome of the **Reichstag** (p. 146), the German Parliament building.

In what's left of your afternoon, visit what used to be called East Berlin, taking in the beautiful neoclassical square, **Gendarmenmarkt,** and exploring the rebuilt **Nikolaiviertel (Nikolai Quarter;** p. 146). After a rest back at your hotel, take in some of Berlin's fabled night life.

On **Day 2,** begin your morning with a tour of **Schloss Charlottenburg** (p. 175), one of the great baroque palaces of Germany. Allow at least 1½ hours for a tour. Nearby you can visit **Die Sammlung Berggruen** (p. 130), with its Picasso collection, if time remains. End your morning with a stroll through Charlottenburg's beautiful formal gardens.

After lunch in a typical Berlin restaurant, head for the **Altes Museum** (p. 131). Even if you don't have time to explore this Museum of Antiquities in depth, view the most famous lady in Berlin, the celebrated colored bust of Queen Nefertiti, dating from 1360 B.C. Highlights of the Egyptian Museum collection will rest on the ground floor here until 2009 (when the collection will be moved to the Neue Museum).

While on Museumsinsel, seeing the Altes Museum, head for the **Pergamon Museum** (p. 132), with its Greek and Roman antiquities. The Pergamon Altar is the highlight of this collection, as is the colossal blue Ishtar Gate which once stood in Babylon in 575 B.C.

Spend the rest of the day going for a refreshing stroll through Berlin's **Tiergarten** (p. 149), the most famous park in Berlin. That evening, take in a cultural presentation at one of Berlin's famous opera houses, perhaps a performance of one of its symphony orchestras. Not into classical music? Then head for the cabaret, old chum.

Day ❸: A Side Trip to Potsdam ⟨★★★⟩

While still based at a hotel in Berlin, take the S-Bahn to the baroque town of **Potsdam,** on the Havel River. While at Germany's answer to Versailles, you can wander for hours, exploring the palaces and gardens of **Sans Souci** (p. 173), which was the former palace of Frederick the Great. After lunch, you can also tour **Schloss Cecilienhof** (p. 175), the former country house of Kaiser Wilhelm II and site of the 1945 Potsdam Conference that included Truman, Stalin, and Churchill.

Return to Berlin by fast train in the afternoon for a final look at Germany's unified capital. Before the day completely fades, pay a visit to the **Kaiser Wilhelm Memorial Church,** in western Berlin (p. 136), and stroll down the **Kurfürstendamm** (known as Ku'Damm), the most famous boulevard in western Berlin.

For something truly typical and evocative, have a mug of beer and regional food in a *Kneipe* (the Berlin equivalent of a London pub). Try **Lutter und Wegner 1811** (p. 167).

Day ❹: Nürnberg ⟨★★⟩

In 6 hours, you can take a train from Berlin to Nürnberg, deep in the heart of Franconia. This ancient city, heavily

Suggested Germany Itineraries

Germany in 1 Week ![1]

Days 1–2: Berlin
Day 3: Potsdam
Day 4: Nürnberg
Days 5–6: Munich
Day 7: Ludwig's Castles

Germany in 2 Weeks ![2]

Day 8: Augsburg
Day 9: Nördlingen & Dinkelsbühl
Day 10: Rothenburg
Day 11: Heidelberg
Days 12–13: Cologne
Day 14: Frankfurt

Germany For Families

Days 1–2: Berlin
Days 3–4: Munich
Day 5: Ludwig's Castles
Day 6: Rothenburg
Day 7: Heidelberg

The Fairy-Tale Road

Day 1: Frankfurt
Day 2: Hanau, Gelnhausen, Fulda
Day 3: Lauterbach, Alsfeld, Neustadt,
       Homburg, Kassel
Day 4: Münden, Göttingen
Day 5: Sababurg, Bad Karlshafen, Höxter, Bodenwerder

Day 6: Hameln
Day 7: Bremen

0   50 mi
0   50 km

Mountain ▲

bombed in World War II, makes an ideal stopover on the way to Munich. After checking into a hotel and enjoying a lunch of Nürnberg-style bratwurst (finger-sized sausages), head in the afternoon for the **Germanisches Nationalmuseum** (p. 239), the city's premier attraction. The National Museum is strong on the works of native son Albrecht Dürer, whose paintings are reason enough for a visit.

If time remains, visit the **Kaiserburg** (p. 240) on a hilltop at the northern edge of the Altstadt (Old City). Until 1571 it was the official residence of German kings and emperors. You might also get a look at **St.-Lorenz-Kirche** (p. 241), across the Pegnitz River, dating from 1270. It's the most appealing of Nürnberg's churches.

Days ❺ & ❻: Munich ⭐⭐⭐

Take an early morning train to Munich (trip time: 2 hr.), so you can more or less get in a full day of sightseeing. For orientation purposes, walk over to the main square of Munich, **Marienplatz** (p. 322), where at three times during the day you can witness a miniature "tournament" on its **Glockenspiel,** the city's clock tower. Climb or take an elevator to the top of the Rathaus tower here. This is the old city hall building, and from its peak, you'll have a panoramic sweep of the Munich skyline.

While you're in the area, stop at **Frauenkirche** (p. 332), Munich's largest church, rebuilt in the Gothic style. For lunch that day, dine at **Viktualienmarkt,** Munich's most famous open-air market and one of the greatest such food markets in Europe.

After lunch, spend 2 hours at **Alte Pinakothek** (p. 323), one of the world's greatest art museums, especially strong in European artists from the 14th to the 18th centuries.

To cap your afternoon, stroll through the beautiful **Englischer Garten** (p. 333),

and don't be surprised to meet some local residents in the nude. For your night fun, follow the oom-pah-pah sounds to the **Hofbräuhaus** (p. 342), the world's most famous beer hall.

On **Day 6,** visit the **Deutsches Museum** (p. 326) in the morning. This German Museum of Masterpieces of Science and Technology is the largest technological museum in the world. It even shelters the first automobile (a Benz from 1886). Allow at least 2 hours for a visit. After lunch, plan on spending the afternoon at **Schloss Nymphenburg** (p. 329), the summer palace of the Wittelsbach dynasty. Allow at least 2½ hours, with time reserved for a stroll through the famous Nymphenburg gardens or park. One of the highlights here is an array of ornate sleighs and coaches once used by "Mad" King Ludwig of Bavaria.

After a return to town, consider attending a cultural performance at the **Cuvilliés Theater** (p. 341), the most beautiful rococo theater in the world.

Day ❼: Ludwig's Castles ⭐⭐⭐

It's easier and more luxurious to rent a car in Munich and drive to Germany's two most famous castles at **Neuschwanstein** (p. 291) and **Hohenschwangau** (p. 291). You can also travel by train to Füssen, 119km (74 miles) southwest of Munich, where you can then take the bus to Neuschwanstein, a distance of 7km (4 miles) east of Füssen. However, you'll spend so much time in travel that you'll have time to visit only one castle that day.

If you're that rushed, make it Neuschwanstein, as it's the true fairy-tale castle of King Ludwig. Hohenschwangau is not as glamorous or as spectacular. Tours of Neuschwanstein take an hour. But because of the rush of visitors to the area, there are often long delays in summer. After your castle tour, return to Munich and travel back to Berlin by train.

3 Germany in 2 Weeks

With 2 weeks to explore Germany, you aren't that rushed and have some breathing room. You can see a bit of the best regions, including the star attractions of the Romantic Road and the medieval city of **Rothenburg,** as well as the university city of **Heidelberg** and the cathedral city of **Cologne,** the greatest stopover along the Rhineland. The tour comes to an end at **Frankfurt,** Germany's transportation hub, where you can make rail and plane connections to virtually anywhere in the world.

Days ❶–❼
Follow itineraries as outlined above.

Day ❽: Augsburg
For this part of the trip, you'll need a car. The trip can be done by public transportation, but you'll lose precious sightseeing hours going from place to place. If you rent a car, it's better to do so in Munich before setting out to visit Ludwig's castles (see above).

From our last stopover at Füssen, head north along one of the great scenic attractions of Germany, the **Romantic Road** (see chapter 8).

Make Augsburg your first stopover. It lies 68km (42 miles) northwest of Munich and the Romantic Road's biggest town and gateway to the Bavarian Alps. Arriving by midmorning, you can take in the **Church of St. Ulrich and St. Afra** (p. 285) before lunch, visiting such attractions in the afternoon as **Fuggerei** (p. 285) and the cathedral of Augsburg, **Dom St. Maria** (p. 285).

Day ❾: Nördlingen ✿ & Dinkelsbühl ✿
On **Day 9,** check out of your hotel at Augsburg and continue north toward the medieval city of **Rothenburg,** one of the greatest attractions of Germany. Your first stopover can be in **Nördlingen** (p. 278), one of the most famous medieval towns along the Romantische Strasse, with many 14th- and 15th-century buildings. Walk its streets, stopping in to visit **St. Georgskirche** (p. 280), dating from the 15th century. If you got a late start, you can enjoy lunch here at **Meyers-Keller**

(p. 279), or else you can continue to **Dinkelsbühl** (p. 276), which is still surrounded by medieval walls and towers. Check into one of the old inns here for the night and explore its cobblestone streets that appear as if in a time capsule.

Day ❿: Rothenburg ✿✿✿: Germany's Greatest Medieval City
In the morning of **Day 10,** continue north along the Romantic Road to **Rothenburg ob der Tauber,** where you can check into a hotel—you'll need the entire day to explore this medieval city, beginning with its ancient **ramparts** (p. 274). First, call on the **Rathaus** (p. 275), where from its Gothic tower you'll have a panoramic view of the town. There are other attractions, including the **Reichsstadtmuseum** (p. 275) and **St. Jakobskirche** (p. 276), but the chief attraction of Rothenburg is the city itself. You can wander its ancient cobblestone streets for hours and still discover something new. For lunch we suggest you rent a bike and cycle along the Tauber River until you find a suitable place for a picnic. Overnight in Rothenburg and spend an hour or two more wandering its streets, as they appear even more mysteriously medieval when lit after dark.

Day ⓫: The University City of Heidelberg ✿✿✿
Leave Rothenburg early in the morning and head west for an overnight stopover in the city of Heidelberg. Called "everybody's favorite town" in Germany, Heidelberg, on the Neckar River, can be explored in a day if you move fast

enough. Check into a hotel in the Alt-stadt (Old Town) for atmosphere and wander its cobblestone streets at your leisure.

If you arrive early enough, spend at least 2 hours exploring **Heidelberg Castle** (p. 441), taking in the panoramic view of the town and its surrounding river valley. Follow this with a boat ride on the Neckar (p. 442) and a visit to the **Kurpfälzisches Museum** (p. 443).

Cap your evening by spending it in one of the fabled and historic student drinking clubs, our favorite being **Zum Roten Ochsen** (p. 444).

Days ⑫ & ⑬: The Cathedral City of Cologne 🎠🎠🎠

From Heidelberg, head north along the Rhine, stopping in one of the Rheingau towns for lunch, our favorite spot being **Rüdesheim** (p. 516), surrounded by vineyards.

Continue north into **Cologne** for the midafternoon. After checking into a hotel for the night of **Day 12,** head for the major attraction of town, the **Kölner Dom** or Cologne Cathedral (p. 539). At night hit one of the city's famous old beer taverns for drinks and dinner, a favorite being **Früh am Dom** (p. 540).

On the morning of **Day 13,** launch an exploration of the highlights of the city, beginning with a morning visit to **Museum Ludwig** (p. 541), with one of

the world's largest collection of the works of Pablo Picasso, among other attractions.

Follow this with a visit to Cologne's oldest museum, **Wallraf-Richartz Museum/ Foundation Corboud** (p. 542), with its amazing exhibition of Gothic works.

After a Rhineland lunch, continue sightseeing at the **Museum Schnütgen** (p. 542), which contains Cologne's best collection of religious art and sculpture.

After an afternoon shopping stroll through the old city, where you can buy a bottle of the famous Eau de Cologne, consider an evening performance of the **Kölner Philharmonie** (p. 545).

Day ⑭: Frankfurt 🎠🎠🎠: Your Exit from Germany

After checking out of your hotel in Cologne, head southwest to the city of Frankfurt. You should arrive in time to check into a hotel and enjoy lunch. Spend the afternoon wandering its rebuilt Old Town, **Altstadt** (p. 480), and visiting **Goethe-Haus** (p. 480).

Later you can visit one of Germany's greatest art galleries, the **Städel Museum** (p. 481), with its collection of European old masters.

End your night with a dinner in a typical restaurant. In the morning you can take the train, or else fly out of Frankfurt, perhaps after promising yourself another trip to Germany in the future.

---

4 Germany for Families

Germany offers many attractions that kids enjoy. And if pacing yourself with enough museum time is a concern, rest easy: many museums in Germany, especially in Munich, have exhibitions that fascinate children of all ages.

Our suggestion is to spend 1 week in Germany as follows: 2 days in **Berlin,** 2 days in **Munich,** and the final 3 days visiting towns and castles that your kids will swear were created by Walt Disney himself—namely, **Ludwig's fairy-tale castles** in Bavaria; **Rothenburg,** a medieval city along the Romantic Road that looks like a stage setting; and, finally, everybody's favorite German town, **Heidelberg,** with its famous castle and other attractions.

Days ❶ & ❷: Berlin ✿✿✿:
Your Gateway to Germany

On **Day 1,** arrive as early as possible to get in a full day of sightseeing, as time is rushed. Before launching any specific sightseeing, take yourself and your kids to the **Brandenburger Tor** or Brandenburg Gate (p. 143), a gate that is the very symbol of Berlin. After a look around, head down Berlin's major boulevard, the famous **Unter den Linden** (see "Frommer's Favorite Berlin Experiences" box on p. 138), filled with great Prussian architecture and world-class museums.

Unter den Linden turns into Karl-Liebknecht-Strasse, leading into **Alexanderplatz,** the heart of old East Berlin in the Cold War days (p. 97). You can take your kids for an elevator ride on the **Fernsehturm** (p. 142), or TV tower, the second-highest structure in Europe, for a view of the united city.

Before lunch, pay a visit to the **Pergamon Museum** on Museumsinsel (p. 132), where your kids are likely to be awed by such famous displays as the Pergamon Altar.

Secure the makings of a picnic lunch and head for the 167-hectare (412-acre) **Tiergarten** (p. 149), the former hunting grounds of Prussian rulers.

After lunch, hop over to see the multimedia extravaganza, **The Story of Berlin** (p. 138), telling in pictures and films the saga of the 8 centuries of the city's turbulent history. Allow 2 hours for a visit.

To cap the afternoon, take your brood on a boat tour of the **River Spree** (p. 152) that cuts across the once-divided city. Have dinner that night in a typical Berlin restaurant.

On **Day 2,** visit the **Reichstag** (p. 146) for a climb up its dramatic dome. Arrive before 8:30am to beat the crowds. After your assault on this monument, head for the **Zoologischer Garten Berlin** (p. 150), Germany's oldest zoo, housing some 13,000 animals, many of them quite rare and all in open natural habitats. You can also visit the adjoining aquarium.

After lunch, take an afternoon visit to **Potsdam** on the Havel River. Potsdam is only 24km (15 miles) southwest of Berlin. It's reached by frequent trains, taking 23 minutes from the Bahnhof Zoo. You can spend the rest of the day exploring **Sans Souci Palace** (p. 173) and its adjacent gardens. There is something here for everyone to see, even kids who bore easily. Head back to Berlin on the train for your final night before taking an early morning flight to Munich.

Days ❸ & ❹: Munich ✿✿✿:
Gateway to Bavaria

On **Day 3,** head for the **Marienplatz** (p. 322) in the center of Munich, where if you arrive at the right hour you can treat your kids to a miniature tournament staged with enameled copper figures on the town's clock tower, **Glockenspiel.** Later, head for the **Deutsches Museum** (p. 326), the German Museum of Masterpieces of Science and Technology, on an island in the Isar River. The largest technological museum in the world is a very hands-on museum with buttons to push, levers to crank, and gears to turn—kids will love it. Allow 2 hours for a visit and plan to have lunch on-site at the museum's affordable restaurant.

In the afternoon, plan a family visit to **Schloss Nymphenburg** (p. 329), the summer palace of the Wittelsbachs. Children delight in the fantasy coaches and sleighs of Ludwig II and enjoy walks through the 200-hectare (500-acre) park. Return to Munich for the night.

In the morning of **Day 4,** take the kids to the **Bavaria Film Studio** (p. 335), Europe's largest filmmaking center. Children love the Bavaria Action Show with its simulated fistfights and fire stunts. Allow 1½ hours for a tour.

Follow this with a visit to the fabled royal **Residenz** (p. 328), where the Wittelsbachs lived from 1385 to 1918. Some very young children might be a bit bored with these stately halls, but as an adult you wouldn't want to visit Munich without seeing it.

After a stroll through the **Englischer Garten** (p. 333), treat yourself and your kids to a lunch of *Weisswurste,* those little white sausages for which Munich is known. The best ones are served at **Don-isl** (p. 318).

In the afternoon, visit **Münchner Stadtmuseum** (p. 331), where children are entertained by an array of carousel animals, marionettes, and hand puppets from around the world. That can be followed with a visit to the **Hellabrunn Zoo** in Tierpark Hellabrunn, lying 6km (4 miles) south of Munich and reached by U-Bahn to Thalkirchen. Hundreds of animals roam here in their natural habitat.

To cap your visit to Munich, take the entire family to **Zum Alten Markt** (p. 316), a moderately priced restaurant on a small square off Munich's largest outdoor food market. In summer, tables are set outside, and it makes for a festive evening as you bid farewell to Munich.

Day ❺: Ludwig's Castles ❋❋❋
On **Day 5,** rent a car in Munich and set out south, deep into Bavaria, to explore the fairy-tale castles of "Mad" King Ludwig: **Neuschwanstein** (a must) and **Hohenschwangau** (if time remains). Kids find that Neuschwanstein evokes a Disney architectural fantasy and delight in touring its lofty precincts, especially when it's reached by horse-drawn carriage. In the afternoon, the 12th-century Hohenschwangau can also be explored. This is where Ludwig spent a "joyless" childhood. You can return to Munich for

the night or else find lodgings in **Füssen** (coverage begins on p. 286).

Day ❻: Rothenburg ❋❋❋
The next morning, **Day 6,** from your base either in Munich or Füssen, drive north or northwest, respectively, to Rothenburg ob der Tauber, the most glorious stopover along the Germany's Romantic Road. This is the best-preserved medieval city in Europe. With your kids in tow, you can wander for hours along its ancient streets, stopping in at the **Kriminalmuseum** (p. 275) or visiting the picture-book **Rathaus** (town hall; p. 275). Rothenburg is encircled by ramparts, and kids delight in walking along them, taking in the medieval tower gates. At some point along the way, stop at one of the kiosks selling *Schneeballen* (snowballs). These are round pastries covered with sugar and sold all over town as a local specialty. Spend the night in Rothenburg.

Day ❼: Heidelberg ❋❋❋
On **Day 7,** journey west to the city of Heidelberg. You can arrive in time to tour the **Altstadt** or old town, beginning at **Marktplatz,** the main market square. Allow at least 1½ hours to walk about the ancient streets and count yourself lucky if you're here on one of the market days (either Wed or Sat), as the entire city is more festive then.

After a lunch in one of Altstadt's student taverns, head up the hill to **Heidelberg Castle** (p. 441) for its stunning views and exploration, allowing about 2 hours for the entire jaunt. In the remaining part of the afternoon, take a **boat ride on the Neckar River** (p. 442). Overnight in Heidelberg.

You can drive to such transportation hubs as Munich in the east or Frankfurt in the north for your return flight.

5 The Fairy-Tale Road

To tour the Märchenstrasse is to take a trip though the land immortalized by the Brothers Grimm. In the gnarled forests and half-timbered cottages, you can still conjure up wicked witches, along with fairies, wizards, dwarfs, and goblins. The Grimm brothers were the earliest scholars of their country's folklore; they traveled to far-flung corners of Germany in the early 19th century to record the tales they heard. Their compendium, *Kinder- und Hausmärchen (Grimm's Fairy Tales),* is the world's second-most frequently translated book, after the Bible.

Today, you can follow the Fairy-Tale Road, a 595km (369-mile) route from Hanau, near Frankfurt, where the Brothers Grimm were born, to Bremen, where the "Bremen Town Musicians" lived. The route goes through some of the prettiest medieval villages in the country. To complete this tour, it's best to rent a car in Frankfurt, as the local public transportation is not adequate for what we've outlined. If you'd like to explore the Fairy-Tale Road in more depth, see chapter 17.

Day ❶: Arrive in Frankfurt ⊛⊛⊛

Take a flight that arrives in Frankfurt as early as possible on **Day 1.** Check into your hotel and enjoy a coffee and a German pastry at a local cafe.

Although Frankfurt was heavily bombed in World War II, there is a lot of the old here—though mostly rebuilt. Head for the **Römerberg,** the heart of the old city where Charlemagne once erected his fort. Visit the **Römer** (p. 481), with its Imperial Hall, exhibiting a portrait gallery of German emperors. Nearby is the **Goethe-Haus** (p. 480), former home of Germany's most famous writer.

Later you can follow in the footsteps of Goethe and wander for at least 2 hours in the **Altstadt** (Old Town).

For lunch, we'd recommend **King Kamehameha Suite** (p. 475), a neoclassical villa that is a bar, cafe, and restaurant during the day.

In the afternoon, see the impressive array of European paintings from various schools in the **Städel Museum** (p. 481). If time remains, explore the **Liebighaus** (p. 481), one of the great sculpture galleries of Europe.

Day ❷: From Hanau to Fulda ⊛

In your rented car, leave Frankfurt in the morning and drive to the town of **Hanau** (p. 573), 20km (13 miles), east of Frankfurt, on the River Main. It was in Hanau that Jakob (1785–1863) and Wilhelm (1786–1859) Grimm were born.

Appropriately, the Fairy-Tale Road starts at a monument to the story-telling brothers at Neustadter Marktplatz. The memorial, erected in 1898, is about all that will interest you in this traffic-clogged suburb of Frankfurt. Hanau was heavily bombed in World War II.

From Hanau, go along B43 about 20km (13 miles) northeast to **Gelnhausen** (p. 574), where the remains of the imperial palace evoke memories of the emperor, Friedrich Barbarossa, and his lover, the beautiful Gela. Barbarossa constructed the castle here on an island in the 12th century.

Continue another 20km (13 miles) to **Steinau an der Strasse** (p. 577), where the Grimm brothers spent their carefree youth. Visit the Amtshaus, the Renaissance palace, and see a performance at the fairy-tale puppet theater. Performances are held most Saturdays and Sundays at 3pm, though shows are not always guaranteed. Half-timbered buildings line cobblestone streets, and the surrounding woods might have been the home of Snow White. In the center of the main square is a memorial fountain honoring the brothers.

Continue north another 30km (20 miles) on B40, following the signs to **Fulda** (p. 578), noted for its baroque architecture, as exemplified by the bishops' palace on Schlossstrasse, overlooking the city. The prince-bishops were guardians of the tomb of St. Boniface, the apostle of Germany. Fulda's cathedral dates from 1704, and pilgrims still worship at the tomb of St. Boniface, in a crypt beneath the main altar. Consider staying overnight in Fulda.

Day ❸: Lauterbach ℱ to Kassel

Leave Fulda in the morning and take B254 into the Vogelsberg Mountains, going via Grossenlüder to **Lauterbach,** 24km (15 miles) northeast of Fulda. (In one of the Grimms' tales, the Little Scalawag loses his sock in Lauterbach.) The town is known for its medieval half-timbered houses and its two castles, Eisenbach and Riedesel. After your visit, follow Route 254 northwest to **Alsfeld,** a town of half-timbered houses and cobblestone streets. Its 1512 Altes Rathaus (town hall) is a showpiece.

Follow the route along the Schwalm River, which the Germans call *Rotkäppchenland,* or Little Red Riding Hood country. Signs point to **Neustadt,** with its circular tower, from which Rapunzel might have let down her golden tresses. Continue north through Schwalmstadt for 29km (18 miles) to **Homberg.**

From Homberg, follow the signs for 39km (24 miles) north to **Kassel** (p. 582), where you'll want to spend the night. The Waldeck Region and the Reinhards Forest around Kassel were the birthplace of many legends about witches, sleeping princesses, strange beasts, and magic spells. These tales had a profound influence on the Grimm brothers, who lived in Kassel from 1798 to 1830. The **Bruder Grimm Museum,** at Schone Aussicht 2, contains letters, portraits, and mementos.

Day ❹: Münden ℱ to Göttingen

Leaving Kassel, go along B3 for some 15km (10 miles) north to **Münden** (p. 587) (known more properly as Hann-Münden). The Fulda and Werra rivers meet here. In the town center are some 700 half-timbered houses built in many styles. Also in Münden is the tombstone of the much-maligned Doctor Eisenbart (a Grimm character), who is remembered every year at a folk festival.

From Münden you can detour from the Fairy-Tale Road, taking the E45 Autobahn to **Göttingen** (coverage begins on p. 618). This is an ideal place to spend the night.

One of the great university centers of Germany, Göttingen is imbued with a lively student life and retains a certain air of medieval romanticism. You can spend hours wandering its narrow streets and looking at its enchanting half-timbered houses, evocative of a story by the Brothers Grimm.

Start your voyage of discovery in its **Marktplatz,** or Market Square, with a statue of the little goose-girl, "the most kissed statue in the world." You can visit the **Altes Rathaus** (old town hall) on the square and later spend an hour wandering through the **Stadtisches Museum** (p. 620), with its fascinating look at the history and culture of Lower Saxony. Visit one of the student taverns after dark, perhaps dining at the **Ratskeller** (p. 619), the cellar tavern of the town hall.

Day ❺: Sababurg to Bodenwerder

Return to the Fairy-Tale Road by going back to Münden and then heading north on Route 80. About 10km (6 miles) north of Münden, in the village of Veckerhagen, go left and follow the signs to **Sababurg** (p. 588).

Right outside the village of Sababurg lies **Dornröschenschloss Sababurg,** Hofgeismar (𝄓 **05671/8080**), a park and castle said to be the setting of the Sleeping Beauty legend. You'll almost start to believe the tale when you see the Italianate turrets of the castle. The park is said to be the oldest zoological garden in the world.

After viewing the castle, take the road back to the Weser Valley village of Oberweser and make a left turn onto B80 heading north. After some 13km (8 miles), you reach the spa of **Bad Karlshafen** (p. 589), a resort noted for its baroque buildings.

Continue north on Route 80 (which becomes Rte. 83) to **Höxter** (p. 590), the easternmost town in Westphalia. Among its many Renaissance and baroque buildings, the town's most visited attraction is **Dechanei (the Deanery).** You can take Corveyer Allee from Höxter for about 3km (2 miles) to **Corvey,** one of the oldest Benedictine abbeys in Germany, planned by Charlemagne and constructed by his son, Ludwig the Pious, in 822.

Follow the Weser River north for some 30km (20 miles) to the town of **Bodenwerder** (p. 591) (www.bodenwerder.de), the birthplace of Lügen Baron von Münchhausen. Lügen Baron (1720–97) was one of the most colorful characters who ever lived along the Fairy-Tale Road.

The baron grew up near the Rathaus, or town hall, at which the **Münchhausen-Erinnerungszimmer (Münchhausen Memorial Room),** Münchhausenplatz 1, D-37619 (© **05533/40-50**) has been installed.

Day ❻: Hameln ✿ of Pied Piper Fame

After a night in Bodenwerder, head northwest on Route 83 for **Hameln** (coverage begins on p. 592).

Immortalized by the Brothers Grimm, and even Goethe and Robert Browning, this is the setting for the famous Pied Piper folk tale. Pied Piper, of course, was the world's most famous rat-catcher, luring the town's children away, never to be heard from again. It's a romantic old town that invites a day's exploration. Rat figures in every conceivable form are for sale in the local shops. Explore its **Gothic Münster** (p. 594), or church, and take in such attractions as the **Rattenfängerhaus (Rat-Catcher's House)** where you can also order lunch (p. 594). Shop for souvenirs and absorb the atmosphere, overnighting in one of the town's inns.

Day ❼: Bremen ✿✿, the Final Stopover

After a night in Hameln, take Route 83 northwest to the A30 Autobahn and continue west beyond Osnabrück until you connect with the E37 Autobahn heading northwest to the port of **Bremen** (coverage begins on p. 600).

In this "ancient town by the gray river," you can spend the day exploring its many attractions. Begin at the **Marktplatz** (p. 605), the heart of town and the main square, with its towering statue of Roland, the port's protector.

Wander at leisure, taking in such attractions as the **Schötting,** a 16th-century guild hall, and the **Haus der Bürgerschaft,** home of Bremen's Parliament. The town's cathedral is **Dom St. Petri.** You can also visit its **Focke-Museum,** one of the best regional museums of Germany. Call on its **Rathaus** (town hall), take in some shopping, and walk the rampart promenade, **Wallanlagen.** (Coverage of all these attractions begins on p. 605.) Overnight in Bremen. The following morning return to Frankfurt for your flight home.

5

Berlin

Berlin's history is dark, not only as Hitler's nerve center of Nazi horror, but also as the battleground of the Cold War. But with its field of new skyscrapers, hip clubs, and fashion boutiques, postmillennium Berlin has recast itself as the Continent's capital of cool.

However, make no mistake, Berlin is not exactly escaping the past, as the opening of the Jüdisches Museum Berlin (Jewish Museum), a paean to German Jewry, testifies. Instead, Berlin is reconciling itself to its notorious history and moving with confidence into its future. As one hip young Berliner, Joachim Stressmann, told us: "We don't know where we're going, but we know where we've been, and no one wants to go back there."

The reunited city of Berlin is once again the capital of Germany. Berlin was almost bombed out of existence during World War II, its streets reduced to piles of rubble, its parks to muddy swampland. But the optimistic spirit and strength of will of the remarkable Berliners enabled them to survive not only the wartime destruction of their city, but also its postwar division, symbolized by the Berlin Wall.

Today, structures of steel and glass tower over streets where before only piles of rubble lay, and parks and gardens are again lush. Nonetheless, even in the daily whirl of working, shopping, and dining along the Ku'Damm, Berliners encounter reminders of less happy days: At the end of the street stands the Kaiser Wilhelm Memorial Church, with only the shell of the old neo-Romanesque bell tower remaining. In striking contrast is the new church, constructed west of the old tower in 1961 and nicknamed "lipstick and powder box" by Berliners because of its futuristic design.

Before the war, the section of the city that became East Berlin was the cultural and political heart of Germany, where the best museums, finest churches, and most important boulevards lay. The walled-in East Berliners turned to restoring their museums, theaters, and landmarks (especially in the Berlin-Mitte section), while West Berliners built entirely new museums and cultural centers. This contrast between the two parts of the city is still evident, though east and west are coming together more and more within the immense, fascinating whole that is Berlin.

1 Orientation

ARRIVING

BY PLANE   **Tegel** is the city's busiest airport, serving most flights from the West. **Schönefeld,** the airport in the eastern sector, is used primarily by Russian and eastern European airlines. Private bus shuttles among the two airports operate constantly, so you can make connecting flights at a different airport. For information on the two airports, call © **01805/000186,** or visit www.berlin-airport.de.

The Legendary Tempelhof Airport Closes

Tempelhof Airport in Berlin, famous as the symbol of the Berlin Airlift, is scheduled to close in October 2008. With its passing, one of the few examples of Nazi-era architecture fades. Its closing will make way for the expansion of the Berlin-Schönefeld International Airport, a former military base, which will be turned into the vastly enlarged Berlin-Brandenburg International Airport.

Lufthansa (© 800/399-3880; www.lufthansa-usa.com) offers direct flights from Washington, D.C., to Berlin. Transatlantic passengers from several other North American cities are routed through the airline's hubs at Frankfurt and Munich.

Delta (© 800/241-4141; www.delta.com) has flights to Berlin-Tegel in the evening from New York's JFK airport. However, daily flights, depending on the season or on business, are not always a sure thing, so you'll need to check with a travel agent or the airline itself.

The best and most convenient service into Berlin is available aboard **British Airways** (© 800/247-9297; www.ba.com), which efficiently funnels dozens of daily flights from North America to Germany, including five a day into Berlin-Tegel, through its vast terminals at London-Heathrow. Connections to Berlin are available from at least 40 gateways in the U.S. and Canada, more than those offered by any other airline. Frequent transatlantic price wars keep fares to Berlin aboard BA lower than you may have thought, especially in off season. Stopovers in London can be arranged at minimal cost, and deeply discounted hotel packages are available in either Berlin or London, at rates that are significantly less than what you'd have paid if you'd arranged them yourself. And if you opt for passage in business class (BA calls it "Club Class"), you'll ride on the most comfortable, and one of the largest, airline seats in the industry, in a configuration that can be transformed into something approaching a bed.

Berlin-Tegel Airport (© 01805/000186; www.berlin-airport.de) is 8km (5 miles) northwest of the city center. Public transportation by bus, taxi, or U-Bahn is convenient to all points in the city. BVG bus nos. X9 and 109 run every 10 to 15 minutes from the airport to Bahnhof Zoo in Berlin's center, departing from outside the arrival hall; a one-way fare is 4€ ($6.40). A taxi (© 800/0261026) to the city center costs about 24€ ($38) and takes 25 to 40 minutes. No porters are available for luggage handling, but pushcarts are free. The **Jetexpressbus TXL,** operated by Berlin's public transport provider, BVG, leaves the airport for Friedrichstrasse and Unter den Linden (trip time: 20–25 min.), at a cost of 3€ ($4.80). The first departure from Alexanderplatz urban rail (S-Bahn) and metro (U-Bahn) station is at 4:52am (Sat–Sun at 5:12am). The last bus leaves Tegel Airport for the city center daily at 11:07pm. Otherwise, buses run back and forth at 10-minute intervals from 6am to 7pm Monday to Friday and then at 20-minute intervals 7 to 11pm. On Saturday, they run every 20 minutes from 6am to 11pm; on Sunday, they run at 20-minute intervals from 6 to 10am, 10-minute intervals 10am to 7pm, and then 20-minute intervals again from 7 to 11pm.

The main terminal has a **visitor information counter** where you can get a free map of the city. The counter is open daily 5am to 10pm. Facilities at the terminal include money-exchange centers, luggage-storage facilities (and locker rentals), a police station, auto-rental kiosks, dining facilities, and a first-aid center. Shops sell gifts, film, and travel paraphernalia.

Berlin-Schönefeld Airport (℡ **01805/000186;** www.berlin-airport.de/EN), once the main airport for East Berlin, now receives many flights from Asia, as well as Russia and other European countries. It lies in Brandenburg, 19km (12 miles) southeast of the city center. The city center is a 55-minute ride on the S-Bahn. You can also take bus no. 171 from the airport to Rudow, where you transfer to the U-Bahn. Either means of transport costs 3€ ($4.80).

BY TRAIN   As Berlin strengthens its role as Germany's capital, increasing numbers of trains are speeding their way into town. All points of the country, especially Frankfurt, Munich, and Bonn, maintain excellent rail connections, with high-tech, high-speed improvements being made to the country's railway system virtually all the time. One recent major improvement is that Berlin and the great port of Hamburg are now 15 minutes closer, thanks to high-speed (250kmph/155 mph) InterCity Express service (the trip is now 2 hr., 8 min.). Since reunification, Berlin has improved the facilities of railway stations in both the western zone (Bahnhof Zoologischer Garten) and eastern zone (Berlin Ostbahnhof), installing improved S-Bahn links to interconnect them. The station you'll use depends on the destination or origin of your train, or the location of your hotel within the city. Some trains, but not all, make arrivals and departures from both stations. A third station, Berlin Lichtenberg, within the city's eastern half, is used for trains pulling in from small towns. For information about any railway station, call ℡ **01805/996633.** A new megastation, **Lehrter Bahnhof,** recently opened in Berlin-Mitte, within a 5-minute walk of the Reichstag. It incorporates the lines that lead to the three other railway stations mentioned above, eliminating the need for cross-town commutes among the city's railway stations.

BY BUS (COACH)   Regularly scheduled buses operate from 250 German and continental cities, including Frankfurt, Hamburg, and Munich. Long-distance bus companies servicing Berlin include **Haru-Reisen** (℡ **030/35195220**) and **Bayern Express & P. Kühn** (℡ **030/86096240**).

Arrivals and departures are at the **ZOB Omnibusbahnhof am Funkturm,** Masurenalle, Charlottenburg. Taxis and bus connections are available at the station and at the U-Bahn, at the nearby Kaiserdamm station.

BY CAR   From Frankfurt, take the E451 north until it connects with the E40 going northeast. Follow this autobahn past Jena and then head north on the E51 into Berlin. From Nürnberg, also take the E51 into Berlin. From Dresden, take the E55 north to Berlin. Expect heavy traffic on the autobahns on weekends and sunny days when everybody is out touring.

VISITOR INFORMATION

For visitor information, head for **Berlin Hauptbahnhof** (the central rail station), open daily 8am to 10pm. There's another tourist office at Neues Krarnzler Eck, along the Kurfürstendamm, the popular shopping boulevard, open Monday to Saturday 10am to 8pm, Sunday 10am to 6pm. Other offices are at the south wing of the Brandenburg Gate, open daily 10am to 6pm; in the Berlin Pavilion at the Reichstag, open April to October daily 8:30am to 8pm, and November to March daily 10am to 6pm. The central phone number for all tourist information is ℡ **030/250024** (www.berlin-tourism.de). The staff will make hotel reservations for you and book tickets for major events and sightseeing tours.

Berlin Today & Tomorrow

Berlin is living up to its reputation as a dynamic, exciting hub of activity as never before. The city's nightlife is among Europe's best and wildest. And since the German government relocated here from Bonn, Berlin is bidding to become the reborn capital not only of Germany, but of all Europe.

As befits a capital, the city has undergone a major face-lift. More than $150 billion was invested in new streets, buildings, and railways. The former East Berlin is rapidly being restored and gentrified, particularly in the **Mitte (central)** district. Here, luxury hotels and shopping arcades compete with the glitter—and litter—of the **Ku'Damm** (short for Kurfürstendamm, a wide boulevard at the center of activity in the western part of Berlin). The reopening of the Hotel Adlon (p. 112), overlooking the Brandenburg Gate, is particularly notable, evoking the restoration of Unter den Linden and the return to some of its prewar glory; Adlon, at one time, was the most important hotel not only in Berlin, but in all of Germany. **Prenzlauer Berg,** a blue-collar eastern neighborhood that escaped the worst of the wartime bombing, is now a chic district of cafes and boutiques. The downside of all this for Berliners has been the sharp increase in real estate prices, as well as the inconvenience of living in the world's largest construction site.

Many of Berlin's famous buildings have also been restored. The rebuilt **Reichstag** (p. 146) has a glittering glass dome; upon the building stands not the old glowering imperial hunter, but the national symbol, the eagle (locals refer affectionately to the statue as "the fat hen"). The **Oranienburger Strasse Synagogue** (commonly known as Neue Synagoge Berlin–Centrum Judaicum/The New Synagogue; p. 145), wrecked on Kristallnacht and finished off by Allied bombers, has been rebuilt to its previous splendor. Likewise, **Berliner Dom (Berlin Cathedral;** p. 143) and the five state museums on **Museumsinsel (Museum Island;** p. 131) have been returned to their original glory.

Visitors unfortunately often overlook Berlin's **natural attractions.** Few metropolitan areas are blessed with as many gardens, lakes, woodlands, and parks—all of which cover an amazing one-third of the city. First-time visitors are often surprised to learn that small farms with fields and meadows still exist within the city limits.

CITY LAYOUT

Berlin is one of the largest and most complex cities in Europe. Because it's so spread out, you'll need to depend on public transportation. No visitor should try to explore more than two neighborhoods a day, even superficially.

The center of activity in the western part of Berlin is the 4km-long (2½-mile) **Kurfürstendamm,** called the Ku'Damm by Berliners, who seem to have a habit of irreverently renaming every street and building in the city. Along this wide boulevard you'll find the best hotels, restaurants, theaters, cafes, nightclubs, shops, and department stores. It's the most elegant and fashionable spot in Berlin, but, like much of the

---

Tips **Finding an Address**

As for the numbering of streets in Berlin, keep in mind that the city sometimes assists you by posting the range of numbers that appears within any particular block, at least within major arteries such as the Kurfürstendamm. These numbers appear on the street signs themselves, which is a great help in finding a particular number on long boulevards. You won't find these numbers on street signs of smaller streets, however. Although some streets are numbered with the odds on one side and the evens on the other, many (including the Ku'Damm) are numbered consecutively up one side of the street and back down the other.

---

city, it combines chic with sleaze in places. Walkers can stop off at one of the popular cafes lining the boulevard.

From the Ku'Damm, you can take Hardenbergstrasse, which crosses Bismarckstrasse and becomes Otto-Suhr-Allee, which will lead to the **Schloss Charlottenburg** area and its museums, a major sightseeing area. The **Dahlem Museums** are in the southwest of the city, often reached by going along Hohenzollerndamm.

The huge **Tiergarten** is the city's largest park. Running through it is **Strasse des 17 Juni,** which leads to the famed **Brandenburg Gate** (just south of the Reichstag). On the southwestern fringe of the Tiergarten is the **Berlin Zoo.**

The Brandenburg Gate is the start of eastern Berlin's most celebrated street, **Unter den Linden,** the cultural heart of Berlin before World War II. It runs from west to east, leading to **Museumsinsel (Museum Island),** where the most outstanding museums of eastern Berlin, including the Pergamon Museum, are situated.

Unter den Linden crosses another major artery, **Friedrichstrasse.** If you continue south along Friedrichstrasse, you'll reach the former location of **Checkpoint Charlie,** a famous border site of the Cold War days. No longer a checkpoint, it now has a little museum devoted to memories of the Berlin Wall.

Unter den Linden continues east until it reaches **Alexanderplatz,** the center of eastern Berlin, with its towering television tower, or Fernsehturm. A short walk away is the restored **Nikolaiviertel (Nikolai Quarter),** a neighborhood of bars, restaurants, and shops that evoke life in the prewar days.

MAPS   Good maps of Berlin can be purchased at bookstores or news kiosks, such as the Europa Press Center (a magazine and newspaper store in the Europa Center). One of the best maps is the **Falk map,** which offers full-color detail and comprehensive indexes (consequently, it's sometimes awkward to unfold and refold). Be sure to obtain an up-to-date map showing the most recent changes.

NEIGHBORHOODS IN BRIEF

Visitors who knew Berlin during the Cold War are amazed at the way traffic now zips between sectors that once were rigidly segregated by border guards. Today, your taxi will blithely drive beneath the Brandenburg Gate or along the Friedrichstrasse, without regard to barriers that once used to be virtually impenetrable. **Note:** For a map detailing Berlin neighborhoods, see the Berlin map in the color insert at the beginning of this book. Below are some names you're likely to hear as you navigate your way through the reunited city.

In the Western Zone

Charlottenburg Despite being renamed by Berlin wits as Klamottenburg (Ragsville) after the bombings of World War II, this is still the wealthiest and most densely commercialized district of western Berlin. Its centerpiece is Charlottenburg Palace. One of the most interesting subdivisions of Charlottenburg is the neighborhood around **Savignyplatz,** a tree-lined square a short walk north of the western zone's most visible boulevard, Kurfürstendamm. Lining its edges and the streets nearby are a profusion of bars, shops, and restaurants, an engaging aura of permissiveness, and an awareness that this is the bastion of the city's prosperous bourgeoisie.

Dahlem Now the university district, Dahlem was originally established as an independent village to the southwest of Berlin's center.

Ku'Damm In the 1950s and 1960s, during the early stages of the Cold War, the Ku'Damm emerged as a rough-and-tumble boomtown, bristling with boxy-looking new construction and permeated with a maverick sense of parvenu novelty. Since reunification, when vast neighborhoods within Mitte opened for real estate speculation and instant gentrification, the Ku'Damm has reinvented itself as a bastion of capitalistic and corporate conservatism, with a distinct sense of old and established money that's waiting for public perceptions to grow bored with the novelties that have been associated with the opening of the former East Berlin. The poignancies of the Weimar Republic and the Cold War are not lost, however, even upon the corporate sponsors of the big-money real estate ventures that line the Ku'Damm. If you look at the Hochhaus entrance of the Europa Center, on the Tauentzienstrasse side,

whose glossy chrome-trimmed interior decor may remind you of an airport waiting lounge, you'll find a plaque honoring the long-ago site of the private home of Weimar statesman Gustav Stresemann, which used to stand at 12A Tauentzienstrasse. Immediately adjacent to that plaque is an artfully graffitied chunk of the former Berlin Wall, encased in Plexiglas like an irreplaceable work of ancient archaeology. It is dedicated to the people who lost their lives trying to escape over the Wall during the peak of the Cold War.

Grunewald Many newcomers are surprised by the sheer sprawl of Grunewald's 49 sq. km (19 sq. miles) of verdant forest. The area serves as a green lung for the urbanites of Berlin. It lies southwest of the city center.

Hansaviertel This neighborhood, northwest of Tiergarten park, contains a series of residential buildings designed by different architects (including Le Corbusier, Walter Gropius, and Alvar Aalto).

Kreuzberg Originally built during the 19th century to house the workers of a rapidly industrializing Prussia, this has traditionally been the poorest and most overcrowded of Berlin's districts. Today, at least 35% of its population is composed of guest workers from Turkey, Greece, and the former Yugoslavia. Prior to reunification, the district evolved into the headquarters for the city's artistic counterculture. Since reunification, however, the fast-changing neighborhoods within Mitte, especially Hackesche Höfe (see below) have offered stiff competition.

Schöneberg Like Kreuzberg, it was originally an independent suburb of workers' housing, but after the war it was rebuilt as a solidly middle-class neighborhood that also happens to include the densest concentration of

Ich bin ein Berliner—But What Is a Berliner?

John F. Kennedy's historic speech on a visit to Berlin in June of 1963 became a famous utterance and made him the most popular American ever to visit the city (see Kennedy Museum, p. 140).

But the question might be asked, "Just what is a Berliner?"

No one could ever accuse the Germans of being too lighthearted or frivolous. Indeed, they rank as among the most reserved in Europe. They take pleasure in neatness, in precision, in the established order of things, and even their language has changed little over the centuries. Instead of creating new words for new concepts or objects for example, the Germans are more apt to string together words they already know.

There's little doubt that Berliners are Germans through and through, and are even Prussian on top of that, but they are also known for their dry wit and humor. They have what's called *Schnauze,* a Texas-like attitude that says everything in Berlin is bigger and better—a trait they share with the Bavarians. According to one joke, a Bavarian boasted that Bavaria was better than Berlin because it had the Alps. He then smugly asked a Berliner whether Berlin had any mountains that compared.

"No" answered the Berliner calmly, looking his rival squarely in the eyes. "But if we did, you can be sure they'd be higher than yours."

With a population of almost 3.5 million people, Berlin is the most densely populated city in Germany. It also has the largest non-German population

gay bars and clubs (between Nollendorfplatz and Victoria-Luise-Platz).

Spandau Set near the junction of the Spree and Havel rivers, about 10km (6 miles) northwest of the city center, Spandau boasts a history of medieval grandeur. Though it merged with Berlin in 1920, its Altstadt (old city) is still intact. The legendary Spandau prison was demolished in the early 1990s.

Tiergarten Tiergarten (which means "Animal Garden") refers to both a massive urban park and, to the park's north, a residential district. The park was originally intended as a backdrop to the grand avenues lain out by the German kaisers. The neighborhood contains the Brandenburg Gate, the German Reichstag (Parliament), the Berlin Zoo, and some of the city's grandest museums.

In the Eastern Zone

Mitte (Center) Closed to capitalist investment for nearly 50 years, this monumental district in the heart of Berlin is the one that's on every speculator's mind these days. It was originally conceived as the architectural centerpiece by the Prussian Kaisers. Its fortunes declined dramatically as the Communist regime infused it with starkly angular monuments and architecturally banal buildings. Although some of Mitte's grand structures were destroyed by wartime bombings, unification has exposed its remaining artistic and architectural treasures. The district's most famous boulevard is Unter den Linden. Famous squares within the district include Pariser Platz (the monumental square adjacent to the Brandenburg Gate), Potsdamer Platz (see below), and Alexanderplatz (see below).

of any German city, with foreign nationals making up more than 10% of the total residents. One of the first and biggest tides of immigration brought the Huguenots in the 17th century. With them came their language; and food still evident in Berlin today—a *Boulette*, for example, is a meatball that can be traced to the Huguenots and is today considered a Berlin specialty.

In more recent times, newcomers to Berlin have included large numbers of Turkish, Yugoslavian, Greek, and Polish immigrants. Turks are the largest minority in Berlin, numbering more than 120,000. They live mainly in the precincts of Kreuzberg, Neukolln, and Wedding. Although problems occasionally arise because of differences in cultural backgrounds, Berlin on the whole enjoys a greater harmony than elsewhere in Germany. Decades of isolation have helped forge a sense of community spirit. Years of living with the Wall during the Cold War have bred tolerance and determination.

As for the Berliner wit, it's most evident in a penchant to nickname everything in sight. The Kongresshalle, for example, built as the American contribution in a 1957 architectural competition, is irreverently called the "pregnant oyster," while the new church next to the Gedächtniskirche is known as the "lipstick and powder puff," and a large global fountain in front of the Europa Center is the "wet dumpling."

Alexanderplatz The former East German regime threw up lots of rather ugly modern buildings and defined Alexanderplatz as the centerpiece of its government. Today, the large and sterile-looking square is dominated by the tallest structure in Berlin, the Sputnik-inspired TV tower.

Hackesche Höfe A warren of brick-sided factories during the 19th century, it's evolving into one of the city's most visible counterculture strongholds. Part of this derives from the fact that it wasn't too badly mangled by the former East German regime. Another factor in its renaissance involves a thirst by cutting-edge, youthful Berliners to recolonize what used to be the heart of the GDR. You'll sense the rising real-estate values and combined aspects of Paris's Latin Quarter and New York's Greenwich Village.

Museumsinsel (Museum Island) This island in the Spree River hosts a complex of museums housed in neoclassical buildings that always seem to be under renovation. Its most famous museum, the Pergamon, contains magnificent reconstructions of ancient temples.

Nikolaiviertel Near the Alexanderplatz, the Nikolaiviertel is the most perfectly restored medieval neighborhood in Berlin, a triumph of the restoration skills of the former East German regime.

Potsdamer Platz Before World War II, this was the thriving heart of Berlin. Blasted into rubble by wartime bombings, it was bulldozed into a no man's land when the Wall went up on its western edge. After reunification, it was transformed into the biggest building site in Europe, out of which emerged a glittering, hypermodern square dominated by such corporate giants as Daimler-Chrysler. It's often cited as a symbol of the corporate culture of a reunited Germany.

Prenzlauerberg This former working-class neighborhood northeast of Berlin-Mitte morphed into the center of creativity in the 1990s. While it has mellowed out a bit, it is still one of Berlin's hottest quarters and boasts a thriving nightlife, particularly along and around Kollwitzplatz and Kastanienallee. Trendy clothing boutiques and art galleries share sidewalks with hip restaurants and bars, and the area has a fairly prominent gay and lesbian scene. In clement weather, people-watching, with a pilsner, at one of Prenzlauerberg's many sidewalk cafes and restaurants is an entertaining way to spend an afternoon, and it won't take long to comprehend why this is one of the most popular (and expensive) places for 20- and 30-somethings to live in Berlin.

2 Getting Around

BY PUBLIC TRANSPORTATION

The Berlin transport system consists of buses, trams, and U-Bahn (underground) and S-Bahn (elevated) trains. The network is run by the **BVG,** or Public Transport Company Berlin-Brandenburg. Public transportation throughout the city operates from about 4:30am to 1:30am daily (except for 68 night buses and trams, and U-Bahn lines U-9 and U-12). For information about public transport, call © **030/19449,** or visit **www.bvg.de.** For a plan of Berlin's **U-Bahn and S-Bahn system,** see the inside front cover of this guide.

The BVG *Einzelfahrschein* (standard ticket) costs 2.10€ to 2.70€ ($3.40–$4.30) and is valid for 2 hours of transportation in all directions, on all forms of public transport, transfers included. A 24-hour ticket for the entire city costs 6€ to 6.30€ ($9.60–$10). Only standard tickets are sold on buses.

Tram tickets must be purchased in advance. All tickets should be kept until the end of the journey; otherwise you'll be liable for a fine of 40€ ($64). Unless you buy a day pass, don't forget to time-punch your ticket into one of the small red boxes prominently posted at the entrance to city buses and underground stations. Standard tickets, valid for all public transport within the city of Berlin, are available at all BVG and S-Bahn and U-Bahn ticket counters.

If you're going to be in Berlin for 3 days, you can purchase a 25€ ($39) **Berlin-Potsdam Welcome Card,** which entitles holders to 72 free hours on public transportation in Berlin and Brandenburg. You'll also get free admission or a price reduction of up to 50% on sightseeing tours, museums, and other attractions, and a 25% reduction at 10 theaters as well. The card is sold at many hotels, visitor information centers, and public-transportation sales points. It's valid for one adult and three children under the age of 14.

Two **excursion bus lines** make some beautiful scenic spots accessible. Bus no. 218 operates from the Theodor-Heuss-Platz U-Bahn station (near the radio tower) via Schildhorn, Grunewald Tower, and Wannsee Beach to the Wannsee S-Bahn station, and bus no. 216 and 218 runs from the Wannsee S-Bahn station to Pfaueninsel.

BY TAXI

Taxis cruise restlessly along the major boulevards, indicating their availability by an illuminated roof light. The meter begins ticking at 2.50€ ($4). Within the city center, each kilometer costs around 1.50€ ($2.40), depending on the time of day. Prolonged taxi rides that you arrange to distant suburbs are factored at a per-kilometer rate of 1€ ($1.60). Staff members at hotels and restaurants can easily summon a cab for you, in some cases simply by throwing a switch on their phone. Otherwise, dial © **030/21-02-02** or 030/26-10-26.

BY CAR

U.S. companies have outlets in Berlin. If possible, you should make reservations in advance. You'll find **Hertz** at Berlin-Tegel Airport (© **030/51489300**) and at Friedrichstrasse 50-55 (© **030/2424440**). **Avis** is also at Berlin-Tegel (© **030/ 60915710**) and at Budapesterstrasse 43 (© **030/2309370**).

In general, we don't recommend driving in Berlin. Traffic is heavy, and parking is difficult to come by. Use the excellent public transportation instead.

PARKING   If you're driving into Berlin, chances are that you'll want to safely store your car once you arrive. Many hotels offer parking facilities; otherwise, you'll find parking garages that remain open throughout the day and night. Those located near the Ku'Damm and the Europa Center include the **Parkhaus Metropol,** Joachimstaler Strasse 14–19; **Parkhaus Los-Angeles-Platz,** Augsburger Strasse 30; **Parkhaus Europa Center,** Nürnberger Strasse 5–7; and **Parkhaus am Zoo,** Budapesterstrasse 38. Charges start at 3€ ($4.80) per hour.

CITY DRIVING   One problem that often infuriates drivers in Berlin is that it's almost impossible to turn left on major avenues (except at major intersections in the east) because of the positioning of metal barriers and tram lines. Oversize signs tell you to drive straight on. Drivers have to make a right-hand turn, swing around the block, and then proceed straight across the tram lines wherever a traffic light will allow.

Beginning in 2008, vehicles with high emissions of noxious substances will be banned from the inner city of Berlin. This restriction at present applies to only 7% of the number of vehicles registered. Drivers must display emission control stickers on their cars or face a fine of 40€ ($64). Stickers come in three colors—red (Class 2), yellow (Class 3), and green (Class 4). By 2010 only Euro Class 4 with a green sticker will be allowed within the city. For more information, refer to www.berlin.de.

BY BICYCLE

Berlin marks biking trails along major streets, especially in the leafy neighborhoods of the former West Berlin. A bike is also ideal for exploring old East Berlin, a city still in redevelopment. One of the best companies for rentals is **Bikes & Jeans** in Mitte at Friedrichstrasse 129 (© **030/447-6666;** www.fahrrad-countrybar.de.vu), renting bikes for 15€ ($24) for 24 hours.

Another good place for bike rentals is **Fahrradstation,** Auguststrasse 29A (© **030/ 22508070;** S-Bahn: Hackescher Markt), open Monday to Friday 10am to 7:30pm, and Saturday 10am to 6pm. A 24-hour rental costs 15€ to 30€ ($24–$48).

FAST FACTS: Berlin

American Express Reiseland American Express offices are at Bayreuther Strasse 37 (© **030/21476292;** U-Bahn: Wittenbergplatz), open Monday to Friday 9am to 7pm and Saturday 10am to 1pm; and at Friedrichstrasse 172 (© **030/ 2017400;** U-Bahn: Friedrichstrasse), open Monday to Friday 9am to 6pm and Saturday 10am to 1pm.

Business Hours Most **banks** are open Monday to Friday 9am to either 1 or 3pm. Most other **businesses** and **stores** are open Monday to Friday 9 or 10am to either 6 or 6:30pm and Saturday 9am to 4pm. Some stores close late on Thursday (usually 8:30pm).

Currency Exchange You can exchange money at all airports, major department stores, any bank, and American Express offices (above).

Dentists & Doctors The tourist office (see "Visitor Information," earlier in this chapter) keeps a list of English-speaking dentists and doctors in Berlin. In case of a medical emergency, call © **030/310031.** For a dental emergency, call © **030/89004333.**

Drugstores If you need a pharmacy *(Apotheke)* at night, go to one on any corner. There you'll find a sign in the window giving the address of the nearest drugstore open at night; such posting is required by law. A central pharmacy is **AlexAApotheke,** Grunerstrasse 20 (© **030/27581640;** U-Bahn: Alexanderplatz). It's open Monday to Friday 9am to 10pm and Saturday 10am to 10pm.

Embassies & Consulates See "Fast Facts: Germany" in the appendix.

Emergencies To call the police, dial © **110.** To report a fire or to summon an ambulance, dial © **112.**

Hospitals Hotel employees are usually familiar with the locations of the nearest hospital emergency room. In an emergency, call © **112** for an ambulance.

Hot Lines If you're the victim of rape or sexual assault, call **LARA,** Tempelhoferufer 14 (© **030/2168888**). For problems relating to drug use or drug addiction, call the drug help line at © **030/19237.** Gays seeking legal or health-related advice should call **Schwüles Uberfall** (© **030/2163336**). Gays can also call **Mann-o-Meter** (© **030/2168008**) for information about anything to do with gay life or gay events in Berlin or the rest of Germany. All of the above are staffed with some English speakers.

Internet Access To keep in touch, visit **Easy Internet Café,** Kurfürstendamm 224 (© **030/88-70-79-70;** U-Bahn: Kurfürstendamm; bus: 109 or 129), open Monday to Saturday 6:30am to 2am. Easy Internet also has several other locations throughout the city, including at Karl-Marx Strasse 78, Schlosstrasse 102, and Rathausstrasse 5. Call for more information.

Laundry & Dry Cleaning Deluxe and first-class hotels offer laundry service, but prices tend to be high. You'll find laundromats *(Wascherei)* and dry-cleaning outlets *(Reiningung)* all over town. Ask at your hotel for options.

Lost Property For items lost on the bus or U-Bahn, go to **BVG Fündbüro,** Potsdamerstrasse 180–182 (℃ **030/19449;** U-Bahn: Kleistpark); it's open Monday to Thursday 9am to 6pm and Friday 9am to 2pm. For items lost on the S-Bahn, go to **S-Bahn Berlin GmbH,** Invalidenstrasse 19 (℃ **030/29743333;** U-Bahn: Friedrichstrasse), Monday, Wednesday, or Thursday 10am to 4pm, Tuesday 10am to 6pm, or Friday 8am to noon. The general lost-property office, **Zentrales Fündbüro,** is at Platz der Luftbrücke 6 (℃ **030/75603101;** U-Bahn: Platz der Luftbrücke). Hours are Monday and Tuesday 7:30am to 2pm, Wednesday noon to 6:30pm, and Friday 7:30am to noon.

Post Office You'll find post offices scattered throughout Berlin, with particularly large branches positioned at Bahnhof Zoo, Hardenbergplatz (U-Bahn: Zoologischer Garten), Tegel and Schönefeld airports, the Hauptbahnhof (main railway station), and in the town center at Joachimstalerstrasse 10. With a limited number of exceptions, most post offices in Germany are open Monday to Friday from 8am to 6pm and Saturday from 8am to 1pm. None of them receive direct telephone calls from the public, but if you're interested in postal rates and procedures, call ℃ **0180/23333,** or click on **www.deutschepost.de.** Unlike the old days, German post offices no longer offer the use of pay telephones for long-distance calls and no longer send international telegrams. (A limited number, however, offer telegram service for destinations within Germany.) When you enter a German post office, know in advance that the yellow-painted windows are for issues about the mail and that the blue-painted windows are for issues associated with money orders and banking rituals. If you just want to buy a stamp for mailing a letter, it's usually more convenient to buy it at any of thousands of small stores, newsstands, or tobacco shops throughout the country that stock them.

Radio Radio programs in English can be heard on 87.9 FM (or 94 FM on cable), 1197 AM for the American Forces Network, and 30 FM (87.6 FM on cable) for the BBC.

Safety One unfortunate side effect of reunification has been an increase in muggings, bank robberies, hate crimes, and car break-ins. Residents of Berlin sometimes feel unsafe at night, especially in the dimly lit streets of Kreuzberg. Nonetheless, Berlin is still much safer than most large American cities. In case of a robbery or an attack, report the problem immediately to the police. You'll need a police report for any insurance claims.

Taxis See "Getting Around," above.

Toilets A restroom is called a *Toilette* and is often labeled wc, with either F (for *Frauen,* "women") or H (for *Herren,* "men"). Public facilities are found throughout Berlin and at all terminals, including the Europa Center on Tauentzienstrasse. It's customary to tip attendants at least .25€ (40¢).

Water The tap water in Berlin, as in all German cities, is safe to drink. However, most Berliners prefer to ask for bottled water, either carbonated or noncarbonated.

3 Where to Stay

Berlin is the scene of frequent international trade fairs, conferences, and festivals, and during these times, vacancies in the city will be hard to find. The greatest concentration of hotels, from the cheapest digs to the most expensive, lies in the center near the **Kurfürstendamm (Ku'Damm),** the main boulevard of western Berlin. Most good-value pensions and small hotels are in the western part of the city; note that many such accommodations are in older buildings where plumbing is rarely state of the art.

The business convention crowd still anchors primarily in the west, as do the hordes of summer visitors on whirlwind tours of Europe. **Eastern Berlin** often attracts Germans from other parts of the country who want a glimpse of the Berlin that was shut away behind the Wall for so long. The eastern sector still doesn't have the visitor structure and facilities of the west, although several first-class and deluxe hotels have opened there, notably the Grand, Adlon, and Hilton.

Travelers can also head for hotels in **Grunewald,** close to nature in the Grunewald Forest, or **Charlottenburg,** near Olympic Park. If you like biking, jogging, and breathing fresh air and don't mind the commute into central Berlin for shopping and attractions, you'll enjoy both these areas.

Tegel Airport is only 20 minutes from Berlin by taxi, but if you have a very early departure or late arrival, and want the added security of an airport hotel, you can check into **Mercure Airport Hotel Berlin Tegel,** Kurt-Schumacher-Damm 202, 13405 Orsteil-Reinickendorf (𝒞 **030/41060;** fax 030/4106700). Doubles are medium-size and furnished in standard motel-chain format. The rate for a double is 140€ ($224). There's also a restaurant on-site, plus a free shuttle service that runs back and forth between the hotel and airport. American Express, Diners Club, MasterCard, and Visa are accepted.

ON OR NEAR THE KURFÜRSTENDAMM
VERY EXPENSIVE
Brandenburger Hof 𝄴𝄴𝄴   This hotel lies on a dignified street in the commercial heart of the city and dates from 1991, when it was built in the classic Bauhaus style beloved by so many Germans. As a Relais & Châteaux property, it offers better food and service than most hotels of its price range. Rooms range from medium size to spacious and are among the most stylish in the city. The decor, with torchier lamps, black-leather upholstery, and platform beds, may appear a touch minimalist, but everybody will appreciate the original artworks that adorn the walls. Another bonus is the state-of-the-art security system and the French doors that open up onto balconies on all but the top floor.

Eislebener Strasse 14, 10789 Berlin. 𝒞 **030/214050.** Fax 030/21405100. www.brandenburger-hof.com. 82 units. 240€–325€ ($384–$520) double; from 395€ ($632) suite. Rates include continental breakfast. AE, DC, MC, V. Parking 21€ ($34). U-Bahn: Kurfürstendamm or Augsburger Strasse. S-Bahn: Zoologischer Garten. **Amenities:** 2 restaurants; piano bar; room service; massage; babysitting; laundry service; dry cleaning. *In room:* TV, Wi-Fi, minibar, hair dryer.

⌒Tips Dialing Germany

Remember that the phone numbers in this book contain an initial 0 in the German city code. That 0 is only used within Germany. Omit it when calling from abroad.

Concorde Berlin Its 17-story limestone exterior near the Kurfürstendamm has already changed the skyline of western Berlin. The location is only 100m (328 ft.) from the landmark Kaiser Wilhelm Memorial Church. The famous Berlin architect, Jan Kleihues, went for understated elegance in the hotel design, which features minimalist interiors in warm colors and modern art on the walls. The bedrooms are the largest in Berlin. Like the public rooms, they are elegantly understated in design and most comfortable with warm colors and beautiful hardwoods. The suites, both junior and regular, are among Berlin's finest and most luxurious, each imbued with grand style.

Augsburger Strasse 41, 10789 Berlin. ℂ 030/8009990. Fax 030/80099999. 311 units. 450€ ($720) double; 1,170€ ($1,872) suite. AE, DC, MC, V. U-Bahn: Zooligischer Garten or Kurfürstendamm. Parking 25€ ($40). **Amenities:** Restaurant; bar; health club; business center; room service; laundry service; dry cleaning. *In room:* A/C, TV, Wi-Fi, minibar, hair dryer, safe.

Grand Hotel Esplanade 𝒜𝒜𝒜 Strikingly contemporary, this luxe hotel lies in a quiet and verdant neighborhood near several foreign embassies, some concert halls, and the massively expanding Potsdamer Platz. Thanks to river views and a swath of park, you might get the feeling that you're far from the city. It competes effectively with other Berlin hotels in its class, with a well-conceived collection of modern art. It is, in fact, the hyper-contemporary alternative to the more traditional Kempinski (see below). The starkly contemporary, bright, sun-flooded, and cheerful rooms pay strict attention to sound insulation. Corner rooms are among the most spacious and have some of the best views of the surrounding area.

Lützowufer 15, 10785 Berlin. ℂ 413/2412541. Fax 030/254788222. www.esplanade.de. 386 units. 139€–224€ ($222–$358) double; from 229€ ($366) suite. AE, DC, MC, V. Parking 20€ ($32). U-Bahn: Kurfürstenstrasse, Nollendorfplatz, or Wittenbergplatz. **Amenities:** 3 restaurants; 2 bars; indoor heated pool; whirlpool; sauna; solarium; fitness center; room service; babysitting; laundry service; dry cleaning; nonsmoking rooms; rooms for those w/limited mobility. *In room:* A/C, TV, Wi-Fi, minibar, hair dryer, safe, bathrobes.

Kempinski Hotel Bristol 𝒜𝒜𝒜 This hotel reigns as one of Berlin's most prestigious and visible hotels, enjoying a reputation equivalent to some of the best hotels in the world. But the emergence of such luxe Berlin-Mitte properties as Adlon (p. 112) and the Regent (p. 114) has shaken the Kempinski crown. It occupies a bulky, boxy-looking building that was originally erected during the peak of the Cold War, but with an interior that has benefited from ongoing improvements and renovations. The staff is superbly trained, and the shamelessly rich-looking decor is more opulent and better designed than that of many comparably priced competitors. Rooms contain high-quality reproductions of English and Continental antiques, and enough insulation to retain an almost reverential hush.

Kurfürstendamm 27, 10719 Berlin. ℂ 800/426-3135 in the U.S., or 030/884340. Fax 030/8836075. www. kempinski.com. 302 units. 330€–420€ ($528–$672) double; from 458€ ($733) suite. Children 11 and under stay free in parent's room. AE, DC, MC, V. Parking 25€ ($40). U-Bahn: Kurfürstendamm. **Amenities:** 2 restaurants; 2 bars; indoor heated pool; fitness center; sauna; steam room; solarium; salon; room service; massage; babysitting; laundry service; dry cleaning; nonsmoking rooms; rooms for those w/limited mobility. *In room:* A/C, TV, Wi-Fi, minibar, hair dryer, safe.

Steigenberger Berlin 𝒜𝒜 One of Berlin's most visible luxury hotels lies on a formal, gracefully proportioned plaza a few steps from the Kaiser Wilhelm Memorial Church. Originally built behind a nondescript facade in 1981, it caters to a demanding clientele of relatively conservative clients. This place represents western Berlin's sense of the status quo more visibly than virtually any other hotel in town. Public areas

Where to Stay & Dine in Western Berlin

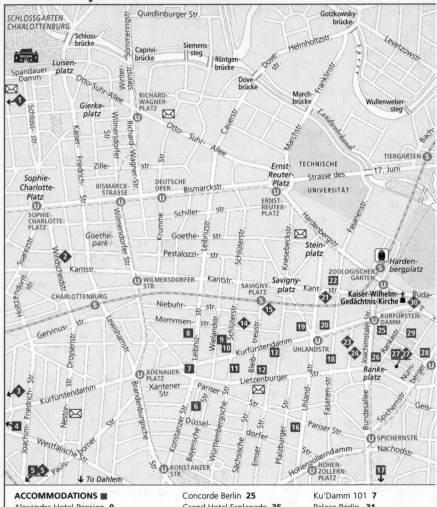

DINING ◆

Alt-Luxemburg **2**
Ana e Bruno **1**
Arlecchino **23**
Daitokai **32**
Die Quadriga **27**
First Floor **31**
Funkturm Restaurant **3**
Hard Rock Cafe **24**
Hugos **30**

Kaefer's Restaurant Dachgarten **37**
Lubitsch **15**
Marjellchen **14**
Paris Bar **21**
Paris-Moskau **36**
Vivaldi **5**

| 0 | 1/4 mi |
| 0 | 0.25 km |

⊠ Post Office
Ⓢ S-Bahn
Ⓤ U-Bahn
🚉 Train station

are large, well-designed, open spaces with high ceilings. Overall, expect a sense of bustling conservatism, plush and contemporary comfort, and corporate Europe at its most deeply entrenched. Rooms, for the most part, are medium in size, each maintained in good condition with tasteful modern decor and generous-size beds.

Los-Angeles-Platz 1, 10789 Berlin. © 800/223-5652 in the U.S. and Canada, or 030/21270. Fax 030/2127117. www.berlin.steigenberger.com. 397 units. 135€–327€ ($216–$523) double; from 669€ ($1,070) suite. Children 11 and under stay free in parent's room. AE, MC, V. Parking 19€ ($30). U-Bahn: Kurfürstendamm. **Amenities:** 3 restaurants; 2 bars; indoor heated pool; fitness room; sauna; solarium; room service; massage; babysitting; laundry service; dry cleaning; nonsmoking rooms; rooms for those w/limited mobility. *In room:* A/C, TV, Wi-Fi, minibar, hair dryer, safe.

EXPENSIVE

Bleibtreu Hotel ⊛　The facade of this trend-conscious hotel isn't easily recognizable from the street, as the tiny lobby is accessible via an alleyway that leads past an avant-garde garden and a big-windowed set of dining and drinking facilities. The setting is the labyrinthine premises of what was built long ago as a Jugendstil-era apartment house. Rooms are small, minimalist, and furnished in carefully chosen natural materials. Extras include dataports and cordless phones. Tables spill from the cafe into the tiny garden, where shrubs and flowers are surrounded with smooth-polished pieces of colored glass—a definite conversation piece.

Bleibtreustrasse 31, 10707 Berlin (1 block south of the Kurfürstendamm). © 030/884740. Fax 030/88474444. www.bleibtreu.com. 60 units. 124€–227€ ($198–$363) double. Children 11 and under stay free in parent's room. AE, DC, MC, V. U-Bahn: Uhlandstrasse. **Amenities:** 2 restaurants; bar; gym; steam bath; room service; massage; laundry service; dry cleaning; nonsmoking rooms; rooms for those w/limited mobility. *In room:* TV, Wi-Fi, minibar, hair dryer, safe.

Savoy ⊛　If you don't demand the full-service facilities of the grander choices, this is the hotel for you. In general, rooms are a bit small, but they are comfortable nonetheless, with such amenities as double-glazed windows and fine furnishings. Bathrooms are decent in size, maintained spotlessly, and contain tub/shower combos. For a nightcap, try the cozy **Times Bar** (p. 167).

Fasanenstrasse 9–10, 10623 Berlin. © 800/223-5652 in the U.S. and Canada, or 030/3-11-0-30. Fax 030/3-11-03-333. www.hotel-savoy.com. 125 units. 146€–277€ ($234–$443) double; 178€–317€ ($285–$507) suite. Children 11 and under stay free in parent's room. AE, DC, MC, V. Parking 8€ ($13). U-Bahn: Kurfürstendamm. **Amenities:** Restaurant; bar; sauna; theater ticket desk; car rental; room service; babysitting; laundry service; dry cleaning; nonsmoking rooms. *In room:* TV, Wi-Fi, minibar, hair dryer, trouser press, safe.

MODERATE

Art Nouveau ⊛ *(Finds)*　On the fourth floor of an Art Nouveau apartment house, this little-known hotel is an atmospheric choice. Even the elevator is a historic gem of the upmarket and desirable neighborhood. Established in the late 1970s, Art Nouveau is fully renovated. The well-furnished and comfortable rooms are pleasantly decorated and high ceilinged and are filled with excellent beds and well-kept bathrooms equipped with tub/shower combos. Rooms in the rear are more tranquil, except when the nearby schoolyard is full of children at play. At an honor bar in the lobby, guests keep track of their own drinks. A generous breakfast is the only meal served.

Leibnizstrasse 59, 10629 Berlin. © 030/3277440. Fax 030/32774440. www.hotelartnouveau.de. 20 units. 126€–176€ ($202–$282) double; 176€–236€ ($282–$378) suite. Rates include continental breakfast. AE, MC, V. Parking 4€ ($6.40). U-Bahn: Adenauerplatz. **Amenities:** Laundry service; dry cleaning; all nonsmoking rooms. *In room:* TV, hair dryer.

Askanischer Hof ⊛ *(Value)*　On the Ku'Damm, which was the heart of West Berlin in the Cold War era, this hotel still exudes an old-fashioned charm that we find most appealing. It is not for those who get off on *moderno*. To testify to its age, vintage photos of long-ago guests line the walls, and there is a lot of Victorian clutter. Nonetheless, it has attracted such past guests as the very hip David Bowie, so it must be doing something right.

The hotel prides itself on offering spacious, even elegant rooms, while maintaining a typical decor of Berlin, which has long ago faded at most hotels. The hotel dates from the end of the 19th century, and it miraculously survived the war. Bedrooms are most comfortable, evoking some of the charm of the 1920s. Those overlooking the Ku'Damm are double glazed to cut down on traffic noise.

Kurfürstendamm 53, D-10707 Berlin. (℗ **030/881-8033.** Fax 030/881-7206. www.askanischerhof.de. 16 units. 118€–185€ ($189–$296) double; 165€–220€ ($264–$352) suite. AE, MC, V. Free parking. U-Bahn: Adenauer Platz. **Amenities:** Breakfast room; nonsmoking rooms. *In room:* TV, minibar, safe.

Hollywood Media Hotel ⋆ *(Finds)*   Germany has never seen a hotel quite like this.
The two replicas of the golden Oscars guarding the door set the tone for Berlin's first cinema hotel. The soundproof rooms are all dedicated to the big heroes or the beautiful divas of the screen—from Marilyn Monroe to John Wayne, from Audrey Hepburn to Humphrey Bogart. Right on the famed shopping street and the former "main street" of West Berlin, the movie-inspired hotel plays up film tie-ins, going from *High Noon* to *In the Heat of the Night.* The most spacious and the best accommodations here are apartments with a kitchenette, balcony, or terrace, each dedicated to a classical movie with a film scene painted directly on the wall. The hotel even has a 100-seat cinema. Rooms are medium to spacious in size, each comfortably and elegantly furnished with full, first-rate bathrooms. Accommodations are spread across six floors.

Kurfürstendamm 202, 10719 Berlin. (℗ **030/889100.** Fax 030/88910280. www.filmhotel.de. 182 units. 115€–169€ ($184–$270) double; 195€–480€ ($312–$768) apt for 2. Rates include buffet breakfast. AE, MC, V. Parking 17€ ($27). Bus: 109, 119, or 219. U-Bahn: Uhlandstrasse. **Amenities:** Breakfast room; bar; fitness room; laundry service; dry cleaning; nonsmoking rooms; rooms for those w/limited mobility. *In room:* A/C, TV, Wi-Fi, minibar, hair dryer, safe.

Hotel Domus *(Value)*   Clean, streamlined, and unpretentious, this government-rated
three-star hotel dates from 1975 and lies in one of Berlin's most attractive districts in Wilmersdorf, a short walk from St. Ludwig's Church. Most of the accommodations come with a small private bathroom. The occupants of two rooms share an adjoining bathroom with toilet and shower stall. It's a favorite of business travelers, who appreciate its good value and respectability. As such, it has a high proportion of single rooms. Rooms are well designed, well scrubbed, and although not particularly large, very comfortable, each with a neat bathroom that is quite spacious, with either shower or tub. There are virtually no extras on-site, except soundproof windows and a charming breakfast room.

Uhlandstrasse 49, 10719 Berlin. (℗ **030/8803440.** Fax 030/88034444. www.hotel-domus-berlin.de. 70 units. 120€–150€ ($192–$240) double; 140€–155€ ($224–$248) suite. Rates include buffet breakfast. Discounts sometimes available Fri–Sun, depending on bookings. AE, DC, MC, V. Parking 10€ ($16). U-Bahn: Hohenzollernplatz or Spichernstrasse. **Amenities:** Breakfast room; bar; nonsmoking rooms. *In room:* TV, Wi-Fi, hair dryer.

Kronprinz Berlin   This hotel is located away from Berlin's center at the far western
edge of the Ku'Damm. In spite of its many discreet charms and features, it remains relatively little known or publicized. All rooms have balconies and fine appointments (often tasteful reproductions of antiques). If you want a little extra comfort, ask for one of the Bel-Etage rooms. Many guests congregate in the garden, under the chestnut trees, in summer.

Kronprinzendamm 1, 10711 Berlin. ℭ 030/896030. Fax 030/8931215. www.kronprinz-hotel.de. 80 units. 150€–215€ ($240–$344) double; 225€–275€ ($360–$440) suite. Children 12 and under stay free in parent's room. Rates include buffet breakfast. AE, DC, MC, V. Parking 13€ ($21). U-Bahn: Halensee. Bus: 110, 119, 129, or 219. **Amenities:** Breakfast room; bar; babysitting; laundry service; dry cleaning; nonsmoking rooms; rooms for those w/limited mobility. *In room:* TV, minibar, hair dryer, safe.

Ku'Damm 101 ℛ   On the main drag of the former West Berlin, this boutique hotel is one of the best. Of course, you have to be pleased with its clean, almost stark lines and minimalist palette. At the western end of the Kurfürstendamm, in the district of Wilmersdorf, the hotel is both a winner and a charmer. The midsize bedrooms represent the latest in contemporary aesthetic and lifestyle, with comfortable furnishings and state-of-the-art bathrooms. You breakfast above the rooftops of Berlin, after being treated, if you wish, to everything from ear acupuncture to Shiatsu body treatments the day before in the on-site spa. The interior design in both the public and private rooms is harmonious, using high quality materials and the latest high-tech innovations.

Kurfürstendamm 101, 10711 Berlin. ℭ 030/5200550. Fax 030/520055555. www.kudamm101.com. 170 units. 119€–250€ ($190–$400) double. AE, MC, V. Parking 14€ ($22). U-Bahn: Adenauer-Platz. **Amenities:** Lounge bar; gym; spa; breakfast-only room service; laundry service; dry cleaning; nonsmoking rooms; rooms for those w/limited mobility. *In room:* A/C, TV, hair dryer, safe.

INEXPENSIVE

Alexandra Hotel Pension   This three-floor hotel is comfortable, centrally located, and quiet. The building dates from 1900 and was converted into a hotel in the 1920s. Certain rooms are lined with photographs of old Berlin—perfect for acquainting yourself with what to look for as you tour the streets of the city. Most rooms have modern furniture and well-kept bathrooms with shower units.

Wielandstrasse 32, 10629 Berlin. ℭ 030/8812107. Fax 030/88577818. www.alexandra-berlin.de. 13 units. 52€–179€ ($83–$286) double. Rates include buffet breakfast. AE, MC, V. S-Bahn: Savignyplatz or Olivaerplatz. **Amenities:** Breakfast room; lounge; babysitting; laundry service; dry cleaning; nonsmoking rooms. *In room:* TV, Wi-Fi, hair dryer.

Bogota   Since 1964, when a quartet of separate hotels on four floors was combined into a cohesive whole, this hotel has been a local favorite for the frugal traveler. Typical for older Berlin apartment houses, rooms come in various shapes and sizes, but all have been recently restored. Guest rooms are well cared for and comfortable, the best opening onto an inner courtyard.

The building more or less withstood World War II bombardments. Constructed in 1911, it had been a famous address known for its frequent parties, at which a young Benny Goodman appeared on occasion. The famous entrepreneur, Oskar Skaller, lived here and was known for his collection of Impressionist paintings, including works by van Gogh. What is now the lounge and TV room was once the office of the infamous director, Hans Hinkel, of the Reich Chamber of Culture. Charlie Chaplin named the title character in his film *The Great Dictator* after Hinkel.

Schlüstrasse 45, 10707 Berlin. ℭ 030/8815001. Fax 030/8835887. www.hotelbogotaberlin.com. 130 units, 60 with bathroom (12 with shower but no toilet). 64€–77€ ($102–$123) double without bathroom; 89€–118€ ($142–$189) double with full bathroom. Rates include continental breakfast. AE, DC, MC, V. Parking 13€ ($21). U-Bahn: Adenauerplatz or Uhlandstrasse. S-Bahn: Savignyplatz. Bus: 109. **Amenities:** Breakfast room; lounge. *In room:* TV, hair dryer.

Hotel-Pension Bregenz   This dignified pension occupies the fourth and sunniest floor of a four-story, century-old apartment building, accessible by elevator. The owner, Mr. Zimmermann, works hard to maintain the cleanliness and charm of his comfortably furnished, relatively large rooms. Double doors help minimize noise from the public corridors. The staff gladly assists guests in reserving tickets for shows and tours.

Bregenzer Strasse 5, D-10707 Berlin. (C) **030/8814307.** Fax 030/8824009. www.hotelbregenz-berlin.de. 14 units, 11 with bathroom (shower only). 60€ ($96) double without bathroom; 85€ ($136) double with bathroom. Rates include continental breakfast. MC, V. Parking 8€ ($13). U-Bahn: Adenauerplatz. S-Bahn: Savignyplatz. **Amenities:** All non-smoking rooms. *In room:* TV, minibar, hair dryer, safe.

Hotel-Pension Funk 🌟 *(Finds)* Lying on a back street of the Kurfürstendamm in western Berlin, the home of actress Asta Nielson has been restored and turned into first-rate and affordable accommodations. Nielson, a Danish born-star (1881–1972), became one of the stellar lights of the silent era, her beauty praised by Guillaume Apollinaire. She was offered her own studio in Nazi Germany by Josef Goebbels, but turned down the offer. Many original features of her home have been preserved, including decorative ceilings and Art Nouveau windows. All the midsize bedrooms are modernized and comfortably furnished.

Fasanenstrasse 69, 10719 Berlin. (C) **030/8827193.** Fax 030/883329. www.hotel-pensionfunk.de. 14 units. 52€–113€ ($83–$181) double. Rates include buffet breakfast. MC, V. U-Bahn: Kurfürstendamm or Uhlandstrasse. **Amenities:** Breakfast room. *In room:* TV on request.

Pension München This pension occupies only part of the third floor of a massive four-story elevator building erected as an apartment house in 1908. It offers a simple but tasteful decor of modern furnishings accented with fresh flowers. Rooms are clean, with contemporary furniture and prints and engravings by local artists. Each comes with a compact, shower-only bathroom. Look for sculptures by the owner in some of the public areas.

Güntzelstrasse 62 (close to Bayerischer Platz), 10717 Berlin. (C) **030/8579120.** Fax 030/85791222. www.hotel-pension-muenchen-in-berlin.de. 8 units. 78€–98€ ($125–$157) double. AE, DC, MC, V. Parking 6€ ($9.60). U-Bahn: Güntzelstrasse. *In room:* TV.

Pension Nürnberger Eck *(Value)* This reliable pension in Charlottenburg is refreshingly old-fashioned. It occupies the second floor of a four-story building on a relatively quiet side street near Europa Center. Rooms are large, with high ceilings, massive doors and, in many cases, reproductions of Biedermeier-style furniture, including comfortable beds, plus small shower bathrooms. This is the kind of place where Sally Bowles from *Cabaret* might have stayed.

Nürnberger Strasse 24A (near the Europa Center), 10789 Berlin. (C) **030/2351780.** Fax 030/23517899. www.nuernberger-eck.de. 8 units, 5 with bathroom. 70€ ($112) double without bathroom; 70€–92€ ($112–$147) double with bathroom. Rates include continental breakfast. MC, V. Parking 6€ ($9.60). U-Bahn: Augsburgerstrasse. **Amenities:** Breakfast room; room service; laundry service. *In room:* TV.

NEAR THE MEMORIAL CHURCH & ZOO
VERY EXPENSIVE

Palace Berlin 🌟🌟 Although it isn't at the level of the Kempinski or the Grand Hotel Esplanade, this well-managed hotel outranks such landmarks as the Berlin Hilton and the Steigenberger Berlin. Don't be surprised by its boxy exterior (ca. 1968) that rises immediately adjacent to the Europa Center. Inside, thanks to dozens of improvements, the setting is very comfortable and, at times, even opulent. The soundproof rooms range in size from medium to spacious. All have fine beds, superb lighting, quality carpeting, and conservatively traditional styling. Known as "new deluxe rooms," the most comfortable accommodations are on the third, fourth, and fifth floors.

In the Europa Center, Budapesterstrasse 45, 10787 Berlin. ⓒ **800/457-4000** in the U.S., or 030/25020. Fax 030/25021161. www.palace.de. 282 units. 190€–355€ ($304–$568) double; 305€ ($488) junior suite; 465€ ($744) suite. AE, DC, MC, V. Parking 23€ ($37). U-Bahn: Zoologischer Garten. **Amenities:** 2 restaurants; 2 bars; indoor heated pool; fitness center; spa; sauna; solarium; room service; massage; nonsmoking rooms; 1 room for those w/limited mobility. *In room:* A/C, TV, Wi-Fi, minibar, hair dryer, trouser press, safe.

EXPENSIVE

Art'otel 🖈 *(Finds)*
Chic, discreet, and avant-garde, this is unlike any other Berlin hotel. The location is ideal, in the heart of cosmopolitan Berlin, with the Ku'Damm action virtually outside the front door. The decor, strictly minimalist, includes touches from top designers. You'll find Philippe Starck bar stools, Arne Jacobsen chairs, and artwork by Berliner Wolf Vostell. Modernists will be at home here, amid chrome-legged furnishings and pedestal tables that look like cable spools. Traditionalists might not be so pleased. Rooms are all comfortable, with soundproofing, large beds, and tasteful lighting. The service here is among Berlin's finest. On weekends, there is a minimum stay of 2 nights required.

Joachimstalerstrasse 29, 10719 Berlin. ⓒ **030/884470.** Fax 030/88447700. www.artotels.com. 133 units. 92€–230€ ($147–$368) double. Rates include buffet breakfast with champagne. AE, DC, MC, V. Parking 14€ ($22). U-Bahn: Kurfürstendamm. **Amenities:** Restaurant; bar; room service; laundry service; dry cleaning; babysitting; nonsmoking rooms; rooms for those w/limited mobility. *In room:* A/C, TV, Wi-Fi, minibar, hair dryer.

Hecker's Hotel
For years, this establishment enjoyed a reputation as a small, private hotel, but now it's expanded. Though not in the same league as the Art'otel (see above), it's still a good choice, conveniently located near the Ku'Damm and the many bars, cafes, and restaurants around Savignyplatz. The original 42 rooms are smaller than the newer units, which are medium size. The rather severe and somewhat somber modern style may not suit everyone—certainly not those seeking romantic ambience—though the sterility is balanced by up-to-date comfort and top-notch maintenance.

Grolmanstrasse 35, 10623 Berlin. ⓒ **030/88900.** Fax 030/8890260. www.heckers-hotel.de. 69 units. 140€–280€ ($224–$448) double; 350€–500€ ($560–$800) suite. AE, DC, MC, V. Parking 13€ ($21). U-Bahn: Uhlandstrasse. Bus: 109 from Tegel Airport to Uhlandstrasse or 119 from Tempelhof Airport. **Amenities:** Restaurant; bar (roof dining in summer); room service; laundry service; nonsmoking rooms; 1 room for those w/limited mobility. *In room:* A/C, TV, fax, Wi-Fi, minibar, hair dryer, safe.

MODERATE

Ambassador Berlin 🖈
This hotel is an attractive choice if you'd like to lodge near the Ku'Damm. Rooms are, for the most part, spacious and comfortable for families and include traditional furnishings. Bathrooms are rather small, and only a fifth have showers; the rest have tubs. Soundproof windows are always a relief in noisy central Berlin. The hotel is sometimes overrun with large groups.

Bayreutherstrasse 42–43, 10787 Berlin. ⓒ **030/219020.** Fax 030/21902380. www.sorat-hotels.com. 218 units. 136€–200€ ($218–$320) double; 156€–210€ ($250–$336) suite. Rates include buffet breakfast. Children 11 and under stay free in parent's room. AE, DC, MC, V. Parking 13€ ($21). U-Bahn: Wittenbergplatz. **Amenities:** Bar; massage; babysitting; laundry service; dry cleaning; nonsmoking rooms. *In room:* A/C, TV, Wi-Fi, minibar, hair dryer.

Hotel Sylter Hof Berlin
This hotel, built in 1966, offers rich trappings at good prices. The main lounges are warmly decorated in Louis XV style, with chandeliers, provincial chairs, and antiques. Well-maintained rooms—mostly singles—may be too small for most tastes but are good for business travelers. All the compact, tiled bathrooms are equipped with tub/shower combos.

Kurfürstenstrasse 116, 10787 Berlin. ✆ **030/21200.** Fax 030/2120200. www.sylterhof-berlin.de. 178 units. 139€ ($222) double; from 164€ ($262) suite. Rates include buffet breakfast. AE, DC, MC, V. Parking 12€ ($19). U-Bahn: Wittenbergplatz. Bus: 100, 129, 146, or 185. **Amenities:** Restaurant; bar; coffee bar; nightclub next door; laundry service; dry cleaning. *In room:* TV w/pay movies, Wi-Fi, minibar, hair dryer.

INEXPENSIVE

Arco Hotel   Although some of its competitors are more visible and more heavily promoted, this four-story hotel is one of the most consistently reliable and fairly priced gay-friendly hotels in Berlin. It occupies part of a 1900 Berlin apartment building. Rooms are mostly white, well scrubbed, and well organized, with tasteful, albeit simple, artwork and furnishings; each has a small, tub/shower bathroom. A garden in back hosts breakfasts during clement weather. A polite and hardworking staff is alert to the location of emerging neighborhood bars and restaurants. Much of its business includes repeat guests.

Geisbergstrasse 30, 10777 Berlin. ✆ **030/2351480.** Fax 030/21475178. www.arco-hotel.de. 20 units. 85€–97€ ($136–$155) double. Rates include breakfast buffet. AE, DC, MC, V. Parking 10€ ($16). U-Bahn: Wittenbergplatz, Viktoria-Luise-Platz, or Nollendorferplatz. **Amenities:** Breakfast room; lounge; laundry service. *In room:* TV, hair dryer, safe.

IN GRUNEWALD

Schlosshotel im Grunewald ❀❀❀   With only 54 gemlike rooms, this is one of the most historic and plushest hotels in Berlin. It was built in the 19th century by a friend and advisor of Kaiser Wilhelm II, who entertained him from time to time on the premises. For anyone who can afford it and prefers a stay in the city's verdant suburbs, the experience can be elegant, historic, and charming. Service is superb and invariably cheerful. Although changes have been made to the decor, its original inspiration was by German-born fashion superstar Karl Lagerfeld. The structure's monumental staircase, minstrel's gallery, and other Belle Epoque trappings remain, but Mr. Lagerfeld's contributions have added an undeniable gloss to the hotel's interior. Beds are sumptuous, with great pillows, fine linen, and elegant fabrics.

Brahmsstrasse 10, 14193 Berlin-Grunewald. ✆ **030/895840.** Fax 030/89584800. www.schlosshotelberlin.com. 54 units. 300€–450€ ($480–$720) double; from 600€ ($960) suite. Rates include buffet breakfast. AE, DC, MC, V. S-Bahn: Grunewald. **Amenities:** 2 restaurants; bar; indoor heated pool; health club; spa; sauna; salon; room service; massage; babysitting; laundry service; dry cleaning; nonsmoking rooms; rooms for those w/limited mobility. *In room:* A/C, TV, minibar, hair dryer, safe.

IN BERLIN-MITTE
VERY EXPENSIVE

Berlin Hilton ❀   The Regent and Westin Grand are finer hotels, attracting some of the Hilton's former clients, but this durable landmark remains strong. Set within one of the city's most expensive and desirable neighborhoods, Gendarmenmarkt, this deluxe hotel was the first to open in what was East Berlin following the collapse of the Berlin Wall. Today, it's the third-largest hotel in the city and one of the most popular, with enough accessories and facilities within its seven floors to keep you busy for a week. Thanks to all the visual distraction in the lobby, you may even have a vague sense that you're in a resort hotel that's eager to meet the needs of both large groups and business travelers. Rooms are conservatively modern and very comfortable, with double-glazed windows, comfortable beds, and bedside controls. At least half overlook the twin churches of the dramatic Gendarmenmarkt.

Mohrenstrasse 30, 10117 Berlin. © **800/445-8667** in the U.S. and Canada, or 030/20230. Fax 030/20234269. www.hilton.com. 589 units. 289€–349€ ($462–$558) double; 364€–489€ ($582–$782) suite. Weekend packages available. AE, DC, MC, V. Parking 20€ ($32). U-Bahn: Stadtmitte. **Amenities:** 5 restaurants; bar; indoor heated pool; health club and spa; Jacuzzi; sauna; salon; room service; massage; babysitting; laundry service; dry cleaning; nonsmoking rooms; rooms for those w/limited mobility. *In room:* A/C, TV, Wi-Fi, minibar, hair dryer, safe.

Grand Hyatt Berlin 𝄐𝄐𝄐

This is the most exciting, best-designed, and most iconoclastic hotel in Berlin, a government-rated five-star mecca. Don't expect rococo frills: Interior designer Hannes Wettstein permeated this hotel with a minimalist simplicity that may remind you of a Zen temple. Ceilings soar toward surreal-looking inverted pyramids, upstairs hallways run off into futuristic-looking infinities, and light derives from rambling expanses of glass or translucent slabs of alabaster. The large and sunflooded rooms are among the hotel's best features. Suites are often commandeered by fashion photographers as backgrounds for cutting-edge fashion layouts. *Hint:* Ask about upgrading your accommodations to the Regency Grand Club.

Marlene-Dietrich-Platz 2, 10785 Berlin. © **030/25531234.** Fax 030/25531235. www.berlin.grand.hyatt.com. 344 units. 305€–490€ ($488–$784) double; from 570€ ($912) suite. AE, DC, MC, V. Parking 20€ ($32). U-Bahn: Potsdamer Platz. **Amenities:** 3 restaurants; cafe; bar; indoor heated pool; health club; spa; Jacuzzi; sauna; business center; room service; babysitting; laundry service; dry cleaning; rooms for those w/limited mobility. *In room:* A/C, TV, Wi-Fi, minibar, coffeemaker, hair dryer, safe.

Hotel Adlon 𝄐𝄐𝄐

Berlin's most historic hotel is a phoenix, freshly risen from the ashes of 1945. No other hotel sits as close to the Brandenburg Gate, at the top of an avenue that's reasserting its claim on the city's sense of chic. Grand and historic, and permeated with the legends of the glamour and tragedies that befell it during various eras of its life, it was originally built by legendary hotelier Lorenz Adlon in 1907, and then reopened with a well-publicized flourish in 1997. Public areas, some of them illuminated with lavishly detailed stained-glass domes, contain coffered ceilings, mosaics, inlaid paneling, and lots of Carrara marble. Rooms are mostly large and have lots of state-of-the-art electronic extras. Those on the top floor offer the best views but are a bit more cramped and lack some extras.

Unter den Linden 77, 10117 Berlin. © **800/426-3135** in the U.S., or 030/22610. Fax 030/22-61-22-22. www.hotel-adlon.de. 394 units. 450€–550€ ($720–$880) double; 900€–1,600€ ($1,440–$2,560) junior suite; from 1,300€ ($2,080) suite. AE, DC, MC, V. Parking 28€ ($45). S-Bahn: Unter den Linden. **Amenities:** 3 restaurants; bar; indoor heated pool; health club; spa; room service; babysitting; laundry service; dry cleaning; nonsmoking rooms; rooms for those w/limited mobility. *In room:* A/C, TV, Wi-Fi, minibar, hair dryer, safe, Jacuzzi and sauna (in some suites).

Hotel de Rome 𝄐𝄐𝄐

If you're a movie star and always stayed at the Hotel Adlon (see above), at last you have an alternative choice if you like your living lush and plush. Rocco Forte hotels has taken an 1889 former central bank of old East Berlin and turned it into an exceptional five-star rated hotel, although the Adlon still reigns supreme. The renovation has been nothing short of spectacular—the underground vault, for example, was turned into a swimming pool. If you get a front room, you'll be overlooking the famous square, Bebelplatz, where Nazis staged the famous book burning of 1933. Most of the bedrooms rest under tall ceilings and are superbly contemporary with all the latest comforts. The grand Opera Court under a glazed ceiling is an idyllic spot for afternoon tea.

Behrenstrasse 37, D-10117 Berlin. © **030/460-6090.** Fax 030/460-60-92000. www.hotelderome.com. 146 units. 450€–520€ ($720–$832) double; from 750€ ($1,200) suite. AE, DC, MC, V. Parking 25€ ($40). S-Bahn: Unter den Linden. **Amenities:** Restaurant; bar; indoor heated pool; gym; spa; children's amenities (from comic books to special toiletries); business services; room service; babysitting; laundry service; dry cleaning. *In room:* A/C, TV, Wi-Fi, minibar, hair dryer, trouser press, safe.

Where to Stay & Dine in Berlin-Mitte

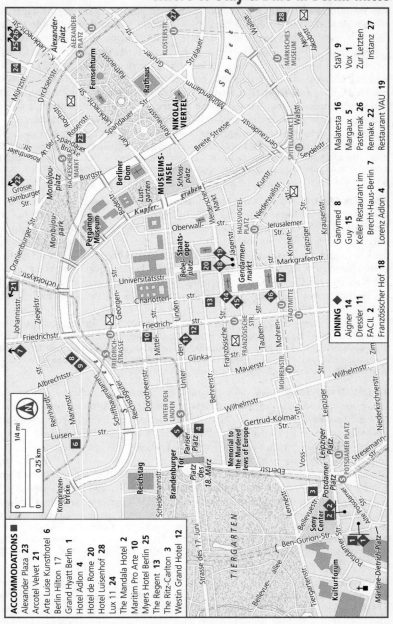

ACCOMMODATIONS ■
Alexander Plaza **23**
Arcotel Velvet **21**
Arte Luise Kunsthotel **6**
Berlin Hilton **17**
Grand Hyatt Berlin **1**
Hotel Adlon **4**
Hotel de Rome **20**
Hotel Luisenhof **28**
Lux 11 **24**
The Mandala Hotel **2**
Maritim Pro Arte **10**
Myers Hotel Berlin **25**
The Regent **13**
The Ritz-Carlton **3**
Westin Grand Hotel **12**

DINING ◆
Aigner **14**
Dressler **11**
FACIL **2**
Französischer Hof **18**
Ganymed **8**
Guy **15**
Keller Restaurant im
Brecht-Haus-Berlin **7**
Lorenz Adlon **4**
Malatesta **16**
Margaux **5**
Pasternak **26**
Remake **22**
Restaurant VAU **19**
StäV **9**
Vox **1**
Zur Letzten
Instanz **27**

The Regent 🌟🌟🌟   This hotel lacks the historical pedigree of its major competitor, the rebuilt Adlon (see above), but the Regent is Berlin's most sumptuous address. One of Berlin's most opulent hotels, it was built in 1996 on the site of a bombed-out parking lot, about a block from the Gendarmenmarkt. From the look of things, you'd never realize the venue is modern, as everything about it evokes Versailles and an undeniable sense of well-established and very plush prosperity. Decor, illuminated with light from two separate courtyards, includes Viennese crystal chandeliers and antiques from throughout Europe, giving you the sense that you've entered a private and very upscale home. Rooms are furnished with timeless taste and elegance.

Charlottenstrasse 49, 10117 Berlin. 📞 888/201-1806 in the U.S., or 030/20338. Fax 030/20336119. www.regent hotels.com. 195 units. 335€–395€ ($536–$632) double; from 655€ ($1,048) suite. AE, MC, V. Parking 20€ ($32). U-Bahn: Französischestrasse. **Amenities:** Restaurant; bar; health club; spa services; Jacuzzi; room service; massage; babysitting; laundry service; dry cleaning; nonsmoking rooms; rooms for those w/limited mobility. *In room:* A/C, TV, Wi-Fi, minibar, hair dryer, safe.

The Ritz-Carlton 🌟🌟🌟   One of Berlin's most glamorous and prestigious hotels opened at the Potsdamer Platz. The building evokes the Art Nouveau heyday of the New York skyscrapers constructed in the 1920s. The club-level rooms and the suites, of course, are the most luxurious way to stay here, but even the standard guest rooms are luxuriously furnished and decorated. The hotel is full of grace notes, such as afternoon tea served in the lobby lounge by an open fireplace; live jazz or blues featured in the hotel bar, the Curtain Club; and an indoor pool. The dining facilities are among the finest in town, featuring a creative European cuisine, with lots of Italian influences.

Potsdamer Platz 3, 10785 Berlin. 📞 800/241-3333 in the U.S., or 030/337777. Fax 030/7775555. www.ritzcarlton. com. 302 units. 345€–570€ ($552–$912) double; 500€ ($800) junior suite; from 695€ ($1,112) suite. AE, DC, MC, V. Parking 25€ ($40). U-Bahn: Potsdamer Platz. **Amenities:** 3 restaurants; bar; indoor heated pool; fitness center; spa; Jacuzzi; sauna; room service; laundry service; dry cleaning; nonsmoking rooms; rooms for those w/limited mobility. *In room:* A/C, TV, kitchen (in suites), minibar, coffeemaker (in suites), hair dryer, safe.

Westin Grand Hotel 🌟🌟🌟   A monument to "capitalistic decadence," as they used to say during the Cold War era, amazingly, this hotel was constructed on socialist soil by the East German government. Now under management by the Westin group and devoid of its original sense of stiffness, it's one of Berlin's finest hotels. Belle Epoque features blend with contemporary styling. Guest rooms come in a wide range of styles, from beautifully appointed standard doubles all the way up to the lush-looking Schinkel Suite. Rooms contain beds with wonderfully soft linens, down pillows, and comforters, as well as terry-cloth robes, tub/shower combos, and fresh flowers.

Friedrichstrasse 158–164, 10117 Berlin. 📞 888/625-5144 in the U.S., or 030/20270. Fax 030/20273362. www. westin.com/berlin. 359 units. 229€–329€ ($366–$526) double; 499€ ($798) junior suite; from 599€ ($958) apt suite. AE, DC, MC, V. Parking 25€ ($26). U-Bahn: Französischestrasse. S-Bahn: Friedrichstrasse. **Amenities:** 3 restaurants; bar; indoor heated pool; fitness club; spa; Jacuzzi; sauna; solarium; salon; room service; massage; babysitting; laundry service; dry cleaning; nonsmoking rooms; rooms for those w/limited mobility. *In room:* A/C, TV, Wi-Fi, minibar, hair dryer, iron.

EXPENSIVE

Alexander Plaza 🌟   A short walk from both Alexanderplatz and the historic district of Hackescher Höfe, this hotel originated in 1897 as an office building. In 1997, it was converted into one of the neighborhood's most charming and best-managed hotels. A labyrinth of hallways opens into rooms with unique floor plans. Each has parquet floors, high ceilings, and neo-Biedermeier blond-wood furniture. The executive rooms are very large. Low-end rooms are smaller and less dramatic, but still very comfortable. The staff here is among the most attentive in Berlin.

Rosenstrasse 1, 10178 Berlin. © **800/223-5652** for reservations in the U.S. and Canada, or 030/240010. Fax 030/24001777. www.hotel-alexander-plaza.de. 92 units. 125€–235€ ($200–$376) double; 185€–330€ ($296–$528) suite. AE, DC, MC, V. Parking 15€ ($24). S-Bahn: Hackescher Markt. **Amenities:** Restaurant; bar; health club; sauna; solarium; steam room; room service; nonsmoking rooms. *In room:* A/C, TV, Wi-Fi, minibar, hair dryer.

Arcotel Velvet ✪ *Finds*
With its Andy Warhol–inspired decor, this hotel stands in what used to be a Cold War no man's land. Enveloped by a vibrant artist and designer scene, the hotel lies right in the midst of some of Mitte's hippest cafes, bars, and restaurants. Its glass facade conceals a comfortably modern hotel that employs minimalist design and innovative concepts in its use of modern equipment, soft furnishings, and tasteful materials. All the beautifully designed bedrooms are stylish and inviting. The on-site restaurant, Lutter & Wegner, is run by Joe Laggner, a legendary star of Austrian innkeeping, and he serves a sublime regional cuisine. That's not all: The Velvet Bar is as hip as Paris Hilton and is a Mitte hot spot, known for its to-die-for cocktails.

Oranienburger Strasse 52, 10117 Berlin. © **030/2787530.** Fax 030/278753800. www.arcotel.at. 85 units. 118€– 230€ ($189–$368) double. AE, DC, MC, V. S-Bahn: Oranienburger Strasse. **Amenities:** Restaurant; bar; room service; laundry service; dry cleaning; nonsmoking rooms; rooms for those w/limited mobility. *In room:* A/C, TV, Wi-Fi, minibar, hair dryer.

The Mandala Hotel ✪
Built in 1999, this 11-story establishment is one of the most posh and elegant hotels in the pivotal Potsdamer Platz neighborhood. The hotel's exterior is sheathed in steel and warmly textured Italian brick. Each of the units inside is configured as a suite and is upholstered in discreetly plush fabrics, decorated with top-of-the-line stone, tile, or marble, and ringed with big windows that flood the postmodern interiors with sunlight. The upper levels, including the lounge, Qiu, one floor above lobby level, are spacious and opulent, in vivid contrast to the discreet and nonflamboyant scale of the reception area. One of this hotel's most charming features is its fifth-floor restaurant, **FACIL** (p. 122).

Potsdamer Strasse 3, 10785 Berlin. © **030/590050000.** Fax 030/590050500. www.themandala.de. 167 units (all suites). 270€–580€ ($432–$928) double; 1,850€ ($2,960) superdeluxe room. AE, DC, MC, V. Parking 18€ ($29). U-Bahn: Potsdamer Platz. **Amenities:** Restaurant; lounge; health club; spa; 2 saunas; solarium; room service; babysitting; laundry service; dry cleaning; nonsmoking rooms. *In room:* A/C, TV, Wi-Fi, minibar, hair dryer, safe.

Maritim ProArte ✪
This is a more luxe version of Art'otel (p. 110). Set about a block from Unter den Linden, this hotel was built as an avant-garde architectural showcase in the mid-1970s by the then-East German government. Today, despite frequent renovations, it still evokes a jazzy, *moderno,* and vaguely dated kind of architecture that features lots of chrome and stainless steel. There's a bustle here, however, thanks in part to a hardworking and polite staff, and a regular clientele of business clients and conventioneers. Avant-garde artwork is exhibited throughout, and Philippe Starck created some of the furniture. Rooms are individually designed, soothing, uncluttered, and comfortable.

Friedrichstrasse 151 (across from Friedrichstrasse station), 10117 Berlin. © **030/20335.** Fax 030/20334090. www. maritim.de. 403 units. 140€–312€ ($224–$499) double; from 240€ ($384) suite. AE, DC, MC, V. Parking 20€ ($32). S-Bahn: Friedrichstrasse. **Amenities:** 3 restaurants; bar; indoor heated pool; fitness studio; sauna; solarium; room service; babysitting; laundry service; dry cleaning; nonsmoking rooms; rooms for those w/limited mobility. *In room:* A/C, TV, Wi-Fi, minibar, hair dryer, safe.

MODERATE

Arte Luise Künsthotel ✚ *Finds*   Its name translates as "home for artists." No, it's not a communal crash pad for the bohemian fringe, but a choice and select boutique hotel where a different German artist designed and individually furnished each of the guest rooms. Under historic preservation, the hotel is in a restored 1825 city palace. Clients from the arts, media, and even the political or business world are drawn to this unusual hostelry. Each room comes as a total surprise, and, of course, you're treated to some of each artist's work, which runs the gamut from Andy Warhol–like pop to classicism. Some units evoke modern minimalism, whereas others are much more quirky.

Luisenstrasse 19, 10119 Berlin. ⓒ **030/284-480**. Fax 030/2844-84-48. 46 units, 29 with bathroom. www.luise-berlin.com. 79€–110€ ($126–$176) double without bathroom; 124€–150€ ($198–$240) double with bathroom; 130€–180€ ($208–$288) suite. AE, DC, MC, V. Parking 15€ ($24). U-Bahn: Friedrichstrasse. **Amenities:** Restaurant/bar next door; laundry service; dry cleaning; all nonsmoking rooms. *In room:* A/C (in some), TV, Wi-Fi, minibar (in suites), safe (in suites).

Hotel Luisenhof ✚   This is one of the most desirable small hotels in eastern Berlin. It lies within a severely dignified house, built in 1822. Its five floors of high-ceilinged rooms have been outfitted in a conservative and traditional style, a welcome escape from modern Berlin. The upgraded units range in size from small to spacious, but all are equipped with fine beds and individual fax machines. The neighborhood around this hotel, like many other parts of the once-dour eastern zone, is undergoing a rapid renovation.

Köpenicker Strasse 92, 10179 Berlin. ⓒ **030/2462810**. Fax 030/24628160. www.luisenhof.de. 27 units. 120€–250€ ($192–$400) double; 150€–350€ ($240–$560) suite. Rates include breakfast. AE, DC, MC, V. Parking 8€ ($13). U-Bahn: Märkisches Museum. **Amenities:** Restaurant; bar; room service; laundry service; dry cleaning; nonsmoking rooms; 1 room for those w/limited mobility. *In room:* TV, minibar, hair dryer.

Lux 11 ✚ *Finds*   In the hip central Mitte district, among fashionable art galleries and trendy media firms, this is an oasis of charm, comfort, and style. In a chic minimalist style, its bedrooms occupy a monolithic space, with a modern, glamorous decor. The open bathrooms are furnished in honey-colored wood and concrete. Lux 11 is the latest creation from that dynamic minimalist duo, Claudio Silvestrin and his wife, Giuliana Salmaso. In the basement is the Aveda Spa, and there's even a "micro" department store operated by a former buyer for Quartier 206, a posh fashion emporium in Berlin.

Rosa-Luxemburg-Strasse 9–13, 10178 Berlin. ⓒ **030/9362800**. www.designhotels.com. 72 units. 149€–205€ ($238–$328) double; 230€–266€ ($368–$426) suite. AE, MC, V. Parking 20€ ($32). U-Bahn: Weinmeisterstrasse. **Amenities:** Restaurant; cafe; bar; health club; spa; sauna; department store; salon; room service; laundry service; dry cleaning; nonsmoking rooms. *In room:* A/C, TV, kitchenette, beverage maker, hair dryer.

Myers Hotel Berlin *Value*   Spared from the 1945 bombings, this classical building from the 19th century has been renovated and turned into a good-value hotel that is comfortable, well maintained, and immaculate. Nostalgia and charm are combined with modern amenities. Guest rooms, midsize to spacious, come with a well-appointed bathroom with the latest fixtures, including tub and shower. The hotel offers several charming features, including a lobby bar with parquet flooring and chairs and tables that look as if they came from Old Havana. Drinks are also served on the garden roof terrace.

Metzer Strasse 26, 10405 Berlin. ⓒ **030/440140**. Fax 030/44014104. www.myershotel.de. 99€–195€ ($158–$312) double. Rates include breakfast. AE, MC, V. Free parking. U-Bahn: Senefelderplatz. Bus: 143. **Amenities:** Breakfast room; tearoom; nonsmoking rooms; rooms for those w/limited mobility. *In room:* TV, minibar, hair dryer, iron, safe.

IN CHARLOTTENBURG
MODERATE

Propeller Island City Lodge ★ *Finds*   Associated with a record producer and song-writing studio (Propeller Island GmbH), this hotel occupies three high-ceilinged floors of an old-fashioned apartment house originally built in the 1880s. Each of the guest rooms is radically different in its decor and theme, and each may delight or appall you with its quirks. Therapie is an all-white, minimalist room whose mood changes with the color of the lighting, which you can adjust at will. Flying Bed places a mattress as an iconic temple at the top of an inclined ramp, giving your bed a cultish importance. And the accommodation known as Galerie features a round bed, a pedal-operated mechanism that can spin the bed on a pivot, and empty picture frames wherein you can superimpose your fantasies. Weirdest of all (and not recommended by us) is the Coffin Room, where cult freaks can sleep in either of two (well-ventilated) closed coffins for a night of Gothic pensiveness . . . or whatever.

Note: This hotel's eccentricities (think installation art/sleeping quarters) means room types simply do not fit into traditional single, double, or suite categories; in some units, multiple guests can stay in the same rooms or units can be connected and feature access to shared or private kitchen and bathroom facilities. Call or visit the website for details on each room's configuration and sleeping situation.

Albrecht-Achilles-Strasse 58, Charlottenburg, 10709 Berlin. ⓒ 030/8919016 (daily 8am–noon) or 0163/2565909 (all other hours). Fax 030/8928721. www.propeller-island.de. 30 units, 24 with bathroom. Rooms 75€–200€ ($120–$320) per person. Each additional person 15€ ($24) per night. DC, MC, V. U-Bahn: Adenauerplatz. **Amenities:** Breakfast room; nonsmoking rooms. *In room:* No phone.

---

4 Where to Dine

If it's true that optimism and appetite go hand in hand, Berliners must be among the most optimistic people in Europe. But just because Berliners like to eat doesn't mean that they like to spend a lot on food. Locals know that you can often have a memorable dinner here in an unheralded wine restaurant or sidewalk cafe. Rising food costs in the east, however, mean that in the new Berlin, the eastern section can no longer be viewed as a bargain basement in the food department.

Examples of typical dishes are the Berliner *Schlachteplatte* (cold plate), pigs' trotters cooked with sauerkraut and pea purée, and *Eisbein* (pickled knuckle of pork with sauerkraut). Venison, wildfowl, and wild boar also appear frequently, as do carp and trout, along with an infinite variety of sausages.

But Berlin does not limit itself to traditional cuisine. A new wave of restaurants has swept across the city, from east to west. More and more are going ethnic, serving everything from Indonesian or French to Thai or Japanese. Eastern European wines are now almost as popular as those from Germany itself.

Note: If a restaurant bill says *Bedienung,* then a service charge has already been added, so just round up to the nearest euro.

ON OR NEAR THE KURFÜRSTENDAMM
VERY EXPENSIVE

Die Quadriga ★★★ MODERN CONTINENTAL   This is the kind of place so hushed, so "correct," and so seamlessly upscale that even when the president of Germany shows up (as he does in an informal and unofficial capacity), it barely makes a ripple in the smooth and well-rehearsed service rituals. The setting is a cherry-paneled room on the lobby level of a hotel (the Brandenburger Hof) that's a long urban trek from the restaurant's namesake, the four-horsed statue atop the Brandenburg Gate, in faraway Berlin-Mitte. Meals are served atop snowy linen to no more than 28 clients at a time, each seated on a chair designed in 1904 by Frank Lloyd Wright. Wines are available by the bottle or by the glass, and menu items vary with the season and the inspiration of the chef. The best examples might include Arctic codfish flavored with lemon thyme and served with a potato risotto; foie gras accompanied by Riesling grapes and Perigord truffles; strips of sole with Dublin Bay prawns served with exotic root vegetables; and saddle of venison stuffed with walnuts, black pudding, and pine nuts.

In the Hotel Brandenburger Hof, Eislebener Strasse 14. © **030/214050.** Reservations required well in advance. Main courses 30€–35€ ($39–$46); fixed-price menus without wine 75€–112€ ($120–$179); 7-course menu with 6 different wines 220€ ($352). AE, MC, V. Tues–Fri noon–2pm; Mon–Sat 7–10:30pm. Closed 2 weeks in Jan and 2 weeks in Aug. U-Bahn: Kurfürstendamm or Augsburgerstrasse.

Hugos ★★★ MEDITERRANEAN   In the Hotel InterContinental Berlin, this is the hot, chic restaurant of a united capital. *Der Feinschmecker,* Germany's leading magazine for traveling, eating, and drinking in style, named it Restaurant of the Year for 2005. Today it seems to be even better than it was when it earned that designation. Choice delicacies are created daily by Thomas Kammeier, one of Berlin's leading masters of the kitchen. You get not only superb food, but a panoramic view from your dining table as well. Backed up by an exquisite, albeit expensive, wine list, this Michelin-starred restaurant is filled with exquisite nuances in its market-fresh cuisine.

Appetizers range from simple to complex, but each is delicious as exemplified by glazed foie gras with mango or a risotto with Périgord truffles and quail-egg croutons. For a main dish, try the codfish with chicory salad, fresh oranges, and virgin olive oil, or else the braised pork cheek with a red-wine-and-shallot sauce.

In the Hotel InterContinental Berlin, Budapesterstrasse 2. © **030/26021263.** Reservations required. Main courses 28€–55€ ($45–$88); fixed-price menus 85€–130€ ($136–$208). AE, DC, MC, V. Mon–Sat 6–11:30pm. Closed July 17–Aug 16. U-Bahn/S-Bahn: Zoologischer Garten.

EXPENSIVE

Paris Bar ★ FRENCH   This French bistro has been a local favorite since it cheered up the postwar years in dismal bombed-out Berlin. It's crowded with elbow-to-elbow tables like a Montmartre tourist trap but is a genuinely pleasing little place on the see-and-be-seen circuit, close to the Theater des Westens. The food is invariably fresh and well prepared, but not particularly innovative.

Kantstrasse 152. © **030/3138052.** Reservations recommended. Main courses 12€–25€ ($19–$40). AE, MC, V. Daily noon–2am. U-Bahn: Uhlandstrasse.

MODERATE

Arlecchino ★ ITALIAN   One of the best Italian restaurants in Berlin not only serves a good cuisine but is one of the most affordable restaurants in its neighborhood. It attracts both homesick Italian expats as well as serious Berlin foodies. The cooks are definitely from the sunny Mediterranean, as reflected by their succulent pastas which are homemade and served fresh daily. In fact, you can easily fill up on a platter of one of these pastas, including penne with bacon and fresh tomatoes or tagliatelle with salmon. Another worthy pasta dish is fettuccine with spinach and mushrooms. Excellent wines also appear on the *carte*—you can, for example, order a fine wine by the glass or a full liter. The staff speaks English and is both friendly and competent.

Meinekestrasse 25. © **030/8812563.** Reservations recommended. Main courses 9.50€–18€ ($15–$29). MC, V. Daily noon–10pm. U-Bahn: Uhlandstrasse.

Kaefer's Restaurant Dachgarten CONTINENTAL   When a team of cutting-edge architects redesigned the most famous building in Berlin, the Reichstag (Parliament House), they added a restaurant on the uppermost floor, just behind the soaring dome that has inspired so many photographs. The setting is metallic looking and edgy. Lines to get in can be overwhelming, mingling sightseers and diners in the same queues, so here's our advice on how to short-circuit the potential wait: Phone in advance for a dining reservation and note the reservation number an attendant will give you. Head for the Reichstag's entrance for those with limited mobility, on the building's west side, facing the Platz der Republik, give the attendant your number, and then ride an elevator directly to the restaurant, avoiding the lines of sightseers coming just to admire the building's dome.

Included in the price of your meal will be a close-up view of the dome and the rest of the building's interior. Frankly, a visit here for breakfast may be your best bet, when there's a businesslike aura that's consistent with this building's august role as a Teutonic icon. Views sweep from the dining room out over what used to be known as East Berlin. The lunch menu is more "Berliner" than the Continental/Asian evening menu. Lunchtime menus include house-style meatballs with coleslaw and potato salad and grilled steaks and wursts. Dinners are a bit more exotic, focusing on such dishes as fried filet of duck with Austrian-style scalloped potatoes, Asian asparagus, and water chestnuts; and filet of turbot with a purée of truffles and herb-flavored risotto.

In the Reichstag, Platz der Republik. (C) 030/22629900. Reservations necessary. Breakfast 9€–25€ ($14–$39); main courses lunch 14€–21€ ($22–$34), dinner 17€–30€ ($27–$48); fixed-price dinners 68€–89€ ($109–$142). AE, DC, MC, V. Daily 9am–4:30pm and 6:30–9:30pm (last food order). S-Bahn: Unter den Linden.

Marjellchen 𝒞 EAST PRUSSIAN   This is the only restaurant in Berlin specializing in the cuisine of Germany's long-lost provinces of East Prussia, Pomerania, and Silesia. Ramona Azzaro, whose East Prussian mother taught her many of the region's famous recipes, is the creative force. Amid a Bismarckian ambience of vested waiters and oil lamps, you can enjoy a savory version of red-beet soup with strips of beef, East Prussian potato soup with shrimp and bacon, *Falscher Gänsebraten* (pork spare ribs stuffed with prunes and bread crumbs "as if the cook had prepared a goose"), marinated elk, and *Mecklenburger Kümmelfleisch* (lamb with chives and onions). This is the type of food Goethe and Schiller liked. Of course, Marjellchen isn't the place to go if you want to keep tabs on your cholesterol intake.

Mommsenstrasse 9. (C) 030/8832676. Reservations required. Main courses 11€–24€ ($18–$38). AE, DC, MC, V. Daily 5pm–midnight. Closed Dec 23, 24, and 31. U-Bahn: Adenauerplatz or Uhlandstrasse. Bus: 109, 119, or 129.

INEXPENSIVE

Hard Rock Cafe (Kids) AMERICAN   This is the local branch of the familiar worldwide chain that mingles rock-'n'-roll nostalgia with American food. Menu choices range from a veggie burger to a "pig" sandwich (hickory-smoked pork barbecue) that you might find in rural Georgia. The food is unexceptional, but service is friendly, and most kids will be happy to eat here. After enough sauerkraut and wurst, kids may want a familiar American hamburger, and this place dispenses them by the truckload.

Meinekestrasse 21. (C) 030/884620. Reservations accepted for groups of 10 or more. Main courses 10€–22€ ($16–$35). AE, MC, V. Sun–Thurs noon–11pm; Fri–Sat noon–1am. U-Bahn: Kurfürstendamm.

Lubitsch CONTINENTAL   Lubitsch is deeply entrenched in the consciousness of many local residents, and it's considered, in some quarters, to have a degree of conservative chic. Menu items include lots of cafe drinks, with glasses of wine priced at 4.50€ to 7€ ($7–$11) and steaming pots of afternoon tea. If you drop in for a meal, expect platters of chicken curry salad with roasted potatoes, Berlin-style potato soup, braised chicken with salad and fresh vegetables, a roulade of suckling pig, and Nürnberger-style wursts. Count on a not-so-friendly staff, a black-and-white decor with Thonet-style chairs, and a somewhat arrogant environment that, despite its drawbacks, is very Berliner.

Bleibtreustrasse 47. ℰ 030/8823756. Reservations not necessary. Main courses 8€–18€ ($12–$29); business lunch 30€ ($48). AE, DC, MC, V. Mon–Sat 10am–midnight; Sun 6pm–1am. U-Bahn: Kurfürstendamm.

NEAR THE MEMORIAL CHURCH & ZOO
VERY EXPENSIVE

First Floor ✿✿ REGIONAL GERMAN/FRENCH   This is the showcase restaurant within one of the most spectacular hotels ever built near the Tiergarten. Set one floor above street level, it features a perfectly orchestrated service and setting that revolve around the cuisine of a master chef. Winning our praise are such dishes as a filet of sole with mussels and fennel, or saddle of venison veal in a spicy crust. Also delectable is the breast of guinea fowl with goose liver on a chervil purée. Starters include fried goose liver with a compote of papaya and Canadian lobster with couscous and crustacean gravy.

In the Palace Berlin, Budapesterstrasse 42. ℰ 030/25-02-10-20. Reservations recommended. Main courses 28€–45€ ($45–$72); 3-course fixed-price menu 40€ ($64); 4-course fixed-price menu 67€ ($107); 5-course fish menu 96€ ($154); truffle menu 138€ ($221). AE, DC, MC, V. Tues–Sat noon–3pm and 6:30–11pm. U-Bahn: Zoologischer Garten.

EXPENSIVE

Daitokai ✿ JAPANESE   Think of this restaurant as a less institutionalized Benihana's, where vermilion carp lanterns illuminate the labyrinth of reflecting pools. Chefs prepare the meals before your eyes at several long tables. This *teppanyaki* restaurant offers some of the city's finest grilled steak—tender, juicy, and never overcooked. The seafood and vegetables are served with an artistic flair, and the fish is always fresh and beautifully presented. The flawless service features kindly, almost overly polite waitresses in kimonos. To dine here inexpensively and still eat well, take advantage of the set luncheons.

Europa Center. ℰ 030/2618099. Reservations recommended. Main courses 12€–43€ ($19–$69); fixed-price meals 28€–65€ ($45–$104). AE, DC, MC, V. Daily noon–3pm and 6pm–midnight. U-Bahn: Zoologischer Garten.

NEAR THE TIERGARTEN

Paris-Moskau INTERNATIONAL   The grand days of the 19th century are alive and well at this restaurant in the beautiful Tiergarten area, where good dining spots are scarce. Menu items are both classic and cutting edge. The fresh tomato soup is excellent. Some dishes—such as grilled filet of beef in mushroom sauce—are mundane, but other, lighter dishes with delicate seasonings are delightful. We recommend the grilled North Sea salmon with herbs accompanied by basil-flavored noodles. The chef should market his recipe for saffron sauce, which accompanies several dishes. You'll receive attentive service from the formally dressed staff.

Alt-Moabit 141. ℰ 030/3-94-20-81. Reservations recommended. Main courses 21€–29€ ($34–$46); fixed-price menus 60€–85€ ($96–$136). AE, DC, MC, V. Daily 6–11:30pm. S-Bahn: Anhalter Bahnhof.

IN GREATER CHARLOTTENBURG
VERY EXPENSIVE

Alt-Luxemburg ✰✰ CONTINENTAL/FRENCH/GERMAN   Karl Wannemacher is one of the most outstanding chefs in eastern Germany. Known for his quality market-fresh ingredients, he prepares a seductively sensual plate. Everything shows his flawless technique, especially the potato-crusted sea bass with a spinach-and–balsamic vinegar sauce, or the roast duck breast with a honey-and-chili sauce. Filet of beef is delectably flavored with a mustard-seed sauce, and poultry breast comes with a Périgord truffle sauce. Featured desserts include a bread roll stuffed with Armagnac mousse served with Armagnac ice cream and spicy prune, or else chocolate soup with a nougat macaroon and mocha ice cream. Alt-Luxemburg offers a finely balanced wine list, and service is both unpretentious and gracious.

Windscheidstrasse 31. © 030/323-87-30. Reservations required. Fixed-price 4-course menu 64€ ($102), 5-course menu 70€ ($112). AE, DC, MC, V. Mon–Sat 5–11pm. U-Bahn: Sophie-Charlottenplatz.

EXPENSIVE

Ana e Bruno ✰ ITALIAN   This is one of Berlin's most charming Italian restaurants, turning out a delectable cuisine that takes full advantage of the freshest ingredients and produce in any season. *Nuova cucina* is emphasized here more strongly than traditional Italian classics, and the chefs like to experiment. The combinations of food yield delicious and harmonious medleys. Expect such dishes as homemade pasta with Norcia truffles and goose-liver sauce, or venison in a radish sauce with chestnuts and a quince purée. You might also go for the superb marinated lobster with Borlotti beans, lemon, and tomato. Regular customers and gourmets keen on experimenting always seem satisfied with the results. A large wine selection, mostly reasonable in price, complements the menu.

Sophie-Charlotten-Strasse 101. © 030/3257110. Reservations recommended. Main courses 22€–36€ ($35–$58); fixed-price menus 58€–100€ ($93–$160). AE, MC, V. Tues–Sat 6:30–10:30pm. S-Bahn: West End.

MODERATE

Funkturm Restaurant *Kids* INTERNATIONAL   This restaurant at the radio tower's 65m (213-ft.) midway point provides both good food and sweeping, high-altitude views. You'll first have to pay 2€ ($3.20) for adults, 1€ ($1.60) for children for the elevator ride up. Inside the restaurant's metallic, glossy interior, every table sits near a window, which is entertaining for kids. Menu items include saddle of lamb with vegetables, pepper steak, and seafood. If you just want to enjoy the view without the food, consider paying 4€ ($6.40) for a ride up to the observation platform near the top of the 136m (446-ft.) tower (2€/$3.20 for children). Kids delight in ascending this radio tower. The higher platform is open daily 10am to 11:30pm. For information about the tower and its upper-tier observation platform, call © **030/30382996.**

Messedamm 22. © 030/30382900. Reservations not necessary. Main courses 8€–18€ ($13–$29); buffet dinner 25€ ($40). AE, DC, MC, V. Tues–Sun 11:30am–11pm. U-Bahn: Kaiserdamm.

IN GRUNEWALD

Vivaldi ✰ FRENCH   This restaurant is the culinary showcase of one of the most unusual small hotels in Berlin, a neo-Renaissance palace built in 1912 by an advisor to Kaiser Wilhelm II. Vivaldi serves, with panache, some of the most elegant hotel food in Berlin, within a paneled and antiques-strewn setting that's as grand as anything you're likely to find in Europe. Most diners opt for one of two fixed-price menus, although there's also a limited a la carte list. Your best bet is to look for the day's suggestion. On our most recent visit, we were tantalized by the cannelloni of leek with iced crab and the grilled turbot with chanterelles and lobster jus. You can also count on the sauté of Bresse rabbit with morels. The chefs take special care with their roast suckling pig with truffled vegetables and a lavender sauce.

In the Schlosshotel im Grunewald, Brahmsstrasse 10. ℭ **030/895840.** Reservations recommended. Main courses 28€–49€ ($45–$78). AE, DC, MC, V. Tues–Sat noon–2pm and 6–10pm. S-Bahn: Grunewald.

IN BERLIN-MITTE
VERY EXPENSIVE
Lorenz Adlon ⍟⍟⍟ CONTINENTAL   This is the most elaborate and formal restaurant in Berlin, with superb cuisine, a discreetly wealthy clientele that tries hard to keep their names out of the newspapers, and a decor that evokes the grandest imperial days of the European (especially French) monarchs. It occupies a site one floor above the lobby of the also-recommended luxe hotel, with windows that overlook the Brandenburg Gate, richly oiled walnut paneling, black-and-white marble, and draperies that seem like monumental works of art in their own right. If the dining room is crowded, you can also opt for seating in either of two smaller and somewhat cozier rooms, the Kaminzimmer and the Bundeszimmer. Your meal might begin with a carpaccio of pickled kingfish served with couscous and pink grapefruit, or a roulade of saddle of rabbit served with eggplant "caviar" and saffron; then move on to a platter that celebrates duck, and as such is piled high with breast of duck, a thigh of duck en confit, and braised duck liver and Swiss chard.

In the Hotel Adlon, Unter den Linden 77. ℭ **030/22611906.** Reservations recommended. Fixed-price menus 105€–265€ ($168–$424). AE, DC, MC, V. Tues–Sat 7–10:30pm. Closed mid-July to mid-Aug. U-Bahn: Unter den Linden.

EXPENSIVE
FACIL ⍟⍟⍟ CONTINENTAL   At vast expense, in the infrastructure of the Mandala Hotel (p. 115), a crane lifted a vast tonnage of glass, steel, and garden supplies to the hotel's fifth-floor terrace. Don't expect a view of the city skyline, as you'll probably get something even better: a verdant oasis of Zen-like calm smack in the middle of one of Berlin's most frenetic neighborhoods. A glass roof, tightly closed for midwinter views of the falling rain and snow, opens dramatically during clement weather for a view of the moon and stars. All this is available only to about 48 diners placed at 14 tables. Service from the well-trained staff is formal, alert, and attentive.

A medley of extremely sophisticated menu items changes with the seasons and the inspiration of the chef, but may include such starters as lukewarm octopus with clams or gnocchi with cèpes (flap mushrooms). The freshest of fish is shipped in, and the chef grabs the best of the catch, fashioning the bounty into Atlantic turbot with fresh fennel and an anchovy sauce or else sea bass with bouillabaisse salad. Meat and poultry dishes also use quality ingredients, and our favorites are the black feather fowl with kohlrabi and dumplings or the lobster with roasted vegetables.

In the Mandala Hotel, Potsdamer Strasse 3. ℭ **030/590051234.** Reservations recommended. Main courses 18€–40€ ($29–$64); fixed-price menus 75€–110€ ($120–$176). AE, DC, MC, V. Mon–Fri noon–3pm and 7–11pm. Closed Jan 1–25 and July 27–Aug 9. U-Bahn: Potsdamer Platz.

Guy ⍟ INTERNATIONAL   At this top-notch restaurant, anticipate a strong sense of gastronomy as theater. Proceed to any of three separate balconies, each supporting at least one row of artfully decorated tables. The effect can be compared to the balconies and private boxes of an old-fashioned opera house. The cuisine is very haute, even to the point of seeming experimental. Examples change monthly but might include white halibut with lobster and green asparagus or sea bass with fresh artichokes and a bouillabaisse foam. Baked crayfish appears with caramelized fennel and an orange sauce or else you can order a carpaccio of venison with foie gras and lime vinaigrette.

Jägerstrasse 59–60. (C) **030/20-94-26-00.** Reservations recommended. Main courses 22€–28€ ($35–$45); fixed-price lunches 17€–22€ ($27–$35), dinners 59€–79€ ($94–$126), dinners with wine 96€–138€ ($154–$221). AE, MC, V. Mon–Fri noon–3pm and 6pm–1am; Sat 6pm–1am. U-Bahn: Stadtmitte or Französischer Strasse.

Margaux 👁👁👁 CONTINENTAL   Chef Michael Hoffmann will dazzle your palate with his seductive, inventive dishes and his brilliant wine cellar. Several food magazines have named this the best gourmet restaurant in Berlin. Only a few steps from the Brandenburg Gate, the restaurant has a stunning, modern interior, designed by the noted architect Johanne Nalbach. The exceptional food, such as the steamed char served with ravioli stuffed with pulverized "tete de veau" or the pigeon stuffed with olives and served with a wine and thyme jus, is made from only the highest-quality ingredients.

Unter den Linden 78. (C) **030/22-65-26-11.** www.margaux-berlin.de. Reservations required. Main courses 23€–42€ ($37–$67); fixed-price menus 75€–125€ ($120–$200). AE, DC, MC, V. Mon–Sat 7–10:30pm. S-Bahn: Unter den Linden.

Remake 👁👁 INTERNATIONAL   Wait till you try Cristiano Reinzner's licorice-scented scallops mated with a cherry sorbet. A horrible combination you say, until you taste this talented chef's experimental dishes prepared with culinary flair learned at the futurist cooking school of El Bulli, in Spain (hailed as that country's best). Scallops might also appear in a pumpkin-and–passion fruit sauce. Another divine creation is the chef's quail breast with bitter chocolate foam and berry reduction. If not that, perhaps you'll go for the plump raw oysters on coffee jelly with white chocolate foam and a black-olive cracker. A specialty is saddle of venison with artichoke chips, with a "remake" of *tagliatelle alla pesto*. The chic restaurant lies off Oranienburgerstrasser, in the Mitte district, in a series of small rooms with exposed brick and "spider" chandeliers hanging over tiled floors.

32 Grosse Hamburger Strasse. (C) **030/200-54-102.** Reservations required. Main courses 24€–40€ ($38–$64); fixed-price menus 80€–140€ ($128–$224). AE, MC, V. Mon–Sat 7–11pm. U-Bahn: Weinmeister Strasse.

Restaurant VAU 👁👁 INTERNATIONAL   This restaurant is the culinary showcase of Master Chef Kolja Kleeberg. Choices include terrine of salmon and morels with rocket salad; crispy pikeperch; salad with marinated red mullet, mint, and almonds; crisp-fried duck with marjoram; ribs of suckling lamb with thyme-flavored polenta; and desserts such as woodruff soup with champagne-flavored ice cream. The wine list is international and well chosen.

Jägerstrasse 54-55 (near the Four Seasons Hotel and the Gendarmenmarkt). (C) **030/202-9730.** Reservations recommended. Main courses 22€–38€ ($35–$61). AE, DC, MC, V. Mon–Sat noon–2:30pm and 7–10:30pm. U-Bahn: Hausvoigteiplatz.

Vox 👁 INTERNATIONAL/SUSHI   This is one of the most exciting and creative restaurants in Berlin, far outshining any competition within the vast architectural complex at Potsdamer Platz. One of Switzerland's best design teams created the minimalist decor, with lots of visual emphasis on a mostly stainless steel, open-to-view kitchen. Here, a team of uniformed chefs concoct artfully presented platters of braised gooseliver with apple-flavored vinaigrette; filet of lamb cooked in a wood-burning oven with goat cheese, pepper oil, and Mediterranean vegetables; rotisserie-cooked breast of Barbary duck with mango chutney; and roasted sturgeon on a frothy sauce of white rosemary. The culinary philosophy here combines Mediterranean with Asian cuisines in ways you may not expect. One corner of the restaurant features the best sushi bar in Berlin. The venue is enhanced by an attentive and very hip staff, some of whom shuttle between the restaurant and a stylish cocktail lounge that features jazz and blues every night, beginning at 10pm. During clement weather, tables spill out onto the terrace, beneath verdant rows of linden trees.

In the Grand Hyatt Berlin, Marlene-Dietrich-Platz 2. (C) 030/25531772. Reservations recommended. Main courses lunch 11€–20€ ($18–$32), dinner 16€–31€ ($26–$50); platters of sushi 12€–31€ ($19–$50); 3-course fixed-price menu 49€ ($78), 4 courses 59€ ($94). AE, DC, MC, V. Restaurant daily noon–2:30pm and 6:30pm–midnight. Bar daily 6pm–2am. U-Bahn: Potsdamer Platz.

MODERATE

Aigner REGIONAL/AUSTRIAN Habsburg Austria lives on here. In the late 1990s, the Dorint chain bought the furnishings from one of Vienna's oldest cafes, the Aigner, and moved them into the ground floor of one of Berlin's most modern hotels. The result is a black-and-white Jugendstil setting replete with Thonet chairs. There's a lot of ambience here, thanks partly to a location that overlooks the Gendarmen-markt; the staff provides old-fashioned service with a modern flair. The restaurant's signature dish is *Tafelspitz,* the boiled-beef-with-horseradish dish. Here, it's served in a big brass kettle with both haunch and shoulder of beef, with lots of soup, vegetables, savoy cabbage, crème fraîche, and apple-flavored horseradish. Other choices include Argentine pepper steak with Béarnaise sauce or else a crusty baked pikeperch with a warm cucumber salad and arugula pesto. Veal dumplings is an old-fashioned dish, served with beets and chive-laced mashed potatoes.

In the Sofitel Berlin am Gendarmenmarkt, Charlottenstrasse 50–52. (C) 030/203751850. Reservations recommended. Main courses 15€–27€ ($24–$43). AE, DC, MC, V. Daily noon–midnight. U-Bahn: Stadtmitte.

Ganymed FRENCH There's nothing trendy or immediately fashionable about this restaurant, which occupied these premises beginning in 1929 and stalwartly continued doing business within East Berlin throughout the Cold War. The setting includes two formal dining rooms, one with an ornate plaster ceiling of great beauty, the other a more modern, big-windowed affair that overlooks the Spree. Food arrives in worthy portions, with plenty of flavor. Many Berlin restaurants have abandoned soups altogether, but the chefs here continue to turn out that old Berlin favorite, green-pea soup, although the ginger-flavored carrot soup is more up-to-date. Our favorite start is lobster blinis on vanilla cream, though you might be tempted by one of the intriguing salad combos. Fish and poultry dishes are equally alluring, including garlic-flavored rack of lamb with rata-touille and deer filet with Duchesse potatoes. Sometimes fish is roasted and served with a Chablis sauce. For dessert, why not the Grand Marnier parfait with orange sauce?

Schiffbauerdamm 5. (C) 030/28599046. Reservations recommended. Main courses 16€–34€ ($26–$54); fixed-price menu 87€ ($139). AE, DC, MC, V. Daily noon–midnight. U-Bahn: Friedrichstrasse.

Malatesta ITALIAN Flavorful Italian food, served within an all-black-and-white venue whose rectilinear simplicity might remind you of a spartan version of a sushi bar, is the heartbeat of this likable Italian restaurant. The aura is high style rather than cozy, with an emphasis on the kind of offhanded hip you might have expected in Milan or Rome. The menu reflects whatever is fresh and succulent at the time, with dishes crafted anew almost every day. Three enduring specialties, however, include tagliatelle with asparagus, fried squid (calamari), and fresh tomatoes; filet of beef with black truffles; and pasta made with ricotta cheese, pesto, and balsamic vinegar. Specialties from throughout Italy are the draw here, with no particular emphasis on northern, southern, or central Italian cuisine over any of the country's other regions.

Charlottenstrasse 59. ℂ **030/20945070.** Reservations recommended. Main courses 15€–19€ ($23–$30). AE, MC, V. Mon–Sat 12:30pm–1:30am. U-Bahn: Stadtmitte.

Zur Letzten Instanz GERMAN   Reputedly, this is Berlin's oldest restaurant, dating from 1525. Zur Letzten Instanz has supposedly been frequented by everybody from Napoleon to Beethoven. Prisoners used to stop off here for one last beer before going to jail. The place is located on two floors of a baroque building just outside the crumbling brick wall that once ringed medieval Berlin. Double doors open on a series of small woodsy rooms, one with a bar and ceramic *Kachelofen* (stove). At the back, a circular staircase leads to another series of rooms, where every evening at 6pm, food and wine (no beer) are served. The menu is old-fashioned, mainly limited to good, hearty fare in the best of the Grandmother Berlin tradition of staples.

Waisenstrasse 14–16 (near the Alexanderplatz). ℂ **030/2425528.** Reservations recommended. Main courses 11€–18€ ($18–$29). AE, DC, MC, V. Mon–Sat noon–1am; Sun noon–11pm. U-Bahn: Klosterstrasse.

INEXPENSIVE

Dressler CONTINENTAL   No other bistro along Unter den Linden re-creates Berlin's prewar decor and style as successfully. Designed to resemble an arts-conscious bistro of the sort that might have entertained tuxedo-clad clients in the 1920s, it's set behind a wine-colored facade and outfitted with leather banquettes, black-and-white tile floors, mirrors, and film memorabilia from the great days of early German cinema. Waiters scurry around in vests and aprons, carrying trays of everything from caviar to strudel, as well as three kinds of oysters and hefty portions of lobster salad. You can always drop in to ogle the racks of elegant pastries, consuming them with steaming pots of tea or coffee. Otherwise, more substantial menu items include turbot with champagne vinaigrette, pheasant breast with Riesling sauce, local salmon trout with white-wine sauce and braised endive, stuffed breast of veal, and calves' livers with apples.

Unter den Linden 39. ℂ **030/2044422.** Reservations recommended. Main courses 11€–25€ ($18–$40); fixed-price menu 11€ ($17) for 2 courses, 15€ ($24) for 3 courses. AE, DC, MC, V. Daily 8am–midnight. S-Bahn: Unter den Linden.

Französischer Hof *Value* GERMAN   If you want a reasonable meal in a relaxed atmosphere, this is the place. Französischer Hof fills two floors connected by a Belle Epoque staircase, evoking a century-old Parisian bistro. The kitchen may not be the finest, but ingredients are fresh and deftly handled. You can begin with the delectable selection of fish canapés. Saddle of lamb is always admirably done, although you may prefer the rather theatrical flambéed filet Stroganoff with almond-studded dumplings. More recent menu items include such starters as pumpkin cream soup or a duck terrine followed by pork medallions in a beer sauce.

Jägerstrasse 56. ℂ **030/20177170.** Reservations recommended. Main courses 18€–21€ ($28–$34). AE, DC, MC, V. Daily 11am–midnight. Closed Dec 24. U-Bahn: Hausvogteiplatz.

StäV *Finds* RHENISH   For years, this upscale tavern entertained the politicians and journalists whose business involved the day-to-day running of the German government from Germany's former capital of Bonn. Although its owners at first opposed the reinauguration of Berlin as the German capital, when the switch was made, they valiantly pulled out of the Rhineland and followed their clientele to new digs, within a 5-minute walk of the Brandenburg Gate, near the Friedrichstrasse Bahnhof. The only beer served is Kölsch, a brew more closely associated with the Rhineland than any other beer. Rhenish food items include a mass of apples, onions, and blood sausage known as *Himmel und Ärd* ("heaven and hell"); braised beef with pumpernickel and raisin sauce; and Rhineland sauerbraten with noodles. Other items, many influenced by the culinary traditions of Berlin, include braised liver with bacon and onions, a crisp version of Alsatian pizza known as *Flammenküche,* and a potato cake topped with apples and shredded beets or with smoked salmon and sour cream.

8 Schiffbauerdamm. Ⓒ **030/282-3965.** Reservations recommended. Main courses 6€–10€ ($9.60–$16). AE, DC, MC, V. Daily 10am–1am. U-Bahn: Friedrichstrasse.

IN KREUZBERG
EXPENSIVE

Horváth ⒶⒶ INTERNATIONAL   The hot new dining ticket of Berlin is this restaurant opened on the site of that former celebrity favorite Exil, where David Bowie partied and Andy Warhol painted. In the Kreuzberg district, it is installed in a 19th-century front room, a showcase for the savory viands of Chef Wolfgang Müller. Celebrities, including the mayor of Berlin, continue to frequent these airy, hyper-avant-garde dining rooms, enjoying dishes that are inspired by recipes from Bavaria to Bangkok. Over chilled elderberry soup, you can decide on your next course—perhaps stuffed shoulder of veal with artichoke hearts, olives, pine nuts, and a mushroom-flavored risotto. Finish off with, perhaps, the passion-fruit tart with marinated fruit and a coconut-flavored lime sauce.

44A Paul-Lincke-Ufer. Ⓒ **030/6128-9992.** Reservations recommended. Main courses 16€–26€ ($26–$42); 5-course fixed-price menu 41€ ($66), 10 courses 69€ ($110). No credit cards. Tues–Sun 6pm–midnight. U-Bahn: Kottbusser Tor.

IN PRENZLAUER BERG

Pasternak Ⓐ Ⓕinds RUSSIAN   Its setting, a pink-walled dining room within a distinguished-looking 150-year-old building adjacent to a synagogue in what used to be the eastern zone, evokes nostalgia in many of its patrons. Menu items read like what the characters in a Dostoevsky novel might have ordered: borscht, blinis, chicken Kiev, pork skewers with pomegranate and walnut sauce, Russian-style ravioli *(taig Taschen)* stuffed with spinach and cheese, beef Stroganoff, and Russian-style hot apple tart. Expect generous portions, an evocative setting, and the kind of clients who don't necessarily remember the former Russian regime in Berlin with any particular distaste. You might get the vague suspicion that some, in fact, might even miss it.

Knaackstrasse 22–24, Prenzlauer Berg. Ⓒ **030/4413399.** Reservations recommended. Main courses 10€–15€ ($16–$24). AE, MC, V. Daily 11am–1am. U-Bahn: Senefelderplatz.

5 Exploring Berlin

SIGHTSEEING SUGGESTIONS FOR FIRST-TIME VISITORS

IF YOU HAVE 1 DAY   Get up early and visit the **Brandenburg Gate,** symbol of Berlin, then walk down **Unter den Linden** and have coffee and pastry at one of the cafes along the edges off this boulevard. Visit the **Gemäldegalerie** to see some of the world's greatest masterpieces. Afterward, go explore **Schloss Charlottenburg,** one of

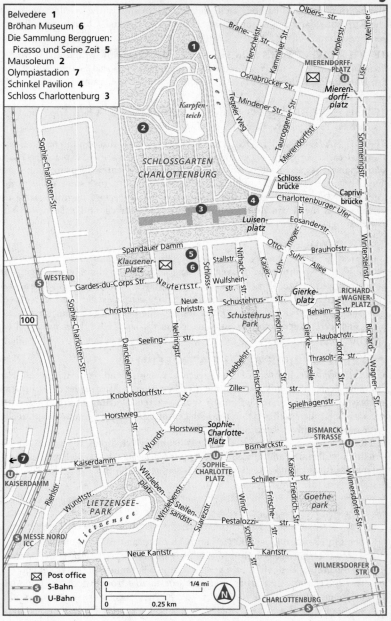

Belvedere **1**
Bröhan Museum **6**
Die Sammlung Berggruen:
  Picasso und Seine Zeit **5**
Mausoleum **2**
Olympiastadion **7**
Schinkel Pavilion **4**
Schloss Charlottenburg **3**

Olbers- str.

Brahe-
Herschelstr.
Kammiher Str.
Keplerstr.
Meitner-
Lise-

MIERENDORFF-
PLATZ

Osnabrücker Str.

*Mieren-
dorff-
platz*

Mindener Str.

Tegeler Weg

Tauroggener Str.

Mierendorffstr.

Sömmeringstr.

Spree

*Karpfen-
teich*

SCHLOSSGARTEN
CHARLOTTENBURG

Schloss-
brücke

Caprivi-
brücke

Charlottenburger Ufer

Wintersteinstr.

Luisen-
platz

Eosanderstr.

Otto- meyer-
str.

Loh- Suhr-

Brauhofstr.

Spandauer Damm

Klausener-
platz

Stallstr.
Nithack-

Kaiser-

Allee

WESTEND

Gardes-du-Corps Str.

Neufertstr.

Wulfsheim-
str.

*Gierke-
platz*

RICHARD-
WAGNER-
PLATZ

100

Sophie-Charlotten-Str.

Christstr.

Neue
Christstr.

Schusterhus-

Friedrich-

Behaim-

Wilmers-

Richard-

*Schustehrus-
Park*

Gierke-
zeile

Haubachstr.

Seeling-

str.

Danckelmann-

Nehringstr.

Hebbelstr.

Thrasolt-

dorfer-
str.

Wagner-

Knobelsdorffstr.

Zille-

str.

Fritschestr.

Spielhagenstr.

Str.

Horstweg

Wundt-

Horstweg

*Sophie-
Charlotte-
Platz*

Bismarckstr.

BISMARCK-
STRASSE

KAISERDAMM

Kaiserdamm

Witzleben-
platz

Witzlebenstr.

SOPHIE-
CHARLOTTE-
PLATZ

Schiller-

Kaiser-
Friedrich-

Wilmersdorfer Str.

Riehlstr.

Wündtstr.

Steifen-
sandstr.

Suarezstr.

Wind-
scheid-

Fritsche-

str.

*Goethe-
park*

*LIETZENSEE-
PARK*

Lietzensee

Pestalozzi-

Kantstr.

MESSE NORD/
ICC

Neue Kantstr.

str.

WILMERSDORFER
STR.

CHARLOTTENBURG

✉ Post office
Ⓢ S-Bahn
Ⓤ U-Bahn

| 0 | | 1/4 mi |
| 0 | 0.25 km | |

N

the finest examples of baroque architecture in Germany. In the evening, walk along the Kurfürstendamm, visit the **Kaiser Wilhelm Memorial Church,** and dine in a local restaurant.

IF YOU HAVE 2 DAYS   On Day 2, visit the **Pergamon Museum** on Museum Island; be sure to see the Pergamon Altar. Explore the **National Gallery** and the **Jewish Museum,** and then head for Alexanderplatz. Take the elevator up for a view from its TV tower.

IF YOU HAVE 3 DAYS   On Day 3, go to **Potsdam** (see "A Side Trip: Potsdam & Its Palaces," later in this chapter).

IF YOU HAVE 4 OR 5 DAYS   On Day 4, take a walk through the restored Nikolai Quarter. In the afternoon return to Charlottenburg Palace and explore the **Historical Apartments** and in the evening visit the **Europa Center** for drinks and dinner. On Day 5, see some of the sights you might have missed. Take some walks through Berlin and stop at the Cold War's **Checkpoint Charlie,** with its museum. If time remains, visit the **Berlin Zoo,** stroll through the **Tiergarten,** and attend a cabaret in the evening.

THE TOP MUSEUMS

The great art collections of old Berlin suffered during and after World War II. Although many paintings were saved by being stored in salt mines, many larger works were destroyed by fire. Part of the surviving art stayed in the east, including a wealth of ancient treasures that remind us of the leading role played by German archaeologists during the 19th and early 20th centuries. The paintings that turned up in the west, and were passed from nation to nation in the late 1940s, have nearly all been returned to Berlin.

CHARLOTTENBURG PALACE & MUSEUMS

Charlottenburg lies just west of the Tiergarten. Plan on spending the day here; the area contains several museums as well as the royal apartments. After seeing the main attractions, you can enjoy a ramble through **Schlossgarten Charlottenburg.** These formal gardens look much as they did in the 18th century. A grove of cypresses leads to a lake with swans and other waterfowl.

North of the palace stands the **Mausoleum,** which holds the tombs of King Friedrich Wilhelm II and Queen Luise—sculpted by Rauch—as well as several other interesting funerary monuments of the Prussian royal family.

The Best Sightseeing Deal

The CityTourCard gives you free entry to more than 50 museums in Berlin, a free trip up the Fernsehturm (Berlin Television Tower), and reduced fare on BVG tours. The card is sold at all BVG and S-Bahn (urban rail) ticket counters and at some 200 hotels, and it's also available from automatic vending machines run by the BVG. Ticket holders may take children ages 5 and younger free. The cost is 23€ ($37) for 72 hours. For more information, visit www.citytourcard.com.

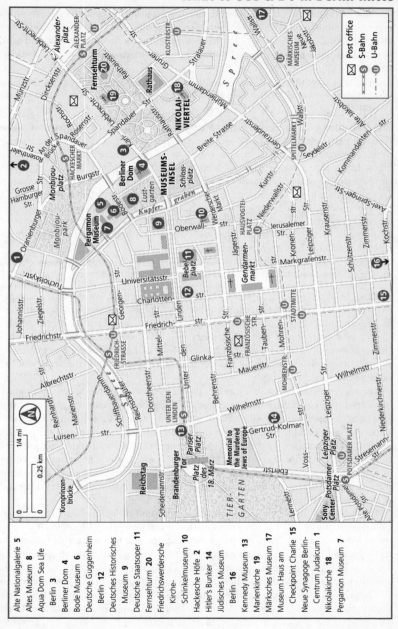

Bröhan Museum   This wonderful museum specializes in decorative objects of the Jugendstil (Art Nouveau) and Art Deco periods (1889–1939), with exquisite vases, glass, furniture, silver, paintings of artists belonging to the Berlin Secession, and other works of art, arranged in drawing-room fashion, including an outstanding porcelain collection.

Schlossstrasse 1a. ℂ **030/3269-0600.** www.broehan-museum.de. Admission 5€ ($8) adults, 4€ ($6.40) students, free for children 12 and under. Tues–Sun 10am–6pm. U-Bahn: Sophie-Charlotte-Platz. Bus: 109 or 309 to Schloss Charlottenburg.

Die Sammlung Berggruen: Picasso und Seine Zeit (The Berggruen Collection: Picasso and His Era) ✸ *Finds*   One of the most unusual private museums in Berlin has accumulated the awesome collection of respected art and antiques dealer Heinz Berggruen. A native of Berlin who fled the Nazis in 1936, he later established antiques dealerships in Paris and California before returning, with his collection, to his native home in 1996. The setting is a renovated former army barracks designed by noted architect August Stüler in 1859. Although most of the collection is devoted to Picasso, there are also works by Cézanne, Braque, Klee, and van Gogh. Some 60 or more works in all, the Picasso collection alone is worth the trip, ranging from his teenage efforts to all of his major periods.

Schlossstrasse 1. ℂ **030/326-9580.** Admission 8€ ($13) adults, 4€ ($6.40) students and children. Tues–Sun 10am–6pm. U-Bahn: Richard-Wagner-Platz, followed by a 10-min. walk. Bus: 129, 145, or 210.

Schloss Charlottenburg ✸✸   Schloss Charlottenburg, one of the finest examples of baroque architecture in Germany, was built by Sophie Charlotte. This beautiful and intelligent woman, a patron of philosophy and the arts, was the wife of Friedrich III, Elector of Brandenburg, who, on January 18, 1701, crowned himself Friedrich I, "King in Prussia." He dared not call himself "King of Prussia" because some parts of Prussia were still dominated by Poland. He nearly bankrupted the state with his extravagant ways.

The residence was begun as a summer palace but got out of hand, eventually growing into the massive structure you see today. When you pass through the heavy iron gates and enter the courtyard, you'll immediately encounter a baroque equestrian statue of Friedrich I himself, by Andreas Schlüter. The main entrance to the palace is directly behind, marked by the 48m (157-ft.) cupola capped by a gilded statue of Fortune. Inside, you'll find a columned rotunda with stucco reliefs depicting the virtues of Prussian princes in mythological terms. From this vestibule, you can take guided tours of the Historical Apartments. English translations of the guide's lecture are sold at the ticket counter.

The main wing of the palace contains the apartments of Friedrich and his "philosopher queen." Of special interest in this section is the **Reception Chamber.** This large room is decorated with frieze panels, vaulted ceilings, and mirror-paneled niches. The tapestries on the walls (1730) are based on Plutarch's *Lives;* included are such classical scenes as Pericles in battle and the sacrifice of Theseus on Delos. At the far end of the west wing is the **Porcelain Chamber,** containing a fine collection of Chinese porcelain.

The **wing,** known as the Knobelsdorff-Flügel and built from 1740 to 1746, contains the apartments of Friedrich the Great. Today, these rooms serve as a museum of paintings, many of which were collected or commissioned by the king—the finest are on the upper floor. Works by Watteau include *The Trade Sign of the Art Dealer Gersaint,* purchased by Friedrich in 1745 for the palace's music hall. Also note the decoration on the walls and ceilings.

At the far eastern end of the Schloss is the **Schinkel Pavillon,** a summerhouse in the Italian style. Karl Friedrich Schinkel, the leading architect of the day, constructed this villa in 1825. Today, it holds a small but noteworthy museum, containing paintings, drawings, and sketches from the early 1800s. Some of the sketches are by Schinkel himself, who was both an architect and an artist.

At the far end of Schlossgarten Charlottenburg is the **Belvedere,** close to the Spree River. This former royal teahouse contains exquisite Berlin porcelain, much of it from the 1700s.

Luisenplatz. ℭ 030/320-91-275. www.spsg.de. Combined ticket for all buildings and historical rooms 12€ ($19) adults, 9€ ($14) children 13 and under and students. Palace Tues–Fri 9am–4pm, Sat–Sun 10am–4pm; museum Tues–Fri 10am–6pm; gardens (free admission) daily 6:30am–8pm (Nov–Feb until 6pm). U-Bahn: Richard-Wagner-Platz. Bus: 145 or 204.

MUSEUMSINSEL MUSEUMS

Alte Nationalgalerie ℛ   This museum is known for its collection of 19th-century German and French Impressionists. The museum also has the world's largest collection of the works of one of the best known of all Berlin artists, Adolph von Menzel (1815–1905). We especially like his *Das Balkonzimmer.* Other paintings include a galaxy of art representing the romantic and classical movements as well as the Biedermeier era, the latter especially well represented by Caspar David Friedrich and Schinkel. Allow at least an hour and a half to take in canvasses by everybody from Pissarro to Cézanne, from Delacroix to Degas, and from van Gogh to Monet. We are especially fond of the works of Max Liebermann and Max Beckmann. The collection would have been far greater than it is had not the Nazis either sold or destroyed so many early-20th-century works they viewed as "degenerate."

Bodestrasse 1–3. ℭ 030/20905577. www.alte-nationalgalerie.de. Admission 8€ ($13) adults, 4€ ($6.40) students, free for children 16 and under. Tues–Sun 10am–6pm (Thurs until 10pm). S-Bahn: Hackescher Markt or Friedrichstrasse. Tram: 3, 4, 5, 12, 13, 15, or 53. Bus: 100, 157, or 378.

Altes Museum   Karl Friedrich Schinkel, the city's greatest architect, designed this structure, which resembles a Greek Corinthian temple, in 1822. On its main floor is the **Antikensammlung (Museum of Antiquities),** a collection of Greek and Roman antique decorative art. Some of the finest Greek vases of the black-and-red-figures style, from the 6th to the 4th century B.C., are here. The best-known vase is a large Athenian amphora (wine jar) found in Vulci, Etruria. It dates from 490 B.C. and shows a satyr with a lyre and the god Hermes. One of several excellent bronze statuettes, the Zeus of Dodone (470 B.C.) shows the god about to cast a bolt of lightning. You can

---

Whatever Became of Queen Nefertiti?

There is no more famous woman of antiquity in all of Berlin than the celebrated colored bust of Queen Nefertiti, dating from about 1360 B.C. and discovered in 1912. It is often used in color ads to symbolize Berlin itself. For years she lingered in the Ägyptisches Museum in Charlottenburg. With old guidebooks, visitors still go there to get a look at her. But she was shipped out with the closure of this museum in 2005. Queen Nefertiti now resides on the ground floor of the **Altes Museum,** where she arrived in September 2005. Here she will remain, along with highlights from the collection of the Egyptian Museum, until she relocates to the Neue Museum in 2009.

Moments **A New Wall**

Berliners aren't likely to forget the **Berlin Wall** any time soon, but just in case, their government has reconstructed a partial stretch of the Wall at Bernauer Strasse and Ackerstrasse (U-Bahn: Bernauer Strasse), at a cost of 1.43 million euros. The 70m-long (230-ft.) memorial consists of two walls that include some of the fragments of the original wall (those fragments not bulldozed away or carried off by souvenir hunters). The memorial is mostly made of mirrorlike stainless steel. Slits allow visitors to peer through. A steel plaque reads, "In memory of the division of the city from 13 August 1961 to 9 November 1989." Critics have called the construction "a sanitized memorial," claiming it does little to depict the 255 people shot trying to escape.

---

also see a rare portrait of Cleopatra (from Alexandria). In the Brandenburg-Prussian art collection is an exceptional bronze statue of the goddess Luna descending through an "arch of the sky." The Prussians called it "the pearl of the collection."

Museumsinsel am Lustgarten. ℂ **030/20-90-55-55.** Admission 8€ ($13) adults, 4€ ($6.40) students, free for children 16 and under. Tues–Sun 10am–6pm (Thurs until 10pm). U-Bahn/S-Bahn: Friedrichstrasse. Bus: 100 to Lustgarten, 147, 157, or 358.

Bode Museum 𝒜𝒜𝒜   One of the great museums of Germany, long closed for restoration, is now open with enlarged exhibits, better lighting, and more viewer-friendly exhibitions. It contains a vast array of museums, including the **Egyptian Museum** 𝒜𝒜𝒜, the Papyrus Collection, the Museum of Late Ancient and Byzantine Art, the Sculpture Collection, the **Picture Gallery** 𝒜𝒜, the Museum of Prehistory, the Children's Gallery, and the extensive Cabinet of Coins and Medals.

In the Egyptian Collection, exhibits range in size from the huge sphinx of Hatsheput (1490 B.C.) to fragments of reliefs from Egyptian temples. Of special interest is the **Burial Cult Room** 𝒜𝒜, where coffins, mummies, and grave objects are displayed along with life-size X-ray photographs of the mummies of humans and animals.

Nearby is the Papyrus Collection, displaying about 25,000 documents of papyrus, ostraca, parchment, limestone, wax, and wood in eight different languages.

The Museum of Late Ancient and Byzantine Art has displays of early Christian sarcophagi, Coptic and Byzantine sculpture, icons, and even gravestones dating from the 3rd through the 18th century. The rich Sculpture Collection exhibits magnificent pieces from ancient churches and monasteries, including a sandstone pulpit support by Anton Pilgram (1490) carved in the shape of a medieval craftsman.

The Picture Gallery is devoted in part to masterpieces from the Dutch and German schools of the 15th and 16th centuries, as well as great works by Italian, Flemish, Dutch, French, and British painters of the 14th to the 18th centuries.

Monbijoubrucke, Bodestrasse 1–3, Museumsinsel. ℂ **030/266-3666.** Admission 8€ ($13) adults, 4€ ($6.40) students and children. Fri–Wed 10am–5pm; Thurs 10am–10pm. U-Bahn: Friedrichstrasse.

Pergamon Museum 𝒜𝒜𝒜   Pergamon Museum houses several departments, but if you have time for only one exhibit, go to the **Department of Greek and Roman Antiquities,** housed in the north and east wings of the museum, and enter the central hall to see the **Pergamon Altar** 𝕲𝕲𝕲 (180–160 B.C.), which is so large that it has a huge room all to itself. Some 27 steps lead from the museum floor up to the colonnade. Most fascinating is the frieze around the base. It shows the struggle of the Olympian gods against the Titans and is strikingly alive, with figures that project as much as a foot from the background. If you explore farther, you'll find a statue of a goddess holding a pomegranate (575 B.C.), found in southern Attica, where it had been buried for 2,000 years. It was so well preserved that flecks of the original paint are still visible on her garments. Many visitors come here to see the fabled **Market Gate of Miletus** 𝕲𝕲𝕲, a Roman gate built around A.D. 120 in the Aegean coastal city of Miletus (now part of Turkey). Regrettably, it is in restoration until 2015. Nonetheless, museum officials have put up a transparent wall that contains the dust and noise but still allows visitors to view this world-class attraction.

The **Near East Museum** 𝕲, in the south wing, contains one of the largest collections anywhere of antiquities from ancient Babylonia, Persia, and Assyria. Among the exhibits is the Processional Way of Babylon with the **Ishtar Gate** 𝕲𝕲𝕲, dating from 575 B.C. You can also visit the throne room of Nebuchadnezzar. Cuneiform clay tablets document a civilization that created ceramics, glass, and metal objects while Europe was still overrun with primitive tribes. The museum's upper level is devoted to the **Museum of Islamic Art.** Of special interest are the miniatures, carpets, and woodcarvings.

Bodestrasse 1–3. ⓒ **030/2090-55-77**. www.smb.museum. Admission 8€ ($13) adults, 4€ ($6.40) students, free for children 16 and under. Tues–Sun 10am–6pm (Thurs until 10pm). U-Bahn/S-Bahn: Friedrichstrasse. Tram: 1, 2, 3, 4, 5, 13, 15, or 53.

TIERGARTEN MUSEUMS

Bauhaus-Archiv Museum für Gestaltung (Bauhaus Design Museum)   The

Bauhaus Museum houses a permanent exhibition of photos and architectural designs relating to the Bauhaus school. Even if you're not a student of architecture, this museum is fascinating; it will bring you closer to the ideas and concepts that inspired modern design.

Klingelhoferstrasse 14. ⓒ **030/2540020**. www.bauhaus.de. Admission Sat–Mon 7€ ($11) adults, 4€ ($6.40) 11 and under; Wed–Fri 6€ ($9.60) adults, 3€ ($4.80) 11 and under. Wed–Mon 10am–5pm. U-Bahn: Nollendorfplatz.

Erotik-Museum   This "museum" lies on the corner of the seediest-looking block in

Berlin. You start out on the third floor and work your way down. Believe it or not, this is now Berlin's fifth-most visited museum. The museum shelters some 5,000 sexual artifacts from around the world, including many Indian and Asian miniatures of erotic positions, even large carved phalli from Bali, along with such relics as African fertility masks. Life-size dioramas explore such topics as S&M and fetishism. There are some Chinese wedding tiles from the 18th and 19th centuries that were supposed to provide sexual education to a newly married couple. The museum in its exhibits also honors the "queen of the Rubber Willy" herself, Beate Uhse, a household name in Germany until her death in 2001. Her life is documented from her Luftwaffe days to pictures of her at the helm of a large speedboat. This septuagenarian opened the world's first shop devoted to "marital hygiene," ultimately championing the right to sell contraceptives, and headed the world's largest sex-related merchandising business. Downstairs are video cabins filled with middle-aged men in raincoats and a "sex superstore."

Joachimstaler Strasse 4. ⓒ **030/8860666**. Admission 5€ ($8) adults, 4€ ($6.40) students and seniors. Mon–Sat 9am–midnight; Sun 1pm–midnight. U-Bahn/S-Bahn: Zoologischer Garten.

Ode to the Murdered Jews of Europe

You might call it "concrete memory." A few hundred yards from Checkpoint Charlie, the **Stiftung Denkmal für die ermordeten Juden Europas (Memorial to the Murdered Jews of Europe)** now occupies a vast site in the center of Berlin, with 2,711 gravestonelike columns. Located in the former East Berlin, just south of the Brandenburg Gate, the memorial was opened on May 10, 2005, 2 days after the 60th anniversary of V-E Day, signaling the ending of World War II in Europe. The official address is Stresemannstrasse 90 (© **030/26394336**). The memorial lies at the edge of the Grosser Tiergarten between Ebertstrasse and Wilhelmstrasse. Take the S-Bahn to Unter den Linden. Admission is free.

Peter Eisenman was the architect who designed the controversial site, filled with claustrophobic pathways through the slabs, some of which are 4.5m (15 ft.) long. The American architect deliberately placed many of the dark gray slabs, with their knife sharp edges, off-kilter, evoking tombstones in an unkept graveyard. Wandering through the memorial is like getting lost in a maze. James Young, a professor at the University of Massachusetts, called it "the Venus' flytrap of Holocaust memorials."

Under heavy guard, the memorial is open 24 hours a day. Underneath the monument are four large rooms containing exhibits that document Nazi crimes against humanity.

Filmmuseum Berlin *★*   A thematic and chronological tour through the saga of the much-troubled German cinema is on show here. The link between Berlin and Hollywood is one of the main focuses of the collection, which is supplemented with special exhibitions. Currently, the museum also owns some 9,000 German and foreign films, both silents and talkies. The collection here owns a million stills of scenes, portraits, and productions along with 30,000 screenplays, 20,000 posters, and 60,000 film programs. Germany's only world-class star, Marlene Dietrich, comes alive again in one wing. Berlin acquired part of her extensive estate of memorabilia in 1993. On display are such costumes as her famous "naked" pearl dress, which gave the illusion of transparency, and the swan's down coat designed by Jean Louis. Photos, costumes, props, letters, and documents recall the remarkable life of this diva, who startled the world with her performance in Josef von Sternberg's *Der Blaue Engel* in 1930. Highlights of other films include props from *Das Cabinet des Dr. Caligari*, the most famous German film of the Weimar Republic. One room is devoted to the controversial Leni Riefenstahl, the star director of the fascist era, whose key films *Triumph des Willens* and *Olympia* established her as one of the world's major filmmakers and the leading exponent of Nazi propaganda.

Potsdamer Strasse 2. © **030/30090372**. www.filmmuseum-berlin.de. Admission 6€ ($9.60) adults; 4.50€ ($7.20) students, seniors, and children 15 and under. Tues–Sun 10am–6pm (Thurs until 8pm). U-Bahn/S-Bahn: Potsdamer Platz.

Gemäldegalerie (Picture Gallery) *★★★*   This is one of Germany's greatest art museums. Several rooms are devoted to early German masters, with panels from altarpieces dating from the 13th to 15th centuries. Note the panel, *The Virgin Enthroned with Child* (1350), surrounded by angels that resemble the demons in the works of Hieronymus Bosch. Eight paintings make up the Dürer collection, including several portraits.

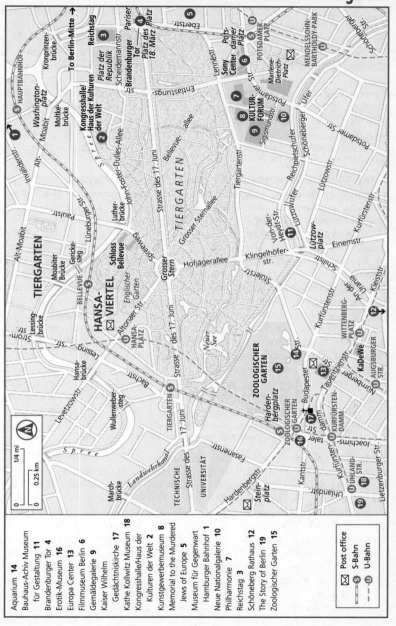

Most of the great European masters are represented. The Italian collection contains five Raphael Madonnas, along with works by Titian *(The Girl with a Bowl of Fruit)*, Fra Filippo Lippi, Botticelli, and Correggio *(Leda with the Swan)*. There are early Netherlandish paintings from the 15th and 16th centuries (van Eyck, van der Weyden, Bosch, and Brueghel) as well. Several galleries are devoted to 17th-century Flemish and Dutch masters, with no fewer than 15 works by Rembrandt, such as his famous *Head of Christ*. *The Man with the Golden Helmet,* long famous as a priceless Rembrandt, was proven in 1986 to be by another hand. This remarkable painting is now accepted as a fine independent original.

Stauffenbergstrasse (entrance is at Mattäiskirchplatz 4). (℗ **030/20-90-55-55**. www.smb.spk-berlin.de/gg. Admission 8€ ($13) adults, 4€ ($6.40) students, free for children 16 and under. Tues–Sun 10am–6pm (Thurs until 10pm). U-Bahn: Potsdamer Platz. Bus: 200 or 347.

Kaiser-Wilhelm Gedächtniskirche (Kaiser Wilhelm Memorial Church)   There is no more evocative site in the western sector of Berlin to remind us of the horrors of war. The massive red-sandstone church that originally stood here was dedicated in 1895 as a memorial to Kaiser Wilhelm II. In 1945, during the closing months of World War II, a bomb dropped by an Allied plane blasted it to pieces, leaving only a few gutted walls and the shell of the neo-Romanesque bell tower. After the war, West Berliners decided to leave the artfully evocative ruins as a reminder of the era's suffering and devastation. In 1961, directly at the base of the ruined building, they erected a small-scale modern church designed by Egon Eiermann. Always irreverent, Berliners, noting the avant-garde architecture and geometric design of the new church, nicknamed it "the lipstick and powder box." Its octagonal hall is lit solely by thousands of colored glass windows set into a honeycomb framework. On its premises, you can visit a small museum with exhibitions and photographs documenting the history of the original church and the destructive ravages of war. The new church can hold up to 1,200 worshippers, and 10-minute religious services—conceived for office workers heading home—are held there every day at 5:30 and 6pm. Between June and August, English-language services are conducted daily at 9am, and free organ concerts are presented here every Saturday year-round at 6pm.

Breit-Scheidplatz. (℗ **030/2185023**. www.gedaechtniskirche-berlin.de. Free admission. Ruined church Mon–Sat 10am–4pm; new church daily 9am–6pm. U-Bahn: Zoologischer Garten or Kurfürstendamm.

Käthe-Kollwitz-Museum   This museum has been called a personalized revolt against the agonies of war. Many works express the sorrow of wartime separation of mother and child, inspired in part by the artist's loss of a son in World War I and a grandson during World War II. Berlin-born Käthe Kollwitz (1867–1945) was an ardent pacifist and socialist whose works were banned by the Nazis. The first woman ever elected to the Prussian Academy of the Arts, she resigned her position in 1933 to protest Hitler's rise to power. Her husband, Karl Kollwitz, was a physician who chose to practice among the poor on a working-class street (now called Kollwitzstrasse). In 1943, Allied bombing drove Käthe to the countryside near Dresden, where she died in 1945 while a guest of the former royal family of Saxony in their castle at Moritzburg.

The lower floors of the museum are devoted to woodcuts and lithographs, the upper floors to particularly poignant sculptures. *Note:* The collection is closed twice a year for special exhibits.

Fasanenstrasse 24. (℗ **030/8825210**. www.kaethe-kollwitz.de. Admission 5€ ($8) adults, 2.50€ ($4) students and children. Wed–Mon 11am–6pm. U-Bahn: Kurfürstendamm or Uhlandstrasse. Bus 109, 110, 204, or 249.

Previews of Coming Attractions

In November of 2007, the German Parliament agreed to provide $650 million to finance the reconstruction of Berlin's old city palace. The actual job will cost $810 million, with the State of Berlin making up the difference in expenses. The palace dates from the Middle Ages, and in 1701 it became the major residence of the kings of Prussia. Allied bombs virtually leveled it in 1945, and the new East German Communist rulers wiped out all trace of it, because to them it suggested capitalistic imperialism. In its place they erected the dull Palace of the Republic in the 1970s.

Kunstgewerbemuseum (Museum of Applied Arts) This museum, set to reopen in the winter of 2009, displays applied arts and crafts from the Middle Ages through the 20th century. Its outstanding exhibition is the Guelph Treasure, a collection of medieval church articles in gold and silver. The basement rooms show contemporary design from the Bauhaus school to Charles Eames and Memphis. Venetian glass, Italian majolica, German Renaissance goldsmiths' work, and 18th-century porcelain figurines are also displayed. Notable are such Art Nouveau works as a translucent opal-and-enamel box by Eugène Feuillâtre. A cafeteria inside is open from 10am to 4:30pm.

Mattäiskirchplatz (opposite the Philharmonie), Tiergartenstrasse 6. ℂ **030/2662902.** www.smb.spk-berlin.de. Admission 8€ ($13) adults, 4€ ($6.40) students, free for children 16 and under. Tues–Fri 10am–6pm; Sat–Sun 11am–6pm. U-Bahn: Potsdamer Platz. Bus: 129 from Ku'Damm to Potsdamer Brücke.

Museum für Gegenwart Hamburger Bahnhof This Museum of Contemporary Art opened in 1996 north of the Spree River in the old Hamburger Bahnhof, the oldest train station in Berlin. The structure was the terminus of the 290km (180-mile) train run from Hamburg. Today, the 19th-century station no longer receives trains but is a premier storehouse of postwar art, a sort of Musée d'Orsay of Berlin. Traces of its former function are still evident, including the high roof designed for steam engines. The modern art on display is some of the finest in Germany; the nucleus of the collection was donated by the Berlin collector Erich Marx (no relation to Karl). You can view everything from Andy Warhol's now-legendary *Mao* to an audiovisual Joseph Beuys archive. The museum houses one of the best collections of the work of Cy Twombly in the world because the curator, Heiner Bastian, was once his assistant. Other works are by Rauschenberg, Lichtenstein, and Dan Flavin. Beuys is also represented by 450 drawings.

Invalidenstrasse 50–51. ℂ **030/398734-11.** www.hamburgerbahnhof.de. Admission 8€ ($13) adults, 4€ ($6.40) students, free for children 16 and under. Tues–Fri and Sun 10am–6pm; Sat 11am–8pm. U-Bahn: Zinnowitzer Strasse; S-Bahn: Lehrter Bahnhof. Bus: 123, 147, 240, or 245.

Neue Nationalgalerie (New National Gallery) ℱ In its modern glass-and-steel home designed by Ludwig Mies van der Rohe (1886–1969), the Neue Nationalgalerie is a sequel of sorts to the art at Dahlem. It contains a continually growing collection of modern European and American art. You'll find works of 19th-century artists, with a concentration on French Impressionists. German art starts with Adolph von Menzel's paintings from about 1850. The 20th-century collection includes works by Max Beckmann and Edvard Munch and E. L. Kirchner's *Brandenburger Tor* (1929), as well as paintings by Bacon, Picasso, Ernst, Klee, and American artists such as Barnett

Moments   **Frommer's Favorite Berlin Experiences**

Strolling Along Unter den Linden and the Kurfürstendamm. You can't know Berlin until you've strolled the Ku'Damm, that glossy, store-lined showcase of Western capitalism, or Unter den Linden, the Prussian centerpiece of the Berlin-Mitte district.

Kneipen **Crawling.** This is the Berlin version of "pub crawling." Whether you want breakfast or a beer at 4am, there's always a *Kneipe* waiting to claim you, no matter what neighborhood you're in.

Looking for a Touch of Culture. The baton of the late Herbert von Karajan is no longer raised, but the Berlin Philharmonic is still one of the world's leading orchestras.

Wandering the Nikolai Quarter. A symbol of Berlin's desire to bounce back after war damage, this charming 16th-century neighborhood has been completely rebuilt. Period taverns and churches make it ideal for a leisurely stroll down narrow streets illuminated by gas lanterns.

Picnicking in the Tiergarten. What better place for a picnic than the former hunting grounds of the Prussian electors? Wander through this 167-hectare (412-acre) park until you find the ideal spot, but first stop off at Kaufhaus des Westens (KaDeWe; p. 158), a sixth-floor food emporium at Wittenbergplatz, 20 minutes away, for the makings of a memorable meal.

Newman. There's food service in the cafe on the ground floor, open 10:30am to 5:45pm when the museum is open.

Potsdamerstrasse 50 (just south of the Tiergarten). ℂ **030/266-2651.** www.neue-nationalgalerie.de. Admission 8€ ($13) adults, 4€ ($6.40) students, free for children 16 and under. Tues–Sun 10am–6pm (Thurs until 10pm). S-Bahn: Potsdamer Platz; U-Bahn: Mendelssohn-Bartholdy-Park.

The Story of Berlin   This multimedia extravaganza portrays 8 centuries of the city's history through photos, films, sounds, and colorful displays. Beginning with the founding of Berlin in 1237, it chronicles the plague, the Thirty Years' War, Frederick the Great's reign, military life, the Industrial Revolution and the working poor, the Golden 1920s, World War II, divided Berlin during the Cold War, and the fall of the Wall. Lights flash in a media blitz as you enter the display on the fall of the Wall, making you feel like one of the first East Berliners to wonderingly cross to the West. Conclude your tour on the 14th floor with a panoramic view over today's Berlin. Allow at least 2 hours to see the museum. Though the displays are a bit jarring and the historical information is too jumbled to be truly educational, the museum does leave a lasting impression.

Ku'Damm-Karree, Kurfürstendamm 207–208 (at the corner of Uhlandstrasse). ℂ **030/88720100.** Admission 9.80€ ($16) adults, 8€ ($13) students, 3.50€ ($5.60) children 6–13, 21€ ($34) family ticket. Daily 10am–8pm (you must enter by 6pm). U-Bahn: Uhlandstrasse.

OTHER MUSEUMS & SIGHTS
Berlinische Galerie   Modern art, photography, and architectural models from 1870 to the present day are sheltered under one roof here in a museum that displays

everything from the grotesque portraits of George Grosz to the works of Dadaists. The collection of fine art alone comprises some 5,000 works, mostly paintings, including everything from the Berlin Secessino movement to abstract expressionism. Since reunification, a number of works was acquired from artists in eastern Berlin. The Collection of Graphic Art offers some 15,000 works, including the complete printed graphic works of Otto Dix. The Photographic Collection ranges from early daguerreotypists to 21st-century works. Some 300,000 plans and drawings, plus some 2,500 architectural models, form the Architecture Collection.

Alte Jakobstrasse 124–128. © 030/7890-2600. www.berlinischegalerie.de. Admission 6€ ($9.60). Wed–Mon 10am–6pm. U-Bahn: Kochstrasse.

Brücke Museum 🗡🗡   Some of our all-time favorite German artists, especially Ernst Kirchner (1880–1938), have a museum devoted to their work. The art movement, Die Brücke, originated in Dresden in 1905 and rejected the emerging modern trends of the 20th century, turning once again to landscapes, folk art, and other retrograde sources for inspiration. This school was an influential predecessor to 20th-century expressionism. Although exhibits change, this museum presents an extensive collection of these expressionist works, including art by Max Kaus, Walter Gramatte, Otto Herbig, and Anton Kerschbaumer. Today, the Brücke Museum owns around 400 paintings and sculptures of the era, along with thousands of prints, watercolors, and drawings, although not all the treasure trove can be displayed at the same time.

Bussardsteig 9. © 030/8312029. www.bruecke-museum.de. Admission 4€ ($6.40) adults, 3€ ($4.80) children 5–13. Wed–Mon 11am–5pm. U-Bahn to Fehrbelliner Platz, then bus no. 115.

Dahlem Museen 🗡🗡   After extensive reorganizing, this complex of museums, occupying one mammoth structure in the heart of Dahlem's Freie Universität, contains institutions devoted to everything from ethnological collections to Far Eastern art.

Occupying most of the main building is the **Ethnologisches Museum** 🗡🗡🗡, which is the one to visit if you have to skip the rest. This is the greatest ethnological collection on earth, totaling some 500,000 artifacts from all continents, even prehistoric America. Art and artifacts are displayed from Africa, the Far East, the South Seas, and South America. Many of the figures are ritualistic masks and are grotesquely beautiful. The Incan, Mayan, and Aztec stone sculptures alone equal the collections of some of the finest museums of Mexico. The best part is the collection of authentic boats from the South Pacific. The museum displays an intriguing assemblage of pre-Columbian relics, including gold objects and antiquities from Peru. The museum's Department of Music allows visitors to hear folk music recordings from around the globe.

In the same complex is the **Museum for Asian Art,** which now includes both the Far Eastern collection as well as the Museum of Indian Art. **Museum für Ostasiatische Kunst (Museum of Far Eastern Art)** 🗡🗡 is a gem of a museum devoted primarily to Japan, Korea, and China, with artifacts dating back to as far as 3000 B.C. Launched in 1906 as the first Far Eastern museum of art in Germany, this museum is one of Europe's finest in presenting an overview of some of the most exquisite ecclesiastical and decorative art from the Far East. It is the equal of or better than similar collections in Paris. In essence, the museum represents the loot acquired during a massive "shopping expedition" the Germans took to Asia, where they even managed to garner the 17th-century imperial throne of China, all lacquered and inlaid with mother-of-pearl. The Japanese woodblock prints, each more exquisite than the next, are reason enough to visit.

Germany's greatest collection of Indian art is on exhibit in the same building at the **Museum für Indische Kunst,** covering a span of 40 centuries. It's an international parade of some of the finest art and artifacts from the world of Buddhism, representing collections from such lands as Burma, Thailand, Indonesia, Nepal, and Tibet.

Outside the Dahlem museum complex, and only a 5-minute walk away, **Museum Europäischer Kulturen** is devoted to the German people themselves—not the aristocrats but the middle class and the peasant stock who built the country. It is a true "museum of the people." The exhibits go back 4 centuries, tracing how artisans and homemakers lived and worked. Household items are displayed along with primitive industrial equipment such as a utensil for turning flax into linen. Furnishings, clothing, pottery, and even items used in religious observances are shown, along with some fun and whimsical exhibits, including depictions of pop culture from the 1950s through the 1980s.

Lansstrasse 8. (©) 030/8301438. Admission 8€ ($13) adults, free for students and children 16 and under. Tues–Fri 10am–6pm; Sat–Sun 11am–6pm. U-Bahn: Dahlem-Dorf.

Kennedy Museum   John F. Kennedy's famous *Ich bin ein Berliner* speech inspired this new museum near the Brandenburg Gate and the Reichstag. The museum documents this beloved president and his iconic family, with such artifacts ranging from the president's black Hermes attaché case to Jackie Kennedy's signature pillbox hat. Naturally, there are artifacts from Kennedy's historic visit to Berlin in June of 1963. The museum's collection includes one of the most comprehensive compilations of Kennedy photographs and both private and official documents.

Pariser Platz 4A. (©) 030/3100-7788. www.thekennedys.de. Admission 7€ ($11) adults, 3.50€ ($5.60) students, free for children 16 and under. Daily 10am–6pm. S-Bahn: Unter den Linden. Bus: 100 or 200.

Martin-Gropius-Bau   This museum is dedicated to the architect, Martin Gropius, who was the uncle of the far more famous Walter Gropius of the Baushaus movement. Martin Gropius designed the building in the Renaissance style, and it was originally an arts-and-crafts museum. Since reunification the building has become one of the most beautiful exhibition halls in Berlin. Today it is a venue for changing exhibitions of art and culture, ranging from Aztec sculptures from Mexico to set designs for the films of Stanley Kubrick, including *Clockwork Orange.*

Niederkirchnerstrasse 7. (©) 030/254860. Admission varies with the event. Wed–Mon 10am–8pm. U-Bahn: Kochstrasse or Potsdamer Platz.

Museum für Naturkunde ★★   Five new halls were designed and reconstructed in 2007 in this museum, which was inaugurated in 1889 by Emperor Wilhelm II. In a modern exhibit hall, the most stunning attraction is the **Brachiosaurus Brancai** ★★★, the world's tallest mounted dinosaur skeleton, a beast that lived some 150 million years ago and was discovered in Tanzania in 1909. The reptile's bones are presented in accordance with the latest scientific findings.

The exhibition features a total of seven dinosaurs "running" as a group. Adjoining halls feature a scientific Jurassic Park filled with prehistoric reptiles. An original fossil of the ancient bird Archaeopteryx went on display for the first time in 2007. You can also see the biggest collection of **meteorites** ★ in Germany, including the gigantic iron meteorite found in Namibia. Large dioramas depict the fauna of the Bavarian Alps and an Icelandic bird colony from 1918 (one of the first of its kind ever designed).

Marker Identifies Hitler's Bunker

For the first time since World War II, the notorious bunker of the Third Reich was marked publicly. The Führer Bunker, as it was called, was where Hitler staged his last stand, committing suicide on April 30, 1945, as Soviet troops encircled the bunker. Stalin had issued orders to bring Hitler to Moscow alive.

"History can be good or bad, but even if it's about a devil, people must be informed of history," said former SS Staff Sgt. Rochus Misch, a Hitler bodyguard who lived in the bunker with him and attended the unveiling of the marker in June of 2006.

For decades, Berlin officials refused to mark the site, fearing it would become a place of pilgrimage for neo-Nazis. Misch dispelled the widely circulated myth that the bunker had 12 floors and an underground highway that Hitler used to cruise the city underground. The bunker was constructed in 1935 and was fortified by walls 4.2m (14 ft.) thick. The bunker is not intact under the parking lot that covers it. Soviet soldiers blew up most of the bunker in the 1980s, and the foundation and walls were filled with rubble. The marker bears graphics, photographs, and a chronology of events in both German and English. The location of the bunker is at the corner of In den Ministergarten and Gertrude Kolmar Strasse near the Potsdamer Platz.

Part of Berlin's Humboldt University, the museum owns 25 million objects and exhibits, and is one of the most significant institutions of its type in the world.

Invalidenstrasse 43. © 030/20-93-85-91. www.naturkundemuseum-berlin.de. Admission 6€ ($9.60) adults, 3.50€ ($5.60) children 14 and under. Tues–Fri 9:30am–5pm; Sat–Sun 10am–6pm. Tram: 6, 8, or 50.

Olympiastadion Built in 1936 by Werner March for the XI Summer Olympic Games, the Olympiastadion, which seats 100,000 people, was the first in Europe to supply all the facilities necessary for modern sports. Hitler expected to see his "master race" run off with all the medals in the 1936 Olympics, but his hopes were dashed when an African American, Jesse Owens, took four golds for the U.S. team.

The stadium area covers a total of 136 hectares (336 acres), but the main attraction is the arena. The playing field in its center lies 14m (46 ft.) below ground level. For a panoramic view of Berlin, take the elevator to the top of the 80m (262-ft.) platform, where the Olympic bell hangs. Sporting or cultural events are still presented here about once a week during spring, summer, and autumn. For ticket sales and information for sporting events within the stadium, call the **Herta-Berlin Soccer Club (Herta-BSC)** at © 030/3009280. For information about the occasional live concerts, call **Conzert Concept** at © 030/810750.

Olympischer Platz 3. © 030/30688100. Admission 3€ ($4.80) adults, 2€ ($3.20) children 5 and under. Mar–Oct daily 10am–7pm; Nov–Feb daily 10am–4pm. U-Bahn: Olympia-Stadion.

Schöneberg Rathaus This former political and administrative center of West Berlin is of special interest to Americans. It was the scene of John F. Kennedy's memorable (if grammatically shaky) *Ich bin ein Berliner* speech on June 26, 1963. Berliners have renamed the square around the building the John-F.-Kennedy-Platz. From the 72m (236-ft.) tower, a Liberty Bell replica is rung every day at noon. Most visitors come here to climb the tower for a panoramic view of Berlin. This Freedom Bell, a gift from the American people in 1950, symbolized U.S. support for the West Berliners during the Cold War. The document chamber contains a testimonial bearing the signatures of 17 million Americans who gave their moral support to the struggle.

John-F.-Kennedy-Platz. ℂ **030/75600.** Free admission. Rathaus daily 10am–6pm; tower daily 10am–5pm. Tower closed Nov–Mar. U-Bahn: Rathaus Schöneberg.

EXPLORING BERLIN-MITTE

The best street for strolling in eastern Berlin is the famous **Unter den Linden,** beginning at Brandenburg Gate.

Alexanderplatz, named for Russian Czar Alexander I, was the center of activity in the old East Berlin. This square has brightened considerably since reunification, though aesthetically speaking it's got a long way to go. Neon lights and bright murals now coexist alongside the dull and fading GDR-era structures, and street musicians and small markets give the area new life.

The massive 335m (1,100-ft.) **Fernsehturm (TV tower;** ℂ **030/2423333)** on Alexanderplatz is the second-highest structure in Europe. It's worthwhile to take the 40-second elevator ride to the observation platform, 186m (610 ft.) above the city. From this isolated vantage, you can clearly distinguish most landmarks, and on the floor above, you can enjoy cake and coffee in the revolving Tele-Café. The elevator to the top costs 9.50€ ($15) for adults and 4.50€ ($7.20) students and children. The tower is open daily March to October 9am to midnight and November to February daily 10am to midnight.

At the foot of the Fernsehturm stands Berlin's second-oldest church, the brick Gothic **Marienkirche (St. Mary's Church),** Karl-Liebknecht-Strasse 8 (ℂ **030/2424467),** dating from the 15th century. Inside you can see the painting *Der Totentanz (The Dance of Death),* painted in 1475, and then discovered in 1860 beneath a layer of whitewash in the church's entrance hall. Also worth seeing is the marble baroque pulpit carved by Andreas Schlüter (1703). The cross on the top of the church annoyed the Communist rulers of the former East Germany—its golden form was always reflected in the windows of the Fernsehturm. The church is open Monday to Thursday 10am to noon and 1 to 6pm, Friday to Sunday noon to 4pm.

(Moments **Night of Shame**

Best visited at night, as it is more evocative then, **Bebelplatz** is a square along Unter den Linden, in Berlin-Mitte, approached just before you reach Staatsoper. Here is an eloquent memorial to the notorious Nazi book burning that took place here on the night of May 10, 1933. Through a window set in the pavement, you can look below to a small library lined with empty bookshelves. Some 25,000 books were burned, all by authors considered enemies of the Third Reich. Nearby is a plaque with the prophetic words of the poet Heinrich Heine. In 1820 he wrote, "Where books are burned, in the end people will burn."

> **Tips** **The Heartbeat of Berlin**
>
> The Potsdamer Platz Arcades contain 140 specialty shops, restaurants, and cafes, inviting you to shop and relax in a civilized urban atmosphere. One of the most visited attractions at the center is the **Sony Center am Potsdamer Platz** (☎ 030/2575-500), with two cinemas—the CineStar Multiplex and the CineStar IMAX 3-D. The 10-story office building offers a panoramic view that embraces the Philharmonie, the Kulturforum, and the Tiergarten. Around Marlene-Dietrich-Platz, prominent companies offer an entire range of leisure and entertainment facilities. They include the Berlin IMAX-Theater, the Stella Musical-Theater, the Grand Hyatt Hotel, the Madison City Suites, the Berlin Casino, and the Cine-Max cinema center.

At Rosenthaler Strasse 40–41, the trendy rebuilt **Hackersche Höfe** has risen from the ashes of World War II to become a chic place for dining, drinking, going to the theater, or patronizing fashionable boutiques and art galleries. Originally these Hacke warehouses were constructed beginning in 1905 as shining examples of Berlin's take on Art Nouveau industrial architecture. Heavily damaged in Allied bombing raids, all nine interconnecting courtyards are new again, with shiny white tiles interspersed with Moorish mosaic designs. Also at this location are a theater and a movie house.

Berliner Dom The cathedral of Berlin took some devastating hits in the British serial bombardments of Berlin in 1940, but it was restored to some of its former glory in the postwar decades, reopening in 1993. Unlike many European capitals where the cathedral is among the top two or three attractions, you can safely miss Berlin's Dom without feeling cultural deprivation. That said, the best way for an overview of this 19th-century cathedral is from the **Dome Gallery** ✿, reached after climbing 270 steps. From here, you get a good glimpse of the Dom's ceiling and the rest of its much-restored interior. The reconstruction of this cathedral into its classic form was completed in 1822. Its most notable features include a wall altar with the 12 Apostles by Karl Friedrich Schinkel and the magnificent Sauer organ containing 7,000 pipes.

The stained-glass windows are especially stunning, depicting such scenes as the Resurrection, as symbolized by an angel holding a palm branch. The tombstones of Prussian royals are displayed in the crypt, the most impressive tombs being those of Frederick I and his queen, Sophie Charlotte. *Tip:* The best time to visit is for one of the organ concerts, conducted year-round, usually on Saturday at 6pm. An announcement is printed within the church listing hours of all ecclesiastical and musical events.

In the Lustgarten, Museumsinsel. ☎ 030/20269136. www.berliner-dom.de. Admission 5€ ($8) adults, 3€ ($4.80) students and seniors, free for ages 13 and under. Mon–Sat 9am–7pm; Sun noon–7pm (until 6pm in winter). S-Bahn: Alexanderplatz or Hackescher Markt.

Brandenburger Tor (Brandenburg Gate) ✿✿ This triumphal arch—now restored—stands in the very heart of Berlin and once was the symbol of the divided city. In the heyday of East Germany, the structure was integrated into the Berlin Wall, which followed a north-south axis as it made its wicked way to the Potsdamer Platz. Six Doric columns hold up an entablature that was inspired by the Propylaea of the Parthenon at Athens. Surrounded by the famous and much-photographed Quadriga of Gottfried Schadow from 1793, the gate was designed by Carl Gotthard Langhans in 1789. Napoleon liked the original Quadriga so much he ordered them taken down and shipped to Paris, but they were returned to Berlin in 1814. In Berlin's heyday before World War II, the gate marked the grand western extremity of the "main street," Unter den Linden. In the Room of Silence, built into one of the guardhouses, visitors still gather to meditate and reflect on Germany's past.

Unter den Linden. Free admission. Room of Silence daily 10am–6pm. S-Bahn: Unter den Linden. Bus: 100.

Deutsche Guggenheim Berlin ⭐ This state-of-the-art museum is devoted to modern and contemporary art. The exhibition space is on the ground floor of the Berlin branch of Deutsche Bank. The Guggenheim Foundation presents several exhibitions at this site annually and also displays newly commissioned works created specifically for this space by world-renowned artists. The bank supports young artists from the German-speaking world by purchasing their works and displaying them throughout the company's offices and public spaces. Exhibitions have ranged from the most avant-garde of modern artists to Picasso, Cézanne, and Andy Warhol.

Unter den Linden 13–15 (at the intersection with Charlottenstrasse). ✆ **030/2020930**. www.deutsche-guggenheim-berlin.de. Admission 4€ ($6.40) adults, 3€ ($4.80) children; free Mon. Daily 11am–8pm (Thurs until 10pm). S-Bahn: Unter den Linden.

Deutsches Historisches Museum From the Neanderthals to the Nazis, the entire saga of German history is presented. The collection includes extensive posters and documents of the history of the workers' movement as well as a few remains from the former *Zeughaus* (arsenal) collection, which, before World War II, had been the largest collection of militaria from the history of Brandenburg and Prussia. The museum also owns tons of the old GDR Communist art (naturally all the workers are depicted with smiling faces). There is a permanent exhibition on German history in the main building, with temporary exhibitions in an annex. The museum has added a new wing designed by famous architect I. M. Pei. A transparent glass wall bridges the gap between the new wing and the original structure, an 18th-century arsenal for the Prussian army. The stunningly modern new wing offers 290,625 sq. m (27,000 sq. ft.) of space, which will be used for some of the city's most fascinating traveling exhibits.

Under den Linden 2. ✆ **030/203040**. www.dhm.de. Admission 5€ ($8). Daily 10am–6pm. U-Bahn: Friedrichstrasse.

Friedrichswerdersche Kirche–Schinkelmuseum This annex of the Nationalgalerie is located in the deconsecrated Friedrichswerdersche Kirche, which was designed in 1828 by Karl Friedrich Schinkel (1781–1841). It lies close to Unter den Linden, not far from the State Opera House. The twin Gothic portals of the old church shelter a bronze of St. Michael slaying a dragon. Inside, the museum is devoted to the memory of Schinkel, who designed many of Berlin's great palaces, churches, and monuments. Memorabilia and documents record his great accomplishments. There are also exhibitions of neoclassical sculptures, portraits, and tombs by Johann Gottfried Schadow, Christian Daniel Rauch, Friedrich Tieck, and Berthel Thorvaldsen, the Danish sculptor.

Werderscher Markt. ✆ **030/2081323**. Free admission. Daily 10am–6pm. U-Bahn: Hausvogteiplatz.

Jüdisches Museum Berlin (Jewish Museum Berlin) ⭐⭐ Europe's largest Jewish Museum presents the panorama of German-Jewish history, its cultural achievements, and its horror. The history of German Jewry is portrayed through objects, works of art, and documentation. The most talked-about museum in Berlin, the Jewish Museum is housed in a building that is one of the most spectacular in the entire city. Called "the silver lightning bolt," it was designed by architect Daniel Libeskind. To some viewers, the building plan and the scarring in the zinc-plated facade suggest a shattered Star of David. Oddly shaped windows are haphazardly embedded in the building's exterior.

Inside, the spaces are designed to make the visitor uneasy and disoriented, simulating the feeling of those who were exiled. A vast hollow cuts through the museum to mark what is gone. When the exhibits reach the rise of the Third Reich, the hall's walls, ceiling, and floor close in as the visitor proceeds. A chillingly hollow Holocaust Void, a dark, windowless chamber, evokes much that was lost.

The exhibits concentrate on three themes: Judaism and Jewish life, the devastating effects of the Holocaust, and the post–World War II rebuilding of Jewish life in Germany.

The roots of this museum were in an older museum opened in 1933 shortly before Hitler's rise to power. That collection of art and Judaica was shut down by the Gestapo in 1938, and all of its holdings were confiscated.

The on-site Liebermanns Restaurant features a world cuisine, with an emphasis on Jewish recipes—all strictly kosher.

Lindenstrasse 9–14. ⓒ 030/25993300. www.juedisches-museum-berlin.de. Admission 5€ ($8), free for children 6 and under, 10€ ($16) family ticket for 2 adults and up to 4 children. Daily 10am–8pm (Mon until 10pm). U-Bahn: Hallesches Tor or Kochstrasse. Bus: M29, M41, or 265.

Märkisches Museum

The full cultural history of Berlin is displayed in one of the most prominent buildings on the banks of the Spree; 42 rooms contain collections of artifacts from excavations, plus such art treasures as Slav silver and Bronze Age finds. You can learn about Berlin's theaters and literature, the arts in Berlin and Brandenburg, and the life and work of Berlin artisans. Most visitors like the array of mechanical musical instruments that can be played Sunday at 3pm, for an extra 1€ ($1.60).

Am Källnischen Park 5. ⓒ 030/308660. Admission 4€ ($6.40) adults, 2€ ($3.20) children. Tues–Sun 9am–5pm. U-Bahn: Märkisches Museum. Bus: 147, 240, or 265.

Museum Haus am Checkpoint Charlie

Exhibits in this small building evoke the tragic events connected with the former Berlin Wall. You can see some of the instruments of escape used by East Germans, including chairlifts, false passports, hot-air balloons, and even a minisub. Photos document the construction of the Wall, the establishment of escape tunnels, and the postwar history of both parts of Berlin from 1945 until today, including the airlift of 1948 to 1949. One of the most moving exhibits is the display on the staircase of drawings by school children, who, in 1961 to 1962, were asked to depict both halves of Germany in one picture. Close to Checkpoint Charlie, and straddling the two sides of Friedrichstrasse, is a memorial of large wooden crosses, some 1,000 in all, that commemorate would-be escapees shot or killed near the Wall from 1961 to 1989.

Friedrichstrasse 43–45. ⓒ 030/2537250. www.mauermuseum.de. Admission 13€ ($20) adults, 7.50€ ($12) students, free for children 16 and under. Daily 9am–10pm. U-Bahn: Kochstrasse or Stadtmitte. Bus: 129.

Neue Synagoge Berlin–Centrum Judaicum (The New Synagogue)

Originally consecrated on Rosh Hashanah in 1866 and capped with what's remembered as one of the most spectacular domes in Berlin, this synagogue was vandalized in 1938 during *Kristallnacht*, torched by Berliners in 1944, blasted by Allied bombs in 1945, and finally, after about a decade of further deterioration, demolished by the Communist East Germans in the 1950s. During its heyday, with 3,200 seats and a design inspired by the Moorish architecture of the Alhambra in Granada, Spain, it was the largest synagogue in Germany. In recent times, it was partially rebuilt, and capped with a gilded dome that's visible for many surrounding blocks. Inside, there's a replica, using some of the original carvings, of some of the original synagogue's entrance vestibules and anterooms, within which are exhibitions detailing the events that transpired in this building since its original construction. The bulk of the synagogue was never rebuilt. In its place is a gravel-covered plot of land where markers indicate the original layout of the building. If you visit, you'll gain a disturbing and unnerving insight into the destruction of a way of life that used to be and a sense of the passion with which Berlin's Jewish and German communities commemorate the memory of their murdered kinfolk.

Oranienburgerstrasse 28–30. ⟨⟩ **030/88028300.** www.cjudaicum.de. Admission 7€ ($11) adults, 5€ ($8) students and children 13 and under. Apr–Sept Sun and Mon 10am–8pm, Tues–Thurs 10am–6pm, Fri 10am–5pm; Mar and Oct Sun–Mon 10am–8pm, Tues–Thurs 10am–6pm, Fri 10am–2pm; Nov–Feb Sun–Thurs 10am–6pm, Fri 10am–2pm. Guided tours in German Sun 2 and 4pm; Wed 4pm (Mar–Oct only); call to request English tours (not always available). Last entrance 30 min. before closing. S-Bahn: Oranienburgerstrasse or Hackescher Markt.

Reichstag (Parliament) 𝄐   The night of February 17, 1933, was a date that lives in infamy in German history. On that night, a fire broke out in the seat of the German house of parliament, the Reichstag. Historians still debate whether it was set by the Nazis, but in any event, the German Communist Party was blamed. That was all the excuse Hitler's troops needed to begin mass arrests of "dissidents and enemies of the lawful government." Because of this mysterious fire, democracy came to an end in Germany. The Reichstag was in for even greater punishment as it faced massive Allied bombardment in World War II.

Today, the Reichstag is back and is once again the home of the country's parliament in the wake of the collapse of the Berlin Wall and subsequent reunification in 1990. The building still evokes the neo-Renaissance style it had when it opened in 1894. It's crowned by a new glass dome designed by Sir Norman Foster, the famous English architect. You can go through the west gate for an elevator ride up to the dome, where a sweeping vista of Berlin opens before you. There's both an observation platform and a rooftop restaurant (but the view is better than the food).

Platz der Republik 1. ⟨⟩ **030/22732152.** Free admission. Daily 8am–midnight (last entrance 10pm). S-Bahn: Unter den Linden. Bus: 100.

THE HISTORIC NIKOLAI QUARTER

The historic **Nikolaiviertel** (U-Bahn: Klosterstrasse) was restored in time for the city's 750th anniversary in 1987. Here, on the banks of the Spree River, is where Berlin was born. Many of the medieval and baroque buildings in the neighborhood were completely and authentically reconstructed after World War II. Subsequently, some of the city's old flavor has been recaptured here.

The area is named for the **Nikolaikirche (Church of St. Nicholas),** Nikolaikirchplatz, off Spandauerstrasse (⟨⟩ **030/24724529**). The church, the oldest in Berlin, was originally constructed in the 14th century on the remains of a 13th-century Romanesque church. The restored building now displays the finds of postwar archaeological digs; during the reconstruction, 800-year-old skeletons were found. It's open daily from 10am to 6pm. Admission to the church and tower is free.

> **Moments** In Memory of . . .
>
> At the corner of Lewetzov and Jagow streets is a **Jewish War Memorial** to the many Berliners who were deported—mostly to their deaths—from 1941 until the end of the war in 1945. The memorial is a life-size sculpture of a freight car with victims being dragged into it. Behind it is a 15m (50-ft.) structure listing the dates of the various death trains and the number of prisoners shipped out. The memorial stands on the site of a former synagogue destroyed by the Nazis.

OTHER ARCHITECTURAL SIGHTS

Just north of the Tiergarten is the **Hansaviertel,** or Hansa Quarter (U-Bahn: Hansaplatz). The architecture of this area was an outgrowth of the great INTERBAU 1957 (International Builder's Exhibition), when architects from 22 nations designed buildings for the totally destroyed quarter. The diversity here is exciting: Fifty architects took part, including Gropius, Niemeyer, and Duttman.

Le Corbusier also submitted a design for an apartment house for INTERBAU 1957, but the structure was so gigantic that it had to be built near the **Olympic Stadium** (U-Bahn: Olympia-Stadion). The **Corbusier House,** called *Strahlende Stadt* (radiant city), is one of Europe's largest housing complexes—its 530 apartments can house up to 1,400 people. Typical of the architect's style, this tremendous building rests on stilts.

The architects of rebuilt Berlin were also encouraged to design centers for the performing arts. One of the most controversial projects was the **Kongresshalle (Congress Hall),** on John-Foster-Dulles-Allee, in the Tiergarten, just west of Brandenburg Gate (S-Bahn: Unter den Linden). This building was conceived as the American contribution to INTERBAU 1957. The reinforced concrete structure has an 18m-high (60-ft.) vaulted ceiling that reminds some viewers of an oversize flying saucer. Berliners immediately christened it "the Pregnant Oyster." The building today is used mainly for conventions. More successful was the **Philharmonie,** new home of the Berlin Philharmonic, at Matthäikirchstrasse, and its adjacent chamber-music hall, next to the Tiergarten. The tentlike roof arches up in a bold curve, and the gold-colored facade glitters.

One of the city's tallest buildings sits in the midst of the city's busiest area. The 22-story **Europa Center,** just across the plaza from the Kaiser Wilhelm Memorial Church at Breitscheidplatz (U-Bahn: Kurfürstendamm), is the largest self-contained shopping center and entertainment complex in Europe. This town-within-a-town opened in 1965 on the site of the legendary Romanisches Café, once a gathering place for actors, writers, and artists in the flamboyant 1920s. Berliners dubbed it "Pepper's Manhattan," after its owner, K. H. Pepper. In addition to three levels of shops, restaurants, nightclubs, bars, and cinemas, it contains dozens of offices, a parking garage, and an observation roof. At the Tauentzienstrasse entrance, you can find two pieces of the former Berlin Wall. The building is open daily 9am to midnight (to 10pm in winter). Admission to the observation roof is 3€ ($4.80).

SIGHTS IN THE ENVIRONS

Haus der Wannsee-Konferenz   This was the site of one of the most notorious conferences in history: a meeting of Nazi bureaucrats and SS officials to plan the annihilation of European Jewry. The minutes of the Wannsee Conference were kept by Adolf Eichmann, the sallow-faced SS functionary who later mapped out transport logistics for sending millions of Jews to their deaths.

The villa is now a memorial to the Holocaust. It includes a selection of photographs of men, women, and children who were sent to concentration camps. This exhibit is not for the squeamish. Nearly all the pictures on display are official Nazi photographs, including some of Nazi medical experiments. As noted at the trials at Nürnberg, "No government in history ever did a better job of photographing and documenting its crimes against humanity."

Am Grossen Wannsee 56–58. ℂ **030/8050010.** www.ghwk.de. Free admission. Daily 10am–6pm. S-Bahn: Wannsee, then bus 114.

Jüdischer Friedhof (Jewish Cemetery)   This famous Jewish cemetery was opened in 1880. It contains 110,000 graves of Jewish residents of Berlin. Many distinguished artists, musicians, scientists, and religious leaders are buried here. Some tombs are of Jewish soldiers who fought for Germany in World War I. A memorial honors Jewish victims murdered during the Nazi era. You may have a hard time finding the cemetery on your own, so we recommend a taxi.

Herbert-Baumstrasse 31, Weissensee (a suburb east of Berlin). ℂ **030/9253330.** Free admission. Apr–Oct Sun–Wed 8am–5pm, Fri 8am–3pm; Nov–Mar Sun–Thurs 8am–4pm, Fri 8am–3pm. Tram: 2, 12, 23, or 24, or taxi.

Sachsenhausen Gedenkstätte (Sachsenhausen Memorial & Museum)   Just north of Berlin, Sachsenhausen was one of the most notorious death camps of the Nazi empire and was liberated by Allied troops in 1945. The freedom was short lived. The Soviet secret police turned it into a prison camp, and the misery and death continued for another 5 years.

The largest prison camp in East Germany, Sachsenhausen was home to some 12,000 inmates from 1945 to 1950, when the prison was shut down. Mass graves of the former prisoners were discovered here only in 1990. A museum has opened on the site documenting the tragic history of two totalitarian regimes, the Nazi and Soviet enslavements. Exhibits show that, during World War II, Sachsenhausen was the administrative headquarters for all the concentration camps, winning the praise of the dreaded SS chief, Heinrich Himmler.

The SS learned its methods of mass killing at this camp. Most of the 30,000 or so victims of the Nazi regime were prisoners of war and included Stalin's oldest son. The Soviet prisoners included 6,000 Nazi officers and other functionaries. After the war, Russian soldiers who contracted sexually transmitted diseases from German women were also sent here.

Strasse der Nationen 22, Oranienburg (35km/22 miles north of Berlin). ℂ **03301/2000.** www.stiftung-bg.de. Free admission. Mar 15–Oct 14 daily 8:30am–6pm; Oct 15–Mar 14 daily 8:30am–4:30pm. Take S-Bahn 1 from Friedrichstrasse to Oranienburg, the last stop; from there, it's a 25-min. walk (it's signposted).

Spandau Zitadelle (Spandau Citadel)   This citadel stands at the confluence of the Spree and Havel rivers in northwestern Berlin. The Hohenzollern electors of Brandenburg used it as a summer residence, and, in time, it became the chief military center of Prussia. The citadel has been besieged by everybody from the French to the Prussians. The Juliusturm (Julius Tower) and the Palas, constructed in the 13th to

> **Kids   Fun for Kids**
>
> Children love the **Berlin Zoo-Aquarium** (see below). Its most famous residents, the giant pandas, are perennial favorites. The zoo also has playgrounds and a children's section, where the animals welcome a cuddle. Another place to take the kids is **Grips-Theater**, Altonaerstrasse 22 (© **030/ 39747477**; U-Bahn: Hansaplatz), known for its bright, breezy productions. Children are sure to enjoy the music and dancing (if not the simple German-language dialogue). Tickets cost 6€ to 18€ ($9.60–$29). Call for current productions. Most performances begin at 7:30pm, although there are some matinees as well, depending on the production. The theater is closed from late June to mid-August.

15th centuries, are the oldest buildings in Berlin still standing. The main building, accessible by footbridge, houses a local-history museum.

Am Juliusturm. © **030/3549440**. Admission 4.50€ ($7.20) adults, 2.50€ ($4) students. Tues–Fri 9am–5pm; Sat–Sun 10am–5pm. U-Bahn: Zitadelle.

BERLIN'S PARKS & ZOO

The huge **Botanischer Garten (Botanical Garden),** Königin-Luise-Strasse 6–8 (© **030/83850100;** www.bgbm.org/bgbm; S-Bahn: Botanischer Garten or Rathaus Steglitz), near the Dahlem Museums, has vast collections of European and exotic plants. The big palm house is one of the largest in the world. A large arboretum is here, as well as several special collections such as a garden for blind visitors and another with water plants. Admission is 5€ ($8) for adults, 2.50€ ($4) for children 6 to 14, and free for children 5 and under. The gardens are open daily April and August 9am to 8pm; May, June, and July 9am to 9pm; September 9am to 7pm; March and October 9am to 6pm; February 9am to 5pm; and November to January 9am to 4pm; the museum is open year-round daily from 10am to 6pm.

Tiergarten ℱ is the largest green space in central Berlin, covering 2.5 sq. km (just under 1 sq. mile), with more than 23km (14 miles) of meandering walkways. It was originally laid out as a private park for the electors of Prussia by a leading landscape architect of the day, Peter Josef Lenné. The park was devastated during World War II, and the trees that remained were chopped down for fuel, as Berliners shivered through the winter of 1945 and 1946. Beginning in 1955, trees were replanted, and walkways, canals, ponds, and flowerbeds were restored to their original patterns. The park is popular with joggers and (sometimes nude) sunbathers. Inside the park is the Berlin Zoo (see below).

Among the park's monuments is the **Siegessäule (Victory Column),** a golden goddess of victory perched atop a soaring red-granite pedestal. The monument stands in the center of the wide boulevard (Strasse des 17 Juni) that neatly bisects the park. A 48m-high (157-ft.) observation platform can be reached by a climb up a 285-step spiral staircase (there's no elevator). It's open April to October Monday to Friday 9:30am to 6:30pm, Saturday and Sunday 9:30am to 7pm; November to March Monday to Friday 10am to 5pm, Saturday and Sunday 10am to 5:30pm. Admission is 2.20€ ($3.50) for adults and 1.50€ ($2.40) for students and children 17 and under. For information, call © **030/3912961.**

Zoologischer Garten Berlin (Berlin Zoo-Aquarium) ✯, Hardenbergplatz 8 (© **030/254010;** www.zoo-berlin.de; U-Bahn/S-Bahn: Zoologischer Garten), founded in 1844, is Germany's oldest zoo. It occupies almost the entire southwest corner of the Tiergarten. Until World War II, the zoo boasted thousands of animals—many were familiar to Berliners by nickname. By the end of 1945, however, only 91 had survived. Today, more than 13,000 animals live here, many of them in large, open natural habitats. The most valuable residents are the giant pandas. The zoo also has Europe's most modern birdhouse, with more than 550 species.

The aquarium is as impressive as the adjacent zoo, with more than 9,000 species of fish, reptiles, amphibians, insects, and other creatures. Crocodiles, Komodo dragons, and tuataras inhabit the terrarium within. You can walk on a bridge over the reptile pit. There's also a large collection of snakes, lizards, and turtles. The glass-roofed "hippoquarium" is a new attraction.

Individual admission to either the zoo or aquarium is 12€ ($19) for adults, 9€ ($14) for seniors and students, and 6€ ($9.60) for children 5 to 15. A combined ticket costs 18€ ($29) for adults, 14€ ($22) for seniors and students, and 9€ ($14) for children 5 to 15 . The zoo is open daily April to September 9am to 6:30pm, October 9am to 6pm, November to February 9am to 5pm, and March 9am to 5:30pm. The aquarium is open year-round daily 9am to 6pm.

AquaDom & Sea Life Berlin, Spandauer Strasse 3 (© **030/992-800;** www.sea life.de; U-Bahn: Hackescher Markt), is hardly the greatest aquarium in Europe, but it has some unique features. The tanks begin on the River Spree and then flow into the Wannsee, a Berlin lake, before heading to the ocean. Thus, you go from fresh water to saltwater. Along the way you meet some 4,000 marine creatures from the octopus to the hound shark, even sea horses. After a Sea Life visit, you can go to the AquaDom to view the largest free-standing aquarium in the world. In Berlin it's home to a vast collection of rainbow-hued tropical fish. At the end of your visit, you take a dramatic glass elevator through a silo-shaped "fish tank" to the exit. Admission is 16€ ($25) for adults, 12€ ($18) for children 3 to 14, and free for children 2 and under. It's open April to September daily 10am to 7pm, October to March daily 10am to 6pm.

6 Organized Tours

WALKING TOURS

For an excellent introduction to Berlin and its history, try one of the walking tours offered by **Berlin Walks** (© **030/3019194;** www.berlinwalks.de). **"Discover Berlin"** is a 3-hour introductory tour that takes you past the New Synagogue, the Reichstag, and the Brandenburg Gate, among other major sites. This walk starts daily at 10am and 2:30pm (in winter at 10am only). **"Infamous Third Reich Sites"** focuses on the sites of major Nazi buildings in central Berlin, such as Goebbels' Propaganda Ministry and Hitler's New Reichschancellery; it starts Wednesday and Sunday at 10am and Saturday at 2:30pm in summer, less frequently in the off season. **"Jewish Life in Berlin"** takes you through the prewar Jewish community; sights include the Old Cemetery and the former Boys' School. The tour starts May to September Monday at 10am. One of the most intriguing tours is **"Berlin—Nest of Spies,"** which takes you to some of the most infamous sites associated with both the Nazis and the Communist takeover of East Germany. Lasting 4 hours, this tour is conducted May to September only on Tuesday and Saturday at 12:30pm. For all tours, reservations are unnecessary—simply meet the guide, who will be wearing a Berlin Walks badge, outside the

---

(*Finds*) **Safari Tours in That Sardine Can on Wheels**

A trend devoted to Communist kitsch is sweeping this once-divided capital. Germans call it *Ostalgie,* meaning nostalgia for the East during the Cold War. They celebrate it as Americans do the '50s. Years after the fall of the so-called German Democratic Republic, East Berlin is making a comeback. One social critic called it "a profound longing for a golden time that never was." Some Berlin entrepreneurs are even offering self-guided "safari tours" in the Trabi, that "sardine can on wheels," built in East German factories between 1955 and 1991. The car was constructed mostly of plastic. The "Trabi Safari" starts at Gendarmenmarkt and Markgrafenstrasse, costing from 25€ to 40€ ($40–$64) per passenger for a tour that lasts 1½ hours. You're taken to the famous Cold War sites of East Berlin, most of which are off the beaten path. For reservations, call (*C*) **030/2759-2273** or visit www. trabi-safari.de.

---

main entrance to Bahnhof Zoologischer Garten (Zoo Station), at the top of the taxi stand. Tours (in English) last from 2½ to 6 hours, and cost 12€ ($19) for those 26 and over, 10€ ($16) for those 14 to 25, and free for children 13 and under (with an adult). Berlin Walks also offers a tour to Potsdam, starting every Sunday at 10am from May to September. **"Discover Potsdam"** lasts 5 to 6 hours, and costs 15€ ($24) for those 26 and over, 12€ ($19) for those 14 to 25, and free for children 13 and under.

BUS TOURS

Berlin is a far-flung metropolis with interesting neighborhoods that are often separated by extended areas of parks, monumental boulevards, and Cold War wastelands. Because of these factors, organized bus tours can be the best way to navigate the city.

Some of the best are operated by **Severin+Kühn,** Kurfürstendamm 216 ((*C*) **030/ 8804190;** www.severin-kuehn-berlin.de; U-Bahn: Kurfürstendamm), located on the second floor of a building across from the Kempinski Hotel. This agency offers a half-dozen tours of Berlin and its environs. Their 2-hour **"Berlin City Tour"** departs April to October daily every half-hour from 10am to 6pm. Tickets cost 20€ ($32) per person. The tour passes 14 important stops in Berlin, including the Europa Center, the Brandenburg Gate, and Potsdamer Platz; provides taped audio commentary in eight languages; and offers the option of getting on and off the bus at any point during the hour. Retain your ticket stub to reboard the bus.

Severin+Kühn also offers the 3-hour **"Big Berlin Tour,"** which departs daily at 10am and 2pm and costs 22€ ($35) per person. This tour incorporates more sites than their 14-Stops-City Tour. All tours include a live guide who delivers commentaries in both German and English.

One of the more intriguing tours visits Potsdam, site of the famed World War II conference and of Sans Souci Palace, former residence of Frederick the Great. The price is 37€ ($59) per person. Departures are Tuesday, Thursday, Saturday, and Sunday at 10am; May and October, there are additional departures Friday to Sunday at 2:15pm.

BOAT TOURS

It may not be the obvious choice for transportation in Berlin, but a boat ride can offer visitors a good change of pace. The networks of canals that bisect the plains of what used to be known as Prussia were an engineering marvel when they were completed in the 19th century. Today, transport through the lakes, locks, and canals around Berlin retains its nostalgic allure and affords unusual vistas that aren't available from the windows of more conventional modes of transport. Berliners boast that their city has more bridges than Venice. Local waterways include the Spree and Havel rivers—ranging in size from narrow channels to large lakes—as well as many canals. You can take short tours that offer close-up views of the city or daylong adventures along the Spree and Havel; the latter often turn into beer-drinking fests.

The city's best-known boat operator is **Stern und Kreisschiffahrt,** Pushkinallee 15 (© **030/5363600;** www.sternundkreis.de). Since Germany's reunification, this company has absorbed the piers and ferryboats of several of its former East German counterparts. The resulting entity is ready and able to take you on waterborne cruises that incorporate sights that were once restricted to Berlin's eastern zone.

The most popular of the cruises, "Historische Stadtfahrt," takes you for a 1-hour ride along the banks of the Spree, the river that helped build Berlin. Departing at 30-minute intervals March to October daily between 10:30am and 5pm, they take in river-fronting views of the city's central core, beginning at a point in the Nikolaiviertel, close to Berlin's imposing 19th-century cathedral, on the Am Palast Ufer (U-Bahn: Nikolaiviertel).

More comprehensive are the 4-hour tours along the river Spree and some of its canals. Originating at the Treptow quays (S-Bahn: Treptow Park), they depart late March to October daily at 9:45am and again at 2pm. These trips offer good views of the exteriors of the Reichstag, the Pergamon Museum, the Königliche Bibliothek (Royal Library), and the monumental heart of what used to be known as East Berlin.

Tours depart from the Jannowitz Brücke (U-Bahn: Jannowitz Brücke). Reservations are usually necessary for all boat rides described above. Rides operate only from late March to late October, depending on the tour, although there might be a special river tour offered around Christmas if demand warrants. Tours lasting 1 hour cost 8.50€ ($14) per person; tours lasting 4 hours cost 18€ ($28) per person. Students and children between the ages of 6 and 15 receive discounts of 50%, and children 5 and under ride for free. Prices and actual itineraries change seasonally; call for more details.

7 Sports & Outdoor Pursuits

BIKING

The best place to rent bikes in Berlin is at **Fahrradstation GmbH,** Bergmannstrasse 9 (© **030/2151566;** U-Bahn: Platz der Luftbrücke), in Kreuzberg. Rentals cost 15€ ($24) per day or 50€ ($80) per week. Oddly enough, rentals of 3-speed, 7-speed, and 21-speed (racing) bikes all cost the same; consequently, a cyclist can rent whichever degree of high-tech savvy he or she prefers. The city maintains a labyrinth of bike paths, marked by red bricks on the walkways, through the central core of Berlin and in its parks, especially the Tiergarten. The best places for biking are the Tiergarten in central Berlin and farther afield in the Grunewald Forest (S-Bahn: Grunewald).

JOGGING

Head for the vast and verdant leafiness of the **Grunewald,** on the city's western edge, which is crisscrossed with pedestrian and bike paths. This area is appropriate for very long endurance tests. Closer to the center is the **Tiergarten,** which allows you to soak up a little history on your morning jog thanks to its many monuments and memorials. The grounds of **Schloss Charlottenburg** are also good for jogging.

SPECTATOR SPORTS

Among Berliners, **füssball (soccer)** is the most popular sport. For information about which teams are playing, ask your hotel receptionist or refer to a daily newspaper or the weekly magazine *Berlin Programm.*

SWIMMING

Berlin is hardly a beach resort, but each summer the banks of many of the canals are covered with sand on which rest deck chairs under rainbow-hued umbrellas. In essence, a series of mini–city beaches is created. The best of these is **Bundespresse Strand,** Kapelle-Ufer 1 (© **030/2809-9119;** www.derbundespressestrand.de), across from the Reichstag in the center of Berlin. It offers two swimming pools, live music, and a glass pavilion for rainy days.

The bar here is the best known "beach bar" in Berlin; if you're hungry, it offers, in addition to beer and cocktails, freshly made salads and grilled meats. On Thursday evenings, salsa music is a feature, and on Sunday, beginning at 3pm, a dance is staged. From May until the end of summer volleyball is offered—free until 5pm, 12€ ($19) thereafter. The location is on the site of the old Berlin Wall in once "forbidden" territory. In summer it's open daily 10am until late at night (no set closing hour; U-Bahn: Friedrichstrasse).

Perched on the top floor of the Europa Center's parking garage (Parkhaus Europa Center), the health and exercise club called **Thermen,** Nürnberger Strasse 7 (© **030/ 2575760;** U-Bahn: Wittenbergplatz), offers an array of heated pools, saunas, massage facilities, and solariums. You'll pay 17€ ($27) for a 3-hour use of these facilities, but most visitors find that unless they're terribly rushed and plan on just a quick dip, it's more practical to buy a full-day pass for 19€ ($30). They'll give you a key to lock up your valuables. It's a good idea to bring your own bathing suit, but if you don't have one, an attendant will drag one out of a tattered inventory in back. Know in advance that men and women share the same saunas, and in Germany, no one seems particularly adverse to sweating nude in a communal setting. Massages go for 24€ ($38) per 30-minute session and should be reserved in advance. Hours are Monday to Saturday 10am to midnight and Sunday 10am to 9pm.

For outdoor swimming during the hot months, head to one of Europe's largest lake beaches at **Wannsee.** Take the S-Bahn to Nikolaisee and follow the hordes of bathers heading toward the water's edge.

TENNIS & SQUASH

A well-respected outfit that features access to indoor tennis and squash courts is **Sport Center Buschkrug,** Buschkrugallee 84 (© **030/6066011;** U-Bahn: Grenzallee). Depending on the time of day you arrive, indoor tennis courts rent for between 16€ and 25€ ($26–$40) per hour, and indoor squash courts rent for between 15€ and 19€ ($24–$30) per hour. Know in advance that the most expensive and most sought-after playing times are between 5 and 9pm, presumably when local residents need to work off steam after a day at the office. A worthy competitor is Berlin's **Squash & Tennis Center,** Treuenbrietzenerstrasse 36 (© **030/4153011;** U-Bahn: Wittenau, then bus no. 124 or X-21), which charges a bit less—18€ to 26€ ($29–$42) per hour for use of one of its half-dozen tennis courts and 9€ to 13€ ($14–$21) for use of one of its 10 squash courts per hour, depending on when you opt to play. Advance reservations at both of the above-mentioned clubs are recommended.

8 Shopping

The **Ku'Damm (Kurfürstendamm)** is the Fifth Avenue of Berlin. It's filled with quality stores but also has outlets hustling cheap souvenirs and T-shirts. Although Berliners themselves shop on the Ku'Damm, many prefer the specialty stores on the side streets, especially between **Breitscheidplatz** and **Olivaer Platz.** You may also want to check out **Am Zoo** and **Kantstrasse.**

Another major shopping street is the **Tauentzienstrasse** and the streets that intersect it: **Marburger, Ranke,** and **Nürnberger.** This area offers a wide array of stores, many specializing in German fashions for women. Stores here are often cheaper than on the Ku'Damm. Also on Tauentzienstrasse (near the Ku'Damm) is Berlin's major indoor shopping center, the **Europa Center** (© 030/264-97-940), with around 75 shops, as well as restaurants and cafes. At the end of this street lies the **KaDeWe,** the classiest department store in Berlin and the biggest in continental Europe.

A new, upmarket version of the Europa Center is the **Uhland-Passage,** at Uhlandstrasse 170, which has some of the best boutiques and big-name stores in Berlin. Shoppers interested in quality at any price should head to **Kempinski Plaza,** Uhlandstrasse 181–183, a pocket of posh, with some of the most exclusive boutiques in the city. Haute-couture women's clothing is a special feature here. More trendy and avantgarde boutiques are found along **Bleibtreustrasse.**

If you're looking for serious bargains, head to **Wilmersdorferstrasse,** with a vast number of discount stores, although some of the merchandise is second rate. Try to avoid Saturday morning, when it's often impossibly overcrowded.

In eastern Berlin, not that long ago, you couldn't find much to buy except a few souvenirs. All that has changed now. The main street, **Friedrichstrasse,** offers some of Berlin's most elegant shopping. Upmarket boutiques—selling everything from quality women's fashions to Meissen porcelain—are found along **Unter den Linden.** The cheaper stores in eastern Berlin are around the rather bleak-looking **Alexanderplatz.** Many specialty and clothing shops are found in the **Nikolai Quarter.** The largest shopping mall in eastern Berlin, with outlets offering a little bit of everything, is at the **Berliner Markthalle,** at the corner of Rosa-Luxemburg-Strasse and Karl-Liebknecht-Strasse.

Most stores in Berlin are open Monday to Friday 9 or 10am to 6 or 6:30pm. Many stay open late on Thursday evenings, often to 8:30pm. Saturday hours are usually 9 or 10am to 2pm.

ANTIQUES

Astoria   Astoria, whose buyers frequently scour the antiques markets of France, England, and Germany, pays homage to the decorative objects of the 1920s and 1930s. You'll find antique mirrors, lamps, tables, and jewelry here, as well as a handful of reproductions. Bleibtreustrasse 42. © **030/8838181.** S-Bahn: Savignyplatz.

Harmel's   Most of Harmel's inventory was gathered in England and France, a commentary on the relative scarcity of genuine German antiques because of wartime bombing. The carefully chosen collection stresses furniture, jewelry, and accessories from the Victorian and Edwardian eras. Damaschkestrasse 24. © **030/3242292.** U-Bahn: Adenauerplatz.

Kunstsalon   Don't expect everything in this shop to be tasteful. Instead, you'll find the kind of rococo art objects that Liberace might have used in a stage set, or that a hip Berliner nightclub or brothel might buy as a means of creating instant kitsch. Everything is a castoff from previous productions of the Komische Oper (Comic Opera), including both the stage props and the costumes. Come here for the wigs, gowns, and waistcoats that clothed the partygoers during *The Merry Widow,* the candelabra that lit up Violetta when she died in *Traviata,* and the associated trash and treasures that evoke smiles from virtually anyone who understands their origin. The store also sells CDs, posters, and reproductions of rare portraits of Garbo, Dietrich, and Charlie Chaplin with Pola Negri during a holiday they enjoyed at the nearby Adlon Hotel in 1929. Unter den Linden 41. ℭ 030/20450203. S-Bahn: Under den Linden.

L. & M. Lee ⟨★   This is one of several sophisticated antiques stores on the Kurfürstendamm's eastern end. The inventory includes mostly German-made porcelain, silver, and glass from the early 20th century, and an assortment of 19th-century pieces from other European countries. Kurfürstendamm 32. ℭ **030/8817333.** U-Bahn: Uhlandstrasse.

ART GALLERIES

Arndt & Partner Berlin   Among the first art galleries to establish itself after the collapse of the Berlin Wall, Arndt & Partner has focused on the discovery of new artists and the emergence of new trends since its inception. The gallery houses the works of today's emerging artists, and of established ones as well. In 2006, the gallery received upgrades, with the addition of a second floor, allowing for larger exhibitions and museum-size installations, and a lounge where film artists can share their work with the viewing public. Zimmerstrasse 90–91. ℭ **030/2808123.** www.arndt-partner.de. U-Bahn: Kochstrasse.

Galerie Brusberg ⟨★   One of Germany's most visible and influential art galleries, Galerie Brusberg was established in 1958 by Dieter Brusberg. The gallery has handled the work of Max Ernst, Salvador Dalí, Paul Delvaux, Henri Laurens, Pablo Picasso, and René Magritte, plus German artists Altenbourg, Antes, and Klapheck. Long before unification, it promoted painters of the old Eastern Bloc, notably Bernhard Heisig, Harald Metzkes, and Werner Töbke. No one will mind if you drop in just for a look. Kurfürstendamm 213. ℭ **030/8827682.** www.brusberg-berlin.de. U-Bahn: Uhlandstrasse.

Galerie Pels-Leusden and Villa Grisebach Auktionen ⟨★   This building, constructed in the 1880s by architect Hans Grisebach as his private home, is a historic monument in its own right. Two floors are devoted to 19th- and 20th-century art, mainly German. Prices begin at around 100€ ($160) for the least expensive lithograph and go much higher. The building also functions as headquarters and display area for an auction house. Sales are held every spring and fall. Fasanenstrasse 25. ℭ **030/ 8859150.** U-Bahn: Uhlandstrasse.

Galerie Thomas Schulte ⟨★   Established in 1991 in the wake of the reunion of Berlin, this quickly became one of Germany's leading international galleries. Focusing on contemporary conceptual art since 1960, the gallery displays the works of well-known artists such as Robert Mapplethorpe, Richard Deacon, and Rebecca Horn. The gallery, located on the first floor, welcomes visitors Tuesday through Saturday, noon to 6pm. Charlottenstrasse 24. ℭ **030/206-08990.** www.galeriethomasschulte.de. U-Bahn: Stadtmitte.

KW Institute for Contemporary Art ⟨★   Located on the site of what was once a margarine factory, this building has been transformed into one of the city's major

Finds **Treasures in the Barn District**

At the very heart and soul of Berlin's fashion and art revival is the **Scheuen-viertel,** or "Barn District" (S-Bahn: Hackescher Markt). The name comes from a period in the 17th century when hay barns were built far from the city center for fear of fires. In time, the city's growth overtook the area, and it became Berlin's Jewish quarter. For some reason, many of its oldest build-ings survived World War II bombing assaults.

The remains of a grand 1909 shopping arcade—which occupies most of the block formed by Oranienburger, Rosenthaler, Grosse Hamburger Strasse, and Sophienstrasse—have been turned into a series of galleries, studios, and theaters. Worth a visit is **Tacheles,** Oranienburger Strasse 54–56 (© **030/2826185;** S-Bahn: Hackescher Markt), or "talking turkey" in Yiddish. It's an alternative arts center.

The more prestigious galleries are found along Auguststrasse. **Galerie Wohnmaschine,** Tucholskystrasse 35 (© **030/30872015;** www.wohnmaschine. de; S-Bahn: Oranienburger Strasse), became the area's first gallery when it opened in 1988. Some of the best artists in the city are on exhibit here, most of them of a conceptual or minimalist bent.

Johanna Petzoldt, Sophienstrasse 9 (© **030/2826754;** U-Bahn: Weinmeis-terstrasse), sells handicrafts from the old Erzebirge region, including wooden toys and assorted curiosities, such as scenes fitted into a matchbox.

centers of contemporary art. The institute houses no permanent collection of its own, and is instead considered a testing ground for emerging artists, with five floors of exhi-bition space and six artists' studios. The courtyard on the grounds, which once lay in ruins, has been refurbished to provide an airy space for visitors to stroll or sit and chat. Check out the Café Bravo Pavilion, which is an art exhibit in itself. Auguststrasse 69. © 030/243-4590. www.kw-berlin.de. U-Bahn: Weinmeister Strasse.

BOOKSHOPS

This literate and culture-conscious city boasts lots of bookshops catering to a multi-lingual clientele. An outfit richly stocked with works from German publishing houses is **Literaturhaus Berlin,** Fasanenstrasse 23 (© **030/8872860;** U-Bahn: Uhland-strasse). The leading gay bookstore of Berlin, containing both erotica and upscale literature in several different languages, is **Prinz Eisenherz,** Lietzenburgerstrasse 9A (© **030/3139936;** S-Bahn: Wartenberg). Since its opening in 1999, **Pro qm,** Alm-stadtstrasse 48–50 (© **030/2472-8520;** www.pro-qm.de; U-Bahn: Rosa-Luxemburg-Platz) has been known as one of Berlin's best bookstores for publications on art, architecture and design, and pop culture. As a testament to its success, the shop has relocated to a new spacious building. This new structure was designed by architects to not only accommodate a larger inventory, but primarily to facilitate discussion and movement among patrons.

CHINA & PORCELAIN

KPM ✸✸✸ This prestigious emporium was founded in 1763, when Frederick the Great invested his personal funds in a lackluster porcelain factory, elevated it to royal status, and gave it a new name: **Königliche Porzellan-Manufaktur (Royal Porcelain Factory)**. It was Prussia's answer to Meissen, in Saxony. Since then, the factory has become world famous for its artistry and delicacy. Each exquisite, hand-painted, hand-decorated item is carefully packed for shipment to virtually anywhere in the world. Patterns, for the most part, are based on traditional 18th- and 19th-century designs. All objects carry a distinctive official signature, an imperial orb, and the letters KPM. There's also an array of high-quality trinkets for visitors.

You can visit the **factory** itself at Wegelystrasse 1 (© **030/390090;** U-Bahn: Tiergarten). Guided tours let you look at the craftsmanship of the employees, and you can buy pieces here. Tours are provided once a day from Monday to Thursday at 10am. The charge is 8€ ($13), which is applied to any purchase. Children 15 and under are prohibited, as are video cameras and photography. Kurfürstendamm 27 (in the Kempinski Hotel Bristol). © **030/88672110.** U-Bahn: Kurfürstendamm.

Rosenthal ⭐⭐⭐   Head here for contemporary Rosenthal designs from Bavaria. In addition to Rosenthal porcelain, you'll find Boda glassware and elegantly modern tableware. Kurfürstendamm 226. © **030/8856340.** U-Bahn: Kurfürstendamm.

COMMIE RELICS

Mondos Arts   As the memories of Berlin's division fade more and more, nostalgia for the era of Soviet rule is popping up in this ever-evolving city. This tiny shop is chock full of relics from the Eastern Bloc period and kitschy items commemorating the old days—good or bad—of Communism. There is an eclectic variety of unique items to choose from here, from items emblazoned with the images of Marx, Lenin, and Rosa Luxemburg, to bottles of Soviet-era beer. Ampelmännchen, the ubiquitous red-and-green man on eastern traffic crossings, serves as the store's unofficial mascot, with the symbol adorning all sorts of items. There's a wide variety of DVDs to choose from, including the propaganda-tinged films of East Berlin. Schreinerstrasse 6. © **030/420-10778.** www.mondosarts.de. U-Bahn: Samariter Strasse.

DEPARTMENT STORES

Corner Berlin ⭐ *(Finds)*   This creation of a former movie producer and a former cosmetics executive is not really a department store, not really a boutique. "It's what it is," one of the owners enigmatically proclaimed. That means you can expect a little of everything: fashion accessories, jewelry, beauty products, gifts, electronics, art, vintage furniture, food, drink, books, and magazines. Almost every item on display is made exclusively in Germany. 40 Französischestrasse 40. © **030/20670940.** U-Bahn: Französischestrasse.

Departmentstore Quartier 206   Located in the center of Berlin, this exclusive shopping center is not just about the merchandise. Housed in a building designed by the renowned architect I. M. Pei's firm, this Art Deco–style glass-and-marble structure contains 8,000 sq. m (86,111 sq. ft.) of retail space. Shopping here is top-notch, and you'll find such luxury brands as Louis Vuitton, Gucci, and Yves Saint Laurent. Friedrichstrasse 71. © **030/2094-6800.** www.quartier206.com. U-Bahn: Stadtmitte.

Galeries Lafayette ⭐   Paris in Berlin is found at this modern department store, right off Friedrichstrasse, designed by Jean Nouvel with a spectacular interior. The opening of this store has made Friedrichstrasse, the "street of spies" in the Cold War era, one of the most fashionable shopping areas in eastern Europe. Its French food department evokes what is meant by "died and gone to heaven." Französischestrasse 23. © **030/209480.** U-Bahn: Französischestrasse.

Kaufhaus des Westens (KaDeWe) ✿✿✿   This huge luxury department store, known popularly as KaDeWe (pronounced *kah*-day-vay), was established nearly a century ago. It's best known for its sixth-floor food department, where more than 1,000 varieties of German sausages are displayed along with delicacies from all over the world. Even the most jaded epicure should find delight here with its wide range of sausages and the tastiest herring sandwiches in Berlin. Sit-down counters are available. After fortifying yourself here, you can explore the six floors of merchandise. KaDeWe is more than a department store—one shopper called it a "collection of first-class specialty shops." Tauentzienstrasse 21. ℭ **030/21210.** U-Bahn: Wittenbergplatz.

Wertheim   This centrally located store is good for travel aids and general basics. It sells perfumes, clothing for the entire family, jewelry, electrical devices, household goods, photography supplies, and souvenirs. It also has a shoe-repair section. Shoppers can fuel up at a large restaurant with a grand view over half the city. Kurfürstendamm 231. ℭ **030/880030.** U-Bahn: Kurfürstendamm.

DESIGN

Bauhaus Archive   The shop at the landmark Bauhaus Archive Museum of Design offers a stunning variety of items in contemporary styles, some designed by artists of the Bauhaus movement. More than 250 items, which incorporate not only design, but also utility, are available for the home and office. Profits from the shop support the Bauhaus Archive in its quest to both sustain its current collections and obtain new acquisitions. Klingelhöferstrasse 14. ℭ **030/254-0020.** www.bauhaus.de. U-Bahn: Nollendorfplatz.

FASHION

Bleibgrün   It's small, it's fashionable, and it's sought after by well-dressed and well-heeled women from Berlin and its suburbs. And best of all, the staff is charming and helpful. Come here for access to things that are terribly chic and contemporary, including dresses by Jean-Paul Gaultier, Paul Smith, Marithé François Girbaud, and a handful of other currently fashionable trendsetters. Bleibtreustrasse 29–30. ℭ **030/ 8821689.** S-Bahn: Savignyplatz.

Sonia Rykiel   This stylish showcase is the only shop in Germany devoted exclusively to Ms. Rykiel, the successful French fashion mogul. She designed the store's interior herself. Beware—even a Sonia Rykiel T-shirt is expensive. There are a children's shop and a women's shop. Kurfürstendamm 186. ℭ **030/8821774.** U-Bahn: Adenauerplatz.

Triebel   This elegant store offers everything you may need for a weekend retreat at a private hunting lodge, such as clothing, shoes, boots, and sporting equipment. If you dream of looking like the lord of a Bavarian manor in a loden coat and feather-trimmed hat, or if you've been invited on a fox hunt, come here first. The inventory includes a selection of hunting rifles and shooting equipment. Schönwalder Strasse 12, Spandau. ℭ **030/3355001.** U-Bahn: Rathaus Spandau. S-Bahn: Spandau.

Werner Scherer ✿   The arrival of this upscale menswear emporium symbolized to some extent the rebirth of the Unter den Linden as a glamorous shopping destination. Set on the street level of the Hotel Adlon, it's the showplace of Munich-based designer Werner Scherer, who makes the kinds of clothes that millionaires love to buy. Expect access to the best-made shirts we've ever seen, silk neckties, and curiosities that include bomber jackets crafted from a mixture of silk and linen, and buttery soft black leather coats. Despite its high prices, the shop does a roaring business with the glam crowd,

---

Finds Calling All Ceramics Lovers

As ceramics lovers learn more and more about the late Hedwig Bollhagen, a great ceramics artist who died in 2001, they are making their way to her **Ceramics Studio** in the little village of Marwitz outside Berlin. The location is at Hedwig-Bollhagen Strasse 4 (𝄢 **03304/39800**), reached on the A111 Autobahn toward Hamburg. The unmistakable and brightly colored geometric patterns of her tableware, with its HB monogram, are appearing in more and more collections around the world. Under the East German Communists, her Bollhagen ceramics were unavailable in the West for decades. The workshop here is open Wednesday 9am to 5pm and Saturday 10am to 2pm. You can purchase seconds at prices beginning at 10€ ($16). Free tours in German are offered the last Wednesday of every month at 1pm.

---

many of whom wouldn't consider buying their shirts anywhere else. Unter den Linden 77. 𝄢 **030/22679893**. S-Bahn: Unter den Linden.

JEWELRY

Treykorn 𝄐 _(Finds)_   This outlet displays the most avant-garde jewelry in Berlin. Owners Andreas and Sabine Treykorn provide a showcase for more than three dozen of the boldest and often most controversial jewelry artisans in the city. Although some pieces sell in the thousands, there are many selections in a more affordable price range. Savignyplatz 13-Passage. 𝄢 **030/31802354**. S-Bahn: Savignyplatz.

KITCHENWARE

VMF   Its inventory is a restaurant owner's fantasy, with appealing kitchen gadgets that cooks will love. Be warned that most appliances here are incompatible with North American electric current. But if you're interested in glassware (from Nachtmann and Eich), stoneware, kitchen cutlery, or Hümmel and Goebel porcelain figurines, you'll find this place fascinating. Kurfürstendamm 229. 𝄢 **030/66006971**. U-Bahn: Kurfürstendamm.

MARKETS

Berliner Trödelmarkt   This flea market is near the corner of the Bachstrasse and the Strasse des 17 Juni, at the western edge of the Tiergarten, adjacent to the Tiergarten S-Bahn station. It's the favorite weekend shopping spot of countless Berliners, who come here to find an appropriate piece of nostalgia, a battered semi-antique, or used clothing. The market is held every Saturday and Sunday 10am to 5pm. Strasse des 17 Juni. 𝄢 **030/26550096**. S-Bahn: Tiergarten.

MILITARY FIGURES

Berliner Zinnfiguren   A mecca for collectors since 1934, this shop carries an impressive inventory of German-language books on military history and more than 10,000 different pewter figurines of soldiers from many different imperial armies, including the Franco-Prussian War of 1870. Also included are hand-painted models of Roman and ancient Greek foot soldiers. Flat, hand-painted pewter figures are sold only in sets of 12 or more. Knesebeckstrasse 88. 𝄢 **030/3157000**. www.zinnfigur.com. S-Bahn: Savignyplatz.

MUSIC

Musik Riedel   Most of the professional musicians of Berlin have a working familiarity with this well-established store, as it's been selling musical instruments and sheet music since 1910. Regardless of how esoteric your tastes, you're likely to find the score to whatever it is that interests you—sometimes in used folios that have some historic interest in their own right. You can also find a good selection of CDs. Uhlandstrasse 38. 𝄞 030/8827395. U-Bahn: Uhlandstrasse.

PERFUME

Harry Lehmann   This is the kind of shop where German mothers and grandmothers might have bought their perfume between the two world wars. Don't expect a standardized list of the big names you'd find at a duty-free airport shop. Most scents are family recipes, distilled from flowers, grasses, and leaves. The reasonable prices may surprise you—10 grams (⅓ oz.) for as little as 5€ ($8). Coming here is a cheap and amusing way to experience the scents of a Prussian spring. Kantstrasse 106. 𝄞 030/3243582. U-Bahn: Wilmersdorferstrasse.

PUNK MEMORABILIA

Kaufhaus Schrill   Few stores mingle junkiness and kitsch with such artful abandon. Stock here would gladden any punk rocker's heart, especially if he or she were on the lookout for Elvis-era memorabilia, hair barrettes that glow in the dark, and jewelry that may appeal to Courtney Love for her date with a group of bikers. Don't expect anything tasteful—that isn't its style. Partly because of that, and partly because the place evokes a vivid sense of the long-ago rebelliousness of the '60s, the place is something of an icon for counterculture youth. Bleibtreustrasse 46. 𝄞 030/8824048. S-Bahn: Savignyplatz.

SCULPTURE

Gipsformerei der Staatlichen Museen Preussischer Kulturbesitz (Plaster Works of the State Museums of Prussia) ✫ *Finds*   This company has duplicated the world's great sculptures as plaster casts since 1819. Today, there's an inventory of more than 6,500 of them, everything from busts of Queen Nefertiti to a faithful reproduction of the Farnese Bull. Objects can be crated and shipped around the world. Sophie-Charlotten-Strasse 17. 𝄞 030/3267690. S-Bahn: Westend.

SHOES

Trippen   Founded on the concept that economic success does not need to come at the cost of social responsibility, Trippen produces shoes that are both environmentally friendly and trendy. The creative team behind the company constantly strives to produce artistic and stylish designs, but not at the expense of the environment. As a means of challenging the disposable nature of the fashion industry, Trippen continues to sell their previous collections, even while putting out new designs each season. Rosenthaler Strasse 40–41. 𝄞 030/2839-1337. www.trippen.com. U-Bahn: Weinmeisterstrasse.

SHOPPING ARCADES

One of the many surprising aspects of the rebuilt and redesigned Potsdamer Platz is the **Potsdamer Platz Arkaden** (U-Bahn/S-Bahn: Potsdamer Platz), one of the most comprehensive shopping malls in Berlin. In a deliberate rejoinder to more outdated Ku'Damm malls, such as the Europa Center, it contains more than 100 shops scattered over three levels.

9 Berlin After Dark

In Berlin, nightlife runs around the clock, and there's plenty to do at any time. Berlin has a monthly English language newspaper, *The Ex-Berliner,* providing a witty, informative guide to the city's culture and entertainment. This magazine is available at newsstands and tourist offices. Tourist offices also distribute a free magazine called *New Berlin* providing tips and recommendations to visitors. The German-language *Berlin Programm* is available at newsstands. The most detailed listings are found in *zitty,* a biweekly publication in German.

THE PERFORMING ARTS
OPERA & CLASSICAL MUSIC

Berliner Philharmonisches Orchester (Berlin Philharmonic Orchestra) ★★★ The Berlin Philharmonic, directed by Claudio Abbado, is one of the world's premier orchestras. Its home, **the Philharmonie,** in the Kulturforum, is a significant piece of modern architecture; you may want to visit even if you do not attend a performance. None of the 2,218 seats are more than 30m (100 ft.) from the rostrum. The box office is open Monday to Friday 3 to 6pm and Saturday and Sunday 11am to 2pm. You can place orders by phone at © **030/25488999.** If you're staying in a first-class or deluxe hotel, you can usually get the concierge to obtain seats for you. Herbert-von-Karajan-Strasse 1. © 030/254880. www.berlin-philharmonic.com. Tickets 20€–85€ ($32–$136); special concerts 53€–138€ ($85–$221). U-Bahn: Potsdamer Platz.

Deutsche Oper Berlin ★ This opera company performs in Charlottenburg in one of the world's great opera houses, a notable example of modern theater architecture that seats 1,885. The company tackles Puccini favorites, Janáček rarities, or modern works, and has a complete Wagner repertoire. A ballet company performs once a week. Concerts, including Lieder evenings, are also presented on the opera stage. Bismarckstrasse 35. © 030/3438401. www.deutscheoperberlin.de. Tickets 12€–112€ ($19–$179). U-Bahn: Deutsche Oper. S-Bahn: Charlottenburg.

Deutsche Staatsoper (German State Opera) ★ The German State Opera performs in the Staatsoper Unter den Linden. This was for years the showcase of the opera scene of East Germany. Originally constructed in 1743 and destroyed in World War II, the house was rebuilt in the 1950s, reproducing as closely as possible the original designs of Georg Knobelsdorff. Some of the world's finest operas, as well as concerts and ballets, are presented here. The opera house will close in 2010 for a 3-year renovation. The box office is open Monday to Friday 11am to 7pm, Saturday and Sunday 2 to 7pm. Unter den Linden 7. © 030/20-35-40. www.staatsoperberlin.de. Tickets: concerts 10€–38€ ($16–$61); opera 5€–160€ ($8–$256). U-Bahn: Französischestrasse. S-Bahn: Friedrichstrasse.

Komische Oper Berlin The Komische Opera has become one of the most highly regarded theater ensembles in Europe, presenting many avant-garde opera productions as well as ballet and musical theater. The box office is open Monday to Saturday 11am to 7pm and Sunday 1pm until 1½ hours before the performance. Behrensstrasse 55–57. © 030/202600. www.komische-oper-berlin.de. Tickets 8€–93€ ($13–$149). U-Bahn: Französischestrasse. S-Bahn: Friedrichstrasse or Unter den Linden.

Konzerthaus Berlin This 1821 building was created by Friedrich Schinkel. It offers two venues for classical concerts: the Grosser Konzertsaal for orchestra and the Kammermusiksaal for chamber music. Its organ recitals are considered the finest in

Germany. Performances are often daring and innovative. The Deutsches Sinfonie-Orchester is also based here. In the Schauspielhaus, Gendarmenmarkt. (✆ **030/203090**. www.konzert haus.de. Tickets 10€–99€ ($16–$158). U-Bahn: Französischestrasse.

THEATER

Berlin has long been known for its theater. Even if you don't understand German, you may enjoy a production of a familiar play or musical.

Perhaps the most famous theater is the **Berliner Ensemble,** Am Bertolt-Brecht-Platz 1 (✆ **030/28408155;** U-Bahn/S-Bahn: Friedrichstrasse), founded by the late playwright Bertolt Brecht. His wife, Helene Weigel, played an important role in the theater's founding and was the ensemble's longtime director. Works by Brecht and other playwrights are presented here. Seats are reasonably priced, ranging from 6€ to 40€ ($9.60–$64).

The most important German-language theater in the country is **Schaubühne am Lehniner Platz,** Kurfürstendamm 153 (✆ **030/890023;** U-Bahn: Adenauerplatz), at the east end of the Ku'Damm, near Lehniner Platz. There are three different stages here. Tickets range from 10€ to 38€ ($16–$61).

Theater des Westens, located between the Berlin Zoo and the Ku'Damm at Kantstrasse 12 (✆ **030/319030;** U-Bahn/S-Bahn: Zoologischer Garten), specializes in plays, musical comedies, and the German equivalent of Broadway extravaganzas. The theater was built in 1896. Performances are held Tuesday to Saturday at 8pm and Sunday at 7pm. Saturday matinees are occasionally available. Ticket prices range from 20€ to 110€ ($32–$176).

THE CLUB & MUSIC SCENE
CABARET

Very popular among visitors to Berlin is the kind of nightspot depicted in the musical *Cabaret,* with floor-show patter and acts that make fun of the political and social scene. Cabaret life in between-the-wars Berlin inspired writers such as Christopher Isherwood, among many others. These emporiums of schmaltz have been reborn in the former East Berlin—though the satire may be a bit less biting than it was during the Weimar Republic. Today's cabaret shows may remind you of Broadway block-busters, without much of the intimacy of the smoky and trenchant cellar revues of the 1930s.

Die Stachelschweine   Since the beginning of the Cold War, the "Porcupine" has poked prickly fun at the German and American political scenes. The performance is delivered in rapid-fire German and evokes the legendary Berliner sense of satire, which can often be scathing in its humor. Although you need to understand German to really appreciate what goes on here, you'll still recognize some of the names (George W., Dick Cheney, Al Gore, and Hillary), and there's likely to be a deliberately corny selection of popular ditties ("Life is a cabaret, old chum") thrown in. Shows take place Tuesday to Friday at 8pm and Saturday at 8 and 9:30pm. The box office is open Tuesday to Friday 11am to 2pm and 3 to 7:30pm, and Saturday 10am to 2pm and 3 to 8:45pm. It's closed in July. Tauentzienstrasse and Budapesterstrasse (in the basement of Europa Center). (✆ **030/2614795.** Cover 12€–26€ ($19–$42). U-Bahn: Kurfürstendamm.

Friedrichstadt Palast   For access to talent that includes multilingual comedians and singers, jugglers, acrobats, musicians, plenty of coyly expressed sexuality, and lots of costume changes, consider an evening here. Although show times may vary with whatever revue is featured at the time of your visit, they tend to begin Tuesday to

Saturday at 8pm, with additional performances every Saturday and Sunday at 4pm. Friedrichstrasse 107. © 030/23262326. www.friedrichstadtpalast.de. Cover Fri–Sat 21€–70€ ($34–$112), Sun–Thurs 17€–60€ ($27–$96). U-Bahn/S-Bahn: Friedrichstrasse.

Wintergarten Varieté   The largest and most nostalgic Berlin cabaret, the Wintergarten offers a variety show every night, with magicians, clowns, jugglers, acrobats, and live music. The most expensive seats are on stage level, where tiny tables are available for simple suppers costing from 13€ to 24€ ($21–$38). Balconies have conventional theater seats, but staff members pass frequently along the aisles selling drinks. Shows usually begin Wednesday to Saturday at 8pm, Sunday at 6pm. Rarely, most often in summer, shows might also be presented on Monday and Tuesday. All times are subject to change, so call ahead. Shows last around 2¼ hours. Potsdamer Strasse 96. © 030/25008888. Cover Fri–Sat 25€–55€ ($40–$88), Sun–Thurs 15€–45€ ($24–$72). U-Bahn: Kurfürstenstrasse.

DANCE CLUBS

Clärchens Ballhaus   This landmark in old East Berlin has reemerged. It became a legend, opening in 1913 right before "The Great War" and miraculously surviving until the end of World War II. Today a hot DJ and live bands rage through the night, with occasional tango dancers or whatever—even Johann Strauss music. Gypsy street musicians are a favorite. Everybody from wild Turks out for a night on the town to elderly East Berlin couples fill the joint. Nazi officers once used the top floor as a private club. It's usually open from 7 to 11pm, but not every night so call before heading here. 24 Augustrasse. © 030/282-9295. S-Bahn: Oranienburger Strasse.

Delicious Doughnuts   This club for acid jazz and other delights still keeps its old name, though it no longer sells doughnuts. A scarlet red decor and black-leather booths have given it a more sophisticated ambience. A pocket-size dance floor is just part of the allure, along with a hot DJ. Rosenthalerstrasse 9. © 030/28099274. Cover Wed–Sat 5€ ($8). U-Bahn: Rosenthaler Platz.

Sage Club ★   This is one of Berlin's trendiest clubs, with a trio of dance areas and a special VIP section with a pool "reserved for the privileged," such as Mick Jagger. This club is like a party tour for the *Sex and the City* crowd. Patrons have done everything and everybody. The music blaring away is rock, funk, "big beat," soul, indie, and house. In the rear is a much frequented wooden courtyard. It's open Thursday to Sunday 7pm to 5am. Köpenicker Strasse 76. © 030/2789830. Cover 5€–11€ ($8–$18). U-Bahn: Heinrich-Heine-Strasse.

SO36 ★ *Finds*   The lines begin to form here about 30 minutes before the place opens, but they move quickly as Berliner hipsters get into the spirit of one of the city's more witty and unconventional clubs. Its name derives from the postal code for this district before World War II. Inside, you'll find two very large rooms, a stage, an ongoing rush of danceable music, and a scene that combines a senior prom in the high school gym with some of the more bizarre aspects of Berlin nightlife. Lots of women come here, both gay and straight, and there's a higher percentage of heterosexual men than you might have expected along this strip of bars in Kreuzberg. If you're lucky enough to be in town for the once-per-month Turkish drag night, you'll find one of the most amusing drag shows in Berlin, where Fatima the belly dancer is likely to be male, beguiling, and well versed in the satirical aspects of life in a Turkish harem. The club is open most nights, based on an evolving schedule, 10:30pm to at least 4am. Oranienstrasse 190, Kreuzberg. © 030/61401306. Cover 4€–21€ ($6.40–$37). U-Bahn: Görlitzer Bahnhof.

2BE-Club   A hip rendezvous, this club contains an inner patio that's like a big tent plus a dance floor where hip-hop and reggae blast the night away. On the walls the scenes evoke the Caribbean with swaying palms. It's open only Friday and Saturday and is strictly for a late-night crowd who begin showing up after 11pm. Women enter free until midnight. Bornimerstrasse 6. ℭ 030/89068410. Cover 15€ ($24). U-Bahn: Oranienburger Tor.

LIVE MUSIC

A Trane   This small and smoky jazz house is an excellent choice for beginning or ending an evening of barhopping in the neighborhood. It features musicians from all over the world. It's open daily at 8pm; music begins around 10pm. Closing hours vary. Pestalozzistrasse 105. ℭ 030/3132550. Cover 8€–15€ ($13–$24). S-Bahn: Savignyplatz.

Knaack-Klub   This four-story club features a live-music venue, two floors of dancing, and a games floor with billiards. There are usually four live rock shows a week, with a fairly even split between German and international touring bands. Show days vary. There's dancing on Wednesday, Friday, and Saturday nights. Hours are nightly from 9pm. Greifwalderstrasse 224. ℭ 030/4427060. Cover 5€–10€ ($8–$16). S-Bahn: Alexanderplatz.

Oxymoron   This is a good example of Berlin's crop of hypertrendy, high-visibility hangouts where the food is served almost as an afterthought to an exhibitionistic/ voyeuristic scene that can be a lot of fun and, in some cases, intriguing. The setting is a high-ceilinged room with old-fashioned proportions and enough battered kitsch to remind you of a coffeehouse in Franz Josef's Vienna. Local wits refer to it as a *Gesamtkunstwerk*—a self-obsessed, self-sustaining work of art that might have been appreciated by Wagner. Most nights after around 11pm, a slightly claustrophobic, much-used annex room—all black with ghostly flares of neon—opens for business as a dance club, usually with a clientele that's about 75% hetero and 100% iconoclastic. If live bands appear at all, it will usually be on a Thursday. It's open daily 11am to 2am. In the courtyard of the complex at Rosenthaler Strasse 40–41. ℭ 030/28391886. Cover 8€–11€ ($13–$18). S-Bahn: Hackescher Markt.

Quasimodo ⍟   This is the top Berlin jazz club. Although many different styles of music are offered here, including rock and Latin, jazz is the focus. Local acts are featured on Tuesday and Wednesday, when admission is free. Summer visitors should check out the Jazz in July festival. The club is open Tuesday to Saturday 9pm to 3am, with shows beginning at 10pm. Kantstrasse 12A. ℭ 030/3180456. Cover Thurs–Sat 7€–24€ ($11–$38). U-Bahn: Zoologischer Garten.

Wild at Heart   This club, with its kitschy knickknacks, colored lights, and wine-red walls, is dedicated to the rowdier side of rock, featuring hard-core punk, rock, and rockabilly bands from Germany and elsewhere. Live performances take place Wednesday to Saturday nights. It's open Monday to Friday 8pm to 3am, Saturday and Sunday 8pm to 10am (yes, you may miss breakfast). Wienerstrasse 20. ℭ 030/6119231. Cover 8€–10€ ($13–$16) for concerts only. U-Bahn: Görlitzer Bahnhof.

DRAG SHOWS

Chez Nous   The famous show at Chez Nous is played to an essentially straight crowd in a mock Louis XIV setting. Some of the world's best drag show acts appear here, from a sultry, boa-draped star from Rio de Janeiro to a drag queen who looks like a gun moll from the 1940s. Shows are Tuesday to Thursday and Sunday at

8:30pm, Friday and Saturday at 8:30 and 11pm. Marburgerstrasse 14. © **030/2131810.** Cover 20€ ($32); cover includes 1 drink. U-Bahn: Wittenbergplatz.

GAY & LESBIAN BERLIN

Traditionally, lesbian and gay life centered on the **Nollendorfplatz** (U-Bahn: Nollendorfplatz), the so-called "Pink Village." There is a history of homosexuality here at the **Schwules Museum,** Mehringdamm 61 (© **030/69599050**), open Wednesday to Monday from 2 to 6pm (7pm Saturday). Admission is 5€ ($8) adults, 3€ ($4.80) students. The state-supported **SpinnbodenLesbenarchiv & Bibliothek,** Anklamerstrasse 38 (© **030/4485848;** www.spinnboden.de), caters to all sorts of lesbian cultural events. **Mann-o-Meter,** Motzstrasse 5 (off Nollendorfplatz; © **030/2168008**), is a gay information center.

Today, Motzstrasse is the location of many gay and lesbian bars, including **Tom's** and **Prinzknecht.**

In the latter half of June, the Lesbisch-Schwules Stadtfest (Lesbian and Gay Men's Street Fair) takes place at Nollendorfplatz. This is topped in size, though not in exuberance, the last week in June by the Christopher Street Day parade, when 200,000 people congregate to have fun and drop inhibitions.

Kumpelnest 3000   Gay or straight, you're welcome here. All that's asked is that you enjoy a kinky good time in what used to be a brothel. This crowded and chaotic place is really a bar now, but there's also dancing to disco classics. Berliners often show up here for early-morning fun after they've exhausted the action at the other hot spots. Open daily 7pm to 5am, even later on weekends. Lützowstrasse 23. © **030/2616918.** U-Bahn: Kurfürstenstrasse.

Prinzknecht   It's large, brick-lined, and mobbed with ordinary guys who just happen to be gay and who just happen to be involved in computers, media, the building trades, and show business. The combination can be unpretentious and a lot of fun, especially when frothy pink Hemingways are bought by friends for friends and the stories start getting raunchy. If you want a place that manages to be both high-class and earthy, within walking distance of lots of other gay options, this might be appropriate. It's open daily 3pm to 3am. Fuggerstrasse 33. © **030/23627444.** U-Bahn: Viktoria-Luise-Platz.

SchwuZ   If you hadn't been warned in advance, you might not even know that this is a nightclub, hidden as it is behind the conventional-looking facade of the Café Sundström. You'll descend into a battered-looking warren of basement rooms, outfitted in a surreal combination of glossy stainless steel that alternates with structural beams and cinder block. The mostly gay, mostly male, and mostly under 35-year-old crowd comes to dance the night away, every night from 11pm until around 4am. There are two separate dance floors, one with cutting-edge, the other with more traditional, dance music. Mehringdamm 61. © **030/6290880.** www.schwuz.de. Cover 5€–8€ ($8–$13). U-Bahn: Mehringdamm.

The Sharon Stonewall Bar   Don't you love the name? The bar honors one of Hollywood's most gay-friendly actresses as well as the Greenwich Village bar where the gay revolution was launched. The atmosphere is so congenial and laid-back that straights, in addition to gays and lesbians, frequent its easy-going loungy atmosphere in the central Mitte district. The friendly owners are from Australia, and the room is filled with comfortable, cozy couches. On some occasions, the bar sponsors theme nights honoring gay and lesbian icons, with the odd DJ. The bartender makes the best strawberry daiquiris in town, and those martinis are extra dry (stirred, not shaken). It's open Sunday to Thursday 8pm to 2am, Friday and Saturday 8pm to 4am. Happy hour is Monday to Thursday 8 to 9:30pm. Linienstrasse 136. ℭ 030/24085502. U-Bahn: Oranienburger Tor. S-Bahn: Oranienburger Strasse.

Tom's Bar   Tom's becomes crowded after 11pm with young gay men. Most of the clients show up here in rugged-looking T-shirts, flannel, jeans, and/or black leather, evocative of a Tom of Finland drawing. Upstairs, the porno action is merely on the screen; downstairs it's real. Tom's is open daily 10pm to 6am. Monday nights feature two-for-one drinks. There's a cover charge for special occasions only. Motzstrasse 19. ℭ 030/2134570. U-Bahn: Nollendorfplatz.

THE BAR & CAFE SCENE
BEER GARDENS & WINE CELLARS
Historischer Weinkeller   This squat and unpretentious inn may be the site of one of your more intriguing evenings in Berlin. The setting is a highly atmospheric vaulted cellar. You can order beer or one of more than 100 German wines, as well as main courses priced at 9€ to 15€ ($14–$24). If you plan to dine, make reservations in advance. During summer months, an outdoor rustic beer garden is open. The inn is open Tuesday to Friday 4 to 11pm, Saturday and Sunday noon to 11pm. Alt-Pichelsdorf 32 (about 1.5km/1 mile west of the Olympiastadion). ℭ 030/36432619. U-Bahn: Olympia-Stadion.

Joe's Wirthaus zum Löwen   This cozy pub in the city center is attractively decorated with traditional Teutonic accessories. Even in winter, when you're snug and warm inside, you get the feeling you're sitting out under the chestnut trees. The kitchen offers good plain German food, including Bavarian specialties and some Italian dishes. It's open daily 11am to 1am; the best time to come here is 7pm to midnight. Hardenbergstrasse 29 (opposite the Kaiser Wilhelm Memorial Church). ℭ 030/2621020. U-Bahn: Zoologischer Garten.

THE BEST BARS
Green Door   No, the name wasn't taken from one of the 20th century's most famous porno flicks, *Behind the Green Door*. There is actually a green door here at this intimate, cozy, and classic cocktail lounge. But like the famous movie itself, there is a '70s-retro feel to the place. Exotic cocktails perfectly prepared by the waitstaff are one of the best features of this place, and all of them have such names as Hot Kiss or Burning Bush. We'd rank their martinis as among the best in town. It's open Monday to Thursday 6pm to 3am, Friday and Saturday 6pm to 4am. Winterfeldstrasse 50. ℭ 030/2152515. U-Bahn: Nollendorfplatz.

Harry's New York Bar   Harry's is an aggressively stylized bar with minimalist decor, pop art, and photographs of all the American presidents. It's modeled after the famous watering hole, Harry's New York Bar, in Paris. Its drink menu is a monument to the oral traditions of the International Bar Flies (IBF) Society and includes such favorites as Mizner's Dream (created in 1962 for the Boca Raton Hotel Club in Florida) and the 1964 classic the Petrifier (ingredients unlisted), for two. The menu lists almost 200 drinks, as well as a limited selection of food. It's open 24 hours a day, 7 days a week. In the Grand Hotel Esplanade, Lützowufer 15. ℭ 030/25478821. U-Bahn: Nollendorfplatz, Wittenbergplatz, or Kurfürstenstrasse.

Juleps New York Bar   The roaring '20s and the turbulent '30s of America are evoked at this speakeasy-type bar with bare brick walls. The only thing they don't have is Prohibition, as the liquor flows. We counted more than 120 different cocktails on the drink menu alone. On a tree-lined street in Charlottenburg, this is a warm, intimate, and welcoming place, with a long oaken bar. If you're hungry, check out those big and yummy bacon cheeseburgers, dig into pasta, or order chicken satays. The kitchen even turns out fabulous desserts such as Mississippi mud cake. The mojitos here are as good as those in Cuba. It's open Sunday to Thursday 5pm to 1am, Friday and Saturday 5pm to 2am. Giesebrechtstrasse 3. © **030/8818823.** U-Bahn: Adenauerplatz.

Newton Bar   There have been more reviews about Berlin's Newton Bar than virtually any other watering hole in town. You may be rejected at the door by a bouncer who disapproves of your sense of style. Here's what you'll get if you're admitted: a high-ceilinged, well-proportioned room that evokes 1960s modernism at its best and a deeply ingrained sense of the well-heeled and socially conscious bourgeoisie looking for like-minded people. It's condemned for its sense of *chicki-miki* (self-conscious chic) by clients of counterculture bars in less expensive neighborhoods. But regardless of how you feel, you can't help but be intrigued by a huge black-and-white mural (photographed by Helmut Newton) that sweeps an entire runway of naked fashion models across your field of vision, and service rituals inspired by Old Prussia. It's open daily 10am till at least 3am, with cocktails priced 9€ to 10€ ($14–$16). Charlottenstrasse 57. © **030/20295421.** U-Bahn: Stadtmitte.

Reingold   This bar is elegant and chic, stretching along the length of a long and narrow room. The overall effect has been called "Manet meeting Hopper." An aquarium seems de rigueur for Berlin bars, but the one here is modest. The beautiful people descend nightly to see and be seen. It's open daily from 7pm to 1am. Novalisstrasse 11. © **030/28387676.** U-Bahn: Friedrichstrasse.

Times Bar   The cozy and intimate Times Bar has a quiet charm reminiscent of a wood-paneled private library in someone's home. The bar is dedicated to the *Times* (of London), whose latest edition is often displayed in the window. Guests sit in leather-upholstered chairs and read English-language newspapers. Menu items range from lobster soup to ice cream. It's open daily 11am to 2am. In the Savoy hotel, Fasanenstrasse 9–10. © **030/311030.** U-Bahn: Zoologischer Garten.

Victoria Bar   One of our favorite lounge retreats is this stylishly retro bar behind blacked-out windows just a stone's throw from Potsdamer Platz in the heart of Berlin. In sophisticated surroundings, you can enjoy an excellent list of cocktails or order a sandwich if you're hungry (with choices running from barbecued beef to cucumber). The walnut tables and long bar are good points for a rendezvous with a friend. "People come here to escape the hustle and bustle," said the bartender. The tequila drinks are from Mexico, the tropical fruit punches from the Caribbean. Reduced drink prices are served Monday to Saturday 6:30 to 9:30pm or all day Sunday. Hours are Sunday to Thursday 6:30pm to 3am, Friday and Saturday 6:30pm to 4am. Potsdamer Strasse 102. © **030/25759977.** U-Bahn: Potsdamer Platz.

FINDING A *KNEIPE*

A *Kneipe* is a cozy rendezvous place, the equivalent of a Londoner's local pub. The typical Berliner has a favorite *Kneipe* for relaxing after work and visiting with friends, and there are hundreds in Berlin.

Lutter und Wegner 1811 ⊀   This place was named after a gastronomic and social landmark, Lutter und Wegner, a hangout for actors in the 19th century. You can have a drink in the stand-up bar or make reservations in advance to dine. Try the local specialty, *Königsberger Klopse,* with potatoes and a fresh salad. We also recommend the Wiener schnitzel or pot roast with horseradish and *Sekt* (German sparkling wine). The wide selection of drinks ranges from single-malt Scotch whiskeys to Italian grappas. Main courses range from 17€ to 25€ ($27–$40). The restaurant is open daily 6pm to midnight; the bar is open daily 6pm to 2am or even later, depending on business. In summer, you can sit on a terrace and observe the passing parade. Schlüterstrasse 55. ⓒ 030/8813440. S-Bahn: Savignyplatz.

CAFE LIFE

At its mid-19th-century zenith, Berlin was famous for its cafes. Max Krell, an editor, once wrote: "Cafes were our homeland. They were the stock exchange of ideas, site of intellectual transactions, futures' market of poetic and artistic glory and defeat." They've changed with the times, but cafes are still going strong in Berlin—particularly, these days, in what used to be East Berlin. In the heart of the old East German capital is a complex of about 100 bars, shops, and restaurants, called **Die Hackenschen Höfe** (S-Bahn: Hackescher Markt). This stylish minimall attracts hip counterculture denizens who wander between galleries, boutiques, and fashionable cafes. It has become one of the most prominent places in the city to go drinking.

Cafe Aedes   Tucked away within what were once small 19th-century factories, this is a trendy and convivial cafe with a counterculture clientele that's very, very hip to the changing face of Berlin and its cultural scene. The decor includes lots of shimmering glass and free-form concrete, and the clientele includes a mixed collection of merchants, artists, performers, writers, and businesspeople. Whiskey with soda costs 8€ ($10), platters of simple food range from 8€ to 13€ ($13–$21). Beef consommé, salmon steaks with mango sauce, pasta with tuna and fresh tomatoes, and vegetarian salads are what it's all about—that and ongoing dialogues. Daily hours are 10am to midnight. Rosenthaler Strasse 40–41. ⓒ 030/2858275. U-Bahn: Weinmeisterstrasse.

Café Einstein ⓕ   This legendary cafe became famous for its mellow house-roasted *Kaffee* and *Kuchen* (freshly made cakes). It became so good, in fact, that it spawned a chain of swanky coffee bars across Berlin. But we always like to go to the original, which is decorated like a gilded cafe in Vienna. It's as grand as a ballroom and is found in an old townhouse mansion. We often drop in for an elaborate breakfast, which usually costs us 10€ ($13) each. You can also return later in the day for a wide range of dishes, going from prosciutto from Italy (also Italian cheeses) to such New Yorker favorites as smoked salmon, bagels, and cream cheese. We think the *Apfelstrudel* is among the best in Berlin with its paper-thin pastry sheets and amber-colored fresh fruit. Ask for it *mit Sahne* (with cream). It's open 9am to 1am daily. Kurfürstenstrasse 58. ⓒ 030/2615096. U-Bahn: Wittenbergplatz.

Café Silberstein   From the outside, this place looks like an art gallery, but once inside, you'll see that it's an artsy cafe, one of Berlin's trendiest, with sushi, ambient music, and an ultra-hip clientele. This is one of the best places to enjoy "new Berlin" in the formerly grim eastern sector. It's open daily 10am to 4am. Oranienburger Strasse 27. ⓒ 030/2812095. U-Bahn: Oranienburger Tor.

Cafe Wintergarten in Literaturhaus Berlin ⓕ   Set within a Tuscan-style brick villa that was built in 1885, 1 block south of the Ku'Damm, a few steps from the Käthe-Kollwitz-Museum, this cafe is part of a private foundation that's devoted to the promotion—through lectures and research—of German literature. In addition to a prestigious and respectable bookshop that fills the building's basement, it contains lecture halls, offices that have links to Germany's academic community, and exhibition space for temporary exhibitions that cost from 3€ to 5€ ($4.80–$8). The best way to unlock the secrets of this place is to head for the cafe and restaurant, with tables that fill two old-fashioned Berliner-style rooms and spill into a much sought-after garden during clement weather. If you're hungry, the cheerful, old-Berliner-style staff will serve platters of noodles with cheese, rigatoni with beef strips, Argentine steaks with herbs and parsleyed potatoes, and cucumber and tuna salads. It's open daily 9:30am to 1am. Fasanenstrasse 23. ℂ 030/8825414. U-Bahn: Kurfürstendamm.

Dachgarten   This cafe is installed in the dome of the Reichstag (p. 146). Sad to say, the food is hardly the city's finest, although we find the setting and panorama so overpowering we recommend a visit, if only for coffee and pastry. If you are a customer here, you can also avoid the long lines of people waiting to enter the dome; restaurant patrons can head for the separate entrance that opens into the Reichstag directly from the Platz der Republik. (It's technically known as the "handicapped entrance.") An elevator will whisk you up to the Dachgarten restaurant. The cafe was stylishly redesigned by Sir Norman Foster, and it looks like a modern art museum. Even the Reichstag *Küchenchef* admits most diners come for the view and not the continental menu. A waiter recently confided to us, "Come back in the morning for breakfast. We get the least complaints about the food then." Main courses cost from 19€ to 30€ ($30–$48), with fixed-price menus going for 68€ to 89€ ($109–$142). The Dachgarten is open daily 9am to 4:30pm and 6:30pm to midnight. Platz der Republik, Tiergarten. ℂ 030/22629900. U-Bahn: Unter den Linden.

GAMBLING THE NIGHT AWAY

Casino Berlin   This is an exclusive club on the 37th floor of the Park Inn Hotel, opening onto a panoramic view of Berlin at night. Games of chance include American roulette, blackjack, and French roulette. Nearly 100 slot machines are found on the ground floor, which is very Las Vegas. The 37th floor gaming club costs 5€ ($8) to enter and is open daily from 3pm to 3am. Alexanderplatz 8. ℂ 030/23894144. U-Bahn: Alexanderplatz.

Spielbank Berlin   It's brassy, it sparkles with lots of chrome, and the staff is about as jaded as any you'll find in a city that's legendary for its jaded citizens. The setting is a high-ceilinged, scarlet affair that might remind you of an airport. The basement is devoted to slot machines; the upper floors (Casino Royale) to a battery of more sophisticated gambling devices that include roulette and baccarat. Men must wear a necktie for access to the Casino Royale, but not to the basement-level slot machines. The cover charge of 5€ ($8) is refunded in the form of a casino chip. There are no maximum bets—the amount you lose, or can bet on any one play, depends on your credit rating with the casino. The slot machines are accessible daily 11:30am to 3am; the rest of the complex is available for bets daily 2pm to 3am. A passport is required to enter the casino; you must be over 18 to enter and gamble. Marlene Dietrich Platz 1 (Potsdamer Platz). ℂ 030/255990. Cover 5€ ($8). U-Bahn: Potsdamer Platz.

10 A Side Trip: Potsdam & Its Palaces ⭐⭐⭐

24km (15 miles) SW of Berlin, 140km (87 miles) NE of Leipzig

The best day trip from Berlin is to the baroque town of Potsdam on the Havel River. It's often been called Germany's Versailles. World attention focused on Potsdam July 17 to August 2, 1945, when the Potsdam Conference helped shape postwar

Europe. The town has many historic sights and was beautifully planned, with large parks and a beautiful chain of lakes formed by the river. The palaces and gardens of **Sans Souci Park,** which lies to the west of Potsdam's historic core, are the major attractions here. A mile northwest of Sans Souci is the **Neuer Garten** on the Heiliger See, which contains the **Schloss Cecilienhof.**

ESSENTIALS

GETTING THERE   By Train   Potsdam Hauptbahnhof is on the major Deutsche Bundesbahn rail lines, with 29 daily connections to the rail stations in Berlin (23 min. to Bahnhof Zoo and 54 min. to Ostbahnhof). There are also 14 trains daily to and from Hannover (3–3½ hr.), and 15 daily trains to and from Nürnberg (6–6½ hr.). For rail information and schedules, call ℂ **01805/996633.**

Potsdam can also be reached by S-Bahn Lines S1 and S7 from Berlin, connecting at Wannsee station with lines R1, R3, and R4. Travel time on these lines from Berlin to Potsdam is 30 minutes. For more information, call **BVG Berlin** (ℂ **030/19449**).

By Bus   Verkehrsverbund Potsdam provides regional bus service with frequent connections between Berlin and Potsdam at Wannsee station (bus no. 118) in Berlin. For travel information and schedules, call **BVG Berlin** (ℂ **030/19449**).

By Car   Access is via the E30 Autobahn east and west or the E53 north and south. Allow about 30 minutes to drive here from Berlin.

VISITOR INFORMATION   Contact **Potsdam–Information,** Am Neuen Markt 1 (ℂ **0331/275580**), open April to October Monday to Friday 9:30am to 6pm, Saturday and Sunday 9:30am to 4pm; November to March Monday to Friday 10am to 6pm, Saturday and Sunday 9:30am to 2pm.

GETTING AROUND   By Public Transportation   Ask at the tourist office about a **Potsdam Billet,** costing 5.50€ ($8.80) and good for 24 hours on the city's public transportation system. In Potsdam, **bus no. 695,** leaving from the rail station, will deliver you to the Potsdam palaces.

By Boat   Because the area around Potsdam is surrounded by water, boat tours in fair weather are a popular diversion. Call **Weisse Flotte Potsdam,** at ℂ **0331/2759210,** for more information.

WHERE TO STAY

Hotel Bayrisches Haus 𝄞𝄞𝄞 *(Finds*   The most tranquil and luxurious retreat in Potsdam today lies just a 15-minute drive from the center. In 1847, King Frederick William ordered the construction of this Bavarian-style chalet in a forest. Miraculously spared from the ravages of war, it has been successfully converted into an exceedingly comfortable residence of charm and grace. With its elegant atmosphere, it is the only luxury hotel in Potsdam and the only one that's rated five stars by the government. The spacious guest rooms are studies in design, comfort, and luxury. From the fireplace in winter to the panoramic terrace in summer, this is the way to live in Potsdam if you can afford it.

Im Wildpark 1, 14471 Potsdam (6km/3¾ miles southwest of Potsdam; take Zeppelinstrasse from the center). ℂ **800/ 735-2428** from the U.S., or 0331/55050. Fax 0331/5505560. www.bayrisches-haus.de. 33 units. 155€–230€ ($248–$368) double; 230€–340€ ($368–$544) suite. Rates include breakfast. AE, DC, MC, V. Free parking. **Amenities:** Restaurant; bar; fitness center; spa facilities; sauna; salon; room service; babysitting; laundry service; dry cleaning; nonsmoking rooms; rooms for those w/limited mobility. *In room:* TV, Wi-Fi, minibar, hair dryer, safe.

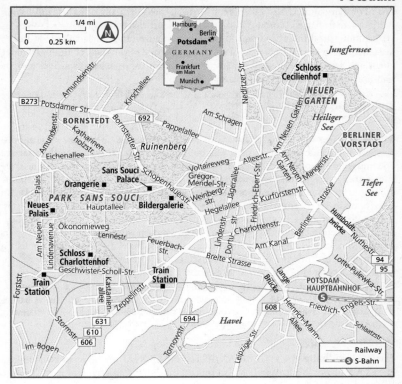

NH Hotel Voltaire ★★

This hotel is a radical renovation of the Brühlsche Palace, formerly a dour and crumbling relic built in 1732. Only the palace's baroque facade has been retained. The site belongs to the NH chain. Rooms are scattered over three floors and, in almost every case, overlook the quiet, pleasant garden in back. The rooms here are far better furnished and more elegantly appointed than those within its closest rival, Schlosshotel Cecilienhof (see below), although the latter has a richer history. The decor, in fact, is so sophisticated here that the Voltaire accurately labels itself as "a designer hotel." Some of the accommodations are large enough to be used as triples, with each guest having enough room to move about. Many families book suites here, although some of the regular rooms are large enough to accommodate extra beds. An added feature is the roof terrace, where you're treated to a panoramic view over Potsdam.

Friedrich-Ebert-Strasse 88, 14467 Potsdam. ✆ **0331/23170.** Fax 0331/2317100. www.nh-hotels.com. 143 units. 92€–120€ ($147–$192) double; from 120€ ($192) suite. AE, DC, MC, V. Parking 14€ ($22). Tram: 92. **Amenities:** Restaurant; 2 bars; health club; Jacuzzi; whirlpool; sauna; solarium; bike rental; room service; babysitting; laundry service; dry cleaning; nonsmoking rooms; rooms for those w/limited mobility. *In room:* TV, Wi-Fi, minibar, beverage maker (in some units), hair dryer, iron, trouser press, safe.

Relexa Schlosshotel Cecilienhof ★★ (Finds)

Many visitors to Potsdam don't realize that they can stay in the palace where Truman and Churchill met Stalin during the

1945 Potsdam Conference. The hotel is better located than any other in Potsdam, or Berlin for that matter, standing in the famous Neuer Garten, bordering a lake about a 15-minute stroll from Sans Souci. The German government originally converted a residential wing of this former royal residence into one of the most charming country hotels and retreats in eastern Germany. Guest rooms are midsize to spacious and are traditionally furnished and well-maintained.

Neuer Garten, Potsdam 14469. ℂ **0331/37050.** Fax 0331/292498. www.relexa-hotels.de. 41 units. 160€–200€ ($256–$320) double; 240€ ($384) suite. AE, DC, MC, V. Parking 8€ ($13). **Amenities:** Restaurant; jogging track; sauna; room service; laundry service; dry cleaning. *In room:* TV, minibar, hair dryer.

Steigenberger Maxx Hotel Sanssouci Potsdam 𝒦 *Finds*   Not your typical businessperson's chain hotel, this is more of a boutique-type establishment, with its terrace opening onto the park and palace of Sans Souci. Many guests prefer to stay in Potsdam during their Berlin visit because of the easy commute. You're given free transportation for your commute between the two cities. Like another hotel in Berlin (Hollywood Media), the Maxx leans heavy on movie theme rooms, using stills, props, and photos from old Hollywood or else from the nearby Babelsberg studio where German films were made in the heyday of UFA, which produced them. The designers wanted to re-create a British or American style hotel from the 1930s and 1950s. In elegant, tasteful, and comfortable surroundings, the guest rooms are midsize to spacious and decorated in dark wood and earthy tones, with cane furniture.

Allee nach Sanssouci 1, 14471 Potsdam. ℂ **0331/90910.** Fax 033/9091909. www.steigenberger.de. 137 units. 90€–130€ ($144–$208) double; 150€–184€ ($240–$294) suite. AE, MC, V. Parking 15€ ($24). Tram: 96. Bus: 606 or 631. **Amenities:** 2 restaurants; bar; spa; sauna; bike rentals; massage; babysitting; laundry service; dry cleaning; nonsmoking rooms; rooms for those w/limited mobility. *In room:* A/C, TV, minibar, hair dryer.

WHERE TO DINE

Friedrich-Wilhelm 𝒦𝒦𝒦 GERMAN/INTERNATIONAL   The finest restaurant to open since before World War II is also romantically scenic and tranquil in addition to serving the city's finest gourmet cuisine. In winter a fireplace blazes, with summer guests retreating to an open-air terrace to enjoy the breezes. The cuisine is market fresh, creative, and wonderfully delicate, though you pay a lot for what you get. Even though operating in an inland city, the chefs seem to obtain remarkably fresh-tasting fish such as seabass or halibut. The menu frequently changes so we can't recommend any specialties but the chefs seem skilled at all they turn out, especially if inspired by the Mediterranean kitchen. Perhaps you'll sample such delights as sturgeon, goose liver, breast of pigeon, or lobster.

In the Hotel Bayrisches Haus, Im Wildpark 1. ℂ **0331/55050.** Reservations required. Main courses 18€–35€ ($29–$56); fixed-price menus 62€–110€ ($99–$176). AE, DC, MC, V. Tues–Sat 6–10pm. Lies 6km (3¾ miles) southwest of Potsdam.

Juliette 𝒦 FRENCH TRADITIONAL/INTERNATIONAL   At last, Potsdam has a world-class restaurant. The cozy and intimate Juliette lies in the center of the restored Holländisches Viertel (Dutch Quarter), 3 blocks north of the Altar Markt. You'll feel at home the moment you enter this restored old house, with its blazing fireplace, low ceilings, and tiny little windows. There is no more romantic choice in the city. Most of the excellent waiters are from France. Menu items include saddle of boar in cranberry sauce, fresh grilled fish, and some wonderful chicken dishes. All the desserts are freshly made on-site.

Jägerstrasse 39. ℂ **0331/2701791.** Reservations required. Main courses 22€–26€ ($35–$42); fixed-price menus 52€–85€ ($83–$136). AE, MC, V. Daily noon–11pm. Tram: 94 or 96.

Specker's Gaststätte zur Ratswaag ✹✹ CONTINENTAL   One of Potsdam's most prestigious and sought-after restaurants happens to be one of its oldest, within a thick-walled country-baroque building set midway between Potsdam's railway station and its historic core. The clients who file in here for the inventive cuisine of Chef Gottfried Specker tend to be deeply involved in the whirlwinds swirling around whatever political event happens to be gripping Germany at the time of your visit. Expect business-suited representatives from municipal and national bureaucracies, often lunching or dining with representatives from the European Union, all within a sometimes reverentially hushed ambience that reflects the basic conservatism of many of the guests. Within a decor noted for thick walls, rich paneling, and mementos that evoke the glory days of Prussia, you'll dine on cuisine that changes with the seasons, the availability of local ingredients, and the inspiration of the chef. As such, it's likely to change at intervals of every 10 to 14 days. Expect a celebration of whatever's fresh (asparagus, strawberries, game, and some kinds of fish are good examples) and ongoing specialties that include, among others, a terrine of wild mushrooms and gooseliver; medallions of sea wolf in a Riesling-flavored foie gras sauce; a clear oxtail soup, loaded with flavor and garnished with spinach leaves; cream of wild mushroom soup; poached crayfish on a bed of black (squid-ink-flavored) risotto; and breast of guinea fowl with a mango-flavored cream sauce.

Am Neuen Markt 10. ✆ 0331/2804311. Reservations recommended. Main courses 16€–24€ ($26–$38); fixed-price menu 35€–70€ ($56–$112). AE, MC, V. Tues–Sat noon–3pm and 6–11pm. S-Bahn: Potsdam Hauptbahnhof.

Villa Kellermann ITALIAN   One of the most talked-about restaurants in Potsdam is in an 1878 villa, once occupied by author Bernhardt Kellerman. The Italian cuisine here attracts a diverse clientele from finance and the arts. Your meal might include marinated carpaccio of sea wolf; ravioli stuffed with cheese, spinach, and herbs; John Dory in butter-and-caper sauce; or an array of veal and beef dishes. The wine list is mostly Italian.

Mangerstrasse 34–36. ✆ 0331/291572. Reservations recommended. Main courses 17€–19€ ($27–$30); fixed-price menus 33€–56€ ($53–$90). AE, DC, MC, V. Tues–Sun noon–10pm. Bus: 695.

EXPLORING THE PARKS & PALACES

A British air raid on April 14, 1945, destroyed much of the old city center, but the major attraction, Sans Souci Park and its palaces, survived.

Neuer Garten   On Heiliger See (Holy Lake), in the northern part of Potsdam, lies the Neuer Garten. The nephew and successor to Frederick the Great, Frederick William II, had these gardens laid out. Set between the park and the palace, this lovely baroque garden is well maintained, and it's a delight to take a walk into it, enjoying the flowerbeds, the well-trimmed hedges and arbors, and the fountains in decorated basins. The tract of land was walled in during the 18th century so that the king and his consort could walk in peace without "peeping Toms" intruding on their privacy.

On Heiliger See, about .5km (1 mile) northwest of Sans Souci. ✆ 0331/9694200. Free admission. Same hours as Sans Souci (see below). Bus: 695.

Sans Souci Palace ✹✹✹   Sans Souci Park, with its palaces and gardens, was the work of many architects and sculptors. The park covers an area of about 1.6 sq. km (⅔ sq. mile). Its premier attraction is the palace of Frederick II ("the Great"), **Sans Souci,** meaning "free from care." Frederick was one of the most liberal and farsighted of the Prussian monarchs. He was a great general, but he liked best to think of himself as an enlightened patron of the arts. Here he could get away from his duties, indulge his intellectual interests, and entertain his friend Voltaire. The style of the buildings he had constructed is called "Potsdam rococo" and is primarily the achievement of Georg Wenzeslaus von Knobelsdorff.

Sans Souci Palace (© **0331/9694200**), with its terraces and gardens, was inaugurated in 1747. The long, one-story building is crowned by a dome and flanked by two round pavilions. The elliptically shaped Marble Hall is the largest in the palace, but the music salon is the supreme example of the rococo style. A small bust of Voltaire commemorates Voltaire's sojourns here. Sans Souci Palace can only be visited with a guide. *Tip:* It is best (especially in summer) to show up before noon to buy your tickets for the palace tour. At busy times, all the slots for the rest of the day can be completely filled by noon. The palace is open April to October Tuesday to Sunday 10am to 6pm, and November to March Tuesday to Sunday 10am to 5pm. Guided tours (in English) of the palace cost 8€ to 12€ ($13–$19) for adults, 5€ to 8€ ($8–$13) for students and children 6 to 18, free for children 5 and under.

Bildergalerie (Picture Gallery), Östlicher Lustgarten (© **0331/9694181**), was built between 1755 and 1763. Its facade is similar to that of Sans Souci Palace, and the interior is one of the most flamboyant in Germany. The collection of some 125 paintings features works by Italian Renaissance and baroque artists along with Dutch and Flemish masters. Concerts of the Potsdam Park Festival take place here. The Bildergalerie is open April 1 to October 31 Tuesday through Sunday from 10am to 6pm. The Bildergalerie can be visited with or without a guide, and the crush of visitors here is nowhere near as intense as at Sans Souci Palace. Entrance without a guided tour costs 3€ ($4.80) for adults, 2.50€ ($4) for students and children 8 to 18, and free for children 7 and under. Guided tours are available only for groups and by appointment.

West of the palace is the **Orangerie** (© **0331/9694280**), built between 1851 and 1864. It was based on Italian Renaissance designs. Its purpose was to shelter southern plants during the cold months. In the central core is the Raphael Hall, which holds 47 copies of that master's paintings. In addition, you can visit five lavishly decorated salons. The Orangerie is open May 15 to October 15 Tuesday through Sunday from 10am to 5pm. The Orangerie must be visited with a guide. Though not as severe a situation of overcrowding as you'll find at Sans Souci Palace, you should still try to get your tickets before noon, especially in midsummer. Guided tours cost 4€ ($6.40) for adults, 2.50€ ($4) for students and children 8 to 18, and free for children 7 and under.

The largest building in the park is the extravagant **Neues Palais** (© **0331/9694361**), built between 1763 and 1769, at the end of the Seven Years' War. Crowning the center is a dome. The rococo rooms, filled with paintings and antiques, were used by the royal family. The most notable chamber is the Hall of Shells, with its fossils and semiprecious stones. At the palace theater, concerts take place every year April to November. The Neues Palais is open April 1 to October 31, Saturday to Thursday from 10am to 6pm. During other months, it's open Saturday to Thursday from 10am to 4pm. Neues Palais must be visited with a guide, costing 6€ ($9.60) for adults, 5€ ($8) for children 8 to 18, and free for children 7 and under.

Zur historischen Mühle. © 0331/9694200. Apr 1–Oct 31 Tues–Sun 10am–6pm; Nov 1–Mar 31 Tues–Sun 10am–5pm. Tram: 94 or 96. Bus: 605, 606, or 695.

Schloss Cecilienhof   This palace was completed in the style of an English country house. Kaiser Wilhelm II had it built between 1913 and 1917 for Crown Prince Wilhelm. The palace was occupied as a royal residence until March 1945, when the crown prince and his family fled to the West. In addition to the regular guided tour, offered in summer, there's a tour of the private rooms of Crown Prince Wilhelm and Princess Cecilie on the upper story. The tour takes place at 11am and 2pm. Note that you can lunch and spend the night here, if you wish.

Cecilienhof was the headquarters of the 1945 Potsdam Conference, attended by the heads of the Allied powers, including Truman, Stalin, and Churchill. You can visit the studies of the various delegations and see the large round table, made in Moscow, where the actual agreement was signed. In winter you have to take a guided tour; in summer you can go with a guide or wander about on your own.

In Neuer Garten. (C) **0331/9694244.** Admission (with tour included) 6€ ($9.60), 5€ ($8) students, free for children 5 and under. The palace can be visited in summer without a guide for 5€ ($8) adults, 4€ ($6.40) students, free for children 5 and under. Apr–Oct Tues–Sun 10am–6pm; Nov–Mar Tues–Sun 10am–5pm. Bus: 692.

Schloss Charlottenhof (R)   This palace was built between 1826 and 1829 by Karl Friedrich Schinkel, Germany's greatest master of neoclassical architecture. He also designed most of the furniture inside. The nearby **Roman Baths** are on the north of the artificial lake known as Maschinenteich (Machine Pond). These baths, constructed between 1829 and 1835, were built strictly for the nostalgic love of antiquity and have no practical purpose.

South of Okonomieweg. (C) **0331/9694228.** Admission 4€ ($6.40) adults, 3€ ($4.80) for persons 17 and under. May–Oct Tues–Sun 10am–6pm. Tram: 91.

Saxony & Thuringia

Traveling in regions of the former East Germany can still be an adventure. Once difficult to visit, famous cities are still being restored and are inviting visitors from the west. These include Dresden, destroyed during World War II and poignantly restored, at least in part; Leipzig, where Johann Sebastian Bach spent most of his musical life as cantor (choirmaster) of St. Thomas Church; Meissen, famous for exquisite porcelain; and Weimar, glowing from its recent designation as a European City of Culture. In addition, unspoiled scenery and medieval towns such as Quedlinburg invite you to wander off the beaten track.

Since reunification, many visitors have come from around the world to explore the political landscape and to honor the memory of the intellectual giants who once made East Germany their home—Goethe, Luther, Bach, Schiller, and Brecht, among others. Hotels are being built and tourist facilities developed. But the traveler should still take care in this rapidly changing terrain. The state of politics here is sometimes erratic and unpredictable, and the economy is weaker than in western Germany.

Eastern Germany is a region in transition. The best guess is that it will yet take 10 to 15 more years before eastern Germany's infrastructure is comparable to western Germany's. The upside of this means that you'll find some of Germany's most unspoiled countryside and untouched villages, where rural traditions that have disappeared from most of western Europe still linger. A visit can provide you with unforgettable new experiences and stories to tell your grandchildren.

Getting around eastern Germany is easier than ever. Some 1,600km (1,000 miles) of autobahns and about 11,000km (7,000 miles) of secondary highways cut across the region. Train schedules are a bit smoother these days because the German government has incorporated the former East German system into its vast national network.

This section of Germany is still in transition, long after the reunification. Outside Dresden or Leipzig, you can still see many old towns that have not succumbed to the Americanization you can find in most of western Germany. Drenched in history and medieval legend, the towns of Weimar and Wittenberg, home to Goethe and Martin Luther, give you a view of Germany that has been swept away in the more modern parts of the country.

1 Weimar ★★

260km (161 miles) SW of Berlin, 22km (14 miles) E of Erfurt

Weimar, a beautiful 1,000-year-old town on the edge of the Thuringian Forest, is an important destination for those interested in German history and culture. Unlike many cities in the former East Germany, Weimar retains much of its old flavor: Many of its important historical monuments were spared bombing in World War II. Its

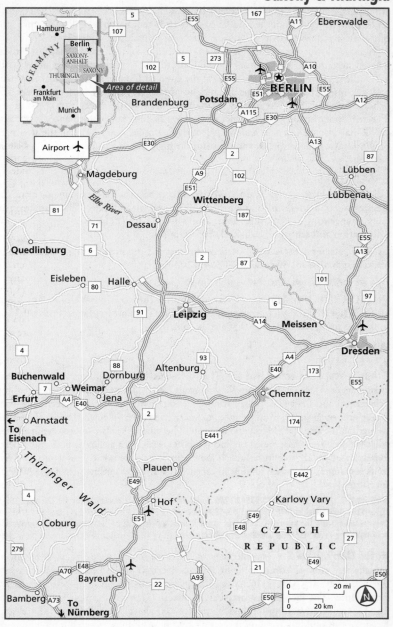

atmospheric, narrow, winding streets, lined with houses with high-pitched gabled roofs, seem left over from the Middle Ages. A 19th-century writer called Weimar "one of the most walkable towns of Europe," and it still fits into that category.

Weimar's history as a cultural center is centuries old. Lucas Cranach the Elder worked here in the 16th century. From 1708 to 1717, Bach was court organist. In 1775, the great Goethe came to reside at the court of Dowager Duchess Anna Amalia and her son, Charles Augustus II, and he attracted such notables as Herder and Schiller. Later in the 19th century, Franz Liszt was musical director of the National Theater; under his auspices, Wagner's *Lohengrin* had its first performance. It was also in Weimar that the German national assembly met in February 1919, in the aftermath of World War I, to draw up the constitution for what was to be called the Weimar Republic.

ESSENTIALS

GETTING THERE   By Train   Weimar Hauptbahnhof is on the major Deutsche Bundesbahn rail lines, which link Erfurt and Leipzig with Dresden. There are frequent daily connections in both directions. Trains from Berlin travel via Leipzig. For rail information and schedules, call © **01805/996633.**

By Bus   Regional buses to all parts of the city and the surrounding area are run by **Verkehrsgesellschaft Weimar** (© **03643/24200**).

By Car   Access is via the E40 Autobahn east and west.

VISITOR INFORMATION   Head for **Tourist-Information Weimar,** Am Markt 10 (© **03643/7450;** www.weimar.de). The office is open Monday to Friday 9:30am to 6pm, Saturday and Sunday 9:30am to 2pm.

WHERE TO STAY
EXPENSIVE

Grand Hotel Russischer Hof 𝕽   The Russischer Hof was built in 1805 by Russian aristocrats for their visits to the Weimar court. Such luminaries as Turgenev, Tolstoy, Schumann, and Liszt have passed through its doors. It sports a dark-green-and-white facade and opens onto an important square in the center of town. Inside, the pastel-colored public areas are elegant and intimate. The small to midsize rooms are in a somewhat lackluster modern annex behind the hotel, each with a shower unit and a decor loosely based on 18th-century French motifs. Even if you're not a guest, consider a visit to its restaurant, Anastasia, serving an excellent Thuringian cuisine with some Austrian specialties.

Goetheplatz 2, D-99423 Weimar. © **03643/7740.** Fax 03643/774840. www.russischerhof.com. 126 units. 165€–285€ ($264–$456) double; 247€–555€ ($395–$888) suite. AE, DC, MC, V. Parking 13€ ($21). Bus: 1 or 7. **Amenities:** Restaurant; cafe; bar; exercise room; sauna; solarium; room service; massage; babysitting; laundry service; nonsmoking rooms; 1 room for those w/limited mobility. *In room:* A/C, TV, Wi-Fi, minibar, hair dryer, trouser press, safe.

Hotel Elephant 𝕽𝕽   The Elephant is Weimar's most famous hotel, although it's actually not quite as comfortable or well accessorized as the Leonardo Hotel. Many celebrities have stayed here, including Tolstoy and Bach; the most notorious guest was Adolf Hitler. The Elephant became best known in Germany through Thomas Mann's novel *Lotte in Weimar* (published in English as *The Beloved Returns*). The elegant facade of this building (ca. 1696) is set off by a beautifully weathered terra-cotta roof, a series of elongated bay windows stretching from the second to the third floors, and, best of all, a frontage onto the old marketplace, which contains a dried-up fountain

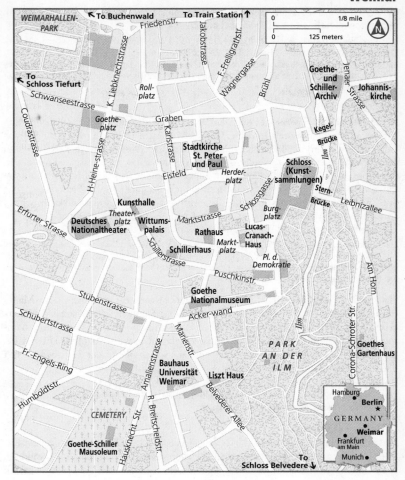

Weimar

WEIMARHALLEN-PARK

To Buchenwald
To Train Station
Friedenstr.
Jakobstrasse
F.-Freiligrathstr.
Wagnergasse
Brühl
Goethe- und Schiller-Archiv
Jenaer Strasse
Johannis-kirche

To Schloss Tiefurt
Schwanseestrasse
Coudrastrasse
K. Liebknechtstrasse
Roll-platz
Goethe-platz
Graben
Karlstrasse
H.-Heine-strasse
Stadtkirche St. Peter und Paul
Eisfeld
Herder-platz
Kegel-Brücke
Ilm
Schloss (Kunst-sammlungen)
Stern-Brücke
Leibnizallee

Erfurter Strasse
Kunsthalle
Theater platz
Deutsches Nationaltheater
Wittums-palais
Schillerstrasse
Marktstrasse
Schlossgasse
Burg-platz
Rathaus
Lucas-Cranach-Haus
Schillerhaus
Markt-platz
Pl. d. Demokratie
Puschkinstr.
Am Horn

Stubenstrasse
Goethe Nationalmuseum
Acker-wand
Ilm
Corona-Schröter Str.

Schubertstrasse
Fr.-Engels-Ring
Humboldtstr.
Amalienstrasse
Marienstr.
R. Breitscheidstr.
Bauhaus Universität Weimar
Liszt Haus
Belvederer Allee
PARK AN DER ILM
Goethes Gartenhaus

CEMETERY
Hausknecht Str.
Goethe-Schiller Mausoleum
To Schloss Belvedere

0 1/8 mile
0 125 meters

Hamburg
Berlin ★
GERMANY
Weimar
Frankfurt am Main
Munich

---

dedicated to Neptune. An Art Deco decor and bold color schemes make the rooms dramatically appealing.

Markt 19, D-99423 Weimar. ☏ **03643/8020.** Fax 03643/802610. www.starwoodhotels.com. 99 units. 125€–245€ ($200–$392) double; 211€–295€ ($338–$472) junior suite; 235€–555€ ($376–$888) suite. AE, DC, MC, V. Parking 13€ ($21). Bus: 5 or 7. **Amenities:** 2 restaurants; bar; lounge; room service; babysitting; laundry service; dry cleaning; nonsmoking rooms; 1 room for those w/limited mobility. *In room:* TV, Wi-Fi (in some), minibar, hair dryer, safe.

Leonardo Hotel ★★★ Ironically, credit for the excellence of this hotel's construction and the lavishness of its materials goes to the former East German government, which designed and built it shortly before reunification. The hotel stands beside Goethe Park, a swath of greenery with posh residences and embassies left over from the Weimar Republic. The lobby is dramatic, with sun-flooded skylights and glass walls. Rooms are small but comfortable. The midsize to spacious bathrooms are the best in town, each with a tub/shower combo.

Belvederer Allee 25, D-99425 Weimar. © 03643/7220. Fax 03643/7222111. www.leonardo-hotels.com. 294 units. 91€–155€ ($146–$248) double; 245€–645€ ($392–$1,032) suite. AE, DC, MC, V. Parking 12€ ($19). Bus: 1. **Amenities:** Restaurant; 3 bars; indoor heated pool; health club; sauna; room service; massage; babysitting; laundry service; dry cleaning; nonsmoking rooms; rooms for those w/limited mobility. *In room:* A/C, TV, Wi-Fi, minibar, hair dryer, trouser press (in some).

INEXPENSIVE

Amalienhof Hotel *Value*   Though not as roomy and comfortable as the preceding choices, this hotel is more affordable. Originally built in 1826 as a private villa, it was enlarged in the early 1990s, with a modern annex just across the street. Reception and breakfast facilities are in the older of the two buildings; if you're assigned a room in the annex, you'll be given a key to the annex's front door. Rooms in the annex are modern in decor and styling; rooms in the hotel's original core are Biedermeier. The hotel has a convenient location, directly south of Goethe National Museum, within an easy walk of the town's historic core and major attractions. The breakfast buffet, the only meal served here, is generous.

Amalienstrasse 2, D-99423 Weimar. © 03643/5490. Fax 03643/549110. www.amalienhof-weimar.de. 32 units. 77€–105€ ($123–$168) double; 95€–115€ ($152–$184) suite. Rates include buffet breakfast. AE, MC, V. Free parking. Bus: 1. **Amenities:** Breakfast room; lounge; nonsmoking rooms; 1 room for those w/limited mobility. *In room:* A/C, TV, coffeemaker, hair dryer.

Thuringen   This affordable hotel in the center of town near the railway station dates from 1897 but has been completely renovated in modern style. The small rooms are clean and simply but adequately furnished, each with a compact shower-only bathroom. The focal point of the public areas is a glassed-in winter garden. The hotel is known for its *gutbürgerlich* (home-style) cookery, which one reader described as "just like my Saxon mother used to cook."

Brennerstrasse 42, D-99423 Weimar. © 03643/903675. Fax 03643/903676. www.hotel-thueringen-weimar.de. 36 units. 77€–87€ ($123–$139) double. Rates include buffet breakfast. AE, MC, V. Free parking. Bus: 1 or 7. **Amenities:** Restaurant; lounge; room service. *In room:* TV, no phone.

WHERE TO DINE

Hotel Elephant ★★ GERMAN/INTERNATIONAL   There are two restaurants in this previously recommended hotel. The more formal, **Anna Amalia,** is modern, sky lit, and airy, with spacious tables, a garden terrace, and good service. Its German and international dishes are the very best in the city. The chefs have an unerring sense of flavor and proportion as well as a fertile imagination. They use only the best ingredients available at the local markets. Filet Stroganoff, pork medallions, and sauerbraten are among the menu items. Goethe, Schiller, Bach, Liszt, and Wagner all wined and dined here.

You can reach the historic **Elephantenkeller (Elephant Cellar)** by a flight of stone steps at a separate entrance. It's decorated in a rustic style, with square travertine columns. The best dishes at this informal restaurant are the traditional Thuringian platters. An autumn specialty is *Zwiebelmarkt* salads, made from onions from the famous October onion market, a tradition dating from 1653.

Am Markt 19. © 03643/8020. Reservations recommended. Main courses 23€–28€ ($37–$45); fixed-price dinner 60€ ($96). AE, DC, MC, V. Anna Amalia summer daily 11am–3pm and Tues–Sat 7:30–11pm, winter Sat–Sun 11am–3pm and Tues–Sat 7:30–11pm. Elephantenkeller Mon–Tues noon–3pm and daily 6pm–midnight. Closed July 1–Aug 25. Bus: 1 or 12.

The Thuringian Forest: Germany's Green Heart

"There is indeed no forest on all the earth as beautiful as the Thuringian," wrote the Danish novelist Martin Anderson Nexö. Trekkers and nature lovers have long extolled the scenic beauties of this region, which has often been called "the green heart of Germany." The *Thuringer Wald* 🟊🟊 was the former stomping ground of such philosophers and artists as Goethe, Schiller, Martin Luther, Ludwig Bechstein, and Bach.

The mountains within the forest, though not nearly as tall as the German Alps, are geological highlights. The highest peaks, around 985m (3,230 ft.), are composed of gneiss, porphyry, and granite; the foothills are made of softer strata of sandstone and sedimentary limestone.

The scenic, 160km (100-mile), northwest-to-southeast ramble known as the Thuringian High Road was one of the most popular destinations anywhere for East German schoolchildren and campers before reunification. You can take a lowland driving version by following Route 88 between Eisenach and Ilmenau, a city that Goethe loved.

Just as attractive as the region's scenic beauty are the dozens of unspoiled, charming medieval villages that pepper the landscape. **Dornburg** has a series of three palaces, perched high above the Saale River. **Altenburg,** directly south of Leipzig, is the home of a hilltop castle. Finally, **Arnstadt,** founded in 704, is the oldest town in the Thuringian Forest. It lies just beyond Erfurt. Today, the town's medieval walkways and buildings are being restored to their former glory.

Ratskeller THURINGIAN   A flight of stairs leads into a pair of dining rooms. The first is vaulted and white, the second more modern, paneled, and with a prominent bar. Everything is correct and proper. You may begin with gooseliver on toast, followed with schnitzel, goulash with mixed salad, or pork cutlets prepared four different ways. These dishes aren't dazzling, but they're very satisfying. The venison, when in season, is excellent, and the wild boar and duck in red-wine sauce is reason enough for a meal here.

Markt 10. © **03643/850573.** Reservations recommended. Main courses 9€–17€ ($14–$27). Fixed-price menus 15€–25€ ($24–$40). AE, MC, V. Daily noon–midnight. Bus: 7 or 71.

Shakespeares INTERNATIONAL   Set in the town's center, a few steps from the Rathaus (Town Hall), this restaurant offers well-prepared food, a bar area, angular modern decor, and big windows that overlook a garden strewn with tables for warm-weather dining. Menu items are well prepared and flavorful, and include salads, soups, risottos, fresh shellfish, and several kinds of grilled fish, some of them served with a Riesling sauce. Main courses may feature savory ragouts of chicken, lamb, or veal; noodles in cream sauce studded with ham and cheese; veal cutlets; and Wiener schnitzels. In addition to the street-level dining room, a small-scale auditorium (Kulturstadt Neurotika) is in the restaurant's cellar. Most of what's presented inside is scheduled for Friday and Saturday nights, with an occasional Sunday-afternoon jazz concert. Entrance to most concerts and plays costs around 15€ ($24) per person.

Windischenstrasse 4–6. © 03643/901285. Reservations recommended. Main courses 22€–24€ ($35–$38). No credit cards. Daily 11am–midnight.

EXPLORING WEIMAR

Weimar enjoys a scenic location on the Ilm River, set against the backdrop of the Ettersberg and Vogtland hills. The city has many popular sights, but perhaps the best thing to do here is simply wander about on foot. A walk at night through the old streets that once felt the footsteps of Goethe, Bach, Wagner, and Schiller is particularly rewarding.

The town's main square, the **Marktplatz,** or market square, retains the old flavor of the city. Instead of breakfast at your hotel, visit one of the bakeries near the square and create your own breakfast, as many locals do. The daily produce market still takes place on the Marktplatz (7am–4pm). The painter Lucas Cranach the Elder lived here during his last year, from 1552 to 1553. Today, you can view the **Lucas Cranach the Elder House** from the outside, richly decorated and bearing a coat of arms of the Cranach family. A modern gallery is inside the house but is open only Thursday and Friday from noon to 8pm, Saturday 11am to 3pm.

For a midday break from sightseeing, we suggest a visit to Park an der Ilm or **Goethe Park,** flanking the river. Goethe himself landscaped this park. It sports numerous 18th-century pavilions and is the best place in Weimar for a picnic.

If you've had a little too much Schiller and Goethe, flee the inner city and escape to **Bauhaus Universität** on Marienstrasse, just across the footpath in front of the Bauhaus building. Here you can meet Weimar students, nearly all of whom speak English.

In the evening, head for one of the smoky beer halls near **Herderplatz,** keeping in mind that Nietzsche, who spent the last 3 years of his life here, discovered them long before you.

Bauhaus-Museum   In 1919, Walter Gropius founded his Staatliche Bauhaus here, so it's only fitting that a museum has been established in Weimar as a testament to the elegance of modernism that was launched in the city. The Bauhaus architectural school of design was noted especially for its program that synthesized technology, craftsmanship, and design aesthetics. It was to sweep the world. From the Bauhaus school rose such towering artists as Klee, Kandinsky, and Feininger. The golden era of Bauhaus is re-created in arts and crafts, graphics, paintings, and representative works of some of the outstanding painters or teachers of the era. A school once flourished here, in the center of town, until 1925.

At Theaterplatz, across from the Deutsches Nationaltheater. © 03643/545401. www.klassik-stiftung.de. Admission 4.50€ ($7.20) adults, 3.50€ ($5.60) students, free for children 5 and under. Daily 10am–6pm. Bus: 1, 2, 3, 5, 6, or 7.

Goethe Gartenhaus 🟊🟊   In a park on the Ilm River stands a plain cottage with a high-pitched roof. Goethe selected this house as his first residence when he came to Weimar. Even after he moved to other quarters, he still came here in summer to find peace and tranquillity. He described the park around him as "infinitely beautiful," and so it remains today.

Im Park an der Ilm. © 03643/545375. www.klassik-stiftung.de. Admission 3.50€ ($5.60) adults, 2.50€ ($4) students, free for children 5 and under. Apr–Oct daily 9am–6pm; Nov–Mar daily 10am–4pm. Bus: 1, 10, or 12.

Goethe Nationalmuseum 🟊🟊🟊   Weimar's principal attraction is the house where Johann Wolfgang von Goethe (1749–1832) lived from 1782 to 1832. It's a typical example of a baroque German nobleman's house. There are 14 exhibition rooms, some pretty much as Goethe and his wife, Christiane Vulpius, left them. The library contains more than 5,000 volumes. The writer's mineral collection is here also, as well as much original art. Although Goethe's reputation rests today on his writing, he had wide-ranging interests, including an interest in science (he was an early advocate of the belief in the common origin of all animal life). He died in Weimar on March 22, 1832.

Am Frauenplan 1. ⓒ 03643/545347. www.klassik-stiftung.de. Admission 6.50€ ($10) adults, 5€ ($8) students, free for children 5 and under. Apr–Sept Tues–Sun 9am–6pm; Oct–Mar Tues–Sun 9am–4pm. Bus: 1, 2, 5, 6, or 8.

Kunstsammlungen zu Weimar

This structure was begun under the guidance of Goethe in 1789 and completed in 1803. The previous castle burned down in 1774; only a tower survived. In one of the wings is a series of galleries dedicated not only to Schiller and Goethe, but also to two other famous names associated with Weimar: Johann Gottfried Herder (1744–1803), the German critic and philosopher who was a pioneer of the *Sturm und Drang* ("Storm and Stress") literary movement, and Christoph Martin Wieland (1733–1813), the poet and critic who wrote the satirical romance *The Republic of Fools*. The museum has a shop, which is open April to October Tuesday to Sunday 9am to 6pm.

The ground floor displays works by Lucas Cranach the Elder. On some of the upper floors, you can see exhibits from Walter Gropius's Bauhaus school, which started in Weimar. The primary aim of this movement was to unify arts and crafts within the context of architecture. Its appeal came from the changing sensibilities of the Industrial Age, as well as from the need for inexpensive construction techniques in an era of rising costs and exploding demand for housing. Followers around the globe may have been impressed, but not the good people of Weimar. They "tolerated" Gropius's school until 1925, and then bombarded it in the press until it finally moved to Dessau. There it stayed until the Nazis closed it in 1933, claiming it was a center of "Communist intellectualism."

Burgplatz 4. ⓒ 03643/545401. www.klassik-stiftung.de. Admission 5€ ($8) adults, 4€ ($6.40) children. Self-parking 1€ ($1.60) hourly. Apr–Oct Tues–Sun 10am–6pm; Nov–Mar Tues–Sun 10am–4pm. Bus: 1.

Liszt-Haus

Franz Liszt (1811–86), the Hungarian composer and pianist, spent the last period of his life here. You'll find several mementos, both personal and musical, from the composer's life, including letters exchanged between Liszt and his son-in-law, as well as the piano at which he played and taught his pupils. The house was once the home of the royal gardeners of Weimar.

Marienstrasse 17. ⓒ 03643/545401. www.klassik-stiftung.de. Admission 2.50€ ($4) adults, 2€ ($3.20) students, .50€ (80¢) children 6–18, free for children 5 and under. Apr–Oct Wed–Mon 10am–6pm. Closed Nov–Mar. Bus: 1, 4, or 6.

Neues Museum Weimar

This is eastern Germany's first museum devoted to modern art, an artistic field frowned upon by the former Communist regime with its more traditional (read: 19th-c.) tastes. The exhibitions are frequently changed or alternated, so you never know what you'll be viewing at any given time. The restored building was constructed in 1869 but radically overhauled to accommodate its new role. The museum was opened to coincide with the naming of Weimar as cultural capital of Europe in 1999. Its permanent exhibition includes works of American minimal and conceptual art as well as pieces by Italian painters and expressive works of the new "wild painters" of Germany, as they are called. In addition, such major artists as Anselm Kiefer and Keith Haring are represented extensively.

Weimarplatz 5 (directly north of center, on the square adjoining Rathenauplatz). (C) **03643/545401.** www.klassik-stiftung.de. Admission 3.50€ ($5.60) adults, 2.50€ ($4) students, free for children 5 and under. Apr–Oct Tues–Sun 11am–6pm; Nov–Mar Tues–Sun 11am–4pm. From the heart of town, Goetheplatz, walk north for 10 min.

Schillerhaus *ﾐﾐ*   After his friend Goethe, Friedrich von Schiller (1759–1805) is the greatest name in German literature. He lived here with his family from 1802 to 1805 and wrote his last works here, including *Wilhelm Tell.* The attic rooms have been furnished as they were in Schiller's day.

Schillerstrasse 9. (C) **03643/545350.** www.klassik-stiftung.de. Admission 4€ ($6.40) adults, 3€ ($4.80) students and children 6–18, free for children 5 and under. Apr–Oct Wed–Mon 9am–6pm; Nov–Mar Wed–Mon 9am–4pm. Bus: 1, 2, 3, 5, 6, 7, or 8.

Schloss Belvedere (Château of Belvedere)   The baroque Schloss Belvedere was a favorite retreat of Anna Amalia and the "enlightened" Weimar set. It has an orangery, along with the open-air theater and an English-style park. Inside the château are displays of dainty rococo art and a collection of historical coaches.

Belvederer Allee. (C) **03643/545931.** Admission 4€ ($6.40) adults, 3€ ($4.80) seniors and students, free for children 5 and under. Apr–Oct Tues–Sun 10am–6pm. Bus: 12. From Weimar, follow the Belvedereschlossallee south for 3km (2 miles).

Schlossmuseum   This is a special art museum often overlooked by the hurried visitor but appreciated by art lovers who care to seek out its special treasures. Its collection of European art ranges from the Reformation period to the 20th century. The museum sprawls across three floors, with main works on the first floor, including paintings by Lucas Cranach. On the second floor is an exhibition of more German works, paintings done in the age of Goethe, and various pieces of Romantic art. There is an exceptional collection of religious icons from the 19th and 20th centuries. In the graphic collection are exhibitions of the works of the great masters such as da Vinci, Dürer, or Rembrandt.

Burgplatz 4. (C) **03643/545960.** Admission 5€ ($8) adults, 4€ ($6.40) students and seniors, free for children 5 and under. Apr–Oct Tues–Sun 10am–6pm; Nov–Mar Tues–Sun 10am–4pm. Bus: 1, 5, 6, 8, or 10. From Markt, the market square in the town center, head east along Am Markt for 5 min.

Wittumspalais   If you follow Rittergasse to the end, you will come upon the 1767 Wittumspalais. This was once the residence of Dowager Duchess Anna Amalia, who presided over the German Enlightenment, which brought a stark rationalism to literature and the arts. The old ducal dower house is devoted to mementos of the movement.

Am Palais 3. (C) **03643/545401.** Admission 4€ ($6.40) adults, 3€ ($4.80) students and seniors, free for children 5 and under. Apr–Oct Tues–Sun 10am–6pm; Nov–Mar Tues–Sun 10am–4pm. Bus: 1, 2, 3, 4, 5, or 6.

MORE SIGHTS

In the **cemetery,** south of the town center, Am Posseckschen Garten, lies the controversial **Denkmal der März Gefallenen,** a monument to the revolutionaries whose merciless and needless slaughter in 1919 (by government forces) so affected the ultra-liberal Gropius and his Bauhaus followers. But most interesting today is the **Goethe-Schiller Mausoleum,** once the family vault of the Weimar dynasty, where Goethe and Schiller, friends in life, lie side by side in death. It was built in 1825 through 1826 in accordance with plans drawn up by Coudray, who consulted Goethe on the design and construction. Schiller was entombed here in 1827 and Goethe in 1832, both in oak coffins. Admission is free. Visiting hours are March to October Wednesday to

Monday 9am to 1pm and 2 to 5pm, and November to February Wednesday to Monday 10am to 1pm and 2 to 4pm. A Russian-style **chapel** is on the south side of the mausoleum. It was built in 1859 for Maria Pavlovna, daughter-in-law of Duke Carl August.

BUCHENWALD CONCENTRATION CAMP & MEMORIAL SITE The Buchenwald bus (no. 6) from Weimar's Hauptbahnhof goes 6km (4 miles) northwest of Weimar to **Gedenkstätte Buchenwald** (© 03643/4300). An estimated 250,000 Jews, Slavs, Gypsies, homosexuals, political opponents, prisoners of war, Jehovah's Witnesses, social misfits, criminals, and others were confined here from 1937 until the camp's liberation by the U.S. Army in 1945. Officially, Buchenwald was a work camp, so far fewer people were killed here than at other concentration camps.

Nonetheless, 56,000 people died here; many, many thousands of others were sent on from here to other death camps; and a quarter of a million people, from more than 30 nations, suffered unspeakable pain as prisoners here. Furthermore, atrocities practiced in Buchenwald have made its very name synonymous with human perversity. Medical experiments on prisoners were common here, and prisoners, ironically, did not get nearly the amount of care and protection that animals in the SS men's zoo received. This is also the concentration camp from which famed author and Nobel Peace Prize–winner Elie Wiesel was liberated. (For more about his experiences at Buchenwald, read his bestselling book, *Night*.)

Buchenwald's sad history continued when Soviet occupation forces used the site as an internment camp from 1945 to 1950, where over 7,000 people died and were buried in mass graves.

Today, Buchenwald is a haunting sight. Only fragments of the camp have been preserved, as much of it has vanished by deliberate destruction and through the wear and tear of many years. The clock in the gate building reflects the time of the liberation by the U.S. Army in 1945. The gate has JEDEM DAS SEINE ("to each his own") inscribed upon it: It is one of the only Nazi concentration camps with a gate that was not inscribed with ARBEIT MACHT FREI ("work will make you free"). All but a few buildings have been replaced with eerie black rocks filling in the foundations (which you can still see) of old barracks and more. The storehouse (as well as some other buildings) still exists in its original form, and the museum inside reflects both the Soviet and the Nazi past of the camp.

A well-planned and -executed monument/memorial lies about 1km (⅔ mile) from the remnants of the camp itself, with its own parking lot. The monument has several facets (sculpture, bell tower, and so on) built over the graves of more than 3,000 Buchenwald victims.

You can visit Buchenwald April to October Tuesday to Sunday 10am to 6pm, and November to March Tuesday to Sunday 10am to 4pm. Last admission is 30 minutes before closing. Admission is free.

SHOPPING

A visit to Weimar's antiques stores offers a chance to buy porcelain, silver, crystal, and furniture that survived the devastation of World War II. An attractive source for mostly 18th- and 19th-century German antiques, with everything from farmhouse-rustic to the kind of high-style pieces you might have expected at Frederick the Great's Sans Souci, can be found at **Franz Christof Antiquitäten,** Schlossgasse 4 (© 03643/902333). Also appealing is **Thiersch Antiquitäten,** Bräuhausgasse 15 (© 03643/402540).

WEIMAR AFTER DARK

A good national theater, live music venues, and dance clubs provide a variety of choices for evening entertainment. The city's bars and outdoor cafes are good places to drink and talk. Just walk down Schillerstrasse or along the Theaterplatz. All of the bars and cafes in this area carry free copies of *Schlagseite* and *Boulevard,* local entertainment papers. *Takt* is another good resource; you can save 3€ ($4.80) by picking it up in the tourist office (see "Visitor Information," earlier in this chapter), the only place it's free.

Weimar's main performance venue is the **Deutsches Nationaltheater,** Theaterplatz 2A (© **03643/755334**), where Franz Liszt and Richard Strauss once conducted. Call the box office or the tourist office for information about schedules. Tickets cost 8€ to 55€ ($13–$88).

C-Keller Galerie, Markt 21 (© **03643/502755**), combines an art gallery with a cafe that serves beer, wine, tea, and light meals. It's a popular place to unwind. The gallery has works for sale by local, national, and European artists. The cafe is open daily noon to 1:30am. The most popular and animated dance club in Weimar isn't exactly cutting edge—it's more like Hannover than Hamburg or Berlin. But if you're interested in a medley of disco favorites from the '70s and '80s, head for **Bistro Corona,** Goetheplatz 5 (© **03643/801756**). This is both a bar and a restaurant open Monday to Friday 8:30am to 11pm, Saturday 10am to 2am, and Sunday 10am to 9pm. The best nights for music and dancing are Friday and Saturday when a 5€ ($8) cover is imposed.

SIDE TRIPS FROM WEIMAR
ERFURT ⚘

The small city of Erfurt, on the Gera River and first mentioned in 742, is one of the most visited cities of eastern Germany because it still exudes the spirit of a medieval market town. Erfurt is filled with historic houses, bridges, winding cobblestone alleys, and church spires reaching toward the skyline, as well as decorative and colorful Renaissance and baroque facades. The city emerged from World War II relatively unscathed and remains one of the best places to see what yesterday's Germany looked like. Nearly everything of interest is concentrated in the Altstadt (Old Town) area. It's well worth your time to take 2 or 3 hours to walk around this city of "flowers and towers."

Why flowers? Erfurt is a center of the German horticultural trade. It's also Europe's largest vegetable seed producer. One of Europe's biggest horticultural shows, the Internationale Gartenbauaustellung, is held here in the Cyriaksburg Park every year from the end of March to September.

GETTING THERE   You can reach Erfurt after a 24km (15-mile) train ride from the Weimar Hauptbahnhof; there are frequent connections. For rail information and schedules, call © **01805/996633.** Access by car is via the E40 Autobahn and State Highway 4. The **Erfurt Tourist-Information** center is at Bendiktsplatz 1 (© **0361/ 66400;** www.erfurt.de). From April to December, it's open Monday to Friday 10am to 7pm, Saturday 9am to 6pm, and Sunday 10am to 4pm. January to March, it's open Monday to Saturday 10am to 6pm and Sunday 10am to 4pm.

Where to Stay
Mercure Erfurt Altstadt   Erfurt's most up-to-date hotel, in the heart of town, is also its best. It was built as a sophisticated enlargement of a *Gasthaus* (inn) from the

1300s. The medieval part—meticulously conserved and restored—faces onto a side street, the Futterstrasse. Otherwise, the hotel is modern, restrained, and tasteful. Most rooms correspond to middle-to-upscale chain-hotel standards. An additional 13 retain the wood paneling and architectural quirks of their original medieval construction and are more interesting. All accommodations are equipped with a small bathroom with a shower stall.

One of the town's best restaurants, Zum Rebstock, is in the old wing of the hotel. The restaurant was part of the original structure and has since been painstakingly restored. It serves German and international dishes.

Meienbergstrasse 26–27, D-99084 Erfurt. (℃) 0361/59490. Fax 0361/5949100. www.accorhotels.com. 141 units. 110€–160€ ($176–$256) double; 200€ ($320) suite. Rates include continental breakfast. AE, DC, MC, V. Parking 10€ ($16). **Amenities:** Restaurant; bar; sauna; solarium; steam room; room service; babysitting; laundry service; dry cleaning; nonsmoking rooms; 1 room for those w/limited mobility. *In room:* TV, Wi-Fi, minibar, coffeemaker, hair dryer, iron.

Radisson SAS Hotel Erfurt   This is one of the town's better addresses. It hasn't fully escaped its East German Cold War boxy architectural quality, but the SAS group has poured tons of money into it to upgrade it and has given it a lot more than a face-lift. Its modern rooms are comfortable but a bit cramped. Bathrooms are very compact, containing tub/shower combinations and inadequate shelf space. The location is halfway between the station and the town center. The on-site restaurant serves first-rate Thuringian meals as well as some international dishes. The restaurant's lounge and bar is a popular rendezvous point.

Juri-Gagarin-Ring 127, D-99084 Erfurt. (℃) 0361/55100. Fax 0361/5510210. www.radisson.com. 284 units. 70€–155€ ($112–$248) double; 165€–495€ ($264–$792) suite. Rates include buffet breakfast. AE, DC, MC, V. Parking 12€ ($19). **Amenities:** Restaurant; bar; lounge; fitness room; wellness center; sauna; steam room; room service; laundry service; dry cleaning; nonsmoking rooms; rooms for those w/limited mobility. *In room:* A/C, TV, minibar, hair dryer.

Where to Dine

Alboth's Restaurant im Kaisersaal ✿✿ INTERNATIONAL   Set within part of a sprawling and stately looking building in the heart of town, this is the most formal and most gastronomically ambitious in town. Much of its decor evokes the lavish aesthetic of the late 18th century, with plush upholsteries and tones of cream, champagne, and gold. Come here for artfully prepared dishes, each richly nouvelle (or *neuen*) in their presentation, each reflecting seasonal variations as interpreted by Claus Alboth, chef and namesake. Perhaps the best way to handle the gastronomy here involves ordering one of the set-price meals, one of which focuses on Thuringian regional dishes with updated, modern twists (ravioli stuffed with blood sausage and liverwurst, for example). Expect a changing array of dishes, the best examples of which include lamb stew in red wine with farmer's cheese, lobster, and champagne soup; roasted wild goat with port-wine sauce; sweetbreads in puff pastry; gooseliver with asparagus-flavored cream sauce; and a chocolate charlotte with raspberries and apricots.

Futterstrasse 15–16. (℃) 0361/5688207. Reservations recommended. Main courses 24€–26€ ($38–$42); fixed-price menus 35€–145€ ($56–$232). AE, MC, V. Tues–Sat 6:30–9:30pm.

Exploring Erfurt

Well-preserved patrician mansions built in both the Gothic and Renaissance styles are the town's dominant feature. Many of the narrow streets are lined with old half-timbered houses. One of Erfurt's curiosities is the **Krämerbrücke** (**Shopkeepers' Bridge;** www.kraemerbruecke.de), which has spanned the Gera since the 14th century. It has houses on both sides, nearly three dozen in all, and is filled with bookstalls, cafes, and antiques shops. You'll certainly want to spend some time here browsing.

The ecclesiastical center is the **Domberg,** where two Catholic churches stand side by side, their 15th-century walls almost closing in on each other. The **Dom (Cathedral; ℂ 0361/6461265),** on Domplatz, was begun in the 12th century and later rebuilt in the 14th century in the Gothic style. Its stained-glass windows above the choir date from 1370 to 1420 and are unusual in Germany because they depict scenes of everyday life. The interior of the cathedral is richly baroque, but it also has some notable works from 1160: a Romanesque altar of the Virgin and the statue-candelabra known as "the Wolfram." Note also the 13th-century tombstone of the count of Gleichen and his two wives. One local legend says that the second woman wasn't his wife at all, but a Saracen beauty from the Holy Land who, under mysterious circumstances, saved his life. The Dom is open May to October Monday to Friday 9 to 11:30am and 12:30 to 5pm, Saturday 9 to 11:30am and 12:30 to 4:30pm, and Sunday 2 to 4pm; November to April, hours are Monday to Saturday 10 to 11:30am and 12:30 to 4pm, and, in addition to Sunday Masses (usually conducted at 9 and 11am), it's open to tourists on Sunday from 2 to 4:30pm.

Its neighbor is the Gothic **Church of St. Severi** (ℂ 0361/576960), a "hall-type" church with five naves. Don't miss seeing its extraordinary font, a masterpiece of intricately carved sandstone, rising practically to the roof. You may also look for a notable sarcophagus of the saint (ca. 1365) in the southernmost aisle. St. Severi is linked to the Dom by a 70-step open staircase. It's open May to October Monday to Friday 9am to 12:30pm and 1:30 to 5pm, and November to April Monday to Friday 10am to 12:30pm and 1:30 to 4pm. It's closed January and during most of February.

The most beautiful churches are the Romanesque **Peterskirche,** dating from the 12th and 14th centuries, and the 13th-century **Predigerkirche,** of the Order of Mendicant Friars. There are also three early medieval churches: **Agidienkirche, Michaeliskirche,** and **Allerheiligengeistkirche.** The tourist office (see above) will give you a map pinpointing all these. Most can be reached on foot.

EISENACH ✿

This town lies on the northwestern slopes of the Thuringian Forest, at the confluence of the Nesse and Horsel rivers, 48km (30 miles) west of Erfurt. Eisenach, once a center of the East German auto industry, is not particularly charming, but it does have one of the region's finest castles and a few sights associated with Luther and Bach, who were both born here. Half-timbered houses ring its ancient market square.

GETTING THERE   Many trains from Erfurt (see above) arrive every day. For rail information and schedules, call ℂ **01805/996633.** Access by car is via the A4 Autobahn east and west. For tourist information, contact **Eisenach-Information,** Markt 9 (ℂ **03691/79230**), open Monday to Friday 10am to 6pm, and Saturday 10am to 4pm. Here you can pick up a map with the locations of all the tourist sites.

Where to Stay & Dine

Hotel Kaiserhof ✿   Much of the elegance of the late 1800s is still evoked here in the lobby and in the dining room especially. Both are stellar examples of the stately looking German Landhaus architecture. Rooms are generally spacious and tastefully renovated, each with comfortable furnishings and midsize bathroom with a combination tub/shower.

Wartburgallee 2, D-99817 Eisenach. © **03691/88890.** Fax 03691/203653. www.kaiserhof-eisenach.de. 64 units. 112€–131€ ($179–$210) double. Rates include buffet breakfast. AE, DC, MC, V. Free parking. Bus: 3. **Amenities:** 2 restaurants; bar; lounge; solarium; steam room; room service; laundry service; dry cleaning; nonsmoking rooms; rooms for those w/limited mobility. *In room:* A/C, TV, minibar, hair dryer, trouser press.

Exploring Eisenach

Eisenach is best known as the site of **Schloss Wartburg** ✦, Wartburg Foundation at the Wartburg (© **03691/2500;** www.wartburg-eisenach.de; bus: 3, 10, or 13), reached only after a rigorous climb up a 180m (590-ft.) hill. Hitler called Wartburg Castle "the most German of German castles" and engaged in a battle with local authorities to take down its cross and replace it with a swastika. This ancient castle belonged to the land-graves of Thuringia and once hosted the medieval *Minnesinger* poets, immortalized by Wagner in *Tannhäuser*. This was also where Martin Luther hid upon his return from the Diet of Worms in 1521, so he could complete his translation of the Bible—he is said to have "fought the Devil with ink" at Wartburg. The castle has now been turned into a regional museum. Admission to the palace, museum, and the room within the castle where Luther lived and worked is 7€ ($11) for adults and 4€ ($6.40) for students and children ages 6 to 18. Admission is free for children 5 and under. It's open March to October daily 8:30am to 8pm, November to February daily 9am to 5pm. The last ticket is sold 1 hour prior to closing.

Eisenach is the birthplace of Johann Sebastian Bach (1685–1750). **Bachhaus,** Am Frauenplan 21 (© **03691/79340;** www.bachhaus.de; bus: 3, 7, 11, or 13), contains many mementos of the Bach family, along with a collection of musical instruments. Admission costs 6€ ($9.60) for adults, 3.50€ ($5.60) for students and children 6 to 18. Children 5 and under enter free. It's open daily 10am to 6pm.

If you're a die-hard Luther fan, you can also visit the **Lutherhaus,** Lutherplatz 8 (© **03691/29830;** www.lutherhaus-eisenach.de; bus: 1 or 5). Martin Luther stayed here as a schoolboy; today, it contains a series of exhibitions illustrating his life. Admission is 3.50€ ($5.60) for adults, 3€ ($4.80) for seniors, and 2€ ($3.20) for students and children 6 to 18. Children 5 and under enter free. It's open daily 10am to 5pm.

2 Leipzig ✦

164km (102 miles) SW of Berlin, 111km (68 miles) NW of Dresden, 126km (78 miles) NE of Erfurt

If you have limited time and have to choose between Dresden and Leipzig, make it Dresden. But if you can work Leipzig into your itinerary, you'll be richly rewarded. More than any other city in former East Germany (except Berlin, of course), Leipzig brings you into the Germany of today. This once-dreary city is taking on a new life and vitality; a visit here can be absolutely invigorating. Glassy skyscrapers and glitzy nightlife add a cosmopolitan flavor you don't encounter in much of the rest of the region. The approximately 20,000 students who study in the area (as Nietzsche, Goethe, and Leibniz once did) help add a spark. One resident put it this way: "Our grunge and metal bands are just as good as those of Berlin, and our cafes just as super-cool."

Leipzig is also famous for more traditional music. Johann Sebastian Bach is closely associated with Leipzig, Mozart and Mendelssohn performed here, and Wagner was born here in 1813.

Because of its strategic value as a rail center, both the RAF and the U.S. Air Force bombed the city heavily in World War II, but it's been rebuilt, more or less successfully. It still has some narrow streets and houses from the 16th and 17th centuries, as well as some Jugendstil (Art Nouveau) flair. And Leipzig is again a major rail terminus. From its Hauptbahnhof—the largest in Europe, with 26 platforms—lines radiate to the chief German cities and the rest of the Continent.

ESSENTIALS

GETTING THERE **By Plane**   The **Leipzig-Halle International Airport** lies 11km (7 miles) northwest of the city center. About 50 airlines link Leipzig with major German cities, such as Munich and Frankfurt, and also some Continental destinations. For **airport information,** call ℂ **0341/2241155** (www.leipzig-halle-airport. de). A train called the Airport Express runs from the airport to the Hauptbahnhof every 30 minutes from 5am to midnight. The fare costs 5€ ($8) for adults and 3.50€ ($5.60) for children. Taxis are also available, meeting all arriving planes, but the 25- to 30-minute ride to the city center will cost around 30€ ($48) each way for up to four passengers.

By Train   The **Leipzig Hauptbahnhof,** Willy-Brandt-Platz, lies on the major Deutsche Bundesbahn rail line, with frequent connections to German cities. Seventeen trains arrive daily from Berlin (trip time: 1 hr., 40 min., to 2 hr., 50 min.); 23 trains from Dresden (1 hr., 35 min., to 2 hr.); and 15 trains from Frankfurt (3–4 hr.). For information and schedules, call ℂ **01805/996633.** The **Hauptbahnhof** has recently been restored and contains many cafes, shops, and restaurants; it's one of the most happening places in Leipzig.

By Bus   Long-distance bus service to such cities as Berlin is provided by **Leipziger Verkehrsbetriebe.** Buses depart from the east side of the main rail station. For information and schedules, call ℂ **0341/19449.**

By Car   Access is via the Halle-Dresden Autobahn east and west or the E51 Autobahn north and south.

VISITOR INFORMATION   Contact the **Tourist-Information** office at Richard Wagner Strasse 1 (ℂ **0341/7104265;** www.leipzig.de), Monday to Friday 10am to 6pm, Saturday and Sunday 9am to 4pm. The office can supply a map pinpointing the major sights. This place becomes a beehive of activity at the time of the annual trade fairs.

SPECIAL EVENTS   Upon arrival, be sure to drop in at the tourist office and see if any festivals are taking place. For a week every year, in October, for example, during the **Leipziger Jazztages,** the churches, student clubs, and opera house fill with jazz music.

GETTING AROUND   A public transit system of trams, light railways, and buses provides frequent service to all parts of the city. An S-Bahn (light railway) serves the suburbs, arriving and leaving from the Hauptbahnhof in the center of Leipzig.

WHERE TO STAY
EXPENSIVE
Hotel Fürstenhof ✸✸✸   This hotel, located in the former residence of a Leipzig banker, is the best in Leipzig, a government-rated five-star hotel. Its interior has been redecorated to reflect the building's original, almost-forgotten neoclassical theme. A corps of English and Swedish designers has outfitted the rooms in a modern interpretation of

Leipzig

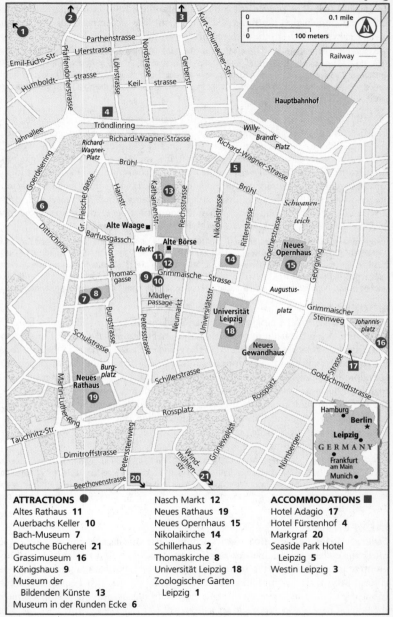

ATTRACTIONS ●

Altes Rathaus **11**
Auerbachs Keller **10**
Bach-Museum **7**
Deutsche Bücherei **21**
Grassimuseum **16**
Königshaus **9**
Museum der
  Bildenden Künste **13**
Museum in der Runden Ecke **6**

Nasch Markt **12**
Neues Rathaus **19**
Neues Opernhaus **15**
Nikolaikirche **14**
Schillerhaus **2**
Thomaskirche **8**
Universität Leipzig **18**
Zoologischer Garten
  Leipzig **1**

ACCOMMODATIONS ■

Hotel Adagio **17**
Hotel Fürstenhof **4**
Markgraf **20**
Seaside Park Hotel
  Leipzig **5**
Westin Leipzig **3**

neoclassical style. The rejuvenated bathrooms, also the nicest in town, have deluxe toiletries and combination tub/showers. The ballroom (the Serpentinensaal) and a monumental staircase date from the 19th century.

Tröndlinring 8, D-04105 Leipzig. © **0341/1400.** Fax 0341/1403700. www.starwoodhotels.com 92 units. 120€–310€ ($192–$496) double; 229€–630€ ($366–$1,008) junior suite. AE, DC, MC, V. Parking 18€ ($29). Tram: 15. **Amenities:** 2 restaurants; 2 bars; indoor heated pool; health club; Jacuzzi; sauna; room service; babysitting; laundry service; dry cleaning; nonsmoking rooms; 1 room for those w/limited mobility. *In room:* A/C, TV, minibar, hair dryer, safe.

Westin Leipzig 𝕽𝕽 Rising 27 floors, this is one of the tallest landmarks in "new" Leipzig and one of eastern Germany's leading hotels. In this luxe category, we prefer the greater charm and comfort of the Fürstenhof (see above), although the Westin is fine in every way. Close to the railway station, it is the largest hotel in Leipzig, a businessperson's favorite, and also a popular venue for conventions. Don't expect lots of atmosphere or personal service. All the guest rooms, ranging from small to spacious, are renovated. Bathrooms are midsize with tub/shower combos. The hotel offers more diverse dining and drinking options than its competitors, everything from a *Bierstube* with Saxon cookery to a *teppanyaki* grill with sushi and sashimi.

Gerberstrasse 15 (5 min. from Altes Rathaus), D-04105 Leipzig. © **800/327-0200** in the U.S. and Canada, or 0341/9880. Fax 0341/9881229. www.westin.com/leipzig. 447 units. 114€–230€ ($182–$368) double; 229€–410€ ($366–$656) suite. Special offers on weekends. AE, DC, MC, V. Parking 11€ ($18). Tram: 4 or 6. **Amenities:** 3 restaurants; 3 bars; indoor heated pool; health club; sauna; solarium; salon; room service; massage; laundry service; nonsmoking rooms; rooms for those w/limited mobility; 2 bowling lanes. *In room:* TV, Wi-Fi, minibar, hair dryer, safe.

MODERATE
Seaside Park Hotel Leipzig Less than a kilometer (about half a mile) from the city center, this is the latest reincarnation of a hotel that opened in 1913 near the central rail depot. Back then it was hailed as the grandest first-class hotel in the city. Today the competition is too keen for it to retain that title. The hotel lies behind a facade of soundproof windows that is government protected as a historical monument. It caters mainly to business travelers but also welcomes vacationers to its well-furnished, midsize to spacious guest rooms, decorated in an Art Deco style with well-equipped bathrooms, mostly with tub/shower combinations. Fine dining characterizes the two restaurants here. Our favorite part of the hotel is a reconstruction of the famous Orient Express dining room.

Richard-Wagner Strasse 7, Leipzig D-04109. © **0341/98520.** Fax 0341/9852750. www.parkhotelleipzig.de. 288 units. 125€–150€ ($200–$240) double; from 250€ ($400) suite. Rates include breakfast. AE, DC, MC, V. **Amenities:** 2 restaurants; bar; health club; whirlpool; sauna; solarium; room service; massage; laundry service; dry cleaning; nonsmoking rooms; rooms for those w/limited mobility. *In room:* A/C, TV, Wi-Fi, minibar, hair dryer, trouser press (in suites), safe.

INEXPENSIVE
Galerie Hotel Leipzig Hof *(Finds* Behind a baroque facade, this offbeat choice offers funky but comfortable rooms. It appeals to artists and students as well as a group of patrons who used to be called "bohemians." Each small to midsize bedroom is furnished in a rather minimalist style. The saving grace is that Leipzig artists contributed paintings or sculpture to make each bedroom unique—hence, the name of the hotel. There is also an on-site art gallery.

Hedwigstrasse 1-3, 04315 Leipzig. © **0341/69740.** Fax 0341/6974150. www.leipziger-hof.de. 73 units. 85€–155€ ($136–$248) double; 165€ ($264) junior suite. AE, DC, MC, V. Tram: 1, 3, or 8. Parking 7€ ($11). **Amenities:** Spa; whirlpool; sauna; laundry service; dry cleaning; art gallery. *In room:* TV, minibar, hair dryer.

Hotel Adagio *Kids*   This is a restored and greatly refurbished 1882 building in a tranquil location between the Neues Gewandhaus and the Grassimuseum. Each mid-size guest room is individually furnished with such themes as the Roaring 1920s. The bathrooms that come with the 1920s guest rooms contain the largest tubs in the city. The hotel staff gives a special welcome to families traveling with children.

Seeburgstrasse 96, Leipzig D-04103. ℂ **0341/216690**. Fax 0341/9603078. www.hotel-adagio.de. 32 units. 85€–90€ ($136–$144) double; 140€–160€ ($224–$256) suite. Rates include buffet breakfast. AE, DC, MC, V. **Amenities:** Breakfast room; bar; room service; laundry service; dry cleaning; nonsmoking rooms; rooms for those w/limited mobility. *In room:* TV, hair dryer.

Markgraf *Value*   Stay here for its affordable price—not any luxurious living. What you get are small yet comfortable rooms. Platform beds with thin mattresses prevail, and there are many blond-wood furnishings. In its modest category, this is one of the best deals in town, all modern and sleek. Maintenance and service rate high points. The hotel lies just a short walk or tram ride south of the city center.

Körnerstrasse 36, 04107 Leipzig. ℂ **0341/303030**. Fax 0341/3030399. www.markgraf-leipzig.de. 54 units. 109€ ($174) double; 129€ ($206) suite. AE, DC, MC, V. Parking 10€ ($16). Tram: 10 or 11 from the Hauptbahnhof. **Amenities:** Gym; sauna; room service; massage; laundry service; dry cleaning. *In room:* TV, Wi-Fi, minibar, safe.

WHERE TO DINE
EXPENSIVE
Auerbachs Keller *✿* SAXON/INTERNATIONAL   This is the famous restaurant and tavern where Goethe staged the debate between Faust and Mephistopheles in his play *Faust*. The cellar dates from 1530 and has a series of 16th-century murals representing the *Faust* legend. The chefs prepare mainly regional Saxon dishes, along with some international selections. Some of the most tempting offerings are filet of veal, beef, or saddle of lamb, prepared with special sauces and served with seasonal vegetables. The menu changes every 2 months. You can also order from a fine selection of wines and beers. Guests have a choice of the stately looking Historic Rooms (dinner only) or the sprawling, Germanic-looking Big Room, with a different menu and paneling and high ceiling to evoke an upscale beer tavern. Between 11:30am and 6pm Monday to Saturday, visitors can see the Historic Rooms for a charge of 1€ ($1.60).

Mädlerpassage (off the market square, close to the Altes Rathaus), Grimmaischestrasse 2–4. ℂ **0341/216100**. www.auerbachs-keller-leipzig.de. Reservations recommended. Historic Rooms main courses 15€–35€ ($24–$56); fixed-price menus 30€–75€ ($48–$120); Big Room main courses 9€–25€ ($14–$40). AE, MC, V. Historic Rooms Mon–Sat 6pm–midnight; Big Room daily 11:30am–midnight. Tram: 4 or 6.

Stadtpfeiffer *✿✿✿* INTERNATIONAL   The most prestigious and best-recommended restaurant in Leipzig occupies a glassed-ringed dining room that seems to glow golden light out into the angular, concrete-and-glass urban landscape it occupies. As such, it's a welcome spot of warmth and humanity in an otherwise anonymous-looking landscape. Inside, you'll find impeccably detailed service rituals and a sublime cuisine, almost a defiant contrast to a restaurant scene that until now wasn't anywhere near as sophisticated, urban, and international as what you'll find here. Depending on the day of your visit, a delightful meal here might include mussels in puff pastry; lightly smoked freshwater fish with bacon; pan-fried shrimp with fennel; various preparations of lobster; fresh fish, perhaps prepared with olives and demi-glace; and desserts which might feature a gratin of figs with almond-flavored ice cream.

In the Gewandhaus, Augustusplatz 8. ℂ **0341/2178920**. Reservations required. Fixed-price menus 88€–108€ ($141–$173). AE, MC, V. Tues–Sat 6pm–midnight.

MODERATE

Kaiser Maximillian ✶✶ MEDITERRANEAN   You may have some of your best meals in Leipzig here, especially if you like Italian and French-inspired dishes from the Mediterranean. In a sophisticated setting with modern appointments, this restaurant, with its black-leather seats and hip waitstaff, is found in the center of Leipzig in the Urban Department Store between the new market and the street leading to the university.

Business people in the area drop in for a quick lunch, but in the evening the ambience is more mellow and ideal for long, lingering meals over wine, especially if you order from the fixed-price gourmet menus. The candles glow as you feast on the offerings of the expert chefs who have a talent for sauces and for creating harmonious flavor combinations. Fish is a specialty, appearing as pikeperch with a calf's head sauce or haddock with a purée of nettles. Anglerfish is a tasty treat with cheeks of beef. You may not want to dine in such an experimental fashion, settling for more familiar meat dishes such as a loin of pork with asparagus and new potatoes, or else saddle of lamb with bell peppers and a creamy polenta. The dessert chef wins our heart with his fresh rhubarb ragout with homemade vanilla ice cream.

Neumarkt 9–19. ✆ 0341/35533333. Reservations required. Main courses 25€–30€ ($40–$48); fixed-price lunch 13€–16€ ($21–$26); 5-course set dinner menus 46€–60€ ($74–$96). AE, DC, MC, V. Mon–Sat noon–3pm and 6pm–midnight.

INEXPENSIVE

Apels Garten GERMAN/SAXON   Its name commemorates the site of a 400-year-old garden, no longer in existence. Today, you'll find a modern mid-1980s building with a conservatively decorated street-level restaurant known for its home-style German food. Specialties include Leipzig-style onion soup or wild-duck soup with homemade noodles, roast goose with potatoes and vegetables, grilled *Wurst* with potatoes and red cabbage, and sauerbraten with onions and red cabbage. The cuisine is more robust than refined; it's very filling.

Kolonnadenstrasse 2. ✆ 0341/9607777. Reservations recommended. Main courses 8€–16€ ($13–$26); fixed-price lunch 12€–21€ ($19–$34), dinner 17€–26€ ($27–$42). AE, MC, V. Mon–Sat 11am–11pm; Sun 11am–3:30pm. Tram: 4, 6, 8, 10, 11, or 13.

Thuringer Hof SAXON/THURINGIAN   Martin Luther used to dine here—that's how old this mellow place is. It's been serving hearty regional fare since 1454. Goethe used to drop in, as did the composer Robert Schumann. By 1865 it became known as the Thüringer Hof and had 1,200 seats, making it one of the most famous restaurants of Germany, as fabled as the Hofbräuhaus in Munich. The restaurant had to be rebuilt after World War II, and the Luther Hall section was completely duplicated. Showing wear and tear in the 1990s, it was rebuilt once again. The tradition is still maintained. There's even a glass-roofed courtyard. Good food is the rule of the day. Some of the recipes sound as if they are the same that Luther himself ate. We're talking Thuringian potato soup with sausage slices or pickled beef with raisin sauce and Thuringian dumplings. Purple cabbage comes with many dishes. Among the courses we'd recommend are spicy pork goulash with cream mushrooms or rare filets of lamb in a garlic sauce with potato croquettes. Hearty eaters will go for the grill platter for two—breast of chicken, venison steak, pork medallions, and home-fried potatoes.

Burgstrasse 19. ✆ 0341/9944999. Reservations recommended. Main courses 8€–17€ ($13–$27). AE, DC, MC, V. Daily 11am–midnight.

Zill's Tunnel SAXON   This is one of the city's most atmospheric restaurants, serving tasty and reasonably priced food, including massive consumption of regionally brewed beer, to hungry diners and drinkers. The restaurant is not a real tunnel, though its barrel-ceilinged ground floor tavern suggests that. The location is at the marketplace opposite the old city hall. Today's restaurant is the end result of a once-popular eatery established here in 1841. You can also dine upstairs in the more formal wine restaurant, with its open fireplace and antiques. In addition to international vintages, there are some good value Meissen wines. The menu is in German and very traditional, including such long-time favorites as pork schnitzel with potatoes or Norwegian filet of salmon, even tender beef tournedos in a pepper sauce. Desserts are rich, wholesome, and prepared fresh daily, as are the homemade soups for appetizers.

Barfussgasschen 9. ℂ **0341/9602078.** Reservations recommended upstairs. Main courses 9€–15€ ($14–$24); fixed-price menus 26€–28€ ($42–$45). AE, DC, MC, V. Daily 11:30am–midnight.

EXPLORING LEIPZIG

Goethe, who was a student in Leipzig, called the city *klein Paris* (miniature Paris). We wouldn't go quite that far, but Leipzig definitely has its charms. One of the best things to do is explore the handsomely restored Art Nouveau **Arkaden** (arcades) that thread through the historic city center core. Mädler Mall is Leipzig's finest arcade. This is the site of the famous **Auerbachs Keller** (p. 193), the setting for one of the scenes of Goethe's *Faust*. A bronze group of characters from *Faust,* sculpted in 1913, beckons you down a stone staircase into the cellar restaurant.

A gateway leads to **Nasch Markt,** which occupies the space behind the Altes Rathaus. Walk around the front of the Altes Rathaus to find yourself within Am Markt, the city's best-known square, at the edge of which stands the **Königshaus.** Originally built in the late 1700s on the site of an even older building, the Königshaus at one time functioned as the city's official guesthouse for VIPs; it housed both Napoleon and Richard Wagner during their sojourns here.

Neues Rathaus on Burgplatz was erected on the site of the old Pleissenburg, the citadel where Martin Luther held a momentous disputation in 1519. The best place in Leipzig for people-watching is on **Petersstrasse,** below Markt.

THE TOP ATTRACTIONS

Altes Rathaus ⊛   The 16th-century town hall stands on the 12th-century Renaissance Markt. Allied bombs rained down on the building, but it has been carefully restored. Inside, you'll find the Stadtgeschichtliches Museum (Museum of City History), chronicling the city's history, both cultural and political.

Markt 1. ℂ **0341/9651320.** www.stadtgeschichtliches-museum-leipzig.de. Admission 4€ ($6.40) adults, 3€ ($4.80) students and children 6–18. Tues 2–8pm; Wed–Sun 10am–6pm. Tram: 4 or 6.

Bach-Museum   The reconstructed Bose House stands in the shadow of the Thomaskirche. It was once the home of the Bach family and now contains the largest Bach archives in Germany, as well as many mementos of the composer.

Thomaskirchhof 14. ℂ **0341/9137200.** www.bach-leipzig.de. Free admission. Daily 11am–6pm. Tram: 9.

Grassimuseum ⊛   This museum is a three-in-one delight in an Art Deco building updated by the celebrated British architect, David Chipperfield. The Ethnological Museum, Musical Instruments Museum, and Arts and Crafts Museum are found under one roof.

We'd go to the Museum für Völkerkunde for its stunning exhibitions of the antique art of Southeast Asia, if for no other reason. From Oceania to Australia, from Indonesia to Europe and the Americas, the exhibits cover all continents and take in Russian displays as well, even displaying artifacts from the Arctic Ocean. In the Musikinstrumentenmuseum you can see one of the largest collections of musical instruments in the world, including the oldest known clavichord, built in 1543 in Italy. Most of the instruments, including lutes, flutes, and spinets, date from the Renaissance era. Recorded sounds from the instruments can be heard as you look them over. Finally, the Museum für Kunsthandwerk is rich in the treasures of Eastern Germany, not only exquisite porcelain (among the world's finest) but tapestries, handicrafts, and even examples of the famous Bauhaus design.

Johannisplatz 5–11. ℂ 0341/21420. www.grassimuseum.de. Museum für Völkerkunde 4€ ($6.40); Musikinstrumentenmuseum 4€ ($6.40); Museum für Kunsthandwerk 4€ ($6.40). Combination ticket for all three 12€ ($19). Museum für Völkerkunde Tues–Fri 10am–6pm, Sat–Sun 10am–5pm; Musikinstrumentenmuseum Tues–Sun 11am–5pm; Museum für Kunsthandwerk Tues and Thurs–Sun 10am–6pm, Wed 10am–8pm.

Museum der Bildenden Künste ⟨⟨ The 2,700 paintings and sculptures in this museum include works by Dürer, Rubens, Rembrandt, Rodin, and van Eyck. In the museum's new home, designed like a glass cube, is one of eastern Germany's most impressive art collections. On exhibit is art ranging from the medieval period in Germany up to modern art in the United States of today. The most important art is the work of Lucas Cranach the Elder, including 16th-century portraits. Tintoretto weighs in with his *Resurrection of Lazarus,* and there are many paintings from the German schools of the 19th and 20th centuries. Impressive pieces of sculpture are by such older masters as Rodin as well as Berthel Thorvaldsen, the most famous sculptor to come out of Denmark.

Katharinenstrasse 10. ℂ 0341/216990. www.mdbk.de. Admission 7€ ($11) adults, 5€ ($8) students and children 4–14, free for children 3 and under. Tues and Thurs–Sun 10am–6pm; Wed noon–8pm.

Museum in der Runden Ecke This museum could hardly have been imagined during the Cold War. The building was the headquarters of the dreaded Stasi, the East German Ministry for State Security. Exhibits detail how Stasi operated within East Germany through various methods, most interesting of which show the tools of espionage, such as hidden cameras and letter-opening (and resealing) machines. Other exhibits show the extent of the massive spying, with entire floors devoted to handwriting samples from Leipzig's citizens and extensive personal files on various members of the population. One exhibition, called "The Power and Banality of the East German Secret Police," documents the meticulous and paranoid methods by which the police monitored every exchange of information in the country. They constantly seized private letters and listened in on phone conversations—at times monitoring up to 2,000 calls at once. The exhibition also traces the steps local people took to throw off the Communist regime and end Stasi terror. On the nights of December 4 and December 5, 1989, local citizens seized the building. Leipzig is called *Heldenstadt,* or "city of heroes," for its role in toppling the government of East Germany.

Dittrichring 24 (north of Thomaskirche). ℂ 0341/9612443. www.runde-ecke-leipzig.de. Free admission. Daily 10am–6pm. Tram: 1, 2, 4, 6, 15, 17, 21, or 24 to Goerderlerring or Thomaskirche.

Schillerhaus In this small farmhouse in Gohlis, a suburb about 20 minutes from the center of Leipzig, Friedrich von Schiller (1759–1805) wrote his "Ode to Joy" in

Singing Through the Centuries: the St. Thomas Boys' Choir

In recent times while the Vienna Boys' Choir enjoyed worldwide fame, Leipzig's St. Thomas Choir (Thomanerchor) languished in obscurity in the eastern zone. Now all that is changing. Any musical expert can tell you that the Leipzig choir has plenty of talent, and as it tours more widely in Europe, its fame will no doubt grow.

The choir has been here since the 13th century. The boys sang on every occasion in the Middle Ages—city celebrations, the installation of bishops, and even executions. Today, the setting for this venerable musical force is **Thomaskirche.** Choirboys still follow an almost medieval regime within a distinctive subculture that's a world unto itself. Each newcomer is assigned a "mentor" from among the trusted older members of the choir, and all members are required to eat, sleep, study, and rehearse according to a semi-monastic regimen. The most famous member was none other than Johann Sebastian Bach. He wrote his great cantatas for this choir and was cantor (choirmaster) for 27 years.

1785. Beethoven incorporated the poem into the great final movement of his Ninth Symphony.

Menckestrasse 42, Gohlis. ⓒ 0341/5662170. www.stadtgeschichtliches-museum-leipzig.de. Admission 3€ ($4.80) adults, 2€ ($3.20) students and children 4–14, free for children 3 and under. Apr–Oct Tues–Sun 10am–6pm; Nov–Mar Wed–Sun 10am–4pm. Tram: 4 to Menckestrasse.

Thomaskirche (St. Thomas Church) ⚐   Leipzig's most famous resident, Johann Sebastian Bach (1685–1750), was cantor here from 1723 until his death. He spent his most creative years as choirmaster at this church and is buried just in front of the altar. Both Mozart and Mendelssohn performed in the Thomaskirche as well, and Wagner was christened here in 1813. The church was built on the site of a 13th-century monastery and was heavily restored after World War II. Its high-pitched roof dates from 1496. When not touring, the city's Thomanerchor (St. Thomas Boy's Choir) presents concerts every Sunday morning and Friday evening.

Thomaskirchhof 18 (just off Marktplatz). ⓒ 0341/9602855. Free admission. Daily 9am–6pm. Tram: 4, 6, 8, 10, 11, or 13.

Zoologischer Garten Leipzig *Kids*   This zoo breeds animals to help conserve endangered species. It was founded in 1878, and it is internationally known for breeding carnivores. The biggest aquarium in eastern Germany outside Berlin is also here.

Pfaffendorfer-Strasse 29. ⓒ 0341/5933385. www.zoo-leipzig.de. Admission 13€ ($21) adults, 11€ ($18) students, 9€ ($14) children 4–14, 34€ ($39) family ticket; free for children 3 and under. Nov–Mar daily 9am–5pm; Apr and Oct daily 9am–6pm; May–Sept daily 9am–7pm. Tram: 12.

MORE SIGHTS & ACTIVITIES

The German Museum of Books and Scripts, the **Deutsche Bücherei,** Deutscher Platz 1 (ⓒ **0341/22710;** www.d-nb.de; tram: 21), is the central archive of German literature. You can visit it for free from Monday to Friday 8am to 10pm, and Saturday 9am to 6pm, but only with an advance phone call. The archive was established in 1912 to

Europe's Second-Oldest Coffeehouse

Ever since 1696, Coffe Baum, Kleine Fleischergasse 4 (© 0341/9610060; www. coffe-baum.de), has entertained the artistic luminaries of Leipzig, including Wagner, Schumann, and Liszt. Reportedly, even the Emperor Napoleon dropped in for a "cuppa." Still going strong after all these years, the cafe dispenses its traditional *Kaffe und Kuchen* (coffee and cake). Many patrons come just for the desserts, including a buttermilk strawberry mousse on mango foam with frozen apricots in chocolate. You can also order full meals here, with main dishes costing from 20€ to 23€ ($32–$37). Typical dishes include milk-fed lamb in garlic sauce or filet of cod poached in Nolly Prat wine with a Dijon mustard–and-caper sauce. Upstairs is a museum with displays of the history of Saxon coffee. Hours are daily 10am to 7pm.

showcase the fine art of German printing and bookbinding. It's said to possess every item of German literature ever published. It also has a copy of *Iskra,* the Bolshevik newspaper that Lenin came here to print secretly in 1900.

Contrary to popular belief, Thomaskirche isn't the oldest church in Leipzig. That distinction belongs to **Nikolaikirche,** on Nikolaistrasse, erected in 1165. Many works by Bach, including the *St. John Passion,* were first performed here.

If the weather is fair, head for the **Leipzig University Tower,** near Nikolaikirche. This metal-and-glass tower overlooks street performers who take over on summer weekends. It's the greatest free show in Leipzig. (Well, not exactly free—the performers will pass the hat at the end of their acts.) Just beware of the skateboard warriors, who make walking about a bit perilous. The **Universität Leipzig,** founded in 1409, has contributed greatly to the cultural growth of the city. The East German government rechristened it Karl Marx University, but the old name was restored in 1990. **Augustusplatz** is the ideal center to rub elbows with the thousands of students who study here.

To escape the fumes and noise of the city, head for such "green lungs" as **Johanna-park,** on Karl-Tauchnitz-Strasse, or one of the wildly overgrown cemeteries by the **Völkerschlachtdenkmal.** On hot days, the fountains in **Sachsenplatz** are popular for splashing about.

SHOPPING

Leipzig has emerged as the art-buying capital of the former East Germany. Galleries hold rich inventories of paintings and sculpture by artists whose works were once unknown to western consumers. **Galerie für Zeitgenössische Kunst,** Karl-Tauchnitz-Strasse 11 (© 0341/140810), is a privately owned art gallery that displays international art, showing about 14 exhibitions a year. It charges 3€ ($4.80) for adults, 2€ ($3.20) for students and children 10 to 18 (free for those 10 and under).

If you're looking for examples of the antique furniture and art objects that many Leipzigers have dragged down from their attics since reunification, head for any of the dozen or so antiques dealers conducting business within the town's core. **Neumarkt Passage** has several antiquarian bookshops. With more than 150 different outlets, including restaurants and cafes, the **Hauptbahnhof,** Willy-Brandt-Platz, is a shopper's delight, one of the best shopping experiences not just in Leipzig, but in this entire part of Germany.

LEIPZIG AFTER DARK

Leipzig's active nightlife offers something for everyone. The area around the Markt is full of bars, cafes, and other entertainment options; it's a good place to kick off your search for a nightspot.

THE PERFORMING ARTS   The **Leipziger Oper** is one of Germany's most acclaimed opera companies. Its home is the **Neues Opernhaus** (it's sometimes referred to simply as "Oper Leipzig"), Augustusplatz 12 (© **0341/1261275;** tram: 4, 7, 8, 10, or 11), opposite Das Gewandhaus (see below). Part of its space is devoted to the **Kellertheater** (© **0341/1261275**), a small-scale theater that presents small-ensemble, progressive performances of all types. The box office for both the main opera house and the Kellertheater is open Monday to Friday 10am to 8pm, and Saturday 10am to 4pm. Tickets to the theater are 10€ to 32€ ($16–$51) for adults, with students getting up to one-third off, depending on the performance. Call the box office, or ask at the tourist office, for information. Tickets to the opera cost 10€ to 60€ ($16–$96); tickets to the Kellertheater cost 15€ to 45€ ($24–$72), depending on the performance.

The home of the famous **Gewandhaus Orchestra** ✦ is a modern concert hall built in 1981, **Das Gewandhaus** (© **0341/1270280;** tram: 4, 7, or 15), which faces the Neues Opernhaus across Augustusplatz. Founded in 1781, the orchestra saw some of its greatest days under the baton of Felix Mendelssohn, who died in Leipzig in 1847. Other notable conductors have included Wilhelm Furtwängler, Bruno Walter, and Kurt Masur. Concerts, ballets, organ recitals, and other events are staged here. Tickets usually range from 15€ to 45€ ($24–$72).

The main venue for theater in Leipzig is the **Schauspielhaus,** Bosestrasse 1 (© **0341/ 1268168;** tram: 1, 2, 4, 6, 15, 17, 21, or 24), home to several arts companies that jointly stage an eclectic mix of theatrical and musical productions. Tickets cost from 7€ to 27€ ($11–$43) for adults, half price for students. The box office is open weekdays noon to 7pm, Saturday 10am to 1pm, and 1 hour before show time.

DANCE CLUBS   Leipzigers like to dance, and the downtown area offers several animated nocturnal venues. Appealing to a youngish crowd is **Nachtcafé,** Petersstrasse 39–41 (© **0341/2114000**). Open only on Monday and Wednesday nights from 9pm till around 3am and Saturday nights from 10pm till around 5am, it plays soul, house, funk, blues, and whatever's hip and contemporary in London and L.A., with music provided by a crew of DJs who are well known locally. Entrance is 5€ ($8), except for women under 24, who invariably talk their way in free. Attracting a young, raffish crowd is **Spizz,** Marktplatz 9 (© **0341/9608043**). Cramped, crowded, sweaty, hot, and usually convivial, they play jazz, boogie-woogie, reggae, pop, and disco music from the '80s and '90s. Entrance costs 10€ ($16) per person. It's open only Friday and Saturday nights from 11pm till around 5am.

LIVE MUSIC   Built against the old city wall, **Moritzbastei,** Universitätsstrasse 9 (© **0341/702590;** tram: 4, 6, 15, or 20), is a jaunty-looking, all-in-one entertainment complex that houses at least two stages for the presentation of concerts and cabarets, a labyrinthine pub with lots of different areas for drinking, carousing, and dancing, and a cafe. It's popular with students. Depending on the night of the week and the time you show up, you'll find either live bands or DJs playing Afro-pop, heavy metal, and rock mixed with contemporary dance music. Some aspect of this complex opens daily from 10am, but the nighttime energy only gets wound up Wednesday to Saturday from 8pm to 5am, when it charges a cover that ranges from 4€ to 12€ ($6.40–$19). Sometimes, in midsummer, films (foreign and German-language) are shown in an open-air terrace in a kind of "be-in" communal venue that will remind you of your college years.

For more blues, jazz, and the occasional presentation of German-language satire and cabaret, head to **Pfeffermühle,** Thomaskirchhof 16 (© **0341/9603253;** tram: 4, 6, 8, 10, 11, or 13), on Monday night, when the bands start up at 10pm. Other nights, people gather to drink and talk. The courtyard here is very popular during warm weather.

GAY BARS & CLUBS   The friendly, ultra-cool bar **RosaLinde,** Langestrasse 11 (© **0341/8796982**), is the central focus of gay nightlife in Leipzig. It's open Sunday to Thursday as a bar from 5 to 11pm; Friday and Saturday, it functions as a cafe, bar, and dance club from 5pm till 3am, with music beginning around 9pm. Come here for a drink and the chance to mingle with conventional, not particularly fetishistic gay men (and to a lesser degree, lesbians) in their 20s and 30s. Another popular gay hangout is **Blaue Trude,** Sternwartenstrasse 14 (© **0341/2126679;** tram: 4, 7, 12, or 15), which functions as a bar every night 7pm to 5am, and as a gay (mostly male) dance club every Tuesday to Saturday from around 11pm to 5am. Admission is free.

VARIETY   Recommended only for visitors who really understand fluent, and highly ironic, German-language nuances, **Schaubühne Lindenfels,** Karl-Heine-Strasse 50 (© **0341/484620;** tram: 1, 2, 4, 6, 15, 17, 21, or 24), offers alternative theater and cinema in a laid-back cafe/bar complex and is open daily 10am to 2am. Admission to movies, which are shown almost nightly, costs between 5€ to 8€ ($8–$13) per person. Admission to theater productions costs from 7.50€ to 13€ ($12–$21) per person. Depending on the seasonal lineup, they're presented Thursday to Saturday and sometimes Sunday.

SIDE TRIPS FROM LEIPZIG
LUTHERSTADT WITTENBERG

This is the city associated with **Martin Luther** (1483–1546), leader of the German Reformation, and it attracts pilgrims from all over the world. Wittenberg's other famous son was humanist Philipp Melanchthon (1497–1560), a Protestant reformer and scholar, and a friend of Luther's and later of Calvin's. Luther and Melanchthon are honored with statues in front of the Rathaus. Wittenberg is a handsome enough city, but a stop here isn't a must unless you're particularly interested in Luther.

Wittenberg lies 68km (42 miles) northeast of Leipzig and 100km (62 miles) southwest of Berlin. Access by car is via the A9 Autobahn north and south, Route 187 east, and Highway 2 north and south. The Wittenberg Bahnhof is on the major Deutsche Bundesbahn rail line (Halle-Berlin), with frequent connections. It's an hour by train from Leipzig. For travel information, contact **Wittenberg-Information,** Schlossplatz 2 (© **03491/498610**). November to February, it's open Monday to Friday from 10am to 4pm, Saturday from 10am to 2pm, and Sunday from 11am to 3pm. March to October, it's open Monday to Friday from 9am to 6pm, Saturday from 10am to 3pm, and Sunday from 11am to 4pm. In January and February, it's closed on weekends.

Both Luther and Melanchthon are buried in the **Schlosskirche,** Friedrichstrasse 1A (© **03491/402585**), which dates from the 15th century but was rebuilt in the 19th. It was on the Schlosskirche doors that Luther nailed his "Ninety-Five Theses" in 1517. The bronze doors were added in 1858 and bear the Latin text of the theses. The church is open November to April, Monday to Saturday 10am to 4pm and Sunday 11:30am to 4pm; May to October, it's open Monday to Saturday 10am to 5pm and

Sunday 11:30am to 5pm. Services are held Sunday at 10am and Wednesday at noon. There's a 30-minute organ concert every Tuesday at 2:30pm. Admission to the church and to its concerts is free; a brief audio guided tour, conducted in either German or English, costs 3€ ($4.80). For further information contact the tourist office at ℂ **03491/498610.**

Part of an Augustinian monastery in which Luther lived has been turned into the **Lutherhalle Wittenberg,** Collegienstrasse 54 (ℂ **03491/42030**). The parish church here, where Luther preached, dates from the 14th century. An oak tree marks the spot outside the Elster gate where Luther publicly burned his papal bull (edict) of excommunication in 1520. Hours are November to March Tuesday to Sunday 10am to 5pm, April to October daily 9am to 6pm. Admission costs 5€ ($8) for adults, 3€ ($4.80) for students and children ages 7 to 18, free for children 6 and under.

You can also visit the **Stadtkirche,** the "Mother Church of the Reformation," Judenstrasse 35 (ℂ **03491/403201**), where Luther did the majority of his preaching. Sections date from the 13th century, making it the oldest structure in Wittenberg. The altar is by Lucas Cranach the Elder, who was once bürgermeister of Wittenberg and a friend to Luther. It's open November to April Monday to Saturday 10am to 4pm and Sunday 11:30am to 4pm; hours for May to October are Monday to Saturday 9am to 5pm and Sunday 11:30am to 5pm. Admission is free.

Where to Stay & Dine
Grüne Tanne ⟨ *Value*   In the city of Martin Luther, only a traditional, atmospheric hotel will do for some visitors. On the outskirts of town, this is a former knight's manor with a history going back 4 centuries. The estate is a warm, inviting, and cozy country manor, with a tradition of welcoming guests since 1871. The hotel maintains a shuttle between the train station and the inn. The guest rooms are midsize and comfortably and tastefully furnished, and the suites are spacious and beautifully maintained. The on-site restaurant is worth a visit even if you're a nonguest: It serves traditional German food. In the summer, dining overflows onto the terrace, and the entire place assumes a festive atmosphere.

Am Teich 1, D-06896 Wittenberg. ℂ **03491/6290.** Fax 03491/629250. www.gruenetanne.de. 40 units. 59€–79€ ($94–$126) double; 105€–135€ ($168–$216) suite. Rates include buffet breakfast. AE, DC, MC, V. Free parking. **Amenities:** Restaurant; nonsmoking rooms. *In room:* TV, hair dryer.

QUEDLINBURG ⟨
In 1994, UNESCO cited Quedlinburg as "an extraordinary example of a medieval European city" and added it to its list of World Heritage Sites.

Quedlinburg, which survived World War II intact, is nestled at the foot of a rock pinnacle and crowned by a castle and an abbey church. Its origins go back to a Saxon settlement in the early 10th century. Here you'll see the church of St. Servatius, an architectural masterpiece, as well as a well-preserved castle and cobbled lanes with half-timbered houses dating from the 16th and 17th centuries. In fact, Quedlinburg has over 1,600 half-timbered buildings, more than any other town in the country.

There are three trains a day from Leipzig (travel time: 3 hr.). Call ℂ **01805/ 996633** for information and schedules. Access by car is along B6. For tourist information, contact **Quedlinburg-Information,** Markt 2 (ℂ **03946/905624;** www. quedlinburg-info.de), open April to September Monday to Friday 9am to 7pm, Saturday and Sunday 10am to 3pm; and October to March Monday to Friday 9:30am to 6pm, and Saturday 10am to 2pm. Begin your tour in the **Altstadt (Old Town),** site of the **Markt (Marketplace).** The **Rathaus (Town Hall),** in the Renaissance style of the 1600s, was originally built in 1310. The statue (ca. 1420) on the left of the facade is of Roland, Charlemagne's knight. The buildings on the other three sides of the Markt are from the 1600s and 1700s. Branching off the square are small cobblestone lanes right out of the Middle Ages. The area around Breitstrasse has several colorful alleyways.

Take the ramp up to the castle to the broad terrace that offers a panoramic view of the medieval town. Here, on the site of the original 9th-century church, stands Quedlinburg's major attraction, the **Stiftskirche St. Servatius** ⋆⋆, Schlossberg 1 (© **03946/709900**), an architectural masterpiece of the Romanesque era. The church was started in 1070 but wasn't consecrated until 1129. Craftsmen from northern Italy created the friezes and capitals above the central nave. Three aisles with diagonal rib vaulting divide the crypt beneath the chancel. The aisles are adorned with frescoes depicting scenes from the Bible.

The church is filled with treasures, including a treasury *(Domschatz)* with manuscripts dating from the 10th century. In 1990, a number of ecclesiastical artifacts that had disappeared after the war turned up in Texas, when the heirs of a U.S. Army officer tried to sell them. The purloined treasures have been returned and are now on permanent display. The church is open May to October Tuesday to Saturday 10am to 6pm, Sunday noon to 6pm; and November to April Tuesday to Saturday 10am to 4pm and Sunday noon to 5pm. Admission is 4€ ($6.40) for adults, 3€ ($4.80) for students and children ages 6 to 18. It's free for children 5 and under.

Burgberg Schloss, Schlossberg 1 (© **03946/2730**), was once part of an abbey. A Saxon stronghold in the 10th century, the castle was expanded from the late 16th to the mid–17th centuries. The complex includes the Schlossmuseum, with 16th- and 17th-century Italian and Flemish paintings as well as exhibits on the town's history. You can also visit a Princes' Hall from the mid-1700s and the throne room. The castle is open April to October daily 10am to 6pm, and in the off season Saturday to Thursday 10am to 4pm. Admission is 3€ ($4.80) for adults, 2€ ($3.20) for children ages 6 to 18, and free for children 5 and under.

Where to Stay

Hotel Zum Brauhaus *(Value*   This is the most atmospheric place to stay in town; it's attached to an old brewery that had been allowed to slumber for decades. In a restored half-timbered house, the hotel offers attractively furnished bedrooms, ranging in size from small to medium. Many of the wooden timbers have been exposed, giving it an old-fashioned look. In spite of its antique look, everything is modern inside. The staff will grant you half board for 15€ ($24) at its brewery restaurant, Brauhaus Lüdde (see below).

Carl-Ritter-Strasse 1 06484 Quedlinburg. © **03946-901481.** Fax 03496/901483. www.hotel-brauhaus-luedde.de. 51 units. 80€–89€ ($128–$142) double; 100€ ($160) suite. MC, V. **Amenities:** Restaurant; bar. *In room:* TV.

Ringhotel Schlossmühle ⋆⋆   Set in the medieval center, this government-rated four-star hotel has emerged as the finest in Quedlinburg. It combines a historic core with a modern addition. Ancient traditions and a modern ambience are perfectly wed here, creating a special atmosphere. Guest rooms are midsize to spacious and are completely up-to-date, each one tastefully furnished and comfortably decorated, with a midsize bathroom and a tub/shower combo. On-site are two restaurants, offering a variety of regional and international dishes, the best in Quedlinburg. The hotel is better accessorized than its nearest competition, Romantik Hotel am Brühl (see below).

Kaiser-Otto-Strasse 28, D-06484 Quedlinburg. © **03946/7870.** Fax 03946/787419. www.schlossmuehle.de. 77 units. 96€–110€ ($154–$176) double; 130€–160€ ($208–$256) suite. AE, DC, MC, V. Parking 10€ ($16). **Amenities:** Restaurant; bar; Jacuzzi; sauna; solarium; massage; library; nonsmoking rooms; rooms for those w/limited mobility. *In room:* TV, minibar, hair dryer.

Romantik Hotel am Brühl ⭐⭐   Romantic and tranquil, and set behind a richly historic brick and half-timbered facade, this hotel is run by the Schmidt family. Guest rooms come in a variety of shapes and sizes, as do the bathrooms. All rooms are well furnished with first-rate mattresses and fine linens; some open onto castle views. Virtually all major attractions are within walking distance.

Billungstrasse 11, D-06484 Quedlinburg. © **03946/96180.** Fax 03946/9618246. www.hotelambruehl.de. 46 units. 100€–145€ ($160–$232) double; 145€–165€ ($232–$264) suite. Rates include buffet breakfast. AE, DC, V. Free parking. **Amenities:** Restaurant; lounge; sauna; solarium; room service; laundry service; nonsmoking rooms; 1 room for those w/limited mobility. *In room:* TV, Wi-Fi, minibar, hair dryer, safe.

Zur Goldenen Sonne   This hotel, which dates from 1671, is a good traditional choice. It stands near the Mathildenbrunne, a landmark fountain. The building's wood-beam construction is typical of this part of Germany. The small rooms are cozily furnished in rustic style, and each is equipped with a small, shower-only bathroom. In summer, the garden is popular with locals and visitors.

Steinweg 11 (a 5-min. walk from the railway station), D-06484 Quedlinburg. © **03946/96250.** Fax 03946/962530. www.hotelzurgoldenensonne.de. 27 units. 79€–92€ ($126–$147) double. Rates include buffet breakfast. AE, MC, V. Free parking. **Amenities:** Restaurant; bar; lounge; nonsmoking rooms; rooms for those w/limited mobility. *In room:* TV, minibar.

Where to Dine

Brauhaus Lüdde GERMAN   The best place for a good regional meal and the best beer is this restored old brewery. The Lüdde brewery was once known throughout the Harz Mountains, but shut down in 1966. After reunification, one of the Lüdde relatives took it over and converted the rotting buildings into a good hotel, brewery, and restaurant. The beer comes in four varieties, the most famous being Pubarschknall, a brown beer. In summer a beer garden flourishes between the main house and the old horse stables. Menus change seasonally but expect good, hearty cooking consisting of regional fare.

Blasiistrasse 14. © **03946/705206.** Reservations not required. Main courses 6€–18€ ($9.60–$29). MC, V. Mon–Sat 11am–midnight; Sun 11am–10pm.

Ratskeller GERMAN/INTERNATIONAL   This longtime favorite is within walking distance of the railway station. Wine buffs should order the rare Saxon wine. The food is hearty and regional. Many of the meat and game specialties are served with wine sauerkraut and dumplings. In season, venison is likely to be on the menu.

Markt 1 (in the Rathaus). © **03946/2768.** Reservations recommended. Main courses 12€–50€ ($19–$80). AE, DC, MC, V. Thurs–Tues 11:30am–10:30pm. Closed Jan.

3 Dresden ⭐⭐⭐

198km (123 miles) S of Berlin, 111km (69 miles) SE of Leipzig

Dresden, once known as "Florence on the Elbe," was celebrated throughout Europe for its architecture and art treasures. Then came the night of February 13, 1945, when Allied bombers rained down phosphorus and high-explosive bombs on the city, which had no military targets. By morning, the Dresden of legend was but a memory. No one knows for sure how many died, but the number is certainly in the tens of thousands,

> **(Value** **Dresden for Less**
>
> The Dresden City-Card, which costs 21€ ($34) and is good for 48 hours, is a great deal for short-term visitors. The card gives you unlimited access to all public trams, buses, and ferries, plus free access to 12 of the city's best museums. There are also reductions on charges for certain sightseeing tours and some cultural events. The tourist office sells the card, and it's also available at the front desks of most hotels.

and perhaps more. If you're interested in the subject, you might want to read Kurt Vonnegut's novel *Slaughterhouse Five*.

Today, Dresden is undergoing a rapid and dramatic restoration, and it is once again a major sightseeing destination. Dresden boasts beautiful churches and palaces, as well as many world-class museums—among the finest in all of Germany.

In 2006, Dresden celebrated its 800th anniversary.

ESSENTIALS

GETTING THERE   By Plane   The **Dresden-Klotsche** airport lies 10km (6 miles) north of the city center. The airport is served by Lufthansa and most international carriers, with regularly scheduled flights from 11 German cities and other major European cities. For flight information, call © **0351/8813360** or visit www.dresden-airport.de. A rail line that's linked to Dresden's S-Bahn network stretches from the airport to the city's main station, requiring 20 minutes' transit each way, and a one-way fare of 1.80€ ($2.90). A taxi from the airport to the center of Dresden costs about 20€ ($32).

By Train   Dresden has two main rail stations, the **Hauptbahnhof,** on Wiener Platz, and the **Dresden-Neustadt,** at Schlesischer Park. Tram no. 3 connects the two. The city is served by the Deutsche Bundesbahn rail line, with frequent connections to major and regional cities. From Berlin, 15 trains arrive daily (trip time: 2–2½ hr.); 12 trains pull in from Frankfurt (trip time: 5 hr.). For rail information and schedules, call © **01805/996633.**

By Car   Access is via the E50 Autobahn from the west or the E4 Autobahn from the north (Rostock, Berlin) or south.

VISITOR INFORMATION   The **Information-Center,** Ostra-Allee 11 (© **0351/ 49192100**), is open year-round Monday to Friday 10am to 6pm, Saturday 10am to 4pm. Here you can book your accommodations and purchase a map of Dresden, get information booklets in English, and obtain tickets for theater, opera, and concerts. The city has a second branch of its tourist office at the Schinkelwache, Theaterplatz (same phone), that maintains the same hours, year-round, and performs the same services as the branch on Pragerstrasse noted above. Unlike the Pragerstrasse branch, however, the Schinkelwache branch is open on Sunday from 10am to 4pm.

GETTING AROUND   By Public Transportation   If you plan to see more than the historic core of Dresden, you can use the bus and tram lines. A ride of four stops or fewer costs 1.80€ ($2.90), or you can purchase a 24-hour pass for 4.50€ ($7.20). Maps and tickets are sold at automated dispensers outside the main rail station. Service is curtailed after midnight, though most major lines operate every hour. Dresden's S-Bahn reaches the suburbs.

Dresden

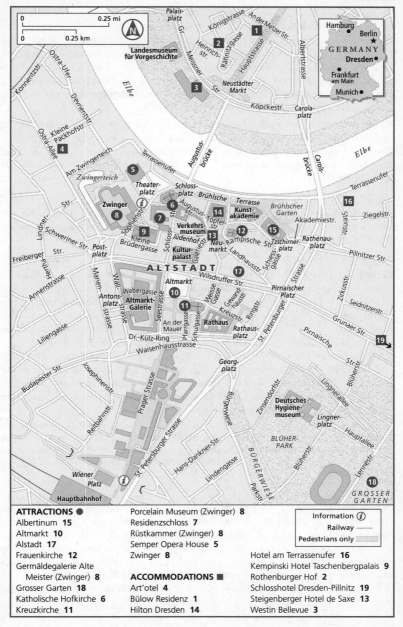

0   0.25 mi
0   0.25 km

Landesmuseum
für Vorgeschichte

Palais-
platz

Königstrasse

An der Metzer Str.

1

Heinrich-
str.

Rähnitzgasse

2

Hauptstrasse

Albertstrasse

3

Neustädter
Markt

Köpckestr.

Carola-
platz

Elbe

Carols-
brücke

Elbe

Terrassenufer

Steinstr.

Ziegelstr.

Ostra-Ufer

Kommerzstr.

Devrientstr.

Ostra-Allee

Kleine
Packhofstr.

4

Am Zwingerteich

Zwingerteich

Terrassenufer

Augustus-
brücke

5

Theater-
platz

Schloss-
platz

Brühlsche   Terrasse

Brühlscher
Garten

16

Akademiestr.

Zwinger

8

7

6

Augustus-
str.

Kunst-
akademie

14

Topfer-
Str.

Verkehrs-
museum

13

Jüdenhof

12

15

Tzschirner-
platz

Rathenau-
platz

Pillnitzer Str.

Sophienstr.

Schloss-str.

Galeriestr.

9

Kleine
Brüdergasse

Post-
platz

Neu-
markt

Rampische   Str.

Landhausstr.

Schless-
gasse

Kultur-
palast

ALTSTADT

Wilsdruffer Str.

17

Pirnaischer
Platz

St. Petersburger Str.

Zirkusstr.

Seidnitzerstr.

Schweriner Str.

Lindner-

Str.

Freiberger   Str.

Marien-

strasse

Wall-
strasse

Altmarkt

10

Weisse
Gasse

Gewand-
hausstr.

Kreuzstr.

Ringstr.

Pirnaische

Grunaer Str.

Annenstrasse

Herha-

Webergasse

Altmarkt-
Galerie

11

An der
Mauer

Pfarrgasse

Schulgasse

Rathaus

Rathaus-
platz

Str.

Str.

Blüherstr.

Lennéstr.

Antons-
platz

Seestrasse

Dr.-Külz-Ring

Waisenhausstrasse

Georg-
platz

Liliengasse

Budapester Str.

Josephinenstr.

Prager Strasse

Bürgerwiese

Zinsendorfstr.

Lingnerallee

Deutsches
Hygiene-
museum

Lingner-
platz

Hauptallee

BLÜHER-
PARK

18

GROSSER
GARTEN

Reitbahnstr.

St. Petersburger Strasse

Hans-Dankner-Str.

Lindengasse

BÜRGERWIESE

Parkstr.

Blüherstr.

Wiener
Platz

Hauptbahnhof

19

Hamburg
Berlin
GERMANY
Dresden
Frankfurt
am Main
Munich

ATTRACTIONS ●
Albertinum **15**
Altmarkt **10**
Alstadt **17**
Frauenkirche **12**
Germäldegalerie Alte
   Meister (Zwinger) **8**
Grosser Garten **18**
Katholische Hofkirche **6**
Kreuzkirche **11**

Porcelain Museum (Zwinger) **8**
Residenzschloss **7**
Rüstkammer (Zwinger) **8**
Semper Opera House **5**
Zwinger **8**

ACCOMMODATIONS ■
Art'otel **4**
Bülow Residenz **1**
Hilton Dresden **14**

Information ⓘ
Railway ——
Pedestrians only ▒

Hotel am Terrassenufer **16**
Kempinski Hotel Taschenbergpalais **9**
Rothenburger Hof **2**
Schlosshotel Dresden-Pillnitz **19**
Steigenberger Hotel de Saxe **13**
Westin Bellevue **3**

By Funicular   Dresden has two funiculars. The busier and more accessible of the two is the **Standseilbahn,** which links the suburb of Loschwitz to a hillside residential area, Weisser Hirsch. More remote, with less frequent runs, is the **Schwebebahn,** which links Loschwitz with Oberloschwitz on Saturday and Sunday only, carrying passengers to the viewing site at Loschwitzhöhe, which gives you an excellent view of the city. This funicular was the first of its kind in the world, built from 1898 to 1900. Fares on either funicular cost 1.80€ ($2.90) each way. For operating hours and more details, contact the transportation office at ✆ **0351/8571011.**

By Ferry   Five ferries service Dresden, each operated by the same authorities that maintain the city's network of trams and buses. One is a vehicular ferry across the River Elbe between Dresden-Kleinzschachwitz and the Pillnitz Castle. To reach its departure point, take tram no. 1 from Postplatz. For more information, call ✆ **0351/8571011.**

WHERE TO STAY

Since reunification and the amazing increase in tourism, Dresden's hotel prices have soared, as has the demand for rooms. Even so-called "budget" hotels can command 130€ ($208) a night for a double.

VERY EXPENSIVE

Kempinski Hotel Taschenbergpalais ⋘⋘⋘   Few hotels of post-reunification Germany have sparked as much pride among local citizens as this one. Its history dates from the early 18th century, when the elector of Saxony built a baroque castle for his favorite mistress, the Countess Cosel, who, for mysterious reasons, was later banished from his court. For 250 years, the palace was the pride of Dresden, a site visited almost as much as the Zwinger. Only the surreal remains of a massive marble staircase survived the bombs, but now the historic Taschenberg Palace is back better than ever.

A real-estate developer spent $175 million on transforming the ruin into Dresden's finest hotel, restoring the five-story baroque, sculpture-dotted facade to its original opulence. Rooms are the most luxurious in town. Those on the west and north sides overlook the Zwinger or the Opera.

Taschenberg 3, D-01067 Dresden. ✆ **0351/49120.** Fax 0351/4912812. www.kempinski-dresden.de. 214 units. 236€–419€ ($378–$670) double; from 334€ ($534) suite. AE, DC, MC, V. Parking 15€ ($24). Tram: 5 or 8. **Amenities:** 2 restaurants; 2 bars; indoor heated pool; health club; spa; sauna; solarium; room service; massage; babysitting; laundry service; dry cleaning; nonsmoking rooms; 1 room for those w/limited mobility. *In room:* A/C, TV, Wi-Fi, minibar, hair dryer, safe.

EXPENSIVE

Bülow Residenz ⋘⋘⋘   We prefer staying at the Bülow Residenz, a charming, gracious boutique hotel and one of the most luxurious in eastern Germany, to the Hotel Taschenbergpalais. This hotel, with a restored facade from the 1700s, has been a success since its opening in the early 1990s. The formal lounge, with its plush seating, sets the tone, and the garden patio is the perfect place to be on a summer day. Individually decorated rooms are unusually spacious compared to most in Dresden. Oversize beds and contemporary redwood furnishings offer a restful ambience. Bathrooms have tub/shower combinations. The sumptuous German-style 19€ ($30) breakfast buffet is well worth it; check the Web for special rates, as many packages include breakfast and/or a pair of nearly-impossible-to-obtain Semperoper tickets (p. 215).

Rähnitzgasse 19 (near the Opera), D-01097 Dresden. © **0351/80030.** Fax 0351/8003100. www.buelow-residenz.de. 30 units. 250€ ($400) double; 310€–520€ ($496–$832) suite. AE, DC, MC, V. Parking 10€ ($16). Tram: 3, 4, 8, or 11. **Amenities:** Restaurant; bar; babysitting; laundry service; dry cleaning; nonsmoking rooms. *In room:* TV, minibar, hair dryer, safe.

Hilton Dresden ⓕ   This hotel is one of the best in the region, though lacking the romance and glamour of the Hotel Taschenbergpalais or the intimacy and charm of the Bülow (see above). Its conservative mansard-roofed facade blends harmoniously with the baroque buildings on the nearby Neumarkt. A glassed-in passageway connects the hotel to a 19th-century building, the Sekundogenitur, which contains two restaurants and an array of banqueting and conference rooms. Rooms are midsize, conservatively modern, and well maintained. Bathrooms are small and have tub/shower combinations. Double-glazed windows cut down on noise. The best rooms face the Frauenkirche.

An der Frauenkirche 5, D-01067 Dresden. © **800/445-8667** in the U.S. and Canada, or 0351/86420. Fax 0351/8642725. www.hilton.com. 333 units. 167€–243€ ($267–$389) double; 272€–382€ ($435–$611) suite. AE, DC, MC, V. Parking 20€ ($32). Tram: 3, 5, 7, 8, or 12. **Amenities:** 7 restaurants; 2 bars; lounge; indoor heated pool; health club; whirlpool; sauna; solarium; car-rental desk; salon; room service; babysitting; laundry service; nonsmoking rooms; 1 room for those w/limited mobility. *In room:* TV, Wi-Fi, minibar, fridge (in some), coffeemaker (in some), hair dryer, iron (in some), trouser press (in some), safe.

Romantik Hotel Pattis ⓕⓕⓕ   Lying outside Dresden center in the Kemnitz section, 4km (2½ miles) to the northwest, this is one of the most romantic and atmospheric hotels in all of eastern Germany. It originated as a mill, but by 1870 it had become a popular day trip for the rich folk of Dresden who came here to go boating on a lake and also to dance the waltz in its ballroom. The property fell into decline after World War II but was rescued by the Pattis family, who reconstructed the original house, which is surrounded by a large, landscaped park. All the spacious rooms and suites are beautifully furnished, cozy, and comfortable with high-quality furnishings and fabrics. On-site is a gourmet restaurant. Begin the evening with a drink in the cozy bar or else in the library in front of a crackling open fire.

Merbitzerstrasse 53, 01157 Dresden-Kemnitz. © **0351/42550.** Fax 0351/4255255. www.pattis.de. 47 units. 130€–205€ ($208–$328) double; 190€–350€ ($304–$560) suite. AE, DC, MC, V. Bus: 94. Parking 5€ ($8) indoors. **Amenities:** 2 restaurants; bar; room service; fitness center; wellness center; sauna; steam room; laundry service; dry cleaning. *In room:* TV, minibar, hair dryer, safe.

Steingenberger Hotel de Saxe ⓕⓕ   In the 18th century a famous hotel once stood on this spot, opening onto views of the Neumarkt. Today a new chain-linked luxury hotel has risen on the spot to grace the skyline of Dresden. Directly opposite the fabled Frauenkirche, the hotel was reconstructed in the grand baroque style with rows of dormer windows. The rooms are luxuriously furnished and most comfortable, definitely a hotel of the 21st century in spite of its old-fashioned architecture. Even the simplest rooms are called "superior," although if you're willing to pay more you can get a deluxe room with even better appointments.

Neumarkt 9, 01067 Dresden. © **0351/43860.** Fax 0351/4386-888. 185 units. 129€–185€ ($206–$296) double; 375€–395€ ($600–$632) suite. AE, DC, MC, V. Parking 18€ ($29). **Amenities:** Restaurant; bar; room service; laundry service; health club; nonsmoking rooms; rooms for those w/limited mobility. *In room:* A/C, TV, Wi-Fi, minibar, hair dryer, safe.

Westin Bellevue ⓕ   The Bellevue, which we'd rank just under the Hilton, stands by the most attractive part of the Elbe. If you look out the hotel's windows or from its terraces to the opposite riverbank, you'll know you're in the spot where Canaletto painted his magnificent scenes. The ornate walls of a pair of courtyards that survived the 1945 bombings have been integrated into the structure and are now a protected monument. Some rooms overlook the courtyards; others are in modern wings that often open onto the Elbe. Whether you stay in the old part or in the new, you'll find well-appointed rooms.

Grosse Meissner Strasse 15, D-01097 Dresden. ℂ **0351/8050.** Fax 0351/8051609. www.westin.com/bellevue. 343 units. 160€–299€ ($256–$478) double; from 399€ ($638) suite. AE, DC, MC, V. Parking 15€ ($24). Tram: 4 or 5. **Amenities:** 2 restaurants; cafe; bar; tearoom; indoor heated pool; health club; sauna; solarium; shopping arcade; salon; room service; babysitting; laundry service; dry cleaning; all nonsmoking rooms; rooms for those w/limited mobility. *In room:* A/C, TV, Wi-Fi, minibar, hair dryer.

MODERATE

Art'otel ⟨ *Finds* The six floors of this dramatic postmodern hotel are the most self-consciously "arty" of any hotel in Dresden. They were designed by Denis Santachiara, whose work has been heralded in Munich, Milan, New York, and Paris. One floor is an art gallery that focuses on striking contemporary paintings and sculpture by German artists. The stylish guest rooms are well furnished and comfortable, each with a neat, efficiently organized private bathroom, mainly with tub/shower combinations. The staff is very conscious of cutting-edge trends in German cities.

Ostra-Allee 33, D-01067 Dresden. ℂ **0351/49220.** Fax 0351/4922777. www.artotels.com. 174 units. 134€–200€ ($214–$320) double; from 160€ ($256) suite. Rates include buffet breakfast. AE, DC, MC, V. Parking 15€ ($24). Tram: 11. **Amenities:** Restaurant; cafe; bar; gym; sauna; solarium; room service; nonsmoking rooms; rooms for those w/limited mobility. *In room:* A/C, TV, Wi-Fi, minibar, coffeemaker (in some), hair dryer.

Hotel am Terrassenufer Comfortable and reasonably priced, this hotel was built in the 1960s as a student dormitory. In the 1990s, it was renovated and enlarged into the streamlined 12-story hotel you see today. Set on the riverbank, a short walk from Dresden's historic core, it offers large, airy, big-windowed rooms with lots of sunlight and compact bathrooms with shower.

Terrassenufer 12, D-01069 Dresden. ℂ **0351/4409500.** Fax 0351/4409600. www.hotel-terrassenufer.de. 196 units. 109€–150€ ($174–$240) double; 144€–240€ ($230–$384) suite. AE, DC, MC, V. Tram: 3, 7, or 9. Parking 6€ ($9.60). **Amenities:** Restaurant; bar; room service; laundry service; dry cleaning; nonsmoking rooms. *In room:* A/C, TV, minibar, hair dryer.

Rothenburger Hof ⟨⟨ Beautifully renovated, this time-honored and traditional hotel, which first opened its doors in 1685, is once again claiming its regal position as a small luxury hotel. A family-run hotel, it is in Neustadt, the area rebuilt after a great fire in the late 1680s. It's within an easy walk of the historical monuments of the Old City. It's much more comfortable today than when it first opened because so many modern improvements have been made, including the addition of a swimming pool, sauna, Turkish bath, and solarium, plus a garden terrace and an elevator. The midsize rooms are traditionally furnished and comfortable, with freshly renovated, tiled bathrooms with tub and shower. Guest room furnishings are tasteful reproductions of antiques.

Rothenburger Strasse 15–17, D-01099 Dresden. ℂ **0351/81260.** Fax 0351/8126222. www.rothenburger-hof.de. 39 units. 99€–160€ ($158–$256) double; 170€–185€ ($272–$296) suite. Rates include buffet breakfast. AE, MC, V. Parking 5€ ($8). Tram: 11. **Amenities:** Garden terrace; indoor heated pool; fitness center; sauna; solarium; children's playground; room service; laundry service; dry cleaning; Turkish bath; nonsmoking rooms; rooms for those w/limited mobility. *In room:* TV, kitchen (in 13 units), minibar.

Schlosshotel Dresden-Pillnitz 🏛🏛 (Finds) Set within a few steps of Schloss Pillnitz (Pillnitz Castle), about 8km (5 miles) east of downtown Dresden, this historic building functioned as a restaurant as early as 1760, often feeding the courtiers and service personnel doing business with the castle. In 1999, the Zepp family poured time and money into its restoration. Today, the upper floors are devoted to well-maintained, discreetly tasteful guest rooms, each with big windows, well-crafted furniture, and comfortable beds. The lower floors contain a cafe, a reception hall, and a high-ceilinged restaurant with excellent food.

August-Böckelstiegel-Strasse 10, D-01326 Dresden-Pillnitz. ℭ **0351/26140.** Fax 0351/2614400. www.schlosshotel-pillnitz.de. 45 units. 115€–135€ ($184–$216) double; 200€–240€ ($320–$384) suite. Rates include buffet breakfast. Free parking. AE, MC, V. **Amenities:** Restaurant; cafe; laundry service; nonsmoking rooms; rooms for those w/limited mobility. *In room:* TV, minibar, hair dryer.

WHERE TO DINE
EXPENSIVE

Lesage 🏛🏛 GERMAN/INTERNATIONAL   One of the city's best restaurants is oddly positioned in the "Transparent Factory of Volkswagen," a stunning glass structure where you can witness new models of cars being assembled by workers in white lab jackets. The elegant restaurant itself is tucked away near the entrance. Begin with such delights as a crayfish torte with a vanilla-laced tomato sauce or a salad of baked fontina cheese, pears, and *bresaola*. You might follow with a veal shank with fresh asparagus or orange slices, or else pillowy cheeks of veal with lentils and black salsify. Perhaps saddle of young wild boar with cabbage and roast dumplings will appear on the menu. If you wish, you can drive off in a new Phaeton.

Lennestrasse 1. ℭ **0351/4204-250.** Reservations required. Main courses 18€–24€ ($29–$38). AE, DC, MC, V. Tues–Sun noon–2:30pm and 6pm–midnight.

Rossini 🏛 ITALIAN   Rossini offers Italian cuisine in a stylish setting, one floor above the lobby of the Dresden Hilton. Menu items might include chicken-liver pâté in Marsala wine; a buffet of Sicilian antipasti, carpaccio of swordfish marinated in Marsala vinaigrette, Parma ham with coarse bread, and a tapenade of olives; Sicilian-style fish soup; or grilled lamb with anchovy sauce. Dessert may be cassata made with ricotta cheese and candied fruit, or a *granita* (sorbet) of oranges and lemons floating on white wine.

In the Dresden Hilton, An der Frauenkirche 5. ℭ **0351/8642855.** Reservations recommended. Main courses 18€–27€ ($29–$43). AE, DC, MC, V. Daily 6–11:30pm. Tram: 4 or 8.

MODERATE

Alte Meister 🏛 CONTINENTAL   Established in 2001, this is the first restaurant directly within the Zwinger that anyone can remember for a very long time. Although it has its own entrance (on Theaterplatz directly opposite the entrance to the Opera House), it's close to its namesake, the Zwinger's Alte Meister collections. Within a high-ceilinged and stately room that evokes the imperial grandeur of Renaissance Saxony, you'll enjoy well-flavored and traditional food items with touches of elegance. The best examples include cream of carrot soup, studded with chunks of braised rabbit liver; soft goat cheese with toast and a ragout of tomatoes; grilled prawns served with chicory salad; and carpaccio of pressed veal with a tomato-and-mushroom salad. Main courses include filet of sea bass served with a curried version of coconut-laced vegetables; breast of free-range chicken with a sauté of Gorgonzola-flavored spinach; and a combination platter that contains, on the same plate, roasted saddle of rabbit and a braised filet of lamb.

Theaterplatz 1A–B. (℃ **0351/4810426.** Reservations recommended. Main courses 9.50€–21€ ($15–$33). AE, MC, V. Daily 10am–1am. Bus: 91.

Brauhaus am Waldschlösschen GERMAN
This is a replica of the old-fashioned beer halls and beer gardens that played such an important role in Dresden's past. Around 250 diners and drinkers can cram into a series of dining rooms, and another 800 can be accommodated within the sprawling garden (open Apr–Oct). Expect heaping platters of such favorites as roast pork shank, sautéed fish with parsley and onions, schnitzels, soups, *Wursts,* and roasts. Live music, usually from a jazzy pianist, is presented Monday to Saturday 8pm to midnight. Beer (Waldschlösschen) is brewed on the premises and comes in several degrees of darkness.

Am Brauhaus 8B (in the Neustadt district, 5km/3 miles northeast of the city center). (℃ **0351/6523900.** Reservations required. Main courses 6€–16€ ($9.60–$26). AE, DC, MC, V. Daily 11am–1am. Tram: 11. Bus: 91.

Italienisches Dörfchen ITALIAN/INTERNATIONAL
Italienisches Dörfchen is a stately looking neoclassical building that was erected in 1911 on the site of the cluster of cottages ("the Italian Village") that once housed the mostly Italian crews of laborers building the nearby monuments of the Saxon kings. Today, it contains a quartet of restaurants, each with a different theme. The best way to decide which to patronize is to wander through the formal premises of the building and inspect them. Choices include the **Biersaal,** whose painted ceiling evokes the 18th century; the neoclassical **Weinzimmer,** a formal, rather uncomfortable and fussy-looking room outfitted in red; and the **Bellotto,** an upscale Italian eatery on the top floor. There's also the **Kurfürstenzimmer,** an area that serves both Saxon and international food. Supplementing the four dining options is **Café,** a graceful-looking antique room with windows that overlook the river. Prices in all four of the restaurants are about the same, but if you're interested just in coffee, tea, a drink, and/or pastries, you'd be best advised to head directly for the cafe.

Theaterplatz 2. (℃ **0351/498160.** Reservations not necessary. Main courses 8€–18€ ($13–$29). AE, DC, MC, V. Daily 10am–midnight. Tram: 4 or 8.

INEXPENSIVE

Ayers Rock 𝄄 *Finds* AUSTRALIAN
The success of this likable restaurant is proof of the growing sophistication of Dresden. It was named and modeled after the geological oddity in central Australia that deeply impressed the owner during a holiday there. Lighthearted and breezy, the place serves almost 300 kinds of cocktails, as well as some brands of German and Aussie beer on tap. Menu items are inspired by what's cooking "down under" and include a savory version of lamb with green-bean stew, grilled veal shank, fresh asparagus with strips of chicken breast, and roebuck steak with mushrooms and glass noodles. After 8:30pm, the bar area gets crowded with the young at heart and singles.

Münzgasse 8. (℃ **0351/4901188.** Reservations not necessary. Main courses 12€–24€ ($19–$38). AE, DC, MC, V. Daily 11am–2am. Tram: 1, 2, or 4.

Bräuhaus Watzke GERMAN
One of Dresden's most famous and atmospheric beer halls lies 6.5km (4 miles) west of the city center, on a site overlooking the Elbe. Established in 1898, it confirms that while governments in Germany may rise and fall, beer halls will remain intact. If the weather is clement, you can opt for a seat within the sprawling garden, where hardworking waitresses carry impossibly heavy loads of beer mugs and heaping platters to the long tables. Inside, the venue is appropriately

woodsy looking and *gemütlich* (cozy). Anything you drink here (including beers of the month) will have been brewed on the premises, with modern equipment that was installed in 1996. Regardless of which kind of beer you pick, a half-liter costs 2.70€ ($4.30). It's never bottled in individual containers, only in kegs, and it's almost never available anywhere except here and within a limited handful of other restaurants nearby. Menu items are appropriately hearty and include *Meltzer Schnitzel,* a filet of veal dredged in malt and fried, or *Watzke Bierfleische,* a ragout of beef stewed in dark aromatic beer. Salads, soups, and fish dishes are just as tasty.

Kötzschenbroder Strasse 1. ℂ 0351/852920. Reservations not necessary. Main courses 6€–17€ ($9.60–$27). AE, MC, V. Daily 11am–midnight. Tram: 4 or 13.

Café Schinkelwache CONTINENTAL   Designed like a miniature Ionic-style temple, this is one of Dresden's architectural gems. Noted architect Karl Friedrich Schinkel built this sandstone structure in 1832 to house soldiers and guards. In 1995, it was rebuilt and reconfigured into the cafe you see today. Its interior is cozier and on a smaller scale than you'd imagine from a look at its stately facade. During clement weather, tables and parasols spill onto the terrace surrounding the building. Menu selections include pastries, meal-size salads, soups, cold platters, toasts, and at least two full-fledged dishes of the day. Wine, beer, and coffee are the preferred drinks.

Theaterplatz 2. ℂ 0351/4903909. Reservations recommended. Pastries 3€–5€ ($4.80–$8); platters 11€–18€ ($18–$29). AE, MC, V. Daily 10am–midnight. Tram: 8 or 11.

Sophienkeller im Taschenbergpalais ✦ *Moments* GERMAN   The food here approximates the hearty medieval feasts you might have expected in the Royal Saxon Court, albeit in a more sanitary form. Your happiness in these deep but bustling cellars depends on where you happen to sit. Four distinct areas are available, but the ones we prefer, and the ones that are the most authentically historic, are the Grosses and Kleines Zunfi Gewölbe, where flickering candles, set beneath vaulted ceilings, provide most of the illumination. Waitresses in traditional dirndls haul steaming platters of crispy suckling pig from the spit with wine-flavored cabbage, a juicy chicken filet with fresh spinach and hearty Gorgonzola cheese, or venison goulash with dumplings. Tantalizing regional appetizers include a Saxon potato soup with fried slices of *Bockwurst* sausage or a smoky fish soup with fresh chervil and shrimp. It's a bit theme-ish, especially in its emphasis on 18th-century costumes, and at least part of its energy is devoted to the care and feeding of large tour groups, but the food is hearty and flavorful and the ambience can be very romantic.

Taschenberg 3. ℂ 0351/497260. Reservations recommended. Main courses 8€–15€ ($13–$24); fixed-price menus 22€–35€ ($34–$55). AE, DC, MC, V. Daily 11am–1am. Tram: 4 or 11.

EXPLORING DRESDEN

Frauenkirche (Church of Our Lady) ✦✦, at Neumarkt (ℂ 0351/4981131; www. frauenkirche-dresden.org), was built between 1726 and 1743 and once was known throughout Europe for its 93m (305-ft.) dome. On the night of February 13, 1945, it was bombed by Allied planes, and during the Cold War remained the most evocative ruins in Dresden. The East German government deliberately let the blackened hulk stay as it was as a reminder of the horrors of modern warfare. Today the church has been rebuilt and was reconsecrated for the 800th anniversary of the founding of Dresden on October 30, 2005. The original pieces from the pile of rubble left over from 1945 were used, along with other materials. This is one of the most important Protestant churches in Germany, with its famous dome restored. In 2002, the duke of Kent came to

Dresden to hand over a new dome cross, with a dimension of 8m (26 ft.), a symbol of reconciliation between Great Britain and Germany. The German chancellor, Gerhard Schröder, participated in the ceremony, the transfer taking place 55 years after the destruction of Dresden by Allied bombers. Admission is free, and hours are daily from 10am to 4pm (tram no. 4 or 8).

Residenzschloss, the Dresden Royal Palace, stands at Schlossplatz (© **0351/ 49142000**), behind its Renaissance facade. This was the former royal palace on which construction was begun in 1709 and where Napoleon once stood. It was destroyed by British bombers in 1945. Sections are open for visits, which cost 12€ ($19) and are led Wednesday to Monday 10am to 6pm. In the Georgenbau rooms are historical exhibits about Dresden, including the rebuilding of the palace. You enter through the impressive main entrance, Georgentor, with its towering statue of Georg, the Saxon count. From April to October, the Hausmann Tower or Hausmannsturm can be climbed for a panoramic vista over Dresden and the Elbe. The chief attraction here is the **Grünes Gewölbe (Green Vaults)** ***, a dazzling collection of 16th- to 18th-century treasures: rococo chests, ivory carvings, jewelry, intricately designed mirrors, and priceless porcelain. Many pieces were created by the craftspeople of local guilds; others were acquired from the far corners of the earth. It's open from mid-March to mid-November (tram no. 2, 4, or 8).

The restored **Katholische Hofkirche (Catholic Court Church)** **, Schlossplatz (© **0351/4844712**), is the largest church in Saxony. It was built by the son of August the Strong, Frederick Augustus II, who ruled from 1733 to 1763. The church's facade has 38 biblical and historical figures in the high baroque style. Inside, you can see the crypt with the tombs of 49 rulers of Saxony and a box allegedly containing the heart of August the Strong. On the main floor you can see a beautiful stone pulpit by the royal sculptor, Balthasar Permoser (1651–1732), one of the leading sculptors of his time in Saxony. There's also an 18th-century church organ. Admission is free. This church, also known as the Cathedral of St. Trinitas, is open Monday to Friday 8:30am to 6pm, Saturday 10am to 4pm, and Sunday 1:30 to 4pm. Guided tours, conducted only in German and priced at 3€ ($4.80) per person, are conducted Monday to Thursday at 2pm and Saturday at 1 and 2pm (tram no. 4 or 8).

Kreuzkirche (Church of the Cross) * (© **0351/4393920**) stands at the **Altmarkt,** or old market square. This church is the home of the Kreuzchor, the famous boys' choir of Dresden. Free concerts are conducted every Saturday at 5pm, unless the choir is traveling. The church's architecture is a combination of baroque and Art Nouveau. The present building is from the late 18th century, although a church stood here as early as the 13th century. You can also see the reconstructed **Rathaus (Town Hall)** and the 18th-century **Landhaus** at the Altmarkt. Very little of it is open to viewing and its tower is also closed. However, you can appreciate its facade. Take tram no. 4 or 8.

Of Dresden's many parks and gardens, the best and most popular is the **Grosser Garten,** to the southeast of the Altstadt. This park, which was mapped out in 1676, contains a zoo and a botanical garden. In the center is a minor *Lustschloss* (pleasure palace) built in 1670 that's most appealing when viewed from the outside; just don't plan a casual visit during the occasional midsummer concerts conducted there (you'll spend most of your time fighting your way through the crowd, rather than admiring the palace!). For more information, contact the tourist office.

THE MAJOR MUSEUMS

Albertinum ⭑⭑⭑   This imposing imperial structure houses one of Germany's great galleries. It's named for the Saxon King Albert, who, between 1884 and 1887, converted this former royal arsenal into a home for a vast collection of art and precious jewelry.

On the upper two floors is the **Galerie Neue Meister** ⭑⭑⭑, a collection of 19th- and 20th-century art and sculpture, from Corot to Otto Dix. We are especially fond of the desolate and haunting landscapes of Caspar David Friedrich, the German Romantic artist. Impressionists and post-Impressionists are well represented, including Gauguin, Degas, Manet, Monet, Corinth, Liebermann, Klimt, and van Gogh. Antifascist artists, whose works were either destroyed or banned in the Nazi era, are also on display. In the sculpture collection, the works of more than 5 millennia are presented, ranging from the ancient cultures of the Mediterranean and the Near East to virtually all epochs of European artistic developments, dating from the early Middle Ages.

Warning: At press time in 2008, this fabled museum was closed for extensive renovations. When you arrive in Dresden, check on its status before heading here.

Brühl Terrace. ⓒ **0351/49142000.** Admission 6€ ($9.60) adults, 3.50€ ($5.60) students and children 6–18, free for children 5 and under. Wed–Mon 10am–6pm. Closed 2 weeks in Jan. Tram: 1, 3, 5, 7, or 8 to Rathenau Platz.

Zwinger ⭑⭑⭑   Augustus the Strong, elector of Saxony (also king of Poland), built this baroque masterpiece, modeled after Versailles, in 1719. Here he staged tournaments and kept dozens of concubines. His physique was called Herculean, his temperament Rabelaisian, but he also had a great love for the arts. Today, this artfully symmetrical complex of buildings holds a collection of museums. The damage caused by the British air raid in 1945 was so devastating that some locals feared the Zwinger would remain a ruin forever. However, it's been restored and it's back in business, welcoming new generations of art lovers.

M. D. Pöppelmann (1662–1736) initially conceived the Zwinger as the forecourt of the castle. In the center of the large quadrangle are formal gardens, fountains, and promenades, forming a deep curving bay enclosed by pavilions. Notable are the Wall-pavilion in the center of the semicircular arched gallery in the west end and the **Nymphenbad (Bath of Nymphs)** ⭑⭑ with its graceful fountains and mythological figures by Balthasar Permoser, who helped Pöppelmann in the construction of the Zwinger. On the northeast side is a Renaissance-style building, added in 1846 by Gottfried Semper (1803–79). Semper's two-story pavilions are linked by one-story galleries. The architectural critic Sir Nikolaus Pevsner once wrote: "What exultation in these rocking curves, and yet what grace! It is joyful but never vulgar; vigorous, boisterous perhaps, but never crude."

The most important museum in the complex is the **Gemäldegalerie Alte Meister** ⭑⭑⭑, which has its entrance at Theaterplatz 1. This gallery, one of the best on the Continent, has as its showpiece Raphael's *Sistine Madonna.* You'll also find Giorgione's *Sleeping Venus,* Antonello da Messina's *The Martyrdom of St. Sebastian,* Titian's *Tribute Money,* and many famous works by Veronese, Tintoretto, Correggio, and Annibale Carracci. You'll also see Flemish, Dutch, and German paintings by Van Dyck, Vermeer, Dürer, and Rembrandt, among others. The Rubens collection includes his spectacular *Neptune,* full of rearing horses, and an exquisite *St. Jerome.* Admission is 7€ ($11) adults, 4.50€ ($7.20) children.

(Moments A Cruise on the Elbe

You can take a cruise on the historic Elbe River from central moorings below the Brühl Terrace. Sächsischer Dampfschiffahrt (© 0351/866090) offers a 4½-hour cruise along the Elbe from Dresden to Rathen, a German village at the border of the Czech Republic. These trips take you through some of the finest river scenery in eastern Germany, including an area known as "Swiss Saxony," one of Germany's most popular natural wonders. It's a land of table-shaped outcrops, isolated pillars, deep gorges, and sheer sandstone cliffs. The upper reaches of the Elbe flow in wide curves through these fantastically shaped rock formations. Between March and early November, boat departures occur daily, at 11am. Because each leg of this waterborne journey requires 4½ hours, you'll have to block out an entire day for this experience if you opt for round-trip transport by boat. Alternatively, you can opt for one-way transit by boat, with a return back to Dresden from Rathen by train, a 40-minute ride. Trains depart at 30-minute intervals throughout the day between Rathen and Dresden. Boat passage, each way, costs 20€ ($32); rail transport, each way, costs 9€ ($14). While you're cruising, look for the Blaues Wunder (Blue Wonder), one of Dresden's most celebrated bridges, completed in 1893 and never destroyed during the wartime bombings. It is a beautiful expression of the bridge-building genius that flourished here at the turn of the 20th century.

Rüstkammer (Armory) displays a vast collection of weaponry from the 15th to 18th centuries, including halberds, shields, cannons, and suits of armor for both men and horses. The Porzellansammlung displays the finery produced by the porcelain factories of Dresden during the 350 years since their founding. Admission is 3€ ($4.80) adults, 2€ ($3.20) children 13 and under.

Theaterplatz 1. (© 0351/49142000. www.skd-dresden.de. Day ticket valid 24 hr. for entrance to 11 of Dresden's top museums and monuments, available at any of the individual museums within the Zwinger, costs 12€ ($19) for adults, 7€ ($11) for students and children 6–18, free for children 5 and under. All 4 Zwinger sites are open Tues–Sun 10am–6pm. Tram: 1, 2, 4, 7, 8, 11, 12, or 14. Bus: 82 or 94 to Postplatz.

BUS TOURS

Responding to the flood of visitors coming to see the city's historic core, **Stadtrundfahrt Dresden**, Königstrasse 6 (© 0351/8995650), has organized a flotilla of red-and-white buses that feature—via prerecorded descriptions and headsets—running commentary in eight languages. Daily from April to October from 9:30am to 5pm, buses depart at 30-minute intervals for circular tours of the city that incorporate overviews of all the major monuments. From November to March service is only from 10am to 3pm. Visitors can hop on or off the bus at any of 19 points along the way, and they can even postpone some of the stops until the following day. Each tour begins at the Schlossplatz, adjacent to the Augustusbrücke. Additional stopovers include the Zwinger, the Grünes Gewölbe, the Frauenkirche, and many of the parks, gardens, and architectural highlights of the city. The price is 19€ ($30) per adult, with no discounts for students; children 13 and under are free when accompanied by an adult.

SHOPPING

Perhaps because of Dresden's destruction in the final days of World War II, there's an emphasis here on collecting the high-quality antiques that remain. You'll find many antiques dealers in the city. Most of the inventory has been culled from homes and estate sales in the relatively unscathed surrounding hamlets. The most interesting shops in Dresden, and many of the most glamorous ones, line either side of the **Königstrasse.** Here, look for a roster of handcrafted goods and gift items. An especially convenient antiques gallery is **Antikitäten,** on the lobby level of the Kempinski Hotel Taschenbergpalais, Am Taschenberg (℡ **0351/49120**).

The oldest manufacturer of porcelain in Dresden is **Wehsener Porzellan,** 5km (3 miles) southeast of the center at Dohnaerstrasse 72 (℡ **0351/4707340;** bus: 72 or 76 from the main railway station). Its hand-painted objects are the most charming and interesting in Dresden. Anything you buy can be shipped.

And don't overlook the city's role as a purveyor of modern painting and sculpture. The best of the art galleries is **Galerie am Blauen Wunder,** Pillnitzer Landstrasse 2 (℡ **0351/2684020**).

Weihnachtsland am Zwinger, Kleine Brüdergasse 5 (℡ **0351/8621230**), is the best-stocked and most interesting gift shop in Dresden, with a year-round emphasis on Christmas, New Year's, and Easter ornaments that are handmade in the nearby Erzgebirge region. Look for pieces of delicate Plauener Spitze lace that's designed to hang on hooks affixed by suction cups to the glass of your windows—it's easy to transport, and some pieces can be acquired for less than 6€ ($9.60). There are also elaborately detailed Easter eggs, carved wooden figurines in the shapes of either soldiers or angels, and framed still lifes and landscapes made from assemblages of dried flowers.

Other shops line **Prager Strasse** with its department stores, **Altmarkt,** and **Wilsdruffer Strasse.** Tony shops and boutiques are found along **Hauptstrasse.**

Count yourself lucky if you're in Dresden for the celebrated **Weihnachtsmarkt** ✶✶, the oldest Christmas market in Germany, a tradition since 1434. Handmade regional crafts, delicious homemade foods such as cakes and cookies, and dozens of other goodies are featured in the Altmarkt. The blown-glass tree decorations from Lauscha are particularly stunning and virtual heirlooms since they never go out of style.

DRESDEN AFTER DARK

Dresden is Saxony's cultural center. There's always a variety of options for nightlife here, whether you're looking for drama, classical concerts, punk-rock shows, dancing, or just a good place to drink.

THE PERFORMING ARTS   Between the Elbe River and the Zwinger, on the western side of Theaterplatz, stands the **Semperoper (Semper Opera House)** ✶✶✶, one of the most exquisite opera houses in the world, Theaterplatz 2 (℡ **0351/4911705;** www.semperoper.de; tram: 1, 2, 4, 7, 8, 11, 12, 14, or 17). Both Wagner and Weber conducted here. Gottfried Semper, the same architect who mapped out the famous picture gallery in the Zwinger, designed the building. Restorers have brought the Renaissance-style two-tiered facade and the interior of the building back to life. Careful attention was paid to the replacement of Semper's original paintings and decorations. More important, the fine acoustics for which the opera house was known have been reestablished. Good seats can be had for 20€ to 120€ ($32–$192). *Note:* Seats are *extremely* difficult to get; purchase your tickets as far in advance as possible. The opera company takes a vacation mid-July to mid-August.

The **Dresden Philharmonic** appears at the **Kulturpalast,** in the Altmarkt (© **0351/4866306;** tram: 3 or 5). Tickets cost 14€ to 50€ ($22–$80). Concerts, sometimes with accompaniment by ballet recitals, are also performed during June and August in the courtyards of the Zwinger.

For musical theater, come to the **Staats Operette,** Pirnaer Landstrasse 131, about 5km (3 miles) southeast of the city center (© **0351/2079929;** tram: 4), which mainly performs works from the 19th and early 20th centuries. The box office is open Sunday 1 hour before the show, Monday 11am to 4pm, Tuesday to Friday 11am to 7pm, and Saturday 4 to 7pm. Tickets cost 5€ to 24€ ($8–$38).

The classical stage for drama in the city is **Schauspielhaus,** Postplatz (© **0351/4913555;** tram: 1, 2, 4, 7, 8, 11, 12, or 14), where dramas by Goethe, Schiller, and Shakespeare (in German) are performed. Performances usually start at 7:30pm. The box office is open Monday to Friday 10am to 6:30pm, Saturday and Sunday 10am to 2pm. Tickets cost 10€ to 28€ ($16–$45). The Schauspielhaus box office also handles tickets and inquiries for the **Residenztheater im Schloss,** Schlossplatz (© **0351/491350;** tram: 4 or 8), a small theater focusing on modern drama and small-ensemble pieces. The cost is 10€ to 60€ ($16–$96). Both theaters are closed from July to mid-August.

For a family theater experience, check out **Theater Junge Generation,** Meissner Landstrasse 4 (© **0351/429120;** tram: 1; bus: 94), which interprets Shakespeare and fairy tales in a way that both kids and parents can enjoy. The box office is open Monday to Saturday 10am to 6pm, and 1 hour before performances. Ticket prices are 5€ to 12€ ($8–$19). In summer, some members of the troupe bring their acts outdoors, usually to the courtyard in front of the Staffhof, an imposing building originally intended as a stable.

Tickets for classical concerts, dance, and opera are available from the tourist office branch within the **Schinkelwache,** Theaterplatz (© **0351/4903909;** tram: 4 or 8), a historic building that was originally a guardhouse for the nearby castle.

BARS At **Brazil Restaurant & Bar Gastronomie,** Kleine Brüdergasse 5 (© **0351/8621200;** tram: 1, 2, 4, or 11), you're likely to experience culture shock when you cross the street between the Zwinger and this Brazilian bar and restaurant where the music is hot and the food is spicy. Platters of food—roasted filet of pork is a specialty—are priced at 12€ to 18€ ($19–$29), although some specialty items, such as roasted rattlesnake, cost up to 46€ ($74). Most clients, however, just opt for a drink at the serpentine bar. Live music begins every night around 9pm. Brazil is open daily 11am to 2am.

At **Las Tapas,** Münzgasse 4 (© **0351/4960108;** tram: 1, 2, 4, or 14), within a stone-floored room modeled after an Iberian *tasca* (wine tavern), you'll find small tables and a stand-up bar area, where up to 40 kinds of Spanish-style marinated mushrooms, sausages, Serrano hams, salted almonds, baked artichokes, and prawns in bacon are displayed behind glass. Priced at 3€ to 8€ ($4.80–$13), they go well with beer or the Spanish wines sold here. More substantial platters, priced at 12€ to 20€ ($19–$32), include lamb tenderloins with eggplant and spits of marinated pork tenderloin served with sherry sauce. It's open daily 11am to between 1 and 2am, depending on business.

A once run-down but now gentrified nightlife destination that assembles about 20 different bars, art galleries, and restaurants into one historic site is **Kunsthof,** 70

Alaunstrasse (© **0351/8036723**), where a series of hip cafes, art galleries, and affordable restaurants line the edges of an interior courtyard. A particularly appealing bar, tapas bar, and restaurant within the complex is the Spain-inspired **El Perro** (© **0351/8036723**).

CLUBS Dance clubs that are known to virtually every 20-something resident of Dresden include **DownTown** (© **0351/8115592**) and **Groove Station** (© **0351/8029594**), set immediately adjacent to one another at Katharinenstrasse 11 and 13 (tram: 7 or 8). Clients can move freely from one to the other of this pair of cramped, sometimes convivial bars, where music rocks and rolls at high volumes and suds flow freely. Both are at their peak capacity on Friday and Saturday nights. Monday is gay and lesbian night, and on Sunday there's dinner and dancing. Both of them are open daily from 9pm "until everybody leaves." A single cover charge, ranging from 9€ to 15€ ($14–$24), depending on the night of the week, applies to both clubs.

Projekttheater Dresden, Louisenstrasse 47 (© **0351/8107600;** tram: 7 or 8), a publicly funded organization, usually, but not always, gives a live jazz performance Tuesday to Sunday at 9pm and also maintains separate areas for the presentation of avant-garde films, lectures, and art exhibitions. Don't expect a nightclub-style cabaret, as no drinks are served. Tickets, available 1 hour before show time, cost 11€ ($18) each. Call to see if there is a performance scheduled.

For an insight into Germany's newest crop of political satirists, head for the irreverent premises of **Herkules Keule,** Sternplatz 1 (© **0351/4925555;** tram: 1, 2, 4, 7, 8, or 11). Although it was well known during the heyday of the former GDR, its sometimes scathing pronouncements have reached their sharpest and shrillest since reunification. Come here if your knowledge of German is extremely good and if you're prepared for caustic, occasionally bitchy humor that touches on everything from politics to sex. Shows are presented Monday to Friday at 7:30pm and Saturday at 6 and 9pm. Admission is 9€ to 19€ ($14–$30), depending on the night of the week.

A SIDE TRIP TO THE SPREEWALD & SORB COUNTRY

For a fascinating side trip, head about an hour's drive north of Dresden to the history-rich Sorb country of Spreewald (Forest of the Spree), which has nearly 260 sq. km (101 sq. miles) of woodland, pastures, and canals. The flat, water-soaked landscape has an eerie beauty, and legends abound about spirits that inhabit the thick forests. Over a period of at least 1,000 years, the people of the region channeled the marshlands into a network of canals, streams, lakes, and irrigation channels, building their houses, barns, and chapels on the high points of otherwise swampy ground. Ethnologists consider this area a distinctive human adaptation to an unlikely landscape, and biologists appreciate the wide diversity of bird and animal life that flourishes in the lush and fertile terrain.

The area is inhabited by the Sorbs, descendants of Slavic tribes that settled here in the 6th century. They speak a language similar to Czech and Polish. The Nazis targeted the Sorbs, outlawing their language and killing many of them. It's estimated that there are still 100,000 Sorbs living in Germany, 30,000 of whom inhabit the Spreewald. They grow vegetables and fruit in a protected landscape, using labor-intensive methods even today.

The Spreewald is at its most appealing in early spring and autumn, when the crowds of sightseers depart and a spooky chill descends with the fog over these

Finds **Schloss Lübbenau Reclaimed**

Nestled deep in the Spreewald and a short walk to the boats that transport you around this region's canal network (see above) is **Schloss Lübbenau,** Schlossbezirk 6, D-0322 Lübbenau (© **03542/8730;** www.schloss-luebbenau. de; 112€–162€/$179–$259 doubles, 132€–200€/$211–$320 suites; rates include breakfast; closed first 2 weeks of Jan). Owned by the Lynar family since 1621, the castle was seized by the Nazis and later controlled by the communist government. During World War II, the property was owned by Count Wilhelm Friedrich zu Lynar, one of the key members of a conspiracy to assassinate Hitler during World War II. The attempt was unsuccessful, and the count was executed in 1944. His family fled to West Germany and later to Portugal, but they returned to reclaim their property after Germany's reunification in 1990. Today, the castle has been restored and converted into a splendid 46-room hotel and restaurant. The cozy guest rooms feature antique furnishings and the overall feel is relaxed, unpretentious luxury in a historical setting. Adjacent to the hotel, you'll find the charming and casual Orangerie, a bright, Portuguese tile-lined cafe and restaurant reflecting the Lynar family's connection to Portugal. One entire side of the long airy space features tall windows facing the lush trees of the Spreewald. The Orangerie serves traditional German and Saxon cuisine and is open May to October; hours vary. Call © **03542/8730** for details.

—*Caroline Sieg*

primeval forests and shallow medieval canals. To get here from Dresden, take Autobahn 13 north until you come to the first turnoff to Lübbenau or the second turnoff, 10km (6 miles) farther, to Lübben. From either hamlet, drive toward the *Hafen* (port). From there, tour companies will take you through the canals via a shallow-draft boat propelled by a long pole, like a Venetian gondola. The guide is often a woman in traditional dress. Several waterside cafes along the canals serve food and drink.

Boat tours cost about 20€ ($32) per person for a 2½-hour excursion through the waterways of the Sorb Country. Few people speak English. The boat-tour companies operate only April to early October, with departures scheduled every day between 9am and 4pm. The companies include Fährmannsverein "Lustige Gurken," Hafen 1 (© **03546/7122**), in Lübben; and, in Lübbenau, Spreewaldmädels, Dammstrasse 77 (© **03542/2225**).

If you're interested in paddling around the Spreewald on your own, head for **Bootsverleih Gebauer,** Lindenstrasse, Lübben (© **03546/7194**), where canoes cost around 12€ ($19) for a 2-hour rental.

The tourist office in Lübben, the main point of departure for most Spreewald cruises, is on Ernst von Houwald Damm 16 (© **03546/2433**). The tourist office in Lübbenau, a secondary point of departure, is at Ehm Welk Strasse 15 (© **03542/ 3668**).

4 Meissen ★

25km (16 miles) NW of Dresden, 174km (108 miles) S of Berlin, 85km (53 miles) E of Leipzig

This "city of porcelain" is most often visited on a day trip from Dresden, although since reunification, it now has suitable accommodations for those who'd like to spend the night and get acquainted with the area.

Meissen lies on both banks of the Elbe, with the Altstadt on the left bank. It's a very old town, dating from A.D. 929. Since 1710, Meissen has been known around the world as the center for the manufacturing of Dresden china. The early makers of this so-called "white gold" were virtually held prisoner here because the princes who ruled the city wanted to keep their secrets to themselves. Today, shoppers can find the greatest selection of porcelain in all Germany. However, not wanting to undercut their distributors in such cities as Munich or Berlin, Meissen porcelain manufacturers keep their prices about the same as elsewhere.

ESSENTIALS

GETTING THERE   By Train   Meissen Bahnhof is on the Deutsche Bundesbahn rail line, with connections departing for Dresden at 30- to 45-minute intervals throughout the day and evening. For rail information, call ✆ **01805/996633.**

By Bus   Regional buses connecting Dresden with Meissen are operated by **Verkehrsgesellschaft Meissen.** Consult the tourist office in Meissen for a schedule of connections or ask at the tourist office in Dresden.

By Car   Access is via the E40 Autobahn from Dresden or the E49 from Leipzig.

By Boat   If you're in Dresden in summer, you can go to Meissen by boat in about an hour and enjoy the scenery along the Elbe. The **Sächsischer Dampfschiffahrt,** Hertha Lindner Strasse 10 (✆ **0351/866090**), leaves daily between May and late October at 9:45am from Dresden's Brühl Terrace, the fortified embankment on the other side of the Hofkirche. Boats arrive in Meissen 2 hours later. Waterborne returns to Dresden from Meissen depart at 2:45pm.

VISITOR INFORMATION   Contact **Tourist-Information Meissen,** Markt 3 (✆ **03521/41940**), November to March Monday to Friday 10am to 5pm and Saturday 10am to 3pm (closed Sat in Jan); April to October, hours are Monday to Friday 10am to 6pm, and Saturday and Sunday 10am to 4pm.

WHERE TO STAY

Welcome Park Hotel ★   This is the only first-rate hotel in town. For decades, Meissen didn't have a suitable hotel, but this Art Nouveau villa filled the void in the early 1990s. You can request a room in the original villa, although most accommodations are in the more sterile modern annexes. A suite on the top floor under the eaves is perfect for romantic couples. Most rooms open onto panoramic vistas.

Hafenstrasse 27–31 (on the Elbe, directly across the water from the castle), D-01662 Meissen. ✆ **03521/72250.** Fax 03521/722904. www.welcome-hotel-meissen.de. 97 units. 100€–145€ ($160–$232) double; 180€–210€ ($288–$336) suite. AE, DC, MC, V. Parking 10€ ($16). **Amenities:** Restaurant; bar; indoor heated pool; fitness center; whirlpool; sauna; solarium; room service; massage; laundry service; dry cleaning; nonsmoking rooms; rooms for those w/limited mobility. *In room:* A/C, TV, minibar, hair dryer.

WHERE TO DINE

Romantik Restaurant Vincenz Richter ★ GERMAN/SAXON   This charming, hearty, and traditional restaurant is in a vine-sheathed 1523 building. It has a hardworking, devoted staff and a cozy setting of Germanic charm. The bar stocks an impressive inventory of local wines, and the kitchens serve ample portions of Saxon food.

An der Frauenkirche 12 (uphill from Meissen's Marktplatz). © 03521/453285. Reservations recommended. Main courses 12€–18€ ($19–$29); fixed-price menu 33€ ($53). AE, DC, MC, V. Tues–Sat noon–11pm; Sun noon–6pm.

EXPLORING MEISSEN

Towering over the town is the Gothic-style **Dom** ☆, Domplatz 7 (© 03521/ 452490), one of the smallest cathedrals in Germany, built between 1260 and 1450. Until the year 1400, the bishops of the diocese of Meissen had their seat next to the cathedral. Later, Saxon rulers were buried here, the first in 1428. Inside are works of art, including a painting by Lucas Cranach the Elder, along with rare Meissen porcelain. The cathedral has been Protestant since the 16th century. Admission costs 2.50€ ($4) per person. A 30-minute German-language guided tour, departing at virtually any time you specify, costs 5€ ($8) per person. Hours are April to October daily 9am to 6pm, and November to March daily 10am to 4pm.

Sharing the castle quarter with the cathedral is **Albrechtsburg Castle** ☆, Domplatz 1 (© 03521/47070), where the first Meissen porcelain was made. Construction of the castle began in 1471 and went on intermittently until 1525. From 1710 to 1864 it was the site of the Meissen Porcelain Manufactory. It is open March to October daily 10am to 6pm, and November to February daily 10am to 5pm (closed weekdays 2 weeks in Jan). Admission is 5€ ($8) for adults, 2.50€ ($4) for children 6 to 16, and free for children 5 and under.

But the prime attraction in town is the **Porzellan-Manufaktur** ☆, Talstrasse 9 (© 03521/4680). At this factory, you can see how the centuries-old process of making Meissen china is still carried on, using the same traditional designs. You can rent a prerecorded audio device, priced at 9€ ($14), which will direct you (in any of several languages) on a self-guided tour lasting between 30 and 60 minutes, depending on how fast you move through the premises. You can visit the on-site **Porcelain Museum,** with 3,000 pieces, plus the workshop. Other than the cost of the guided tour, admission is free. The factory, its museum, and the audio machines are available May to October daily 9am to 6pm, and November to April daily 9am to 5pm.

SHOPPING   Porzellan-Manufaktur (see above) has recently crafted, hand-painted porcelain, which they'll ship home for you. However, don't expect prices to be much cheaper than in other German cities. The same organization also maintains a shop, with basically the same prices, in the center of Meissen at Burgstrasse 6 (© 03521/ 458015).

Franconia & the German Danube

The Renaissance swept across all of Germany, but it concentrated its full force on that part of northern Bavaria that had once been a Frankish kingdom. Franconia today contains many of Germany's greatest medieval and Renaissance treasures. Its hillsides are dotted with well-preserved medieval castles, monasteries, and churches. From the region's feudal cities sprang some of Germany's` most significant artists—Albrecht Dürer, Lucas Cranach the Elder, Veit Stoss, Adam Krafft. Today, Franconia draws music lovers to its annual **Mozart Festival** in Würzburg (see chapter 8) and **Wagner Festival** in Bayreuth (p. 46).

Franconia owes much of its beauty to the limestone range on the southern edge of the province. Between these hills and the edge of the Bavarian Forest is the upper **Danube,** which begins about 30km (20 miles) from Regensburg. The Danube gradually builds force from the smaller streams flowing out of the Alps and Swabian Jura, and by the time it reaches the Austrian border, at Passau, it's large enough to carry commercial ships and barges. Although not as important to the German economy as the Rhine, the Danube was responsible for the growth of several influential towns.

Franconia's countryside is equally compelling, especially the forest called **Frankenwald.** This scenic region stretches from the Bohemian Forest on the border of the Czech Republic in the east to the fringes of Frankfurt in the west. The most beautiful part is Frankisches Schweiz, the "Switzerland of Franconia," bounded by Bamberg on the west, Bayreuth in the east, and Kulmbach in the north.

OUTDOORS IN FRANCONIA The best **hiking** is in the northern parts of the province. Even the Germans, who rush to the Bavarian Alps, often overlook the some 25,000 hiking trails in Franconia. Local tourist officials have details of the best hikes in their area. Most trails are found in Germany's largest park, **Altmühltal Nature Park,** and in the Frankenwald.

You can also explore Franconia by **bike.** At all area train stations, you can rent a mountain bike for 10€ ($16) per day, half price with a valid train ticket. Local tourist offices have information on the best biking routes. The **Danube Bicycle Path** cuts right through Regensburg; cyclists can ride along its 650km (400 miles) from the river's source to Passau. The Regensburg tourist office (see "Visitor Information," under Regensburg, later in this chapter) is the best source when organizing a biking trip. You can even go as far as Vienna. The **Five Rivers Bicycle Path** is a 3- to 5-day circular route through the valleys of the Danube, Naab, and Vils. This path links Regensburg with Amberg and Nürnberg.

1 Bayreuth ⟨★

230km (143 miles) N of Munich, 64km (40 miles) E of Bamberg, 92km (57 miles) NE of Nürnberg

Bayreuth lies in a wide valley on the upper basin of the Roter Main River. In the town's early years, the counts of Andechs-Meranien gave it the protection of a fortified castle. In the Middle Ages, Bayreuth became the property of the Hohenzollerns and grew into one of the leading centers of this part of Germany. It's now the capital of the district of upper Franconia.

Bayreuth is forever associated with **Richard Wagner** (1813–83). The town is worth a visit for its baroque and rococo architectural treasures, even if you're not interested in its favorite son, but most people come here because it's the home of the annual Wagner opera festival, and the premier location for Wagnerian performance in the world.

Wagner's "endless melody" is still said to pervade Bayreuth. The composer's early success caught the eye of Ludwig II, king of Bavaria. With the king's support, Wagner opened his first **Festspielhaus** in 1876, in an old residence in Bayreuth; later he built and designed a new Festspielhaus, suited especially for his own operas. Wagner not only composed the music for his music dramas but also wrote the librettos and designed the sets. *Tristan and Isolde* remains perhaps his most daring opera; his best known is the four-opera *Ring of the Nibelungs*.

ESSENTIALS

GETTING THERE   By Train   The **Bayreuth Hauptbahnhof** is on the main Nürnberg-Pegnitz-Bayreuth and Bayreuth-Weiden rail lines, with good connections. Express trains arrive from Nürnberg every hour. For information, call ✆ **0180/5996633.**

By Bus   Long-distance bus service to Berlin and Munich is provided by **Bayern Express & P. Kuhn Berlin GmbH.** For information, call ✆ **030/86096240.** Local and regional buses in the area are run by **OVF Omnibusverkehr Franken GmbH** in Bayreuth (✆ **0921/789730**).

By Car   Access by car is via the A9 Autobahn from the north and south.

VISITOR INFORMATION   Contact **Tourist-Information,** Luitpoldplatz 9 (✆ **0921/88588;** www.tourismus.bayreuth.de), Monday to Friday 9am to 6pm and Saturday 9am to 2pm. From May to October, it is also open Sunday 10am to 2pm.

GETTING AROUND   Many streets within the historic core of Bayreuth are exclusively reserved for pedestrians, and that, coupled with the city's small size, makes walking between points of interest both easy and efficient. Whereas the centerpiece of the old town is Marktplatz, the geographical landmark of the new town is the Hauptbahnhof. Buses no. 1 through 12 crisscross the town, and of those, about half follow a route that moves between those two points. If in doubt, ask someone at the tourist office or waiting at a bus stop. One-way bus fares for points within the town and its outskirts cost 1.70€ ($2.70).

WHERE TO STAY
EXPENSIVE
Goldener Anker ⟨★★   This inn is popular locally and has a similar comfort level to the Bayerischer Hof. It has hosted distinguished composers, singers, and conductors for more than 200 years. The framed photographs on the time-seasoned, oak-paneled walls are museum treasures. The guest book includes signatures of such notables as

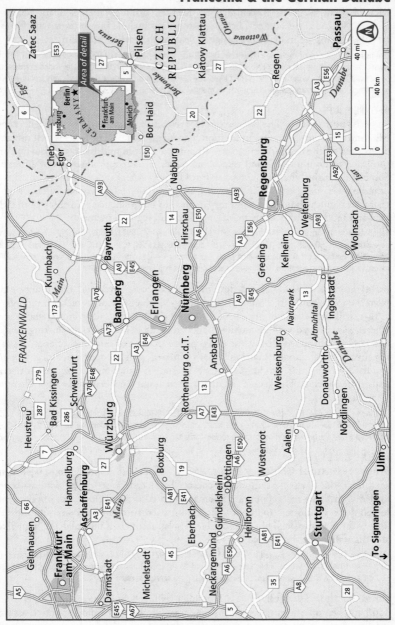

Richard Strauss, Arturo Toscanini, Fritz Kreisler, Bruno Walter, William Saroyan, Lauritz Melchior, and Patrice Chereau. Furnishings include fine antiques and Oriental rugs. Rooms are individually designed, each with a small bathroom.

Opernstrasse 6 (next door to the Markgräfliches Opernhaus), 95444 Bayreuth. © 0921/65051. Fax 0921/65500. www.anker-bayreuth.de. 42 units. 140€–198€ ($224–$317) double; 450€ ($720) suite. Rates include continental breakfast. AE, DC, MC, V. Parking 10€ ($16). Closed Dec 20–Jan 15. Bus: 7. **Amenities:** Restaurant; room service; babysitting; laundry service; nonsmoking rooms. *In room:* TV, hair dryer.

MODERATE

Bayerischer Hof ⊛ The Bayerischer Hof remains a special favorite of Wagner fans, who find it the most convenient location for arriving by rail. The hotel is well run and offers some of the best service in town. Rooms range from midsize to spacious and are furnished in both modern and traditional pieces, usually reproductions of antiques. Some of the furnishings are shipped in from France; others are in the more functional Scandinavian modern style. The hotel dining facilities have even more charm and character than the hotel itself, and they're open to nonresidents, who enjoy both classical and modern dishes from an international and regional menu.

Bahnhofstrasse 14 (in front of the train station), 95444 Bayreuth. © 0921/78600. Fax 0921/7860560. www. bayerischer-hof.de. 50 units. 98€–120€ ($157–$192) double; 265€ ($424) suite. AE, DC, MC, V. Parking 11€ ($18). **Amenities:** Restaurant; bar; indoor heated pool; sauna; room service; babysitting; laundry service; nonsmoking rooms; rooms for those w/limited mobility. *In room:* TV, minibar, hair dryer.

Hotel Lohmühle ⊛ Located next to the Mühlbach River and a 5-minute walk from the town center, this hotel opened in 1979, when one of its oldest buildings (a 17th-c. half-timbered mill once used for tanning hides and later grinding grains into wheat) was enlarged with an architecturally compatible (new-but-old-looking) annex and radically upgraded. Today, the two separate sections of this hotel offer an appealing mix of old-fashioned Franconia that's softened with modern amenities, a polite and hardworking staff, and lots of regional charm. Guest rooms are cozy, comfortable, and rustic looking. The hotel's restaurant is recommended separately in "Where to Dine," below.

Badstrasse 37, 95444 Bayreuth. © 0921/53060. Fax 0921/5306469. www.hotel-lohmuehle.de. 42 units. 105€–168€ ($168–$269) double. Children age 8 and under stay free in parent's room. AE, DC, MC, V. Parking 5€ ($8). **Amenities:** Restaurant; bar; nonsmoking rooms. *In room:* TV, minibar.

INEXPENSIVE

Brauerei-Gasthof Goldener Löwe ⊛ *Value* This is an unpretentious, well-managed inn—the town's best affordable choice. The facade is set off by window boxes loaded with flame-red geraniums. Rooms have a Bavarian theme, with checker-patterned down comforters and light-grained pinewood trim. Guest rooms and shower-only bathrooms are small but comfortable. The atmosphere is informal and homelike, and the staff is very hospitable.

Kulmbacher Strasse 30, 95445 Bayreuth. © 0921/746060. Fax 0921/47777. www.goldener-loewe-bayreuth.de. 13 units. 75€–105€ ($120–$168) double; 90€–110€ ($144–$176) suite. Rates include continental breakfast. AE, DC, MC, V. Free parking. Bus: 2. **Amenities:** Dining room; bar; room service. *In room:* TV.

Hotel-Gasthof Spiegelmühle This high-ceilinged building, which dates from 1555 and was once a working mill, is now transformed into a modest and unassuming little hotel, kept clean and comfortable. In spite of its lack of pretensions, well-known conductors and singers often stay here during the festival. Many of the rooms are small but quite adequate, each with a compact, shower-only bathroom.

Kulmbacher Strasse 28, 95445 Bayreuth. © 0921/41091. Fax 0921/47320. www.hotel-spiegelmuehle.de. 13 units. 80€–95€ ($128–$152) double. Rates include continental breakfast. AE, DC, MC, V. Free parking. Bus: 6. **Amenities:** Breakfast room; bar; beer garden; room service; nonsmoking rooms. *In room:* TV, coffeemaker, hair dryer.

WHERE TO DINE
EXPENSIVE
Jagdschloss Thiergarten ❧ CONTINENTAL   No one makes a pilgrimage to Bayreuth for its restaurants, but this one stands out. The building, which lies outside the center of town, was constructed as a private hunting lodge and has a hexagonal baroque tower. The cuisine is in the culinary traditions of France, Italy, and Germany. Menu items might include lobster risotto with basil, stuffed halibut with caviar sauce and kohlrabi noodles, and terrine of sweetbreads. There's an impressive wine list.

The establishment is also a cozy hotel with eight large rooms boasting all the modern accoutrements. Doubles run 140€ to 180€ ($224–$288), including breakfast.

Oberthiergärtner Strasse 36 (6km/4 miles south of Bayreuth center). © 09209/9840. Fax 09209/98429. Reservations recommended. Main courses 12€–26€ ($19–$42); fixed-price menus 36€ ($58) for 3 courses, 42€ ($67) for 4 courses. AE, MC, V. Daily noon–2pm and 6–10pm. Bus: 11.

MODERATE
Gendarmerie ❧ FRENCH/FRANCONIAN   Within the town center itself, the previously recommended Bayerischer Hof contains the town's most intriguing dining choices. The hotel has a selection of restaurants offering both French and Franconian cooking. The Hans-Sachs-Stube, an air-conditioned replica of an old inn, has walls covered with pictures of famous opera singers who have performed in Bayreuth or dined here. You can also dine at the hotel's bistro, Spanische Stube. The best cuisine, however, is found at the Gendarmerie, the main a la carte restaurant. The food is superbly precise and refined here, combining inventive French dishes with the best of Franconian fare. Each dining room has a different decor, although the seasonally adjusted menu is the same in all three.

Bahnhofstrasse 14 (in front of the train station). © 0921/78600. Reservations recommended. Main courses 12€–22€ ($19–$35); fixed-price menu 17€ ($27). AE, DC, MC, V. Daily 7am–1am.

INEXPENSIVE
Oskar's (Value) FRANCONIAN/INTERNATIONAL   It's cozy, it's popular, and it offers some of the best value in a town that's not particularly noted for reasonable prices. Set in the heart of town, Oskar's has a large central dining room, designed like a greenhouse and flooded with sunlight, and a trio of smaller, cozier *Stuben* that have wood paneling and a sense of updated Franconian tradition. Menu items include lots of old-fashioned Franconian favorites, such as loin of beef with horseradish sauce and Bayreuther-style *Klos* (potato dumplings), roasted pork, schnitzels, baked salmon, and sauerbraten. There's also a short list of pastas, soups, and salads. Whenever a particular vegetable or fruit comes into season, expect lots of emphasis on it in the list of daily (or weekly) specials.

Maximilianstrasse 33. © 0921/5160553. Reservations not necessary. Main courses 6.50€–16€ ($10–$26). MC, V. Mon–Sat 8am–1am; Sun 9am–1am.

Restaurant Lohmühle FRANCONIAN   Set in the previously recommended hotel, this cozy and well-managed restaurant is partially contained in what was built in the 1600s as a mill. The rest is in a modern (but antique-looking) extension that was added in the late 1970s. Today, views from its tables encompass the Mühlbach

River, and its cuisine focuses on the specialties of Franconia, particularly in the use of freshwater fish such as carp and trout. The fish are kept in large holding tanks and aquariums, and can be prepared in virtually any way you specify.

In the Hotel Lohmühle, Badstrasse 37. ℭ **0921/53060.** Reservations recommended. Main courses 10€–18€ ($16–$29). AE, DC, MC, V. June–Aug and Nov–Dec Mon–Sat noon–2pm and 6–10pm, Sun noon–2pm; Jan–May and Sept–Oct Mon–Fri 6–10pm, Sat noon–2pm and 6–10pm, Sun noon–2pm.

THE BAYREUTHER FESTSPIELE

The Richard Wagner opera festival takes place between mid-July and the end of August. If you arrive in Bayreuth then, you may think that the entire town has turned out to pay homage to the great composer, who built his opera house here, lived here, and was buried here following his death in Venice.

Tickets to the festival operas are almost impossible to obtain (there's an 8-year waiting list) but can sometimes be booked as part of a package tour. Tickets cost 50€ to 210€ ($80–$336). *Warning:* During the 5 weeks of the festival, hoteliers raise their rates quite a bit. Always firmly establish the rate before booking a room and make reservations far in advance.

EXPLORING BAYREUTH

Altes Schloss Eremitage (Hermitage) ⍟   The margraves of Bayreuth also had a pleasure palace outside the city, reached via a road lined with chestnut trees that were planted in honor of Frederick the Great. Georg Wilhelm built it in 1718 as a retreat. The castle is set in a park, full of formal as well as English-style gardens. In them, you can see the New Palace of the Hermitage, built around 1750. Its columns are covered with polychrome pebbles in mosaic style, a unique structural element in German architecture. A part of the palace becomes a cafe in summer and sometimes hosts painting exhibitions.

On Rte. 22, 5km (3 miles) northeast of Bayreuth toward Weiden. ℭ **0921/759690.** Gardens free; palace 3€ ($4.80) adults, free for those 17 and under. Gardens daily 24 hr. Palace Apr–Sept daily 9am–6pm; Oct 1–15 daily 10am–4pm. Bus: 22 (runs every 20 min. during the day).

Festspielhaus   The operas of Wagner are dispensed like a musical Eucharist to Wagnerian pilgrims at the Festspielhaus, at the northern edge of town. The theater, designed by the composer himself, is not a beautiful building, but it's an ideal Wagnerian facility, with a huge stage capable of swallowing up Valhalla, and excellent, beautifully balanced acoustics throughout the auditorium. Because of the design, the orchestra never overwhelms the singers. The festival was opened here in 1876 with the epic *Ring* cycle. When the composer died in Venice, his wife, Cosima, took over. In the post–World War II era, Wagner's grandsons, Wolfgang and Wieland, have produced the operas, with exciting avant-garde staging and the best musicians and singers from all over the world.

Am Festspielhügel 2–3. ℭ **0921/78780.** Guided tour 5€ ($8). Tours offered in German only; English leaflets are available. Apr–Sept Tues–Sun at 10, 10:45am, 2:15, and 3pm; Oct and Dec–Mar Tues–Sun at 10:45am and 2:30pm. Tours may not be given during rehearsals or at festival time. Bus: 5.

Franz-Liszt-Museum   Wagner's father-in-law was Franz Liszt (1811–86), the great Hungarian-born composer and piano virtuoso who revolutionized piano playing. His daughter, Cosima, married Wagner. Liszt is buried in the Bayreuth cemetery. The museum, which opened on October 22 (Liszt's birthday) in 1993, shows the room where the composer died. It also displays memorabilia related to his life and work.

Wahnfriedstrasse 9. ℂ 0921/5166488. Admission 1.60€ ($2.60). Sept–June daily 10am–noon and 2–5pm; July–Aug daily 10am–5pm. Bus: 2 to Villa Wahnfried.

Markgräfliches Opernhaus ⟨⚹⟩

This is the only authentic baroque theater in Germany. It's still in its fine original condition. Behind its weathered wooden doors is a world of gilded canopies and columns, ornate sconces, and chandeliers. The house was built under the auspices of the Margravine Wilhelmine, who was known for her taste and her cultivation of the arts; her name has been given to a special baroque style called *Wilhelmian*. Her brother, Frederick the Great, formally opened the theater in 1748. Up until that time, operas (notably those of Telemann) had been performed in the court theater. Today, the opera house, which seats 520, is used for Bayreuth's other festival: the **Franconian Weeks' Festival,** usually held late in May. Concerts are also given during the summer.

Opernstrasse. ℂ 0921/7596922. Guided tours (in German only) 5€ ($8) adults, free for children. Apr–Sept daily 9am–6pm; Oct–Mar daily 10am–4pm. Bus: 2.

Neues Schloss (New Palace)

The well-preserved Neues Schloss in the center of town also shows the influence and enlightened taste of the talented and cultured Wilhelmine (1709–58). This baroque palace dates from the mid–18th century. The apartments of Wilhelmine and her husband, Margrave Friedrich, are decorated in a late-rococo style with period furnishings.

Ludwigstrasse (1 block from the Markgräfliches Opernhaus). ℂ 0921/759690. Guided tours (in German, with English leaflets available) 5€ ($8) adults, free for ages 17 and under. Tours given Apr–Sept daily 9am–6pm; Oct–Mar Tues–Sun 10am–4pm. Bus: 2.

Richard-Wagner-Museum (Wahnfried) ⟨⚹⟩

This was Wagner's residence from 1874 until the time of his death in 1883, and the house remained in his family until 1966. Only the front of the original Wahnfried—which means "illusory peace"—remains intact. On display is a wide range of Wagner memorabilia, including manuscripts, pianos, furnishings, artifacts, and even a death mask. If you walk to the end of the garden, fronting the rotunda, you'll see the graves of the composer and his wife.

Richard-Wagner-Strasse 48 (south of the town center). ℂ 0921/757280. www.wagnermuseum.de. Admission 4.50€ ($7.20) adults, 2€ ($3.20) students at festival time (4€/$6.40 and 2€/$3.20 the rest of the year). Apr–Oct daily 9am–5pm (to 8pm Tues and Thurs); Nov–Mar daily 10am–5pm. Bus: 2.

2 Bamberg ⟨⚹⟩⟨⚹⟩

238km (148 miles) NW of Munich, 61km (38 miles) NW of Nürnberg, 97km (60 miles) NE of Würzburg

This little city is one of the gems of Franconia, although visitors often pass it by. Bamberg is set in the rolling Franconian hills where the Regnitz River flows into the Main. It's loaded with attractions, including numerous architectural treasures, and suffered very little damage in World War II.

In the Middle Ages, Bamberg was a powerful ecclesiastical center. Originally, it was two towns divided by the river: the ecclesiastical town of the prince-bishopric, of which it was the capital for 800 years, and the secular town of the burghers. Bamberg's architecture reflects more than 1,000 years of building, with styles ranging from Romanesque to Gothic, Renaissance to baroque, up to the eclecticism of the 19th century. There are narrow cobblestone streets, ornate mansions and palaces, and impressive churches.

Today, Bamberg and beer go together like barley and hops. The town has been called "a beer drinker's Eden" (there are more breweries here than in Munich). The average Bamberger drinks 190 liters (50 gal.) of beer a year, making the rest of the German people look like teetotalers by comparison. Beer lovers come from afar for Rauchbier, a smoked beer first brewed in 1536.

ESSENTIALS

GETTING THERE   By Train   The **Bamberg Bahnhof** is on the Stuttgart-Hof and the Berlin-Munich rail lines, with frequent connections in both directions. Most visitors arrive from Nürnberg (see "Nürnberg (Nuremberg)," below) in just 1 hour. There are direct trains running from Bayreuth to Bamberg. For information and schedules, call © **01805/996633.**

By Car   Access is via the B22 from Würzburg or the A73 from Nürnberg.

VISITOR INFORMATION   Contact the **Bamberg Tourist Information Office,** Geyerswöthstrasse 3 (© **0951/2976200;** www.bamberg.info). Office hours are April to December Monday to Friday 9:30am to 6pm, Saturday 9:30am to 2:30pm, and Sunday 9:30am to 2:30pm.

GETTING AROUND   A well-run network of buses fans out from the Zentralomnibusbahnhof on Promenadestrasse, next to the railway station. A single ride for Zone 1 costs 1.20€ ($1.90); a single ride for Zone 1 and 2 goes for 2.10€ ($3.40). For more information, head to I Punkt (© **0951/9685872**) in the railway station, open Monday to Thursday 7am to 7pm and Friday 7:30am to noon. Bus maps and tickets can be purchased at the station or from machines at stops along the route.

WHERE TO STAY
EXPENSIVE
Bamberger Hof Bellevue 🖈   This hotel plays second fiddle to the Welcome Hotel Residenzschloss (see below), but the service and accommodations of both are roughly on par. A great old palace of stone, crowned by a tower and facing a little park, it's good for soaking up the mellow atmosphere of yesteryear. Try to book one of the large rooms with sitting areas. Each unit is well furnished and attractively maintained, most often with a generous-size bathroom with tub/shower combo.

Schönleinsplatz 4, 96047 Bamberg. © 0951/98550. Fax 0951/985562. www.bambergerhof.de. 50 units. 165€–185€ ($264–$296) double; 195€–450€ ($312–$720) suite. Rates include buffet breakfast. AE, DC, MC, V. Parking 15€ ($24). Bus: 8 or 12. **Amenities:** Restaurant; bar; lounge; room service; laundry service; dry cleaning; nonsmoking rooms; rooms for those w/limited mobility. *In room:* TV, minibar, hair dryer.

Romantik Hotel-Weinhaus Messerschmitt 🖈🖈   This hotel in the heart of the city, beloved by traditionalists, is Bamberg's most romantic choice. However, some of its antique appeal as an old German inn has been diminished by the addition of 50 new bedrooms in a modern wing. These are the most up-to-date and among the most comfortable in town. The main building of the hotel remains one of the oldest structures in the area, dating from 1422. The present exterior is 18th century, a gabled expanse of pale blue and yellow with baroque-style window frames. Inside, the mellow decor includes paneling, ceramic ovens, and antiques. Many of the beds have meticulously crafted headboards. The owner and his staff are very helpful.

Langestrasse 41, 96047 Bamberg. © 0951/297800. Fax 0951/2978029. www.hotel-messerschmitt.de. 69 units. 130€–170€ ($208–$272) double; 220€ ($352) junior suite. Rates include buffet breakfast. AE, DC, MC, V. Parking

8€ ($13). **Amenities:** Restaurant; lounge; sauna; steam room; Jacuzzi; nonsmoking rooms; 1 room for those w/limited mobility. *In room:* TV, minibar.

Welcome Hotel Residenzschloss ᚷᚷ   This elegant hotel, a blend of old and new, is the best choice in town. It lies on a bank of the Regnitz, near the Altstadt and across from the Bamberg Symphony Orchestra building. The building, with its ocher-colored baroque walls, was constructed by the local archbishop in 1787 as a hospital. Today, the original hospital chapel continues to host local weddings. A less glamorous modern annex is connected to the main building by a glass-sided breezeway. The annex contains perfectly functional rooms, but those in the main building are midsize to spacious and decorated in a classical elegant style with supremely comfortable furnishings.

Untere Sandstrasse 32, 96049 Bamberg. ℭ 0951/60910. Fax 0951/6091701. www.residenzschloss.com. 180 units. 137€–192€ ($219–$307) double; 285€–330€ ($456–$528) suite. Rates include buffet breakfast. AE, DC, MC, V. Parking 8€ ($13). Bus: 26. **Amenities:** 2 restaurants; bar; gym; sauna; solarium; steam room; room service; babysitting; laundry service; dry cleaning; nonsmoking rooms; 1 room for those w/limited mobility. *In room:* TV, Wi-Fi, minibar, hair dryer.

MODERATE
Barock Hotel am Dom ᚷ *(Value)*   This hotel offers some of the same style, tradition, and romance of the pacesetters above, but at a better price. Advance reservations are recommended. The owners have retained every detail of the original ornamented facade and renovated key areas of the interior. The result is a winning combination of baroque elements in a well-lit modernized building. Guest rooms are attractively furnished, if a bit cramped, as are the shower-only bathrooms. The comfort level and maintenance are high. Rates include a nourishing breakfast served in the old cellar, with tables under the plastered stone vaulting.

Vorderer Bach 4, 96049 Bamberg. ℭ 0951/54031. Fax 0951/54021. www.barockhotel.com. 19 units. 93€–100€ ($149–$160) double. Rates include buffet breakfast. AE, DC, MC, V. Bus: 8 or 12. **Amenities:** Breakfast room; lounge. *In room:* TV, minibar, hair dryer.

Hotel National   The National is still a favorite, though it no longer enjoys the renown it used to. Modernization has removed some of its quaint charm, and it lacks the style of the Romantik Hotel-Weinhaus Messerschmitt (see above), but the price is right and the rooms are first rate, each with a tidily kept bathroom, most often with a tub/shower combination. With its black mansard roof, iron balconies, baroque and classical detailing, and opulent public rooms, the hotel is attractive, if small. It has well-maintained and traditionally furnished rooms that tend to provide a comfortable stay.

Luitpoldstrasse 37, 96052 Bamberg. ℭ 0951/509980. Fax 0951/22436. www.hotel-national-bamberg.de. 41 units. 90€–110€ ($144–$176) double; 110€–120€ ($176–$192) suite. Children 7 and under stay free in parent's room. Rates include buffet breakfast. AE, DC, MC, V. Parking 7€ ($11). Bus: 5. **Amenities:** Restaurant; bar; room service; laundry service; dry cleaning; nonsmoking rooms. *In room:* TV, Wi-Fi, minibar, hair dryer.

INEXPENSIVE
Hotel Garni Graupner   This hotel continues a tradition started in the 14th century of accepting overnight guests. It's your best bet if you find the properties listed above a bit pricey. You can usually get a room here, perhaps with a view over the Altstadt, and it will be clean and decent, although short on charm. If the main hotel is full, guests are directed to the lackluster 1960s annex, about 8 blocks away, across the canal. It offers 10 modern rooms for the same price charged in the main hotel. The same family also owns a rose-garden cafe a stone's throw from the cathedral.

Langestrasse 5, 96047 Bamberg. © 0951/980400. Fax 0951/9804040. www.hotel-graupner.de. 30 units, 26 with bathroom. 70€ ($112) double without bathroom; 75€–88€ ($120–$141) double with bathroom; 95€ ($152) junior suite. Rates include buffet breakfast. AE, MC, V. Parking 3€–6€ ($4.80–$9.60). Bus: 1, 2, 4, 8, or 16. **Amenities:** Breakfast room; cafe; lounge; nonsmoking rooms. *In room:* TV, hair dryer.

WHERE TO DINE

Historischer Brauereiausschank Schlenkerla FRANCONIAN Diners congregate here much as they did in 1678, when the place was a brewery. The decor is rustic, with long wooden tables and smallish chairs. The price is right, and the *gemütlich* (cozy) atmosphere is genuine. Unpretentious Franconian fare is served, including local dishes such as *Bierbrauervesper* (smoked meat and sour-milk cheese) and *Rauchschinken* (smoked ham). Wash them down with the hearty malt, Rauchbier, which has an intense smoky aroma and flavor.

Dominikanerstrasse 6. © 0951/56060. Main courses 6€–10€ ($9.60–$16). No credit cards. Wed–Mon 9:30am–11:30pm. Closed Jan 7–21. Bus: 26.

Romantik Restaurant-Weinhaus Messerschmitt ✦ FRANCONIAN/INTERNATIONAL You can dine better here, and in a more refined atmosphere, than anywhere else in town. This pleasant restaurant is more than 160 years old. The cuisine is presented simply but is remarkably well made. Menu items vary, depending on what ingredients are available. Freshwater fish (kept in an aquarium) and game are two of the specialties. You may find some of the offerings, such as eels in dill sauce, a bit too authentic, but the Franconian duck is a terrific choice.

Langestrasse 41. © 0951/297800. Main courses 16€–28€ ($26–$45). AE, DC, MC, V. Daily 11am–11pm. Bus: 1 or 2.

EXPLORING BAMBERG

Alte Hofhaltung, a Renaissance imperial and Episcopal palace, with a courtyard surrounded by late-Gothic framework buildings, dominates the center square. **Altes Rathaus** ✦ is the strangest town hall in Germany. Determined not to play favorites between the ecclesiastical and secular sections of the city, the town authorities built this Gothic structure on its own little island in the middle of the Regnitz River, halfway between the two factions—a true middle-of-the-road (or river) political stand. From the island, you get the best view of the old fishermen's houses along the banks in the section called "Little Venice."

Alte Hofhaltung The palace lies on the north side of Bamberg's great cathedral. Although stripped of a lot of its former glory, it is still an impressive half-timbered pile in the Gothic style, with a spacious courtyard and Renaissance styling. Sometimes special events are staged in this courtyard. Ask at the tourist office for more information. Inside the palace are the remains of the original 11th-century Diet (Assembly) hall. The palace is noted for its lovely rooms, such as the frescoed Kaisersaal, the main banqueting hall, or Chinesisches Kabinet, the latter salon known for its walls of marquetry. Don't miss the rose garden.

The building itself is more intriguing than its on-site Historisches Museum (Historical Museum), filled with artifacts, documents, and maps of the history of Bamberg. To fully appreciate this museum, you must either be fluent in German, be writing a book on the history of Bamberg, and/or view the city as the place of origin of your ancestors.

Domplatz 8. © 0951/5190746. Admission 3.10€ ($5). May–Oct Tues–Sun 9am–5pm.

Kaiserdom (Imperial Cathedral) 🍂🍂 This cathedral on a hillside was begun in 1215 in Romanesque and early-Gothic style. It has a double chancel, the eastern one raised on a terrace to compensate for the slope. The massive towers at the four corners of the church dominate Bamberg's skyline. The interior contains some fine religious art. Best known is the 13th-century equestrian statue, the **Bamberger Reiter,** which represents the idealized Christian king of the Middle Ages. Among the many tombs is that of Emperor Heinrich II, who erected the original cathedral. Sculptor Tilman Riemenschneider labored more than a decade over this masterpiece of a tomb, as well as the one devoted to the emperor's wife, Kunigunde (who was suspected of adultery, commemorated in a scene on the tomb). In the west chancel is the only papal tomb north of the Alps, containing the remains of Pope Clement II, who died in 1047. The rich cathedral treasury may be seen in the adjoining **Diözesanmuseum.**

Domplatz. 🕾 **0951/502330.** Free admission. May–Oct Mon–Fri 9:30am–6pm, Sat 9:30–11:30am and 12:45–6pm, Sun 12:30–1:45pm and 2:45–6pm; Nov–Apr Mon–Sat 9:30am–5pm, Sun 12:30–1:45pm and 2:45–5pm. Diözesanmuseum 3€ ($4.80) adults, 2€ ($3.20) students and children ages 8–14, free for children 7 and under. Diözesanmuseum Tues–Sun 10am–5pm. Bus: 10.

Neue Residenz 🍂 Opposite the Alte Hofhaltung is the 17th-century Neue Residenz, a much larger palace of prince-bishops, showing both Renaissance and baroque influences, and the site of one of the most famous unsolved mysteries in Germany. In 1815, a corpse found beneath the windows of the palace turned out to be the body of Marshal Berthier, Napoleon's chief of staff, who retired here after Napoleon was exiled to Elba. No one knows if Berthier was murdered or committed suicide. Upstairs are works by German masters. On the second floor are the former **Imperial Apartments,** with Gobelin tapestries, parquet floors, and baroque furnishings. The **Emperors' Hall** has portraits and frescoes.

Domplatz 8. 🕾 **0951/519390.** Admission 4€ ($6.40) adults, 3€ ($4.80) children. Apr–Sept daily 9am–6pm; Oct–Mar daily 10am–4pm. Bus: 10.

SHOPPING

The primary shopping district in Bamberg is by the cathedral, where you will find stores of all kinds, including more than a dozen antiques shops and numerous galleries. An antiques store that has it all, **Sebok,** Untere Königstrasse 21 (🕾 **0951/202593**), offers paintings, books, furniture, fine jewelry, silver, glass, toys, watches, clocks, and more. Auctions are held every 2 months, with the summer auction falling in July. If you're interested in local ceramics, go to **Topferladen,** Untere Brücke 1 (🕾 **0951/56913**), where you'll find ceramic candleholders, cups, dinnerware, vases, and garden statuary.

BAMBERG AFTER DARK

Sinfonie an der Regnitz, Mussstrasse 1 (🕾 **0951/9647200**), is home to the Bamberg Symphony Orchestra from September to May. From the last week in June to mid-July, there's a summer festival with weekend symphonic concerts. Tickets are 20€ to 40€ ($32–$64).

Hofburg Repertory Theater performs at the **E. T. A. Hoffman Theater,** E.T.A.-Hoffmann-Platz 1 (🕾 **0951/873030**). Its season runs September through July. The productions range from 18th-, 19th-, and 20th-century classics to contemporary musicals. The box office is open daily 10am to 6pm and 1 hour before showtime. In June and July, the company moves outdoors, performing a series of German-language dramas in the courtyard of the Alte Hofhaltung (see above). Tickets for both indoor and outdoor performances are 16€ to 29€ ($26–$46), but students with a valid ID card pay half price. For more information about these and other cultural events in Bamberg, contact the Tourist Information Office (see "Visitor Information," above).

A young crowd gathers at **Jazzclub,** Obere Sandstrasse 18 (© **0951/55225**), to listen to punk, Goth, and alternative music on Tuesday and Thursday nights from 9pm to 1am, when the cover is 5€ ($8) mid-September to April; the club opens its cellar for live jazz on Friday and Saturday 9pm to 2am, when the cover is 9€ to 16€ ($14–$26), depending on the group. Tickets to virtually any cultural or sporting event in Bamberg are available from the city's largest ticket agency, **BVD Bamburger Ticket Agency,** Langestrasse 22 (© **0951/980820**), open Monday to Friday 9am to 6pm and Saturday 9am to 1pm.

Another option for whiling away the after-dark hours is a visit to **Haas Säle,** Obere Sandstrasse 7 (© **0951/51935329**), where you'll find a battered-looking pub with a small stage which presents, depending on the night of the week, flamenco dancing, short plays, or political satire. Disco music follows the show. There's almost never a cover charge and everything is usually spontaneous and pulled together on short notice.

3 Nürnberg (Nuremberg) ★★

169km (105 miles) NW of Munich, 225km (140 miles) SE of Frankfurt, 204km (127 miles) NE of Stuttgart

When this city celebrated its 900th birthday in 1950, the scars of World War II were still fresh. Nürnberg was once a masterpiece of medieval splendor, but that legacy was lost in the ashes of war. With the exception of Dresden, no other German city suffered such devastation in a single air raid. On the night of January 2, 1945, 525 British Lancaster bombers rained fire and destruction on this city, the ideological center of the Third Reich.

Nürnberg today has regained its vitality and is now a symbol of postwar prosperity. The city swarms with people, both longtime residents and the *Gastarbeiter* (foreign workers), who have flooded the city in recent years—many from the old Soviet Bloc countries to the east. For most of the year, the city is thronged with visitors, too. It's a notable industrial center, still associated with its traditional gingerbread products and handmade toys. The first pocket watches, the Nürnberg eggs, were made here in the 16th century.

Centuries of art and architecture made Nürnberg a treasure. During the 15th and 16th centuries, Nürnberg enjoyed a cultural flowering that made it the center of the **German Renaissance,** bringing together Italian Renaissance and German Gothic traditions. In the artists' workshops were found such great talents as Veit Stoss, Peter Vischer, Adam Krafft, Michael Wolgemut and, above all, Albrecht Dürer. Koberger set up his printing press here, and Regiomontanus built an astronomical observatory. Here, too, flourished the guilds of the Meistersingers, composed of prosperous artisans; Wagner made their most famous member, Hans Sachs, the hero of his opera *Die Meistersinger von Nürnberg.*

Many of Nürnberg's most important buildings, including some of the finest churches in Germany, have been restored or reconstructed. The old part of the city, the **Altstadt,** lies mainly within a pedestrian zone. Today's visitors can see the ruins of the ramparts that once surrounded the city as well as more modern sites, such as the **Justice Palace,** where the War Crimes Tribunal sat in 1946.

Visitors can also see the **Zeppelinfeld arena,** the huge amphitheater where, from 1927 to 1935, Hitler staged those dramatic Nazi rallies that were immortalized by

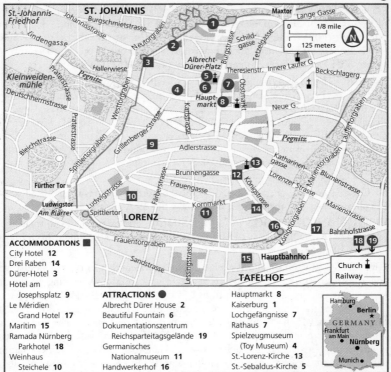

Leni Riefenstahl in *Triumph des Willens (Triumph of the Will)*. Hitler's architect, Albert Speer, constructed what has been called a "concrete mecca," whose grounds today have been turned into a park with apartment blocks, a trade fair, and a concert hall. Speer's Congress Hall, larger than the Colosseum in Rome, has become a recording studio and warehouse.

ESSENTIALS

GETTING THERE **By Plane** **Nürnberg Flughafen** is 6km (4 miles) north of the city center. Despite its relatively small size (it's only the ninth busiest in Germany), this airport is served by 14 airlines, with flights to dozens of European destinations. These are supplemented by charter flights. For information and schedules, call ✆ **0911/93700** or visit **www.airport-nuernberg.de**.

By Train The **Nürnberg Hauptbahnhof** lies on several major German rail lines, with frequent connections to big cities and many smaller regional towns. Travel time to Frankfurt is 2 hours; to Berlin, 6 hours; and to Munich, 2 hours. For information and schedules, call ✆ **01805/996633.**

By Bus Long-distance bus service from such cities as Munich and Frankfurt is provided by **Deutsche Touring GmbH** (✆ **0911/221940**). Long-distance bus service from other cities within Germany is provided by, among others, **Bayern Express**

(© 030/86096240). Regional service to neighboring towns within Franconia is offered by **OVF Omnibusverkehr Franken GmbH,** Nelson Mandela Platz 18 in Nürnberg (© **0911/430570**). For information on these or any other bus line coming into Nürnberg (or anywhere else in Franconia), contact one of the city's largest travel agents, **TUI Reise Center,** Lorenzerstrasse 19 (© **0911/2270000**).

By Boat   The Main-Danube Canal links together the Rhine, the Main, and the Danube. For information about the canal itself, call the **Hafener-Waltung Nürnberg** (© **0911/642940**). For information about riverboat tours on the canal and the rivers that feed it, contact **Neptun (NPS) GmbH** (© **0911/60046261;** www.neptun-personenschifffahrt.de). Between May and September, the company offers, from Nürnberg, a daily water excursion to Forchheim, 4 hours away, each way. The cost of 20€ ($32) round-trip allows several hours for stamping around the streets of Forchheim before returning the same day to Nürnberg.

By Car   From Munich, take the A9 Autobahn north; from Frankfurt, head southeast along the A3 Autobahn; from Berlin, take the A9 Autobahn south.

VISITOR INFORMATION   Contact **Tourist Information,** Hauptmarkt 18 (© **0911/2313222**), Monday to Saturday 9am to 6pm and also Sunday from May to October 10am to 4pm.

GETTING AROUND   Nürnberg has a **subway** system that consists of an east-west and a north-south line that intersects at the Hauptbahnhof. Depending on the distance you travel, one-way fares cost from 1.90€ to 8.40€ ($3.10–$13). A Day Ticket Solo, valid for the entire transportation network for 24 hours, costs 3.80€ ($6.10). Principal stops within Nürnberg's medieval core include Lorenzkirche and Weisser Turm. For more information, call © **0911/2834646.** But **walking** between two points at opposite ends of the old town—the Hauptbahnhof (main railway station) and the Kaiserburg (the base of the city's medieval castle)—will take you only about 30 minutes and will lead you through the heart of the city's medieval core and past most of its historic monuments. To summon a **taxi,** call © **0911/19410.**

WHERE TO STAY
EXPENSIVE
Le Méridien Grand Hotel 🟊🟊🟊   This old-world palace is the best place to stay in Nürnberg. The Grand is a solid six-story blockbuster built "when hotels were really hotels"—that is, before World War I. Rooms are the finest and most spacious in town. Furnishings are first rate and stylish, and the roomy bathrooms are exceedingly well maintained, with deluxe toiletries and tub/shower combos. Many have a private sitting area.

Bahnhofstrasse 1–3 (across from the Hauptbahnhof), 90402 Nürnberg. © **800/367-8340** in the U.S., or 0911/ 23220. Fax 0911/2322444. www.lemeridien.com. 186 units. 270€–330€ ($432–$528) double; 430€–1,000€ ($688–$1,600) suite. AE, DC, MC, V. Parking 12€ ($19). U-Bahn: Hauptbahnhof. **Amenities:** Restaurant; bar; indoor heated pool; gym; sauna; solarium; salon; room service; laundry service; dry cleaning; nonsmoking rooms; rooms for those w/limited mobility. *In room:* A/C (in some), TV, minibar, hair dryer, iron.

Maritim 🟊🟊   Maritim attracts those who prefer modern convenience to old-world charm. It used to be the city's most stylish hotel, until the Méridien chain upgraded the Grand. Rooms are of good size—although not as spacious as the Grand's—with large beds and many extras, such as large bathrooms with tub/shower combos. Try an upper-floor room for a panoramic view over Nürnberg's medieval fortifications and busy traffic artery.

Frauentorgraben 11, 90443 Nürnberg. © **0911/23630.** Fax 0911/2363823. www.maritim.de. 316 units. 198€–310€ ($257–$403) double; 268€–437€ ($429–$699) suite. Rates include breakfast. AE, DC, MC, V. Parking 15€ ($24). U-Bahn: Hauptbahnhof. **Amenities:** Restaurant; bar; coffee shop; indoor heated pool; gym; sauna; solarium; steam bath; room service; laundry service; dry cleaning; nonsmoking rooms; 1 room for those w/limited mobility. *In room:* A/C, TV, Wi-Fi, minibar, hair dryer, safe.

Ramada Nürnberg Parkhotel ✦ The Ramada is not as grand as Le Méridien Grand Hotel or even the Maritim (see above), but it's close to the top of the heap. This hotel is one of the most modern in town; it looks like a four-story collection of concrete cubes set up on stilts. Inside, it's flooded with natural light, with many windows offering views of the landscaped park around it. For the most part, both the guest rooms and combination tub/shower bathrooms are roomy; the furnishings, though not terribly stylish, are comfortable and inviting. Three rooms are specially designed for travelers with disabilities. The hotel is directly connected to the Meistersingerhalle, where concerts and conventions take place.

Münchenerstrasse 25 (5-min. drive from city center), 90478 Nürnberg. © **0911/47480.** Fax 0911/4748420. 200 units. 135€–310€ ($216–$496) double; 240€–340€ ($384–$544) suite. Rates include buffet breakfast. Children 11 and under stay free in parent's room. AE, DC, MC, V. Parking 10€ ($16). Tram: 9. Bus: 36. **Amenities:** Restaurant; bar; indoor heated pool; sauna; solarium; room service; laundry service; dry cleaning; nonsmoking rooms; rooms for those w/limited mobility. *In room:* TV, Wi-Fi, minibar, coffeemaker (in some), hair dryer, safe.

MODERATE

Drei Raben ✦ *(Finds* An offbeat choice, this is the first theme hotel ever established in Nürnberg. The Three Ravens (its English name) offers individually decorated bedrooms, each chamber decorated according to a local legend. One room is devoted to Dürer, and another to a modern day saga—Nürnberg's famous soccer team. The most unusual junior suite is called "Legend and Bathtub Enchantment," for up to three guests. Standing in the middle of the room is an enchanting bathtub. Less expensive are the standard rooms, which are equally comfortable but lacking the drama of the theme rooms. As a startling entrance, the reception area is decorated with pods to evoke the film *2001: A Space Odyssey.* The location is a 5-minute walk from the Hauptbahnhof, the main train station.

Königstrasse 63, 90402 Nürnberg. © **0911/274380.** Fax 0911/232611. www.hotel3raben.de. 25 units. 120€ ($192) standard room; 150€ ($240) theme room; 185€ ($296) junior suite. AE, DC, MC, V. **Amenities:** Bar; laundry service; room service; nonsmoking rooms. *In room:* TV, Wi-Fi.

Dürer-Hotel ✦ The Dürer has steadily grown in prestige since it opened in the late '80s. It stands beside the birthplace of its namesake, right under the castle and near all the major sightseeing attractions. The guest rooms have some modern furniture but overall have a cozy, antique charm. The bathrooms are well kept and midsize with tub/shower combinations. The only meal served is breakfast, but you're only a short walk from restaurants and cafes.

Neutormauer 32, 90403 Nürnberg. © **0911/2146650.** Fax 0911/214665555. www.duererhotel-nuernberg.de. 107 units. 140€–200€ ($224–$320) double; 160€–220€ ($256–$352) suite. Rates include buffet breakfast. AE, DC, MC, V. Parking 10€ ($16). Tram: 6 or 9. Bus: 36 or 46. **Amenities:** Breakfast room; bar; lounge; fitness center; sauna; steam bath; room service; nonsmoking rooms; 1 room for those w/limited mobility. *In room:* TV, minibar, hair dryer (in some).

Hotel Am Josephsplatz ✦✦ *(Finds* In the historic center of the city, this restored hotel is installed in a building dating from 1675. However, its interior has been completely modernized with all the latest gadgetry, and there are such extras as a winter garden and a rooftop sun terrace. A family-style atmosphere prevails, and the historic ambience was preserved during wholesale renovations. Miraculously the building survived massive damage during the heavy bombings of WWII. Bedrooms are beautifully furnished with antique styling including draped beds and swag curtains. If you prefer less traditional rooms, there are some that are decorated in a more modern style. The restaurant on-site serves a classic Franconian cuisine.

Josephsplatz 30-32, Nürnberg 90403. © 0911/214470. Fax 0911/21447200. www.hotel-am-josephsplatz.de. 36 units. 99€–140€ ($158–$224) double; 129€–179€ ($206–$286) apt. Rates include buffet breakfast. AE, V. Parking 8€–15€ ($13–$24). **Amenities:** Fitness center; sauna; solarium; nonsmoking rooms. *In room:* TV, fridge, minibar, safe.

INEXPENSIVE

City Hotel *Value*   This serviceable, if unspectacular, hotel provides a great low-cost choice. It occupies the third, fourth, and fifth floors of an old-fashioned building on a wide pedestrian thoroughfare. Take a small elevator upstairs to the third-floor reception area, where the efficient owner will show you one of her simple, cramped, but immaculate rooms. The tiny bathrooms have shower stalls.

Königstrasse 25–27 (near St.-Lorenz-Kirche), 90402 Nürnberg. © 0911/225638. Fax 0911/203999. 20 units. 65€–100€ ($104–$160) double. Rates include continental breakfast. AE, DC, MC, V. Parking 12€ ($19). Closed for 2 weeks after Christmas. U-Bahn: Lorenzkirche. **Amenities:** Breakfast room; lounge. *In room:* TV, hair dryer.

Weinhaus Steichele *&*   This small and charming hotel retains its old-fashioned allure. It's located on a tranquil street but not far from the bustling activity of the train station, just outside the city wall. The building is a beautifully balanced and handcrafted structure of heavy stone blocks with a curved sloping roofline. Any overflow of guests spills into a modern annex next door that blends harmoniously with the older building. Rooms are decorated in a rustic Bavarian style, each with a small but efficiently organized shower-only bathroom.

Knorrstrasse 2–8 (near Jakobsplatz), 90402 Nürnberg. © 0911/202280. Fax 0911/221914. www.steichele.de. 49 units. 100€–170€ ($160–$272) double. Rates include buffet breakfast. AE, DC, MC, V. Parking 10€ ($16). U-Bahn: Weisser Turm. **Amenities:** Restaurant; breakfast room; rooms for those w/limited mobility. *In room:* TV, hair dryer.

WHERE TO DINE
EXPENSIVE
Essigbrätlein *&&&* FRANCONIAN/CONTINENTAL   This is the best restaurant in Nürnberg, dwarfing all other competition. The city's most ancient restaurant, dating from 1550, was originally a meeting place of wine merchants. Its upscale cuisine is reason enough to visit the city in the first place. The cuisine is so inventive and refreshing, with many nouvelle recipes, that we view this as worth a detour. The chef firmly believes in market-fresh ingredients. Look for an ever-changing menu based on seasonal availability. The traditional specialty is roast loin of beef (what the name of the restaurant means in German).

Weinmarkt 3. © 0911/225131. Reservations required. All main courses 28€ ($36); fixed-price 3- and 4-course lunch 45€–50€ ($72–$80); 4- and 6-course dinner 75€–90€ ($120–$144). AE, DC, MC, V. Tues–Sat noon–1:30pm and 7–9:30pm. Closed Jan 1–15 and 2 weeks in Aug (dates vary). U-Bahn: Karstadt.

MODERATE
Heilig-Geist-Spital *Value* FRANCONIAN   You wouldn't want to get much more Franconian than this. Heilig-Geist-Spital, Nürnberg's largest historical wine house, in

business for 650 years, is entered through an arcade above the river. The main dishes are typical Franconian fare, hearty and filling. Carp is a specialty, as is pork knuckle—we're sure no one has altered this recipe since the days of Dürer himself. In season, you can order leg of venison with noodles and berries. The wine list is abundant and excellent.

Spitalgasse 16. ℂ 0911/221761. Reservations recommended. Main courses 9€–15€ ($14–$24). AE, MC, V. Daily noon–11pm. Bus: 46 or 47.

Weinhaus Steichele ✸ FRANCONIAN/BAVARIAN   Steichele's walls are covered with polished copper pots, antique display cases lit from within, and hanging chandeliers carved into double-tailed sea monsters and other mythical beasts. Try roast shoulder of pork with potato balls and sauerkraut; or paprika-coated baked ham in an onion sauce, served with french fries and a salad. The wine list is superb. Surely if former patron Hermann Hesse returned today, he would notice no major alteration in the cuisine. Amid all the change in Nürnberg, this place still respects former times.

Knorrstrasse 2. ℂ 0911/202280. Reservations recommended. Main courses 6€–18€ ($9.60–$29). AE, DC, MC, V. Mon–Sat 11am–midnight; Sun 11am–3pm. U-Bahn: Weisser Turm.

INEXPENSIVE

Bratwurst-Häusle FRANCONIAN   This is the most famous bratwurst eatery in the city—stop here for lunch as you explore historic Nürnberg. Prices are kept at a 1970s level, but portions are as large as ever. In winter, you'll find an open hearth to warm you; in summer, this is a refreshingly cool retreat from the heat. Expect a cheerful, mostly non-English-speaking staff, a savory collection of soups (including potato soup and liver dumpling soup), and a strong emphasis on such garnishes as potato salad and sauerkraut.

Rathausplatz 1 (opposite the Rathaus). ℂ 0911/227695. Reservations recommended. Main courses 6.50€–10€ ($10–$16). AE, MC, V. Mon–Sat 10am–10:30pm. U-Bahn: Lorenzkirche.

Historische Bratwurst-Glöcklein ✸ *Kids* FRANCONIAN   Nürnbergers refer to it as their *Bratwurst locale* (local bratwurst), and it's the only serious rival to Bratwurst-Häusle (see above). The kitchen prepares a traditional Nürnberg-style bratwurst with sauerkraut and boiled potatoes, all served on tin plates. Because beer goes perfectly with wurst, you'll enjoy sampling some of the brews on tap while admiring the craftsmanship of the room, which dates from the Middle Ages. Ham hocks are an additional specialty. Be careful or you'll spend your entire afternoon on the sun terrace—it's that tempting.

Im Handwerkerhof, Königstrasse 5. ℂ 0911/227625. Reservations recommended. Main courses 6.20€–11€ ($9.90–$18). No credit cards. Mon–Sat 10:30am–9pm. U-Bahn: Hauptbahnhof.

EXPLORING NÜRNBERG

You can easily spend a full day here seeing the sights. Begin at the central market square, **Hauptmarkt,** the most colorful place in Nürnberg, filled with kiosks stacked tall with fresh produce brought in from the countryside. Nearly all the city's attractions lie nearby within the **medieval fortifications,** parts of which still remain. Between the main wall (which has rampart walks) and the secondary wall once ran the waters of a protective moat. At the "corners" of the Altstadt are the massive stone towers, still intact, of the city gates. The remains of dozens of other gateway towers still exist along the ramparts. Crowning the northern periphery of the Altstadt is the **Kaiserburg.**

The best example of Nürnberg's aesthetic passion is the **Beautiful Fountain** on Marktplatz. This stone pyramid, 18m (60 ft.) high, dates from 1396 and is adorned with 30 figures arranged in four tiers. Within it is enclosed the symbol of Nürnberg, the journeyman's ring.

At some point in your day, wander over to **Handwerkerhof,** near the main train station. In this mall, you can see artisans creating the products for which Nürnberg has been known since the Middle Ages: glassware, pewter (often in the form of beer mugs), intricate woodcarvings, and toys.

If you're interested in a famous landmark of World War II, visit the **Justizgebäude,** Fürtherstrasse 22 (U-Bahn: Bärenschanze), where the "Judgment of Nürnberg" took place. Here, in Room 600, the surviving leaders of the Third Reich stood trial in October 1946 for crimes against humanity. Afterward, 10 were hanged. The building still serves as a courthouse, and you'll have to ask the guard at the door if you can enter.

Albrecht Dürer House ☆

The town's most popular shrine is the Albrecht Dürer House, just a short walk up the cobblestoned Bergstrasse, from the Dürer Monument and St. Sebald Church. Typical of the half-timbered burghers' houses of the 15th century, the structure is the only completely preserved Gothic house in Nürnberg. The first floors are sandstone, surmounted by two half-timbered stories and a gabled roof with a view of the town below. Exhibits inside the house are devoted to Dürer's life and works. Many of the rooms are furnished with important historical pieces and contain original etchings and woodcuts, plus copies of Dürer's paintings.

Am Tiergartnertor, Albrecht-Dürer-Strasse 39. ✆ 0911/2312568. www.museen.nuernberg.de. Admission 5€ ($8) adults, 2.50€ ($4) students and children 6–15, free for children 5 and under. July–Sept daily 10am–5pm (Thurs until 8pm); Oct–June Tues–Sun 10am–5pm (Thurs until 8pm). Tram: 4. Bus: 36.

Dokumentationszentrum Reichsparteitagsgelände ☆

In the north wing of the unfinished Kongresshalle, the memories of the Nazi Party Congress rallies of 1934 and 1935 live on. Since the end of World War II, the city of Nürnberg has been virtually synonymous with the most famous set of war trials during the 20th century: the Nürnberg Trials. Beginning on November 20, 1945, 21 leading Nazi war criminals were tried in Courtroom 600 before the Allied International Military Tribunal for conspiracy and crimes against world peace, the rules of warfare, and humanity. The trials became a milestone in judicial history as a birthplace for a new law of nations: For the first time in history, sentences were pronounced according to the principle of the personal responsibility of the individual. Extraordinary, too, is that the site of these renowned war trials is also the former site of the Nazi Party rally grounds. Faced with the historical legacy of National Socialism, the trials were deliberately set in Nürnberg in order to make a statement.

You can visit the **Documentation Center Nazi Party Rally Grounds** to gain a greater understanding of the events in Nürnberg that shaped world history. Regular 1-hour guided tours to Courtroom 600 are conducted year-round, but only on Saturday and Sunday from 1 to 4pm, and only in rapid-fire German, for a price of 2.50€ ($4) per person, with advance reservations. Included are permanent and changing exhibitions, plus visits to the rally grounds. In addition, the Documentation Center considers academic and pedagogical tasks to be an integral part of its education work. One example of this is the International Study Forum, presenting film programs as well as talks and discussions with groups to assess their opinions before and after their visits to the exhibition. Political and peace education are central to the Documentation Center's vision, as is the study of human rights.

Albrecht Dürer & the German Renaissance

If Dürer's father had had his way, his son would have become a goldsmith. Fortunately, that didn't happen. Albrecht Dürer (1471–1528) began his artistic career as apprentice to Michael Wolgemut, then the leading artist in Nürnberg, in 1486. There he learned to excel in woodcutting and engraving. Almost everyone is familiar with the sketch he made of praying hands—it's been reproduced so often it's become a greeting-card cliché.

Dürer was not content to stay in Nürnberg. In 1490, he embarked on a series of travels that eventually took him to Italy, where he came into contact with the artists of the Renaissance. On his return to Nürnberg, he brought their ideas back with him. Dürer was thus largely responsible for pulling art north of the Alps out of the medieval world and into the new era.

A restless man, Dürer was always probing into the world about him; he produced several theoretical works on art, on architecture, and on the science of proportion. At one point he even invented a mechanical device for drawing a picture that was a first step toward the principle of the photographic camera.

Dürer was one of the first major world masters to paint an acknowledged self-portrait. In fact, he painted three; his very first known drawing is a sketch of himself at the age of 13. These paintings show clearly how he saw the artist's role, and the importance of his own mission. The last self-portrait (in the Alte Pinakothek in Munich) shows Dürer in an almost Christ-like stance, representing the artist as an elevated figure concerned with the expression of universal ideas. Other important paintings of his include the portrait of *Charlemagne* at the Germanisches Nationalmuseum in Nürnberg and his *Four Apostles,* commissioned for the Nürnberg Rathaus.

The Kongresshalle opens onto Lake Grosser Dutzendteich. Across the lake stands Zeppelinwiese, a field that's the site of the Tribüne, that mass mammoth marble platform from which Hitler ranted at more than 100,000 spectators enthralled by his violent denunciations.

Bayernstrasse 110. (℃) 0911/2315666. www.museen.nuernberg.de. Admission 5€ ($8) adults, 2.50€ ($4) students and children, family card 11€ ($18). Mon–Fri 9am–6pm; Sat–Sun 10am–6pm. S-Bahn: 2 to Dutzendteich. Tram: 9. Bus: 36 or 55.

Germanisches Nationalmuseum (Germanic National Museum) ⟨⟨⟨   The largest museum of German art and culture is just inside the south section of the medieval city walls. It covers the entire spectrum of German craftsmanship and fine arts from their beginnings to the 20th century. The prehistoric and early historical section contains finds from the Stone Age and from the burial sites of the Merovingians. The extensive painting and sculpture sections include works by Albrecht Dürer and Veit Stoss, a sculptor and woodcarver known for his "nervous" angular forms and realism. The boundless variety and richness of German handicrafts is fully evident in this museum. There's also an important library and archive here.

Kartäusergasse 1 (near the Hauptbahnhof). © 0911/13310. www.gnm.de. Admission 6€ ($9.60) adults, 4€ ($6.40) children. Tues and Thurs–Sun 10am–6pm; Wed 10am–9pm (free admission after 6pm Wed). U-Bahn: Opernhaus.

Kaiserburg *☝* "The Burg" looms above the city from its hilltop at the northern edge of the Altstadt. From 1050 to 1571, it was the official residence of the German kings and emperors, including Frederick Barbarossa. The castle is divided into three complexes: the Kaiserburg (Imperial Castle), the Burgraves' Castle, and the Municipal Buildings of the Free City.

The oldest portion is the **Pentagonal Tower** (1050). It probably dates from the previous palace of the Salian kings, over which the Burgraves' Castle was constructed. Although the **Burgraves' Castle** has been in ruins since it was destroyed by fire in 1420, the remains offer visitors a look into the layout of a feudal castle. The watchmen and guards used the heavy ramparts with the parapet walks and secret passages to protect the burgraves and the emperors, who lived in the inner core of the castle complex.

Kaiserburg, grouped around the inner court within the ramparts of the Burgraves' Castle, was the residence of the kings and emperors of Germany. Most of the buildings were constructed during the 12th century and centered on the once magnificent Palas, built by Konrad III in 1138. The great Knights' Hall on the ground floor and the Imperial Hall on the floor above look much as they did when King Frederick III rebuilt them in the 15th century, with heavy oak beams and painted ceilings. The rooms are decorated with period Gothic furnishings. Adjoining the Palas is the Imperial Chapel—actually two chapels, one above the other in cross section but united at the center by an open bay. Thus, the emperor could worship to the same liturgy with his court in the upper chapel while the lesser members of his retinue worshiped in the lower.

The third set of buildings, outside the Burgraves' Castle, was erected by the council of Nürnberg in the 14th and 15th centuries, when it took over the responsibility of protecting the emperor. This section includes the imperial stables (now a youth hostel), the massive bastions of the fortress, the Tiefer Brunnen (Deep Well), and the castle gardens. Even more impressive than the fortress is the view of the roofs and towers of Nürnberg from its terraces.

The complex also includes the new **Kaiserburg Museum** (© 0911/2009540), which contains antique weaponry, armor, and paintings, and explains the history of the castle.

Burgstrasse 13. © 0911/2446590. Admission (including all parts of the castle) 6€ ($9.60) adults, 4€ ($6.40) students, free for children 16 and under. Apr–Sept daily 9am–6pm; Oct–Mar daily 10am–4pm. Bus: 36 or 46.

Lochgefängnisse   Under the Altes Rathaus is a medieval prison with its original cells and torture chamber, a gruesome attraction. Opposite the torture chamber lie the remnants of a room that once hid the city council's treasures and important documents during wars and emergencies. An underground passage from the dungeons to the outside world existed from 1543 until 1945, when bombing rendered it impassable.

Rathausplatz. © 0911/2312690. www.museen.nuernberg.de. Admission 3€ ($4.80) adults, 1.50€ ($2.40) children. Tues–Sun 10am–4:30pm. Closed weekends Nov–Mar; closed Jan. Bus: 36, 46, or 47.

Spielzeugmuseum (Toy Museum) *Kids*   Nürnberg is a major toy center, so it's only fitting that the city devote a museum to this industry. Toys, both hand- and machine-made, fill three floors. Some date from medieval times. The collection of old dollhouses is vastly amusing, as is a mechanical Ferris wheel. You'll often see adults here (even without children).

Karlstrasse 13–15. (✆) 0911/2313164. www.museen.nuernberg.de. Admission 5€ ($8) adults, 2.50€ ($4) students and children, 11€ ($17) family ticket (2 parents with 1 or more children). Tues–Fri 10am–5pm; Sat–Sun 10am–6pm. Bus: 36.

St.-Lorenz-Kirche 🎔

Across the Pegnitz River is the largest and stateliest church in Nürnberg. Begun in 1270, it took more than 200 years to complete, but the final result is one of Gothic purity, inside and out. The twin towers flank the west portal. The portal's sculptures depict the theme of redemption, from Adam and Eve through the Last Judgment. Upon entering the church, note the color and detail in the stained-glass rosette above the portal. Much of the church's stained and painted glass dates from the 15th century. The interior is punctuated by pillars that soar upward to become lost in the vaulting shafts above the nave. Each pillar is adorned with sculptures carrying on the theme introduced at the entrance. The oldest of these is *Mary with Child,* created around 1285. The sculptures urge you toward the single east choir, the last portion of the church to be completed (1477). *The Angelic Salutation* (1519), carved in linden wood by Veit Stoss, is suspended from the roof of the church just behind the Madonna Chandelier. To the left of the altar is the Gothic Tabernacle, hewn from stone by Adam Krafft (1496), its upthrusting turret repeating the vertical emphasis of the church. Above the high altar is another masterpiece by Stoss, a carved crucifix.

Lorenzer Platz 10. (✆) 0911/2446990. Free admission. Mon–Sat 9am–5pm; Sun 1–4pm. U-Bahn: Lorenzkirche.

St.-Sebaldus-Kirche

Consecrated in 1273, this church is a fine example of 13th-century transition from Romanesque to German Gothic styles. The nave and west choir are late Romanesque, with a narrow chancel containing a simple altar and an ancient bronze baptismal font. The larger east choir, consecrated in 1379, is pure Gothic and contains the church's most important treasures. Between the two east pillars is a huge 16th-century crucifixion group dominated by a life-size crucifix by Veit Stoss. Just behind the altar is the elaborate shrine of St. Sebald, whose remains are encased in a monument cast in brass by Peter Vischer in 1519. It's supported by an array of snails and dolphins and adorned with a host of statuettes. The nave of the church also holds several important **works of art** 🎔🎔, including 14th-century statues of St. Catherine and St. Sebald and the *Madonna with a Halo* (1440).

Albrecht-Dürer-Platz 1. (✆) 0911/2142500. Free admission. Jan–Mar daily 9:30am–4pm; Apr–May and Oct–Dec daily 9:30am–6pm; June–Sept daily 9:30am–8pm. Sun services 8:30 and 10am. U-Bahn: Lorenzkirche.

SHOPPING

Located near the railway station in the center of the city, **Handwerkerhof** (U-Bahn: Hauptbahnhof) is a crafts mall in a medieval castle setting, where Franconian artisans create and sell a wide range of handicrafts. It's open March 20 to December 23, weekdays 10am to 6:30pm and Saturday 10am to 4pm. In December, it also opens Sunday 10am to 6:30pm.

At **Kistner,** Weinmarkt 6 ((✆) **0911/203482;** U-Bahn: Lorenzkirche), you can step back in time. This wonderful store is full of antique books, prints, and engravings, including some by Dürer, Rembrandt, and other masters. The owner, Herr Kistner, is an expert in the field.

Villeroy & Boch, Königstrasse 13 ((✆) **0911/223182;** U-Bahn: Lorenzkirche), sells sets of china, crystal ware, and porcelain trinkets.

The largest department store in the city, **Karstadt,** Königstrasse 14 (© **0911/2130;** U-Bahn: Lorenzkirche), carries clothing, housewares, and other home furnishings.

Adding variety to prudence, **Condomi,** Ludwigstrasse 57 (© **0911/232784;** U-Bahn: Weisser Turm), sells condoms in various colors, textures, flavors, and scents. It also has postcards and T-shirts.

NÜRNBERG AFTER DARK

A theater complex offering quality productions of drama and opera, the **Staatstheater Nürnberg,** Richard-Wagner-Platz 2–10 (© **0180/1344276** for tickets; U-Bahn: Opernhaus), houses the Kammerspiele, Opernhaus, and Schauspielhaus. *Note:* Until November 2008, the theater will be closed for some extensive renovations. Before that reopening, performances will take place in the **Kongresshalle** in the former Nazi Party Grounds at Zeppelin Wiese on the eastern outskirts of Nürnberg and in the Tafelhalle, Aussere Sulzbacher Strasse (© **911/2315297**). The box office is open Monday to Friday 9am to 6pm; tickets are 9€ to 59€ ($14–$94). Students get 25% off, and the general public can check on discounted seats at the box office 1 hour before each performance. For tickets to this venue, call the number listed above or contact the town's largest ticket-selling agency (it's within a large department store and sells tickets to virtually every cultural and sporting event in the region), Fanatix Kartenvorverkauf im Saturn (© **0911/777744**).

Touring cabaret acts play at the **Loni-Übler-Haus,** Marthastrasse 60 (© **0911/ 541156;** U-Bahn: Hauptbahnhof), on Saturday and Sunday at 8pm. The box office is open Tuesday to Friday 9am to 10pm, and tickets are 10€ to 50€ ($16–$80). The city's premier outdoor venue, **St. Katarina,** is located in the ruins of the Katharinenkirche, Katherinenkloster 1 at Peter-Vischer-Strasse (U-Bahn: Lorenzkirche). It hosts concerts by an eclectic mix of international musical acts. The events within this evocative outdoor ruin are, by necessity, subject to sudden cancellations because of inclement weather. With that in mind, contact the above-mentioned Fanatix Kartenvorverkauf im Saturn (© **0911/777744**) for information about tickets and scheduling.

A garden house glowing in blue light marks the rear entrance to **Starclub,** Maxtorgraben 33 (© **0911/551682;** U-Bahn: Rathenauplatz), known as the "House of 11 Beers" for its 11 home brews. Beers start at 3€ ($4.80), accompanied by baguette sandwiches at 4.50€ ($7.20) and other cheap snacks. Students come around for backgammon and darts or animated conversation on the patio out front. It's open Sunday to Wednesday 7pm to 1am, Thursday 7pm to 2am, and Friday and Saturday 7pm to 3am. An artists' hangout, **Treibhaus,** Karl-Grillenberger-Strasse 28 (© **0911/ 223041;** U-Bahn: Weisser Turm), opens early for big breakfasts that run 3€ to 15€ ($4.80–$24), and offers soup, salad, and sandwich specials from 4€ to 7€ ($6.40–$11) throughout the day. At night, it dims the lights and keeps serving drinks. It's open Monday to Friday 8am to 1am, Saturday and Sunday 9am to 1am. Food is served until 10:30pm, and breakfast is served all day.

Another low-key arts scene, **Café Ruhestörung,** Tetzelgasse 21 (© **0911/221921;** U-Bahn: Lorenzkirche or Rathenauplatz), offers some of the best people-watching in the city. Just sit on the patio and order a drink or a sandwich and watch the world stroll by. Draft beers are 2.50€ to 4€ ($4–$6.40). It's open Monday to Friday 7:30am to 2am, Saturday 8:30am to 3am, and Sunday 9am to 2am.

At **Mach 1,** Kaiserstrasse 1–9 (© **0911/2406602;** U-Bahn: Lorenzkirche), Thursday and Friday move from disco to hip-hop, warming up for Saturday's big house party. Cover is 8€ ($13) on Thursday, 9€ ($14) on Friday, and 11€ ($18) on Saturday. Hours are Thursday to Saturday 10pm to 5am.

A popular gay bistro, **Cartoon,** An der Sparkgasse 6 (© **0911/227170;** U-Bahn: Lorenzkirche), serves beer, wine, and light meals Monday to Saturday 2pm to midnight and Sunday 2 to 11pm. For later hours, hit the dance clubs, all of which have both gay and straight clientele.

4 Regensburg ★★

122km (76 miles) NE of Munich, 100km (62 miles) SE of Nürnberg, 114km (71 miles) NW of Passau

Regensburg is one of Germany's best preserved cities, relatively undamaged by World War II bombings. Despite this, it remains somewhat obscure to many foreign visitors. Even if you don't have time to explore the city's museums or the interiors of its many historical monuments, try to take in the view of the Danube from one of its bridges, especially at sunset.

Regensburg started as a Celtic settlement, called Radespona, around 500 B.C. The Romans later took it over, renamed it Castra Regina, and made it their center of power on the upper Danube. From the 7th century, the town was the center from which Christianity spread over southern Germany. The architecture of Regensburg testifies to its long history and past grandeur, which reached its peak by the beginning of the Gothic era. Its buildings and towers offer an unspoiled glimpse into history, and many of its ancient structures are still in active use today. The best example is the **Stone Bridge,** built in 1146 on 16 huge arches, in continuous service for more than 800 years.

ESSENTIALS

GETTING THERE   By Train   The **Regensburg Hauptbahnhof** is on major rail lines, including Passau-Regensburg-Nürnberg and Munich-Landshut-Regensburg, with frequent connections in all directions. From Munich, more than 20 trains arrive daily (trip time: 1½ hr.), and from Frankfurt, 18 trains daily (trip time: 3½ hr.). The trip from Nürnberg takes only 1 hour, 15 minutes; from Passau (see "Passau," later in this chapter), 1½ hours. For rail information and schedules, call © **01805/996633.**

By Bus   Regional buses service the nearby towns. For information about routes, scheduling, and prices of buses operating within the region, contact the **Regensburger Verkehrsverbund (RVV;** © **0941/463190)** for information. For bus runs to such cities as Munich or Nürnberg, service is provided by **Watzinger** (© **0941/784930**).

By Car   Access by car is via the A3 Autobahn from east and west and the A93 from north and south.

VISITOR INFORMATION   Contact **Tourist-Information,** Altes Rathaus (© **0941/5074410**). Hours are year-round Monday to Friday 9am to 6pm, Saturday and Sunday 9am to 4pm; between November and March, Sunday hours are 9:30am to 2:30pm.

GETTING AROUND   You can walk around the center of Regensburg and see the highlights. To get from the Hauptbahnhof to the town's medieval core (Altstadt) take any of the bright yellow Altstadt buses that line up along Maximilianstrasse, next to the station. One-way fare is .80€ ($1.30). Buses run at 6-minute intervals every Monday to Friday 8:30am to 8:30pm. There's no service on Saturday and Sunday. If you wish to go farther afield, you'll find an adequate system of bus routes fanning out from the railway station to the outer suburbs. A single ride costs 1.80€ ($2.90), and buses run 6am to midnight daily. A 24-hour ticket costs 3.80€ ($6.10). A list of bus routes is available at the railway station at the Presse & Buch kiosk.

WHERE TO STAY

Bischofshof am Dom 🌟🌟   A longtime favorite, appealing to traditionalists, this hotel was constructed as an ecclesiastical academy by the bishops of Regensburg in 1810. Today it blends 19th-century monastic with modern secular. Many of the units have hosted princes, even emperors. Rooms are attractively furnished, although the bathrooms with tub/shower combos, though well maintained, are a bit small. Part of the hotel takes in a piece of a Roman gateway. Behind the building is one of Regensburg's most popular sun terraces. Guests can also sit in the hotel's *Weinstube* (wine bar) or in one of the 350 seats in the beer garden. The beer comes from a brewery dating from 1649.

Krauterermarkt 3, 93047 Regensburg. ⓒ **0941/58460**. Fax 0941/5846146. www.hotel-bischofshof.de. 55 units. 135€–155€ ($216–$248) double; 200€ ($320) suite. Rates include breakfast. AE, DC, MC, V. Parking 8€ ($13). Bus: 1. **Amenities:** Restaurant; bar; nonsmoking rooms; 1 room for those w/limited mobility. *In room:* TV, dataport, minibar, hair dryer.

Hotel Orphée 🌟🌟   You get one hotel here but three different houses and three different living experiences. Our preferred choice is the splendid baroque mansion, Grand Hotel Orphée, which is sumptuous with beautifully restored bedrooms at Untere Bachgasse 8, right next door to the Restaurant Orphée. You'll live in the grand style of old Germany with elaborately carved and inlaid baroque doors, period door frames with hand-wrought hinges, and ornate ceilings, along with state-of-the-art bathrooms. If you're romantic, opt for one of the rooms in the attic with baroque roof beams and panoramic views over the roofs of the town.

The Petit Hotel Orphée at Wahlenstrasse 1 is the coziest of the lot. It's installed in the former home of a prosperous family of merchants. Rooms here are individually furnished but with antique washstands and Turkish tiles. In some respects, this is the prettiest hotel of the lot.

A final hotel, Country Manor Orphée, Andreasstrasse 26, lies across an old stone bridge, north of the Danube. The hotel is installed on the second floor of a 16th-century salt warehouse, which has been turned into a cultural center with a cinema, restaurant, and artists' studios. Ten enticing apartments are rented, six of which have a little patio overlooking the banks of the Danube. Each unit has its own kitchenette and a vaguely Mediterranean look.

Grand Hotel Orphée at Untere Bachgasse 8, 93047 Regensburg; Petit Hotel Orphée at Wahlenstrasse 1, 93047 Regensburg; Country Manor Orphée at Andreasstrasse 26, 93059 Regensburg. ⓒ **0941/596020** for Grand Hotel Orphée and Petit Hotel Orphée; ⓒ **0941/59602300** for Country Manor Orphée. Fax 0941/59602199 for Grand Hotel Orphée and Petit Hotel Orphée; 0941/59602399 for Country Manor Orphée. www.hotel-orphee.de. 25 units in Grand Hotel Orphée, 15 units in Petit Hotel Orphée, 10 units in Country Manor Orphée. 120€–195€ ($192–$312) in Grand Hotel Orphée; 95€–175€ ($152–$280) in Petit Hotel Orphée; 130€–150€ ($208–$240) in Country Manor Orphée. AE, DC, MC, V. Rates include breakfast. **Amenities:** Restaurant; bar. *In room:* TV (in some rooms), kitchenette (in some units).

Parkhotel Maximilian 🌟   The next best thing to staying in one of "Mad" King Ludwig's palaces is to check into the Parkhotel Maximilian, an exquisite neo-rococo building. Its facade and public areas have been classified a public monument. The main salon, with a ceiling supported by columns of polished red stone, continues the theme of 18th-century opulence coupled with 21st-century convenience. Guest rooms are attractively furnished, and each comes with a roomy private bathroom with a tub/shower combo.

Maximilianstrasse 28, 93047 Regensburg. © 0941/56850. Fax 0941/52942. www.maximilian-hotel.de. 52 units. 149€–170€ ($238–$272) double. Rates include continental breakfast. AE, DC, MC, V. Parking 4€–8€ ($6.40–$13). Free parking on weekends. Bus: 1, 2, 3, or 6. **Amenities:** Restaurant; cafe; room service; laundry service; dry cleaning; nonsmoking rooms; rooms for those w/limited mobility. *In room:* TV, Wi-Fi, minibar, hair dryer.

Straubinger Hof *(Finds* This attractive, unpretentious hotel is little publicized, but bargain hunters should seek it out. The small rooms are simple but satisfactory, with lots of sunlight and angular, somewhat spartan furniture, and a tiny bathroom containing a shower.

Adolf-Schmetzer-Strasse 33 (15-min. walk east of the cathedral), 93055 Regensburg. © 0941/60030. Fax 0941/794826. www.hotel-straubinger-hof.de. 60 units. 65€–90€ ($104–$144) double. Rates include breakfast. AE, DC, MC, V. Free parking. Bus: 1. **Amenities:** Dining room; lounge; nonsmoking rooms; rooms for those w/limited mobility. *In room:* TV, minibar, hair dryer.

WHERE TO DINE

Gänsbauer *(k* BAVARIAN/INTERNATIONAL   For elegant dining, visit Gänsbauer, one of the best restaurants in the city. The setting is mellow and old-fashioned, but the cuisine is strictly neue Küche (cuisine moderne) with a Continental influence. Well-known Bavarian dishes are given a lighter touch here, and only the freshest ingredients are used. The baby turbot in Pernod sauce is superb. The desserts are often exotic. The restaurant occupies a 500-year-old building with an open space where you can sit in fair weather.

Keplerstrasse 10. © 0941/57858. Reservations recommended. Main courses 18€–39€ ($29–$62); fixed-price dinners 64€–93€ ($102–$149). AE, DC, MC, V. Mon–Sat 6–10:30pm. Bus: Fischmarkt.

Restaurant & Bistro Rosenpalais *(kkk* INTERNATIONAL   Positioned on the eastern fringe of Regensburg's historic core, this restaurant occupies a gracefully proportioned 18th-century baroque villa with an exterior painted in tones of bright pink and cream. This building has had stints as a private home as well as an upscale *Lustschloss* (wine tavern), a tradition it continues in two separate venues today. One floor above street level, you'll find the more formal venue, the restaurant, consisting of two high-ceilinged and somewhat restrained dining rooms, one of which is shaped like an octagon. Here, menu items are as posh and esoteric as you'll find anywhere in the area, with seasonal variations that might include marinated calves' livers with tomato-and-basil vinaigrette, a very generously sized crayfish salad, cream of spinach soup garnished with braised mussels, a perfectly braised filet of tuna with mango-studded couscous and bok choy, and venison cutlets with Bavarian herbs and seasonings.

Less formal and esoteric cuisine is served in the somewhat more extroverted street-level bistro, where among the salads, pastas, and old-fashioned Teutonic and Continental specialties you'll find sole meunière, wurst with sauerkraut, pepper steak with french fries, and French onion soup with a crusty top layer of Emmenthal cheese.

Minoritenweg 20. © 0941/5997579. Reservations recommended. Main courses 13€–28€ ($21–$45); fixed-price menus 33€–69€ ($53–$110). MC, V. Tues–Sat 11:30am–2pm and 6pm–1am.

EXPLORING REGENSBURG

Regensburg is a city of churches; it was once the focal point from which Christianity spread throughout Germany and even into central Europe via the Danube. The most

Moments **Cruising the Danube**

One reason for visiting this *Dreiflüssestadt* (town of three rivers) on the Austrian frontier is for a boat tour along the Danube and its tributaries, the Inn and the Ilz. Trips range from a 45-minute three-river tour to a steamer cruise downriver to Vienna. The cruises depart from Fritz-Schäffer Promenade. Many passengers prefer to go by boat, and then take a train back.

You may also be tempted to board one of the passenger ferries that makes runs (Apr–Oct only) every day from Passau downstream to the Austrian city of Linz. The trips take 5 hours each way, cost 22€ ($35) per person, and depart every day except Monday from the city's riverfront piers at 9am and noon.

If you're interested in gaining even greater insights into life along the Danube, you can continue by train from Linz to Vienna, buying a ferryboat, train, and hotel package priced at a reasonable 274€ ($438) per person, which will include round-trip transit by boat and train to Vienna, via Linz, from Passau, and 1 night's stay at a four-star hotel in Vienna. For information about either the day trip to Linz or the overnight sojourn in Vienna, contact the **Donau-Schiffahrt Line** (www.donauschiffahrt.de) through its local representative, Würm & Höck, Höllgasse 26, D-94032 Passau (© 0851/ 929292).

majestic of these churches is the towering **Dom St. Peter's** ⟨₭⟩, Domplatz (© 0941/ 5865500; bus: 1, 6, or 11), which was begun in the 13th century on the site of an earlier Carolingian church. Because it was constructed with easily eroded limestone and green sandstone, this French Gothic edifice is constantly being restored. The massive spires of the two western towers, added in the mid–19th century, were almost completely replaced in 1955 with a more durable material. The well-preserved **stained-glass windows** ⟨₭₭⟩ in the choir (14th c.) and south transept (13th c.) are impressive. Most of the pillar sculptures in the aisles of the nave were made in the cathedral workshop in the mid–14th century. The townsfolk call the two little sculptures in the niches on opposite sides of the main entrance *The Devil* and *The Devil's Grandmother*. The cathedral is home to a famous boys' choir, the **Chor Dompatzen,** which performs every Sunday morning at 10am Mass. The performance is open to all. From May to October, the cathedral is open Monday to Saturday 8am to 6:30pm and Sunday noon to 6pm; November to April, hours are Monday to Saturday 8am to 4pm and Sunday noon to 4pm. Admission is free.

You can also visit the cathedral treasures at the **Domschatzmuseum,** Krauter-markt 3 (© 0941/57645; bus: 1, 6, or 11, or the Altstadt bus), which displays goldsmiths' work and splendid textiles from the 11th to 20th centuries. Entrance is through a portal in the north aisle of the cathedral. It's open April to October Tuesday to Saturday 10am to 5pm and Sunday noon to 5pm; December to March, generally only Friday and Saturday 10am to 4pm and Sunday noon to 4pm; and closed in November. The charge is 2€ ($3.20) for adults and 1€ ($1.60) for students and children 17 and under. You can also buy a combination ticket to the Domschatzmuseum and the

Diözesanmuseum St. Ulrich (see below) that costs 3€ ($4.80) for adults and 4€ ($6.40) for a family ticket. (Admission to the cloister isn't included with this ticket.)

The permanent collection of the **Diözesanmuseum St. Ulrich** is on exhibit in the former Church of St. Ulrich, an early-Gothic building to the side of the cathedral, Domplatz 2 (© **0941/51688;** bus: 1, 2, 6, or 11). Sculptures, paintings, and goldsmiths' work form a representative selection of religious art in the diocese from the 11th to the 20th centuries. Of particular interest are works on loan from the monastic foundations of the diocese. The museum is open April to October Tuesday to Sunday 10am to 5pm. Admission is free.

Crossing the cathedral garden, you enter the **cloister** with its Romanesque Aller Heiligenkapelle (All Saints' Chapel) and Sankt Stephan Kirche (St. Stephen's Church). The ancient frescoes on the walls of the chapel depict liturgical scenes from All Saints' Day. The 11th-century church of St. Stephen contains an altar made of a hollowed limestone rock with openings connecting to early Christian tombs. You can only visit the cloister and St. Stephen's Church on one of the guided tours, which are given (in English) from May to October Monday to Saturday at 10, 11am, and 2pm, Sunday and holidays at noon and 2pm; November to April, hours are Monday to Saturday at 11am and Sunday and holidays at noon. The charge is 3€ ($4.80) adults, 1.50€ ($2.40) students and children, and free for children 5 and under.

Of all the remnants of Roman occupation of Regensburg, the ancient **Porta Praetoria,** behind the cathedral, is the most impressive, with its huge stones piled in the form of an arched gateway. Through the grille beside the eastern tower you can see the original level of the Roman street, nearly 3m (10 ft.) below—which is why you often have to step down into the churches of Regensburg.

Of the four **Museen de Stadt Regensburg (City Museums of Regensburg),** the most important is **The Historisches Museum** ⭐, Dachauplatz 2–4 (© **0941/5072448;** bus: 1, 2, or 3), one of the most notable museums in east Bavaria. Its displays show major developments in the history of the region from the earliest days up to the present. You'll see relics of the Roman period, such as a stone tablet marking the establishment of a garrison at Regensburg in the 2nd century. There's also a stone altar to the Roman god Mercury, as well as several Christian tombstones. The museum is open Tuesday, Wednesday, Friday, and Saturday 10am to 4pm, Thursday 10am to 8pm. Admission is 2.20€ ($3.50) for adults; 1.10€ ($1.80) for students, seniors, and children 8 to 18; 4.40€ ($7) for a family ticket; and free for children 7 and under.

No town hall in Germany is preserved better than Regensburg's **Altes Rathaus** ⭐, Rathaus Platz (© **0941/5073440;** bus: 1, 6, or 11, or the Altstadt bus). This Gothic structure, begun in the 13th century, contains a Reichssaal (Imperial Diet Hall), where the Perpetual Diet sat from 1663 to 1806. In the basement of the Rathaus are the dungeons, with the torture chamber preserved in its original setting. The Altes Rathaus is open daily, with guided tours Monday to Saturday every 30 minutes 9:30am to noon and 2 to 4pm; Sunday and holidays, every 30 minutes 10am to noon. Know in advance that all of the above-mentioned tours are in rapid-fire, colloquial German, with the exception of a single English-language tour, conducted daily at 3:30pm. For information about tours of the Rathaus, contact either the tourist office (p. 243) or the number noted above.

REGENSBURG AFTER DARK

The town's cultural center, **Alte Mälzerei,** Galgenberger Strasse 20 (© **0941/75738**), hosts concerts and theater productions, as well as a run-down bar and beer garden that serves cheap drinks daily 2pm to 1am. The only late-night bar in town, **Wunderbar,** Keplerstrasse 11 (© **0941/53130;** bus: Altstadt bus), serves drinks until 3am, 7 nights a week.

Historische Wurstküche, Thundorferstrasse 3 (© **0941/466210**), celebrated its 853rd birthday in 2008, making it the oldest operating fast-food joint in all of Germany. It's still the best place in town for those delicious Regensburger sausages, which are cooked over beechwood fires in the small kitchen. A total of six of them, served with sauerkraut and fresh bread, costs 7€ ($11). It's located next to the Steinerne Brücke, and tables have a river view. At various times the river has risen to flood the joint. It is open April to October daily from 8am to 7pm, and from November to March only, Sunday 8am to 3pm.

At **Scala,** Gesandtenstrasse 6 (© **0941/52293;** bus: Altstadtbus), three bars hem in the dance floor and attract an under-35 crowd. It's open Wednesday to Sunday 11pm to 3am (until 4am Fri–Sat). Admission is 3€ to 5€ ($4.80–$8).

5 Passau ⋆⋆

191km (119 miles) E of Munich, 117km (73 miles) SE of Regensburg

For years, Passau languished in a lost corner of West Germany. But since reunification, the beauty and nostalgia of this old city has been rediscovered. With its romantic river setting and stately streets, Passau is a city of great harmony. Located at the confluence of the Danube and two of its tributaries, the Ilz and Inn rivers, Passau's bustling port is worth a visit in itself.

ESSENTIALS

GETTING THERE   By Train   Because Passau is a German border station, **Inter-City** trains stop here, with frequent daily arrivals from such cities as Nürnberg, Munich, and Vienna. The other major rail links include Frankfurt-Nürnberg-Passau-Vienna and Nürnberg-Regensburg-Passau, with frequent connections. Trip time from Nürnberg is 2 to 3 hours; from Frankfurt, 4½ to 6 hours; from Munich, 2 hours; from Regensburg, 1 hour, 10 minutes; and from Vienna, 3¼ hours. For rail information and schedules, call © **01805/996633.**

By Bus   No long-distance buses serve Passau. However, buses service the outskirts of the city. For schedules (in German), call **RBO (Regional Bus Ostbayern GmbH)** at © **0851/756370.**

By Car   Access is by the A3 Autobahn from the north or south.

VISITOR INFORMATION   Contact the **Tourist Information Office,** Rathausplatz 3 (© **0851/955980**). Hours are April to October Monday to Friday 8:30am to 6pm, Saturday and Sunday 9am to 4pm; November to March, Monday to Thursday 8:30am to 5pm and Friday 8:30am to 4pm.

GETTING AROUND   Local inner-city buses, clearly marked CITY-BUS, run through Passau and make stops at both the Rathaus (Town Hall) and the Hauptbahnhof (railway station) every 15 minutes, charging a per-person rate of 1.50€ ($2.40). They connect all the attractions recommended below. They operate Monday to Friday 8am to 6pm and Saturday 8am to 4pm. There's no service on Sunday. Call the tourist office for scheduling information.

WHERE TO STAY
EXPENSIVE
Holiday Inn ❀   The Holiday Inn, integrated into the city's largest shopping center, is rather sterile, but it's the best hotel in Passau. Although the guest rooms are in a standard chain-hotel format, they are the most comfortable in town, each with a mid-size bathroom with tub/shower combination.

Bahnhofstrasse 24 (across from the Hauptbahnhof), 94032 Passau. ⓒ 0851/59000. Fax 0851/5900529. 129 units. www.holiday-inn.com. 100€–183€ ($160–$293) double; 195€ ($312) suite. AE, DC, MC, V. Parking 10€ ($16). Bus: City-Bus. **Amenities:** 2 restaurants; bar; indoor heated pool; health club; sauna; solarium; room service; laundry service; nonsmoking rooms; 1 room for those w/limited mobility. *In room:* A/C, TV, Wi-Fi, minibar (in some), coffeemaker (in some), hair dryer, trouser press (in some).

Schloss Ort ❀   For old-fashioned charm with the comfort of today, you can seek lodging in a castle whose origin goes back to the 1200s. The bedrooms are the most spacious in town, opening onto the River Inn. Many prefer one of the bedrooms with 19th-century four-poster beds, although modern furnishings have been scattered throughout as well. Even if you don't stay here, you might want to patronize the on-site restaurant which overflows onto a garden terrace in fair weather, with tables overlooking the Inn. The restaurant doesn't serve on Mondays and in winter.

Ort 11, 94032 Passau. ⓒ 0851/34072. Fax 0851/31817. www.schlosshotel-passau.de. 18 units. 97€–136€ ($155–$218) double; 142€–199€ ($227–$318) suite. DC, MC, V. Parking 4€ ($6.40). **Amenities:** Restaurant; bar; nonsmoking rooms. *In room:* TV.

MODERATE
Altstadt-Hotel ❀ *Finds*   The waters of the Danube, the Ilz, and the Inn converge just a few steps from this hotel. You could stay just for the view, but it's also a well-run, well-priced hotel. Guests who could afford the Holiday Inn seek out this little charmer for its ambience. Rooms are comfortably furnished in traditional style; some overlook the confluence of the rivers. All rooms come with an average-size and tidily kept bathroom with a modern shower. In summer, guests can enjoy meals on the terrace. The hotel has opened an annex, **Zum Laubenwirt,** lying 30m (100 ft.) from the main building. In 15 rooms that are also comfortably furnished and well equipped, it offers bathrooms with shower and such in-room amenities as a dataport, minibar, and hair dryer. Doubles range from 75€ to 80€ ($120–$128), including a buffet breakfast.

Bräugasse 23–29, 94032 Passau. ⓒ 0851/3370. Fax 0851/337100. www.altstadt-hotel.de. 35 units. 115€–125€ ($184–$200) double; 155€ ($248) suite. Rates include buffet breakfast. AE, DC, MC, V. Parking 8€ ($13) in underground garage. Bus: City-Bus. **Amenities:** Restaurant; bar; nonsmoking rooms. *In room:* TV, Wi-Fi, minibar, hair dryer.

Passauer Wolf ❀   This hotel on the Danube lies behind an elegant baroque facade. It isn't as up-to-date as the Holiday Inn but has better food and more character. Rooms are modern and comfortable and service is efficient. Bathrooms are compact, functional boxes that are well maintained but come with shower stalls instead of tubs. The hotel's Passauer Wolf Restaurant is one of the most distinguished in town.

Rindermarkt 6, 94032 Passau. ⓒ 0851/931510. Fax 0851/9315150. 40 units. www.hotel-passauer-wolf.de. 99€–149€ ($158–$238) double. Rates include breakfast. AE, DC, MC, V. Parking 9€ ($14). Bus: City-Bus. **Amenities:** Restaurant; lounge; room service; laundry service; dry cleaning; nonsmoking rooms; rooms for those w/limited mobility. *In room:* TV, minibar, hair dryer.

Weisser Hase ❀ *Value*   This inn straddles the peninsula between the Danube and Inn rivers in the heart of Passau. Completely up-to-date, the "White Rabbit" (its English name) has been accommodating wayfarers since the 1500s. Some prefer this hotel to the more highly rated Passauer Wolf because it provides better value for your money. The guest rooms are midsize and neatly organized with functional furniture that is nonetheless comfortable; each comes with an average-size tiled bathroom with a modern shower unit. There's also a *Weinstube* with Bavarian-Austrian decor—carved wood and provincial chairs.

Ludwigstrasse 23 (off Ludwigsplatz, halfway between the Dom and the Hauptbahnhof), 94032 Passau. © 0851/92110. Fax 0851/9211100. www.weisser-hase.de. 108 units. 125€–150€ ($200–$240) double; 160€–198€ ($256–$317) suite. Rates include buffet breakfast. AE, DC, MC, V. Parking 11€ ($18). Bus: City-Bus. **Amenities:** Restaurant; lounge; sauna; solarium; nonsmoking rooms. *In room:* TV, hair dryer (in some), safe (in some).

INEXPENSIVE

Hotel König   Although the location isn't as scenic as that of the Altstadt-Hotel (see above), this hotel sits at the edge of a spit of land separating the Danube and Inn rivers. Behind massive stucco-covered buttresses and a salmon-colored facade, the interior is comfortably up-to-date. Each well-scrubbed room has pinewood accents. The best open onto views of the Danube or the Inn. The private bathrooms are compact, each with some shelf space and a shower unit.

Untere Donaulande 1, 94032 Passau. © 0851/3850. Fax 0851/385460. www.hotel-koenig.de. 40 units. 85€–140€ ($136–$224) double. Rates include buffet breakfast. AE, DC, MC, V. Parking 10€ ($16). Bus: City-Bus. **Amenities:** Restaurant (next door); bar (next door); lounge; sauna; solarium; nonsmoking rooms; rooms for those w/limited mobility. *In room:* TV, minibar, hair dryer.

Wilder Mann &   The most historic hotel in Passau has origins that may date to the 11th century. On the waterfront market square next to the ancient town hall, the hotel has hosted everybody from the Empress Elizabeth ("Sissi") of Austria to the moon-walking U.S. astronaut Neil Armstrong. The midsize to spacious rooms are furnished in a richly baroque style, each with a well-maintained private bathroom with a tub/shower. Dining in the elaborately old-fashioned and candlelit restaurant is one of the best reasons to stay here. On-site is the small Passauer Glasmuseum devoted to German glass.

Am Rathausplatz, 94032 Passau. © 0851/35071. Fax 0851/31712. www.wilder-mann.com. 49 units. 80€–100€ ($128–$160) double; 200€ ($320) suite. AE, DC, MC, V. **Amenities:** Restaurant; room service; nonsmoking rooms. *In room:* A/C, TV (in some).

WHERE TO DINE

Another dining option is the **Passauer Wolf hotel** (see above), which has one of the better restaurants in town. It serves classic dishes and regional specialties.

Blauer Bock FRANCONIAN/GERMAN   Set in the heart of Passau, adjacent to the Danube, this nostalgia-laden building was constructed in 1374 and is one of the oldest buildings in town. Part of its allure derives from a woodsy, dark-paneled interior that reeks of 19th-century coziness. This, coupled with a riverside terrace with 250 seats, replete with views of the passing river traffic, makes it a great choice for a snack, meal, or drink. Menu items are simple, traditional, and straightforward. The best examples include *Leberknödel* (liver-dumpling) soup and pork shank, slow-cooked for hours, served with a local version of dumplings and sauerkraut. A tasty and time-tested main course, prepared only for two diners at a time, is a roasted and pickled leg of pork with sauerkraut, potatoes, and dumplings. At least four kinds of beer, each brewed within the city limits of Passau by any of several local brewers, are available on tap at any time. Bottled beers from the town's other local brewers are also available.

Also on the premises are four simple, conservatively decorated bedrooms, each with minibar and TV, and renting for 65€ to 88€ ($104–$141) double, 89€ to 130€ ($142–$208) triple. Laundry service and room service are also available.

Höllgasse 20. ℂ 0851/34637. Reservations recommended. Main courses 5.50€–12€ ($8.80–$19); fixed-price lunches 5.50€–9€ ($8.80–$14), dinners 10€–15€ ($16–$24). AE, DC, MC, V. Daily 7am–11pm.

Heilig-Geist-Stift-Schenke BAVARIAN/AUSTRIAN   Each year we hope for a first-class restaurant in Passau, but until that great day comes, this little inn, born in 1358, remains the top choice, with hearty, stick-to-your-ribs fare. In summer, you can sit in a beautiful wine garden under chestnut trees. Indoors, the dining room has an open fireplace, decorated with old tools used to press grapes. The restaurant has its own vineyard, and you can order its wines under the label "Grüner Veltliner." The ancient kitchen serves low-cost regional dishes, including boiled rump steak Austrian-style and roast suckling pig. Passauer Schlosserbaum is a dessert specialty (the waiter will explain). Bavarian, Austrian, and international dishes are featured.

Heiliggeistgasse 4. ℂ 0851/2607. Reservations recommended. Main courses 9.50€–17€ ($15–$27). MC, V. Thurs–Tues 10am–midnight. Closed Jan.

Peschl Terrasse *Value* FRANCONIAN   Named after the beer (Peschl) served in many variations here, this popular eatery is known for copious portions of straightfor-ward and traditional food that tastes especially marvelous when accompanied with beer. There's a cavernous main dining room, three small areas for private parties, and a sunny Danube-fronting outdoor terrace that's invariably the most popular place on warm summer evenings. The establishment has been in the hands of the same family since 1855, and since then, lots of suds have been swilled and spilled within its folk-loric-looking premises. Menu items include roasted shank of veal or pork, usually served with sauerkraut, dumplings, and/or potatoes; cream of potato soup; fish goulash; heaping platters of sausages; terrine of venison; pigs' trotters sauerbraten; and schnitzels of pork, chicken, or veal.

Rosstränke 4. ℂ 0851/2489. Reservations not necessary. Main courses 10€–20€ ($16–$32). MC, V. Tues–Sun 10am–midnight.

EXPLORING PASSAU

The **Altstadt** is built on a rocky spur of land formed by the confluence of the Inn and the Danube. To best appreciate its setting, cross the Danube to the **Veste Oberhaus,** St. Georg Berg 125, a medieval Episcopal fortress towering over the town and the river. Note how arches join many of the houses, giving them a unity of appearance. As you view the town, you can sense that the architecture here is more closely allied to northern Italy and the Tyrolean Alps than to cities to the north. The fortress houses a museum of regional history (ℂ 0851/4933512), going back to medieval times. It's open March to November Monday to Friday 9am to 5pm, and Saturday and Sunday 10am to 6pm. Admission is 5€ ($8) for adults, 4€ ($6.40) for children, and 10€ ($16) for a family ticket. Take the shuttle bus to the castle.

Dominating the town are the twin towers of the **Dom (St. Stephen's Cathedral),** Domplatz 9 (ℂ 0851/39241; bus: City-Bus). The original Gothic plan is clear despite its 17th-century reconstruction in grand baroque style. Its most unusual fea-ture is the octagonal dome over the intersection of the nave and transept. The interior of the cathedral is mainly Italian baroque—almost gaudy, with its many decorations and paintings. Of particular interest is the choir, which remains from the Gothic period. A newer addition is a huge organ, said to be the largest church organ in the world, built in 1928 and placed in an 18th-century casing. Thirty-minute concerts are given May to October Monday to Saturday at noon; there's a second performance on Thursday at 7:30pm. The noon concerts cost 3.50€ ($5.60) for adults and 1€ ($1.60) for students and children 13 and under. The cost of the Thursday 7:30pm concert varies based on your seat, and runs 5€ to 8€ ($8–$13) for adults, 3€ to 4€ ($4.80–$6.40) for children. The Dom is open Monday to Saturday 8 to 11am and 12:30 to 6pm. Admission is free.

Below the cathedral, on the bank of the Danube, are the **Marktplatz** and the 13th-century **Rathaus,** with a facade decorated with painted murals depicting the history of the town. Inside, the huge knights' hall contains two large 19th-century frescoes illustrating incidents from the legend of the Nibelungen. The Town Hall has a Glock-enspiel in its tower that plays at 10:30am, 2 and 7:25pm; on Saturday there's an additional performance at 3pm.

PASSAU AFTER DARK

Combining quality drama with a dramatic setting, the **Stadttheater Company** is housed in the **Stadttheater Passau,** Gottfried-Schäfer-Strasse (© **0851/9291913**), a beautiful baroque opera house built by the local prince-bishops. Call for performance schedules and ticket prices. Summertime brings drama, pantomime, opera, jazz, and classical concerts to town, scheduled as part of the **Europäische Wochen (European Weeks) Festival,** which runs June to late July. Call © **0851/560960** for information; for schedules, tickets, or reservations, contact the **Kartenzentrale der Europäischen Wochen Passau** (© **0851/752020;** fax 0851/4903424; www.passau.de).

Home to Passau's popular cabaret company, **Theater im ScharfrichterHaus,** Milchgasse 2 (© **0851/35900;** www.scharfrichter-haus.de), is open September to July. It also hosts a series of jazz concerts throughout the year. Contact the theater for schedules, prices, and ticket availability. Tickets cost 18€ to 25€ ($29–$40).

Café Innsteg, Innstrasse 15 (© **0851/51257**), housed in a bungalow hanging over the Inn River, offers the town's most scenic setting in which to relax with a drink. Like every other cafe/bar in town, it's open from midmorning until 1am. **Café Kowalski,** Oberer Sandstrasse 1 (© **0851/2487**), is less dramatic but also has balcony views of the river. Underground, across the river, **Joe's Garage,** Lederergasse 38 (© **0851/31999**), is a friendly student dive named after a Frank Zappa album.

6 Ulm ★★

97km (60 miles) SE of Stuttgart, 138km (86 miles) W of Munich

Visit Ulm for its architectural heritage and its history—not for great shopping, nightlife, or even an exciting local life. The city (situated at a strategic spot on the Danube) is a bit sleepy, smug, and satisfied with its monuments, especially its undeniably magnificent cathedral. Ulm's importance as a commercial river port has made it a prosperous city ever since the Middle Ages. Today, Ulm is a center of scientific and technological research, as befits the birthplace of Albert Einstein, who started life here in 1879. The old, narrow alleyways of the Altstadt lead to a modern city of riverbank promenades, beer gardens, spacious squares, and pedestrian zones.

ESSENTIALS

GETTING THERE   By Train   The **Ulm Hauptbahnhof** is on several major and regional rail lines, with frequent connections in all directions. More than 40 trains per day arrive from Munich (trip time: 1 hr., 15 min.) and some 50 or more from Stuttgart (1 hr., 10 min.). Daily trains also arrive from Cologne (3 hr., 12 min.). From Frankfurt (2 hr., 20 min.), you can take an ICE (InterCity-Express), the fastest and most comfortable way to travel by rail. For rail information and schedules, call ℭ **01805/996633.**

By Bus   There are no buses from major cities; local buses service only satellite towns—mostly bedroom communities of Ulm.

By Car   Access by car is via the A8 Autobahn east and west or the A7 north and south. It takes about 1½ hours to drive to Ulm from Munich and about 3 hours to drive from Frankfurt.

VISITOR INFORMATION   Tourist-Information, Münsterplatz (ℭ **0731/ 1612830;** www.tourismus.ulm.de), is open Monday to Friday 9am to 6pm and Saturday 9am to 1pm. From May to October, it's also open Sunday 10:30am to 2:30pm.

GETTING AROUND   Ulm's only tram line runs east-west, connecting the suburban *Messe* (convention center) with the main Hauptbahnhof (railway station) and Söflingen. Ulm's historic core, Altstadt, lies within an easy walk from the Hauptbahnhof. Bus nos. 3, 7, and 8 radiate from the station to the suburbs. Buses and trams run at intervals of between 10 and 30 minutes, depending on the time of day and day of the week, and cost from 1.50€ to 2.10€ ($2.40–$3.40) depending on the distance you travel.

WHERE TO STAY

Hotel am Rathaus & Reblaus   This is the most atmospheric place to stay in town, lying in back of the landmark Rathaus (Town Hall) in the Old Town. It consists of both the main hotel and an equally charming half-timbered Reblaus, the annex. The owner of the hotel is a collector, filling the public areas with antiques, old paintings, and even 19th-century dolls. Try for a bedroom facing the front, since its windows open onto the towering spire of the famous cathedral. Bedrooms have a scattering of antiques, and all have modern appointments as well, with good lighting and crisp white sheets. Hand-painted Bavarian cupboards add more decorative touches throughout the rooms.

Kronengasse 8–10, 89073 Ulm. ℭ **0731/968490.** Fax 0731/9684949. www.rathausulm.de. 34 units. 86€–125€ ($138–$200) double; 155€ ($248) family room (maximum 5 persons). AE, DC. Closed late Dec to mid-Jan. Free parking. **Amenities:** Breakfast room; nonsmoking rooms. *In room:* TV, Wi-Fi.

Maritim Hotel Ulm ★★★ *Kids*   A first-class hotel, this 16-story city-center choice is the grandest hotel in and around Ulm, which until the 1990s never had a first-rate hotel. All guest rooms are large, furnished with first-rate pieces and deluxe mattresses, and have roomy bathrooms with tub/shower combinations. The hotel advertises itself as a home away from home, but few homes look like this palace, and even fewer have the facilities of this monument. The hotel is also the most family-friendly in Ulm; it's the only one to offer rooms big enough for extra beds, babysitting services, and a pool.

Basteistrasse 40, 89073 Ulm. ℭ **0731/9230.** Fax 0731/9231000. www.maritim.de. 287 units. 149€–213€ ($238–$341) double; from 260€ ($416) suite. AE, DC, MC, V. **Amenities:** 2 restaurants; bar; indoor heated pool; gym; room service; babysitting; laundry service; dry cleaning; nonsmoking rooms; rooms for those w/limited mobility. *In room:* A/C, TV, minibar, hair dryer.

Neu-Ulm Mövenpick Hotel   This hotel beside the Danube contains rather bland, but well-maintained, rooms. Many feature views of the river. Guest rooms are in a

---

Finds   Farther Up the Danube: Sigmaringen

Schloss Sigmaringen (© 07571/729230; www.hohenzollern.com), one of the most impressive castles in Germany, lies about 100km (60 miles) southwest of Ulm, dramatically situated on a rock above the Danube. Inside, the rooms are filled with period furniture, porcelain objects, and works of art. The castle also holds displays of 15th- and 16th-century paintings and one of the biggest private collections of arms in Europe. Schloss Sigmaringen is open February to April and November daily 9:30am to 4:30pm, May to October daily 9am to 4:45pm, and December and January only by private arrangements. Admission is 6€ ($9.60) for adults and 2.80€ ($4.50) for children 6 to 18; children 5 and under enter free. To get to Sigmaringen from Ulm, take a train on the Ulm-Freiberg line, or drive southwest on the B311 and then west on the B32. From the north, take the B313 or 88. There are also trains from Stuttgart.

---

standard chain format, but each is midsize and furnished comfortably. All units contain a compact and well-organized tiled bathroom with a tub/shower. The English-speaking staff is helpful.

Silcherstrasse 40, 89231 Neu Ulm. © 0731/80110. Fax 0731/85967. www.moevenpick-hotels.com. 135 units. 95€–130€ ($152–$208) double; 125€ ($200) junior suite; from 185€ ($296) suite. AE, DC, MC, V. Parking 10€ ($16). Bus: 2, 3, or 7. **Amenities:** Restaurant; cafe; bar; room service; laundry service; dry cleaning; nonsmoking rooms; rooms for those w/limited mobility. *In room:* TV, minibar, hair dryer.

WHERE TO DINE

Zunfthaus der Schiffleute BAVARIAN/SEAFOOD   Built some 6 centuries ago between the Danube and the Blau, this landmark building is the classic restaurant in the old town of Ulm. It was once the guild headquarters for local fishermen. For a long time it was the pub of fishermen, who told tall tales about how the Danube used to flood and the fish would swim right up to the kitchen door where they were caught and put on the grill. Fresh fish is still a specialty here, but you can also order a number of well-prepared meat specialties, including delectable veal, roast beef, or entrecôte. A number of freshly made soups and hors d'oeuvres (including carpaccio) are prepared daily. Finish with a velvety chocolate mousse.

Fischergasse 31. © 0731/64411. Reservations not needed. Main courses 9.80€–20€ ($16–$32). AE, MC, V. Daily 11am–midnight.

Zur Forelle ⊛ SWABIAN/GERMAN   So authentically historic and so renowned as a bastion of Germanic *Gemütlichkeit* (coziness) is Zur Forelle that whenever a celebrity arrives in town, their hosts entertain them here. (Noteworthy visitors have included Albert Einstein and Herbert von Karajan.) Named after the trout that appear in succulent versions on the menu, it contains three antique, half-paneled dining rooms, an outdoor terrace with a view of the river and Ulm's historic core, masses of geraniums in its exterior window boxes, and a history of feeding hungry diners that goes back at least 375 years. Food items arrive in generous portions and reflect the best old-fashioned German cooking of the region, with special emphasis on fish. Your meal might begin with Ulm-style herb-and-salmon soup, spicy fish soup with garlic, or a platter of pickled seasonal vegetables. Main courses include beef and liver stew with roasted potatoes and green salad; filet of beef with fresh mushrooms and an herb-flavored cream sauce, served with house-made noodles and green salad; a mixed grill that offers roasted sausage, sliced pork, and hash-brown potatoes on one platter; roasted Barbary duckling in a reduction of port wine; and a wide choice of fish based on whatever is available that day from the local fish market.

Fischergasse 25. (C) **0731/63924.** Reservations recommended. Main courses 11€–22€ ($18–$35); fixed-priced menus 22€–48€ ($35–$77). AE, MC, V. Daily 11:30am–3pm and 5–10pm.

EXPLORING ULM

If you approach the town from the Stuttgart-Munich autobahn, you'll miss the best view. So sometime during your visit, you should cross the Danube into Neu Ulm for a look at the gables and turrets of the Altstadt, which line the north bank of the river. Here is the **Fishermen's Quarter,** with its little medieval houses and tree-shaded squares. Nearby are the elaborate Renaissance patrician houses and the Gothic Renaissance **Rathaus.**

Rathaus   The Rathaus was built in 1370 as a warehouse but has served as the town hall since 1419. It contains some ornate murals dating from the mid–16th century. On the south gable hang coats of arms of cities and countries with which Ulm is linked by commerce. On the east gable is an astronomical clock from 1520. Above the staircase is a reproduction of A. L. Berblinger's flying machine from 1811. Known as "the tailor of Ulm," he was one of the first people to make a serious attempt at flight.

Marktplatz 1. (C) **0731/1610.** Free admission. Mon–Wed 7am–4:30pm; Thurs 7am–6pm; Fri 7am–noon. Bus: 4, 5, 6, or 9.

Ulmer Museum 𝄐   This museum contains an important collection of arts and crafts produced in Ulm and upper Swabia from medieval times onward. There are also exhibitions of both ancient and modern art and artifacts, ranging from the region's prehistory up to the 20th century, with works by Klee, Kandinsky, and Picasso.

Marktplatz 9 (near the cathedral). (C) **0731/1614300.** Admission 3.50€ ($5.60) adults, 2.50€ ($4) students, free for children 14 and under; free for all Fri. Tues–Wed and Fri–Sun 11am–5pm; Thurs 11am–8pm. Bus: 2, 5, or 6.

Ulm Münster 𝄐𝄐𝄐   Before you even get close to the city, you'll see the towering Ulm Münster on the skyline. Its 162m (531-ft.) steeple is the tallest of any cathedral in the world, and the Ulm Münster itself is second only to Cologne Cathedral in size. Without the pews, the nave of the church could hold nearly 20,000 people, more than twice the population of Ulm at the time the cathedral was begun in 1377. When Ulm joined the Protestant movement in 1531, work on the building was suspended. It was not to be continued until 1844, and wasn't completed until 1890. Miraculously, the cathedral escaped serious damage during World War II.

The exterior is almost pure German Gothic, even though bricks were often used in the walls along with the more typical stone blocks. The unusual feature of the Münster is that its architects placed as much emphasis on horizontal lines as on the vertical. Before entering, stop to admire the main porch whose three massive arches lead to two 15th-century doors. This section dates from the 14th and 15th centuries and contains a wealth of statues and reliefs.

The five aisles of the cathedral lead directly from the hall below the tower through the nave to the east chancel. The conspicuous absence of a transept heightens the emphasis on the chancel and also increases the length of the nave. Huge pillars towering into steep arches enclose each of the five aisles. The ceiling is swept into net-vaults so high that any of Germany's church steeples could sit comfortably beneath them. The nave is so large that, even with pews, it can accommodate more than 11,000 people at one service.

The most remarkable treasure of the cathedral is the **Chorgestühl** ௸௸௸ or choir stalls, which are some of the finest examples in Germany of woodcarving. Jorg Syrliun the Elder created these between 1469 and 1474. He depicted personages from the Bible facing those from the pagan era.

You can climb the tower as far as the third gallery (768 steps) to look out on the town and surrounding countryside over the Danube plain as far as the Alps.

Münsterplatz 1. ℂ 0731/9675023. Münster free; tower 4€ ($6.40) adults, 2.50€ ($4) children. Buy tickets an hour before the climb. Nov–Feb daily 9am–4:45pm; Mar and Oct daily 9am–5:45pm; Apr–June and Sept daily 8am–6:45pm; July–Aug daily 8am–7:45pm. Bus: 2, 7, or 9.

ULM AFTER DARK

The best beer hall in town is **Barfusser,** Lautenberg 1 (ℂ **0731/6021110**), a brew-pub that also makes its own pretzels. A beer garden overlooks the Danube. If you'd like to go on a tavern crawl, you can walk **Neue Strasse** down to the river. But if you have a beer at every place, you may not even make it to the river.

8

The Romantic Road

The aptly named Romantic Road, or Romantische Strasse, is one of Germany's most popular tourist routes. The road stretches for 290km (180 miles) between Würzburg in the north and Füssen in the foothills of the Bavarian Alps. On the way is a series of medieval villages and 2,000-year-old towns. Frankfurt and Munich are convenient gateways for exploring the road by car, coach, or rail.

Another way to tour the route is by **bicycle.** Cyclists can begin at Würzburg and follow the bike path along the Main River. Tourist offices along the road provide cycling maps and other helpful information. Campgrounds are generally 10 to 20km (6–12 miles) apart. Bikes can be rented at any train station along the Romantic Road for 5€ to 10€ ($8–$16) per day with a valid train ticket.

The Romantic Road is more than just a scenic route—it's also a powerful marketing organization composed of 26 municipalities, each of which would love to welcome you for a visit. The Romantic Road Association will provide information on sights and attractions and mail information packs in English. Contact the **Touristik Arbeitsgemeinschaft Romantische Strasse,** Segringer Strasse 19, 91550 Dinkelsbühl (© **9851/551387;** www. romantischestrasse.de).

THE TOWNS OF THE ROMANTIC ROAD Every town on the road has its special charms and attractions—and its drawbacks. **Rothenburg,** for example, is a perfect museum town but is overwhelmed with tourists. **Dinkelsbühl** is less perfect—it doesn't do as good a job of transporting you into the past—but at least it has a life of its own, independent of tourists. **Nördlingen** is less romantic even than Dinkelsbühl but is more real. **Augsburg** is Bavaria's third-largest city (after Munich and Nürnberg) but still has a rich medieval past. **Würzburg,** traditionally the first town on the route, is the bustling center of the Franconian wine region and home to one of Germany's greatest palaces.

BUS TOURS OF THE ROMANTIC ROAD April to October, a deluxe motorcoach, with toilets and reclining seats, departs from Frankfurt daily at 8am, stopping on the main squares of 30 towns en route, pulling into Füssen at 7pm. One-way transit between Frankfurt and Füssen costs 99€ ($158), but you can get off the bus and reboard it later at any town en route. Buses also run the other way, from Füssen to Frankfurt, following more or less the same schedule. Make advance reservations with **Deutsche Touring Frankfurt** (© **069/7903501;** www.deutsche-touring.com), Am Römerhof 17, 60486 Frankfurt.

1 Würzburg ✸✸

280km (174 miles) NW of Munich, 119km (74 miles) SE of Frankfurt, 109km (68 miles) NW of Nürnberg

For Germans, the south begins at Würzburg, one of the loveliest baroque cities in the country and the best place to start driving the Romantic Road. This young and lively city on the Main has a population of some 50,000 students, who give it a German version of *joie de vivre.* It's also a center of the Franconian wine region.

Würzburg remained faithful to the Roman Catholic Church throughout the Reformation. It's been called "the town of Madonnas" because of the more than 100 statues of its patron saint that adorn the house fronts. The best known of these statues is the baroque *Patrona Franconiae,* also known as the "Weeping Madonna," which stands among other Franconian saints along the buttresses of the 15th-century Alte Mainbrücke, Germany's second-oldest stone bridge.

On March 16, 1945, Würzburg was shattered by a bombing raid. In a miraculous rebuilding program, nearly every major structure has been restored.

ESSENTIALS
GETTING THERE By Train The **Würzburg Hauptbahnhof** lies on several major and regional rail lines, with frequent connections to all major German cities. From Frankfurt, 30 trains arrive per day (trip time: 1½ hr.); from Munich, 20 trains (2½ hr.); from Nürnberg, 30 trains (1 hr., 10 min.); and several trains from Berlin (5 hr., 50 min.). For rail information and schedules, call © **01805/996633.**

By Bus For bus service along the Romantic Road, see "Bus Tours of the Romantic Road," above.

By Car Access is via the A7 Autobahn from north and south or the A3 Autobahn from east and west. The A81 Autobahn has links from the southwest.

VISITOR INFORMATION Contact the **Tourist Information Office,** in the Falcon House, Am Marktplatz 9 (© **0931/372398**). It's open April to December Monday to Friday 10am to 6pm, and Saturday and Sunday 10am to 4pm; January to March, hours are Monday to Friday 10am to 4pm, Saturday 10am to 1pm.

SPECIAL EVENTS For Mozart lovers, the highlight of the cultural year is the annual **Mozart Festival,** staged in June. Fans of Wolfgang Amadeus from around the world, especially Americans and Europeans, flock to this festival. The venue for most of the Mozart concerts is the glorious baroque palace, the Residenz (see below). For information, contact the tourist office (see above). Many visitors book tours that feature the Mozart festival; the best are conducted by **Allegro Holidays** (© **800/838-6860;** www.allegroholidays.com).

GETTING AROUND The quickest and most efficient means for covering the central core of Würzburg is by tram (streetcar). A single fare is 1.50€ ($2.40), or else you can purchase a ticket, good for 24 hours at any station, for 4.10€ ($6.60). The same fare applies to buses, which also serve the city. For information about routes and schedules, call © **0931/361352.**

WHERE TO STAY
EXPENSIVE
Hotel und Weinrestaurant Schloss Steinburg ✸ *Finds* This turreted castle and its outbuildings sprawl high on a hill overlooking Würzburg. The castle foundations date from the 13th century, but what you see was largely rebuilt around 1900. It's an

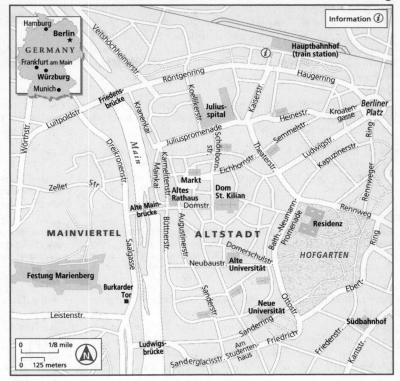

ideal choice for motorists, offering a tranquil setting and reasonable rates. From the terrace, guests can view the Main River, acres of vineyards, and the web of rail lines that carry cargo far into the distance. Rooms have a country nostalgia and come with small tiled bathrooms with showers or tubs.

Auf dem Steinberg, 97080 Würzburg. ℰ 0931/97020. Fax 0931/97121. www.steinburg.com. 52 units. 155€–205€ ($248–$328) double. Rates include buffet breakfast. AE, DC, MC, V. Free parking. Take Rte. 27 3km (2 miles) toward Fulda. **Amenities:** Restaurant; lounge; indoor heated pool; sauna; room service; babysitting; laundry service; dry cleaning. *In room:* TV, hair dryer, safe.

Premier Hotel Rebstock ✵✵   Housed in a palace that dates from 1408, this impressive hotel is not as stylish as the Maritim (see below), but it appeals to those nostalgic for a taste of old Germany. Today it is part of the Best Western chain. Through a classical doorway, you enter a wide foyer with carved wooden doors and an old Spanish sea chest. The interior is tasteful. Guest rooms are equipped with bathrooms containing tub/shower combos. A winter garden with a fountain and chimney replaces an old courtyard.

Neubaustrasse 7, 97070 Würzburg. ℰ 800/528-1234 in the U.S., or 0931/30930. Fax 0931/3093100. www.rebstock. com. 72 units. 176€–213€ ($282–$341) double. Children 11 and under stay free in parent's room. AE, MC, V. Parking 10€ ($16). Tram: 1, 3, or 5. **Amenities:** 2 restaurants; bar; lounge; car rental; room service; babysitting; laundry service; dry cleaning; nonsmoking rooms. *In room:* TV, Wi-Fi, minibar, coffeemaker, hair dryer, iron, safe.

MODERATE

Franziskaner *(Value)*   For homespun cleanliness, this 1909 hotel is a winner—and the price is right, too. You'll receive a hearty welcome from the staff. The lobby has attractive black panels surrounded with natural wood; the breakfast room has fine large windows looking out to the greenery beyond. All of the rooms are well furnished, each with an immaculate bathroom, mostly with tub/shower combos. The hotel serves only breakfast.

Franziskanerplatz 2, 97070 Würzburg. ✆ 0931/35630. Fax 0931/3563333. www.hotel-franziskaner.de. 43 units. 110€–130€ ($176–$208) double. Rates include buffet breakfast. AE, MC, V. Tram: 1. **Amenities:** Restaurant; breakfast room. *In room:* TV, hair dryer.

Hotel Maritim *(★★★)*   Nothing in Würzburg matches this hotel for comfort and style, not even its closest contender, Premier Hotel Rebstock (see above). The Maritim, built in 1983, has 20 rooms with views over the Main River and is linked to the city convention center. A baroque-style mansard roof tops its modern and imposing yellow facade. Rooms are comfortable, each with a midsize, tiled bathroom with tub/shower combination.

Pleichertorstrasse 5, D-97070 Würzburg. ✆ 0931/30530. Fax 0931/3053900. www.maritim.de. 287 units. Fri–Sun 105€–134€ ($168–$214) double, 162€ ($259) suite; Mon–Thurs 160€–179€ ($256–$286) double, 259€ ($414) suite. Rates include buffet breakfast. AE, DC, MC, V. Parking 9€ ($14). Tram: 2 or 4. **Amenities:** Restaurant; bar; indoor heated pool; sauna; solarium; steam room; room service; laundry service; dry cleaning; nonsmoking rooms; rooms for those w/limited mobility. *In room:* A/C, TV, Wi-Fi, minibar, hair dryer.

Zur Stadt Mainz *(★)* *(Finds)*   Dating from the 1400s, when it was known as the Raven, this is one of the most romantic and atmospheric of Franconian inns. Owners Margarethe and Anneliese Schwarzmann are known for their hospitality and excellent cuisine. The midsize rooms are furnished in a cozy, old-fashioned Franconian style, with comfortable beds, tasteful furnishings, and small bathrooms with shower only. The breakfast buffet is the most generous and the best in town.

Even if you're not a guest, consider visiting their restaurant, where many of the traditional dishes come from a historic cookbook. Apple strudel lures afternoon coffee drinkers.

Semmelstrasse 39, 97070 Würzburg. ✆ 0931/53155. Fax 0931/58510. www.hotel-stadtmainz.de. 15 units. 110€ ($176) double; 130€ ($208) triple; 160€ ($256) quad. Rates include breakfast buffet. AE, DC, MC, V. Parking 9€ ($14). **Amenities:** Restaurant. *In room:* TV, hair dryer.

INEXPENSIVE

Schönleber   You'll find this family hotel in the central part of historic Würzburg. The ground floor is rented to boutiques that monopolize the two enormous arched windows facing the sidewalk. The upper floors offer smallish but comfortable rooms. Bathrooms are cramped and most have showers (some have tubs). The staff is friendly and helpful.

Theaterstrasse 5, 97070 Würzburg. ✆ 0931/3048900. Fax 0931/30489030. www.hotel-schoenleber.de. 54 units, 27 with bathroom. 65€ ($104) double without bathroom; 70€–100€ ($112–$160) double with bathroom. Rates include buffet breakfast. AE, DC, MC, V. Parking 8€ ($13). Closed Dec 22–Jan 6. Tram: 1, 2, 3, or 5. **Amenities:** Breakfast room. *In room:* TV, hair dryer, trouser press.

St. Josef *(★)* *(Value)*   St. Josef has the best inexpensive accommodations in the Altstadt. Its owner has been successful in bringing it up-to-date. Rooms, though small, are pleasantly furnished and well maintained, each equipped with an efficiently organized bathroom with shower unit. Fresh flowers add a personalized touch to this well-run establishment.

Semmelstrasse 28–30, 97070 Würzburg. (C) **0931/308680.** Fax 0931/3086860. www.hotel-st-josef.de. 33 units.
85€–95€ ($136–$152) double; 124€ ($198) triple. MC, V. Parking 8.50€ ($14). Tram: 1, 2, 3, or 5. **Amenities:**
Restaurant; lounge; nonsmoking rooms. *In room:* TV, minibar, hair dryer.

WHERE TO DINE

Try the local specialty, *Zwiebelkuchen,* which is like a quiche Lorraine, and also look
for another specialty, *Meerfischle* (a well-seasoned stew made from saltwater fish).
White Franconian wine goes well with the local sausage.

Backöfele FRANCONIAN/GERMAN   Because this place is a short walk from
both the Residenz and the Rathaus, you'll probably eat here at least once while in
Würzburg. Even the locals don't really know whether to call it a beer hall, a wine cellar, or a restaurant. Regardless, the place serves well-prepared traditional food in huge
quantities. Two specialties include lamb chops with fresh potatoes and fresh vegetables
and pikeperch with noodles and a salad.

Ursulinergasse 2. (C) **0931/59059.** Reservations recommended. Main courses 9€–15€ ($14–$24). AE, MC, V.
Mon–Sat noon–1am; Sun noon–midnight. Tram: 1 or 4.

Ratskeller Würzburg *(Value* FRANCONIAN/INTERNATIONAL   This 500-year-
old Ratskeller (part of the Rathaus) serves tasty Franconian fare at reasonable prices.
Country cookery is an art here, as you'll discover if you order the boiled beef with
horseradish sauce and noodles. Other specialties include marinated salmon with
potato pancakes, pikeperch in a white-wine sauce, and medallions of pork gratin with
cheese. Game is featured in season. Ask about local beer and Franconian white wines.

Langgasse 1 (near the Alte Mainbrücke). (C) **0931/13021.** Reservations required Sat–Sun. Main courses 13€–17€
($21–$27); 4-course set menu 25€ ($40). AE, DC, MC, V. Daily 11:30am–2:30pm and 5:30–10:30pm. Tram: 1, 2, 3, or 5.

Weinhaus Zum Stachel *(F* FRANCONIAN/INTERNATIONAL   No other wine
house in Würzburg is as old as this one, dating from 1413. Seats and walls have been
burnished by the clothing of many hundreds of drinkers and diners during the past
500 years. The portions are generous. Try the veal *cordon bleu,* tender pepper steak
aromatically flavored with cognac, or more prosaic rump steak with onions. Some
dishes, such as chateaubriand, are so elaborate that they're prepared only for two. The
chef is proudest of his freshwater fish prepared according to old family recipes. In
summer, you can dine in a vine-draped outdoor courtyard. Wines are from the restaurant's own vineyards.

Gressengasse 1. (C) **0931/52770.** Reservations required. Main courses 15€–22€ ($24–$35); fixed-price menus
30€–49€ ($48–$78). No credit cards. Mon–Sat 11am–midnight. Tram: 1, 3, 4, or 5.

Wein- und Fischhaus Schiffbäuerin *(F Finds* SEAFOOD   One of the best dining
spots in the region is this combined wine house/fish restaurant, across the river in an
old half-timbered building on a narrow street, about 1 minute from the old bridge.
The house specializes in freshwater fish such as pike, carp, char, tench, trout, wels, and
eel. Most of these dishes are priced per 100 grams (3½ oz.). Soup specialties are fish,
snail, and French onion.

Katzengasse 7. (C) **0931/42487.** Reservations recommended. Main courses 15€–28€ ($24–$45). No credit cards.
Tues–Sun noon–2:30pm; Tues–Sat 6–10pm. Closed mid-July to mid-Aug. Tram: 3 or 4.

EXPLORING WÜRZBURG

In spring and summer, the liveliest place in town is the **Markt (central marketplace).**
Here street performers entertain and vendors hawk their wares, ranging from fresh
fruit to souvenir trinkets. You can also stroll down the traffic-free **Schönbornstrasse,**

with its modern boutiques and cafes. The wine merchants here sell *Bocksbeutels,* the green, narrow-necked wine bottles native to the region. It's said that the shape came about because wine-drinking monks found it the easiest to hide under their robes.

Dom St. Kilian   This cathedral, begun in 1045, is the fourth-largest Romanesque church in Germany. The high-baroque stucco work was done after 1700. The imposing row of bishops' tombs begins with that of Gottfried von Spitzenberg (ca. 1190), who was one of the first prince-bishops to rule over the town. Look for three sandstone tombstones by Riemenschneider, constructed between 1502 and 1506. The Dom is dedicated to St. Kilian, an Irish missionary to Franconia in the 7th century.

Domstrasse (at the end of Schönbornstrasse). ℭ **0931/3211830.** Free admission. Easter–Oct Mon–Sat 10am–5pm, Sun 1–6pm; Nov–Easter Mon–Sat 10am–noon and 2–4:30pm, Sun 12:30–1:30pm and 2:30–6pm.

Festung Marienberg (Marienberg Fortress) ⋇   Festung Marienberg, located across from the Altstadt, over the stone bridge, was the residence of the local prince-bishops from 1253 to 1720. The combination of age and wartime destruction has taken a serious toll on its thick walls and once-impenetrable ramparts. But what remains is worth a visit. The 8th-century **Marienkirche,** one of the oldest churches in Germany, stands within its walls.

In the former arsenal and Echter bulwark, to the right of the first courtyard, is the **Mainfränkisches Museum (Main-Franconian Museum)** (ℭ **0931/205940**), housed here since 1946. It's the historical museum of the former Bishopric of Würzburg and Dukedom of Franconia as well as the provincial museum of lower Franconia. On display is a collection of important sculptures by the great, flamboyant Gothic master, Tilman Riemenschneider (1460–1531), called "the master of Würzburg." The sculptor came to live here in 1483 and was the town's mayor in 1520 and 1521. Never a totally decorative artist, Riemenschneider concentrated on the reality of people's appearances, highlighting their hands, faces, and clothing. The museum also displays paintings by Tiepolo and sandstone figures from the rococo gardens of the prince-bishops' summer palace. A tribute to one of the few industries of the city, winemaking, is paid in the press house, which contains historic casks and carved cask bases and a large collection of glasses and goblets.

Fürstenbaumuseum (ℭ **0931/43838**) is situated in the restored princes' wing of the fortress. Here you can glimpse the living quarters and conditions of the prince-bishops up to 1718. The urban-history section offers a stroll through 1,200 eventful years of Würzburg's history, including an exhibit relating to the discovery of X-rays by Wilhelm Conrad Röntgen in 1895. A model of the town shows its appearance in 1525, and another shows the destruction after the bombing of 1945.

Festung Marienberg. ℭ **0931/205940.** www.mainfraenkisches-museum.de. Admission: Mainfränkisches Museum 3€ ($4.80) adults, 1.50€ ($2.40) students, and free for children 13 and under; Fürstenbaumuseum 3€ ($4.80) adults, 1.50€ ($2.40) students, and free for children 13 and under. Combination ticket for both museums 4€ ($5.20). Mainfränkisches Museum Apr–Oct Tues–Sun 10am–5pm; Nov–Mar Tues–Sun 10am–4pm. Fürstenbaumuseum Apr–Oct Tues–Sun 10am–5pm. Tours of the fortress (in English and German) Apr–Oct Tues–Sun 10am–4pm; 2€ ($2.60). Bus: 9.

Residenz (Schloss und Gartenverwaltung Würzburg) ⋇⋇   The Residenz of Würzburg is the last and finest of a line of baroque castles built in Bavaria in the 17th and 18th centuries. This horseshoe-shaped edifice was begun in 1720 to satisfy Prince-Bishop Johann Philipp Franz von Schönborn's passion for elegance and splendor. Its design was the joint effort of the best Viennese, French, and German architects working under the leadership of Balthasar Neumann (1687–1753). An architect and an engineer, Neumann was known for his technical virtuosity and the harmony of his compositions. This castle shows a unity of purpose and design unusual in structures of such size.

At the center of the castle is the masterful *Treppenhaus* (staircase). The high, rounded ceiling above is decorated with a huge fresco by Tiepolo. At its center, Apollo is seen ascending to the zenith of the vault. The surrounding themes represent the four corners of the world, the seasons, and signs of the zodiac. The painting appears to be overflowing onto the walls of the upper hall.

The other important attraction is the court chapel, in the southwest section. Neumann placed the window arches at oblique angles to coordinate the windows with the oval sections, thus creating a muted effect. The rectangular room is divided into five oval sections, three with domed ceilings. Colored marble columns define the sections, their gilded capitals enriching the ceiling frescoes by Johann Rudolf Byss. At the side altars, Tiepolo painted two important works: *The Fall of the Angels* on the left and *The Assumption of the Virgin* on the right.

During the summer, a **Mozart festival** is held in the upper halls. For information, call ℂ **0931/372336.**

Residenzplatz 2, Tor B. ℂ 0931/355170. Admission 5€ ($8) adults; 4€ ($6.40) students, children, and seniors. Apr–Oct daily 9am–6pm; Nov–Mar daily 10am–4:30pm. Guided tours in English (included in admission) 10am and 3pm. Tram: 1 or 5.

WÜRZBURG AFTER DARK

Much of Würzburg's nightlife takes place in its numerous *Weinstuben* (wine cellars). For music and cultural happenings, scan the flyers posted in the *Studentenhaus* (student center) on Am Exerzierplatz at Münzstrasse.

The city's oldest jazz club, **Omnibus,** Theaterstrasse 10 (ℂ **0931/56121;** bus: 14 or 20), has been packing it in for live acts for nearly 3 decades. This cellar-level joint is also where people come to drink and play chess. It's open Monday to Thursday 8pm to 1am, and Friday and Saturday 9pm to 3am. Cover charges for performances range from 8€ to 16€ ($13–$26). A place for a cheap meal or a drink, **Standard,** Oberthurstrasse 11a (ℂ **0931/51140;** bus: 14 or 20), is open daily 9:45am to 2am. It occasionally has a live band on the weekend. **Kult Statt Kneipe,** Landwehrstrasse 10 (ℂ **0931/53143;** tram: 1, 3, or 5), keeps the stereo cranking. It's open Monday to Friday 9am to 1am (Thurs until 2am), Saturday 10am to 2am, and Sunday 10am to 1am.

The **Weinstuben Juliusspital,** Juliuspromenade 19 (ℂ **0931/54080**), is a top address for wine connoisseurs, with an array of characteristic Franconian vintages. Meals are also served. It's open daily 10am to midnight.

2 Miltenberg ⋆

29km (18 miles) S of Mespelbrunn, 71km (44 miles) W of Würzburg

This riverside town, along with Amorbach (see below), is located to the west of the traditional route of the Romantic Road, but it's very popular and well worth a visit. Miltenberg is sleepy, traditional, and full of half-timbered buildings. If you're looking for a medieval town but you want to avoid the tour-bus hordes that overrun places like Rothenburg (see "Rothenburg ob der Tauber," later in this chapter), Miltenberg is for you.

The town, which is still enclosed within walls and gate towers, is attractively situated under a steep wooded hill crowned by a castle. Its municipal charter dates from 1237, but it was actually settled centuries earlier by the Romans. The best way to appreciate Miltenberg's charm is on a fast drive-through, with a pedestrian detour through its charming **Marktplatz** 𝔽. Here, on steeply sloping terrain centered on a Renaissance-era red-sandstone fountain and a wealth of flowers, you'll find a phalanx of half-timbered houses, and one of the oldest inns in Germany, the **Haus zum Riesen.**

ESSENTIALS

GETTING THERE   By Train   Three or four trains per day arrive from Würzburg, 90 minutes away, and about a dozen come every day from the important railway junction of Aschaffenburg, 45 minutes away. For railway information, call ℂ **01805/ 996633.**

By Car   From the north, take Route B469 into town (it's signposted). From Würzburg, take the A3 west and then minor roads.

VISITOR INFORMATION   The **tourist office,** Engelplatz 69 (ℂ **09371/404119**), offers English-language pamphlets describing brief self-guided walking tours through the town. It's open Monday to Friday 9am to 5pm. May to October, it's also open Saturday 10am to 1pm.

WHERE TO STAY

Haus zum Riesen Hotel 𝔽   This awesomely historic hotel is permeated with a polite sense of modern management. Its origins date from 1190, just before it hosted Frederick Barbarossa during his expeditions in this part of Germany. During the Thirty Years' War, it housed VIPs from both sides, depending on who was in control. Today, this hotel is the most evocative in town, graced with charmingly old-fashioned rooms, usually with beamed ceilings. Bathrooms range from midsize to spacious, most often with a tub/shower combo. However, the place is more famous as a restaurant than as a hotel (see review below).

Hauptstrasse 97, 63897 Miltenberg. ℂ 09371/3644. www.riesen-miltenberg.de. 14 units. 80€–105€ ($128–$168) double; 125€ ($200) suite. Rates include breakfast. No credit cards. **Amenities:** Restaurant; bar; lounge; room service. *In room:* Hair dryer.

Hotel Altes Bannhaus 𝔽   This medieval hotel on the town's main street is behind a severely dignified stone facade that's graced with an elaborate iron bracket. It treads the fine line between authentically historical and merely dowdy. Overall, its vaulted stone cellars and massive masonry are charming. Rooms are more angular and modern looking than the authentically antique public areas. Each has functional furniture, small windows, and small shower-only bathrooms.

Hauptstrasse 211, 63897 Miltenberg. ℂ 09371/3061. Fax 09371/68754. www.altes-bannhaus.de. 10 units. 95€–100€ ($152–$160) double. Rates include continental breakfast. AE, DC, MC, V. **Amenities:** Restaurant; room service. *In room:* TV, minibar, hair dryer.

WHERE TO DINE

Gasthaus zum Riesen GERMAN   Although this restaurant is associated with the hotel above, it is run separately at a nearby address, lying 90m (300 ft.) away. Inside, the dining room is an antique that often features old-fashioned dishes, such as bear steak, imported from Russia. From the kitchen come such German granny favorites as either potato soup or liver dumpling soup, as well as a dish that we've seen in no other restaurant in Germany, *Ochsenfetzen* ("torn-apart ox"). This delicacy—the subject of many articles in culinary reviews and based on authentic medieval scholarship—uses brisket of beef marinated for 2 weeks in marinades that change every other day. You can also order such rib-sticking fare as loin of pork with mushrooms, or a platter piled high with pork filets, turkey filets, German sausages, rösti (hash browns), and freshly made salads. Most diners order freshly made crepes or ice cream for dessert.

99 Hauptstrasse. ℂ 09371/989948. www.riesen-miltenberg.de. Main courses 8€–16€ ($13–$26). Daily 11am–3:30pm and 7:30–11pm. AE, MC, V.

EXPLORING MILTENBERG

Park your car in the first convenient parking lot and walk into the center of town—don't attempt to drive. Other than the above-mentioned Marktplatz, the main attraction in town is **Schloss Miltenberg** ℛ. (Be warned in advance that this castle is sometimes identified simply as "Miltenberg.") Don't expect a rich tour of a medieval-looking interior, as all but a fraction (a cafe) of the castle's inside has been closed for a long-standing series of renovations. You can visit the courtyard, however, and climb to the top of a watchtower for a sweeping view over the surrounding forest. The courtyard, the tower, and the cafe that's associated with the site are open only May to October Tuesday to Friday 2 to 5:30pm, Saturday and Sunday 1 to 5:30pm. Admission costs 1.50€ ($2.40) adults and 1€ ($1.60) for children 11 and under.

During your exploration of Miltenberg, don't overlook the oldest and most historic bar in town, a 500-year-old hangout that locals refer to simply as **Weinhaus,** Marktplatz 185 (ℂ **09371/5500**). Here, every evening between 5:30pm and midnight, you can order any of the local vintages, at a per-glass price of 2€ to 6€ ($3.20–$9.60).

3 Amorbach ℱ

11km (7 miles) S of Miltenberg, 92km (57 miles) SW of Würzburg

This little town shouldn't take up too much of your time, but it does offer a few rewarding sights, notably the Abteikirche of St. Maria. It also has one of the finest hotels in the region. As you wander about Amorbach's center, note how local homeowners have dotted the half-timbered facades with flower boxes.

ESSENTIALS

GETTING THERE   By Train or Bus   Three or four trains arrive every day from Würzburg (trip time: 90 min.), and 12 arrive from Aschaffenburg (trip time: 45 min.). For railway information, call ℂ **01805/996633.** However, there are no direct trains. Passengers must arrive first in Miltenberg for a change of trains before proceeding on to Amorbach.

By Car   From Miltenberg, follow Route 469 south for 11km (7 miles).

VISITOR INFORMATION   The **Stadt Verkehrsamt,** at the Rathaus, Marktplatz 1 (ℂ **09373/20940**), is open May to September Monday to Friday 9:30am to noon and 2:30 to 5:30pm, Saturday 10am to 1pm. In October, hours are Monday to Friday 9:30am to noon and 3 to 5pm. From November to April, it is open Monday to Friday 10am to noon and 3 to 5pm.

WHERE TO STAY & DINE

Der Schafhof Amorbach ℛℛℛ   The most romantic and carefully manicured hotel in the district lies within what was originally a Benedictine monastery (ca. 1450) and rebuilt in 1721 in a country-baroque style. The more historic rooms lie within the former abbey; more modern, better-equipped units are within a well-built modern annex. Our favorites lie under the eaves of the main building and are crisscrossed with a labyrinth of hand-hewn ceiling beams. Rooms are stylish and comfortably outfitted in a plush but conservative style, each with a midsize tiled bathroom with a tub/shower combo.

Local gourmets fawn on the sublime cuisine served in the hotel's **Abtstube,** the finest restaurant in the district, specializing in regional and Mediterranean cuisine. Main courses range from 16€ to 19€ ($26–$30).

Otterbachtal, 63916 Amorbach. (🕿 09373/97330. Fax 09373/4120. www.schafhof.de. 24 units. 135€–180€ ($216–$288) double; 220€–285€ ($352–$456) suite. Rates include breakfast. AE, DC, MC, V. From Amorbach, follow N47 (the Niebelungenstrasse) west for 5km (3 miles). **Amenities:** 2 restaurants; lounge; sauna; solarium; room service; laundry service. *In room:* TV, minibar, hair dryer, safe (in some).

EXPLORING AMORBACH

Much of the fun of a visit to Amorbach lies simply in wandering through the streets of the old town, where half-timbered medieval buildings, some of them a bit artfully askew, still evoke old Germany.

The town's most important monument is the **Abteikirche St. Maria** *✿*, Kirchplatz (🕿 09373/971545). This impressive church underwent at least a half-dozen enlargements and alterations between the 8th and the 18th centuries, but it still retains a degree of charm and cohesiveness. The interior is a mass of ornate baroque stucco, centering on one of the most impressive baroque-era organs in Germany. Entrance is free, but a guided tour, conducted in German or English, costs 3€ ($4.80) per person. It's open March 15 to November 8 Monday to Saturday 9:30am to 5:45pm and Sunday 11am to 5:45pm; November 9 to March 14 daily 10:30am to 12:30pm and 1:30 to 4pm.

A small museum, **Sammlung Berger (The Berger Collection),** Wolkmannstrasse 2 (🕿 09373/99081), holds around 17,000 teapots, many from the U.S. and Britain. Part of the funding of this museum comes from a local teapot manufacturer, whose wares are sold in the museum shop. Entrance is 4€ ($6.40). It's open only April to October, Tuesday to Sunday 11am to 5pm.

The ruined remains of **Wildenberg Castle,** Odenwald (🕿 09373/20940), lie 5km (3 miles) southeast of Amorbach. Originally built 1,000 years ago, it's now little more than a jumble of impressive medieval-looking rock piles. The restored watchtower, however, can be climbed every Sunday 11am to 5pm. Admission is free. The view over the Odenwald Forest is excellent.

4 Bad Mergentheim *✿*

47km (29 miles) S of Würzburg, 106km (66 miles) NE of Stuttgart

Most of this spa town's fame derives from its role during and after the Renaissance as the home, beginning in 1525, of the Teutonic Knights, one of the most durable orders of feudal knights. From their base in Bad Mergentheim, they received tributes and pledges of allegiance from as far away as Lithuania. The knights' way of life ended abruptly in 1809, when Napoleon forcibly disbanded the order, consequently threatening the very existence of the town.

But Bad Mergentheim's fortunes were reversed in 1826, when a shepherd discovered rich mineral springs a short walk north of the town center during the time when Germany's spas were expanding at a rapid pace. The water turned out to be the strongest sodium-sulfate water in all of Europe; it was said to have health-giving properties, especially in the treatment of digestive disorders. With the knights gone, the little town had discovered the key to its future prosperity.

ESSENTIALS

GETTING THERE **By Train or Bus** Access by train is easier and more convenient than by bus. From Würzburg, trains arrive almost every hour (trip time: 40 min.). From Stuttgart, they arrive at intervals of 90 to 120 minutes (trip time: 90 min.). For information about **railway schedules,** call © **01805/996633.** For bus service along the Romantic Road, see "Bus Tours of the Romantic Road," at the beginning of this chapter.

By Car From Würzburg, head south along Route 19.

VISITOR INFORMATION The Tourist Office, called **Kultur und Verkehrsamt,** is at Marktplatz 3 (© **07931/57131**). April to October, it's open Monday to Friday 9am to 5pm, Saturday 10am to 4pm, and Sunday 10am to 2pm. November to March, it is open Monday to Friday 9am to noon and 2:30 to 5pm.

WHERE TO STAY & DINE

Haus Bundschu ⭐ *Finds* Though nowhere near as highly rated as the Victoria (see below), this is a cozy, affordable nest that some prefer to properties with more facilities. Inviting, understated, and cozy, this hotel was built about 2 decades ago in a style that incorporated a masonry-covered courtyard, lots of exposed wood, and touches of Romantic Road nostalgia. It's within a 5-minute walk of the town center. Rooms are sunny, with big windows, and well-maintained, each with a midsize bathroom with tub/shower combination.

Cronbergstrasse 15, 97980 Bad Mergentheim. © **07931/9330.** Fax 07931/933633. www.hotel-bundschu.de. 51 units. 78€–100€ ($125–$160) double. Rates include breakfast. AE, DC, MC, V. **Amenities:** Restaurant; bar; lounge. *In room:* TV, minibar, hair dryer, iron.

Hotel Victoria ⭐⭐⭐ The best hotel in town occupies a stately, five-story, ocher-colored building. Inside, the color scheme is an oft-repeated and very pleasing combination of champagne, beige, yellow, and black. Rooms are modern and plush, with lots of concealed, very elegant lighting and comfortable furnishings. All accommodations have a roomy bathroom stylishly outfitted with deluxe fixtures, toiletries, and a tub/shower combination. The on-site restaurant, Zirbelstube, is the finest in the area and is definitely the place to dine even if you're not a guest. However, you should call for a reservation.

Poststrasse 2–4, 97980 Bad Mergentheim. © **07931/5930.** Fax 07931/593500. www.victoria-hotel.de. 78 units. 105€–155€ ($168–$248) double; 180€–230€ ($288–$368) suite. Half board 30€ ($48) extra per person. Rates include breakfast. AE, DC, MC, V. Parking 6€ ($9.60) per day. **Amenities:** 2 restaurants; bar; lounge; health spa; room service; massage; laundry service; dry cleaning. *In room:* TV, minibar, hair dryer.

EXPLORING BAD MERGENTHEIM

The best way to see the town is to wander through its historically evocative streets, most of which radiate from the meticulously restored **Marktplatz.** Schloss Park leads to the spa establishments on the right bank of the Tauber. The Kursaal is a pump room with both a visitor center and bathing facilities.

The most impressive structure in town, noted for its relatively large size, is the somewhat sterile and barren-looking **Münster Kirche Sankt Johannes,** Ledermarkt 12 (© **07931/98600**), which was begun around 1250 and completed several centuries later. It's open daily 9am to dusk; entrance is free. More appealing is the medieval castle that once served as the Teutonic Knights' home base, the **Deutschordenschloss,** site of the **Deutschordensmuseum,** Schloss 16 (© **07931/52212;**

Finds   An Excursion to Stuppach

The agrarian village of **Stuppach** (pop. 500), located 11km (7 miles) south-east of Bad Mergentheim, is the site of one of the region's most important artistic treasures, the *Stuppacher Madonna* by Matthias Grünewald (ca. 1475–1528). This dark, brooding work is diametrically opposed to the lighter motifs of such contemporaneous artists as Dürer. It's the artistic centerpiece of the village's only church, the **Fahrkirche Maria Krönung,** Kirchplatz (✆ **07931/2605**), which can be visited, without charge, in winter daily from 10am to 3pm and in summer daily from 10am to 5:30pm (closed Jan).

www.deutschordensmuseum.de). Inside is a sweeping retrospective of chivalry's preconceptions and preoccupations, with all the requisite displays of suits of armor and weapons. Surprisingly, this medieval order of knights has been restored and now serves as a religious and charitable organization. Note the corner towers in the inner courtyard, which are furnished with Renaissance spiral staircases. The museum is open April to October Tuesday to Sunday 10:30am to 5pm, and November to March Tuesday to Saturday 2 to 5pm and Sunday 10:30am to 5pm. Entrance is 4.20€ ($6.70) for adults, 3.20€ ($5.10) for seniors and students, 1.50€ ($2.40) for children 6 to 14, and free for children 5 and under.

A second-tier attraction that's a lot less worthwhile than a walk through the town itself is the **Wildpark Bad,** Bad Mergentheim Game Preserve (✆ **07931/41344**), 5km (3 miles) east of the town center. It contains wild animals in cages and roaming within natural environments. Mid-March to October, it's open daily 9am to 6pm. Entrance is 8.50€ ($14) for adults, 5.50€ ($8.80) for children.

5 Weikersheim

10km (6 miles) E of Bad Mergentheim, 40km (25 miles) S of Würzburg

The architecture of this riverside town is consistently 18th century; it's one of the most stylistically unified towns on the Romantic Road. Weikersheim also boasts one of the mightiest castles on the Romantic Road.

ESSENTIALS

GETTING THERE   By Train or Bus   Trains pull into Weikersheim from Würzburg at intervals of 60 to 120 minutes throughout the day (trip time: 40 min.). From Stuttgart, they arrive at intervals of 90 to 120 minutes (trip time: 90 min.). For information about railway schedules, call the station at ✆ **01805/996633.** For bus service along the Romantic Road, see "Bus Tours of the Romantic Road," at the beginning of this chapter.

By Car   Take the B232 from Bad Mergentheim.

VISITOR INFORMATION   The **Tourist Office** at Marktplatz 7 (✆ **07934/ 10255**) is open April to October Monday to Friday 9:30am to 5:30pm, and November to March Monday to Thursday 9am to 5pm and Friday 9am to 1pm.

WHERE TO STAY & DINE

Flair Hotel Laurentius ♔   The most appealing hotel in town is an old-fashioned monument to the art of hospitality. It's an ideal stopover along the Romantic Road, for either a meal or an overnight stay. Its vaulted, street-level area is the site of a cozy restaurant and wine bar. Upstairs, a series of high-ceilinged rooms contain a pleasing, unpretentious mix of attractive reproductions and genuine antiques. Bathrooms are quirkily old-fashioned, but not without charm, each with a tub/shower combination. Suites have whirlpool tubs and panoramic flatscreen televisions.

Marktplatz 5, 97990 Weikersheim. ℂ **07934/91080.** Fax 07934/910818. www.hotel-laurentius.de. 14 units. 95€–110€ ($152–$176) double; 158€–298€ ($253–$477) suite. Rates include breakfast. AE, DC, MC, V. Free parking. **Amenities:** Restaurant; cafe; bar; sauna; room service; laundry service. *In room:* TV, minibar (in suites), hair dryer, iron.

EXPLORING WEIKERSHEIM

During its formative years, the very existence of the town was dependent on its castle, **Schloss Weikersheim,** Schlossstrasse (ℂ **07934/992950;** www.schloss-weikersheim. de). It was begun in 1586 and completed a century later in a severely dignified style that had nothing to do with the baroque style then popular in other parts of Germany. When Count Ludwig II reestablished Weikersheim as his family's main residence, he ordered that the old moated castle be replaced with a new Renaissance palace.

You can visit the castle's interior daily April to October 9am to 6pm and November to March 10am to noon and 1 to 5pm; admission is 5€ ($8) adults and 2.50€ ($4) for students, seniors, and children. A family ticket is 13€ ($21). Its architectural and decorative highlight is the **Rittersaal (Knight's Hall)** ♔♔, which was completed in 1603 and shows the transition between the baroque and the earlier Renaissance style. This is the most sumptuous banqueting hall ever built in Germany. Note the bas-reliefs of game animals lining the walls. The entrance doorway is carved with a scene of a battle against the Turks. The gigantic chimney piece is adorned with an allegory illustrating the motto, "God gives luck." The castle contains one of the most remarkable collections of **antique furnishings** ♔♔ of any castle in Germany, a treasure trove stretching out for 2 centuries beginning in 1550. Also, allow some time to wander through the well-preserved **gardens.**

To one side of the castle is the **Marktplatz,** a semicircular market square that opens onto sweeping vistas. It was laid out in the early 18th century.

6 Creglingen

19km (12 miles) E of Weikersheim, 40km (25 miles) S of Würzburg

The history of Creglingen goes back more than 4,000 years. Originally, it was an important Celtic stronghold. Later on, around the year 1000, it was mentioned in written sources as a wine-growing site. By 1349, the town had gained the right to call itself a "city." Around the same time, Creglingen became an important pilgrimage site, thanks to the legend of a local farmer who claimed to have seen Jesus and a phalanx of angels plowing his fields.

Today, Creglingen is one of the quietest hamlets along the Romantic Road, with a tiny but colorful inner core of buildings that evoke the Germany of long ago and a charming but substandard set of accommodations, usually in local farmhouses. The surrounding countryside is called "The Lord God's Little Land"—locals believed that it resembled the Garden of Eden. You may think so too, if you explore the local streams and lakes, where anglers fish for pike, carp, trout, eel, or perch.

ESSENTIALS

GETTING THERE   By Train or Bus   Rail connections from Würzburg arrive about once every 2 hours, pulling into the hamlet of Steinach, about 19km (12 miles) from Creglingen. At the station, an employee will call a local taxi to take you into Creglingen. For railway information, call the information service for local train lines at © **01805/996633.** For bus service along the Romantic Road, see "Bus Tours of the Romantic Road," at the beginning of this chapter.

By Car   Follow the signs west from Weikersheim.

VISITOR INFORMATION   Tourist information is at Torstrasse 2 (© **07933/ 631**); it's open Monday to Friday 9am to 4:30pm.

WHERE TO STAY

Accommodations are not plentiful in Creglingen; most visitors are merely passing through. You might find a small B&B operating in summer, but don't count on it. Consider the city of Würzburg (p. 258) for food and lodgings.

EXPLORING CREGLINGEN

Creglingen is home of one of the most quirky museums in Germany, the **Fingerhut-museum (Thimble Museum),** Kohlesmühle 6 (© **07933/370**), where the largest collection of thimbles in Europe has been accumulated. Some of them are bone rings dating from prehistoric times; others are made of brass that was smelted in Creglingen during the Middle Ages. It's open April to October Tuesday to Sunday 10am to 12:30pm and 2 to 5pm; hours for November, December, and March are Tuesday to Sunday 1 to 4pm. Admission is 1.50€ ($2.40).

The most important local attraction is the **Herrgottskirche (Chapel of Our Lord).** The chapel was built by the counts of Hohenlohe around 1525. Its enormous altarpiece, a 19m (33-ft.) structure showing the ascension of Mary, was decorated in the 16th century. All the artist's sensitivity is translated into the expression of the Virgin. The work is set in a filigree shrine specially constructed to catch the day's changing light effects. The chapel can be visited daily April to October 9:15am to 5:30pm, and November to March Tuesday to Sunday 10am to noon and 1 to 4pm. Admission is 2€ ($3.20). For more information, contact the tourist office (© **07933/508**), which is set 3km (2 miles) south of Creglingen within the Gerrgottstal Valley. It's clearly posted from the village center.

7 Rothenburg ob der Tauber ★★★

117km (73 miles) NE of Stuttgart, 51km (32 miles) SE of Würzburg

If you have time for only one town on the Romantic Road, make it Rothenburg. Admittedly, if you arrive at Rothenburg's Bahnhof, at the northeast corner of town, you may find it hard to believe that this is the best-preserved medieval city in Europe. Contemporary life and industry have made an impact, and as you leave the station, you'll initially see factories and office buildings. But don't be discouraged. Inside those undamaged 13th-century city walls is a medieval town seemingly untouched by the passage of time.

The only drawback to this gem is that it suffers from serious overcrowding, especially in summer. (The Rothenburg locals go so far as to put bumper stickers on their cars proclaiming in German, "I'm not a tourist—I actually live here.") Ironically, Rothenburg, for centuries, was impoverished and forgotten. It was first mentioned in

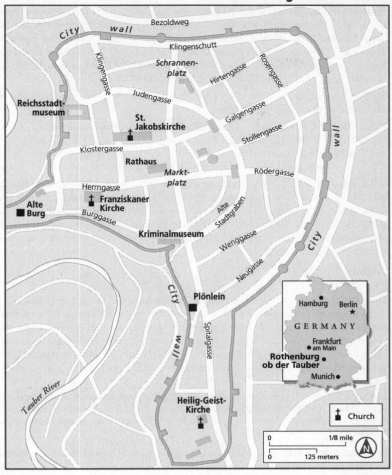

written records in 804 as Rotinbure, a settlement above ("ob" in German) the Tauber River. The town grew to be a free imperial city, reaching its apex of prosperity under Bürgermeister Heinrich Toppler in the 14th century.

ESSENTIALS

GETTING THERE   By Plane   The nearest regional airport is Nürnberg (see chapter 7); from there it's a 2-hour train ride to Rothenburg.

By Train   You can reach Rothenburg via a daily train from Frankfurt (trip time: 3 hr.), from Hamburg (trip time: 5½ hr.), or from Berlin (trip time: 7 hr.). Rothenburg lies on the Steinach-Rothenburg rail line, with frequent connections to all major German cities, including Nürnberg and Stuttgart. For information, call (£) **01805/996633.**

By Bus   For bus service along the Romantic Road, see "Bus Tours of the Romantic Road," at the beginning of this chapter. Regular long-distance buses service Rothenburg from Frankfurt, Würzburg, Augsburg, and Munich, as well as Füssen. For information and reservations, call the Frankfurt number (✆ **069/790-3261** in Frankfurt). Regional bus service is provided by **OVF Omnibusverkehr Franken GmbH,** Nelson-Mandela-Platz 18, D-90159 Nürnberg (✆ **0911/430570**).

By Car   Access by car is via the minor road south from Creglingen or by the A7 Autobahn on the Würzburg-Ulm run.

VISITOR INFORMATION   Contact **Rothenburg Tourismus Service,** Marktplatz (✆ **09861/404800**). November to April, it's open Monday to Friday 9am to noon and 1 to 5pm, and Saturday 10am to 1pm; May to October, it's open Monday to Friday 9am to noon and 1 to 6pm, Saturday and Sunday 10am to 3pm.

SPECIAL EVENTS   The cultural event of the year is the **Meistertrunk festival,** held May 13 to May 16; it celebrates the entire history of the town, with more than 1,000 participants in costume. Concerts, historical exhibitions, a parade, and a play about the Burgermeister Nusch's wager (see the Reichsstadtmuseum listing, below) are the festival's highlights. The play is also staged in July and October. For details, contact the visitor information office.

WHERE TO STAY
EXPENSIVE
Burg Hotel ⍟   Although not as fancy as the Eisenhut (see below), this inn is full of German charm. It lies at the end of a cul-de-sac in an old-fashioned timbered house that overlooks the Tauber Valley—just the kind of place Red Riding Hood might have visited to see Grandma. Parking is in the barn of a former Dominican monastery. Rooms are spread across three floors (no elevator). There are many extras, including spacious bathrooms with showers and large mirrors. Any room is likely to please, but for the best views, ask for no. 7, 12, or 25.

Klostergasse 1–3, 91541 Rothenburg ob der Tauber. ✆ **09861/94890.** Fax 09861/948940. www.burghotel.rothen burg.de. 15 units. 90€–170€ ($144–$272) double; from 170€ ($272) suite. Rates include buffet breakfast. MC, V. Parking 9€ ($14). **Amenities:** Nonsmoking rooms; rooms for those w/limited mobility. *In room:* TV, dataport, minibar, hair dryer, safe.

Eisenhut (Iron Helmet) ⍟⍟⍟   Eisenhut is the most celebrated inn on the Romantic Road and one of the finest small hotels in Germany. It's also rather expensive, but it's worth the money. If this hotel has a problem, it might be its popularity. The staff always appears overworked. The hotel is composed of four medieval patrician houses joined together. Rooms range from medium to spacious, and all are unique. Yours may contain hand-carved and monumental pieces, or a tufted satin headboard for a 1940s Hollywood touch. All are enhanced by bedside controls, spacious bathrooms with tub/shower combinations, and ample closet space.

Herrengasse 3–5, 91541 Rothenburg ob der Tauber. ✆ **09861/7050.** Fax 09861/70545. www.eisenhut.com. 79 units. 156€–225€ ($250–$360) double; 299€–350€ ($478–$560) suite. AE, DC, MC, V. Parking 9€ ($14). Closed Jan 3–Feb 28. **Amenities:** Restaurant; piano bar; beer garden; room service; laundry service; dry cleaning; nonsmoking rooms. *In room:* TV, Wi-Fi, minibar, hair dryer.

Hotel Mittermeier ⍟⍟⍟   This is the most tranquil and atmospheric hotel in town, and it also serves the most highly rated cuisine. You may want to dine here even if you're not a guest. Lying only a kilometer (⅔ mile) from the center of town, this is an old-fashioned Bavarian inn but it's been completely modernized. Each of its bedrooms is individually decorated in a combination of modern and traditional furnishings. Bathrooms are state of the art, with robes, makeup mirrors, and designer toiletries among other amenities. Guests settle into a soft armchair in the library or else use the high-speed wireless Internet access in the public areas. Almost every guest patronizes the hotel's deluxe restaurant (see review below). The concierge is particularly helpful in offering tour advice, ranging from wine tasting in Würzburg to strolls around the town walls of Dinkelsbühl.

Vorm Würzburger Tor 7–9, 91541 Rothenburg ob der Tauber. © 09861/94540. Fax 09861/945-49-41. www.mittermeier. rothenburg.de. 27 units. 70€–145€ ($112–$232) double; 169€ ($270) junior suite; 198€ ($317) suite. AE, DC, MC, V. Parking 7€ ($11). **Amenities:** Restaurant; bar; business services; room service; laundry service; dry cleaning; babysitting; nonsmoking rooms. *In room:* A/C, TV, Wi-Fi, hair dryer.

Romantik Hotel Markusturm 🏵🏵 This is one of Rothenburg's charming nuggets, without the facilities and physical plant of the Eisenhut, but a winner in its own right. When this hotel was constructed as a customs house in 1264, one of Rothenburg's defensive walls was incorporated into the building. Some rooms have four-poster beds, and about half the bathrooms have tub/shower combos. The individual decorations range from contemporary to antique (Biedermeier or Empire, for example). Dare you ask for a room called an "Oasis of Dreams" done in Laura Ashley? Many guests request room no. 30, a cozy attic retreat. The hotel employs one of the most helpful staffs in town.

Rödergasse 1, 91541 Rothenburg ob der Tauber. © 09861/94280. Fax 09861/9428113. www.markusturm.de. 25 units. 125€–190€ ($200–$304) double. Rates include buffet breakfast. AE, DC, MC, V. Parking 8€ ($13). **Amenities:** Room service; babysitting; laundry service; dry cleaning; nonsmoking rooms. *In room:* TV, hair dryer.

MODERATE
Hotel Reichs-Küchenmeister 🏵 We are very partial to this hotel, one of the town's oldest structures. Although it sustained damage in a World War II firestorm, a massive, thoroughly sensitive restoration has rendered it both stylish and well equipped. Rooms are furnished with regional wooden furniture; some contain minibars. Bathrooms are a bit small, but maintenance is tidy and each comes with a tiled shower. Seventeen less expensive rooms are in a less desirable annex across the street.

Kirchplatz 8 (near St. Jakobskirche), 91541 Rothenburg ob der Tauber. © 09861/9700. Fax 19861/970-409. www.reichskuechenmeister.com. 45 units. 75€–135€ ($120–$216) double; 130€–170€ ($208–$272) suite for 2; 150€–215€ ($240–$344) suite for 5. Rates include buffet breakfast. AE, DC, MC, V. Parking 5€ ($8) in the lot; 6.50€ ($10) in the garage. **Amenities:** Restaurant; wine bar; whirlpool; sauna; solarium; Turkish bath; nonsmoking rooms. *In room:* TV, minibar (in some), hair dryer, safe.

INEXPENSIVE
Bayerischer Hof This little B&B doesn't even try to compete with the grand inns of the town. The Bayerischer Hof stands midway between the Bahnhof and the medieval walled city. Petra and Harald Schellhaas welcome guests to their clean, well-furnished accommodations. The exterior looks somewhat sterile, but the inside of the hotel is full of cozy Bavarian touches such as traditionally painted furniture. Rooms and shower-only bathrooms are small, but the housekeeping is excellent and the staff is most hospitable.

Ansbacherstrasse 21, 91541 Rothenburg ob der Tauber. © 09861/6063. Fax 09861/86561. www.bayerischerhof. com. 9 units. 62€–105€ ($99–$168) double. Rates include continental breakfast. MC, V. Free parking. Closed Jan. **Amenities:** Restaurant/bar. *In room:* TV.

Gasthof Goldener Greifen   Don't expect glamour and glitz here—just home-style warmth and comfort. Located in a 1374 patrician house, this hotel stands next door to the prestigious Baumeisterhaus restaurant. Guest rooms are simple but cozy and comfortable, most with either a shower-only bathroom, or a tub/shower combo. The staff is willing to help in any way. You can order your morning coffee in the garden amid roses and geraniums.

Obere Schmiedgasse 5 (off Marktplatz), 91541 Rothenburg ob der Tauber. ⓒ **09861/2281.** Fax 09861/86374. www.gasthof-greifen-rothenburg.de. 21 units, 20 with bathroom. 60€ ($96) double with bathroom including tub/shower combo; 77€–102€ ($123–$163) double with shower only. Rates include buffet breakfast. AE, MC, V. Free parking. Closed Dec 22–Jan 5. **Amenities:** Room service; laundry service; coin-operated laundry; dry cleaning. *In room:* TV (in most), no phone.

WHERE TO DINE
EXPENSIVE
Hotel Mittermeier Restaurant ⋆⋆⋆ FRANCONIAN/INTERNATIONAL   One of the great restaurants along the Romantic Road, this hotel is the domain of Christian Mittermeier, whose original take on Franconian cuisine is a gastronomic beacon. He is an inventive chef who can regale you with the subtlety and flavor of his cooking, based on only the freshest of ingredients. With its garden terrace, the restaurant offers inviting service and near faultless cuisine. Lunch menus are often ignored by chefs who concentrate on dinner. Not so here. Such lunch dishes are offered as slices of bison rib-eye on wild garlic with risotto or "on-the-skin" roast pikeperch with a potato and poppy seed roulade. You can finish off with a delectable caramel rhubarb cake. Dinner is even more elaborate, with such heavenly delights as a Ligurian fish soup with Tahiti vanilla, Norway lobster, and fresh mint. Main dishes tend to be sublime, including a roasted ridge of suckling pig on leaf spinach or else truffled filet of salmon with crayfish in puff pastry. We still remember the parfait of passion fruit with fresh raspberries and rose-water sorbet.

Vorm Würzburger Tor 7–9. ⓒ **09861/94540.** Reservations required. Main courses 18€–32€ ($29–$51); 4-course fixed-price menu 79€ ($126), 5-course 97€ ($155). AE, DC, MC, V. Tues–Sat noon–2pm and 6–9:30pm.

MODERATE
Ratsstube FRANCONIAN   This restaurant enjoys a position right on the market square, one of the most photographed spots in Germany. It's a bustling center of activity throughout the day—a day that begins when practically every Rothenburger stops by for coffee. Inside, a true tavern atmosphere prevails with hardwood chairs and tables, vaulted ceilings, and pierced copper lanterns. Downstairs you'll find a wine bar offering live music nightly. The a la carte menu of Franconian wines and dishes includes sauerbraten and venison, both served with fresh vegetables and potatoes. For dessert, you can order homemade Italian ice cream and espresso. This is a longtime favorite of those who prefer typical Franconian cookery without a lot of fuss and bother. If you arrive at 9am, the staff will serve you an American breakfast.

Marktplatz 6. ⓒ **09861/55-11.** Reservations recommended. Main courses 7€–23€ ($11–$37). MC, V. Mon–Sat 9am–10pm; Sun 9am–6pm.

EXPLORING ROTHENBURG
For an excellent view, take a walk on the **town ramparts** ⋆. The wall tour, from the massive 16th-century Spitaltor (at the end of the Spitalgasse) to the Klingentor, takes about a half-hour. To fortify yourself for this walk, you can stop at one of the many kiosks in town selling the local pastry called *Schneeballen* (snowballs), a round, sugar-coated pastry that's fattening but delicious.

If you want to escape the tourist hordes, you can rent a bike at **Rad und Tat,** Bensenstrasse 17 (© **09861/87984**), for about 10€ ($16) per day. Get a map from the tourist office and head out along the Tauber River with a picnic lunch.

Kriminalmuseum (Criminal Museum)   The only museum of its kind in Europe, the Kriminalmuseum is housed in a structure built in 1395 for the Order of the Johanniter, who cared for the sick. The building was redone in 1718 in the baroque style; it's the only example of baroque architecture in town. The museum's four floors provide an insight into the life, laws, and punishments of medieval days. You'll see chastity belts, shame masks, a shame flute for bad musicians, and a cage for bakers who baked bread too small or too light.

Burggasse 3–5. © 09861/5359. www.kriminalmuseum.rothenburg.de. Admission 3.80€ ($6.10) adults, 2.60€ ($4.20) students, 2.20€ ($3.50) children 6–17. Apr–Oct daily 9:30am–6pm; Nov and Jan–Feb daily 2–4pm; Dec and Mar daily 10am–4pm.

Rathaus (City Hall) ☆   Rothenburg's town hall has an older Gothic section from 1240 and a newer Renaissance structure facing the square. From the 50m (160-ft.) tower of the Gothic hall is a great **view** ☆ of the town. The tower was first used as a sentry's lookout, but after a fire destroyed the Gothic hall's twin (where the Renaissance hall now stands) in 1501, it became a lookout for fire. Guards rang the bell every quarter-hour to prove that they were awake and on the job.

The new Rathaus, built in 1572 to replace the portion destroyed in the fire, is decorated with intricate friezes, an oriel extending the building's full height, and a large stone portico opening onto the square. The octagonal tower at the center of the side facing the square contains a grand staircase leading to the upper hall. On the main floor is the large courtroom.

Marktplatz. © 09861/404-92. Admission: Rathaus free; tower 1€ ($1.60) adults, .50€ (80¢) children. Rathaus Mon–Fri 8am–6pm. Tower Apr–Oct daily 9:30am–12:30pm and 1–5pm; Dec daily noon–3pm; Nov and Jan–Mar Sat–Sun and holidays noon–3pm.

Reichsstadtmuseum (Imperial City Museum)   The historical collection of Rothenburg is housed in this 13th-century Dominican nunnery. The cloisters are well preserved, and you can visit the convent hall, kitchen, and apothecary. The museum collection includes period furniture and art from Rothenburg's more prosperous periods, including the original glazed elector's tankard, and a new section of archaeological objects from prehistoric times up to the Middle Ages. Among the artistic exhibits is the 1494 *Rothenburg Passion* series, 12 pictures by Martinus Schwartz that depict scenes from the suffering of Christ. You can also see the works of English painter Arthur Wasse (1854–1930), whose romantic pictures manage to capture the many moods of the city. Finally, there's a Jewish section, with gravestones from the Middle Ages and some religious objects.

But perhaps the most remarkable object on display is an enormous tankard that holds 3.5 liters—more than 6 pints. You'll find echoes of its story all over the city. In 1631, during the Thirty Years' War, the Protestant city of Rothenburg was captured by General Tilly, commander of the armies of the Catholic League. He promised to spare the town from destruction if one of the town burghers could drink down the huge tankard full of wine in one draught. Bürgermeister Nusch accepted the challenge and succeeded, thus saving Rothenburg. Look for the clock on the Marktplatz with mechanical figures representing this event.

Klosterhof 5. © 09861/939043. www.reichsstadtmuseum.rothenburg.de. Admission 3€ ($4.80) adults, 2€ ($3.20) students and children 6–18, 5€ ($8) family ticket. Apr–Oct daily 10am–5pm; Nov–Mar daily 1–4pm.

St. Jakobskirche (Church of St. Jacob)   The choir of this Gothic church dates from 1336. In the west gallery is the **Altar of the Holy Blood** 𝆺𝅥𝆺𝅥, a masterpiece by the famous Würzburg sculptor Tilman Riemenschneider (ca. 1460–1531). The work was executed between 1499 and 1505, to provide a worthy setting for the Reliquary of the Holy Blood. This relic, venerated in the Middle Ages, is contained in a rock-crystal capsule set in the reliquary cross (ca. 1270) in the center of the shrine. The scene on the altar beneath *The Last Supper* immediately makes a strong impact on the viewer. Christ is giving Judas the morsel of bread, marking him as the traitor. The apostle John is leaning on Christ's bosom. The altar wings show the entry of Christ into Jerusalem (on the left) and Christ praying in the Garden of Gethsemane (on the right). The altar casing is the work of Erhard Harschner, Rothenburg's master craftsman. The fine painted-glass windows in the choir date from the late-Gothic period. To the left is the tabernacle (ca. 1400), a place of sanctuary for condemned criminals.

Klostergasse 15. © 09861/700620. Admission 1.50€ ($2.40) adults, .50€ (80¢) children. Apr–Oct Mon–Sat 9am–5:30pm, Sun 11am–5:30pm; Dec daily 10am–5pm; Nov and Jan–Mar daily 10am–noon and 2–4pm.

SHOPPING
Kunstwerke Friese, Grüner Markt 7 (© **09861/7166**), specializes in cuckoo clocks and also carries Hümmel figurines, pewter beer steins, music boxes, and dolls. It's Christmas every day at **Weihnachtsdorf (Christmas Village),** in the market square, which is filled with shops carrying everything from clothing and accessories to cuckoo clocks, but the real attractions are locally made toys and Christmas ornaments. If you collect teddy bears, you'll love **Teddyland,** Herrengasse 10 (© **09861/8904**), which stocks more than 5,000 of them, the largest teddy bear population in Germany. Bear images are printed on everything from T-shirts to bags and watches.

ROTHENBURG AFTER DARK
At the **Figurentheater,** am Burgtor at Herrengasse 38 (© **09861/3333**), puppet shows are presented year-round Monday to Saturday at 8pm, and June 15 to September, also at 3pm. The evening shows cost 8€ ($13) for adults, 7€ ($11) for students, and 6€ ($9.60) for children 13 and under. Matinee tickets are 6€ ($9.60) for adults, with student and children's tickets costing 5€ ($8) and 4€ ($6.40), respectively.

The most idyllic place to go in the evening is **Unter den Linden,** at Kurze Steige 7B (© **09861/5909**), a cafe-bar on the River Tauber. You reach it by going under the arch at St. Jakobskirche and following Klingengasse through the town gate, heading down a path to Detwang. The cafe is open April to October, daily 10am to 10pm, but it shortens its hours in winter, depending on weather.

8 Dinkelsbühl ⍟

93km (58 miles) SW of Nürnberg, 14km (71 miles) NE of Stuttgart, 105km (65 miles) SE of Würzburg

Still surrounded by its medieval walls and towers, Dinkelsbühl is straight out of a Brothers Grimm story, even down to the gingerbread, one of the town's main products. Behind the 10th-century walls, the town retains a quiet, provincial attitude despite its many visitors. The cobblestone streets are lined with fine 16th-century houses, many with carvings and paintings depicting biblical and mythological themes.

ESSENTIALS
GETTING THERE   By Train   The nearest train station is in Ansbach, which has several trains daily from Munich, Nürnberg, and Stuttgart. From Ansbach, Dinkelsbühl

can be reached by bus. Train rides from Munich or Frankfurt take about 2½ to 3 hours, depending on the connection. For rail information, call © **01805/996633.**

By Bus   For bus service along the Romantic Road, see "Bus Tours of the Romantic Road," at the beginning of this chapter. Regional buses link Dinkelsbühl with local towns. There are three to five buses a day to Rothenburg and five to six buses a day to Nördlingen.

By Car   Take B-25 south from Rothenburg.

VISITOR INFORMATION   Contact **Stadt Verkehrsamt,** Marktplatz (© **09851/ 9-02-40),** open May through October Monday to Friday 9am to 6pm, Saturday 10am to 1pm and 2 to 4pm, and Sunday and holidays 10am to noon; November to April hours are Monday to Friday 10am to 1pm and 2 to 5pm, and Saturday 10am to noon.

SPECIAL EVENTS   This dreamy village awakens once a year for the **Kinderzeche (Children's Festival),** which is held for 10 days in July. This festival commemorates the saving of the village by its children in 1632. According to the story, the children pleaded with conquering Swedish troops to leave their town without pillaging and destroying it—and got their wish. The pageant includes concerts given by the local boys' band dressed in historic military costumes. For more information, check out **www.kinderzeche.de.**

WHERE TO STAY & DINE

Blauer Hecht ⚘   This inn, one of the best in town, is also a brewery/tavern. In honor of its longtime role, beer is still brewed in its backyard. Now a chain hotel, it has been considerably modernized and updated. The elegant building dates from the 17th century and has three hand-built stories of stucco, stone, and tile. Although it's centrally located, rooms are tranquil. Most are medium in size, although there are some small singles. Each unit contains a neatly kept and efficiently organized private bathroom with a tiled shower.

Schweinemarkt 1, 91150 Dinkelsbühl. © **09851/5810.** Fax 09851/581170. www.blauer-hecht.de. 46 units. 90€–95€ ($144–$152) double; 115€ ($184) suite. Rates include continental breakfast. AE, MC, V. Free parking. **Amenities:** Restaurant/bar; indoor heated pool; sauna; solarium; steam bath; laundry service; nonsmoking rooms. *In room:* TV, minibar, safe.

Deutsches Haus ⚘   For those seeking tradition, these are the finest rooms in town. The facade of Deutsches Haus, which dates from 1440, is rich in painted designs and festive woodcarvings. Each room in this casually run hotel is cozy and comfortable, but different—you may find yourself in one with a ceramic stove or in another with a Biedermeier desk. Rooms come with a neatly tiled tub/shower combination. Even if you don't stay here, you may want to dine in the **Altdeutsches Restaurant,** one of the finest in Dinkelsbühl. It's intimate and convivial, and serves Franconian and regional specialties.

Weinmarkt 3, 91550 Dinkelsbühl. © **09851/6058.** Fax 09851/7911. www.deutsches-haus-dkb.de. 18 units. 119€ ($190) double; 139€ ($222) suite. Rates include continental breakfast. AE, MC, V. Parking 8€ ($13). Closed Jan 8–Feb 1. **Amenities:** Restaurant. *In room:* TV, minibar, hair dryer.

Eisenkrug ⚘⚘   The sienna walls of this centrally located hotel were built in 1620. Today, the Eisenkrug's forest-green shutters are familiar to everyone in town. Many celebrate family occasions at the hotel restaurant, enjoying the cafe with alfresco tables in warm weather. The stylish rooms are wallpapered with flowery prints and filled with engaging old furniture. An additional nine rooms are in an equally fine guest-house nearby. All rooms in the newer wing are rather standardized and modern look-ing. The older rooms offer more charm, although some tend to be smaller. Some of the beds are canopied. Bathrooms range from small to spacious, mostly with a tub/shower combination.

Zum kleinen Obristen serves a gourmet international cuisine. The chef takes an indigenous Franconian-Swabian approach, with many innovative touches. The supe-rior wine cellar has some really unusual vintages.

Dr. Martin-Luther-Strasse 1, 91550 Dinkelsbühl. © 09851/57700. Fax 09851/577070. www.hotel-eisenkrug.de. 13 units. 91€ ($146) double. Rates include continental breakfast. MC, V. Free parking. **Amenities:** 2 restaurants. *In room:* TV, minibar, hair dryer, safe.

EXPLORING DINKELSBÜHL

Dinkelsbühl is a lively, wonderfully preserved medieval town, full of narrow, cobble-stone streets. You may begin exploring at the 14th-century gateway, **Rothenburger Tor,** and then head down the wide Martin Luther Strasse to the market square. Along the way you can take in the town's fine collection of early Renaissance burghers' houses. Dinkelsbühl's main attraction is the late-Gothic **Georgenkirche,** on Markt-platz, built between 1448 and 1499. The church contains a carved Holy Cross altar and pillar sculptures, many from the 15th century. The best evening activity here is to take a walk around the ramparts. There's a night watchman making the rounds about town, as in medieval times.

9 Nördlingen ⟨★

130km (81 miles) NW of Munich, 95km (59 miles) SW of Nürnberg

Nördlingen is one of the most irresistible medieval towns along the Romantic Road. It's still encircled by well-preserved fortifications from the 14th and 15th centuries. Things are rather tranquil around Nördlingen today; nonetheless, the town still employs sentries to sound the reassuring message, *"So G'sell so"* (all is well), as they did in the Middle Ages.

The area wasn't always so peaceful. The town sits in a gigantic crater called the Ries. Once thought to be the crater of an extinct volcano, it is now known that the Ries was created by a meteorite at least half a mile in diameter. It struck the ground some 15 million years ago at more than 161,000kmph (100,000 mph). Debris was hurled as far as Slovakia, and all plant and animal life within a radius of about 150km (100 miles) was destroyed. Today the Ries is the best-preserved and most scientifically researched meteorite crater on earth. The American astronauts from *Apollo 14* and *Apollo 17* did their field training in the Ries in 1970. Contact the **Rieskrater-Museum** (see below) for tours of the crater.

ESSENTIALS

GETTING THERE   By Plane   The nearest major airport is in Nürnberg; from there you can make either bus or rail connections to Nördlingen.

By Train   Nördlingen lies on the main Nördlingen-Aalen-Stuttgart line, with fre-quent connections in all directions. Call © **01805/996633** for schedules and more information. Nördlingen can be reached from Stuttgart in 2 hours, from Nürnberg in 2 hours, and from Augsburg in 1 hour.

By Bus   For bus service along the Romantic Road, see "Bus Tours of the Romantic Road," at the beginning of this chapter.

By Car Access by car is via the A7 Autobahn north and south and Route 29 from the east. From Dinkelsbühl, take Route 25 south.

VISITOR INFORMATION Contact the **Verkehrsamt,** Marktplatz 2 (℃ **09081/ 84116**), open Easter to October Monday to Thursday 9am to 6pm, Friday 9am to 4:30pm, and Saturday 9:30am to 1pm; November to Easter, hours are Monday to Thursday 9am to 5pm, and Friday 9am to 3:30pm.

WHERE TO STAY

Kaiser Hotel Sonne ⚐ The Sonne is in a bull's-eye position next to the cathedral and the Rathaus. It has a heady atmosphere from having entertained so many illustrious personalities since it opened as an inn in 1405. Among its guests have been emperors; kings; princes, including Frederick III, Maximilian I, and Charles V; the great poet Goethe; and, in more recent times, American astronauts. Many of the rooms contain hand-painted four-poster beds. Each is midsize to spacious, and most are tastefully and comfortably furnished, with excellent bathrooms, mostly with tub/shower combinations.

Marktplatz 3, 86720 Nördlingen. ℃ **09081/5067.** Fax 09081/23999. www.kaiserhof-hotel-sonne.de. 43 units, 35 with bathroom. 86€ ($138) double without bathroom; 120€ ($192) double with bathroom; 140€ ($224) suite. Rates include breakfast and parking. AE, DC, MC, V. **Amenities:** Restaurant; bar; room service; babysitting; laundry service; dry cleaning. *In room:* TV, minibar, hair dryer.

NH Klösterle Nördlingen ⚐⚐ The accommodations here are the best and most luxurious in town. This historic, white-sided, red-roofed building was originally constructed as a monastery in the 1200s. Since then, its ziggurat-shaped gables and steep roof have been an essential part of Nördlingen's medieval center. The hotel offers elevator access and a hardworking, polite staff. Guest rooms have dark-wood fixtures, lots of electronic extras, and larger-than-expected bathrooms with tub/shower combinations.

Beim Klösterle 1, 86720 Nördlingen. ℃ **09081/87080.** Fax 09081/8708100. www.nh-hotels.de. 98 units. 115€–145€ ($184–$232) double. Rates include buffet breakfast. AE, DC, MC, V. Parking 10€ ($16). **Amenities:** 2 restaurants; bar; indoor heated pool; fitness center; sauna; solarium; room service; massage; laundry service; dry cleaning; nonsmoking rooms. *In room:* TV, minibar, hair dryer, iron, safe.

WHERE TO DINE

Meyers-Keller ⚐ CONTINENTAL The conservative, modern decor here seems a suitable setting for the restrained neue Küche style of the talented chef and owner, Joachim Kaiser. The cuisine changes according to the availability of ingredients and the inspiration of the chef; typical selections are likely to include roulade of sea wolf, salmon with baby spinach and wild rice, and John Dory with champagne-flavored tomato sauce. There's also an impressive array of European wines, many reasonably priced.

Marienhöhe 8. ℃ **09081/4493.** Reservations required. Main courses 16€–24€ ($26–$38); fixed-price menu 35€–119€ ($56–$190). AE, MC, V. Fri–Sun, Tues and Wed 11:30am–2pm and 6–10pm; Thurs 6–10pm. Local bus to Marktplatz.

EXPLORING NÖRDLINGEN

You can walk around the town on the covered parapet on top of the perfectly preserved walls. Along the way, you'll pass 11 towers and five fortified gates. At the center of the circular Altstadt, within the walls, is **Rübenmarkt.** If you stand in this square on market day, you'll be swept into a world of the past—the country people here have preserved many traditional customs and costumes, which, along with the ancient houses, evoke a living medieval city. Around the square are a number of buildings, including the Gothic **Rathaus.** An antiquities collection is displayed in the **Stadtmuseum,** Vordere Gerbergasse 1 (© **09081/2738230**), which is open March to October Tuesday to Sunday 1:30 to 4:30pm. Admission is 3€ ($4.80) for adults and 2€ ($3.20) for children.

St. Georgskirche ⚜, on the square's northern side, is the town's most striking sight and one of its oldest buildings. This Gothic Hall Church dates from the 15th century. Plaques and epitaphs commemorating the town's more illustrious 16th- and 17th-century residents decorate the fan-vaulted interior. Although the original Gothic altarpiece by Friedrich Herlin (1462) is now in the Reichsstadtmuseum in Rothenburg, a portion of it, depicting the Crucifixion by Nikolaus Gerhart van Leydeu, remains in the church. Above the high altar stands a more elaborate baroque altarpiece. The church's most prominent feature, however, is the 90m (300-ft.) French Gothic tower, called the "Daniel." At night, the town watchman calls out from the steeple, his voice ringing through the streets. The tower is accessible daily April to October from 9am to 8pm, and admission is 1.55€ ($2.50) for adults and 1€ ($1.60) for students and children. It's free to visit the church, which is open Easter to October Monday to Friday 9:30am to 12:30pm and 2 to 5pm, and Saturday and Sunday 9:30am to 5pm.

Rieskrater-Museum, Hintere Gerbergasse (© **09081/2738220**), documents the impact of the meteorite that crashed into the earth here on the Alb plateau nearly 15 million years ago. Hours are Tuesday to Sunday 10am to noon and 1:30 to 4:30pm. Admission is 4€ ($6.40) for adults and 1.50€ ($2.40) for students and children ages 6 through 11; free for children 5 and under.

10 Donauwörth

40km (25 miles) N of Augsburg, 11km (7 miles) S of Harburg, 95km (59 miles) NW of Munich

Visitors come to Donauwörth for its architecture and sense of history rather than for specific attractions. The town is located on what was the last navigable point on the Danube, which led to its becoming a key stop on the trade route between Augsburg and Nürnberg. Its attempted capture by the Imperial Party in 1608 led directly to the division of Germany into warring Protestant and Catholic military alliances, leading to the Thirty Years' War.

The oldest part of town sits on an island in the middle of the stream, access to which is via the oldest surviving gate in town, the **Riederstor,** which funnels traffic along the island's most historic and evocative street, the **Reichsstrasse.** Donauwörth was badly damaged in World War II bombing raids in 1945, but it has been carefully restored. Parts of the town's fortifications have survived.

ESSENTIALS
GETTING THERE   By Train   Trains arrive from Augsburg at 30-minute intervals throughout the day (trip time: 35–45 min.). Trains also come hourly from Munich (trip time: 90 min.). For information, call © **01805/996633.**

By Bus   For bus service along the Romantic Road, see "Bus Tours of the Romantic Road," at the beginning of this chapter.

By Car   From Augsburg, follow Route 2 north. From Nördlingen, take Route 25.

VISITOR INFORMATION   Tourist-Information is at Rathausgasse 1 (© **0906/ 789151**), open Monday to Friday 9am to 5pm.

WHERE TO STAY & DINE

Posthotel Traube ⋆ This hotel dates from the 1600s with a guest list that included Goethe and Mozart. Despite its modern conveniences, there's still the definite sense of old Mittel Europa here, thanks to a somewhat creaky staff and a no-nonsense approach to innkeeping. Rooms are nostalgically outfitted with engravings and prints of old-fashioned Germany. This is a comfortable choice with midsize to spacious bedrooms. Perhaps some of the furnishings show too much wear and tear, but tradition-minded guests like it here. Each bathroom is midsize to roomy, most often with a tub/shower combination.

On the premises is a restaurant that serves solid, reliable dishes, not inventive in any way, but hearty and filling. These Franconian recipes have been around for a few generations.

Kapellstrasse 14–16, 86609 Donauwörth. (©) 0906/706440. www.posthoteltraube.de. 43 units. 85€–90€ ($136–$144) double. Rates include continental breakfast. MC, V. **Amenities:** Restaurant; cafe/lounge; sauna; massage. *In room:* TV, hair dryer.

EXPLORING DONAUWÖRTH

The **Heiligeskreuz** or Church of the Holy Cross, a large 1720 baroque building with concave interior galleries, dominates the town. It's an outstanding example of the distinctive churches built and decorated in the school of Wessobrunn, which flourished in the 17th and 18th centuries and often employed elaborate stucco decorations.

The site that draws the greatest numbers of visitors is the **Käthe-Kruse-Puppen-Museum,** Pflegstrasse 21A (© 0906/789170). Inside, you'll find a small-scale collection of the dolls and dollhouses that were designed by master artisan Käthe-Kruse, whose most prolific period during the 1950s and 1960s has been called a high point in the history of doll making. May to September, it's open Tuesday to Sunday 11am to 5pm; November to March it is open Wednesday, Saturday, and Sunday 2 to 5pm; April and October, hours are Tuesday to Sunday 2 to 5pm. Entrance costs 3€ ($4.80) for adults, half price for children 11 and under.

11 Augsburg

68km (42 miles) NW of Munich, 80km (50 miles) E of Ulm, 160km (100 miles) SE of Stuttgart

Augsburg's 2,000 years of history have made it one of southern Germany's major sightseeing attractions. It's the Romantic Road's largest town and serves as a gateway to the Alps and the south.

Augsburg was founded under Emperor Tiberius in 15 B.C., though little remains from this period. On the other hand, the wealth of art and architecture from the Renaissance is staggering. Augsburg has hosted many distinguished visitors and boasts an array of famous native sons, including painters Hans Holbein the Elder and the Younger and playwright Bertolt Brecht. In 1518, Martin Luther was summoned to Augsburg to recant his 95 theses before a papal emissary. Today, Augsburg, with a population of about 250,000, is an important industrial center and Bavaria's third-largest city, after Munich and Nürnberg.

ESSENTIALS

GETTING THERE **By Train** About 90 Euro and InterCity trains arrive here daily from all major German cities. For information, call © 01805/996633. There are 60 trains a day from Munich (trip time: 30–50 min.) and 35 from Frankfurt (3–4½ hr.).

By Bus   For bus service along the Romantic Road, see "Bus Tours of the Romantic Road," at the beginning of this chapter.

By Car   Access is via the A8 Autobahn east and west. From Donauwörth, take Route 2 south.

VISITOR INFORMATION   Contact **Tourist-Information,** Schiessgrabenstrasse 14 (© **0821/502070**), open Monday to Friday 9am to 6pm, and also Saturday at Rathausplatz, 10am to 1pm.

GETTING AROUND   Public transportation in Augsburg consists of four tram lines and 31 bus lines. They operate daily from 5am to midnight.

WHERE TO STAY
EXPENSIVE
Steigenberger Drei Mohren ✹✹   The original "Three Moors," dating from 1723, was one of the most renowned hotels in Germany before its destruction in a 1944 air raid. In 1956, it was reconstructed in a modern style in four- and five-story buildings. It remains the premier hotel in town despite competition from the Romantik Hotel Augsburger Hof (see below). The drawing room contains a slatted natural-wood ceiling and walls, along with a room-wide mural of Old Augsburg. Guest rooms are comfortable and inviting, with thick carpets, double-glazed windows, and large bathrooms with tub/shower combinations. Doubles vary in size and appointments, ranging from smaller, somewhat cramped quarters to more spacious accommodations.

Maximilianstrasse 40, 86150 Augsburg. © **800/223-5652** in the U.S. and Canada, or 0821/50360. Fax 0821/157864. www.augsburg.steigenberger.de. 106 units. 151€–181€ ($242–$290) double; 235€–650€ ($376–$1,040) suite. Children 11 and under stay free in parent's room. AE, MC, V. Parking 14€ ($22). Tram: 1. **Amenities:** 2 restaurants; bar; staff can arrange golf; car rental; room service; babysitting; laundry service; dry cleaning; nonsmoking rooms. *In room:* A/C (in some), TV, Wi-Fi, minibar, hair dryer, trouser press (suites only).

INEXPENSIVE TO MODERATE
Dom Hotel ✓*Value*   The Dom Hotel lacks the decorative flair of its competitors, but it is a peaceful, comfortable hotel. That, combined with the moderate rates, makes this one of the most appealing choices in town. The 15th-century half-timbered structure rises imposingly beside Augsburg's famous cathedral. Rooms on most floors are medium in size, although we prefer the smaller attic accommodations, where you can rest under a beamed ceiling and enjoy a panoramic sweep of the rooftops of the city. Accommodations come with neatly tiled and efficiently organized compact bathrooms with tub/shower combinations. Breakfast is the only meal served; during warm weather, it can be enjoyed in a garden beside the town's medieval fortifications.

Frauentorstrasse 8, 86152 Augsburg. © 0821/343930. Fax 0821/34393200. www.domhotel-augsburg.de. 52 units. 91€–130€ ($146–$208) double; 116€–150€ ($186–$240) suite. Rates include buffet breakfast. AE, DC, MC, V. Free parking in lot; 7€ ($11) in garage. Tram: 2. **Amenities:** Breakfast room; indoor heated pool; Internet access; exercise room; sauna; solarium; massage; laundry service; nonsmoking rooms. *In room:* TV, minibar, hair dryer, safe.

Privat Hotel Riegele ✓*Value*   The Schmid family welcomes you into their little hotel opposite the Hauptbahnhof (the main rail station). They run a neat, tidy hotel with midsize-to-spacious bedrooms, each with comfortably modern furnishings that are renewed as needed, along with highly polished, tiled private bathrooms. On-site is the Braus Bräustüble, a tavern patronized by locals as well as visitors for its hearty reginal dishes. The breakfast buffet is one of the most generous in town.

Augsburg

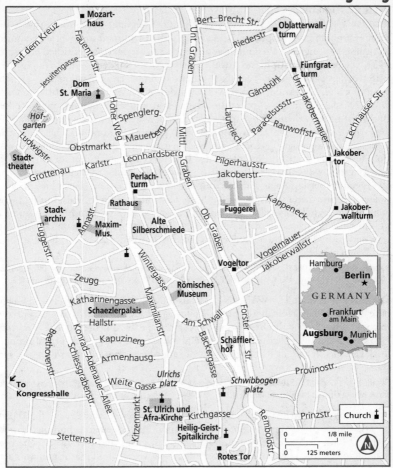

Viktoriastrasse 4, 86150 Augsburg. ☏ **0821/509000.** Fax 0821/517746. www.hotel-riegele.de. 28 units. 89€–130€ ($142–$208) double; extra bed 25€ ($40). AE, DC, MC, V. Free parking. **Amenities:** Restaurant; bar; room service; laundry service. *In room:* TV, Wi-Fi.

Romantik Hotel Augsburger Hof
This is a favorite for its traditional, romantic atmosphere. Originally built in 1767, the hotel has thick, solid walls and exposed beams and timbers. Rooms are modern but not as romantic as the hotel's name suggests. They range from small to spacious. Some bathrooms seem crowded in as an afterthought, but each is beautifully maintained and contains a shower. Rooms overlooking the tranquil inner courtyard are more expensive than ones facing the street.

Auf dem Kreuz 2, 86152 Augsburg. ☏ **0821/343050.** Fax 0821/3430555. www.augsburger-hof.de. 36 units. 90€–140€ ($144–$224) double. Rates include buffet breakfast. AE, DC, MC, V. Parking 7€ ($11). Tram: 2. **Amenities:** Restaurant; lounge; sauna; room service; laundry service; dry cleaning; nonsmoking rooms; rooms for those w/limited mobility. *In room:* TV, minibar, hair dryer.

WHERE TO DINE

August ✹✹ INTERNATIONAL By virtually everyone's accounting, this is the most gastronomically sophisticated and sought-after restaurant in town, with a social and culinary pedigree that's nothing short of spectacular. Having flourished here since 1989, it's positioned within an artfully contemporary dining room that's outfitted with wooden panels and a decor that's otherwise almost entirely painted in different tones of white. With windows that overlook a view of the nearby cathedral, it contains only 20 seats and enough space between them for artful (conversational) indiscretions. But whereas many rituals here, especially the service, are conducted the old-fashioned way, the cuisine is the often inspired and innovative work of Chef Christian Grünewald, whose light textured emphasis on seasonal vegetables has elicited praise from local and national media. Be warned in advance that if you opt for the set-price menu here, it will contain no fewer than 15 courses, and be configured either as an all-vegetarian version or as a meat, fish, and vegetable version, depending on your wishes. Specific menu items change with the availability of ingredients, but examples are likely to include cannelloni stuffed with a braised combination of black trumpet mushrooms and apples; fresh goose liver with mandarin oranges, almonds, white carrots, and celery sauce; and a manioc-based risotto flavored with chives, black truffles, and Emmenthaler cheese.

Frauentorstrasse 27. ℂ 0821/35279. Reservations strongly recommended. Main courses 30€–36€ ($48–$58); set-price menu 90€ ($144). AE, MC, V. Wed–Sat 7–10pm. Closed 2 weeks in Jan and 2 weeks in Sept–Oct. Tram: 2.

Die Ecke ✹ FRENCH/SWABIAN This is the town's finest dining choice. Guests have included Hans Holbein the Elder, Wolfgang Amadeus Mozart, and, in more contemporary times, Rudolf Diesel (as in the engine) and Bertolt Brecht. The *Weinstube* ambience belies the skilled cuisine. A pâté of pheasant might precede breast of duckling. The filet of sole in Riesling is a classic, and the seasonal venison dishes, a specialty, are the best in town.

Elias-Holl-Platz 2. ℂ 0821/510600. Reservations required. Main courses 16€–32€ ($26–$51); 4-course fixed-price dinner 48€ ($77), 8-course 68€ ($109). AE, DC, MC, V. Daily 11:30am–2pm and 5:30–10pm. Tram: 2.

Fuggerei Stube GERMAN/SWABIAN This affordable restaurant can fit 60 people at a time into its large, *gemütlich* dining room. Expect generous portions of well-prepared food such as sauerbraten, pork schnitzel, game, and fish dishes. The beer foaming out of the taps here is Storchenbräu; most visitors find that it goes wonderfully with the conservative German specialties that are this establishment's forte.

Jakoberstrasse 26. ℂ 0821/30870. Reservations recommended. Main courses 10€–20€ ($16–$32). AE, MC, V. Tues–Sun 12:30–2:30pm; Tues–Sat 5:30–11pm. Tram: 1.

Welser Kuche SWABIAN/BAVARIAN Come to the Welser Kuche for a medieval feast on wooden tables. *Knechte* and *Mägde* (knaves and wenches) serve the traditional menu in 16th-century costumes. Fixed-price menus, called "Welser Feast," are eaten with a dagger and your fingers for cutlery. Stone walls, knotty-pine paneling, and stucco arches frame the wooden tables. Recipes here are from a cookbook, discovered in 1970, that belonged to Philippine Welser (1527–80), baroness of Zinnenburg and wife of Habsburg Archduke Ferdinand II. Meals last about 3 hours. Sometimes parties of two or four can be seated at the last minute, but reservations should be made as far in advance as possible.

Maximilianstrasse 83 (close to the rail station). ℂ 08231/96110. Reservations required. Feasts 41€ ($66) for 6 courses, 46€ ($74) for 8 courses; rates do not include drinks. AE, DC, MC, V. Daily 8–11pm. Tram: 2.

EXPLORING AUGSBURG

Extending southward from the Rathaus is the wide **Maximilianstrasse** ✿, lined with shops and old burghers' houses and studded with fountains by the Renaissance Dutch sculptor Adrien de Vries.

Church of St. Ulrich and St. Afra ✿
Near the southern end of Maximilianstrasse is the Hercules Fountain, and behind it, the most attractive ecclesiastical compound in Augsburg. The churches of St. Ulrich and St. Afra were constructed between 1476 and 1500 on the site of a Roman temple. As a tribute to the 1555 Peace of Augsburg, which recognized two denominations, one Roman Catholic and the other Lutheran, these two separate churches—Catholic St. Afra and Protestant St. Ulrich—stand next to each other. The churches are mainly 15th-century Gothic with baroque overlays. St. Afra is the most elaborate, with a magnificent altar and finely carved baroque railings bordering the entrance. St. Ulrich is the former monastery assembly hall, taken over by the Lutherans. The shared crypt contains the tombs of the two namesake saints. The lance and saddle of St. Ulrich are displayed in the sacristy.

Ulrichplatz 15. ✆ 0821/345560. Free admission. Daily 9am–5pm. Tram: 1.

Dom St. Maria
The cathedral of Augsburg has the distinction of containing the oldest stained-glass windows in the world. These Romanesque windows, dating from the 12th century, are in the south transept and depict Old Testament prophets in a severe but colorful style. They are younger than the cathedral itself, which was begun in 944 and partially Gothicized in the 14th century. The 11th-century bronze doors, leading into the three-aisle nave, are adorned with bas-reliefs of a mixture of biblical and mythological characters. The cathedral's interior, restored in 1934, contains side altars with altarpieces by Hans Holbein the Elder and Christoph Amberger. You'll find the ruins of the original basilica in the crypt beneath the west chancel.

Hoher Weg. ✆ 0821/3166353. Free admission. Mon–Sat 7am–5pm; Sun noon–5pm. Tram: 1.

Fuggerei ✿
During the 15th and 16th centuries, Augsburg became one of Europe's wealthiest communities, mainly because of its textile industry and the political and financial clout of its two banking families, the Welsers and the Fuggers. The Welsers have long since faded away. But the founders of the powerful Fugger family have established themselves permanently by an unusual legacy, the Fuggerei, set up in 1519, by Jakob Fugger the Rich, to house poorer Augsburgers. It's Europe's oldest welfare housing.

The basic features, laid down in 1521, are still in force today. The nominal rent of 1€ ($1.60) per annum (formerly one Rhenish guilder) has not changed in more than 450 years (the city council determines who gets the break—it's based on need). The only obligation is that tenants pray daily for the souls of their founders. The Fuggerei is a miniature, self-contained town with its own gates, which are shut from 10pm to 5am and guarded by a night watchman. Franz Mozart, a master Mason fallen on hard times—and great-grandfather of Wolfgang Amadeus Mozart—once lived at Mittlere Gasse 14.

The Fugger Foundation owns the Fuggerei. A house at Mittlere Gasse 13, next to the one once occupied by Mozart's ancestor, is now the Fuggerei's **museum.** The rough 16th- and 17th-century furniture, wood-paneled ceilings and walls, and cast-iron stove, as well as other objects of everyday life, show what it was like to live here in earlier times.

At the end of Vorderer Lech. (© 0821/3198810. www.fuggerei.de. Museum 2€ ($3.20) adults, 1€ ($1.60) students and children. Museum Apr–Oct daily 8am–8pm; Nov–Mar daily 9am–6pm. Tram: 1.

Rathaus   In 1805 and 1809, Napoleon visited the Rathaus, built by Elias Holl in 1620. Regrettably, the building was also visited by an air raid in 1944, leaving it a mere shell of what had once been a palatial eight-story monument to the glory of the Renaissance. Its celebrated "golden chamber" was left in shambles. But now, after a costly restoration, the public can again visit the Rathaus on walking tours that offer a view of the golden chamber (celebrated for its imposing portals, gold-leaf coffered ceilings, and huge wall frescoes), as well as other rooms.

Am Rathausplatz 2. (© 0821/3242120. Admission 2€ ($3.20) adults, 1€ ($1.60) children 7–14, free for children 6 and under. Daily 10am–6pm. Tram: 1.

Schaezlerpalais   The Schaezlerpalais, a 60-room mansion built between 1765 and 1770, has an amazing art collection. Most of the works in the collection are by German artists of the Renaissance and baroque periods, including Hans Holbein the Elder and Hans Burgkmair. One of the most famous paintings is Albrecht Dürer's portrait of Jakob Fugger the Rich. Rubens, Veronese, Tiepolo, and others are also represented. The palace-gallery also has a rococo ballroom, with gilded and mirrored wall panels and a ceiling fresco, *The Four Continents*. On April 28, 1770, Marie Antoinette danced the night away here.

Maximilianstrasse 46 (facing the Hercules Fountain). (© 0821/3244102. Admission 7€ ($11) adults, 5.50€ ($8.80) children. Wed–Sun 10am–4pm. Tram: 1.

AUGSBURG AFTER DARK

Kongresshalle, Güggingerstrasse 10 ((© 0821/3242348; tram: 1), presents concerts by the local ballet and opera companies and the chamber and symphony orchestras. Call for schedules, prices, and reservations. It's closed in August. The internationally renowned **Mozart Festival** is held in Augsburg every September. Contact the Tourist-Information office (see above) for details. In the courtyard of the Fugger Palace, the city hosts a **musical theater** production each June and July. Tickets run 12€ to 35€ ($19–$56). Information and reservations are available by calling the tourist office.

Maximilianstrasse, the main shopping street, continues to be the focus of nightlife after the shops close, with its many cafes. **Brauereigasthaus Drei Königinnen,** Meister-Veits-Gässchen 32 ((© 0821/158405; tram: 2 or 4), doubles as an art gallery, has a pleasant beer garden that's open 1:30 to 10pm, and has a main restaurant/bar that closes at 8pm. Another garden/bar combo that keeps the same hours is **Thorbräu,** Wertachbrucker-Tor-Strasse 9 ((© 0821/36561; tram: 2 or 4). **Liliom,** Unterer Graben 1 ((© 0821/33724; tram: 2 or 4), is equipped with a good stereo system to go with drinks and conversation; here, too, local artwork is often available for purchase. The bar is open Monday to Thursday 7pm to 3am and Friday to Sunday 6pm to 1am.

12 Füssen ⭒

92km (57 miles) S of Augsburg, 119km (74 miles) SW of Munich

Füssen is in the foothills of the Bavarian Alps, at the end of the Romantic Road. The town is mainly a base for those going on to the castles at Neuschwanstein and Hohenschwangau, but it has a number of attractive buildings, including a 15th-century castle once used by the bishops of Augsburg as a summer palace. Füssen is also ideally located for excursions into the surrounding countryside.

ESSENTIALS

GETTING THERE   By Plane   The nearest major airport is in Munich.

By Train   Trains from Munich and Augsburg arrive frequently throughout the day. For information, call ℂ **01805/996633.** Train time from Munich is 2½ hours; from Frankfurt, it's 6 to 7 hours.

By Bus   For bus service along the Romantic Road, see "Bus Tours of the Romantic Road," at the beginning of this chapter. Regional service is provided by **Deutsche Touring GmbH,** Frankfurt (ℂ **069/7903501**). This company runs at least 13 buses a day to the royal castles.

By Car   Access by car is via the A7 Autobahn from the north and also the B17 from Augsburg.

VISITOR INFORMATION   Contact the **Kurverwaltung,** Kaiser-Maximilian-Platz 1 (ℂ **08362/93850**). Hours vary but are usually Monday to Friday 8:30am to 6:30pm and Saturday 9am to 2:30pm in summer, and in winter Monday to Friday 9am to 5pm and Saturday 10am to noon.

WHERE TO STAY

Hotel Christine   The Christine is one of the best local choices. The staff spends the long winter months refurbishing the rooms so they'll be fresh and sparkling for spring visitors. Breakfast, the only meal served, is presented on beautiful regional china as classical music plays in the background. A Bavarian charm pervades the hotel, and the small- to medium-size rooms are very cozy, though hardly fit for King Ludwig were he to return.

Weidachstrasse 31 (5-min. ride from the train station), 87629 Füssen. ℂ **08362/7229.** Fax 08362/940554. www.hotel-christine-fuessen.de. 13 units. 100€–140€ ($160–$224) double. Rates include continental breakfast. MC, V. Free parking. Closed Jan 15–Feb 15. **Amenities:** Breakfast room; lounge. *In room:* TV, hair dryer.

Steig Mühle *(Value*   Owners and hosts Gunter and Hedwig Buhmann like things to be cozy—their chaletlike guesthouse is almost a cliché of Bavarian charm. Rooms open onto a view of the lake or mountains, and many have their own balconies. They're furnished in a neat, functional style and kept immaculately clean. Each room comes with a tiny shower-only bathroom. There aren't a lot of frills, but the place offers one of the best values in the area.

Alte Steige 3, 87629 Füssen-Weissensee. ℂ **08362/91760.** Fax 08362/3148. www.steigmuehle.de. 24 units. 60€–64€ ($96–$102) double. Rates include buffet breakfast. No credit cards. Free outside parking, 3€ ($4.80) in garage. From Füssen, take Rte. 310 toward Kempten, a 5-min. drive. **Amenities:** Breakfast room; lounge. *In room:* TV.

WHERE TO DINE

Fischerhütte *✷* SEAFOOD   This restaurant is at the edge of the lake, within sight of dramatic mountain scenery. There are four gracefully paneled, old-fashioned dining rooms, and there's a terrace in summer. As its name (Fisherman's Cottage) suggests, the establishment specializes in seafood. Menu items read like an international atlas: one-half of an entire Alaskan salmon (for two); North Atlantic lobster; a garlicky version of French bouillabaisse; fresh alpine trout, prepared pan-fried or with aromatic herbs in the style of Provence; and grilled halibut. A limited array of meat dishes is also offered, and a selection of succulent desserts. In summer, a beer garden serves simple Bavarian specialties.

Uferstrasse 16 (5km/3 miles northwest of Füssen), Hopfen am See. ℂ **08362/91970.** Reservations recommended. Main courses 10€–22€ ($16–$35). AE, DC, MC, V. Daily 10am–9:30pm.

Zum Schwanen *(Value)* SWABIAN/BAVARIAN   The loyal clients of this small, attractively old-fashioned restaurant enjoy such specialties as homemade sausage, roast pork, lamb, and venison. Service is always helpful and attentive, and the large portions are a good value.

Brotmarkt 4. ⓒ 08362/6174. Reservations required. Main courses 6€–18€ ($9.60–$29). MC, V. Tues–Sun 11:30am–2:30pm; Tues–Sat 5:30–9pm. Closed Nov and 3 weeks in Mar; closed Sun in winter.

EXPLORING FÜSSEN

Füssen's main attraction is the **Hohes Schloss,** Magnusplatz (ⓒ **08362/903164**), one of the finest late-Gothic castles in Bavaria. It was once the summer residence of the prince-bishops of Augsburg. Inside you can visit the Rittersaal or "Knight's Hall," known for its stunning coffered ceiling. There's also a collection of Swabian artwork from the 1400s to the 1700s. The castle is open April to October Tuesday to Sunday 11am to 4pm, with hours reduced from November to March to 2 to 4pm. Admission costs 3€ ($4.80) for adults, free for children 13 and under.

Immediately below the castle lies the 8th-century **St. Mangkirche** and its **abbey** (ⓒ **08362/6190**), which was founded by the Benedictines and grew up on the site where St. Magnus died in 750. In the 18th century it was reconstructed in the baroque style, and in 1803 it was secularized. Free tours of the abbey are given July to September on Tuesday and Thursday at 4pm and on Saturday at 10:30am; in May, June, and October the schedule is Tuesday at 4pm and Saturday at 9:30am; and from January to April tours are on Saturday at 10:30am. In November and December, you might be able to arrange a tour by contacting the tourist office (see above).

Within the abbey complex, signs point the way to the **Chapel of St. Anne,** where you can view the macabre *Totentanz* or "dance of death," painted by an unknown local artist in the early 15th century. It has a certain uncanny fascination. The chapel is open April to October Tuesday to Sunday 10am to 5pm, and November to March Tuesday to Sunday 1 to 4pm. Admission is free. Nearby is the **Museum of Füssen** (**Heimatmuseum;** ⓒ **08362/903145**), which displays artifacts relating to the history and culture of the region, including a collection of musical instruments. It keeps the same hours as the chapel and charges 2.55€ ($4.10) to enter.

The principal shopping spot in town is the **Reichenstrasse,** which was known in Roman times as the Via Claudia. This cobblestone street is flanked with houses from the Middle Ages, most of which have towering gables.

A ROCOCO MASTERPIECE

From Füssen, you can take a fascinating side trip to the **Wieskirche** ✦✦ (ⓒ **08862/ 932930;** www.wieskirche.de), one of the most extravagant rococo buildings in the world, a masterpiece by Dominikus Zimmermann. The Wieskirche is a noted pilgrimage church, drawing visitors from all over the globe. It's located on the slopes of the Ammergau Alps between Ammer and Lech, in an alpine meadow just off the Romantic Road near Steingaden, where there is a visitor information office (ⓒ **08862/200**). The staff at the office can give you a map and confirm that the church is open.

With the help of his brother, Johann Baptist, Zimmermann worked on this church from 1746 to 1754. The ceiling is richly frescoed. It's amazing that so much decoration could be crowded into so small a place. The great Zimmermann was so enchanted with his creation that he built a small home in the vicinity and spent the last decade of his life here. A bus heading for the church leaves Füssen Monday to Friday twice per day (once per day on the weekend). Visitors should check the timetable at the station for bus information or ask at the Füssen tourist office (see above). The trip takes 30 minutes and costs 10€ ($16) round-trip.

13 Neuschwanstein ★★★ & Hohenschwangau ★

7km (4 miles) E of Füssen, 116km (72 miles) SW of Munich

Just east of Füssen are the two "Royal Castles" of Hohenschwangau and Neuschwanstein (www.neuschwanstein.com), among the finest in Germany. Hohenschwangau, the more sedate of the two, was built by Maximilian II in 1836; Neuschwanstein was the brainchild of his son, "Mad" King Ludwig II. The extravagant Ludwig was responsible for two other architectural flights of fancy besides Neuschwanstein: Linderhof, near Oberammergau, and Herrenchiemsee, on an island in Chiemsee (both are covered in chapter 10). Ludwig died under mysterious circumstances in 1886 (see "The Fairy-Tale King" box, below).

After you've fought the crowds to get into these royal castles (in summer, the lines to get in can seem endless), you can spend your remaining time hiking around the surrounding Alpine peaks and valleys for what might be some of the most memorable walks of your life. For one of the grandest panoramas in all of the Alps (in any country), hike up to the **Marienbrücke** (the trail is signposted), which spans the Pöllat Gorge behind Neuschwanstein Castle. If you're properly dressed and have stout boots, continue uphill from the gorge for another hour for the most splendid view possible of "Mad" King Ludwig's fantasy castle.

ESSENTIALS

GETTING THERE   By Bus   Ten buses a day arrive from Füssen (see earlier in this chapter).

By Car   Head east from Füssen along the B17.

VISITOR INFORMATION   Information about the region and the castles is available at the **Kurverwaltung,** Kaiser-Maximilian-Platz 1, Füssen (✆ **08362/93850**). Hours vary but are usually Monday to Friday 8:30am to 6:30pm and Saturday 9am to 2:30pm in summer; in winter, hours are Monday to Friday 9am to 5pm and Saturday 10am to noon. Information is also available at the Kurverwaltung, Rathaus, Münchenerstrasse 2, Schwangau (✆ **08362/938523**), open Monday through Friday from 9am to 5pm and Saturday from 10am to 1pm.

WHERE TO STAY & DINE NEARBY

Hotel Lisl and Jägerhaus   This graciously styled villa and its annex in a historic building across the street are among the better addresses in the area. Most rooms have a view of one or both castles, even from one of the bathroom windows. A few rooms in the main building have been decorated with exclusive wood paneling and carvings. If you're assigned to the annex, never fear, as its rooms are just as fine—or in some cases even better than the main building. Some of the bathrooms in the Jägerhaus are larger than some hotel rooms, and come complete with large tubs and showers. For charm and price, this one is a winner.

Neuschwansteinstrasse 1–3, 87645 Hohenschwangau. ✆ **08362/8870.** Fax 08362/81107. www.neuschwanstein-hotels.de. 47 units. 85€–170€ ($136–$272) double; 180€–220€ ($288–$352) suite. AE, DC, MC, V. Free parking. Closed Dec 21–26. **Amenities:** 2 dining rooms; bar; room service; nonsmoking rooms. *In room:* TV, safe (in some).

Hotel Müller Hohenschwangau   The location of this hospitable inn, near the foundations of Neuschwanstein Castle, makes it alluring. Rooms are comfortable

The Fairy-Tale King

Ludwig II, often called "Mad" King Ludwig (although some Bavarians hate that label), was born in Munich in 1845, the son of Maximilian II. Only 18 years old when he was crowned king of Bavaria, handsome Ludwig initially attended to affairs of state, but he soon grew bored and turned to less subtle pursuits. A loner who never married, Ludwig gradually became more and more obsessed with acting out his extravagant fantasies.

At the baroque palace of **Nymphenburg** (p. 310), the summer residence of the Bavarian rulers, you can still see in the Marstall Royal Stables the richly decorated coaches and sleighs in which young Ludwig loved to travel, often at night, with his spectacular entourage. His crown jewels can be admired in the treasury in the Königsbau wing of the **Residenz** palace, in the heart of Munich (p. 328).

Ludwig had a long association with Richard Wagner and was a great fan and benefactor of the composer. The king had Wagner's operas performed for his own pleasure and watched them in royal and solitary splendor. At Linderhof, the first romantic palace that he built, he even reconstructed the Venus grotto from the Munich opera stage design for *Tannhäuser.*

Ludwig's architectural creations are legendary. To construct his own Versailles, he chose one of Germany's most beautiful lakes, Chiemsee. He called the palace **Herrenchiemsee,** in homage to Louis XIV, the Sun King. Today, visitors can enjoy the castle's Versailles-style Hall of Mirrors and its exquisite gardens (p. 363). **Schloss Linderhof** (p. 378), in the Graswang Valley near Oberammergau, was a smaller creation but became his favorite castle; it was the only one completed by the time of his death.

Nestled in a crag high above the little town of Hohenswangen is the most famous of the royal designer's efforts, the multiturreted Disney-like **Neuschwanstein** (see below). From a distance, the castle appears more dreamlike than real. It's the most photographed castle in Germany. The king's study, bedroom, and living room sport frescoes of scenes from Wagner's operas *Tristan and Isolde* and *Lohengrin.*

Finally, Ludwig's excesses became too much, and he was declared insane in 1886 when he was 41 years old. Three days later, he was found drowned in Lake Starnberg on the outskirts of Munich. He may have committed suicide, or he may have been murdered. A memorial chapel lies on the bank of the lake. Ludwig is buried along with other royals in the crypt beneath the choir of St. Michael's Church.

and inviting, and have a bit of Bavarian charm. Each is midsize and filled with tasteful, comfortable furnishings, along with a small tiled bathroom equipped with a shower. Nature lovers especially enjoy hiking the short distance to nearby Hohenschwangau Castle.

This hotel is your best bet for dining even if you're not a guest. You have a choice of savory Bavarian cuisine or superb international dishes with an emphasis on flambé. In summer, dinners are served on the Alpsee Boathouse's lakeside terrace.

Alpseestrasse 16, 87645 Hohenschwangau. ☏ *08362/81990.* Fax 08362/819913. www.hotel-mueller.de. 41 units. 112€–170€ ($179–$272) double; 187€–250€ ($299–$400) suite. Rates include buffet breakfast. AE, DC, MC, V. Free parking. Closed Jan–Feb. Bus from Füssen stops here. **Amenities:** 4 restaurants; bar; outdoor pool; sauna; Turkish bath; room service; nonsmoking rooms. *In room:* TV, minibar (in some), hair dryer.

VISITING THE ROYAL CASTLES

Be prepared for very long lines (sometimes an incredible 4–5 hr. wait) at the castles during summer, especially in August. On some days, 25,000 people visit. To alleviate the inconvenience of long lines and stress, **RAD Data Communications** (www.rad. com) has installed a network for organizing visits. Under this new system, tickets displaying specific admission times are sold at ticket offices at the entrance to either castle. Visitors can then purchase a ticket and wait for their reserved tour instead of standing in long lines with no definite time set. Entry to the castles is controlled by a computerized turnstile that reads the tickets. Ticketing information for each castle is conveyed to the central ticket office via a microwave link, which links the two castles to an office in the valley below.

HOHENSCHWANGAU ⭐

Not as glamorous or spectacular as Neuschwanstein (see below), the neo-Gothic **Hohenschwangau Castle** nevertheless has a much richer history. The original structure dates from the days of the 12th-century knights of Schwangau. When the knights faded away, the castle began to fade, too, helped along by the Napoleonic Wars. When Ludwig II's father, Crown Prince Maximilian (later Maximilian II), saw the castle in 1832, he purchased it and in 4 years had it completely restored. Ludwig II spent the first 17 years of his life here and later received Richard Wagner in its chambers.

The rooms of Hohenschwangau are styled and furnished in a much heavier Gothic mode than those in Neuschwanstein. Many are typical of the halls of knights' castles of the Middle Ages in both England and Germany. There's no doubt that the style greatly influenced young Ludwig and encouraged the fanciful boyhood dreams that formed his later tastes and character. Hohenschwangau, unlike Neuschwanstein, has a comfortable look about it, more like an actual home than a museum.

Among the most attractive chambers is the **Hall of the Swan Knight,** named for the wall paintings depicting the saga of Lohengrin. Note the Gothic grillwork on the ceiling with the open spaces studded with stars.

Hohenschwangau, Alpseestrasse (☏ **08362/930830**), is open April to September daily 8am to 5:30pm, and October to March daily 9am to 3:30pm. Admission is 9€ ($14) for adults and 8€ ($13) for students and children 12 to 15; children 11 and under enter free. There are several parking lots that serve both castles.

NEUSCHWANSTEIN ⭐⭐⭐

Neuschwanstein was King Ludwig II's fairy-tale castle. Construction lasted 17 years until the king's death, when all work stopped, leaving a part of the interior uncompleted. From 1884 to 1886, Ludwig lived in these rooms on and off for a total of only about 6 months.

The doorway off to the left side of the vestibule leads to the king's apartments. The **study,** like most of the rooms, is decorated with wall paintings showing scenes from Nordic legends. The theme of the study is the Tannhäuser saga. The only fabric in the room is hand-embroidered silk, used in curtains and chair coverings, all designed with the gold-and-silver Bavarian coat of arms.

From the vestibule, you enter the **throne room** through the doorway at the opposite end. This hall, designed in Byzantine style by J. Hofmann, was never completed. The floor is a mosaic design, depicting the animals of the world. The columns in the main hall are made of deep-copper-red porphyry. The circular apse where the king's throne was to have stood is reached by a stairway of white Carrara marble. The walls and ceiling are decorated with paintings of Christ in heaven looking down on the 12 Apostles and six canonized kings of Europe.

The **king's bedroom** is the most richly carved in the entire castle—it took 4½ years to complete this room alone. The walls are decorated with panels carved to look like Gothic windows, as well as with a mural depicting the legend of Tristan and Isolde. In the center is a large wooden pillar, completely encircled with gilded brass sconces. The ornate bed is on a raised platform with an elaborately carved canopy. Through the balcony window you can see the 50m (150-ft.) waterfall in the Pöllat Gorge, with the mountains in the distance.

The fourth floor of the castle is almost entirely given over to the **Singer's Hall,** the pride of Ludwig II and all of Bavaria. Modeled after the hall at Wartburg, the Singer's Hall is decorated with marble columns and elaborately painted designs interspersed with frescoes depicting the life of Parsifal.

The castle is open year-round. In September, visitors have the additional pleasure of hearing Wagnerian concerts along with other music in the Singer's Hall. For information and reservations, contact the tourist office, **Verkehrsamt,** at the Rathaus in Schwangau (© **08362/938523**). Tickets go on sale in early June and sell out rather quickly. The castle can only be visited on one of the guided tours (offered in English), which are given year-round, except November 1; December 24, 25, and 31; January 1; and Shrove Tuesday. April to September, tours are given 9am to 6pm, and October to March, times are 10am to 4pm. Tours leave every 45 minutes and last 35 minutes. Admission is 9€ ($14) for adults, 8€ ($13) for students and seniors over 65, and free for children 14 and under. A combination ticket for both castles is 17€ ($27) for adults and 15€ ($24) for children 14 and under.

Reaching Neuschwanstein involves a steep half-mile climb from the parking lot at Hohenschwangau Castle (see above). This can be a 30-minute walk for the athletic, an eternity for those less so. To cut down on the climb, you can take a bus to Marienbrücke, a bridge that crosses over the Pöllat Gorge at a height of 93m (305 ft.). From that vantage point, you, like Ludwig, can stand and meditate on the glories of the castle and its panoramic surroundings. If you want to photograph the castle, don't wait until you reach the top, where you'll be too close for a good shot. It costs 1.80€ ($2.90) for the bus ride up to the bridge or 1€ ($1.60) to return. From Marienbrücke, it's a 10-minute walk to Neuschwanstein castle. This footpath is very steep.

The traditional way to reach Neuschwanstein is by horse-drawn carriage; this costs 5€ ($8) for the ascent and 2.50€ ($4) for the descent. *Note:* Some readers have complained about the rides being overcrowded and not at all accessible for visitors with limited mobility.

9

Munich

The people of Munich never need much reason to celebrate. If you arrive here in late September, you'll find them in the middle of **Oktoberfest,** which draws more than seven million people every fall and lasts for 16 days, ending on the first Sunday in October. Although Oktoberfest, when beer flows as freely as water, is the most famous of Munich's festivals, the city is actually less inhibited during the more interesting pre-Lenten **Fasching** (see chapter 3). Even the most reserved Germans get caught up in this whirl of colorful parades, masked balls, and revelry.

Munich is a lively place all year long—fairs and holidays seem to follow one on top of the other. But this is no "oom-pah" town. Here you'll find an elegant and tasteful city with sophisticated clubs and restaurants, wonderful theaters, fine concert halls, and fabulous museums. According to various polls, it's also the Germans' first choice as a place to live.

1 Orientation

Munich is just slightly smaller than Berlin or Hamburg. You can explore the heart of Munich on foot, but many attractions are in the environs, so you'll have to rely on a car or public transportation.

ARRIVING

BY PLANE   About 27km (17 miles) northeast of central Munich at Erdinger Moos, the **Munich International Airport** (© **089/97500;** www.munich-airport.de), inaugurated in 1992, is among the most modern, best-equipped, and most efficient airports in the world. The airport handles more than 400 flights a day, serving at least 65 cities worldwide. Passengers can fly nonstop from New York, Miami, Chicago, and Toronto, among other places.

S-Bahn (© **089/41424344**) trains connect the airport with the Hauptbahnhof (main railroad station) in downtown Munich. Departures are every 20 minutes for the 40-minute trip. The fare is 10€ ($16); Eurailpass holders ride free. A taxi into the center costs about 50€ to 60€ ($80–$96). Airport buses, such as those operated by Lufthansa, also run between the airport and the center.

BY TRAIN   Munich's main rail station, the **Hauptbahnhof,** on Bahnhofplatz near the city center, is one of Europe's largest. It contains a hotel, restaurants, shopping, car parking, and banking facilities. All major German cities are connected to this station. Some 20 daily trains connect Munich to Frankfurt (trip time: 3¾ hr.) and 23 to Berlin (trip time: 6¾ hr.). For information about long-distance trains, call © **01805/996633.**

The rail station is connected with the **S-Bahn** rapid-transit system, a 418km (259-mile) network of tracks, providing service to various city districts and outlying suburbs. For S-Bahn information, call © **01805/661010.** The **U-Bahn (subway)** system serving Munich is also centered at the rail station. In addition, buses fan out in all directions.

BY BUS Munich has long-distance bus service from many German and European cities. Depending on their point of origin, buses depart from the section of the Hauptbahnhof called the West-Wing Starnberger Bahnhof, or from the Deutsche Touring Terminal on Arnulfstrasse 3, about a block away. For information about connections, fares, and schedules, call **Deutsche Touring GmbH** at ✆ **089/88989513.** Regional service to towns and villages within Bavaria can be arranged through **Oberbayern Autobus,** Heidemann-Strasse 220 (✆ **089/323040**), or Sareiter Busbetrieb, Maximilianstrasse 39. An affiliate of Oberbayern Autobus, Sareiter Busbetrieb, organizes bus tours to specific tourist destinations around Bavaria and into neighboring Austria, including the castles of King Ludwig, Innsbruck, and Salzburg. Sareiter Busbetrieb can be contacted through the Oberbayern Autobus phone number.

VISITOR INFORMATION

There are two tourist offices in Munich: Bahnhofplatz 2, open Monday to Saturday 9am to 8pm and Sunday 10am to 6pm; and Marienplatz in Neuen Rathaus, open Monday to Friday 10am to 8pm and Saturday 10am to 4pm. For information, call ✆ **089/23-39-65-00** (www.muenchen.de).

CITY LAYOUT

Munich's **Hauptbahnhof,** or rail station, lies just west of the town center and opens onto Bahnhofplatz. From there you can take Schützenstrasse to one of the major centers of Munich, **Karlsplatz** (nicknamed Stachus). Many tram lines converge on this square. From Karlsplatz, you can continue east along the pedestrians-only Neuhauserstrasse and Kaufingerstrasse until you reach **Marienplatz,** which is located deep in the **Altstadt (old town)** of Munich.

From Marienplatz you can head north on Dienerstrasse, which will lead you to Residenzstrasse and finally to **Max-Joseph-Platz,** a landmark square, with the Nationaltheater and the former royal palace, the Residenz. East of this square runs **Maximilianstrasse,** Munich's most fashionable shopping and dining street, and the site of the prestigious Kempinski Hotel Vier Jahreszeiten München. Between Marienplatz and the Nationaltheater is the **Platzl** quarter, where you'll want to head for the nightlife; here you'll find some of the finest (and also some of the worst) restaurants in Munich, along with the landmark Hofbräuhaus, the most famous beer hall in Europe.

North of the old town is **Schwabing,** a former bohemian section whose main street is Leopoldstrasse. The sprawling municipal park grounds, the **Englischer Garten,** are due east of Schwabing.

FINDING AN ADDRESS/MAPS In the Altstadt, "hidden" squares may make finding an address difficult; therefore, you may need a detailed street map, not the more general maps handed out for free by the tourist office and many hotels. Falk publishes the best ones, which contain a detailed street index and are available at nearly all bookstores and at many newsstands.

NEIGHBORHOODS IN BRIEF

Altstadt This part of Munich is the site of the original medieval city. The Altstadt is bordered by the Sendlinger Tor (*Tor* means gate) and Odeonsplatz to the north and south, and by the Isartor and Karlstor to the east and west. The hub is **Marienplatz,** with its Rathaus (Town Hall) and its Glockenspiel performances. You can walk across the district in about 15 minutes.

Schwabing Since 1945, this large northern section of the city has been known as a bohemian district similar to Greenwich Village in New York. **Leopoldstrasse** makes almost a straight axis through its center. The Englischer Garten forms its eastern border, the Studentenstadt is to its north, and Olympiapark and Josephsplatz mark its western border.

Olympiapark Host to rock and pop concerts on weekends, this residential and recreational area was the site of the 1972 Olympics, which is remembered for the terrorist attack by the Arab "Black September" group against Israeli athletes. The 1972 Munich Olympic Games were meant to show the world the bold new face of a rebuilt Munich, showcasing the premises of the innovative Olympic City. The Black September terrorists, however, had different plans. They managed to slip into the compound housing the athletes from Israel and, before the day was over, had slaughtered a total of 11 of Israel's finest athletes, each in place to compete in the Olympic Games. A storm of protest was raised around the world. The games were virtually ruined, and Munich's bright new image was shattered (their police force seemed to make mistake after mistake). Dark memories of the Holocaust were revived at a time when Germany, and Munich specifically, was trying to forget its recent past and show the world that it had moved into a brighter and happier future. For more information, see p. 333.

Museum Quarter Between the Altstadt and Schwabing is the museum district, containing such great museums as the **Alte Pinakothek** (p. 323). Bordered by Briennerstrasse and Theresienstrasse, it covers only 2 blocks, but it can take days to explore in depth if you visit all the wonderful state-owned museums.

Nymphenburg Take the U-Bahn to Rotkreuzplatz, then tram no. 12 to the Nymphenburg district, about 8km (5 miles) northwest of the city center, site of the summer palace of the Wittelsbach dynasty and the famous porcelain manufacturer (p. 310).

2 Getting Around

The best way to explore Munich is by walking. In fact, because of the vast pedestrian zone in the center, many of the major attractions can only be reached on foot.

BY PUBLIC TRANSPORTATION

The city's underground rapid-transit system, the **U-Bahn** or Untergrundbahn network, is modern and relatively noise-free. The aboveground **S-Bahn,** or Stadtbahn, services suburban locations. At the transport hub, Marienplatz, U-Bahn and S-Bahn rails cross each other.

The same ticket entitles you to ride both the U-Bahn and the S-Bahn, as well as **trams (streetcars)** and **buses.** The U-Bahn is the system you'll probably use most frequently. You're allowed to use your Eurailpass on S-Bahn journeys, as it's a state-owned railway. Otherwise, you must purchase a single-trip ticket or a strip ticket for several journeys at one of the blue vending machines positioned at the entryways to the stations.

If you're making only one trip, a **single ticket** will average 2.20€ ($3.50), although it can reach as high as 8.80€ ($14) to an outlying area. A more economical option is the **strip ticket,** called *Streifenkarte* in German. It's good for several rides and sells for 11€ ($14). A trip within the metropolitan area costs you two strips, which are valid

Munich Neighborhoods

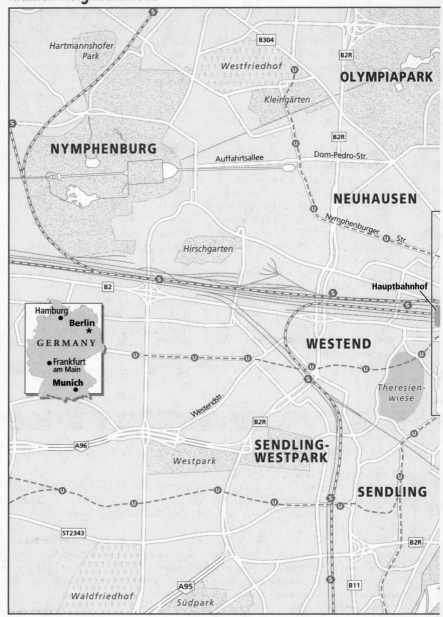

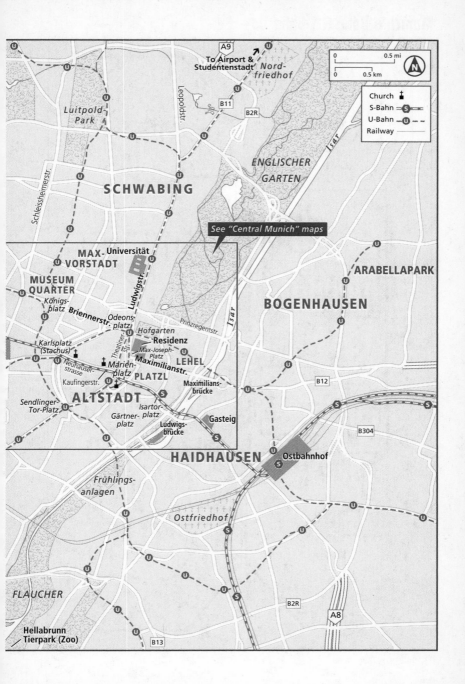

To Airport &
Studentenstadt

A9

Nord-
friedhof

B11

B2R

Isar

Luitpold-
Park

Schleissheimerstr.

Leopoldstr.

ENGLISCHER
GARTEN

SCHWABING

See "Central Munich" maps

MAX- Universität
VORSTADT

ARABELLAPARK

MUSEUM
QUARTER

Königs-
platz

Briennerstr.

Ludwigstr.

Odeons-
platz

Prinzregentstr.

BOGENHAUSEN

Isar

Hofgarten

Residenz

Karlsplatz
(Stachus)

Theaterstr.

Max-Joseph-
Platz

LEHEL

Neuhauser-
strasse

Mārien-
platz

Maximilianstr.

Kaufingerstr.

PLATZL

Maximilians-
brücke

B12

ALTSTADT

Sendlinger-
Tor-Platz

Isartor-
platz

Gärtner-
platz

Ludwigs-
brücke

Gasteig

B304

HAIDHAUSEN

Ostbahnhof

Frühlings-
anlagen

Ostfriedhof

FLAUCHER

B2R

A8

Hellabrunn
Tierpark (Zoo)

B13

0 ____ 0.5 mi
0 ____ 0.5 km
N

Church	†
S-Bahn	Ⓢ
U-Bahn	Ⓤ
Railway	

Munich U-Bahn & S-Bahn

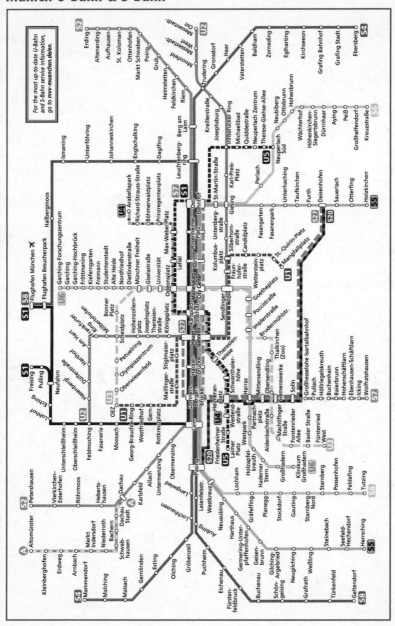

for 2 hours. In that time, you may interrupt your trip and transfer as you like to any public transportation, as long as you travel in one continuous direction. When you reverse your direction, you must cancel two strips again. Children 6 to 14 use the red *Kinderstreifenkarte,* costing 5.20€ ($8.30) for five strips; for a trip within the metropolitan area, they cancel only one strip. Children over the age of 15 pay adult fares. A **day ticket** for 5€ ($8), called a *Tageskarte,* is also a good investment if you plan to stay within the city limits. It's good from the moment of purchase until 4am of the following morning. If you'd like to branch out to Greater Munich—that is, within an 80km (50-mile) radius—you can purchase a day card for 13€ ($20). For public transport information, call ℂ **089/210-33-0.**

BY TAXI

The meter on cabs you hail on the street or find waiting at a taxi stand begins at 2.70€ ($3.50). If you phone for a taxi, 1€ ($1.60) will be added to the fare. For rides within the city of Munich, you'll be charged 1.60€ ($2.60) per kilometer, unless your ride is longer than 10km (6¼ miles), in which event, the per-kilometer rate goes down to between 1.25€ to 1.40€ ($2–$2.30), depending on the distance you travel. Drivers who wait for passengers within their cabs receive a prorated waiting fee of 23€ ($37) per hour. For more information, call ℂ **089/21610** or 089/19410.

BY CAR

It's usually cheaper to rent a car before leaving for Germany (see "Getting There & Getting Around," in chapter 3), though you can also rent one here. Major car-rental companies have easy-to-spot offices at the airport.

If you're already in Munich and plan on making excursions into the Bavarian countryside, it's often more convenient to rent a car in the city center instead of trekking out to the airport. Car-rental companies are listed under *Autovermietung* in the yellow pages of the Munich phone book. Contact **Sixt Autovermietung,** Einsteinstrasse 106 (ℂ **1805/4180050**), to rent a car locally.

Because of heavy traffic, don't attempt to see Munich itself by car. And beware if your hotel doesn't have parking. Parking garages tend to be expensive, often 18€ to 25€ ($29–$40) per night.

BY BICYCLE ⚡

The tourist office sells a pamphlet for .50€ (80¢) called *Rad-Touren für unsere Gäste;* it outlines itineraries for touring Munich by bicycle. One of the most convenient places to rent a bike is **Radius Bikes** (ℂ **089/596113**), at the far end of the Hauptbahnhof, near lockers opposite track 32. The charge is 12€ to 16€ ($19–$26) per 4 hours, or else 14€ to 18€ ($22–$29). Mountain bikes are rented for about 25% more. A deposit of 50€ ($80) is assessed; students and Eurailpass holders receive a 10% discount. Radius Bikes is open May to early October daily 9:30am to 6pm.

FAST FACTS: Munich

Bookstores Most large bookshops in Munich have an English-language section, including **Word's Worth** bookshop, 21a Schellingstrasse (ℂ **089/2809141**).

Business Hours Most **banks** are open Monday to Friday 8:30am to 12:30pm and 1:30 to 3:30pm (many stay open to 5:30pm Thurs). Most **businesses** and **stores** are open Monday to Friday 9am to 6pm and Saturday 9am to 2pm. On *langer Samstag* (the first Sat of the month), stores remain open until 6pm.

Consulates See "Embassies & Consulates" in "Fast Facts: Germany," in the appendix.

Currency Exchange You can get a better rate at a bank than at your hotel. On weekends or at night, you can exchange money at the Hauptbahnhof exchange, open daily 6am to 11:30pm.

Dentists & Doctors For an English-speaking dentist, go to the **Klinik und Poliklinik für Kieferchirurgie der Universität München,** Lindwurmstrasse 2A (© **089/51600;** U-Bahn: Goetheplatz), the dental clinic for the university. It deals with emergency cases and is always open. For 24-hour medical service, go to **Schwabing Hospital,** Kolner Platz 1 (© **089/33040302;** U-Bahn: Scheidplatz).

Drugstores For an international drugstore where English is spoken, go to **Bahnhof Apotheke,** Bahnhofplatz 2 (© **089/594119;** U-Bahn/S-Bahn: Hauptbahnhof), open Monday to Friday 8am to 6:30pm and Saturday 8am to 2pm. If you need a prescription filled during off hours, call © **089/557661** for open locations. The information is recorded and in German only, so you may need to get someone from your hotel staff to assist you.

Emergencies For emergency medical aid, phone © **112.** Call the police at © **110.**

Fax Head for any of the hole-in-the-wall kiosks labeled **Deutsche Telecom.** These include locations on the Marienplatz and in the Hauptbahnhof. Deutsche Telecom phone cards are available in denominations of 6.50€ to 30€ ($10–$48). You can use these to operate self-service fax machines.

Internet Access You can send e-mails or check your messages at the **Easy Internet Café,** Bahnhofplatz 1 (© **089/55999696;** U-Bahn: Hauptbahnhof). It's open daily from 7:30am to 11:45pm. Although this is the most convenient Internet cafe, know that others are found at other strategic locations in central neighborhoods. Ask your hotel desk for the one nearest you.

Laundry & Dry Cleaning A reliable dry-cleaning establishment is **SB Wasch Center,** Parkstrasse 8 (© **089/14079937).** Look in the yellow pages under either *Wascherei* or *Waschsalon* for a coin-operated laundry near your hotel.

Post Office The most central post office is found at Bahnhofplatz (U-Bahn/S-Bahn: Hauptbahnhof), opposite the main train station exit, and is open Monday to Friday 7am to 8pm, Saturday 9am to 4pm, and Sunday 10am to 3pm. You can have your mail sent here *Poste Restante* (general delivery), but include the zip code (80335). You'll need a passport to reclaim mail, and you can't call for information, but must show up in person.

Restrooms The center of Munich has several clean, safe, and well-kept public facilities.

Safety Munich, like all big cities, has its share of crime, especially pickpocketing and purse and camera snatching. Most robberies occur in the much-frequented tourist areas, such as Marienplatz and the Hauptbahnhof, which is particularly dangerous at night. Many tourists also lose their valuables when they carelessly leave clothing unprotected as they join the nude sunbathers in the Englischer Garten.

Television There are two national TV channels, ARD (Channel 1) and ZDF (Channel 2). Sometimes these stations show films in the original language (most often English). The more expensive hotels often have cable TV, with such channels in English as CNN.

3 Where to Stay

There are many rooms available in Munich, though most are costly. Bargains are few and far between—but they do exist.

Portal München Betriebs-GmbH & Co. KG (main tourist office), Fraunhofer-strasse 6 (✆ **0891/2300180;** www.muenchen-tourist.de), open daily 9am to 5pm, is helpful if you arrive without a hotel reservation. Here, Bavarian personnel (most speak English), with some 35,000 listings in their files, will help you find a place to stay. Tell them what you can afford. They'll book you a room and even give you a map with instructions on how to reach it. Keep your receipt. If you don't like the room, go back to the tourist office, and they'll book you another at no extra charge. Reservations are free, but a deposit equal to 10% of the total value of your stay is collected in advance. For direct access to the hotel booking department, call ✆ **089/23396550** or fax 089/23330319.

IN CENTRAL MUNICH
VERY EXPENSIVE

Bayerischer Hof & Palais Montgelas ✮✮✮   Together, the Bayerischer Hof and the 17th-century Palais Montgelas create a Bavarian version of New York's Waldorf-Astoria. This establishment has undergone lavish improvements and is now better than ever, a rival even of the top-ranking Kempinski Hotel Vier Jahreszeiten (see below). It's been a favorite ever since King Ludwig I used to come here to take a bath (the royal palace didn't have bathtubs back then). Rooms range from medium to extremely spacious, and the decor from Bavarian provincial to British country-house chintz. Many beds are four-posters. Palais Montgelas has 20 of the most upscale rooms.

Promenadeplatz 2–6, 80333 München. ✆ 089/21200. Fax 089/2120906. www.bayerischerhof.de. 395 units. 269€–454€ ($430–$726) double; from 1,440€ ($2,304) suite. AE, DC, MC, V. Parking 26€ ($42). Tram: 19. **Amenities:** 3 restaurants; 5 bars; nightclub; spa; rooftop pool and garden; gym; sauna; car rental; room service; massage; babysitting; laundry service; dry cleaning; nonsmoking rooms; sun terrace; 1 room for those w/limited mobility. *In room:* TV, Wi-Fi, minibar, hair dryer, safe.

Charles Hotel ✮✮✮   Set at the edge of the old Botanical Gardens, this luxurious modern hotel is a venture into Munich for the famous Rocco Forte collection of European hotels. A government-rated five-star hotel, the Charles rose in the historic center of Munich, standing in its own tranquil gardens. The spacious bedrooms, each bright and airy, open onto views of the botanical gardens and the more distant Alps. Sleek, contemporary furnishings grace the rooms, which have soundproof doors and windows and three direct line phones. The bathrooms are among Munich's best decorated, with original Nymphenburger porcelain. Wonderful earth colors are used throughout, including camel and moss green.

Sophhienstrasse 28, 80333 München. ✆ 089/5445550. Fax 089/5445552000. www.charleshotel.de. 160 units. 390€–530€ ($624–$848) double; 720€ ($1,152) junior suite; from 960€ ($1,536) suite. AE, DC, MC, V. Parking 24€

Where to Stay & Dine in Central Munich

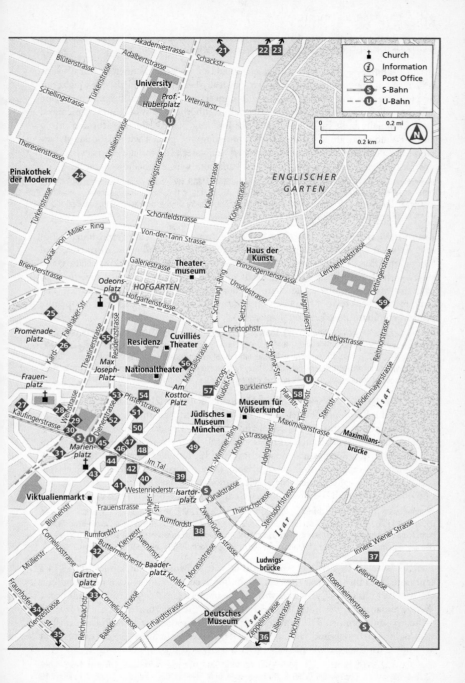

($38). U-Bahn: Karlsplatz. **Amenities:** Restaurant; bar; indoor pool; fitness room; spa; sauna; steam bath; Internet access; room service; laundry service; dry cleaning. *In room:* A/C, TV, minibar, hair dryer, safe.

Hotel Palace 𝄐𝄐 It's tasteful, it's restrained, it's perfectly mannered, and it's very, very aware of how prestigious a stay here can really be. The Hotel Palace is sought out by performers at the nearby theaters and concert halls as a peaceful and nurturing address in Bogenhausen, a stylish residential neighborhood east of Munich's medieval core. Originally built in 1986 as an office building, it was later transformed into a hotel. Public areas are streamlined and contemporary, graced with elaborate hyper-modern balustrades on travertine-sheathed staircases. Rooms are immaculate and upscale, and each comes with a luxurious bathroom with a tub/shower combo.

Trogerstrasse 21, 81675 München. ℂ 089/419710. Fax 089/41971819. www.hotel-palace-muenchen.de. 74 units. 205€–265€ ($328–$424) double; from 430€ ($533) suite. AE, DC, MC, V. U-Bahn: Prinzregentumplatz. **Amenities:** Restaurant; bar; health club; sauna; steam room; room service; laundry service; dry cleaning; nonsmoking rooms; rooms for those w/limited mobility. *In room:* A/C, TV, Wi-Fi, minibar, hair dryer, safe.

Kempinski Hotel Vier Jahreszeiten München 𝄐𝄐𝄐 This grand hotel is not only the most elegant in Munich, it's also Germany's most famous and distinctive, and among the finest in the world. Its tradition stretches back to 1858. Rooms and suites—which have hosted royalty, heads of state, and famed personalities from all over the world—combine the charm of days gone by with modern luxuries. The antique-style beds feature fine linen on sumptuous mattresses. The windows opening onto Maximilianstrasse are double-glazed.

Maximilianstrasse 17, 80539 München. ℂ 800/426-3135 in the U.S., or 089/21250. Fax 089/21252000. www. kempinski-vierjahreszeiten.de. 308 units. 246€–450€ ($394–$720) double; from 720€ ($1,152) suite. AE, DC, MC, V. Parking 20€ ($32). Tram: 19. **Amenities:** Restaurant; 2 bars; indoor heated pool; fitness center; sauna; Turkish bath; solarium; room service; massage; babysitting; laundry service; dry cleaning; nonsmoking rooms; rooms for those w/limited mobility. *In room:* A/C, TV, Wi-Fi, minibar, hair dryer, safe.

Mandarin Oriental 𝄐𝄐𝄐 One of Munich's smaller hotels is also one of its posh-est. Only the Kempinski Hotel Vier Jahreszeiten München and the Bayerischer Hof (see above) outclass this sophisticated and luxurious winner. Located within sight of the Frauenkirche at Marienplatz, the stylish and elegant wedge-shaped 1880s building combines neo-Renaissance, neoclassical, and Biedermeier touches. A marble stair-case sweeps upward to the very comfortable, large rooms, each with specially crafted furniture or original antiques. Many accommodations have private terraces opening onto views of Munich. Bathrooms are well appointed, each with a tub and shower.

Neuturmstrasse 1, 80331 München. ℂ 089/290980. Fax 089/222539. www.mandarinoriental.com. 73 units. 395€–520€ ($632–$832) double; from 630€ ($1,008) suite. AE, DC, MC, V. Parking 20€ ($32). U-Bahn/S-Bahn: Marien-platz. Tram: 19. **Amenities:** 2 restaurants; bar; rooftop pool; fitness room; room service; babysitting; laundry service; dry cleaning; nonsmoking rooms; rooms for those w/limited mobility. *In room:* A/C, TV, Wi-Fi, minibar, hair dryer, safe.

Sofitel Munich Bayerpost 𝄐𝄐 In the heart of Munich, this modern hotel in a traditional building lies near the Hauptbahnhof or central railway station. It combines the architectural style of yesterday with all the modern amenities of today. Built in the Wilhelminian style, the hotel is rated five stars by the government, and it's a bastion of luxury and comfort. The midsize to spacious bedrooms are beautifully furnished with natural materials and tasteful fabrics. The Maisonette Suites on the eighth floor are known for their panoramic views over the city and the Alps beyond.

Bayerstrasse 12, 80335 München. ℂ 089/599380. Fax 089/599481000. www.sofitel.com. 396 units. 149€–179€ ($238–$286) double; 229€–449€ ($366–$718) junior suite; from 564€ ($902) suite. AE, DC, MC, V. Parking 24€

($38). U-Bahn: Hauptbahnhof. **Amenities:** Restaurant; bistro; bar; disco; indoor pool; fitness center; spa; sauna; solarium; business center; room service; laundry service; dry cleaning; rooms for those w/limited mobility. *In room:* A/C, TV, Wi-Fi, minibar, hair dryer, safe.

MODERATE

Advokat Hotel   This hotel occupies a six-story apartment house originally constructed in the 1930s. Its stripped-down, streamlined interior borrows in discreet ways from Bauhaus and minimalist models. One Munich critic said the rooms look as if Philippe Starck had gone on a shopping binge at Ikea. The result is an aggressively simple, clean-lined, and artfully spartan hotel with few facilities. There's no restaurant on the premises and no particular extras to speak of other than a delightful rooftop breakfast. But the prices are reasonable, and the staff is helpful.

Baaderstrasse 1, 80469 München. © **089/216310.** Fax 089/2163190. www.hotel-advokat.de. 50 units. 160€–280€ ($256–$448) double. Rates include buffet breakfast. AE, DC, MC, V. S-Bahn: Isartor. **Amenities:** Breakfast room; nonsmoking rooms. *In room:* TV, Wi-Fi, minibar, hair dryer.

An der Oper   This five-floor hotel, built in 1969, is superbly located for sightseeing or shopping in the traffic-free malls, and it's just steps from the Bavarian National Theater. In spite of its basic decor, there are touches of elegance. Rooms, which range from small to medium, have double-glazed windows, a small sitting area with armchairs, and a table for those who want breakfast in their rooms.

Falkenturmstrasse 11, 80331 München. © **089/2900270.** Fax 089/29002729. www.hotelanderoper.com. 68 units. 180€–270€ ($288–$432) double; 246€–390€ ($394–$624) apt. Rates include buffet breakfast. AE, MC, V. Tram: 19. **Amenities:** Nonsmoking rooms; rooms for those w/limited mobility. *In room:* TV, Wi-Fi, minibar, hair dryer.

Anna Hotel   This building was constructed around 1900 as a four-story office block, and in 2002, when it was converted into this streamlined and stylish hotel, the developers had to evict at least one doctor's office. Today, it's a clean, charming, well-managed hotel with a minimalist and stylish decor that's loaded with wood paneling and warm tones of ocher and russet, with touches of yellow-and-black marble in all the bathrooms. A collection of postmodern sculptures in the lobby is by Stephan Ester, a locally well-known artist. Many of the clients of this hotel are business travelers, who appreciate the stylish and well-choreographed service and the comfortably secure bedrooms. Four of the suites are in a tower that affords exceptional views over the city. The hotel restaurant is open from 7am to 1am, with warm food available every day from noon to midnight.

1 Schützenstrasse, 80335 München. © **089/599940.** Fax 089/59994333. www.annahotel.de. 73 units. 195€–370€ ($312–$592) double; 370€–550€ ($592–$880) tower suite. Rates include continental breakfast and nonalcoholic contents of the minibar. MC, V. Parking 22€ ($35). U-Bahn: Karlsplatz or Hauptbahnhof. **Amenities:** Restaurant; bar; free access to health club and sauna a few buildings away; laundry service; dry cleaning; nonsmoking rooms. *In room:* A/C, TV, Wi-Fi, minibar, hair dryer.

Cortiina *ℛ (Finds*   Built in 2001, this hotel has quickly gained a foothold with loyal business clients, most of whom hail from Germany, Switzerland, Austria, and Great Britain. Rising five stories above a centrally located and historic neighborhood in the heart of Munich, its cozy, warm design may remind you of a high-alpine retreat as imagined by Frank Lloyd Wright. There's a sheathing of intricately crafted dark-stained oak and exposed flagstones in both the public areas and the bedrooms, and a careful allegiance throughout the design to the Chinese principles of feng shui, wherein objects, windows, traffic patterns, and doors are carefully balanced for a maximum of emotional and psychic harmony.

Ledererstrasse 8, 80331 München. © 089/2422490. Fax 089/242249100. www.cortiina.com. 35 units. 196€–266€ ($314–$426) double; 286€–326€ ($458–$522) suite. Rates include continental breakfast. AE, DC, MC, V. Parking 15€ ($24). U-Bahn: Marienplatz. **Amenities:** Breakfast room; bar; honor bar/lounge; room service; babysitting; laundry service; dry cleaning; nonsmoking rooms. *In room:* TV, Wi-Fi, minibar, hair dryer, safe.

Eden-Hotel-Wolff ☆   If you must stay in the train station area, this is your best bet. The hotel is also conveniently located across the street from the Munich terminus of the Lufthansa Airport Bus. The austere stone-clad facade of the Eden-Hotel-Wolff does not reveal the warmth and comfort within. The interior is richly traditional, with chandeliers and dark-wood paneling. Most rooms are spacious, and all are tastefully furnished in a decor that runs the gamut from extremely modern to rustic. Some units are hypoallergenic, with special beds and a private ventilation system. Ask about special weekend rates, which may or may not be available.

Arnulfstrasse 4–8, 80335 München. © **089/551150.** Fax 089/55115555. www.ehw.de. 210 units. 143€–310€ ($229–$496) double; 275€–375€ ($440–$600) suite. 1 child up to age 6 stays free in parent's room. Rates include buffet breakfast. AE, DC, MC, V. Parking 15€ ($24). U-Bahn/S-Bahn: Hauptbahnhof. **Amenities:** Restaurant; bar; spa; fitness room; room service; babysitting; laundry service; nonsmoking rooms. *In room:* TV, minibar, hair dryer, safe.

Excelsior Hotel ☆   This solidly comfortable, government-rated four-star hotel (which is not a member of any chain) near the city's main railway station prides itself on its restored facade, a pale exterior that replicates its original turn-of-the-20th-century design, which was destroyed in wartime bombings. The hotel's bedrooms are quite spacious, outfitted in a tasteful and conservative style. All units contain bathrooms with shower/tub combos. Overall, this is a low-key, discreet, highly Europeanized hotel with a resolute lack of glitter.

Schützenstrasse 11, 80335 München. © **089/55-13-70.** Fax 089/55-13-61-21. www.excelsior-muenchen.de. 114 units. 190€–285€ ($304–$456) double; 315€–355€ ($504–$568) suite. AE, DC, MC, V. Parking 22€ ($35). U-Bahn: Hauptbahnhof. **Amenities:** Restaurant; bar; room service (breakfast-only); laundry service; dry cleaning; nonsmoking rooms. *In room:* A/C, TV, Wi-Fi, minibar, hair dryer.

Hotel Exquisit ☆   One of the most appealing hotels in the Sendlinger Tor neighborhood lies behind a wine-colored facade on a quiet residential street that seems far removed from the heavy traffic and bustle of the nearby theater district. Built in 1988, it has a paneled lobby whose focal point is a lounge that gets busy around 6 or 7pm. Staff members are unusually pleasant, offering a genuine welcome and ushering you up to rooms that are spacious and comfortably furnished. About half overlook an ivy-draped garden, others look over the street.

Pettenkoferstrasse 3, 80336 München. © **089/5519900.** Fax 089/55199-499. www.hotel-exquisit.com. 50 units. 135€–265€ ($216–$424) double; 175€–325€ ($280–$520) suite. Rates include buffet breakfast. AE, DC, MC, V. Parking 15€ ($24). U-Bahn: Sendlinger Tor. **Amenities:** Restaurant; private garden; bar; sauna; room service; laundry service; dry cleaning; nonsmoking rooms. *In room:* TV, Wi-Fi, minibar, hair dryer.

Hotel Mark *(Value*   This hotel near the Hauptbahnhof's south exit is known for comfort and moderate prices. The rooms are functionally furnished, although a bit cramped, but you should sleep in peace. All rooms have soundproof windows. Breakfast is the only meal served.

Senefelderstrasse 12, 80336 München. © **089/559820.** Fax 089/55982333. www.hotel-mark.de. 95 units. 82€–242€ ($131–$387) double. Rates include buffet breakfast. AE, DC, MC, V. Parking 14€ ($22). U-Bahn/S-Bahn: Hauptbahnhof. **Amenities:** Breakfast room; room service; babysitting; laundry service; dry cleaning; nonsmoking rooms. *In room:* TV, Wi-Fi, minibar, hair dryer, safe.

Hotel Olympic ℛ   Built as a private villa around 1900, this hotel represents one of Munich's most appealing conversions of an antique building into a hip and attractive hotel. The lobby occupies a high-ceilinged, Victorian vestibule that retains many of the original details. Breakfast is served in a very large, graciously proportioned dining room, where memories of the grand bourgeoisie of the Industrial Revolution still seem to permeate the woodwork. Rooms are minimalist and all white, much more modern than the ground-floor reception areas, but comfortable and well engineered.

Hans Sachs Strasse 4, 80469 München. ℂ **089/231890.** Fax 089/23189199. www.hotel-olympic.de. 38 units. 155€–200€ ($248–$320) double; 530€–880€ ($848–$1,408) apt. Rates include buffet breakfast. AE, DC, MC, V. Parking 18€ ($29). U-Bahn: Sendlinger Tor. **Amenities:** Breakfast room; lounge; room service; babysitting; laundry service; dry cleaning. *In room:* TV, Wi-Fi, minibar, hair dryer.

Hotel Splendid-Dollmann im Lehel ℛ *(Finds*   Check in here if you want a hotel that's up-to-date yet replete with antiques, fine paintings, quality Oriental carpets, and a sense of Munich's sometimes gracious 18th- and 19th-century past. The venue is an elegant 19th-century town house, fronted with chiseled white-stone blocks, in the upscale neighborhood known as the Lehel district. Inside, an attentive staff welcomes you into a small, boutique-style hotel replete with a library-style bar and many of the decorative accessories of an upscale private home. Bedrooms are cozy, colorful, and well maintained, each with a different theme and reproductions of antique furniture.

Thierschstrasse 49, 80538 München. ℂ **089/238080.** Fax 089/23808365. www.hotel-splendid-dollmann.de. 37 units. 160€–200€ ($256–$320) double; 230€–270€ ($368–$432) suite. Parking 8.50€ ($14). AE, DC, MC, V. U-Bahn: Lehel. **Amenities:** Bar; room service. *In room:* TV, Wi-Fi.

Torbräu ℛ   The foundations of this government-rated four-star hotel in the heart of historic Munich date from the 15th century. Although many vestiges of its folkloric exterior attest to the hotel's distinguished past, the bedrooms are modern and are reasonably comfortable. All units have well-kept bathrooms, mostly with shower-tub combos. In all, the place is a lot more charming than many of its bandbox-modern competitors.

Tal 41, 80331 München. ℂ **089/24-23-40.** Fax 089/24-234-235. www.torbraeu.de. 92 units. 185€–258€ ($296–$413) double; 255€–342€ ($408–$547) suite. Rates include buffet breakfast. AE, MC, V. Parking 15€ ($24). Closed 1 week at Christmas. U-Bahn: Isartor. **Amenities:** 2 restaurants; bar; room service; babysitting; laundry service; dry cleaning; nonsmoking rooms. *In room:* A/C, TV, Wi-Fi, minibar, beverage maker (in some), hair dryer, safe.

INEXPENSIVE

Brack   Because it lies close to the Oktoberfest grounds, it's virtually impossible to get in here during the festival. But at other times of the year, the rejuvenated hotel might be an ideal choice and most affordable. Management has combined both traditional architecture and modern amenities in the same building. Bedrooms are tastefully decorated with a number of comforts such as electrically operated shutters and soundproof windows. Thoughtful extras include free use of bikes along with a map outlining cycle routes.

Lindwurmstrasse 153, 80337 München. ℂ **089/747255.** Fax 089/72015015. www.hotel-brack.de. 50 units. 99€–169€ ($158–$270) double, 119€–189€ ($190–$302) triple. Rates include breakfast. AE, DC, MC, V. U-Bahn: Poccistrasse. Free parking. **Amenities:** Breakfast room; free bikes; Internet access; laundry service. *In room:* TV.

Creatif Hotel Elephant *(Value*   From the outside, the sterile building evokes a student dormitory, but inside the hotel warms considerably—and is, in fact, one of the best deals in the area of the Hauptbahnhof (the main rail station). The use of bright pastels enlivens the atmosphere a bit, and the small bedrooms are well maintained as well as simply though comfortably furnished. Guests are granted 50% off their meals at the Al Teatro Restaurant lying at Schwanthalerstrasse 15, just a 5-minute walk from the hotel.

Lämmerstrasse 6, Leopoldvorstadt, 80335 München. ⓒ 089/555-785. Fax 089/550-1746. www.creatifelephanthotel. com. 40 units. 89€–110€ ($142–$176) double. AE, DC, MC, V. U-Bahn/S-Bahn: Hauptbahnhof. **Amenities:** Breakfast room; Internet access; laundry service. *In room:* TV.

Hotel Biederstein *Finds*   Near the Englischer Garten, this B&B is a charmer on the Munich hotel scene. It is decorated with high-end modern furnishings in a minimalist style and is operated by the same people who run Gästehaus Englischer Garten, one of Munich's most frequently booked small inns (see below). The hotel rents bikes to its guests to ride through the English Garden. Bedrooms are spacious and most of them are priced at the lower end of the scale. A first-rate breakfast is served on the terrace.

Keferstrasse 18, 80802 München. ⓒ 089/3899970. Fax 089/399997389. www.hotel-biederstein.de. 34 units. 103€–275€ ($165–$440) double; 165€–380€ ($264–$608) suite. AE, DC, MC, V. Parking 8€ ($13). U-Bahn: Münchner Freiheit. **Amenities:** Breakfast terrace; room service; babysitting; laundry service; dry cleaning. *In room:* TV, minibar, hair dryer.

Hotel Jedermann *Value Kids*   If you're put off by Munich's high hotel prices, you'll be happy at the Hotel Jedermann. Its central location and good value make it a fine choice, especially for families on a budget (cribs and cots are available). The old-fashioned Bavarian rooms are generally small, but cozy and comfortable, each with a shower-only bathroom. A generous breakfast buffet is served. Staff attitude here, however, needs a major overhaul.

Bayerstrasse 95, 80335 München. ⓒ 089/543240. Fax 089/54324111. www.hotel-jedermann.de. 55 units. 75€–189€ ($120–$302) double; 90€–219€ ($144–$350) triple. Rates include buffet breakfast. MC, V. Parking 10€ ($16). U-Bahn/S-Bahn: Hauptbahnhof. **Amenities:** Breakfast room. *In room:* A/C (in some units), TV, hair dryer, safe (in most units).

Hotel Schlicker *Finds*   This charming traditional hotel dates to 1544 and has been run in a friendly, inviting fashion by the Mayer family since 1897. Although it's situated between a McDonald's and a Burger King, it's also in the heart of Munich, just steps away from the landmark Marienplatz and around the corner from our favorite food market in Germany, Viktualienmarkt. Only the breakfast room suggests that this place was once an ancient inn—the rest of the hotel is modernized. Bedrooms are comfortable and traditional, each midsize.

Tal 8, 80331 München. ⓒ 089/2428870. Fax 089/296059. www.hotel-schlicker.de. 69 units. 118€–174€ ($189–$278) double; 240€–270€ ($384–$432) suite. Rates include continental breakfast. AE, DC, MC, V. Parking 12€ ($19). U-Bahn: Marienplatz. **Amenities:** Breakfast room; room service. *In room:* TV, minibar, safe (in some).

Monaco *Kids*   This hotel, only a few steps from the Hauptbahnhof, became prominent when it was voted the most popular government-rated hotel in all of Germany in 1998. It's as good now as it was way back when. A member of the Small Elegant Hotels of the World, the Monaco is still as highly regarded as it was when it first came to prominence. If we judged a hotel by its generous Bavarian breakfast buffet, we'd rate this one a winner. But its bedrooms, which are spacious, modern, and decorated for comfort, make the Monaco appealing as well. Many rooms can be rented for three guests, making it a favorite with families. Personal service is another feature of this family-run hotel.

Schillerstrasse 9, 80336 Munich. ⓒ 089/545-99-40. Fax 089/550-37-09. www.hotel-monaco.de. 27 units. 60€–220€ ($96–$352) double; 90€–290€ ($144–$464) triple. Extra bed 20€–50€ ($32–$80). Rates include continental breakfast. AE, MC, V. U-Bahn/S-Bahn: Hauptbahnhof. Parking 15€ ($24). **Amenities:** Breakfast room; room service; nonsmoking rooms. *In room:* TV, Wi-Fi.

Pension Westfalia *Ⓡ (Value* This four-story town house (originally built in 1895) near Goetheplatz is one of Munich's best pensions. It faces the meadow where the annual Oktoberfest takes place. Rooms are rather functional and short on extras, but they are well maintained, each with a small shower-only bathroom. Parking on the street, when available, is free.

Mozartstrasse 23, 80336 München. ☎ **089/530377.** Fax 089/5439120. www.pension-westfalia.de. 19 units, 14 with bathroom. 50€–60€ ($80–$96) per person double without bathroom; 68€–82€ ($109–$131) per person double with bathroom. Rates include buffet breakfast. AE, MC, V. U-Bahn: Goetheplatz. Bus: 58. **Amenities:** Breakfast room; nonsmoking rooms. *In room:* TV.

Uhland Garni Located in a residential area, just a 10-minute walk from the Hauptbahnhof, the Uhland could easily become your home in Munich. The stately town mansion, built in Art Nouveau style, stands in its own small garden. The hotel offers friendly, personal service, and rooms are soundproof, snug, traditional, and cozy. Bathrooms contain showers, and only breakfast is served.

Uhlandstrasse 1, 80336 München. ☎ **089/543350.** Fax 089/54335250. www.hotel-uhland.de. 30 units. 82€–185€ ($131–$296) double. Rates include buffet breakfast. AE, DC, MC, V. Free parking. U-Bahn/S-Bahn: Theresienwiese. Bus: 58. **Amenities:** Breakfast room; nonsmoking rooms. *In room:* TV, Wi-Fi (in most), minibar, hair dryer, safe.

IN SCHWABING

Gästehaus Englischer Garten *ⓇⓇ (Kids* This ivy-covered villa oasis of charm and tranquillity, close to the Englischer Garten, provides old-fashioned family atmosphere and is one of our preferred stopovers in Munich. The decor of the small to medium rooms has been called "Bavarian grandmotherly"; furnishings include genuine antiques, old-fashioned but exceedingly comfortable beds, and Oriental rugs. Bathrooms with showers are small and not one of the hotel's stronger features, but their maintenance is first-rate. Fifteen units are across the street in an annex; these are small apartments, each with a bathroom and a tiny kitchenette. Ask for room no. 10, 20, 30, or 90; these are bigger and have better views. In fair weather, breakfast is served in a rear garden.

Liebergesellstrasse 8, 80802 München-Schwabing. ☎ **089/3839410.** Fax 089/38394133. www.hotelenglischergarten. de. 25 units, 16 with bathroom. 71€–120€ ($114–$192) double without bathroom; 120€–180€ ($192–$288) double with bathroom; 103€–174€ ($165–$278) apt. AE, DC, MC, V. Parking 8€ ($13). U-Bahn: Münchner Freiheit. **Amenities:** Breakfast room; babysitting; laundry service; dry cleaning; nonsmoking rooms. *In room:* TV, minibar.

IN HAIDHAUSEN

Preysing *Ⓡ (Finds* If you want a quiet location and don't mind a hotel on the outskirts, consider the Preysing, located across the Isar near the Deutsches Museum. (A short tram ride will bring you into the center of the city.) When you first view the building, a seven-story modern structure, you may feel we've misled you. However, if you've gone this far, venture inside for a pleasant surprise. The hotel's style is agreeable, with dozens of little extras to provide homelike comfort. Fresh flowers are everywhere, the furnishings have been carefully selected, and fresh fruit is supplied daily.

Preysingstrasse 1, 81667 München. ☎ **089/458450.** Fax 089/45845444. www.hotel-preysing.de. 76 units. 155€–245€ ($248–$392) double; from 258€ ($413) suite. Rates include buffet breakfast. AE, DC, MC, V. Parking 12€ ($19). S-Bahn: Rosenheimerplatz. Tram: 18. **Amenities:** Breakfast room; lounge; room service; babysitting; laundry service; dry cleaning. *In room:* A/C, TV, Wi-Fi, minibar, hair dryer.

IN NYMPHENBURG

Kriemhild *Kids*　This is one of the best choices for visitors with kids in tow, as it lies in the suburb of Nymphenburg, one of the most famous attractions of Munich, known for its beautiful gardens and leafy parks. From the front door of this well-run establishment, you and the children can walk over to the entrance to Schloss Nymphenburg (p. 329). For dad, there is also nearby Hirschgarten Park, site of the biggest biergarten in Europe. The government-rated three-star hotel is run exceptionally well with an accommodating staff. The more spacious rooms contain a corner sofa, which can be converted for use as a three- or four-bed family room. In the morning, there's an elaborate buffet breakfast, and at night you can drink beer or wine in a cozy Bavarian-styled *Guntherstube* (beer tavern).

Guntherstrasse 16, 80639 München. ☎ **089/171-1170.** Fax 089/1711-1755. www.kriemhild.de. 18 units. 102€–170€ ($163–$272) double; 118€–178€ ($189–$285) suite. Rates include continental breakfast buffet. AE, MC, V. Free parking. Tram: 16 or 17. S-Bahn: Laim. **Amenities:** Breakfast room; bar; nonsmoking rooms. *In room:* TV, Wi-Fi, minibar, hair dryer.

Laimer Hof *Finds Kids*　This Renaissance villa is in one of the most tranquil and exclusive sections of Munich. Nymphenburg Palace, with its enchanting park, lies within an easy walk from the hotel. The villa from 1886 was turned into a hotel in 1937, but a young couple, Sebastian and Alexandra Rösch, took over and made substantial improvements and renovations, turning it into one of the most desirable private hotels of Munich. The bedrooms are completely modernized and furnished in a traditional way, exuding comfort and tradition. The hotel is popular with families, and many of the rooms can be connected to form one unit. A lavish breakfast buffet is part of the deal. The hotel is also within a short walk of Hirschgarten, Europe's biggest beer garden. Jogging, walking, and riding a bike are popular in the Nymphenburg Park.

Laimer Strasse 40, 80639 München. ☎ **089/178038.** Fax 089/1782007. www.laimerhof.de. 23 units. 105€ ($168) double. Rates include buffet breakfast. AE, MC, V. Free parking. U-Bahn: Rotkreuzplatz, then tram no. 17. Bus: 41. **Amenities:** Breakfast room. *In room:* TV, minibar, safe.

TOP Hotel Erzgiesserei Europe *Finds*　This undiscovered hotel lies in the suburb of Nymphenburg, site of the famous palace, yet you are only a 5-minute U-Bahn ride from the center of Munich. If you'd like a little entertainment, there's an English-language cinema just around the corner. Rated four stars by the government, it is a first-class hotel with sleek, modern rooms tastefully and comfortably furnished. It's run by an efficient staff who welcomes you to their Alt Wuerttemberg restaurant, serving a first-rate international cuisine, tables overflowing into the garden courtyard in summer.

Erzgiessereistrasse 15, Nymphenburg, 80335 München. ☎ **089/126-820.** Fax 089/123-6198. www.topinternational. com. 106 units. 91€–178€ ($146–$285) double. AE, DC, MC, V. Parking 12€ ($19). U-Bahn: Stiglmaierplatz. **Amenities:** Restaurant; bar; room service; laundry service; nonsmoking rooms; rooms for those w/limited mobility. *In room:* TV, Wi-Fi, hair dryer, minibar.

4 Where to Dine

Munich, one of the few European cities with more than one Michelin-rated three-star restaurant, is the place to practice *Edelfresswelle* ("high-class gluttony"). The classic local dish, traditionally consumed before noon, is *Weisswurste,* herb-flavored white-veal sausages blanched in water. Sophisticated international cuisine is popular throughout the city, too. For the location of restaurants in this section, see the "Where to Stay & Dine in Central Munich" map on p. 302.

IN CENTRAL MUNICH
VERY EXPENSIVE

Ederer ☆☆ MODERN INTERNATIONAL   Noted as one of the poshest and most desirable addresses in Munich, and the culinary domain of celebrity chef Karl Ederer, this restaurant occupies an antique building that's noted for its huge windows, several blazing fireplaces, very high ceilings, and an appealing collection of paintings. Inspiration for the menu items covers the gamut of cuisines from Bavaria, France, Italy, the New World, and the Pacific Rim, and as such, they've received lots of rave attention in the German press. The menu changes with the seasons and the whim of the kitchen staff, but might include such starters as marinated sweet-and-sour pumpkin served with shiitake mushrooms, parsley roots, and lukewarm chunks of octopus; or terrine of duckling foie gras with a very fresh brioche and a dollop of pumpkin jelly. Representative main courses include a delectable roasted breast of duckling with stuffing, glazed baby white cabbage, mashed potatoes, and gooseliver sauce; or pan-fried anglerfish with a sauce made from olive oil, lemon grass, and thyme.

Kardinal Faulhaber Strasse 10. ⓒ **089/24-23-13-10.** Reservations required. Main courses 22€–33€ ($35–$53); fixed-price 2-course lunch 27€ ($43), 3-course dinner 48€ ($77), 5-course dinner 85€ ($136). AE, DC, MC, V. Mon–Sat noon–2:30pm and 6:30–10pm. U-Bahn: Marienplatz or Odeonsplatz.

Garden Restaurant ☆ MEDITERRANEAN/INTERNATIONAL   This showcase restaurant within one of Munich's showcase hotels looks like a miniature pastel-colored palace. It's set in a solemnly hushed room filled with blooming plants off the otherwise bustling hotel lobby. Upscale food is served to a cosmopolitan crowd. Menu items are about as cultivated and esoteric as you can find in Munich. Examples include thin noodles with strips of quail and mushroom sauce, and a "land and sea" salad—a bouquet of greens stuffed with gooseliver and fresh mushrooms. One of the most sought-after dishes is filet of Dover sole in lemon-butter sauce, served simply but flavorfully with fresh spinach and boiled potatoes. Desserts are appropriately lavish, and always imaginative. Ever had baked curd cheese ravioli with rhubarb and tonka-bean ice cream?

In the Bayerischer Hof Hotel, Promenadeplatz 2–6. ⓒ **089/2120993.** Reservations recommended. Main courses 18€–35€ ($29–$56). AE, DC, MC, V. Daily noon–3pm and 6–11:30pm. Tram: 19 or 21.

Restaurant Königshof ☆☆☆ INTERNATIONAL/FRENCH   This remains one of Munich's grand hotel dining rooms, with its oyster-white panels of oak, polished bronze chandeliers, silver candelabra, and porcelain. The waiters are polite and skilled and the chefs highly inventive. With each passing year, this venerated restaurant just seems to get better and better. The cuisine is simply dazzling, light, full of flavor, and prepared with only the finest of ingredients. For some of the most discerning foodies in Germany, this restaurant is a must on their gastronomic itineraries.

Sit back and succumb to the exquisite and varied pleasures of the intelligent, graceful cuisine that emerges from the kitchen. Among the favorite dishes we've sampled here are sautéed anglerfish with wild garlic and vine-ripened cherry tomatoes or else turbot with fresh morels. Especially delectable is a saddle of bison with sautéed polenta, eggplant, and young onions. Lobster appears with a delightful vanilla butter, and loin of lamb is aromatically seasoned with fresh herbs.

In the Hotel Königshof, Karlsplatz 25 (Am Stachus). ⓒ **089/551360.** Reservations required. Main courses 36€–46€ ($58–$74); fixed-price menus 90€–130€ ($144–$208). AE, DC, MC, V. Tues–Sat noon–2:30pm and 7–10pm. S-Bahn: Karlsplatz. Tram: 19, 20, or 21.

Restaurant Vue Maximilian *๕* FRENCH/INTERNATIONAL   Restaurant Vue Maximilian is in a quiet and elegant location within walking distance of the opera house. The atmosphere is dignified and refined, the service extremely competent, and the food prepared along classic French lines with imaginative variations, including Asian influences. The menu changes every 4 to 6 weeks. You might begin with crayfish with asparagus and a green parsley mousse, or else a terrine of boiled beef and horseradish. For a main course, try pan-fried filet of char with fresh vegetables or a filet of Bavarian beef with roasted wood mushrooms and truffled celery.

In the Kempinski Hotel Vier Jahreszeiten München, Maximilianstrasse 17. © **089/21250**. Reservations required. Main courses 20€–32€ ($32–$51); 4-course fixed-price menu 82€ ($131). AE, DC, MC, V. Daily noon–3:30pm and 6–11:30pm. Tram: 19.

Schuhbecks in den Südtiroler Stuben *๕๕๕* BAVARIAN/INTERNATIONAL This luxe restaurant is at the very top of all the restaurants of Bavaria, given serious competition only by Tantris (p. 319). Chef Alfons Schuhbeck enjoys well-deserved celebrity. East meets West in his fusion cuisine, which some critics liken to "California freestyle." At the top of his menu, the chef welcomes you with "modest greetings," but there is nothing modest about the cuisine. The menu is forever changing, based on the freshest and best ingredients in any season.

Some of our favorite starters include fish soup made with freshwater fish and crayfish, given added zest with a touch of curry; marinated tuna fish with caviar and vegetable jelly; and the truffle-infused pasta with Parmesan and summer vegetables. We also adore such main dishes as saddle and tongue of veal with pan-fried asparagus and a carrot-and-celery purée, or the combination stuffed rabbit shank and grilled duck breast with Roman flour dumplings.

An Platzl 6–8. © **089/2166900**. Reservations required. Fixed-price menus 78€–123€ ($125–$197). AE, DC, MC, V. Tues–Sat 11am–3pm; Mon–Sat 6–11pm. U-Bahn/S-Bahn: Marienplatz.

EXPENSIVE

Austernkeller *๕* SEAFOOD   This "oyster cellar" is a delight to visitors and locals, with the largest selection of oysters in town, from raw oysters to oysters Rockefeller. A terrific starter is the shellfish platter with fresh oysters, mussels, clams, scampi, and sea snails. Or you may begin with a richly stocked fish soup or cold hors d'oeuvres. French meat specialties are also offered, but the focus is seafood—everything from lobster thermidor to shrimp grilled in the shell. The decor is elegant and refined, and the service is attentive.

Stollbergstrasse 11. © **089/298787**. Reservations required. Main courses 20€–32€ ($32–$51). AE, DC, MC, V. Daily 5pm–1am. Closed Dec 23–26. U-Bahn: Isartor.

La Galleria *๕* ITALIAN   This is one of the most appealing of the several Italian restaurants in Munich's center, taking the greatest risks with experimental Italian cuisine. It provides gracious service and a roster of dishes that change with the availability of ingredients and the inspiration of the chefs. Examples are poached sea wolf with fresh vegetables in fennel sauce, an aromatic guinea fowl scented with lavender, homemade spaghetti with white Italian truffles, herb-flavored risotto with chunks of lobster and braised radicchio (the best we've had in Munich), and roasted soft-shell crabs with a light onion sauce.

Sparkassenstrasse 11. © **089/297995**. Reservations recommended. Main courses 18€–25€ ($29–$40); fixed-price dinners 40€–55€ ($64–$88). AE, DC, MC, V. Mon–Sat noon–2:30pm and 6:30–11:30pm. U-Bahn/S-Bahn: Marienplatz.

Mark's Restaurant *®®®* FRENCH/CONTINENTAL   This restaurant is appropriately elegant with an impeccably trained staff. Lunch is served in a small, cozy enclave off the lobby, Mark's Corner, and is usually limited to a fixed-price menu favored by businesspeople. Dinners are more elaborate, served one floor above street level in a formal dining room that overlooks a monumental staircase and the lobby below. On Sunday and Monday nights only, the formal dining room is closed, and dinner is served in Mark's Corner. Menus change monthly and according to the inspiration of the chef. Many dishes are somewhat experimental but still succeed beautifully, such as filet of beef with a ragout of artichokes and potatoes and deep-fried baby garlic buds; sea wolf with green lentils, bacon, and gooseliver; and filet of beef with horseradish, served with dumplings and savoy cabbage.

In the Mandarin Oriental, Neuturmstrasse 1. ℂ 089/290980. Reservations recommended. Main courses 29€–32€ ($46–$51); fixed-price lunch (in Mark's Corner) 79€ ($126), dinner 100€ ($160). AE, DC, MC, V. Daily noon–2pm and 7–11pm. U-Bahn/S-Bahn: Marienplatz.

Seven Fish *®* SEAFOOD   Some of the best and freshest fish dishes are served at this first-class restaurant lying a short walk from the famous Munich open-air market, Viktualienmarkt. Based on the freshest catch of the day, the menu is forever changing. The smartly executed cuisine was created by two Greek brothers who know their fish. At a small bar, you can enjoy Japanese-style sushi or else sit at one of the main tables, some of which overflow onto the square out front in fair weather.

Gärtnerplatz 6. ℂ 089/2300-0219. Reservations recommended. Main courses 20€–30€ ($32–$48). AE, MC, V. Daily 10am–11pm. U-Bahn: Marienplatz.

MODERATE

Alois Dallmayr *®®* CONTINENTAL   With a history dating from 1700, this is the most famous delicatessen in Germany. After looking at its tempting array of delicacies from around the globe, you'll think you're lost in a millionaire's supermarket—and, in fact, Dallmayr has been a purveyor to many royal courts. Here you'll find Munich's most elegant consumers. The upstairs dining room serves a subtle German version of Continental cuisine, owing a heavy debt to France. The food array is dazzling, ranging from the best herring and sausages we've ever tasted to such rare treats as vine-ripened tomatoes flown in from Morocco and papayas from Brazil. The famous French *poulet de Bresse* (this Bresse chicken is identified throughout Europe as the most flavorful and tender chicken anywhere), beloved of gourmets, is also shipped in. The smoked fish is fabulous, and the soups are superbly flavored, especially the one made with shrimp. If you're dining alone, you may prefer to sit at the counter instead of a table. This bustling restaurant is crowded at lunchtime.

Dienerstrasse 14–15. ℂ 089/213-51-00. Reservations recommended. Main courses 35€–44€ ($56–$70); fixed-price 4-course lunch 72€ ($115), 7-course dinner 118€ ($189). AE, DC, MC, V. Tues–Sat noon–2pm and 7–10pm. Tram: 19.

Café Dukatz in the Literaturhaus *®* INTERNATIONAL/FRENCH   Our hangout in Munich is this cafe/restaurant that pays tribute to the writer Oskar Maria Graf (1894–1967) and is decorated with Graf memorabilia. Jenny Holzer, the New York artist, was called in to carry out the Graf theme. She took sentences from Graf's writings and inscribed them on the cafe's leather benches and on the plates. You'll have to finish your meal to see what Graf had to say. A typical remark: "It must soon be that I am famous." Munich is the center of publishing in Germany, and writers, editors, and readers drop in throughout the day for coffee and cake.

This is no mere coffeehouse, however. The restaurant serves full-fledged meals with some of the Bavarian countryside's finest ingredients. At lunch, try a sandwich such as the baguette with rabbit or the pastrami with sauerkraut. At our most recent dinner, we enjoyed salmon in champagne sauce with fresh oysters. The *Blutwurst* in pastry, with diced apples, was better than the typical *boudin noir* in a French bistro. For dessert, try the pear tart with almond cream.

Salvatorplatz 1. ℂ 089/2919600. Reservations not needed. Main courses 15€–28€ ($23–$44). No credit cards. Mon–Sat 10am–1am; Sun 10am–7pm. U-Bahn: Odeonsplatz.

Café Glockenspiel (Kids) PASTRIES/INTERNATIONAL   This is the most frequented cafe in Munich. It's across from the Rathaus, and a crowd gathers here every day at 10:30am to watch the miniature tournament staged by the clock on the Rathaus facade. In addition to the view, the cafe has strong coffee and freshly made pastries with a limited menu of hot dishes. It also makes a fine place to end your day tour of Munich and to fortify yourself for Munich after dark. Arrive around 5pm for a drink and watch the square morph from daytime to night. It's an ideal place for people-watching, too.

Marienplatz 28. ℂ 089/264256. Main courses 11€–18€ ($18–$29). MC, V. Mon–Sat 10am–1am; Sun 10am–7pm. U-Bahn/S-Bahn: Marienplatz.

Lenbach ℱ CONTINENTAL/ASIAN   Aggressively hip and aesthetically striking, this is one of the most sought-after and iconoclastic restaurants in Munich. It occupies a landmark brick-and-stone building, erected in 1887, that originally functioned as the home and sales outlet for the era's most flamboyant antiques dealer, who frescoed its interior with Renaissance murals. An unusual blend of hypermodern and Renaissance motifs greets clients here, whose path to their table is along a slightly elevated catwalk that evokes a runway where supermodels might strut their stuff before a phalanx of photographers.

Delectable menu items include a rack of Iberian pork with garlic or else boiled veal with risotto and fresh vegetables. Thai curry appears with tiger prawns, or you might order the sea bass with an unusual potato-and-pomegranate risotto. For starters try beef steak tartare with homemade walnut hash browns, or grilled octopus with fresh grapefruit.

Ottostrasse 6. ℂ 089/5491300. Reservations recommended. Main courses lunch 8.50€–15€ ($14–$24), dinner 20€–29€ ($32–$46). AE, DC, MC, V. Mon–Sat 11:30am–2:30pm and 6pm–midnight. U-Bahn: Stachus.

Nürnberger Bratwurst Glöckl am Dom ℱ (Kids) (Value) BAVARIAN   The homesick Nürnberger comes here just for one dish with those delectable little sausages: *Nürnberger Schweinwurst mit Kraut.* You can also find such items as crispy roast pork with bread dumplings and cabbage salad, veal breast stuffed with a potato-and-cucumber salad, or breaded veal escalopes topped with a cream sauce. This old restaurant first opened in 1893. It was rebuilt after World War II, and it is now the coziest and warmest of all the local restaurants. Chairs look almost as if they were hand-carved, and upstairs, reached through a hidden stairway, is a dining room hung with reproductions of Dürer prints. Tables are shared, and food is served on tin plates. Last food orders go in at midnight. A short walk from Marienplatz, the restaurant faces the Frauenkirche.

Frauenplatz 9. ℂ 089/295264. Reservations recommended. Main courses 10€–20€ ($16–$32). MC, V. Daily 10am–1am. U-Bahn: U2 or U3 to Marienplatz.

Kids Family-Friendly Restaurants

Café Glockenspiel (on the Marienplatz) Your kids can down delectable Bavarian pastries while enjoying the miniature "tournament" staged each day near the clock on the Rathaus facade.

Nürnberger Bratwurst Glöckl am Dom (Frauenplatz 9, facing the cathedral) Hot dogs will never taste the same again after your child has tried one of these savory little sausages from Nürnberg.

Tower Restaurant, Olympiapark (p. 333) For a panoramic view of the Alps as well as the Olympic grounds, take your kids here to dine and, later, out onto one of the observation platforms.

Pfistermühle BAVARIAN   The country comes right into the heart of Munich at this authentic and old-fashioned restaurant, a series of charmingly decorated dining rooms in a converted old mill. A warm welcome and a refreshing cuisine await you here. Many of the dishes would be familiar to your Bavarian grandmother, and portions are generous and satisfying. Come here for some of the most perfectly prepared roasts in the city, always served with a selection of fresh vegetables. Instead of these meat courses, you can opt for a fine array of simply prepared fresh fish from the lakes and rivers of Bavaria, especially the delectable salmon trout or brown trout. Most fish dishes come with chive-flecked sour cream and a potato pancake. Finish with a pyramid of vanilla custard served with a fresh berry sauce followed by a glass of wild-cherry schnapps.

In the Platz Hotel, Pfistermühle 4. (C) **089/23703865.** Reservations recommended. Main courses 13€–20€ ($21–$32). AE, DC, MC, V. Mon–Sat noon–11pm. U-Bahn: Marienplatz.

Ratskeller München BAVARIAN   Throughout Germany, you'll find Ratskellers, traditional cellar restaurants in Rathaus (city hall) basements, serving decent and inexpensive food and wine. Munich is proud of its Ratskeller. The decor is typical: dark wood and carved chairs. The coziest tables are in the semiprivate dining nooks in the rear, under the vaulted painted ceilings. Bavarian music adds to the ambience. The menu, generally a showcase of regional fare, includes some international dishes, many of them vegetarian, which is unusual for a Ratskeller. The chef also grills certain dishes that are lighter in content than the usual German fare served in town cellars. Delectable menu items include ocean filet of cod sautéed in butter and served with a German potato salad, or *Schweinshaxe* (roast pork shank), baked with a crunchy crust and served with potato dumplings and red cabbage.

Im Rathaus, Marienplatz 8. (C) **089/2199890.** Reservations required. Main courses 10€–24€ ($16–$38). AE, MC, V. Daily 10am–midnight. U-Bahn/S-Bahn: Marienplatz.

Spatenhaus BAVARIAN/INTERNATIONAL   The Spatenhaus, one of Munich's best-known beer restaurants, offers wide windows overlooking the opera house on Max-Joseph-Platz. You can sit in an intimate, semiprivate dining nook or at a big table. Spatenhaus has old traditions, typical Bavarian food, and generous portions at reasonable prices. If you want to know what all this fabled Bavarian gluttony is about, order the "Bavarian plate," which is loaded with various meats, including pork and sausages. (After that, you'll have to go to a spa.) Other fine choices include grilled filets of lemon sole with a creamy lobster sauce, roast pork with potato dumplings and red cabbage, and grilled salmon with ricotta-stuffed ravioli. Of course, to be loyal, you should order the restaurant's own beer, Spaten-Franziskaner-Bier, with your meal. There's another dining annex on the second floor, open daily from 11:30am to 1am, specializing in an international cuisine that includes brook trout or roast salmon steak with noodles in a lobster sauce, as well as Angus beef with a red-wine sauce with fried potatoes. Main courses in this restaurant annex cost 18€ to 24€ ($29–$38).

Residenzstrasse 12. ℰ **089/2907060.** Reservations recommended. Main courses 14€–25€ ($22–$40). AE, MC, V. Daily 9:30am–12:30am. U-Bahn: Odeonsplatz or Marienplatz.

Vinorant Alter Hof ℱ *Value* FRANCONIAN In a castle in the heart of the city (Marienplatz), this restaurant serves the best Franconian regional cuisine in Munich. In the basement is a wine bar where you can enjoy inexpensive snacks and the best of regional wines. Upstairs a more formal cuisine is served, including an excellently prepared fixed-price menu. This old favorite is decorated in a regional style, and adjusts its menus to take advantage of the best ingredients in any season—game in autumn, fresh asparagus in the spring. Although cooking for the "masses," the chefs manage to create distinctive flavor in their dishes. Desserts are yummy and made fresh daily, great on flavor, and heavy on calories.

Alter Hof 3. ℰ **089/24243733.** Reservations recommended in main restaurant. Main courses 16€–22€ ($26–$35). DC, MC, V. Mon–Sat 11:30am–11:30pm. U-Bahn/S-Bahn: Marienplatz.

Weinhaus Neuner BAVARIAN/INTERNATIONAL This is an *Ältestes Weinhaus Münchens* (Old Munich Wine House), one of the city's landmark taverns. Dating from the late 15th century, it's the only building in Munich with its original Tyrolean vaults. The place brims with warmth and charm. Once young priests were educated here, but after Napoleon brought secularization, it became a wine tavern and a rendezvous for artists, writers, and composers, including Richard Wagner. The casual *Weinstube* is the less formal section and has lots of local atmosphere. New dishes on the menu include mussels with braised lemons and fresh asparagus in a basil sauce. The filet of turbot with fresh mushrooms in a champagne sauce is sublime, as is the carpaccio of filet of beef with fresh herbs and truffle-flavored vinaigrette. Finish off with a homemade sorbet with a pineapple ragout.

Herzogspitalstrasse 8. ℰ **089/2603954.** Reservations recommended. Main courses 18€–24€ ($29–$38); fixed-price lunch 18€–23€ ($29–$37), dinner 37€ ($59). AE, MC, V. Mon–Sat 11:30am–3pm and 5:30pm–midnight. U-Bahn/S-Bahn: Karlsplatz/Stachus.

Zum Alten Markt *Value* BAVARIAN/INTERNATIONAL Snug and cozy, Zum Alten Markt serves beautifully presented fresh cuisine. Located on a tiny square off Munich's large outdoor food market, the restaurant has a mellow charm and a welcoming host, Josef Lehner. The interior decor, with its intricately coffered wooden ceiling, came from a 400-year-old Tyrolean castle. In summer, tables are set up outside. Fish and fresh vegetables come from the nearby market. You may begin with a tasty homemade soup, such as cream of carrot or perhaps black-truffle tortellini in cream sauce with young onions and tomatoes. The chef makes a great *Tafelspitz* (boiled beef). You can also order classic dishes such as roast duck with applesauce or a savory roast suckling pig.

Am Viktualienmarkt, Dreifaltigkeitsplatz 3. ℰ **089/299995.** Reservations recommended. Main courses 13€–18€ ($20–$29). No credit cards. Mon–Sat noon–midnight. U-Bahn/S-Bahn: Marienplatz. Bus: 53.

INEXPENSIVE

Andechser am Dom GERMAN/BAVARIAN   This restaurant and beer hall is set on two floors of a postwar building adjacent to the rear of the Frauenkirche. It serves beer brewed in a monastery near Munich (Andechser) and generous portions of German food. You're welcome to order a snack, a full meal, or just a beer. Menu items are often accompanied with German-style potato salad and green salad and include such dishes as veal schnitzels, steaks, turkey croquettes, roasted lamb, fish, and several kinds of sausages that taste best with tangy mustard. In clement weather, tables are set up on the roof and on the sidewalk in front, both of which overlook the back of one of the city's finest churches.

Weinstrasse 7A. ℂ **089/298481.** Reservations recommended. Main courses 6.50€–15€ ($10–$24). AE, DC, MC, V. Daily 10am–1am. U-Bahn/S-Bahn: Marienplatz.

Bar-Restaurant Morizz CONTINENTAL/THAI/INTERNATIONAL   This is *the* hip gay restaurant of Munich. As estimated by the staff, it has a 70% gay-male clientele; lesbian women and gay-friendly straights make up the rest of the clients. Part of the space is devoted to a sprawling, attractive bar, where red-leather chairs, mirrors, and an impeccably trained staff evoke a 1920s Paris hotel bar. You can enjoy at least 40 single-malt whiskeys, a half-dozen single-barrel bourbons, and a wide array of unusual wines. The adjacent dining room offers an appealing combination of international and Continental food, prepared by a central European staff whose interpretation of Thai cuisine is especially enjoyable. The menu changes weekly. Try the *Vorspeisen-Teller* of mixed Thai specialties; some find the lemon grass almost addictive. Other choices include veal preparations, fresh fish, pastas, and salads (including one garnished with strips of confit of duckling).

Klenzestrasse 43. ℂ **089/2016776.** Reservations recommended. Main courses 12€–16€ ($19–$26). MC, V. Sun–Thurs 7pm–2am; Fri–Sat 7pm–3am. U-Bahn: Fraunhoferstrasse.

Beim Sedlmayr GERMAN   For insights into the cheap but flavorful cuisine that helped build 19th-century Munich, consider a meal at this bustling folkloric tavern near the epicenter of Munich's historic zone, the Viktualienmarkt. Within a woodsy and sometimes harried environment that can get very busy, you can enjoy schnitzels, sauerbraten, salads, and soups with foaming mugs of beer.

Westenriederstrasse 14. ℂ **089/2608444.** Reservations not necessary. Main courses 9€–13€ ($14–$21). No credit cards. Daily 9am–11pm. U-Bahn/S-Bahn: Marienplatz.

Bier- und Oktoberfest Museum 🅐 *Finds* BAVARIAN   Nothing else in Munich is this authentically Bavarian. The Augustiner Brewery operates this museum and restaurant as a nonprofit organization in one of the antique buildings of Munich, going back to 1327. You can first visit the museum and learn a lot about beer and even the famous Oktoberfest festival. After the tour, you're given a voucher for a Bavarian snack and a glass of brew for only 4€ ($6.40). The snack includes the famous Camembert-like cheese of Munich, *Obatzda,* along with *Leberwurst* (liver sausage). Your doctor may not like it, but to go Bavarian all the way you can spread *Schmalz* (chicken fat) over your freshly baked rye bread.

After 6pm you can stick around for the regional Bavarian fare, starting perhaps with a beer-infused goulash and noodles and following with sausage salads or schnitzels and the like. Naturally, everything is washed down with the Augustiner brew.

Sterneckstrasse 2. ℂ **089/2423-1607.** www.bier-und-oktoberfestmuseum.de. Reservations not needed. Main courses 4€–6.90€ ($6.40–$11). No credit cards. Museum Tues–Sat 1–5pm; beer hall Tues–Sat 6pm–midnight. U-Bahn or S-Bahn: Isartor.

Cohen's JEWISH/CENTRAL EUROPEAN   This joint serves food like that available in Munich before the war and the dreaded Holocaust. Come here for the tastes and flavors of another era, everything washed down with Golan wines imported from Israel. We'd visit just to eat Cohen's potato salad, but you can have so much more, including gelfilte fish, latkes, and wonderful goulash dishes. Roast hen appears with couscous, and a delicious green split pea soup is also served. Naturally the matzo ball and noodle soup is delectable. Singers perform on Friday evenings.

Theresienstrasse 31, Maxvorstadt. ℂ 089/280-9545. Reservations recommended. Main courses 9€–12€ ($14–$18). AE, MC, V. Mon–Sat noon–3pm and 6–10:30pm. U-Bahn: Theresienstrasse.

Deutsche Eiche GERMAN   The building was constructed in 1864, and there's been a restaurant with a mostly gay, or at least arts-oriented, clientele since its very debut. In the 1970s, Fassbinder, the noteworthy film director, hung out here a lot, usually dressed entirely in chains and leather. Late in the 1990s, the place was renovated into a less evocative, more streamlined-looking beer hall, still with a healthy percentage of gay clients, with direct access to a 26-room hotel and one of the busiest gay saunas in Munich. Accommodations in the hotel are relatively affordable at 110€ to 135€ ($176–$216) for a double. Each has a TV and telephone and an all-white, efficient-looking collection of furnishings.

However, we recommend the place as a restaurant/bar. Simple beer hall–style food includes escalope of pork with french fries, turkey steak with mushrooms in cream and homemade noodles, and a filet of pork with roasted potatoes and fresh vegetables.

Reichenbachstrasse 13. ℂ 089/2311660. Reservations not necessary. Main courses 10€–16€ ($16–$26). AE, MC, V. Daily 7am–1am. U-Bahn: Fraunhoferstrasse.

Donisl BAVARIAN/INTERNATIONAL   Donisl is one of Munich's oldest beer halls, dating from 1715. Readers have praised this Munich-style restaurant as *gemütlich* (cozy, pleasant), with its relaxed and comfortable atmosphere, although the seating capacity is about 550. In summer, you can enjoy the hum and bustle of the Marienplatz by dining in the garden area out front. The restaurant has two levels, the second of which is a gallery. Most of the staff speaks English. The standard menu offers traditional Bavarian food as well as a menu of weekly changing specials. A specialty is *Weisswurste,* the little white sausage that has been a decades-long tradition of this place. Select beers from Munich's own Hacker-Pschorr Brewery top the evening. A zither player at noon and an accordion player in the evening entertain diners.

Weinstrasse 1. ℂ 089/22-01-84. Reservations recommended. Main courses 6€–8€ ($9.60–$13). AE, DC, MC, V. Daily 9am–midnight. U-Bahn/S-Bahn: Marienplatz.

La Valle ℛ ITALIAN   Right off the Marienplatz in the heart of Munich, this is one of the best restaurants and pizzerias in town. There's an elegant bar for a predinner drink, and your table might be on one of two floors. The interior is decorated in a classic Italian style, and the service from the largely "south of the border" staff is among the finest in the area. Luigi, the owner, is always on hand to provide menu advice, especially about the day's creations of fish, pasta, or meat specialties. For starters, the minestrone is about the best in Munich, as are the pastas, especially the rich spaghetti carbonara. Pizzas come with toppings ranging from cheese and mushrooms to salami. There's always a grilled fish of the day, perhaps king prawns with fresh herbs, each with fresh vegetables. We've found that the best meat dish is the tender veal in a white wine–and-lemon sauce.

Sparkassenstreet 5. © **089/29160676.** Reservations recommended. Small main courses and pizzas 6.80€–13€ ($11–$21); main courses 13€–18€ ($21–$29). AE, MC, V. Daily 11am–12:30am. U-Bahn/S-Bahn: Marienplatz.

Prinz Myshkin VEGETARIAN This popular vegetarian restaurant near the Marienplatz offers freshly made salads, some macrobiotic selections, Indian and Thai vegetarian dishes, as well as vegetarian *involtini* (stuffed roll-ups) and casseroles, soups, and zesty pizzas, many of which are excellent. You can sample such dishes as a potato-zucchini truffle gratin with lamb's lettuce and a honey-nut dressing or else homemade buckwheat crepes filled with spinach, ricotta, and Parmesan cheese in an herb-laced cream sauce. Roulettes of Swiss chard come with roasted nuts, fresh mushrooms, and tofu in an herb-flavored cream sauce, and you can also order tofu Stroganoff with steamed broccoli and carrots.

Hackenstrasse 2. © **089/265596.** Reservations recommended. Main courses 8€–16€ ($13–$26). AE, MC, V. Daily 11am–12:30am. U-Bahn/S-Bahn: Marienplatz.

Weisses Bräuhaus BAVARIAN/RHENISH Weisses Bräuhaus is big, bustling, and Bavarian with a vengeance. Not for the pretentious, this informal place does what it's been doing for centuries: serving home-brewed beer. At one time, the famous salt-trade route between Salzburg and Augsburg passed by its door, and salt traders are very thirsty folk. The front room, with smoke-blackened dark-wood paneling and stained glass, is for drinking and informal eating; the back room is more formal. Sample typical Bavarian dishes such as smoked filet of trout, rich potato soup, roast pork with homemade potato dumplings and cabbage salad, or Viennese veal goulash with mushrooms and cream sauce. You have to share a table, but that's part of the fun.

Tal 7. © **089/299875.** Reservations recommended, especially for the back room. Main courses 8€–20€ ($13–$32). MC, V. Daily 7am–1am. U-Bahn/S-Bahn: Marienplatz.

NEAR THE ISAR, SOUTH OF CENTER

Asam Schlössl BAVARIAN/INTERNATIONAL This Augustiner brewery restaurant offers a relaxed, relatively informal hideaway amid the congestion of Munich. The building was built as a private villa in 1724. Some of the original castlelike design remains, though the structure has been expanded and renovated over the years. All brews offered are products of Augustiner, including both pale and dark versions of *Weissebier,* beer fermented from wheat. Menu items include such typical Bavarian fare as *Böffla-mott* (beef braised in red wine) with *Semmelknödel* (bread dumplings), and a dish beloved by Emperor Franz Josef of Austria, *gesottener Tafelspitz mit frischen Kren,* a savory form of the familiar boiled beef with horseradish.

Maria-Einsiedel-Strasse 45. © **089/7236373.** Main courses 7.50€–20€ ($12–$32). AE, MC, V. Daily noon–1am. U-Bahn: Thalkirchen.

IN SCHWABING

This district, which was called "bohemian" in the 1920s, overflows with restaurants. Many of them are awful, but there are several fine choices, some of which attract a youthful clientele. The evening is the best time for a visit.

VERY EXPENSIVE

Tantris MEDITERRANEAN/INTERNATIONAL Tantris serves Munich's finest cuisine. Chef Hans Haas was once voted the top chef in Germany, and he has refined and sharpened his culinary technique since. The setting is unlikely: a drab commercial area, with bare concrete walls and a garish decor. But inside, you're transported by the fine service and excellent food that's a treat for the eye as well as the palate. The

Beer Gardens

If you're in Munich between the first sunny spring day and the last fading light of a Bavarian-style autumn, head for one of the city's celebrated biergartens. Traditionally, beer gardens were simply tables placed under chestnut trees planted above the storage cellars to keep beer cool in summer. (Lids on beer steins, incidentally, were meant to keep out flies.) It's estimated that today Munich has at least 400 beer gardens and cellars. Food, drink, and atmosphere are much the same in all of them.

Bamberger Haus, Brunnerstrasse 2 (𝄐 **089/3088966;** U-Bahn: Scheidplatz), located northwest of Schwabing at the edge of Luitpold Park, is named after a city noted for mass consumption of beer. The street-level restaurant, **La Terrazza,** serves Bavarian and international specialties: well-seasoned soups, grilled steak, veal, pork, and sausages. If you only want to drink, you might visit the rowdier and less expensive beer hall in the cellar. Main courses in the restaurant range from 9€ to 17€ ($14–$27). Also on-site is the **Cantina Mexicana & Churrascaria Brasil,** serving Mexican and South American dishes, with main courses costing 9€ to 18€ ($14–$29). La Terrazza is open Sunday and Tuesday to Thursday 11am to 1am, Friday and Saturday 11am to 3am. The cantina serves Sunday and Tuesday to Thursday 6pm to 1am, Friday and Saturday 6pm to 3am. American Express, MasterCard, and Visa are accepted.

Englischer Garten, the park lying between the Isar River and Schwabing, is home to several beer gardens. Our favorite is **Biergarten Chinesischer Turm,** Englischer Garten 3 (𝄐 **089/3838730;** U-Bahn: Universität). It's the largest and most popular of its kind in Europe, taking its name from its location at the foot of an easy-to-find pagodalike tower. Beer and Bavarian food, and plenty of it, are what you get here. A glass or mug of beer large

choice of dishes is wisely limited, and the cooking is subtle and original. You may begin with a terrine of smoked fish served with green-cucumber sauce and follow with classic roast duck on mustard-seed sauce or a delightful concoction of lobster medallions on black noodles.

Johann-Fichte-Strasse 7, Schwabing. 𝄐 **089/3619590.** www.tantris.de. Reservations required. Fixed-price 4-course lunch 96€ ($154); fixed-price 5-course dinner 125€ ($200), 8-course dinner 145€ ($232). AE, DC, MC, V. Tues–Sat noon–3pm and 6:30–10:30pm. Closed public holidays, annual holidays in Jan and May. U-Bahn: Dietlindenstrasse.

MODERATE

Bibulus 𝄐 ITALIAN   If you come here in the summer and sit on the outdoor terrace with its garden view, it's easy to believe that you've suddenly been transported to the Mediterranean. The interior is full of streamlined furnishings and dramatic, oversize modern paintings. Menu items come from all over Italy, but the favorites are those from the owner's native Friuli, near Venice. In season there's lavish use of asparagus, arugula, shellfish, rabbit, wild mushrooms, and venison in such alluring preparations as ravioli stuffed with lobster, tagliatelle, rotini, linguini with braised radicchio and shellfish, and, when available, saltimbocca (veal with prosciutto).

enough to bathe in (ask for *ein mass Bier*) costs 11€ ($18). It will likely be slammed down, still foaming, by a server carrying 12 other tall steins. The food is cheap—a simple meal begins at 8€ ($13). Homemade dumplings are a specialty, as are all kinds of tasty sausages. You can also get a first-rate *Schweinebraten* (a braised loin of pork served with potato dumpling and rich brown gravy), which is Bavaria's answer to the better-known sauerbraten of the north. Huge baskets of pretzels are passed around, and they're eaten with *Radi,* the large, white radishes famous in these parts. Oom-pah bands often play, adding to the festive atmosphere. The place is open every day March to November 10am to midnight, but December to February, its hours depend on the weather and the number of patrons.

If you're going to the zoo, you may want to stop at the nearby **Gaststätte zum Flaucher,** Isarauen 8 (ⓒ **089/7232677**; bus: 52), for fun and food. Gaststätte is mellow and traditional, with tables set in a tree-shaded garden overlooking the river. Here you can order the local specialty, *Leberkäs,* a large loaf of sausage eaten with freshly baked pretzels and plenty of mustard. Beer costs from 7€ ($11) for a half-liter mug. Main courses cost from 6.50€ to 17€ ($10–$27). May to October, it's open daily 10am to midnight, but November to April, only Saturday and Sunday 10am to 9pm.

Hirschgarten, Hirschgartenstrasse 1, in Nymphenburg Park, near the palace (ⓒ **089/17999199**; S-Bahn: Laim; tram: 17 to Romanplatz), is the largest open-air restaurant in Munich, with seating for more than 8,000 beer drinkers and merrymakers. Full meals cost 7.50€ to 15€ ($12–$24). A 1-liter stein of Augustiner beer is 10€ ($16). It's open daily 9am to midnight. MasterCard and Visa are accepted. For information on Munich's other favorite drinking spots—beer halls—see "Munich After Dark," on p. 341.

Siegfriedstrasse 11. ⓒ **089/396447**. Reservations recommended. Main courses 16€–23€ ($26–$37); fixed-price lunch menus 12€–17€ ($19–$27), dinner 37€ ($59). AE, DC, MC, V. Mon–Fri noon–2:30pm; daily 6:30–11pm. U-Bahn: Münchner Freiheit.

Der Katzlmacher ⓡ *(finds* ITALIAN Few Italian restaurants would have had the nerve to adopt as their name a pejorative German term referring to Italians. This one did, however, and its sense of humor has helped make it beloved by loyal local fans. The setting is a postwar building near the university, with dining rooms that are evocative of an elegant and rustic mountain lodge high in the Italian Alps. Stylish and theatrical, and filled with well-dressed, prosperous-looking clients, it contains lavishly carved paneling, masses of artfully arranged flowers, and huge amounts of charm. The cooking is based on the culinary traditions of the Marches, Friuli, and Emilia-Romagna, all known for their fine cuisines and agrarian bounty. The owner is Claudio Zanuttigh, who supervises specialties that might include calzone stuffed with spinach and pine nuts, carpaccio of duck breast, a commendable grilled swordfish with red-wine vinaigrette, eel with champagne sauce, and a succulent version of *fritto misto del pesce* (mixed fried fish) based on whatever is in season.

Kaulbachstrasse 58. ℰ **089/348129.** Reservations recommended. Main courses 18€–28€ ($29–$45); fixed-price lunches 16€–27€ ($25–$42), dinners 41€–54€ ($66–$86). MC, V. Mon–Sat noon–3pm and 6:30–11pm. U-Bahn: Universität.

La Bouille FRENCH/MEDITERRANEAN   The kitchen of sunny Provence is celebrated at this restaurant, which opened in 2004 and became an immediate success. In elegant surroundings, you're welcomed with a smile and invited in to peruse the menu. Friendly service, fine French wines, and, most of all, the flavor-filled cooking redolent of olive oil and the aromas of Provence prevail here. Our party recently devoured perfectly prepared dishes that included pigeon with green cabbage, rack of lamb with a fresh olive crust, and a tender and beautifully flavored breast of duck. Save room for one of the artfully crafted desserts.

Neureutherstrasse 15, at Arcisstrasse. ℰ **089/399936.** Reservations recommended. Main courses 18€–23€ ($29–$37); fixed-price menus 48€–58€ ($77–$93). DC, MC, V. Mon–Fri 12:30–2:30pm and 7pm–midnight; Sat 7pm–midnight; Sun 6:30–11pm. U-Bahn: Josephsplatz or Universität.

IN BOGENHAUSEN

Käfer-Schänke GERMAN/INTERNATIONAL   This is a great spot for casual dining with elegant style, in a setting that evokes a chalet. It's located on the second floor of a famous gourmet shop called Käfer. The cuisine roams the world for inspiration—from Lombardy to Asia. You select your hors d'oeuvres from the most dazzling display in Munich. Often Käfer-Schänke devotes a week to a particular country's cuisine. On one visit, we enjoyed the classic soup of the French Riviera (sea bass with fennel). From a cold table, you can choose smoked salmon or smoked eel. Venison, quail, and guinea hen are also regularly featured.

Prinzregentenstrasse 73. ℰ **089/4168247.** Reservations required. Main courses 25€–42€ ($40–$67). AE, DC, MC, V. Mon–Sat noon–11pm. Closed holidays. U-Bahn: Prinzregentenplatz. Bus: 53 or 54.

5 Exploring Munich

Munich is stocked with so many treasures that any visitor who plans to "do" the city in a day or two will not only miss out on many major sights but will also fail to grasp the city's spirit and absorb its special flavor. There are, however, a few vital highlights.

THE TOP ATTRACTIONS
THE CITY CENTER

Marienplatz ℱ is the heart of the Altstadt, or old city. On its north side is the **Neues Rathaus (New City Hall),** built in 19th-century Gothic style. Each day at 11am and also at noon and 5pm in the summer, the Glockenspiel on the facade performs a miniature tournament, with enameled copper figures moving in and out of the archways. You may wish to climb the 55 steps to the top of the Rathaus's tower (an elevator is also available) for a view of the city center. The **Altes Rathaus (Old City Hall),** with its plain Gothic tower, is to the right. It was reconstructed in the 15th century after being destroyed by fire.

South of the square you can see the oldest church in Munich, **St. Peter's.** The **Viktualienmarkt,** just off Marienplatz and around the corner from St. Peter's church, has been a gathering place since 1807. Here, people gossip, browse, and snack, as well as buy fresh country produce, wines, meats, and cheese.

To the north lies **Odeonsplatz,** Munich's most beautiful square. The **Residenz (Royal Palace)** is just to the east, and the **Theatinerkirche** is to the south. Adjoining

Frommer's Favorite Munich Experiences

A Morning at the Deutsches Museum   It would take a month to see all of the largest technological museum in the world, but a morning will at least whet your appetite. Everything is here: the first automobile by Benz (1886), the original V-2 rocket (Hitler's secret weapon), the first diesel engine, and plenty of buttons to push.

An Afternoon at Nymphenburg Palace   The Wittelsbach family considered this the best place to be on a hot afternoon—and so might you. The grounds of Germany's largest baroque palace are filled with lakes, waterfalls, and pavilions.

A Night at the Opera (Cuvilliés Theater)   It's the most beautiful rococo theater in the world: a small, elaborately gilded tier-boxed structure from the mid–18th century.

A Day in the Beer Gardens   Müncheners gather on weekends in summer to down high tankards of beer and watch the world go by, especially at Chinesischer Turm in the Englischer Garten.

the Residenz is the restored **Nationaltheater,** home of the acclaimed Bavarian State Opera and Bavarian National Ballet.

Running west from Odeonsplatz is the wide shopping avenue, Briennerstrasse, leading to **Königsplatz.** Flanking this large Grecian square are three classical buildings constructed by Ludwig I—the **Propyläen,** the **Glyptothek,** and the **Antikensammlungen.** The busy Ludwigstrasse runs north from Odeonsplatz to the section of Munich known as **Schwabing.** This is the Greenwich Village or Latin Quarter of Munich, proud of its artistic and literary heritage. Ibsen and Rilke lived here, as well as members of the Blue Rider group, which influenced abstract art in the early 20th century. Today, Schwabing's sidewalk tables are filled with young people from all over the world.

Isartor (Isar Gate) is one of the most-photographed Munich landmarks. It's located east of Marienplatz at Isartorplatz. This is the only tower left from the fortified wall that once encircled Munich. The other major gate of Munich is the **Karlstor,** once known as Neuhauser Tor, lying northeast of Karlsplatz (also called Stachus) at the end of Neuhauserstrasse. It formed part of the town's second circuit of walls, dating from the 1500s. The Karlstor lost its main tower (built 1302) in an 1857 explosion.

MUSEUMS & PALACES
Alte Pinakothek (Old Picture Gallery) ✿✿✿   This is one of the most significant
art museums in the world. The nearly 900 paintings on display in this huge neoclassical building represent the greatest European artists of the 14th through the 18th centuries. Begun as a small court collection by the royal Wittelsbach family in the early 1500s, the artistic treasure trove grew and grew. Only two floors have exhibits, but the museum is immense; we do not recommend that you try to cover it all in a day. Pick up a floor plan to guide you through the dozens of rooms.

The landscape painter *par excellence* of the Danube school, **Albrecht Altdorfer,** is represented by six monumental works. Works of **Albrecht Dürer** include his final,

What to See & Do in Central Munich

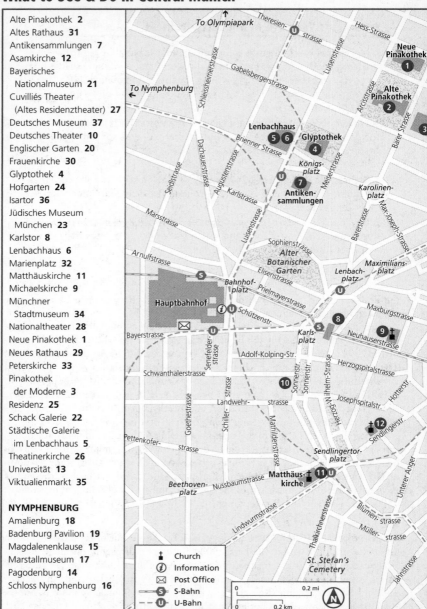

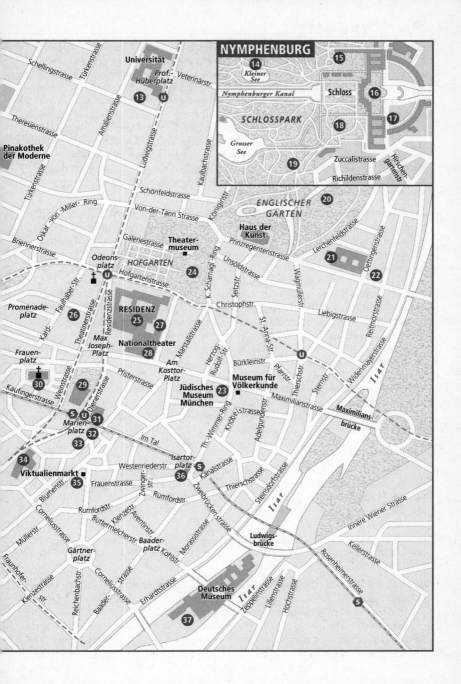

NYMPHENBURG

14 Kleiner See

15

Nymphenburger Kanal

Schloss 16

SCHLOSSPARK

17

18

Grosser See

19

Zuccalistrasse

Richildenstrasse

Schellingstrasse

Türkenstrasse

Universität

Prof.-Huberplatz

Veterinärstr.

13 U

Theresienstrasse

Amalienstrasse

Pinakothek der Moderne

Ludwigstrasse

Kaulbachstrasse

Schönfeldstrasse

ENGLISCHER GARTEN

20

Von-der-Tann Strasse

Königinstr.

Galeriestrasse

Haus der Kunst

Lerchenfeldstrasse

Oettingenstrasse

Oskar--von-Miller- Ring

Theatermuseum

Prinzregentenstrasse

21

Brienerstrasse

Odeonsplatz

HOFGARTEN

24

K. Schanagl--Ring

Unsöldstrasse

Seitzstr.

Wagmüllerstr.

22

Reitmorstrasse

Hofgartenstrasse

Christophstr.

Liebigstrasse

Karlt.--Faulhaber-Str.

Residenzstrasse

Promenadeplatz

26

RESIDENZ

25 27

Max Joseph-Platz

Nationaltheater

28

Am Kosttor-Platz

Marstallstrasse

Herzog--Rudolf-Str.

St.--Anna-Str.

U

Widenmayerstrasse

Isar

Theatinerstrasse

Frauen-platz

Bürkleinstr.

Pfisterstrasse

Jüdisches Museum München

23

Museum für Völkerkunde

Pfarrstr.

Thierschstr.

Sternstr.

Maximilianstrasse

Maximilians-brücke

Kaufingerstrasse

Weinstrasse

30

29

Dienerstrasse

Th.-Wimmer-Ring

Knöbelstrasse

Adelgundenstr.

S U

31

Marien-platz

32

Im Tal

33

34

Isartor-platz

S

Viktualienmarkt

35

Westenriederstr.

36

Kanalstrasse

Zweibrückenstrasse

Steinsdorfstrasse

Isar

Blumenstr.

Frauenstrasse

Zwingerstr.

Thierschstrasse

Rumfordstr.

Cornelliusstrasse

Rumfordstr.

Buttermelcherstr.

Klenzestr.

Aventinstr.

Morassistrasse

Müllerstr.

Gärtner-platz

Baader-platz

Kohlstr.

Ludwigs-brücke

Innere Wiener Strasse

Fraunhofer-str.

Klenzestr.

Reichenbachstr.

Baaderstrasse

Cornelliusstrasse

Erhardtstrasse

Deutsches Museum

37

Isar

Zeppelinstrasse

Lilienstrasse

Hochstrasse

Rosenheimerstrasse

Kellerstrasse

S

and greatest, *Self-Portrait* (1500). Here the artist has portrayed himself with almost Christ-like solemnity. Also displayed is Dürer's last great painting, a two-paneled work called *The Four Apostles* (1526). Works by **Lucas Cranach the Elder** include his *Venus.* Several galleries are given over to Dutch and Flemish masters. There are more **Rubens** here than in any other museum in Europe. **Roger van der Weyden**'s *St. Columbia Altarpiece* (1460–62) measures nearly 3m (10 ft.) across, a triumph of his subtle linear style. Works by **Rembrandt** and **Van Dyck** are also displayed. French, Spanish, and Italian artists can be found in both the larger galleries and the small rooms lining the outer wall. Note *Holy Family* by **Raphael** and *Madonna* by **Leonardo da Vinci.**

Barer Strasse 27. ℂ 089/23805216. www.alte-pinakothek.de. Admission 5.50€ ($8.80) adults, 4€ ($6.40) students and seniors, free for those 14 and under. Admission 1€ ($1.60) for all ages Sun. Tues 10am–8pm; Wed–Sun 10am–6pm. U-Bahn: Theresienstrasse. Tram: 27. Bus: 53.

Bayerisches Nationalmuseum (Bavarian National Museum) 𝓐𝓐   In 1855, King Maximilian II began an institution to preserve Bavaria's historic and artistic treasures. The collection grew so rapidly that it had to be moved to larger quarters several times over the past 100 years. Its current building, near the Haus der Kunst, contains three vast floors of sculpture, painting, folk art, ceramics, furniture, and textiles, as well as clocks and scientific instruments.

After entering the museum, turn right into the first large gallery, the **Wessobrunn Room,** devoted to early church art from the 5th through the 13th centuries. Some of the museum's oldest and most valuable works are here, including ancient and medieval ivories. The most famous is the Munich ivory from about A.D. 400. At the crossing to the adjoining room is the stone figure, the *Virgin with the Rose Bush,* from Straubing (ca. 1300), one of the few old Bavarian pieces of church art influenced by the spirit of mysticism.

The **Riemenschneider Room** is devoted to the works of the great sculptor Tilman Riemenschneider (1460–1531) and his contemporaries. Characteristic of the sculptor's works is the natural, unpainted wood of his carvings and statuary. Note especially the *12 Apostles from the Marienkapelle in Würzburg* (1510), the central group of the high altar in the parish church of Münnerstadt (1490–92), and the figure of St. Sebastian (1490).

The second floor contains a fine collection of stained and painted glass—an art in which medieval Germany excelled. Other rooms include baroque ivory carvings, Meissen porcelain, and ceramics. Also on display are famous collections of 16th- to 18th-century arms and armor, and a collection of antique clocks, some dating from the 16th century.

Prinzregentenstrasse 3. ℂ 089/2112401. www.bayerisches-nationalmuseum.de. Admission 5€ ($8) adults, 4€ ($6.40) students and seniors, free for children 14 and under. Tues–Wed and Fri–Sun 10am–5pm; Thurs 10am–8pm. U-Bahn: Lehel. Tram: 17. Bus: 53.

Deutsches Museum (German Museum of Masterpieces of Science and Technology) 𝓐𝓐𝓐 *Kids*   This is the largest technological museum in the world. Its huge collection of priceless artifacts and historic originals includes the first electric dynamo (Siemens, 1866), the first automobile (Benz, 1886), the first diesel engine (1897), and the laboratory bench at which the atom was first split (Hahn, Strassmann, 1938). There are hundreds of buttons to push, levers to crank, and gears to turn. A knowledgeable, English-speaking staff answers questions and demonstrates how steam engines, pumps, and historical musical instruments work.

Among the most popular displays are those on mining, with a series of model coal, salt, and iron mines, as well as the electrical power hall, with high-voltage displays that actually produce lightning. There are also exhibits on transportation, printing, photography, and textiles, and halls devoted to air-and-space and high-tech themes. Activities include glass-blowing and papermaking demonstrations. The astronomy exhibition is the largest in Europe.

Museumsinsel 1. (C) 089/21791. www.deutsches-museum.de. Admission 8.50€ ($14) adults, 7€ ($11) seniors, 3€ ($4.80) students, free for children 6 and under. Daily 9am–5pm. Closed major holidays. U-Bahn: Fraunhoferstrasse. S-Bahn: Isartor. Tram: 18.

Lenbachhaus *Finds* One of the most unheralded but one of the greatest collections of art is housed in the opulent 1800s mansion of the painter Franz von Lenbach. The collection is chiefly celebrated for its works by the Blaue Reiter (Blue Rider) group, which arose in the city in the years before World War I. The group has a color theory: that blue represents the male principle, austere and spiritual; yellow the female principle, gentle, bright, and sensual; with red standing for what is brutal and heavy. The most evocative painting of that movement is the 1911 *Blue Horse* by Franz Marc. The treasure trove of art here includes works by every artist from Wassily Kandinsky to Andy Warhol. On display is Paul Klee's 1920 *Rose Garden,* an example of what the artist called "polyphonous painting."

No portrait in the gallery is as arresting as that of the *Dancer Aleksandr Sakharov*, painted in 1909 by Alexey von Jawlensky. Sakharov hides behind kohl-rimmed eyes and a voluptuously rouged mouth while wearing a red dress. In 1926 Rudolf Schlichter depicted *Bertolt Brecht* as a common man. Temporary modern exhibits are also presented at this gallery.

33 Luisenstrasse 33. (C) 089/2333200. www.lenbachhaus.de. Admission 6€ ($9.60) adults, 3€ ($4.80) students. Tues–Sun 10am–6pm. U-Bahn: Karolinenplatz.

Pinakothek der Moderne In 2002, one of the world's largest museums devoted to the visual arts of the 19th and 20th centuries opened in Munich, just minutes from the Alte and Neue pinakotheks. This is the vastest display of fine and applied arts in the country as, for the first time, four major collections came together under one roof. This is Munich's version of the Tate Gallery in London or the Pompidou in Paris.

Wander where your interest dictates: the **Staatsgalerie Moderner Kunst (State Gallery of Modern Art)**, with paintings, sculpture, photography, and video; **Die Neue Sammlung,** which constitutes the national museum of applied art featuring design and craftwork; the **Architekturmuseum der Technischen Universität (Technical University's Architectural Museum),** with architectural drawings, photographs, and models; and the **Staatliche Graphische Sammlung (State Collection of Graphics),** with its outstanding collection of prints and drawings.

Whenever we visit, we spend most of our time in the modern art collection, lost in a world of our favorite artists such as Picasso, Magritte, Klee, Kandinsky, even Francis Bacon, de Kooning, and Warhol. The museum also owns 400,000 drawings and prints from Leonardo da Vinci to Cézanne up to contemporary artists. They are presented at alternating exhibits.

The architectural galleries hold the largest specialist collection of its kind in Germany, comprising some 350,000 drawings, 100,000 photographs, and 500 models. The applied arts section features more than 50,000 items, from the beginnings of the Industrial Revolution via Art Nouveau, up to Bauhaus and today's computer culture.

Barerstrasse 40. ℂ **089/23805360.** www.pinakothek.de. Admission 9.50€ ($15) adults; 6€ ($9.60) students, seniors, and children 16 and under; 1€ ($1.60) for all on Sun. Wed and Fri–Sun 10am–6pm; Thurs 10am–8pm. U-Bahn: Odeonsplatz.

Residenz ✸   When one of the Bavarian royals said that he was going to the castle, he could have meant any number of places, especially if he was Ludwig II. But if he said that he was going home, he could only be referring to the Residenz. This enormous palace, with a history almost as long as that of the Wittelsbach family, was the official residence of the rulers of Bavaria from 1385 to 1918. Added to and rebuilt over the centuries, the complex is a conglomerate of various styles. Depending on how you approach the Residenz, you might first see a German Renaissance hall (the western facade), a Palladian palace (on the north), or a Florentine Renaissance palace (on the south facing Max-Joseph-Platz).

The Residenz has been completely restored since its almost total destruction in World War II and now houses the Residenz Museum, a concert hall, the Cuvilliés Theater, and the Residenz Treasury. The **Residenz Museum** (ℂ **089/290671**) comprises the southwestern section of the palace, some 120 rooms of art and furnishings collected by centuries of Wittelsbachs.

The **Ancestral Gallery** is designed like a hall of mirrors, except that instead of mirrors, there are portraits of the Wittelsbach family, set into gilded, carved paneling. The largest room in the museum section is the **Antiquarium,** possibly the finest example of interior Renaissance secular styling in Germany. Frescoes adorn nearly every inch of space on the walls and ceilings. The room is broken into sections by pilasters and niches, each with its own bust of a Roman emperor or a Greek hero. The central attraction is the two-story chimney piece of red stucco and marble, completed in 1600. It's adorned with Tuscan pillars and the coat of arms of the dukes of Bavaria.

On the second floor of the palace, directly over the Antiquarium, is an enormous collection of Far Eastern porcelain. Note also the fine assemblage of Oriental rugs in the long, narrow **Porcelain Gallery.**

If you have time for only one item in the **Schatzkammer (Treasury)** ✸✸, make it the 16th-century Renaissance statue of *St. George Slaying the Dragon.* This equestrian statue is made of gold, but you can barely see the precious metal for the thousands of diamonds, rubies, emeralds, sapphires, and semiprecious stones embedded in it. Both the Residenz Museum and the Schatzkammer are entered from Max-Joseph-Platz on the south side of the palace.

From the Brunnenhof, you can visit the restored **Cuvilliés Theater (Altes Residenztheater)** ✸✸✸. This is Germany's most outstanding example of a rococo tier-boxed theater. Directly over the huge center box, where the royal family sat, is a crest in white and gold topped by a jewel-bedecked crown of Bavaria held in place by a group of cherubs in flight. Court architect François de Cuvilliés designed the theater in the mid–18th century. During World War II, the interior was dismantled and stored. After the war, it was reassembled in the reconstructed building. In summer, this theater is the scene of frequent concerts and opera performances. Mozart's *Idomeneo* was first performed here in 1781.

To the north of the Residenz, the Italianate **Hofgarten,** or Court Garden, is one of the special "green lungs" of Munich. The garden was laid out between 1613 and 1617. It's enclosed on two sides by arcades; in the center is the Hofgarten temple, a 12-sided pavilion dating from 1615.

Max-Joseph-Platz 3. ℂ 089/290671. www.residenz-muenchen.de. Combination ticket for Residenzmuseum and Schatzkammer 9€ ($14) adults, 8€ ($13) seniors, free for students and children 17 and under. Ticket for either Residenzmuseum or Schatzkammer 6€ ($9.60) adults, 5€ ($8) seniors, free for students and children 17 and under. Apr to mid-Oct daily 9am–6pm; mid-Oct to Mar daily 10am–5pm. U-Bahn: Odeonsplatz.

Schack-Galerie To appreciate this florid and romantic overdose of sentimental German paintings of the 19th century, you've got to enjoy fauns and elves at play in picturesque, even magical, landscapes. Such art has its devotees. Obviously, if you're a Picasso Cubist, you'd be better off going elsewhere. But this once-private collection adheres to the baroque tastes of Count Adolf Friedrich von Schack of Schwerin (1815–94), who spent a rich life acquiring works by the likes of Spitzweg, Schwind, Fuerbach, and others, many others—some of whom frankly should have been assigned to the dustbin of art history. Still, in all, we find a visit here fun, at least on a rainy, gray day. It's like wandering back to a lost world.

Prinzregentenstrasse 9. ℂ 089/23805224. Admission 3€ ($4.80) adults, 2€ ($3.20) children. Wed–Sun 10am–5pm. Closed major holidays. Bus: 100.

Schloss Nymphenburg 𝕽𝕽 In summer, the Wittelsbachs would pack up their bags and head for their country house, Schloss Nymphenburg. A more complete, more sophisticated palace than the Residenz, it was begun in 1664 by Elector Ferdinand Maria in Italian-villa style and took more than 150 years to complete. The final palace plan was created mainly by Elector Max Emanuel, who in 1702 decided to enlarge the villa by adding four large pavilions connected by arcaded passageways. Gradually the French style took over, and today the facade is a subdued baroque.

The palace interior is less subtle, however. Upon entering the main building, you're in the **great hall,** decorated in rococo colors and stuccos. The frescoes by Zimmermann (1756) depict incidents from mythology, especially those dealing with Flora, goddess of nymphs, for whom the palace was named. Concerts are still presented here in summer.

From the main building, turn left and head for the **arcaded gallery** connecting the northern pavilions. The first room in the arcade is the Great Gallery of Beauties, painted in 1710. More provocative, however, is Ludwig I's Gallery of Beauties in the south pavilion. Paintings by J. Stieler (1827–50) include the *Schöne Münchnerin (Lovely Munich Girl)* and a portrait of Lola Montez, the dancer whose affair with Ludwig caused a scandal.

To the south of the palace buildings, in the rectangular block of low structures that once housed the court stables, is the **Marstallmuseum.** In the first hall, look for the glass coronation coach of Elector Karl Albrecht, built in Paris in 1740. From the same period comes the hunting sleigh of Electress Amalia, with the statue of Diana, goddess of the hunt. Even the sleigh's runners are decorated with shellwork and hunting trophies.

The coaches and sleighs of Ludwig II are displayed in the **third hall.** His constant longing for the grandeur of the past is reflected in his ornately designed state coach, which was meant for his marriage to Duchess Sophie of Bavaria, a royal wedding that never took place. The coach wasn't wasted, however, because Ludwig often used it to ride through the countryside to one of his many castles, creating quite a picture. The coach is completely gilded, inside and out. In winter, the king would use his state sleigh (also on display), which is nearly as elaborate as the Cinderella coach.

Nymphenburg's park 𝕽 stretches for 200 hectares (500 acres). A canal runs through it from the pool at the foot of the staircase to the cascade at the far end of the

English-style gardens. A number of delightful pavilions are in the park: the **Baden-burg Pavilion,** a bathing pavilion near the lake of the same name; the **Pagodenburg,** decorated in chinoiserie style; and the **Magdalenenklause (Hermitage),** meant to be a retreat for prayer and solitude.

Our favorite is the **Amalienburg** ☆☆ pavilion, whose plain exterior belies the rococo decoration inside. Built as a hunting lodge for Electress Amalia (in 1734), the pavilion carries the hunting theme through the first few rooms and then bursts into salons of flamboyant colors, rich carvings, and wall paintings. The most impressive room is the Hall of Mirrors, a symphony of silver ornaments on a pale-blue background.

Other attractions include the **Porzellansammlung,** or Museum of Porcelain, which is above the stables of the Marstallmuseum. Some of the finest pieces of porcelain in the world, executed in the 18th century, are displayed here, along with an absolute gem—miniature copies in porcelain, done in extraordinary detail, of some of the grand masterpieces in the Alte Pinakothek. Each was commissioned by Ludwig I.

Schloss Nymphenburg 1. ☎ **089/179-080.** www.schloesser.bayern.de. Admission to all attractions 10€ ($16) adults, 8€ seniors, free for students and children 17 and under. Admission to Schloss Nymphenburg only: 5€ ($8) adults, 4€ ($6.40) seniors, free for students and children 17 and under. Admission to Marstallmuseum, Amalienburg, or Porzellansammlung porcelain only: 4€ ($6.40) adults, 3€ ($4.80) seniors, free for students and children 17 and under. Oct–Mar daily 10am–4pm; Apr–Sept daily 9am–6pm. Free parking beside the Marstallmuseum. U-Bahn: Rotkreuzplatz, then tram no. 17 to Botanischergarten. Bus: 41.

MORE ATTRACTIONS
MUSEUMS

Antikensammlungen (Museum of Antiquities) ☆   This collection grew around the vase collection of Ludwig I, who had fantasies of transforming Munich into a second Athens. It was originally called the Museum Antiker Kleinkunst (Museum of Small Works of Ancient Art). Many pieces are small in size but not in value or artistic significance.

The museum's five main-floor halls house more than 650 Greek vases. The oldest, the pre-Mycenaean "goddess from Aegina" (3000 B.C.), carved from a mussel shell, is in Room I. The upper level of the Central Hall is devoted to large Greek vases discovered in Sicily and to Etruscan art. On the lower level is the collection of Greek, Roman, and Etruscan jewelry. (Note the similarities with today's designer fashions.) Also on this level are rooms devoted to ancient colored glass, Etruscan bronzes, and Greek terra cottas.

Königsplatz 1. ☎ **089/59988830.** Admission 3.50€ ($5.60) adults, 2.50€ ($4) students and seniors, free for children 15 and under. Joint ticket to the Museum of Antiquities and the Glyptothek 5.50€ ($8.80) adults, 3.50€ ($5.60) students and seniors, free for children 15 and under. Tues–Sun 10am–5pm (Thurs until 8pm). U-Bahn: Königsplatz.

BMW Welt   Factory tours and a museum to visit are possible at this avant-garde building which stands near Olympic Park. The BMW museum previews the history of the automobile, including the actual models. Visitors touring the factory can see how BMWs are made, including both cars and motorcycles. Plant tours (in English and German) are offered only on weekdays, last 2½ hours, and cost 6€ ($9.60); call in advance for tour schedules and information.

Lerchenauer Strasse 57. ☎ **0180/1118822.** www.bmw-welt.com. Museum admission 12€ ($19) adults, 6€ ($9.60) children and seniors, family ticket 24€ ($38). Tues–Fri 9am–6pm; Sat–Sun 10am–8pm. U-Bahn: Olympiazentrum.

Glyptothek (Museum of Sculpture) ☆   The ideal neighbor for the Museum of Antiquities, the Glyptothek supplements the pottery and smaller pieces of the main museum with the country's largest collection of ancient Greek and Roman sculpture.

Included are the famous pediments from the temple of Aegina, two marvelous statues of *kouroi* (youths) from the 6th century B.C., the colossal figure of a *Sleeping Satyr* from the Hellenistic period, and a splendid collection of Roman portraits.

Königsplatz 3. (℗ 089/286100. Admission 3.50€ ($5.60) adults, 2.50€ ($4) students and seniors, free for children 15 and under; joint ticket to the Museum of Antiquities and the Glyptothek 5.50€ ($8.80) adults, 3.50€ ($5.60) students and seniors, free for children 15 and under. Tues–Sun 10am–5pm (Thurs until 8pm). U-Bahn: U2 to Königsplatz.

Judisches Museum München

The idea was first conceived back in the 1920s. At long last a Jewish museum has become a reality. The collection of permanent and temporary exhibits is part of a municipal building project in the center of Munich. It is a repository of Jewish culture in the city. On three exhibition floors, visitors can gain insights into Jewish life and culture as lived in Munich. On each floor is a study area or learning center and library where visitors can explore issues of interest. Adjacent to Marienplatz and Viktualienmarkt, the complex is part of a large Jewish community center that includes a new synagogue with a cornerstone that was laid in 2003, 65 years after the pogrom and the destruction of Munich's synagogues. On the site of the museum are a bookstore and a cafe/bar. The permanent exhibition of artifacts is located on the lower level.

St. Jakobsplatz 16. (℗ 089/233-96096. www.juedisches-museum.muenchen.de. Admission 8€ ($13) adults, 4€ ($6.40) students and children. Tues–Sun 10am–6pm. U-Bahn/S-Bahn: Marienplatz.

Münchner Stadtmuseum (Municipal Museum) ⚘

Munich's Municipal Museum offers insight into the city's history and people's daily lives. A wooden model shows Munich in 1572. Special exhibitions about popular arts and traditions are presented frequently. The museum's most important exhibit is its *Moriskentanzer* (Moorish Dancers) on the ground floor. These 10 figures, each 60cm (2 ft.) high, carved in wood, and painted in bright colors by Erasmus Grasser in 1480, are among the best examples of secular Gothic art in Germany. The second-floor photo museum traces the early history of the camera back to 1839. Daily at 6:30 and 9pm, the film museum shows two different films from its extensive archives. The collection of historical musical instruments on the fourth floor is one of the greatest of its kind in the world.

St. Jacobs-Platz 1. (℗ 089/23322370. www.stadtmuseum-online.de. Admission 4€ ($6.40) adults, 2€ ($3.20) students and children 6–15, free for children 5 and under, 6€ ($9.60) family ticket; Sun free for everyone. Tues–Sun 10am–6pm. U-Bahn/S-Bahn: Marienplatz.

Neue Pinakothek (New Picture Gallery) ⚘

This museum offers a survey of 18th- and 19th-century art, including paintings by Gainsborough, Goya, David, Manet, van Gogh, and Monet. Among the more popular German artists represented are Wilhelm Leibl and Gustav Klimt. Note particularly the genre works by Carl Spitzweg, whose paintings poke gentle fun at everyday life in Munich.

Barerstrasse 29 (across Theresienstrasse from the Alte Pinakothek). (℗ 089/23805195. www.pinakothek.de. Admission 5.50€ ($8.80) adults, 4€ ($6.40) students and seniors, free for children 15 and under. Thurs–Mon 10am–6pm; Wed 10am–8pm. U-Bahn: Theresienstrasse. Tram: 27. Bus: 53.

Stadtische Galerie im Lenbachhaus ⚘

The State Gallery is in the ancient gold-colored villa of portrait painter Franz von Lenbach (1836–1904). It's devoted both to his work and to that of other artists. Enter through the gardens. You'll first be greeted by a large collection of early pieces by Paul Klee (1879–1940). There's also an outstanding group of works by Kandinsky, leader of the Blue Rider movement in the early 20th century, and many 19th- and 20th-century paintings throughout the villa. The enclosed patio is pleasant for a coffee break.

Luisenstrasse 33. ⓒ 089/23332000. www.lenbachhaus.de. Admission 6€ ($9.60) adults, 3.50€ ($5.60) students and children 6–12, free for children 5 and under. Tues–Sun 10am–6pm. U-Bahn: Königsplatz.

CHURCHES

Munich has many beautiful churches in addition to those listed below. Visitors should not miss the **Asamkirche,** on Sendlinger Strasse (ⓒ **089/23687989;** U-Bahn/ S-Bahn: Sendlingertor), a beautiful rococo church built between 1733 and 1746 and dedicated to St. John of Nepomuk. The **Michaelskirche,** or St. Michael's Church, Neuhauserstrasse 52 (ⓒ **089/2317060;** U-Bahn/S-Bahn: Marienplatz), is the largest Renaissance church north of the Alps. It was built by Duke William the Pious from 1583 to 1597. Lastly, the **Matthäuskirche** (ⓒ **089/593212**), or St. Matthew's Church, Nussbaumstrasse 1 (U-Bahn: Sendlinger Tor), is a modern Evangelical cathedral completed in 1955.

Frauenkirche (Cathedral of Our Lady) ✿

When the smoke cleared from the 1945 bombings, only a fragile shell remained of Munich's largest church. Workmen and architects restoring the 15th-century Gothic cathedral used whatever remains they could find in the rubble, along with modern innovations. The overall effect of the rebuilt Frauenkirche is strikingly simple, yet dignified. The twin towers with their onion domes, which remained intact, have been the city's landmark since 1525. Instead of the typical flying buttresses, huge props on the inside, which separate the side chapels, support the edifice. Twenty-two simple octagonal pillars support the Gothic vaulting over the nave and chancel.

Entering the main doors, your first impression may be the lack of windows (most of them are hidden by the enormous pillars). According to legend, the devil laughed at the notion of hidden windows and stamped in glee at the stupidity of the architect—you can see the strange footlike mark called "the devil's step" in the entrance hall. In the chapel directly behind the high altar is the cathedral's most interesting painting: Jan Polack's *The Protecting Cloak* (1510), showing the Virgin holding out her majestic robes to shelter all humankind. The collection of tiny figures beneath the cloak includes everyone from the pope to peasants.

Frauenplatz 1. ⓒ 089/2900820. Free admission. Sat–Thurs 7am–7pm; Fri 7am–6pm. U-Bahn/S-Bahn: Marienplatz.

Peterskirche (St. Peter's Church)

Munich's oldest church (1180), known locally as Old Peter, has turned over a new leaf—a gold one at that. The white-and-gray interior has been decorated with gilded baroque accents and *trompe l'oeil* medallions. It contains a series of murals by Johann Baptist Zimmermann, but nothing tops the attraction of the bizarre relic in the second chapel on the left: the gilt-covered and gem-studded skeleton of St. Mundita. From its resting place on a cushion, it stares at you with two false eyes in its skull. Jewels cover its rotten teeth, quite a contrast to the fresh roses usually kept in front of the black-and-silver coffin. The church also has a tall steeple, which you can climb, though it lacks an elevator. Colored circles on the lower platform tell you whether the climb is worthwhile: If the circle is white, you can see as far as the Alps.

Rindermarkt 1 (near the Rathaus). ⓒ 089/2604828. Church free; tower 2.50€ ($4) adults, 1.50€ ($2.40) students, .50€ (80¢) children. Mon–Sat 9am–6pm; Sun 10am–7pm. U-Bahn/S-Bahn: Marienplatz.

Theatinerkirche

Named for a small group of Roman Catholic clergy (the Theatines), this church, dedicated to Saint Kajetan, is Munich's finest example of Italian baroque. Two Italian architects, Barelli and Zucalli, began building it in 1662.

François de Cuvilliés the Elder added the facade a century later, and his son finally completed the structure in 1768. Fluted columns that line the center aisle support the arched ceiling of the nave. Above the transept, dividing the nave from the choir, the ceiling breaks into an open dome, with an ornate gallery decorated with large but graceful statues. Nothing detracts from the whiteness of the interior except the dark wooden pews and the canopied pulpit. Since 1954 the church has been under the care of the Dominican Friars.

Theatinerstrasse 22. ℂ **089/2106960.** Free admission. Mon–Fri 10am–1pm and 1:30–4:30pm; Sat 10am–3pm. U-Bahn: Odeonsplatz.

PARKS & ZOOS

Munich's city park, the 18th-century **Englischer Garten** ☞, borders Schwabing on the east and extends almost to the Isar River. This is one of the largest and most beautiful city parks in Germany. It was the brainchild of Sir Benjamin Thompson, the English scientist who spent most of his life in the service of the Bavarian government. You can wander for hours along the walks and among the trees, flowers, and sunbathers. Nude sunbathing is permitted in certain areas of the park (some claim these areas are Munich's most popular tourist attraction). For a break, stop for tea on the plaza near the Chinese pagoda or have a beer at the nearby beer garden. You might also take along a picnic put together at the elegant shop of **Alois Dallmayr,** or less expensive fare from **Hertie,** across from the Hauptbahnhof, from **Kaufhof** at Marienplatz, or from Munich's famous open-air market, the **Viktualienmarkt.**

Hellabrunn Zoo stands in Tierpark Hellabrunn, about 6km (4 miles) south of the city center, at Tierparkstrasse 30 (ℂ **089/625080;** www.zoo-munich.de; U-Bahn: Thalkirchen; bus: 52). It's one of the largest zoos in the world, with hundreds of animals roaming in a natural habitat. A walk through the attractive park is recommended even if you're not a zoo buff. There's a big children's zoo, as well as a large aviary. You can visit the zoo daily 8am to 6pm (in winter, 9am–5pm); admission is 9€ ($14) for adults, 6€ ($9.60) for students and seniors, 4.50€ ($7.20) for children ages 4 to 14, and free for children 3 and under.

THE OLYMPIC GROUNDS

Olympiapark (ℂ **089/30670;** www.olympiapark-muenchen.de; U-Bahn: Olympiazentrum), site of the 1972 Olympic Games, occupies 300 hectares (741 acres) at the city's northern edge. More than 15,000 workers from 18 countries transformed the site into a park of nearly 5,000 trees, 43km (27 miles) of roads, 32 bridges, and a lake. Olympiapark has its own railway station, U-Bahn line, mayor, post office, churches, and elementary school. The planners even broke the city skyline by adding a 293m (961-ft.) television tower in the center of the park.

The area's showpiece is a huge stadium, capable of seating 69,300 spectators and topped by the largest roof in the world—nearly 67,000 sq. m (721,118 sq. ft.) of tinted acrylic glass. The supports for the stadium are anchored by two huge blocks, each capable of resisting about 3.6 million kilograms (4,000 tons) under stress. The roof serves the additional purpose of collecting rainwater and draining it into the nearby Olympic lake.

Olympia Tower, Olympiapark (ℂ **089/30672750**), is open daily 9am to midnight. A ticket for a ride up the tower (on the speediest elevator on the Continent, no less) costs 4.50€ ($7.20) for adults and 2.80€ ($4.50) for children 14 and under. An exclusive dining spot in the tower is the **Tower Restaurant** (ℂ **089/30668585**),

Black September for the Olympics

The 1972 Munich Olympics was meant to celebrate peace among nations; for the first 10 days, these games did. However, in the early morning hours of September 5, eight Palestinian terrorists, later claiming to be part of the "Black September" group, snuck into the Olympic Village. Within a few minutes of entering the quarters of the sleeping Israeli athletes, they had killed two Israelis and taken nine others hostage.

As the ensuing siege played out on TV sets around the world, the terrorists demanded the release of over 200 Arab guerrillas jailed in Israel, as well as safe passage for themselves and their hostages. Few novelists could have conceived the plot (and mistakes by German law enforcement) that ensued, as negotiations helplessly and hopelessly dragged on between the terrorists and West German security officials. In Israel, Golda Meir firmly stood by her government's policy of "not dealing with terrorists." The job of dealing with the terrorists fell upon the shoulders of the West Germans.

By 8:30pm on the day of the attack, the first of three helicopters landed at Olympic Village to fly the terrorists and their hostages out of West Germany via a Lufthansa 737 that was waiting at the military air base at Fürstenfeldbruck, 24km (15 miles) away. Blinded and tied close together, the Israeli athletes, along with their heavily armed captors, were placed into the helicopters and flown away, landing at Fürstenfeldbruck at 10:30pm.

The negotiations between the terrorists and West German security officials suddenly collapsed when a West German sharpshooter hidden in the darkness fired unexpectedly at the terrorists. The Palestinians quickly responded by unleashing automatic fire at the tied and bound Israelis; one tossed a hand grenade into a helicopter, killing all of the remaining hostages. In response, the West Germans unleashed their firepower, killing five of the terrorists and eventually capturing the others.

Mark Spitz, an American Jew and winner of seven gold medals, was flown out of Germany for his own safety as the Olympic Games were suspended for the first time in their history. The world mourned, and in a controversial decision, the Germans continued the games 34 hours later, with mixed reactions from both the world at large and the participating athletes. The presiding officer of the Games, Avery Brundage, issued a famous pronouncement, "The Games must go on!", and so they did.

For more on this tragic event, read or watch the book/documentary movie titled *One Day in September*.

which features a selection of international and German dishes. Food is served daily 11am to 5pm and 6:30 to 10:30pm. A complete dinner costs 30€ to 60€ ($48–$96). The food is decent and fresh, but of secondary consideration—most come here for the extraordinary view, which reaches to the Alps. Four observation platforms look out over Olympiapark. The Tower Restaurant revolves around its axis in 60 minutes, giving guests who linger a changing vista of Munich. Diners Club, MasterCard, and Visa are accepted.

Restaurant Olympiasee is at the base of the tower, Spiridon-Louis-Ring 7 (© 089/ 30672822), serving genuine Bavarian specialties, with meals costing 10€ ($16) and up. The restaurant is open daily 10am to 7pm (until 8:30pm in summer, when it's popular because of its terrace). No credit cards are accepted.

ESPECIALLY FOR KIDS

Of all the museums in Munich, kids will most enjoy the **Deutsches Museum,** Museumsinsel 1 (© 089/21791; S-Bahn: Isartor; tram: 18), which has many hands-on exhibits (p. 326).

On the third floor of the **Münchner Stadtmuseum,** St. Jakobsplatz 1 (© 089/ 23322370; U-Bahn/S-Bahn: Marienplatz), is an array of marionettes and hand puppets from around the world. Another section is devoted to fairground art, including carousel animals, shooting galleries, roller-coaster models, and wax and museum figures. The main exhibit has the oldest-known carousel horses, dating from 1820. For hours and admission fees, see p. 331.

Spielzeugmuseum, in the Altes Rathaus, Marienplatz 15 (© 089/294001; U-Bahn/ S-Bahn: Marienplatz), is a historical toy collection. It's open daily 10am to 5:30pm. Admission is 3.50€ ($5.60) for adults, 1.50€ ($2.40) for children, and 6€ ($9.60) for a family ticket.

For a truly charming experience, go to the **Münchner Marionettentheater,** Blumenstrasse 32 (© 089/265712; U-Bahn/S-Bahn: Marienplatz), which was established in 1858. It stages marionette productions of operas by Mozart and other composers every Wednesday, Thursday, Saturday, and Sunday at 3pm, and every Saturday at 8pm. At matinees, adults pay 8€ ($13) entrance, children cost 6.50€ ($10). At evening shows tickets for adults cost 15€ ($24) and children's tickets go for 10€ ($16). Matinees tend to be more animated and crowded than evening shows and are particularly well suited for younger children ages 4 and up.

Bavaria Film Studio, Bavariafilmplatz 7, Geiselgasteig (© 089/64990; tram: 25 to Bavariafilmplatz), is Europe's largest filmmaking center—Munich's version of Hollywood. Visitors can watch such spine-tingling thrillers as *Adventure in the Devil's Mine* and *Cosmic Pinball.* The 30-minute Bavaria Action Show features a stunt team demonstrating fistfights and fire stunts, tumbling down staircases, and even taking a 30m-high (100-ft.) plunge. Guided 1½-hour tours (book 4 weeks in advance for a tour in English) are given March to October daily 9am to 4pm, November to February daily 10am to 3pm. Admission is 10€ ($16) for adults, 9€ ($14) for students and seniors, 7€ ($11) for children ages 4 to 14, and free for children 3 and under.

Hellabrunn Zoo has a large children's zoo, where kids can pet the animals. For details, see p. 333.

6 Organized Tours

BY BUS

City tours encompass aspects of both modern and medieval Munich, and depart from the main railway station aboard blue-sided buses. Departures, depending on the season and the tour, occur between two and eight times a day, and tours are conducted in both German and English. Most tours don't last more than 2½ hours, with the exception of a scientific odyssey that focuses on the technological triumphs of Munich as witnessed by various museums that include the Deutsches Museum. That experience usually lasts for a minimum of 4 hours, plus the time you spend wandering through museums at the end of your tour. Depending on the tour, adults pay 11€ to 60€ ($18–$96); children 13 and under are charged 6€ to 14€ ($9.60–$22). Advance reservations for most city tours aren't required, and you can buy your ticket from the bus driver at the time you board. Tours leave from the square in front of the Hauptbahnhof, at Hertie's.

To go farther afield and visit major attractions in the environs (such as Berchtesgaden or Ludwig II's castles), contact **Sightseeing Gray Line,** Schützenstrasse 9 (© **089/549-075-60;** U-Bahn/S-Bahn: Hauptbahnhof), open year-round Monday to Friday 9am to 6pm and Saturday 9am to 1pm. (Travel agents in Munich, as well as the concierge or reception staff at your hotel, can also book these tours.) At least a half-dozen touring options are available, ranging from a quickie 1-hour overview of the city to full-day excursions to such outlying sites as Berchtesgaden, Oberammergau, and Hohenschwangau, site of three of Bavaria's most stunning palaces. To participate in tours that cover attractions outside the city limits, advance reservations are required, especially if you want the bus to pick you up at any of Munich's hotels.

BY BIKE

Pedal pushers will want to try Mike Lasher's popular **Mike's Bike Tour,** Hochbrückenstrasse (© **089/255-43-988;** www.mikesbiketours.com). His bike-rental services include maps, locks, child and infant seats, and helmets at no extra charge. English and bilingual tours of central Munich run only March 16 to April 15 and September 1 to November 10 daily at 12:30pm and from April 16 to August 31 daily at 4pm. Customers love Mike's charm. Participants meet under the tower of the old town hall, a gray building on the east end of Marienplatz. Mike, the consummate guide, will be here—whistle in mouth—letting everyone know who he is. The tour veers from the bike paths only long enough for a lunch stop at a beer garden. Fear not, fainthearted: The bikes are new, and the rides are easy, with plenty of time for historical explanations, photo opportunities, and question-and-answer sessions. The cost for a tour, including the bike, is 24€ ($38). It is also possible to rent a bike for 12€ ($19) for same-day return or 21€ ($34) overnight.

ON FOOT

Munich Walk Tours, in English (© **0171/2740204;** www.munichwalktours.de), is a fun way to get to know the city. Munich is shared from various expert points of view; these range from a straight "City Walk," taking in the highlights, to a "Beer and Brewery Tour." The "City Walk" is offered only from January 2 to April 30 and October 17 to November 30 daily 10:45am, lasting 2¼ hours and costing 10€ ($16). The "Beer and Brewery Tour" departs January 2 to April 30 and October 2 to December 31 Monday, Wednesday, and Saturday at 5:30pm; May 1 to September 15 daily 6:15pm; and September 16 to October 1 daily 2:30pm. It lasts 3 hours and costs 18€ ($29). "Hitler's Munich—Third Reich Tour," an intriguing sojourn, is conducted only January 2 to March 31 and November 1 to December 31 Monday and Wednesday to Sunday at 10:30am, and April 1 to June 30 daily 10am. It lasts 2½ hours and costs 12€ ($19). Children 13 and under with an adult go free on these tours. The meeting point for all tours is at the main entrance of the New Gothic Rathaus on Marienplatz. Call to confirm starting times and places to meet or to ask about other tours.

7 Sports & Outdoor Pursuits

BEACHES, POOLS & WATERSPORTS

On hot weekends, much of Munich heads for nearby lakes, the **Ammersee** and the **Starnbergersee,** where bathing facilities are clearly marked. You can also swim at **Maria-Einsiedel,** in the frigid, snow-fed waters of the Isar River. The city has several public swimming pools as well. The largest of these includes the giant competition-size pool in the Olympiapark, the **Olympia-Schwimmhalle** (*©* **089/30672290;** U-Bahn: Olympiazentrum). Admission is 5€ ($8). Information on both sailing and windsurfing is available from the **Bayerischer Seglerverband,** Georg-Brauchle-Ring 93 (*©* **089/15702366**).

JOGGING

Regardless of the season, the most lushly landscaped place in Munich is the **Englischer Garten** (U-Bahn: Münchner Freiheit), which has an 11km (7-mile) circumference and an array of dirt and asphalt tracks. Also appropriate are the grounds of the **Olympiapark** (U-Bahn: Olympiazentrum) or the park surrounding **Schloss Nymphenburg** (U-Bahn: Rotkreuzplatz, then tram no. 17 toward Amalienburgstrasse; bus: 41). More convenient to the center of the city's commercial district is a jog along the embankments of the Isar River.

ROWING

Rowboats add to the charm of the lakes in the **Englischer Garten.** You can rent them at a kiosk at the edge of the Kleinhesseloher See. Rowboat rentals are also on the southern bank of the **Olympiasee,** in the Olympiapark.

SKIING

Because of the proximity of the Bavarian and Austrian Alps, many Munich residents are avid skiers. For information on resorts and getaway snow-related activities, contact the **Bayerischer Seglerverband,** Georg-Brauchle-Ring 93, 80992 München (*©* **089/15702366**).

SPECTATOR SPORTS

Munich loves soccer and has one of Europe's outstanding teams, **Bayern München,** which plays at the Olympic Stadium in Olympiapark. If you want to attend a match, call *©* **089/54818181.**

TENNIS

At least 200 indoor and outdoor tennis courts are scattered around greater Munich. Many can be booked in advance by calling *©* **089/54818181.** For information on Munich's many tennis tournaments and competitions, contact the **Bayerischer Seglerverband,** Georg-Brauchle-Ring 93, 80992 München (*©* **089/15702366**).

8 Shopping

The most interesting shops are concentrated on Munich's pedestrians-only streets, between Karlsplatz and Marienplatz.

ART

Bayerischer Kunstgewerbe-Verein *☆☆*   This is one of Germany's largest, most visible, and most historic art galleries, established in the 1840s as a showcase for local artists. The complex contains an upscale art gallery and a sales outlet, the Ladengeschäft, where attractive crafts are sold at prices that begin at 25€ ($40). Works by more than 400 artists are displayed and sold here. Examples include sculpture in all kinds of media, crafts, textiles, and woven objects. Pacellistrasse 6–8. ℂ 089/2901470. U-Bahn: Karlsplatz.

BOOKS

Hugendubel   Not only is this Munich's biggest bookstore, but it enjoys the most central location. It sells a number of English-language titles, both fiction and nonfiction, and also offers travel books and helpful maps. Marienplatz 22. ℂ 0180/1484484. www.hugendubel.de. U-Bahn/S-Bahn: Marienplatz.

CHINA, SILVER & GLASS

Kunstring Meissen ℱ   During the coldest days of the Cold War, this was Munich's exclusive distributor of Meissen and Dresden china, manufactured behind the Iron Curtain in East Germany. With reunification, Kunstring's exclusive access became a thing of the past. Despite that, the shop still contains one of Munich's largest inventories of the elegant porcelain. Briennerstrasse 4. ℂ 089/281532. U-Bahn: Odeonsplatz.

Rosenthal Studio-Haus ℱℱℱ   Rosenthal, established in 1879 in the Bavarian town of Selb near the Czech border, is one of the three or four most prestigious names in German porcelain. Much (though not all) of the line today focuses on contemporary design, an approach that separates it from the more traditional Nymphenburg, Sevrès, and Limoges. The manufacturer preestablishes prices for Rosenthal patterns and maintains them rigidly, so there are no price breaks at this factory outlet. You will find, however, the widest array of Rosenthal patterns available in Germany. In addition to porcelain, the line includes furniture, glass, and cutlery. Dienerstrasse 17. ℂ 089/222617. U-Bahn/S-Bahn: Marienplatz.

CRAFTS

Bayerischer Kunstgewerbeverein (Bavarian Association of Arts & Crafts) This showcase for Bavarian artisans has excellent handicrafts: ceramics, glasses, jewelry, woodcarvings, pewter, and seasonal Christmas decorations. Pacellistrasse 6–8. ℂ 089/2901470. U-Bahn: Karlsplatz.

Prinoth ⟨Finds⟩   Most of the woodcarvings sold here are produced in small workshops in the folklore-rich Italian South Tyrol. The selection is wide-ranging, and because the shop is 6km (3½ miles) west of Munich's tourist zones, prices are reasonable compared to those of shops closer to the Marienplatz. Guido Schneblestrasse 9A. ℂ 089/560378. U-Bahn: Laimerplatz.

DEPARTMENT STORES

Kaufhof   At one of the largest department stores in town, wander freely among displays that are art forms in their own right. The inventory includes virtually everything, from men's, women's, and children's clothing to housewares, and much more. Marienplatz. ℂ 089/231851. U-Bahn/S-Bahn: Marienplatz.

Ludwig Beck am Rathauseck   Most merchandise here is intended for local residents; however, visitors will also be interested in this four-floor shopping bazaar, which sells handmade crafts from all over Germany, old and new. Items include decorative pottery and dishes, etched-glass beer steins and vases, painted wall plaques, decorative flower arrangements, unusual kitchenware, fashions, textiles, and much more. Am Marienplatz 11. ℂ **089/236910.** U-Bahn/S-Bahn: Marienplatz.

ENGRAVINGS & POSTCARDS

Philatelie und Ansichtskarten *(Finds* This collection looks more like a dusty museum storeroom than a shop. Academics and collectors from throughout Germany phone in special requests for antique engravings and postcards that depict specific settings, personalities, and places. Merchandise, each piece carefully inventoried and stored in cardboard boxes arranged by subject, ranges from sober to schmaltzy. Bahnhofplatz 2. ℂ **089/596757.** U-Bahn: Bahnhofplatz.

EYEGLASSES

Pupille Shelf after shelf of eyeglasses in all styles and sizes reveal why Germans are known for their optical products, which are sold around the world. The country, in effect, is the market leader in eyewear. Some of the most fashionable glasses in Germany are sold here, including selections from name designers such as Chanel. Theatiner Strasse 8. ℂ **089/24243838.** Tram: 19.

FASHION

Bogner Haus Before you head for the slopes, shop here for the latest in ski clothing and styles. Willy Bogner, the filmmaker and Olympic downhill racer, sells this flamboyant attire. The store also sells more formal clothing for men and women. Residenzstrasse 14–15. ℂ **089/2907040.** U-Bahn/S-Bahn: Marienplatz or Odeonplatz.

Frankonia This store, established in 1907, has Munich's most prestigious collection of *Tracht* (traditional Bavarian dress). If you see yourself dressed hunter style, or in traditional Alpine garb, this place can outfit you well. There's a fine collection of wool cardigan jackets with silvery buttons. They carry inventory for both men and women. Maximiliansplatz 10. ℂ **089/2900020.** U-Bahn: Odeonplatz.

Hirmer In the pedestrian zone, this shop has the best collection of German-made and international men's clothing in town. The staff here is especially skilled at helping people select something that looks good on them. The selection comes from such brand names as Boss, Barbour, Rene Lezard, and van Laak. Both business and leisure suits are sold at middle- to upper-bracket prices. They even cater to "big beer bellies." Kaufinger Strasse 22. ℂ **089/236830.** U-Bahn: Marienplatz.

Loden-Frey You can see the twin domes of the Frauenkirche above the soaring glass-enclosed atrium of this shop's showroom. Go here for the world's largest selection of loden clothing and traditional costumes, as well as for international fashions from top European designers such as Armani, Valentino, and Ungaro. Maffeistrasse 7. ℂ **089/210390.** U-Bahn/S-Bahn: Marienplatz.

Maendler This store is divided into a series of boutiques well known to virtually every well-dressed woman in Bavaria. You'll find the creative vision of Joop, New York New York, and Jil Sander here. Looking for that special something for your dinner with the mayor or the president of Germany? Ask to see formal eveningwear by Jean-Paul Gaultier. For something more experimental and daring, head for the branch called **Rosy Maendler,** Maximiliansplatz 12 (same phone; U-Bahn: Odeonplatz; tram: 19), where you'll find a more youthful version of the same store. Theatinerstrasse 7. ℂ **089/24228850.** U-Bahn: Marienplatz.

Wies'n Tracht & Mehr ✦ *Finds*   The milkmaid-style dress, the dirndl, has been making a comeback. In spite of its low-cut bodice, it is considered wholesome. The best selection of dirndls in Munich is offered at this outlet, but prices are not cheap, starting at 400€ ($640). Both new and vintage dirndls are sold here. They are worn with the traditional off-the-shoulder white blouse and often an apron. Tal 19. No phone. www.wiesn-tracht-mehr.de. U-Bahn or S-Bahn: Marienplatz.

FOOD

Dallmayr ✦   What Fortnum & Mason is to London, the venerable Dallmayr is to Munich. Gastronomes as far away as Hamburg and Berlin telephone orders for exotica not readily available anywhere else. Dallmayr's list of prestigious clients reads like a who's who of German industry and letters. Wander freely among racks of foodstuffs: Some are too delicate to survive shipment abroad; others can be shipped anywhere. Dienerstrasse 14–15. ✆ 089/21350. Tram: 19.

JEWELRY & WATCHES

CADA-Schmuck ✦   Herbert Kopp, a jewelry designer, is attracting lots of media attention for his stunning handmade jewelry sold here. His chic wares come in 18-carat gold or sterling silver. There is a large collection of earrings (both small and large) along with necklace and pendants. Maffeistrasse 8. ✆ 089/255427-0. Tram: 19.

Hemmerle ✦✦✦   This is *the* place for jewelry. The original founders of this conservative shop made their fortune designing bejeweled fantasies for the Royal Bavarian Court of Ludwig II. All pieces are limited editions, designed and made in-house by Bavarian craftspeople. The company also designs its own wristwatch, the Hemmerle. Maximilianstrasse 14. ✆ 089/2422600. U-Bahn/S-Bahn: Marienplatz.

PORCELAIN

Porzellan-Manufaktur-Nymphenburg ✦✦✦   At Nymphenburg, about 8km (5 miles) northwest of the heart of Munich, is one of Germany's most famous porcelain factories, on the grounds of Schloss Nymphenburg. You can visit its exhibition and sales rooms, Monday to Friday 10am to 5pm. Shipments can be arranged if you make purchases. A more central branch is in Munich's center at Odeonsplatz 1 (✆ 089/282428; U-Bahn: Odeonsplatz). Nördliches Schlossrondell 8. ✆ 089/1791970. Bus: 41.

TOYS

Münchner Puppenstuben und Zinnfiguren Kabinette *Kids*   This is Germany's oldest miniature pewter foundry, dating from 1796. Many Germans visit Munich every December to purchase traditional Christmas decorations of a type once sold to Maximilian I, king of Bavaria. Managed by matriarchs of the same family, this store is one of the best sources in Germany for miniature houses, furniture, birdcages, and people, all cunningly crafted from pewter or carved wood. Some figures are made from 150-year-old molds that are collector's items in their own right. Anything here makes a great gift not only for a child but also for an adult with a nostalgic bent. Maxburgstrasse 4. ✆ 089/293797. U-Bahn: Karlsplatz.

Obletter's *Kids*   Established in the 1880s, this is one of the largest emporiums of children's toys in Munich. The two floors of inventory contain everything from folkloric dolls to computer games. Karlsplatz 11. ✆ 089/55089510. U-Bahn: Karlsplatz.

9 Munich After Dark

To find out what's happening in Munich, go to the tourist office just outside the Hauptbahnhof (© **089/23396500**) and ask for *Monatsprogramm* (a monthly program guide), costing 1.65€ ($2.70). It contains a complete cultural guide, telling you not only what's being presented—including concerts, opera, special exhibits, and museum hours—but also how to purchase tickets.

THE PERFORMING ARTS

Nowhere else in Europe, other than London and Paris, will you find so many musical and theatrical events. The good news is that seats don't cost a fortune—so count on indulging yourself and going to several performances. You can get good tickets for anything from 10€ to 45€ ($16–$72).

If you speak German, you'll find at least 20 theaters offering plays of every description: classic, comic, experimental, contemporary—take your pick. The best way to find out what current productions might interest you is to go to a theater-ticket agency. Head for **München Tickets** (© **0180/54818181**), where you can purchase tickets to cultural, entertainment, and sporting events within Bavaria, with access to the same computer database. For some sporting events (such as soccer) and musical events (including most of the operas subsidized by the city of Munich), where season tickets and long-term subscriptions reduce availability, you'll have to go to the venue's box office, as organizers tend not to cooperate with outside ticket agencies.

Cuvilliés Theater (Altes Residenztheater) An attraction in itself (see "Residenz," p. 328), this is the most beautiful theater in Germany, and it was completely restored in 2008. The **Bavarian State Opera** and the **Bayerisches Staatsschauspiel** perform smaller works here, in keeping with the tiny theater's more intimate character. Box-office hours are Monday to Friday 10am to 6pm and Saturday 10am to 1pm. Residenzstrasse 1. © **089/2185-19-40** for ticket information. Building tours 5€ ($8).

Bayerischen Staatsoper The **Bavarian State Opera** is one of the world's great companies. The Bavarians give their hearts and souls to opera. Productions here are beautifully mounted and presented, and the company's roster includes some of the world's greatest singers. Hard-to-get tickets may be purchased at the box office Monday to Friday 10am to 6pm and Saturday 10am to 1pm, plus 1 hour before each performance. The Nationaltheater is also the home of the **Bavarian State Ballet.** Nationaltheater, Max-Joseph-Platz 2. © **089/21851920.** www.bayerische.staatsoper.de. Tickets 15€–243€ ($24–$389), including standing room. U-Bahn/S-Bahn: Marienplatz.

Bayerisches Staatsschauspiel (State Theater) This repertory company is known for its performances of the classics: Goethe and Schiller, Shakespeare, and others. The box office, around the corner on Maximilianstrasse, is open Monday to Friday 10am to 6pm, Saturday 10am to 1pm, and 1 hour before performances. Max-Joseph-Platz. © **089/21851920.** www.bayerischesstaatsschauspiel.de. Tickets 15€–60€ ($24–$96). U-Bahn/S-Bahn: Marienplatz.

Deutsches Theater Musicals are popular here, but operettas, ballets, and international shows are performed as well. During Carnival in January and February, the theater becomes a ballroom—the costume balls and official black-tie festivities here are famous throughout Europe. Schwanthalerstrasse 13. © **089/55234444.** www.deutsches-theater.de. Tickets 24€–64€ ($38–$102); higher for special events. U-Bahn/S-Bahn: Karlsplatz/Stachus.

Münchner Kammerspiele (Munich Studio Theater)   Contemporary and classic plays are performed here. The season runs early October to July. You can reserve tickets by phone Monday to Friday 10am to 6pm, but you must pick them up at least 2 days before a performance. The box office is open Monday to Friday 10am to 6pm and on Saturday 10am to 1pm, plus 1 hour before performances. There's also a second, smaller theater called **Werkraum,** Hildegardstrasse 1 (same phone as below), where new works are presented. Maximilianstrasse 28. ⒸⒻ **089/233-966-01.** www.muenchner-kammerspiele.de. Tickets 6€–39€ ($9.60–$62). U-Bahn: Marienplatz. S-Bahn: Isartor. Tram: 19.

Münchner Philharmoniker (Munich Philharmonic Orchestra)   This famous orchestra was founded in 1893. Its music director is Christian Thielemann, and its home is the Gasteig Cultural Center, where it performs in Philharmonic Hall. The center also shelters the Richard Strauss Conservatory and the Munich Municipal Library, and has five performance halls. You can purchase tickets at the ground-level Glashalle, Monday to Friday 9am to 6pm and Saturday 9am to 2pm. The Philharmonic season runs mid-September to July. Gasteig Kulturzentrum in the Haidhausen district, Rosenheimerstrasse 5. ⒸⒻ **089/480-98-55-00.** www.muenchnerphilharmoniker.de. Tickets 10€–51€ ($16–$82). S-Bahn: Rosenheimerplatz. Tram: 18 to Gasteig. Bus: 51.

BEER HALLS

The *Bierhalle* is a traditional Munich institution, offering food, entertainment, and, of course, beer. It is said that Müncheners consume more beer than anyone else in Germany. Bernd Boehle once wrote: "If a man really belongs to Munich, he drinks beer at all times of the day, at breakfast, at midday, at teatime; and in the evening, of course, he just never stops." A half-liter of beer will set you back about 3.50€ ($5.60). For information on outdoor beer gardens, see the "Beer Gardens" box, earlier in this chapter.

Augustinerbräu   This hall's dark-wood panels and carved-plaster ceilings make the place look older than it is. It's been around for less than a century, but beer was first brewed on this spot in 1328 (or so they claim). The long menu changes daily, and the cuisine is not for dieters: It's hearty, heavy, and starchy, but that's what customers want. It's open daily 11am to 11pm. Neuhäuserstrasse 27. ⒸⒻ **089/23183257.** U-Bahn/S-Bahn: Karlsplatz/Stachus. Tram: 19.

Hofbräuhaus am Platzl 👉   The state-owned Hofbräuhaus is the world's most famous beer hall. Visitors with only 1 night in Munich usually come here. The present Hofbräuhaus was built in 1897, but the tradition of a beer house on this spot dates from 1589. This one was the setting for the notorious meeting in which Hitler took control of the tiny German Workers' Party in 1920. Fistfights erupted as the Nazis attacked their Bavarian enemies here in the beer palace.

Today, 4,500 beer drinkers can crowd in here. Several rooms, including a top-floor room for dancing, are spread over three floors. With its brass band (which starts playing at 11am), the ground-floor Schwemme is what you always expected of a beer hall—eternal Oktoberfest. In the second-floor restaurant, strolling musicians entertain, and dirndl-clad servers offer mugs of beer between singalongs. Every night the Hofbräuhaus presents a typical Bavarian show in its Fest-Hall from 7:45pm to midnight. The hall is open daily 9am to midnight. Am Platzl 9. ⒸⒻ **089/221676.** U-Bahn/S-Bahn: Marienplatz.

Max Emanuel Brauerei   Löwenbräu turned this brewery into a beer hall in the 1920s. It still serves steins of beer and platters of filling German grub. On Wednesday and Friday, the second floor plays host to a popular salsa dance club. In the summer they feature a beer garden. The hall is open in the winter daily 5pm to 1am and during the summer daily 11am to 1am. Adalbertstrasse 33. © 089/2715158. www.max-emanuel-brauerei.de. Cover Wed 8€ ($13), Fri–Sat 10€ ($16). U-Bahn: Universität.

Türkenhof This beer hall is not the stereotypical schmaltzy old-Bavaria tourist trap. You'll find cosmopolitan cuisine made by a Greek co-owner and lively, intelligent conversation flowing among the student patrons. It's a big, fun bar created out of a 150-year-old butcher shop, with five varieties of Augustiner beer on tap. It's open Sunday to Thursday 11am to 1am, Friday and Saturday 11am to 3am. Türkenstrasse 78. © 089/2800235. U-Bahn: Universität.

Waldwirtschaft Grosshesselöhe This popular summertime rendezvous, located above the Isar River near the zoo, has seats for some 2,000 drinkers. Music ranging from Dixieland to English jazz to Polish polka is played throughout the week. Entrance is free, and you bring your own food. It's open daily 11am to 11pm (they have to close early because neighborhood residents complain), with live music on Friday to Sunday nights. George-Kalb-Strasse 3. © 089/74994030. S-Bahn: Isartal Bahnhof. Tram: 7.

NIGHTCLUBS & DANCE HALLS

Bayerischer Hof Night Club Here in the extensive cellars of the Bayerischer Hof hotel (p. 301), you'll find some of Munich's most sophisticated entertainment. Within one very large room is a piano bar, where a musician plays Friday and Saturday nights 7 to 10pm. Behind a partition that disappears after 10pm is a bandstand for live orchestras, which play to a crowd of dancing patrons every night from 10pm to 3 or 4am, depending on business. Entrance to the piano bar is free, but there's a cover charge to the nightclub Friday and Saturday nights. Drinks begin at 8€ ($13). The club and bar are open daily 10pm to 3am. Daily happy hour is 7 to 8:30pm, with drinks starting at 5€ ($8). In the Hotel Bayerischer Hof, Promenadeplatz 2–6. © 089/21200. Cover to nightclub Fri–Sat 5€–50€ ($8–$80). Tram: 19.

Café am Hochhaus On any given night the scene shifts here. One night might be boogie and soulful reggae, another night retro and disco. On Sunday there is a gay T-dance, and on Monday night management promises "anything can happen." It's open Monday to Saturday 8pm to 3am. Blumenstrasse 29. © 089/89058152. U-Bahn: Sendlinger Tor.

Nachtgalerie This night gallery contains two dance halls rocking to party music and hip-hop along with house, electro, or even rhythm and blues. The club attracts largely intoxicated crowds in their 20s and 30s. International student parties are often staged here. Expect various theme nights, perhaps one devoted to the sounds of a Caribbean summer. Girls dance with girls, boys with boys, and sometimes boys with girls. The cover is 10€ ($16), but once inside, drinks are cheap—beginning at 2€ ($3.20). Nachtgalerie is open Friday and Saturday 10pm to 5am. Amulfstrasse 17. © 089/32455595. S-Bahn: Hackerbrücke. (At the end of the bridge, veer right and descend the steps.)

Night Flight *Finds* Located amid enormous airfield hangars, this nightclub is designed to highlight the visual effect of airplane departures and arrivals. To get here, you'll have to drive 40km (25 miles) north of the city or take a 30-minute ride on the S-Bahn. There are five bars, a dance floor, and a restaurant. Frenetic dancing to techno music is the main attraction. In summer, dancers cool off and catch their breath on an outdoor terrace, where the main sport is watching the airport. It's open Tuesday to Saturday 10pm to 6am. Franz Josef Strauss Airport, Wartungsallee 9. © 089/97597999. Cover 10€ ($16) S-Bahn: Flughafen.

Oklahoma   File under surreal. German and European bands decked out in cowboy hats and boots struggle with the nuances of an extremely foreign musical form. Even when the results are dead-on mimicry, there's something strange about watching German "cowboys" line dance or lean on the bar while guzzling Spaten. Cover is at the low end of the scale, rising when English and American acts hit the stage. Depending on your mood, this place can be a lot of fun. Pull on your jeans and come on in Tuesday to Saturday 8pm to 1am. Schäftlarnstrasse 156. © **089/7234327.** Cover 10€–12€ ($16–$19). U-Bahn: Thalkirchen.

Rattlesnake Saloon   This is the largest and most popular country-and-western bar in Munich, a sort of C&W honky-tonk with a Bavarian accent. Same owner, same concept as Oklahoma (see above)—the difference is the rib-eye steaks, barbecued pork, chili, and other southern U.S. dishes available to hungry country-music fans. On Wednesday, if you never learned line dancing at home, you can give it a shot here under the watchful eye of a Teutonic instructor. From May to September, there's a biergarten open daily from 10am to 7pm. During irregularly scheduled rockabilly parties, everything is cleared away to create a dance floor. Dress as countrified as you want. Rattlesnake is open Tuesday to Sunday 7pm to 3am. The location is 5km (3 miles) north of the Marienplatz. Schneeglöckchenstrasse 91. © **089/1504035.** Cover 7€–12€ ($11–$19). S-Bahn: Fasanerie.

JAZZ

Jazzclub Unterfahrt   This is Munich's leading jazz club, attracting artists from throughout Europe and North America. Reaching it requires wandering down a labyrinth of underground cement-sided corridors that might remind you of a bomb shelter during the Cold War. Once inside, the space opens to reveal flickering candles, a convivial bar, high ceilings, and clusters of smallish tables facing a stage and whatever singers and musicians happen to be emoting at the time. Off to one corner is an art gallery. The bar here opens daily at 8pm; live music is Tuesday to Sunday 8:30pm to 1am, Friday and Saturday 7:30pm to 3am. Einsteinstrasse 42. © **089/4482794.** Cover 10€–14€ ($16–$22). U-Bahn: Max-Weber-Platz.

Mister B's   This small, dark club hosts a slightly older, mellower crowd than the rock and dance clubs. Blues, jazz, and rhythm-and-blues combos take the stage Thursday to Saturday. It's open Tuesday to Sunday 8pm to 3am. Herzog-Heinrichstrasse 38. © **089/534901.** Cover 5€–9€ ($8–$14). U-Bahn: Goetheplatz.

Schwabinger Podium   This club offers varying nightly entertainment. Oldies and rock 'n' roll dominate some evenings. It's open Sunday to Thursday 8pm to 1am and Friday and Saturday 8pm to 3am. Wagnerstrasse 1. © **089/399482.** Cover 5€ ($8). U-Bahn: Münchner Freiheit.

THE BAR & CAFE SCENE

In addition to the venues listed below, see the review for Café Dukatz in the Literaturhaus on p. 313.

Alter Simpl   Once a literary cafe, Alter Simpl takes its name from a satirical revue of 1903. Today it attracts a wide segment of locals. The real fun happens after 11pm, when the iconoclastic artistic ferment resembles Berlin more than Bavaria. It's open Sunday to Thursday 11am to 3am, Friday and Saturday 11am to 4am. Türkenstrasse 57. © **089/2723083.** U-Bahn: Universität.

Café Puck   A dark-paneled retreat for students, artists, and workers, this cafe plays a variety of roles for its diverse crowd. It's a bar to students; a restaurant to the locals, who like the daily menu of German, American, and Asian dishes; and a hangover cure for artists and young people who creep in after midday for a big American breakfast. There's usually plenty of conversation and someone who wants to practice English, and there are always German- and English-language newspapers. Also, most of their staff speaks fluent English. Café Puck is open daily 9am to 1am. Türkenstrasse 33. ℂ 089/ 2802280. U-Bahn: Universität.

Havana Club   This is not the spicy Cuban club you might expect. Employees may tell you about the bar's brush with fame, when Gloria Estefan made an appearance, but its day-to-day function is as a lively singles bar fueled by rum-based cocktails. It's open Monday to Thursday 6pm to 1am, Friday and Saturday 6pm to 3am, Sunday 7pm to 1am. Herrnstrasse 30. ℂ 089/291884. S-Bahn: Isartor.

Holy Home   Close to Gärtnerplatz, this little hideaway bar is home to Munich's coterie of artists and designers. It's a cozy, welcoming place where patrons in their 20s and 30s often spend hours listening to the home-grown DJs spin their magic. Fresh Augustiner beer is on tap, beginning at 3.20€ ($5.10); mixed drinks cost around 8€ ($13). Hours are Sunday to Wednesday 7pm to 1am, Thursday to Saturday 7pm to 3am. Reichenbachstrasse 21. ℂ 089/2014546. U-Bahn: Sendinger Tor.

Killians Irish Pub/Ned Kelly's Australian Bar   This is a two-in-one venue. If you grow tired of Irish music, you can take a trip "down under" in the adjoining bar. Behind the Frauenkirche, these bars are among the liveliest in Munich, with Irish and Australian beer and food, live music, and broadcasts of major sports events. In one bar, Irish bands play on weekdays, giving way on Saturday and Sunday to rock 'n' roll and rhythm 'n' blues. The Australian menu is more exotic than the more familiar Irish grub. Ever had ostrich curry? Only a minute's walk from the Marienplatz, the location of the bars is in the exact center of Munich. Both bars are open Monday to Thursday 4pm to 1am, Friday and Saturday 11am to 2 or 3am, and Sunday noon to 1am. Frauenplatz 11. ℂ 089/24219899. U-Bahn/s-Bahn: Marienplatz.

K&K Klub   This basement dive looks dirty and grungy. Graffiti artists have decorated its main door. But a mixed crowd often begins their nighttime prowl of Munich by using this place as a launch pad. Some of the best DJs in Munich play electro and house music to the demimonde who show up here. At an adjoining table, we heard a group of young guys organizing a sex party for later in the evening. This *Klub* is not for the faint of heart. It's open Monday to Thursday and Sunday 8pm to 2am, Friday and Saturday 8pm to 3am. Reichenbachstrasse 22. ℂ 089/20207463. www.kuk-klub.de. U-Bahn: Frauenhofer.

Pusser's New York Bar   This is the only European franchise of a small, well-run chain of restaurant-bars based in Tortola, British Virgin Islands. Its nostalgic decor celebrates the British navy of the 18th and 19th centuries. The specialties are Caribbean-inspired dishes and rum-based drinks, such as Pusser's Painkiller (rum, coconut, fresh orange juice, pineapple, and grated nutmeg). The cellar houses a piano bar. It's open daily 6pm to 3am. Falkenturmstrasse 9. ℂ 089/220500. U-Bahn/S-Bahn: Marienplatz.

Sausalitos   For the best margaritas in town, the kind Hemingway used to slurp down in Havana, head to this welcoming Mexican cantina. If you're in your 20s, you'll fit right in. You never know what to expect: perhaps a young man walking around in a leather jockstrap or a blonde beauty showing off her latest nipple piercings. If you're ravenous, order the generous platters of main dishes ranging from 9€ to 13€ ($14–$21), or else opt for drinks costing from 6€ to 9€ ($9.60–$14). During happy hour daily from 5 to 8pm, mixed drinks are half-price. It's open Monday to Thursday and Sunday 11am to 1am, Friday and Saturday 11am to 2:30am. Im Tal 16. © **089/ 24295494.** U-Bahn/s-Bahn: Marienplatz.

Schumann's Bar am Hofgarten　This is Munich's most legendary bar. It has an international fan club, lots of pizzazz, a history that goes back forever, and new premises that have been the subject of many architectural reviews. Some of the staff members here consider the layout, the ample use of green marble, and the wooden paneling evocative of a church. All of that changes, however, when the drinks begin to flow and the crowd gets animated. This night bar is a grand-slam rip-roaring affair that gets very crowded. There's a simple roster of menu items that changes with the season and the outside temperature. Schumann's is open Monday to Friday 5pm to 3am, Saturday and Sunday 6pm to 3am. Odeonsplatz 6–7, at the corner of Galerie Strasse. © **089/229060.** U-Bahn: Odeonsplatz.

Shamrock　At this beer lover's bar, you can compare the great brews of Germany with the best of the Irish exports. There's free entertainment every night at 9pm, when a mixed bag of Irish, rock, country, folk, funk, or blues musicians take to the stage. There are even Irish fiddlers. Should you get hungry, there's a good pizza menu to order from, costing from 6.20€ ($9.90). One of the chefs makes a "wild" chili con carne as well. Located near the university, Shamrock gets a fair share of the student crowd. Hours are Sunday to Thursday 6pm to 1am, Friday and Saturday 6pm to 2am. Trautenwolfstrasse 6. © **089/331081.** U-Bahn: Giselastrasse.

GAY & LESBIAN CLUBS

Munich's gay and lesbian scene is centered around the blocks between the Viktualienmarkt and Gärtnerplatz, particularly on Hans-Sachs-Strasse.

Bau　Macho and swaggering, this gay bar encourages leather, denim, and as many uniforms as can be crammed onto the bodies that surround its street-level bar. Dimly lit and international, it's not as scary as it might look at first. Don't be surprised if you spot several New York City cop uniforms on either level. It's open nightly 8pm to 3am. Müllerstrasse 41. © **089/269208.** U-Bahn: Sendlinger Tor.

Inges Karotte　This is one of the major gathering places for lesbians in Munich, both foreign and domestic. One patron called the clients "a female jungle," a widely diverse group of ages, professions, and interests. Many stylish lesbians show up here escorted by their girlfriends. It's a good atmosphere for drinking and mating. Cocktails begin at 5€ ($8), and happy hour is only from 4 to 6pm. Disco music sometimes rules the night. Hours are Monday to Saturday 6pm to 1am, Sunday 4pm to 1am. Baaderstrasse 13. © **089/2010669.** U-Bahn: Frauenhofer Strasse.

Kr@ftakt　As might be suggested by its name, this is an Internet cafe and the only gay one in Munich. Its clientele, looking for that Internet connection, is both gay and lesbian. Although we've put this listing in the nightlife section because of its late hours, it even serves a late breakfast costing from 4€ ($6.40). If you arrive late enough, you might even call it brunch. There's a happy hour on Wednesday from 7 to 9pm when a beer goes for only 1€ ($1.60). You can also order food here throughout the day, including pasta dishes costing from 6.90€ to 10€ ($11–$16). We get the impression that more gays go here to socialize in a convivial atmosphere than search the Web. It's open Sunday to Thursday 10am to 1am, Friday and Saturday 10am to 3am. Thalkirchenstrasse 4. ℂ **089/21588881**. U-Bahn: Sendlinger Tor.

Nil   It's fun, it's convivial, and it has a clientele somewhat younger than the one at Teddy-Bar across the street (see below). In addition to fit and youthful German men hanging with one another at the octagon-shaped bar, you're likely to see faded stars from German stage and screen, sipping drinks with their men friends, reflecting on the glory days of their youth. Most of the clients come here to drink and mingle, but if you're hungry, platters of food are well prepared and relatively inexpensive at 6€ to 8€ ($9.60–$13). Nil is open daily 3pm to 3am. Hans-Sach-Strasse 2. ℂ **089/265545**. U-Bahn: Sendlinger Tor.

NY Club 𝕲𝕲   Known as New York Discotheque for nearly 2 decades, this club has reinvented itself. Attracting male *fashionistas*, it is now the most stylish and modern gay dance club in town. Guests enjoy two different areas, a beautifully designed lounge or a high-tech dance floor with lots of room for dancing and cruising. Both pastimes are pursued most eagerly here. Look for special events and gay parties by searching the club's website. Sonnenstrasse 25. ℂ **089/62232152**. www.nyclub.de. U-Bahn: Sendlinger Tor. Cover from 5€ ($8); higher for special events.

Teddy-Bar   Gay and neighborly, and ringed with varnished pine and a collection of teddy bears, this is a congenial bar patronized by gay men over 30. It's relatively easy to strike up a conversation, and if you're hungry, there are platters of Bavarian and German food. It's open nightly 6pm to 4am. October to April it opens for brunch at 11am on Sunday. Hans-Sachs-Strasse 1. ℂ **089/2603359**. U-Bahn: Sendlinger Tor.

10 Side Trips from Munich

The **Bavarian Alps** are within easy reach (see chapter 10), or you can head for **Neuschwanstein** (p. 291) to see Ludwig II's fairy-tale castle.

DACHAU CONCENTRATION CAMP MEMORIAL SITE

In 1933, what had once been a quiet little artists' community just 15km (10 miles) from Munich became a tragic symbol of the Nazi era. Shortly after Hitler became chancellor, Himmler and the SS set up the first German concentration camp on the grounds of a former ammunition factory. The list of prisoners at the camp included enemies of the Third Reich, including everyone from communists and Social Democrats to Jews, homosexuals, Gypsies, Jehovah's Witnesses, clergymen, political opponents, some trade union members, and others.

During its notorious history, between 1933 and 1945, more than 206,000 prisoners from 30 countries were imprisoned at Dachau, perhaps a lot more. Some were forced into slave labor, manufacturing Nazi armaments for the war and helping to build roads, for example. Others fell victim to SS doctors, who conducted grotesque medical experiments on them. And still others were killed after Dachau became a center for mass murder: Starvation, illness, beatings, and torture killed thousands who were not otherwise hanged, shot by firing squads, or lethally injected. The death toll was then compounded in December 1944, when a typhus epidemic took thousands of lives within and around the camp; forced marches in and out of the camp claimed thousands of others as well. At least 30,000 people were registered as dead while in Dachau between 1933 and 1945. However, there are many other thousands who were also murdered there, even if their deaths weren't officially logged.

Before Hitler, a Beloved Artists' Colony

Unknown to many, Dachau had a glorious history long before it became infamous in the annals of human cruelty. At the end of the 19th century, it was one of the leading artists' colonies of Germany, and landscape painting was virtually developed in the Dachau moorlands. Women were not yet allowed in the Munich Art Academy but they were educated in the town's private art schools.

If you have time to spare, you can explore Dachau's historic core, including its **Schloss Dachau,** a hilltop Renaissance castle that dominates the town at Schlossplatz (© 08131/87923). All that's left of a much larger palace is a wing from 1715. Stand in the east terrace for a panoramic view of Munich in the distance. The highlight is the grand Renaissance hall, with its scenes of figures from ancient mythology. Chamber concerts are staged here. The on-site brewery hosts the town's beer and music festival annually during the first 2 weeks of August. Charging 2€ ($3.20) for admission, the castle is open April to September Tuesday to Sunday 9am to 6pm, and October to March Tuesday to Sunday 10am to 4pm.

Many paintings from the artists who settled here in the 1800s are still in town, especially the works on display in **Gemäldegalerie,** Konrad-Adenauer-Strasse 3 (© 08131/567516), open Tuesday to Friday 11am to 5pm, Saturday and Sunday 1 to 5pm, charging an admission of 4€ ($6.40).

The SS abandoned the camp on April 28, 1945, and the liberating U.S. Army moved in to take charge the following day. In all, a total of 67,000 living prisoners—all of them on the verge of death—were discovered at Dachau and its subsidiary camps.

Upon entering the camp, **KZ-Gedenkstätte Dachau,** Alte-Roemar-Strasse 75 (© 08131/669970; www.kz-gedenkstaette-dachau.de), you are faced by three memorial chapels—Catholic, Protestant, and Jewish—built in the early 1960s. Immediately behind the Catholic chapel is the Lagerstrasse, the main camp road lined with poplar trees, once flanked by 32 barracks, each housing 208 prisoners. Two barracks have been rebuilt to give visitors insight into the conditions the prisoners endured.

The museum is housed in the large building that once contained the kitchen, laundry, and bathrooms. Photographs and documents show the rise of the Nazi regime and the SS; other exhibits show the persecution of Jews and other prisoners. Every effort has been made to present the facts. The tour of Dachau is a truly moving experience.

You can get to the camp by taking the frequent S-Bahn train S2 from the Hauptbahnhof to Dachau (direction: Petershausen), then bus no. 726 to the camp. The camp is open Tuesday to Sunday 9am to 5pm; admission is free. The English version of a 22-minute documentary film, *KZ-Dachau,* is shown at 11:30am and 3:30pm. All documents are translated in the catalog, which is available at the museum entrance.

10

The Bavarian Alps

Walk into a rustic alpine inn along the German-Austrian border and ask the innkeeper whether he or she is German, and you'll most likely get the indignant response, "Of course not! I'm Bavarian." Some older inhabitants of the region still remember when Bavaria was a kingdom with its own prerogatives, even while it was a part of the German Reich (1871–1918).

The huge province of Bavaria includes not only the Alps but also Franconia, Lake Constance, and the capital city of Munich. This chapter explores the mountainous region along the Austrian border, a world unto itself. The hospitality of this area is famous, and the picture of the plump, rosy-cheeked innkeeper with a constant smile is no myth. Many travelers think of the Alps as a winter vacationland, but you'll find that nearly all the Bavarian resorts and villages boast year-round attractions.

Munich is the major driving gateway, with autobahns leading directly to the Bavarian Alps. If you're beginning your tour in Garmisch-Partenkirchen in the west, you should fly into Munich. However, if your destination is Berchtesgaden in the eastern Alps, the nearest airport is Salzburg, Austria.

OUTDOORS IN THE BAVARIAN ALPS The Bavarian Alps are both a winter wonderland and a summer playground. The **skiing** is the best in Germany. A regular winter snowfall in January and February usually measures from 30 to 50cm (12–20 in.), leaving about 2m (6½ ft.) of snow in areas served by ski lifts. You can reach the great **Zugspitzplatt** snowfield in spring or autumn by a rack railway; it is inaccessible in winter. The Zugspitze, at 2,960m (9,709 ft.) above sea level, is the tallest mountain peak in Germany. Ski slopes begin at a height of 2,650m (8,692 ft.).

The second great ski district in the Alps is **Berchtesgadener Land,** with alpine skiing around Jenner, Rossfeld, Götschen, and Hochschwarzeck. Snow conditions are consistently good until March. You'll find a cross-country skiing center, many kilometers of tracks in first-class condition, natural toboggan runs, an artificial ice run for toboggan and ski-bob (or snow-bike) runs, and artificial ice-skating and curling rinks.

In summer, **alpine hiking** is a major attraction. One of the best areas is the 1,240m (4,067-ft.) **Eckbauer,** lying on the southern fringe of Partenkirchen (the tourist office at Garmisch-Partenkirchen will supply maps and details). Many visitors come to the Alps in summer just to hike through **Berchtesgaden National Park,** bordering the Austrian province of Salzburg. The 2,470m (8,102-ft.) Watzmann Mountain, the Königssee (Germany's cleanest, clearest lake), and parts of the Jenner—the pride of Berchtesgaden's four ski areas—are within the park, which has well-mapped trails through protected areas, leading the hiker through spectacular natural beauty. For more on hiking in the park, contact **Nationalparkhaus,** Franziskanerplatz 7,

83471 Berchtesgaden (*C* **08652/64343**), open daily 9am to 5pm.

From Garmisch-Partenkirchen, serious hikers can embark on full-day or overnight alpine treks, following clearly marked footpaths and staying in isolated mountain huts. Some huts are staffed and serve meals. For truly remote unsupervised huts, you'll be provided with information on how to gain access. For information, ask at the local tourist office or write to the government-subsidized **German Alpine Association,** Am Franziskanerplatz 7, 83471 Berchtesgaden (*C* **08652/ 64343;** www.alpenverein.de), which will also direct you to a privately owned tour operator, the **Summit Club** (www.summit club.de), an outfit devoted to the organization of high-altitude expeditions throughout the world.

For the true outdoorsperson, savor the somewhat touristy facilities of Garmisch-Partenkirchen, and then use it as a base for explorations of the rugged Berchtesgaden National Park. Stay at one of the inns in Mittenwald or Oberammergau and take advantage of a wide roster of outdoor diversions there. Any outfitter will provide directions and link-ups with their sports programs from wherever you stay. Street maps of Berchtesgaden and its environs are usually available for free from the **Kurdirektion (tourist office),** Königsseer Strasse, Berchtesgaden (*C* **08652/9670**), and more intricately detailed maps of the surrounding alpine topography are available for a fee.

Weather permitting, another summer activity is **ballooning,** which can be arranged through **Outdoor Club Berchtesgaden,** Am Gmundberg (*C* **08652/ 97760**).

Anglers will find plenty of **fishing** opportunities (especially salmon, pikeperch, and trout) at Hintersee and the rivers Ramsauer Ache and Königsseer Ache. To acquire a fishing permit, contact the **Kurdirektion** (tourist office; see above) at Berchtesgaden, which will direct you to any of four different authorities, based on where you want to fish. For fishing specifically within the Hintersee, contact tourist officials at the Kurverwaltung, ImTal 2 (*C* **08652/967-0**), at Ramsau, 12km (7½ miles) from Berchtesgaden.

Despite the obvious dangers, **hang gliding** or **paragliding** from the vertiginous slopes of Mount Jenner can be thrilling. To arrange it, contact **Summit Club** (see above).

Practice your **kayaking** or **whitewater rafting** techniques on one of the area's many rivers, such as the Ramsauer, Königsseer, Bischofswiesener, and Berchtesgadener Aches. For information and options, contact the above-mentioned **Outdoor Club Berchtesgaden.**

If you would like to go **swimming** in an alpine lake—not to everyone's taste, due to frigid temperatures—there are many lidos found in the Bavarian Forest.

Of course, there's plenty to do outdoors during the winter as well, including some of the greatest **alpine** and **cross-country skiing** in all of Europe. Call the local "Snow-Telefon" (German only) at *C* **08652/967297** for current snow conditions.

There's also skating between October and February at the world-class ice-skating rink in Berchtesgaden. Less reliable, but more picturesque, is skating on the surface of the Hintersee, once it's sufficiently frozen.

EXPLORING THE REGION BY CAR

Acclaimed as one of the most scenic drives in all of Europe, the **Deutsche Alpenstrasse (German Alpine Road)** ⭐ stretches for some 480km (300 miles) between Berchtesgaden in the east and Lindau on Lake Constance in the west (see chapter 11).

The road goes through or past mountains, lakes, forests, and "castles in the sky." We prefer to take the drive in early spring or early autumn. In winter, mountain passes are often shut down, and even those highways that remain open can be dangerous.

IF YOU HAVE 1 DAY   After your stopover in Munich (see chapter 9), head south along Autobahn A8 (drive in the right lane if you want to avoid the hysterical speeders on the left). Turn south on Route B20 for **Berchtesgaden,** 158km (98 miles) southeast of Munich. After settling in and having lunch, take an afternoon excursion to **Obersalzberg** and **Kehlstein** (you can go by bus).

IF YOU HAVE 2 DAYS   While still based in Berchtesgaden, explore the **Königssee,** to the south (about 2 hr. by boat). This long, narrow lake, famed for its steep banks and dark waters, is one of Europe's most dramatic and romantic sights. In the afternoon, drive west along the alpine road and then north on Route B20 some 20km (12 miles) to **Bad Reichenhall,** one of Germany's most famous spas. Return to Berchtesgaden for the night.

IF YOU HAVE 3 DAYS   Get back on Autobahn A8 toward Munich but turn off at **Prien,** 85km (53 miles) southeast of Munich. The premier attraction here is the Neues Schloss, a fantastic castle begun by Ludwig II in 1878 on the island of Herrenchiemsee. You can find food and lodging at Prien.

IF YOU HAVE 4 DAYS   Get back on the autobahn to Munich, but take a cross-country route (472) toward Bad Tölz, which is one of Bavaria's leading spas, although it lacks any major attractions. Continue west from Bad Tölz along 472 to the town of Bichl, at which point you head south along Route 11 until you reach Benediktbeuern, a distance of 14km (9 miles) from Bad Tölz. Here you'll find **Benediktbeuern,** the most ancient Benedictine monastery in upper Bavaria. Records trace it back to the year 739. After a look, continue 6km (4 miles) south along Route 11 to **Kochel am See,** with its alpine vistas. Follow Route 11 south to the express highway, Route 2, which you then follow about 30km (20 miles) to **Mittenwald** on the Austrian border. Plan an overnight stay.

IF YOU HAVE 5 DAYS   You'll want to spend as much time as possible in **Mittenwald.** Goethe called it a "living picture book"—we think it looks like part of *The Sound of Music* film set. It's also a major center for violin making. Give it at least a morning before driving northwest for 20km (12 miles) on Route 2 to **Garmisch-Partenkirchen,** two towns combined. After checking in, head for the major attraction, the **Zugspitze,** the highest peak in German territory. Wear warm clothing. This could be the highlight of your trip to Bavaria.

IF YOU HAVE 6 DAYS   Leaving Garmisch-Partenkirchen, head north on Route 2 for 20km (12 miles) toward **Oberammergau.** Along the way, you'll pass **Kloster Ettal,** founded in 1330. Its original 10-sided church is a stunning example of the Bavarian rococo style. Some 10km (6 miles) to the west is **Schloss Linderhof,** one of "Mad" King Ludwig's royal residences, built between 1874 and 1878 on the grounds of his hunting lodge. These two attractions will take up most of your day, but you'll still arrive in the little old woodcarver's village of Oberammergau, 11km (7 miles) northeast of Linderhof, in time to wander about. Later, enjoy a hearty Bavarian dinner before turning in to your alpine bed.

1 Berchtesgaden ★★

158km (98 miles) SE of Munich, 18km (11 miles) SE of Bad Reichenhall, 23km (14 miles) S of Salzburg

Ever since Ludwig I of Bavaria chose this resort as a favorite hideaway, the tourist business in Berchtesgaden has been booming. The village is situated below the many summits of Watzmann Mountain—2,713m (8,899 ft.) at its highest point. According to legend, the mountain peaks were once a royal family who were so evil that God punished them by turning them into rocks.

Berchtesgaden is a quiet old alpine village with ancient winding streets and a medieval marketplace and castle square. Its name is often linked with Hitler and the Nazi hierarchy, but this impression is erroneous. Hitler's playground was actually at Obersalzberg, on a wooded plateau about half a mile up the mountain.

ESSENTIALS

GETTING THERE   **By Air**   The nearest airport is **Salzburg Airport** (© 0662/85800). It has regularly scheduled air service to Frankfurt, Amsterdam, Brussels, Berlin, Dresden, Düsseldorf, Hamburg, London, Paris, and Zürich. Major airlines serving the Salzburg airport are **Austrian Airlines** (© 0662/854511), **Lauda Air** (© 0662/854511), **Lufthansa** (© 0180/58384267), and **Tyrolean** (© 0662/854511). From Salzburg you can take a 1-hour train ride to Berchtesgaden, although you'll have to change trains at Freilassing.

By Train   The **Berchtesgaden Bahnhof** lies on the Munich-Freilassing line. Twelve trains a day arrive from Munich (trip time: 1½ hr.). For information, call © 01805/996633 (www.bahn.de). Berchtesgaden has three mountain rail lines—Obersalzbergbahn, Jennerbahn, and Hirscheckbahn—going to mountain plateaus around the resorts. For information, contact **Berchtesgadener Bergbahn AG** (© 08652/95810) and **Obersalzbergbahn AG** (© 08652/2561).

By Bus   Regional bus service to alpine villages and towns around Berchtesgaden is offered by **RVO Regionalverkehr Oberbayern** at Berchtesgaden (© 08652/94480).

By Car   Access by car is via the A8 Autobahn from Munich in the north or Route 20 from the south. The drive from Munich takes about 2 hours.

VISITOR INFORMATION   Contact the **Kurdirektion,** Königsseerstrasse 2 (© 08652/9670). It's open Monday to Friday 8:30am to 5pm and Saturday 9am to noon.

WHERE TO STAY

Alpenhotel Denninglehen ★ *Finds*   Set in a high alpine meadow 6km (3⅔ miles) east of Berchtesgaden, at an altitude of 900m (2,950 ft.) above sea level (Berchtesgaden is 500m/1,640 ft. above sea level), this solid, traditional-looking mountain chalet was built in 1980. Ringed with snow in winter and grassy meadows and flower beds in summer, and within a short schuss from the ski slopes, it's a refreshingly rustic (albeit manicured) getaway for urbanites, with comfortable lodgings, clean air, and views that stretch for miles. Bedrooms are outfitted in either rustic, wood-sheathed contemporary style or more folkloric Bavarian and old-fashioned decor. The bathrooms will hardly dazzle. Although efficient and modernized, they are rather small with a toilet and shower (no tub).

Am Priesterstein 7, 83471 Berchtesgaden/Oberau. © 08652/97890. Fax 08652/64710. www.denninglehen.de. 25 units. 38€–48€ ($61–$77) per person. Rates include continental buffet. MC, V. Closed last week of Dec and Jan

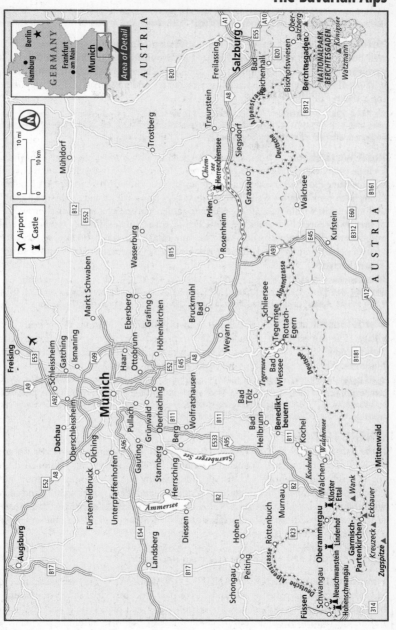

The Bavarian Alps

15–29. From Berchtesgaden, drive along Rte. 305, following signs to Unteran; take Rte. 319, following the signs to Oberau. **Amenities:** Restaurant; bar; indoor heated pool; fitness room; sauna. *In room:* TV.

Hotel Krone *Value*   One of the most appealing bargains in Berchtesgaden is this well-built chalet-inspired hotel. Operated by live-in managers, the Grafe family, and permeated with a sense of alpine thrift and good cheer, it offers cozy rooms sheathed with varnished pine. Each has a balcony or terrace and a compact bathroom containing a shower or tub.

Am Rad 5, 83471 Berchtesgaden. © **08652/94600.** Fax 08652/946010. www.hotel-krone-berchtesgaden.de. 21 units. 42€–52€ ($67–$83) per person. Rates include breakfast buffet. MC, V. Closed Nov 1–Dec 20. **Amenities:** Restaurant; whirlpool; sauna; nonsmoking rooms. *In room:* TV, hair dryer, safe.

Hotel Wittelsbach   Quiet, serene, and sedate, with a loyal clientele that tends to include many elderly guests who return year after year, this is a well-maintained hotel with century-old, four-story premises. It resembles a private, Jugendstil (Art Nouveau) chalet with pink exterior walls, lavish balustrades (most rooms have a private balcony), and a location within a small but verdant garden on one of the major thoroughfares of the town center. Bedrooms are comfortable, quiet, high ceilinged, generously sized, and decorated in tones of pale blue. The only meal offered is breakfast, served within a rustic, charming, *gemütlich* (cozy) room loaded with local artifacts and a sense of Teutonic charm.

Maximilianstrasse 16, 83471 Berchtesgaden. © **08652/96380.** Fax 08652/66304. www.hotel-wittelsbach.com. 29 units. 74€–84€ ($118–$134) double; 100€–130€ ($160–$208) suite. Rates include breakfast buffet. AE, DC, MC, V. Free parking. **Amenities:** Breakfast room; room service; coin-operated laundry. *In room:* TV, minibar.

Vier Jahreszeiten *⋆*   This is an old inn with modern extensions in the heart of the village. The inn has been remodeled and improved over the years and is quite comfortable now. Some of the newer units, with tiny sitting rooms and balconies, resemble suites. There's a terrace for your summer viewing pleasure.

Maximilianstrasse 20, 83471 Berchtesgaden. © **08652/9520.** Fax 08652/5029. www.hotel-vierjahreszeiten-berchtesgaden.de. 59 units. 76€–99€ ($122–$158) double; 105€–142€ ($168–$227) junior suite. Rates include buffet breakfast. AE, DC, MC, V. Free outdoor parking, 8€ ($13) in garage. **Amenities:** Restaurant; bar; lounge; indoor heated pool; sauna; solarium. *In room:* TV, minibar, hair dryer.

WHERE TO DINE

Hubertusstube INTERNATIONAL   You'll get an undeniable sense of Bavarian *Gemütlichkeit* in this richly paneled restaurant, where a trio of old-fashioned dining rooms, each with a century-old history of hospitality, offers well-prepared food and a view of the Alps. Specialties include filets of baby lamb flavored with garlic and served with leaf spinach and gratin potatoes. A small sirloin steak is roasted with a mustard coating, and a good-tasting veal steak is stuffed with ham and cheese and served with a mixed salad. Service is traditional and very polite.

In the Hotel Vier Jahreszeiten, Maximilianstrasse 20. © **08652/9520.** Reservations recommended. Main courses 13€–25€ ($21–$40). AE, DC, MC, V. Daily 11:30am–2pm and 6–11pm.

Panorama Restaurant GERMAN/INTERNATIONAL   The decor includes lots of blond birchwood paneling and touches of pale blue, but virtually no one notices it because the windows encompass a sweeping view of Obersalzberg and the nearby mountains. Recommended dishes include braised trout with almonds; pepper steak; goulash or *Leberknödelsuppe* (liver dumpling soup); veal or pork schnitzels; and a savory version of that traditional rib-sticker, *Schweinshaxen* (pork shank).

In the Alpenhotel Kronprinz, Am Brandholz. (℃ **08652/6070**. Reservations recommended. Main courses 10€–27€ ($16–$43). AE, DC, MC, V. Daily noon–3pm and 6–9pm.

SEEING THE SIGHTS

The Stiftskirche (Abbey Church), dating from 1122, is adjacent to the Königliches Schloss Berchtesgaden. The church is mainly Romanesque, with Gothic additions. One of its ancient twin steeples was destroyed by lightning and rebuilt in 1866. The interior contains many fine works of art; the high altar has a painting by Zott dating from 1669. In the vestry is a small silver altar donated by Empress Maria Theresa of Austria.

Schlossplatz ⚔, partially enclosed by the castle and Stiftskirche, is the most attractive plaza in town. On the opposite side of the square from the church is a 16th-century arcade that leads to **Marktplatz,** with typical alpine houses and a wooden fountain from 1677 (restored by Ludwig I in 1860). Some of Berchtesgaden's oldest inns and houses border this square. Extending from Marktplatz is the **Nonntal,** lined with more old houses, some built into Lockstein Mountain, which towers above the town.

Heimatmuseum, Schloss Aldelsheim, Schroffenbergallee 6 ((℃ **08652/4410;** www. heimatmuseum-berchtesgaden.de), is a minor but charming museum devoted to alpine woodcarving. The craft here predates the more fabled woodcarving at Oberammergau. Some of the best examples in Germany are on display. The museum is open Tuesday to Sunday 10am to 4pm. Admission is 2.50€ ($4) for adults, and free for children 18 and under. It's closed in November.

Königliches Schloss Berchtesgaden   In the Middle Ages, Berchtesgaden grew up around a powerful Augustinian monastery. Its monks introduced the art of woodcarving, for which the town is still noted. When the town became part of Bavaria in 1809, the abbey was secularized and eventually converted to a palace for the royal Wittelsbach family. Now it is a museum, mostly devoted to the royal collection of sacred art, including wood sculptures by the famed artists Veit Stoss and Tilman Riemenschneider. There's also a gallery of 19th-century art, a collection of Italian furniture from the 16th century, and a display of 17th- and 18th-century pistols and guns. Visitors are ushered through about 30 of the castle's showcase rooms as part of tours that depart at 20-minute intervals throughout the day. Tours last an hour each, and are conducted mostly in German, with a smattering of English. (English-language written texts and descriptions of the castle are passed out in advance.) Note that the castle is closed for the last half of August every year, during which time HRH Franz, the duke of Bavaria, heir to the throne of Bavaria and owner of the castle, comes for his summer holiday.

Schlossplatz 2. (℃ **08652/947980.** Admission 7€ ($11) adults, 3.50€ ($5.60) students and seniors, 3€ ($4.80) children 6–17, free for children 5 and under. Mid-May to mid-Oct Sun–Fri 10am–noon and 2–4pm; mid-Oct to mid-May Mon–Fri 11am–2pm. Closed last half of August.

Salzbergwerk Berchtesgaden *Kids*   These salt mines at the eastern edge of town were once owned by the Augustinian monastery. Operations began here in 1517. The deposits are more than 300m (1,000 ft.) thick and are still processed from four galleries or "hills." Visitors are given protective miner's clothing. Older children will enjoy the guided tours that begin with a ride into the mine on a small, wagonlike train. After a nearly 1km (½-mile) journey, visitors leave the train and explore the rest of the mine, sliding down a miner's slide and riding on the underground salt lake in a ferry. The highlight of the tour is the "chapel," a grotto containing unusually shaped salt formations illuminated for an eerie effect. The 1½-hour tour can be taken any time of the year, in any weather.

Bergwerkstrasse 83. ℂ 08652/60020. Admission 14€ ($22) adults, 9€ ($14) students and children 4–16, Family Card 40€ ($64). May–Oct daily 9am–5pm; Nov–Apr daily 11:30am–3pm. Bus: 840.

SIDE TRIPS TO KÖNIGSSEE & OBERSALZBERG

KÖNIGSSEE 𝕽𝕽

This is the "jewel in the necklace" of Berchtesgaden. The waters of this scenic lake appear to be dark green because of the steep mountains that jut upward from its shores. Low-lying land on the lake's northern edge contains a parking lot and a few charming inns and bathing facilities, but mountains enclose the rest of the lake, making it impossible to walk along the shoreline. The only way to explore the water, unless you're like one of the mountain goats you may see above, is by boat. Electric motorboats—no noisy gas-powered launches allowed—carry passengers on tours around the lake throughout the summer and occasionally even in winter.

The most popular spot on Königssee is the tiny flat peninsula on the western bank, the site of a basilica as early as the 12th century. Today the Catholic **Kirche Sankt Bartholomä (Chapel of St. Bartholomew)** is still used for services (except in winter). The clergy must arrive by boat because there's no other way to approach the peninsula.

The adjacent buildings include a fisher's house and a restaurant, which was once a favorite hunting lodge of the Bavarian kings. Here you can sample trout and salmon caught in the crisp, clean waters. At the southern end of the lake you come to the Salet-Alm, where the tour boats make a short stop near a thundering waterfall. If you follow the footpath up the hillside, you'll reach the summer pastures used by the cattle of Berchtesgaden. Just over the hill is **Lake Obersee,** part of Königssee until an avalanche separated them 8 centuries ago. If you prefer a shorter trip, you can take the boat as far as St. Bartholomew and back.

To reach Königssee from Berchtesgaden by car, follow the signs south from the town 5km (3 miles). It's also a pleasant hour's walk or a short ride by electric train or bus from the center of town.

For information about boat excursions, call **Schiffahrt Königssee** at ℂ 08652/ 96360. An entire tour of Königssee requires about 2 hours. There are boats in summer every 15 minutes, so getting off one boat and climbing aboard another is easy if you want to break up the tour. During the summer, the first boat departs every morning at 8am and the last boat leaves at 5:15pm. In winter, boats leave about every 45 minutes beginning at 9:45am. The important stops are at Salet and St. Bartholomä. A round-trip fare for a lake tour is 15€ ($24) for adults and half price for children.

OBERSALZBERG 𝕽𝕽

The drive from Berchtesgaden to Obersalzberg at about 1,000m (3,000 ft.) is one of Bavaria's most scenic routes. Obersalzberg was where Hitler settled down in a rented cottage after his prison term while he completed *Mein Kampf.* After he came to power in 1933, he bought Haus Wachenfeld and had it remodeled into his residence, the Berghof. Obersalzberg became the center for holiday living for Nazis such as Martin Bormann and Hermann Göring.

Today, you can walk around the **ruins of Hitler's Berghof.** This was where the famous 1938 meeting took place between Hitler and British Prime Minister Neville Chamberlain. The result was the Munich Agreement, which Chamberlain so mistakenly declared would bring "peace in our time." The Berghof was destroyed in 1945 by

Bavarian government authorities at the request of the U.S. Army—the Americans did not want a monument to Hitler. One of the only fully remaining structures from the Nazi compound is a guesthouse called the **General Walker Hotel** that was used by U.S. troops stationed in Europe.

An eerily fascinating point of interest is the **Kehlstein (Eagle's Nest)** 🕷🕷, which was erected on a high-altitude site by Bormann, who intended it as a 50th-birthday gift for Hitler. Built on a rocky plateau and never intended as a military installation, its access was made possible by the construction of a 7km (4½-mile) road that was blasted out of solid rock beginning in 1937—an outstanding act of engineering. Ironically, Hitler visited the site very rarely, perhaps three times in all. Unlike Hitler's larger lodgings at Obersalzberg, which were demolished by the Allies at the end of World War II, the original granite-built teahouse on the mountain summit at Kehlstein is still standing. Today it's the site of a restaurant, the **Kehlsteinhaus.** In winter, the site is completely closed because of snow blockages on its access road.

Between April and October, if you want to reach Kehlstein, you can either sign up for an organized tour with Eagle's Nest Tours (see below), or set out by yourself from the railway station at Berchtesgaden. Modern buses operated by the **RVO Bus Company** (for information, call the Berchtesgaden Tourist Office at (✆ **08652/9670**) charge 6€ ($9.60) per person for a round-trip transit from the Berchtesgaden railway station up to the alpine hamlet of **Berchtesgaden-Hintereck.** Here, you'll find some souvenir shops, a documentation center, and a minimuseum showcasing the region's role as a place of rest and relaxation for Hitler. Also at Hintereck, you'll have the option of visiting a bunker and a grim series of rooms used as a military prison by the Nazi regime. Access to the minimuseum, the documentation center, the bunker, and the prison cells at Hintereck costs 5€ ($8) for adults. Access is free for students, children 15 and under, and military personnel. From April to October, they're open daily from 9am to 5pm; from November to March, they're open Tuesday to Sunday 10am to 3pm (closed Jan 1, Nov 1, and Dec 24, 25, and 31).

To continue uphill from Hintereck to Kehlstein, you'll have to transfer to the **Kehlstein Bus** that hauls passengers uphill, past sweeping panoramas, along a tight and winding alpine road, to the base of an elevator shaft that will carry you the remaining way to the Kehlstein. Total transit time from Berchtesgaden to Kehlstein, without stops, is about 50 minutes each way. The Kehlstein bus line operates at roughly 20-minute intervals daily from 9am to 5pm from mid-May to mid-October. Round-trip passage, including the fee for the elevator, costs 18€ ($29) per person (free for children 4 and under). If you're hardy, you can skip the elevator and take a 30-minute uphill climb along a well-marked hiking trail instead. The **restaurant** at the summit, within the Kehlsteinhaus, is open during hours that correspond to the bus access described above.

The Kehlstein road is closed to private traffic. The only option for drivers of private cars involves parking in the lot at Hintereck and then riding the Kehlstein bus to the base of the elevator described above.

If you prefer to visit Kehlstein by guided tour, you'll find worthwhile English-language options at the American-run **Eagle's Nest Tours,** Königseerstrasse 2 ((✆ **08652/ 64971;** www.eagles-nest-tours.com). Tours, including Obersalzberg, Eagle's Nest, and the bunker system as an afternoon history package, are conducted daily mid-May to mid-October, starting at the Berchtesgaden Visitor Center. The service also takes visitors to sights such as the Salt Mines and the Königssee. A 4-hour tour costs 45€ ($72) for adults, 30€ ($48) for children 7 to 12, and is free for children 6 and under. One of the most popular tours offered is the "Sound of Music" tour to nearby Salzburg, which costs 35€ ($56) for adults, 25€ ($40) for children 6 to 12, and free for children 5 and under.

Where to Stay

Hotel zum Türken   The Hotel zum Türken, located in Obersalzberg, is legendary. It's designed in the alpine style and has terraces with views. On its facade is a large painted sign of "the Turk"—legend has it that the first owner was a veteran of the Turkish war. In the 1930s, anti-Nazi remarks led to trouble for the proprietor, Herr Schuster, who was arrested. Afterward Bormann used the building as a Gestapo headquarters; it then fell victim to air raids and looting in April 1945. Herr Schuster's daughter, Therese Partner, was able to buy the ruin from the German government in 1949. There is an old air-raid shelter directly under the hotel that can be visited every day from 9am to 3pm. The small- to medium-size rooms are well maintained, with neatly kept bathrooms. Most rooms have balconies with views of the valley.

83471 Berchtesgaden-Obersalzberg. © 08652/2428. Fax 08652/4710. www.hotel-zum-turken.com. 15 units, 12 with shower or tub. 72€–95€ ($115–$152) double without bathroom; 102€–148€ ($163–$237) double with bathroom. Rates include continental breakfast. AE, DC, MC, V. Free parking. Obersalzberg bus from Berchtesgaden. **Amenities:** Breakfast room; bar; lounge. *In room:* Hair dryer, no phone.

InterContinental Resort Berchtesgaden ✿✿✿   Set against snow-capped mountains, Herman Göring's former rural retreat has been turned into one of the best hotels in the Bavarian Alps. It is just over a rise from the Berghof, the house where Hitler plotted his dirty deeds. You can ski here in the winter or golf and hike, certainly swim, and also go rafting in the summer. The opening of this luxurious spa and retreat on land formerly inhabited by Nazis plotting massive blood and death has generated unfavorable press comment worldwide. But until the Nazis made it their private preserve, the Obersalzberg area was a vacation retreat in the 19th century. So, in a sense, the resort is returning to its origins with the opening of this hotel. The spacious bedrooms are furnished with deluxe styling, comfort, charm, and grace.

Hintereck 1, 83471 Berchtesgaden. © **08652/97550.** Fax 08652/97559999. www.ichotelsgroup.com. 138 units. 223€–285€ ($357–$456) double; from 433€ ($693) suite. AE, DC, MC, V. Parking 15€ ($24). **Amenities:** 3 restaurants; bar; 2 heated pools (1 indoor, 1 outdoor); sauna; health club; business services; salon; room service; babysitting; laundry service; dry cleaning; nonsmoking rooms. *In room:* A/C, TV, minibar, coffeemaker, hair dryer, iron, safe.

2 Bad Reichenhall ✦

135km (84 miles) SE of Munich, 20km (12 miles) SE of Salzburg

The best German spas can call themselves *Staatsbad* (where the standards of maintenance and cleanliness, quality of the waters, and breadth of facilities are high enough for the government to recognize them as among the top-rated spas in the country), and Bad Reichenhall bears that title with pride. This town is the most important curative spa in the Bavarian Alps. Its brine springs, with a salt content as high as 24%, are the most powerful saline springs in Europe, and the town has been a source of salt for more than 2,400 years. The combination of the waters and the pure air has made Bad Reichenhall a recognized spa for centuries.

In 1848, King Maximilian of Bavaria stayed here, popularizing Bad Reichenhall as a fashionable resort. Today, visitors come from all over the world to take the waters, which supposedly treat asthma and other respiratory ailments. Treatment sessions take place almost exclusively in the morning at seven resort institutes, the therapy ranging from simply drinking the water to pneumatotherapy—even electronic lungs for the most serious cases.

ESSENTIALS

GETTING THERE   By Air   The nearest airport is Salzburg (see "Berchtesgaden," earlier in this chapter). From Salzburg, it's a 20-minute train ride into Bad Reichenhall, with trains leaving every hour throughout the day, with a change in Freilassing. There are also frequent bus and rail connections to and from Berchtesgaden, either trip taking about 45 minutes. Buses or trains leave every hour from Berchtesgaden heading for Bad Reichenhall.

By Train   Bad Reichenhall is connected to the airport at Munich (see chapter 9) by frequent train service through Rosenheim. The trip takes about 2½ hours. For information and schedules, call ⟡ **01805/996633** or check out **www.bahn.de**.

By Bus   Regional bus service to and from Bad Reichenhall is provided by **RVO Regionalverkehr Oberbayern** (⟡ **08821/948274**). From the spa, you can take a bus to various stops in the Bavarian Alps, including Berchtesgaden.

By Car   Access is by the A8 Autobahn, from Munich in the north and Salzburg in the south. Exit on Federal Highway 21 into Bad Reichenhall.

VISITOR INFORMATION   For tourist information, go to the **Kur- und Verkehrsverein im Kurgastzentrum,** Wittelsbacherstrasse 15 (⟡ **08651/6060**). It's open Monday to Friday 8:30am to 5pm and Saturday 9am to noon.

WHERE TO STAY

Parkhotel Luisenbad 𝒜𝒜   A world unto itself, Parkhotel Luisenbad is an 1860s hotel with a new wing in a garden setting. Rooms range from medium to spacious. The more modern ones are handsome, with bold colors and tasteful furnishings, but many guests prefer the older, more traditional rooms. Bathrooms are well-maintained, with tub/shower combinations and deluxe toiletries.

Ludwigstrasse 33, 83435 Bad Reichenhall. ⟡ **08651/6040.** Fax 08651/62928. www.parkhotel.de. 83 units. 105€– 215€ ($168–$344) double. Rates include continental breakfast. DC, MC, V. Parking 5€ ($8). **Amenities:** 3 restaurants; bar; lounge; indoor heated pool; sauna; mud baths; room service; massage; laundry service; dry cleaning; nonsmoking rooms. *In room:* TV, minibar, hair dryer, safe.

Salzburger Hof *Value*   This three-story hotel is one of the best deals in town. Its public areas are filled with old Bavarian charm. Best of all are the compact rooms, most of which contain streamlined sofas, beds with built-in headboards, and armchairs around a breakfast table; all open onto tiny balconies. All units contain bathrooms with showers. Price depends on the view.

Mozartstrasse 7, 83435 Bad Reichenhall. ⟡ **08651/97690.** Fax 08651/976999. www.hotel-salzburgerhof.de. 25 units. 76€–96€ ($122–$154) double. Rates include continental breakfast. No credit cards. Parking 2.50€ ($4). **Amenities:** Restaurant. *In room:* TV.

Villa Erika 𝒜 *Finds*   Charming, intimate, and personalized, this Italianate hotel was built in a grandiose Renaissance style in 1898 by an architect who based his inspiration on a small palace he had admired near Venice. Today, with an interior that has been much modernized by its hardworking owner, Anton Oberarzbacher, it welcomes overnight guests into a verdant garden in a location in the heart of Bad Reichenhall. Bedrooms are outfitted in a combination of contemporary and vaguely Jugendstil design, in monochromatic color schemes of red, blue, yellow, or green, with lots of exposed wood. Virtually everyone who stays here opts for the half-board plan. The dining room is open only to residents of the hotel.

Adolf-Schmid-Strasse 3, 83435 Bad Reichenhall. ℂ 08651/95360. Fax 08651/9536200. www.hotel-pension-erika.de. 33 units. 35€–51€ ($56–$82) per person double; 49€–65€ ($78–$104) per person suite. Rates include breakfast. Parking 4€ ($6.40). AE, MC, V. Closed Nov–Feb; in-house restaurant closed Sun year-round. **Amenities:** Restaurant; lounge. *In room:* TV, safe.

WHERE TO DINE

Restaurant die Holzstube GERMAN/ITALIAN/INTERNATIONAL   The old-fashioned tradition and service here attract many regular patrons. In a garden setting, you can watch flowers bloom and enjoy a wide selection of cuisine (with many diet-conscious selections). You may try one of the kitchen's own original recipes—for example, marinated and roasted medallions of venison *Königin Luise,* served with bacon, chanterelles, and whortleberries. A more modern dish is roasted seawater shrimp with a lemon purée and pesto sauce.

In the Parkhotel Luisenbad, Ludwigstrasse 33. ℂ 08651/6040. Reservations recommended. Main courses 15€–23€ ($24–$37); fixed-price menu 27€ ($43). DC, MC, V. Daily noon–2pm and 6–9pm.

EXPLORING BAD REICHENHALL

The climate permits a complete spectrum of outdoor events, from excursions into the mountains for skiing or hiking to tennis tournaments. Gardeners and botanists will enjoy the spa gardens; the sheltered location of the town amid the lofty Alps permits the growth of several varieties of tropical plants, giving the gardens a lush, exotic appearance. There's also a wide choice of indoor activities, from symphony concerts to folklore presentations to gambling in the casino.

The great fire of 1834 destroyed much of the town, but many impressive churches survived. An outstanding example is **St. Zeno,** a 12th-century Gothic church with a later baroque influence. Its most remarkable feature is its painted interior, centering on the carved altarpiece of the *Coronation of the Virgin.*

Bad Reichenhaller Saltmuseum, Alte Saline Reichenhall (ℂ 08651/7002146), a short walk from the Kurgarten, is home of the industry responsible for Bad Reichenhall's growth and prosperity from Celtic times to today. Parts of the old plant still stand, but most of it was reconstructed in the mid–19th century by Ludwig I of Bavaria. The large pumps and huge marble caverns are impressive. Tours run May to October daily 10 to 11:30am and 2 to 4pm, and November to April Tuesday and Friday 2 to 4pm. Admission is 5.90€ ($9.50) for adults and 3.90€ ($6.30) for children.

SHOPPING

Shops are predictably upscale, rather limited in scope, and conservative. Since 1856, **Josef Mack Co.,** Anton-Winkler-Strasse 7 (ℂ 08651/963110), has been the region's best place for medicinal herbs, many grown in the Bavarian Alps.

BAD REICHENHALL AFTER DARK

Most guests looking for a night out head for the **Bayerische Spielbank Casino,** Wittelsbacherstrasse 17 (ℂ 08651/95800), which offers roulette, American roulette, blackjack, and 50 types of slot machines. You must show your passport if you plan to do any gaming. It's open daily 3pm to 2am; admission is 2.50€ ($4). Men must wear jackets and ties. The **theater,** also located here at the Kurgastzentrum, site of the casino, is a setting for operas, operettas, plays, ballets, musicals, symphonies, folkloric evenings, and chamber-music recitals. The tourism office (see "Visitor Information," above) keeps a complete list of events and ticket prices. When weather permits, performances are staged in an open-air pavilion. Tickets are 15€ to 40€ ($24–$64).

If you want to hang out with the locals, go to the **Axel Bar,** a woodsy bar in the Steigenberger Axelmannstein Hotel, Salzburgerstrasse 2–6 (✆ **08651/7770**). Here you can dance to rather sedate disco music interspersed with folk tunes. Good old-fashioned Bavarian beer is the order of the evening at everybody's favorite beer hall, **Burgerbräu,** Waaggasse (✆ **08651/6080**).

3 Chiemsee ⭐

85km (53 miles) SE of Munich, 22km (14 miles) E of Rosenheim, 64km (40 miles) W of Salzburg

Chiemsee, known as the "Bavarian Sea," is one of the most beautiful lakes in the Bavarian Alps. It's surrounded by a serene landscape. In the south, the mountains reach almost to the water. Resorts line the shores of this large lake, but the main attractions are its two islands, **Frauenchiemsee** and **Herrenchiemsee,** where Ludwig II built his palace, Neues Schloss.

ESSENTIALS

GETTING THERE   By Train   Prien Bahnhof is on the major Munich-Rosenheim-Freilassing-Salzburg rail line, with frequent connections in all directions. Ten trains arrive daily from Munich (trip time: 1 hr.). For information, call ✆ **01805/996633** or visit www.bahn.de.

By Bus   Regional bus service is offered by **RVO Regionalverkehr Oberbayern** (✆ **08821/948274**).

By Car   Access by car is via the A8 Autobahn from Munich.

VISITOR INFORMATION   Contact the **Kur- und Verkehrsamt,** Alte Rathaus-Strasse 11, in Prien am Chiemsee (✆ **08051/69050**). It's open Monday to Friday 8:30am to 6pm. From May to September it is also open on Saturday during the same hours.

GETTING AROUND   By Steamer   From the liveliest resort, Prien, on the lake's west shore, you can reach either Frauenchiemsee or Herrenchiemsee via lake steamers. The round-trip fare to Herrenchiemsee is 6.20€ ($9.90), and the round-trip fare to Fraueninchiemsee is 7.30€ ($12). Children 13 and under travel free. The steamers, operated by **Chiemsee-Schiffahrt Ludwig Fessler** (✆ **08051/6090;** www.chiemsee-schifffahrt.de), make round-trips year-round covering the entire lake. Connections can also be made from Gstadt, Seebruck, Chieming, Übersee/Feldwies, and Bernau/Felden. Large boats leave Prien/Stock for Herrenchiemsee May to September daily, about every 20 minutes from 9am to 5pm. The last return is at 6:50pm.

By Bus   Bus service is from the harbor to the DB station in Prien (Chiemsee-Schiffahrt) and around the lake by RVO.

WHERE TO STAY

Bayerischer Hof   The rustic decor creates the illusion that this relatively severe modern hotel is older than it is. Of note is the painted ceiling in the dining room. The rest of the hotel is more streamlined—modern, efficient, and appealing—though the Yachthotel (below) has more style and flair. Nonetheless, rooms are comfortable and bathrooms well equipped, with showers or tubs.

Bernauerstrasse 3, 83209 Prien am Chiemsee. © **08051/6030.** Fax 08051/62917. www.bayerischerhof-prien.de. 46 units. 90€–110€ ($144–$176) double. Rates include buffet breakfast. AE, MC, V. Parking 7€ ($11). Restaurant closed Nov; restaurant and hotel closed last 2 weeks of Jan. **Amenities:** Restaurant; bar; lounge; laundry service; nonsmoking rooms. *In room:* TV, minibar, safe.

Inselhotel zur Linde *(Value)* Set on the highest hillock on the Fraueninsel, this is a solid, richly textured, and historic inn with a tradition of welcoming overnight guests that goes back to 1396. Its premises are scattered among a pair of steep-roofed, old-fashioned Teutonic-looking buildings surrounded with a lush flowering garden and flanked by the island's largest and busiest beer garden. Bedrooms feature high ceilings and are old-fashioned and conservatively outfitted with lace curtains, various tones of beige and champagne, and traditional, Mittel-European style. Don't expect much in the way of amenities here. You'll be comfortable, but other than a telephone, it's fairly gadgetless.

Haus 1, 83256 Fraueninsel im Chiemsee. © **08054/90366.** Fax 08054/7299. www.inselhotel-zurlinde.de. 14 units. 114€–124€ ($182–$198) double. Rates include continental breakfast. MC, V. Closed mid-Jan to mid-Mar. **Amenities:** Restaurant; laundry service.

Yachthotel Chiemsee *(* The boating crowd flocks to this hotel on the western shore of the "Bavarian Sea." This hotel offers attractively furnished rooms, all with balconies or terraces, some opening onto the water. Lakeside rooms are equipped with two double beds and a pullout sofa for groups of four or more. Most rooms are fairly spacious, and all bathrooms contain shower or tub.

Harrasser Strasse 49, 83209 Prien am Chiemsee. © **08051/6960.** Fax 08051/5171. www.yachthotel.de. 97 units. 156€–186€ ($250–$298) double; 220€–360€ ($352–$576) suite. Rates include buffet breakfast. AE, DC, MC, V. Free parking. **Amenities:** Restaurant; bar; indoor heated pool; squash court; whirlpool; sauna; solarium; room service; laundry service; dry cleaning; rooms for those w/limited mobility. *In room:* TV, hair dryer, safe.

WHERE TO DINE

Restaurant Mühlberger *(((* CONTINENTAL A 2-minute drive (or 5-min. walk) from the center of Prien, this is a cozy, relatively modern building whose exposed pine and coziness makes it look older. The thoughtful and hospitable staff present menu items that reflect the diversity of local culinary traditions, and although lots of imagination is shown in the kitchens, some of the recipes evoke strong memories of childhood in many patrons. Examples including *Saibling* (a local freshwater whitefish) served in herb sauce with new potatoes, filet of veal with exotic wild mushrooms and a sauce made from a local white wine, a tender form of veal-based *Tafelspitz* (the boiled-beef dish that's always associated with Vienna and its last emperor, Franz Josef), many well-flavored versions of chicken, and such saltwater fish dishes as tuna steak with a curried tomato sauce or turbot with béarnaise sauce. You may begin a meal here with a terrine of guinea-fowl with pearl onions and end it with a house-made strudel that's layered with wild cherries, vanilla ice cream, and chocolate sauce.

Bernauerstrasse 40. © **08051/966888.** Reservations recommended. Main courses 24€–26€ ($38–$42); fixed-price lunch 35€ ($56), dinner 59€–70€ ($94–$112). MC, V. Thurs–Mon 11:30am–2pm and 6–10pm. Closed 3 weeks in Feb and 2 weeks in Nov.

EXPLORING THE ISLANDS
FRAUENCHIEMSEE

Frauenchiemsee (or Fraueninsel) is the smaller of the lake's two major islands. On its sandy shore is a fishing village that holds an elaborate festival at Corpus Christi (usually late May). Fishing boats are covered with flowers and streamers, fishers are outfitted in

Bavarian garb, and young women of the village dress as brides. As the boats circle the island, they stop at each corner for the singing of the Gospels. The island is also the home of a Benedictine convent, Frauenchiemsee Abbey, founded in 782, which makes it the oldest in Germany. The convent is known for a liqueur called Kloster Likör—it's supposed to be an "agreeable stomach elixir."

You can walk around the island in about 30 minutes to enjoy panoramic views of the lake. **Torhalle** (© **08054/7256**), a summer-only art gallery, is installed in the ancient hall that used to be the gatehouse of the Frauenwörth convent. Admission is 2.50€ ($4) for adults, 1.50€ ($2.40) for students, and free for children 11 and under. The hall is open only May to October daily 11am to 6pm.

HERRENCHIEMSEE ⟨⟨

Herrenchiemsee (or Herreninsel) is home to the fantastic **Neues Schloss** (also known as Königschloss), Herrenchiemsee 3 (© **08051/68870**), begun by Ludwig II in 1878 (see "The Fairy-Tale King," in chapter 8). Never completed, the castle was to have been a replica of Versailles, which Ludwig admired. When work stopped with Ludwig's death in 1886, only the center of the palace had been completed. Nonetheless, the palace and its formal gardens, surrounded by woodlands of beech and fir, remain one of the grandest and most fascinating of Ludwig's constructions.

The palace **entrance** is lit by a huge skylight over the sumptuously decorated staircase. Frescoes depicting the four states of existence alternate with Greek and Roman statues in niches on the staircase and in the gallery above. The vestibule is adorned with a pair of enameled peacocks, Louis XIV's favorite bird.

The **Great Hall of Mirrors** ⟨⟨ is unquestionably the most splendid room, and the most authentic replica of Versailles. The 17 door panels contain enormous mirrors reflecting 33 crystal chandeliers and 44 gilded candelabra. The vaulted ceiling is covered with 25 paintings depicting the life of Louis XIV.

Practically every inch of the **state bedroom** ⟨ has been gilded. On the dais, instead of a throne, is a richly decorated bed, its purple-velvet draperies weighing more than 135kg (300 lb.). Separating the dais from the rest of the room is a carved wooden balustrade covered with gold leaf. On the ceiling, a huge fresco depicts the descent of Apollo, surrounded by the other gods of Olympus. The sun god's features bear a strong resemblance to those of Louis XIV.

The **dining room** is a popular attraction for visitors because of the so-called "little table that sets itself." A mechanism in the floor permitted the table to go down to the room below to be cleared and re-laid between courses. Over the table hangs an exquisite chandelier of Meissen porcelain, the largest in the world and the single-most valuable item in the palace.

You can visit Herrenchiemsee year-round. From April to September, tours run daily 9am to 6pm. Off season, they run daily 9:40am to 4pm. Admission (in addition to the round-trip boat fare) is 7€ ($11) for adults, 6€ ($9.60) for students, and free for children 17 and under.

4 Bad Wiessee ⟨★

53km (33 miles) S of Munich, 18km (11 miles) SE of Bad Tölz

If you've always believed that the best medicine is the worst tasting, you should feel right at home in Bad Wiessee—the mineral springs of this popular spa on the Tegernsee are saturated with iodine and sulfur. However, the other attractions of this small town more than make up for this healthful discomfort. The spa, with a huge lake at its feet and towering Alps rising behind it, is a year-round resort. In summer, swimming and boating are popular; in winter, you can ski on the slopes or skate on the lake. The springs are used for the treatment of many diseases, including rheumatism and heart and respiratory conditions. In spite of its tiny size, Bad Wiessee has sophisticated medicinal facilities, accommodations, and restaurants.

The main season begins in May and ends in October. During these busy times, you should definitely make reservations in advance. Many hotels close in winter, so be warned if you're an off-season visitor. In recent years, the town has become increasingly popular with vacationers from Munich.

From Bad Wiessee, a number of tours are possible, including visits to Munich, Chiemsee, and the castles of Neuschwanstein (p. 291), Herrenchiemsee (p. 363), and Linderhof (p. 378). You can also visit Salzburg and Innsbruck in Austria. The tourism office (see below) will supply details.

ESSENTIALS
GETTING THERE   By Train   Travelers arriving by train disembark at Gmünd, 3km (2 miles) away. At the railway station there, a flotilla of buses (9–11 per day) meets every major train, with easy connections on to Bad Wiessee. For rail information, call ℂ **01805/996633.**

By Bus   Three to five buses depart every day for Bad Wiessee from Munich's Hauptbahnhof, with additional stops along the Zweibrückestrasse, adjacent to Munich's Deutsches Museum (trip time: 90 min.). Round-trip transport costs 19€ ($30) per person. For bus information, call ℂ **08022/19412.**

By Car   Access from either Munich or Salzburg is via the A8 Autobahn. Take the Holzkirchen exit heading toward Bad Wiessee and follow the signs.

VISITOR INFORMATION   For information, go to the **Kurverwaltung,** Adrian-Stoop-Strasse 20 (ℂ **08022/86030**). May to October, the tourism office's hours are Monday to Friday 8am to 6pm, and Saturday 9am to noon. In the off season, hours are Monday to Friday 8am to 5pm.

WHERE TO STAY
Hotel Lederer am See ⍟   This spa and holiday hotel in a large park is one of the most distinguished choices in town. From the balcony of your room, you'll look out onto the Tegernsee and the Lower Bavarian Alps. The atmosphere is pleasant, with dependable service and attractive, well-maintained rooms, ranging in size from medium to spacious. Each unit comes with a midsize bathroom with a tub/shower combination.

Bodenschneidstrasse 9–11, 83707 Bad Wiessee. ℂ 08022/8290. Fax 08022/829200. www.lederer.com. 98 units. 95€–160€ ($152–$256) double. Rates include breakfast. AE, DC, MC, V. Free parking. **Amenities:** Restaurant; bar; lounge; nightclub; indoor heated pool; outdoor tennis court; sauna; solarium; room service; laundry service; dry cleaning. *In room:* TV, hair dryer.

Hotel Rex ⍟   A modern hotel with much charm and character, Hotel Rex is set against a backdrop of the Lower Bavarian Alps. It's an ideal choice for a vacation by the lake. The decorator tried to make the place as warm and inviting as possible. The well-maintained rooms are furnished in Bavarian style and contain bathrooms with showers or tubs.

Münchnerstrasse 25, 83707 Bad Wiessee. ℃ **08022/86200**. Fax 08022/8620100. www.hotel-rex.de. 57 units. 45€– 69€ ($72–$110) per person double. Rates include breakfast. MC, V. Parking 5€ ($8). Closed Nov 1–Apr 14. **Amenities:** Restaurant; bar; lounge; room service; laundry service. *In room:* TV, hair dryer.

Landhaus am Stein This typical Bavarian inn, with geranium-filled balconies and a roof overhang, is a real alpine resort. It attracts scenery lovers in summer and skiers in winter. Rooms range from small to medium in size and are recently refurbished and completely modern; each has a balcony and either a tiled shower or tub bathroom. All rooms are nonsmoking.

Im Sapplfeld 8, D-83707 Bad Wiessee. ℃ **08022/98470**. Fax 08022/83560. www.landhausamstein.de. 17 units. 130€–160€ ($208–$256) double; 190€–240€ ($304–$384) suite. Rates include buffet breakfast. AE, DC, MC, V. Free parking. **Amenities:** Breakfast room; lounge; indoor heated pool; sauna; solarium; steam room; room service; massage; laundry service; dry cleaning. *In room:* TV, minibar, hair dryer, safe.

Park Hotel Resi von der Post *(Value)* This enduring favorite has been around much longer (since the 1950s) than many of its fast-rising competitors. It has been considerably modernized and now has well-furnished, traditional rooms. Bathrooms, although a bit cramped, are well organized, neatly maintained, and equipped with showers. Make reservations early; it's usually booked up for the year by summer.

Zilcherstrasse 14, 83707 Bad Wiessee. ℃ **08022/98650**. Fax 08022/986565. www.hotel-resi-von-der-post.de. 25 units. 82€–99€ ($131–$158) double; from 95€–118€ ($152–$189) suite. Rates include buffet breakfast. AE, DC, MC, V. Parking 5€ ($8). **Amenities:** Restaurant; lounge; room service. *In room:* TV, Wi-Fi, minibar.

Wiesseer Hof This modern, but still traditional, four-story hotel looks like an overgrown chalet. Rooms are snug and cozy in the alpine tradition. Most have balconies, festooned in summer with boxes of geraniums, with views over a lawn dotted with greenery. The tiled bathrooms are small—most with bathtubs, some with showers. The stuccoed wooden walls of the public areas create a *gemütlich* warmth. The hotel also has one wheelchair-accessible room.

Sanktjohanserstrasse 46, 83707 Bad Wiessee. ℃ **08022/8670**. Fax 08022/867165. www.wiesseerhof.de. 48 units. 90€–135€ ($144–$216) double. Rates include buffet breakfast. MC, V. Free parking. **Amenities:** 2 restaurants; bar; lounge; fitness room; spa; sauna; massage; laundry service; dry cleaning; 1 room for those w/limited mobility. *In room:* TV, hair dryer, safe.

WHERE TO DINE

Most visitors dine at their hotels, as Bad Wiessee is known for its hotels, rather than its restaurants. However, you'll find one (but only one) well-recommended restaurant here.

Freihaus Brenner *(R)* CONTINENTAL This restaurant's setting is a cozy, steep-roofed farmhouse whose intricate murals and weathered balconies evoke the old-fashioned Teutonic world. The original building was built in the early 1800s. Burnt to the ground around 1900, it was rebuilt nearby a few years later about 18m (60 ft.) from the main location. Today, young and energetic proprietors keep the recipes fresh and international and the service zippy for clients who enjoy the *gemütlich* setting and the woodsy location overlooking the lake, about a 5-minute drive west from the center of Bad Wiessee. Menu items include selections from every country that borders Germany, including Italy, Switzerland, France, and Austria. There are also some Thai dishes. As far as local fare goes, we recommend roasted duckling with red cabbage and potato salad and the *Wursts,* which come in several varieties and are sometimes served with braised celery and new potatoes.

Freihaus 4. (© 08022/82004. Reservations recommended. Main courses 12€–26€ ($19–$42). MC, V. Daily 9am–10pm (warm food daily noon–2pm and 6:30–10pm).

EXPLORING BAD WIESSEE

Bad Wiessee offers plenty of summer activities, including sailing or windsurfing on the lake, mountain biking, and hiking. A drive up the **Wallberg Road** winds through the Moorsalm pasture to an altitude of 1,000m (3,300 ft.). There's also plenty of golf and tennis. In winter, experienced alpine skiers are drawn to the Wallberg, and there are many cross-country trails as well. Wintertime hiking is also a possibility, as about 100km (62 miles) of paths are cleared of snow. The less athletic can enjoy horse-drawn sleigh rides. Finally, you can also take a **mountain cable car,** which travels 1,530m (5,100 ft.) high.

The town of Bad Wiessee has an old-world charm. It's best explored via the old-fashioned steam train or by taking a carriage ride. During the annual lake festivals in summer, locals don traditional clothing and parade through the town. Worth the trip is the nearby **Tegernsee Ducal palace,** which contains the former monastery of St. Quinn, founded in A.D. 746.

SHOPPING

You'll find Bavarian souvenirs, loden coats, and lederhosen here. If you want to acquire one-of-a-kind woodcarvings, either religious or secular, head for the studio of **Franz Trinkl,** Dr. Scheid Strasse 9A (© **08022/8749**), where you'll find an idiosyncratic collection of artfully carved figurines.

5 Mittenwald ✦

106km (66 miles) S of Munich, 18km (11 miles) SE of Garmisch-Partenkirchen, 37km (23 miles) NW of Innsbruck

The year-round resort of Mittenwald, in a pass in the Karwendel Range, seems straight out of *The Sound of Music.* Especially noteworthy and photogenic are the painted Bavarian houses with overhanging eaves. On the square stands a monument to Mathias Klotz, who introduced violin making to Mittenwald in 1684. The town is a major international center for this highly specialized craft.

ESSENTIALS

GETTING THERE   By Train   Hourly train service runs on the express rail line between Munich and Innsbruck, Austria. From Munich, trip time is 1½ to 2 hours; from Frankfurt, 5 to 6 hours. Call © **01805/996633** for information.

By Bus   Regional bus service from Garmisch-Partenkirchen and nearby towns is frequently provided by **RVO Regionalverkehr Oberbayern** at Garmisch (© **08821/948274** for schedules and information).

By Car   Access by car is via the A95 Autobahn from Munich.

VISITOR INFORMATION   Contact the **Tourist-Information Mittenwald,** Dammkarstrasse 3 (© **08823/33981;** www.mittenwald.de). It's open Monday to Friday 8:30am to noon and 1 to 5pm, and Saturday 9am to noon.

WHERE TO STAY

Die Alpenrose ✦ *(Value)*   This particularly inviting hotel is in the village center at the foot of a rugged mountain. The facade is covered with decorative designs and window boxes. The inn's original 14th-century structure was once part of a monastery. Rooms are in the Alpenrose (the former monastery) and its annex, the Bichlerhof. Try to stay in the main building, where rooms have a great deal of charm, with finely woven fabrics, old-fashioned farmhouse cupboards, and dark-wood paneling. Bathrooms in both buildings are a bit cramped; each has a shower only. The tavern room overlooking the street has many fine features, including handmade chairs, flagstone floors, and a square-tile stove in the center.

Obermarkt 1, 82481 Mittenwald. (Ⓒ) **08823/92700.** Fax 08823/3720. www.hotel-alpenrose-mittenwald.de. 19 units. 66€–85€ ($106–$136) double. Rates include buffet breakfast. AE, DC, MC, V. Free parking. **Amenities:** Restaurant; bar; room service. In room: TV, minibar, hair dryer.

Gästehaus Sonnenbichl (Value)   One of the more modest inns in town, this chalet nevertheless offers good value and comfort. Built in 1977, it resembles a private country home with a view of the village set against a backdrop of the Alps. The small but exceedingly well-kept rooms are freshly decorated in vivid natural colors, and all contain neatly kept bathrooms with tub/shower combinations. Reserve well in advance.

Klausnerweg 32, 82481 Mittenwald. (Ⓒ) **08823/92230.** Fax 08823/5814. www.sonnenbichl-tourismus.de. 18 units. 33€–44€ ($53–$70) per person double; 48€–70€ ($77–$112) per person apt. Rates include buffet breakfast. MC, V. **Amenities:** Breakfast room; sauna; room service. In room: TV, minibar, hair dryer.

Hotel Post 𝒢𝒢   Mittenwald's finest lodging, the Post is the most seasoned and established chalet hotel in the village, dating from 1632, when stagecoaches carrying mail and passengers across the Bavarian Alps stopped here to refuel. A delightful lunch and dinner are served on the sun terrace, with a view of the Alps. Beds are among the most comfortable in town, with duvets and beautiful linen. All the midsize bathrooms are efficiently organized, mostly with shower stalls.

Obermarkt 9, 82481 Mittenwald. (Ⓒ) **08823/9382333.** Fax 08823/9382999. www.posthotel-mittenwald.de. 82 units. 86€–140€ ($138–$224) double; 116€–170€ ($186–$272) suite. Rates include buffet breakfast. MC, V. Free parking. **Amenities:** Restaurant; bar; lounge; indoor heated pool; sauna; room service; massage; nonsmoking rooms. In room: TV, minibar, hair dryer, safe.

WHERE TO DINE

Restaurant Arnspitze 𝒢 BAVARIAN   This traditionally decorated restaurant, in a modern chalet hotel on the outskirts of town, is the best in Mittenwald. The cuisine is solid, satisfying, and wholesome. Try sole with homemade noodles or veal steak in creamy smooth sauce, and then finish with one of the freshly made desserts.

Innsbruckerstrasse 68. (Ⓒ) **08823/2425.** Main courses 17€–22€ ($26–$35). MC, V. Thurs–Mon noon–2:30pm and Wed–Mon 6–9pm. Closed 2 weeks in Apr.

EXPLORING MITTENWALD

Mittenwald's chief attraction is the town itself, its most notable feature being the **painted houses** 𝒢𝒢 that line the main street. The village can be explored in about an hour and a half. In winter it's a picture postcard of snow-laden charm, and in summer a mass of flowering facades with pots of geraniums, clinging to houses with their richly decorated gables.

The town's museum, which contains a workshop, has exhibits that trace the history of violins and other stringed instruments from their invention through various stages of their evolution. The **Geigenbau- und Heimatmuseum,** Ballenhausgasse 3 (Ⓒ 08823/ 25-11), is open Tuesday to Friday 10am to noon and 1 to 5pm, Saturday and Sunday 10am to noon. Admission is 4€ ($6.40) for adults, 3€ ($4.80) students, and 2€ ($3.20) for children. The museum is closed November 6 to December 16.

In the surrounding countryside, the scenery of the Wetterstein and Karwendel ranges constantly changes. Some 130km (80 miles) of hiking paths wind up and down the mountains around the village. You can hike through the hills on your own, take part in mountain-climbing expeditions, or take horse-and-carriage trips and motorcoach tours to nearby villages. The **Karwendelbahn Mittenwald** (© 08823/8480) is a cable car operating in winter and summer, costing 21€ ($34) round-trip and running daily from 9am to 4:30pm. It climbs to a height of 2,244m (7,360 ft.), where numerous ski trails become hiking trails in summer. In winter, the 7km-long (4.3-mile) Dammkar skiing downhill slope offers some of the best skiing and snowboarding in the Bavarian Alps.

In the evening, various inns offer typical Bavarian entertainment, such as folk dancing and singing, zither playing, and yodeling. Concerts during the summer are held in the music pavilion.

SHOPPING

Professional musicians have sought out the classical stringed instruments crafted here for centuries. Prices may be steep, but a visit to **Geigenbau Leonhardt,** Mühlenweg 53A (© **08823/8010**), is educational—even if you're just browsing the array of instruments.

6 Garmisch-Partenkirchen ★★★

97km (60 miles) SW of Munich, 117km (73 miles) SE of Augsburg, 60km (37 miles) NW of Innsbruck

The twin villages of Garmisch and Partenkirchen make up Germany's top alpine resort. In spite of their urban flair, the towns maintain the charm of an ancient village, especially Partenkirchen. Even today, you occasionally see country folk in traditional dress, and you may be held up in traffic while the cattle are led from their mountain-grazing grounds down through the streets of town.

ESSENTIALS

GETTING THERE   By Train   The **Garmisch-Partenkirchen Bahnhof** lies on the major Munich-Weilheim-Garmisch-Mittenwald-Innsbruck rail line, with frequent connections in all directions. Twenty trains per day arrive from Munich (trip time: 1 hr., 22 min.). For information and schedules, call © **01805/996633.** Mountain rail service to several plateaus and the Zugspitze is offered by the **Bayerische Zugspitzbahn** at Garmisch (© **08821/7970**).

By Bus   Both long-distance and regional buses through the Bavarian Alps are provided by **RVO Regionalverkehr Oberbayern,** Finkenstrasse 3, in Garmisch-Partenkirchen (© **08821/948274**).

By Car   Access is via the A95 Autobahn from Munich; exit at Eschenlohe.

VISITOR INFORMATION   Contact the **Verkehrsamt,** Richard-Strauss-Platz 2 (© **08821/180700**). It's open Monday to Saturday 8am to 6pm, and Sunday and holidays 10am to noon.

GETTING AROUND   An unnumbered municipal bus services the town, depositing passengers at Marienplatz or the Bahnhof, from which you can walk to all centrally located hotels. This free bus runs daily every 15 minutes from 6am to 8pm.

WHERE TO STAY

EXPENSIVE

Grand Hotel Sonnenbichl 𝒢𝒢   The most upscale hotel in the area is on the hillside overlooking Garmisch-Partenkirchen, 1.5km (1 mile) from the city center and 3km (2 miles) from the Bahnhof. It has excellent views of the Wetterstein mountain range and the Zugspitze (from front rooms only; rear rooms open onto a forested hillside). Bedrooms are well kept and range from midsize to spacious; some accommodations contain showers instead of bathtubs. The decor is generally Art Nouveau.

Burgstrasse 97, 82467 Garmisch-Partenkirchen (take Rte. 23 toward Oberammergau). ℂ **08821/7020.** Fax 08821/702131. www.sonnenbichl.de. 93 units. 168€–198€ ($269–$317) double; 245€–470€ ($392–$752) suite. Rates include buffet breakfast. AE, DC, MC, V. Free parking. **Amenities:** 2 restaurants; bar; indoor heated pool; fitness center; whirlpool; sauna; solarium; room service; massage; laundry service; dry cleaning. *In room:* TV, hair dryer, safe.

MODERATE

Atlas Posthotel 𝒢   The history and identity of Garmisch are bound up in events that took place at this hotel in the heart of town. It began as a tavern in 1512. During the Thirty Years' War, it sheltered refugees from besieged Munich. In 1891, it was bought by the Berlin beer baron who invented Berliner Weissen, which quickly became one of the most popular brands in Garmisch. Rooms range from spacious to rather small and cozy, successfully mingling Bavarian antique charm with modern comforts. Bathrooms are beautifully kept, containing tub/shower combos.

Marienplatz 12, 82467 Garmisch-Partenkirchen. ℂ **08821/7090.** Fax 08821/709205. www.clausings-posthotel.de. 44 units. 89€ ($142) double. Rates include buffet breakfast. AE, MC, V. Parking 3€ ($4.80). **Amenities:** 2 restaurants; bar; room service. *In room:* TV, Wi-Fi, minibar, hair dryer.

Post-Hotel Partenkirchen 𝒢   The Posthotel Partenkirchen, which was founded in 1492, is one of the town's most prestigious hotels. In recent years, it has even surpassed its major rival, the Reindl's Partenkirchner Hof (see below). You'll experience old-world living in stylish, U-shaped rooms containing Bavarian baroque carved furnishings and antiques. The sunny balconies overlook a garden and offer a view of the Alps. Rooms are generally medium size, though some are quite spacious, and each comes with a midsize bathroom with tub/shower combo.

Ludwigstrasse 49, 82467 Garmisch-Partenkirchen. ℂ **08821/93630.** Fax 08821/93632222. www.post-hotel.de. 59 units. 100€–150€ ($160–$240) double; 170€–230€ ($272–$368) suite. Rates include buffet breakfast. MC, V. Parking 7€ ($11). **Amenities:** Breakfast room; bar; skiing; mountain climbing; room service; laundry service. *In room:* TV, minibar, hair dryer, safe.

Waxenstein 𝒢 *Finds*   One of the most delightful places to recharge your batteries is not in Garmisch itself, but in Grainau, lying in a sunny spot, 2km (1¼ mile) from the center. The hotel opens onto panoramic views of the Zugspitze. The bedrooms and suites are spacious and elegantly furnished. Even if you're not an overnight guest, but touring the area, consider a visit to their Toedt's Restaurant, which serves market-fresh ingredients with excellent regional cooking.

Höhenrainweg 3, 82491 Grainau. ℂ **08821/9840.** Fax 08821/8401. www.waxenstein.de. 41 units. 120€–155€ ($192–$248) double; 175€–195€ ($280–$312) suite. Rates include breakfast. AE, DC, MC, V. **Amenities:** Restaurant; bar; outdoor pool; fitness center; sauna; room service; laundry service. *In room:* TV, Wi-Fi, hair dryer, minibar, safe.

INEXPENSIVE

Gasthof Fraundorfer *Finds*   The family-owned Gasthof Fraundorfer is on Partenkirchen's main street, just a 5-minute walk from the old church. Its original style

Hiking in the Bavarian Alps

Hiking is Bavaria's favorite pastime. Locals believe firmly in the emotional and spiritual benefits of walking and hill climbing and tend to hit the trails the moment the snows melt.

The tourist office in Garmisch-Partenkirchen will point you to hiking trails of varying degrees of difficulty, all clearly marked with signs. The office also offers a brochure outlining the half-dozen best trails. You don't have to be an Olympic athlete to enjoy them. Most hikes will take an energetic person 4 to 5 hours, but some of them are shorter and easy enough for children.

An easily accessibly destination is the 1,240m (4,070-ft.) **Eckbauer** peak, which lies on the southern fringe of Partenkirchen. The easy trails on its lower slopes are recommended for first-time alpine hikers. You can even take a chairlift to the top, where, in real Bavarian style, the *Bergasthof* (a guesthouse or cafe, usually in a high-altitude and rural location) will serve you a glass of buttermilk. In less than an hour, you can descend on relatively easy trails through a forest. The cable car stretching from Garmisch to the top of the Eckbauer departs year-round from the Eckbauerbahn (© **08821/ 3469**), adjacent to the ski stadium in Garmisch. Round-trip costs 11€ ($18) for adults, 6.50€ ($10) for children ages 6 to 16, and free for children 5 and under.

More demanding are the slopes of the rugged **Alpspitz** region, which begins about a mile southwest of Garmisch. The area is interlaced with wildflowers, unusual geology, alpine meadows, and a network of cable cars and hiking trails spread over a terrain ranging in altitude between 1,200m (4,000 ft.) and 1,800m (6,000 ft.). The highest trails are around the summit of the Alpspitz at 2,600m (8,528 ft.).

One of the most appealing ways to gain a high-altitude panorama over this region is to take a trip up the Alpspitz. Begin your journey at the Kreuzeckbahn/Alpspitzbahn cable car terminus, a mile south of Garmisch. The cable car will carry you uphill along the Kreuzeckbahn for a 4-minute ride across a jagged landscape to the lowest station of the Hochalm cable

has not been changed, so it retains the character of bygone days. There are three floors under a sloping roof, with a facade brightly decorated with murals depicting a family feast. You'll be in the midst of village-centered activities, near shops and restaurants. Rooms are furnished in a traditional alpine manner. Two rooms have four-poster beds; all have firm mattresses. Some larger units are virtual apartments, suitable for up to five guests. Bathrooms are compact with shower stalls. The Gästehaus Barbara is in back, with 20 more beds, including a *Himmelbett* (heaven bed), which is loaded with soft, feather-stuffed pillows and comforters.

Ludwigstrasse 24, 82467 Garmisch-Partenkirchen. © **08821/9270.** Fax 08821/92799. www.gasthof-fraundorfer.de. 32 units. 78€–100€ ($125–$160) double; 115€–188€ ($184–$301) family room for 2–5 people. Rates include buffet breakfast. MC, V. Free parking. **Amenities:** Restaurant; solarium; room service (breakfast only); laundry service; dry cleaning. *In room:* TV, kitchenettes (in apts), hair dryer, safe.

car. Here the Hochalmbahn will carry you uphill for another 4 minutes to the top of the Osterfelderkopf, 1,950m (6,500 ft.) above sea level. Cable cars for both stages of this trip depart at 30-minute intervals daily 8:15am to 5:15pm. After your visit to the Osterfelderkopf summit, you can return to Garmisch via a different route, a direct downhill descent via the Alpspitzbahn, a 10-minute ride above jagged gorges, soaring cliffs, and grassy meadows.

Round-trip passage along this three-tiered alpine itinerary costs 21€ ($34) for adults and 16€ ($26) for children 6 to 15; it's free for children 5 and under. These fares and times of departure can fluctuate. For the latest details, call either the information service for the above-mentioned cable cars (**© 08821/7970**) or check with the Garmisch **Verkehrsamt (tourist office)** on Richard-Strauss-Platz 2 (**© 08821/720688**).

From Garmisch-Partenkirchen, many other peaks of the Wetterstein range are accessible as well, via the 10 funiculars ascending from the borders of the town. From the top of the 1,780m (5,840-ft.) **Wank** to the east, you get the best view of the plateau on which the villages of Garmisch and Partenkirchen sit. This summit is also a favorite with the patrons of Garmisch's spa facilities because the plentiful sunshine makes it ideal for the *Liegekur* (deck-chair cure).

Another hearty hike is through the **Partnachklamm Gorge** 👀, a canyon with a roaring stream at the bottom and sheer cliff walls rising on either side of the hiking trail. Take the Graseck Seilbahn from its departure point at the bottom of the gorge, less than 1km (½ mile) south of Garmisch's ski stadium, and get off at the first station, which is adjacent to a cozy hotel, the **Forsthaus Graseck** (**© 08821/54006**). The 3-minute cable car ride costs 3.50€ ($5.60) per person each way (free for hotel guests) and operates from 7am to 10pm, midnight on weekends. You may want to get a meal or drink at the hotel first.

Haus Lilly   Many visitors appreciate this spotlessly clean guesthouse. It wins points for its large breakfasts and the personality of its smiling owner, Maria Lechner, whose English is limited but whose hospitality transcends language. Each small room comes with a comfortable bed and free access to a kitchen. Bathrooms are small and have shower stalls.

Zugspitzstrasse 20–22 (a 15-min. walk from the Bahnhof), 82467 Garmisch-Partenkirchen. © 08821/52600. 8 units. 70€ ($112) double, triple, or quad. Rates include buffet breakfast. No credit cards. Free parking. **Amenities:** Breakfast room; lounge; room service. *In room:* TV, hair dryer.

Hotel Hilleprandt *⁄Value*   This cozy, tranquil chalet is a great budget choice, lying 450m (1,500 ft.) from the train station. Its wooden balconies, attractive garden, and backdrop of forest-covered mountains give the impression of an old-time alpine building. However, a complete renovation has brought streamlined modern comfort. Rooms are small but comfortable, each with a private balcony and tiled tub/shower bathroom.

Riffelstrasse 17 (near Zugspitze Bahnhof and Olympic Ice Stadium), 82467 Garmisch-Partenkirchen. ℂ 08821/943040. Fax 08821/74548. www.hotel-hilleprandt.de. 13 units. 42€–53€ ($67–$85) double; from 60€ ($77) suite. Rates include buffet breakfast. MC, V. Free parking. **Amenities:** Restaurant; breakfast room; lounge; fitness center; Jacuzzi; sauna; sun bed; room service; massage; laundry service; dry cleaning. *In room:* TV, hair dryer, safe.

Reindl's Partenkirchner Hof ℛ   Reindl's opened in 1911 and has continuously attracted a devoted following. Owners Bruni and Karl Reindl maintain a high level of luxury and hospitality in this Bavarian retreat. The annexes, the Wetterstein and the House Alpspitz, have balconies, and the main four-story building has wraparound verandas, giving each room an unobstructed view of the mountains and town. Rooms are among the most attractive in town. The best are suites with panoramic views of mountains or the garden. Fine carpeting and rustic pine furniture add to the allure.

Bahnhofstrasse 15, 82467 Garmisch-Partenkirchen. ℂ 08821/943870. Fax 08821/94387250. www.reindls.de. 63 units. 55€–75€ ($88–$120) per person double; 77€–135€ ($123–$216) suite. Rates include breakfast. DC, MC, V. Parking 10€ ($16). Closed Nov 10–Dec 15. **Amenities:** 2 restaurants; bar; lounge; indoor heated pool; health club; sauna; room service; laundry service; dry cleaning. *In room:* TV, Wi-Fi, minibar, hair dryer.

WHERE TO DINE
EXPENSIVE

Reindl's Restaurant ℛℛ INTERCONTINENTAL   One of the best places to eat in Partenkirchen is Reindl's, a first-class restaurant in every sense of the word. The seasonal menu offers modern cuisine as well as regional Bavarian dishes. Two notable appetizers are the scampi salad *Walterspiel* with fresh peaches, lemon, and tarragon, and the homemade gooseliver pâté with Riesling jelly. For a main dish, try *coq au Riesling* (chicken in wine) with noodles or veal roasted with *Steinpilzen*, a special mushroom from the Bavarian mountains. For dessert, try either the Grand Marnier sabayon with strawberry and vanilla ice cream or something more spectacular: a *Salzburger Nockerl* (a dessert soufflé made with egg white, sugar, butter, and flour) for two.

In the Partenkirchner Hof, Bahnhofstrasse 15. ℂ 08821/943870. Reservations required. Main courses 12€–22€ ($19–$35). DC, MC, V. Daily noon–2:30pm and 6:30–11pm. Closed Nov 5–Dec 15.

MODERATE

Alpenhof ℛ *(Value* INTERNATIONAL   Alpenhof is widely regarded as one of the finest restaurants in Garmisch, as are the hotel dining rooms at the Posthotel Partenkirchen and Reindl's Partenkirchner Hof. The cuisine here is grounded in tradition. Robert Laepold offers a variety of Bavarian specialties, as well as trout meunière or pikeperch with a savory peppercorn sauce. Locals love the roast duck with red cabbage and potato dumplings. For dessert, try a soufflé with exotic fruits. In summer, the outside tables are lovely, but in winter you can retreat to the cozy interior, which is flooded with sunlight from a greenhouse.

Am Kurpark 10. ℂ 08821/59055. Reservations recommended. Main courses 9€–20€ ($14–$32). MC, V. Daily 11am–2pm and 6–10pm.

Joseph-Naus-Stub'n ℛ GERMAN/CONTINENTAL   One of the most charming dining spots in town lies on the lobby level of a prominent and very visible hotel, the Zugspitze, which, with its traditional alpine design, evokes a very large mountain chalet on steroids. Within a country-baroque decor that manages to be elegant and woodsy, but with a definite sense of almost ladylike grace, you can enjoy some of the most upscale and sophisticated cuisine in town. Menus change with the season, but the best examples include selections from an oft-changing array of oysters, crabs, North Sea sole and flounder, trout, and zander, each prepared in a different way every night or according to your specifications. During the autumn and winter, the focus is on game dishes, including filets of venison.

In the Zugspitze Hotel, Klammstrasse 19. © 08821/9010. Reservations recommended Fri–Sat nights. Main courses 11€–20€ ($18–$32); fixed-price menus 26€ ($42) for 3 courses, 55€ ($88) for 6 courses. Daily 5:30–10pm; Sun noon–2pm. AE, DC, MC, V.

Spago MEDITERRANEAN/INTERNATIONAL   Its decor successfully mixes elements from Spain, Italy, and southern France into a hybrid, ocher-toned mélange of the three, and the clientele tends to include a higher percentage of American expatriates from the nearby Army base than any other restaurant in town. Set within a 5-minute walk from the railway station, this is a place well accustomed to the tastes and preferences of a clientele from everywhere, and it's relatively easy to strike up a conversation at the bar. Its menu includes pastas; burgers; steaks; a flavorful version of chicken breast in a crust of crushed cornflakes, served with wok-fried vegetables and basmati rice; spinach-flavored lasagna; and even a mixed grill inspired by the wide-open spaces of the (mythical) American West, served with baked beans, baked potatoes, and sour cream.

Partnachstrasse 50. © 08821/966-555. Reservations not necessary. Main courses 9€–26€ ($14–$42). AE, DC, MC, V. Daily 10am–11pm.

INEXPENSIVE

Café Riessersee BAVARIAN/INTERNATIONAL   This cafe/restaurant on the shores of a small emerald-green lake is the ideal place to stop after you explore the Zugspitze. It's a great place for a leisurely lunch or afternoon coffee with cakes, ice cream, and chocolates, but it's worth visiting for the Bavarian dinner dishes as well. Dinner main courses center on fresh fish served from a big aquarium-style holding tank. Seasonal dishes are based on, for example, wild game, fresh fruits and wild berries, and forest mushrooms. During *Spargel* (asparagus) season, there is a menu devoted entirely to asparagus. The priciest main course, 50€ ($80), features the most elaborate mixed grill in the region—succulent cuts of beef, pork, veal, and chicken (don't worry, this price is not indicative of the rest of the menu!).

Riess 6 (3km/2 miles from the center of town). © 08821/95440. Main courses 8€–20€ ($13–$32). AE, MC, V. Daily 11am–9pm.

EXPLORING THE AREA

Garmisch-Partenkirchen is a center for winter sports, summer hiking, and mountain climbing. The symbol of the city's growth and modernity is the **Olympic Ice Stadium,** built for the 1936 Winter Olympics and capable of holding nearly 12,000 people. On the slopes at the edge of town is the **Ski Stadium,** with two ski jumps and a slalom course. In 1936, more than 100,000 people watched the events in this stadium. Today it's still an integral part of winter life in Garmisch—the World Cup Ski Jump is held here every New Year's Day.

The town and its environs offer some of the most panoramic views and colorful buildings in Bavaria. The pilgrimage **Chapel of St. Anton,** on a pinewood path at the edge of Partenkirchen, is all pink and silver, inside and out. Its graceful lines are characteristic of the 18th century, when it was built. In the park surrounding the chapel, the **Philosopher's Walk** ⭐ is a delightful spot to wander, just to enjoy the views of the mountains around the low-lying town.

This area has always attracted German romantics, including "Mad" King Ludwig (see the box "The Fairy-Tale King," on p. 290). Perhaps with Wagner's music ringing in his ears, the king ordered the construction of a hunting lodge here in the style of a Swiss chalet but commanded that the interior look like something out of *The Arabian Nights*. The lodge, **Jagdschloss Schachen,** is still here. It can only be reached after an arduous climb. The tourist office will supply details. Mid-June to mid-September, tours to the lodge usually leave from the Olympic Ski Stadium at 11am and 2pm, but check before you go.

TO THE TOP OF THE ZUGSPITZE ⭐⭐⭐

From Garmisch-Partenkirchen, you can see the tallest mountain in Germany, the **Zugspitze,** 2,960m (9,709 ft.) above sea level. Ski slopes begin at a height of 2,650m (8,692 ft.). For a panoramic view of both the Bavarian and the Tyrolean (Austrian) Alps, go all the way to the summit. There are two ways to reach the Zugspitze from the center of Garmisch. The first begins with a trip on the cog railway, the Zugspitzbahn, which departs from the back of Garmisch's main railway station daily every hour from 8:15am to 2:15pm. The train travels uphill, past lichen-covered boulders and coursing streams, to a high-altitude plateau, the Zugspitzplatt, where views sweep out over all Bavaria. At the Zugspitzplatt, you'll transfer onto a cable car, the Gletscher Seilbahn, for a 4-minute ride uphill to the top of the Zugspitze. There, far-reaching panoramas, a cafe and restaurant, a gift shop, and many alpine trails await. Total travel time for this itinerary is about 55 minutes, but you may want to linger at the first stop, the Zugspitzplatt, before continuing up.

The other way to get to the summit is to take the Zugspitzbahn for a briefer trip, disembarking 14km (9 miles) southwest of Garmisch at the lower station of the Eibsee Seilbahn (Eibsee Cable Car), next to a clear alpine lake. The cable car will carry you from there directly to the summit of the Zugspitze, for a total transit time of about 38 minutes. The Eibsee Seilbahn makes its run at least every half-hour 8:30am to 4:30pm (July–Aug to 5:30pm).

Round-trip tickets allow you to ascend one way and descend the other, in order to enjoy the widest range of spectacular views. May to October, round-trip fares are 47€ ($75) for adults, 33€ ($53) for ages 16 to 18, and 28€ ($45) for children 6 to 15. November to April, round-trip fares are reduced to 37€ ($59) for adults, 27€ ($43) for ages 16 to 18, and 23€ ($37) for ages 6 to 15. Year-round, family fare for two adults and a child costs 104€ ($166). For more information, contact the **Bayerische Zugspitzbahn,** Olympiastrasse 27, Garmisch-Partenkirchen (© **08821/7970;** www. zugspitze.de).

SHOPPING

Your best bets are in the traffic-reduced Ludwigstrasse in Partenkirchen and in the almost traffic-free zone from Richard-Strauss-Platz to Marienplatz in Garmisch. A vast array of stores sells boots, boutique items, clothing, jewelry, art, antiques, and more. If you like traditional Bavarian dress but don't want to spend a lot of money, head for **Loisachtaler,** Burgstrasse 20 (© **08821/52390**). Here, Petra Ostler has assembled the area's finest collection of secondhand clothing. Take your pick: a Jägermeister loden coat, an alpine hat with pheasant feathers, or a cast-off dirndl. They all look like new.

GARMISCH-PARTENKIRCHEN AFTER DARK

You can test your luck at the town's casino, **Spielbank Garmisch-Partenkirchen,** Am Kurpark 10 (© **08821/95990**). Admission costs 2.50€ ($4) per person, and you must be 18 or over (you must present a passport). The casino is open daily 3pm to 2am. Beginning at 8pm, blackjack tables are open. Friday and Saturday, games of seven-card stud poker are arranged (book in advance). Men must wear a jacket and tie.

If you'd like to meet the locals at night, head for one of the taverns for a beer. All major hotels have bars, but for a change of pace, go to the **Irish Pub,** Rathausplatz 8 (© **08821/3938**), and order a Guinness. This pub, in the center of town, attracts one of the most convivial crowds in the area.

Many hotels have dance floors that keep the music pumping into the wee hours, but for dancing of a different sort, check out the summer program of **Bavarian folk music and dancing,** held every Saturday night mid-May to September in the Bayern-halle, Brauhausstrasse 19. During the same season Saturday to Thursday, **classical concerts** are held at the Garmisch park bandstand. On Friday, these live shows move to the Partenkirchen bandstand. Check with the local tourist office (see "Visitor Information," earlier in this section) for details about these programs as well as a 5-day **Johann Strauss Festival** held in June.

7 Oberammergau ★

95km (59 miles) SW of Munich, 20km (12 miles) N of Garmisch-Partenkirchen

Oberammergau is best known for its famous Passion Play, which is staged only every 10 years; the next one will take place in 2010. Surely the world's longest-running show, it began in 1634 when the town's citizens took a vow to give dramatic thanks after they were spared from the devastating plague of 1633.

However, a visit to Oberammergau is ideal at any time, even without the performance. The town is in a wide valley surrounded by forests, green meadows, and mountains. It offers first-class hotels and cozy inns, and has long been known for the skill of its woodcarvers. Numerous hiking trails lead through the nearby mountains to hikers' inns. You can also simply go up to the mountaintops on the Laber cable railway or the Kolben chairlift.

Oberammergau also offers opportunities for tennis buffs, minigolf players, cyclists, swimmers, hang-gliding enthusiasts, and canoeists. The recreation center, Wellenberg, with open-air pools, fountains, sauna, solarium, and restaurant, is one of the Alps' most beautiful. The surrounding Ammer Valley is a treasure trove for explorers. And Oberammergau is often used as a base for visiting Linderhof Castle, the Benedictine monastery at Ettal, or the fairy-tale Neuschwanstein and Hohenschwangau castles (see chapter 8).

ESSENTIALS

GETTING THERE **By Train** The **Oberammergau Bahnhof** is on the Murnau-Bad Kohlgrum-Oberammergau rail line, with frequent connections in all directions. Through Murnau, all major German cities can be reached. Daily trains arrive from Munich in 2 hours and from Frankfurt in 7 hours. For rail information and schedules, call © **01805/996633** or visit www.bahn.de.

By Bus Regional bus service to nearby towns is offered by **RVO Regionalverkehr Oberbayern** in Garmisch-Partenkirchen (© **08821/948274**). An unnumbered bus goes back and forth between Oberammergau and Garmisch-Partenkirchen.

By Car   Many visitors drive here; the trip takes 1½ hours from Munich and 5½ hours from Frankfurt. Take the A95 Munich-Garmisch-Partenkirchen Autobahn and exit at Eschenlohe.

VISITOR INFORMATION   Contact the **Oberammergau Tourist Information Office,** Eugen-Papst-Strasse 9A (© **08822/92310**). It's open Monday to Friday 8:30am to 6pm, and Saturday 9am to noon and 1 to 5pm.

WHERE TO STAY & DINE

The cost of accommodations in Oberammergau includes a universally imposed *Kurtaxe* (special tax) of 1.30€ ($1.55). This entitles visitors to a card providing small discounts at local attractions.

Alte Post   Since 1612 this provincial, chalet-style inn has been in the center of the village. It has a wide overhanging roof, green-shuttered windows painted with decorative trim, a large crucifix on the facade, and tables set on a sidewalk under a long awning. It's the village's social hub. The interior has a storybook charm, with a ceiling-high green ceramic stove, alpine chairs, and shelves of pewter plates. The rustic rooms range in size from cozy to spacious and have wood-beamed ceilings and wide beds with giant posts; most have views. All the small bathrooms are tiled, with shower units.

Dorfstrasse 19, 82487 Oberammergau. © **08822/9100**. Fax 08822/910100. www.ogau.de. 32 units. 65€–105€ ($104–$168) double. Rates include buffet breakfast. AE, DC, MC, V. Free parking. **Amenities:** Restaurant; nonsmoking rooms. *In room:* TV.

Hotel Café-Restaurant Friedenshöhe *(Value*   This villa enjoys a beautiful location. It's one of the town's best bargains, although for quality, it's not in the same league as the Böld or the Parkhotel Sonnenhof (see both below). It once hosted Thomas Mann. Rooms range from rather small singles to spacious doubles. They're furnished in tasteful modern style and are well maintained, each with a compact, tiled bathroom with shower unit. Opt for one of the corner rooms if possible (they're bigger). Bathrooms tend to be too small but do contain showers. There's an indoor terrace with a panoramic view.

König-Ludwig-Strasse 31, 82487 Oberammergau. © **08822/94484**. Fax 08822/4345. www.friedenshoehe.de. 16 units. 60€–80€ ($96–$128) double. Rates include buffet breakfast. AE, DC, MC, V. Closed Nov–Dec 14. **Amenities:** Restaurant; bar. *In room:* TV (on request).

Hotel Der Schilcherhof *(Value*   This hotel is divided among three different old-fashioned and charming structures, each built between 1861 and 1938. This is old, and rather courtly, *Deutschland.* With its surrounding gardens, the Schilcherhof offers good-value rooms, all of which contain midsize, shower-only bathrooms. In summer, the terrace overflows with festive, beer-drinking patrons. Nearby is the Ammer River, which flows through the village. Although the house is built in the old style, with wooden front balconies and tiers of flower boxes, it has a fresh look.

Bahnhofstrasse 17, 82487 Oberammergau. © **08822/4740**. Fax 08822/3793. www.hotel-schilcherhof.de. 26 units. 64€–84€ ($102–$134) double. Rates include full breakfast. AE, MC, V. Parking 5€ ($6.50). Closed Nov 15–Christmas. **Amenities:** Breakfast room; bar; lounge; room service. *In room:* TV, Wi-Fi, hair dryer, no phone.

Hotel Restaurant Böld *𝓡*   This well-designed chalet hotel steadily improves in quality and now is among the town's premier choices, in a neck-to-neck race with Parkhotel Sonnenhof (see below). It lies only a stone's throw from the river. Rooms are well furnished; most have balconies. All of the accommodations are equipped with a midsize bathroom with shower stalls.

König-Ludwig-Strasse 10, 82487 Oberammergau. © 08822/9120. Fax 08822/7102. www.hotel-boeld.de. 57 units. 79€–125€ ($126–$200) double; from 135€ ($216) suite. Rates include buffet breakfast. AE, MC, V. Free outdoor parking; 6€ ($9.60) in garage. **Amenities:** Restaurant; bar; whirlpool; sauna; solarium; room service; nonsmoking rooms; rooms for those w/limited mobility. *In room:* TV, minibar, hair dryer.

Hotel Wolf *(Value)*   An overgrown Bavarian chalet, Hotel Wolf is at the heart of village life. Its facade, like others in the area, has an encircling balcony, heavy timbering, and window boxes spilling cascades of geraniums. Inside, it retains some local flavor, although concessions to modernity have been made, such as an elevator. Rooms range from small to medium, and five are singles. The small, tiled bathrooms with showers are spotless.

Dorfstrasse 1, 82487 Oberammergau. © 08822/92330. Fax 08822/923333. www.hotel-wolf.de. 32 units. 110€–135€ ($176–$216) double. Rates include buffet breakfast. DC, MC, V. Free parking. **Amenities:** Restaurant; bar; outdoor pool; sauna; solarium; room service. *In room:* TV, Wi-Fi, hair dryer.

Parkhotel Sonnenhof *(Kids)*   Short on charm and alpine rusticity, this modern hotel still has a lot going for it. It's far enough from the summer crowds to offer guests peace and tranquillity, but it's still within walking distance of the center. The hotel overlooks the Ammer River and a beautiful *Pfarrkirche* (parish church). Rooms are well maintained, filled with first-class comforts, and have balconies with an alpine vista, often of Oberammergau's mountain, the Kobel. Each of the efficiently organized, midsize bathrooms comes with tub or tub/shower combo. All rooms are nonsmoking.

König-Ludwig-Strasse 12, 82487 Oberammergau. © 08822/9130. Fax 08822/3047. www.parkhotellerie-sonnenhof.de. 61 units. 110€–145€ ($176–$232) double; 125€–160€ ($200–$256) suite. AE, DC, MC, V. Free parking. **Amenities:** 3 restaurants; bar; indoor heated pool; fitness center; sauna; 2 children's centers; massage; babysitting; laundry service; dry cleaning; nonsmoking rooms. *In room:* TV, minibar (in some), hair dryer, safe.

Schlosshotel Linderhof *(Finds)*   This hotel has gables, shutters, and half-timbering in the style of a Bavarian chalet. The famous palace (see "Side Trips from Oberammergau," below) is only about 350m (1,150 ft.) away. Rooms are dignified and high ceilinged, with tasteful hints of 19th-century gentility but with modern conveniences, such as bathrooms with showers and tubs.

Linderhof 14 (near the palace), 82488 Ettal. © 08822/790. Fax 08822/4347. www.schlosshotel-linderhof.com. 29 units. 95€–120€ ($152–$192) double. Rates include breakfast. AE, DC, MC, V. Free parking. **Amenities:** Restaurant; bar; lounge. *In room:* TV, fridge, hair dryer.

Turmwirt *(Finds)*   This cozy Bavarian-style 18th-century inn offers small, snug rooms, many with private balconies opening onto mountain views. Each comes with a small but well-maintained private bathroom with a tub/shower combo. The present building was constructed in 1889 and has since been altered and renovated many times, including a substantial enlargement in 1968. It's an intricately painted green-shuttered country house with a well-maintained homelike interior. The owners consist of three generations of the Glas family, who often present Bavarian folk evenings.

Ettalerstrasse 2 (5 min. from the town center), 82487 Oberammergau. © 08822/92600. Fax 08822/1437. www.turmwirt.de. 22 units. 96€–110€ ($154–$176) double. Rates include buffet breakfast. AE, DC, MC, V. Free parking. **Amenities:** Restaurant; breakfast room; lounge; room service; laundry service; dry cleaning; nonsmoking rooms. *In room:* TV, minibar, hair dryer, safe.

EXPLORING OBERAMMERGAU

Oberammergau has much to offer. Consider taking an excursion to either the **Berg Laber,** the mountain which rises to the east of the town, or **Berg Kolben,** to the west. Berg Laber, slightly more dramatic, is accessible via an enclosed cable-gondola

(© **08822/4770**) that offers a sweeping alpine view. The 10-minute ascent costs 15€ ($24) per person. The top of Berg Kolben is accessible via a two-passenger open-sided chairlift (© **08822/4760**), with exposure to high winds that is a lot more primal. The cost is 12€ ($19) round-trip. Both are open mid-July to mid-October and mid-December to March daily 9am to noon and 1 to 4:30pm.

Aside from the actors in the Passion Play, Oberammergau's most respected citizens are **woodcarvers,** many of whom have been trained in the village woodcarver's school. In the **Pilatushaus,** Ludwig-Thoma-Strasse (© **08822/949511**), you can watch local carvers, as well as painters, sculptors, and potters, as they work. June to October, their hours are Monday to Friday 1 to 6pm and Saturday 10am to 12:30pm. Many examples of their art are throughout the town, on painted cottages and inns, and in the churchyard.

Heimatmuseum, Dorfstrasse 8 (© **08822/94136**), has a notable collection of 18th-, 19th-, and 20th-century Christmas crèches, all hand carved and painted. It's open mid-May to mid-October Tuesday to Sunday 2 to 6pm; in the off season (Apr through mid-May and mid-Oct to Oct 29), hours are Saturday only 2 to 6pm. Admission is 6€ ($9.60) for adults, 1€ ($1.60) for students and children ages 6 to 16, and free for children 5 and under. The museum is closed from October 29 to March 29.

When strolling through the village, note the **frescoed houses** named after fairy-tale characters, such as the "Hansel and Gretel House" and "Little Red Riding Hood House." The citizens of Oberammergau have a long tradition of painting frescoes on their houses, most often based on scenes from fairy tales. The most famous frescoed house is **Pilatushaus** on Ludwig-Thoma-Strasse (see above), which today is a home to artisans. The frescoes here are the most beautiful in town, the creation of Franz Seraph Zwinck, who was the greatest of the town's fresco artists. They were known as *Lüftmalerei* painters. Zwinck based his fresco not on a fairy tale, but on a depiction of Jesus Christ coming before Pilate—hence the name of the house, Pilatushaus.

SIDE TRIPS FROM OBERAMMERGAU
SCHLOSS LINDERHOF 𝒜𝒜

Until the late 19th century, a modest hunting lodge, owned by the Bavarian royal family, stood on a large piece of land 13km (8 miles) west of the village. But in 1869, "Mad" King Ludwig struck again, this time creating a French rococo palace in the Ammergau Mountains. This is his most successful creation. Unlike his palace at Chiemsee (see "Chiemsee," earlier in this chapter), Schloss Linderhof was not meant to copy any other structure. And unlike the Neuschwanstein palace (p. 291), its concentration of fanciful projects and designs was not limited to the palace interior. In fact, the gardens and smaller buildings at Linderhof are, if anything, more elaborate than the two-story main structure.

Our favorite rooms are on the second floor, where ceilings are much higher because of the unusual roof plan. Ascending the winged staircase of Carrara marble, you'll find yourself at the **West Gobelin Room (music room),** with carved and gilded paneling and richly colored tapestries. This room leads directly into the **Hall of Mirrors,** where the mirrors are set in white-and-gold panels, decorated with gilded woodcarvings. The hall's ceiling is festooned with frescoes depicting mythological scenes.

In the popular style of the previous century, Ludwig laid out the **gardens** 𝒜𝒜 in formal parterres with geometrical shapes, baroque sculptures, and elegant fountains. The front of the palace opens onto a large pool where, from a gilded statue in its center, a jet of water sprays 32m (105 ft.) into the air.

Finds Shopping for Woodcarvings

Oberammergau's woodcarvings are among the most sought after in the Germanic world, and many an example has graced the mantelpieces and shelves of homes around the globe. Most subjects are religious, deriving directly from 14th-century originals; however, to cater to the demands of modern visitors, there's been an increased emphasis lately on secular subjects, such as drinking or hunting scenes. Competition is fierce for these woodcarvings, many of which are made in hamlets and farmhouses throughout the region. Know before you buy that even some of the most expensive "handmade" pieces might have been roughed in by machine before being finished off by hand.

The **Holzschittschule (Woodcarving School)** (© 08822/3542) has conditions of study that may remind you of the severity of the medieval guilds. Students who labor over a particular sculpture are required to turn it in to the school, where it's either placed on permanent exhibition or sold during the school's once-a-year sell-off, usually over a 2-day period in July.

Baur Anton, Dorfstrasse 27 (© 08822/821), has the most sophisticated inventory of woodcarvings. The shop employs a small cadre of carvers who usually work from their homes to create works inspired by medieval originals. The outgoing and personable sales staff is quick to admit that the forms of many of the pieces are roughed in by machine, but most of the intricate work is completed by hand. Pieces are crafted from maple, pine, or linden (basswood). Prices start at 9€ ($14). Carvings are in their natural grain, stained, or polychromed (some of the most charming), and in some instances, are partially gilded.

The park also contains several other small but exotic buildings, including a **Moorish Kiosk** where Ludwig could indulge his wildest Arabian nights fantasies. He would retreat here by himself for hours, smoking a *chibouk* (a Turkish tobacco pipe) and dreaming of himself as an Asian prince. The pavilion is a mammoth artificial grotto that is amazingly realistic, although Ludwig ordered many changes made to its design. The cavelike grotto was created out of artificial rock that looks real, complete with stalagmites and stalactites and three separate chambers.

Schloss Linderhof, Linderhof 12, 82488 Ettal (© 08822/92030; www.linderhof.de), is open to the public throughout the year and makes an ideal day trip from Munich, as well as from Oberammergau. It's open April to September daily 9am to 6pm. From October to March, the grotto and Moorish Kiosk are closed, but the castle is open daily 10am to 4pm. Admission in the summer is 7€ ($11) for adults, 6€ ($9.60) for students, and free for children 14 and under. In winter, admission is 6€ ($9.60) for adults, 5€ ($8) for students, and free for children 14 and under.

Buses run between Oberammergau (from the railway station) and Schloss Linderhof seven times per day, beginning at 10:25am; the last bus leaves Linderhof at 6:58pm. Round-trip fare is 11€ ($18). For bus information, call **RVO Bus Company** (© 08821/948274) at their regional office in Garmisch-Partenkirchen. Motorists from Oberammergau should follow the signs to Ettal, about 5km (3 miles) away, and then go another 5km (3 miles) to Draswang; from there follow the signs to Schloss Linderhof.

KLOSTER ETTAL 𝆑

Kloster Ettal, on Kaiser-Ludwig-Platz at Ettal (© **08822/740;** www.kloster-ettal.de), lies in a lovely valley sheltered by the steep hills of the Ammergau. Duke Ludwig the Bavarian founded this abbey in 1330. Monks, knights, and their ladies shared the honor of guarding its statue of the Virgin, attributed to Giovanni Pisano. In the 18th century, the golden age of the abbey, there were about 70,000 pilgrims here every year.

The **Church of Our Lady,** within the abbey, is one of the finest examples of Bavarian rococo architecture in existence. The impressive baroque facade was built from a plan based on the designs of Enrico Zuccali. Around the polygonal core of the church is a two-story gallery. Visitors stand under a vast dome and admire the **fresco,** painted by John Jacob Zeiller in the summers of 1751 and 1752.

The abbey stands 3km (2 miles) south of Oberammergau, along the road to Garmisch-Partenkirchen. Admission is free, and it's open daily 8am to 7pm year-round. Buses from Oberammergau leave from the Rathaus and the Bahnhof once per hour during the day, with round-trip fare 8€ ($13). Call the **RVO Bus Company** in Garmisch-Partenkirchen (© **08821/948274**) for information.

11

Lake Constance (Bodensee)

Mild climate and plentiful sunshine make Lake Constance (*Bodensee* in German) a top vacation spot for lovers of sun and sand, as well as for sightseers and spa-goers. The hillsides that slope to the water's edge are covered with vineyards and orchards and are dotted with colorful hamlets and busy tourist centers. Cruise ships and ferries link every major center around the lake. Although the lake's 260km (160-mile) shoreline is shared by three nations—Austria, Germany, and Switzerland—the area around the lake is united in a common cultural and historical heritage.

Lake Constance is actually divided into three lakes, although the name is frequently applied only to the largest of these, the Obersee. The western end of the Obersee separates into two distinct branches: the Überlingersee is a long fjord, while the Untersee is more irregular, jutting in and out of marshland and low-lying woodland. The two branches are connected by a narrow channel—which is actually the upper Rhine.

The lake offers a wealth of **activities,** including swimming, sailing, windsurfing, diving, and rowing. You can swim either in the cold waters of the lake itself, or in one of the heated lakeside pools. The Eichwald Lido at Lindau boasts a 1km-long (½-mile) "beach," with plenty of lawns for sunbathing German-style. The other popular place for lakeside swimming at a heated pool is the Jakob Lido at Constance. One of the best ways to see the lake is to cycle around it. You can rent **bicycles** at all the major train stations, including Lindau and Konstanz.

Sailing on Lake Constance is a major attraction. Some boatyards and sailing schools rent boats; you'll be asked to show some proof of proficiency (a certification from a sailing school, for example). Or you can rent rowboats and motorboats at all major hotels along the lake.

From Munich, motorists should take the B12, via Landsberg and Kempten, to reach the lake. Drivers from Frankfurt head south along the A81 Autobahn to Memmingen, transferring to B18. The nearest international airport to Lake Constance is at Zürich, 79km (49 miles) southwest of the town of Konstanz. The Munich airport is about 225km (140 miles) north of the lake.

1 Lindau ★★

179km (111 miles) SW of Munich, 32km (20 miles) S of Ravensburg

Lindau dates from the end of the 9th century. It was a free imperial town of the Holy Roman Empire from the Middle Ages to 1804, when it became a part of Bavaria. For centuries, it was a center of trade between Bavaria and Switzerland.

Its unique setting on an island at the eastern end of Lake Constance made Lindau a prime tourist attraction. Today this garden city is under landmark protection and has outgrown its boundaries and spread to the shores of the mainland. It now caters to the tourist's every whim, from sunbathing to baccarat. Lindau is a charming city.

You can wander at will through the maze of winding narrow streets lined with houses that have stood the test of time. At the harbor stand two **lighthouses:** One, Mangturm, was built in the 1200s, the other in 1856. Each tower is some 37m (120 ft.) tall and can be climbed by the athletic via narrow spiral staircases. The reward is a panoramic vista of the Alps, both Swiss and Austrian. Another interesting building is the 15th-century **Rathaus.**

ESSENTIALS

GETTING THERE   Lindau is connected to the mainland by a road bridge and a causeway for walkers and trains. It's a transportation link between the western part of Lake Constance and the towns of Austria and Switzerland, which lie directly across the water. Regional flights come in to the Friedrichshafen airport (see "Essentials" in section 2). The nearest major airport is Zürich.

By Train   The Lindau Bahnhof is on the major Basel-Singen-Radolfzell-Lindau and Lindau-Kissleg-Memmingen-Buchloe rail lines, with frequent connections in all directions. Call ℭ **01805/99-66-33,** or visit www.bahn.de for information.

By Bus   Regional bus service along Lake Constance is offered by **RAB Regionalverkehr Alb-Bodensee GmbH** in Lindau (ℭ **08382/509220**).

By Ferry   Five to seven ferries per day (depending on the season) link Lindau with Konstanz. Before reaching Lindau, boats stop at Meersburg, Mainau, and Friedrichshafen; the entire trip takes 3 hours. Call the tourist office for information and schedules.

By Car   Access by car from Munich is via autobahns A96 and B31.

VISITOR INFORMATION   Tourist-Information is at Ludwigstrasse 68 (ℭ **08382/26-00-30**). The office is open May to September Monday to Friday 9am to 1pm and 2 to 7pm, Saturday and Sunday 2 to 7pm; from October to April it is open Monday to Friday 9am to 1pm and 2 to 5pm.

WHERE TO STAY

Hotel Bayerischer Hof ★★★   This old-world hotel outshines all its competitors in Lindau. It opens onto the lakeside promenade and looks almost like a hotel on the Mediterranean. The atmosphere and service here are first-rate. The large rooms are Lindau's finest, each well furnished with traditional styling, and the bathrooms contain tub/shower combos. Most have good views; the less desirable units overlook a narrow thoroughfare.

Seepromenade, 88131 Lindau. ℭ **800/223-5652** in the U.S. and Canada, or 08382/91-50. Fax 08382/91-55-91. www.bayerischerhof-lindau.de. 97 units. 175€–314€ ($280–$502) double; 291€ ($466) junior suite; 445€–469€ ($712–$750) suite. Children 9 and under stay free in parent's room. Rates include buffet breakfast. AE, DC, MC, V. Parking 11€ ($17). **Amenities:** 2 restaurants; bar; lounge; outdoor heated pool; health club; sauna; steam room; room service; massage; laundry service; dry cleaning; nonsmoking rooms; rooms for those w/limited mobility. *In room:* TV, Wi-Fi, minibar, hair dryer, iron, safe.

Hotel-Garni Brugger *Value*   This modest, charming little hotel is the best affordable choice in Lindau. It's pleasingly proportioned, with a gabled attic and French doors that open onto the balconies in the back. The small rooms are up-to-date, furnished in a functional modern style, with lots of light; each comes with a small, tiled bathroom with shower. The winter garden is filled with potted plants. The location is an easy walk from the lake and casino.

Lake Constance

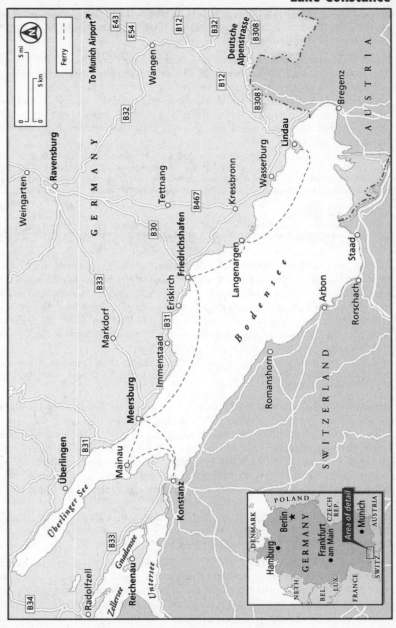

Bei der Heidenmauer 11, 88131 Lindau. ℭ **08382/9-34-10**. Fax 08382/41-33. www.hotel-garni-brugger.de. 23 units. 86€–98€ ($138–$157) double. Additional bed 26€ ($42). Rates include buffet breakfast. AE, DC, MC, V. Parking 7€ ($11). **Amenities:** Breakfast room; lounge. *In room:* TV, minibar.

Hotel Reutemann und Seegarten ★★   Located next to its parent, the superior Bayerischer Hof, this hotel has two villas. The Reutemann has large rooms and bathrooms with showers and huge tubs. The Seegarten, with little flower-filled balconies and trailing vines, has spacious and handsome rooms, especially those with lake views (which cost more, naturally). Bathrooms at Seegarten are smaller, with either tub/shower combos or shower stalls. Both villas have their own waterfront gardens with furniture for sunbathing.

Seepromenade, 88131 Lindau. ℭ **08382/91-50**. Fax 08382/91-55-91. www.bayerischerhof-lindau.de. 64 units. 125€–226€ ($200–$362) double. Children 9 and under stay free in parent's room. AE, DC, MC, V. Parking 11€ ($18). **Amenities:** Restaurant; lounge; heated outdoor pool; fitness center; sauna; steam room; room service; massage; babysitting; laundry service; dry cleaning; nonsmoking rooms. *In room:* TV, Wi-Fi, minibar, hair dryer, iron, safe.

WHERE TO DINE

Hotel Villino ★★ *Finds* ITALIAN/ASIAN   In the suburb of Hoyren, this hotel is better known for its excellent Italian restaurant than for its bedrooms. Only dinner is served, in a comfortable room decorated in high-tech Milanese style. The elegant menu includes pesto-laced spaghetti, Sicilian-style fish soup, a heaping platter of scampi served with stuffed squid and fresh tomatoes, anglerfish and lobster fried with cardamom, and a particularly succulent version of leg of lamb with garlic sauce. A fine Asian menu features sushi, Thai soup, and such dishes as filet of veal or pikeperch with Asian spicing.

The establishment maintains 16 rooms, priced at 150€ to 240€ ($240–$384) each, plus one suite at 390€ ($624). Each unit has a private balcony, minibar, TV, and telephone. Rates include breakfast, and parking is free.

Hoyren (1km/½ mile east of Lindau's center), Hoyerberg 34. ℭ **08382/93-450**. Fax 08382/93-45-12. www.villino.de. Reservations recommended. Main courses 34€ ($54); fixed-price 4-course menu 86€ ($138), 5-courses 96€ ($154). MC, V. Tues–Sun 6pm–midnight.

Hoyerberg Schlössle ★★★ FRENCH   This fine hotel lies about a 15-minute drive from the Altstadt (old town). The inner dining room is beautifully decorated, with a view of the mountains and lake. You can also dine on the two terraces. Continental delicacies include cream of scampi soup, Bodensee pikeperch stuffed with champagne-flavored herbs, and Allgäuer saddle of venison with small flour dumplings and French beans. Meals here are memorable; the chef has great flair and doesn't oversauce the food. In the afternoon the restaurant serves as a cafe, offering light snacks and drinks.

Hoyerbergstrasse 64, at Lindau-Aeschach. ℭ **08382/2-52-95**. www.hoyerbergschloessle.de. Reservations required for dinner. Main courses 22€–29€ ($35–$46); fixed-price menu 64€–80€ ($102–$128). AE, DC, MC, V. Restaurant Wed–Sun noon–2pm and Tues–Sun 6–10pm; cafe Tues–Sun 2–4:30pm. Closed Feb.

Zum Sünfzen GERMAN/BAVARIAN   This 14th-century, all-wood restaurant at the end of Maximilianstrasse serves good, reasonably priced food. Dishes range from roast pork with vegetables to filet of venison. Fresh fish from Lake Constance is a specialty. The food is the type you might be served in a middle-class private home along the lake.

Maximilianstrasse 1. ℭ **08382/58-65**. Reservations recommended. Main dishes 10€–25€ ($16–$40). AE, DC, MC, V. Daily 10am–2pm and 6–9pm.

EXPLORING LINDAU

A tour of this *Ferieninsel* (holiday island) begins with the **old harbor,** seen from the lakeside promenade. The **Mangturm,** the old lighthouse, stands on the promenade as a reminder of the heavy fortifications that once surrounded the city. It also marks where Lindau was once divided into two islands. The harbor entrance is marked by the 33m (108-ft.) **New Lighthouse** and the **Bavarian Lion,** standing guard as yachts and commercial ships pass by below.

Hauptstrasse, in the center of the town, is the main street of the Altstadt. The most easily recognizable building is the **Altes Rathaus,** erected in 1422. The stepped gables are typical of the period, but the building's facade also combines many later styles of architecture. The interior, once used as a council hall, is the town library. Frescoes represent scenes from a session of the 1496 Imperial Diet.

Just north of Hauptstrasse is the town's most familiar landmark, the round **Diebsturm (Thieves' Tower),** with its turreted roof. Next to it is the oldest building in Lindau, the 11th-century **St. Peter's Church,** which houses a war memorial chapel. In the church is a group of frescoes by Hans Holbein the Elder.

Returning to Hauptstrasse, which cuts through the exact center of the island, follow the street eastward to the **Haus zum Cavazzen,** Am Marktplatz (© **08382/94-40-73**), the handsomest patrician house on Lake Constance. It holds the municipal art collection. Included are exhibits of sculpture and painting from the Gothic, Renaissance, and baroque periods. Some of the rooms are furnished with period pieces showing how wealthy citizens lived in the 18th and 19th centuries. Among the rarities is a collection of mechanical musical instruments. This attraction is open April to October Tuesday to Friday and Sunday 11am to 5pm, plus Saturday 2 to 5pm. Admission is 2.50€ ($4) adults, 1€ ($1.60) students and children 6 to 15; for a guided tour there is an extra charge of 2€ ($3.20) per person.

Passing across Am Marktplatz and by the Collegiate Church and St. Stephen's Church, both baroque, you come to the strange pile of rocks known as **Heathen's Wall,** dating from Roman times. Beyond this is the **Stadtgarten (Town Garden)** which, although peaceful during the day, livens up at night when the wheels of the town's casino begin to spin.

OUTDOOR PURSUITS

For decades it was possible to rent bikes at the train station, but no more. Today, rentals are available at **Unger's Fahrradverleih,** Insel Graben 14 (© **08382/943688**), close to the train station. The price ranges from 6€ to 15€ ($9.60–$24) per day. The outfitter is open Monday to Friday 9am to 1pm and 2 to 6pm, Saturday 9am to 1pm and 3 to 6pm, and Sunday 9am to 1pm. Lindenhofpark is the most scenic area (it's also ideal for a picnic).

The town has three lakeside **beaches,** all open in summer Monday to Friday 10:30am to 7:30pm and Saturday and Sunday 10am to 8pm. The biggest beach is **Eichwald,** about a half-hour walk away along Uferweg (to the right if you're facing the harbor); or take bus no. 1 or 2 to Anheggerstrasse, then bus no. 3 to Karmelbuckel. Admission is 3€ ($4.80) for adults, 1€ ($1.60) for children. To reach **Lindenhofbad,** take bus no. 1 or 2 to Anheggerstrasse, then bus no. 4 to Alwind. Admission is 4€ ($6.40) for adults and 2€ ($3.20) for children. If you're driving, follow the signs to B31; stay on B31 until you see the exit marked Schachen.

You can rent **windsurfers** at **Kreitmeir,** In der Grub 17 (© **08382/23330**), for 15€ ($24) per hour. At the little dock next to Lindau's rail bridge, you can rent a **paddleboat** for 10€ ($16), a motorboat for 20€ ($32), or an electric boat for 17€ ($27) from **Bootsvermietung Hodrius** (© **08382/29-77-71**).

SHOPPING

Michael Zeller is known throughout Bavaria for a twice-yearly **Internationale-Bodensee-Kunstauktion (art auction)** held in the spring and fall (dates vary) and a much smaller auction in December. His year-round store, **Michael Zeller,** 3 Bindergasse (© **08382/9-30-20;** www.zeller.de), has Lindau's best selection of watercolors, engravings, and prints, along with jewelry, porcelain, and furniture. For the best selection of pottery, head for **Angelika Ochsenreiter,** Ludwigstrasse 29 (© **08382/2-38-67**), which has teapots, cups, dishes, and animal figures.

LINDAU AFTER DARK

Lindau's casino, **Chelles Alle 1** (© **08382/27-740**), offers slot machines from noon to 2am and blackjack and roulette from 3pm to 2am (until 3am Friday to Saturday). The bet ceiling is 12,000€ ($19,200) for roulette. Admission is 2.50€ ($4), and a passport is required as proof of age. Men should wear a jacket and tie.

2 Friedrichshafen

22km (14 miles) W of Lindau, 20km (12 miles) S of Ravensburg

Friedrichshafen is at the northeastern corner of the Bodensee, near the lake's widest point. This mostly modern city was almost completely rebuilt after World War II. It has one of the longest waterfront exposures of any town along the lake. Besides that, the town's highlights are two interesting museums and the dome-capped **Schlosskirche,** the premier reminder of Friedrichshafen's baroque past.

ESSENTIALS

GETTING THERE   By Air   The **Friedrichshafen** airport (© **07541/28401**) lies 5km (3 miles) north of town. Flights to Friedrichshafen come in from Frankfurt, Vienna, Cologne, London's Stanstead Airport, and Berlin. For access to flights deriving from cities not mentioned above, consider flying into Zürich's airport, which lies about 100km (60 miles) away.

By Train   Friedrichshafen is the largest railway junction along the northern edge of the Bodensee and is a major transfer point for rail passengers going on to other cities and resorts along the lake. The town has two railway stations, the **Stadtbahnhof** (© **07541/31390**), in the center, and the **Hafenbahnhof** (© **07541/372717**), along the Seestrasse, about 1km (¾ mile) away. Both of these stations are interconnected by bus nos. 1, 2, 4, 6, and 7. Trains arrive from Ulm and Stuttgart at intervals of 1 to 1½ hours throughout the day. For information and schedules, call © **01805/99-66-33.**

By Bus   Regional bus service along Lake Constance is provided by **RAB Regionalverkehr Alb-Bodensee GmbH** in Lindau (© **08382/509220**).

By Car   Friedrichshafen is easily reached from Stuttgart and Munich. From Stuttgart, follow Autobahn 8 east to the city of Ulm, then turn south onto Route 30 into Friedrichshafen. From Munich follow Autobahn 96 west/southwest to Lindau, then head west on Route 31 along Lake Constance to Friedrichshafen.

By Boat April to October, about eight lake steamers travel between Friedrichshafen and Lindau, Bregenz (Austria), and Konstanz. For departure times and details, call **BSB** © **07541/9238389.** A ferry runs year-round between Friedrichshafen and Romanshorn, Switzerland (trip time: 40 min.) and costs 7€ ($11) for adults and 3.50€ ($5.60) for children ages 6 to 15.

VISITOR INFORMATION The city's **Tourist Information Office** is at Bahnhofplatz 2 (© **07541/30010;** www.friedrichshafen.de). It's open May to September Monday to Friday 9am to 6pm, Saturday 9am to 1pm; October and April Monday to Thursday 9am to noon and 2 to 5pm, and Friday 9am to noon; and November to March Monday to Thursday 9am to noon and 2 to 4pm, and Friday 9am to noon.

WHERE TO STAY
Buchhorner Hof 𝕽 This charming lakeside hotel, the best in town, provides a compromise between the luxurious, modern comfort of larger hotels and the traditional hospitality of smaller inns. It's housed in Friedrichshafen's oldest building. Rooms are well furnished, and each comes with a midsize modern bathroom with tub/shower combination. The restaurant serves adequate fare at lunch and dinner, and the bar is a cozy retreat.

Friedrichstrasse 33, 88045 Friedrichshafen. © **07541/20-50.** Fax 07541/3-26-63. www.buchhornerhof.de. 96 units. 100€–260€ ($160–$416) double; 255€ ($408) suite. AE, DC, MC, V. Parking 10€ ($16). **Amenities:** Restaurant; bar; health spa; 2 whirlpools; sauna; solarium; steam room; bike rental; room service; laundry service; dry cleaning; nonsmoking rooms; rooms for those w/limited mobility. *In room:* TV, Wi-Fi, minibar, hair dryer.

Hotel Goldenes-Rad Located in the pedestrian center in the middle of town, this traditional hotel is a short walk from Lake Constance, the ferry, and the Zeppelin Museum. Rooms are comfortable and modern, with showers and cosmetic mirrors. The location is not very car-friendly; however, the hotel does have a parking lot nearby. The English-speaking staff is courteous and helpful.

Karlstrasse 43, 88045 Friedrichshafen. © **800/528-1234** or 07541/28-50. Fax 07541/28-52-85. www.goldenes-rad.de. 70 units. 119€–129€ ($190–$206) double; 129€–189€ ($206–$302) suite. Rates include buffet breakfast. AE, DC, MC, V. Parking 5€ ($8). **Amenities:** Restaurant; lounge; fitness center; sauna; bike rental; room service; massage; laundry service; dry cleaning; nonsmoking rooms. *In room:* TV, Wi-Fi, minibar, hair dryer, safe.

Seehotel 𝕽 *Finds* This is one of the most appealing hotels in town, almost in the same league as the Buchhorner Hof. It's right beside the Seepromenade. The small rooms are decorated sensibly, even stylishly. Some have air-conditioning; most have views of the water. All the bedrooms have midsize bathrooms, mostly with tub/shower combinations. The staff is sensitive and well trained.

Bahnhofplatz 2 (near the railway station), 88045 Friedrichshafen. © **07541/30-30.** Fax 07541/30-31-00. www. seehotelfn.de. 132 units. 129€–185€ ($206–$296) double; 176€–272€ ($282–$435) suite. AE, DC, MC, V. Free outside parking, 11€ ($18) inside. **Amenities:** Restaurant; bar; health spa; sauna; steam room; room service; laundry service; dry cleaning; nonsmoking rooms. *In room:* A/C (in some), TV, Wi-Fi, minibar, hair dryer, safe.

WHERE TO DINE
Hotel-Restaurant Maier 𝕽 *Finds* INTERNATIONAL/GERMAN In the center of the hamlet of Fischbach, at the edge of the lake, this hotel is best known for its restaurant. Local diners appreciate the generous, well-prepared dishes, the attentive service, and the sweeping views over the lake. One dining room is contemporary and modern, the other a re-creation of a traditional *Stube* in the mountains. Some of the best items on the menu include chicken breast in lemon sauce, pork filet with herbs and a sweet-pepper sauce, or else pork filet with fresh mushrooms and roasted onions.

Rebirth of the Zeppelin

The zeppelin fell out of favor in 1937 when the *Hindenburg* blew up in New Jersey, but its postmillennium sibling glides peacefully over Lake Constance. (Don't worry. The new zeppelin is much smaller and rises with inert helium gas, not the explosive hydrogen used by the *Hindenburg*.) The airship, named *Bodensee*, can climb to 2,325m (7,750 ft.). The newer vessel carries 12 passengers and a crew of two, as opposed to the *Hindenburg*, which carried 100 aboard. Cruising at approximately 54kmph (34 mph) over the scenic lake, it takes passengers on hour-long flights scheduled daily, costing 355€ ($568) per person Monday to Friday, or 390€ ($624) on weekends. For more information and takeoff points along the lake, visit **www.zeppelinflug.de**.

The hotel contains 49 rooms, each with TV, minibar, and telephone. Doubles cost 85€ to 150€ ($136–$240) and include breakfast and free parking. Most rooms are air-conditioned.

Poststrasse 1–3, Fischbach (6km/4 miles west of Friedrichshafen). ✆ **07541/40-40**. www.hotel-maier.de. Reservations recommended. Main courses 10€–23€ ($16–$37). AE, DC, MC, V. Sat–Thurs 11:30am–2pm; daily 5:30–10pm.

Restaurant Kurgarten INTERNATIONAL   Depending on the time of day, this place might look like a cafe, a bar, or a restaurant. It has a beautiful view over its own garden and the lake, and there's a wide range of tasty menu items. Vegetarian choices include mushrooms stuffed with spinach and zucchini stuffed with ratatouille. Other good options include an Argentine beefsteak with herb butter and grilled scampi on noodles with slices of local vegetables and salad.

Olgastrasse 20. ✆ **07541/3-20-33**. Reservations not necessary. Main courses 10€–25€ ($16–$40). MC, V. Daily 11:30am–11pm.

EXPLORING FRIEDRICHSHAFEN

The best thing to do in town is to stroll the lake-fronting **Seepromenade,** with its sweeping view that extends on clear days all the way to the Swiss Alps. Cycling along the broad Seestrasse is also a delight. A kiosk within the Stadtbahnhof rents bikes for 8€ to 10€ ($13–$16) a day.

The town's architectural highlight is the 17th-century **Schlosskirche,** Schlossstrasse 33 (✆ **07541/21308**). The palatial ecclesiastical buildings that were once part of the church's monastery were converted in the 1800s into a palace for the kings of Württemberg. Today, they're privately owned. The church is well worth a visit, but it's open only Easter to October daily 9am to 6pm.

Zeppelin-Museum (✆ **07541/38010**; www.zeppelin-museum.de), in the Hafenbahnhof, Seestrasse 22, is a tribute to Count Ferdinand von Zeppelin. Around 1900, this native of Konstanz invented and tested the aircraft that bore his name. The museum has a re-creation of the giant and historic zeppelin *Hindenburg,* including a full-scale replica of its passenger cabins. The famous blimp exploded in a catastrophic fire in New Jersey in 1937, possibly because of sabotage. The museum also has memorabilia associated with zeppelins and their inventor. May to October, it's open Tuesday to Sunday 9am to 5pm; November to April, hours are Tuesday to Sunday

10am to 5pm. Admission is 8€ ($13) for adults and 3.50€ ($5.60) for children 16 and under.

Of interest to students of educational techniques is Friedrichshafen's **Schulmuseum,** Friedrichstrasse 14 (© **07541/32622**), which traces the development of education between 1850 (when classes were taught by monks and nuns) and 1930 (when education was the responsibility of the German state). The museum is near the Schlosskirche in the historic heart of town. Look for reconstructions of schoolrooms from periods in the 19th and 20th centuries. April to October, it's open daily 10am to 5pm; November to March, hours are Tuesday to Sunday 2 to 5pm. Admission is 3€ ($4.80) for adults and 1€ ($1.60) for children.

3 Meersburg ⭐

190km (118 miles) S of Stuttgart, 143km (89 miles) SE of Freiburg

Like the towns of Italy's Lake District, this village on the northern shore of Lake Constance cascades in terraces down the hillside to the water. The heart of Meersburg is a pedestrian area. You can drive into town as far as the Neues Schloss, where you must leave your car and continue on foot. In the center, the streets become narrow promenades and steps wander up and down the hillside. From the dock, large and small boats set out for trips on the water. Many watersports are available. One charming feature of Meersburg is the town watchman who still makes nightly rounds, keeping alive an ancient tradition.

ESSENTIALS

GETTING THERE   By Plane   Regional flights come into the Friedrichshafen airport, 20km (12 miles) from Meersburg. The nearest international airport is at Zürich, 80km (50 miles) away.

By Train   The nearest rail station is in **Überlingen,** 14km (9 miles) away, on the Basel-Singen-Radolfzell-Lindau rail line, with frequent connections in all directions. Call © **01805/99-66-33** for more information. From Überlingen station, buses depart for Meersburg at 30-minute intervals every day from 6:15am to 9:45pm, charging 8€ ($13) each way. Buses are marked either MEERSBURG or FRIEDRICHSHAFEN but always bear no. 7395 on the front.

By Bus   Buses arrive about every 30 minutes throughout the day from Friedrichshafen. Regional bus service along Lake Constance is provided by **RAB Regionalverkehr Alb-Bodensee GmbH** in Friedrichshafen (© **07541/30130**).

By Ferry   Regular ferry service goes to the town of Konstanz.

By Car   Access by car is via the A7 Autobahn from the north or Highway B31. You can drive from Munich in about 3 hours, from Frankfurt in about 4½ hours, and from Stuttgart in about 2 hours.

VISITOR INFORMATION   For tourist information, contact the **Meersburg Tourismus,** Kirchstrasse 4 (© **07532/44-04-00**). May to October, it's open Monday to Friday 9am to 12:30pm and 2 to 6pm; November to May, it's open Monday to Friday 9am to noon and 2 to 4:30pm.

SPECIAL EVENTS   The surrounding vineyards produce excellent wine, and on the second weekend in September, winemakers around the lake come to Meersburg for the **Lake Constance Wine Festival.**

WHERE TO STAY

Gasthof zum Bären *(★ (Value*   This picture-book hotel in the heart of town offers the best value in Meersburg. There's an ornately decorated corner tower, purple wisteria covers most of the facade, and window boxes overflow with red geraniums. The hotel was built in 1605 on the foundations of a building from 1250 (the cellar of the original Bären is still here). Its small rooms are attractive, snug, and cozily furnished.

Marktplatz 11, 88709 Meersburg. © **07532/4-32-20.** Fax 07532/43-22-44. www.baeren-meersburg.de. 20 units. 82€–108€ ($131–$173) double. Rates include buffet breakfast. No credit cards. Parking 6€ ($9.60). Closed mid-Nov to mid-Mar. **Amenities:** Restaurant. *In room:* TV.

Hotel Garni Eden   Built in 1971, this modern and contemporary-looking, white-walled chalet is a 5-minute uphill walk from the lake's edge. Most visitors come for rest, relaxation, and calm, spending quiet time reading in their rooms or on their private terrace or balcony, strolling around the lake, or exploring Meersburg—its flower-filled center (and its restaurants) lies about 450m (1,500 ft.) away. Bedrooms have simple, angular furniture and a well-scrubbed sense of tidiness. Other than breakfast, no meals are served, but in light of the many restaurants within a very short walk, no one seems to care.

Menizhoferweg 4, 88709 Meersburg. © **07532/43050.** Fax 07532/430533. www.hotel-meersburg.de. 19 units. 90€–139€ ($144–$222) double. Rates include continental breakfast. AE, MC, V. Free parking. **Amenities:** Breakfast room; nonsmoking rooms. *In room:* TV, minibar, hair dryer, safe.

Romantik Hotel Residenz am See *(★★★*   In an idyllic waterfront setting, this hotel is not only the town's best, with the best cuisine, but it's enveloped by vineyards, and its rooms open onto panoramic vistas of the Bodensee. Most of the Romantik hotels in the chain are traditional German, but this one is contemporary in styling, with tasteful, elegantly furnished rooms, both public and private. Rooms, ranging from midsize to spacious, are individually furnished, each most comfortable with a first-rate bathroom with tub and shower. Even if you're not a guest, consider dining here, though you should call first for a reservation. As befits its lakeside setting, fish is the chef's specialty, especially pikeperch. It's a choice little gem, so reserve early in the peak of the summer.

Uferpromenade 11, 88709 Meersburg. © **07532/80040.** Fax 07532/800-470. www.romantikhotels.com. 24 units. 155€–225€ ($248–$360) double; 245€–295€ ($392–$472) suite. Rates include breakfast. AE, MC, V. **Amenities:** Restaurant; bar; room service; laundry service; dry cleaning. *In room:* TV, Wi-Fi, minibar, hair dryer.

Seehotel Off *(★ (Finds*   Unique on the lake, this little charmer lies on the waterfront near vineyards. Its lake terrace and winter garden are just some of the special features of the domain of Elisabeth Off and her husband, Michael Off, a master chef. Most of the attractively furnished, midsize bedrooms have a view of the lake, often from a private balcony. This is a very eco-sensitive hotel—for example, all units can be insulated from electricity so as to avoid any "electrosmog." Throughout the hotel its furnishings are modern, harmonious, and well balanced, and about a dozen rooms are designed according to feng shui principles. An on-site health center features everything from aromatherapy to Reiki.

Uferpromenade 51, 88709 Meersburg. © **07532/44740.** Fax 07532/447444. www.hotel.off.mbo.de. 19 units. 86€–164€ ($138–$262) double; 135€–179€ ($216–$286) suite. DC, MC, V. Parking 8€ ($13). **Amenities:** Restaurant; winter garden; outdoor pool; spa; lake terrace. *In room:* TV, Wi-Fi.

Seehotel zur Münz   If you want to save some money, and don't need glamour or a romantic atmosphere, consider checking in here. This is the simplest of our recommendations, but it's well maintained, decent, and comfortable in every way. Only a pedestrian walkway and an iron railing separate this hotel from the tree-lined lake-front. The ambience within lets you forget urban bustle. The rooms are neatly kept, all with bathrooms with tub/shower combos.

Seestrasse 7, 88709 Meersburg. © **07532/43590.** Fax 07532/77-85. www.seehotel-zur-muenz.de. 11 units. 80€–130€ ($128–$208) double. Rates include buffet breakfast. MC, V. Parking 5€ ($8) covered, 3€ ($4.80) uncovered, 8€ ($13) in garage. **Amenities:** Breakfast room. *In room:* TV.

Weinstube Löwen *&* Weinstube Löwen is a centuries-old, charming inn on the market square. Its facade has green shutters, geranium-filled window boxes, and vines reaching the upper windows under the steep roof. The Fischer family has updated its interior while keeping a homelike ambience. All but a few rooms have been modernized in a streamlined functional style. They are a bit cramped, however.

Marktplatz 2, 88709 Meersburg. © **07532/4-30-40.** Fax 07532/43-04-10. www.hotel-loewen-meersburg.de. 21 units. 80€–120€ ($128–$192) double. Rates include buffet breakfast. AE, MC, V. Parking 4.50€ ($7.20). **Amenities:** Restaurant; room service; laundry service; dry cleaning; nonsmoking rooms. *In room:* TV, safe.

WHERE TO DINE

Winzerstube zum Becher *&* REGIONAL/GERMAN   Year after year this little independently run restaurant manages to serve better food than any hotel in town. If you've come to Germany with images of a handcrafted Weinstube that radiates warmth, then you should dine here. A pea-green tile oven tucked away in a corner provides heat in winter. The chairs are not that comfortable, but the rest of the flowered, paneled, and happily cluttered room provides a cozy atmosphere. The specialty of the chef is onion-flavored Swabian *Zwiebelrostbraten* with *Spätzle*, along with a host of other specialties, including fresh fish from Lake Constance. A superb fixed-price dinner cuts down on the cost. The restaurant also offers drinks (mostly wine from their own winery) and snacks.

Höllgasse 4, near the Altes Schloss. © **07532/90-09.** Reservations required. Main courses 12€–28€ ($19–$45); fixed-price lunches 25€–33€ ($40–$53), dinners 36€–60€ ($58–$96). AE, DC, MC, V. Tues–Sun 10am–2pm and 5pm–midnight. Closed 3 weeks in Jan.

EXPLORING MEERSBURG

After you enter the town through the ancient **Obertor (Upper Gate),** you'll be on Marktplatz. Here lies the 16th-century **Rathaus,** which contains a typical German Ratskeller. Leading off from this is **Steigstrasse,** the most interesting artery, passing between rows of half-timbered houses whose arcades serve as covered walkways above the street.

Nearby, at Schlossplatz, the **Altes Schloss** *&* ((© **07532/80000)** dates from 628 and is the oldest intact German castle. All the relics of a warring age are here—clubs, flails, armor, helmets, and axes—along with 30 fully furnished rooms, decorated with pieces from various epochs. The bishops of Konstanz lived in this castle until the 18th century, when they moved to the Neues Schloss (see below). The baron of Lassberg, an admirer of medieval romance, then took over and invited Annette von Droste-Hülshoff (1797–1848), his sister-in-law and Germany's leading female poet, to come as well. She had the castle turned into a setting for artists and writers. You can visit her luxuriously furnished chambers, as well as the murky dungeons and the castle museum with its medieval jousting equipment. The castle is open March to October daily 9am to 6:30pm, and November to February daily 10am to 6pm. Admission is 6.50€ ($10) for adults, 5€ ($8) students, and 3.50€ ($5.60) for children. Next to the castle is **Castle Mill** (1620), with a 9m (30-ft.) wooden water wheel, the oldest of its kind in Germany.

Finds **A Taste of Honey**

Just 10km (6 miles) from Meersburg is the famous Wallfahrtskirche at Birnau (© **07556/9-20-30**), 5km (3 miles) southeast of Überlingen. This pilgrimage basilica, which dates from the mid–18th century, was built in rococo style, with rose, blue, and beige marble predominating. A celebrated statuette—the Honigschlecker, or "honey-taster"—shows a baby sucking a finger as he's yanked out of a nest of bees. It's to the right of the St. Bernard altarpiece. The church is open daily 7:30am to 7pm. Admission is free.

You go from the medieval to the baroque when you enter the **Neues Schloss,** Schlossplatz (© **07532/4404900**). The leading architect of the 18th century, Balthasar Neumann, was responsible for some of the castle's design. Ceiling paintings and frescoes were done by prominent artists and craftsmen. Elegant stucco moldings grace the ceilings and walls. The Spiegelsaal, or Hall of Mirrors, is the setting for an international music festival in summer. On the top floor is the **Dornier Museum** (© **07532/431115**), which traces the history of Germany's aircraft and aerospace industries. Admission is 4.50€ ($7.20) for adults and 1.50€ ($2.40) for children 12 and under. It's open April to October daily 10am to 1pm and 2 to 6pm.

On the promenade below stands the **Great House,** which dates from 1505. It now holds ticket offices for the railway and steamer lines on Lake Constance. Regular ferry service to Konstanz leaves from the dock on the outskirts of town.

OUTDOOR PURSUITS

Rock-strewn beaches lie west of the town center; here you can go swimming or just soak up the sun for free. But the amenities are better at the **Beheiztes Freibad,** Uferpromenade 9–11 (© **07532/4402850**), a 5-minute walk east of the harbor. Here you can lie on the grass on a strip of sand adjacent to the lake, or immerse yourself in any of three outdoor swimming pools. A sauna is also on-site, plus refreshment stands and a small restaurant. Entrance to the compound costs 3.50€ ($5.60) for adults, 2€ ($3.20) for students, and 1.50€ ($2.40) for children; it's free for children 3 and under. Hours are Monday to Thursday 10am to 10pm, Saturday 10am to 11pm, Sunday 8am to 9pm.

MEERSBURG AFTER DARK

Spiegelsaal (Hall of Mirrors), in the Neues Schloss at Schlossplatz, is the splendid backdrop for an annual international chamber-music festival. It takes place from the end of April through May. You may hear, for example, baroque ensembles, a string quartet, and a pianist playing the works of Schumann. Tickets start at 16€ ($26). Call © **07541/2033300** for information.

The **Konstanz Stadttheater,** the oldest theater in Germany, dating from 1609, moves to its summer theater in Meersburg during July and August. For more details about the Meersburg program offerings, call © **07531/13-90-01-01** or 07531/900154.

Other than the cultural offerings mentioned above, after dark in Meersburg means taking a romantic stroll along the Uferpromenade bordering the lake and visiting one of the bars or *Bierhalles.* The most charming and traditional place for a drink is at the **Winzerstube zum Becher,** which also is our preferred choice for dining (see above), although you can visit just for drinks. On the Market Square, another fun place to go in the evening is the **Weinstube Löwen** (see above), a delightful, centuries-old inn covered in vines. If you like your drinks enjoyed with a lake view, head for the **Seehotel Off,** Uferpromenade (© 07532/44740), fronting the Bodensee. It's especially romantic around here at night.

4 Konstanz (Constance) ⚓

179km (111 miles) S of Stuttgart, 76km (47 miles) NE of Zürich

Crowded against the shores of Lake Constance by the borders of Switzerland, the medieval town of Konstanz had nowhere to grow but northward across the river. Today this resort city lies on both banks of the Rhine, as the river begins its long journey to the North Sea. Its strategic position made Konstanz the most important city on the lake. Nowadays tourists come to enjoy the shops, the largest beach in the area, and the magical beauty of nearby **Mainau Island.**

ESSENTIALS

GETTING THERE   By Train   Konstanz is on the main Konstanz-Singen-Villingen-Offenburg rail line, the Schwarzwaldbahn, with frequent connections to the major cities of Germany. For information, call © 01805/99-66-33.

By Bus   Regiónal bus service around Konstanz is provided by **SBG Südbaden Bus GmbH** at Radolfzell (© 07732/9-94-70).

By Boat   Ferry service and lake cruises operate between Konstanz, Mainau Island, Meersburg, Lindau, and Bregenz. The operator is **Bodensee-Schiffsbetriebe,** Hafenstrasse 6 (© 07531/36-40-389).

By Car   Access by car is via the B33.

VISITOR INFORMATION   Contact **Tourist-Information,** Bahnhofplatz 13 (© 07531/13-30-30). April to October, the office is open Monday to Friday 9am to 6:30pm, Saturday 9am to 4pm, and Sunday 10am to 1pm; hours November to March are Monday to Friday 9:30am to 12:30pm and 2 to 6pm.

WHERE TO STAY

Barbarossa ⚓ *Kids*   The Wiedemann family welcomes you to this time-tested favorite which has both modern and traditional architectural elements. Rooms come in a wide array of options, from a small, simple single to a large double. All the accommodations have been modernized and are comfortably furnished. Rooms are individually decorated and many have their own themes, such as Romeo and Juliet for romantic stopovers or Barbarossa for more "warlike" guests. A number of family rooms are also rented, suitable for three to four guests.

Obermarkt 8, 78462 Konstanz. © 07531/128990. Fax 07531/12899-700. www.barbarossa-hotel.com. 55 units. 105€–120€ ($168–$192) double; 110€–130€ ($176–$208) family unit. AE, DC, MC, V. **Amenities:** Restaurant; bar; room service; laundry service; Internet access; nonsmoking rooms. *In room:* TV.

Buchner Hof   Though located in Petershausen, this hotel is just a short walk from most points of interest. The pleasantly furnished rooms range from small to medium. Some bathrooms have showers only, others tub/shower combos. The hotel is named after composer Hans Buchner, who became organist at the town cathedral in 1510 and was one of the first musicians to arrange and catalog the wealth of Gregorian chants found in the region.

Buchnerstrasse 6 (in Petershausen, across the Rhine from Konstanz), 78464 Konstanz. ℭ 07531/8-10-20. Fax 07531/81-02-40. www.buchner-hof.de. 13 units. 110€–140€ ($176–$224) double. Rates include buffet breakfast. AE, DC, MC, V. Free outdoor parking; 10€ ($16) in garage. Closed Dec 23–Jan 7. **Amenities:** Breakfast room; sauna; solarium; laundry service; dry cleaning. *In room:* TV, minibar, hair dryer.

Steigenberger Inselhotel 𝕽𝕽𝕽   The Insel started life as a Dominican monastery in the 13th century; now it's the single finest place to stay along the German side of the lake. It has a prime location—on an island, with its own lakeside gardens and dock. The white step-gabled building holds an inner Romanesque cloister. Most of the spacious doubles have a living-room look, with sofas, armchairs, and tidy bathrooms with tub/shower combos.

Auf der Insel 1, 78462 Konstanz. ℭ 800/223-5652 in the U.S. and Canada, or 07531/12-50. Fax 07531/125-250. www.konstanz.steigenberger.com. 102 units. 224€–278€ ($358–$445) double; 310€–400€ ($496–$640) suite. Rates include buffet breakfast. AE, DC, MC, V. Parking 7€ ($11). **Amenities:** 2 restaurants; bar; fitness room; sauna; solarium; room service; babysitting; laundry service; dry cleaning; nonsmoking rooms; rooms for those w/limited mobility; lake facilities. *In room:* TV, Wi-Fi, minibar, hair dryer, safe.

WHERE TO DINE

Casino Restaurant am See 𝕽 INTERNATIONAL   If you happen to lose at roulette during one of your outings in Konstanz, you can revive your spirits (and drink a few, too) on the lakeside terrace of this casino restaurant. The view is lovely and the food first-rate. The restaurant offers a good choice of dishes; try the fresh fish or saddle of lamb. The food is complemented by a good wine cellar.

Seestrasse 21. ℭ 07531/81-57-65. Reservations required. Jacket required for men in the casino. Main courses 8€–30€ ($13–$48); fixed-price menu 38€ ($61). AE, DC, MC, V. Sun–Thurs 6pm–1am; Fri–Sat 6pm–3am.

NEARBY DINING

Schwedenschenke *(Finds* GERMAN/SWEDISH   Visitors sometimes make a pilgrimage to Mainau Island in Lake Constance for a meal in this old-fashioned restaurant. The chef's specialty is assorted lake fish, including perch, pikeperch, and trout. You can also try Hungarian goulash, Swedish meatballs in cream sauce, and *Tafelspitz* (boiled beef with horseradish sauce).

Mainau Island. ℭ 07531/30-31-56. Reservations recommended. Main courses lunch 10€–26€ ($16–$42), dinner 18€–32€ ($29–$51). AE, DC, MC, V. May–Sept daily 9am–11pm; Mar–Apr and Oct Sun–Wed 11am–6pm, Fri–Sat 9am–11pm. Bus: 4 from the center of Konstanz.

EXPLORING KONSTANZ

The best way to see Konstanz is from the water. The **shoreline** 𝕽 is fascinating, with little inlets that weave in and out around ancient buildings and city gardens. Several pleasure ships offer tours along the city shoreline and across the lake to Meersburg and several other destinations. Contact **Bodensee-Schiffsbetriebe,** Hafenstrasse 6 (ℭ **07531/3640389;** www.bsb-online.com). The timetable for ferries changes every month, so check locally. The cost is 7€ to 13€ ($11–$21) with a car, 2.50€ ($4) without a car. For information, contact **Stadtwerke Konstanz** (ℭ **07531/8030;** http://sw.konstanz.de).

During the summer, outdoor concerts are presented in the **city gardens.** Below the gardens is the **Council Building,** where the Council of Constance met. The building was originally constructed as a storehouse in 1388 but came to be used for meetings. The hall was restored in 1911 and decorated with murals depicting the history of the town. On the harbor in front is an **obelisk** erected in memory of Count Ferdinand von Zeppelin, the citizen of Konstanz who invented the dirigible in the late 19th century.

The towers of the Romanesque **basilica** rise behind the city garden. Begun in 1052, this church took centuries to complete. The neo-Gothic spire was added only in 1856. During the Council of Constance, the members of the synod met here. From the top tower, a view opens onto the lake and the city.

MAINAU ISLAND 🟊🟊 The unusual, almost tropical island of Mainau lies 6km (4 miles) north of Konstanz, in the arm of the Bodensee known as the Überlingersee. Here, palms and orange trees grow and fragrant flowers bloom year-round, practically in the shadow of the snow-covered Alps. The Baden princes discovered long ago that the island, protected from harsh winter winds, enjoys a freak microclimate where vegetation can grow year-round; the most delicate of tropical plants are given greenhouse protection, however. In the center of this botanical oasis is an ancient castle, once a residence of the Knights of the Teutonic Order, now owned by Swedish Count Lennart Bernadotte. Only the island's gardens and parks can be visited by the public. They're open daily March to October 7am to 8pm; in winter, hours are shortened to 9am to 6pm.

There are four restaurants on the island but no overnight accommodations. You can reach Mainau either by tour boat from Konstanz or by walking across the small footbridge connecting the island to the mainland, north of the city. Admission is 14€ ($22) for adults, 7.50€ ($12) for students, 4.50€ ($7.20) for children, and free for children 11 and under. For more information, call © **07531/3030** or visit www.mainau.de.

OUTDOOR PURSUITS If you'd like to go biking along the lake, visit **Velotours,** Ernst-Sachs-Strasse 1 (© **07531/9-82-80**), where rentals cost from 14€ ($17) per day. Bike tours are available. The shop is open March to October daily 8am to 5pm.

SHOPPING

The main commercial artery, **Hussenstrasse,** has the best shopping options in this cosmopolitan town. **Jacqueline,** Hussenstrasse 29 (© **07531/2-29-90**), has stylish garments for women who seek a more mature look. Men can find tuned-in fashion, both formal and sporty, at **Pierre,** Hussenstrasse 3 (© **07531/22-150**), and **Holzherr,** Rossgartenstrasse 32 (© **07531/128730**).

KONSTANZ AFTER DARK

Classical music offerings throughout the year are numerous. The concert season of the **Bodensee Symphony Orchestra** (© **07531/90-08-10**) runs September to April, and a **summer music festival** is held mid-June to mid-July. There's also an **outdoor music festival** on the island of Mainau for 3 days in July. Contact the visitor information office (see above) for tickets, schedules, and venues. In May, the **Bodensee Festival** (© **07541/20-33-300**) offers a mix of classical concerts and theatrical productions, presented at various locations around the shores of the lake. Tickets are 15€ to 40€ ($24–$64).

Plays have been staged at the **Stadttheater Konstanz,** Konzilstrasse 11 (© **07531/ 90-01-50**), Germany's oldest active theater, since 1609. It has its own repertory company. In July and August, the company moves to its summer theater in Meersburg (see "Meersburg," earlier in this chapter). Ticket prices depend on the production.

In the main room of the **Konstanz Casino,** Seestrasse 21 (© **07531/81-57-0**), try your luck at blackjack, seven-card stud poker, or roulette. Slot machines are in a side room. Entry requires a passport as proof of age, and there's a cover of 3€ ($4.80). Men are required to wear jackets and ties. The casino is open daily 2pm to 3am and until

4am Friday and Saturday. There's a restaurant on the premises (see "Where to Dine," above), open from 6pm to midnight.

On weekends, the **Theatercafé,** Konzilstrasse 3 (© **07531/9785456**), plays a mix of hip-hop and house late into the night. Good Dixieland jazz and country are found at **Hafenhalle,** Hafenstrasse 10 (© **07531/2-11-26**), every Sunday. Call for details.

Two **music festivals** featuring contemporary rock, jazz, and cabaret music are held during the summer. An international menagerie of bands descends on the town in late June and early July for a series of concerts held in huge tents. Ticket prices are 15€ to 29€ ($24–$46), with a few free shows, too. Throngs of revelers flood the town on September 1 for the annual **Rock Am See Festival** (© **07531/9-08-80;** www.koko.de), where a 55€ ($88) ticket buys you admission to an all-day event that draws international stars.

5 Reichenau ⊛

10km (6¼ miles) NW of Konstanz

In the more southerly of the two arms that stretch westward from the Bodensee, Reichenau is a small historic island that was only recently connected to the mainland by a causeway. By the end of the 800s, it was the site of three separate monasteries, the oldest of which had been established in 724. Later, Reichenau became a political force within the Holy Roman Empire. Today, much of the island is devoted to cultivating vegetables and salad greens, and consequently has a sedate aura, much prized by escapists looking for a quiet getaway.

ESSENTIALS

GETTING THERE   By Train   Reichenau's railway station lies midway between the larger railway junctions of Radolfzell (to the west) and Konstanz (to the east). Trains from throughout Germany and Switzerland make frequent stops at both those cities, from which passengers heading to Reichenau can transfer onto a small railway line that makes runs at hourly intervals on to Bahnhof Reichenau. Buses from Bahnhof Reichenau to Insel Reichenau (the city's historic core) take 10 minutes each way. For information, call © **01805/99-66-33.**

By Bus   Bus service to Reichenau is limited and inconvenient. For information, call **SBG GmbH** (© **07732/9-94-70**).

By Car   From Konstanz, motorists should take Route 33 east to Reichenau.

By Boat   For information about the ferryboats that ply the waters between Reichenau and the German lakeside hamlet of Allensbach, running April to October only, call © **07533/98848.**

VISITOR INFORMATION   The tourist office is the **Verkehrsbüro,** Pirmimstrasse 145 (© **07534/92070**). May to September, it's open Monday to Friday 8:30am to 12:30pm and 1:30 to 6pm, Saturday 9am to noon; October to April, hours are Monday to Friday 8:30am to noon and 2 to 5pm.

WHERE TO STAY

Seehotel Seeschau ⊛   This comfortable, well-maintained hotel is set directly beside the lake. It features good-size rooms with upscale reproductions of antique furniture and, in many cases, views over the lake. Bathrooms are neatly kept, with tub/shower combinations. This hotel is especially appealing in the midsummer, when the flowers around its windows burst into bloom.

An der Schiffslände 8, 78479 Reichenau. ⓒ **07534/257.** Fax 07534/72-64. www.seeschau.mdo.de. 23 units. 128€– 180€ ($205–$288) double; 230€ ($368) suite. Rates include continental breakfast. AE, DC, MC, V. Free parking. **Amenities:** 2 restaurants; bar; room service; babysitting; nonsmoking rooms. In room: TV, minibar, hair dryer, Jacuzzi.

Strandhotel Löchnerhaus *ℛ* This is a good, well-managed hotel, just a stone's throw from the lakefront and its own boat pier. It's set within a pleasant garden and offers bathrooms with tub/shower combinations and well-maintained rooms, many of which have private verandas or terraces and lake views.

Schiffslände 12, 78478 Reichenau. ⓒ **07534/80-30.** Fax 07534/582. www.strandhotel-reichenau.de. 42 units. 170€–310€ ($272–$496) double. Rates include buffet breakfast. AE, DC, MC, V. Parking 8€ ($13). Closed Nov–Feb. **Amenities:** Restaurant; lounge; boat rental; laundry service; dry cleaning. In room: TV, minibar, hair dryer, iron, safe.

WHERE TO DINE

Restaurant Strandhotel Löchnerhaus GERMAN/INTERNATIONAL This restaurant, with its hardworking, kindly staff, is the traditional favorite of many locals. The modern-style dining room has lake views. Menu items include sea bass cooked either in Riesling sauce or in a potato crust, whitefish from the Bodensee, rack of lamb with horseradish and mint, grilled meats such as steak, and a savory version of goulash.

Schiffslände 12. ⓒ **07534/80-30.** Reservations recommended. Main courses 16€–22€ ($26–$35). AE, DC, MC, V. Daily noon–2pm and 6–9pm. Closed Nov–Feb.

EXPLORING REICHENAU

The island is divided into three separate villages (Oberzell, Mittelzell, and Niederzell), each of which is centered on the remains of a medieval monastery. The most impressive of these is the **Münster St. Maria und Markus,** Burgstrasse (ⓒ **07534/249**), in Mittelzell. Originally founded in 725, it became one of the most important centers of learning in the Carolingian era. It reached its peak around 1000, when it was the home of about 700 monks. The structure is beautiful in its simplicity. Entrance is free, but a visit to the treasury costs 1€ ($1.60). The church is open daily year-round 9am to 6pm; its treasury is open only May to October Monday to Saturday 11am to noon and 3 to 4pm. While you're in the vicinity, notice the **Krautergarten (Herb Garden),** in the shadow of the cathedral on the Hermann Contractus Strasse. It emulates the herb and vegetable gardens maintained by monks in the Middle Ages.

The hamlet of Niederzell is home to **Stiftskirche St. Peter and St. Paul,** Egino-Strasse (no phone). If it's not open when you arrive, the tourist office will call someone to unlock the gates for you. In 1990, during restorations of the church's apse, a series of Romanesque frescoes were uncovered and are now on view.

The nearby hamlet of Oberzell houses **Stiftskirche St. George,** Seestrasse (no phone). Rising abruptly from a cabbage field, it has a severely dignified, very simple facade and a series of charmingly naive medieval frescoes inside. It's open daily 9am to 6pm. Admission is free.

A final site worth a stop is the **Heimatmuseum,** in the Stadthaus, Ergat 1, in Mittelzell (no phone). This is a showcase for the handicrafts and folklore that developed on Reichenau and the surrounding region. It's open April to October Thursday to Sunday 10:30am to 4:30pm, plus November to March only Saturday and Sunday 2 to 5pm. Entrance costs 3€ ($4.80) adults, 1.50€ ($2.40) children. For further information, contact the local tourist office (see above).

SHOPPING

For a sampling of the many wines produced within the Bodensee region, head for **Winzer Vereins,** Munsterplatz (✆ **07534/293**), where you'll be able to see rack upon rack of local vintages. You can even try a single glass to decide if you want to buy a bottle.

REICHENAU AFTER DARK

Those seeking a "night on the town" often drive over to Konstanz nearby. Life is considerably quieter in the more demure Reichenau after dark. Most visitors who come in summer prefer to sit out on one of the lakeside terraces—called *Terrassen am See* in German—enjoying the beer, the company, and mostly the romantic views of the town at night. The best of these are at the two previously recommended hotels, **Seehotel Seeschau** and **Strandhotel Löchnerhaus.** When the weather is foul, the best place for a drink is the **Kaminstube,** also at the Seehotel Seeschau.

6 Überlingen ⊘★

40km (25 miles) N of Konstanz, 46km (29 miles) E of Ravensburg, 24km (15 miles) W of Friedrichshafen

Locals call the town of Überlingen, founded in the 1200s, a German version of Nice because of its sunny weather and lakeside location. It's also one of the best-preserved medieval sites along the Bodensee.

ESSENTIALS

GETTING THERE   By Train   Rail passengers are funneled through nearby Friedrichshafen, from where a smaller rail line goes through Überlingen to Radolfzell. Trains run in either direction along that line at hourly intervals throughout the day. Überlingen's railway station lies on the extreme western edge of town. For rail information, call ✆ **01805/99-66-33.**

By Bus   Regional bus service along Lake Constance is provided by **RAB Regionalverkehr Alb-Bodensee GmbH** in nearby Weingarten (✆ **0751/509220**).

By Car   Überlingen is off Route 31, just northwest of Konstanz. From Stuttgart via Ulm, take Route 30 south then Route 31 west at Friedrichshafen. From Munich, follow Autobahn 96 west/southwest to Lindau, then Route 31 west to Friedrichshafen and Überlingen.

By Boat   April to October, 8 to 10 ferryboats a day carry passengers to Überlingen from Konstanz (trip time: 1 hr., 20 min.) for 9€ ($14) each way. For information, call the **Weiss Flote,** an armada of lake steamers maintained by the BSB Bodensee Schiffsbetriebe GmbH (✆ **07531/3640389**). No cars are carried on any of these ferries.

VISITOR INFORMATION   Tourist information is available at Landungsplatz 14 (✆ **07551/991122**), May to September Monday to Friday 9am to 6pm, Saturday 10am to 3pm, and Sunday 10am to 1pm; November to March Monday to Wednesday and Friday 9am to noon and 1 to 4pm, Thursday 9am to noon and 1 to 6pm; and April and October Monday to Friday 9am to noon and 1 to 5pm, and Saturday 10am to 3pm.

WHERE TO STAY & DINE

Landgasthöf zum Adler   In the confines of a bucolic hamlet (Lippertsreute), this hotel/restaurant occupies two antique buildings, the older of which was built 300 years ago. Rooms are cozy, unpretentious, and appealingly (and artfully) rustic. All rooms contain bathrooms with tub/shower combinations.

The restaurant serves heaping, well-prepared portions of German/Swabian dishes such as *Spanferkel* (roast suckling pig), *Zwiebelrostbraten* (onion-flavored roast beef), and Bodensee whitefish prepared with white-wine sauce. Main courses cost 10€ to 19€ ($16–$30). It's open Friday to Wednesday from 11:30am to 2:30pm and Friday to Tuesday from 5pm to midnight.

Hauptstrasse 44, Lippertsreute (10km/6¼ miles north of the center), 88662 Überlingen. (€ **07553/8-25-50.** Fax 07553/82-55-70. www.landgasthofzumadler.de. 16 units. 66€–102€ ($106–$163) double. Rates include breakfast. MC, V. Parking 5€ ($8). Closed Nov. **Amenities:** Restaurant; breakfast-only room service; laundry service; dry cleaning. *In room:* TV, hair dryer.

Parkhotel St. Leonhard 𝕲𝕲   Set on a hilltop, this hotel allows urban visitors to rest and recharge. The woodsy-looking chalet is flanked by more angular, modern annexes. Rooms are of good size, modern, conservative, comfortable, and well designed with some bathrooms containing tub/shower combinations, others with only showers. The kitchen succeeds admirably in serving both regional and international cuisine in three nonpretentious restaurants. The food is consistently good and is prepared with market-fresh ingredients. Main courses cost 8€ to 22€ ($13–$35).

Obere St. Leonhard-Strasse 71 (1.5km/1 mile north of the center), 88662 Überlingen. (€ **07551/80-81-00.** Fax 07551/80-85-31. www.parkhotel-sankt-leonhard.de. 170 units. 145€–180€ ($232–$288) double; 290€–490€ ($464–$784) suite. Rates include buffet breakfast. AE, MC, V. Free parking. **Amenities:** 3 restaurants; bar; indoor heated pool; 3 tennis courts; health club; sauna; babysitting; laundry service; dry cleaning; nonsmoking rooms. *In room:* TV, minibar, hair dryer.

Schäpfle 𝕲 *Finds*   With bedrooms opening onto balconies, most of which are decorated in a romantic style with fully Eiderdowns and draped fabrics, this hotel has a lot of character. In the heart of the resort, the hotel might as well be in the country, with its rustic design touches and a slightly old-fashioned aura in spite of the up-to-date furnishings. Bedrooms are spread across two buildings, one opening right on the lake. Guests and locals gather in the on-site tavern, serving specialties of southern Germany.

Jakob-Kessenringstrasse 14, 88662 Überlingen. (€ **07551/63494.** Fax 07551/67695. www.schaepfle.de. 32 units. 60€–65€ ($96–$104) double. No credit cards. **Amenities:** Restaurant; bar; room service; laundry service; nonsmoking rooms. *In room:* TV.

EXPLORING ÜBERLINGEN

The most important of the city monuments is the **Münster** 𝕲, a surprisingly large medieval structure that required 200 years to build. The larger of its two towers functioned during wars as a military watchtower and was later capped with an eight-sided Renaissance lantern. The severely dignified exterior is offset by an elaborate and intricate Gothic interior. Take special notice of the main altarpiece, carved in the early 1600s by Jorg Zurn. It is open daily 8am to 6pm. Entrance is free.

On the opposite side of the square is Überlingen's **Rathaus** 𝕲, built in the late 1400s. Most of its interior is devoted to municipal offices, except for the Ratsaal, whose vaulted ceiling and lavishly paneled walls make it the most beautiful public room in town. Notice the coats of arms representing various factions of the Holy Roman Empire. Hours are Monday to Friday 9am to noon and 2:30 to 5pm; in summer, they are also open Saturday 9am to noon. Entrance is free.

The city maintains a **Heimatmuseum (Museum of Folklore)** within one of its most prized buildings, the Reichlin-von-Meldegg Haus, Krummeberggasse 30 (€ **07551/991-079**). This building artfully emulates the style of the Florentine Renaissance. Inside you can also visit both a chapel and a lavishly ornate rococo ballroom. The building and its museum are open May to October Tuesday to Saturday 9am to 12:30pm and 2 to 5pm, and Sunday 10am to 3pm. Admission is 3€ ($4.80) adults, 1€ ($1.60) children, and free for children 5 and under.

Also look for the **Franziskanerkirche,** Spitalgasse. Especially striking is the contrast between this church's severely dignified exterior and its lavishly baroque interior. It is open daily 8am to noon and 2 to 5pm.

The townspeople of Überlingen took great care to ornament the medieval fortifications that protected them from outside invaders. The best preserved of these walls is the **Stadtmauer,** which in recent times was landscaped into a graceful ramble lined with trees and shrubbery. It's part of the encircling walls that flank the north and east sides of town.

Along the waterfront promenade, Seepromenade, with a view of the faraway Swiss Alps, is the **Greth,** one of the largest old buildings in town and originally a market and storage vault for corn. Today it houses the city's tourist office.

Überlingen is also the site of one of the best-known medical clinics on the Bodensee. The **Buchinger Clinic,** Willhelmbeckstrasse 27 (© **07551/8070**), is expensive, aristocratic, and exclusive. Good spa treatments are available in two of the town's hotels, the Kur und Gasthaus Routher and the Gasthaus Seepark.

7 Ravensburg

20km (12 miles) N of Friedrichshafen, 32km (20 miles) N of Lindau

Ravensburg isn't on Lake Constance, but it's nearby and makes a good side trip. The town boasts one of the most impeccably preserved medieval cores in the region. During the 1400s, the linen trade made Ravensburg into one of the richest towns in Germany, but economic stagnation set in during the 1600s as a result of the Thirty Years' War. Today, this quiet town is a tourist's delight.

ESSENTIALS
GETTING THERE   By Train   Most passengers change trains in nearby Ulm. From Ulm, trains depart at hourly intervals for Friedrichshafen, stopping en route in Ravensburg (trip time: 1 hr.). For information call © **01805/99-66-33.**

By Bus   Most bus routes into Ravensburg start at nearby villages and hamlets. For information, call © **0751/2766.**

By Car   From Stuttgart, follow Autobahn 8 east to the city of Ulm, then turn south onto Route 30 directly into Ravensburg. From along Lake Constance, you can take routes B33, B30, or 467 north to Ravensburg.

VISITOR INFORMATION   Head to the **Stadtverkehrsamt,** Kirchestrasse 16 (© **0751/82800**). It's open Monday to Friday 9am to 5:30pm and Saturday 10am to 2pm.

WHERE TO STAY
Hotel-Gasthof Obertor *(Value*   This is the town's best choice for frugal travelers. This hotel was built in the 12th century as a farmhouse and is almost as old as the town. It has a lovely garden terrace in front and a park in the back. Rooms vary greatly in size and personality, so you may want to take a peek at a couple before deciding which to take. Turn-of-the-20th-century antiques abound, mostly made of cherrywood—typical of the Bodensee area.

Markstrasse 67, 88212 Ravensburg. $\textcircled{C}$ **0751/3-66-70.** Fax 0751/3-66-72-00. www.hotelobertor.de. 31 units. 106€–125€ ($170–$200) double; from 160€ ($256) suite. Rates include breakfast. AE, DC, MC, V. Free outdoor parking, 7€ ($11) in the garage. **Amenities:** Restaurant; wine bistro; whirlpool; sauna; room service; massage; babysitting; laundry service; dry cleaning; nonsmoking rooms. *In room:* TV, Wi-Fi, hair dryer.

Romantik Hotel Waldhorn ✸✸ The most appealing hotel in Ravensburg occupies a late-18th-century building and a more modern annex. Because both buildings lie within the town's all-pedestrian zone, it's easy to get a sense of the relaxed local lifestyle. Rooms are comfortable and cozy, and the staff is very charming. All rooms have a midsize to large bathroom with a tub/shower combination. Das Rebleutehaus, one of the hotel's restaurants, serves Swabian specialties such as *Spätzle* and large ravioli stuffed with meat and spinach.

Marienplatz 15, 88212 Ravensburg. $\textcircled{C}$ **0751/3612-0.** Fax 07151/3612-100. www.waldhorn.de. 40 units. 135€– 150€ ($216–$240) double; 190€ ($304) suite. Rates include buffet breakfast. AE, MC, V. Parking 8€ ($13). **Amenities:** 2 restaurants; lounge; room service; babysitting; laundry service; dry cleaning; nonsmoking rooms; rooms for those w/limited mobility. *In room:* TV, Wi-Fi, minibar (in some), hair dryer, safe.

WHERE TO DINE

Romantik Hotel Waldhorn Restaurant ✸✸✸ MODERN INTERNATIONAL This sophisticated restaurant is run by celebrity chef Albert Bouley. The stylish, gracefully antique dining room has massive ceiling beams. The Asian-influenced cuisine is among the most subtle, celebrated, and exotic in Germany. Menu items combine Eastern and Western culinary traditions with verve and zest, and change according to the seasons and the inspiration of the much-praised chef. You can order such delectable dishes as tender, well-flavored medallions of lamb with miso, lemon zest, and a mint tempura. Grilled sole is a wake-up to the palate with its exotic flavorings of chili and tamarind. If you want to become both a gourmet and a gourmand, opt for the fixed-price menu. Although it changes nightly, it usually features such inspired dishes as salad of breast of duck in lemon oil with a ragout of shrimp, lobster, and mussels seasoned with fresh herbs; sole with gooseliver and fresh asparagus; and filet of stag with goat cheese. Desserts are spectacular.

Marienplatz 15. $\textcircled{C}$ **0751/36120.** Reservations recommended. Main courses 20€–32€ ($32–$51); fixed-price 7-course dinner menu 98€ ($157). AE, DC, MC, V. Tues–Sat 11:30am–2pm and 6–10:30pm.

EXPLORING RAVENSBURG

You'll appreciate that cars are banned from the narrow labyrinth of alleyways within Ravensburg's historic core. Two of the most evocative streets are **Untere Breite Strasse** and **Charlottenstrasse,** both of which lie near the town's central square. Lining the Marienplatz are the late-Gothic **Rathaus;** the 14th-century **Kornhaus,** once one of the largest corn exchanges in the region and now the town's library; and the **Waaghaus,** originally built in the 1400s as a warehouse for municipal supplies and now a bank. Look also for the old city **watchtower** and the Renaissance-era **Lederhaus,** the town's post office.

Also on the Marienplatz is the **Karmelitenklosterkirche.** Originally a monastery in the 14th century, it later housed a mercantile association devoted to the promotion of the linen trade. The complex's church can be visited every day from 8am to 6pm. Nearby, at the corner of Kirchstrasse and the Herrenstrasse, is the **Liebfrauenkirche,** the parish church of Ravensburg. Deceptively simple on the outside, the 14th-century structure has been radically but authentically reconstructed on the inside. Look for remnants of original stained glass and a heavy somberness reminiscent of the Middle Ages.

Moments Scaling the Ramparts

Part of Ravensburg's allure is its well-preserved network of medieval fortifications, studded with defensive towers. The most visible is the 52m (171-ft.) Mehlsack Tower, adopted as the municipal symbol of Ravensburg itself. You can climb to its heights by means of 240 heavily worn, circular steps, but only on Sunday from April to October, 10am to 2pm. Entrance is 1€ ($1.60). Two other defensive towers can be spotted from the Marienplatz. These are the Obertor, the oldest gate in the city walls, accessible via Marktstrasse, and the Grünerturm (Green Tower), covered with moss-colored ceramic tiles, many of which date from the 14th century. Neither the Grünerturm nor the Obertor can be visited.

Ravensburg's only noteworthy museum is its **Heimatmuseum,** devoted to local folklore and handicrafts. It lies within the Volkhaus, Torplatz 7 (for information contact the tourist office), and is open Tuesday to Friday 2 to 8pm, Saturday and Sunday 2 to 3pm. Admission is free.

A SIDE TRIP TO WEINGARTEN

An important archaeological excavation is located within the agrarian hamlet of Weingarten, a sleepy village 5km (3 miles) north of Ravensburg. To reach the village, take bus no. 1 or 2 from Marienplatz. In the 1950s, teams of archaeologists discovered one of the richest troves of German graves in the country. Artifacts from the dig lie in the **Alamannen Museum,** located in Kornhaus, Karlstrasse 28 (© **0751/405125**). It's open Tuesday to Sunday 3 to 5pm (Thurs until 6pm). Admission is 3€ ($4.80).

Weingarten is also home to the largest baroque church in Germany, the **Weingarten Basilica** (© **0751/56-12-70**), which rises to about 60m (200 ft.). It was established in 1056 by the wife of a prominent official in the Guelph dynasty. Inside is one of the holiest relics in Germany, a mystical vial, which, according to legend, contains several drops of Christ's blood. The relic was entrusted to the convent by the sister-in-law of William the Conqueror, the Guelph Queen Juditha. Another highlight of the church is the organ, one of the largest in the country. Its installation required 13 years, beginning in 1737. Also noteworthy are the ceiling frescoes by Cosmas Damian Asam, one of the leaders of the Baroque School. The church is open daily 8am to 6pm.

Finally, if you can manage to schedule your visit for the day after Ascension (the Thurs 40 days after Easter), you can witness the *Ludfreitag,* a massive **procession** of pilgrims, at the head of which are more than 2,000 horsemen. The breeding of horses for this procession is a matter of quiet pride among local farmers.

For information on Weingarten, call the **tourist office** at Münsterplatz (© **0751/ 40-51-27**).

12

The Black Forest (Schwarzwald)

The Black Forest covers a triangular section roughly 145km (90 miles) long and 40km (25 miles) wide in southwestern Germany. The pine- and birch-studded mountains here are alive with fairy-tale villages, spas, and ski resorts. The peaks in the southern part of the forest reach as high as 1,525m (5,000 ft.) and are excellent for skiing in winter and hiking or mountain climbing in summer. The little lakes of Titisee and Schluchsee are popular for boating, swimming, and ice skating. Fish abound in the streams and lakes.

GETTING TO THE BLACK FOREST International airports serve the area from Stuttgart (see chapter 13) and the Swiss city of Basel, which is 70km (43 miles) from Freiburg im Breisgau, the "capital" of the Black Forest. Trains run north and south through the Rhine Valley, with fast, frequent service to such Black Forest towns as Freiburg and Baden-Baden. Motorists should take the A5 Autobahn, which runs the length of the Schwarzwald. From Lake Constance (see chapter 11), continue along Route 13 for 65km (40 miles) until you reach the Black Forest.

EXPLORING THE REGION BY CAR Roads through the forest are excellent, especially the **Schwarzwald Hochstrasse** (Black Forest High Rd. or Ridgeway, Rte. B500), which runs almost the entire length of the region, from Baden-Baden to Freudenstadt, then resumes at Triberg and goes on to Waldshut on the Rhine. While taking this scenic road, you'll have many opportunities to park your car and explore the countryside or to turn off on one of the side roads leading to hospitable villages, ancient castles, and rolling farmlands.

1 Freiburg im Breisgau ★ ★

208km (129 miles) SW of Stuttgart, 70km (44 miles) N of Basel (Switzerland), 280km (174 miles) S of Frankfurt

The largest city in the Black Forest region is often overlooked because of its out-of-the-way location. When approached from the Rhine plain on the west, Freiburg is silhouetted against towering mountain peaks, which are only an hour from the town by funicular or car.

Because of its climate, Freiburg is a year-round attraction and sports center. The city is in the path of warm air currents that come up from the Mediterranean through the Burgundy Gap. In early spring, the town usually bursts into bloom while the surrounding mountain peaks remain covered with snow. In the fall, the smell of new wine fills the narrow streets even as snow falls on nearby peaks.

ESSENTIALS

GETTING THERE By Train Frequent trains connect Freiburg to major airports in Basel (Switzerland) and Stuttgart. Daily trains arrive from Frankfurt (trip time: 2 hr.)

and Hamburg (trip time: 8 hr.), as well as from Berlin and Zürich, Switzerland. For information, call ℂ **01805/996633.**

By Bus   Long-distance bus service is provided by **Südbaden Bus GmbH,** Central Bus Station, Freiburg (ℂ **0761/3680388**), with service from Freiburg to EuroAirport Basel-Mulhouse; and by **EuroRegioBus** (ℂ **0761/3680388**), which has a bus between Freiburg and the French cities of Mulhouse and Colmar.

By Car   Access by car is via the A5 Autobahn north and south.

VISITOR INFORMATION   For tourist information, contact **Freiburg Information,** Rathausplatz 2–4 (ℂ **0761/3881880**). The office is open June to September Monday to Friday 8am to 8pm, Saturday 9:30am to 5:30pm, and Sunday 10am to noon; and October to May Monday to Friday 8am to 6pm, Saturday 9:30am to 2:30pm, and Sunday 10am to noon.

GETTING AROUND   Freiburg is well served by buses and trams, the latter running in the inner city. A one-way fare costs 2€ ($3.20); a 24-hour day pass is 4.80€ ($7.70). A family pass, good for two adults and up to four children, is sold for just 8€ ($13). For schedules and information, or to buy passes, go to Plus-Punkt, Salzstrasse 3 (ℂ **0761/4511500**), in the Altstadt. Hours are Monday to Friday 8am to 7pm and Saturday 8am to 2pm. Most of the city's public transportation network shuts down from 12:30 to 5:30am.

WHERE TO STAY

Best Western Premier Hotel Victoria   This is a bastion of Black Forest hospitality, and the location is among the best in town. Founded in 1875, it lies 200m (656 ft.) from the main rail station near the cathedral. Although it is a historical hotel, it is thoroughly modernized and "green," using many energy-saving devices such as toilet tissue from recycled paper and solar panels to provide much of its heat. The bedrooms are beautifully designed and furnished, with every gadget from electronic key card locks to in-room movies.

Eisenbahnstrasse 54, 79098 Freiburg. ℂ **0761/207340.** Fax 0761/20734444. www.victoria.bestwestern.de. 63 units. 138€–161€ ($221–$258) double. AE, DC, MC, V. Parking 10€ ($16). **Amenities:** Bar; barber/salon; room service; laundry service; nonsmoking rooms; units for those w/limited mobility. *In room:* TV, Wi-Fi, hair dryer.

Colombi-Hotel 𝒦𝒦𝒦   The Colombi is the most luxurious hotel in town, and its white walls and angular lines make it easy to spot. Despite its downtown location, the hotel is quiet and peaceful. Many business conferences take place here, but the Colombi caters to independent travelers as well. Rooms are well furnished and appointed; the suites are especially luxurious, and all guest rooms contain bathrooms with tub/shower combinations.

Rotteckring 16, 79098 Freiburg. ℂ **0761/21060.** Fax 0761/31410. www.colombi.de. 116 units. 245€–275€ ($392–$440) double; 290€–305€ ($464–$488) junior suite; 400€–850€ ($640–$1,360) suite; 350€ ($455) apt. AE, DC, MC, V. Parking 14€ ($22). Tram: 10, 11, or 12. **Amenities:** 3 restaurants; cafe; bar; indoor heated pool; health club; spa; sauna; salon; room service; babysitting; laundry service; dry cleaning. *In room:* A/C, TV, minibar, hair dryer, safe.

Kühler Krug   This cozy inn is better known for its dining than for its rooms, although it makes a good choice for a family-run hotel, lying only 2km (1¼ miles) from the center in the suburb of Günterstal. Fixed-price menus range from 18€ to 35€ ($29–$56). A classic regional cuisine with a modern twist is served, with the chefs specializing in fish, which is not just thrown on the grill, but often served with

The Black Forest

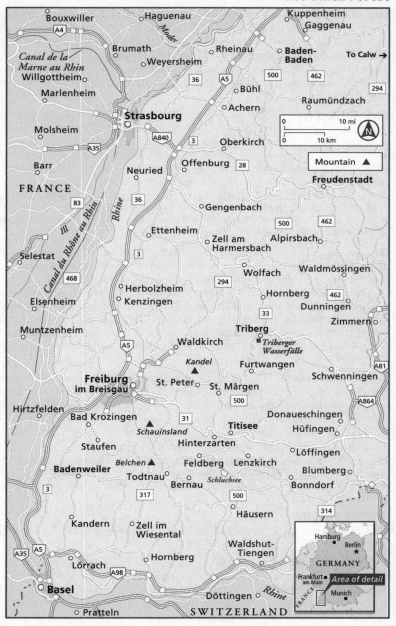

Bouxwiller
Haguenau
Kuppenheim
Gaggenau

Moder

Brumath
Rheinau
Baden-Baden
To Calw →

Weyersheim

Canal de la Marne au Rhin
Willgottheim

36
A5
500
462

Marlenheim
Bühl
294

Strasbourg
Achern
Raumündzach

Molsheim

0 ____ 10 mi
0 ____ 10 km

N

A35
A840
3
Oberkirch

Barr
Offenburg
28
Mountain ▲

FRANCE
Neuried
Freudenstadt

83
36
Gengenbach

Rhine
500
462

Ettenheim
Zell am Harmersbach
Alpirsbach

468
3
Wolfach
Waldmössingen

Ill
Herbolzheim
294
Hornberg
462

Elsenheim
Kenzingen
33
Dunningen

Canal du Rhône au Rhin
Triberg
Zimmern

Muntzenheim
Waldkirch
Triberger Wasserfälle

A5
Kandel ▲
Furtwangen
A81

Freiburg im Breisgau
St. Peter
St. Märgen
Schwenningen

Hirtzfelden
500
A864

Bad Krozingen
31
Donaueschingen

▲ *Schauinsland*
Titisee
Hüfingen

Staufen
Hinterzarten

Badenweiler
Belchen ▲
Feldberg
Lenzkirch
Löffingen

3
Todtnau
Schluchsee
Blumberg

317
Bernau
500
Bonndorf

Kandern
Zell im Wiesental
Häusern
314

A35 A5
Hornberg
Waldshut-Tiengen

Lörrach
A98

Basel
Döttingen
Rhine

Pratteln
SWITZERLAND

Hamburg
Berlin ★

GERMANY

Frankfurt am Main
Area of detail

FRANCE
Munich

405

creative sauces such as fresh salmon in a saffron foam. In autumn, many game dishes are offered, including wild rabbit in a hazelnut sauce. The bedrooms upstairs are small to medium in size, comfortably furnished, and well maintained. Walkers and hikers in the Black Forest sing the praise of this old-fashioned inn.

Torplatz 1, 79100 Freiburg-Günterstal. ℂ 0761/29103. Fax 0761/29782. www.booking.com/hotel/de/kuhler-krug.en. html. 85€ ($136) double. MC, V. Free parking. **Amenities:** Restaurant; bar; room service; laundry service; nonsmoking rooms. *In room:* TV.

Park Hotel Post ⟨ℛ⟩   This baroque hotel, with an elaborate zinc cap on its octagonal turret, is within walking distance of Freiburg's major attractions and the rail station. This has been one of the top hotels in town for a long time, although its services and style aren't as good as the Colombi's. The attractively furnished rooms come in a variety of shapes and sizes and are among the most comfortable in town. Bathrooms have tub/shower combinations. Breakfast is the only meal served.

Eisenbahnstrasse 37, 79098 Freiburg. ℂ 0761/385480. Fax 0761/31680. www.park-hotel-post.de. 44 units. 129€–189€ ($206–$302) double; 199€–319€ ($318–$510) apt. Rates include buffet breakfast. AE, MC, V. Parking 8€ ($13). Tram: 10, 11, or 12. **Amenities:** Breakfast room; lounge; room service; laundry service; dry cleaning. *In room:* TV, Wi-Fi, minibar, hair dryer.

Rappen ⟨Finds⟩   This charming inn in the pedestrians-only Altstadt has a lot more cozy Black Forest ambience than its nearby competitors. It's marked with a wrought-iron hanging sign, little dormer windows in its steep roof, window boxes, and shutters. Rooms are small and simply but comfortably furnished; the most desirable have views of the cathedral. Bathrooms are a bit cramped and contain either a tub or shower.

Münsterplatz 13, 79098 Freiburg. ℂ 0761/31353. Fax 0761/382252. www.hotelrappen.de. 18 units, 13 with bathroom. 80€ ($128) double without bathroom; 124€ ($198) double with bathroom. Rates include buffet breakfast. AE, MC, V. All trams stop 20m (60 ft.) behind the hotel. **Amenities:** Restaurant; room service; nonsmoking rooms. *In room:* TV, Wi-Fi.

Zum Roten Bären ⟨ℛ⟩   One of the oldest buildings in Freiburg, with parts dating from 1120, this is also said to be the oldest inn in Germany. A modern wing blends in pleasantly. The interior is delightfully decorated, emphasizing original construction elements along with scattered pieces of antique furniture. Rooms are well styled and furnished, all with bathrooms with showers or tubs. Try for a room in the older section, which has more tradition and atmosphere.

Oberlinden 12, 79098 Freiburg. ℂ 0761/387870. Fax 0761/3878717. www.roter-baeren.de. 25 units. 149€–169€ ($238–$270) double; 190€ ($304) suite. Rates include buffet breakfast. AE, DC, MC, V. Parking 9€ ($14). Tram: 1. **Amenities:** Restaurant; sauna; room service; laundry service; dry cleaning. *In room:* TV, minibar (in some), hair dryer, safe (in some).

WHERE TO DINE

Even if you're not staying at the **Kühler Krug,** recommended above, consider it for lunch or dinner.

Die Hans-Thoma-Stube ⟨ℛℛ⟩ REGIONAL/FRENCH   This is one of the most acclaimed restaurants in the area, with a sumptuous setting and gracious and skillful service. Choice ingredients, masterful preparation, and creative presentation delight both the eye and the palate. The menu changes seasonally but may include filet of turbot with fresh mushrooms and a Madeira jus served with green asparagus, or else a tournedos filet of veal with delectable truffles. There are two 18th-century-style dining rooms.

In the Colombi Hotel, Rotteckring 16. © **0761/21060.** Reservations required. Main courses 29€–45€ ($46–$72); fixed-price lunches 25€–34€ ($40–$54), dinners 55€–99€ ($88–$158). AE, DC, MC, V. Daily noon–3pm and 7–11pm. Tram: 10, 11, or 12.

Eichhalde *ŘŘ* FRENCH/GERMAN   This notable French bistro lies in the Herden district, a 20-minute walk from the center. It gets a lot of neighborhood patronage. Fixed-price lunches and dinners are available. The chef has steadily built up a local reputation, and the cuisine is based on the clever handling of first-rate, often luxurious ingredients. The gooseliver terrine comes with a discreet touch of port aspic, and the sea bass is enticingly served with a fresh thyme sauce. For lighter appetites, the turbot salad with mustard sauce brims with flavor.

Stadtstrasse 91. © **0761/54817.** Reservations required. Main courses 18€–25€ ($29–$40); fixed-price menus 24€–54€ ($38–$86). MC, V. Sun and Wed–Fri noon–2pm; Wed–Mon 6–10pm. Bus: 14.

Markgräfker Gif GERMAN   This is a restaurant and *Weinstube* that serves a savory cuisine with market-fresh ingredients. The former city mansion of the von Kagenneck family, this neoclassical villa has been restored and is today an elegant setting for dining with both antiques and modern art. Fresh, local products are used whenever available. The wine list is limited but choice. Dishes range from asparagus-stuffed ravioli to sautéed butterfish laced with ginger. For dessert, try the elderberry ice cream if featured.

Gerberau 22. © **0761/32540.** Reservations recommended. Main courses 15€–25€ ($24–$39). AE, DC, MC, V. Tues–Fri noon–2pm and 6–10pm; Sat–Sun noon–2:30pm and 6–10pm.

Oberkirchs Weinstube *Value* GERMAN   The innkeeper provides excellent regional cooking and comfortable rooms in this traditional establishment. The setting, on a colorful square, is pure picture postcard. The main Weinstube is old, with a monumental ceiling-high ceramic stove made with ornate decorative tiles. You get good old-fashioned food here—tasty soups, meat dishes, and poultry—and large helpings. Some of the best-tasting dishes include fried fresh trout from the Black Forest or else poached salmon in a Béarnaise sauce. Boiled beef is offered with a horseradish sauce, or else you can order medallions of turkey breast in an orange-pepper sauce. In season, you might want to try young pheasant. In the rear is a modern complex fronting an open patio with a fish pond.

The Weinstube also has 26 excellent rooms, all with private bathrooms or showers. Doubles cost 142€ to 170€ ($227–$272), with continental breakfast included.

Münsterplatz 22. © **0761/2026868.** Fax 0761/2026869. www.hotel-oberkirch.de. Reservations recommended. Main courses 12€–23€ ($19–$37). AE, MC, V. Mon–Sat noon–2pm and 6:30–9:30pm. Closed for 2 weeks in Jan. Tram: 1, 4, or 6.

EXPLORING FREIBURG

Augustiner Museum *Ř*   The Augustiner Museum is housed in the former church and monastery of the Order of St. Augustine. It contains the town's finest collection of art, including religious art spanning more than 1,000 years. Among the treasures are some of the cathedral's original stained-glass windows, as well as the most important of its medieval gold and silver treasures, brought here for safekeeping. Among the best works in the collection are *The Snow Miracle* by Mathias Grünewald and works by Hans Baldung Grien, who was a pupil of Albrecht Dürer. There's also a rich collection of fine late-Gothic wooden sculpture, as well as Art Nouveau glass objects.

Augustinerplatz. © **0761/2012531.** www.augustinermuseum.de. Free admission (except special exhibits). Tues–Sun 10am–5pm. Guided tours Wed 12:30pm, Sun 11am. Tram: 1.

Freiburg Cathedral 🖈🖈   This cathedral is one of the great masterpieces of Gothic art in Germany. Its unique spire is of filigree stonework; the steeple sits on an octagonal belfry, which holds a historic 4,500kg (5-ton) bell dating from 1258. Although begun in 1200 in the Romanesque style, by the time it was completed in 1620, the builders had incorporated various Gothic styles.

Upon entering by the south door, you'll be in the transept facing an early-16th-century sculpture of the adoration of the Christ Child by the Magi. If you turn left into the nave, you'll see at the far end of the aisle, by the entrance to the tower, a fine 13th-century statue of the Virgin flanked by two adoring angels. The high altar has an altarpiece built between 1512 and 1516 by Hans Baldung Grien. Resting against one of the Renaissance pillars along the aisle is a carved 16th-century pulpit, with stairs winding around the curve of the column. The figures below the stairs are likenesses of the townspeople, including the sculptor.

In the aisles are 14th-century stained-glass windows. The oldest stained glass, dating from the 13th century, is in the small round windows of the south transept. Some pieces, however, have been removed to the Augustiner Museum and replaced by more recent panels.

Münsterplatz. 🕾 **0761/202790.** Admission: cathedral free; tower 2€ ($3.20) adults, 1€ ($1.60) students, free for children 14 and under. Cathedral year-round Mon–Sat 9am–6pm, Sun 1–6pm. Tower May–Oct Mon–Sat 9:30am–5pm, Sun 1–5pm; Nov–Apr Wed–Sat 9:30am–5pm. Tram: 4, 5, or 6.

Museum für Neue Kunst   This modern art collection was formerly housed in the Augustiner Museum. Painting and sculpture, beginning with examples of German expressionism, Neue Sachlichkeit, and other classic modern works, especially by artists of southwest Germany, are displayed here.

Marienstrasse 10A. 🕾 **0761/2012581.** www.museen.freiburg.de. Admission 2€ ($3.20) adults, 1€ ($1.60) students, free for children 6 and under. Tues–Sun 10am–5pm. Tram: 1, 4, 5, or 6.

MORE SIGHTS IN THE ALTSTADT

In Münsterplatz, across from the cathedral, is the **Kaufhaus (Customs House),** the most colorful building in Freiburg. This Gothic structure, with oriel windows at each end, was originally an ancient emporium, to which a balcony was added in 1550. Above the massive supporting arches, the facade is decorated with the statues of four emperors of the Habsburg dynasty, of whom all but one visited Freiburg during his reign. Unfortunately, the inside cannot be visited.

FREIBURG AFTER DARK

An impressive entertainment complex, the **Konzerthaus,** hosts a variety of events, ranging from classic music to theater to pop concerts. In June and July, huge tents are raised to house the annual **Zeltmusik festival,** which emphasizes jazz but includes other musical styles as well. Summer also brings a series of **chamber-music concerts** to the Kaufhaus, in Münsterplatz, and a program of **organ recitals** to the Freiburg Cathedral. Information about all venues and events listed above, including program schedules and ticket sales, is available from **Freiburg Information** (see above).

The city also has a thriving bar and club scene that goes on into the wee hours. **Jazzhaus,** Schnewlinstrasse 2 (🕾 **0761/2923446;** tram: 1, 4, 5, or 6), hosts pop, folk, blues, and jazz shows by international, regional, and local bands. The club is open Wednesday to Sunday 7pm until 1am, with a cover of 10€ to 29€ ($16–$46). Until 8pm, the **Café Atlantik,** Schwabentorring 7 (🕾 **0761/33033;** tram: 1), serves up

---

Moments   **An Excursion to the Upper Black Forest**

From Freiburg, you can make a 145km (90-mile) 1-day circuit through one of the most scenic parts of the Black Forest, returning in time for dinner. Along the way, you'll pass a trio of the highest summits in the Black Forest and two of the region's most beautiful lakes.

Head immediately south to **Schauinsland** along Route 317, a narrow twisting road. At the car park, you can climb some 100 steps to the belvedere tower for a panoramic view of the area.

Continuing south, you reach **Belchen Mountain,** which rises to a height of 1,414m (4,640 ft.). From where the road ends, it is an easy 20-minute hike to the summit. On a clear day, you can look out from the observation platform here and take in a panoramic sweep of the Rhine plain, plus a view of the Alps from Säntis to Mont Blanc.

Continue east to the hamlet of Todtnau, where visitors can walk up a footpath to **the Falls of Todtnau,** about a mile away. Back at Todtnau, continue east along Route 317 to Feldberg. Here a chairlift takes visitors to the 1,425m (4,750-ft.) **Seebuck** peak, which is crowned by the Bismarck monument and offers another sweeping panoramic view of the Black Forest.

On the road again, follow Route 317 east until it becomes Route 500 heading south to **Schluchsee,** one of the loveliest lakes of the area and the most important body of water in the Black Forest.

After a visit here, head north along Route 500 to the hamlet of **Lenzkirch,** from which you'll have a view of Lake Titisee. The road then continues to the resort of **Titisee** itself (see below). After a visit you can return to Freiburg by heading west along Route 31.

---

spaghetti platters for 3.50€ to 7€ ($5.60–$11), but later on, it's mainly a bar, occasionally with a band. It's open Saturday to Thursday 11am to 2am, Friday 11am till 3am.

Hausbräuerei Feierling, Gerberau 46 (© **0761/243480;** tram: 1 or 2), is a brewpub, with a beer garden across the street. It's open daily 11am to midnight. Those who want a dark, smoky bar should head to the local Irish pub, the **Isle of Innisfree,** Augustinerplatz 2 (© **0761/22984;** tram: 1, 4, 5, or 6), which sometimes has live music. **Cafe Brasil,** Wannerstrasse 21 (© **0761/289888;** tram: 1, 5, or 6), has a tropical feel. It's open daily 10am to 1am.

2 Badenweiler *⭐*

35km (22 miles) S of Freiburg, 240km (150 miles) W of Stuttgart

Badenweiler is one of the smallest and most charming spa towns in the Black Forest. It's also the site of the best-preserved Roman baths north of the Alps. Town authorities here are intent on keeping their community spotless, squeaky clean, and steeped in Black Forest myth and legend. Badenweiler is located halfway between Freiburg and Basel, near the Swiss border.

ESSENTIALS

GETTING THERE   By Train   With no railway station in Badenweiler, rail passengers should first go to Freiburg, then switch onto any of the dozen or so daily trains that carry them to the town of Müllheim. From there, it's easiest to take a taxi the 8km (5 miles) east to Badenweiler. (Taxis make special efforts to line up whenever trains arrive.) The one-way charge is 12€ to 16€ ($19–$26) to anywhere in Badenweiler, a distance of 4km (2½ miles). If, by any chance, there are no taxis in line, you can call for one at ℂ **07631/2255.**

Buses also line up at Müllheim's railway station, charging 3.50€ ($5.60) for the short ride to Badenweiler. Bus no. 111 heads to Badenweiler and beyond, with departures scheduled every 60 to 75 minutes, depending on the time of day.

By Bus   Unless you're coming into Badenweiler from one of the nearby communities, bus travel is not convenient.

By Car   From the A5 Autobahn, which runs north to south between Karlsruhe and Basel, exit at the Müllheim/Badenweiler exit, then follow the signs to Badenweiler.

VISITOR INFORMATION   Head for **Kur-Touristik,** Ernst-Eisenlohr-Strasse 4 (ℂ **07632/799300**), which is open daily 10am to 1pm (closed Sat–Sun Oct–Mar).

WHERE TO STAY

Hotel Ritter 𝕽   Informal and personal, this hotel is composed of a trio of buildings. The oldest and most traditional looking is a 150-year-old chalet that contains the least expensive rooms. Newer and somewhat more comfortable lodgings lie within a pair of relatively new annexes. Rooms are cozy, simple, and modern, with clean bathrooms containing tub/shower combos.

Friedrichstrasse 2 (a 10-min. walk west from the center), 79410 Badenweiler. ℂ **07632/8310.** Fax 07632/831299. www.hotelritter.de. 75 units. 198€–242€ ($317–$387) double; 264€ ($422) suite. Rates include breakfast. Half board is included for 2 or more nights; otherwise, it costs 25€ ($40) per person. AE, MC, V. Free parking. **Amenities:** Restaurant; bar; indoor heated pool; health club; spa; Jacuzzi; sauna; room service; massage; babysitting; laundry service; dry cleaning; nonsmoking rooms. *In room:* TV, minibar, hair dryer, safe.

Hotel Römerbad 𝕽𝕽𝕽   This is the best, most elaborate, and most historic spa and hotel in town, attracting urbanites in need of R&R from throughout Germany. The staff is steeped in an old-world sense of courtliness. The clientele has included Nietzsche, Thomas Mann, and Andy Warhol. The domes, mansard roofs, and balconies of this bone-white structure inspire a comparison to an elaborate wedding cake. Inside, the hotel combines opera-house grandeur with antiques, ornate ceiling medallions, and touches of gilt. Rooms are traditionally furnished, often spacious, and beautifully maintained, with sumptuous beds and bathrooms containing tub/shower combos.

The Römerbad is also known for its seasonal concerts. Music lovers throughout the country seek out the hotel's concert hall, built in the early 1800s as a shelter for horses and carriages. A series of **classical or jazz concerts,** each performed over a period of about 4 days, is presented three or four times a year. For information, contact the hotel directly.

Schlossplatz 1, 79410 Badenweiler. ℂ **07632/700.** Fax 07632/70200. www.hotel-roemerbad.de. 76 units. 198€–308€ ($317–$493) double; 206€–326€ ($330–$522) junior suite; 256€–392€ ($410–$627) suite. Rates include breakfast. AE, DC, MC, V. Parking 10€ ($16). **Amenities:** 2 restaurants; bar; indoor thermal pool; 2 outdoor tennis courts; health club; spa; sauna; solarium; room service; massage; babysitting; laundry service; nonsmoking rooms. *In room:* TV, Wi-Fi, hair dryer, safe.

Moments Bathing as the Romans Did

The springs that pour water into the spa facilities here are very little changed since Roman days, a fact that the local resort, the **Cassiopeia Therme,** Kaiser-strasse 5 (© **07632/799200**), won't let you forget. It offers mud packs, massage, sauna, and steam bath treatments. The well-preserved Roman baths, originally built in A.D. 75, still stand today within the Kurpark, or spa gardens. The Roman baths can only be visited as part of a guided tour, offered mostly in German but with some English commentary, every Monday at 10am. For information and advance reservations, contact the spa directly. The modern-day baths, which include a large indoor swimming pool filled with the thermally heated waters as well as a series of steam rooms and saunas, are open daily from 9am to 10pm. The cost, per person, for access to the thermally heated swimming pool is 11€ ($18) between 9am and 6pm, and 7€ ($11) between 6 and 10pm. Use of the saunas and steam rooms costs an additional 5€ ($8) per person. A family ticket, priced at 27€ ($43), is available anytime during the spa's opening hours and allows access to the pool, saunas, and steam rooms for two adults and three children under age 18.

Hotel Schwarzmatt ☆☆   Although it ranks behind the Römerbad, this hotel is a consistently popular choice, thanks to its lack of pretension and hardworking, English-speaking staff. The modern, three-story building is adorned with flower boxes along its balconies and flanked by verdant evergreens. The comfortable rooms range from medium to large; all have elegant beds and immaculate bathrooms, with tub/shower combos.

Schwarzmattstrasse 6A (a short walk east of the town center), 79410 Badenweiler. © **07632/82010**. Fax 07632/820120. www.schwarzmatt.de. 41 units. 210€–370€ ($336–$592) double; 310€–390€ ($496–$624) suite. Rates include buffet breakfast. AE, MC, V. Free outdoor parking; garage parking 10€ ($16). **Amenities:** Restaurant; bar; lounge; indoor heated pool; room service; laundry service; dry cleaning; nonsmoking rooms. *In room:* TV, minibar, hair dryer, safe.

WHERE TO DINE

Romantik Hotel Zur Sonne ITALIAN/GERMAN   This hotel is more renowned among locals for its cuisine than for its rooms. The *Weinstube* decor includes old paneling and timbers. Menu items feature a savory mixture of German and Italian cuisine, including braised guinea fowl with arugula; carpaccio of veal with arugula and shaved Parmesan cheese; lobster cocktail; at least four kinds of fresh fish; and ravioli stuffed either with lobster and sage, or with ham and ricotta, according to your tastes. In springtime, a menu category is devoted exclusively to variations on asparagus.

The hotel offers 43 comfortable units with bathrooms containing tub/shower combos, costing 115€ to 140€ ($184–$224).

Moltkestrasse 4. © **07632/75080**. Reservations recommended. Main courses 18€–29€ ($29–$46); fixed-price menu 39€–65€ ($62–$104). AE, DC, MC, V. Daily noon–2pm and 6–9pm.

Schwarzmatt REGIONAL/INTERNATIONAL   There's nothing about this restaurant that's homelike or traditional. Instead, you'll find an airy, high-ceilinged, modern decor with views out over the garden. The well-prepared food consists of

Black Forest specialties, as well as such international dishes as steaks, pastas, salads, and casseroles. The menu is ever-changing but always good. The kitchen staff is skillful and the service professional. Every afternoon from 3 to 5pm, there's a buffet with an impressive assortment of regional and international cakes and other treats served with coffee.

In the Hotel Schwarzmatt, Schwarzmattstrasse 6. (© 07632/82010. Main courses 26€–32€ ($42–$51); fixed-price menu 30€–59€ ($48–$94). AE, MC, V. Daily noon–2pm and 7–10pm.

EXPLORING THE AREA

The town offers a wide range of hiking trails through the Black Forest, the most exhilarating of which is a trek to the **Schloss Bürgeln,** 7846 Schliengen (© **07626/237**), 20km (12 miles) south of Badenweiler and accessible by car (follow the signs from Badenweiler's center). Schloss Bürgeln was built in 1764 by order of the abbot of St. Blasein and offers a commanding view of the surrounding countryside; on a clear day, you can see Basel, the Vosges of France, and the bend in the Rhine as it flows into Switzerland. Especially noteworthy are the verdant gardens around the castle. The castle can only be visited March to November, and only on guided tours (in German and English) daily at 11am and 2, 3, 4, and 5pm. *Note:* If a concert is scheduled, there is no 5pm tour. Adults pay 5€ ($8), and children 11 and under are 2.50€ ($4).

3 Titisee ⟨★

53km (33 miles) E of Freiburg, 160km (99 miles) W of Stuttgart

Titisee is the quintessential German retreat, favored by thousands for its ability to soothe, relax, and refresh the spirit and body. This small lakeside resort, which can be traversed on foot within about 12 minutes, offers access to all the natural bounty of the Schwarzwald. Well-marked hiking trails lead up the hillsides. Motorized vehicles are forbidden on the lake, for the sake of swimmers and general tranquillity. Nearby rises the Feldberg, at 1,525m (5,000 ft.) the highest point in the Black Forest.

Titisee has a year-round population of 2,000, although on busy summer days when visitors come in from nearby cities such as Freiburg, the population can easily swell to three times that amount. More facilities are available at the more workaday community of Neustadt, about 6km (4 miles) away.

ESSENTIALS

GETTING THERE   By Train   From Freiburg, trains arrive at intervals of every 30 minutes (trip time: 45 min.). The Titisee rail station is on Parkstrasse. For information call © **01805/996633.**

By Bus   Bus connections into Titisee are mostly limited to rural hamlets within the surrounding Schwarzwald. For information, call the local bus company at their office in Neustadt, **Südbaden Bus GmbH,** at © **07651/9365880.**

By Car   Titisee is set near the junction of highways B31 and B317, clearly marked from the larger towns that surround it. Driving time from Freiburg is 45 to 60 minutes, depending on traffic; from Stuttgart the trip takes 90 minutes.

VISITOR INFORMATION   Contact the tourist office at Strandbadstrasse 4 (© **07651/98040;** www.titisee.de). May to October, it's open Monday to Friday 9am to 6pm, and Saturday and Sunday 10am to 1pm; November to April, it's open Monday to Friday 9am to noon and 1:30 to 5pm.

WHERE TO STAY

Hotel Brügger am See *(Value* This is one of the most affordable spa hotels around the waterfront. Its allure lies in its relaxation and beauty treatments. The building is a modified chalet, with balconies and an all-window dining room. Rooms are contemporary and mostly a good size, with exceedingly comfortable furnishings and bathrooms containing tub/shower combos.

Strandbadstrasse 14, 79822 Titisee. ℂ **07651/8010.** Fax 07651/8238. www.hotel-brugger.de. 65 units. 112€–156€ ($179–$250) double. Rates include buffet breakfast. Half board 25€ ($40) per person. MC, V. Parking 7€ ($11). **Amenities:** Restaurant; bar; lounge; indoor heated pool; health spa; salon; room service; massage; laundry service; dry cleaning. *In room:* TV, Wi-Fi, hair dryer, safe.

Parkhotel Waldeck *(Value* This hotel is extremely popular, and for good reason—it offers tremendous value and numerous luxuries. A richly decorated interior with Oriental rugs, hexagonal floor tiles, and a beamed and paneled wooden ceiling is very welcoming, as are the bright faces of the helpful staff. The exterior is sheltered against a pine-covered hillock. The small rooms are colorful and comfortable. All bathrooms contain tub/shower combos.

Parkstrasse 6, 78922 Titisee. ℂ **07651/8090.** Fax 07651/80999. www.parkhotelwaldeck.de. 66 units. 51€–72€ ($82–$115) per person double; 78€–95€ ($125–$152) per person suite. Rates include buffet breakfast. AE, DC, MC, V. Parking in garage 7€ ($11). **Amenities:** Restaurant; bar; lounge; indoor heated pool; health club; 4 saunas; solarium; room service; coin-operated laundry; nonsmoking rooms. *In room:* TV, minibar, hair dryer, safe.

Trescher's Schwarzwaldhotel am See *** This sprawling hotel in the center of the resort is the most comprehensive in Titisee, with three massive annexes, each bordering a flower-filled courtyard constructed on a platform built directly into the waters of the lake. The spacious rooms are graceful and conservatively decorated, all with bathrooms with tub/shower combos.

Seestrasse 10, 79822 Titisee-Neustadt. ℂ **07651/8050.** Fax 07651/8186. www.schwarzwaldhotel-trescher.de. 84 units. 155€–230€ ($248–$368) double; 230€–350€ ($368–$560) suite. Rates include breakfast buffet. AE, DC, MC, V. Parking 14€ ($22). **Amenities:** Restaurant; bar; indoor heated pool; health club; sauna; solarium; room service; babysitting. *In room:* TV, minibar, hair dryer, safe.

WHERE TO DINE

Trescher's Schwarzwaldhotel am See * INTERNATIONAL/BLACK FOREST The formal dining room in this hotel (recommended above), with picture windows opening onto the lake, is the best choice for dining in Titisee. Many of the chef's specialties are regional. Recommended appetizers include melon with Black Forest ham and carpaccio of beef with Parmesan. As for main courses, the Black Forest trout is delectably broiled and served with parsley potatoes, and there's also a hunter's plate, Black Forest style, with *Spätzle* (dumplings). A good authentic regional choice is the boiled calves' heads and tongues, served in an onion–red wine sauce. For dessert, try the Black Forest Cherry Bomb.

Seestrasse 10. ℂ **07651/8050.** Reservations required. Main courses 18€–35€ ($29–$56); fixed-price menu 38€ ($61). AE, DC, MC, V. Daily 11:30am–2pm and 6:30–9pm.

WHERE TO STAY & DINE NEARBY

Just 5km (3 miles) west of Titisee, or 30km (20 miles) east of Freiburg, lies **Hinterzarten,** one of the major pockets of posh within the Black Forest. You may want to retreat here instead of Titisee, as Hinterzarten is more tranquil and luxurious. In the town center stands **St. Oswald's,** a church constructed in 1146.

Hotel Reppert ✿   Although not rated as highly as the Park Hotel Adler (below), this is a good second choice, a luxurious and traditional hotel in a sunny and central location in a church meadow fronting the village pond. Its many rooms open onto balconies, each shaded by an umbrella. All units come with tub/shower combinations. A rich, warm ambience inhabits the comfortable, well-furnished rooms. The lobby is filled with antiques.

The regional/international food served here is exceedingly good and the salad buffet is the best and freshest in the area.

Adlerweg 21–23, 79856 Hinterzarten. © 07652/12080. Fax 07652/120811. www.reppert.de. 43 units. 206€–290€ ($330–$464) double; 268€–298€ ($429–$477) suite. Rates include half board. AE, DC, MC, V. Garage parking 9€ ($14). Closed Nov 7–Dec 10. **Amenities:** Restaurant; lounge; 3 pools (heated outdoor, heated indoor, and indoor seawater); health club; 2 Jacuzzis; sauna; steam room; room service; babysitting; laundry service; dry cleaning; all nonsmoking rooms. *In room:* TV, Wi-Fi, minibar, hair dryer, safe.

Park Hotel Adler ✿✿✿   This is one of the Black Forest's great inns. Chic and country estate–like with a wealth of leisure facilities, the inn suggests luxury at every turn. It's in the middle of a lovely 4-hectare (10-acre) park. Rooms are sumptuously appointed and beautifully maintained, and many are quite spacious. Beds are so comfortable you won't want to get out of them, and the beautiful bathrooms are equipped with tub/shower combos. The hotel's family ownership dates from 1446.

The Wirtshus attracts serious foodies with finely honed cuisine that ranges from Black Forest specialties such as calves' heads, to international favorites such as filet of sole with scallops in a mushroom cream sauce. For dessert, try the strawberry mousse.

Adlerplatz 3, D-79856 Hinterzarten. © 07652/1270. Fax 07652/127717. www.parkhoteladler.de. 146 units. 205€–260€ ($328–$416) double; 295€–380€ ($472–$608) junior suite; 335€–555€ ($536–$888) suite; 265€–285€ ($424–$456) apt. Rates include buffet breakfast. AE, DC, MC, V. Parking 9€ ($14). **Amenities:** 2 restaurants; bar; indoor heated pool; health spa; Jacuzzi; sauna; steam room; salon; room service; babysitting; laundry service; dry cleaning; nonsmoking rooms. *In room:* TV, Wi-Fi (in some), minibar, hair dryer, safe.

EXPLORING THE AREA

You won't find museums or monuments at this outdoorsy resort, but the cold, clear waters of Lake Titisee are among the most sought-after in the region. The premier bathing spot is **Schwimmbad Titisee,** Strandbadstrasse (© 07651/8272), which combines the chlorinated waters of the town's largest swimming pool with access to a sandy beach adjacent to the lake, complete with cabanas, showers, and refreshment stands. Entrance to the complex costs 4€ ($6.40) for adults, 2.50€ ($4) for students and children. It's open from mid-May to September daily 9am to 7pm (closed Oct to mid-May).

Except for a handful of medium-size steamers that slowly circumnavigate the lake (see below), local ordinances allow only rowboats, foot-operated paddleboats, and electric (not gas-operated) motorboats on the water's surface, a rule that keeps noise, pollution, and rowdiness to a minimum. You can rent rowboats and paddleboats for 6€ to 9€ ($9.60–$14) per half-hour. About a half-dozen purveyors of these rental craft line the edges of the Seestrasse, the town's main lakefront promenade; the two best are **Drubba** (© 07651/981200) and **Schweizer-Winterhalder** (© 07651/8214).

Schweizer-Winterhalder also operates **lake steamers,** which provide a more comfortable excursion. June to September, they depart during the day at hourly intervals from the company's pier. Trips last about 25 minutes and are priced at 4€ ($6.40) per person.

Spa clients within Titisee head for the facilities within the **Hotel Brügger,** am See, Strandbadstrasse 14 (© **07651/8010**), which are open to residents of other hotels. In nearby Neustadt, the **Kneipp-Kur** (© **07651/1270**), in the Kurpark, offers an equivalent spa facility, with treatments for cardiac and vascular disorders, rheumatism, and intestinal diseases.

Shoppers and boaters head to the stores that line the lakefront **Seestrasse.** In the early evening, a Bavarian-style marching band promenades along the lakefront, its members stopping at various hotels en route.

4 Triberg ⟨⋆

138km (86 miles) SW of Stuttgart, 48km (30 miles) NE of Freiburg

Triberg, deep in the heart of the Black Forest, is home to the highest waterfall in the country. It also claims to be the birthplace of the cuckoo clock, so if you're in the market for a traditional timepiece, this is the place to find it. You'll also find many little shops selling woodcarvings, music boxes, and other local crafts. **Warning:** Triberg is virtually overrun with tour buses in summer, and the traffic tie-ups on the road to Triberg can be horrendous.

ESSENTIALS

GETTING THERE   By Plane   The nearest major airport is at Stuttgart, 2½ hours away by train.

By Train   Trains arrive daily from Munich (trip time: 4½ hr.) and from Frankfurt (trip time: 3 hr.). The **Triberg Bahnhof** is on the Konstanz-Singen-Villingen-Offenburg-Schwarzwaldbahn rail line, with frequent connections in all directions. Call © **01805/996633** for schedules and information.

By Bus   Regional bus service in the Black Forest area is provided by **SBG Südbaden Bus GmbH,** located in the nearby town of Furtwangen (© **07723/19449**).

By Car   Access is via the A5 Autobahn north and south; exit at Offenburg and then follow the signs along Route 33 south.

VISITOR INFORMATION   Contact the tourist office, Wallfahrtstrasse 4 (© **07722/866490**), open year-round daily 10am to 5pm.

WHERE TO STAY

Romantik Parkhotel Wehrle ⟨⋆⟨⋆   This is the finest and most traditional inn in the area. Built in the early 1600s, Parkhotel Wehrle was acquired around 1730 by the family that has owned it ever since. Its lemon-yellow walls and gabled mansard roof occupy one of the most prominent street corners in town. The main house offers an old-world atmosphere, but forest-loving vacationers often request accommodations near the woods in a separate chalet, where a pool and breeze-filled balconies create a modern sylvan retreat. The good-size rooms are beautifully furnished and individually decorated, sometimes with antiques.

Gartenstrasse 24 (1.5km/1 mile from the train station), 78098 Triberg. © **07722/86020.** Fax 07722/860290. www.parkhotel-wehrle.de. 50 units. 129€–210€ ($206–$336) double; from 285€ ($456) suite. Rates include buffet breakfast. AE, DC, MC, V. Free parking outdoors; 6€ ($9.60) in garage. **Amenities:** 3 restaurants; bar; 2 pools (1 outdoor, 1 heated indoor); health club; spa; room service; laundry service; dry cleaning; nonsmoking rooms. *In room:* TV, Wi-Fi, hair dryer, safe.

Moments Wunderhiking in the Black Forest

You can see the loveliest parts of the Black Forest by hiking the ancient trail of the cuckoo-clock traders. Really. The trail follows the route of the traders who, centuries ago, carried the famous Black Forest clocks across Europe. On the village-to-village journey, you pass through deep, fragrant pinewoods and sunny pastures where farmhouses are set scenically on hillsides.

The circle trail starts at Triberg, with its waterfalls. An arrangement with a series of hotels along the trail, beginning with the **Parkhotel Wehrle** (see below), allows you to hike with only a small rucksack; vans haul your luggage on to the next hotel. You can hike from 1 to 10 days and more if you have the time (but most hikers have their fill long before this). Distances for a day's hike between hotels range from 20km to 27km (12–17 miles).

Clearly marked signs guide you across this easy trail, and the Parkhotel Wehrle provides a road map and detailed road descriptions (in English) to set you on your way. Restaurants and farmhouses offering food and refreshment are not far apart, and the area is quite safe, even for a woman walking alone.

Römischer Kaiser _Value_ You get old-style charm here, and old-style prices, too. This comfortable, charmingly preserved hotel has been owned by several generations of the same family since 1840. The exterior has lots of exposed wood. Rooms come in a wide range of shapes and sizes, but all are pleasant and well maintained. Bathrooms are roomy, with showers or tubs.

Sommerauerstrasse 35 (1.5km/1 mile outside Triberg), 78098 Triberg-Nussbach. © 07722/96940. Fax 07722/969429. www.roemischer-kaiser.com. 27 units. 62€–74€ ($99–$118) double. Rates include buffet breakfast. AE, DC, MC, V. Free parking. Closed Nov 15–Dec 7. **Amenities:** Restaurant; lounge. _In room:_ TV, hair dryer.

WHERE TO DINE

Parkhotel Wehrle _&_ CONTINENTAL   People come from great distances to eat at this famous restaurant. Meals are accompanied by the ticking of a stately grandfather clock; meanwhile, the clientele relaxes in the comfort of cane-bottomed French-style armchairs. The cuisine is intelligent and imaginative, with a focus on natural flavors. Even simple dishes have a certain flair. Try the trout or saddle of venison with juniper-berry cream sauce and _Spätzle._ A traditional dessert is apples baked with pine honey and flambéed with _Kirschwasser,_ a black cherry brandy. Some of the game specialties are prepared for two.

Marktplatz. © 07722/86020. Reservations required. Main courses 21€–35€ ($34–$56); fixed-price 3-course menu 21€ ($34). AE, DC, MC, V. Daily noon–2pm and 7–10pm.

EXPLORING THE AREA

Triberg is the home of the highest waterfall in Germany, **Wasserfelle Gutach (Gutach Falls)** _&_, which drops some 160m (525 ft.), spilling downhill in seven misty and poetically evocative stages. They're only accessible on foot. To get here you park your car in a designated area in the town center, near the Gutach Bridge, and then walk along a clearly signposted trail. Signs point to DEUTSCHLAND'S HOCHSTE WASSERFELLE

(Germany's Highest Waterfall), which requires, round-trip, about an hour of moderately difficult hill climbing. Seeing the falls is possible only between April and late October. (The rest of the year, snowfalls make trails dangerously slippery, and access to the falls is closed.) At the bottom of the falls are some souvenir shops; a cafe and restaurant that serves bracing, rib-sticking German food and portions of Black Forest cake; and a kiosk that collects an entrance charge of 2.50€ ($4) for adults and .90€ ($1.50) for students and children ages 8 to 15.

Schwarzwald-Museum of Triberg, Wallfahrstrasse 4 (© **07722/4434;** www.schwarzwaldmuseum.com), brings the olden days of the Black Forest vividly to life, with displays of dresses, handicrafts, furnishings, bird music boxes, and, of course, clocks and clock making. You can also see a working model of the famed Schwarzwaldbahn railway; opened in 1873, it led to the development of Triberg as an international winter sports and health resort. There is also a mineral exhibit of the area, and Europe's largest barrel organ collection. The museum is open daily May to September 10am to 6pm, and October to April 10am to 5pm. Admission is 4.50€ ($7.20) adults and 2.50€ ($4) students and children ages 5 to 17. Children 4 and under enter free.

One of the most beautiful churches in the Black Forest, the **Wallfahrtskirche Maria in der Tannen (Church of Our Lady of the Fir Trees),** Clemens-Maria-Hofbauer Strasse (© **07722/4566**), lies on the western edge of town, an 8-minute walk from the center. Built during the 18th century, it has superb baroque finishings, including a remarkable ornate pulpit. It's open daily, year-round, from 8am to 7pm. Entrance is free.

After a visit to the church, consider driving to the **Freilichtmuseum Schwarzwälder** in the hamlet of Gutach (© **07831/93560**), which lies 17km (11 miles) north of Triberg. Here, you'll find a collection of looms and paraphernalia related to the weaving industry that in some cases are as much as 4 centuries old. In summer, guides demonstrate weaving techniques on some of the looms. The museum is open April to October daily from 9am to 6pm. Admission costs 6€ ($9.60) for adults and 3€ ($4.80) for students and children ages 5 to 18. A family ticket is 13€ ($21). From the A5, turn off at the Offenburg exit and follow B33 toward Gengenback, Hausach, and Triberg. At Hausach, turn right toward Gutach.

A 15km (10-mile) drive south of Triberg is the **Deutsches Uhrenmuseum (German Clock Museum),** Gerwigstrasse 11, in the hamlet of Furtwangen (© **07723/920800**). To get here, drive for 20 minutes west along the B500, following the signs to Furtwangen.

Finds **Stop for Clocks**

You may want to make a stop along the B33 between Triberg and Hornberg at the **Haus der 1000 Uhren (House of 1,000 Clocks),** An der Bundesstrasse 33, 78098 Triberg-Gemmelsbach (© **07722/96300;** www.hausder1000uhren.de). You'll recognize the shop immediately by the giant cuckoo clock and water wheel in front. A painter of clock faces, Josef Weisser, launched the business in 1824; today his great-great-grandson owns the place. The shop is open Easter to October Monday to Saturday 9am to 5pm and Sunday 10am to 4pm. It ships to the United States and Canada and takes all major credit cards. There's another branch in the center of Triberg, near the entrance to the waterfall.

It's open daily November to March 10am to 5pm and April to October 9am to 6pm. Admission is 4€ ($6.40) for adults and 3€ ($4.80) for children. This museum presents a history of timepieces, including displays of a wide variety of Black Forest clocks, some from the early 18th century. Many are elaborate and complicated. Look for the mechanical music automata and the cuckoo clocks.

5 Freudenstadt

92km (57 miles) N of Freiburg

One of the most important transportation hubs in the northern tier of the Black Forest is Freudenstadt, a riverside town known for clear air, streaming sunshine, and a sense of cleanliness and conservatism. Originally founded in 1599 by Duke Friedrich I of Württemberg, Freudenstadt provided a home at the time for Protestants fleeing religious persecution within Carinthia, in southern Austria. French troops set most of the town ablaze in the closing days of World War II, but it was completely rebuilt, close to the original plans, by 1950.

ESSENTIALS

GETTING THERE   By Train   Trains from Frankfurt arrive hourly throughout the day (trip time: 3½ hr.). Ten trains per day arrive from Munich (trip time: 4½ hr.). Freudenstadt has two railway stations, the **Stadtbahnhof,** an older and smaller station in the center of town, and the **Hauptbahnhof,** about .6km (1 mile) south of the center. Most trains stop at both. For information on trains throughout Germany and Europe, call © **01805/996633.**

By Bus   Bus travel tends to be convenient only for those coming from surrounding hamlets. Buses stop at both the Bahnhofplatz and the Marktplatz. For information, call © **07441/860130.**

By Car   Driving from Stuttgart, following the B28, takes about 15 minutes; from Karlsruhe via the B462, about 30 minutes.

VISITOR INFORMATION   The **Tourist Information Office** is at Marktplatz 64 (© **07441/8640;** www.freudenstadt.de). It's open Monday to Friday 10am to 5pm, Saturday 10am to 3:30pm (until 1pm in winter), and Sunday 11am to 1pm.

WHERE TO STAY

Hotel Bären   This establishment's cozy interior, lined with old panels and capped with heavy ceiling beams, may remind you of the inside of a prosperous local farmhouse. Rooms are cozy, traditionally decorated, and well maintained, containing tub/shower combinations. The staff is charming and polite, conveying a nostalgic sense of traditional Germany.

The hotel is perhaps best known for its restaurant, which serves well-prepared Swabian food with main courses costing 12€ to 28€ ($19–$45).

33 Langestrasse (near the Marktplatz), 72250 Freudenstadt. © 07441/2729. Fax 07441/2887. www.hotel-baeren-freudenstadt.de. 36 units. 95€–160€ ($152–$256) double. MC, V. Free parking. **Amenities:** Restaurant; lounge; room service; laundry service; dry cleaning. *In room:* TV, hair dryer.

Hotel Hohenried im Rosengarten ⚙   This three-story hotel is designed to look like a modern version of an alpine chalet. The garden contains more than 2,000 well-tended rose bushes. The comfortable and contemporary-looking rooms overlook a golf course and stately trees. In summertime, the balconies are adorned with geranium-filled flower boxes. All the accommodations come with neatly tiled bathrooms with shower units. The staff is polite and speaks English.

Zeppelinstrasse 5–7 (1.5km/1 mile south of Freudenstadt's center), 72250 Freudenstadt. © **07441/2414.** Fax 07441/2559. www.hotelhohenried.de. 25 units. 99€–168€ ($158–$269) double. AE, MC, V. Bus: 14. **Amenities:** Restaurant; bar; lounge; indoor heated pool; health club; sauna; room service; laundry service; dry cleaning; nonsmoking rooms; rooms for those w/limited mobility. *In room:* TV, Wi-Fi, hair dryer.

WHERE TO DINE

Jägerstüble SWABIAN/GERMAN   Like most of the buildings around it, this is an excellent re-creation of a medieval house that was severely damaged during World War II. Inside, foaming mugs of beer and hardworking waitresses in folkloric costumes contribute to an unpretentious re-creation of the Germany of another era. The hearty and savory dishes include *Eisbein* (veal shank) with sauerkraut, farmers' omelets, venison steak prepared with garlic and red wine, and goulash of venison.

Marktplatz 12. © **07441/2387.** Reservations recommended. Main courses 12€–18€ ($19–$29). MC, V. Tues–Sat 8am–11pm; Sun 8am–6pm.

Warteck ☆ SWABIAN/GERMAN   One of the most durable restaurants in Freudenstadt opened in 1951 in a location that's a 3-minute walk from the town's Marktplatz. A pair of charming dining rooms are lined with flowers and outfitted in tones of ocher and turquoise. You'll enjoy savory, relatively formal cuisine that includes braised oxtail with herbs and vegetables, roasted pigeon, and a preparation of sweetbreads for which the chef is especially well known. Fish crops up often on the menu, often simply braised and served in an herb-enriched butter sauce. Everything here is in good taste, with lots of elegant, low-key charm. The restaurant lies within a cozy, government-rated three-star hotel with 13 well-furnished doubles, costing from 80€ to 90€ ($128–$144), including breakfast.

Stuttgarterstrasse 14. © **07441/91920.** Fax 07441/919293. www.warteck-freudenstadt.de. Reservations recommended. Main courses 18€–35€ ($29–$56); fixed-price menus 37€–39€ ($59–$62). AE, DC, MC, V. Wed–Mon noon–2pm and 6–10pm. Closed 2 weeks during Jan and Nov.

WHERE TO STAY & DINE NEARBY

If you want to experience the Schwarzwald at its most isolated and remote, consider a stay at either of the following two hotels, which are positioned south and north of the hamlet of Baiersbronn, respectively. Baiersbronn lies 6km (4 miles) northwest of Freudenstadt. Trains arrive in Baiersbronn about once an hour from Stuttgart and Karlsruhe, stopping in Baiersbronn before continuing south for another 6km (4 miles) to Freudenstadt. Local buses (marked BAIERSBRONN) depart from the Marktplatz in Freudenstadt for Baiersbronn, but there are only about four per day, and they won't take you anywhere near either of the two hotels. For the short distance involved, it's a lot more convenient to take any of the taxis lined up in Freudenstadt's Marktplatz.

Hotel Bareiss ☆☆   This deluxe resort hotel is equivalent in most ways to the Hotel Traube Tonbach (see below) but a bit less formal and a lot less stiff. It provides a soothing, carefully orchestrated, well-manicured environment, where peace, quiet, and access to the surrounding forest are fiercely guarded. You'll find lots of urban refugees on-site, recuperating from stressful careers. Rooms are spacious, carefully maintained, conservatively modern, and very comfortable. All have views over the forest and have bathrooms with tub/shower combos.

Gärtenbühlweg 14, 072270 Baiersbronn/Mitteltal. (✆ **07442/470.** Fax 07442/47320. www.bareiss.com. 127 units. 176€–216€ ($282–$346) double; 292€–378€ ($467–$605) suite; 207€–274€ ($331–$438) apt. All rates are per person. Rates include buffet breakfast. AE, DC, MC, V. Parking 9€ ($14). From the center of Baiersbronn, head south following signs pointing to Hotel Bareiss for 10km (6 miles). **Amenities:** 3 restaurants; bar; 4 heated pools (2 indoor); tennis court; health club; sauna; bike rental; salon; room service; massage; babysitting; laundry service; dry cleaning; nonsmoking rooms. *In room:* A/C (in some), TV, Wi-Fi, minibar, hair dryer, safe.

Hotel Traube Tonbach 👁👁👁 This is the grande dame of Black Forest resorts. In 1957, this establishment was massively enlarged into the stately, multibalcony resort you see today and immediately attracted one of the grandest resort clienteles in Germany. Set closer to Baiersbronn (only about a mile north of town) than its competitor, the Bareiss (see above), the Traube Tonbach prides itself on its conservatism, its strictly enforced sense of peace and quiet, and the glamour of its very upscale clientele. Rooms are good size, solid, well built, quiet, and very, very comfortable. All bathrooms are neatly appointed with tub/shower combinations. Ask the staff for advice on nearby hiking trails.

Ortsteil Tonbach, Tonbachstrasse 237, 72270 Baiersbronn. (✆ **07442/4920.** Fax 07442/492692. www.traubetonbach.de. 170 units. 127€–182€ ($203–$291) double; 245€ ($392) suite. Rates include breakfast. Half board 18€ ($23) per person. AE, DC, MC, V. Parking 5€–7.50€ ($8–$12). **Amenities:** 4 restaurants; bar; lounge; 3 heated pools (2 indoor); tennis court; health club; whirlpool; sauna; steam room; room service; massage; babysitting; laundry service; dry cleaning; nonsmoking rooms; bowling alley. *In room:* A/C (suites only), TV, Wi-Fi, minibar, hair dryer, safe.

EXPLORING FREUDENSTADT

Freudenstadt's appeal is its location in the midst of the best hiking, skiing, and camping country in the Black Forest. It's one of the best centers for exploring the fabled **Schwarzwald Hochstrasse** 👁👁. This highway stretches for 80km (50 miles) from Baden-Baden to Freudenstadt and can be traveled in 1½ hours (although most tourists prefer to take much longer due to the many charming shops and cafes along the way). Many points along the route approach a height of 1,000m (3,300 ft.) and you'll find a number of belvederes and car parks where you can take in the view. Along the route are dozens of winter ski slopes.

In summer, visitors hike in the country's largest nature preserve, the **Parkwald** 👁👁 abutting Freudenstadt. The park is riddled with miles of walking trails. You can pick up excellent trail maps at the Freudenstadt tourist office (see above) before setting out, either in winter or summer.

Unlike many German towns, Freudenstadt has no castle overshadowing it, but it certainly does have an enormous castle square. This plot of land, the largest **Marktplatz** 👁 in Germany, was laid out in the 16th century for a castle that was never built. History's loss is today's gain. The market square that greets the visitor to Freudenstadt is a maze of lawns and concrete, broken by patches of flowers and kiosks. The buildings surrounding the square are mainly postwar because the air raids and fires of World War II almost completely destroyed the city. A few of the old Renaissance structures on the square have been reconstructed, up to their neat little archways and gabled roofs.

The town takes pride in its **Stadtkirche,** Marktplatz (✆ **07441/6554**), dating from the 17th century. The unusual L-shaped architecture of the church brings the two main aisles together at right angles. Over the entrance stand identical towers, topped with rounded domes and narrow spires. The church's most important treasure is the 12th-century reading desk, supported by carved and painted likenesses of the Evangelists. It's open daily 10am to 5pm. Entrance is free.

Freudenstadt doesn't have any other museums or attractions worth mentioning, with the exception of a small regional folk and crafts museum, the **Heimatmuseum,** in the Stadthaus, Marktplatz (© **07441/6177**). It's open Monday to Friday 9 to 11am and 3 to 5pm, Sunday 10am to noon. Entrance is free.

FREUDENSTADT AFTER DARK

In lieu of any real nightlife, locals head for a local *Stube,* or beer hall, for a "night on the town." Most of these drinking places are within hotels, and two of the best are at the previously recommended Hotel Bären and the Jägerstüble (see above), the latter serving the largest mugs of beer in town. In winter, you can find beer drinkers gathered around the old tile stove of the **Ratskeller,** Marktplatz 8 (© **07441/952805**). If you like this place, you can opt to order platters of traditional Swabian dishes, including *Zwiebelrostbraten* (onion-flavored roast beef), served with sauerkraut, that seem to go especially well with the beer.

6 Calw

20km (13 miles) S of Pforzheim, 66km (41 miles) N of Freudenstadt

Many residents of other parts of Germany call Calw (the *w* is silent) the most appealingly folkloric town in the Black Forest. Hermann Hesse, who was born here in 1877, described Calw as "the most beautiful place I know."

ESSENTIALS

GETTING THERE   By Train   Trains arrive at Calw's Bahnhof at hourly intervals from both Stuttgart and Karlsruhe. Both cities are about an hour away. For railway information, call © **01805/996633.**

By Bus   Buses that travel between Horb, Nagold, and Pforzheim make stops at Calw's Bahnhofplatz. For information, call © **07051/96890.**

By Car   Calw lies midway between Pforzheim and Nagold, along Highway B463. From the A8 Autobahn, exit at the signs indicating Calw.

VISITOR INFORMATION   The **Tourist Information office** in Calw is at Marktbrücke 1 (© **07051/968810;** www.calw.de). It's open year-round Monday to Friday 9am to 12:30pm and 2 to 5pm, and also May to October Saturday 9:30am to 12:30pm.

WHERE TO STAY

Hotel Kloster Hirsau   The best place for overnighting lies right outside of town 2km (1¼ miles) to the north in the direction of Hirsau. Parts of the foundation of this historic hotel date from 1092, when the site functioned as a monastery that was noted for housing overnight visitors. Today, the establishment retains its medieval touches and antique charm. The good-size rooms have lots of Schwarzwald-inspired features, including pinewood trim and reproductions of traditional furniture. Bathrooms are tidily kept with tub/shower combos. The oldest, most atmospheric, and charming bedrooms are nos. 114 to 235.

Ortsteil Hirsau, Wildbacher Strasse 2, 75365 Calw. © **07051/96740.** Fax 07051/967469. www.hotel-klosterhirsau.de. 40 units. 109€–124€ ($174–$198) double. Rates include breakfast. Half board 18€ ($29) per person. AE, MC, V. Free parking; parking in garage 8€ ($13). **Amenities:** Restaurant; lounge; indoor heated pool; tennis courts; health club; sauna; salon; nonsmoking rooms. *In room:* TV, minibar, hair dryer, safe (in some).

Moments Off the Beaten Trail

The environs of Calw also merit some attention if you have the time. Of exceptional interest is the hamlet of **Zavelstein**, which is signposted in Calw. Follow the road south for 5km (3 miles). A drive to this little hamlet is especially spectacular in late March and April, when the meadows blossom with edelweiss and crocuses. You may want to continue south in the direction of Talmühle-Seitzental, where you'll see a sign pointing along a twisting road leading to **Neubulach** (© 07053/969510). Until it closed in the mid-1920s, this was one of the most active silver mines in the Black Forest. Long after it was abandoned, the medical profession learned that its dust-free interior was beneficial in the treatment of asthma. A therapy center is now located inside. The mine's ancient shafts can be visited on guided tours given April to November daily from 10am to 4pm, costing 4.50€ ($7.20) for adults and 2.50€ ($4) for children.

WHERE TO DINE

Ratsstube *Value* SWABIAN/INTERNATIONAL   This is the most popular and reliable restaurant in town, not to be confused with the more down-market and sudsier Ratskeller, whose entrance lies a few feet away. The Ratsstube, built in the early 1800s, has two separate dining rooms, each evocative of a bygone Germany. It's very rustic and ethnic German; very little English is spoken by the staff. The interior is a labyrinth of masonry-sided rooms. The well-prepared but not particularly innovative dishes include *Zwiebelrostbraten* (roast beef with onions), filet of sole in wine sauce, stingray in black-butter sauce, trout with almonds or meunière style, and an array of sausages served with cabbage and roasted potatoes. Service is competent.

Marktplatz 12. © 07051/92050. Reservations recommended. Main courses 10€–14€ ($16–$22). MC, V. Daily 11:30am–9pm (last order).

Restaurant Klosterschanke SWABIAN/INTERNATIONAL   Cozy and historically authentic, this restaurant occupies a trio of dining rooms with beamed and/or vaulted ceilings, which, in some cases, are hundreds of years old. Menu items include fresh house-marinated sardines, rack of lamb with white beans, *Zwiebelrostbraten,* monkfish braised in olive oil with herbs, and several kinds of schnitzel. Although the food never reaches the sublime, it's always fresh and competently prepared.

Wildbader Strasse 2. © 07051/96740. Reservations recommended. Main courses 16€–24€ ($26–$38); fixed-price menu 18€–20€ ($29–$32). MC, V. Daily lunch noon–2pm; *Kaffe mit Kuchen* (coffee and cakes) 2–6pm; dinner 6–10pm.

EXPLORING CALW

Calw's allure derives from its impressive and meticulously maintained roster of late-17th- and early-18th-century houses, whose half-timbered facades add an undeniable charm to such sites as the Marktplatz. The town's most prominent bridge, the 14th-century **Niko-lausbrücke,** in the center, merits a stroll in admiration of its carefully chiseled masonry.

The birthplace of Herman Hesse, the **Hesse Haus,** Marktplatz 30 (© 07051/7522), is a literary shrine for scholars and fans. Entrance is 5€ ($8) adults, 3€ ($4.80) students and children. The only other formal attraction in town is a small-scale folklore museum called **Palais Vischer,** Bischofstrasse 48 (© 07051/167260). It's open April to October Saturday and Sunday 2 to 5pm. Admission is 1.50€ ($2.40) adults, free for children 11 and under.

7 Pforzheim

35km (22 miles) S of Karlsruhe, 53km (33 miles) SW of Stuttgart

Set at the northern edge of the Black Forest, at the junction of three rivers (the Würm, the Enz, and the Nagold), Pforzheim is one of the Schwarzwald's largest settlements. It was founded by the Romans as a fortified camp and developed into an important mercantile center during the Middle Ages. Key industries have traditionally included the crafting of jewelry and clock making. Although it was severely damaged by bombs during World War II, Pforzheim is a worthwhile site for an overnight stay between forays into the Black Forest.

ESSENTIALS

GETTING THERE   By Train   Trains pull into Pforzheim at least once an hour from Munich (trip time: 3 hr.), Frankfurt (trip time: 2 hr.), and Stuttgart (trip time: 1½ hr.). The railway station lies within an 8-minute walk of the center. For information, call ☎ **01805/996633.**

By Bus   Bus travel to Pforzheim is a lot less practical than rail travel. The bus stop is at Leopoldplatz, in the town center.

By Car   Pforzheim lies beside the high-speed A-8 Autobahn that stretches between Munich and Karlsruhe. Transit from Stuttgart takes between 45 and 90 minutes; from Munich, around 2½ hours; and from Frankfurt, around 2 hours.

VISITOR INFORMATION   Head to **Stadinformation,** Marktplatz 1 (☎ **07231/ 393700;** www.pforzheim.de), open Monday to Friday 10am to 6pm, and Saturday 10am to 1pm.

WHERE TO STAY

Hotel Royal   Equivalent in most ways to the Parkhotel (see below), the Royal's only drawback is its location on the outskirts of town. It was built in 1995 in a two-story, modern format. Rooms are small to medium size, contemporary, sunny, comfortable, clean, and utterly without pretension. All bathrooms contain showers or tubs. The staff is polite and well trained.

Wilhelmbeckerstrasse 3A (1.5km/1 mile north of the center), 75179 Pforzheim. ☎ **07231/14250.** Fax 07231/142599. www.hotel-royal-pforzheim.de. 43 units. 115€–117€ ($184–$187) double. Rates include breakfast and free parking. AE, DC, V. Bus: 29. **Amenities:** Restaurant; bar; free admission to nearby sauna and fitness center; room service; laundry service; dry cleaning; nonsmoking rooms. *In room:* TV, minibar, hair dryer, safe.

Parkhotel ⊛   Set in the center of town, the four-story, contemporary Parkhotel is the meeting place for most of the civic and charitable organizations in Pforzheim. Inside, you'll find a streamlined, tasteful decor with lots of exposed wood and stone. Rooms are good size, airy, and comfortable, with bathrooms containing tub/shower combinations.

Deimlingerstrasse 36, 75175 Pforzheim. ☎ **07231/1610.** Fax 07231/161690. www.parkhotel-pforzheim.de. 208 units. 132€–162€ ($211–$259) double; from 182€ ($291) suite. Rates include breakfast buffet. Free parking. AE, DC, MC, V. **Amenities:** 2 restaurants; bar; cafe; health club; Jacuzzi; sauna; steam room; room service; babysitting; laundry service; dry cleaning; nonsmoking rooms; rooms for those w/limited mobility. *In room:* A/C, TV, Wi-Fi, minibar, hair dryer, trouser press (in most), safe.

WHERE TO DINE

Parkrestaurant GERMAN   This well-managed restaurant offers solid home-style cuisine, a view over the Stadt Theater and the banks of the Enz River, and a polite, well-trained staff. We prefer this place to the Galarestaurant, its more upscale sibling

Finds Medieval Excursion from Pforzheim

One of the Schwarzwald's most evocative sights lies 18km (11 miles) to the northeast of Pforzheim, within the agrarian hamlet of Maulbronn. **Kloster Maulbronn** (© 07043/926610) has been called the best-preserved medieval monastery north of the Alps. Most of its more than 30 stone-sided buildings were constructed between 1150 and 1390, within an encircling wall that protected the monks and their allies from outside attackers. The most visible of the buildings is the compound's **church,** which combines aspects of Romanesque and Gothic architecture, and which influenced the design of later structures throughout central and northern Europe. Look for the complicated **irrigation system,** still intact, which distributed water to key elements within the compound. Most visitors arrive by car or taxi from the center of Pforzheim, although there's also a bus that departs for Maulbronn from Pforzheim's Leopoldplatz at 50-minute intervals throughout the day. The monastery is open March to October daily 9am to 5:30pm, and November to February Tuesday to Sunday 9:30am to 5pm. Admission is 5.50€ ($8.80) adults, 2.80€ ($4.50) students and children.

within the same hotel. Menu items include schnitzels, stews, roulades and grills, soups, salads, and hearty, regional desserts layered with chocolate and whipped cream.

In the Parkhotel, Deimlingerstrasse 36. © 07231/16101. Reservations not necessary. Main courses 10€–22€ ($16–$35); fixed-price menu 64€ ($102). AE, DC, MC, V. Daily noon–2pm and 6–11:30pm.

EXPLORING PFORZHEIM

Allied bombs demolished much of Pforzheim in World War II. Of the limited number of buildings that have been restored to their former grandeur, **Sankt Michaelerskirche (St. Michael's Church),** Schlossberg 10 (© 07231/102484), is the most dramatic. It was built in stages between the 1200s and 1400s and combines aspects of both Romanesque and Gothic architecture. It's open daily 8:30am to 6pm. A fine example of a more modern church is the **Stadtkirche,** on Melanchthonstrasse (no phone), in the town center across from the Parkhotel. Rebuilt from the town's rubble during the 1950s, this is a symbol of Pforzheim's rebirth from the devastation of World War II.

For insights into the role that clock making has traditionally played in Pforzheim, head for the city's **Technisches Museum,** Bleichstrasse 81 (© 07231/392869; www. technisches-museum.de), where souvenirs and mementos of the clock-making trade commemorate humankind's painstaking efforts to organize time. On the premises is a reconstruction of a clock-making studio from the early 1800s. The museum is open every Wednesday 9am to noon and 3 to 6pm, and every second and fourth Sunday 10am to 5pm. Admission is free, although donations are appreciated.

The equally nostalgic **Schmuckmuseum,** Jahnstrasse 42 (© 07231/392126; www.schmuckmuseum.de), is devoted to Pforzheim's jewelry-making trade. Its collection includes ornaments from the 3rd century B.C. to modern times. The museum is open Tuesday to Sunday 10am to 5pm. Admission is 3€ ($4.80).

If you're passionate about botany or gardening, you may enjoy a visit to the **Alpengarten (Alpine Garden),** Auf dem Berg 6 (© 07231/70590), in which about 100,000 varieties of high-altitude plants are grown in a natural-looking milieu. Set adjacent to the banks of the Würm River, about 3km (2 miles) south of Pforzheim's center, it's open March to November Monday to Friday 9am to noon and 2 to 6pm, Saturday 9am to 2pm. Admission costs 3€ ($4.80). To reach it from Pforzheim, follow the signs to Würm.

8 Baden-Baden ★★

111km (69 miles) W of Stuttgart, 111km (69 miles) NE of Freiburg, 174km (108 miles) S of Frankfurt

In the 19th century, European nobility rediscovered Baden-Baden, where the bath-conscious Roman emperor Caracalla once came to ease his arthritic aches. Swanky clients such as Queen Victoria, Kaiser Wilhelm I, Napoleon III, Berlioz, Brahms, and Dostoyevsky helped make Baden-Baden the most elegant and sophisticated playground in Germany. Tolstoy set a scene in *Anna Karenina* here, though he gave the town a different name. Today, the clientele may have changed, but Baden-Baden still evokes an aura of 19th-century privilege, combined with the most up-to-date facilities.

Baden-Baden is the ideal choice for sports and outdoor enthusiasts. Golf, tennis, and horseback riding are all popular. Lovers of horse racing will enjoy the international racing season each August at Iffezheim Track. The surrounding countryside is filled with hiking and mountain climbing options. During the winter, Baden-Baden is a convenient center for skiing: After a day on the slopes, you can return to a soothing swim in a thermal pool and a night out at the casino.

ESSENTIALS

GETTING THERE   By Train   Baden-Baden is on major rail lines connecting Frankfurt and Basel, and Stuttgart and Munich. There are 20 trains daily from Stuttgart (trip time: 1¼ hr.); 25 from Munich (trip time: 4 hr., 10 min.), and 45 from Frankfurt (trip time: 3 hr.). For information, call © 01805/996633. The railway station is at Baden-Oos, north of town; regrettably, it's an expensive 20-minute taxi ride from the town center.

By Car   Access to Baden-Baden is via the A5 Autobahn north and south or the A8 Autobahn east and west. The drive south from Frankfurt takes 2 hours; from Munich, it's about 4 hours.

VISITOR INFORMATION   For information, contact **Tourist-Information,** Schwarzwaldstrasse 52 (© 07221/275200; www.baden-baden.com), Monday to Saturday 9am to 6pm and Sunday 9am to 1pm. After the morning shift on Sunday in the tourist office, information can be obtained in the Drinking House from 2 to 5pm.

GETTING AROUND   Baden-Baden is serviced by a network of buses whose routes coincide at the Leopoldplatz, in the center. Bus no. 201, which runs at 10-minute intervals, interconnects most of the important sites with the railway station, about 5km (3 miles) from the center. One-way fare is 2€ ($3.20), and a day pass, good for 24 hours of unlimited public transport for two adults and two children, is 5€ ($8).

WHERE TO STAY
VERY EXPENSIVE
Brenner's Park-Hotel & Spa ★★★   This sumptuously furnished hotel is one of the finest in the world, far outdistancing the two Steigenberger properties (see below).

It lies in a large private park facing the River Oos and Lichtentaler Allee. The spa facilities here, Baden-Baden's best, are a major draw. Some of its international habitués wouldn't dare let a year go by without an appearance at this glamorous place. Rooms and suites are the last word in luxurious appointments. Beds are sumptuous, and bathrooms are state of the art.

Schillerstrasse 4–6, 76530 Baden-Baden. © **07221/9000.** Fax 07221/38772. www.brenners.com. 100 units. 335€–530€ ($536–$848) double; 630€–1,400€ ($1,008–$2,240) suite. AE, DC, MC, V. Parking 19€ ($30). Bus: 201. **Amenities:** 2 restaurants; bar; lounge; indoor heated pool; fitness center; spa; sauna; solarium; salon; room service; massage; babysitting; laundry service; dry cleaning; nonsmoking rooms; rooms for those w/limited mobility. *In room:* A/C (in some), TV, Wi-Fi, minibar, hair dryer, safe.

EXPENSIVE

Der Kleine Prinz 🙊 *(Finds*   This small hotel is in a century-old baroque building in the central pedestrian zone, a short walk from the casino and the thermal baths. Two elegant city mansions were combined to form the most personalized, cozy, and intimate nest at the spa. Norbert Rademacher, who owns the hotel with his wife, has had 25 years experience in the United States as director at the Waldorf-Astoria and the New York Hilton. Each of the good-size rooms has its own special feature: an open fireplace, a tower, a balcony, or a whirlpool bathtub. Personalized service adds to the attractiveness of this intimate, immaculate hotel.

Lichtentalerstrasse 36, 76530 Baden-Baden. © **07221/346600.** Fax 07221/38264. www.derkleineprinz.de. 45 units. 199€–299€ ($318–$478) double; 325€–850€ ($520–$1,360) suite. Rates include buffet breakfast. AE, MC, V. Parking 16€ ($26). **Amenities:** Restaurant; bar; room service; Internet access; babysitting; laundry service; dry cleaning; nonsmoking rooms; rooms for those w/limited mobility. *In room:* A/C, TV, minibar, hair dryer.

Hotel Belle Epoque 🙊🙊   This is one of the most charming hotels in Baden-Baden, and it's operated by the same people who run the romantic Der Kleine Prinz (see above). Constructed as a private home in 1870, this gem lives up to its namesake. Each room is different, medium in size, and luxuriously furnished with swag draperies, lace curtains, and either antiques or reproductions. All bathrooms come equipped with tub/shower combinations. The owners will, if possible, give you the style of furnishings you request—Empire, Louis XV, Louis XVI, Biedermeier, Victorian, or Louis Philippe.

Maria-Viktoria-Strasse 2C, 76530 Baden-Baden. © **07221/300660.** Fax 07221/300666. www.hotelbelleepoque.de. 16 units. 215€–299€ ($344–$478) double; 325€–695€ ($520–$1,112) suite. Rates include buffet breakfast. Parking 16€ ($26). AE, DC, MC, V. Bus: 204. **Amenities:** Lounge; Internet access; room service; laundry service; dry cleaning. *In room:* A/C, TV, minibar, hair dryer, Jacuzzi (suites only).

Privathotel Quisisana 🙊🙊   Although Brenner's Park-Hotel and even the Steigenberger properties are far superior (see above and below), this runner-up is more tranquil. It's set in a spacious park, 8 minutes away from the town center on foot. Some of the most up-to-date health facilities in the Black Forest are here. You can spend an early morning in group calisthenics, for example, followed by treatments with any of a dozen skin- and muscle-toning techniques. One of the more unusual facilities is the *Tepidarium,* where a room is warmed to body temperature as you sit and listen to meditation music. All rooms are suites and well kept, spacious, and well appointed, furnished with both traditional and modern styling and with bathrooms containing tub/shower combinations.

Bismarckstrasse 21, 76530 Baden-Baden. © **07221/3690.** Fax 07221/369269. www.privathotel-quisisana.de. 45 units. 230€–400€ ($368–$640) double. Rates include buffet breakfast. AE, MC, V. Free parking. Bus: 216. **Amenities:** Restaurant; bar; indoor heated pool; health club; small spa; Jacuzzi; sauna; room service; babysitting; laundry service; dry cleaning. *In room:* TV, Wi-Fi, hair dryer, safe.

Steigenberger Badischer Hof 🔒🔒   A Baden-Baden landmark, this famed traditional hotel isn't quite as highly rated as Brenner's (see above), but it's neck and neck
with its sibling, the Europäischer Hof (see below). Badischer Hof is on a busy street
in the center of town, but in the back you'll find an elegant garden with a wide
balustraded terrace, flowerbeds, and a lawn around a stone fountain. The hotel began
its career in 1809 as a social center for famous personalities, who came here for "the
season." The four-story-high colonnaded hallway, with its great staircase and encircling balustraded balconies, is the hotel's most distinguishing feature. The well-furnished rooms are priced according to size and view. Many have private balconies, and
all have bathrooms with tub/shower combos. Each is elegantly appointed with tasteful fabrics and comfortable beds. Those in the monastery have thermal water piped
into the bathrooms.

Langestrasse 47, 76530 Baden-Baden. 🕻 800/223-5652 in the U.S. and Canada, or 07221/9340. Fax 07221/
934470. www.steigenberger.com. 139 units. 180€–270€ ($288–$432) double; 326€ ($522) suite. Rates include buf-
fet breakfast. Half board 34€ ($54). AE, MC, V. Parking 13€ ($20). Bus: 201. **Amenities:** Restaurant; bar; lounge; 3
heated pools (1 outdoor and 2 indoor); health club; Jacuzzi; sauna; solarium; salon; room service; babysitting; laundry service; dry cleaning; nonsmoking rooms. *In room:* A/C (suites only), TV, minibar, hair dryer, safe (in some).

Steigenberger Europäischer Hof 🔒🔒   This is the liveliest and most social of the
centrally located hotels, with a far more bustling atmosphere than Brenner's or the
other Steigenberger (see above). The elegant Europäischer Hof is adjacent to the Oos
River, which runs at the edge of the Kurpark. The hotel has a pair of joined structures
that were built back when spacious living facilities were more affordable. Its colonnaded central hallway is stunning. Many suites and rooms open onto balconies. The
staff is a bit too formal for our tastes, but highly efficient.

Kaiserallee 2 (opposite the Kurgarten and the casino), 76530 Baden-Baden. 🕻 800/223-5652 in the U.S. and
Canada, or 07221/9330. Fax 07221/28831. www.steigenberger.com. 128 units. 208€–278€ ($333–$445) double;
778€–978€ ($1,245–$1,565) suite. Rates include buffet breakfast. AE, MC, V. Parking 18€ ($29). Bus: 201. **Ameni-
ties:** Restaurant; bar; fitness center; sauna; salon; room service; babysitting; laundry service; dry cleaning; nonsmoking rooms. *In room:* A/C (in some), TV, Wi-Fi, minibar, hair dryer, safe (in some).

MODERATE
Haus Reichert   The five-floor 19th-century Haus Reichert is an inviting place in a
central location, not far from the casino. Rooms are of good size, high ceilinged, and
comfortable, though little of the original furniture or detailing has survived the many
renovations. All of the neatly kept bathrooms contain tub/shower combinations. Most
are priced at the lower end of the scale given below.

Sophienstrasse 4, 76530 Baden-Baden. 🕻 07221/9080. Fax 07221/29534. www.hausreichert.de. 25 units. 100€–
155€ ($160–$248) double. Rates include continental breakfast. AE, DC, MC, V. Parking 6€ ($9.60). Bus: 201. **Ameni-
ties:** Breakfast room; lounge; indoor heated pool; sauna; room service; laundry service; dry cleaning. *In room:* TV,
minibar, hair dryer, safe.

INEXPENSIVE
Hotel am Markt *(Value*   On the old marketplace, this hotel is far removed from the
grander social life of Baden-Baden and its deluxe palace hotels. But though it may be
at the bottom of the pecking order, it's number one in town for economy. The location is first rate, with the quiet interrupted only by chimes from the church across the
square. A tiny terrace cafe in front has petunia-filled window boxes. The hotel offers
small, simply furnished, comfortable rooms.

Marktplatz 18, 76530 Baden-Baden. ℭ **07221/27040.** Fax 07221/270444. www.hotel-am-markt-baden.de. 27 units, 12 with bathroom or shower. 62€–65€ ($99–$104) double without bathroom or shower; 78€–80€ ($125–$128) double with bathroom or shower. Rates include buffet breakfast. MC, V. Parking 3€ ($4.80). Bus: 201. **Amenities:** Breakfast room; laundry service; dry cleaning; all nonsmoking rooms. *In room:* TV.

WHERE TO DINE

Le Jardin de France 𝕱𝕱𝕱 MODERN/FRENCH   The most highly recommended and most elegant restaurant in Baden-Baden lies in a baronial-looking building in the center of town. It features the kind of haute cuisine and elegance that qualifies it as one of Germany's best restaurants. Defining itself as a "small corner of France set within Germany," it's enhanced by the creative cuisine and service of Alsatian-born Stephan and Sophie Bernhard. Within an extremely comfortable milieu of antiques, masses of flowers, and the sense that you're within a historic monument, you'll be confronted with menu items that many critics from throughout Germany have defined as memorable. During clement weather, an outdoor terrace provides alternative seating. You might begin with freshwater whiting in puff pastry with a horseradish-flavored cream sauce and winter vegetables; a rosette of scallops with vanilla-flavored olive oil, bay leaves, and artichoke hearts; fried scallops of foie gras with pineapple, fava beans, and essence of balsamic vinegar; and crayfish poached in a bouillon of Sancerre, essence of orange, and caviar. Main courses include a thick-cut slice of turbot with compote of carrots, Bresse chicken with cinnamon sauce and a purée of chestnuts, and lacquered pigeon with cumin-flavored maple syrup and a purée of sweet potatoes. Plan on spending an evening tableside.

Lichtentalerstrasse 13. ℭ **07221/3007860.** Reservations required. Main courses 27€–42€ ($43–$67). AE, DC, MC, V. Wed–Sun noon–2pm; Tues–Sun 7–9:30pm. Closed July 15–25.

Münchner Löwenbräu GERMAN/BAVARIAN   Though Baden-Baden has many fine restaurants dispensing haute cuisine, this isn't one of them—the food here is simple and affordable. The terrace is beneath a copse of clipped and pruned linden trees, and the indoor dining room, with its curved glass walls, is up a flight of stone steps at the rear. Many kinds of German sausage are offered, along with Bavarian specialties and a wide selection of cheeses. Regional devotees order pork knuckles fresh from the "pork-knuckle grill." Regulars often ask for the "Löwenbräu platter of bites," which is a hearty plate with everything from black pudding to sliced pork. For dessert, we suggest the apple fritters. The restaurant also has a popular beer garden.

Gernsbacher Strasse 9 (in the Altstadt). ℭ **07221/22311.** Main courses 8€–22€ ($13–$35). AE, DC, MC, V. Daily 10am–11pm. Bus: 201.

Park-Restaurant 𝕱 FRENCH/ALSATIAN   Park-Restaurant serves some of the best food in the center of Baden-Baden, although its cuisine is not quite as refined as that of Zum Alde Gott (see below) on the outskirts. This is one of the renowned spa dining rooms of Europe, and the cuisine and service are definitely worth the high price. The emphasis is on French (Alsatian) dishes. Specialties include pâté of quail and gooseliver, and roast saddle of venison or lamb noisettes with tarragon sauce. For dessert, try an ice-cream soufflé.

In Brenner's Park Hotel, Schillerstrasse 6 (at the corner of Lichtentaler Allee). ℭ **07221/9000.** Reservations required. Main courses 35€–43€ ($56–$69). AE, DC, MC, V. Daily 7–11pm. Bus: 201.

Stahlbad 𝕱 CONTINENTAL   Stahlbad is a luxury restaurant with an elegant decor. Although its food may not be as good as Park-Restaurant's (see above), it's the most tranquil and charming choice in the center of town, mainly because of its garden terrace. The owner, Frau Uschi Mönch, welcomes you in the dining room. The decor and atmosphere evoke a tavern, with prints, copper vessels, antique pewter plates, mugs, and engravings. Continental specialties are pepper steak and venison steak (in hunting season), fresh fish, and lobster thermidor (very expensive). The homemade fettuccine Alfredo with white truffles (in season) is as good as any you'll have in Rome.

Augustaplatz 2. ℂ **07221/24569.** Reservations required. Main courses 17€–30€ ($27–$48). AE, DC, MC, V. Tues–Sun noon–2pm and 6–10pm. Bus: 201.

DINING AT NEUWEIER

Many of Baden-Baden's visitors dine at the satellite resort of Neuweier, 10km (6 miles) southwest via Fremersbergstrasse.

Zum Alde Gott 🞶🞶 BADISCHER   This is where true gourmets come to dine. In an attractive and very old wine cellar, Wilfried Serr, the most distinguished chef in the Baden-Baden area, mixes his palette of flavors with astounding skill and imagination. Wild game in season is a fine art here. Try also the Black Forest trout or the sea bass. There are only 12 tables, and the ambience is bright and cheerful. An added bonus is an open-air terrace.

Weinstrasse 10. ℂ **07223/5513.** Reservations required. Main courses 24€–35€ ($38–$56). DC, MC, V. Fri–Wed noon–3pm and 6:30–11pm. Bus: 216.

EXPLORING BADEN-BADEN

Caracalla-Therme   These baths have been made more pleasing visually by the addition of a round colonnaded extension with splashing and cascading pools. You can decide on your own bath temperature here. Medicinal treatment includes mud baths, massages, and whirlpools. The slightly radioactive water, rich in sodium chloride, comes from artesian wells 1,800m (5,900 ft.) under the Florentiner Mountain. Its temperature is around 160°F (71°C). Bathers usually begin in cooler pools, working up to the warm water. The baths also have a sauna area, with foot baths and sun baths; sauna temperatures go from 185° to 200°F (85°–93°C). You must wear bathing suits in the pools, but everyone goes nude in the saunas.

Römerplatz 1. ℂ **07221/275940.** Admission 15€ ($24) for 2 hr., 17€ ($27) for 3 hr., 17€ ($22) for 4 hr. Daily 8am–10pm. Bus: 201.

Friedrichsbad   Friedrichsbad, also known as the Old Baths, was built from 1869 to 1877 at the behest of Grand Duke Friedrich von Baden. Following the Roman-Irish method, it takes about 2 hours to have the complete program, which involves a shower, two saunas 130° to 160°F (54°–71°C), a brush massage soaping, thermal steam baths, and three freshwater baths ranging from warm to 60°F (16°C). After a 30-minute period of rest and relaxation, you're supposed to feel rejuvenated. Other types of therapy, including massage, electrotherapy, and hydrotherapy, are also offered. Massages are 6.50€ ($10) for cream massage, 22€ ($35) for a 30-minute neck and back massage, and 45€ ($72) for a 1-hour full-body massage.

Römerplatz 1. ℂ **07221/275920.** Admission 21€ ($34) without soap-brush massage, 29€ ($46) with soap-brush massage. Daily 9am–10pm.

Sammlung Frieder Burda 🞶🞶🞶   One of Germany's most extensive collections of modern art has opened in an airy Richard Meier–designed building standing at the edge of a park. Its primary focus is on the works of postwar German expressionists.

(Moments **Ambling on the "Ohs"**

The center of Baden-Baden activity is **Lichtentaler Allee** ⊛⊛, the park promenade along the bank of the Oosbach River (affectionately called the Oos—pronounced *Ohs*), which runs through the center of town. As you stroll along this
walk, you'll be amazed at the variety not only of exotic shrubs and trees but
also of the rhododendrons, azaleas, and roses. At the north end of the park, on
the banks of the stream, are the buildings of the **Kurgarten,** including the classical Kurhaus, used as an entertainment complex.

The scion of a famous publishing family, Frieder Burda spent nearly 4 decades amass-
ing this amazing collection of some 580 works of contemporary art ranging from
George Baselitz to Sigmar Polke, from Max Beckmann to Gerhard Richter. Our
favorite is anything by Ernst Ludwig Kirchner. Not all the works are German—note
the late *oeuvre* by Picasso or the examples of American abstract expressionism, works
by Willem de Kooning, Mark Rothko, or Jackson Pollock.

Lichtentaler Allee 8B. (℃ **07221/398980.** www.sammlung-frieder-burda.de. Admission 9€ ($14) adults; 7€ ($11)
students, children, and seniors. Tues–Fri 11am–6pm; Sat–Sun 10am–6pm.

Trinkhalle (Pump Room)   The spa gardens contain the Pump Room, where visitors can sip the water. The loggia of the hall is decorated with frescoes depicting Black
Forest legends. The springs of Baden-Baden have been recognized for more than
2,000 years, and their composition is almost the same today as when the Romans built
their baths here in the 3rd century.

Kaiserallee 3. No phone. Free admission. Apr–Oct daily 10am–6:30pm. Bus: 201.

THE CASINO

Spielbank   Open year-round, this is the oldest casino in Germany, popular for
more than 200 years. Dostoyevsky is said to have written *The Gambler* after he lost his
shirt, and almost his mind, at the tables here. The casino rooms were designed in the
style of an elegant French château. Jackets and ties for men are mandatory, as is
eveningwear for women. To enter during gambling hours, you must possess a valid
passport or identification card and be at least 21 years old.

The historic gaming rooms may be viewed daily 9:30am to noon on a tour costing
5€ ($8) for adults, 3€ ($4.80) for children 15 and under. For those who want to
gamble later, a full day's ticket is available for 3€ ($4.80). The minimum stake is 5€
($8), but visitors are not obligated to play. Hours are daily 2pm to 2am (Fri–Sat until
3am).

Kaiserallee 1. (℃ **07221/30240.** Bus: 1.

SPORTS & OUTDOOR PURSUITS

For an entirely new perspective on the area, go hot-air ballooning. **Ballooning 2000**
offers rides between the Black Forest and the Vosges. Contact pilot Rainer Keitel
((℃ **07223/60002**) for details. A 2-hour champagne breakfast trip over the Rhine Valley goes for 253€ ($405) per person.

For a more up-close and personal experience, **rock climbing** at all levels and alti-
tudes can be enjoyed on the Battert rocks directly over the city. For a climber's guide,

contact the **German Alpine Club,** Rathausplatz 7 (© **07221/17200**). You can also walk the 8km (5-mile) nature trail from the Strouzda chapel via Friesenberg to Fremersberg.

Horse races and horseback riding provide additional entertainment in Baden-Baden. Most races take place at the racetrack at Iffezheim, 30km (19 miles) from Baden-Baden, but for tickets and information about the races, contact their organizers, the **Internationaler Club,** Lichtentaler Allee 8 (© **07229/1870**). Highlights of Baden-Baden's racing season, of which the Internationaler Club is the primary architect, occur during Spring Meeting (a week in late May and early June) and Grand Week (the last 8 days of Aug). If you prefer to actually ride a horse instead of watching others do it, you can ride on a 1km (⅔-mile) outdoor track at **Equestrian Hall,** Gunzenbachstrasse 4A (© **07221/301862**) for 30€ ($48) per hour of instruction.

Many other outdoor sports are offered as well. The local 18-hole course in Fremersberg is one of the most scenic in Europe; contact the **Baden-Baden Golf Club** at © **07221/23579.** Monday to Friday greens fees are 45€ ($72), Saturday and Sunday 60€ ($96).

For tennis, contact either **Tennis-Halle 365,** Rheinstrasse 197 (© **07221/67808**), which maintains indoor and outdoor tennis courts; or **Tennis Club Rot Weiss,** at Lichtentaler Allee 5 (© **07221/24141**), which offers only outdoor tennis courts. At either complex, outdoor courts are available daily late April to October (weather permitting) from 8am to an hour before sundown for around 5€ ($8) per hour. At Tennis-Hallee 365, indoor courts (available daily, year-round, pending the availability of space and advance reservations, 7am to 10pm) cost 20€ ($32) per 50-minute session.

Swimmers can exercise and splash around at the **Bertholdbad,** on the Ludwig-Wilhelm-Strasse 24 (© **07221/277581**). The complex contains a *Hallenbad* (indoor heated pool) that's open to the general public Tuesday to Friday 7:45 to 9am and 1 to 8pm (Wed until 9pm), Saturday 7:45am to 3pm, and Sunday 7:45 to 1pm; and a *Friebad* (outdoor swimming pool) that's open mid-May to mid-September daily from 9am to 7pm. Daily entrance to the compound costs 3.50€ ($5.60) for adults and 2.50€ ($4) for students and children 8 to 18.

SHOPPING

A flower-flanked pedestrian zone includes **Sophienstrasse** and **Gernsbacher Strasse,** streets lined with upscale boutiques, among the most expensive in Germany. Women's clothing by one of Germany's most emulated designers is available at **Escada Boutique,** Sophienstrasse 18 (© **07221/390448**). Another shop, **Münchner Moden,** Lichtentalerstrasse 13 (© **07221/31090**), carries women's designs in loden-colored wool during autumn and winter and offers Austrian and Bavarian silks, linens, and cottons during warmer months. The best men's store, **Herrenkommode,** Sophienstrasse 16 (© **07221/29292**), is a bit more international, focusing on Renee Lazard.

BADEN-BADEN AFTER DARK

Baden-Baden has a busy annual schedule of concert, dance, and dramatic performances. The centerpiece for most of the resort's cultural activities is the oft-photographed **Kurhaus,** Kaiserallee 1 (© **07221/9070**). Originally built in the 1870s as the focal point of the resort, the Kurhaus does not contain spa facilities, as its name implies, but is rather a catch-all entertainment complex. In the same building is Baden-Baden's casino, the **Spielbank** (see "The Casino," above).

The **Theater am Goetheplatz,** Goetheplatz (© **07221/932700**), is a well-maintained and beautiful baroque-style theater that presents opera, ballet, and drama productions. It opened auspiciously with the world premiere of the Berlioz opera *Beatrice et Benedict* in 1862. Every summer, the verdant core of Baden-Baden is home to several outdoor concerts, many of which focus on jazz or classical music, often informal late-afternoon or early-evening affairs organized on short notice by the tourist office. More elaborate concerts, many of them performed by the town's resident orchestra, the **Philharmonic Orchestra of Baden-Baden,** are part of the resort's **Musikalischer Sommer Festival,** usually conducted during an 8-day period in mid-July. Although the Baden-Baden Philharmonic is likely to perform mostly within the echoing interior of one of the largest concert halls in Germany, the **Festspielhaus,** in the Alter Bahnhof (see below for ticket information), smaller events are likely to crop up within venues scattered throughout the town. For tickets to any cultural or musical event within Baden-Baden, contact either the tourist office (© **07221/275200**), which sells tickets on its premises, or the **Ticket Service Trinkhalle,** in the Trinkhalle on Kaiser Alee (© **07221/932700**).

After a long slumber, Germany's most famous spa is percolating once again. Attracting visiting celebrities, the bar at **Medici,** Augustaplatz 8 (© **07221/2006**), has become the most fashionable in town. The late-night, designer-jeans crowd flocks to the lively but riotously noisy **Bombay Rooms,** Kaiserallee 4 (© **07221/3974370**), for drinks and fun, later heading downstairs to Max's to dance the night away.

Bars in the resort hotels often have low-key entertainment. Try the **Jockey Bar,** in the lobby of the Steigenberger Badischer Hof (© **07221/9330**), or the **Oleander Bar** in Brenner's Park Hotel, Schillerstrasse 4–6 (© **07221/9000**).

13

Heidelberg, Stuttgart & the Neckar Valley

Ancient castle ruins in the midst of thick woodlands, quiet university towns, busy manufacturing centers—you'll find all these in the countryside of southwestern Germany. The area extends along the Neckar River from Heidelberg past medieval towns and modern cities as far as Tübingen. The Neckar flows between the Black Forest and the Schwäbische Alb region. Although the river is open to commercial shipping vessels as far as Stuttgart, much of the valley has remained unspoiled. The castles that rise around every bend in the river were once home to the German royal families of Hohenstaufen and Hohenzollern. Today, castles and country palaces sometimes offer bed and board to travelers.

1 Heidelberg ★★★

120km (74 miles) NW of Stuttgart, 20km (12 miles) SE of Mannheim, 88km (55 miles) S of Frankfurt

Summertime in Heidelberg, according to the song from *The Student Prince,* is a time for music and romance. Today, it's also a time when droves of visitors invade this beautiful city. Heidelberg was not leveled by air raids in World War II and therefore still has original buildings from the later Middle Ages and early Renaissance. Modern Heidelberg centers on Bismarckplatz at the foot of the Theodore-Heuss-Brücke; in this part of the city, you'll find many of the best hotels and restaurants, and the tall buildings and shopping plazas contrast with the Altstadt nearby. Across the Neckar are sports grounds, a zoo, and a large botanical garden.

Heidelberg is, above all, a university town and has been since 1386. Students make up much of the population. The colorful atmosphere that university life imparts to the town is felt especially in the old student quarter, with its narrow streets and lively inns. This oldest university in Germany is officially named **Ruprecht-Karl-University,** honoring both its founder, Elector Ruprecht I of the Palatinate, as well as the man who, in 1803, made it the leading university in the state of Baden, Margrave Karl Friedrich. The school was founded after the Great Schism of 1378, when conflicting claims to the papacy created unrest and German teachers and students fled the Sorbonne in Paris.

ESSENTIALS

GETTING THERE **By Plane** The nearest major airport is Frankfurt (see chapter 14), with a direct bus link to Heidelberg. The shuttle bus between Frankfurt and Heidelberg costs 20€ ($32) per person. Call ℭ **0621/651620** for shuttle information.

Moments **Exploring on Two Wheels**

Unique in Germany, the **Neckar Valley Cycle Path** ☆ allows you to ride all the way from the source of the Neckar in Villingen-Schwenningen, 375km (233 miles) to the confluence of the Rhine at Mannheim. The path is marked with a signpost showing a green bicycle and a red wheel mark. The route follows the river the whole way, though many cyclists go only as far as Heidelberg. Along the way, you'll pass castles, manor houses, vineyards, country inns, and such old towns as Rottweil and Esslingen. Most cyclists average about 50km (30 miles) per day on the trail.

By Train　Heidelberg's **Hauptbahnhof** is an important railroad station, lying on the Mannheim line, with frequent service to both regional towns and major cities. From Frankfurt, 56 trains arrive per day (trip time: 1 hr.); from Stuttgart, 35 trains (trip time: 45 min.). Travel time to and from Munich is about 3½ hours. For information, call ℂ **01805/996633.**

By Bus　Regional bus service is provided by **BRN Busverkehr Rhein-Neckar** at Heidelberg (ℂ **06221/60620**).

By Car　Motorists should take the A5 Autobahn from the north or south.

VISITOR INFORMATION　Contact **Tourist-Information,** Willy-Brandt-Platz 1 (ℂ **06221/19433**). It's open April to October Monday to Saturday 9am to 7pm, and Sunday 10am to 6pm; and November to March Monday to Saturday 9am to 6pm. Here, visitors can purchase a **Heidelberg Card,** which provides discounts on attractions and free use of public transportation. Cards valid for any consecutive 2-day period cost 14€ ($22) per person; cards valid for any consecutive 4-day period go for 21€ ($34) per person. A family card is available as well. Valid for two adults and two children 15 and under for any consecutive 2-day period, it sells for 28€ ($45) and carries the same provisions.

GETTING AROUND　Heidelberg is crisscrossed with a network of trams and buses, many of which intersect at the Bismarckplatz in the town center. Bus nos. 41 and 42 travel frequently between the railway station and the Universitätsplatz. The Altstadt stretches on either side of the Hauptstrasse between the Bismarckplatz and the Universitätsplatz. Bus or tram fares cost 2.20€ ($3.50) for a single ride.

WHERE TO STAY

If you want to stick with the familiar, you can stay at the **Crowne Plaza Heidelberg,** Kurfürstenanlage 1 (ℂ **06221/9170**), in the center of town, offering all the comforts of a top-tier hotel but lacking any Heidelberg atmosphere. Doubles cost 250€ ($400).

VERY EXPENSIVE

Der Europäische Hof-Hotel Europa ☆☆☆　This glamorous hotel is by far Heidelberg's best. It fronts the city park in the heart of town, within walking distance of the castle and the university. Its interior is like that of a gracious home, with antiques, crystal chandeliers, and Oriental rugs. Some rooms and several suites face a quiet inside garden; front rooms in the oldest section tend to be noisy (from traffic). Nineteen have whirlpool tubs. The most dramatic recent improvement has been the addition of the Panorama Spa Club and the latest fitness equipment.

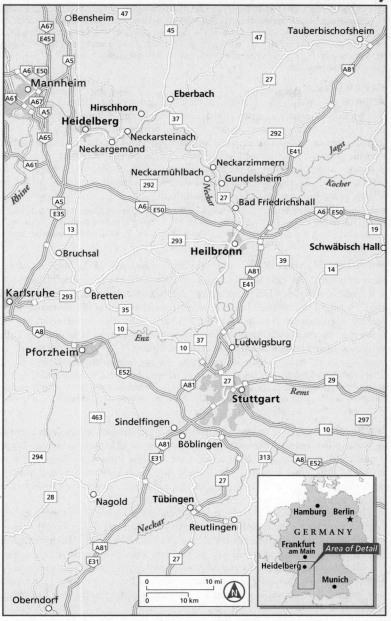

Friedrich-Ebert-Anlage 1, 69117 Heidelberg. © **800/223-4541** in the U.S. and Canada, or 06221/5150. Fax 06221/ 515506. www.europaeischerhof.com. 118 units. 318€–366€ ($509–$586) double; 380€–428€ ($608–$685) junior suite; 520€–592€ ($832–$947) 2-room apt. AE, DC, MC, V. Parking 15€ ($24). Tram: Bismarckplatz. **Amenities:** 2 restaurants; bar; indoor heated pool; spa; sauna; solarium; steam bath; shopping arcade; room service; babysitting; laundry service; dry cleaning; nonsmoking rooms; rooms for those w/limited mobility. *In room:* A/C, TV, Wi-Fi, minibar, hair dryer, trouser press, safe.

EXPENSIVE

Arthotel *Finds* This is a carefully restored and very hip designer hotel lying in the Altstadt. It attracts a trendy crowd, often young, and is imbued with sophistica-tion and taste. Special features include a big roof terrace with panoramic views and an inner courtyard for open-air drinking and dining. You are in the heart of Heidelberg, near the Old Bridge across the Neckar and in a position just below the famous castle. A pedestrian area is found on the street in front, ideal for shopping and sightseeing. Bedrooms and suites are as modern as tomorrow, with simple yet elegant furnishings, including soothing pastels and oak parquet floors.

Grabengasse 7, 69117 Heidelberg. © **06221/650060.** Fax 06221/65006100. www.arthotel.de. 24 units. 125€–198€ ($200–$317) double; 255€–350€ ($408–$560) suite. AE, MC, V. Parking 12€ ($19). **Amenities:** Restaurant; bar; rooftop terrace; room service; laundry service; dry cleaning. *In room:* A/C, TV, Wi-Fi, beverage maker (in some), hair dryer, safe.

Heidelberg Marriott Hotel This hotel sits on the banks of the Neckar, just a few minutes from the Altstadt and the main train station. Although it doesn't have the flair and traditional style of Der Europäische Hof (above), it's far superior to its nearest rival, Holiday Inn Crowne Plaza. The exit from the autobahn is only minutes away, making it convenient for motorists. Rooms are comfortably furnished, many with views over the river or the hills beyond. As a special service, the hotel operates a shut-tle service to and from Frankfurt International Airport.

Vangerowstrasse 16, 69115 Heidelberg. © **06221/9080.** Fax 06221/908660. www.marriott.com. 248 units. 127€–246€ ($203–$394) double; 390€–698€ ($624–$1,117) suite. AE, DC, MC, V. Parking 17€ ($27). Tram: 2. **Amenities:** 2 restaurants; bar; lounge; indoor heated pool; health club; spa; sauna; solarium; room service; massage; babysitting; laundry service; dry cleaning; nonsmoking rooms; rooms for those w/limited mobility. *In room:* A/C, TV, Wi-Fi, minibar, coffeemaker, hair dryer.

Hip Hotel *Finds* This boutique hotel is the only designer inn in town to surpass Arthotel in modern flair. Both attract a similar clientele of *fashionistas* to their elegant, sophisticated precincts. Hip, incidentally, means "Hyper Individual Place" in this con-text. The little hotel is part of the historic inn, Zum Güldenen Schaf, which for decades has been operated by the welcoming Kischka family, who are known for their historic menus and theme evenings.

The hotel is installed in this 250-year-old building, but don't expect antique, creaky rooms. Everything is fresh and contemporary—Claudia and Karim Kischka traveled the world picking up furnishings and accessories for the bedrooms. Each room is also individually designed and named for some of the most famous cities in the world, including New York, Tokyo, Marrakesh, and Amsterdam. If you're a little commie-ori-ented, you can opt for the Havanna Room, where a huge blow-up of Che Guevara will "guard" the activities in your bed at night. There's even a room with beamed ceil-ings inspired by the city of Heidelberg itself.

Hauptstrasse 115, 69117 Heidelberg. © **06221/20879.** Fax 06221/160409. www.hip-hotel.de. 15 units. 140€–210€ ($224–$336) double; 210€–240€ ($336–$384) suite. AE, DC, MC, V. Parking 11€ ($18). **Amenities:** Restaurant; bar; room service; laundry service. *In room:* A/C, TV, Wi-Fi, minibar.

Heidelberg

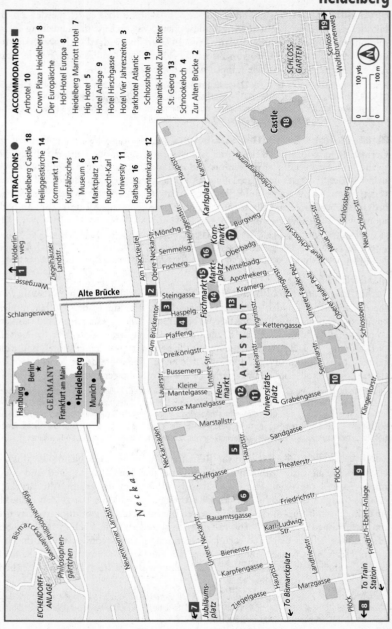

ACCOMMODATIONS ■

Arthotel **10**
Crown Plaza Heidelberg **8**
Der Europäische
Hof-Hotel Europa **8**
Heidelberg Marriott Hotel **7**
Hip Hotel **5**
Hotel Anlage **9**
Hotel Hirschgasse **1**
Hotel Vier Jahreszeiten **3**
Parkhotel Atlantic
Schlosshotel **19**
Romantik-Hotel Zum Ritter
St. Georg **13**
Schnookeloch **4**
Zur Alten Brücke **2**

ATTRACTIONS ●

Heidelberg Castle **18**
Heiliggeistkirche **14**
Kornmarkt **17**
Kurpfälzisches
Museum **6**
Marktplatz **15**
Ruprecht-Karl
University **11**
Rathaus **16**
Studentenkarzer **12**

Hotel Hirschgasse 🏰🏰 This historic country-home-style hotel, nestled on the hillside of a historic lane adjoining Philosopher's Way, is tops in Heidelberg for its tranquil and romantic setting. It dates from 1472 and has lodged such impressive figures as Mark Twain and Otto von Bismarck. Rooms are all suites decorated in Laura Ashley designs, and all come equipped with tub/shower combos.

Hirschgasse 3, 69120 Heidelberg. ℂ 06221/4540. Fax 06221/454111. www.hirschgasse.de. 20 units. 150€–195€ ($240–$312) junior suite; 195€–245€ ($312–$392) deluxe suite; 245€–340€ ($392–$544) salon suite. AE, DC, MC, V. Free parking. Bus: 34. **Amenities:** 2 restaurants; lounge; room service; babysitting; laundry service; dry cleaning; nonsmoking rooms. *In room:* TV, Wi-Fi, minibar, hair dryer, safe, Jacuzzi.

Romantik-Hotel Zum Ritter St. Georg 🏰 A glorious old inn right out of the German Renaissance, the Zum Ritter is a well-preserved rarity, although it's inferior to the Hirschgasse (above) in comfort and antique charm. Built in 1592 by Frenchman Charles Bèlier, it's now listed among the major sightseeing attractions of this university town. There are no public lounges. Many rooms are somewhat cramped, but beds are comfortable and the bathrooms have been renewed. All units contain bathrooms with tub/shower combos.

Hauptstrasse 178, 69117 Heidelberg. ℂ 06221/1350. Fax 06221/135230. www.ritter-heidelberg.de. 37 units. 144€–176€ ($230–$282) double; 206€–246€ ($330–$394) suite. AE, DC, MC, V. Bus: 11, 12, 41, or 42. **Amenities:** 3 restaurants; room service; laundry service; dry cleaning; all nonsmoking rooms. *In room:* TV, minibar, hair dryer.

MODERATE

Parkhotel Atlantic Schlosshotel 🏰 This grand hotel lies a 20-minute walk from the center on the wooded outskirts of Heidelberg, near the castle. It offers modern comfort in annexes built around the core of an older villa. Guests are assured calm and comfort and can take advantage of the many woodland trails extending through the Neckar Valley. This hotel's setting makes it the best in its price range; hotels in the city center, unless soundproof, get a lot of traffic noise. The room decor is lackluster, but they're comfortable, and contain bathrooms with tub/shower combos.

Schloss-Wolfsbrunnen-Weg 23, 69118 Heidelberg. ℂ 06221/60420. Fax 06221/604260. www.parkhotel-atlantic.de. 23 units. 95€–100€ ($152–$160) double; 105€–145€ ($168–$232) suite. Rates include buffet breakfast. AE, DC, MC, V. Free parking. Bus: 11, 12, or 33. Head east from the Hauptbahnhof, along Kurfürstenanlage, going through the tunnel and take the 2nd turn, bringing you to Heidelberg Castle; continue straight beyond the castle to the hotel. **Amenities:** Breakfast room; lounge; room service; laundry service; nonsmoking rooms. *In room:* TV, Wi-Fi, minibar.

Zur Alten Brücke 🏰 Next to the Restaurant Wirtshaus zum Nepomuk, this discovery is in an early-18th-century townhouse that has been restored and much improved over the years. The hotel takes its name from the nearby Alte Brücke, a famous bridge spanning the Neckar. Even though the building is a golden oldie, the small hotel is most up-to-date, with renewed plumbing and bright, modern, airy bedrooms furnished comfortably and tastefully in a modern style. Each of the bedrooms has a different floor plan, and each has a panoramic view—some overlook the river, others Heidelberg Castle. The suites here are some of the most romantic in town, especially the roomy penthouse ones. Each comes with a bamboo floor, designer beds, a large bathroom, and a great view.

Obere Neckarstrasse 2, 69117 Heidelberg. ℂ 06221/739130. Fax 06221/7391320. www.hotel-zur-alten-bruecke.de. 16 units. 139€–159€ ($222–$254) double; from 199€ ($318) suite. Rates include buffet breakfast. No credit cards. Parking 12€ ($19). **Amenities:** Restaurant; bar. *In room:* TV.

INEXPENSIVE

Hotel Anlage *(Value* This is one of Heidelberg's best affordable hotels, located in the heart of the city, on the street leading up to the castle. It occupies one wing of a lavishly built, late-19th-century palace. Rooms are cozy and have bathrooms containing tub/shower combinations.

Friedrich-Ebert-Anlage 32, 69117 Heidelberg. © 06221/5850960. Fax 06221/585096130. www.hotel-anlage.de. 19 units. 79€–98€ ($126–$157) double; 109€–135€ ($174–$216) triple. Rates include continental breakfast. AE, DC, MC, V. Parking 7€ ($11). Bus: 11 or 33. **Amenities:** Breakfast room; lounge; room service; laundry service; dry cleaning. *In room:* TV.

Hotel Vier Jahreszeiten This hotel is a worthy choice for any of the four seasons. It's located near the starting point for many interesting walks. Several famous student inns (drinking taverns patronized mainly by students of the university at Heidelberg, although open to all) and the castle are also nearby. The hotel has been improved over the years; the rooms are comfortable, with bathrooms equipped with tub/shower combinations. The price and the location here are hard to beat.

Haspelgasse 2 (near the Alte Brücke), 69117 Heidelberg. © 06221/24164. Fax 06221/163110. www.4-jahreszeiten.de. 22 units. 95€–130€ ($152–$208) double. Rates include continental breakfast. AE, DC, MC, V. Parking 8€ ($13). Bus: 21, 34, or 42. **Amenities:** Breakfast room. *In room:* TV.

Schnookeloch *(Value* This is one of the most historic old taverns of Heidelberg, dating from 1703 when the winner of the latest student duel would retire here with his friends to celebrate with lots and lots of beer. Things might get a little raucous here on weekends, and if you're bothered with noise, you might want to seek lodgings elsewhere. Otherwise, you'll find small- to medium-size bedrooms upstairs that are beautifully maintained, modernized, and most comfortable. Even if you're not a guest, consider stopping in for a beer or a full meal. Regional specialties such as sausages and schnitzels dominate the menu, with an occasional fish dish thrown in.

Haspelgasse 8, 69117 Heidelberg. © 06221/138080. Fax 06221/1380813. www.schnookeloch.de. 11 units. 99€–110€ ($158–$176) double; 130€ ($208) triple. AE, MC, V. Parking 8€ ($13). **Amenities:** Restaurant; bar; room service; laundry service. *In room:* TV.

WHERE TO DINE
VERY EXPENSIVE

Kurfürstenstube *(★★* FRENCH One of the finest choices for dining in Heidelberg is in the ground-floor wing of this deluxe hotel. The wood-paneled grill room is attractively decorated with provincial furnishings—real Old Heidelberg with coffered ceilings, wood paneling, and lots of nostalgic kitsch. The menu is in English, but the cuisine is mainly French, with both fixed-price and a la carte meals. Only the highest quality seasonal ingredients are used. Dishes are creative, refined, and balanced, as evoked by such main courses as grilled filet of turbot with crayfish, grilled filets of sole on a ragout of artichokes and bell pepper, or saddle of lamb poached in pinot noir with a chorizo-and-potato ragout. Another good dish is filet of pikeperch on fresh green asparagus with a saffron risotto and champagne risotto. The wine list is the most impressive in town.

In Der Europäische Hof-Hotel Europa, Friedrich-Ebert-Anlage 1. © 06221/5150. Reservations required. Main courses 29€–32€ ($46–$51); fixed-price menus 80€–130€ ($128–$208). AE, DC, MC, V. Daily noon–2:30pm and 6:30–11:30pm. Tram: Bismarckplatz.

Schwarz Das Restaurant *(★★★* GERMAN/MEDITERRANEAN Almost from the moment it opened, this beautifully designed restaurant on the 12th floor of the

Print Media Academy was hailed by the press as the finest place for serving the best cuisine in the city. From its lofty perch, Schwarz Das opens onto the most panoramic views. The restaurant also features the town's most elegant aperitif bar, even a smoker's lounge. The darling of critics, Manfred Schwarz earned his reputation by cooking for numerous state guests to Germany. Here he is turned loose to let his culinary imagination run wild, using superb products turned into refined dishes. His gourmet fixed-price menus, ranging from three to seven courses, are changed every month. Who knows what is to be featured at the time of your visit? Let's just say he's big on truffles and caviar, along with luxe products. You might start with a terrine of Scottish wild salmon with watercress, followed with superb main courses such as baked filet of veal with morels and crayfish, or roasted brook trout and Canadian lobster on a squid salad in a basil-and-tomato vinaigrette.

Kurfürstenanlage 60. ⓒ 06221/757030. Reservations required. Main courses 26€–34€ ($42–$54); fixed-price menus 75€–98€ ($120–$157). AE, DC, MC, V. Tues–Sat 6–10pm. Closed Jan 1–9 and Aug 2–22.

EXPENSIVE

Simplicissimus 🍴🍴 FRENCH   This elegant spot is ideal for a gourmet rendezvous, and in summer it features an outdoor courtyard for dining. Johann Lummer, one of the finest chefs in Heidelberg, prepares a cuisine moderne with consummate skill. *Gourmet* magazine said that Herr Lummer "paints with food," and we agree. Not only are his dishes delectable, but their presentation is equally pleasing. The menu varies but is likely to include fresh mushrooms in cream sauce with homemade noodles, or crayfish with fresh melon and herb-flavored cream sauce.

Ingrimstrasse 16. ⓒ 06221/183336. Reservations required. Main courses 20€–25€ ($32–$40); fixed-price menus 35€–65€ ($56–$104). MC, V. Tues–Sat 6pm–midnight; Sun noon–3pm. Closed 1 week in late Aug, 1 week in Sept, and 2 weeks in Jan. Bus: 11, 12, 33, 35, or 41.

MODERATE

Goldene Sonne 🍴 GERMAN/CONTINENTAL   One of the most reliable restaurants in Heidelberg, enjoying favor with both residents and visitors, is this long-time favorite restaurant in the center of the historic city. The chefs do not aspire to greatness, but their menus burst with freshness and originality, and they use quality ingredients to concoct their appealing dishes.

Among hors d'oeuvres, we've succumbed to their mixed salad of fresh greens with a truffle-nut dressing and grated Parmesan. Other worthy appetizers include giant shrimp served in a potato straw basket or beef carpaccio. Alternatively, you might start with one of the homemade soups, made fresh daily, featuring the likes of cream of asparagus with salmon or French tomato soup with a tempura of giant shrimp. The chefs are strong on their meat dishes, including a juicy rump steak with Pommery mustard sauce and roast potatoes, and they also excel at their fresh fish dishes, including snapper with risotto and grilled vegetables. At least three dishes a day appeal to vegetarians, including eggplant lasagna. Desserts are limited but carefully made, including a three-plate sorbet based on in-season fresh fruits.

Hauptstrasse 170–172. ⓒ 06221/8935764. Reservations recommended. Main courses 18€–23€ ($28–$37); fixed-price menu 35€ ($56). MC, V. Tues–Sun noon–3pm and 6pm–midnight.

Kurpfälzisches Museum Restaurant GERMAN   This quiet culinary oasis at the museum makes a good stopover for lunch. The setting is baroque and very grand, with one enormous dining hall and two satellite dining rooms. You can order such dishes as rump steak Madagascar with green pepper while you enjoy the view of the little garden and splashing fountain. The food is satisfying, though hardly gourmet.

Hauptstrasse 97. ℂ 06221/24050. Reservations required. Main courses 11€–22€ ($18–$35). AE, DC, MC, V. Daily noon–2:30pm and 6–10pm. Bus: 1 or 35.

Romantik-Hotel Zum Ritter St. Georg ⊛ GERMAN/INTERNATIONAL   This restaurant (in one of Heidelberg's most famous Renaissance buildings) is popular with students and professors, who know that they can get not only German cooking here but also the wonderful Dortmunder Actien-Bräuerei beer. You dine either in the first-class Rittersaal (Great Hall) or in the smaller Councillors' Chamber. We like the elegant larger room, with its sepia ceilings, wainscoting, and Oriental rugs. The house specialty is saddle of Odenwald venison for two (in season); when this dish is offered, locals flock here. We recommend starting with the game soup St. Hubertus with brandy foam, and ending with the crêpes suzette.

Hauptstrasse 178. ℂ 06221/1350. Reservations recommended. Main courses 15€–22€ ($24–$35); fixed-price menus 27€–40€ ($43–$64). AE, DC, MC, V. Daily noon–2pm and 6–10pm. Bus: 10, 11, or 12.

Zur Herrenmühle ⊛ GERMAN/INTERNATIONAL   The service at this family-owned restaurant, located in a 17th-century house with thick walls and antique paneling, is equaled only at the Kurfürstenstube (see above), and the sophisticated maitre d' adds both glamour and an appropriate theatricality. The classical cuisine is based on fresh ingredients. Try the rack of lamb with herbs and homemade green noodles, or the roast roebuck with a vinegar-and-honey sauce. The desserts, such as the sorbet flavored with blood oranges served with a parfait of mandarin oranges, make better use of fresh fruit than any other place in town.

Hauptstrasse 239. ℂ 06221/602909. Reservations recommended. Main courses 15€–22€ ($24–$35); fixed-price menu 35€ ($56). AE, DC, MC, V. Tues–Sat 6pm–midnight. Closed last 2 weeks of Mar. Bus: 33.

INEXPENSIVE
Dorfschänke ⊛ Finds GERMAN   Hidden down a back street in the Neuenheim section, this is one of the simplest restaurants in Heidelberg, and its affordable prices make it popular with students. Okay, so it doesn't have tablecloths—just plain wooden tables—but it's been packed since 1908, so its cooks must be doing something right. The specialty is *Flammkuchen,* a regional dish from Alsace. It's like a square pizza with onions and cheese but no tomato sauce. It's a real tasty treat, as are the garlic-studded lamb and the steak served with bubbling mozzarella cheese, spinach, and fried potatoes. Tables are placed outside in summer.

Lutherstrasse 14. ℂ 06221/419041. Reservations recommended on Fri–Sat for dinner. Main courses 8€–15€ ($13–$24). No credit cards. Daily 5pm–midnight.

EXPLORING HEIDELBERG
TOURING HEIDELBERG CASTLE ⊛⊛⊛   You can reach the huge red-sandstone Heidelberg Castle (ℂ 06221/538421), set amid woodlands and terraced gardens, by several routes. You can drive up the winding Neue Schlossstrasse past the old houses perched on the hillside, or walk. Walking is the most rewarding approach because of the constantly changing scenic view of the town and surrounding countryside. You can take the more gradual slope from the Klingentor, or make the shorter walk up the steep Burgweg from Kornmarkt. The Klingentor, the much easier walk, takes about 20 minutes. The steep Burgweg walk, from Kornmarkt in the center of town, can take a good 30 or 40 minutes, depending on your stamina.

(Moments **Boating in the Neckar**

Heidelberg is an ideal point from which to explore the romantic Neckar Valley. From April to early October, you can take a boat tour along the river as far as Neckarsteinach. There are usually four or five round-trips daily, and you need not return on the same boat. Boats are operated by the **Rhein-Neckar-Fahrgastschiffahrt GmbH,** Stadthalle, Heidelberg (℡ **06221/20181;** www.rnf-schifffahrt.de). Trips between Heidelberg and Neckarsteinach cost 15€ ($24) round-trip, and those between Heidelberg and Hirschhorn (which operate June 17–Sept 12) cost 17€ ($27) round-trip. The same families have been working the Neckar since the early 1600s.

The castle is a dignified ruin, but even in its deteriorated state, it's one of the finest Gothic-Renaissance castles in Germany. Entering at the main gate, the huge **Gun Park** is to your left, from which you can gaze down upon Heidelberg and the Neckar Valley. Straight ahead is the **Thick Tower,** or what remains of it after its 8m (26-ft.) walls were blown up by the French in the late 17th century. Leaving Gun Park via Elizabeth's Gate (erected by Friedrich V in 1615 for his Scottish wife, the daughter of James I), you come to the Bridge House and the bridge crossing the site of the former moat.

Along the north side of the courtyard stretches the stern **palace of Friedrich IV** *Ϟϟ,* erected 1601 to 1607. The palace is less damaged than other parts of the castle, and its rooms are almost completely restored, including the gallery of princes and kings of the German empire from the time of Charlemagne. The ancient bell tower, at the northeast end of the Altan, dates from the early 1500s.

At the west end of the terrace, in the cellars of the castle, is the **Wine Vat Building** *Ϟ,* built in the late 16th century and worth a visit for a look at the Great Cask, symbol of the abundant and exuberant life of the Rhineland-Palatinate. This huge barrel-like monstrosity, built in 1751, is capable of holding more than 208,000 liters (55,000 gal.) of wine.

To the east, connecting the palace of Friedrich IV to the **Ottheinrich Building,** itself an outstanding example of German Renaissance architecture, is the **Hall of Mirrors Building,** constructed in 1549—a Renaissance masterpiece. Only the shell of the original building remains, enough to give you an idea of its former glory, with arcades and steep gables decorated with cherubs and sirens.

Next to Ottheinrich's palace is the Chemist's Tower, housing the **Pharmaceutical Museum** *Ϟ* (℡ **06221/25880**), with utensils and laboratory equipment from the 18th and 19th centuries. Entrance is free to those who paid admission already to enter the castle precincts. Admission to the castle is 3€ ($4.80) for adults and 1.50€ ($2.40) for children.

A 1-hour guided tour of the castle costs 4€ ($6.40) for adults and 2€ ($3.20) for children. Tours are frequent, especially in summer, and some are conducted in English. The castle is open March to November daily 9:30am to 6pm; December to February daily 10am to 5pm.

EXPLORING THE ALTSTADT   All the important sights of Heidelberg lie on or near the south bank of the Neckar. However, you should cross to the north side of the river (via the 18th-c. Karl Theodore Bridge) for the best overall view. **Philosophenweg**

(Philosopher's Way), halfway up the hill on the north bank, offers an especially fine vista.

In the town itself, a tour of the main attractions begins with **Marktplatz** in front of the **Rathaus.** On market days, the square is filled with stalls of fresh flowers, fish, and vegetables. At the opposite end of the square is the late-Gothic **Heiliggeistkirche,** built around 1400, the largest Gothic church in the Palatinate. For nearly 300 years, the church was the burial place of the electors, but most of the graves were destroyed in the French invasion late in the 17th century. Around the corner is the famous old mansion **Romantik-Hotel Zum Ritter St. Georg** (p. 438).

Kurpfälzisches Museum (Museum of the Palatinate) 🔦   This museum is housed in a baroque palace. It contains a large collection of painting and sculpture from 6 centuries. Notable is the Riemenschneider Altar from Windsheim (1509), showing Christ and the 12 Apostles. There's also an archaeological collection with a cast of the jawbone of the 500,000-year-old Heidelberg Man and a section on the history of the Palatinate. The restaurant is a great lunch stop (p. 440).

Hauptstrasse 97. ⓒ 06221/5834020. Admission 3€ ($4.80) adults, 1.80€ ($2.90) students and children 17 and under. Tues–Sun 10am–6pm. Bus: 11, 12, 35, 41, or 42.

Studentenkarzer (Student Jail)   The walls and even the ceilings of this prison are covered with graffiti and drawings, including portraits and silhouettes. The last prisoners (unruly and drunken students) were held here in 1914. Ring the caretaker's bell for admission.

Augustinergasse 2. ⓒ 06221/543554. Admission 3€ ($4.80) adults, 2.50€ ($4) students and children 14 and under. Apr–Sept Tues–Sun 10am–6pm; Oct Tues–Sun 10am–4pm; Nov–Mar Tues–Sat 10am–4pm. Bus: 10 or 12.

SHOPPING

The main shopping street is the traffic-free **Hauptstrasse,** which is filled with stores selling glass, crystal, handicrafts, and other items. Heidelberg is also known for its markets, including the one held on Wednesday and Saturday mornings at Marktplatz and another held Tuesday and Friday mornings at Friedrich-Ebert-Platz. One Saturday a month, based on a flexible schedule that corresponds to the events being presented in the city's convention center, a giant *Flohmarkt* (flea market) sprawls along the Kirchheimer Weg, on the city's southwestern edge, beginning at the Messeplatz. Come here for a streetside collection of junk, knickknacks, and castaways from another era.

A city of this size has lots of stores from which to choose. **Gätschenberger,** Hauptstrasse 6 (ⓒ **06221/144817;** tram: 1 or 5), is known for its array of fine linens and embroideries for bed, bathroom, and table.

Spiess & Walther, Friedrich-Ebert-Anlage 23a (ⓒ **06221/22233;** bus: 12), features exclusive designs in contemporary furniture, antiques, and textiles. For all items in leather, stop by **Leder-Meid,** Hauptstrasse 88 (ⓒ **06221/22570;** tram: 1 or 3; bus: 35 or 41), which sells the crafts of German and other manufacturers. Some of the best women's clothing in Heidelberg is inventoried at **Caroline,** just around the corner from the entrance to the Hotel Europäischer Hof, at Friedrich-Ebert-Anlage 1 (ⓒ **06221/ 602963**). Come here for casual but elegant sportswear, and also for upscale formal wear.

If you want more variety under one roof, go to either branch of Heidelberg's best department store, **Kaufhof,** Hauptstrasse 24 (ⓒ **06221/5040;** tram: 1 or 5) or Bergheimerstrasse 1 (ⓒ **06221/9160;** tram: 1 or 5).

HEIDELBERG AFTER DARK

Nights here are alive with the youthful enthusiasm of Heidelberg's students. Early evenings often start in the bars along Hauptstrasse; then late nights get rolling in the clubs around Marktplatz.

THE PERFORMING ARTS   The main performance stage is **Theater der Stadt,** Theaterstrasse 4 (✆ **06221/582000;** bus: 41 or 42), where nightly entertainment includes plays, opera, and dance productions. From June 24 to August 13, the **Schlossfest-Spiele** festival brings opera, classical music, jazz, and theater to venues around the area, including Heidelberg Castle. Contact **Herdelberler Ticket Service,** Theaterstrasse 4 (✆ **06221/5820000**), for tickets.

HISTORIC STUDENT DRINKING CLUBS   Heidelberg's most famous and revered student tavern, **Zum Roten Ochsen (Red Ox Inn)** ✮, Hauptstrasse 217 (✆ **06221/ 20977;** bus: 33), opened in 1703. For six generations, it has been in the Spengel family; they have welcomed everybody from Bismarck to Mark Twain. It seems that every student who has attended the university has left his or her mark (or initials) on the walls. The series of rooms, where revelers sit at long oak tables under smoke-blackened ceilings, is arranged in horseshoe fashion; the U part has a pianist who sets the musical pace. As the evening progresses, the songs become louder and louder. A mug of beer costs 2.50€ ($4) and up, wine is 3.50€ ($5.60) per glass. Meals go from 9€ to 17€ ($14–$27). The tavern is open Monday to Saturday 5pm to midnight; from April to October, it is also open from 11:30am to 2pm. It's closed mid-December to mid-January.

Next door is **Zum Sepp'l,** Hauptstrasse 213 (✆ **06221/23085;** bus: 11 or 33), open since 1634, the second-most famous drinking club in Heidelberg. It's also filled with photographs and carved initials of former students, along with memorabilia that ranges from old Berlin street signs to Alabama license plates. The building itself dates from 1634. Meals cost 8€ to 18€ ($13–$29). A mug of beer goes for 2.50€ ($4). There's live piano music Monday, Tuesday, Friday, and Saturday from 7pm to midnight. When the university is closed, the activity dies down considerably. It's open Monday to Friday noon to 11pm, and Saturday and Sunday 11:30am to 3:30pm and 5pm to midnight.

BARS & CAFES   **Max Bar,** Marktplatz 5 (✆ **06221/24419;** bus: 11 or 33), is a beer drinker's bar, but you can also get a baguette or croissant to soak up some of the alcohol. There's indoor and patio seating. It's open daily 8am to 1am. When you tire of beer and want a more spirited drink, wander over to **Sonder Bar,** Unterestrasse 13 (✆ **06221/25200;** bus: 41 or 42), which stocks more than 150 brands of whiskey, 10 kinds of vodka, and sundry other potions, besides its 11 types of beer. It's open daily 2pm to 2am (Fri–Sat until 3am).

Catch up on the latest news and trends at **Café Journal,** Hauptstrasse 162 (✆ **06221/161712;** bus: 41 or 42), where drinkers linger over beer while scanning newspapers and magazines from all over Europe and the United States. The cafe is open daily 8am to midnight. **Hard Rock Cafe,** Hauptstrasse 142 (✆ **06221/22819;** bus: 41 or 42), has a branch here, open 10am to 1am.

LIVE MUSIC & CLUBS   Once-sleepy Heidelberg now has a thriving music scene. A welcome addition on the scene for salsa lovers is **Havana Cocktailbar-Restaurant,** Neckarstaden 24 (✆ **06221/3893430**), adding some Latino zest to this university town. Tapas and mojitos, along with some 100 cocktails, brighten the evening, as does the live piano music. The trendy **Print Media Lounge,** Kurfürstenanlage 60 (© **06221/653949**), has opened across from the rail station. Serving full meals, it's mainly known for its music and exotic cocktails. There's soul, funk, and jazz on Sundays; DJs play on Friday and Saturday nights.

2 Hirschhorn, Eberbach & Heilbronn

From April to early October, you can take a boat tour in the Neckar Valley as far as Neckarsteinach and back (see "Boating in the Neckar," above). You can also see the many attractions along the banks of the Neckar by car, driving eastward along the right bank of the river.

HIRSCHHORN ✿

This medieval town, 26km (16 miles) east of Heidelberg, is known as the gem of the Neckar Valley. Overlooking the town and the river from a fortified promontory is the 18th-century **Hirschhorn Castle.** The castle defenses are from the 14th century, and wall paintings from that period can be seen in the chapel. The castle is now a hotel and restaurant (below). For a view of the sharp bend of the Neckar below the town, climb to the top of the tower.

GETTING THERE Access by car is via Route 45 east from Heidelberg. Hirschhorn lies on the Neckarelz-Heidelberg rail line with frequent local service between the two towns. For information, call © **01805/996633.**

WHERE TO STAY & DINE

Schloss-Hotel ✿   This hotel, in a hilltop castle looming over the center of town, offers rooms with river views and collections of antiques. Some are in a guesthouse annex, but those in the castle have more space, style, and tradition. Central heating and an elevator have been installed. Bathrooms are neatly kept with tub/shower combinations. The restaurant, which serves traditional dishes, is open to nonresidents as long as they phone in advance. Specialties include roast pork loin with fresh asparagus or rump steak with hollandaise sauce.

Auf Burg Hirschhorn (on Rte. B37), D-69434 Hirschhorn. © **06272/92090.** Fax 06272/3267. www.schlosshotel-hirschhorn.de. 25 units. 105€–132€ ($168–$211) double; 142€ ($227) suite. Rates include buffet breakfast. AE, MC, V. Free parking. Closed mid-Dec to Jan. **Amenities:** Restaurant; lounge; room service. *In room:* TV, minibar.

EBERBACH

The imperial city of Eberbach, established in 1227, is 11km (7 miles) farther along the Neckar, at a point where the river twists to make a wide bend to the south. Its castle, which dates all the way from 1190, was mostly destroyed in the 15th century, but its ivy-covered ruins attract many visitors today. The old Pfarrhof, the medieval center of the town, is within the city walls.

Eberbach was once heavily fortified, and the remains of three castles (all of them in ruins) once stood here. Today you can walk along its ancient streets and take in views of the facades of its historic houses.

Begin your tour at the **Alter Markt,** or old market square. The most colorful facade here is the frescoed **Hotel Karpfen,** Alter Market 1. Many visitors can be seen photographing what the Germans called its *sgraffito* (frescoed) facade.

You can visit the tourist office in the historic **Haus Thalheim,** Kellereistrasse 36 (© **06271/4899**). This is the house, or so it is believed, where Great Britain's future Queen Victoria was conceived. Victoria's parents were on an extended holiday, living in Haus Thalheim, 9 months prior to her birth. In a controversial claim, some local historians assert that Victoria was actually born aboard the family's yacht moored in the Neckar. The same historians also claim, for reasons having to do with public relations and anti-German sentiment among the British at the time, that soon thereafter, the family took their newborn daughter to England and announced that Victoria had actually been born on British soil. The debate continues, quietly, in Eberbach.

Upstairs, above the tourist office, is the headquarters of the **Naturpark Informationszentrum,** the organization that dispenses maps and advice about hiking or walking through the enveloping Odenwald forest. They'll tell you about overnight shelters, give you a list of guesthouses, and outline the carefully marked footpaths leading through the forest. These offices are open May to October Monday to Friday 8:30am to noon and 2 to 5pm, Saturday 10am to noon; from November to April, they're open Monday to Thursday 8:30am to noon and 2 to 5:30pm, Friday 8:30am to noon.

Every Saturday from May to October, beginning at 10:30am, departing from the tourist office, there's a 1-hour guided walking tour, in English and German, of Eberbach's old town.

Burg Eberbach (Eberbach Castle) lies about 1km (⅔ mile) from the town center; it's a steep, uphill climb. It is only a ruin, a jumble of once-fortified walls and arches that visitors can wander through without charge, at any hour of the day or night. Views from the base of the ruin are panoramic.

From **Burg Eberbach,** signs point to a forest path that leads, after an additional 90-minute relatively flat walk, to **Katzenbuckl.** Here, you'll see the **Turm Katzenbuckl,** a tower built during the Victorian age of the "Grand Tour" that marks the highest point in the Odenwald Forest. The stone-sided tower (a 19th-c. mock-medieval folly) is open without charge day and night. Views are also panoramic. From Eberbach to Katzenbuckl requires a total walk of 2 hours, a distance of about 6km (3¾ miles).

GETTING THERE Routes 37 and 45 connect to the A5 Autobahn heading north and south or the A6 going east and west. From Heidelberg, head east along Route 37. Eberbach lies on the Neckarelz-Heidelberg rail line, with frequent service. Call © **01805/996633** for information.

VISITOR INFORMATION Contact the **Tourist Office** at Leopoldplatz 1 (© **06271/87242**), open May to October Monday to Friday 8:30am to 5pm, and Saturday 10am to noon; November to April, the office is open Monday to Thursday 8:30am to 5pm, and Friday 8:30am to noon.

WHERE TO STAY & DINE

Hotel zum Karpfen ⚜ This is the best and most colorful hotel in town. On its facade are authentic sgraffiti (scratched-on paintings) that depict the story of Eberbach. The building is more than 2 centuries old. Each room contains a bathroom with tub/shower combination. The old-world restaurant serves well-prepared meals.

Am Alten Markt 1, 69412 Eberbach. © **06271/71015.** Fax 06271/71010. www.hotel-karpfen.com. 50 units. 88€–105€ ($141–$168) double; 130€ ($208) suite. Rates include buffet breakfast. AE, MC, V. Free parking. **Amenities:** Restaurant (closed Tues); lounge; room service. *In room:* TV, hair dryer.

HEILBRONN

Heilbronn is a major commercial and cultural center. It was made an imperial city by Emperor Karl IV in 1371; however, documents show that a Villa Heilbrunna existed here in A.D. 741. The town owes its name to a holy spring that bubbled up from beneath the high altar at **St. Killian's Church,** the city's most important monument. The old city was largely destroyed in World War II, but the church has been rebuilt in its original Gothic and High Renaissance style. The church's 64m (210-ft.) tower is the earliest example of Renaissance architecture in Germany. Inside are excellent original woodcarvings, preserved during the war, including an elaborate choir and an altar.

Opposite the church is the reconstructed **Rathaus,** a combination of Gothic and Renaissance architecture. On its balcony is an astronomical clock dating to 1580. It was designed by the best-known horologist of the time, Isaak Habrecht, who created the famous clock inside the cathedral at Strasbourg, France.

Some 4,000 hectares (9,800 acres) of wooded parkland surround the city, accessible by footpaths and nature trails.

GETTING THERE   Access by car is via the A6 Autobahn east and west and the A81 north and south. From Heidelberg, drive south along Route 45, and then take A6 east. Heilbronn lies on the major Stuttgart-Würzburg rail line with frequent service. Call ✆ **01805/996633** for information. Bus service to Stuttgart is provided by **Regional Bus Stuttgart GmbH** at Heilbronn (✆ **07131/78560**). For local transport information, call Heilbronner Verkehrsverbund at ✆ **07131/888860.**

TOURIST INFORMATION   Contact the **Stadtisches Verkehrsamt,** Kaiserstrasse 17 (✆ **07131/562270**), Monday to Friday 10am to 6pm, and Saturday 10am to 4pm.

WHERE TO STAY

Insel-Hotel ✿   The leading first-class choice in town and the finest hotel in the area, Insel is on an island (*Insel* in German) in the river, right in the heart of Heilbronn. Its midsize to spacious rooms are well furnished, each with a good-size tiled bathroom with tub/shower combination. Many of the rooms have private balconies opening to a view of the weeping willows in the hotel's private park. The hotel's recreational facilities include an indoor heated pool.

The front terrace of the hotel is the virtual nerve center of town, with locals stopping in to order a beer and catch up on all the gossip. The in-house restaurant is also an excellent choice, even if you're a nonguest. The chefs specialize in Swabian dishes that include onion-flavored roast beef and homemade *Spätzle.*

Friedrich-Ebert-Brücke, 74072 Heilbronn. ✆ 07131/6300. Fax 07131/626060. www.insel-hotel.de. 120 units. 135€–165€ ($216–$264) double; 190€–300€ ($304–$480) suite. AE, DC, MC, V. Free parking. **Amenities:** Restaurant; bar; indoor heated pool; fitness room; sauna; solarium; room service; massage; babysitting; laundry service; dry cleaning; nonsmoking rooms. *In room:* TV, Wi-Fi, hair dryer.

WHERE TO DINE

Ratskeller GERMAN/SWABIAN   This is your best bet for dining in Heilbronn. It's an authentic Ratskeller, unlike so many others, but it's been given the modern treatment, with upholstered banquettes and wrought-iron grillwork. The rib-sticking fare here is solid and reliable. Main dishes include goulash, pepper steak with French fries and salad, and grilled sole. Fish specialties and vegetarian meals are also featured. There's an impressive wine list, although many diners consider the "wine of the cellar" (house wine) perfectly adequate.

Im Rathaus, Marktplatz 7. ✆ 07131/84628. Reservations recommended. Main courses 9€–18€ ($14–$29). AE, MC, V. Mon–Sat 11am–11pm. Closed 10 days in Sept.

3 Stuttgart ⟨⋆

203km (126 miles) SE of Frankfurt, 222km (138 miles) NW of Munich, 126km (78 miles) SE of Heidelberg

Unlike many prosperous industrial centers, Stuttgart is not a city of concrete—two-thirds of the land inside the city limits is devoted to parks, gardens, and woodland. Yet Stuttgart is one of Germany's largest manufacturing cities, the home of Mercedes, Porsche, and Zeiss optical equipment. It's also the site of international trade fairs and congresses.

As a cultural center, Stuttgart is without peer in southwestern Germany. The Stuttgart Ballet is known throughout the world, and its State Opera and Philharmonic Orchestra are also highly regarded. In addition, Stuttgart boasts an abundance of theater groups, cultural festivals, and museums, and is also the largest wine-growing city in Germany.

The name "Stuttgart" comes from a stud farm owned by one of the dukes of Swabia, son of Emperor Otto the Great. By 1427, Stuttgart had become the capital and residence of the counts of Württemberg. The city expanded under the reign of Kaiser Wilhelm I (1816–64). At the turn of the 20th century, it had a population of 175,000. By World War I, Stuttgart's landmass extended to the Neckar River.

During World War II, bombing attacks leveled 60% of Stuttgart's buildings. Not one of its landmarks or historic structures survived intact. After the war, Stuttgart became the capital of the newly formed state of Baden-Württemberg (many still call it by its former name, Swabia). Stuttgart's population today is about 600,000.

ESSENTIALS

GETTING THERE   By Plane   The **Stuttgart Echterdingen Airport** (✆ 0711/9480) is 14km (9 miles) south of the city near Echterdingen. The airport has connections with most major German and European cities. Trip time from Frankfurt is 50 minutes; from Hamburg or Berlin, 1¼ hours. The commuter train to Stuttgart leaves from below the arrivals level of Terminal 1. Trains depart every 20 minutes, taking 27 minutes. A one-way fare is 3.10€ ($5). A taxi to the city center costs from 30€ ($48).

By Train   Stuttgart has rail links to all major German cities, with frequent connections. The train station is directly north of the historic area. Twenty-seven daily trains run from Munich (trip time: 2–3 hr.), and 19 trains run from Frankfurt (trip time: 1½–2 hr.). For information, call ✆ **01805/996633.**

By Bus   Long-distance bus service into Stuttgart from cities outside Germany, including London, Paris, Vienna, and Amsterdam, is maintained by **Deutsche Touring GmbH** (✆ 0711/2730962; www.touring.de). Passengers coming into Stuttgart from other cities within Germany almost always opt to take the train.

By Car   Access by car is via the A8 Autobahn east and west, or the A81 north and south.

VISITOR INFORMATION   Information about transportation, sightseeing, and hotels is available at the **Touristik-Zentrum,** Königstrasse 1A (✆ **0711/22280;** www.stuttgart-tourist.de), which is open year-round Monday to Friday 9am to 8pm and Saturday 9am to 6pm; it also has Sunday hours November to April from 1 to 6pm, and May to October from 11am to 6pm.

GETTING AROUND   A single ride between points that fall within Stuttgart's historic core on the city's bus or subway system costs 1.90€ ($3.10). Rides to the outer

Stuttgart

ATTRACTIONS ●
Altes Schloss and Württembergisches Landesmuseum **9**
Liederhalle **8**
Neues Schloss **10**
Rathaus **11**
Staatsgalerie **6**
Staatstheater **7**

ACCOMMODATIONS ■
Alter Fritz **1**
Am Schlossgarten **5**
City Hotel **13**
Der Zauberlehrling **12**
Hotel Mack & Pflieger **2**
Hotel Stuttgart 21 **3**
Hotel Wörtz-Zur Weinsteige **14**
Steigenberger Hotel Graf Zeppelin **4**

Church ⚰
Information ⓘ
Post Office ✉

suburbs, depending on where you travel, range from 2.35€ to 6.30€ ($3.80–$10). Often, the most economical way of handling multiple rides on the system involves buying a *Tageskarte* (day ticket), which costs 5.60€ ($9); it's valid for a day of unlimited transport within the city core and also within zones 1 and 2. A 1-day pass that's valid for transport within the entire network (in other words, the city center and zones 1–5) sells for 12€ ($18). An exceptional bargain is its 3-day equivalent, available only to temporary residents of a local hotel or guesthouse, selling for 9.90€ ($16) within the city center and zones 1 (central Stuttgart) and 2 (immediate suburbs), and for 13€ ($21) for rides anywhere within the network. For more information about the city's transport system, its routes, and its prices, call © **0711/19449.**

WHERE TO STAY

No matter when you come to Stuttgart, you'll probably find an international trade fair in progress, from the January glass-and-ceramics exposition to the December book exhibition. (Stuttgart is also southern Germany's most important publishing center.) Good accommodations may be difficult to find at almost any time, so you should always reserve in advance.

EXPENSIVE

Am Schlossgarten 𝒜𝒜𝒜   The Steigenberger Graf Zeppelin (see below) is the market leader in Stuttgart, attracting the Porsche crowd, but this government-rated five-star hotel wins the race for charm and tranquillity. Its location is in a landscaped park, although it is close to the Königstrasse shopping zone. Listed as one of the "Leading Hotels of the World," it's only a few minutes from the central train station on foot. The epitome of luxury living in Stuttgart, it is an oasis of charm and grace, with the town's most enjoyable hotel dining and drinking facilities.

Bedrooms and suites are elegant with individual character, tasteful fabrics, comfortable furnishings, and deluxe bathrooms with tub and shower. The on-site Zirbelstube offers a grand cuisine under the direction of Bernhard Diers and his team of talented chefs. Innovation and craftsmanship mark the cuisine. In summer the Restaurant am Schlossgarten with its outdoor tables is one of the most romantic places for dining in Stuttgart. There is also a wine bar serving an innovative Mediterranean cuisine, with perhaps the finest wine *carte* in Stuttgart.

Schillerstrasse 23, 70173 Stuttgart. © **0711/20260.** Fax 0711/2026888. www.hotelschlossgarten.com. 116 units. 274€–305€ ($438–$488) double; 348€ ($557) junior suite; from 418€ ($669) suite. AE, DC, MC, V. Parking 16€ ($26). **Amenities:** 3 restaurants; cafe; business services; Internet room; laundry service; dry cleaning; nonsmoking rooms. *In room:* A/C, TV, Wi-Fi, minibar, hair dryer, safe.

Hilton Garden Inn Stuttgart Neckar Park 𝒜𝒜   At long last Stuttgart has a Hilton, although it lies east of the center and across the river in the leafy suburb of Bad Cannstatt with its Kur Park. As German Hiltons go, this is one of the more modest choices, but it's first class in all respects, ranging from the comfort of its bedrooms to the quality of its food and service. It is especially popular with commercial travelers in Stuttgart on automobile business.

All the bedrooms are built to the highest modern standards with all the latest gadgets. Furnishings are tasteful with modern sophistication, and the sleek bathrooms come with tub/shower combos. We especially enjoy the Palm Beach restaurant on the ground floor, with its cocktails, light Mediterranean food, and typical American dishes. A special feature is a 24-hour Pavilion Pantry stocked with snacks, drinks, and "everything you forgot."

Mercedesstrasse 75, 70372 Stuttgart-Bad Cannstatt. © **0711/900550.** Fax 0711/90055100. http://hiltongarden inn.hilton.com. 150 units. 220€–285€ ($352–$456) double. AE, DC, MC, V. **Amenities:** Restaurant; food and drink lounge; fitness center; children's programs; business center; room service; laundry service; dry cleaning; nonsmoking rooms; rooms for those w/limited mobility. *In room:* A/C, TV, Wi-Fi, minibar, beverage maker, hair dryer, iron, safe.

Steigenberger Hotel Graf Zeppelin 👫👫   This is the best hotel for those who come to wheel and deal with Stuttgart businesspeople. Although situated at the train station, it's not only attractive but dignified and stylish, once you get past its plain postwar exterior. The spacious soundproof rooms are colorfully decorated, all with tidily kept bathrooms with tub/shower combinations.

Arnulf-Klett-Platz 7, 70173 Stuttgart. © **800/223-5652** in the U.S. and Canada, or 0711/20480. Fax 0711/2048542. www.stuttgart.steigenberger.com. 195 units. 135€–255€ ($216–$408) double; 305€–355€ ($488–$568) suite. AE, DC, MC, V. Parking 18€ ($21). U-Bahn: Hauptbahnhof. **Amenities:** 3 restaurants; bar; indoor heated pool; spa; Jacuzzi; sauna; room service; babysitting; laundry service; dry cleaning; nonsmoking rooms; 1 room for those w/limited mobility. *In room:* A/C, TV, minibar, hair dryer, trouser press, safe (suites only).

MODERATE

Alter Fritz   Pleasant, conservative, quiet, and isolated in a verdant location about a mile north of the center of Stuttgart, this imposing stone-sided building dates from 1903, when it was constructed at the edge of a wooded stretch of land known as Killesberg Park. Many visitors opt for at least some exposure to the great outdoors, often with morning jogs or brisk walks through the footpaths in the park. The building's interior was radically modernized in the mid-1980s, leaving a clean, efficient, and blandly modern collection of public areas flooded with sunlight and, in many cases, views of the park.

The cuisine has French and international overtones. Residents of the hotel dine in a room devoted exclusively to them; nonresidents eat in a cozy dining room known as Der Kleine Fritz.

Feuerbacher Weg 101, Killesberg 70192. © **0711/135650.** Fax 0711/1356565. www.alter-fritz-am-killesberg.de. 10 units. 95€–125€ ($152–$200) double. Rates include continental breakfast. No credit cards. Free parking. Bus: 43. **Amenities:** Restaurant; laundry service. *In room:* TV, minibar.

Der Zauberlehrling 👫 *(Finds*   This offbeat choice is quirky and funky, with a lot of bohemian charm. Each of its individually designed bedrooms conjures up a theme, ranging from the Suite of 1,001 Nights to Seventh Heaven. Likewise, the decor in minimalist settings roams the world—perhaps the Hermitage, a country estate in some far and distant land with ruby-red brocades and sultry salons. As you enter Paddington, you're brought back to antiques from Queen Victoria's times, with Miss Marple looking down from above. The most modern of all is the Media Suite, with its high-tech efficiency where communication is everything. The managers claim that this chamber is "the place for new messages from all over the world, and maybe even the universe." If you want to perform dirty deeds in private while in Stuttgart, behind carefully concealed doors, we suggest that you won't be exposed if you check into the Black Box.

The name of this hotel, "The Sorcerer's Apprentice," comes, of course, from that old ballad by Goethe, although many people know it better from the classic Disney film.

Rosenstrasse 38, 70182 Stuttgart. © **0711/2377770.** Fax 0711/237775. www.zauberlehrling.de. 9 units. 145€–280€ ($232–$448) double; from 350€ ($560) suite. AE, MC, V. Parking 12€ ($19). U-Bahn: Schlossplatz. **Amenities:** Restaurant; bar; room service; laundry service. *In room:* TV, minibar, fan.

Hotel Wörtz-Zur Weinsteige *Value*   The amber lights of a *Weinstube* (wine bar) welcome visitors to this local favorite in Stuttgart, which has the best rooms and the best food of all local hotels in this price range. The small rooms are paneled and sometimes have massive hand-carved armoires; all are soundproof. The *Weinstube* evokes the feeling of a remote corner of Swabia—it's perfect for relaxing after a long trip. The hotel is known for its garden terrace.

Hohenheimerstrasse 28–30, 70184 Stuttgart. ℂ 0711/2367000. Fax 0711/2367007. www.hotel-woertz.de. 32 units. 110€–145€ ($176–$232) double. Rates include buffet breakfast. AE, DC, MC, V. Parking 4€–6€ ($6.40–$9.60). U-Bahn: Dobelstrasse. **Amenities:** Restaurant; lounge; room service; nonsmoking rooms; 1 room for those w/limited mobility. *In room:* TV, hair dryer, safe.

INEXPENSIVE

City Hotel *Finds*   The City is a bed-and-breakfast-type hotel, within walking distance of the sights in the city center. It offers pleasantly furnished but hardly spectacular rooms equipped with private showers (no tubs) and direct-dial telephones. The generous breakfast buffet, the only meal served, is offered in a sunny winter garden.

Uhlandstrasse 18 (directly west of Charlottenplatz), 70182 Stuttgart. ℂ 0711/210810. Fax 0711/2369772. www.cityhotel-stuttgart.de. 31 units. 99€–115€ ($158–$184) double. Rates include buffet breakfast. AE, DC, MC, V. Free parking. U-Bahn: Olgaeck. **Amenities:** Breakfast room; lounge; nonsmoking rooms; 1 room for those w/limited mobility. *In room:* TV, Wi-Fi, minibar.

Hotels Mack & Pflieger   These two hotels share the same management and basically the same design. Set within a few steps of one another just a short walk from the railway station, they were built in stages between around 1960 and 1980. Each rises between three and four stories and has roughly the same decor and architectural style. All the rooms are small and somewhat basic, but are nonetheless completely adequate and comfortable. Bathrooms are small with a shower or a tub.

Kriegerstrasse 7 (Hotel Mack) and Kriegerstrasse 11 (Hotel Pflieger), 70191 Stuttgart. Mack: ℂ 0711/292942; fax 0711/2536919; www.hotel-mack-stuttgart.de. Pflieger: ℂ 0711/221878; fax 0711/293489; www.hotel-pflieger.de. 54 units. 79€–120€ ($126–$192) double. Rates include buffet breakfast. AE, DC, MC, V. Free parking. U-Bahn: Hauptbahnhof. **Amenities:** Breakfast room; bar; lounge; nonsmoking rooms; rooms for those w/limited mobility. *In room:* TV.

Hotel Stuttgart 21 *Value*   This hotel, though not as centrally located as the City Hotel, offers more style and better rooms. Other benefits are a nicely tiled indoor pool with a sauna and a manicured garden where a waiter will take your drink order. Rooms are well maintained and inviting. Most are medium in size, although some are quite small. All contain showers.

Friedhofstrasse 21, 70191 Stuttgart. ℂ 0711/25870. Fax 0711/2587404. www.bestwestern.com. 90 units. 98€–130€ ($157–$208) double; 120€–300€ ($192–$480) suite. Rates include buffet breakfast. AE, DC, MC, V. Free parking. U-Bahn: Turlenstrasse/Burgerhospital. **Amenities:** Restaurant; lounge; indoor heated pool; sauna; solarium; steam bath; room service; massage; babysitting; laundry service; nonsmoking rooms. *In room:* TV, Wi-Fi, minibar, coffeemaker, hair dryer.

WHERE TO DINE

Wielandshöhe *INTERNATIONAL*   Vincent Klink, one of the most celebrated chefs in Germany, runs the greenest restaurant in Stuttgart. He focuses on food raised without pesticides or chemical additives. Every month, he changes the menu, posting the new *carte* like a work of art. Klink is an inventive chef, and he has an almost sensual approach to food, giving his cuisine a seductive charm that can wake up a terminally jaded palate. You're likely to be captivated by such dishes as braised rye bread with fresh oysters or baked venison with herbs, and especially the rack of veal with sweetbreads and fresh morels. The thornback ray filet with capers and Amalfi lemons might well be the best version of this dish you ever order. If featured, start with his minestrone with olives and basil; it should win an award.

Alte Weinsteige 71. ☎ **0711/6408848.** Reservations required. 4-course menu 74€ ($118); 6-course menu 98€ ($157). AE, DC, MC, V. Wed–Sat noon–2pm and 6:30–9pm. Tram: U-6 or U-9 from the center of Stuttgart.

Zeppelin-Stüble SWABIAN   Although many restaurants in Stuttgart have abandoned true Swabian cuisine for more international fare, the chefs here still turn out the old-fashioned specialties preferred by locals. In this elegantly appointed restaurant furnished with Swabian antiques, each dish uses fresh, seasonal ingredients. Such Swabian specialties as *Rostbraten* (roast beef) and *Maultaschen* (a type of ravioli made with a variety of fillings) are offered. The kitchen does an excellent *Schwäbischer* sauerbraten (a Swabian version of marinated beef) with *Spätzle* and salad. Other specialties include seared salmon steak with dill sauce and strips of calf's liver in a red wine–and–onion sauce.

In the Steigenberger Hotel Graf Zeppelin, Arnulf-Klett-Platz 7. ☎ 0711/2048184. Reservations recommended. Main courses 14€–25€ ($22–$40). AE, DC, MC, V. Mon–Sat 11:30am–2:30pm and 6–10:30pm; Sun 11:30am–2:30pm. U-Bahn: Hauptbahnhof.

Zur Weinsteige ⍟ INTERNATIONAL   The interior of this restaurant celebrates German handicrafts. Everything looks handmade, from the hand-blown leaded glass in the small-paned windows to the carved columns and tables and chairs. International cuisine, with a number of Swabian specialties, is offered. In summer, you can sit among the grapevines stretching over the sun terrace. Also worth seeing is the wine cellar, well stocked with the best regional wines and a wide selection of German and international wines. You can buy wine directly from the hotel's vineyards. Next to the cellar is a room for sitting and tasting.

In the Hotel Wörtz, Hohenheimerstrasse 30. ☎ **0711/2367000.** Fax 0711/2367007. Reservations recommended. Main courses 16€–27€ ($26–$43); fixed-price lunch 15€ ($24), dinners 30€–75€ ($48–$120). AE, DC, MC, V. Tues–Sat noon–2pm and 6–10pm. Closed holidays, 3 weeks in Jan, and 2 weeks in Aug. S-Bahn: Dobelstrasse.

EXPLORING STUTTGART

Many of the most remarkable structures in today's Stuttgart are of progressive design, created by such architects as Ludwig Mies van der Rohe, Walter Gropius, Hans Scharoun, and Le Corbusier. The **Liederhalle,** Schloss-Strasse, constructed in 1956 of concrete, glass, and glazed brick, is fascinating inside and out. The hall contains three auditoriums.

The town's older section is clustered around **Schillerplatz** and the statue of the great German poet and dramatist, Schiller. **Neues Schloss,** on Schlossplatz, can be visited only by group tour. It was originally constructed between 1746 and 1807 and rebuilt beginning in 1958. Today, it houses state government rooms. The modern **Rathaus** faces the old Marktplatz, where flowers, fruit, and vegetables are sold in open stalls.

For the best view of Stuttgart, climb to the top of the 510m (1,673-ft.) **Birkenkopf,** west of the city. The hill was created from the debris of Stuttgart dumped here after World War II. After the 20-minute walk to the top, you'll be rewarded by a view of the city and the surrounding Swabian Hills, covered with vineyards and woods.

Between April and October, every day at 11am, the local tourist office organizes an English- and German-language guided tour through the city's historic core. Beginning on the sidewalk in front of the tourist office (Königstrasse 1A; ☎ **0711/2228240**) and lasting for 90 minutes, it costs 8€ ($13). There's no discount for students or most age groups, but children 4 and under can tag along for free. A longer and more comprehensive walking tour, conducted entirely in German, is organized from the same location (May–Dec only) every Saturday at 10am. With a duration of 2½ hours, it's priced at 10€ ($16), no charge for children 4 and under.

For insights into the areas surrounding Stuttgart's historic core, you might be interested in a guided bus tour of the city and its suburbs. Conducted year-round, in German and English, and departing every day at 1:30pm, the 2½-hour tour costs 20€ ($32) for adults, 17€ ($27) for students, and 12€ ($19) for children ages 6 to 12; children 5 and under ride free. Be warned that this tour requires a minimum number of participants and will be canceled if there aren't enough candidates, so advance reservations are important.

Altes Schloss and Württembergisches Landesmuseum (Old Castle and Württemberg Regional Museum) ⟨⟩   One of Stuttgart's oldest standing structures, this huge ducal palace was originally a moated castle built in the 13th century and was later redone in the 16th century in Renaissance style. Now it houses the Württembergisches Landesmuseum, which traces the art and culture of Swabia from the Stone Age to the present. The most valuable items include a survey of European glass through the ages, the ducal art chamber, and the crown jewels. The museum also houses a large collection of Swabian sculptures; an exhibition of clocks, coins, and musical instruments; the famous treasures of the tomb of the Celtic prince of Hochdorf (ca. A.D. 530); and a collection from the Merovingian period in the early Middle Ages.

Schillerplatz 6. ℂ 0711/2793498. www.landesmuseum-stuttgart.de. Admission 4.50€ ($7.20), 3€ ($4.80) students, free for children 13 and under. Tues 10am–1pm; Wed–Sun 10am–5pm. U-Bahn: Schlossplatz.

Fernsehturm (Television Tower)   This 217m (712-ft.) tower, capped with a red-and-white transmitter, soars above a forested hillock south of Stuttgart. It was designed and built in 1956 using radically innovative applications of aluminum and prestressed reinforced concrete, and served as a prototype for larger towers in Toronto and Moscow. A restaurant is at the tower's base, and a cafe, bar, restaurant, observation platform, and information about the tower's construction are at the top of a 150m (492-ft.) elevator. Food is served daily 10am to 8pm. Look outside for the mobile platforms used by window washers.

Jahnstrasse 120, Stuttgart-Degerloch (south of the city, just off B3). ℂ 0711/232597. www.fernsehturm-stuttgart. com. Admission 5€ ($8) adults, 3€ ($4.80) children. Daily 9am–10:30pm. Tram: 15.

Gottlieb Daimler Memorial   The life and the work of Gottlieb Daimler, the inventor, is revealed here, along with the first models of the Daimler ever made. It was at this spot that the first internal combustion engine was brought to perfection in 1883. Car buffs enjoy looking at some of the tools mechanics used to perfect the cars that led to the creation of the chic Mercedes line of vehicles. Blueprints and models are also shown. In the re-created workshop you can see models of Daimler and Wilhelm Maybach's first horseless carriage and the ground-breaking "grandfather clock" engine.

Taubenheimer Strasse 13, Bad Cannstatt-Stuttgart. ℂ 0711/569399. Free admission. Tues–Sun 10am–4pm. U-Bahn: Kursaal.

Mercedes-Benz Museum ⟨⟩   This museum honors the oldest automobile factory in the world and the invention of the motorcar by Carl Benz and Gottlieb Daimler. Nearly 75 historical vehicles are shown, including a Daimler Reitwagen from 1885, the first motor-bicycle. You can also see Daimler's first Mercedes of 1902. Racecars on display date from 1899 and include the Blitzen-Benz, the Silver Arrow, the Sauber Mercedes, the Indy car, and some vehicles built especially to achieve speed records.

Mercedesstrasse 100, Stuttgart-Bad Cannstatt. (ℭ 0711/1730000. www.museum-mercedes-benz.com. Admission 8€ ($13); free for children 14 and under. Tues–Sun 9am–6pm. S-Bahn: 1 to Gottlieb-Daimler-Stadion; then walk to the entrance of the plant, where you'll be taken on a special bus to the museum.

Porsche Museum 𝒢 Opening in 2008, a much-expanded Porsche Museum lets you see around 80 of these legendary cars that trace the history of this highly prized automobile. Ferdinand Porsche set up his own business on Porsche Square in Zuffen-hausen in 1931, launching a business that would become world famous for its sporty serial autos and racing cars. Surprisingly, the Volkswagen was also launched here in 1936 and called the "Beetle" or "Rounded Porsche."

On exhibit are such prizes as the first Porsche-branded car, a Boxster precursor from 1948; as well as the Formula 1 champions of the mid-1980s and the 911 GTI that won the Le Mans competition in 1998. You can also see the Porsche 904 Carrera GTS Coupé from 1964, the first car with a plastic body. That was the same year that the great Porsche 911 was introduced.

You can also call and make reservations to tour the factory to see how an entire sports car comes together. Gigantic robotic claws lower finished bodies onto drive-trains and chassis, and you'll see how fenders, engines, and dashboards come together to make the 911s or Boxsters.

Porschestrasse 1. (ℭ 0711/91125685. Free admission. Factory tours in English Mon–Fri 10am. Museum Mon–Fri 9am–4pm; Sat–Sun 9am–5pm. S-Bahn: Neuwirtshaus/Porscheplatz.

Staatsgalerie (State Gallery of Stuttgart) 𝒢 The city's finest art museum exhibits works spanning some 550 years. However, the best collection is from the 19th and 20th centuries, especially the works of the German expressionists—Kirchner, Bar-lach, and Beckmann—as well as representatives of the Bauhaus school and Blue Rider group, such as Klee and Feininger. There are also examples of French art of the 19th and 20th centuries and of the European and American postwar avant-garde.

Konrad-Adenauer-Strasse 30–32. (ℭ 0711/470400. Admission 4.50€ ($7.20) adults, 3€ ($4.80) students, free for children 13 and under. Tues–Sun 10am–6pm (Thurs until 9pm); until midnight the 1st Sat of each month. U-Bahn: Staatsgalerie.

SHOPPING

Home to clothing designers Hugo Boss and Ulli Knecht, Stuttgart has its fair share of boutiques that range from interesting to elegant. **Klett Passage,** across from the train station, is an underground mall full of upscale shops. If you follow the Königsstrasse from the station for about half a mile, you'll likely find anything you want in one of the retail stores that line the street. There are somewhat more expensive boutiques along the Calwer Strasse, especially in the gleaming chrome-and-glass arcade, **Calwer Passage.** Bargains galore can be found at the Saturday morning **flea market** on the Karlsplatz between the old castle and the new palace, where clothes, books, furniture, household items, art, and just about anything else are likely to turn up.

In business since 1723, **Tritschler,** Am Marktplatz 7 (ℭ 0711/1204574; U-Bahn: Charlottenplatz), stocks glass, porcelain, and fine china as well as cutlery and decora-tive housewares. **Pavillon,** Eberhardstrasse 31–33 (ℭ 0711/243134; U-Bahn: Rathaus), specializes in silver from the 19th and 20th centuries, and also sells glass, crystal, Meis-sen porcelain, and a few paintings.

The city's largest bookstore, **Wittwer,** Königstrasse 30 (© **0711/25070;** S-Bahn: Hauptbahnhof), carries many books in English and has tables placed throughout the store so that you can comfortably scan potential purchases. For a bit of everything, head to the city's largest department store, **Breuninger,** Marktstrasse 1–3 (© **0711/ 2110;** U-Bahn: Charlottenplatz), where glass elevators whisk you through several floors of housewares, furnishings, and fashion.

STUTTGART AFTER DARK

Listings of the various cultural events, as well as tickets, are available from the tourist office (see "Visitor Information," earlier in this section). The magazine *Lift,* available at newsstands, lists all the happenings around Stuttgart.

THE PERFORMING ARTS Staatstheater, Oberer Schlossgarten (© **0711/ 202090;** S-Bahn: Hauptbahnhof), is the leading cultural venue in Stuttgart. The theater consists of the Grosses Haus for opera and ballet, the Kleines Haus for theater, and the Kammer-Theater, which puts on experimental works. This is home to the world-class **Stuttgart Ballet,** established by the American choreographer John Cranko in the 1960s and now led by Reid Anderson. It also houses the respected **Staatsoper (State Opera).** Tickets are 8€ to 115€ ($13–$184) and can be purchased at the Staatstheater box office (closed Aug).

Classical and other concerts may be heard in the three halls of the **Liederhalle,** Berliner Platz 1–3 (© **0711/2027710;** U-Bahn: Liederhalle/Berlinerplatz), which is home to the **Stuttgarter Philharmoniker,** under the baton of Gabriel Feltz, and the **Radio Symphony Orchestra.** Tickets for all concerts are on sale at **SKS Russ,** Charlottenplatz 17 (© **0711/1635321;** U-Bahn: Charlottenplatz). Prices are 8€ to 32€ ($13–$51).

THE BAR, CAFE & CLUB SCENE   Start your evening with a drink at **Amadeus,** Charlottenplatz 17 (© **0711/292678;** U-Bahn: Charlottenplatz), where students and locals gather. It's open Monday to Thursday 3pm to 2am and Friday and Saturday 11am to 4am.

For a trendier locale, and one where you're likely to meet counterculture Stuttgart (complete with purple hair and piercings in unpredictable places), head to **Palast der Republik,** Friedrichstrasse 27 (© **0711/2264887;** U-Bahn: Keplerstrasse), a century-old bar that has tended to draw an arts-conscious crowd throughout its long history. DJs play funk and soul. It's open Monday to Wednesday 11am to 2am, Thursday to Saturday 11am to 3am, and Sunday 3pm to 1am. **Café Stella,** Hauptstätter Strasse 57 (© **0711/6402583;** U-Bahn: Österreichischerplatz), is a see-and-be-seen kind of place that serves drinks and food; it hosts local jazz bands, on a varying schedule, several times a month. Sunday brunch is a particularly stylish venue for the hip and hipster wannabes.

4 Tübingen ★★

47km (29 miles) S of Stuttgart, 153km (95 miles) NE of Freiburg

Though it's often compared to Heidelberg, this quiet old university town on the upper Neckar has a look and personality all its own. Gabled medieval houses are crowded against the ancient town wall at the bank of the river. In summer, students pole gondola-like boats up and down the river. This far upstream, the Neckar is too shallow for commercial vessels, so Tübingen has been spared the industrial look of a trading community.

Progress has not passed the city by, however. In spite of its medieval aspect, it has a new residential and science suburb in the shadow of the Schönbuch Forest north of the city, with medical facilities, research institutes, and lecture halls affiliated with the university. The buildings of the old university, founded in 1477, are north of the botanical gardens. The humanist Melanchthon taught here in the 16th century, and later on Schiller, Hegel, and Hölderlin were students.

ESSENTIALS

GETTING THERE   By Air   The nearest major airport, at Stuttgart, has good connections to Tübingen, including a direct bus link.

By Train   The Stuttgart-Tübingen rail line offers frequent service. Tübingen also has good rail ties to other major cities in Germany, including Frankfurt (trip time: 3½ hr.), Berlin (trip time: 11 hr.), and Hamburg (trip time: 8½ hr.). For information, call © 01805/996633.

By Bus   Because of Tübingen's position astride some of the major rail lines of central Europe, most visitors get here from other parts of Germany by train. But if you're committed to the idea of bus transport in and out of town, contact **Deutsche Touring GmbH** in Frankfurt (© 069/7903501) for information about the buses that service Tübingen and its surrounding region.

By Car   Access is via Route 27 west from the A8 Autobahn running east and west, or via Route 28 east from the A81 Autobahn running north and south.

VISITOR INFORMATION   Contact the **Verkehrsverein,** An der Eberhardsbrücke (© 07071/91360), open Monday to Friday 9am to 7pm and Saturday 9am to 5pm. From May to September, the office is also open on Sunday from 2 to 5pm.

WHERE TO STAY

Hotel am Bad *(Value*   This hotel, located in the center of one of Tübingen's well-maintained public parks, offers woodland calm not far from the city center. Its rambling rose-colored exterior complements the masses of red flowers on the sun terrace. Rooms are modest and a bit small but still comfortable, all containing bathrooms with tub/shower combos.

Europastrasse Freibad 2, 72072 Tübingen. © 07071/79740. Fax 07071/75336. www.hotel-am-bad.de. 35 units. 92€–115€ ($147–$184) double. Rates include buffet breakfast. AE, MC, V. Free outdoor parking; 6.50€ ($10) in garage. Closed Dec 20–Jan 4. **Amenities:** Breakfast room; bar; room service; laundry service; dry cleaning; nonsmoking rooms; 1 room for those w/limited mobility. *In room:* TV, Wi-Fi, minibar, hair dryer.

Hotel am Schloss *(★ (Finds*   One of the most charming and atmospheric hotels in town is a group of steep-gabled antique buildings in the town's historic core; each is accented in summer with window boxes loaded with flowers, and the oldest dates to 1491. You'll register in the main building and be assigned a room, and if it's within either of the two very old, and very historic, outbuildings, you'll get a key for access to their respective entrances. None of the three buildings has an elevator, but each has thick walls, and each has benefited from a recent renovation that retains the old-fashioned charm while adding modern conveniences and a scattering of simple, traditional, and noncontroversial furnishings.

The main building contains at least half of the hotel's accommodations, as well as its restaurant, where Swabian food is served daily at both lunch and dinner (closed Tues Oct–Apr). Main courses range from 10€ to 20€ ($16–$32). An enduring specialty is

Maultaschen, a traditional regional dish resembling large ravioli that are stuffed with a mixture of spices and minced meats. Staff here is cordial but no-nonsense and hardworking.

Burgsteige 18, 72070 Tübingen. ℂ **07071/92940.** Fax 07071/929410. www.hotelamschloss.de. 35 units. 104€–128€ ($166–$205) double. Rates include buffet breakfast. AE, DC, MC, V. Parking 6.50€ ($8.45). **Amenities:** Restaurant; bar; laundry service; dry cleaning. *In room:* TV, minibar (in some), hair dryer, safe (in some).

Krone Hotel 🎯   The town's most prestigious hotel is located right off the river, in the heart of Tübingen. It's traditional and conservative, with a homey atmosphere. The decor includes a generous use of antiques or fine reproductions. Rooms are personalized; many are decoratively tiled, and all contain bathrooms with tub/shower combos.

Among hotel dining rooms, the Krone Restaurant serves some of the most sophisticated fare in town. Both international dishes and regional specialties are available; complete meals range from 30€ to 45€ ($48–$72).

Uhlandstrasse 1, 72078 Tübingen. ℂ **07071/13310.** Fax 07071/133132. www.krone-tuebingen.de. 47 units. 129€–159€ ($206–$254) double; 169€–199€ ($270–$318) suite. Rates include buffet breakfast. AE, DC, MC, V. Free parking. Closed Dec 23–31. **Amenities:** Restaurant; lounge; room service; laundry service; dry cleaning; non-smoking rooms; rooms for those w/limited mobility. *In room:* TV, Wi-Fi, hair dryer, safe (in some).

WHERE TO DINE

Restaurant Museum 🎯 *Value* INTERNATIONAL/SWABIAN   This is one of Tübingen's foremost restaurants. It's a pleasant place to dine on international specialties such as Marseille snail soup, or regional dishes such as Swabian medallions of veal. The lunches here are considered by many locals (including students) to be not only the best in town but also the best value.

Wilhelmstrasse 3. ℂ **07071/22828.** Reservations recommended. Main courses 9€–22€ ($14–$35) fixed-price menus 16€–19€ ($26–$30). AE, MC, V. Daily 11am–3pm and 6pm–midnight.

Restaurant Rosenau 🎯🎯 GERMAN/SWABIAN   This restaurant, near the botanical gardens, offers the finest food in the town center, though it does not measure up to the Gasthof Waldhorn (below). Landgasthof Rosenau is like a roadhouse with a cafe annex. The owner serves modern cuisine along with superb Swabian specialties, listed under the gutbürgerlich selections. Try the tasty and filling Swabian hot pot with *Spätzle* (dumplings) and fresh mushrooms or the delectable veal steak with morels. Desserts are often elaborate. In fair weather, guests can order drinks out in the sun.

Beim Neuen Botanischen Garten. ℂ **07071/68866.** Reservations recommended. Main courses 13€–23€ ($21–$37); fixed-price 3-course lunch 19€ ($30), 4-course dinner 50€ ($80). AE, DC, MC, V. Tues–Sun 11am–midnight.

NEARBY DINING

Gasthof Waldhorn 🎯🎯🎯 GERMAN/FRENCH   The finest restaurant in the area is not in Tübingen but on its outskirts, at Tübingen-Bebenhausen. It's decorated like an elegant manor house. Herr and Frau Schulz offer a light German and French cuisine based on regional ingredients, backed up by an impressive wine list (with many half bottles). With a chef who combines inventiveness and solid technique, this is one restaurant that truly deserves its stars. The menu changes daily but may include trout terrine and wild venison with forest mushrooms, along with the in-season vegetable. The dessert specialty is a soft cream concoction flavored with rose hips. Behind the house, the garden has five tables for summer dining.

Schönbuchstrasse 49 (6km/4 miles from the town center). ℂ 07071/61270. Reservations required. Main courses 24€–36€ ($38–$58); fixed-price menu 78€ ($125). No credit cards. Wed–Sun noon–1pm and 6:30–9pm. Closed 2 weeks in Aug.

EXPLORING TÜBINGEN

The Neckar River runs through Tübingen. With landfill, the city created a long and narrow island in the river's center. This island is reached by walking across a wide bridge, called Eberhardsbrücke. Locals enjoy the tree-shaded promenade **Platanenallee** ☘☘, which, in warm weather, is filled with strollers. From there, you get a panoramic view of the town, with its willows and houses reflected in the river. Towering above the other buildings is the **Schloss Hohentübingen (Renaissance castle),** which is now used by the university. It's worth climbing up to the castle for the dramatic view from the terraces.

The narrow streets of the Altstadt wind up and down the hillside, but they all seem to lead to **Marktplatz** ☘, where festive markets are held on Monday, Wednesday, and Friday. You'll feel as if you're stepping into the past when you come upon country people selling fruit and vegetables in the open square. Facing the square is the **Rathaus** ☘, which dates from the 15th century but also has more recent additions, including the 19th-century painted designs on the facade.

On a hillside above Marktplatz is **Stiftskirche,** Holzmarkt, the former church of the Stift, an Augustinian monastery. The monastery became a Protestant seminary in 1548, and its church became the Collegiate Church. Worth seeing inside are the tombs of the dukes of Württemberg in the chancel and the 15th-century French Gothic pulpit and rood screen. The church is open daily 9am to 5pm. You can climb the **tower** (enter on the left of the chancel) for a panoramic view. The chancel and tower are open Tuesday to Friday 10:30am to 5pm, and Saturday and Sunday 2 to 5pm. Admission to the tower is 2€ ($3.20) for adults and 1.50€ ($2.40) for children.

Hölderlinturm, Bursagasse 6 (ℂ **07071/22040**), lies at the end of a walk by the Neckar River. This was the home of the lyric poet Friedrich Hölderlin, who resided here with the Zimmer family from the onset of his mental illness at age 36 until his death in 1843, at age 73. Hölderlin is not well known outside Germany, but we highly recommend that you read a few of his poems in translation. Most tours of the museum are in German, but you can request one in English. The house is open Tuesday to Friday 10am to noon and 3 to 5pm, Saturday and Sunday 2 to 5pm. Admission is 2.50€ ($4) adults, 1.50€ ($2.40) students and children.

TÜBINGEN AFTER DARK

Student-inspired nightlife makes this old town very young at heart. Just head into the Marktplatz at night and follow the sound of partying. You can order a beer and read the comics hanging on the walls of **Marktschenke,** Am Markt 11 (ℂ **07071/22035**), then join the students spilling outside into the square. Daily hours are 9am to 1am; Friday and Saturday it closes at 2am. Or start your evening in the ancient **Boulanger,** Collegiumsgasse 2 (ℂ **07071/23345**), where you could offer to pick up Hegel's bar tab, which has gone unpaid for more than 200 years. **Ammerschlag,** Ammergasse 13 (ℂ **07071/51591**), is a cramped and smoky hole-in-the-wall dive that has live music one Sunday a month, ranging from blues to rap. Hours are daily 3pm until 1am.

Better-suited for drinks and gossip than dancing is the cramped, but fun, hole-in-the-wall **Blauer Turm Lounge,** Friedrichstrasse 21 (ℂ **07071/360390**), which is open Tuesday to Thursday from 6pm to 1am, Friday and Saturday from 6pm to 3am, and Sunday from 6pm to midnight. Look for Tuesday night "chillouts after work," Wednesday night swing, and live DJs every Friday and Saturday. Entrance is free.

A final option is **Music Club Nice,** Schlachthausstrasse 9 (✆ **07121/204550**). Configured like a hip but disorganized cubbyhole bar, it focuses on live and recorded hip-hop and techno music. It's open nightly, but music is only played Friday and Saturday nights from 10pm to 3am. Entrance costs up to a maximum of 5€ ($8), but depending on the musical venue and time of your arrival.

5 Schwäbisch Hall ⋆⋆

97km (60 miles) NE of Stuttgart, 138km (86 miles) W of Nürnberg

Technically, this medieval town is not in the Neckar Valley; however, if you skip it in your travels through this region, you'll have missed one of southwestern Germany's treasures. Schwäbisch Hall is located in the heart of the forests of the Schwäbische Alb, where it clings to the steep banks of the Kocher River, a tributary of the Neckar. The houses of the Altstadt are set on terraces built into the hillside; from the opposite bank they appear to be arranged in steps, overlooking the old wooden river bridges.

ESSENTIALS

GETTING THERE   By Train   Trains run daily from Stuttgart and Nürnberg into the Bahnhof Schwäbisch Hall. For information, call ✆ **01805/996633.**

By Bus   Regional bus service in the area is offered by **Stuttgart GmbH.** Call ✆ **0791/930090** for schedules and information.

By Car   Access is via the A6 Autobahn running east and west, or Route 14 from the east and Route 19 from the north.

VISITOR INFORMATION   The **Verkehrsverein,** Am Markt 9 (✆ **0791/751385**), is open October to April Monday to Friday 9am to 5pm; from May to September, hours are Monday to Friday 9am to 6pm, and Saturday and Sunday 10am to 3pm.

WHERE TO STAY & DINE

Der Adelshof ⋆   The Adelshof is in an attractive stone building, much of it dating from 1400. Its advantage is its location, right in the center of town. Rooms are clean and comfortable, if a bit small, all equipped with bathrooms containing tub/shower combinations. The refurbished, 500-year-old Kellerbar has become one of the town's most popular bars.

Am Markt 12 (on Marktplatz), 74523 Schwäbisch Hall. ✆ 0791/75890. Fax 0791/6036. www.hotel-adelshof.de. 46 units. 105€–145€ ($168–$232) double; 150€ ($240) suite. Rates include breakfast. AE, DC, MC, V. Parking 5€ ($8). **Amenities:** Restaurant/bistro; bar; sauna; massage; laundry service; dry cleaning; nonsmoking rooms. *In room:* TV, hair dryer.

Hotel Hohenlohe ⋆⋆   The Hohenlohe is on the left bank of the Kocher River, in the historic Freie Reichsstadt district opposite the town center. Rooms are pleasant and compact, with bright color accents. Most of the accommodations open onto scenic views, and all of them have a combination tub/shower. Breakfast is served on an open-view roof deck. The restaurant offers regional meals; a cafeteria and a bar are also on the premises.

Am Weilertor 14, 74523 Schwäbisch Hall. ✆ 0791/75870. Fax 0791/758784. www.hotel-hohenlohe.de. 114 units. 139€–198€ ($222–$317) double; 295€–360€ ($472–$576) suite. Rates include buffet breakfast. AE, DC, MC, V. Parking 7€ ($11) inside, free outside. **Amenities:** 2 restaurants; cafeteria; bar; 3 heated pools (1 outdoor, 2 indoor);

fitness center; sauna; solarium; room service; massage; nonsmoking rooms; rooms for those w/limited mobility; bowling alley. *In room:* TV, Wi-Fi, minibar, hair dryer, safe.

EXPLORING SCHWÄBISCH HALL

The **Marktplatz** ⚜⚜ here is the most attractive in Germany. Fine half-timbered patrician houses flank the sloping square; at the lower end stands the baroque Rathaus. In the center is a 16th-century Gothic fountain adorned with statues of St. Michael with St. George and Samson. The Marktplatz is the scene of festive occasions, such as the annual Kuchenfest, celebrating the ancient salt industry that grew around the salt springs in Schwäbisch Hall.

On the north side of Marktplatz, facing the Rathaus, are 54 large, imposing, delicately curved stone steps leading to **Michaelskirche.** This cathedral is a 15th-century Gothic church with a 12th-century tower. Many pews date from the 15th century, as does St. Michael's altarpiece in the side chapel. The church is open March to November 14 Monday noon to 5pm, and Tuesday to Friday 10am to 5pm; November 15 to February, hours are Monday noon to 2pm, and Tuesday to Sunday 11am to 3pm. It costs 1€ ($1.60) to visit the church tower.

14

Frankfurt

The thriving industrial metropolis of Frankfurt, Germany's fifth-largest city and Goethe's hometown, may well be your first glimpse of Germany.

Most international flights land at Frankfurt's huge airport, and its massive 19th-century railway station is the busiest in Europe. Frankfurt is a heavily industrial city, with more than 2,450 factories operating around the *Furt* (ford) on the Main River, where the Frankish tribes once settled. As the home of the Bundesbank, Germany's central bank, Frankfurt is also the country's financial center. It's been a major banking city ever since the Rothschilds opened their first bank here in 1798. Frankfurt also has a leading stock exchange.

Frankfurt's international trade fairs in spring and autumn bring some 1.5 million visitors to the city and its *Messe Frankfurt* (fairgrounds) often cause a logjam at hotels. Fairs include the Motor Show, the Textile Fair, the Chemical Industries Fair, and the Cookery Fair. But the best known is the International Book Fair, which draws some 5,500 publishers from nearly 100 countries and is the most important meeting place in the world for the acquisition and sale of book rights and translations.

If all roads used to lead to Rome, today they seem to converge on Frankfurt, making it the hub of a great network of European traffic routes. Frankfurt today is both a much visited business center and a worthy tourist destination with a distinct personality.

1 Orientation

GETTING THERE

BY PLANE Flughafen (© **069/6900;** www.airportcity-frankfurt.de) lies 11km (7 miles) from the city center at the Frankfurter Kreuz, the intersection of two major expressways, A3 and A5. This airport, continental Europe's busiest, serves more than 290 destinations in about 110 countries worldwide. It's also Germany's major international gateway. All major German airports can be reached via Frankfurt. Flying time from Frankfurt to Berlin and Hamburg is 70 minutes; to Munich, 60 minutes. For status of flights coming in and out of the Frankfurt airport, call © **069/6900.**

At the **Airport Train Station** beneath Terminal 1, you can connect to German InterCity trains and S-Bahn commuter trains to Frankfurt and nearby cities. Terminal 2 is linked to Terminal 1 by a people-mover system, Sky Line, which provides quick transfers.

For information about S-Bahn trains and regional trains departing from the Frankfurt airport to other points in and near Frankfurt, or for information about trains headed from the Frankfurt airport to more distant destinations, call © **01805/ 996633** (11861 in Germany; www.bahn.de). S-Bahn line S-8 between the airport and

Frankfurt center runs every 10 minutes and deposits passengers at the main rail station in 11 to 15 minutes. A one-way ticket costs 4.50€ ($7.20). Purchase tickets before boarding.

BY TRAIN   Frankfurt's main rail station, the **Hauptbahnhof,** the busiest in Europe, is the arrival point for some 1,600 trains per day carrying about 255,000 passengers. A train arrives from most major cities of Germany every hour until 8pm. Many other European cities also have direct rail links with Frankfurt. For travel information, ticket reservations, and seat information, call **Deutsche Bahn** (© **01805/996633** or 11861 in Germany) or visit **www.bahn.de.**

BY BUS   Frankfurt has long-distance bus service to about 800 German and European cities. Buses depart from the south side of the Hauptbahnhof. For information, contact **Deutsche Touring GmbH, Am Römerhof 17** (© **069/7903501**).

BY CAR   The A3 and A5 autobahns intersect at Frankfurt. The A3 comes in from the Netherlands, Cologne, and Bonn, and continues east and south to Würzburg, Nürnberg, and Munich. The A5 comes from the northeast (Hannover and Bad Hersfeld) and continues south to Heidelberg, Mannheim, and Basel (Switzerland). From the west, the A60 connects with the A66, which leads to Frankfurt and the inner city, hooking up with the A3. Road signs and directions are frequently posted.

VISITOR INFORMATION

The **tourist office** is in two locations: at the Hauptbahnhof, opposite the main entrance (© **069/21-23-88-00;** www.frankfurt-tourismus.de), open Monday to Friday 8am to 9pm, and Saturday and Sunday 9am to 6pm; and in Römerberg 27 (© **069/212-38800**), open Monday to Friday 9:30am to 5:30pm, and Saturday and Sunday 10am to 4pm.

CITY LAYOUT

Most of Frankfurt's sights, nightlife, restaurants, and hotels lie in the **Stadtmitte (town center).** However, chances are you'll cross the Main River to visit the applewine taverns in the **Sachsenhausen** area as well. It is also possible that you'll seek out both restaurants and hotels in the increasingly fashionable **Westend.** Most of the other areas of Frankfurt probably will not concern you, unless you're hunting for intriguing restaurants in the **Nordend (North End)** or even in the **Ostend (East End).**

Most of the heart of Frankfurt can be covered on foot. Nearly all the main sights lie within the boundaries of the old town walls, which today form a stretch of narrow parkland, almost a perfect half-moon around the **Altstadt** or old city. Once one of the great old towns of Europe, the Altstadt was blasted in two horrendous air raids in 1944. Some of its buildings have been sympathetically reconstructed in the old style.

A good place to start exploring Frankfurt is at the **Römerberg,** or historical core of the city. This is actually the site where Charlemagne erected his fort. In medieval times, the Römerberg was the marketplace of Frankfurt.

The most important building in the Stadtmitte is the red-sandstone church of **St. Bartholomäus,** often called "the Dom" although it isn't a cathedral. It was the venue for the coronation of the Holy Roman emperors even though it didn't have cathedral status.

Directly to the east of Römerplatz stands the glaring modern building, **Kultur-Schirn,** a cultural center where various exhibitions are held. It is a controversial postmodern structure that meets with ridicule among Frankfurters, who like their architecture traditional.

Frankfurt

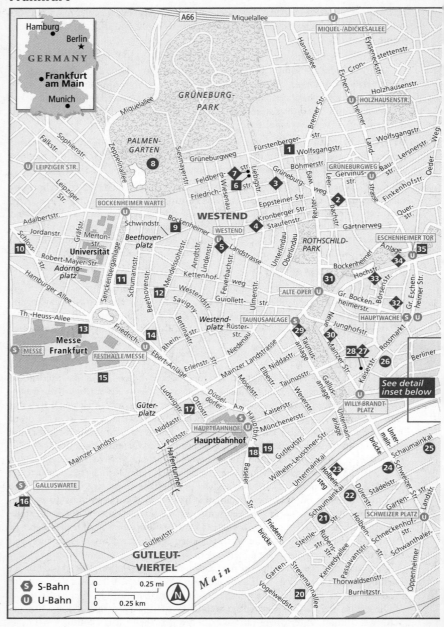

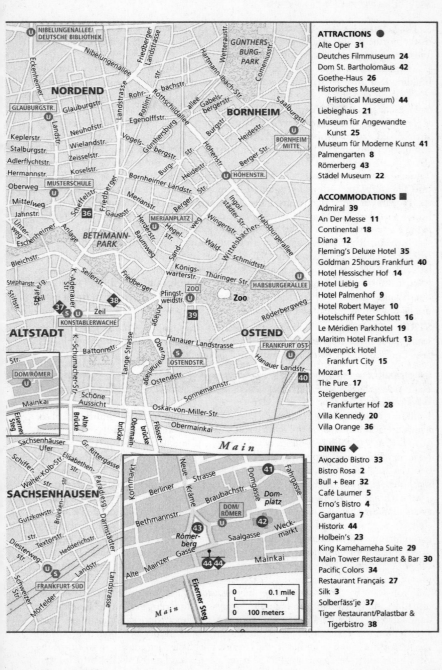

465

The **Goethe-Haus** and **Goethe-Museum** are only a short walk north of the center in the northern Altstadt. To the north of this is **Zeil,** the Fifth Avenue of Germany and one of Europe's greatest shopping streets.

Another landmark of the Stadtmitte is **Hauptwache,** an 18th-century baroque building that is a virtual Times Square of Frankfurt, as it lies at the junction of both the U-Bahn and the S-Bahn lines. Northwest of the Hauptwache is the **Börse,** the stock exchange of Frankfurt.

The Hauptbahnhof, at the western edge of the center of town, opens onto a large street called **Am Hauptbahnhof.** As you walk out of the station, Düsseldorferstrasse will be on your left and Baselerstrasse on your right, heading south toward the Main River. You have a choice of three streets heading east to the center of the **Altstadt:** Taunusstrasse, Kaiserstrasse, and Münchner Strasse. Münchner Strasse leads directly into **Theaterplatz,** with its opera house. Taunusstrasse goes to three of the major Altstadt squares in the southern part of the city: **Goetheplatz, Rathenauplatz,** and (most important) the **Hauptwache,** with its rail connections. In this section of Frankfurt, along Kaiserstrasse, some of the best shops are found.

The **Main River** flows slightly south of the Altstadt. Many bridges, including the Alte Brücke and the Obermainbrücke, cross this important waterway. On the south bank of the Main is a popular district, **Alt-Sachsenhausen,** center of the apple-wine taverns (more about them later). For other major attractions, you'll have to branch out, heading east to the Frankfurt Zoo or northwest to the Palmengarten (both easily reached by public transportation).

STREET MAPS   Arm yourself with a detailed street map, not the general overview handed out by the tourist office. Maps are sold at most bookstores and news kiosks. See "Bookstores" in "Fast Facts: Frankfurt," below.

2 Getting Around

BY PUBLIC TRANSPORTATION

Frankfurt is linked by a network of fast, modern subways, trams, and buses, all of which are administered by the **RMV (Rhein-Main Verkehrsverbund),** Mannheimer Strasse 15 (© **01805/768-4636;** www.rmv.de). All methods of public transport can be used within their respective fare zones at a single price, which includes transfers between any of them. Tickets are purchased at green, coin-operated automatic machines *(Fahrscheine)* that are lined up adjacent to each of the points of departure. The machines accept all denominations of coins and bills up to 50€ ($80), but be aware that any change you receive will be in coins, so try to use the smallest bills possible. Zone charts and additional information in six languages are displayed on all the automatic machines. Except for bus travel (where you have the option of paying the driver directly for your passage), be sure to buy your ticket before you board any of the public transport conveyances of Frankfurt. If you're caught traveling without the proper ticket, you may be fined 40€ ($64).

If you want to simplify the ticket-buying process, both for public transport and museum admissions within Frankfurt, consider the purchase of a **Frankfurter Tageskarte (Frankfurt Card)** from either of the city's tourist offices. These cards allow unlimited travel anywhere within the greater Frankfurt area, plus transport on the shuttle bus going to and from the airport, plus half-price admission to any of the city's museums. The cost is 8.70€ ($14) for a 1-day card and 13€ ($20) for a 2-day card. Children age 14 and under go free when traveling with an adult. *Warning:* The card expires on midnight of the day of purchase (or midnight the following day, for the 2-day card). Use after that can subject you to a fine. For more information, contact the tourist office.

For more information about Frankfurt's public transportation system, call **RMV,** the city transport office, at © **01805/7684636,** or visit www.rmv.de and look for the information listed in English.

BY TAXI

There's no surcharge for calling for a taxi; dial © **069/792020,** 230033, or 250001. Otherwise, you can get a cab either by standing at any of the city's hundreds of clearly designated taxi stands or by hailing one that has an illuminated dome light. Taxis charge by the trip and by the carload, without surcharge for pieces of luggage. Some are suitable for carrying up to six passengers, others for a maximum of only four. Regardless of their size, the initial fee you'll pay for a Frankfurt taxi is 2€ ($3.20) plus 1.60€ ($2.60) per kilometer for rides between 6am and 10pm; from 10pm to 6am, the basic rate is 2.50€ ($4) plus 1.70€ ($2.70) per extra kilometer.

BY RENTAL CAR

The big rental companies each maintain offices at the airport and at central locations throughout Frankfurt. The most reliable are **Avis,** whose downtown branch is inside the Hauptbahnhof (© **069/27997010**), and **Hertz,** whose offices are in the Hauptbahnhof (© **069/230484**) and at the airport (© **069/69593244**). Also recommended is **Europcar,** which maintains offices at the Hauptbahnhof (© **069/2429810**) and at the airport (© **069/697970**).

FAST FACTS: Frankfurt

American Express The office is on Theodor-Heuss-Allee 112 (© **069/97970**), some 4km (2.5 miles) from the city center (S-Bahn: Westbahnhof). Offices are open Monday to Friday 9:30am to 6pm and Saturday 10am to 1pm.

Bookstores The best English-language bookstore is **British Bookshop,** Börsenstrasse 17 (© **069/280492;** U-Bahn/S-Bahn: Hauptwache). It's open Monday to Friday 9:30am to 7pm and Saturday 9:30am to 6pm.

Currency Exchange There are multiple facilities for the exchange of international currencies at the Frankfurt airport.

Dentists & Doctors For an English-speaking dentist or doctor, call © **069/19292** to arrange an appointment.

Drugstores For information about pharmacies open near you, call © **069/ 19292.** Otherwise you can go to Kissel-Apotheke, Mörfelder Landstrasse 235 (© **069/68974730**).

Emergencies Dial © **110** for the police; © **112** for a fire, first aid, and ambulance; and © **069/6607271** for emergency dental service.

Internet Access Head for **CyberRyder,** Tongegasse 31 (© **069/91396754;** www. cyberyder.de), open Monday to Friday 9:30am to 10pm, Saturday 10am to 10pm, and Sunday noon to 10pm. Internet connections cost 1.60€ ($2.10) for 15 minutes. There are several other Internet cafes in Frankfurt as well; the best place to search for Internet cafes is along Elizabethstrasse, across from the Hauptbahnhof in central Frankfurt.

Luggage Storage & Lockers Lockers can be rented and luggage stored at the Hauptbahnhof.

Post Office There's a post office at the Hauptbahnhof (*℃* **069/97511004**), open Monday to Friday 6:30am to 9pm, Saturday 8am to 6pm, and Sunday and holidays 11am to 6pm.

Safety Frankfurt is a relatively safe city, but you should still stay alert at all times. Stay out of the area around the Hauptbahnhof at night, as muggings are frequent.

Toilets There are many decent public facilities in central Frankfurt, especially in the Altstadt.

3 Where to Stay

Frankfurt is notorious for room shortages during busy trade fairs. If you have the bad luck to arrive when one of them is scheduled, you may find all the more central hotels fully booked. To find an available room, head to one of the tourist offices or book online at www.frankfurt-tourismus.de.

Even without the fairs, Frankfurt is one of the world's great commercial hubs, so businesspeople pour into the city at all times of the year. Hotels, for the most part, are expensive. However, you can sometimes negotiate a rate decrease on weekends when the business clients don't predominate. Hotels also tend to be booked well in advance, so reservations are important.

Nearly all the major hotels in the city center are convenient to the train station, the business district, and the fairgrounds. Of course, you can take a taxi, but walking time is often no more than 20 minutes to where you're going.

IN THE CENTER
VERY EXPENSIVE
Hotel Hessischer Hof 𝕬𝕬𝕬   Frankfurt hotels don't get much better than this. If it wasn't for the Steigenberger Frankfurter Hof (see below), it would be the top-ranking hotel in the city. A private and traditional place with an elegant atmosphere, this boxy, nine-story hotel has luxe style and amenities all the way. The hotel is located opposite the trade-fair building. The relatively modest postwar exterior doesn't prepare you for the spacious and glamorous interior. Many of the bedrooms are furnished with antiques. In the older building in front, accommodations are traditionally furnished with chandeliers strung from high ceilings, antique furnishings, and 19th-century lithographs. Rooms here are not quite as elegant as those at the Frankfurter Hof and Meridien. But in the newer wing, *Nordflugel,* the bedrooms outrank even the stiffest Frankfurt competitors.

Friedrich-Ebert-Anlage 40, 60325. *℃* **069/75400.** Fax 069/75402924. www.hessischer-hof.de. 117 units. 281€–561€ ($450–$898) double; 359€–2,151€ ($574–$3,442) suite. Children 12 and under stay free in parent's room. AE, DC, MC, V. Parking 20€ ($32). S-Bahn: Platz der Republik. **Amenities:** Restaurant; bar; fitness equipment; room service; massage; babysitting; laundry service; dry cleaning; nonsmoking rooms; 1 room for those w/limited mobility. *In room:* A/C, TV, Wi-Fi, minibar, hair dryer, safe.

Le Méridien Parkhotel 🕸🕸   Le Meridien Parkhotel provides warmth and personal attention to its guests, mainly from the world of commerce, who can walk over in a few minutes to the fairgrounds. It opens onto a verdant, parklike square. The hotel has been built in two sections—an ornately decorated 1905 palace and a sleek but duller 1970s boxy wing. We prefer the older, more traditional rooms in the *palais,* though they are more expensive than those in the annex. *Palais* accommodations have a luxurious atmosphere and are individually designed. Annex units are larger, however, with high ceilings and built-in furnishings.

Wiesenhüttenplatz 28–38 (near the Hauptbahnhof), 60329. ℂ 866/500-8320 in the U.S. and Canada, or 069/26970. Fax 069/2697884. www.lemeridien-frankfurt.com. 300 units. 211€–275€ ($338–$440) double; 375€–670€ ($600–$1,072) suite. AE, DC, MC, V. Parking 20€ ($32). S-Bahn: 8. **Amenities:** Restaurant; bar; nearby golf course; squash and racquetball courts; spa; sauna; solarium; car-rental desk; business center; room service; babysitting; laundry service; dry cleaning; nonsmoking rooms; rooms for those w/limited mobility. *In room:* A/C, TV, Wi-Fi, minibar, hair dryer, trouser press, safe.

Steigenberger Frankfurter Hof 🕸🕸🕸   This is the most famous, most prestigious, and most legendary hotel in Frankfurt, with service and a historic setting that's unmatched anywhere else in town. The only hotel in Frankfurt that really measures up is our favorite, the Hessischer Hof (see above), but the restaurant (Restaurant Français, p. 474) is better here. The highly visible five-story flagship of one of Germany's most elegant hotel chains, it was established in 1872 behind a landmark stone facade that's very central, very prominent, and very grand. Its rooms are in high demand by visiting dignitaries, especially during the book fair, when guests as prominent as the former king of Greece have been denied a room. Public areas are discreet and plush; bedrooms high ceilinged, sun flooded, and gracefully furnished. Some of the more traditional rooms have valuable antiques, but those in the Bethmann Wing have a 1970s aura with bland blond-wood furnishings. Its art collection, including Gobelin tapestries, French antiques, and 18th-century portraits, is noteworthy.

Am Kaiserplatz, 60311. ℂ 800/223-5652 in the U.S. and Canada, or 069/21502. Fax 069/215900. www.frankfurterhof.steigenberger.de. 321 units. 290€–399€ ($464–$638) double Mon–Thurs, 180€–219€ ($288–$350) double Fri–Sun; 590€–1,320€ ($944–$2,112) suite. Parking 20€ ($32). AE, DC, MC, V. U-Bahn: Willy-Brandt-Platz. **Amenities:** 4 restaurants; bar; health club; sauna; solarium; steam bath; business center; room service; babysitting; laundry service; dry cleaning; nonsmoking rooms; rooms for those w/limited mobility. *In room:* A/C, TV, fax, Wi-Fi, minibar, hair dryer, trouser press, safe.

EXPENSIVE

An Der Messe 🕸   This quiet charmer is the choice of seasoned and discriminating visitors to Frankfurt. It's just a 5-minute walk from the university, the banking district, and the fairgrounds. The staff does much to make guests feel comfortable. Rooms are large and stylishly furnished; many have an Asian motif. A half-dozen singles are rented, but they're hard to come by unless you reserve well in advance.

Westendstrasse 104, 60325. ℂ 069/747979. Fax 069/748349. www.hotel-an-der-messe.de. 46 units. 130€–330€ ($208–$528) double. Rates include buffet breakfast. AE, DC, MC, V. Underground garage parking 13€ ($21). Tram: 16 or 19. **Amenities:** Breakfast room; room service; babysitting; laundry service; dry cleaning; nonsmoking rooms. *In room:* TV, Wi-Fi, minibar, hair dryer, trouser press.

Fleming's Deluxe Hotel 🕸🕸🕸   In a prime position in the center of the city, this dazzling hotel takes you by elevator up to its rooftop terrace for panoramic views over Frankfurt and the Taunus Hills in the distance. In its furnishings and appointments, it is worthy of its government-granted five stars. Top-quality materials, including textiles, come in warm earth colors such as amber or Bordeaux red. A sophisticated sense of modern design is evident throughout, especially in the glamorous rooms and suites. It's the little things that count, including safes large enough to hold a laptop. We find their health center one of the best of the hotels of Frankfurt.

Eschenheimer Tor 2, 60313 Frankfurt. ✆ **069/4272320.** Fax 069/42723999. www.flemings-hotel.com. 113 units. 252€–272€ ($403–$435) double; 437€ ($699) suite. Rates include breakfast. AE, DC, MC, V. U-Bahn: Eschenheimer Tor. **Amenities:** Restaurant; bar; health club; business center; room service; laundry service; dry cleaning; rooms for those w/limited mobility; nonsmoking rooms. *In room:* A/C, TV, Wi-Fi, minibar, hair dryer, safe.

Maritim Hotel Frankfurt 𝒢𝒢   This is one of the largest hotels in Germany, with a layout that almost defines it as a small town within a city. Set behind a curved, mostly glass eight-story facade, it's the only hotel in Frankfurt with direct access, via a covered walkway, to the trade fairgrounds. Expect well-orchestrated, but somewhat anonymous, comforts at this Bauhaus-industrial behemoth, and a location that requires a bit of a hike, or a taxi ride, to more scenic and historic neighborhoods of Frankfurt. Bedrooms may be neutral in their cultural references, but they are very comfortable (writing desks are big if you need to set up a small office) and are more stylish than those at the Marriott across the street.

Theodor-Heuss-Allee 3, 60486. ✆ **069/75780.** Fax 069/7578-1000. www.maritim-hotels.de. 543 units. 115€–381€ ($184–$610) double; 340€–670€ ($544–$1,072) suite. AE, DC, MC, V. Parking 22€ ($35). U-Bahn: Messe Frankfurt. **Amenities:** 2 restaurants; 2 bars; indoor heated pool; fitness club; sauna; solarium; room service; massage; nonsmoking rooms; rooms for those w/limited mobility. *In room:* A/C, TV, Wi-Fi, minibar, hair dryer, safe.

The Pure 𝒢𝒢 *(Finds*   There's nothing else like this hotel in all of Frankfurt. A new concept in hotel design, the Pure carries modernism to its extremes. Near the main rail station, you wander into this daringly avant-garde hotel and encounter a lobby that evokes the set of Kubrick's *A Clockwork Orange.* You would never believe that this was a loft back in the 1800s. Even the light here changes throughout the day, in a soothing white in the morning turning to orange by evening. Bright, clear materials were used throughout, including both white lacquer and white leather. This idea of "space without borders" (as the hotel puts it) continues into the all-white bedrooms with leather-upholstered headboards and parquet flooring.

Niddastrasse 86, 60329 Frankfurt. ✆ **069/7104570.** Fax 069/710457177. www.the-pure.de. 50 units. 140€–400€ ($224–$640) double. AE, DC, MC, V. Parking 15€ ($24). **Amenities:** Bar; fitness room; sauna; steam bath; room service; laundry service; dry cleaning. *In room:* A/C, TV, Wi-Fi, minibar, hair dryer, safe.

Villa Orange 𝒢𝒢 *(Finds*   This hotel resulted from the radical renovation of a century-old building with lots of architectural character. A team of architects and decorators with taste and talent created a conservative and elegant decor that combines lots of natural hardwoods into the kind of cozy nest in which a business or leisure traveler would feel very comfortable. Overall, the hotel is comfortable, intimate, tasteful, and well mannered—a fine alternative to one of the megahotels.

Hebelstrasse 1, 60318 Frankfurt. ✆ **069/405840.** Fax 069/40584100. www.villa-orange.de. 38 units. 155€–275€ ($248–$440) double. Rates include buffet breakfast. AE, MC, V. Free parking. U-Bahn: Musterschule or Merienplatz. **Amenities:** Bar; babysitting; laundry service; dry cleaning; nonsmoking rooms. *In room:* A/C, TV, Wi-Fi, beverage maker, hair dryer.

MODERATE

Gubermühle 𝒢𝒢 *(Finds*   When Goethe was a young man and this building was a romantic villa, he met his first love here. After years of being dilapidated, this building, which originally was a 16th-century flour mill, has emerged as a favorite address for the *chicky-micky (fashionistas).* All signs of Goethe's day are now gone except for the first-rate Biergarten overlooking the Main River. To honor the writer, the chefs still serve his favorite dish, veal *Tafelspitz* (boiled), with a green sauce made with nine fresh herbs. For those who want to stay over, the guest rooms are imbued with a sense of the romantic, with beautiful furnishings including French beds and bathrooms in Belgian marble. Each individually decorated bedroom is in a country house style.

Deutschhermufer 105, 60594 Frankfurt am Main. © 069/965-2290. 20 units. 140€ ($224) double, 700€ ($1,120) suite. AE, MC, V. U-Bahn: Römer. **Amenities:** Restaurant; beer garden; room service; laundry service; nonsmoking rooms. *In room:* A/C, TV, Wi-Fi, minibar, safe.

INEXPENSIVE

Admiral *Kids*   This hotel is a favorite with families, who like its location near the zoo, a short haul from the center of Frankfurt. The rooms are plainly but comfortably furnished with a natural-wood, Scandinavian-style decor. The bathrooms are small, each with a shower stall. Only breakfast is served.

Hölderlinstrasse 25, 60136 Frankfurt. © 069/448021. Fax 069/439402. www.hoteladmiral.de. 47 units. 65€–82€ ($104–$131) double. Rates include buffet breakfast. AE, DC, MC, V. Parking 10€ ($16). U-Bahn: Zoologischer Garten (Zoo). **Amenities:** Bar; nonsmoking rooms. *In room:* TV, Wi-Fi, minibar, safe.

Continental   The choice of many businesspeople, this hotel is near the Hauptbahnhof. Founded in 1889, it enjoyed its heyday in the Belle Epoque era. The rooms are modern and comfortable, though the shower-only bathrooms are small. Around the corner are lively bars, but serenity prevails inside. The windows have been soundproofed to keep out traffic noise.

Baselerstrasse 56, 60329 Frankfurt. © 069/42729990. Fax 069/232914. www.hotelcontifrankfurt.de. 88 units. 50€–72€ ($80–$115) double. AE, DC, MC, V. Parking 15€ ($24). U-Bahn/S-Bahn: Hauptbahnhof. **Amenities:** Restaurant; nonsmoking rooms. *In room:* TV, hair dryer.

Hotelschiff Peter Schlott *Finds*   This 1950s riverboat, now permanently moored at the Frankfurt suburb of Höchst, has some of the smallest, but most evocative, hotel rooms in the area. The style is reminiscent of life at sea: Everything is tiny and cramped, and mattresses are a bit thin. But the unusual nature of the accommodations helps soften any disagreeability, and the waters of the Main lap soothingly beneath your portholes. You'll have to exercise caution on this ship's narrow and steep staircases. If you have enormous amounts of luggage, consider a stay in a more conventional hotel.

Mainberg, 65929 Frankfurt. © 069/3004643. Fax 069/307671. www.hotel-schiff-schlott.de. 19 units, all with washbasins, 10 with shower, none with toilet. 65€ ($104) double without shower; 91€ ($146) double with shower. Rates include continental breakfast. AE, DC, MC, V. S-Bahn: Höchst. **Amenities:** Restaurant. *In room:* No phone.

IN WESTEND
VERY EXPENSIVE

Radisson SAS Frankfurt   This futuristic hotel comes as a surprise in conservative Frankfurt. Rising 19 floors, it appears like a glass cube suspended in a shining blue disc. Located next to the Frankfurt Messe Exhibition Center, it lies near the autobahn, only 15 minutes from the airport. The famous designer, Adam D. Tihany, created public spaces in a style called "industrial luxe." Architectural whimsies include such features as his iconic suspended wine tower. His partner, Mateo Thun, painted the 15 various floors in pinks, oranges, and even blood reds. Pick your room theme— At Home (in dark chocolate tones); Chic (felt covers in anthracite and burgundy); Fashion (yards of Missoni fabric and oversize headboards); and Fresh (Warhol-inspired flower prints on bright blue carpets). A spectacular surprise is the health club's gargantuan pool facing the Manhattanlike skyline of Frankfurt.

Franklinstrasse 65, 60486 Frankfurt am Main. © **069/7701550.** Fax 069/77015510. www.frankfurt.radissonsas. com. 428 units. 235€–295€ ($376–$472) double; 410€–1,050€ ($656–$1,680) suite. AE, DC, MC, V. Parking 22€ ($35). S-Bahn: Westbahnhof. Train: 17. **Amenities:** 2 restaurants; 2 bars; indoor heated pool; fitness center; sauna; solarium; steam bath; business center; room service; massage; babysitting; laundry service; dry cleaning; nonsmoking rooms; rooms for those w/limited mobility. *In room:* A/C, TV, Wi-Fi, beverage maker, hair dryer, trouser press, safe.

EXPENSIVE

Hotel Palmenhof ☞   A short walk from the botanical gardens, this is a five-story Art Nouveau building. Some of the original architectural features have been preserved. The facade is very grand, a reddish sandstone Romantic-era pile from 1890. It stands across from the Cafe im Literaturhaus, a wining-and-drinking spot that seduces authors away from book fairs. The interior has such architectural features as skylights beaming light down onto a Belle Epoque set of furnishings. Rooms have somewhat fussy furnishings but are well kept and often contain high ceilings.

Bockenheimer Landstrasse 89–91, 60325 Frankfurt. © **069/7530060.** Fax 069/75300666. www.palmenhof.com. 46 units. Mon–Thurs 155€–175€ ($248–$280) double, 230€–255€ ($368–$408) suite; Fri–Sun 75€–90€ ($120–$144) double, 155€ ($248) suite. AE, DC, MC, V. Parking 15€ ($24). U-Bahn: Westend. **Amenities:** Breakfast room; room service; laundry service; dry cleaning. *In room:* TV, Wi-Fi, minibar, hair dryer, safe.

MODERATE

Hotel Liebig ☞ *(Finds*   The aura within this upscale B&B is small scale, intimate, and luxurious, with an intensely "decorated" look that could have been lifted directly from the pages of a Laura Ashley (or Versace) catalogue. As such, it presents a welcome change for business travelers looking for something more personalized and less anonymous than what's available within one of the blockbuster hotels closer to the fairgrounds. The town house that contains it was built in 1905 and still retains its ornate maroon sandstone facade, its curving interior staircase, and proportions that hint at its origins as an upscale private home. The full bathrooms are handsomely decorated and spotlessly maintained.

Liebigstrasse 45, 60323 Frankfurt am Main. © **069/2418299.** Fax 069/24182991. www.hotelliebig.de. 20 units. 115€–195€ ($184–$312) double; 190€–290€ ($304–$464) suite. Parking 14€ ($22). AE, MC, V. U-Bahn: Westend. **Amenities:** Breakfast room; garden; nonsmoking rooms. *In room:* A/C, TV, minibar, safe.

Hotel Robert Mayer ☞ *(Finds*   This is one of the most artfully decorated hotels in town. It's within walking distance of Frankfurt's trade fair complex. Though the building dates from 1905, the rooms date from 1994, when the manager hired 11 lesser known artists to decorate them; each imposed his or her vision on one of the bedrooms. You may find a thought-provoking jumble of furniture inspired by Frank Lloyd Wright or an anonymous Milanese postmodernist piece set adjacent to pop art. Creature comforts, however, remain high.

Robert-Mayer-Strasse 44, 60486 Frankfurt am Main. © **069/970910.** Fax 069/97091010. www.arthotel-frankfurt.de. 11 units. 130€–240€ ($208–$384) double. Rates include continental breakfast. AE, DC, MC, V. U-Bahn: Bockenheimer Warte. *In room:* TV.

INEXPENSIVE

Diana *(Value*   Spotless and homey, the Diana is a bargain. It's a copy of a private villa, with a drawing room and an intimate breakfast salon, located on a pleasant residential street. The small bedrooms are rather lackluster, but comfortable and clean, each with a neat little bathroom with a shower stall.

Westendstrasse 83, 60325 Frankfurt am Main. $\mathcal{C}$ **069/9074420.** Fax 069/90744277. 26 units. 86€–110€ ($138–$176) double; 105€–135€ ($168–$216) triple. Rates include continental breakfast. AE, DC, MC, V. Parking 8€ ($13). U-Bahn: Westend. Bus: 17. **Amenities:** Breakfast room. *In room:* TV.

Mozart $\mathcal{R}$ (Value   Perhaps the best small hotel in Frankfurt, the Mozart stands on the periphery of the Palmengarten, right off busy Fürstenbergerstrasse. Everything inside—walls, furniture, and bed coverings—is white or pink. Rooms are small but comfortable, each with a tidily kept shower-only bathroom. The breakfast room, with its crystal chandeliers and Louis XV–style chairs, could pass for an 18th-century salon.

Parkstrasse 17 (near the Alte Oper), 60322. $\mathcal{C}$ **069/1568060.** Fax 069/1568061. www.mozart-frankfurt.de 35 units. 95€–145€ ($152–$232) double (185€/$296 during trade fairs). Rates include continental breakfast. AE, DC, MC, V. Closed Dec 24–Jan 1. U-Bahn: Holzhausenstrasse. Bus: 36. **Amenities:** Breakfast room. *In room:* TV, minibar.

ACROSS THE MAIN
VERY EXPENSIVE

Villa Kennedy $\mathcal{RRR}$ On the south bank of the Main River, this luxurious five-star hotel opened in a trio of newly constructed buildings surrounding the 1904 Villa Speyer. It lies close to the center of Frankfurt's Left Bank nightlife district, Sachsenhausen, with its vibrant bars and restaurants. Along with the Pure, Villa Kennedy is the epitome of Teutonic cool. "We are more than a crash pad," the manager assured us. "We are a way of life."

The hotel respects the past but is as modern as the 21st century. Surprisingly for a midcity hotel, the villa is set in landscaped gardens. The bedrooms are spacious and among the swankiest in town, with beautiful furnishings, subtle lighting, wooden floors, and full-length mirrored walls; the suites are the pride of Frankfurt, fit for a visiting president. Off the central courtyard and garden is the colonnaded Gusto, a first-class restaurant serving both German and international cuisine. Guests and nonresidents alike meet in JFK's Bar & Lounge.

Kennedy Allee 70, 60596 Frankfurt am Main. $\mathcal{C}$ **069/717120.** Fax 069/717122430. www.villakennedy.com. 163 units. 550€–590€ ($880–$944) double; from 685€ ($1,096) suite. AE, DC, MC, V. Parking 15€ ($24). U-Bahn: Schweitzer Platz. **Amenities:** Restaurant; bar; indoor heated pool; gym; spa; steam room; room service; laundry service; dry cleaning; nonsmoking rooms; rooms for those w/limited mobility. *In room:* A/C, TV, Wi-Fi, minibar, trouser press, safe.

IN THE EAST END
MODERATE

Goldman 25hours Frankfurt $\mathcal{R}$ (Finds   Artists and media types tend to favor this hotel with its often mischievous design, including lamps that are penguin replicas wearing shades on their heads. After work, its bar scene becomes boisterous and is the place to be seen. The designers of this place loved color and saturated the hotel with it—and they're not afraid to use purple. A *fashionista* told us, "I always stay here because it's cool and sexy." Think of it as an urban retreat for night owls, with individually decorated bedrooms that are stylishly comfortable, very avant-garde.

Hanauer Landstrasse 127, 60314 Frankfurt am Main. $\mathcal{C}$ **069/40586890.** Fax 069/4058689890. 49 units. 125€ ($200) double. AE, DC, MC, V. U-Bahn: Zoo. **Amenities:** Restaurant; bar; room service; laundry service. *In room:* A/C, TV, Wi-Fi, minibar, hair dryer, safe.

EUROPA QUARTER
MODERATE

Mövenpick Hotel Frankfurt City $\mathcal{R}$ In the heart of the Europa Quarter, this government-rated, four-star, first-class hotel stands next to the trade fairgrounds, 2km

(1¼ miles) from the city center. It's suitable choice for both vacationers and business travelers. Its midsize to spacious bedrooms are among the most modern in the city, and we're especially fond of the apple-green furnishings and the use of such trendy colors as ocher and burgundy. Aphorisms from the works of Goethe appear above the headboards, and many of the furnishings are made from the increasingly rare zebrawood.

Den Haagerstrasse 5, 60327 Frankfurt am Main. © 069/7880750. Fax 069/788075888. www.moevenpick-hotels. com. 288 units. 89€–155€ ($142–$248) double; 159€–205€ ($254–$328) junior suite. AE, DC, MC, V. U-Bahn: Hauptbahnhof. **Amenities:** Restaurant; bar; fitness center; solarium; room service; laundry service; dry cleaning; rooms for those w/limited mobility. *In room:* A/C, TV, Wi-Fi, minibar, hair dryer, safe.

ON THE OUTSKIRTS
EXPENSIVE

Hotel Amadeus *(★ (Finds* Set within the leafy residential suburb of Bergen-Enkheim, an easy 15-minute tram ride northeast from central Frankfurt, this is a warm and friendly hotel with well-designed accommodations and a stature as one of the leading architectural highlights of its neighborhood. It features a soaring, atrium-style lobby fronted with glass, marble floors, and three wings that join together in a design that emulates an airplane propeller. The staff here is especially charming, and on-site is a cozy bar that stays open late, a restaurant that attracts residents of the surrounding community, and a concierge who knows how to get things done.

Röntgenstrasse 5, 60338 Frankfurt am Main. © 06109/3700. Fax 06109/370720. www.hotel-amadeus-frankfurt.de. 160 units. 165€–188€ ($264–$301) double Mon–Fri; 68€–98€ ($109–$157) double Sat–Sun. AE, MC, V. Free parking. Tram: U-7. **Amenities:** Restaurant; bar; access to nearby fitness center; babysitting; laundry service; dry cleaning. *In room:* A/C, TV, minibar, hair dryer, iron, safe.

4 Where to Dine

Almost overnight, without much of the world being aware, the city of Frankfurt has become one of Europe's great dining capitals. Everybody knows it for its banking and business, but serious gourmets also descend on the city, which offers one of Europe's most varied cuisines. It still doesn't have as eclectic a mixture of cuisine as New York (which has virtually every cuisine served on Earth), but Frankfurt is getting there.

For years, visitors to the famous book fair always came home to tell visitors, "You can't get a decent meal in Frankfurt." That wasn't even true way back then, and it's gross libel today. Still fighting to overcome a terrible culinary reputation, Frankfurt now ranks with Berlin and Munich as a dining mecca.

See the map on p. 464 for restaurant locations.

IN THE CENTER
VERY EXPENSIVE

Restaurant Français *(★★★* FRENCH   This restaurant is very stylish, and very conscious of maintaining the top-notch standards usually associated with upscale hotel restaurants in Paris. It occupies a duet of stately rooms, outfitted in tones of imperial blue and gold, on the lobby level of Frankfurt's most prestigious hotel. Don't think you can go slumming if you drop in for a bite here. Jackets and (preferably) ties are recommended for gentlemen. Menu items are cultivated, posh, and beautifully prepared and presented—the descriptions alone will make you drool. Look for brilliant combinations, such as Alsatian goose liver with smoked eel and apple sorbet, or else caviar with an iced cucumber gratinée. As for main courses, sample such delights as lobster with passion fruit or else milk-fed lamb from the Pyrenées with a hint of cumin.

In the Steigenberger Frankfurter Hof, Am Kaiserplatz. © **069/21502.** Reservations required. Main courses 29€–50€ ($46–$80); fixed-price 8-course menu 117€ ($187). AE, DC, MC, V. Mon–Fri noon–2:30pm and 6:30–10:30pm. U-Bahn: Willy-Brandt-Platz.

Tiger Restaurant/Palastbar & Tigerbistrot ★★★ INTERNATIONAL This

restaurant is Frankfurt's finest. No one expected a restaurant associated with a cabaret (Tigerpalast, p. 487) to be this exceptional, but when Michelin first granted it a star in 2000, the city took notice. This basement-level dining room, which is covered in whimsical murals that might have been painted by a latter-day Jean Cocteau, has welcomed Joan Collins, Siegfried & Roy, lots of CEOs of local corporations, and most of the high-ranking ministers of the local government.

Menu items are intensely cultivated and impeccably presented. Try the sea bass with a mild pepper crust with chanterelles, risotto, and baked calves' head ravioli, or the sole rolls with Périgord truffle with fried artichokes and potato foam. Further culinary acrobatics include poached German beef with a potato risotto and fried artichokes in an herb sauce. Meals in the Palastbar & Tigerbistrot are less elaborate and cheaper, served under the vaulted brick ceiling of what was built as a warehouse about a century ago. Examples include vegetarian paella in saffron sauce or breast of chicken stuffed with tomato, sage, and Parma ham, served with an eggplant mousse and potato gnocchi.

Heiligkreuzgasse 16–20. © **069/92002250.** Reservations required. Main courses in restaurant 34€–54€ ($54–$86); main courses in Palastbar & Tigerbistrot 26€–37€ ($42–$59); fixed-price menus in restaurant 49€–100€ ($78–$160). AE, DC, MC, V. Restaurant Tues–Sat 6pm–1am; Palastbar & Tigerbistrot Tues–Sun 5pm–1am. U-Bahn: Konstablerwache.

EXPENSIVE

Avocado Bistro ★★★ FRENCH/MEDITERRANEAN Chic, upscale, and

soothing, this bistro has lots of fresh flowers and an atmosphere that manages to be both grandly bourgeois and artsy at the same time. It's a suitable venue for either a seduction or a sales pitch, the kind of place meant for celebrations and champagne. Menu items change with the seasons. Food selections on any given night are limited, but you're almost assured that every item is fresh and carefully chosen by the chef. Inventiveness and solid technique go hand in hand here. Tempting starters might include half-cooked sea bass with olive oil and mustard corns, or roast breast of quail flavored with sesame. Main-course temptations are likely to be breaded veal with walnuts and cognac, or baked salmon in a fine pastry and champagne sauce. Filet of turbot is served roasted in caraway and served with a Dijon mustard sauce.

Hochstrasse 27. © **069/292867.** www.restaurant-avocado.de. Reservations required. Main courses 27€–35€ ($43–$56); fixed-price lunch 30€ ($48), dinner 57€ ($91). AE, MC, V. Tues–Sat noon–2:30pm; Mon–Sat 6pm–10:30pm. U-Bahn: Opernplatz.

MODERATE

King Kameha Suite ★★ INTERNATIONAL Frankfurt *fashionistas* con-

verge on this sophisticated enclave in a wonderfully preserved neo-classical villa with a sweeping marble staircase. "We're whatever you want us to be," the manager told us. Perhaps he was referring to the multipurpose role of his establishment—chic lounge, bar, cafe, restaurant, and, yes, even a nightclub. In a historic building across from the opera house, the dining room is on the second floor.

Exceptional products are featured with a finely honored technique. The cooking has flair and imagination, including such dishes as braised cheek of veal with morels or else young goat with salsify and polenta. A lot of grill specialties are featured, and the pastas are homemade, including ravioli of wild garlic filled with sautéed mushrooms.

Taunusanlage 20. ℂ 069/71035277. Reservations required for dining. Main courses 18€–23€ ($29–$37). AE, DC, MC, V. Mon–Fri 11:30am–3pm and 6–11pm; Sat 6–11pm; Sun 10am–3pm. S-Bahn: Tanusanlage.

Main Tower Restaurant & Bar ⍟ EUROPEAN   Set on the semicircular 53rd floor of one of the tallest buildings in Frankfurt, this is Frankfurt's most architecturally unusual restaurant. It offers a starkly modern environment (steel tables, minimalist chairs), where the main aesthetic intrigue lies in views that extend for miles in all directions. The long line of diners who ascend every day for lunch, dinner, and after-work cocktails makes up one of the most diverse clientele in town, including grandmothers showing the view to their offspring, media hipsters affiliated with the building's TV stations, and newcomers trying to figure out the geography of Frankfurt.

The chefs don't try to get by on the view alone. Their cuisine is hardly the most imaginative in the city, but it is solid and reliable, and prepared with fresh ingredients. Appetizers range from a smoked salmon with a pesto sauce to a carpaccio of beef with eggplant. Some of the best dishes include baby goat with parsley and caraway or scallops with potato and balsamico.

Neue Mainzer Strasse 52–58. ℂ 069/3650-4777. Reservations required. Main courses 18€–30€ ($29–$48); fixed-price menus 57€–98€ ($91–$157). AE, MC, V. Tues–Thurs 5:30pm–1am; Fri–Sat 5:30pm–2am. U-Bahn: Willy-Brandt-Platz.

Pacific Colors ⍟ CALIFORNIAN   This intensely dramatic lobby-level restaurant in Frankfurt's most avant-garde hotel boasts a New Age design in (what else?) Pacific tones of sea green and blue, with big-windowed views over the trees and walkways of the Friedberger Anlage Park. The food is what keeps gastronomes coming back—particularly those with a fondness for a Mediterranean-inspired cuisine that manages to be both airy and earthy. As conceived by culinary artist Manfred Breuer, the exact composition of the menu changes about every 3 months, but the best examples include a seafood medley—a trio of red snapper, white fish, and prawns served with spicy chili-laced noodles and a coriander syrup. The steak is also sumptuous, a filet mignon with an olive-and-potato tapenade.

In the lobby of the Hilton Hotel, Hochstrasse 4. ℂ 069/1338000. Reservations recommended. Main courses 21€–31€ ($34–$50). AE, DC, MC, V. Daily 6:30–11:30pm. U-Bahn: Eschenheimer Tor.

INEXPENSIVE

Bull + Bear INTERNATIONAL/MEDITERRANEAN   The decor here may remind you of a glass-sided cube, thanks to soaring ceilings and a glittery, metallic look that evokes the waiting room of an international airport. The room's focal point is a shimmering circular bar that's illuminated with pin lights and spotlights, perhaps a high-tech version of a pagan temple. Many of the office workers in this intensely commercial neighborhood have been here at least once for lunch, and to a lesser extent, dinner. Well-prepared menu items include club sandwiches, tortellini stuffed with ricotta and spinach, saddle of lamb with Provençal vegetables, and a wide selection of grilled Angus steaks.

Bull + Bear also serves as a singles bar and a late-night dance spot. In the basement, there's a dance floor that's usually mobbed, especially on Friday and Saturday, with a young, hip, after-work crowd. A live DJ plays house, techno, and trance music; the cover charge is 8€ ($13). Drinks start at 5€ ($8) each during happy hour, which is every day from 4 to 7pm.

Am Börsenplatz/Schillerstrasse 11. 🕾 **069/13388733.** Reservations recommended for parties of 6 or more. Main courses 10€–22€ ($16–$35); lunch salads, sandwiches, and platters 7€–14€ ($11–$22). AE, DC, MC, V. Mon–Thurs 10am–1am; Fri–Sat 9am–3am. U-Bahn/S-Bahn: Hauptwache.

Historix HESSIAN   This restaurant on the ground floor of Frankfurt's Historisches Museum is almost like an exhibition itself—one featuring the age-old art of regional Hessian cooking. Naturally, it attracts exhausted museumgoers looking for a respite from too much culture, but because of its low prices and well-prepared cuisine, it also has diners who may not have visited the museum in many years, if at all. There's a strong emphasis on maintaining a setting that looks historic and authentic to the Hessian tradition of wine and apple-cider cellars, but the modern world is very much apparent through big, plate-glass windows that let in sunlight and a view of passersby in the old town outside. Traditional Hessian dishes such as pork schnitzel with green sauce, *Tafelspitz*, Frankfurter *Hacksteak* (chopped steak), and roasted pork shank with green sauce taste fabulous with the tart and acidic flavor of hard cider.

In the Historisches Museum, Saalgasse 19. 🕾 **069/294400.** Reservations recommended. Main courses 5€–14€ ($8–$22). MC, V. Daily 11am–11pm. U-Bahn: Römer.

Solberfäss'je 🖈 *(Finds* HESSIAN   Cramped, old-fashioned, and gregarious, this restaurant is firmly committed to maintaining its role as the kind of beer bar and working-class restaurant that thrived in this neighborhood a century ago, when its clientele included mostly the horse-cart drivers delivering supplies to homes and stores along the nearby Zeil. Food items focus on schnitzels, sauerbratens, *Rouladens* of beef, and the kinds of roasted knuckles and joints that dyed-in-the-wool beer lovers savor, and which have been associated with *Bierkellers* since anyone can remember. These include roasted shanks of lamb, veal, pork, beef, and turkey, each of which emerges savory and crackling from the ovens. There are also three versions of *Eisbein* (pork knuckle), either roasted, smoked, or steamed. Rainer Sänger is your hardworking, English-speaking host. The restaurant's name, in Hessian dialect, refers to a medieval technique of preserving meat in barrels filled with salt.

Grosse Friedberger Strasse 8. 🕾 **069/296767.** Reservations recommended. Main courses 10€–15€ ($16–$24). AE, DC, MC, V. Mon–Sat 10am–midnight. U-Bahn: Konstabler Hauptwache.

IN WESTEND
VERY EXPENSIVE

Erno's Bistro 🖈🖈🖈 FRENCH   A chic midtown rendezvous despite being cramped and claustrophobic, Erno's draws everybody from visiting film stars to bank executives. Under its former chef and namesake, Erno Schmitt, this restaurant became the first in Frankfurt to earn a Michelin star. He's gone, but Valéry Mathis's food seems to improve every year, and we actually like this bistro better than before. Frankfurt foodies recommend the people-watching possibilities, the fine service, and the sense of theatrical flair.

The kitchen serves fish brought fresh by air from European waters. The chef offers both cuisine moderne and what is known as *cuisine formidable.* The most exciting (and expensive) appetizer is artichokes in puff pastry with sautéed potatoes and foie gras. For a main course, try pigeon with duck liver in a savory truffle sauce. Another excellent choice is filet of venison coated with truffles and served with a smooth and creamy savoy cabbage. A most recommendable main course is a braised leg of rabbit so tender it falls off the bone. It is served on a bed of lentils and diced carrots infused with a dash of curry. Also delicious is rack of lamb with a ragout of white beans and sea bass with beets and a truffle sabayon.

Liebigstrasse 15 (between the Alte Oper and the Palmengarten). © 069/721997. Reservations required. Main courses 42€–46€ ($67–$74). AE, MC, V. Mon–Fri noon–2pm and 7–10pm. Closed mid-June to mid-July. U-Bahn: Westend.

Gargantua ✸✸✸ CONTINENTAL   One of the Westend's genuinely stylish restaurants, Gargantua evokes an upscale and somewhat snobbish 1920s-era bistro in Paris. Set on a verdant street corner with outdoor tables separated from the sidewalk by a wrought-iron fence, it's outfitted in tones of green and white. The guiding force behind the cuisine is a local food writer and columnist, Klaus Trebes, who, with his wife, Monika, usually directs the restaurant in a discreet, well-versed way that includes a sophisticated knowledge of German, Italian, and Austrian wines. Patrons expect— and receive—a near-perfect dining experience. Flavors, textures, and colors combine to delight in such dishes as a creamy soup with black sausage and Perigord truffles, or a zesty risotto with radicchio, squid, and spicy chorizo sausage. The chef is at his best when he prepares guinea fowl braised with cinnamon or rack of veal with a morel cream sauce. Rib-eye steak comes with a vegetable flan and rosemary potatoes, or else you can sample Arctic cod with young cabbage.

Liebigstrasse 47. © 069/720718. Reservations required. Main courses 28€–34€ ($45–$54); fixed-price dinners 60€–85€ ($96–$136). AE, DC, MC, V. Mon–Fri noon–2:30pm and 6pm–1am; Sat 6pm–1am. U-Bahn: Westend.

EXPENSIVE

Bistro Rosa CONTINENTAL   From the outside, Bistro Rosa's gingham curtains and brass rails evoke a saloon. From the inside, the venue resembles a French bistro, complete with caricatures of pigs that bear vague resemblances to Toulouse-Lautrec, Goethe, and some of Germany's politicians. Although pork occasionally appears on the menu, a better bet may be duck breast with orange sauce. You don't have to wait for the holiday season to enjoy those old-time German favorites, such as roast goose with red cabbage and chestnuts, or roasted lamb in an herb-flavored crust. A more unusual dish is the breast of pheasant, a real delicacy, served with pineapple. Desserts include chocolate mousse or crème brûlée. In summer, a narrow terrace, separated from a parking lot with ivy-covered lattices, provides outdoor seating.

Grünebergweg 25. © 069/721380. Reservations recommended. Main courses 25€–45€ ($40–$72). No credit cards. Mon–Sat 6:30pm–midnight. U-Bahn: Westend.

INEXPENSIVE

Café Laumer *Finds* GERMAN/AUSTRIAN   There are many cafes scattered throughout Frankfurt, but this one is proud of literary antecedents that are a bit deeper, broader, and more authentic than those that are cited by some of its competitors. No one will mind if you adopt this place as a cafe, but if you want full-fledged meals, they're available as well, but only until its regrettably early closing every day at 7pm. Menu items include crisp schnitzels, freshly made salads, grilled steaks with peppercorn sauce, roulades of beef or pork stuffed with herbs and bread crumbs, and when it's available, good-tasting fresh game and fish dishes. Framed honorariums on the walls of this place refer to its most historically famous client, a prominent scholar of Hegel and Marx, musicologist and philosopher Theodor Adorno (1903–69), who used to come here every day in the 1930s for coffee and conversation before moving on to professorships at Oxford and Princeton.

Bockenheimer Landstrasse 67. © **069/727912**. Reservations recommended for meals. Main courses 5.50€–9.80€ ($8.80–$16). MC, V. Mon–Sat 7:30am–7pm; Sun 9am–7pm. U-Bahn: Westend.

ACROSS THE MAIN
MODERATE
Holbein's 𝒢 INTERNATIONAL   In the courtyard of the Städel, entered from Holbeinstrasse, this is an elegant choice for dining on a carefully crafted cuisine. Its decor has been likened to dining in a jewel box with a backdrop of paintings by old masters. The service is among the most efficient in town. Marvelously fresh ingredients are cooked with admirable care and precision. You might begin with a mix of Kombucha tea and prosecco on ice before digging into the well-chosen array of poultry, fish, and meat dishes. The range is from the most tender of Argentine filet mignon to grilled Canadian lobster in vanilla foam.

Holbeinstrasse 1. © **069/66056666**. Reservations required. Main courses 18€–29€ ($29–$46); fixed-price menu 45€ ($72). AE, MC, V. Tues–Sun 10am–midnight. U-Bahn: Schweizer-Platz.

IN THE EAST END
VERY EXPENSIVE
Silk 𝒢𝒢 *(Finds* FUSION/AUSTRO-GERMAN   It's like wandering into a vehicle about to set off on some space odyssey. Actually, it's a "bed restaurant." The chic patrons, mostly in their 20s and 30s, are barefoot, semi-reclining on white-leather beds while they're served sublime food. Dining areas are bathed in iridescent light in harmonious color moods. The waterbed is a special delight, surrounded by a virtual aquarium. All guests dine at the same time, with the reception beginning at 7:30pm and dinner service following at 8pm and lasting for most of the evening.

The prix-fixe menu consists of several courses. Definitely plan to make an evening of it if you dine here. The experimental cuisine is presented with equally innovative music in the background. Only fresh seasonal ingredients are used, and Mediterranean diversity meets Asian minimalism, as you sample such delights as a succulent lobster spiked with mango, Serrano ham, and lemon grass. Perhaps you'll have a rack of lamb with a sauerkraut risotto (a first for many diners), or else corn ravioli with pumpkin-seed oil, or smoked salmon with marinated fresh fennel. The restaurant is also a night club, open Friday and Saturday 9pm to 6am. The restaurant lies in the Fechenheim district, east of the center, a 10-minute tram ride.

Karl Benz Strasse 21. © **069/900200**. Reservations required. 10-course fixed-price menu 88€ ($141). AE, MC, V. Tues–Sat 7pm–2am. Tram: 11 or 12.

INEXPENSIVE
Das Leben ist Schön ITALIAN   In spite of its name, this is a pocket of Little Italy in Frankfurt, lying on the east side of the Main. The chefs turn out the best pizzas, each with a paper-thin crust, in this sector of the city. Guests share wooden tables, reading the day's specials from a blackboard. Each person at the table seems to get to know each other quickly, and the place becomes festive as the night wears on. Stills from Fellini films or Italian families line the walls, making for a homelike aura.

Hanauer Landstrasse 198. © **069/430570**. Main courses 6€–18€ ($9.60–$29). MC, V. Daily 6pm–1am. U-Bahn: Zoo.

5 Exploring Frankfurt

When bombs rained down on Frankfurt in 1944, nearly all the old half-timbered buildings were leveled. In what seemed like record time, residents of Frankfurt rebuilt their city into a fine mélange of modern and traditional architecture and faithfully restored some of their most prized old buildings as well.

Although Frankfurt doesn't have the monuments or museums to equal Munich or Berlin, its museums and exhibition halls still lure some two million visitors annually. As the cultural director of the city of Frankfurt, Dr. Hans Bernhard Nordhoff, told us, "We offer you everything from Goethe to Andy Warhol, from *Tyrannosaurus Rex* to the female ideal of Botticelli."

Many of the grandest museums lie along the Main on the south bank—often called "Museum Embankment," in itself a dazzling array of contemporary architecture even before you go inside to look at the exhibits.

See the map on p. 464 for the location of Frankfurt's major attractions.

The easiest way to sightsee in Frankfurt is to take a cruise on the Main River aboard one of the vessels operated by **Primus-Line,** Mainkai 36 (© **069/133837**). Boats leave from the North Bank of the Main at Mainkai during the day, offering a 50-minute excursion for 6.70€ ($11) or a 100-minute excursion for 8.70€ ($14). The trip gives you a preview of the skyline of Frankfurt.

THE TOP ATTRACTIONS
ALTSTADT ⟨★★⟩

Allow about half a day to explore the old town, which was once one of the greatest and most historic in Germany before World War II bombing raids turned it to dust. Its specific attractions include the **Goethe Haus,** which was the birthplace of Germany's greatest writer in 1749. Goethe spent his early life wandering around the Altstadt, and you can follow in his footsteps.

Among the more intriguing sights is the **Dom** (detailed below), which was consecrated in 1239. This cathedral was chosen to serve as the electoral site for the kings of the Holy Roman Empire in 1356. Ten imperial coronations took place here between 1562 and 1792.

Among other attractions are the **Römer,** an interconnected trio of medieval patrician's houses, which functioned as the city hall of Frankfurt as early as 1405. Today it is still the official seat of Frankfurt's lord mayor. The Römerberg is the historic core of the old Altstadt, famous for its magnificent half-timbered houses reconstructed after bombings, according to their original plans.

At the northern edge of the Altstadt is **An der Hauptwache,** named for the old guardhouse *(Hauptwache)* which stands upon it. This square is the heart of modern Frankfurt. Underneath is the Hauptwache U-Bahn station with a modern shopping promenade.

Goethe-Haus ⟨★⟩ This house, where Johann Wolfgang von Goethe (1749–1832) was born, has been a shrine for Goethe enthusiasts since it opened to the public in 1863. One observer wrote that the postwar restoration was carried out "with loving care and damn-the-expense craftsmanship." The house is decorated in various styles, all reflecting the fashion trends of the 18th century: neoclassical, baroque, and rococo. You can view the library, where Goethe's father worked and often watched the street for the return of his son. A portrait of the severe-looking gentleman hangs behind the door of his wife's room.

On the second floor is an unusual astronomical clock built around 1749 and repaired in 1949 to run for another 200 years. The picture gallery contains paintings collected by Goethe's father. These works, mainly by contemporary Frankfurt artists, influenced Goethe's artistic views for a great part of his life. You can also see one of

Goethe's most important childhood possessions, a puppet theater, which played a significant role in his novel *Wilhelm Meister*.

Annexed to the house, the **Frankfurter Goethe-Museum** has a library of 120,000 volumes and a collection of about 30,000 manuscripts, as well as 16,000 graphic artworks and 400 paintings associated with Goethe and his works.

Grosser Hirschgraben 23–25. (*C*) **069/138800**. www.goethehaus-frankfurt.de. Admission 5€ ($8) adults, 2.50€ ($4) students, 1.50€ ($2.40) children 7–18, free for children 6 and under. Mon–Sat 10am–6pm; Sun and holidays 10am–5:30pm. U-Bahn/S-Bahn: Hauptwache.

Liebieghaus ☆☆☆ The building is an 1896 villa. Its collection includes objects from ancient Egypt, classical Greece and Rome, and medieval and Renaissance Europe. Highlights include a small 8th-century-B.C. bronze horse and Roman copies of the *Torso* of Polycletus, Praxiteles's *Satyr*, and Myron's *Athena*. Although the most ancient artifacts generate the most excitement, the medieval section is also fascinating. Look for the *Virgin and Child* created in Trier in the 11th century, the head of Barbel von Ottenheim (attributed to van Leyden in 1462), the Riemenschneider *Madonna*, Andrea della Robbia's altarpiece of the Assumption, and the 16th-century *Black Venus with Mirror*.

Schaumainkai 71. (*C*) **069/21238617**. www.liebieghaus.de. Admission 7€ ($11) adults; 5€ ($8) seniors and students; free for children 11 and under. Tues and Thurs–Sun 10am–5pm; Wed 10am–8pm (last entrance is at 4:30pm, even on Wed). Tram: 15 or 16 to Otto-Hahn-Platz.

Städel Museum ☆☆☆ This is Frankfurt's most important art gallery, containing a fine collection of most European schools of painting. The first floor features French Impressionists such as Renoir and Monet, along with German painters of the 19th and 20th centuries. Note in particular Kirchner's *Nude Woman with Hat*. Also on the first floor is Tischbein's *Portrait of Goethe in the Campagna in Italy*. If you're short on time, go directly to the second floor to view the outstanding collection of Flemish primitives, 17th-century Dutch artists, and 16th-century German masters such as Dürer, Grünewald, Memling, Elsheimer, and many others. One of the most impressive paintings is Jan van Eyck's *Madonna* (1433). Lucas Cranach the Elder is represented by a large winged altarpiece and his rather impish nude *Venus*. Recent acquisitions include Jean Antoine Watteau's *L'Ile de Cythère* (1709). In the Department of Modern Art are works by Bacon, Dubuffet, Tapies, and Yves Klein.

Schaumainkai 63 (on the south bank of the Main). (*C*) **069/6050980**. www.staedelmuseum.de. Admission 10€ ($16) adults, 8€ ($13) children 12–16, 18€ ($29) family ticket, free for children 11 and under. English audio guide 4€ ($6.40). Tues, Fri, and Sun 10am–6pm, Wed–Thurs 10am–9pm. U-Bahn: Schweizer Platz.

Römerberg ☆

The Altstadt (U-Bahn/S-Bahn: Hauptwache) centers on three Gothic buildings with stepped gables, known collectively as the **Römer**, Römerberg (*C* **069/21234814**). These houses were originally built between 1288 and 1305 and bought by the city a century later for use as the Rathaus. The second floor of the center house is the **Kaisersaal (Imperial Hall)**, lined with the romanticized 19th-century portraits of 52 emperors; 13 of them celebrated their coronation banquets here. You can visit this hall daily 10am to 1pm and 2 to 5pm. An hourly tour costing 2€ ($3.20) is obligatory. Tours are conducted in English and German and tickets can be purchased at the entrance to the Römer.

The elaborate facade of the Römer, with its ornate balcony and statues of four emperors, overlooks **Römerplatz (Römerberg Square)**. On festive occasions in days gone by, the square was the scene of oxen roasts that featured flowing wine. Today, unfortunately, the Fountain of Justitia pours forth only water, but oxen are still roasted on special occasions.

Dom ⟨★⟩

The dominant feature of the Altstadt is the 15th-century, red-sandstone tower of the **Dom St. Bartholomäus,** in whose chapels the emperors of the Holy Roman Empire were elected and crowned for nearly 300 years. The church was constructed between the 13th and 15th centuries on the site of a Carolingian building. It is most noted for its **west tower** or Westturm ⟨★★⟩, which is greatly ornamented and crowned by a polygonal gable. It's topped by both a lantern and a dome. Surprisingly, the cathedral was not completed until 1877, but it was based on plans created by the Dom's original architect, Madern Gerthener. Destroyed by Allied bombs in 1944, it was rebuilt in 1953. One of its chief treasures is its **choir stalls** ⟨★⟩, which represent brilliant Upper Rhine craftsmanship, dating from around the mid–14th century. In the north chancel, look for **Maria Schlafaltar (Altar of Mary Sleeping),** dating from 1434. It is the only altar remaining from the church's original interior. The Dom is open daily, at no charge, from 9am to noon and 2 to 6pm.

In the cloister is the **Dom Museum** (☎ **069/13376186**) which, among other things, exhibits robes of the imperial electors. These robes, which are still quite sumptuous, were worn at coronation ceremonies. The oldest vestments date from the 1400s. Walk west of the cathedral to an "archaeological garden" called **Historischer Garten,** with ruins of both Roman and Carolingian fortifications. Hours are Tuesday to Friday 10am to 5pm and Saturday and Sunday 11am to 5pm. Admission is 2€ ($3.20) for adults and 1€ ($1.60) for children.

OTHER TOP MUSEUMS

Deutsches Filmmuseum (German Film Museum) ⟨★⟩

This is the finest film museum in Germany. Old films from the collection are shown continuously on the second floor. The rooms downstairs chronicle the history of the filmmaking industry. Exhibits include Emile Reynaud's 1882 Praxinoscope, Edison's Kinetoscope from 1889, and a copy of the Lumière brothers' Cinematograph from 1895. There are also models illustrating how special effects are shot, including those in the original *King Kong*.

Schaumainkai 41, at the corner of Schweizerstrasse. (☎ **069/21238830**. www.deutschesfilmmuseum.de. Admission 2.50€ ($4) adults, 1.30€ ($2.10) students and children; film screenings 5.50€ ($8.80) adults, 4.50€ ($7.20) students, 2.30€ ($3.70) children. Tues, Thurs–Fri, and Sun 10am–5pm; Wed 10am–8pm; Sat 2–8pm. U-Bahn: Schweizer Platz.

Historisches Museum (Historical Museum) ⟨★⟩

Since this dignified museum was established in a stately looking building near Town Hall in 1878, its curators have systematically added exhibits that showcase the history and culture of Frankfurt. Collections include examples of gold and silver plateware and jewelry; pottery and porcelain; paintings, lithographs and photographs; and scaled-down models of the Altstadt at various periods of its development.

Saalgasse 19. (☎ **069/21235599**. www.historisches-museum.frankfurt.de. Admission 4€ ($6.40) adults, 2€ ($3.20) children 6–18, free for children 5 and under. Tues–Sun 10am–6pm; Wed 10am–9pm. U-Bahn: Römer.

Museum für Angewandte Kunst (Museum of Applied Arts) ⟨★⟩

More than 30,000 objects from across Europe and Asia are exhibited here. Two buildings house the collection: a 19th-century villa and a 1985 structure designed by New York architect Richard Meier. The museum has an outstanding collection of German rococo furnishings (called *Mainzer Meistermobel*) created in Mainz. The glassware is a highlight, with some Venetian pieces from the 15th century. On the second floor, the Far East and Islamic department has a rich collection of Persian carpets and faience dating from the 9th century. One of Germany's finest porcelain collections is here as well.

Schaumainkai 17. (C) 069/21234037. www.museumfuerangewandtekunst.frankfurt.de. Admission 5€ ($8) adults, 2.50€ ($4) students and children 7–18, free for children 6 and under. Tues and Thurs–Sun 10am–5pm; Wed 10am–9pm. U-Bahn: Schweizer Platz.

Museum für Moderne Kunst (Museum of Modern Art)   This museum opened in 1991 in a building created by Hans Hollein, the Viennese architect. The structure is designed like a boat, but in spite of its somewhat bizarre shape, the gallery has a bright, spacious air. (Some critics claim the dazzling architecture is more interesting than the exhibits.) Major artists since the 1950s are displayed here, including Roy Liechtenstein (see his *Brush-stroke*), Andy Warhol, and George Segal, with his *Jazz Combo*.

Domstrasse 10 (in the center of the Altstadt, near Römerberg). (C) 069/21230447. www.mmk-frankfurt.de. Admission 7€ ($11) adults, 3.50€ ($5.60) students, free for children 5 and under, free for all last Sat of each month. Tues and Thurs–Sun 10am–5pm; Wed 10am–8pm. U-Bahn: Römer. Tram: 11 to Domstrasse.

PARKS

Frankfurt has a lot of parks. Locals like to point out that while the city has no Central Park as New York does, it is itself a central park. A botanic city ring has replaced the enclosing city walls of old Frankfurt. Along the Main is a park landscape where you'll see bankers taking their lunch break beneath statues of heroes from the past.

The Palmengarten ♔, Siesmayerstrasse 61 ((C) 069/21233939; U-Bahn: Westend; bus: 32), is a park and a botanical garden. During the last decade, the gardens have been renewed and the conservatories and historic greenhouses completely reconstructed. You can admire a perennial garden, an expanded rock garden, and a beautiful rose garden. A huge gallery that serves as an exhibition hall for flower shows and other botanical exhibitions surrounds the 1869 palm house. In recent years, new conservatories have been added: The Tropicarium is a complex for tropical vegetation; the Sub-Antarctic House displays plants from southern Chile, Argentina, and New Zealand; and the Entrance Conservatory houses insectivorous plants and bromeliads. Collections of orchids, palms, succulents, water lilies, and many others are also on display.

Admission to the botanical garden is 5€ ($8) for adults and 2€ ($3.20) for children, or 9.50€ ($15) for a family ticket. It's open daily March to October 9am to 6pm, and November to February 9am to 4pm. In the park area, there's a small lake where people can row boats. In summer, concerts are given in the band shell; evening events include open-air dancing, jazz, and fountain illumination. There are some facilities for food. For guided tours in English call (C) 069/21233391.

Bethmann Park, with its Chinese gardens, is another interesting park. It lies immediately to the northeast of Stadtmitte, and is reached by bus no. 30 or tram no. 12.

SPORTS & OUTDOOR PURSUITS
JOGGING

A pretty jogging route is along the quays of the River Main, using both sides of the river and the bridges to create a loop. Another choice is the centrally located Gruenberg Park, with walkways that are suitable for jogging.

TENNIS

Few of the tennis courts in Frankfurt allow nonmembers to play. A noteworthy exception is the **Tennisplatz Eissporthalle,** Am Bornheimer hang, 60486 Frankfurt

(© 069/21239308 or 069/21230810; www.eissporthalle-ffm.de; U-Bahn/S-Bahn: Eissporthalle), which has a half-dozen courts. They're open May to October daily 8am to sundown. The cost is 10€ ($16) per hour.

6 Shopping

When it comes to shopping, Frankfurt has everything. The specialty shops here are so much like those in the United States that visitors from America will feel right at home. Most stores are open Monday to Friday 9 or 10am to 6 or 6:30pm, and Saturday 9 or 10am to 2pm.

In Frankfurt, the shopping scene is divided into different regions. On "the Golden Mile," the **Zeil,** a pedestrian zone between the Hauptwache and Konstablerwache, you'll find department stores, clothing shops, shoe stores, and furniture outlets. Once one of the most famous shopping streets on the Continent, the Zeil was destroyed in the war and hasn't regained all of its former prestige, though it has the highest sales of any shopping area in Germany. Still the Fifth Avenue of Germany and one of Europe's best places to shop, the shopping on the Zeil now faces too much competition to enjoy the prestige it once had. In the 14th century, it was a cattle market. Nearby is the **Kleinmarkthalle,** a covered market with international grocery products.

The **Hauptwache,** in the center of Frankfurt, has two shopping areas, one above and one below ground. Groceries, book dealers, flowers, clothing, tobacco, photo supplies, recordings, and sporting equipment abound. In the Hauptwache-Passage are restaurants, travel agencies, and banks.

Schillerstrasse, another pedestrian zone, lies between Hauptwache and Eschenheimer Turm, near the stock exchange. Walking from Schillerstrasse northeast toward Eschenheimer Tor, you'll pass many elegant boutiques and specialty shops.

Southwest of the Hauptwache is the Alte Oper. You can reach it by taking either the **Goethestrasse,** with exclusive stores evocative of Paris or Milan, or the parallel **Grosse Bockenheimerstrasse,** traditionally nicknamed Fressgasse or "Pig-Out Alley." Most wine dealers, delis, and butcher shops here look back on a long and venerable past. **Opernplatz** has a variety of restaurants and cafes.

West of the Hauptwache is Rossmarkt, leading to **Kaiserstrasse.** It passes the **BFG skyscraper,** which has three floors of exclusive retail stores, boutiques, and restaurants, and directly connects the downtown area to the Hauptbahnhof. Kaiserstrasse is also known for its large selection of stores selling clothing, audio and photography equipment, and stainless-steel ware. The heart of the fur trade in Frankfurt is **Düsseldorfer Strasse,** opposite the Hauptbahnhof. Most book dealers are located around the Hauptwache and **Goetheplatz.** Antiques, old books, etchings, and paintings on **Braubachstrasse** can be found near the Römer, at the Dom, and on Fahrgasse.

Art and antiques are the domain of **Alt-Sachsenhausen,** an appealing and original neighborhood. The **Frankfurt Flea Market** takes place here every Saturday 8am to 2pm along the Main River on the Sachsenhausen side. To get here, walk from the Römer toward the river and cross the Eisener Steg bridge.

ART GALLERIES

Galerie Adler   This is the most avant-garde gallery in Frankfurt, presenting all media from paintings to photographs and video to plastic. It features a talented array of fresh faces, both young Frankfurters and international artists. Various exhibitions are staged throughout the year. Hanauer Landstrasse 134. © 069/43053962. U-Bahn: Zoo.

DEPARTMENT STORES

Karstadt   A Frankfurt shopping tradition along the Golden Mile, this vast store offers clothes and shoes for every mood. It also caters to a wide range of budgets. Families with small children may want to check out the selection of toys, and foodies take delight in the food hall in the basement, with tidbits from all over the globe. On the ground floor is a selection of jewelry and cosmetics, among other items. Zeil 90. (*) 069/929050. U-Bahn: Konstablerwache.

Kaufhof   This department store accurately touts its one-stop shopping. On its seven floors it's got just about everything—porcelain, accessories, clothes, jewelry, glassware, and a food hall. Tired of shopping? Retreat to the top-floor restaurant, which has one of Frankfurt's most panoramic views. Zeil 116–126. (*) 069/21910. U-Bahn: Hauptwache.

FASHION

For basics, check out the vast array of clothing at the previously recommended department stores.

Kleidoskop   Even though this shop specializes in secondhand clothing, much of it appears to be new. For those who like designer labels, there is an array of Gucci, Armani, Prada, and other big names—all up for grabs at cut-rate prices. Oeder Weg 56. (*) 069/550837. U-Bahn: Eschenheimer Tor.

JEWELRY

House of Silver   This little shop set in the midst of the apple-wine taverns of Sachsenhausen is a discovery. Savvy Frankfurter collectors go here to indulge their taste in silver jewelry. The store is small, but the range is wide, going from classic motifs to more modern lines. Schweizer Strasse 73. (*) 069/627681. U-Bahn: Schweizer Platz.

Renekirn Juweliere & Ohrmacher   Formerly known as Christ Jewelers, this is one of Europe's largest jewelry and watch retail stores. On two floors there is an array of almost every bauble known to man (and woman), including sparkling studs, rings, and bracelets, along with necklaces and even dashing wrist and pocket watches. All items can be altered to fit. Check out the top-quality selection of pearls from the South Pacific. Kaiserstrasse 1. (*) 069/138820. U-Bahn: Hauptwache.

PORCELAIN

Höchster Porzellan Manufacture GmbH   This gilt and blue-painted showroom contains one of Germany's largest inventories of what's been created by Höchst Porcelain for more than 150 years. Quality of the "white gold" is almost flawless, and the prestige level of virtually anything associated with this outfit is about as good as it gets in Frankfurt today. (Even Goethe's mother collected the stuff, praising its virtues to her impressionable and articulate young son.) If the object of your desire lies on the sale table, there may be a markdown to 60% off retail prices. You can request particular color schemes for whatever object you select, as long as it's within the historical/aesthetic framework of the era when the original item was produced. Look in particular for illustrated platters inspired by the Struwwelpeter legends, beloved by children in Mittel Europa for generations. Palleskestrasse 32. (*) 069/3009020. S-Bahn: Höchst.

Mitsukoshi   The more frequently visited half of this shop is devoted to one of the most complete inventories of Meissen porcelain in Frankfurt. The other half contains a relentlessly upscale assortment of luxury goods made by, among others, Gucci. Widely publicized by journalists in Tokyo and Osaka, this shop is an essential stop for most of the Japanese travelers visiting Frankfurt. As such, most of the staff members speak fluent Japanese, and when tour buses arrive, there are likely to be mobs of Asian clients. Part of the second floor contains a "museum" with copies of antique Meissen candelabra and tureens, any of which can be duplicated if you have enough money and time to wait for their eventual delivery. Bethmannstrasse 56. © 069/9218870. U-Bahn: Willy-Brandt-Platz.

7 Frankfurt After Dark

For details of what's happening in Frankfurt, you can pick up copies of *Journal Frankfurt* at newsstands throughout the city. Also listing events are *Frizz* and *Strandgut*, both free and available at the tourist office.

To purchase tickets for many major cultural events, go to the tourist office at the Hauptbahnhof. Or you can head for a bona-fide ticket agent, one of the biggest in Frankfurt, for tickets to concerts, plays, and sporting events throughout town. **Best Tickets** lies in the ZeilGalerie (Shop no. 47), 112–114 Zeil (© **069/20228** or 069/91397621).

Of course, one of the greatest ways to spend an evening in Frankfurt is at one of the *Apfelwein* (apple-wine) taverns across the south bank of the Main in the district of Sachsenhausen.

THE PERFORMING ARTS

Theater der Stadt Frankfurt, Untermainanlage 11 (© **069/1340400;** U-Bahn: Willy-Brandt-Platz), has three stages. One belongs to the **Frankfurt Municipal Opera,** whose productions have received worldwide recognition in recent years. Two stages are devoted to drama. If your German is adequate, you may want to see a performance of **Städtische Bühnen/Schauspiel** (© **069/1340400**), a forum for classic German plays as well as modern drama. A variety theater, **Kunstlerhaus Mouson Turm,** Waldschmidtstrasse 4 (© **069/40589520;** U-Bahn/S-Bahn: Merianplatz), hosts plays, classical music concerts, and dance programs almost every night of the week. Tickets run 6€ to 44€ ($9.60–$70).

Alte Oper   The old opera house is still the pride of Frankfurt, even though opera is no longer presented here. This building was reopened in 1981, following its reconstruction after World War II bombings. The original structure had been officially opened in 1880 by Kaiser Wilhelm I. At that time, it was hailed as one of the most beautiful theaters in Europe. Today the Alte Oper is the site of frequent symphonic and choral concerts. The box office is open Monday to Friday 8:30am to 8:30pm, and Saturday 9:30am to 2pm. Opernplatz. © 069/13400. www.alteoper.de. Tickets 35€–75€ ($56–$120). U-Bahn: Alte Oper.

English Theatre   This English-language theater was founded by the actress Judith Rosenbauer, who is still its artistic director. It began in a Sachsenhausen backyard but was later moved to this location, compliments of the city of Frankfurt. Musicals, comedies, dramas, and thrillers are produced. During the season (Sept–July), performances are Tuesday to Saturday at 7:30pm and Sunday at 6pm. The box office is open Monday from noon to 6pm, Tuesday to Friday from 11am to 6:30pm, Saturday from 3 to 6:30pm, and Sunday from 3 to 5pm. Kaiserstrasse 34. © 069/24231620. www.english-theatre.org. Plays 19€–30€ ($30–$48); musicals 27€–42€ ($43–$67). S-Bahn: Hauptbahnhof.

Oper Frankfurt/Ballet Frankfurt   This is Frankfurt's premier showcase for world-class opera and ballet. Acclaimed for its dramatic artistry, the **Frankfurt Opera** is under the charge of conductor Sylvain Cambreling. The world-renowned **Frankfurt Ballet** is directed by William Forsythe. The box office is open Monday to Friday 8am to 8pm, and Saturday 8am to 6pm. Willy-Brandt-Platz (between the Hauptbahnhof and the Innenstadt). ℂ 069/1340400. www.oper-frankfurt.de. Opera and ballet 9€–130€ ($14–$208). U-Bahn: Willy-Brandt-Platz.

THE CLUB & MUSIC SCENE
CABARET
Tigerpalast The most famous and sought-after cabaret in Frankfurt, this was named after co-founder Johnny Klinke's Chinese zodiac birth year (the Tiger). Klinke founded the club with Margarita Dillinger in the late 1980s. Shows are presented in a not very large blue-and-black theater, where guests sit at tiny tables to see about eight different artists per show. The acts usually include four Italian acrobats, three Russians who jump into one another's arms from dizzying heights, an East Indian shadow puppeteer who imitates the likenesses of famous German and U.S. politicians, a Mexican juggler, and a Ukrainian ballet artist who dances to the melodies of Edith Piaf. A tiger, a panther, and a sea lion all make carefully choreographed appearances as well, each presented with an emphasis on razzmatazz, nostalgia, and schmaltz. Each show lasts 2 hours with breaks for drinks and snacks, and each is presented as child-approved, family-style entertainment without nudity. Two restaurants are associated with this cabaret (p. 475). Shows are Tuesday through Thursday 7 and 10pm, Friday to Saturday 7:30 and 10:30pm, and Sunday 5 and 9pm. Heiligkreuzgasse 16–20. ℂ 069/9200220. www.tigerpalast.de. Tickets 50€–54€ ($79–$86); half price for children 11 and under. Drinks from 10€ ($16). U-Bahn: Konstabler Wache.

DANCE CLUBS
In a 16-square-block area in front of the Hauptbahnhof, you'll find a rowdy kind of entertainment, what the Germans call *erotische Spiele.* Doormen will practically pull you inside to view porno movies, sex shows, sex shops, and dance clubs teeming with prostitutes. **Warning:** This area can be dangerous—don't come here alone. For less lurid activities in a safer environment, head to the live-music clubs, dance clubs, bars, and cafes across the Main River in the **Sachsenhausen** district. Most gay bars and clubs are located in a small area between Bleichstrasse and Zeil.

Cocoon Club ℛ Frankfurt's best dance club is presided over by Sven Väth, the most celebrated DJ in Germany. Joining Väth on Friday and Saturday nights are top acts from around Europe, and the joint pulsates with life at this time. The dance club is huge, and there are three bars. Since the Cocoon is only open Friday and Saturday, on other nights the action centers on the more subdued Micro Club Restaurant, which features a continental and Asian fusion cuisine as well as dancing to electronic music. Fashion shows and live acts are also featured at the Micro. The Micro offers jazz, funk, soul, and R&B. The Cocoon is open Friday and Saturday 9pm to 6am; the Micro is open Tuesday to Thursday 7pm to 3am, and Friday and Saturday 7pm to 6am. Carl-Benz-Strasse 21. ℂ 069/5069-6948. Cover at Cocoon 15€ ($24). S-Bahn: Haltestelle Ostendstrasse.

King Kamehameha Club The launch of this club on a street once filled with abandoned warehouses helped make the industrial East End of Frankfurt a chic after-dark address. Called "King Ka" by its loyal devotees, the club remains the hottest weekend address in this part of Frankfurt. On Thursday nights a live band is usually presented, with DJs taking over on Friday and Saturday nights. The club is open only from Thursday to Saturday 10pm to 4am. Hanauer Landstrasse 192. ℂ 069/4800370. U-Bahn: Zoo.

Living xxl   On Friday and Saturday night it seems that half of Frankfurt—both gay and straight—is here dancing the night away. The club is one of the largest bars and restaurants in Germany, with a widely mixed clientele. The most action and dancing are on Friday and Saturday nights. The location is in the Eurotower, the headquarters of the European Central Bank. The terraced interior is architecturally dramatic. The compound opens Monday to Friday at 11:30am, but closing times can vary from 11pm to 4am. On Saturday it is open 7pm to 5am. Kaiserstrasse 29. ℂ 069/242937-0. U-Bahn: Seckbacher Landstrasse.

The Odeon Club ℱ   This club is housed in the beautiful Bethmann Pavilion dating from 1808. One of the most frequented clubs in Frankfurt, it draws a widely varied crowd, depending on the night of the week—student night on Thursday, a 30s-to-40s crowd on Friday, and dance music on Saturday, which draws a younger crowd in their 20s to the R&B music as well as hip-hop and soul. The ground floor offers two bars and a spacious dance floor, with more tranquil seating in the winter garden. For those who want to sit, talk, and cuddle, there is the upper floor bar with its many cushions. The Odeon is open only on Monday 5pm to 4am, Thursday 9pm to 4am, and Friday and Saturday 10pm until dawn. Seilerstrasse, 34 City Center. ℂ 069/ 285-055. Cover 5€ ($8). U-Bahn: Konstabler Wache.

LIVE MUSIC

Der Jazzkeller   This basement club, established in 1952, is one of the most famous and atmospheric jazz clubs in Germany. Its reputation is as solid as the 200-year-old redbrick walls that surround it. The place has played host to such jazz luminaries as Louis Armstrong, Dizzy Gillespie, and Gerry Mulligan. Thursday and Saturday, live music usually begins at 10pm. On nights when there is no live music, the club becomes a late-night pub. It's open Tuesday to Sunday 9:30pm to 3am. Kleine Bockenheimer 18A (near Goethestrasse). ℂ 069/288537. Concerts 5€–15€ ($8–$24). U-Bahn/S-Bahn: Alte Oper.

Sansibar   In summer one of the most popular bars is in the industrial East End on the "wrong side" of the Main River. This is one of the best open-air roof bars and lounges in Frankfurt, with panoramic views of the city. Guests lounge on bamboo chairs, the better heeled sipping champagne while blue-collar workers drink beer. Sansibar is open April 30 to September 30 Monday to Saturday 7pm to 3am. Hanauer Landstrasse 190. ℂ 069/91396147. U-Bahn: Zoo.

Sinkkasten   At this live-music institution, regulars show up regardless of who's playing. Rock, reggae, blues, pop, jazz, and African music bands may be found here, except on Thursday, Saturday, and late Friday, when the club turns disco. Come early to beat the crowd, or risk being turned away. It's open Sunday to Thursday 9pm to 2am, Friday and Saturday 9pm to 3am. Brönnerstrasse 5–9. ℂ 069/280385. Dance club 5€–8€ ($8–$13), concerts 6€–20€ ($9.60–$32). U-Bahn/S-Bahn: Konstablerwache.

GAY FRANKFURT

Lucky's Manhattan   Best described as a gay cafe and bar wrapped into one, Lucky's also has aspects of a conservative tearoom. Most folks come here to drink beer or apple wine, or perhaps to nibble on the limited array of toasts and crepes. It's a worthwhile place to begin an evening on the town. Lucky's operates Sunday through Thursday 3pm to 1am, and Friday and Saturday 3pm to 2am. Schäfergasse 27. ℂ 069/28-49-19. U-Bahn/S-Bahn: Konstablerwache.

Pulse   This is a cafe with an active bar trade; a clientele that's mostly fashionable, male, and gay; and a throbbing Valentine-hued decor of red, black, and gray. Come here for breakfasts after a late night out, salads, sandwiches, and late-night platters that include mini-quiches. Menu items cost from 4€ to 18€ ($6.40–$29); mixed drinks are from 8€ to 11€ ($13–$18), unless they're alcohol-free (such as the Safe Sex on the Beach), when they go for 8€ ($13). Some nights, house and garage music begins after 10pm, transforming the place into something that you may define as a dance club with food service. Pulse is open Monday to Saturday 11am to 1am (till 3 or 4am Sat), and Sunday 9:30am to 1am. Bleichstrasse 38A. ✆ 069/13886802. U-Bahn: Konstablerwache.

Zum Schwejk   This is one of the coziest and most traditional-looking pubs in town, with a mostly gay clientele and a kind of gruff friendliness that's conducive to striking up dialogues with fellow patrons. Some of the staff are kindly beer-hall ladies from way, way back, and there's absolutely no emphasis on twinky life or youth culture. What we mean is, if you're in your 40s and looking for conviviality, this place, replete with its wood paneling and *bierhall* flavor, is a good choice. No food is served, but the beer is cold and frothy, and the place has the potential to become your "regular" hangout in Frankfurt. It's open Sunday to Thursday 11am to 1am, and Friday and Saturday 11am to 2am. Schäfergasse 20. ✆ 069/29-31-66. U-Bahn/s-Bahn: Konstablerwache.

BARS & CAFES

Balalaika   For one of the most charming evenings Frankfurt can offer up, head to Sachsenhausen—not for an *Apfelwein* tavern, but to visit this shoebox-size club. It is the domain of Anita Honis, an American from Harlem, who imbues the club with her personal charm and her music. Several times a night she'll bring out her guitar and entertain guests while perched on a wooden bar stool. Balalaika is open Sunday to Thursday 8pm to 2:30 or 3am, and Friday and Saturday 8pm to 4am. Schifferstrasse 3. ✆ 069/612226. Bus: 30 or 36.

Café Karin   The mayor of Frankfurt first steered us to this place, claiming that "the real Frankfurter" patronizes this cafe. "Come here for a preview of German culture," His Honor told us. With its art-filled walls, old wooden tables, and daily newspapers (which some patrons read for hours), it's a place to relax and linger. Perhaps every hour or so a waiter may come over, but don't count on it. We like to hit this place for breakfast and then later stop off for a nightcap around midnight. It's open Monday to Thursday 9am to 1am, Friday and Saturday 9am to 2am, and Sunday 10am to 7pm. Grosser Hirschgraben 28. ✆ 069/295217. U-Bahn: Hauptwache.

Jimmy's Bar   To impress that really big client, take him or her to Frankfurt's most elegant bar in its most elegant hotel, Hessischer Hof (p. 468). Against a backdrop of gentle piano music, you can drink your Tom Collins in style with the city's smoothest service. The bartenders seem able to fill all requests, no matter how unusual. Jimmy's is open daily 8pm to 4am. Hessischer Hof, Friedrich-Ebert-Anlage 40. ✆ 069/75400. S-Bahn: Platz der Republik. Bus: 32 or 33.

Luna   This hip bar is always packed with Frankfurt's young professionals drinking cocktails and listing to the cool jazz playing in the background. The bartenders perform gymnastics (reminiscent of the Tom Cruise film *Cocktail*) in making such drinks as grasshoppers, juleps, champagne fizzes, and tropical coladas. Drink prices start at 6€ ($9.60). The place is packed on weekends. Hours are Monday to Thursday 7pm to 2am, Friday and Saturday 7pm to 3am. Stiftstrasse 6. ✆ 069/294774. U-Bahn: Hauptwache.

8 Side Trips from Frankfurt

Picturesque Aschaffenburg and some of the leading spas of Germany lie on Frankfurt's doorstep. Another memorable side trip is to Mainz (p. 511).

ASCHAFFENBURG

40km (25 miles) SE of Frankfurt, 77km (48 miles) NW of Würzburg

Aschaffenburg was originally a Roman settlement on the right bank of the Main River and later became an important town in the Middle Ages. In recent years, it's grown industrially, but even with 250 garment manufacturers, the town has remained peaceful and provincial. Its many parks and shady lanes make it a fitting gateway to the streams and woodlands of the Spessart Hills. Weekly fairs are held on the square, where fishers along the banks of the Main sell seafood straight from their buckets. Many traditional shops are in a pedestrian zone, with lamps, fountains, and flowers.

ESSENTIALS

GETTING THERE   By Train   The **Aschaffenburg Bahnhof** is on the major Nürnberg-Würzburg-Frankfurt line and on the regional Maintal Aschaffenburg–Mittenburg-Wertheim line, with frequent connections in all directions. From Frankfurt, 45 trains arrive daily (trip time: 30–45 min.). For information, call © **01805/996633.**

By Bus   There is no direct bus service between Frankfurt and Aschaffenburg.

By Car   Access by car is via the A3 Autobahn east and west.

VISITOR INFORMATION   Contact **Tourist-Information,** Schlossplatz 1 (© **06021/395800**). It's open April to September Monday to Friday 9am to 6pm and Saturday 9am to 1pm.

GETTING AROUND   Aschaffenburg and the immediate region around it are served by a network of green-painted buses whose junction point is the Hauptbahnhof, the city's main railway station. Because many of the streets within the city's historic core are reserved for pedestrians, many sightseers take bus no. 1, 4, 5, or 8 between the Hauptbahnhof and the Stadthalle (town hall), immediately adjacent to the Altstadt. Buses run daily 5:30am to 9pm. Rides within the central zone cost 1.40€ ($2.30) per person each way. An all-day ticket goes for 2.60€ ($4.20). For information, call the city tourist office (© **06021/395800**).

WHERE TO STAY

Hotel Dalberg   Built in 1994, this hotel occupies a prominent site that's within a 5-minute walk from Aschaffenburg's historic core and its pedestrian zone. Rising behind an all-white, four-story facade, it offers cozy, well-designed rooms, each with a tiled shower. On the premises you'll find a rustic-looking *Weinstube* (wine bar) serving regional cuisine and drinks from a bar.

Pfaffengasse 12–14, 63739 Aschaffenburg. © **06021/3560.** Fax 06021/219894. www.hotel-dalberg.de. 26 units. 95€–220€ ($152–$352) double. Rates include continental breakfast. AE, MC, V. Bus: 1 or 4. Parking 11€ ($18). **Amenities:** Restaurant; bar. *In room:* TV, minibar.

Hotel Post   This is the town's premier hotel, offering greater comfort than its rivals. Close to the heart of town and built in 1919, rooms are well maintained and decorated in traditional style. Some units come with a tub and shower, others only a shower. The dining room is a stylized version of an old posting inn; it includes an original mail coach, timbered walls and ceiling, and lead-glass windows. Reasonably priced Franconian meals are served here.

Goldbacherstrasse 19–21, 63739 Aschaffenburg. ⓒ **06021/3340.** Fax 06021/334144. www.post-ab.de. 69 units. 116€–150€ ($186–$240) double; 139€–173€ ($222–$277) junior suite. Rates include buffet breakfast. AE, DC, MC, V. Parking 4€ ($6.40). Bus: 1, 3, 4, 6, or 10. **Amenities:** Restaurant; room service; indoor heated swimming pool; sauna; solarium; babysitting; laundry service; nonsmoking rooms; rooms for those w/limited mobility. *In room:* A/C, TV, minibar, hair dryer.

WHERE TO DINE
Meals are also offered at the two hotels listed above.

Schlossweinstuben FRANCONIAN/BAVARIAN   One of the most alluring corners of this historic castle is its popular wine cellar. Here you'll find a wide variety of German wines to complement the conservative but well-prepared menu items. A meal may begin with liver-dumpling soup, and then follow with a game specialty (depending on the season). The selection of very fresh fish is likely to include trout and pike. There is no pretension to this cuisine—it's just hearty, rib-sticking fare.

Schloss Johannisburg. ⓒ **06021/12440.** Reservations recommended. Main courses 14€–36€ ($22–$58). No credit cards. Tues–Sun 11am–midnight. Bus: 1, 3, or 4.

EXPLORING ASCHAFFENBURG
The best park in Aschaffenburg is **Schönbusch Park,** Kleine Schönbuschallee 1 (ⓒ **06021/625478;** bus: 4), located 3km (2 miles) across the Main. It's a marvel of planning, using the natural surroundings as a setting for formal 18th-century gardens, shady lanes, temples, and gazebos. At the edge of the mirror-smooth lake is a small neoclassical castle, really a country house, once used by the electors of Mainz. The house is open April to September Tuesday to Sunday 9am to 6pm. Admission is 3€ ($4.80) for adults, 2€ ($3.20) for students, and free for children 14 and under. In summer, it's possible to rent a small boat to go on the lake. There's also a cafe/restaurant open daily 8am to 8pm.

The most impressive castle in Aschaffenburg is the huge Renaissance **Schloss Johannisburg** ⚑, Schlossplatz 4 (ⓒ **06021/386570;** bus: 1, 4, or 8), reflected in the waters of the Main. Erected from 1605 to 1614, it became the residence of the rulers of the town, the prince-electors of Mainz. The red-sandstone castle is almost perfectly symmetrical, with four massive lantern towers surrounding an inner courtyard. April to September, the castle is open Tuesday to Sunday 9am to 6pm; October to March, hours are Tuesday to Sunday 10am to 4pm. Admission is 4€ ($6.40) for adults and 3€ ($4.80) for children 14 and under. While here you can visit the Schlossweinstuben (see above). From the castle gardens you can reach the **Pompeianum,** built by Bavaria's King Ludwig I as a replica of the Castor and Pollux palace discovered among the ruins of Pompeii. The Pompeianum is open April to mid-October Tuesday to Sunday 9am to 6pm. Admission is 4€ ($6.40) for adults, 3€ ($4.80) for students, and free for children 14 and under. The combination ticket **Schloss Johannisburg and Pompeianum** is 6€ ($9.60) for adults, 5€ ($8) for children 14 and under.

Stiftskirche St. Peter and St. Alexander, Stiftsgasse 5 (ⓒ **06021/22420;** bus: 1, 4, or 10), has stood on its hill overlooking the town for 1,000 years. Its architecture has changed over the centuries, however, with remodeling and reconstruction, and today it stands as a combination of Romanesque, Gothic, and baroque. Its most precious treasure is the painted retable *The Lamentation of Christ,* by Mathias Grünewald. The interior is decorated with several paintings of the school of Lucas Cranach, as well as a marble-alabaster pulpit by Hans Juncker. One of the oldest pieces is a Roman-style crucifix from A.D. 980. Adjacent to the north side of the church is a Romanesque cloister from the 13th century. The church is open Wednesday to Monday 11am to 5pm. Admission is free, but a tour costs 2.50€ ($4) adults, 1.50€ ($2.40) students and children, and 5€ ($8) for a family ticket.

WIESBADEN ℛ
40km (25 miles) W of Frankfurt, 151km (94 miles) SE of Bonn

This sheltered valley, between the Rhine and the Taunus mountains, has held a spa since Roman times. Today, Wiesbaden competes with Baden-Baden for the title of Germany's most fashionable resort. Its success is based partly on its 26 hot springs, with temperatures of 117° to 150°F (47°–66°C), and partly on its proximity to Frankfurt's transportation centers, which gives the spa a distinctly international flavor.

Wiesbaden is also a major cultural center. Every spring it plays host to the International May Festival of music, dance, and drama. The major concert halls are in the **Kurhaus,** a lively, multiroomed structure centered on a cupola-crowned hall. In addition to concerts, the complex hosts plays and ballets, plus a variety of social gatherings, such as international conferences, congresses, exhibitions, and trade fairs. It also holds a casino, a lively restaurant, and an outdoor cafe.

For more active visitors, Wiesbaden offers horseback riding, a golf course, swimming, tennis, and hiking. The streets of the city are nice to stroll, as is the **Kurpark,** which has a lake surrounded by old shade trees. It's especially beautiful at night, when the water reflects the lights of the spa and the huge fountains are lit. The park stretches for about a kilometer (½ mile) northward along the Kuranlagen, ending in a fancy residential quarter, the Sonnenberg.

ESSENTIALS
GETTING THERE   By Train   Trains run between Frankfurt airport and Wiesbaden about every hour, leaving from the airport's lower level (trip time: 30 min.). Tickets can be purchased at machines in the station area or at the airport's railway ticket counter. There's also frequent service from the center of Frankfurt on S-Bahn S-1 and S-9 (trip time: 30–40 min.). For information, call © **01805/996633.**

By Car   Wiesbaden lies at a major crossroads, with access via the A3 Autobahn from the north and south, connecting with the A66 Autobahn from the west and east. Travel time by car from Frankfurt is about 20 to 30 minutes, depending on traffic. From the Frankfurt airport to Wiesbaden by car is about 20 minutes.

VISITOR INFORMATION   The **Verkehrsbüro,** Marktstrasse 6 (© **0611/ 1729780;** www.wiesbaden.de), is open daily 9am to 6pm.

GETTING AROUND   The Hauptbahnhof is the junction point for most of the city's bus lines. Buses are blue-sided, and charge, depending on the distance within the city limits you travel, 2.20€ to 4.20€ ($3.50–$6.70) for rides to most points in town. City buses operate Monday to Friday between 5am and midnight, at intervals of between 10 and 15 minutes, with less frequent service on Saturday and Sunday. Kirchgasse and Langgasse are two of the most prominent streets in the pedestrian zone, but the closest point to catch a bus to either of them is in front of the Stadttheater.

THERMAL BATHS   **Kaiser Friedrich's Therme,** Langgasse 38–40 (© **0611/ 1729660**), is big, modern, and well maintained. These baths are famous within Germany for their ability to soothe the aches and pains of arthritis, gout, indigestion, and other ailments induced by age and everyday stress. The saunas and thermally heated swimming pools are open daily from 10am to 10pm (until midnight Fri). Admission costs 3.50€ ($5.60) per hour in summer, going up to 5€ ($8) per hour in winter. Remember that the venue here involves at least partial nudity (in the saunas, perhaps with a towel, although in the pools, it's usual to wear a bathing suit) for both men and women, who mingle freely within the facilities. Tuesday, however, is reserved only for women. The thermal baths sit within a centrally positioned park whose landscaping includes hundreds of seasonal flowers.

WHERE TO STAY
Very Expensive
Hotel Nassauer Hof 𝕶𝕶𝕶   The superluxurious Nassauer Hof is among the most appealing hotels in town. Often referred to as the "grande dame" of Wiesbaden, its spacious rooms have up-to-date conveniences like soundproof windows, elegant furnishings, and comfortable appointments. Bathrooms contain tub/showers, deluxe beauty products, and robes. The hotel stands in the city center, within walking distance of the Kurhaus, Spielbank, theaters, and shopping area.

Kaiser-Friedrich-Platz 3–4, 65183 Wiesbaden. ⓒ 800/223-6800 in the U.S., or 0611/1330. Fax 0611/133632. www.nassauer-hof.de. 169 units. 238€–348€ ($381–$557) double; from 460€ ($736) suite. AE, DC, MC, V. Parking 18€ ($29). Bus: 5, 18, or 25. **Amenities:** 2 restaurants; bar; indoor heated pool; fitness center; spa; sauna; solarium; room service; babysitting; laundry service; nonsmoking rooms; rooms for those w/limited mobility. *In room:* A/C, TV, Wi-Fi, minibar, hair dryer.

Expensive
Hotel Klee am Park 𝕶𝕶 *(Value)*   We highly recommend this hotel to those who find the older, more luxurious Nassauer Hof a bit too monumental. Klee am Park is a square, modern hotel in a tranquil setting, surrounded by its own informal gardens. The theater, casino, and shopping area are nearby. Rooms have French doors opening onto balconies; some have sitting areas large enough for entertaining. Bathrooms are midsize and contain tubs and showers.

Parkstrasse 4, 65189 Wiesbaden. ⓒ **0611/90010.** Fax 0611/9001310. www.klee-am-park.de. 60 units. 148€–188€ ($237–$301) double. AE, DC, MC, V. Free parking. Bus: 8. **Amenities:** Cafe/restaurant; bar; terrace; room service; laundry service; dry cleaning; nonsmoking rooms; rooms for those w/limited mobility. *In room:* TV, minibar, hair dryer.

Moderate
Admiral Hotel *(Value)*   The centrally located Admiral is a favorite of traditionalists and one of Wiesbaden's best values. Readers consistently praise the owners (a retired U.S. Army officer and his German-born wife) for their hospitality. Rooms are furnished in a charmingly old-fashioned way, often with brass beds. Bathrooms are small yet clean and contain showers. The hotel offers health food.

Geisbergstrasse 8, 65193 Wiesbaden (a 5-min. walk from the Kurhaus). ⓒ **0611/58660.** Fax 0611/521053. www.admiral-hotel.de. 28 units. 79€–139€ ($126–$222) double; 98€–149€ ($157–$238) triple. Rates include buffet breakfast. AE, DC, MC, V. Parking 14€ ($22). Bus: 1 or 8. **Amenities:** Breakfast room; laundry service; dry cleaning; nonsmoking rooms. *In room:* TV, hair dryer.

Hotel Klemm   This hotel occupies a late-19th-century Jugendstil villa with solid stone walls. Although the setting is well scrubbed and respectable, it has touches of genteel shabbiness that seem to go well with the nostalgia that permeates this part of Wiesbaden. This place enjoys many repeat visitors. Rooms are simple but comfortable and well kept, with shower-only bathrooms. They serve breakfast only.

Kapellenstrasse 9, 65193 Wiesbaden (near the Kurhaus). ⓒ **0611/5820.** Fax 0611/582222. www.hotel-klemm.de. 60 units. 110€–180€ ($176–$288) double. AE, DC, MC, V. Bus: 1, 2, or 8. *In room:* TV, minibar, hair dryer.

pentahotel Wiesbaden ⚘ Lots of businesspeople stay here instead of staying in Frankfurt, as it's only 20 minutes from the Frankfurt airport. Because of its location outside of the center, the hotel is more suited for motorists who don't want to face the traffic of Wiesbaden. Think of it as a good roadside motel, one that is almost equally convenient for visiting Wiesbaden or Frankfurt. Rooms are modern and comfortably furnished. If you want the old spa ambience of Wiesbaden, then opt for Klee am Park or Hotel Nassauer Hof.

Abraham-Lincoln-Strasse 17, 65189 Wiesbaden. ⓒ **0611/7970.** Fax 0611/797731. www.pentahotels.com. 205 units. 120€ ($192) double; 250€ ($400) suite. AE, DC, MC, V. Parking 14€ ($22). Bus: 5 or 28. **Amenities:** Restaurant; bar; room service; babysitting; laundry service; dry cleaning; nonsmoking rooms. *In room:* A/C, TV, Wi-Fi, minibar, hair dryer.

Inexpensive

Hotel am Landeschaus This hotel in central Wiesbaden is one of the spa's best reasonably priced hotels. It's completely modern, but also warm, cozy, and inviting. Rooms are well kept, with small, shower-only bathrooms. Guests can enjoy drinks in a rustic ale tavern on-site.

Mortitzstrasse 51, 65185 Wiesbaden (within walking distance of the railroad station). ⓒ **0611/996660.** Fax 0611/996666. 15 units. 81€–115€ ($130–$184) double. Rates include buffet breakfast. MC, V. Parking 7€ ($11). Closed Dec 22–Jan 5. Bus: 10, 14, or 16. **Amenities:** Tavern; nonsmoking rooms. *In room:* No phone.

WHERE TO DINE

Ente Restaurant ⚘⚘⚘ CONTINENTAL/MEDITERRANEAN This restaurant serves the best food in town, and the innovative chef makes sure that meals are as pleasing to the eye as they are to the palate. The light, modern cuisine features weekly changing specialties; typical offerings include crispy duck from the oven with savoy cabbage and rhubarb sauce. Roast duck liver is served with a mango-and-pistachio pesto. Another good dish is an asparagus ragout with morels and a vanilla froth. Desserts, especially the lemon soufflé with strawberries and the mountain-honey ice cream, are reason enough to visit. Ente also has one of the best wine lists in Europe, including many moderately priced bottles. A boutique, delicatessen, wine cellar, and bistro are attached.

In the Hotel Nassauer Hof, Kaiser-Friedrich-Platz 3–4. ⓒ **0611/133666.** Reservations required. Main courses 32€–37€ ($51–$59); fixed-price dinners 75€–115€ ($120–$184). AE, DC, MC, V. Mon–Sat noon–2:30pm and 6–10:30pm. Bus: 5, 18, or 25.

Käfer's INTERNATIONAL Käfer's directs two restaurants within one at the stately and prestigious Kurhaus. The more appealing of the two is Käfer's Bistro, a replica of the kind of bustling, upscale, well-run bistro you may find in Lyon or Paris. In an adjoining room is the airier, quieter, and more self-consciously formal Casino Restaurant. The menu and prices are the same as in the bistro, but the atmosphere is calmer and, frankly, a bit more stuffy. Men are required to wear a jacket and tie. Menu items change every 4 weeks. Examples may include smoked salmon served with a rösti pancake, crème fraîche, and chives; Canadian lobster with yogurt-flavored cocktail sauce and lemon; penne pasta with pesto sauce and grilled giant prawns; vegetarian dishes; and in springtime, asparagus with filet mignon, bacon, or salmon steak. Dessert may be a mousse, flavored with three kinds of chocolate.

In the Kurhaus, Kurhausplatz 1. ⓒ **0611/536200.** Reservations recommended. Main courses 16€–28€ ($26–$45). AE, MC, V. Daily 11:30am–1am. Bus: 1, 2, or 8.

Restaurant M. AUSTRIAN/INTERNATIONAL Set on the street level of the Hotel de France, a stately-looking structure built in 1880, this is a well-managed, stylish, and upscale brasserie that attracts goodly numbers of actors, politicians, and in-the-know yuppies who appreciate good food and—by the animated dialogues popping up around the main dining room—conversation. Within a champagne-colored decor that includes memorabilia from upscale cigar companies, movie stills from the '30s and '40s, African hunting trophies, and, among others, large photos of the Manhattan skyline, you can enjoy mostly Austrian food with international touches, all of it prepared by the "M" within the restaurant's name, Markus Seegert. Menu items include arugula salads with apple relish and grilled strips of perch; tomato soup flavored with fresh basil; grilled shrimp with garlic and a dash of balsamic vinegar; well-seasoned lentils ringed with slices of Sardinian goat cheese; scallops of veal on a bed of lettuce accompanied with cherry tomato and pine nut risotto; and grilled Pacific tuna with Thai-style mango chili and buttermilk-and-herb risotto. The hotel that contains this restaurant, incidentally, is a four-star, well-scrubbed place with 37 rooms and doubles priced from 132€ to 282€ ($211–$451). Each room has a TV, telephone, minibar, and a safe, and contemporary decor with touches of soft red and wood paneling.

In the Hotel de France, Taunusstrasse 49. (€) **0611/204-8765**. Reservations recommended. Main courses 18€–28€ ($29–$45). AE, DC, MC, V. Mon–Sat noon–2pm and 6:30–10:30pm. Bus: 1.

WIESBADEN AFTER DARK

"Rien ne va plus" is the call when the ball starts to roll on the gaming tables at the **Spielbank Wiesbaden,** Im Kurhaus, Kurhausplatz 1 (€) **0611/536100;** bus: 1, 8, or 16). The casino is open daily 3pm to 3am and admission is 2.50€ ($4). Roulette, blackjack, and poker are featured. It's located at the end of Wilhelmstrasse, one of the most famous streets in Wiesbaden. To enter, you must present a passport or an identification card. You must be 18 to enter and gamble, and men must wear jackets and ties.

Music and **theater** flourish in Wiesbaden throughout the year. For information on performances during your visit, check the Wiesbaden tourist office (see "Visitor Information," above). For information about any of the conference and cultural facilities in the **Kurhaus** compound, including the casino and theater, call (€) **0611/17290.**

Hessisches Staatstheater, Christian-Zais-Strasse (€) **0611/1321;** bus: 1), built in 1894 by Emperor Wilhelm II, is one of the most beautiful theaters in Germany. From September 15 to June 30 it presents a program of operettas, musicals, ballets, and plays. Tickets are 6€ to 49€ ($9.60–$78).

An important event is the **International May Festival.** The festival features concerts, classical in-house drama productions, and a wide selection of guest performances by internationally renowned theater companies. For information and tickets, call (€) **0611/1321.**

Park Café, Wilhelmstrasse 36 (€) **0611/3413246;** bus: 1), incorporates a cafe, brasserie, and a nightclub. It's sprawling and often very busy. The cover ranges from 8€ to 12€ ($13–$19), and it's open daily 9pm to 4am.

BAD HOMBURG ⚓

16km (10 miles) N of Frankfurt, 45km (28 miles) NE of Wiesbaden

Bad Homburg is one of Germany's most attractive spas, still basking in the grandeur left over from turn-of-the-20th-century Europe. The spa's saline springs are used to treat various disorders, especially heart and circulatory diseases. The town has been a popular watering spot since Roman times. Royalty from all over the world have visited. King

Chulalongkorn of Siam (Thailand) was so impressed that he built a Buddhist temple in the Kurpark. Czar Nicholas I erected an onion-domed Russian chapel nearby. The name of the town was popularized by England's Edward VII when, as Prince of Wales, he visited the spa and introduced a new hat style, which he called the "homburg." The town became the gaming capital of Europe when the Blanc brothers opened the casino in 1841.

The **Spa Park** is a verdant, carefully landscaped oasis in the middle of an otherwise rather commercial-looking town. The actual spa facilities are in the **Kaiser Wilhelms Bad im Kurpark** (© **06172/178178**). They're open daily 9am to 11pm. Tuesdays are reserved for women only. Entrance to the facilities is 40€ ($64) per person for 4 hours, 60€ ($96) for a full-day admission. Patrons have access to a wide range of facilities, including thermally heated pools, saunas, steam baths, and herb-enriched hot-water baths. Massage facilities and special mud baths require additional fees. The immaculately tended gardens in the surrounding Kurpark are filled with brooks, ponds, arbors, and seasonal flowers. The town center has a sprawling pedestrian-only district with many shops, restaurants, and cafes.

ESSENTIALS

GETTING THERE By Train Visitors from Frankfurt usually opt to take the S-5 train, which runs from Frankfurt's main railway station to Bad Homburg for a cost of 6€ ($9.60) each way. The trip takes about 20 minutes. Call © **01805/996633** for information.

By Car Access by car from the north or south is via the A5 Autobahn, exiting at Bad Homburg.

VISITOR INFORMATION For information, go to the **Verkehrsamt im Kurhaus,** Louisenstrasse 58 (© **06172/178110;** www.bad-homburg.de). It's open Monday to Friday 8:30am to 6:30pm and Saturday 10am to 2pm.

GETTING AROUND Public transport in Bad Homburg is provided by a network of green-and-white buses, with main junction points that are the Hauptbahnhof, a 10-minute walk southwest of the city center, and in front of the Kurhaus, in the city center. Buses, which run daily 4:30am to midnight, charge 2€ ($3.20) per ride.

WHERE TO STAY
Expensive
Maritim Kurhaus-Hotel   As sleek and up-to-date as this hotel near the spa facilities is, the Steigenberger Bad Homburg far outclasses it. Double rooms feature king-size beds; singles have queen-size beds. All rooms are plush. Some rooms have balconies or terraces, permitting wide-angle views over the greenery of the surrounding park; many have tall bay windows.

Kurpark, Ludwigstrasse, 61348 Bad Homburg. © 06172/6600. Fax 06172/660100. www.maritim.de. 158 units. 84€–245€ ($134–$392) double; 155€–265€ ($248–$424) suite. AE, DC, MC, V. Parking 16€ ($26). Bus: 1, 2, 3, 4, 11, or 12. **Amenities:** Restaurant; bar; indoor heated pool; sauna; solarium; room service; babysitting; laundry service; dry cleaning; nonsmoking rooms. *In room:* TV, dataport, minibar, hair dryer, safe.

Steigenberger Bad Homburg   This is the resort's best and most prestigious hotel. Europe's high society used to stroll here in days of yore, and an ambience of luxury still prevails. Rooms are beautifully furnished, each with individually adjustable air-conditioning and extra-long beds. The spacious bathrooms contain deluxe luxury items, sumptuous robes, and combination tub/showers. All rooms are soundproof.

Kaiser-Friedrich-Promenade 69–75 (opposite the spa gardens and casino), 61348 Bad Homburg. © **800/223-5652** in the U.S. and Canada, or 06172/1810. Fax 06172/181630. www.bad-homburg.steigenberger.com. 169 units. 155€–260€ ($248–$416) double; from 284€ ($454) suite. AE, DC, MC, V. Parking 18€ ($29). Bus: 1, 2, 3, 4, 11, or 12. **Amenities:** Restaurant; bistro; bar; fitness room; sauna; solarium; steam bath; business center; room service; babysitting; laundry service; dry cleaning; nonsmoking rooms. *In room:* A/C, TV, Wi-Fi, minibar, hair dryer, safe.

Moderate
Parkhotel Bad Homburg *Value*   This is your best bet for a moderately priced spa vacation. This hotel has an enviable location in the middle of the Kurpark's well-maintained gardens, near the thermal springs. Although its design is modern and angular, its edges are softened with window boxes. Rooms are conservatively furnished. Bathrooms are well kept and contain a combination tub/shower. On the premises are a bar and a sunroom. One of the hotel's restaurants serves a savory Italian cuisine, the other offering excellent Asian fare.

Kaiser-Friedrich-Promenade 53–55, Am Kurpark, 61348 Bad Homburg. © **06172/8010.** Fax 06172/801400. www.parkhotel-bad-homburg.de. 124 units. 152€–218€ ($243–$349) double; 162€–228€ ($259–$365) suite. Rates include buffet breakfast. AE, DC, MC, V. Parking 10€ ($16). Tram: 5. **Amenities:** 2 restaurants; bar; fitness room; Jacuzzi; sauna; solarium; bicycle rental; room service; babysitting; laundry service; dry cleaning; nonsmoking rooms; rooms for those w/limited mobility. *In room:* TV, minibar, safe.

Inexpensive
Das Hardtwald Hotel *⚓*   This hotel, resembling a chalet set in a forest, is an ideal retreat near the spa gardens. In spring, flowers overflow from its window boxes. The comfortably furnished rooms overlook the forest and come with a compact tiled bathroom with tub and shower or only shower. The chef in the excellent, flower-filled dining room uses only the freshest ingredients to prepare his well-known international and German dishes. In summer, tables are set on the large patio. Next to the hotel is a stable where you can rent horses.

Philosophenweg 31 (a 20-min. walk from the center of town), 61350 Bad Homburg. © **06172/9880.** Fax 06172/82512. www.hardtwald-hotel.de. 43 units. 105€–150€ ($168–$240) double. Rates include buffet breakfast. AE, DC, MC, V. Bus: 3. **Amenities:** 2 restaurants; bar; room service; laundry service; dry cleaning; nonsmoking rooms. *In room:* TV, minibar, hair dryer, safe.

Haus Daheim *Value*   This light-blue corner building is one of the finest small hotels in town, with a loyal following of repeat business. The comfortable rooms have firm beds, plus tiled bathrooms with shower. Admittedly a modest choice compared to the hotels reviewed above, but for value, it's hard to beat. All rooms are soundproof.

Elisabethenstrasse 42 (a short walk from the Kurhaus), 61348 Bad Homburg. © **06172/677350.** Fax 06172/67735000. 19 units. 99€–165€ ($158–$264) double. Rates include buffet breakfast. AE, DC, MC, V. Parking 12€ ($19). Tram: 5. **Amenities:** Breakfast room; nonsmoking rooms. *In room:* TV, minibar, hair dryer, safe.

WHERE TO DINE
Casino-Restaurant FRENCH/GERMAN   Until a few years ago, this was the only restaurant in Germany that directly adjoined the gaming tables of a casino. And while not in the same class as Sängers, it's also one of the finest restaurants in town. The dining room is decorated in a formal, vaguely English style. It offers attentive service and a winning combination of light French and German cuisine. Head chef Herr Finkenwirth begins each workday searching for fresh, seasonal ingredients at the local markets. Lobster is a popular choice. Although the main kitchen service stops at 10:30pm; there's a reduced menu until 12:30am.

Im Kurpark. © **06172/170170.** Reservations required. Jacket and tie required for men. Main courses 15€–20€ ($24–$32); fixed-price menus 29€–36€ ($46–$58). AE, DC, V. Daily 6pm–12:30am. Tram: 5.

Sängers Restaurant 🏵🏵🏵 FRENCH   Local food lovers and spa devotees crowd this restaurant to enjoy the highly personal and inventive cuisine, the best in the spa. The two elegant dining rooms are outfitted in the style of 18th-century England. Menu items may include carpaccio of turbot with Iranian caviar, gooseliver terrine served with brioche and gelatin of wild berries, a foam-capped celery soup with quail eggs, roast breast of duck on a bed of rhubarb, and a succulent array of desserts.

Kaiser-Friedrich-Promenade 85 (near the Steigenberger Bad Homburg). (*C*) **06172/928839**. Reservations required. Main courses 26€–33€ ($42–$53); 4-course set menu 73€ ($117); 6-course set menu 98€ ($157). AE, MC, V. Mon–Sat noon–2pm and 7–11pm. Closed 2 weeks in July. Bus: 1, 4, 11, or 12.

EXPLORING BAD HOMBURG

Bad Homburg Palace   This palace was the residence of the landgraves of Hesse-Homburg from its construction in 1680 until the mid–19th century. Its builder, Prince Frederick II von Homburg, preserved the White Tower from the medieval castle that stood on the site. In the late 19th century, the palace became a summer residence for Prussian kings and, later, German emperors. After World War I, the state assumed ownership. The interior contains 18th-century furniture and paintings, including a bust of Prince Frederick II by Andreas Schlüter, Germany's greatest baroque sculptor. The former "telephone room of the empress" features *Cleopatra* by Pellegrini.

Schlossverwaltung (a few blocks from the spa gardens). (*C*) **06172/9262148**. Admission 4€ ($6.40) adults, 2.50€ ($4) children. Tues–Sun 10am–4pm. Bus: 1, 4, or 11.

Taunus Therme   A large recreation area, Taunus Therme boasts several pools, a sauna, a solarium, and a health center, plus TVs, cinemas, and two restaurants.

Seedammweg. (*C*) **06172/40640**. Admission Mon–Fri 13€ ($21) for 2 hr., 17€ ($27) for 4 hr., 24€ ($38) for all day; Sat–Sun and holidays 15€ ($24) for 2 hr., 26€ ($42) for all day; free for children 3 and under. Sun–Tues 9am–11pm; Wed–Sat 9am–midnight. Bus: 6.

BAD HOMBURG AFTER DARK

Spielbank Im Kurpark ((*C*) **06172/17010**; tram: 5), called the "Mother of Monte Carlo," is the spa's major attraction. This casino opened way back in 1841 and helped make Bad Homburg famous. Roulette, blackjack, and baccarat are the games here. Passports are required for entrance (you must be 18 to enter and gamble), and men must wear jackets and ties. Admission is 2.50€ ($4); hours are daily 2:30pm to 3am.

The town's favorite beer hall and *Weinstube* is **Zum Wasserweibehen,** Am Mühlberg 57 ((*C*) **06172/29878**; bus: 1, 4, or 11). About 1.5km (1 mile) east of the town center, you'll find another folkloric place, **Zum Ruppe Karl,** Hamburgerstrasse 6 ((*C*) **06172/42484**; bus: 2 or 12), whose home-style cuisine is enhanced by the establishment's homemade apple wine. The **Kurhaus** also contains a handful of bars, cafes, and shops that usually stay open late.

BAD NAUHEIM 🏵

35km (22 miles) N of Frankfurt, 64km (40 miles) NE of Wiesbaden

Like many spas throughout Germany, Bad Nauheim's popularity increased in the early part of the 20th century, when the railroad became a convenient and inexpensive means of transportation. Still going strong today, this resort at the northern edge of the Taunus Mountains is a center for golf, tennis, and ice skating, as well as the starting point for hiking up the 236m (774-ft.) **Joannisberg,** which towers over the town.

The warm carbonic-acid springs of the spa are used to treat heart and circulatory disorders and rheumatic diseases. The **Kurpark** is attractive, well maintained, and

---

Fun Fact **Elvis in Bad Nauheim**

Many famous guests have visited this spa, including Otto von Bismarck (1859) and Richard Strauss (1927). Franklin D. Roosevelt spent about 2 years here with his family when he was a small child. Locals believe that Bad Nauheim was spared destruction during World War II, even though a Nazi radio transmitter was installed here, because President Roosevelt had fond memories of the place.

Real fame came to the spa when a private named Elvis Presley arrived and found a home off base, right next to the Kurhaus. The singer was stationed in nearby Friedberg/Hessen at Ray Barracks Kaserne from October 1958 to March 1960, and his presence had an electrifying effect on the German youth scene. It was here that Elvis fell in love with Priscilla. She was 14 at the time, and when she first arrived at the plain, old-fashioned villa where he lived, the street was full of German girls, waiting by the sign AUTOGRAPHS BETWEEN 7 AND 8PM ONLY. After that first meeting, she saw him once more, and when he returned to the States, he vowed to send for her.

Elvis wasn't the only famous American to visit. Newspaper magnate William Randolph Hearst was in the habit of coming here every year with his mistress, Marion Davies, and a dozen or so of her women friends—Hearst would have the women chauffeured around the countryside in style. He firmly believed Bad Nauheim's physicians were the answer to his minor heart problem. Here he had his notorious meeting with Mussolini in 1931 ("a marvelous man"), and from here he flew to Berlin to meet Hitler in 1934. He claimed that he had done "much good" in advising Hitler to drop his persecution of the Jews, but afterward he spent most of his life trying to live down his image as a supporter of the Nazi cause.

---

filled with promenaders all summer long. The impressive **bathhouse** is the single largest complex of Jugendstil architecture in Germany. The **Sprudelhof (fountain court),** at the center, stretches from the Hauptbahnhof to the Kurpark and all the way to the Kurhaus. All the important sights, including the bathhouse complex, can be visited in half a day. The resort has a busy activity calendar, with concerts twice daily, along with operas, plays, dances, and fashion shows.

ESSENTIALS

GETTING THERE **By Train** Bad Nauheim can easily be reached from Frankfurt. Trains arrive at least once per hour (every 30 min. during rush hours) during the day (trip time: 30 min.). Service is on the Weatherman line between Frankfurt and Giessen. For information, call ✆ **01805/996633.**

By Car Access is via the A5 Autobahn from the north and the south. Driving time from Frankfurt is about half an hour.

VISITOR INFORMATION For information, go to the **Verkehrsverein,** Neue Kurolonnade (✆ **06032/929920;** www.bad-nauheim.de). It's open Monday to Friday 10am to noon and 2 to 6pm, Saturday noon to 4pm, and Sunday 11am to 4pm.

WHERE TO STAY

Best Western Hotel Rosenau   This is one of the better choices at the resort. The Rosenau is an updated version of a German manor house, with white walls and a red-tiled hip roof. Inside, the decor is one of light-toned wood and pastel colors. Rooms are modern and attractive, with combination tub/shower. All rooms are soundproof.

Steinfurther Strasse 1 (west of Grosser Teich, the town lake), 61231 Bad Nauheim. ℭ **800/780-7237** in the U.S. and Canada, or 06032/96460. Fax 06032/9646666. www.bestwestern.com. 54 units. 125€ ($200) double Mon–Thurs; 90€ ($144) double Fri–Sun. Rates include continental breakfast. AE, DC, MC, V. Free parking. Closed Dec 27–Jan 8. **Amenities:** 2 restaurants; bar; fitness room; sauna; solarium; bicycle rental; car rental; room service; babysitting; laundry service; dry cleaning; nonsmoking rooms. *In room:* A/C, TV, minibar, hair dryer, iron, trouser press.

Dolce Bad Nauheim ⭐⭐   This hotel is the finest in town, with better amenities than the Rosenau. It's in the middle of the park that rings the resort's thermal springs. Its public areas are filled with green plants and arching windows. Rooms, with big sliding glass windows and balconies, provide calm, quiet, and conservative comfort. Bathrooms are luxurious and contain deluxe luxury items and combination tub/showers. Special diets and vegetarian menus are available.

Elvis-Presley-Platz 1, 61231 Bad Nauheim. ℭ **06032/30-30.** Fax 06032/303419. www.amkurpark.dolce.com. 159 units. 109€–244€ ($174–$390) double; 279€–299€ ($446–$478) suite. Rates include continental breakfast. AE, DC, MC, V. **Amenities:** 2 restaurants; cafe; bar; English pub; indoor heated pool; fitness room; spa; sauna; solarium; walking trail; biking trail; business center; room service; massage; babysitting; laundry service; dry cleaning; all nonsmoking rooms; rooms for those w/limited mobility. *In room:* TV, Wi-Fi, minibar, hair dryer, safe.

WHERE TO DINE

Rosengarten INTERNATIONAL   This restaurant is known as one of the best in town, and while the cooking is not innovative, we are impressed with its honesty and freshness. The flavorful dishes may include cream of tomato and young-vegetable soup, roast breast of young hen, and filet of salmon with fresh herbs, plus several different pork and game dishes, depending on the season. There are no pretensions here.

In the Hotel Rosenau, Steinfurther Strasse 1. ℭ **06032/96460.** Main courses 10€–22€ ($16–$35). AE, MC, V. Tues–Sun noon–2pm and 6–10pm. Closed Dec 27–Jan 30.

15

The Rhineland

Few rivers can claim such an important role in the growth of a nation as the Rhine. The Rhine rises in Switzerland and ultimately flows through the Netherlands in its progress to the sea, but most of its 1,370km (850 miles) snake through the mountains and plains of Germany. For more than 2,000 years, it has been a chief trade route, its deep waters enabling modern seagoing vessels to travel downstream from the North Sea as far as Cologne.

From its earliest times, the Rhine has also been a main road for religious, intellectual, and artistic ideas. It has been called a "triumphal avenue of the muses," and a trip along its banks today reveals endless treasures.

From Mainz north to Koblenz, the winding river cuts through steep vine-covered hillsides dotted with towns whose names are synonymous with fine German wine. Here you'll find the dramatic Lorelei, the legendary rock from which a siren lured men to their doom. The saga of *The Nibelungenlied*, the best known of the Rhine legends, is associated with the topography from the Siebenge-birge (the Seven Mountains) near Bonn, where Siegfried slew the dragon, to the city of Worms, where Brunhild plotted against the dragon-slayer.

The Rhine is also the home of many of Germany's largest and most modern cities. **Cologne (Köln)** and **Düsseldorf** vie for trade and tourism. Cologne is also a common starting point for boat tours of the river.

Roadways along the Rhine tend to be heavily trafficked, so allow adequate time. Main roads hug both the left and right banks of the river, and at many points you'll come across car-ferries that can take you across. The most scenic stretch for driving is the mid-Rhine, between Koblenz and Mainz. EuroCity and Inter-City trains connect all the major cities, including Cologne, Düsseldorf, Bonn, and Mainz. Rail service also extends as far north as Hamburg and as far south as Munich.

1 Speyer ★

93km (58 miles) S of Mainz, 21km (13 miles) SW of Heidelberg

One of the oldest Rhine cities, Speyer celebrated its 2,000th jubilee in 1990. It became a significant religious center early on when the Diet of Speyer, in 1529, united the followers of Luther in a protest against the Church of Rome.

ESSENTIALS
GETTING THERE By Train Trains reach Speyer only by connections at Mannheim. The trip from Frankfurt takes 1 to 1½ hours; from Munich, 3½ to 4 hours. Call ℂ **01805/996633** for schedules (11861 in Germany; www.bahn.de).

Watch on the Rhine

The Rhine carries more freight than any other river in Europe, and its once famous salmon were caught at the rate of 250,000 annually. But by the 1950s the river had simply become too poisonous for the fish to survive. By the 1970s and 1980s, the fabled Rhine was called "the sewer of Europe." That has now changed and the salmon are back. Billions of euros spent on water-treatment plants led to a cleaner river. However, the salmon you see today heroically leaping about aren't the same salmon of yore. The new salmon were brought in from Ireland, France, Scotland, and Scandinavia. Therefore, we must rely on old cookbooks to tell us of the glorious taste of the salmon Rhinelanders once enjoyed. One species of small crab is not as welcome. This alien amphipod that came from the Danube is now spreading to all the major rivers of Germany, including the Rhine, devouring native species at a rapid rate, and reducing biodiversity.

By Bus   About one bus per hour arrives from Heidelberg. Regional service is provided by **BRN Busverkehr Rhein-Neckar GmbH** at Ludwigshafen (© **0621/12003;** www.brn.de).

By Car   You can drive from Frankfurt in about an hour, from Munich in about 4 hours. Access is by the A61 Autobahn east and west connecting with Route 9 south.

VISITOR INFORMATION   For information, go to the **Verkehrsamt,** Maximilianstrasse 13 (© **06232/142392;** www.speyer.de). It's open November 1 to March 31 Monday to Friday 9am to 5pm, and Saturday 10am to noon; and April to October Monday to Friday 9am to 5pm, Saturday 10am to 3pm, and Sunday 10am to 2pm.

GETTING AROUND   A blue-and-white City Shuttle bus runs from the Speyer Hauptbahnhof through the town to Festplatz near the cathedral, east of the Altstadt. It connects most major hotels and restaurants. The bus comes every 10 minutes, and the service runs daily 7am to 7pm. The trip costs 1€ ($1.60).

WHERE TO STAY

Goldener Engel   This centrally located inn lies near the Gothic town gate at Maximilianstrasse, adjoining one of Speyer's finest restaurants, Zum Alten Engel (see below), and is the most atmospheric choice in town. Imbued with lots of character in the spirit of old Rhinelander hotels, the Goldener Engel comes complete with many traditional touches and antiques such as baroque free-standing clothes closets. In contrast, the midsize bedrooms are completely modern and up-to-date, with well-maintained private bathrooms with showers and tubs.

Mühlturmstrasse 5–7, 67346 Speyer. © 06232/13260. Fax 06232/132695. www.goldener-engel-speyer.de. 46 units. 92€–110€ ($147–$176) double. Rates include buffet breakfast. AE, DC, MC, V. **Amenities:** Breakfast room; bikes available for guests. *In room:* A/C, TV.

Rhein-Hotel Luxhof   This hotel is imbued with an unusual character. It's modern in style, but somehow retains the spirit of a rambling country inn. The blandly decorated rooms are well designed and compact, often featuring small sitting areas that open onto tiny balconies. All come equipped with bathrooms containing tub/shower combos.

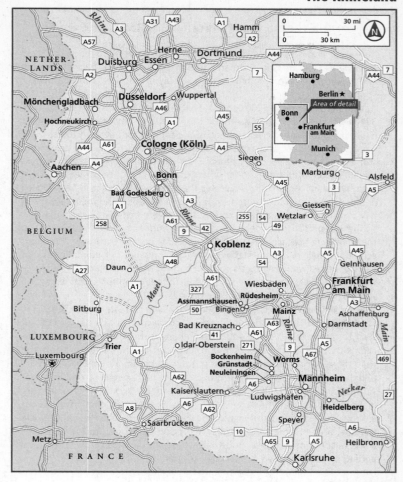

At the Rhine Bridge, just outside the town, 68766 Hockenheim. © **06205/3030.** Fax 06205/30325. www.luxhof.de. 45 units. 99€–118€ ($158–$189) double. Rates include buffet breakfast. AE, DC, MC, V. Free parking. **Amenities:** Restaurant; lounge; beer garden; health club; sauna; solarium; laundry service; nonsmoking rooms; 1 room for those w/limited mobility. *In room:* TV, Wi-Fi, minibar (in some), safe (in some).

WHERE TO DINE

Backmulde *(★ (Finds* FRENCH/SEAFOOD Backmulde is owned by Gunter Schmidt, who serves not only seafood and French cuisine, but a few modernized Rhineland-Palatinate recipes. You can savor such unusual delicacies as gratinéed oysters in champagne sabayon, quail stuffed with well-seasoned sweetbreads, or a meltingly tender roast lamb with freshly picked spinach.

Karmeliterstrasse 11–13. © **06232/71577.** Reservations required. Main courses 24€–30€ ($38–$48); fixed-price menus 32€–68€ ($51–$109). AE, DC, MC, V. Tues–Sat 11:30am–2:30pm and 7–11:30pm. Closed 3 weeks late Aug to mid-Sept.

(Moments   Cruising the Mythically Rich Rivers of Germany

Increasing numbers of travelers are opting for views of some of the most legendary panoramas in Germany directly from the deck chairs of yachts and cruise ships. We recommend two deeply entrenched competitors for your dollars.

Viking River Cruises, 5700 Canoga Ave., Woodland Hills, CA 91367 (© 800/ 304-9616; www.vikingrivers.com), is the world's largest river cruise line. It maintains a total of 14 river cruisers, each designed for between 100 and 230 passengers. Efficient and, in some cases, infused with touches of luxury, the cruises traverse the muddy waters of the Rhine between Amsterdam and Basel (Switzerland), traveling for between 5 and 12 nights. For views of Germany's eastern regions, cruises along the Elbe usually begin in Magdeburg and end in Decin, on the border of the Czech Republic, and focus heavily on day trips through the majestic core of such revered cities as Dresden.

The per-person rate, depending on the onboard accommodations and the season, ranges from $212 to $342 per day double occupancy. Onboard attendants deliver commentaries in several languages (including English) of the sights and monuments en route. Food is served at tables for between four and eight diners, cruise-ship style. All meals, onboard lodgings, and shore excursions are included in the price.

Peter Deilman Cruises, 1800 Diagonal Rd., Suite 170, Alexandria, VA 22314 (© 800/348-8287; www.deilmann-cruises.com), maintains a higher ratio of staff to guests than Viking, and the company is noted for ships with staterooms that are a bit more posh and luxurious, and a bit more expensive, than those of competitors. Per-person rates, per diem, range between $295 and $650, double occupancy. Rhine cruises usually begin or end in either Amsterdam or Mainz, last for between 9 and 17 days, and in some cases meander up part of the Mosel Valley as well. Deilman also offers cruises along such history-filled rivers as the Po, the Saône, the Rhône, and the Danube, and in some cases, offers the option of back-to-back cruises that traverse some of Europe's industrial canals, beginning in Amsterdam and ending on the Black Sea about 3 weeks later.

Kutscherhaus 🍴 GERMAN/RHINELANDER   You're transported back to old Germany at this beer garden, once a depot for *Kutschen* (stagecoaches) in the 1890s. Its gabled, half-timbered architecture is an inviting oasis, with climbing vines and plenty of summer flowers. The food is regional, hearty, and filling, and served in generous portions. Begin with appetizers such as a smoked salmon or cream soup with garden vegetables. Main courses feature fresh ingredients and are well prepared, including *loup de mer* (sea bass) or filet of halibut, perfectly grilled rump steak, or a delicious plate of herring with a creamy sauce.

The inn has three attractive, modern bedrooms, costing 75€ to 115€ ($120–$184) for a double. Each room comes with private bathroom, TV, and minibar, and rates include breakfast.

Am Fischmarkt 5A, 67346 Speyer. ℭ **06232/70592.** Main courses 13€–17€ ($21–$27); fixed price menus 19€–40€ ($30–$64). AE, DC, MC, V. Fri–Tues 11:30am–2pm and 6–11pm.

Zum Alten Engel *(★ Value* RHINELANDER   Zum Alten Engel, one of the finest restaurants in Speyer, is animated, loud, convivial, and extremely popular. To reach it, you'll descend a flight of antique masonry steps to a century-old brick-vaulted cellar, flickering with candles and awash with German antiques. Set in Speyer's historic core, and much in demand among locals, it specializes in hearty regional cuisine accompanied by the perfect glass of wine—more than 180 kinds of wine from around Germany and the world are available. Menu items usually include hearty gutbürgerlich fare of the kind many locals remember from their childhoods. The best examples of this old-fashioned "home-and-hearth" cookery include fried sausages, liver dumplings, a Rhenish version of sauerbraten, pepper steak, veal cutlets, and at least two different preparations of lamb.

Mühlturmstrasse 7. ℭ **06232/70914.** Reservations required. Main courses 8€–22€ ($13–$35). MC, V. Mon–Sat 11:30am–2:30pm and 6–11pm; Sun 5–11pm. Closed 2 weeks in Aug.

EXPLORING SPEYER

Nothing brings back the medieval German empire as much as the **Kaiserdom (Imperial Cathedral)** *★★* in Speyer (ℭ **06232/1020**), the greatest building of its time. This cathedral, consecrated in the early 11th century, is the largest Romanesque edifice in Germany. Having weathered damage by fires, wars, and restorations, the cathedral was finally brought back to its original shape during a restoration that ran from 1957 to 1961. When you enter the church through the single west door set in a stepped arch, you're at once caught up in the vastness of its proportions; the whole length of the nave and east chancel opens up, lit by the muted daylight from above. The church contains the royal tombs of four emperors, three empresses, and four German kings, as well as a row of bishops' tombs. It is open April to October Monday to Friday 9am to 7pm, Saturday 9am to 6pm, and Sunday 1:30 to 6pm; off-season hours are daily from 9am to 5pm.

Other attractions include **Historisches Museum der Pfalz (Palatinate Historical Museum;** ℭ **06232/13250),** whose main attraction is the Domschatz or Cathedral treasury. Inaugurated in 1910, this museum is housed in a castle with four wings and lies next to the cathedral. In all, there are 300,000 artifacts here related to the history of the Palatinate and the city of Speyer. Relics date from prehistorical times, with a strong emphasis on the Roman and medieval eras.

On-site is the **Wine Museum,** with exhibits showing how the Romans produced their *vino.* The world's oldest bottle of wine (ca. A.D. 300) is also exhibited. Objects found in tombs of former emperors under the Dom are exhibited in the treasury. The most celebrated exhibit is the Bronze Age *Golden Hat of Schifferstadt.* This is a golden, cone-shaped object used in religious celebrations in ancient times. The entrance to the Historisches Museum is on Domplatz. Hours are Tuesday to Sunday 10am to 6pm, Wednesday 10am to 8pm. Entrance is 4€ ($6.40) adults, 3€ ($4.80) children 16 and under.

The **Technik-Museum (Museum of Technology),** Geibstrasse 2 (ℭ **06232/67080**), is housed in a former 1913 aircraft hanger. Here you can view a vast array of airplanes, locomotives, vintage automobiles, fire engines, and even automatic musical instruments.

For us, the biggest thrill is going inside a 20-ton U-boat once used to terrorize Allied shipping in the Atlantic.

Annexed to the museum is the **Marine Museum,** displaying a rich collection of historical model ships. Part of the attraction is a monumental 3-D IMAX cinema. Entrance to the two museums costs 13€ ($20) for adults, 11€ ($17) for children 15 and under. It's open daily 9am to 6pm.

Dreifaltigkeitskirke (Trinity Church), on Grosse Himmelsgasse, dates from 1701 to 1717 when it was constructed in an elaborate baroque style. One of the most richly adorned and decorated churches along the Rhine, and the only elaborate, baroque-style church that still exists in the Rhine-Main-Neckar region, the interior contains a two-story gallery with a splendid balustrade of wooden capped vaulting painted by artisans. Johann Peter Grabner, architect to the court of Palatinate, designed the church. Check with the Speyer tourist office to see if the church is open on the day of your visit.

Speyer was one of the most important centers of Jewish culture along the Rhine, although precious little of that settlement remains today. However, some ruins from the old **Jewish quarter** can still be seen behind the Palatinate Historical Museum. Enter the ruins from Judengasse and pay the entry fee at the gatehouse (© **06232/ 291971).** The east wall of the ancient synagogue is the Judenbad (called *Mikwe* in Hebrew), a 12th-century ritual bathhouse for women. The masons who constructed the Dom also built this bathhouse, the oldest and best-preserved relic of its kind in the country and a poignant, nostalgic reminder of a vanished culture. The site is open from April to October daily 10am to 5pm, costing 2€ ($3.20) admission.

2 Worms (★

45km (28 miles) S of Mainz, 43km (27 miles) SW of Darmstadt

Before the Romans came, Germanic peoples had made Worms their capital. Here, Siegfried began his legendary adventures, recorded in *The Nibelungenlied.* Later on, Martin Luther arrived under less than desirable circumstances. He was "invited" to appear before the Imperial Diet at Worms, and after refusing to retract his grievances against the Church of Rome, Holy Roman Emperor Charles V declared him an outlaw. A huge monument to Luther and other giants of the Reformation has been erected.

Worms also makes an excellent base for a tour of the **Deutsche Weinstrasse,** an 80km (50-mile) route through local wine towns (see "A Driving Tour of the German Wine Road," below).

ESSENTIALS

GETTING THERE   By Plane   The nearest airport is at Frankfurt (see chapter 14), 69km (43 miles) away. From Frankfurt, you can drive to Worms in a rented car. Take A5 south to A3 west to A65 south.

By Train   Worms enjoys good rail connections to major German cities. It lies on the main Mainz-Mannheim line. At Mannheim, one train per hour runs south in to Speyer (trip time: 30 min.). For rail information and schedules, call © **01805/996633** (11861 in Germany; www.bahn.de).

By Bus   Regional bus service for the area is provided by **BRN Busverkehr Rhein-Neckar GmbH** (© **06241/207312)** in Worms.

By Car   From Mainz (see section 3, below), continue south along Route 9.

VISITOR INFORMATION   For tourist information, go to the **Verkehrsverein,** Neumarkt 14 (© **06241/25045;** www.worms.de). It's open year-round Monday to Friday 9am to 6pm; from April to October, it's also open Saturday 9:30am to 1:30pm.

GETTING AROUND   A network of cream-colored buses traverses most neighborhoods of the town and its suburbs. The city's main junction point is the Hauptbahnhof. Buses run 6am to midnight and charge 2.10€ ($3.40) and 3.20€ ($5.10) depending on how far you go, paid directly to the driver.

WHERE TO STAY

Central Hotel Worms *Value*   One of the best small hotels in the city, this is a modest and unassuming choice. Innkeeper Alexandra Hill rents comfortably furnished but rather small rooms. All contain bathrooms with tub/shower combos. The reception staff speaks English, and the hotel has an ideal central location, within walking distance of all major historic monuments.

Kämmererstrasse 5, 67547 Worms. © **06241/64570.** Fax 06241/27439. www.centralhotel-worms.de. 19 units. 80€–90€ ($128–$144) double. Rates include buffet breakfast. AE, DC, MC, V. Parking 5€ ($8). Closed Dec 22–Jan 22. Bus: 2, 4, or 5. **Amenities:** Breakfast room; lounge; nonsmoking rooms; rooms for those w/limited mobility. *In room:* TV.

Dom-Hotel   This is an ideal choice for the in-and-out traveler. The all-purpose hotel is a postwar structure built in a complex of shops and boutiques. Rooms are a little boxy and functionally furnished, but all are well maintained and contain bathrooms with tub/shower combos.

Am Obermarkt 10 (about a block from the cathedral), 67547 Worms. © **06241/9070.** Fax 06241/23515. www.dom-hotel.de. 60 units. 105€–125€ ($168–$200) double; 140€ ($224) apt. Rates include buffet breakfast. AE, DC, MC, V. Free parking. Bus: 2. **Amenities:** Restaurant; lounge; laundry service; dry cleaning; nonsmoking rooms. *In room:* TV, minibar, hair dryer.

Parkhotel Prinz Carl *✦✦*   At long last Worms has a hotel that befits its status as such an important and historic German city. Architecturally distinguished in the old Rhinelander style with step gables, it is completely modernized inside, decorated in a warm, elegant style. There are five different room categories ranging from standard to deluxe, but all of the accommodations are furnished comfortably and tastefully, with sleek contemporary bathrooms containing tubs and showers. In the morning, guests enjoy the most generous breakfast buffet in town. The formal restaurant features first class and international specialties backed up with an impressive wine list from the Rhineland itself.

Prinz-carl-Anlage 10, 67547 Worms. © **06241/3080.** Fax 06241/308309. www.parkhotel-prinzcarl.de. 90 units. 119€ ($190) double; 139€ ($222) junior suite; 149€ ($238) deluxe studio. AE, DC, MC, V. **Amenities:** Restaurant; bar; room service; babysitting; laundry service; dry cleaning; nonsmoking rooms; rooms for those w/limited mobility. *In room:* A/C, TV, Wi-Fi, minibar, hair dryer, safe.

WHERE TO DINE

Rôtisserie Dubs *✦* CONTINENTAL   The prices are a bit steep for the area, but you're paying for imaginative cookery and quality ingredients. Despite rustic ceiling beams and the massive stonework of the fireplace, Rôtisserie Dubs has a feeling of elegant airiness. The light Continental cuisine adds to that impression. Owner Wolfgang Dubs features such French-inspired dishes as salmon in champagne marinade and delicately seasoned pike-and-cabbage soup. His steak in snail sauce is worth the trip outside of town (it may not sound appealing but it's quite sublime).

Kirchstrasse 6. (𝒞) **06242/2023.** Reservations required. Main courses 26€–44€ ($42–$70). MC, V. Wed–Mon noon–2:30pm and 6pm–midnight. At Rheindurkheim, take Rte. 9 north for 8km (5 miles).

EXPLORING WORMS

Towering physically and historically above all the other ancient buildings of the city is the majestic **Dom St. Peter** 𝕬𝕬, Lutherring 9 ((𝒞) **06241/6151;** bus: 2). This basilica is a fine example of High Romanesque style. The east choir, with a flat facade and semicircular interior, is the oldest section, dating from 1132. It was designed as the sanctuary, where the clergy performed the rites of divine service. The chancel glows with the gold and marble of the pillared enclosure of the **baroque high altar** by the famous 18th-century architect Balthasar Neumann. This opulent work was so large that there was no place for a proper transept. In Gothic times the choir stalls stood in the apse, but later they were built into the transept. The interior has a quiet elegance, with little decoration other than the rosette window and several memorial slabs and monuments. Well worth seeing is the highly decorated 14th-century **side chapel of St. Nicholas,** with its Gothic baptismal font and new stained-glass windows. This was the setting of history's famous Diet of Worms, an assembly of august figures of the Catholic hierarchy, an imperial court that banished Martin Luther into exile when he refused to renounce his so-called "heretical doctrine." (Luther adamantly maintained that religious truth exists in scripture, not in papal power or edicts.) The cathedral is open for visitors April to October daily 9am to 6pm, and November to March daily 9am to 5pm.

North of the Altstadt is the restored **old Jewish quarter** (bus: 2). Before World War II, Worms had one of the oldest Jewish communities in Germany. The still-functioning **synagogue,** Hintere Judengasse 6 ((𝒞) **06241/8534700**), which dated from the 11th century, was destroyed in 1938 and has since been rebuilt. The synagogue is open November to March daily 10am to noon and 2 to 4pm, and April to October 10am to 12:30pm and 1:30 to 5pm. Inside, you'll find the **Raschi-Haus Museum** (same phone; www.worms.de), containing memorabilia from the original synagogue and references to the Holocaust. The museum is open November to March daily 10am to 12:30pm and 1:30 to 4:30pm, and April to October Tuesday to Sunday 10am to 12:30pm and 1:30 to 5pm. Admission is 1.50€ ($2.40) adults, .80€ ($1.30) children 13 and under. A staff member inside will point you in the direction of the **Judenfriedhof (Jewish cemetery)** 𝕬, off the Lutherring, one of the oldest and largest in Europe, with hundreds of tombstones, some more than 900 years old.

WORMS AFTER DARK

The city's most important showcase for music, classical drama (in German only), and opera is the **Städtisches Spiel und Festhaus** (ca. 1962), Rathenaustrasse 11 ((𝒞) **06241/ 22525;** bus: 2).

Don't expect raucous nightlife in Worms. Our best advice, if you want a drink in the town center, is to head for the **Judengasse** (bus: 2), a street with a denser collection of nightlife options than any other in town. One of the most appealing is the **Affenhaus,** Judengasse 17 ((𝒞) **06241/22216**), which opens for business every day at 10am, carrying on into the wee hours.

A DRIVING TOUR OF THE GERMAN WINE ROAD 𝕬𝕬

Germany's oldest designated tourist route, the **Deutsche Weinstrasse,** runs south for 80km (50 miles) from Bockenheim, a small town 14km (8½ miles) west of Worms, to

Schweigen-Rechtenbach on the frontier with France. This is a land of old castles (most in ruins) and venerable vineyards. Most of the wines produced here are whites, with special emphasis on clear, aromatic Rieslings and Weissburgunders. The area also abounds in old Rhineland-Palatinate inns and wine taverns, serving hearty local specialties such as *Sauerbraten* (beef marinated in wine vinegar).

Armed with a map (available at the Worms tourist office), you can set out to explore the area beginning in the north at **Bockenheim.** From Bockenheim, follow Route 271 directly south to Grünstadt, where signs point the way to the village of **Neuleiningen,** 10km (6 miles) away. The locals here are known rather unflatteringly as *Geesbocke* or "billy goats," a reference to their longtime poverty—goats (supposedly) were the only livestock they could afford. Today they bear the label with a certain pride. While here, sample the local fare at **Alte Pfarrey,** Untergasse 40, Neuleiningen (© 06359/86066), where fixed-price menus cost 68€ ($109). It is open Wednesday to Sunday noon to 1:30pm and 6:30 to 9pm.

From here, Highway 271 leads south to Kallstadt, a distance of 10km (6 miles), where our next stopover at **Bad Dürkheim** is signposted. Here you can view the remains of the **Monastery of Limburg,** once one of the most significant Romanesque structures in the country. The best restaurant is **Weinrefugium,** Schlachthausstrasse 1A (© 06322/8910980), which charges 29€ to 35€ ($46–$56) for fixed-price menus of regional food. It is open Wednesday to Sunday 1 to 2:30pm and 6 to 9:30pm.

Route A65 and B9 en route to Kaiserslautern, west of Bad Dürkheim, leads to **Frankenstein Schloss,** a castle from the Middle Ages (now in ruins). Local legend claims it was this *Schloss* that inspired Mary Shelley's classic monster.

A journey 8km (5 miles) south along 271 leads to the **Deidesheim,** the medieval seat of the bishops of Speyer. The grounds that surround their former Schloss, now a picturesque ruin, have been turned into a lovely park. Some of the wine road's most charming half-timbered buildings are found on the main square, Marktplatz. Deidesheim is your best bet for wine tastings in this area. Our favorite place is the **Basserman-Jordan Wine Estate,** Kirchgasse 10 (© 06326/6006), dating from 1775. On-site is a **Museum of Historical Wines,** a collection containing wines from every year up until 1880. Admission is free and you can visit the estate Monday to Friday from 8am to 6pm and Saturday from 10am to 3pm.

The most elegant hotel in the neighborhood is the very stylish **Deidesheimer Hof,** Am Marktplatz 1 (© 06326/96870; www.deidesheimerhof.de), where doubles cost 125€ to 290€ ($200–$464). Inside are two restaurants, the **Schwarzer Hahn,** where fixed-price menus go from 90€ to 180€ ($144–$288), and the more artfully rustic **St.-Urban,** which charges 50€ ($80) for fixed-price menus.

From Deidesheim, continue along Route 271 for another 15 minutes, following the signs to **Neustadt-an-der-Weinstrasse,** the largest town on the Weinstrasse, lying at the foot of the Haardt hills. Pass quickly through its ugly suburbs to reach the heart of the old town, with its narrow, often-crooked streets. There are some 2,000 hectares (5,000 acres) of vineyards within the town limits, and the main streets are lined with taverns and wine shops. For wine tastings, visit **Weingut Probsthof,** Probstgasse 7 (© 06321/6315). Open Monday to Saturday from 8am to 6pm, this estate offers tastings for 8€ ($13). If you prefer *Sekt* (sparkling wine), the cost rises to 9€ ($14).

From Neustadt, you can drive 5km (3 miles) south to historic **Schloss Hambach** (© 06321/30881), half a mile outside the village of Hambach. It's open March to November daily 10am to 5:30pm; admission is 4.50€ ($7.20).

An 8km (5-mile) drive south takes you into the sleepy hamlet of **St. Martin,** which for our money is the loveliest village along the wine road, filled with antique houses draped with flowering vines. A castle here, whose nostalgic ruins still tower over St. Martin, happens to have the best food and lodging along the wine road. Its name is **St. Martiner Castell,** Maikammer Strasse 2 (✆ **06323/9510;** www.hotelcastell.de), and each of its 26 rooms rents for around 98€ ($157) double occupancy, with breakfast included. In its restaurant, main courses are 10€ to 22€ ($16–$35) and fixed-price menus are 38€ to 67€ ($61–$107).

Yet another 5km (3 miles) south (the road is signposted) takes you to **Gleisweiler,** a wine-producing hamlet known as the warmest village in Germany. Fig trees flourish in its rich soil and almost subtropical climate.

From Gleisweiler, it's 13km (8 miles) south along Route B38 to **Annweiler,** site of **Burg Trifels** ✿✿ (✆ **06346/8470),** the Rhineland's most fabled castle, set imperiously on a jagged crag. In 1193, Richard the Lionhearted was captured and imprisoned here until he was bailed out with a huge ransom. From the panoramic peak, you can also view the ruins of Scharfenberg Castle and Anebos Castle to the south. Burg Trifels is open January to March and October to November daily 9am to 5pm, April to September daily 9am to 6pm, and closed in December. The last ticket (4€/$6.40) is sold 30 minutes prior to closing.

The most idyllic place for food and lodging in the area is **Landhaus Herrenberg,** Lindenbergstrasse 72, 76829 Landau-Nussdorf (✆ **06341/60205;** www.landhaus-herrenberg.de), 3km (1¾ miles) north of Landau in der Pfalz, a 15-minute drive east of Annweiler. This is a movie cliché of a charming country inn along the wine road, although its nine rooms are contemporary and well appointed, costing 89€ ($142) a night. The owners, the Lergenmüller family, have won awards for their red wines. Naturally, their bottles are the wines of choice in the excellent on-site regional restaurant, which offers three- or four-course menus for lunch Friday to Wednesday; meals cost from 35€ ($56). The inn is closed 3 weeks in January. American Express, MasterCard, and Visa are accepted.

The B38 leads next to **Klingenmünster,** a journey of only 8km (5 miles) south. From here, a sign points the way to the ruins of **Burg Landeck,** reached after a 30- to 40-minute stroll through a chestnut-tree forest. At the end, the castle ruins stand at one of the most scenic spots along the wine road, with views extending as far as the Black Forest.

From here, B38 goes yet another 8km (5 miles) to reach **Bad Bergzabern,** an old spa, without equal for its old half-timbered houses.

From Bad Bergzabern, a 10km (6-mile) drive along Highway B38 (the final lap of your journey) will deliver you to **Schweigen-Rechtenbach,** a village at the French frontier. In the summer of 1935, local vintners constructed a gargantuan stone arch, the **Deutsches Weintor (German Wine Gate),** marking the southern end of this oft-traveled tourist route. From a gallery atop the gate, you can view miles of vineyards and even see a panorama of the Vosges in France. Visitors can cross the border, some 230m (754 ft.) from the arch, to sample the vintages on the French side as well, as there are no border formalities here. You can follow a trail known as the Weinlehrpfad (wine inspection path), going on for 1.5km (1 mile) until you reach the vineyards at the hamlet of Sonnenberg. This is one of the most rewarding walks along the wine route.

In Schweigen-Rechtenbach, one of the best values for lodging is found in the town center at **Am Deutschen Weintor,** Bacchusstrasse 1 (✆ **06342/7335;** www.hotel garni-amdeutschenweintor.de), which charges 52€ to 75€ ($83–$120) for a double room, breakfast included. We suggest getting a meal at the **Hotel Schweigener Hof,** Hauptstrasse 2 (© **06342/9250**), open daily 11:30am to 3pm and 5 to 9pm. A fixed-price lunch or dinner is 15€ to 21€ ($24–$34); wine is extra.

3 Mainz (⋆

13km (8 miles) S of Wiesbaden, 82km (51 miles) NW of Mannheim, 40km (25 miles) SW of Frankfurt

Mainz is located on the left bank of the Rhine, across from the Rhine's intersection with the Main River. It is thought that there may have been wine-producing vines in the area even before the coming of the Romans in 38 B.C., although it was from that time that the regions of the Rheingau and Rheinhessen became widely known for fine viticulture.

At the beginning of the Christian era, a bridge connected the settlement on the Rhine's left bank and the Roman fortifications opposite. In the 8th century, the town became a primary archbishopric. Over the centuries, church politics and a series of wars shuffled control of the city back and forth between the French (who called it "Mayence") and various German factions. Today Mainz is a bustling city, with a prosperous trade in wine and other businesses.

Most visitors will be interested in the relatively compact **Altstadt,** which has been restored tastefully and carefully.

ESSENTIALS

GETTING THERE   By Plane   The nearest airport is at Frankfurt (see chapter 14). There is direct rail service from the airport (S-14 train) via Wiesbaden to Mainz. For information, call the Mainz Railway Station at © **06131/151055.**

By Train   From Frankfurt, an express train takes 30 minutes to reach Mainz, while the S-Bahn arrives in 40 minutes. There are also trains leaving Mainz for Heidelberg and Koblenz (trip time: 1 hr.) or Cologne (trip time: 2 hr.). Daily trains to and from Munich take about 4½ hours. For more rail information, call © **01805/996633** (11861 in Germany; www.bahn.de).

By Bus   Regional bus service is provided by **ORN Omnibusverkehr Rhein-Nahe GmbH,** at Mainz (© **06131/5767470;** www.orn-online.de).

By Car   Access by car to Mainz is via the A60 east and west, and the A63 south and A643 north.

VISITOR INFORMATION   Go to **Touristik Centrale,** Brückenturm am Rathaus (© **06131/286210;** www.info-mainz.de). It's open Monday to Friday 9am to 6pm and Saturday 10:30am to 2:30pm.

GETTING AROUND   Trams and buses fan out across the city from the Hauptbahnhof from 5am until around midnight. Fares start at 2.50€ ($4) and vary depending on how far you go.

SPECIAL EVENTS   The most celebrated merrymaking in festive Mainz is the All Fools capers at **Carnival** each spring, on the Monday and Tuesday before Ash Wednesday, where merrymakers act like fools, jesters, and clowns. This festival is broadcast throughout Germany the way the Macy's parade is throughout the U.S. Each year on the last weekend in June, the **Gutenberg Festival** sponsors festivities as a living memorial to the city's favorite son, the inventor of the movable-type printing press. There's also an annual **Wine Fair** the first week in August and the first week in September. For information, contact the tourist office at © **06131/286210.**

WHERE TO STAY

EXPENSIVE

Hilton Mainz City 𝒜𝒜   Occupying two desirable plots of land near the center of town, the Hilton is one of the most imaginatively designed and strikingly modern hotels along the Rhine Valley. Its twin sections are sheathed in reflective mirrors and soaring spans of steel, and are connected by a glass-sided, covered walkway above the traffic below. The labyrinthine interior has sun-flooded atriums with live plants and acres of marble flooring. The spacious rooms are the most artfully decorated in the region.

Rheinstrasse 68 (a 5-min. walk from the cathedral), 55116 Mainz. ℂ 800/445-8667 in the U.S. and Canada, or 06131/2450. Fax 06131/245589. www.hilton.com. 437 units. 133€–320€ ($213–$512) double; from 274€ ($438) suite. AE, DC, MC, V. Parking 20€ ($32). Bus: 7, 13, 17, 34, or 37. **Amenities:** 3 restaurants; bar; gym; sauna; solarium; room service; babysitting; laundry service; dry cleaning; nonsmoking rooms; rooms for those w/limited mobility; casino. *In room:* A/C, TV, Wi-Fi, minibar, hair dryer.

Hyatt Regency Mainz 𝒜𝒜𝒜   Opening onto the Rhine, this deluxe palace has eclipsed the two Hiltons and now reigns supreme. Sparkling new, it is the best hotel south of Cologne, done in a strikingly modern architectural style. A glittering 21st-century aura prevails in the public rooms, restaurants, and guest accommodations. The room furnishings are tasteful and sleekly sophisticated, with modern art decorating the walls. The more desirable units open onto the Rhine, and these have even larger bathrooms. The public facilities are among the best in this part of Germany, with a wine bar and the Römische Weinstube restaurant, featuring a grand river terrace along the Rhine. In summer a beer garden goes full blast.

Malakoff-Terrasse 1, 55116 Mainz. ℂ 06131/731234. Fax 06131/731235. www.mainz.regency.hyatt.com. 268 units. 170€–250€ ($272–$400) double; from 368€ ($589) junior suite. AE, DC, MC, V. **Amenities:** 2 restaurants; bar; lounge; beer garden; indoor heated pool; fitness center; Jacuzzi; room service; massage; babysitting; laundry service; dry cleaning; nonsmoking rooms; 1 room for those w/limited mobility. *In room:* A/C, TV, Wi-Fi, beverage maker, hair dryer, safe.

MODERATE

Favorite Parkhotel 𝒜   Set in isolated privacy within a park on a hillside above the Rhine and the old city of Mainz, which lies within a 12-minute downhill walk, this three-story hotel was established in the early 1960s, and enlarged in 2005 with a five-story modern wing. It's a respectable, conservative, family-managed hotel. Accommodations in the old wing are actually preferred for their solid sense of comfort, pastel colors, and conservative sense of modernity. Rooms within the new wing are trendier, more artfully contemporary, and more minimalist and monochromic, but still very comfortable. The morning breakfast buffet is very complete, a reflection of the good service and food in the gourmet-conscious Stadtpark Restaurant, and its *Bierkeller*-style cohort, the Bierkutscher. Then, of course, there is an outdoor beer garden, open from May to late September daily from noon to 10pm.

Karl Weiser Strasse 1, 55131 Mainz. ℂ 06131/80150. Fax 06131/801-5420. www.favorite-mainz.de. 121 units. 154€–234€ ($246–$374) double; 224€–265€ ($358–$424) suite. Rates include buffet breakfast. AE, DC, MC, V. Parking 15€ ($24). Bus: 60 or 61. **Amenities:** 2 restaurants; beer garden; indoor heated pool; fitness center; rooftop Jacuzzi; sauna; room service; massage; babysitting; laundry service; dry cleaning; nonsmoking rooms; 1 room for those w/limited mobility. *In room:* TV, Wi-Fi, minibar, hair dryer, iron.

Hotel Mainzer Hof 𝒜   Mainzer Hof is six floors of modernity directly on the Rhine, almost at the point where some of the boats dock. This hotel is a clean-cut, convenient stopover. The medium-size rooms are well furnished and well maintained and have bathrooms with tub/shower combos.

Kaiserstrasse 98 (a 10-min. walk from the Hauptbahnhof), 55116 Mainz. ✆ **06131/288990.** Fax 06131/228255. www.hotel-mainzerhof.de. 80 units. 108€–150€ ($173–$240) double. Rates include buffet breakfast. AE, DC, MC, V. Parking 7€ ($11). Bus: 9. **Amenities:** Restaurant; bar; lounge; sauna; room service; laundry service; dry cleaning; nonsmoking rooms. *In room:* TV, Wi-Fi, minibar, hair dryer.

Mainz City Hilton 🏨🏨   In the historic zone of Mainz, about a 3-block walk from the rail terminus, this Hilton is a bit livelier than its sibling. Although the rooms are about the same in both Hiltons, we prefer the relatively subdued atmosphere here and the more personal staff. We also like the architectural touches, including an ancient wall discovered during reconstruction. The wall was preserved and now frames the courtyard terrace. Rooms are a bit cookie cutter, but tasteful and spacious, each with a deluxe bathroom with a shower stall and deep tub. They're priced according to view and location; those on the top cost the most money because of their panoramic views and balconies. The least desirable are on the lower floors, facing a park.

Munsterstrasse 11, 55116 Mainz. ✆ **06131/2780.** Fax 06131/2782099. www.hilton.com. 128 units. 138€–275€ ($221–$440) double; 191€–310€ ($306–$496) suite. Rates include buffet breakfast. AE, DC, MC, V. Parking 20€ ($32). **Amenities:** Restaurant; 2 bars; exercise room; room service; babysitting; laundry service; dry cleaning; nonsmoking rooms; rooms for those w/limited mobility; cabaret theater. *In room:* A/C, TV, Wi-Fi, beverage maker, minibar, hair dryer, safe.

INEXPENSIVE

Hotel Ibis   This chain hotel is modern and functional, its two chief attractions being its convenient location at the edge of the Old Town and its affordable prices. Bedrooms are small to midsize and are suitably comfortable in a chain-format sort of way. Rooms are climate controlled.

Holzhofstrasse 2, 55116 Mainz. ✆ **016131/2470.** Fax 016131/234126. www.ibishotel.com. 144 units. 75€ ($120) double. AE, DC, MC, V. Free parking. **Amenities:** Bar; laundry service; nonsmoking rooms; rooms for those w/limited mobility. *In room:* A/C, TV, no phone.

WHERE TO DINE

Palatinate is the regional cuisine of the area in which Mainz is located. Palatinate is basic German fare with regional subtleties based on the availability of local ingredients.

Geberts Weinstuben 🍴 *Finds* PALATINATE   This traditional *Weinstube* is housed in one of the oldest buildings in Mainz, with a decor that's almost spartan. But people flock here for the food, not the ambience. Once seated, you're treated to a traditional meal of game, fish, or regional specialties such as goose *à l'orange*. The cuisine includes other hearty regional fare such as roast pork with sauerkraut.

Frauenlobstrasse 94. ✆ **06131/611619.** Reservations required. Main courses 18€–27€ ($29–$43); fixed-price menu 30€ ($48). AE, MC, V. Sun and Tues–Fri 11:30am–2pm and Tues–Sat 6–10pm. Closed mid-July to mid-Aug. Bus: 21 or 70.

Haus des Deutschen Weines GERMAN   Set in Mainz's historic core, immediately adjacent to the Stadttheater, this modern, contemporary-looking restaurant focuses on a savory combination of German food and mostly German wines. Wines run the gamut of virtually every vintage produced within Germany, and the staff is well versed in their compatibility with menu items that include, but are not limited to, fresh or marinated salmon, all kinds of venison (available year-round), a savory version of rump steak, and perfectly grilled fish. Expect lots of emphasis on whatever vegetable is in season at the moment of your arrival. In spring, for example, asparag celebrated with at least a dozen variations served either as starters or as main courses. No one will object if you order just wine and a small platter of food; examples include *Spundekäse*, an age-old recipe that mingles local cheese whipped with onions and cream into a soft paste. It's best served with rough-textured bread and, naturally, wine.

Gutenbergplatz 3. © 06131/221300. Reservations recommended. Main courses 11€–18€ ($18–$29). AE, MC, V. Daily 11:30am–midnight.

L'Angolo ITALIAN   This informal Italian-inspired trattoria is known for its congenial staff and its excellent pizza and pasta. You can also order freshly made salads, with shrimp or prosciutto, and meat dishes with escalopes of either pork or veal. Reasonable prices and a full bar generally keep this place packed.

Augustinerstrasse 8. © 06131/231737. Pizzas and pastas 8€–12€ ($13–$19); meat platters 10€–15€ ($16–$24). No credit cards. Daily 11am–midnight. Bus: 6, 15, or 23.

Weinstube Lösch *(Value* RHINELAND   This old-fashioned *Weinstube* in the heart of the Altstadt has been popular for generations and is rich in tradition. The menu offers regional hot and cold dishes and light salads, plus lots of Rhine wine. The pork schnitzel with mushrooms is particularly savory. Two regional dishes include jagerschnitzel with mushrooms and tzigeunerschnitel with paprika, both served with boiled potatoes and a green salad. Tender rumpsteak is also a huge specialty here. At only 12 tables, they seat 85 guests. Six additional tables are placed out front in summer on the pedestrian mall.

Jakobsbergstrasse 9. © 06131/220383. Reservations recommended. Main courses 11€–21€ ($18–$34). No credit cards. Tues–Sun 5:30–10:30pm. Bus: 6 or 23.

EXPLORING MAINZ

Dom und Diözesan Museum (Cathedral and Diocesan Museum) *

Above the roofs of the half-timbered houses in the Altstadt rise the six towers of St. Martin's Cathedral, the most important Catholic cathedral in the country after Cologne's. It dates from A.D. 975 but was continually rebuilt and restored, reaching its present form mainly in the 13th and 14th centuries. Below the largest dome, a combination of Romanesque and baroque styles, is the transept, separating the west chancel from the nave and smaller east chancel. Many of the supporting pillars along the aisles of the nave are decorated with carved and painted statues of French and German saints.

The cathedral's Diocesan Museum houses a collection of religious art. In it are exhibitions of reliquaries and medieval sculpture, including works by the Master of Naumburg. In the 1,000-year-old cathedral crypt is a contemporary gold reliquary of the saints of Mainz. Among the most impressive furnishings in the sanctuary are rococo choir stalls and an early-14th-century pewter baptismal font.

Domstrasse 3. © 06131/253344. Cathedral free; Diocesan Museum 3.50€ ($5.60) adults, 2€ ($3.20) students and children 15 and under. Cathedral Apr–Sept Mon–Fri 9am–6:30pm, Sat 9am–4pm, Sun 2–5pm; Oct–Mar Mon–Fri 9am–5pm, Sat 10am–3:30pm, Sun 1–3pm. Museum Tues–Sat 9am–5pm. Bus: 1, 7, 13, 17, or 23.

Gutenberg Museum **

This museum is a unique memorial to the city's most famous son. In the rebuilt Gutenberg workshop, visitors can trace the history of printing, beginning with Johannes Gutenberg's hand press, on which he printed his 42-line-per-page Bible from 1452 to 1455. The collections cover the entire spectrum of the graphic arts in all countries, past and present, as well as printing, illustration, and binding. Two Gutenberg Bibles are the most popular exhibits.

Liebfrauenplatz 5 (opposite the east towers of the cathedral). ✆ 06131/122640. www.gutenbergmuseum.de. Admission 5€ ($8) adults, 2€ ($3.20) ages 8–18, free 7 and under. Tues–Sat 9am–5pm; Sun 11am–1pm. Closed Jan. Bus: 54, 57, 60, or 71.

Landesmuseum Mainz (Provincial Museum of the Central Rhineland) ⚡

It's worth a visit here to get a pictorial history of Mainz and the middle Rhineland ranging from prehistoric times to the present. The Lapidarium shows one of the most important collections of Roman monuments in Europe. The most impressive exhibits are the Roman tombstones of soldiers and civilians of the 1st century A.D. and the towering Column of Jupiter, erected in Mainz at the time of Nero, around A.D. 65 to 68. There's a true-to-life replica of the column in front of the Parliament building.

Grosse Bleiche 49–51. ✆ 06131/23295557. www.landesmuseum-mainz.de. Admission 3€ ($4.80), 6€ ($9.60) family ticket, free for children 5 and under; free for all Sat. Tues 10am–8pm; Wed–Sun 10am–5pm. Bus: 6, 15, or 23.

SHOPPING

The city's most active shopping area is **Am Brand,** a short boulevard near the cathedral that's lined with shops on either side (bus: 1 or 54). One of the town's best clothing emporiums is **Peek & Cloppenburg,** Am Brand 38 (✆ **06131/669200**), which sells clothing for men, women, and children, in styles ranging from very formal to chic and casual. For German designer fashions, head to **Sinn,** Markt 19 (✆ **06131/971560**), which carries men's and women's clothing.

Whatever you can't find along the Am Brand will almost certainly be available among the vast inventories of Mainz's most visible department store, **Kaufhof,** Schusterstrasse 41 (✆ **06131/2540;** bus: 54). For a treasure trove of secondhand goods, shop the **Krempelmarkt;** this flea market is held along the banks of the Rhine on the first Saturday of each month, February to October (bus: 54).

Many of Mainz's hotels, restaurants, and banks take an interest in modern art. You might also want to visit the city's most prestigious modern art gallery, **Galerie H. G. Lautner,** Augustinerstrasse 52 (✆ **06131/225736;** bus: 54).

MAINZ AFTER DARK

The cultural center of the city is **Frankfurter Hof,** Augustinerstrasse 55 (✆ **06131/ 220438;** bus: 54), which stages concerts of classical music, jazz, folk, and pop. The center also hosts an annual tent festival featuring an eclectic mix of international performers. Tickets to all events cost 10€ to 75€ ($16–$120). Call for scheduled shows, festival dates and performers, and ticket information.

Although you can buy tickets at the offices of any of the theaters and entertainment venues in Mainz, a more convenient way is to contact the **Ticket Service,** which is a division of the town's tourist office at Brückenturm am Rathaus, 55116 Mainz (✆ **06131/286210;** bus: 54).

In terms of its nightlife, Mainz is sleepy enough to compel many residents to head to Cologne or Düsseldorf after dark. But if you don't want to get out of town too quickly, consider dancing the night away at the **Disco Kuz,** Dagobertstrasse 20 (✆ **06131/286860;** bus: 60 or 61), where you'll find attractive people drinking, dancing, and talking. It's open Wednesday, Friday, and Saturday 10pm until at least 4am, charges a 6€ to 8€ ($9.60–$13) cover, and attracts ages 20 to around 35. The hottest address is **Red Cat,** Emmerich-Josef-Strasse 13 (✆ **06131/225656**), in the heart of town, right off the landmark Schillerplatz. The club is tiny, as is its dance floor, but hip young Mainzers pack the joint anyway. **Chapeau Claque,** Kleine Landgas (✆ **06131/223111;** bus: 9), is a gay bar that's open nightly 6pm to 4am.

4 The Rheingau (★(★(★

Legend says that when God was looking for a place to set up Paradise, the sunny slopes between the Taunus Mountains and the Rhine nearly won the prize. Today the Rheingau is the kingdom of another god: Bacchus. Nearly every town and village from Wiesbaden to Assmannshausen is a major wine producer. The names suddenly seem familiar—Bingen, Johannesburg, Rüdesheim, Oestrich—because they're featured on the labels of many wines.

The Rheingau is also rich in old churches and castles, as well as landmarks. The **Niederwald Monument,** on a hill halfway between Rüdesheim and Assmannshausen—it can be reached by cable car from either town—is a huge statue of Germania, erected by Bismarck in 1883 to commemorate the unification of Germany. Below it, on a small island at the bend of the Rhine, is the **Mäuseturm (Mouse Tower),** where, according to legend, the greedy archbishop of Mainz was devoured by a swarm of hungry mice. But the real attraction of the Rheingau is the cheerful character of the wine villages and their people. Rüdesheim and Assmannshausen are the most visited towns.

ESSENTIALS

GETTING THERE   By Plane   The nearest airport is at Frankfurt (see chapter 14), 50km (30 miles) away.

From the airport, you can rent a car. Otherwise, take the train or bus from Wiesbaden (see the "By Train" or "By Bus" section, below). There are bus links from the Frankfurt airport to Wiesbaden's bus and train transport hubs.

By Train   The main rail station at Rüdesheim is on the Wiesbaden-Koblenz line, with frequent service to regional towns and connections to all major cities. For rail information and schedules, call (✆ **01805/996633** (11861 in Germany; www.bahn. de). Train service from Frankfurt is via Wiesbaden and takes 1 hour.

By Bus   Bus service for the region is provided by **ORN Omnibusverkehr Rhein-Nahe GmbH,** in Wiesbaden (✆ **0611/977580;** www.orn-online.de).

By Car   Access by car is via the A61 Autobahn from the north and Highway 42 connecting with the A671 from the west. From Frankfurt, motorists can take the A66 until they reach the junction with Route B42, which will be signposted and lead them right to Rüdesheim. Motorists heading from Koblenz on the west bank of the Rhine can use the A61 to Bingen, and then follow the signs for the ferryboats that cross the river to Rüdesheim. For information on the ferry service, call (✆ **06722/19433.** From Koblenz, you can also take B42 along the east bank of the river, which will lead directly into Rüdesheim. Route B42 links Rüdesheim with Assmannshausen.

VISITOR INFORMATION   For information about Rüdesheim and Assmannshausen (see below), go to the **Stadt Verkehrsamt,** Geissenheimer 22 in Rüdesheim (✆ **06722/19433**). It's open January to mid-April and November to December Monday to Friday 11am to 5pm, and mid-April to October Monday to Friday 9am to 7pm, Saturday and Sunday 10am to 5pm; Christmas market (the weeks before Christmas), they are also open Saturday and Sunday 11am to 5pm.

RÜDESHEIM (★

With its old courtyards and winding alleyways lined with timbered houses, Rüdesheim is the epitome of a Rhine wine town. The vineyards around the village date back to the Roman emperor Probus. The full-bodied Riesling is produced here, as well as brandy and *Sekt* (sparkling wine). Rüdesheim is also the scene of the annual August wine festival, when the old taverns on the narrow and very touristy **Drosselgasse (Thrush Lane)** are crowded with visitors from all over the world. Drosselgasse has been called "the smallest but the happiest street in the world." From April to November, you can listen to music and dance in these taverns daily noon to 1am.

To prove how seriously Rüdesheimers take their wine, they have opened a wine museum in Bromserburg Castle. The **Rheingau- und Weinmuseum,** Rheinstrasse 2 (*©* **06722/2348;** www.rheingauer-weinmuseum.de), charges 5€ ($8) for adults, and 3€ ($4.80) for children 11 and under; it's open mid-March to October daily 9am to 6pm (last admission 5:15pm). It traces the history of the grape and has an exhibition of wine presses, glasses, goblets, and drinking utensils from Roman times to the present. Wine tastings are 7€ to 15€ ($11–$24) extra, depending on how many samples you drink.

WHERE TO STAY & DINE

Breuer's Rüdesheimer Schloss *ꝏ*   This hotel is the first choice for staying and dining in town. The Breuer family is noted for its wine cellars and plentiful food and drink. The wine cellar dates from 1729. The mostly medium-size rooms are immaculately kept, and a few are even quite spacious, all with bathrooms equipped with tub/shower combos. The hotel staff will help you prepare a tailor-made package of excursions or perhaps a "gastronomic feast" and a musical evening on their premises. German and Rhineland specialties are served here. The chef prides himself on his *Zehnthofplatte,* consisting of regional sausages, smoked pork, grilled knuckle of pork, and sauerkraut.

Steingasse 10, 65385 Rüdesheim. *©* **06722/90500.** Fax 06722/905050. www.ruedesheimer-schloss.de. 26 units. 125€–155€ ($200–$248) double; 155€–175€ ($248–$280) suite. Children 12 and younger stay free in parent's room. Rates include buffet breakfast. AE, DC, MC, V. Free parking. Closed Dec 21–Jan 9. **Amenities:** Restaurant; free bikes; laundry service; dry cleaning; nonsmoking rooms; 1 room for those w/limited mobility. *In room:* TV, minibar, hair dryer, safe.

Gasthof Krancher *Finds*   This is a home-and-hearth choice. Gasthof Krancher has been in the Krancher family for four generations and it's located next to the inn's own vineyards. Naturally, the Kranchers make their own wines, and they'll gladly show you the cellar where they store bottles that have won gold and silver medals. Everything is decorated in a regional motif. Rooms are a bit cramped but are reasonably comfortable. All units contain private bathrooms with showers. From your window you can look out on the vineyards. Local German food, mostly Rhinelander specialties, is served here, with a simple three-course meal costing around 20€ ($32).

Eibinger-Oberstrasse 4 (a 10-min. hike uphill from the town center), 65385 Rüdesheim. *©* **06722/2762.** www. gasthof-krancher.de. Fax 06722/47870. 62 units. 56€–76€ ($90–$122) double. Rates include buffet breakfast. MC, V. Free parking. **Amenities:** Restaurant; lounge. *In room:* TV.

Hotel und Weinhaus Felsenkeller   The beautifully carved timbers on the facade of this 1613 building suggest the traditional aura you'll find inside. A sampling of Rhine wine can be enjoyed in a room with vaulted ceilings and murals with vine leaves and pithy pieces of folk wisdom. In fair weather, guests can eat on the terrace. The hotel serves regional Rhineland cuisine and complete meals, which are huge and cost from 18€ to 43€ ($29–$69). The small, attractively modern, and freshly painted rooms open onto views of the vineyards surrounding the house. Each comes with a small and tidily kept bathroom with tub/shower combo.

Oberstrasse 39–41 (in the center of the old town), 65385 Rüdesheim. ℂ **06722/94250.** Fax 06722/47202. www. ruedesheim-rhein.com. 60 units. 85€–120€ ($136–$192) double; 111€–142€ ($178–$227) triple. Rates include buffet breakfast. AE, MC, V. Free parking. Closed Nov–Easter. **Amenities:** Restaurant; lounge; private garden; non-smoking rooms; rooms for those w/limited mobility. *In room:* TV, hair dryer.

Rüdesheimer Hof *(Value* This village inn, set back from the Rhine, boasts a side garden and terrace where wine tasters gather at rustic tables. Most of the units are roomy and comfortably furnished, all with bathrooms containing tub/shower combos. The atmosphere is informal. If you stay here, you can sample the lifestyle of a Rhine village by mingling with the townspeople, eating the regional food, and drinking the Rheingau wines. Guests dine at cafe tables placed under a willow tree. Food is served daily 11:30am to 9:30pm and meals cost 18€ to 22€ ($29–$35).

Geisenheimerstrasse 1 (a 10-min. walk from the Bahnhof), 65385 Rüdesheim. ℂ **06722/91190.** Fax 06722/48194. www.ruedesheimer-hof.de. 38 units. 82€–119€ ($131–$190) double. Rates include buffet breakfast. AE, DC, MC, V. Free parking. Closed Dec to mid-Feb. **Amenities:** Restaurant; lounge; nonsmoking rooms. *In room:* A/C, TV.

ASSMANNSHAUSEN

This old village at the northern edge of the Rheingau is built on the slopes of the east bank of the Rhine. Its half-timbered houses and vineyards seem precariously perched on the steep hillsides, and the view of the Rhine Valley from here is awe-inspiring. Assmannshausen is known for its fine Burgundy-style wine. It lies 5km (3 miles) north-west of Rüdesheim and 60km (37 miles) west of Frankfurt.

WHERE TO STAY & DINE

Alte Bauernschanke-Nassauer Hof *⊛* The wine-grower owners have turned two of the oldest mansions in town into a hotel and restaurant. The interior decor is luxurious, the comfort fine, and the welcome hearty. Rooms are beautifully furnished in traditional style. All units have bathrooms with tub/shower combos. The restaurant has live folk music every night. Try goulash soup, pepper steak with fresh green beans and french fries, and a bottle of the growers' red wine. Meals cost 22€ to 30€ ($29–$39).

Niederwaldstrasse 23 (near the church, about .5km/¼ mile from the Rhine), 65385 Rüdesheim-Assmannshausen. ℂ **0672249990.** Fax 06722/47912. www.altebauernschaenke.de. 53 units. 82€–115€ ($131–$184) double; 115€–145€ ($184–$232) suite. Rates include buffet breakfast. AE, MC, V. Closed Dec 16–Mar 8. **Amenities:** Restaurant; bar; lounge; room service. *In room:* TV, hair dryer.

Krone Assmannshausen *⊛⊛⊛* This distinguished hotel offers the most luxurious accommodations in the entire Rüdesheim am Rhein district. It's on the banks of the Rhine, surrounded by lawns, gardens, and a pool. Its origins can be traced back 400 years. The inn is a great big gingerbread fantasy with fairy-tale turrets and wooden balconies evocative of the Romantic architecture of the 16th century. A small second-floor lounge is virtually a museum, with framed letters and manuscripts of some of the famous people who have stayed here—Goethe, for one, and also Kaiser Wilhelm II. There's a stack of about 40 autograph books dating from 1893 signed by writers, painters, diplomats, and composers. You may stay in a medieval, Renaissance, or postwar building. The spacious rooms have an old-inn character, with traditional furnishings.

Rheinuferstrasse 10, 65385 Rüdesheim-Assmannshausen. ℂ **06722/4030.** Fax 06722/3049. www.hotel-krone.com. 65 units. 170€–210€ ($272–$336) double; 270€ ($432) junior suite; 350€–560€ ($560–$896) suite. AE, DC, MC, V. Free parking. **Amenities:** Restaurant; outdoor pool; room service; babysitting; laundry service; dry cleaning. *In room:* TV, minibar, hair dryer, Jacuzzi bath (in some), fireplace.

5 Koblenz ⟨★⟩

88km (55 miles) SE of Cologne, 63km (39 miles) SE of Bonn, 100km (60 miles) NW of Frankfurt

Koblenz has stood at the confluence of the Rhine and the Mosel for more than 2,000 years. Its strategic location in the mid-Rhine region has made the city a vital link in the international river trade routes of Europe. The city is surrounded by vine-covered hills dotted with castles and fortresses. Koblenz is also the place where many cruises through the Rhine begin or end.

ESSENTIALS

GETTING THERE   By Plane   The nearest airports are Frankfurt (see chapter 14) and Cologne (later in this chapter). From there, you can rent a car or go by train. See below for train information.

By Train   The **Koblenz Hauptbahnhof** lies on a major rail line, with frequent connections to important German cities. For train information, prices, and schedules, call ℂ **01805/996633** (11861 in Germany; www.bahn.de). Thirty trains per day arrive from Frankfurt (trip time: 2 hr.) and 16 from Berlin (trip time: 8½ hr.). Trains also arrive every 30 minutes from Cologne (trip time: 45 min.–1 hr.).

By Bus   Rail is by far the best way to get to Koblenz, but information on bus service is available by calling ℂ **0261/3038823.**

By Car   Access by car to Koblenz is via the A48 Autobahn east and west, connecting with the A3 north to south.

VISITOR INFORMATION   For information about tours, boat trips on the Rhine, and bus and train connections, contact the **Koblenz Tourist Office,** Bahnhofplatz 17 (ℂ **0261/31304**). It's open Monday to Saturday 9am to 6pm, and Sunday 10am to 6pm.

GETTING AROUND   The city is served by 10 main bus lines. Fare is 1.70€ to 2.25€ ($2.70–$3.60) depending on how far you go, paid on the bus (the bus driver will help you get the proper ticket, though most tourists will stay in the central zone and pay the cheaper fare). A day pass, valid for 1 day's transport within the city limits, sells at the tourist office and costs 5€ ($8).

WHERE TO STAY

Hotel Brenner ⟨★⟩   This hotel is your best bet if you're seeking a moderately priced choice. The small- to medium-size rooms are spotlessly maintained. Each bathroom has a tub/shower combo. The garden retreat is a pleasant spot for getting back to nature.

Rizzastrasse 20–22 (near the Kurfürstl Schloss), 56068 Koblenz. ℂ 0261/915780. Fax 0261/36278. www.hotel-brenner.de. 24 units. 64€–78€ ($102–$125) double. Extra person over age 6 27€ ($43). Rates include buffet breakfast. AE, DC, MC, V. Parking 6€ ($9.60). Bus: 1 or 5 to Christuskirche. **Amenities:** Breakfast room; lounge; nonsmoking rooms. *In room:* TV, minibar, hair dryer.

Hotel Scholz   Scholz is a personally run, well-maintained family hotel offering sparsely furnished units that make for a reasonably priced overnight stopover. Rooms are small, but the beds are comfortable and the bathrooms contain tub/shower combos.

Moselweisserstrasse 121 (a 5-min. bus ride from the town center), 56073 Koblenz. ℂ 0261/94260. Fax 0261/942626. www.hotelscholz.de. 67 units. 78€ ($125) double. Rates include buffet breakfast. AE, DC, MC, V. Free parking. Closed Dec 22–Jan 9. Bus: 6 or 16. **Amenities:** Restaurant; lounge; nonsmoking rooms. *In room:* TV, Wi-Fi.

Kleiner Riesen This is one of the few hotels in central Koblenz that sits directly on the banks of the Rhine. Its rooms are close enough to view the boats as they go by. Within the city proper, only the Mercure is better. The Kleiner Riesen is a large, overgrown, informal chalet, with several lounges and comfortable rooms. All units come equipped with neatly kept bathrooms with tub/shower combos. It's away from town traffic, so it has a peaceful small-town quiet.

Kaiserin-Augusta-Anlagen 18, 56068 Koblenz. Ⓒ **0261/303460.** Fax 0261/160725. www.hotel-kleinerriesen.de. 28 units. 88€ ($141) double. Rates include buffet breakfast. AE, DC, MC, V. Parking 8€ ($13). **Amenities:** Lounge; nonsmoking rooms. *In room:* TV.

Mercure 🌟🌟 Glittering and stylish, the Mercure is easily the best hotel in town. It's perched on a hillock at the edge of the Rhine. Its streamlined architecture contrasts with the century-old trees and ancient stones of the surrounding medieval town. Rooms are well insulated against sound, and each has a neatly kept bathroom with a tub/shower combo. One of the city's loveliest riverside promenades is just a short walk away.

Julius-Wegeler-Strasse 6, 56068 Koblenz. Ⓒ **0261/1360.** Fax 0261/1361199. www.mercure.de. 168 units. 125€–168€ ($200–$269) double; 260€ ($416) suite. 2 children stay free in parent's room. AE, DC, MC, V. Parking 12€ ($19). Bus: 9 or 10. Pets accepted. **Amenities:** 2 restaurants; lounge; fitness center; whirlpool; sauna; solarium; room service; babysitting; laundry service; dry cleaning; nonsmoking rooms; rooms for those w/limited mobility. *In room:* A/C, TV, Wi-Fi (in some), minibar, hair dryer, safe.

WHERE TO DINE

Da Vinci 🌟🌟 MEDITERRANEAN One of the most appealing restaurants in Koblenz is plush and richly accessorized, with backlit bars lighting up like displays in an art museum, plus plenty of polished copper, wood paneling, and leather. And in honor of the restaurant's namesake, it contains replicas—either framed or painted like murals directly onto the walls—of Da Vinci's most famous art. There's a convincing copy of the *Mona Lisa,* plus a replica of *The Last Supper,* which meanders for at least 4.5m (15 ft.) along one wall. Conveniently central, with a location near Centralplatz, the venue focuses on Mediterranean cuisine, but with presentations that are a lot more sophisticated than anything *mamma mia* ever made. The best examples include carpaccio of beef with fresh Parmesan and arugula; grilled quail with forest mushrooms and paprika sauce; a "strudel" stuffed with Italian cured ham, grilled vegetables, olive paste, and mushrooms; terrine of gooseliver with crostini and lentil salad; a salad of braised scallops and assorted shellfish; poached turbot with a sauce made from sparkling wine and vanilla; and roasted rack of lamb with rosemary sauce. Dessert? How about a duet of sweet ravioli stuffed with lemon grass ice cream and drizzled with caramel sauce.

Firmungstrasse 32B. Ⓒ **0261/921-5444.** Reservations recommended. Main courses 10€–22€ ($16–$35). AE, DC, MC, V. Daily 11am–11pm. Bus: 8.

Palais INTERNATIONAL This old building, a former furniture store, has been converted into a cafe set against a backdrop of Art Nouveau styling. The exterior is a 19th-century Victorian facade, and the interior is filled with fine antiques and original paintings. The chefs roam the world borrowing recipes, to create a finely tuned modern cuisine enhanced by attentive service. Try the platterwide Wiener schnitzel or a succulent chicken breast with curry sauce, diced pineapples, and pears. The pastas are succulent, especially the penne with a Gorgonzola sauce, served with an herby garlic bread.

Firmungstrasse 2. Ⓒ **0261/1005833.** Reservations recommended. Main courses 10€–15€ ($16–$24). MC, V. Mon–Sat 8am–1am; Sun 10am–10pm.

(Moments A Lofty Look at the Corner of Germany

For the most panoramic view of Koblenz, go to the point where the two rivers meet. It is called Deutsches Eck, or the "corner of Germany." From the top of the base where a huge statue of Wilhelm I once stood, you can see the Altstadt and across the Rhine to the Festung Ehrenbreitstein.

Weinhaus Hubertus GERMAN Weinhaus Hubertus looks like a timbered country inn. It's the oldest wine tavern in town, dating from 1696. The place offers German wines accompanied by a choice of homemade dishes—soups, sandwiches, and light platters, all designed to go well with the wines offered. The furnishings and decor are family-style, providing a homelike atmosphere. There's a choice here of 100 wines from all over Germany, 30 of these by the glass. In summer, you can enjoy the view of the Altstadt from the terrace.

Florinsmarkt 6 (across from the Old Rathaus). (©) 0261/31177. Reservations recommended. Main courses 7.50€–18€ ($12–$29). MC, V. Wed–Mon 4–10pm. Bus: 1.

EXPLORING KOBLENZ

Koblenz was heavily bombed during World War II, but many of its historic buildings have been restored. The focal point of the Altstadt is the **Liebfrauenkirche (Church of Our Lady),** a 13th-century Gothic basilica built on a Romanesque foundation, with twin towers topped by onion-shaped spires. The early-18th-century **Rathaus** was formerly a Jesuit college. In the courtyard behind the hall is a fountain dedicated to the youth of Koblenz called *Das Schängelchen (The Spitting Boy),* and that's just what he does. At the edge of the old town, near the Deutsches Eck, is Koblenz's oldest, biggest, and most attractive church, **St. Castor's,** originally built in 836, though in its present form it dates mostly from the 12th century.

   Festung Ehrenbreitstein (© 0261/9742441), across the Rhine from Koblenz, can be reached by chairlift between May and September. You can also drive there via the Pfaffendorfer Bridge just south of the Altstadt or take bus no. 8, 9, or 10 from the rail station. The fortress was constructed on a rock and towers 120m (400 ft.) above the Rhine. The present walls were built in the 19th century. From the stone terrace is one of the best views along the Rhine; the panoramic vista includes not only Koblenz but also several castles on the river and many terraced vineyards. To reach the fortress, make the 1.70€ ($2.70) one-way passage across the river from the main Rhine dock. Ferries operate mid-March to late November daily 9am to 5:15pm. The chairlift operates April to October daily 9:30am to 4:30pm. Round-trip tickets cost 6.50€ ($10) for adults, 4.50€ ($7.20) for children 13 and under.

KOBLENZ AFTER DARK

THE PERFORMING ARTS The **Rheinische Philharmonie Orchestra** performs in the **Rhein-Mosel-Halle,** Schlossstrasse 35 (© 0261/300160; bus: 9 or 10), which also hosts other performances. Tickets cost 15€ to 60€ ($24–$96). Call for listings, dates, and prices of other performances. The **Stadttheater (City Theater),** housed in the **Grossehaus,** Dinehartplatz (© 0261/1292804; bus: 9 or 10), stages dramas, comedies, and musicals (in German) September to June. The box office is open daily 9am to noon. Tickets are 20€ to 55€ ($32–$88), but can be higher depending on the event.

BARS A pub-oriented crowd, mostly under 40, hangs out late at night at the previously recommended **Palais,** Firmungstrasse 2, Am Görresplaz (© **0261/1005833**), before heading for one of the many pubs on Florinsmarkt for a nightcap. **Club Abaco** (same phone), in the basement of this building, attracts a mostly 20-ish crowd to dance to the music provided by a live DJ. The club is open Thursday to Saturday from 9pm to 4am, charging a cover that ranges from 5€ to 15€ ($8–$24).

At **Irish Pub Koblenz,** Burgstrasse 7 (© **0261/9737797;** bus: 1), copious amounts of Guinness, Kilkenny, hard cider, and German beers are served as accompaniment to everything from traditional Gaelic songs to progressive rock 'n' roll. Hours are Monday to Thursday 4pm to 1am, Friday 4pm to 2am, Saturday 1pm to 2am, and Sunday 1pm to 1am.

6 Bonn ⸙

72km (45 miles) S of Düsseldorf, 27km (17 miles) S of Cologne, 174km (108 miles) NW of Frankfurt

Until 1949, Bonn was a sleepy little university town, basking in its 2,000 years of history. Then suddenly it was shaken out of this quiet life and made capital of the Federal Republic of Germany. But in 1991, after the reunification of Germany, Berlin again became the official capital.

From the 13th century through the 18th century, Bonn was the capital of the prince-electors of Cologne, who had the right to participate in the election of the emperor of the Holy Roman Empire. The city is also proud of its intellectual and musical history—Beethoven was born here; composer Robert Schumann and his wife, pianist Clara Schumann, lived here; and Karl Marx and Heinrich Heine studied in Bonn's university.

Bonn is also within sight of the **Siebenbirge (Seven Mountains),** a volcanic mountain range rising up on the eastern bank of the Rhine. The local wine produced on these slopes is known as *Drachenblut* (Dragon's Blood) and is better than most German reds.

ESSENTIALS

GETTING THERE   By Plane   The nearest airport is **Flughafen Köln/Bonn** (see "Cologne," later in this chapter). Buses from the airport to Bonn's main rail station run every 30 minutes daily 6am to 10:30pm.

By Train   The **Bonn Hauptbahnhof** is on a major rail line, with connections to most German cities. There are 12 trains daily to Berlin (trip time: 5 hr.), more than 30 trains to Frankfurt (trip time: 2 hr.), and service to Cologne every 15 minutes (trip time: 20 min.). For information, call © **01805/996633** (11861 in Germany; www.bahn.de).

By Bus   Long-distance bus service goes to such cities as Munich, Stuttgart, Aachen, Brussels, and London. For information, call **Deutsches Touring GmbH** in Frankfurt (© **069/7903501**). Regional bus service to Bad Godesberg and nearby towns is provided by **Regionalverkehr Köln GmbH at Meckenheim** (© **0228/7111**).

By Car   Access is by the A565 Autobahn connecting with the A3 Autobahn from the north or south.

VISITOR INFORMATION   Go to the **Bonn Tourist Office,** Windeckstrasse 1 (© **0228/775000;** www.bonn.de), open Monday to Friday 9am to 6:30pm, Saturday 9am to 4pm, and Sunday 10am to 2pm.

GETTING AROUND   If you visit the Reisenzentrum under the Bonn railway station, you can pick up a free map outlining the city's transportation network. The office is open Monday to Saturday 5:30am to 10pm and Sunday 6:30am to 10pm. Bus or S-Bahn/U-Bahn tickets cost 1.50€ to 9.30€ ($2.40–$15). You can also purchase a day ticket costing 5.20€ to 20€ ($8.30–$31).

WHERE TO STAY

Dorint Sofitel Venusberg 🏰🏰🏰   This elegant and intimate hotel, built in a style evocative of a French country home, is surrounded by the beauty of the Venusberg nature reserve, part of the larger Kottenforst. It is the grandest choice for Bonn. About half the units offer private balconies overlooking the hills. Bathrooms are well accessorized, all equipped with tub/shower combos.

An der Casselsruhe 1 (2.5km/1½ miles southwest of Bonn, via Trierer Strasse), 53127 Bonn. © 0228/2880. Fax 0228/288288. www.dorint.de. 85 units. 90€–280€ ($144–$448) double; 365€–409€ ($584–$654) junior suite; 525€–569€ ($840–$910) suite. AE, DC, MC, V. Parking 11€ ($18). **Amenities:** 2 restaurants; piano bar; lounge; nearby health club; Jacuzzi; sauna; solarium; salon; room service; massage; babysitting; laundry service; dry cleaning; nonsmoking rooms; rooms for those w/limited mobility. *In room:* A/C, TV, Wi-Fi, minibar, hair dryer, safe.

Günnewig Bristol Hotel 🏰🏰   This somewhat sterile, Cold War–era concrete-and-glass tower is still the best address in town. The good-size rooms are the best in Bonn, with such extras as trouser presses and double-glazing on the windows, along with fashionable and well-equipped bathrooms with tub/shower combos and robes. The staff is also excellent.

Prinz-Albert-Strasse 2 (near Poppelsdorf Castle), 53113 Bonn. © 0228/26980. Fax 0228/2698222. www.guennewig. de. 116 units. 114€–186€ ($182–$298) double; 230€–390€ ($368–$624) suite. Children 12 and under stay free in parent's room. Rates include American breakfast. AE, DC, MC, V. Parking 14€ ($22). Tram: 61 or 62. **Amenities:** 3 restaurants; bar; lounge; indoor heated pool; sauna; solarium; room service; babysitting; laundry service; dry cleaning; nonsmoking rooms. *In room:* A/C, TV, Wi-Fi (in some), minibar, hair dryer, safe.

Hotel Beethoven   One of the Beethoven's wings faces the Rhine. The hotel's main attraction is a panoramic view of the river traffic from the high-ceilinged dining room, which serves first-class meals. Double-glazed windows prevent urban noises from disturbing the calm in the well-furnished rooms, which range from small to medium. All units have bathrooms with tub/shower combos.

Rheingasse 24–26 (across the street from the Stadttheater, a 10-min. walk from the Hauptbahnhof), 53113 Bonn. © 0228/631411. Fax 0228/691629. www.hotel-beethoven-bonn.com. 59 units. 70€–97€ ($112–$155) double. Rates include continental breakfast. MC, V. Parking 6€ ($9.60). Tram: 62. Bus: 638. **Amenities:** Restaurant; nonsmoking rooms. *In room:* TV, hair dryer.

Hotel Domicil 🏰🏰   This modern and convenient hotel, like the Kaiser Karl (see below), is an oasis of charm and grace in Bonn's rather sterile environment. It's like an exclusive London town house and provides a viable alternative to the Günnewig Bristol (see above). In the front, a glass-and-steel portico stretches over the sidewalk. The interior is one of the most elegant in the capital. The handsomely designed and spacious rooms range from Belle Epoque to Italian modern. All units contain neatly kept bathrooms with tub/shower combos.

Thomas-Mann-Strasse 24–26 (4 blocks north of the cathedral, near the Hauptbahnhof), 53111 Bonn. © 800/780-7234 in the U.S., or 0228/729090. Fax 0228/691207. www.bestwestern.de. 44 units. 131€–222€ ($210–$355) double; 250€ ($400) suite. Rates include buffet breakfast. AE, DC, MC, V. Parking 18€ ($29). U-Bahn: Hauptbahnhof. **Amenities:** Restaurant; bar; Jacuzzi; sauna; car rental; salon; room service; babysitting; laundry service; dry cleaning; nonsmoking rooms. *In room:* TV, minibar, beverage maker, hair dryer, iron, safe, trouser press.

Kaiser Karl ⓡⓡ *(Finds)*   Kaiser Karl is one of Bonn's gems. Like the Domicil (see above), it has more style and atmosphere than other luxury leaders. Constructed in 1905 as a private town house, it was converted in 1983 into a stylish four-story hotel. The attractive decor includes lacquered Japanese screens, English antiques, Oriental carpets, Venetian mirrors, and Edwardian potted palms. Each beautifully furnished room has a bathroom with a tub/shower combo.

Vorgebirgstrasse 56, 53119 Bonn. ⓒ 0228/985570. Fax 0228/9855777. www.kaiser-karl-hotel-bonn.de. 42 units. 140€–420€ ($224–$672) double; from 250€ ($400) suite. Children 6 and under stay free in parent's room. AE, DC, MC, V. Parking 12€ ($19). Bus: 645 or 607. Pets allowed. **Amenities:** Restaurant; lounge; car rental; room service; babysitting; laundry service; dry cleaning; nonsmoking rooms; rooms for those w/limited mobility. *In room:* TV, minibar, hair dryer, safe.

Sternhotel   This is one of the best of Bonn's moderately priced hotels. It offers an informal, cozy atmosphere. Rooms are homey, all with comfortable furnishings and bathrooms equipped with tub/shower combos.

Markt 8 (next to the Rathaus), 53111 Bonn. ⓒ 0228/72670. Fax 0228/7267125. www.sternhotel-bonn.de. 80 units. 99€–185€ ($158–$296) double; 145€–230€ ($232–$368) suite. Rates include buffet breakfast. DC, MC, V. U-Bahn: Uni-Markt. Bus: 624, 625, or 626. **Amenities:** Breakfast room; lounge; nonsmoking rooms; rooms for those w/limited mobility. *In room:* TV, minibar.

WHERE TO DINE

Em Höttche *(Value)* GERMAN   Em Höttche enjoys a long and colorful history, going all the way back to 1389. It's fed thousands over the centuries with its rib-sticking fare—perhaps changing the recipes every 100 years or so. The interior has been restored, with carved-wood paneling, natural brick, old beamed ceilings, decoratively painted plaster, and curlicue chandeliers. Favorite dining spots are tables set inside the walk-in fireplace. On the a la carte list, you'll find specialties for two, including entrecôte. Fresh salmon is often available. Complement your meal with a carafe of local wine—the best buy in the house. However, the drink of choice for most visitors is Kölsch beer, a famous Rhineland beer for which the establishment is well known.

Markt 4 (next to the Rathaus). ⓒ 0228/690009. Reservations not accepted. Main courses 12€–18€ ($19–$29). No credit cards. Daily 11am–1am. Tram: 47. Bus: 618.

Le Petit Poisson ⓡ FRENCH/SEAFOOD   The food here is some of the best in Bonn's center. All ingredients are fresh, and many dishes are temptingly light and contemporary. Try the cream of fish and mushroom soup. Savory meat and game dishes include venison in vermouth sauce. Many diplomats dine here.

Wilhelmstrasse 23A. ⓒ 0228/633883. Reservations recommended. Main courses 25€–30€ ($40–$48); fixed-price dinners 48€–68€ ($77–$109). AE, DC, MC, V. Tues–Sat 6pm–1am. Tram: 61 or 62.

Ristorante Grand'Italia ⓡ ITALIAN/INTERNATIONAL   This is one of the most appealing Italian restaurants along the Rhine. Main courses might include a *filetto della casa* (filet of beef prepared in a "special sauce," the composition of which the chefs won't discuss), *tagliorini* with white truffles, and an autumnal version of roast pheasant. Also look for Roman-style osso buco (veal shank layered with prosciutto), a succulent risotto Milanese, and such desserts as a velvety version of zabaglione.

Bischofsplatz 1 (adjacent to the old market sq.). ⓒ 0228/638333. Reservations recommended. Main courses 17€–23€ ($27–$37). AE, DC, MC, V. Daily noon–2:30pm and 6–11:30pm. Tram: 62 or 66.

Zur Lese GERMAN   This restaurant's polite service and outdoor terrace with a sweeping view over the Rhine attract many local residents, especially in the afternoon, when visitors drop in for coffee, cakes, and glasses of wine after strolling in the nearby Hofgarten. Elegant, well-prepared lunches are also offered. Dinner is served in the cafe. A menu of German specialties (with English translations) includes pork with curry sauce and the chef's superb *Gulasch Lese* (goulash). You can also choose rainbow trout or lobster from the terrace aquarium. The food is home-style and hearty, with no pretense.

Adenauerallee 37. ℂ 0228/223322. Reservations recommended. Main courses 11€–21€ ($18–$34); fixed-price dinner 36€ ($58). AE, DC, MC, V. Restaurant Tues–Sun noon–midnight. Cafe Tues–Sun noon–2pm and 6–10pm.

EXPLORING BONN

The best way to get acquainted with Bonn is to take a **walking tour,** the meeting point of which is the Bonn Tourist Office (see above). Call ℂ **0228/775000** for reservations. Tours lasting 2½ hours cost 14€ ($22) for adults or 7€ ($11) for children 6 to 14, free for children 5 and under, with a family ticket (2 adults and 2 kids) going for 24€ ($38). Tours depart January to April 4 and November 2 to December 15 only on Saturday at 2pm. The "Big City Tour" is conducted on a bus with commentary in English and German, taking in all the scenic highlights and going by the major monuments. The last part of the tour involves a walk through the historic core.

The **government quarter,** along the west bank of the Rhine, is a complex of modern, rather nondescript white buildings. The two most impressive, both along Koblenzerstrasse, are the former residences of the president and chancellor. These empire-style villas are reminiscent of the older Bonn, before it became an international center of diplomatic activity. They are not open to the public. Running north along the Rhine from the government buildings is a tree- and flower-lined promenade, which ends at the **Alter Zoll.** This ruined ancient fortress makes a fantastic viewing point from which visitors can see across the Rhine to the Siebengebirge and the old village of Beuel. These grounds, in essence, have become a city park.

Beethoven House ☆   Beethoven House is Bonn's pride and joy. Beethoven was born in 1770 in the small house in back, which opens onto a little garden. On its second floor is the room where he was born, decorated only with a simple marble bust of the composer. Many of Beethoven's personal possessions are in the house, including manuscripts and musical instruments. In the Vienna Room, in the front of the house overlooking the street, is Beethoven's last piano. The instrument was custom-made, with a special sounding board to amplify sound for the hearing-impaired composer.

Bonngasse 20 (in the old section of town, just north of the marketplace). ℂ 0228/981750. www.beethoven-haus-bonn.de. Admission 5€ ($8) adults, 4€ ($6.40) students and children, 10€ ($16) family ticket. Apr–Oct Mon–Sat 10am–6pm, Sun 11am–6pm; Nov–Mar Mon–Sat 10am–5pm, Sun 11am–5pm. Tram: 62 or 66.

Haus der Geschichte der Bundesrepublik Deutschland (House of History of the German Republic)   All the sweep and drama of Germany's modern history is brought to life in this museum, in artifacts, photographs, and other displays. Exhibits trace the history of Germany after 1945, up to the breakdown of law and order in the eastern sector that led to reunification. The museum made headlines in 2001 when Emilie Schindler, the 93-year-old widow of Oskar Schindler, donated some of her famous husband's documents to the museum. Oskar Schindler was the subject of Steven Spielberg's film *Schindler's List,* one of the best-known movies ever made of the Holocaust. The bequest includes excerpts from the diary of one of hundreds of Jews who Schindler, a German industrialist, saved from the Nazi death camps. The donation also includes a

photo album of the making of the Spielberg movie and a congratulatory letter from then American president Bill Clinton.

Willy-Brandt-Allee 14. © 0228/91650. www.hdg.de. Free admission. Tues–Sun 9am–7pm. U-Bahn: Heussallee/ Museumsmeile.

Kunstmuseum Bonn   One of the major buildings along the new Museum Mile, this triangular structure, flooded with light, contains one of the most important art collections along the Rhine. The highlight is 20th-century art, including works by Rhenish expressionists, most notably August Macke. There are also works by Kirchner, Schmidt-Rottluff, Campen-Donk, Ernst, Seehaus, and Thuar.

Friedrich-Ebert-Allee 2. © 0228/776260. http://kunstmuseum.bonn.de. Admission 5€ ($8) adults, 2.50€ ($4) children, 10€ ($16) family ticket. Tues–Sun 10am–6pm (Wed until 9pm). U-Bahn: Heussallee.

SHOPPING

Not surprisingly, you'll find lots of shops in town specializing in garments suitable for diplomacy and business. Most of the best are on the **Sternstrasse** (S-Bahn: Hauptbahnhof), partly a pedestrian-only street at certain times of day. Fanning out from here, you'll find women's clothing at **Beatrix Moden,** Am Neutor 5 (© **0228/ 634696**), and at **La Belle,** Friedrichstrasse 51 (© **0228/637475**).

Eighteenth-century German and French furniture as well as Biedermeier is found at **Paul Schweitzer,** Loebestrasse 1 (© **0228/362659;** S-Bahn: Godesberger Bahnhof), which also handles Oriental carpets, silver, French glass, and estate jewelry. A market called the **Flohmarkt,** at Rheinaue, Ludwig-Erhard-Strasse (tram: 66), is where you'll find all manner of secondhand goods and collectibles. It's held the third Saturday of each month April to October. A weekly market, **Wochenmarkt,** on the square of the same name, is held Monday to Saturday. You can enjoy a good lunch here, buying cooked food as you walk along inspecting the produce and various flea market items.

BONN AFTER DARK ·

Once a dismal place to go out on the town, Bonn now has a thriving fine-arts community and a brisk nightlife. If you're in the area around the first Saturday in May, don't miss the spectacular annual fireworks display, visible for a distance of 26km (16 miles) south of the city.

THE PERFORMING ARTS   Bonn has always struggled with the perception that it can't compete with the larger arts communities in Hamburg and Berlin, and consequently it compensates (or overcompensates) with an impressive roster of cultural events. One of the most visible is "La Scala of the Rhineland," the **Oper der Stadt Bonn,** Am Boeselagerhof (© **0228/778000;** www.theater-bonn.de; S-Bahn: Hauptbahnhof), where ballet and opera are performed at regular intervals mid-August to June. Box office hours are Monday to Friday 10am to 3:30pm, Saturday 9:30am to noon, and Sunday 10am to 2pm. Tickets are 9€ to 115€ ($14–$184) each, depending on the event.

The **Bonn Symphony Orchestra** performs in Beethovenhalle, Wachsbleiche 16 (© **0228/7222-0;** S-Bahn: Hauptbahnhof), September to June, with occasional free concerts given on Sunday mornings. Otherwise, tickets cost 15€ to 62€ ($24–$99). On a more intimate scale, chamber music is sometimes presented within a small but charming concert hall within the **Beethoven House** (© **0228/981750** for details).

During the Bonner Summer Festival, mid-May to August, an international selection of dance and music groups performs, mostly for free, in open-air locations around the city. Contact ℭ **0228/201030** or 0228/2010345 for details. In addition, the **Beethoven Festival,** a rekindling of both the nostalgia and the music associated with Bonn's greatest musical genius, takes place in late August and September. Contact the visitor information center (see "Visitor Information," above) for information.

Bonn's **Theater-Kasse,** Windeckstrasse 1 (ℭ **0228/775000;** S-Bahn: Hauptbahnhof), is a well-known and highly resourceful ticket agency associated with the city's tourist office. It has access to tickets for virtually every sporting, entertainment, and cultural venue in Bonn. Also call for information on performers, schedules, and prices.

DANCE CLUBS   A weekend-only club, **Sharon,** Oxfordstrasse 20–22 (ℭ **0228/ 656760;** S-Bahn: Hauptbahnhof), is straight out of the 1970s, with dancing to soul and funk under a spinning mirror ball and strobe lights. It's open Friday and Saturday 10pm to 5am, with an 8€ to 10€ ($13–$16) cover.

LIVE MUSIC & CABARET   The **Pantheon Theater,** Bundeskanzlerplatz (ℭ **0228/ 212521;** bus: 610), stages jazz and pop concerts, comedy shows, and political cabaret. Nearly every weekday there is a performance of some sort. Friday and Saturday, the facility becomes a dance club. The box office is open Monday to Friday noon to 6:30pm.

BARS   **Pawlow,** Heerstrasse 64 (ℭ **0228/653603;** S-Bahn: Tanninbusche Sud), has an alfresco terrace. While here, don't let appearances intimidate you—a sometimes fierce-looking crowd with tattoos and body piercings is actually a bored intelligentsia at heart. Pawlow is open daily 10am to 1am (hours are later on weekends).

GAY BARS   The most crowded gay bar is **Boba's Bar,** Josefstrasse 17 (ℭ **0228/ 650685;** S-Bahn: Hauptbahnhof), near the railway station, adjacent to the Rhine. It welcomes a drinking (but not dancing) crowd in their 20s and 30s. It's open Tuesday to Sunday 8pm to 3am and Friday and Saturday 8pm to 5am. There's also **Le Copain,** Berliner Platz 5 (ℭ **0228/639935;** S-Bahn: Berliner-von-Suttner-Platz), which attracts a somewhat older clientele and is open 4pm to 1 or 2am.

7 Bad Godesberg

6km (4 miles) S of central Bonn

Part of greater Bonn, Bad Godesberg is one of the Rhine's oldest spa towns. It's located just opposite the legendary Siebengebirge (Seven Mountains), with a view of the crag, Drachenfels (Dragon's Rock) where, according to legend, Siegfried slew the dragon. You can still see some ancient castle ruins on the hills, such as **Godesberg Castle,** built in the 13th century by the electors of Cologne (its ruins have been incorporated into the Ringhotel Rheinhotel Dreesen, see below). From the promenade along the Rhine, you can watch a flow of boats and barges wending their way up and down the river.

Most of the spa's activities center on the small but elegant 18th-century **Redoute Palace.** Theaters, concerts, and social functions offer a constant whirl of events. Since these events are not permanent, check with the tourist office, which publishes a weekly list of current events happening at the time of your visit.

GETTING THERE   You can reach Bad Godesberg from Bonn by taking tram no. 16 or 63 from Bonn's central rail station (trip time: 20 min.). If you're driving from the center of Bonn, take the B9 (driving time: 20 min.). For information about the town, consult the Bonn Tourist Office (see "Bonn," earlier in this chapter).

WHERE TO STAY

Ringhotel Rheinhotel Dreesen ⟨★⟩   Directly beside the river, a 10-minute ride from the center of Bonn, this noble structure offers rooms opening onto the banks of the river. Across the river, guests can see the national park areas of Siebengebirge and Petersberg. Bedrooms are elegant and comfortable, each tastefully furnished and ranging from midsize to spacious, with first-class bathrooms with tub and shower. Bikes are available for cycling tours along the banks of the Rhine or else in the park. Freshly prepared meals with quality ingredients are served in the on-site bistro and restaurant.

Rheinstrasse 45, 53179 Bad Godesberg. (𝄢 **0228/82020.** Fax 0228/8202153. www.rheinhoteldreesen.de. 72 units. 170€–225€ ($272–$360) double; 200€–240€ ($320–$384) suite. Rates include breakfast. AE, DC, MC, V. Parking 10€ ($16). Tram: 16. **Amenities:** 2 restaurants; bar; 2 pools (1 heated indoor, 1 outdoor); tennis court; fitness center; free bikes; children's activities; car rental; business center; room service; laundry service; dry cleaning. *In room:* A/C, TV, Wi-Fi, minibar, safe.

WHERE TO DINE

Halbedel's Gasthaus ⟨★★⟩ CONTINENTAL   Here, amid many nostalgic souvenirs and antique tables and chairs, the courtly owners will welcome you to their turn-of-the-20th-century villa. The kitchen prides itself on using mostly German-grown produce. The chefs are true artists, using ingredients of superlative quality to create harmonious flavors and textures. Some of the dishes will be familiar; others are imaginative inventions. Perhaps the most experimental dish on the menu is pigeon with a dark chocolate–and-chili sauce. In spite of the sound of it, it is a great flavor to many gourmets. Also reaching heights of culinary bliss is the gooseliver with a brioche that's accompanied with apples and a passionfruit sauce. Lobster tartare appears delectably with avocados and mangos. We are also impressed with the turbot with fresh artichokes and morels.

Rheinallee 47. (𝄢 **0228/354253.** Reservations recommended. Main courses 32€–38€ ($51–$61); fixed-price menu 81€–93€ ($130–$149). AE, MC, V. Tues–Sun 6-10:30pm. Closed July 26–Aug 26. Tram: 16 from Bonn. Bus: 610.

8 Aachen (Aix-la-Chapelle) ⟨★⟩

64km (40 miles) W of Cologne, 80km (50 miles) SW of Düsseldorf

The ancient Imperial City of Aachen (Aix-la-Chapelle), at the frontier where Germany, Belgium, and the Netherlands meet, is inseparably connected with Charlemagne. He selected this spot as the center of his vast Frankish empire. History is important here, but today there's also a youthful *joie de vivre* that attracts young people from all over the world. Visitors also come for the sulfurous hot springs and the magnificent cathedral.

Aachen has an even longer history as a spa than as an imperial city. Roman legionnaires established a military bath here in the 1st century A.D. By the end of the 17th century, Aachen was known as the "Spa of Kings" because royalty from all over Europe came here to take the cure. Its springs are among the hottest in Europe. The treatment includes baths and the *Trinkkur* (drinking the water). The spa gardens are the center of resort activity, with attractive ponds, fountains, and shade trees.

ESSENTIALS

GETTING THERE   By Train   The Hauptbahnhof at Aachen receives some 200 trains a day from all parts of Germany and from Paris, with easy connections from most major cities as well as nearby Cologne (trip time: 45 min.). Frankfurt is 2 hours and 45 minutes away, and Munich, 5 hours and 40 minutes. For information, call ℂ **01805/996633** (11861 in Germany; www.bahn.de).

By Car   Access is by the A4 Autobahn east and west or the A44 north or south. Driving time from Cologne is 50 to 60 minutes, depending on traffic. Frankfurt is 3½ hours away by car; Munich, 6½ hours.

VISITOR INFORMATION   You'll find the **Tourist Office Aachen** on Friedrich-Wilhelm-Platz (ℂ **0241/1802960;** www.aachen.de). Office hours are Monday to Friday 9am to 6pm, Saturday 9am to 3pm, and Sunday 10am to 2pm.

GETTING AROUND   Buses pull into the main railway station in the center of town at Peterskirchhof and Peterstrasse. Tickets are 1.50€ to 6.50€ ($2.40–$10). A 24-hour pass, available at the bus station, offers unlimited travel within Aachen for 6.10€ ($9.80).

WHERE TO STAY

Am Marschiertor *☘ Finds*   This charming hotel stands in the center of Aachen, not far from the Hauptbahnhof and next to the medieval town gate for which it's named. The hotel is quiet, with a courtyard and a view over the Altstadt and cathedral. The lobby and connecting hall are attractive, with antique furniture. The recently refurbished rooms have a cozy atmosphere, and each—generally medium in size—is well appointed and well maintained with bathrooms containing tub/shower combos.

Wallstrasse 1–7, 52064 Aachen. ℂ 0241/31941. Fax 0241/31944. www.hotel-marschiertor-aachen.de. 50 units. 88€–135€ ($141–$216) double. AE, DC, MC, V. Parking 10€ ($16). Bus: 1, 11, or 21. Pets accepted. **Amenities:** Breakfast room; lounge; room service; babysitting; nonsmoking rooms. *In room:* TV, Wi-Fi, hair dryer.

Aquis Grana City Hotel *☘*   Aquis Grana City Hotel is your best bet in the town center. The comfortable rooms offer all the modern extras and range from spacious to medium. All units contain bathrooms with tub/shower combos. The staff is very alert to all your needs. Housekeeping rates an A+.

Büchel 32, 52016 Aachen. ℂ 0241/4430. Fax 0241/443137. www.hotel-aquisgrana.de. 97 units. 88€–230€ ($141–$368) double; 270€–420€ ($432–$672) suite. Children up to 10 stay free in parent's room. AE, DC, MC, V. Free parking. Bus: 1, 11, or 21. **Amenities:** Restaurant; lounge; room service; laundry service; dry cleaning; nonsmoking rooms; rooms for those w/limited mobility. *In room:* TV, minibar, hair dryer, safe.

Hotel Benelux *Value*   The warm and inviting Benelux is within walking distance of many major attractions. It's a small family-run hotel, tastefully decorated and personalized. Americans from the Southwest will feel at home in the lobby/reception area—it has probably the only cactus collection in Aachen. Rooms range from small to medium. All units come equipped with bathrooms containing tub/shower combos.

Franzstrasse 21–23 (5-min. walk from the Hauptbahnhof), 52064 Aachen. ℂ 0241/400030. Fax 0241/40003500. www.hotel-benelux.de. 33 units. 103€–148€ ($165–$237) double. Rates include continental breakfast. AE, DC, MC, V. Parking 8€ ($13). Bus: 5, 25, or 35. **Amenities:** Restaurant; lounge; fitness center; room service; laundry service; nonsmoking rooms. *In room:* A/C, TV, minibar, hair dryer, iron, safe.

Hotel Dorint Sofitel Quellenhof *☘☘☘*   Once a country home for the kaiser during World War I, this has been turned into a charming, welcoming hotel that appeals to traditionalists. Operated by the Dorint chain, the hotel and its spa are reason enough to go to Aachen. Both the public and the private rooms are spacious and beautifully decorated, resting under tall ceilings. An antique and conservatively modern decor is successfully blended. Rooms are furnished comfortably and attractively, each with a private bathroom with tub and shower. Many guests use the hotel as a spa, and it has the Royal Spa with a pool, Turkish bath, Finnish sauna, bio-sauna, ice grotto, and solarium, along with beauty-treatment rooms. The drinking and dining facilities are first class.

Monheimsallee 52, 52062 Aachen. (C) 0241/91320. Fax 0241/9132100. www.accorhotels.com. 185 units. 190€–365€ ($304–$584) double; 220€–530€ ($352–$848) suite. 1 child stays free in parent's room. AE, DC, MC, V. Parking 15€ ($24). Pets allowed. **Amenities:** Restaurant; 2 bars; dance club; indoor heated pool; gym; spa; sauna; solarium; steam room; tour desk; business center; room service; babysitting; dry cleaning; nonsmoking rooms; rooms for those w/limited mobility. *In room:* A/C, TV, Wi-Fi, hair dryer, safe.

WHERE TO DINE

Magellan INTERNATIONAL   Set within a 5-minute walk from Aachen's Rathaus (Town Hall), with a sprawling outdoor terrace that overlooks trees and flowers, this restaurant encompasses cuisine from terrain that its namesake, the famed explorer Magellan, might have visited. The venue is rustic, with thick wooden tables, durable chairs, and a magisterial chandelier that somehow evokes something akin to a Greek Orthodox church. The menu includes choices from Turkey (*mezes*, the succulent and savory dishes like mashed eggplant, olives, and hummus); Italy (pizzas and pastas), Germany (schnitzels and sausages), as well as a wide choice of grilled lamb and beefsteaks.

Pontstrasse 78. (C) 0241/401-6440. Reservations not necessary. Main courses 10€–15€ ($16–$24). MC, V. Daily 10am–1am (Fri–Sat till 2am); last order for hot food at 11pm. Bus: 3 or 13.

Ratskeller INTERNATIONAL   This is a charming, old-fashioned restaurant beloved by many. The less expensive section is the Postwagen, a publike setting that serves platters and drinks in the afternoon. But we prefer the majesty of the brick-and-stone Ratskeller, where a sense of medievalism is enhanced by solid, conservative fare, such as sauerkraut with *Wurst,* minestrone or potato soup, grilled steaks, fricassee of sole, and fresh berries and pastries for dessert.

Markt 40, Am Markt (in the Rathaus). (C) 0241/35001. Reservations recommended. Postwagen: Platters 10€–19€ ($16–$31); 3-course menu 28€ ($45). Ratskeller: Main courses 20€–28€ ($32–$45); fixed-price menus 38€–53€ ($60–$84). AE, DC, MC, V. Postwagen daily 10am–10pm. Ratskeller daily 11am–3pm and 6–10pm. Bus: 2, 11, or 25.

EXPLORING AACHEN

Aachen's Altstadt is small enough to be covered on foot. Marktplatz, in the heart of town, is overshadowed by the Gothic **Rathaus,** which contains the city archives. From here, you can head down one of the most popular and busiest pedestrian precincts in the city, Krämerstrasse, which will lead to **Münsterplatz (Cathedral Square)** and the famous cathedral (see below), one of the masterpieces of architecture in the Western world. Past the cathedral you reach the Elisengarten, bordered on the south by the symbol of Bad Aachen, the **Elisenbrunnen,** a rotunda with a thermal drinking fountain. From Münsterplatz you can go through the great iron gate to the **Fischmarkt,** with old merchants' houses and the Fischpuddelchen fountain with spouting fish.

Wingerstsberg Kurgarten and the **Stadtgarten,** with its thermal bath and casino, lie to the northeast of town, and the **Hauptbahnhof** is on the southern ring, opening onto Römerstrasse.

Couven Museum ⊛   This gracefully designed villa gives you an insight into the decorative traditions of the late 18th and 19th centuries. It has one of the best collections of antique furnishings of any museum in the region. On the ground floor is a reproduction of a small-scale chocolate factory. You'll find treasures, some of them low-key and discreet, virtually everywhere you look.

Huhnermarkt 17. © 0241/4324421. www.couven-museum.de. Admission 5€ ($8) adults, 2.50€ ($4) students and children. Tues–Sun 10am–5pm; 1st Sun of every month 1–5pm. Bus: 4.

Dom (Cathedral) ★★   About A.D. 800, Emperor Charlemagne built the "octagon," the core of the Imperial Cathedral. Within stands the marble *Königsstuhl,* Charlemagne's throne, one of the most venerable monuments in Germany. (Visitors to the cathedral can view the throne only with a guide; request one at the treasury or call ahead.) The Holy Roman emperors were crowned here from 936 to 1531, when Frankfurt became the coronation city.

The cathedral is an unusual mixture of Carolingian (the well-preserved dome), Gothic (the choir, completed in 1414), and baroque (the Hungarian chapel), all united into a magnificent upward sweep of architecture. The **treasury** ★★★, in the adjoining house (entry: Klostergasse), is the most valuable and celebrated ecclesiastical treasure trove north of the Alps. But the cathedral itself holds its own share of wealth. The elaborate gold shrine (1215) in the chancel contains the **relics of Charlemagne** ★★★. The **pulpit** ★★★ of Henry II (ca. 1002) is copper studded with precious gems.

Klosterplatz 2. © 0241/47709127. www.aachendom.de. Cathedral free; treasury 4€ ($6.40) adults, 3€ ($4.80) students and children. Cathedral daily 7am–7pm; treasury Mon 10am–1pm, Tues–Wed and Fri–Sun 10am–6pm, Thurs 10am–9pm. Bus: 1, 11, or 21.

Rathaus   The 14th-century Rathaus was built on the original site of Charlemagne's palace. Part of the ancient palace structure can still be seen in the so-called Granus Tower at the east side of the hall. The richly decorated facade, facing the marketplace, is adorned with the statues of 50 German rulers, 31 of them crowned in Aachen. In the center, standing in relief, are the "Majestas Domini," the two most important men of their time in the Holy Roman Empire, Charlemagne and Pope Leo III.

On the second floor of the Rathaus is the double-naved and cross-beamed Imperial Hall, where coronation banquets took place from 1349 to 1531. Built as the successor to the Carolingian Royal Hall, today it contains exact replicas of the imperial crown jewels, true in size and material to the originals, presently in the Vienna Secular Treasury. On the walls are the Charlemagne frescoes, painted in the 19th century by Alfred Rethel, illustrating the victory of the Christian Franks over the Germanic heathens.

Am Markt. © 0241/4327310. Admission 2€ ($3.20) adults, 1€ ($1.60) students and children. Daily 10am–1pm and 2–5pm. Closed sometimes for official events. Bus: 4 or 11.

Suermondt Ludwig Museum ★   The impressive collection of medieval German sculpture, one of the finest in the land, includes a *Madonna in Robes* (1420) from the Swabian school and a *Virgin and Child* from the 14th-century Tournai school. The second landing has a good collection of primitive Flemish and German works, along with 17th-century Dutch and Flemish paintings. Look for works by Van Dyck and Jordaens. The museum also has modern works, especially from the 1920s and 1930s.

Wilhelmstrasse 18. © 0241/479800. www.suermondt-ludwig-museum.de. Admission 5€ ($8) adults, 3€ ($4.80) children. Tues–Sun noon–6pm (Wed until 9pm). Bus: 3, 4, or 13.

AACHEN AFTER DARK

For information about what's happening in Aachen, pick up a copy of the booklet *Tourist-Information,* published and given away free by the tourist information office. You can also download a copy at www.aachen.de. Alternatively, you can buy a copy of the monthly glossy, *Klenkes,* a magazine available in news kiosks around the city for 2€ ($3.20).

THE PERFORMING ARTS   Classical concerts are presented in the town's convention center, **Kongresszentrum Eurogress,** Mondheimsallee 48 (℃ **0241/91310;** bus: 57), by the local symphony orchestra and by visiting chamber orchestras. The **Theater Aachen** (formerly the Stadttheater), Theaterplatz (℃ **0241/47841;** bus: 33, 34, or 57), hosts opera, theater, and dance recitals. Ticket prices in both places are 14€ to 100€ ($22–$160). If you understand German and want to see experimental theater and plays by Bertolt Brecht, head for the small and rather cramped **Theater 99 Akut,** Gasborn 9–11 (℃ **0241/27458;** bus: 166). Tickets are 19€ to 56€ ($30–$90).

BARS & CAFES   There are at least a half-dozen bars in or around Aachen's Marktplatz. One of the most appealing is the **Martesa Keller,** Martesastrasse (no phone; bus: 13). This cozy, convivial, wood-paneled place offers live music, usually jazz, on most nights (usually Wed–Sat, beginning around 8:30pm) and a bar that opens every night at 6pm. More youth oriented is the **Café Kittel,** Pontstrasse 39 (℃ **0241/ 36560;** bus: 13), which somewhat resembles a greenhouse; its menu concentrates on beer, wine, sandwiches, and quiche. It's open Monday to Thursday 10am to 2am, Friday and Saturday 10:30am to 2am, and Sunday 10am to 1am.

DANCE CLUBS   Friday and Saturday nights, **Rotation,** Pontstrasse 135 (no phone; bus: 13), keeps the dance music cranking until 6am. Other nights, the music provides a background for drinking and socializing. There's no cover charge and no food served. It's open Sunday to Thursday 3pm to 2am.

LIVE MUSIC   It's Irish in conception, but **Wild Rover,** Hirschgraben 13 (℃ **0241/ 35453;** bus: 4 or 33), is a rock club first and foremost. The bands that take the stage nightly range from mainstream to punk. It's open daily 8pm to 1am (on weekends until 3am). A worthy competitor is the **Exil-Bar,** Schlossstrasse 2 (℃ **0241/512345;** bus: 33, 34, or 57), where live music, including jazz and rock, is presented within a small, smoke-filled, and decidedly bohemian venue every night 6pm to 1am. A final nightlife venue is the **Domkeller,** Hof 1 (℃ **0241/34265;** bus: 1, 11, or 21), which offers live blues or jazz on some nights and lots of hubbub every night. It is open Monday to Thursday 10am to 1am and to 3 or 4am Friday and Saturday.

9 Cologne (Köln) ★★★

27km (17 miles) N of Bonn, 40km (25 miles) S of Düsseldorf, 188km (117 miles) NW of Frankfurt

Cologne (Köln), the largest city in the Rhineland, is so rich in antiquity that every time a new foundation is dug, the excavators come up with archaeological finds. Devastating though the World War II bombing was, reconstruction brought to light a period of Cologne's history that had been a mystery for centuries. Evidence showed that Cologne was as important and powerful during the early Christian era as it was during Roman times and the Middle Ages.

Cologne traces its beginnings to 38 B.C., when Roman legions set up camp here. As early as A.D. 50, Emperor Claudius gave it municipal rights as capital of a Roman province. In the early Christian era, a bishopric was founded here and a number of saints were martyred, including the patron of the city, St. Ursula. During the Middle Ages, as Cologne became a center for international trade, Romanesque and Gothic churches were built with prosperous merchants' gold. Today there is much to see from every period of the city's 2,000-year history—from the old Roman towers to the modern opera house. But Cologne is also a bustling modern city and is becoming the fine-art capital of Germany.

Cologne (Köln)

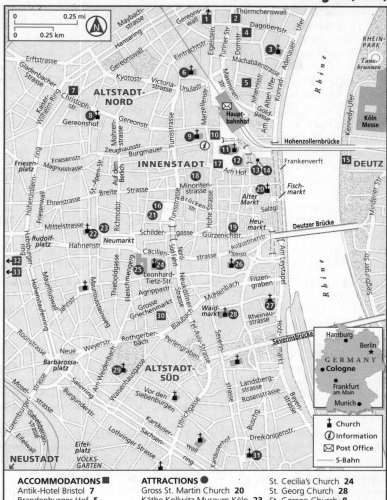

ESSENTIALS
GETTING THERE **By Plane** Cologne and Bonn are served by the same airport, **Flughafen Köln/Bonn Konrad Adenauer** (© **02203/404001**; www.airport-cgn.de), 14km (9 miles) southeast of Cologne. Flights come from most major European cities. Bus no. 170 from the airport to the center of Cologne operates every 12 minutes, from 5am to 7pm. Travel time takes 20 minutes, and the fare is 9€ ($14) per person. A taxi, suitable for up to four passengers, costs from 25€ ($40).

By Train The **Cologne Hauptbahnhof** is in the heart of the city, next to the cathedral. For schedules, call © **01805/996633** (© 11861 in Germany; www.bahn.de). This depot has frequent rail connections to all major German cities and many Continental destinations. There are 18 trains per day from Berlin (trip time: 4 hr., 20 min.), 30 from Frankfurt (trip time: 1 hr., 22 min.), and 25 from Hamburg (trip time: 4½ hr.).

By Bus Cologne is linked to several major cities, including Frankfurt, by bus. For complete information and schedules, call **Deutsche Touring GmbH** (© **0221/ 7598660**; www.deutsche-touring.com). Regional bus service to nearby cities such as Trier (see chapter 16) is provided by **Regionalverkehr Köln GmbH (KVB;** © **0221/ 16370)**.

By Car Cologne is easily reached from major German cities. It's connected north and south by the A3 Autobahn and east and west by the A4 Autobahn.

VISITOR INFORMATION For tourist information, go to the **Köln Tourismus Office,** Unter Fettenhennen 19 (Am Dom; © **0221/22130400**; www.koelntourismus. de), a few steps from the cathedral. October to June, it's open Monday to Saturday 9am to 9pm and Sunday 10am to 6pm; July to September, hours are Monday to Saturday 9am to 10pm and Sunday 10am to 6pm.

GETTING AROUND For 1.50€ to 9.30€ ($2.40–$15), depending on where you're going, you can purchase a ticket allowing you to travel on Cologne's excellent **bus, tram, U-Bahn,** and **S-Bahn** connections. A day ticket, the **Kölner Tageskarte,** which costs 5.20€ ($8.30), allows you to travel throughout the city's transportation network from 9am to 3am. For more information, call © **0221/5470** or go to **www. kvb-koeln.de**.

For a taxi, call © **0221/19410** for a recorded message and then press 1 in reply. Meters start at 2.50€ ($4) and rise 1.45€ ($2.30) per kilometer for rides between 6am and 10pm and 1.55€ ($2.50) per kilometer for rides between 10pm and 6am.

WHERE TO STAY
VERY EXPENSIVE
Excelsior Hotel Ernst 🖈🖈🖈 In spite of increased competition, notably from the Hyatt Regency, Cologne's longtime prestige hotel continues to hold its own as the premier address in Cologne. Founded in 1863, the hotel is known for its Empire-style lobby. The public areas contain old-master paintings, including an original work by Van Dyck. The breakfast room has a Gobelin tapestry. Rooms are spacious with bathrooms containing tub/shower combos.

Trankgasse 1–5, Domplatz, 50667 Köln. © **0221/2701**. Fax 0221/2703333. www.excelsiorhotelernst.de. 152 units. 325€–440€ ($520–$704) double; from 590€ ($944) suite. Rates include continental breakfast. AE, DC, MC, V. Parking 22€ ($35). U-Bahn: Hauptbahnhof. **Amenities:** 2 restaurants; piano bar; fitness center; sauna; steam room; room service; babysitting; laundry service; dry cleaning. *In room:* A/C, TV, Wi-Fi, minibar, hair dryer, safe, bathrobes (in some), Jacuzzi/whirlpool tub (in some).

Grandhotel Schloss Bensberg 🌟🌟🌟   The most romantic place to stay in the area is this restored baroque castle constructed 300 years ago at a point 14km (9 miles) from Cologne. Crowning a hill, it offers panoramic views of the city. This is life on a grand scale, fit for a German prince—indeed, it was a prince, Jan Wellem, who built the castle in the first place.

After lavish renovations, it has been successfully transformed and elegantly furnished with all the modern amenities. Rooms vary in size—after all, this is a castle—but all of them are handsomely equipped with such extras as three phones. Our favorite is no. 307 with its panorama of Cologne and its black marble bathroom with Jacuzzi. The atmosphere is more intimate and friendly than some drafty castle might suggest. It features special grace notes such as a collection of 10,000 wines in the cellar, a state-of-the-art spa, and 66,000 lights around the pool imitating a night sky.

Kadettenstrasse, 51429 Bergisch Gladbach. ℭ **02204/420.** Fax 02204/42888. www.schlossbensberg.com. 120 units. 265€–370€ ($424–$592) double; from 465€ ($744) suite. AE, DC, MC, V. Parking 16€ ($26). **Amenities:** 3 restaurants; bar; indoor heated pool; fitness center; spa; room service; babysitting; laundry service; nonsmoking rooms; rooms for those w/limited mobility. *In room:* A/C, TV, Wi-Fi, minibar, hair dryer, safe.

Hotel im Wasserturm 🌟🌟🌟   When the tallest water tower in Europe was converted into an 11-story deluxe hotel-in-the-round, at a cost of $75 million, one of the most avant-garde and daring reincarnations of an existing structure in all of Germany was born. Even if living in a water tower is not your idea of a good time, check the hotel anyway. It's southwest of the city center, just a mile from the cathedral. The design and decor are ingenious, from the Warhol paintings to the tiled lobby with stunning dark woodwork. The structure is 19th century, but everything else is contemporary. Rooms come in unusual configurations, but each is cleverly designed for comfort, flair, and convenience. Original art and exquisite carpeting fill the spacious rooms, and the bathrooms are deluxe, tiled in mosaics and containing such extras as triptych mirrors, robes, and deep tubs with power showers.

Kaygasse 2, Köln 50676. ℭ **0221/20080.** Fax 0221/2008888. www.hotel-im-wasserturm.de. 88 units. 215€–370€ ($344–$592) double; from 249€ ($398) suite. AE, DC, MC, V. **Amenities:** Restaurant; bar; sauna; solarium; room service; massage; babysitting; laundry service; dry cleaning; nonsmoking rooms. *In room:* A/C, TV, Wi-Fi, minibar, hair dryer, safe.

Hyatt Regency 🌟🌟   This is the most spectacular and up-to-date hotel in Cologne. It's an architectural triumph: a mixture of reddish granite, huge expanses of glass, and a facade that combines Art Deco and neo-Aztec styles. The lobby is dramatic, with a 4m (13-ft.) waterfall. Rooms are stylishly furnished and come with walk-in closets. Many have views of the Rhine and the cathedral on the other side. Bathrooms have private phones, deep tubs with showers, robes, and deluxe toiletries. To get to the Altstadt from here, you can take the Hohenzollernbrücke, a bridge across the Rhine.

Kennedy-Ufer 2A (across the Rhine from the Altstadt, a short walk from the train station), 50679 Cologne-Deutz. ℭ **888/591-1234** in the U.S., or 0221/8281234. Fax 0221/8281370. www.hyatt.com. 306 units. 178€–263€ ($285–$421) double; from 338€ ($541) junior suite. AE, DC, MC, V. Parking 17€ ($27). Tram: 1 or 9. **Amenities:** 2 restaurants; bar; beer garden; indoor heated pool; fitness center; whirlpool; sauna; solarium; steam room; business center; room service; massage; babysitting; laundry service; dry cleaning; nonsmoking rooms; rooms for those w/limited mobility. *In room:* A/C, TV, Wi-Fi, minibar, coffeemaker, hair dryer, safe.

EXPENSIVE
Dom Hotel 🌟🌟   Few hotels in Germany have been so consistently awarded the official government five stars or maintained such a standard of excellence as this old-world hotel right across from the cathedral. We prefer the Excelsior Hotel Ernst (see above),

but there are many clients who will stay nowhere else but the Dom. The hotel's location, in the shadow of the cathedral, assures it a steady clientele. In summer, the side portico overlooking the square is filled with cafe tables. Rooms have all modern conveniences and a wide collection of period furniture. Try for one of the corner units, which are the most spacious and have the best views. To reach the hotel by car, drive into the square to the side of the Dom's flying buttresses.

Domkloster 2A, 50667 Köln. ⓒ 800/543-4300 in the U.S., or 0221/20240. Fax 0221/2024444. www.cologne.le meridien.com. 124 units. 185€–342€ ($296–$547) double; from 300€ ($480) suite. AE, DC, MC, V. Parking 20€ ($32). U-Bahn: Hauptbahnhof. **Amenities:** Restaurant; bar; lounge; business center; room service; massage; babysitting; laundry service; dry cleaning; nonsmoking rooms. *In room:* A/C, TV, minibar, hair dryer, iron, bathrobe, slippers.

MODERATE

Antik-Hotel Bristol 𝕽𝕽   The Bristol is exceptional in that each of its rooms is furnished with genuine antiques, either regal or rustic. There's a different antique bed in almost every room, ranging from French baroque and rococo to something reminiscent of High Rhenish ecclesiastical art; the oldest four-poster dates from 1742. Bathrooms include tub/shower combos. The Bristol stands in a little park, with lots of greenery, flowers, and fountains. It's near a U-Bahn stop and within walking distance of the cathedral.

Kaiser-Wilhelm-Ring 48, 50672 Köln. ⓒ 0221/120195. Fax 0221/131495. www.antik-hotel-bristol.de. 44 units. 118€ ($189) double; from 136€ ($218) suite. Rates include buffet breakfast. AE, DC, MC, V. Parking 15€ ($24). Closed Dec 23–Jan 2. U-Bahn: Christophstrasse. **Amenities:** Breakfast room; bar; room service; massage; babysitting; laundry service; dry cleaning; nonsmoking rooms. *In room:* TV, Wi-Fi, minibar, hair dryer, trouser press, safe.

Chelsea 𝕽 *(Finds*   This is one of Cologne's most chic designer boutique hotels, a favorite of painters, art gallery owners, and other artists. The artfully designed and glamorously contemporary bedrooms have huge, beautifully maintained bathrooms with showers and luxurious tubs. Original pieces of art fill this well-designed hotel. If you'd like more space and don't mind spending extra euros, you can opt for one of the junior suites or apartments. The on-site restaurant and cafe is a sophisticated rendezvous point and features a finely honed blend of art and food. It takes about 20 minutes to walk to the center of town.

Jülicherstrasse 1, Belgisches Viertel 50674, Köln. ⓒ 0221/207150. Fax 0221/239137. www.hotel-chelsea.de. 35 units. 92€–149€ ($147–$238) double; 185€–235€ ($296–$376) junior suite or apt. AE, DC, MC, V. Parking 8€ ($13). U-Bahn: Rudolfplatz. **Amenities:** Restaurant; bar; laundry service. *In room:* TV, Wi-Fi, minibar, hair dryer.

Hopper Hotel et cetera 𝕽 *(Finds*   The unusual name of this hotel provides no clue as to its former role as one of the monasteries of Cologne. Only the statue of a bishop in the lobby evokes any former ecclesiastical role. The interior, which received a radically contemporary overhaul, contrasts dramatically with the older landmark-status exterior. Some of Cologne's finer artists have their works on display in the bedrooms, which are elegantly but a bit sparsely furnished, each with a modern bathroom with tub and shower. The parquet floors are made of eucalyptus, and the units are fitted with handsomely designed cherrywood furnishings. Try to avoid the small so-called "cloister cells," rooms better suited for the monks of old. Two of the double rooms have connecting doors, making them suitable for families. We'd opt for one of the junior suites if available, as they come with such extra amenities as a kitchenette. The top-floor room boasts a roof terrace and deck chair. The hotel lies in the fashionable district of Cologne known as Belgisches Viertel.

Brüsselerstrasse 26, 50674 Köln. Ⓒ/fax **0221/924400**. www.hopper.de. 49 units. 110€–125€ ($176–$200) double; 140€–155€ ($224–$248) suite. Rates include continental breakfast. AE, DC, MC, V. Parking 13€ ($21). U-Bahn: Molttestrasse. **Amenities:** Restaurant; fitness center; sauna. *In room:* TV, minibar, hair dryer, safe.

Hopper Hotel St. Antonius   Named after a statue of St. Antonius that stands in the garden (the owners bought it during a holiday in Portugal), this hotel rises five very modern floors from a location in the heart of Cologne's historic core. You'll register in a lobby sheathed with slabs of gray stone and floored with stone mosaics. The same colors are repeated within the very contemporary-looking bedrooms, with wooden floors, marble-sheathed bathrooms with tubs and showers, and teakwood furniture. This is a well-selected and popular choice with an articulate staff and lots of comfort and style.

Dagobertstrasse 32, 50668 Köln. Ⓒ **0221/16600**. Fax 0221/1660166. www.hopper.de. 54 units. 135€–165€ ($216–$264) double; 160€–200€ ($256–$320) suite. AE, DC, MC, V. Parking 13€ ($21). U-Bahn: Ebertplatz or Dom/Hauptbahnhof. **Amenities:** Restaurant; bar; room service; laundry service; nonsmoking rooms; rooms for those w/limited mobility. *In room:* TV, minibar, kitchenette (in some), safe.

Santo 🎯 *(Finds)*   This hotel comes as a surprise in Cologne because it's so different from its competitors—an oasis of feng shui with an array of orchids and open spaces, plus a beautiful teak bar in the front. Light is the focal point of the architects' philosophy, and the staff is trained in offering individualized hospitality. The hotel is a unique blend of materials, some of it old such as fine oak wood. But it's also as modern as tomorrow with its Kreon lamps creating shifting patterns of light. The bathrooms with shower and tub are laid out in a sleek, contemporary fashion, and the minimalist bedrooms are comfortable with an elegant design that relies on simplicity more than clutter. Only breakfast is provided, but there are many good restaurants nearby.

Dagoberstrasse 22, 50668 Köln. Ⓒ **0221/9139770**. Fax 0221/913977777. www.hotelsanto.de. 69 units. 114€–160€ ($182–$256) double. Rates include continental breakfast. AE, DC, MC, V. Parking 15€ ($24). U-Bahn: Ebertplatz. **Amenities:** Breakfast room; bar; room service; laundry service; nonsmoking rooms. *In room:* A/C, TV, hair dryer.

INEXPENSIVE

Brandenburger Hof   In this family-style hotel, all rooms are small, warm, and equipped with sinks, and there's a well-kept bathroom with combination tub/shower on each floor. A full breakfast, including orange juice and eggs, is served in a cozy room or, in summer, in the garden. The hotel is about 3 blocks from the river and within walking distance of the cathedral.

Brandenburgerstrasse 2–4 (behind the Hauptbahnhof), 50668 Köln. Ⓒ **0221/122889**. Fax 0221/135304. www. brandenburgerhof.de. 45 units, 28 with bathroom. 50€–95€ ($80–$152) double without bathroom, 70€–155€ ($112–$248) double with bathroom; 75€–120€ ($120–$192) triple without bathroom, 85€–195€ ($136–$312) triple with bathroom; 80€–130€ ($128–$208) quad without bathroom. Rates include continental breakfast. No credit cards. Free parking. U-Bahn: Hauptbahnhof. **Amenities:** Breakfast room; lounge.

Coellner Hof *(Value)*   Set within a 10-minute walk north of the cathedral, this six-story, turn-of-the-20th-century building houses a well-maintained, comfortable hotel that has received well-deserved praise from several readers. Public areas are distinguished looking, and some, including the dining room, are richly paneled. Each room is decorated in a conservative, solid style that evokes a baronial German home. The newer bedrooms have been updated in a crisp, comfortable, and clean modern international style that's soothing in its use of neutral, monochromatic colors and dark hardwoods. Bedrooms are larger than the norm in government-rated three-star hotels, and each comes with a small, tiled bathroom with a tub/shower combo.

Hansaring 100, 50670 Köln. © 0221/16660. Fax 0221/1666166. www.coellnerhof.de. 78 units. 79€–195€ ($126–$312) double; on selected weekends 62€ ($99) double. Parking 8€ ($13). Rates include continental breakfast. AE, DC, MC, V. U-Bahn: Ebertplatz. **Amenities:** Bar; restaurant; sauna; laundry service; nonsmoking rooms; rooms for those w/limited mobility. *In room:* TV, hair dryer.

WHERE TO DINE
VERY EXPENSIVE
Hanse Stube 𝕉𝕉 FRENCH One of Cologne's best restaurants, Hanse Stube offers top-drawer service and food better than that served in the dining room of the Dom Hotel. Prodigious talent and imagination go into shaping the cuisine. Unusual and tasty main courses include breast of guinea fowl stuffed with herbs or medallions of venison with savoy cabbage and a sweet-corn potato rösti (hash brown potatoes). Also delectable are a galantine of quail with pigeon breast served with pistachios in aspic, or else a filet of lamb with spinach and a tomato ragout.

On the ground floor of the Excelsior Hotel Ernst, Domplatz. © 0221/2701. Reservations recommended. Main courses 32€–38€ ($51–$61); fixed-price lunch 32€–38€ ($51–$61); tasting menu 85€ ($136). AE, DC, MC, V. Daily noon–2:30pm and 6–midnight. U-Bahn: Hauptbahnhof.

EXPENSIVE
Le Moissonnier 𝕉𝕉 FRENCH This charming brasserie is steeped in the aesthetic and culinary traditions of the early 20th century, with mirrors, cove moldings, dark paneling against ocher-colored walls, bentwood chairs, and tiled floors. Here you'll enjoy the carefully crafted cuisine of Chef Eric Menchon. Menu items change with the season and the inspiration of the chef but are likely to include risotto with almonds and truffle oil; crayfish sautéed in vanilla oil; carpaccio of turbot; and a house specialty that combines braised filet of goose breast with tarragon and strips of goose-liver, and is served with prosciutto-studded mashed potatoes. Salads and fresh fish are all delicious, as are the sauerkraut and a Toulouse-inspired version of cassoulet loaded with pork, small sausages, and white beans.

Krefelder Strasse 25. © 0221/729479. Reservations recommended. Main courses 30€–40€ ($48–$64); 4-course lunch menu 51€ ($82). V. Tues–Sat noon–1:45pm and 7–10:45pm. U-Bahn: Hansaring.

MODERATE
Brauhaus im Walfisch GERMAN/FRENCH Brauhaus im Walfisch isn't easy to find, but it's a good choice for atmospheric dining. This step-gabled inn with a black-and-white timbered facade dates from 1626. More importantly, it serves excellent food. There are many German specialties, often influenced by French cuisine. You might try the sole meunière or venison for two.

Salzgasse 13 (on a narrow street set back from the Rhine, near Heumarkt). © 0221/2577879. Reservations required. Main courses 11€–19€ ($18–$30). No credit cards. Mon–Thurs 5pm–midnight; Fri 3pm–midnight; Sat–Sun 11am–midnight. U-Bahn: Heumarkt.

Das Kleine Stapelhäuschen 𝕉 GERMAN This is one of the most popular wine taverns in Cologne. It's housed in an office building and opens onto the old fish-market square and the Rhine. The two-story dining room and service bar are antique in style. Provincial cabinets hold a varied wine collection. A wide cantilevered wooden staircase leads to mezzanine tables. Though the wine is the main reason for coming here (it's that special), the cuisine is also excellent. A specialty is Rheinischer sauerbraten with almonds, raisins, and potato dumplings. You can also order marinated roast

beef in a dark-brown vinegar sauce with raisins, or else escalope of veal with roast potatoes and a mixed salad.

Fischmarkt 1–3 (a few minutes from the cathedral). ℂ **0221/2577862** or 0221/2577863. Reservations recommended. Main courses 17€–27€ ($27–$43). AE, MC, V. Daily 11:30am–11pm. Closed Dec 22–Jan 10. U-Bahn:
Heumarkt.

Fischer's ✶ *(Finds* INTERNATIONAL   Part of Fischer's appeal is because of the fact
that it's owned and directed by one of Germany's best-known women sommeliers,
Christina Fischer. Don't expect to see her hawking wines on the floor, however. These
days she's more of an *éminence grise,* leaving the day-to-day wine pouring to a staff of
underlings. A 10-minute walk from the cathedral, Fischer's has a large, modern-look-
ing, cream-colored dining room that's lined with wine racks and paintings celebrating
grape harvesting, the production of wine, and its uncorking rituals. The chefs are
proud of the restaurant's policy of combining culinary tenets from both Europe and
Asia, often on the same platter. The finest examples include *Tafelspitz* (boiled beef)
served with potato/arugula salad; sashimi of tuna with bean-sprout salad and lemon
sauce; fried sea bream with strips of foie gras; and roast beef with a comfit of lemons,
braised celery, house-made noodles, and whiskey sauce. In terms of the energy
invested in it by the staff, the wine served here is as important as the food itself. There
are at least 40 kinds of wine available by the glass and more than 700 vintages from
around the world available in bottles.

Hohenstaufenring 53, Ringe. ℂ **0221/3108470.** Reservations required. Main courses 20€–35€ ($32–$56). DC,
MC, V. Tues–Fri noon–2pm; Fri–Sat 6:30–11pm. Tram: 12, 16, or 18.

EXPLORING COLOGNE

One of the best panoramas over the ancient city of Cologne is from within one of the
cars of the Rhein-Seilbahn, the first and only cable car in Europe that was designed to
span a major river. The Rhein-Seilbahn stretches between a point near the zoo, in the
district of Cologne-Riehl, to the Rheinpark in Cologne-Deutz, a total of about 900m
(3,000 ft.). From the air, you'll get a good view of the busy river traffic along the
Rhine. The cable car operates March 15 to November 2 daily 10am to 6pm. A one-
way ticket costs 4€ ($6.40) for adults, 2.40€ ($3.90) for children; a round-trip ticket
costs 6€ ($9.60) for adults, 3.50€ ($5.60) for children. For more information, call
ℂ **0221/5474184.**

THE TOP ATTRACTIONS

Käthe Kollwitz Museum Köln   This is the second museum in Germany devoted
to the works of this major German figure (1867–1945), the country's most celebrated
female artist of the 20th century (and this one has more of her works than its sibling
museum in Berlin). Capturing human emotions, both tender and arresting, the
Berlin-born artist focuses on such subjects as death, hunger, war, love, grief, and even
happiness. In addition to the works of Kollwitz, presented in drawings, sketches, and
sculpture, the museum also has special exhibitions, such as those devoted to Picasso,
William Hogarth, or even contemporary artists.

Neu-Markt 18–24 (in Neu-Markt Galerie, Innenstadt). ℂ **0221/2272363.** www.kollwitz.de. Admission 3€ ($4.80).
Tues–Fri 10am–6pm; Sat–Sun 11am–6pm.

Kölner Dom (Cologne Cathedral) ✶✶✶   This majestic structure is one of the
world's great cathedrals—the spiritual and geographical heart of the city. It's the largest

Beer Taverns

Some of the best inexpensive places to eat (and drink) in Cologne are beer taverns. Come to **Bräuhaus Sion,** Unter Taschenmacher 5–7 (© **0221/2578540;** U-Bahn: Heumarkt; tram: 5 or 7), if you want a traditional local tavern where the beer is good, the wood paneling smoky with time and frequent polishing, and the food portions generous. The main courses are traditional and filling Westphalian fare, and the best dish is *Kölsch Kaviar* (blood sausage with onion rings). On tap is the famed local beer, Kölsch, a light brew with an alcohol content of about 3%. It's served in *Stangen* (rods) about 18cm (7 in.) tall. Main courses are 16€ to 26€ ($26–$42). No credit cards are accepted. It's open daily 10am to 11:30pm, but closed Christmas Eve.

Früh am Dom ⍟, Am Hof 12–14 (© **0221/2613211;** U-Bahn: Hauptbahnhof), is the best all-around choice. Well-cooked meals are served on scrubbed wooden tables, with a different German specialty offered every day of the week. They have a menu in English. A favorite dish is a Cologne specialty of cured smoked knuckle of pork cooked in root-vegetable broth and served with sauerkraut and potato purée; apple purée and dumplings go well with this dish. Also sample a glass of Früh-Kölsch—a top-fermented brew with a dry, inimitable taste and a 1,000-year-old tradition. In summer, there's a beer garden. Meals cost 11€ to 20€ ($18–$32). No credit cards are accepted. The tavern is open 8am to midnight; hot meals are served 11:30am to 11:30pm.

Haus Töller, Weyerstrasse 96 (© **0221/2589316;** U-Bahn: Barbarossaplatz), a 15-minute walk south of the cathedral, has thrived as a brew house since 1876 by selling copious portions of two-fisted Teutonic food and foaming mugs of a local brew, Sion. The menu includes a local specialty, *Schinkenhempsel* (roast leg of pork), served with sauerkraut and roast potatoes. Main courses are 12€ to 20€ ($19–$32); a mug of Sion will set you back 1€ ($1.60). No credit cards are accepted. It's open daily 5pm to midnight.

Gothic cathedral in Germany. From the top of the south tower, you get panoramic views of the city and surrounding area.

Construction began in 1248, in order to house the relics of the three Magi brought to Cologne in 1164 by Archbishop Reinald von Dassel, chancellor to Frederick Barbarossa. After the completion of the chancel, south tower, and north-side aisles (around 1500), work was halted and not resumed until 1823. In 1880, the great enterprise was completed, and unlike many time-consuming constructions that change styles in midstream, the final result was in the Gothic style, true to the original plans.

At the end of the war in 1945, this great cathedral appeared relatively unscathed, even though the entire district around it was leveled. According to legend, Allied bombers used the Dom as a landmark to guide their flights to more strategic military targets and could not bring themselves to destroy such an architectural triumph.

For the best overall view of the cathedral, stand back from the south transept, where you can get an idea of its actual size and splendor. Note that there are no important horizontal lines—everything is vertical. The west side (front) is dominated by two towering spires, perfectly proportioned and joined by the narrow facade of the nave. The first two stories of the towers are square, gradually merging into the octagonal form of the top three stories and tapering off at the top with huge finials. There is no great rose window, so characteristic of Gothic architecture, between these spires— nothing detracts from the lofty vertical lines.

Entering through the west doors (main entrance), you are immediately caught up in the cathedral's grandeur. Although this portion of the church is somewhat bare, the clerestory and vaulting give a feeling of the size of the edifice. The towering windows on the south aisles include the Bavarian windows, donated by King Ludwig I of Bavaria in 1848. Like most windows in the nave, they are colored with pigments that have been burned on rather than stained. In the north aisles are the stained-glass Renaissance windows (1507–09).

In the center of the transept is an elegant bronze-and-marble altar that can be seen from all parts of the cathedral. Behind the high altar, in the chancel, is *The Shrine of the Three Magi* ⊛⊛⊛, the most important and valuable object in the cathedral. It's designed in gold and silver in the form of a triple-naved basilica and decorated with relief figures depicting the life of Christ, the Apostles, and various Old Testament prophets. Across the front of the chancel are two rows of **choir stalls** ⊛ divided into richly carved partitions. The oak choir dates from 1310 and is the largest extant in Germany.

Surrounding the chancel are nine chapels, each containing important works of religious art. The Chapel of the Cross, beneath the organ loft, shelters the oldest full-size cross in the Occident, the painted, carved oak cross of Archbishop Gero (969–76). Directly across the chancel, behind the altar in Our Lady's Chapel, is the famous *Altar of the City Patrons* ⊛⊛⊛ painted by Stephan Lochner (1400–51). When closed, this triptych masterpiece shows the *Annunciation,* and when opened, it reveals the *Adoration of the Magi* in the center, flanked by St. Ursula, the patron saint of Cologne, and St. Gereon.

English-language tours are given Monday to Saturday at 10:30am and 2:30pm, and Sunday at 2:30pm. German-language tours are conducted Monday to Saturday at 11am, 12:30pm, 2pm, and 3:30pm, and every Sunday at 2 and 3:30pm. Tours last an hour and cost 4€ ($6.40) for adults and 2€ ($3.20) for students and children.

Domkloster. ℭ **0221/92584731.** www.koelner-dom.de. Cathedral free. Cathedral tower 2.50€ ($4); Treasury 4€ ($6.40); combination ticket to Treasury and Tower 5€ ($8). Cathedral daily 6am–7:30pm, except during religious services; Cathedral tower and treasury daily 10am–6pm. U-Bahn: Dom/Hauptbahnhof.

Museum für Angewandte Kunst (Museum of Applied Art)   This is a showcase for the arts and crafts of Germany dating from the Middle Ages, with the 20th-century prominently featured. This museum is one of the best of its kind in Germany.

An der Rechtsschule. ℭ **0221/22123860.** Admission 4.20€ ($6.70) adults, 2.60€ ($4.20) children 6–12, free for children 5 and under. Tues–Sun 11am–5pm. U-Bahn: Hauptbahnhof.

Museum Ludwig ⊛⊛⊛   This stunningly upgraded museum is the home of one of the world's largest collections of the works of Pablo Picasso, bested only by the Picassos in Paris and Barcelona. Irene Ludwig, widow of the late German art patron Peter Ludwig, for whom the museum is named, donated numerous Picassos to the museum, including 49 paintings, 29 ceramics, 37 works on paper, 15 relief plates, and 681 graphic prints, which previously had been on loan to the museum.

In 1976, Ludwig first gave more than 300 works of art to Cologne to form the basis of this museum. Some of these paintings are the most celebrated and reproduced Picassos in the world, including *Harlequin with Folded Hands* from 1923 and the disturbingly forceful *Woman with Artichoke* from 1941.

The museum is also home to a great collection of modern art from Dalí to Warhol. The American Pop Art collection that also includes Roy Lichtenstein, Rauschenberg, and Jasper Johns, rivals the Guggenheim in New York. Our two favorites are Dalí's *Railway Station at Perpignan* and Ed Kienholz's *Portable War Memorial*.

Museum Ludwig is also the home of **Agfa-Historama**, which chronicles the art of photography for the past century and a half, with works by all the greats. This collection of historic photographs and cameras is the largest in the world.

Bischofsgartenstrasse 1. Ⓒ 0221/22126165. www.museenkoeln.de/museum-ludwig. Admission 9€ ($14) adults, 6€ ($9.60) students and children. Tues–Sun 10am–6pm; 1st Fri of each month 10am–11pm. U-Bahn: Dom/ Hauptbahnhof.

Museum Schnütgen 🌟🌟   This is Cologne's best collection of religious art and sculpture. It's all displayed in an original setting, Cäcilienkirche (St. Cecilia's Church), which is a fine example of Rhenish-Romanic architecture. The works displayed include several medieval ivories, woodwork, and tapestries, including one showing rosy-cheeked Magi bringing gifts to the Christ Child (1470). There are also many Madonnas, of all sizes and descriptions, carved in stone, wood, and metal.

Cäcilienstrasse 29. Ⓒ 0221/22123620. www.museenkoeln.de. Admission 3.20€ ($5.10) adults, 1.90€ ($3.10) children. Tues–Fri 10am–5pm; Sat–Sun 11am–5pm. U-Bahn: Neumarkt.

Römisch-Germanisches Museum (Roman-Germanic Museum)   The most compelling treasure in this museum is the Dionysos-Mosaik, from the 3rd century A.D., discovered in 1941, when workers were digging an air-raid shelter. This elaborately decorated and colored mosaic was once the floor of an *oecus* (main room) of a large Roman villa. It depicts Dionysus, the Greek god of wine. On the second floor of the museum is an unusual collection of Roman antiquities found in the Rhine Valley, including Roman glass from the 1st through 4th centuries, as well as pottery, marble busts, and jewelry.

Roncalliplatz 4. Ⓒ 0221/22124438. www.museenkoeln.de. Admission 5€ ($8) adults, 3€ ($4.80) children, free for children 5 and under. Tues–Sun 10am–5pm. U-Bahn: Hauptbahnhof.

Wallraf-Richartz Museum/Foundation Corboud 🌟🌟🌟   This is Cologne's oldest museum, begun in the 19th century with a collection of Gothic works by local artists, still one of the main attractions. The Wallraf-Richartz shows art from A.D. 1300 to 1900. Several well-known works from churches are exhibited as well, including the triptych of the *Madonna with the Vetch Flower* (1410). The painting collection represents nearly every period and school, from the Dutch and Flemish masters to the French Impressionists. Stephan Lochner's *Madonna in the Rose Garden* (1450) is a fine example of the German Gothic style, as are his frightening *Last Judgment* and Dürer's *Drummer and Piper*. The museum also houses Germany's largest collection of works by Wilhelm Leibl as well as paintings by Max Ernst, Paul Klee, and Ernst Ludwig Kirchner.

Martinstrasse 39. Ⓒ 0221/22121119. www.museenkoeln.de. Admission 9€ ($14) adults, 6€ ($9.60) students and children 5–16, free for children 4 and under. Wed and Fri 10am–6pm; Thurs 10am–8pm; Sat–Sun 11am–6pm. U-Bahn: Hauptbahnhof.

CHURCHES

Cologne has 12 important Romanesque churches, all within the medieval city wall. Devastated during World War II, they have been almost completely restored and again recapture Cologne's rich early medieval heritage. **St. Panteleon,** Am Pantaleonsberg 2 (U-Bahn: Poststrasse), built in 980, has the oldest cloister arcades remaining in Germany. **St. Gereon,** Gereonsdriesch 2–4 (U-Bahn: Christophstrasse), is elliptically shaped, with a decagon between its two towers. It contains the tomb of St. Gereon and other martyrs, and its crypt still has mosaics from the 11th century. **St. Severin,** Severinstrasse 1 (U-Bahn: Severinstrasse), originated as a late-4th-century memorial chapel; the present church dates from the 13th to the 15th centuries.

The church of **St. Ursula** (1135), Ursulaplatz (U-Bahn: Hauptbahnhof), is on the site of a Roman graveyard. Legend has it that St. Ursula, patron saint of Cologne, was martyred in Cologne with her 11,000 virgin companions in about 451. **St. Maria im Kapitol,** Kasinostrasse 6 (U-Bahn: Heumarkt), is on the site where Plectrudis, wife of Pippin (dim figures of the Dark Ages, significant because Plectrudis is one of the few women who had political power in the area, as she was the daughter of an important land owner), built a church in the early 8th century. The cloverleaf choir of the present structure was modeled on that of the Church of the Nativity in Bethlehem. **St. Aposteln,** Neumarkt 30 (U-Bahn: Neumarkt), and **Gross St. Martin,** on the Rhine in the Altstadt (U-Bahn: Heumarkt), also have the cloverleaf choir design.

St. Georg, Am Waidmarkt (U-Bahn: Poststrasse), the only remaining Romanesque pillared basilica in the Rhineland, contains an impressive forked crucifix from the early 14th century. **Cäcilienkirche (St. Cecilia's Church),** Cäcilienstrasse 29 (U-Bahn: Neumarkt), is the site of the Museum Schnütgen for sacred art (see above). **St. Andreas,** near the cathedral (U-Bahn: Hauptbahnhof), contains a wealth of late Romanesque architectural sculpture. The remaining two Romanesque churches are on the Rhine: **St. Kunibert,** Kunibertskloster 2 (U-Bahn: Hauptbahnhof), and **St. Maria Lyskirchen,** Am Lyskirchen 12 (U-Bahn: Heumarkt), both of 13th-century origin.

SHOPPING

Shopping is not taken quite as seriously here as in Düsseldorf—with one exception. Increasingly, Cologne is emerging as the capital of contemporary art in Germany, and lately the city seems to be brimming with galleries.

ART GALLERIES   We'll recommend the major ones to get you started, but there are many more than we can list here. You might want to walk along **St. Apernstrasse** (U-Bahn: Neumarkt), where many leading art galleries are located. The gallery that launched Cologne as a European art mecca is **Galerie der Spiegel,** Richartstrasse 10 (© 0221/255552; U-Bahn: Hauptbahnhof). Established amid the ruins of the wartime bombings in 1945, it was a focal point for the contemporary art that evolved from the shattered dreams of the postwar years. Since then, it has managed to hold its own against rising competition. **Galerie Greve,** Drususgasse 1–5 (© 0221/2571012; U-Bahn: Dom Hauptbahnhof), changes its exhibits every season, specializing in international postwar avant-garde painting. Another excellent gallery for both modern and experimental art is **Galerie Michael Werner,** Gertrudenstrasse 24 (© 0221/9254620; U-Bahn: Neumarkt), which sells contemporary European, particularly German, painters.

CLOTHING   Looking almost like a modern cathedral, the home of one of Germany's leading retailers of clothing, **Peek & Cloppenburg,** Schildergasse 65 (© 0221/453900), lies under a translucent nave that evokes a large crystal egg, using 6,800

Fun Fact **Cologne Water**

The word *cologne* has been a part of the common language since the introduction many years ago of the scented water called *Kölnisch Wasser* (eau de cologne). **Eau de Cologne,** Glockengasse 4711 (© **0221/57289250;** U-Bahn: Neumarkt), sells the scented water first developed at this address by Italian chemist Giovanni Maria Farina in 1709. Originally employed to hide the stench of aristocrats who rarely bathed, cologne is now simply a sweet-smelling tradition and a cheap way to take home a little piece of Cologne. The smallest 25-milliliter flacon costs a mere 5€ ($8).

---

handmade panels of glass held together by strips of metal and wooden beams. Renzo Piano designed the store in what he termed a "rather classical cubic form." Shoppers behind the diaphanous walls browse through one of Germany's most elegant, but often affordable, selection of clothing. The company has been selling clothing to well-dressed Germans for more than a century.

Long surpassed by Düsseldorf for fashion, Cologne's pedestrian-friendly layout is blossoming with some of the chicest stores along the Rhine. *Fashionistas* are flocking to **Apropos Coeln,** 12 Mittelstrasse (© 0221/272-5190), for the latest from Prada or Jil Sander. Storefronts continue to open in the Friesen district, including the Lebanese-born **Perla Zayek's** namesake boutique at 94 Friesenwall (© **0221/256-022**), or **Atelier Ludvik,** 43 Palmstrasse (© **0221/277-4568**), where you'll find funky, feminine togs by designer Fenja Ludwig.

OUTDOOR MARKETS   If you're interested in the kitschy artifacts that pour out of estate sales, be alert to the flea markets in Cologne's inner city. The most appealing are held within the **Alter Markt** (U-Bahn: Hauptbahnhof), at irregular intervals throughout the year, usually at least once a month (ask at the tourist office). More regular are the outdoor food and vegetable markets, the largest of which is held on the **Wilhelmsplatz,** in the Nippes district (U-Bahn: Florastrasse), Saturdays 8am to at least 2pm.

COLOGNE AFTER DARK

As one of Germany's major cultural centers, Cologne has a variety of fine arts and nightlife options. Many clubs stay open into the early morning hours. You can pick up a copy of *Stadt Revue* or *Kölner* for 3€ ($4.80) each to find out what's happening in the city. If you're interested in attending a sporting, entertainment, or cultural event within Cologne, you can always head to the box office for tickets. More convenient, however, is the well-orchestrated service of **Köln-Ticket,** Grosse Neugasse 2 (© 0221/2801;** U-Bahn: Hauptbahnhof), which has many different event tickets for sale. Depending on the ticket, the service charge is around 5€ ($8).

THE PERFORMING ARTS

The most impressive grouping of theaters in Cologne is within the **Schauspielhaus,** Offenbachplatz (© **0221/22128400;** U-Bahn: Neumarkt), the site of three theaters, each with its own agenda and schedule. Performances range from the avant-garde to the classic. **Der Keller,** Kleingedankstrasse 6 (© 0221/318059; U-Bahn: Ulrepsorte), hosts contemporary plays, usually in German, and dance performances. Tickets are

14€ to 34€ ($22–$54) each; call either the number listed above or **Köln-Ticket** (© **0221/2801**) for schedules and show times.

Kölner Philharmonie   This architectural showcase was completed during the late 1980s. The concert hall features a soaring roof, enviable acoustics, and some of the finest classical music along the country's western tier. The building is the home of two separate orchestras, the **Gürzenich Kölner Philharmoniker** and the **Westdeutscher Rundfunk Orchestra.** Pop and jazz programs are also presented. Performances are given almost every night at 8pm, except Monday. Bischofsgartenstrasse 1. © **0221/204080.** Tickets 17€–130€ ($27–$208). U-Bahn: Hauptbahnhof.

Oper der Stadt Köln   This is the leading opera house of the Rhineland, known for its exciting productions and innovative repertory of classical and contemporary works. Performances take place almost every evening except Tuesday, usually at 7:30pm. Dance programs are also presented. The box office is open Monday to Friday 9am to 6pm and Saturday 9am to 2pm. Offenbachplatz. © **0221/22128400.** Tickets 10€–66€ ($16–$106). U-Bahn/ S-Bahn: Neumarkt.

THE CLUB & MUSIC SCENE
DANCE CLUBS   A combination of live bands and DJs play at the **MTC Music Club,** Zulpicher Strasse 10 (© **0221/2404188**; U-Bahn: Zulpicherplatz), an unpretentious, even somewhat grungy bar with a small stage at one end. Either live or recorded music is played nightly, usually beginning at around 8pm and continuing in an amiable, albeit high-volume and somewhat dysfunctional venue till around 3am. Expect lots of interest in punk-rock exhibitionism. The cover of 8€ ($13) is charged only when the music is live.

One of the city's most dramatic and surreal nightlife options is **E-Werk,** Schanzenstrasse 28 (© **0221/9627910**; U-Bahn: Keupstrasse), a combination of a dance club and a large concert hall. It's housed within what used to be an electrical power plant. Recorded music alternates with live acts. It's open every Friday and Saturday night at 10pm. Cover is 5€ ($8). Concert prices are 15€ to 25€ ($24–$40).

JAZZ CLUBS   **Klimperkasten** (also known as **Papa Joe's Biersalon**), Alter Markt 50–52 (© **0221/2582132**; U-Bahn: Hauptbahnhof), is an intimate jazz and piano bar open from 11am to 3am, with live music every night beginning around 8pm. The jazz is also hot at **Papa Joe's Jazzlokal,** Buttermarkt 37 (© **0221/2577931**; U-Bahn: Heumarkt). Sunday, when the music begins at 4pm and lasts until 1am, is the best day to come. The club is also open for live jazz Monday to Saturday 8pm to 3am. Surprisingly, there's never a cover.

LIVE-MUSIC CLUBS   Several times a week (usually Wed and Sat at 8pm, but with frequent exceptions), the **Underground,** Vogelsanger Strasse 200 (© **0221/542326**; U-Bahn: Venloerstrasse Gürtel), hosts rock groups that include both relatively unknown local acts and high-profile bands. There's a dance club on other nights. This place, in the words of a spokesperson, is "very alternative. If you're 40, you're probably too old to appreciate the music here." A food stand inside prepares pastas, burgers, and breakfast items for late-night (or early morning) hunger pangs. Cover is 8€ to 15€ ($13–$24).

Prime Club (formerly known as Luxor), Luxemburgstrasse 40 (© **0221/924460**; U-Bahn: Barbarossaplatz, offers some kind of live music most nights of the week, except Monday. You'll never know what to expect. The management books unknown, inexperienced bands, some of which show great promise. Hours vary, but usually music starts around 9pm. Cover ranges from 10€ to 20€ ($16–$32).

BARS

A 110-year-old bar, **Päffgen Bräuhaus,** Friesenstrasse 64–66 (© **0221/135461;** U-Bahn: Friesenplatz), serves its Kölsch brand of beer, along with regional cuisine. Seating is available indoors and out. It's open Sunday to Thursday 10am to midnight, Friday and Saturday 10am to 3am. **Altstadt Päffgen,** Heumarkt 62 (© **0221/2577765;** U-Bahn: Heumarkt), also serves the local brew and German dishes, and is open Tuesday to Sunday noon to midnight.

Students who have rediscovered the styles of the 1960s and 1970s lounge amid a decor of lava lamps, futuristic televisions, and other memorabilia at **Hallmacken-reuthur,** Brüsseler Platz 9 (© **0221/517970;** U-Bahn: Rudolfplatz). This is a place to drink, eat a late breakfast (until 4pm), or have a plate of pasta (6–11pm). It's open daily 11am to 1am. A holdover from Cologne's leftist days is **Hotelux,** Von Sandt Platz 10 (© **0221/241136**). Both its food and scarlet decor are self-consciously Soviet. You can eat platters of Russian food, drink Russian beer or more than two dozen brands of Russian vodka, and sit in a garden with greenery that is thankfully apolitical. It's open Sunday to Thursday 6pm to 1am, Friday and Saturday 6pm to 3am. The most sophisticated rendezvous for hip straights and a few gays in Cologne today is **Gloria,** Apostelnstrasse 11 (© **0221/660630;** U-Bahn: Neumarkt). If there's music playing, there's a cover of 5€ to 22€ ($8–$35). The club is open Monday to Thursday 9am to 1am, Friday and Saturday 9am to 3am, and Sunday 11am to 1am.

GAY NIGHTLIFE

Cologne offers more diversions and distractions for gay men and women than any other city in the Rhineland. Head either to the Marienplatz area or the "Bermuda Triangle" (see below). The most central gay bar in the Marienplatz area is **Chains,** Stephansstrasse 4 (© **0221/238730;** U-Bahn: Neumarkt). This one, attracting a mostly male leather and denim crowd, is open 10pm to 2 or 3am. Also see the review of Gloria, above. For more information about gay Cologne, go to **www.anyway-koeln.de**.

If you want to do as the Kölners do, consider a walk through what locals call **"the Bermuda Triangle,"** formed by the locations of the three bar/clubs listed below and positioned around the Rudolfplatz and the Altermarkt. Visited as an ensemble, they provide plenty of insight into the local gay lifestyle. The first is **Schampanja,** Mauritiuswall 43 (© **0221/2409544;** U-Bahn: Neumarkt), a small pub that sometimes books live bands (often punk).

Pay a visit to **Checkpoint,** Pipinstrasse 7 (© **0221/92576868;** www.checkpoint-cologne.de; U-Bahn: Zurticherplatz), a privately owned dispenser of information that performs some of its functions in cooperation with the city's official tourism authorities. It's open Sunday to Friday 5 to 9pm and Saturday 1 to 9pm, and has a staff that's ready, willing, and able to tell you what's up in gay Cologne. They'll even sell you memorabilia.

The first weekend in July is devoted to the city's **Gay Pride Parade,** when as many as 500,000 spectators line the parade route for a glimpse of the floats and marchers. For specifics on the parade, contact Checkpoint (see above) or click on **www.cologne pride.de**.

DRAG ACTS   Cologne isn't prudish when it comes to admiring the female figure, even if that figure is biologically male. For the most sophisticated drag acts in the

Rhineland, head for the **Bar of the Hotel Timp,** Heumarkt 25 (✆ **0221/2581409;** U-Bahn: Heumarkt). This tiny spot opens at 11pm and presents drag acts every night from 1 to 4am (it stays open till 5 or 6am). The cover of 8€ to 14€ ($13–$22) gets you views of such camp heroines as the divine Marlene Dietrich, several European starlets, and even Leni Riefenstahl, the controversial *Wünderkind* of German movies during the Hitler regime. Get here early if you want a good table.

10 Düsseldorf ⭐

40km (25 miles) N of Cologne (Köln), 230km (143 miles) NW of Frankfurt

Düsseldorf is a wealthy city—the richest in Germany. It's big and commercial, full of banks and industrial offices and skyscrapers, but it's also refreshingly clean. Düsseldorf got its start as a settlement on the right bank of the Rhine, but today it's spread out on both sides—the older part on the right, and the modern, commercial, and industrial part on the left. Five bridges connect the two sections, the most impressive being the Oberkassel. Parks and esplanades line the riverbanks. After 85% of the right bank was destroyed in World War II, Düsseldorf followed a modern trend in reconstruction, and today it's the most elegant metropolis in the Rhine Valley.

ESSENTIALS

GETTING THERE   By Plane   Düsseldorf International Airport, 6km (4 miles) north of the city, has regularly scheduled connections to 14 German, 47 European, and 132 international airports. You can fly from Frankfurt to Düsseldorf in just 45 minutes or from Munich or Berlin in an hour. For flight information, call ✆ **0211/4210.**

The airport is linked to the **GermanRail** network. Transfer to the Düsseldorf main rail station is via S-Bahn 7, offering service daily 4:03am to 12:30am, with trains every 20 minutes (trip time: 12 min.). One-way fare is 2.10€ ($3.35). For information, call ✆ **01805/996633.** Regular airport buses also connect the airport with Bonn and Cologne. A taxi ride to central Düsseldorf takes about 20 to 30 minutes and costs from 25€ ($40), depending on traffic.

By Train   The main train station, the **Düsseldorf Hauptbahnhof,** on Konrad-Adenauer-Platz in the southeastern sector, offers frequent connections to all major cities. The trip time to Frankfurt is about 2½ hours; to Munich, about 7 hours. For information, call ✆ **01805/996633.** Düsseldorf also has extensive regional rail links; for information on regional trains or trams, call ✆ **0211/58228.** Luggage-storage facilities are available at the Hauptbahnhof.

By Bus   Access to Düsseldorf is a lot easier by rail than by bus. The region's largest carrier is **Adorf GmbH** (✆ **0211/418970**), most of whose buses service small towns within the Rhineland that don't necessarily have railway stations of their own. Buses usually pull into Düsseldorf at the northern edge of the Bahnhofplatz.

By Car   Access to Düsseldorf is by the A3 Autobahn north and south or the A46 east and west.

VISITOR INFORMATION   For information, go to the **Tourist Office,** Immermannstrasse 65B (✆ **0211/17202844;** www.duesseldorf-tourismus.de), opposite the railway station. It's open Monday to Saturday 9:30am to 7pm and Sunday and national holidays 4 to 8pm. The office also has a hotel reservations service, which charges a one-time booking fee of 5€ ($8), along with a deposit that equals the price of the first night's accommodations. For the tourist office's room reservation services, call ℭ **0211/1720224,** Monday to Saturday 9:30am to 6:30pm.

GETTING AROUND   Düsseldorf is a big, sprawling city, so you'll probably want to rely on public transportation. The city and environs are served by a network of **S-Bahn railways** that fan out to the suburbs, along with **buses, Strassenbahn (trams),** and a **U-Bahn** system. Ask at the tourist office (ℭ **0211/17202844**) about purchasing a **Düsseldorf WelcomeCard,** offering free use of public transportation as well as free entrance to city museums, reductions on city tours, boat rides, and opera and ballet tickets. Valid for 24 hours, the welcome card costs 9€ ($14) for an adult or 18€ ($29) for a group/family card (2 adults plus 2 children up to age 14 or 3 adults). A welcome card valid for 48 hours goes for 14€ ($22) for an adult or 28€ ($45) for a group/family card. A 72-hour card is available for 19€ ($30) for individuals and 38€ ($61) for groups/families.

Taxi meters begin at 3€ ($4.80), after which you'll be billed between 1.28€ to 1.50€ ($2.10–$2.40) per kilometer, depending on the time of day. To call for a taxi in Düsseldorf, dial ℭ **0211/33333.**

WHERE TO STAY
VERY EXPENSIVE
Steigenberger Park-Hotel 𝕽𝕽   This traditional deluxe German hotel has been completely modernized and reequipped to meet modern demands. Its central location, overlooking the Hofgarten Park, is virtually unbeatable, which may explain why it attracts so many conventions and groups. The Steigenberger maintains a high level of service in the old-world style. All rooms, refitted to the latest standards, are cozy and comfortable. Bathrooms have make-up mirrors, robes, and tub/shower combos.

Corneliusplatz 1 (at the beginning of Königsallee, next to the German Opera), 40212 Düsseldorf 1. ℭ 800/223-5652 in the U.S. and Canada, or 0211/13810. Fax 0211/131679. www.steigenberger.de. 134 units. 235€–265€ ($376–$424) double; from 700€ ($1,120) suite. Rates include buffet breakfast. AE, DC, MC, V. Free parking. Tram: 78 or 79. Bus: 778. **Amenities:** Restaurant; 2 bars; lounge; fitness center; sauna; room service; babysitting; laundry service; dry cleaning; nonsmoking rooms. *In room:* A/C (in some), TV, Wi-Fi, minibar, hair dryer, safe.

EXPENSIVE
Ashley's Garden 𝕽𝕽   Posh, upscale, distinguished, and very quiet, this hotel occupies what was built in 1938 as a stately looking villa in the wealthy residential suburb of Golzheim, 5km (3 miles) north of the city center. Set within a 5-minute walk of both the Rhine and the Düsseldorf *Messe* (fairgrounds), it's completely outfitted, in both the bedrooms and the public areas, with English antiques and yard upon yard of Laura Ashley fabrics. The overall feel is that of an English country house. Terraces overlook a pleasant garden. Bedrooms are exceedingly comfortable, beautifully furnished, and spacious for the most part.

Karl-Kleppe-Strasse 20, 40474 Düsseldorf Ortsteil Golzheim. ℭ 0211/5161710. Fax 0211/453299. www.ashleys garden.de. 42 units. 140€–200€ ($224–$320) double. Rates include continental breakfast. AE, DC, MC, V. U-Bahn: Reeserplatz. **Amenities:** Restaurant; bar; lounge; outdoor pool; laundry service. *In room:* TV, Wi-Fi.

Radisson SAS Media Harbour Hotel 𝕽   The architect of this hotel was inspired by the harbor, creating a stunning V-shaped facade of Brazilian slate with panoramic windows. The outer walls not only look transparent, they slant. In the center of Medienhafen, an emerging district south of the center, the hotel offers luxurious and stylish bedrooms, furnished in a dramatically modern style. Its lounge with a fireplace is

Düsseldorf

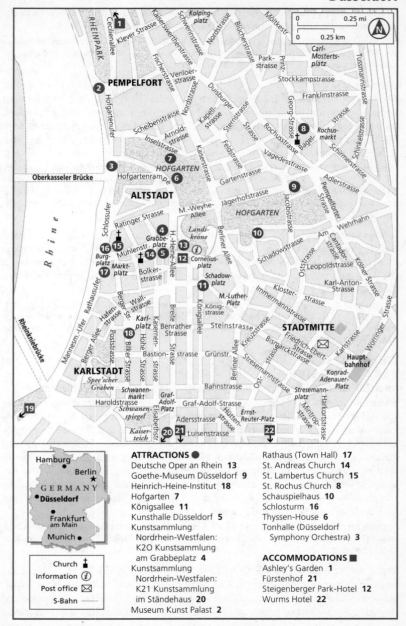

ATTRACTIONS ●
Deutsche Oper an Rhein **13**
Goethe-Museum Düsseldorf **9**
Heinrich-Heine-Institut **18**
Hofgarten **7**
Königsallee **11**
Kunsthalle Düsseldorf **5**
Kunstsammlung
  Nordrhein-Westfalen:
  K2O Kunstsammlung
  am Grabbeplatz **4**
Kunstsammlung
  Nordrhein-Westfalen:
  K21 Kunstsammlung
  im Ständehaus **20**
Museum Kunst Palast **2**

Rathaus (Town Hall) **17**
St. Andreas Church **14**
St. Lambertus Church **15**
St. Rochus Church **8**
Schauspielhaus **10**
Schlosturm **16**
Thyssen-House **6**
Tonhalle (Düsseldorf
  Symphony Orchestra) **3**

ACCOMMODATIONS ■
Ashley's Garden **1**
Fürstenhof **21**
Steigenberger Park-Hotel **12**
Wurms Hotel **22**

a cozy retreat, and the Italian food at Amano is among the best in the city. Both the vacationer and the business traveler will find comfort here.

Hammer Strasse 23, 40219 Düsseldorf. ℂ 800/333-3332 or 0211/311190. Fax 0211/3119110. www.radissonsas. com. 135 units. 169€–370€ ($270–$592) double; 500€ ($800) suite. AE, DC, MC, V. **Amenities:** Restaurant; bar; health center; room service; laundry service; dry cleaning. In room: A/C, TV, Wi-Fi, minibar, hair dryer, safe.

INEXPENSIVE

Fürstenhof   This hotel is a good, safe choice in the center of town. It's modern but not glaringly so and opens onto a tree-filled square. Rooms are handsomely furnished, each ranging in size from medium to spacious. All units contain bathrooms with tub/shower combos, and most of the guest rooms are at the lower end of the price scale. Half the breakfast room is reserved for nonsmoking guests.

Fürstenplatz 3, 40215 Düsseldorf 1. ℂ 0211/386460. Fax 0211/379062. www.fuerstenhof-duesseldorf.de. 43 units. 75€–245€ ($120–$392) double. Rates include buffet breakfast. AE, DC, MC, V. Parking 12€ ($19). Closed Dec 24–Jan 2. Tram: 701, 707, or 708. Bus: 725. Pets allowed. **Amenities:** Breakfast room; lounge; health club; sauna; car rental; room service; babysitting; laundry service; dry cleaning; nonsmoking rooms. In room: A/C, TV, minibar, hair dryer, safe.

Wurms Hotel *(Value*   The Wurms Hotel, set in a five-story stucco building, is a good budget choice, even though it has an expensive room or two. The small rooms are done in dark wood offset by bright bedspreads and curtains. The buffet breakfast is the only meal served. The hotel is a short walk from the central landmark square, Graf-Adolf-Platz.

Scheurenstrasse 23 (near Graf-Adolf-Strasse, about 4 blocks from the Hauptbahnhof), 40215 Düsseldorf. ℂ 0211/ 375001. Fax 0211/375003. www.hotel-wurms.de. 27 units. 75€–395€ ($120–$632) double. Rates include buffet breakfast. MC, V. Parking 8€–15€ ($13–$24). Tram: 734, 741, or 752. Bus: 835. **Amenities:** Breakfast room; lounge; room service. In room: TV, Wi-Fi.

WHERE TO DINE
VERY EXPENSIVE

Im Schiffchen *介介介* FRENCH/SEAFOOD   The chefs at Im Schiffchen deliver a refined, brilliantly realized repertoire of the finest cuisine you'll find in any city along the Rhine. The ingredients that go into the meals are unimpeachably authentic— every tomato, every onion, every fish or piece of meat seems to have been thoroughly evaluated for quality before purchasing. The menu is ever-changing, based on seasonal variations, but you might find homemade gooseliver pâté with green peppercorns, Brittany lobster in chamomile petals, a delectable Norwegian salmon in Vouvray sauce, or lobster cooked in chamomile tea. We could return again and again for the pikeperch cooked aromatically in puff pastry. The desserts are luscious; try the granulated fruit mélange with almond cream.

Kaiserswerther Markt 9 (on the outskirts of the city, at Kaiserswerth). ℂ 0211/401050. Reservations required. Main courses 39€–66€ ($62–$106); fixed-priced 8-course menu 136€ ($218). AE, DC, MC, V. Tues–Sat 7–10:30pm. Tram: 79 to Klemensplatz.

Victorian Restaurant *介介介* CONTINENTAL/INTERNATIONAL   This is the finest restaurant in the city center. The decor features sparkling crystal, black-leather banquettes, and masses of flowers. The food represents the best of both traditional and modern schools. The best examples include heavenly deep-fried zucchini flowers stuffed with lobster mousse and flavored with a sauce of champagne vinegar and coriander, apple salad with slices of gooseliver, and three-vegetable purée. The delectable desserts change with the inspiration of the pastry chef but might include terrine of oranges served with raspberry liqueur and fresh mint.

Nearby is the **Bistro im Victorian,** with a minimalist interior design. The kitchen area is wide open, so you can watch as the fresh ingredients are whipped into meals. Main courses in the Bistro cost from 18€ to 26€ ($28–$41).

Königstrasse 3A. ℂ 0211/8655020. Reservations required for the restaurant, recommended for the bistro. Main courses 34€–39€ ($54–$62); fixed-price menus lunch 40€–45€ ($64–$72), dinner 67€–95€ ($107–$152). AE, DC, MC, V. Mon–Sat noon–3pm and 7–11pm. Tram: 77 or 79.

EXPENSIVE

De' Medici ✿ FRENCH/ITALIAN   De' Medici is elegantly modern, and the chefs make it their goal to startle and amaze diners with zesty flavors. The menu lists an array of tried-and-true dishes, with concessions to whatever was available in the market that day. The marinated sweetbreads over sautéed eggplant or medallions of veal in puff pastry are both unusual and excellent. The fish here is particularly well prepared, including a succulent version of sea bass baked (for two diners) in a salt crust.

Amboss-Strasse 3 (on the outskirts, at Oberkassel). ℂ 0211/594151. Reservations required. Main courses 17€–25€ ($27–$40). AE, DC, MC, V. Mon–Fri noon–2:30pm; Mon–Sat 6–10pm. U-Bahn: Amboss-Strasse.

Rheinturm Top 180 Restaurant ✿ GERMAN/INTERNATIONAL   This futuristic restaurant is set atop the spool-shaped summit of the city's tallest tower (172m/564 ft.) and revolves slowly, affording a 360-degree panorama of Düsseldorf's buildings and parks. Most people come here for the view, but the food is competently prepared and includes grills, game dishes, fish, and soups. Try the slices of smoked duck breast with creamy savoy cabbage or rolls of salmon stuffed with turbot filling and served in Riesling-and-saffron sauce. Vegetarian courses are also featured. Menu items focus on fresh seasonal ingredients, and the menu sometimes celebrates the arrival of fresh asparagus in springtime, as well as fresh fish and fresh game whenever it's in season. A trip to the tower's observation lookout costs 4.50€ ($7.20) for adults, 3€ ($4.80) for children 13 to 17, and 2€ ($3.20) for children 6 to 12; kids 5 and under go free. The tower is open daily 10am to 11:30pm.

Stromstrasse 20. ℂ 0211/8632000. Reservations recommended. Main courses 23€–31€ ($37–$50); fixed-price 4-course dinner 50€ ($80). AE, DC, MC, V. Daily noon–2:30pm and 6:30–11pm. Tram: 704, 709, or 719. Bus: 725.

MODERATE

Zum Schiffchen ✿ RHINELAND   Come here if you're looking for Düsseldorf's most traditional and atmospheric restaurant. Zum Schiffchen, in the heart of the Altstadt, is the city's oldest restaurant. A golden model ship on top of the step-gabled building (which dates from 1628) reminds you of its location, near the river. The interior follows the tavern tradition of scrubbed wooden tables and rustic artifacts. Good, hefty portions of regional cuisine are the rule here. Menu items include such two-fisted German specialties as *Wursts,* sauerbraten, schnitzels, knuckle of pork with roast potatoes, and great emphasis on seasonal specialties like asparagus. The menu is large, and the service by the blue-aproned waiters (called *Köbesse*) is rather hectic. Zum Schiffchen is the perfect place to sample Frankenheim, Düsseldorf's local beer. Over the years, the restaurant has attracted a host of famous diners ranging from Napoleon and Heinrich Heine to Arthur Miller.

Hafenstrasse 5 (a block from the Rhine). ℂ 0211/132421. Reservations required. Main courses 9€–29€ ($14–$46). AE, DC, MC, V. Mon–Sat 11am–10:45pm. U-Bahn: Heinrich-Heine-Allee.

INEXPENSIVE

Im Alten Bierhause RHINELAND   Lying 1.6km (1 mile) from the center, this place is actually more of a wine tavern than a restaurant. The building dates from 1641. Style connoisseurs will recognize it as typical of the Rhine's left bank (as opposed to the right, the left bank has more of a bohemian aura). Traditional German specialties are served here. The house specialty is *Speck-Pfannenkuchen,* a bacon pancake; a similar version is made with marmalade. On Sunday the beer drinkers pile in at 11am. The specialty of the house is that dark and foamy local brew, Altbier.

Alt-Niederkassel 75 (on the outskirts). ℰ 0211/551272. Reservations required. Main courses 8€–23€ ($13–$37). No credit cards. Tues–Sat 3–11:30pm; Sun 11am–11pm. Closed 3 weeks in July-Aug (dates vary). Bus: 834.

Zum Schlüssel GERMAN   As Germanic as the Rhine and set within the pedestrian zone in the heart of town, Zum Schlüssel thrived as a brewery under the name Alt Gatzweiler during the early 20th century, then folded, and was reborn as a smaller-scale brewery. Today, its fermentation vats and elaborate pipes are visible from the wood-sheathed dining room. The beer that arrives in frothy mugs is the Alt Schlüssel brand, available in various degrees of darkness, depending on the season. Menu items are Germanic dishes that complement the beer, and include sauerbratens, schnitzels, *Eisbein* (pork knuckles), homemade soups, freshly made salads, and succulent steaks.

Gatzweilers beer hall, Bolkerstrasse 43–47. ℰ 0211/8289550. Reservations recommended. Main courses 9€–16€ ($14–$26). AE, DC, MC, V. Daily 10am–midnight (Fri–Sat until 1am). U-Bahn: Heinrich-Heine-Allee.

EXPLORING DÜSSELDORF

As in most German cities, there's an **Altstadt (old town),** with a **Marktplatz (marketplace),** a Gothic **Rathaus (town hall),** and a few old buildings and churches. Near the Rathaus on Burgplatz are two of the city's most famous landmarks, the twisted spire of **St-Lambertus Basilika (St. Lambertus Church)** and the **Schlossturm (Castle Tower),** both of 13th-century origin. A short walk to the east takes you to **St-Andreas Basilika (St. Andreas Church).**

The Altstadt has been called "the longest bar in the world" because of the 200-plus bars and restaurants found here. The favorite drink is a top-fermented Altbier (old beer); it's a dark, mellow brew that must be consumed soon after it's made.

A walk up **Königsallee,** called the "Kö" by Düsseldorfers, will give visitors a quick overview of the city and its residents. This street flanks an ornamental canal, shaded by trees and crossed by bridges. One bank is lined with office buildings, the other with elegant shops, cafes, and restaurants. Here you'll see women dressed in the very latest styles. Düsseldorf is the fashion center of Germany. It's known for its Fashion Weeks, which attract designers and buyers from all over Europe.

If you walk up the Kö toward the Trident Fountain at the northern end of the canal, you'll reach the **Hofgarten,** a huge, rambling park. Here you can wander along the walks or sit and relax amid shade trees, gardens, fountains, and statues, almost forgetting you're in the very center of the city. Among the monuments is one to the poet Heinrich Heine. The Hofgarten is a good central point for seeing the city's major attractions—nearly all museums and cultural attractions are on its perimeter. Towering over the Hofgarten is Düsseldorf's most impressive skyscraper, the **Thyssen-House.** Residents call it the Dreischeibenhaus ("three-slice house"), because it actually looks like three huge monoliths sandwiched together. Northeast of the Hofgarten is **St. Rochus,** one of the city's finest modern churches.

Düsseldorf continues its bold march into the 21st century, especially in its once dilapidated but now trendy **MedienHafen** district. Originally this was a flourishing warehouse sector in the 19th century. Today it is often a showcase for avant-garde modern architecture, especially in the office buildings and other works of Frank O. Gehry, winner of the Pritzker prize, the Nobel Prize of architecture. Of course, Gehry's far better known work is his celebrated titanium masterpiece, the Guggenheim Museum in Bilbao, Spain.

Düsseldorf's most striking example of his work is the ensemble of "organic" looking high rises at Neuer Zollhof. This trio of buildings with their wavy lines can easily be spotted along the waterfront. Yachts and luxury cruisers stud the harbor at the foot of the Rhine Tower of MedienHafen. For the best view of these avant-garde buildings, including Gehry's controversial architecture, walk down the water-bordering prome-nade, Am Handelshafen, beginning at the Rhine Tower, heading toward Franziusstrasse.

Goethe-Museum Düsseldorf   The Anton and Katharina Kippenberg Foundation sponsors this literary museum dedicated to Goethe's life and work. It emerged from the Kippenbergs' private collection of some 35,000 items, including autographs, books, busts, paintings, coins, medals, plaques, and china. About 1,000 pieces are shown in the permanent exhibition, including first drafts of well-known poems. The displays present a chronology of Goethe's life and work. There are also exhibits on var-ious topics of the Goethe era.

Schloss-Jägerhof (in the Jägerhof Castle at the Hofgarten), Jacobistrasse 2. (C) 0211/8996262. www.goethe-museum.com. Admission 3€ ($4.80) adults, 1.50€ ($2.40) children. Tues–Fri and Sun 11am–5pm; Sat 1–5pm. Tram: 704 or 707. Bus: 722 or 800.

Heinrich-Heine-Institut   Heinrich Heine (1797–1856) was Germany's greatest lyric poet. More than 10,000 volumes, as well as the manuscript bequest of this Düs-seldorf-born poet, are found here. Born into a Jewish family, Heine nominally con-verted to Christianity so that he could attend law school. He was the author of the famous *Die Lorelei*, and his poems were set to music by Schubert, Schumann, and Hugo Wolf. His work was prohibited during the Nazi era, during which *Die Lorelei* was officially attributed to an unknown author. In the Altstadt, you visit the house where Heine was born. It's at Bolkerstrasse 53 and is marked by a plaque.

Bilkerstrasse 12–14. (C) 0211/8995574. Admission 3€ ($4.80) adults, free for children 17 and under. Tues–Fri and Sun 11am–5pm; Sat 1–5pm. Tram: 704 or 707.

Kunsthalle Düsseldorf   The Kunsthalle Düsseldorf is devoted to contemporary art from the Rhineland and throughout Europe. No other museum in the city keeps up with changing trends in art as well as this one. Visiting exhibits of every shape and size, often bizarre, are displayed here. If time remains, visit the museum's latest attrac-tion, KIT (Kunst im Tunnel). This is an "art tunnel" literally under the museum. Here up-and-coming artists display their work, and exhibitions are frequently changed.

Grabbeplatz 4 (across from the Kunstsammlung Nordrhein-Westfalen, west of the Hofgarten). (C) 0211/8996243. www.kunsthalle-duesseldorf.de. Admission 5.50€ ($8.80) adults, 3.50€ ($5.60) students and children 10–15, free for children 9 and under. Tues–Sat noon–7pm; Sun 11am–6pm. U-Bahn: Heinrich-Heine-Allee.

Kunstsammlung Nordrhein-Westfalen: K2O Kunstsammlung am Grabbe-platz This museum is divided into two museums, but the K20 Grabbeplatz loca-tion is the older and superior art center (see below for the second location). The black glass edifice here is one of the most stunning modern buildings in the city. The most important exhibit is a collection of nearly 100 paintings by Paul Klee, the famous Swiss painter who once taught at Düsseldorf's National Academy of Art. The museum also displays an outstanding exhibition of surrealist art, including Salvador Dalí. Some of the major modern 20th-century artists are on display, including works by everybody from Picasso to Matisse, along with Bonnard, Léger, Johns, and Pollock. You'll also see a series of American masterpieces dating from 1946, as well as some of the lesser known but very celebrated painters of the 20th century, including art by Markus Lüpertz, Per Kirkeby, and Gerhard Richter. Six major temporary exhibits of art land here annually. *Warning:* This museum will be closed until late in 2009 for renovations.

Grabbeplatz 5 (opposite the Kunsthalle). ℂ 0211/8381130. www.kunstsammlung.de. Admission 6.50€ ($10) adults, 4.50€ ($7.20) students and children. Tues–Fri 10am–6pm (until 10pm every 1st Wed of the month); Sat–Sun 11am–6pm. U-Bahn: Heinrich-Heine-Allee.

Kunstsammlung Nordrhein-Westfalen: K21 Kunstsammlung im Ständehaus

This is the second division of the more famous K20 Kunstsammlung (see above). On show at K21 is international art that dates from 1980 and extends into the post-millennium period. It defines itself—and certainly its future—as a museum for the art of the 21st century. This is a museum in the making, and it is expected that its fledgling collection will be beefed up every year as bequests come in. The present collection is augmented by contributing museums who agree to lend great art for a limited period. K21 also displays works from some of the great collections in private hands in Germany. Don't expect all future art to be paintings. As a showplace of the 21st century, photography is embraced, as are moving images on film and video. If you have limited time, head for K20. But if you want to take "pot luck," see what's being displayed at K21. It will certainly be worth your while. *Warning:* K20 is closed until late 2009 for renovations, but K21 will be open on its regular schedule.

Ständehausstrasse 1. ℂ 0211/8381600. www.kunstsammlung.de. Admission 6.50€ ($10) adults, 4.50€ ($7.20) students, 2€ ($3.20) children. Tues–Fri 10am–6pm (until 10pm every 1st Wed of the month); Sat–Sun 11am–6pm. Tram: 703, 706, 712, 713, or 715 to Graf-Adolf-Platz.

Museum Kunst Palast ☝

This is one of the largest and most comprehensive museums in the Rhineland. The painting collection includes works by Rubens, Caspar David Friedrich, and the Die Brücke and Der Blaue Reiter schools. The sculpture collection ranges from the late Middle Ages to the 20th century. There are also some 80,000 prints and drawings, as well as early Persian bronzes and ceramics, a glass collection, textiles from late antiquity to the present, and a design collection.

Ehrenhof 5. ℂ 0211/8924242. www.museum-kunst-palast.de Admission 10€ ($16) adults, 7.50€ ($12) students and children, 20€ ($32) family ticket. Tues–Sun 11am–6pm. Tram: 701, 706, 711, or 715.

SHOPPING

Düsseldorf is a city of high fashion and high prices. Many chic Europeans visit the city just to shop for what's new and hot. The best and trendiest fashions are sold on the opulent east side of the Königsallee. The two largest concentrations of designer shops are found at the **Kö Galerie,** Königsallee 60, and the **Kö Center,** Königsallee 30. Each gallery has some 100 shops. Those not interested in dishing out lots of euros for designer duds should head for the more recently opened **Schadow Arcade,** off Schadowplatz, at the end of the Kö. Fashion here isn't so haute, but neither are the prices. Shoppers spend some 500 million euros in the shops on Schadowstrasse annually—more than is spent on any other street in the country.

ANTIQUES Düsseldorf's historic core contains a fine selection of antiques stores.
Lothar Heubel, Bastionstrasse 27 (© **0211/134103;** U-Bahn: Heinrich-Heine-Allee), specializes in Asian and African antiques, including jewelry, ceramics, and Chinese items from the Han, Ming, and Tang dynasties, mixed in with a handful of antiques from Provence and the south of France.

DEPARTMENT STORES Carsch Haus, Heinrich-Heine-Platz (© **0211/83970;** U-Bahn: Heinrich-Heine-Allee), carries a good selection of fashions, as well as quality home furnishings, jewelry, and other items.

DESIGNER CLOTHING & ACCESSORIES Bogner Shop, Königsallee 6–8 (© **0211/134222**), carries functional sportswear that's meant for action on the golf course, tennis court, and ski slopes. The designers have their workshop on the second floor.

Chanel, Kö Center (© **0211/325935**), offers the company's complete line of products, from clothing to cosmetics and fragrances.

Shoes and more shoes fill the racks at **Walter Steiger Schuhe,** Kö Galerie (© **0211/134104**), the German designer of high-quality, high-fashion footwear. Choose from luggage, handbags, shoes, and other accessories at **Etienne Aigner,** Kö Galerie (© **0211/3230955**). In the boutique of **Louis Vuitton,** Kö Center (© **0211/323230**), leather accessories, luggage, and handbags are sold.

DINNERWARE & KITCHEN ACCESSORIES A diversity of items and styles can be found at **Georg Jensen,** Kö Galerie (© **0211/324281**), the shop of the German designer who redefines silver flatware, bowls, candle sticks, coffee pots, and much more.

FURNITURE & DECORATIVE ACCESSORIES One of Düsseldorf's largest purveyors of Art Deco furniture and art objects is **Arts Decoratifs,** Hohestrasse 20 (© **0211/324553;** U-Bahn: Heinrich-Heine-Allee). Look for lamps, vases, paperweights, and high-quality prewar costume jewelry, some of which could make good souvenirs.

JEWELRY & WATCHES Located in the heart of the designer shopping district, **Wempe Juwelier,** Königsallee 14 (© **0211/324077**), is one of a chain of 23 shops scattered throughout Düsseldorf that carries Swiss watches and jewelry designs in gold, silver, and precious stones.

DÜSSELDORF AFTER DARK
The place to go for nightlife in Düsseldorf is the **Altstadt.** This .8 sq. km (⅓ sq. mile) of narrow streets and alleyways, between Königsallee and the Rhine River, is jam-packed with restaurants, dance clubs, art galleries, boutiques, nightclubs, and some 200 song-filled beer taverns. Düsseldorfers refer to a night cruising the Altstadt as an *Altstadtbummel.*

THE PERFORMING ARTS Classical music has long had an illustrious association with this city, once home to Brahms, Mendelssohn, and Schumann (though there are no specific tourist sites relating to them in Düsseldorf). Therefore, it's not surprising that both the **Düsseldorfer Symphoniker** and its home, **Tonhalle,** Ehrenhof 1 (box office © **0211/8996123;** U-Bahn: Tonhalle), are world famous. The Tonhalle is perhaps Germany's most successful modern concert hall after Berlin's Philharmonie. The highly regarded orchestra gives about a dozen concerts a year, with tickets running 24€ to 75€ ($38–$120). **Deutsche Oper am Rhein,** Heinrich-Heine-Allee 16A

(© **0211/8908211;** U-Bahn: Heinrich-Heine-Allee), is one of the city's renowned opera and ballet companies. Tickets are 11€ to 120€ ($18–$192).

Schauspielhaus, Gustav-Gründgens-Platz 1 (© **0211/85230;** U-Bahn: Heinrich-Heine-Allee), is known all over Germany for its outstanding productions and acting. Performances (in German) take place September to June, and tickets cost 14€ to 44€ ($22–$70).

BARS & BEER HALLS   The oldest brewery-bar in the city is **Bräuerei Schumacher,** Oststrasse 123 (© **0211/8289020;** U-Bahn: Oststrasse), a popular establishment that serves only beer brewed by its parent company. It's open daily 10am to midnight. Two other breweries, each serving beer brewed on the premises, are **Brauerei im Füchschen,** Ratingerstrasse 28 (© **0211/137470;** U-Bahn: Heinrich-Heine-Allee), and **Bräuerei zum Schlüssel,** Bolkerstrasse 43 (© **0211/828955;** U-Bahn: Heinrich-Heine-Allee), both of which also offer platters of German food.

Angel images fill every nook and cranny of **Engelchen** (German for "little angel"), Kurzestrasse 15 (© **0211/327356;** U-Bahn: Heinrich-Heine-Allee), where an alternative arts crowd gathers for conversation and coffee, beer, or mixed drinks. It's open Monday to Friday 11am to 2am and weekends 3pm to 5am.

DANCE CLUBS   Two hot dance spots, **Tor 3,** Ronsdorferstrasse 143 (© **0211/7336497),** and **Stahlwerk,** Ronsdorferstrasse 134 (© **0211/730350),** face each other across the street (U-Bahn: Langenbergerstrasse). Both intersperse recorded dance music with live acts from throughout Europe. Both draw a mixed, fashion-conscious crowd, are open Friday and Saturday from 10pm to about 6am, and charge a cover of 6€ to 14€ ($9.60–$22).

LIVE-MUSIC CLUBS   A popular piano bar, **Bei Tino,** Königsallee 21 (© **0211/326463;** U-Bahn: Königsallee), has music noon to 3am nightly; guests are often allowed to play the piano. **McLaughlin's Irish Pub,** Kurzestrasse 11 (© **0211/324611;** U-Bahn: Heinrich-Heine-Allee), serves Guinness and Murphy's with stew and pies, and presents touring Irish bands on the weekend. It's open Sunday to Thursday 5pm to 1am and Friday and Saturday 11am to 3am.

GAY CLUBS   Most of the gays in Düsseldorf head to the richer and more diverse (and more exciting) gay fleshpots of Köln, but if you want to remain in the city, **Café Rosa Mond,** Lierenfelderstrasse 39 (© **0211/167575;** www.rosamond.de), has a bar and Düsseldorf's widest variety of activities, ranging from an occasional theater piece to a Saturday-night dance hall and even weekly flea market-style auctions. Once you're here, the staff can guide you to other gay venues in the region.

16

The Mosel Valley

The Mosel meanders in a snakelike path through the mountains west of the Rhineland, passing town after town, seemingly with the sole purpose of beautifying the riverbanks. Nearly every village and hill has its own castle or fortress, often surrounded by vineyards.

The Mosel (*Moselle* in French) begins in the hills of France, but its most scenic portion is the last 193km (120 miles) before it enters the Rhine at Koblenz.

Many of the rich and full-bodied Mosel wines are superior to those of the Rhine Valley.

If you enter Germany via France or Luxembourg, the Mosel route is a good way to begin your tour of the German countryside. You'll arrive first at the major city of **Trier** with its significant Roman ruins before weaving through the Hunsrück and Eifel mountains.

1 Cochem ✦

92km (57 miles) NE of Trier, 51km (32 miles) SW of Koblenz

This medieval town, located in one of the best wine regions of the Mosel Valley, is crowded against the left bank of the river by a huge vineyard-covered hill. Because of its large number of inns, Cochem is your best choice for an overnight stopover between Koblenz and Trier.

The town is a typical wine village, with tastings and festivals. But the biggest attraction is **Reichsburg Cochem** ✦ (© 02671/255). The original 1027 castle was almost completely destroyed by Louis XIV's army in 1689. It has since been restored according to the original ground plans, and its medieval ramparts and turrets create a dramatic backdrop for the town. To reach the castle, follow the steep footpath from the center of town; the 15-minute walk is well worth it for the rewarding views of the town and the Mosel below. Although you can visit the grounds anytime, the interior of the castle is open daily mid-March to November 9am to 5pm. Guided tours (in English) are conducted at regular intervals. Admission is 4.50€ ($7.20) for adults, 2.50€ ($4) for students and children, and 13€ ($21) for a family ticket.

ESSENTIALS

GETTING THERE   By Train   The **Cochem Bahnhof** is on the Wasserbillig-Trier-Koblenz rail line, with frequent service between these connecting cities. For information, call © **01805/996633** (11861 in Germany; www.bahn.de).

By Bus   Regional bus service along the Mosel is provided by **RMV Rhein Mosel Verkehrsgesellschaft** (© **01805/7684636;** www.rmv.de) and by **Moselbahn, GmbH** (© **06531/96800**).

By Car   Access is via the A48 Autobahn on the Koblenz-Trier express highway; exit either at Ulmen or at Kaisersesch.

Fun Fact **Thunderbird, It's Not**

Mosel wines have the lowest alcohol content (about 9%) of any white wine in the world. Because of this, they are best enjoyed in their youth.

By Boat   Boat rides on the Mosel River operate between Trier and Cochem. Contact **Gebrüder Kolb,** Briedern/Mosel (© **02673/1515**).

VISITOR INFORMATION   For tourist information, contact the **Verkehrsamt,** Endertplatz 1 (© **02671/60040**), open Monday to Friday 9am to 5pm; from July to October, it is also open Saturday 9am to 5pm and Sunday 10am to noon.

SPECIAL EVENTS   During the last week in May or the first week of June, **Mosel-Wein-Woche** begins, celebrating the region's wines with tasting booths and a street fair. A similar **Weinfest** takes place the last weekend of August. For information on either of these events, contact the tourist office (see above) or the **Weingut Winzer-hof** (© **02671/7297**) for details on dates, activities, and accommodations.

WHERE TO STAY

Alte Thorschenke ⊛   Both a hotel and a wine restaurant, the centrally located Alte Thorschenke is one of the oldest and best-known establishments along either side of the Mosel. The romantically conceived building, with its timbers and towers, was originally built in 1332. It became a hotel in 1960, when a modern wing was added. Most rooms are reached via a cantilevered wooden staircase that has creaked for centuries (there's also an elevator in the rear). Six rooms have four-poster beds; all units contain tub/shower combinations. There's also a romantic Napoleon suite.

Brückenstrasse 3, 56812 Cochem. © **02671/7059.** Fax 02671/4202. www.castle-thorschenke.com. 35 units. 84€–115€ ($134–$184) double; from 115€ ($184) suite. Rates include buffet breakfast. AE, DC, MC, V. Parking 6€ ($9.60) in garage. **Amenities:** Restaurant; room service; laundry service; dry cleaning; nonsmoking rooms. *In room:* TV, minibar, hair dryer.

Lohspeicher   This inn is good for an overnight stopover, although it's better known for serving the best food within Cochem than it is for its rooms. This generously proportioned 1832 building with hand-hewn beams was once a warehouse. Rooms, though generally a bit small, are comfortably furnished, all with bathrooms containing tub/shower combinations. Excellent Rhinelander cuisine is served in the dining room. The team of Ingo, Birgit, and Laura Beth are the warmest hosts in the area.

Obergasse 1, 56812 Cochem. © **02671/3976.** Fax 02671/1772. www.lohspeicher.de. 9 units. 110€–150€ ($176–$240) double. Rates include half board. MC, V. Parking 7€ ($11). Closed Feb. **Amenities:** Restaurant; lounge; nonsmoking rooms. *In room:* TV, hair dryer.

WHERE TO DINE

L'Auberge de Vin ⊛ RHINELANDER   Within the town of Cochem itself, the best food, a traditional cuisine, is served by the Beth family. Their aim is to offer you the finest of their market-fresh shopping every day. Connoisseurs flock here to enjoy soup made with some of the fattest and most delectable snails in Germany. Fresh fish and game dishes, such as venison in autumn, round out the menu. Among the fish courses, you might enjoy the filet of pikeperch with fresh asparagus, or the scallops

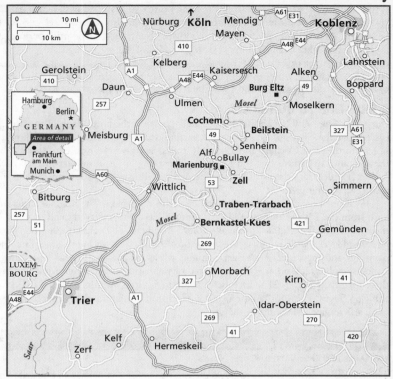

with tomato and noodles in a lobster sauce. Other praise-worthy dishes include breast of pigeon with "smashed" celery in a red-wine sauce, or saddle of lamb with ratatouille.

In the Lohspeicher, Obergasse 1. ℂ 02671/3976. Reservations recommended. Main courses 23€–27€ ($37–$43); fixed-price menus 33€–92€ ($53–$147). MC, V. Thurs–Tues noon–2pm and 6–10pm. Closed: Feb.

Weissmühle im Enterttal GERMAN   Set within Cochem's suburb of Enterttal, this restaurant's fine cuisine is popular with locals. You can dine within either the Müllerstube—a woodsy, antique-looking room that might remind you of an inn high in the Swiss Alps—or in the brighter, sunnier, and larger Sommerrestaurant.

⌒Moments Wine Tasting with the Baron

Guests of the Alte Thorschenke can visit the 500-year-old **Schloss Landesberg,** Ediger-Eller (www.mosel-weinproben.de), about 7km (4½ miles) from Cochem. Here in the old cellars, you can taste some of the best wines produced along the banks of the Mosel. To arrange a visit if you're not staying at the hotel, call ℂ 02675/277.

A trademark dish is fresh trout from the small nearby lake, stuffed with herbs, baked, and kept warm at your table with a hot stone. The inn also rents 36 well-furnished bedrooms, each individually furnished in a rustic country style. The price per person for bed and breakfast ranges from 45€ to 55€ ($72–$88).

Endertstrasse 1. ⓒ 02671/8955. Fax 02671/8207. www.weissmuehle.de. Reservations recommended. Main courses 14€–25€ ($22–$40). MC, V. Daily noon–2pm and 6–9pm. From Cochem's center, drive toward the Autobahn, following the signs for Koblenz/Trier; the inn is on the left of the road, 1.5km (1 mile) northwest of Cochem.

A SIDE TRIP TO BURG ELTZ

Burg Eltz ⓐⓐ (ⓒ 02672/950500), a stately castle on the north bank of the Mosel, is set above the village of Moselkern and surrounded by woodlands. It lies 20km (12 miles) northeast of Cochem and 29km (18 miles) southwest of Koblenz. Access is by the A48 and A61 autobahns and Route 49. A parking lot, Antoniuskapelle, less than 1.5km (1 mile) from the castle, can be reached via Münstermaifeld. A bus runs to the castle every 5 minutes.

This is one of the few intact medieval castles in the region. The original structure, built from the 12th century to the 17th century, has been preserved in all its glory—the romance of the Middle Ages really comes alive here. The castle houses four separate residences, with original medieval furnishings that include some fine old paintings and tapestries. A treasury contains works by goldsmiths and silversmiths, armor, weapons, and other objects acquired by the family over the centuries. The castle is open daily March 21 to October 9:30am to 5:30pm. Admission is 8€ ($13) for adults, 5.50€ ($8.80) for children, and 24€ ($38) for a family ticket. There are two small self-service restaurants in the castle.

2 Beilstein

11km (7 miles) E of Cochem, 111km (69 miles) W of Mainz

This unspoiled medieval wine town on the east bank of the Mosel has an unusual marketplace hewn right into the rocky hillside. Above the town stand the former cloister church and the ruins of the 12th-century Metternich Castle.

ESSENTIALS

GETTING THERE   By Train   The nearest rail station is at Cochem (see above).

By Bus   Service from Cochem and other points along the Mosel is available from RMV Rhein Mosel Verkehrsgesellschaft (ⓒ 01805/7684636; www.rmv.de) and from Moselbahn GmbH (ⓒ 06531/96800; www.moselbahn.de).

By Car   Access by car is via the A48 Autobahn on the Koblenz-Trier run; exit at Kaisersesch.

VISITOR INFORMATION   The nearest information office is at Cochem (see above).

WHERE TO STAY & DINE

Haus Burgfrieden   This hotel's simple but comfortable rooms are outfitted in an uncluttered modern style. They aren't very spacious, but the maintenance is good. All units contain neatly kept bathrooms equipped with tub/shower combinations. On the premises is a dining room featuring international cuisine. Main courses cost 9.50€ to 21€ ($15–$34).

Im Muhlental 17 (a 5-min. walk west of the town center), 56814 Beilstein. ℂ **02673/93639.** Fax 02673/936388. www.hotel-burgfrieden.de. 39 units. 75€–85€ ($120–$136) double. Rates include buffet breakfast. No credit cards. Free parking. Closed Nov–Mar. **Amenities:** Restaurant; lounge. *In room:* TV, safe.

Haus Lipmann 𝒢 *Finds*   You can sample the wines that made Beilstein famous at this popular inn in the town center. The five guest rooms are located in its main house. They're all small, cozy, and very inviting, with tiny bathrooms and showers.

For six generations, the same family has tended the vast riverside vineyards that have won them acclaim. Try their Ellenzer Goldbäumchen or their Beilsteiner Schlossberg. In summer, the most popular place at the inn for drinking and dining is the vine-covered terrace with a statue of Bacchus, overlooking the Mosel. You can also try the antiques-filled tavern or the wood-paneled Rittersaal, with its collection of old firearms and pewter. In the cooler months, fires burn in the tall walk-in fireplace and the tiny open hearth. German food is served.

Marktplatz 3, 56814 Beilstein. ℂ **02673/1573.** Fax 02673/1521. www.hotel-haus-lipmann.com. 5 units. 100€ ($160) double. Rates include buffet breakfast. No credit cards. Free parking. Closed Nov–Mar. **Amenities:** Restaurant; bar; room service. *In room:* TV.

3 Zell an der Mosel

69km (43 miles) NE of Trier, 105km (65 miles) W of Mainz, 35km (22 miles) S of Cochem

This old town, along the east bank of the Mosel, is best known for its excellent wine, Schwarze Katze ("Black Cat"). The grape is king here, as you'll quickly realize if you visit during the annual autumn wine festival. Nearby, on the left bank of the Mosel, 8km (5 miles) from Zell, stands the little wine village of **Alf.** The surroundings are idyllic, especially if you climb up to the Marienburg, which has a fine view over the Mosel and the vineyards of Zell.

ESSENTIALS

GETTING THERE   By Train   The nearest rail station is at Bullay, some 5km (3 miles) away. For information, call ℂ **01805/996633** (11861 in Germany; www.bahn.de).

By Bus   Regional bus service is provided by **RMV Rhein Mosel Verkehrsgesellschaft GmbH** (ℂ **01805/7684636;** www.rmv.de) and **Moselbahn GmbH** (ℂ **06531/96800;** www.moselbahn.de).

By Car   Access by car is via the A1 Autobahn north and south, or via Route 53 east and west.

VISITOR INFORMATION   Go to **Tourist-Information,** in the Rathaus, Marktstrasse 2 (ℂ **06542/96220**), Monday to Friday 9am to 5pm and Saturday 10am to 1pm.

WHERE TO STAY & DINE

Haus Notenau   Solid, comfortable, and well maintained, this three-story building was erected in 1960 on the forested outskirts of town. Your hosts, members of the Saxler family, will offer you a cheerful, no-nonsense stay in rooms that are outfitted with contemporary-looking furniture and pale pastel-color schemes, each quiet, calm, and uncontroversial. Bathrooms are very cramped with showers and tubs. Come here for rest, relaxation, and contemplation. If Haus Notenau is full, additional accommodations are available at its comparably priced sibling, **Haus Brandenburg,** Brandenburger Strasse 1 (𝄌 **06542/5010**). The Notenau does not have its own restaurant, but the staff will direct you to eateries nearby.

Notenau 7–8, 56856 Zell an der Mosel. 𝄌 **06542/5010.** Fax 06542/5280. www.haus-notenau.de. 20 units. 68€ ($109) double. Rates include breakfast. Discounts for stays of more than 3 days. Free parking. AE, MC, V. Bus: From Zell's center, take bus no. 333, direction Bernkastel. **Amenities:** Nonsmoking rooms. *In room:* No phones.

Zur Post   This hotel sits directly on the river. Its small rooms are carpeted, with French doors opening onto balconies. The bathrooms are midsize, each with a tub/shower combination. The owner takes pride in looking after her guests and ensuring their comfort. The restaurant is open for lunch and dinner Tuesday to Sunday, serving German cuisine and an extensive selection of Mosel wines. Enjoy a glass in the warmly decorated *Weinstube* or on the inviting sun terrace as you watch the river traffic go by.

Schlossstrasse 21, 56856 Zell an der Mosel. 𝄌 **06542/4217.** Fax 06542/41693. www.hotel-zur-post-zell.de. 14 units. 75€–85€ ($120–$136) double. Rates include buffet breakfast. AE, DC, MC, V. Free parking. Closed Feb to mid-Mar. **Amenities:** Restaurant; lounge. *In room:* TV, no phone.

4 Traben-Trarbach

60km (37 miles) NE of Trier, 103km (64 miles) W of Mainz, 18km (11 miles) SW of Zell

Thanks to their central location on the Mosel, halfway between Koblenz and Trier, the twin towns of Traben and Trarbach have become the wine capitals of the Mosel Valley. Their gardenlike promenades are viewpoints for annual international speedboat and water-skiing competitions. The **July wine festival** attracts visitors from all over Europe to the old wine cellars and taverns of the towns.

Above Trarbach, on the east bank of the river, are the remains of the 14th-century **Grevenburg Castle,** the scene of hard-fought battles to gain control of its strategic position. On the opposite bank, above Traben, are the ruins of **Mont Royal,** a late-17th-century fortress built by the invading Louis XIV. You can wander about these testimonials to faded grandeur at any time, without charge. Another attraction is the spa resort, **Bad Wildstein,** with its thermal springs.

ESSENTIALS

GETTING THERE   By Train   Rail passengers for Traben-Trarbach can arrive either at Trier or Bullay, then go the rest of the way by bus. Call 𝄌 **01805/996633** (11861 in Germany; www.bahn.de) for schedules and times.

By Bus   Regional bus service among the Mosel River towns is provided by **RMV Rhein Mosel Verkehrsgesellschaft** (𝄌 **01805/7684636;** www.rmv.de) and by **Moselbahn GmbH** (𝄌 **06531/96800;** www.moselbahn.de).

By Car   Access is via the A48 Autobahn (Trier-Koblenz); exit at Wittlich.

VISITOR INFORMATION   For tourist information, contact the **Kurverwaltung und Verkehrsamt,** Bahnhof 5, Traben (𝄌 **06541/83980**), open Monday to Friday 10am to 4pm; from May to October, additional hours are Saturday 11am to 3pm.

WHERE TO STAY & DINE

Hotel Moseltor *(Finds*   You'll find this gay-friendly hotel on the outskirts of town at Im Otsteil Trarbach. Inside this masterpiece of 19th-century fieldstone masonry, a charming combination of new construction and antique elements creates a warm mixture of comfort and convenience. The inviting rooms have neatly kept bathrooms containing tub/shower combinations.

Chef George Bauer's reputation for light cuisine has spread so widely that German urbanites come here for gastronomic weekends (meals cost 25€–38€/$40–$61). The hotel is open year-round, but the restaurant is closed in February and on Tuesday.

Moselstrasse 1, 56841 Traben-Trarbach. © **06541/6551.** Fax 06541/4922. www.moseltor.de. 11 units. 90€–150€ ($144–$240) double. Rates include continental breakfast. AE, DC, MC, V. Parking 7.50€ ($12) in garage. **Amenities:** Restaurant; lounge; room service; nonsmoking rooms. *In room:* TV, hair dryer, trouser press, safe.

Romantik Art Nouveau Hotel Bellevue 🛠🛠   This Art Nouveau castle on the riverbank is one of the finest hotels along the Mosel. It was designed in 1903 by the noted architect Bruno Moehring and features elaborate timberwork, a domed tower, a high-pitched roof, gables, and dormers. Many of the cozy rooms are furnished with antiques. All units contain neatly kept bathrooms with tub/shower combinations. The Clauss-Feist Restaurant is a romantic spot for both breakfast and dinner, with stained-glass windows and an old-German ambience. There's a cozy fireplace as well as an ivy-covered terrace for dining outside.

Am Moselufer, 56841 Traben-Trarbach. © **06541/7030.** Fax 06541/703400. www.bellevue-hotel.de. 60 units. 135€–190€ ($216–$304) double; 160€–300€ ($256–$480) suite. Rates include buffet breakfast. AE, DC, MC, V. Free outdoor parking, 10€ ($16) in garage. **Amenities:** Restaurant; bar; indoor heated pool; fitness center; spa; sauna; Turkish bath; room service; massage; laundry service; dry cleaning. *In room:* TV, minibar, hair dryer, safe.

5 Bernkastel-Kues 🏞

48km (30 miles) NE of Trier, 113km (70 miles) W of Mainz

In a valley full of wine towns, Bernkastel stands out as the most colorful. Half-timbered buildings dating from as early as 1608 surround its old Marktplatz. In the center of the square stands **St. Michael's Fountain,** which flows with wine during the annual September wine festival. Like Traben-Trarbach, this town is split into twin villages on opposite banks of the Mosel.

ESSENTIALS

GETTING THERE   By Train   The nearest rail station is the Wittlich Hauptbahn-hof, 20km (13 miles) west, with a bus or taxi connection to Bernkastel-Kues. For information, call © **01805/996633** (11861 in Germany; www.bahn.de).

By Bus   Regional bus service along the Mosel River is provided by **RMV Rhein Mosel Verkehrsgesellschaft** (© **01805/7684636;** www.rmv.de) and **Moselbahn GmbH** (© **06531/96800;** www.moselbahn.de).

Moments **For a Grand Panorama**

On a rocky promontory, 3km (1¾ miles) to the southeast of the town, stands **Burg Landshut.** Once the domain of the archbishops of Trier, the property dates from the 11th century but long ago fell into ruins. You don't come here for these ruins but for one of the grandest **panoramas** 🛠🛠 in the entire Rhineland and Mosel areas. Even the steepest slopes on the way to this belvedere are covered with vines.

The Taste of the Grape & an Overnight, Too

Since 1156 the Prüm family has operated a winery at this spot. Today **S.A. Prüm Winery,** Uferallee 25–26, 54470 Bernkastel-Wehlen (© **06531/3110;** fax 06531/8555; www.sapruem.com), allows visitors onto the estate for a wine-tasting, costing from 14€ ($22). Reservations are advised. For centuries, the winery has been known for its Rieslings but now offers Weissburgunder/Pinot Blanc, which is a delight. Visits are possible Monday to Friday 10am to noon and 2 to 4pm, and Saturday 10am to 4pm. There is a beautifully decorated guest house of eight spacious bedrooms, furnished in part with antique pieces. A patio garden opens onto the Mosel. Doubles rent for 69€ to 89€ ($110–$142) a night and are equipped with neatly tiled bathrooms with showers. Each unit comes with a TV and dataport, and rates include breakfast. The winery and guest house are closed December to mid-February. American Express, MasterCard, and Visa are accepted.

By Car   Access by car is via the A48 Autobahn on the Koblenz-Trier run; exit at Wittlich.

VISITOR INFORMATION   Contact **Tourist-Information,** Gestade 6, in Bernkastel (© **06531/4023**), open May to October Monday to Friday 8:30am to 12:30pm and 1:30 to 5pm, Saturday 10am to 5pm, and Sunday 10am to 1pm; from November to April, hours are Monday to Thursday 8:30am to 12:30pm and 1 to 5pm, and Friday 8:30am to 3:30pm.

WHERE TO STAY

Doctor Weinstuben   This intricately half-timbered building in the town center dates from 1652. Today it's the most visually arresting hotel in Bernkastel. Transformed into a tavern in 1830, it still has many of its original woodcarvings. Its public areas are traditional, and the cozy (but often too-small) rooms are furnished in a simple, modern style with bathrooms containing tub/shower combinations. Look for the 150-year-old plant called *Blau Regen* (Blue Rain) in the garden.

Hebegasse 5, 54470 Bernkastel-Kues. © **06531/96650.** Fax 06531/6296. www.doctor-weinstuben.de. 29 units. 75€–107€ ($120–$171) double; 110€–139€ ($176–$222) suite. Rates include buffet breakfast. AE, DC, MC, V. **Amenities:** Restaurant; bar. *In room:* TV, minibar, hair dryer.

Hotel Moselpark 🏵🏵   This is a government-rated four-star hotel, the best in the area and also one of the largest. Many of its rivals are mere inns with only a few bedrooms. This three-story hotel also boasts the widest range of leisure facilities and activities in the area, including a fitness studio, dance bar, and large swimming pool. Bedrooms are midsize to spacious and are exceedingly comfortable and well maintained, each coming with a tub/shower combination. You can spend virtually a week on the grounds, treating the place like a resort. Many distractions are right on the grounds, everything from a *Bierstube* to a massage parlor.

Im Kurpark, Bernkastel-Kues 54470. ℂ 06531/5080. Fax 06531/508612. www.moselpark.de. 143 units. 134€– 252€ ($214–$403) double. Rates include buffet breakfast. AE, DC, MC, V. Free parking. **Amenities:** 2 restaurants; *Bierstube;* wine tasting; dance club; indoor heated pool; 4 indoor and 2 outdoor tennis courts; fitness center; sauna; bike rental; room service; massage; babysitting; laundry service; dry cleaning; nonsmoking rooms; rooms for those w/limited mobility. *In room:* TV, dataport, minibar, hair dryer.

Zur Post 🍀   Even though relatively modest, this is the wine-growing town's finest inn. This centrally located hotel was once a stopover for horseback riders on the local postal routes. The well-maintained but small rooms have both traditional and modern furnishings. Bathrooms are both tiny and tidy, containing tub/shower combinations. Public areas include an elegantly crafted stairwell flanked by half-timbered walls and a paneled, beamed dining room.

Gestade 17, 54470 Bernkastel-Kues. ℂ 06531/96700. Fax 06531/967050. www.hotel-zur-post-bernkastel.de. 42 units. 80€–95€ ($128–$152) double; 150€ ($240) junior suite. Rates include buffet breakfast. DC, MC, V. Free parking. Closed Jan. **Amenities:** Restaurant; lounge; sauna; nonsmoking rooms; rooms for those w/limited mobility. *In room:* TV, minibar.

WHERE TO DINE

Waldhotel Sonnora 🍀🍀🍀 CONTINENTAL   One of the most gastronomically spectacular restaurants in Germany is 18km (11 miles) west of Bernkastel-Kues. With only 12 tables, it tends to be fully booked up to 3 months in advance on weekends and 2 weeks in advance for weeknights. (*Hint:* If you want to dine here on short notice, consider lunch instead of dinner, when demand for tables is less intense; it's also easier to get a reservation if you're a guest of the hotel.) If you're lucky enough to snare a reservation for dinner, you may prefer to overnight in one of the hotel's 20 bedrooms. Doubles (ranging from simple to elaborate, though all are conservative) cost from 110€ to 270€ ($176–$432), including breakfast. Each has a TV and telephone, and most contain a minibar.

Menu items are elaborate and concocted from hyper-upscale ingredients through the supervision of Master Chef Helmut Thieltges and his family. Your meal might include ravioli stuffed with gooseliver and served with an essence of oxtail broth; crayfish with a lemon-and-walnut-oil marinade with caviar-flavored cream sauce; and an artichoke-and-apple salad with lobster medallions, mussels, and a curry-flavored coconut sauce. Main courses, depending on the season, might feature turbot strips of sole with grilled lobster with chicory in a lemon-butter sauce; filet of Bresse pigeon with a carrot tart; and a platter of sweetbreads, kidneys, and brains in a mild balsamic vinegar–and-shallot sauce. In late autumn and winter, the venison and other game dishes are delightful. For dessert, consider a warm chocolate quiche with star-fruit terrine, banana-flavored ice cream, and pineapple ragout. The restaurant has one of the most comprehensive wine lists in the area, with vintages from the region, Europe, and the world.

Auf dem Eichelfeld. ℂ 06578/406. www.hotel-sonnora.de. Reservations essential. Main courses 38€–50€ ($61–$80); fixed-price menus 120€–148€ ($192–$237). AE, MC, V. Wed–Sun noon–2pm and 7–9pm. Closed late Dec to late Jan and July 2–16.

6 Trier (Treves) 🍀🍀

124km (77 miles) SW of Koblenz, 143km (89 miles) SW of Bonn, 193km (120 miles) SW of Frankfurt

Augusta Treverorum (Trier) was founded under Augustus in 16 B.C. It eventually became known as Roma Secunda—the second Rome. For nearly 5 centuries, well into the Christian era, Trier remained one of Europe's power centers.

But this city, Germany's oldest, actually dates back much farther. In 2000 B.C., according to legend, the Assyrians established a colony here, and archaeological findings indicate a pre-Roman Celtic civilization. The buildings and monuments still standing today, however, date from Roman and later periods.

Trier lies only 10km (6 miles) from Luxembourg on the western frontier of Germany, where the Ruwer and Saar rivers meet the Mosel. The city is rich not only in art and tradition but also in wine—it's one of Germany's largest exporters.

ESSENTIALS

GETTING THERE   By Train   Trier Hauptbahnhof is on the Wasserbillig-Trier-Koblenz "Moselbahn" line and also the Trier-Saarbrücken line. Trier has frequent regional connections. There are 20 trains per day to Koblenz (trip time: 1 hr., 20 min.), 20 trains to Cologne (trip time: 2 hr., 25 min.), and 20 trains to Saarbrücken (trip time: 1 hr., 20 min.). For information, call © **01805/996633** (11861 in Germany; www.bahn.de).

By Bus   Buses between Trier and Bullay run along the Mosel River, leaving from the main station in Trier at Bussteig 3. Service is provided by **RMV Rhein Mosel Verkehrsgesellschaft** (© **01805/7684636;** www.rmv.de) and **Moselbahn GmbH** (© **06531/96800;** www.moselbahn.de).

By Boat   Boat rides on the Mosel River operate between Trier and Cochem (see "Cochem," earlier in this chapter). Contact **Mosel Personen Schiffahrt Gebrüder Kolb,** Briedern/Mosel (© **02673/1515**).

By Car   Access by car to Trier is via the A1 Autobahn north and south, the A48 east, and Route 51 from the north.

VISITOR INFORMATION   Contact **Tourist-Information,** An der Porta Nigra (© **0651/978080;** fax 0651/9780876; www.trier.de), open January to February Monday to Saturday 10am to 5pm and Sunday 10am to 1pm; March to April Monday to Saturday 9am to 6pm and Sunday 10am to 3pm; May to October Monday to Thursday 9am to 6pm, Friday and Saturday 9am to 7pm, and Sunday 10am to 5pm; November and December Monday to Saturday 9am to 6pm and Sunday 10am to 3pm; and December 24 and 31 10am to 1pm (closed Dec 25–26 and Jan 1).

GETTING AROUND   Most of Trier's attractions are within walking distance of each other, and few visitors need to take the bus. Tickets (purchased on the bus) cost 1.70€ ($2.70) within zone 1 (the city). For information, call © **0651/717273.**

WHERE TO STAY

EXPENSIVE

Mercure Porta Nigra ℛ   The six-story Mercure Porta Nigra combines style, comfort, and location, making it one of the best choices in Trier. Most rooms have sitting areas and ornately tiled bathrooms with tub/shower combos.

Porta-Nigra-Platz 1 (across from the Roman ruins), 54292 Trier. © 0651/27010. Fax 0651/2701170. www.accorhotels.com. 106 units. 124€–170€ ($198–$272) double; 246€ ($394) suite. AE, DC, MC, V. Parking 10€ ($16). Bus: 3. **Amenities:** 2 restaurants; cafe; bar; sauna; solarium; room service; babysitting; laundry service; dry cleaning; nonsmoking rooms; rooms for those w/limited mobility. *In room:* A/C, TV, Wi-Fi, minibar, hair dryer, safe.

Park Plaza ℛℛ   Although the Villa Hügel has a more traditional and tranquil location, the Park Plaza has shot to the top of the line as the finest hotel at which to stay in Trier, based on its amenities and modern comforts. Lying just a 3-minute walk from the Dom, it is stylish, tastefully furnished, and supremely comfortable. Extras include everything from the city's best health club (styled in the Roman tradition) to a winter garden lounge. Bedrooms are superior in styling and design, and there are hypo-allergenic accommodations as well as family rooms with connecting doors. Maids even place a bathrobe and slippers in the state-of-the-art bathrooms with tub-shower combo. Caesar's Restaurant specializes in both a regional and international cuisine.

Nikolaus-Koch-Platz 1, Trier 54290. ⓒ 0651/99930. Fax 0651/9993555. www.parkplaza-trier.de. 150 units. 114€– 160€ ($182–$256) double; 199€–280€ ($318–$448) junior suite. AE, DC, MC, V. Parking 10€ ($16). **Amenities:** Restaurant; bar; spa; room service; laundry service; dry cleaning; nonsmoking rooms; rooms for those w/limited mobility. *In room:* A/C, TV, Wi-Fi, minibar, hair dryer, safe.

pentahotel Trier *(R)*   This hotel is located in the heart of the sightseeing zone, near the old Roman monuments. It may be too sleek and impersonal for some, but it's serviceable in every way. Rooms are spacious, with streamlined modern furnishings and bathrooms containing tub/shower combos.

Kaiserstrasse 29, 54290 Trier. ⓒ **0651/94950.** Fax 0651/9495666. www.pentahotels.com. 127 units. 85€–132€ ($136–$211) double; 115€–230€ ($184–$368) suite. Rates include buffet breakfast. AE, DC, MC, V. Parking 6€ ($9.60) outdoors; 8.50€ ($14) in garage. Bus: 1, 2, or 12. **Amenities:** Restaurant; bar; lounge; room service; babysitting; laundry service; dry cleaning; nonsmoking rooms; rooms for those w/limited mobility. *In room:* A/C (in some), TV, Wi-Fi, minibar, coffeemaker (in some), hair dryer, iron.

Villa Hügel *(R)(R) (Kids)*   This lovely, white, Art Nouveau villa, built in 1914, offers more style and ambience than some of the other hotels, such as the pentahotel Trier. The windows overlook either a private garden with old trees or the city. Rooms are spacious and high ceilinged, and all contain bathrooms with tub/shower combos. Four double rooms are so large that they're almost suites, making them favorites with families.

Bernhardstrasse 14, 54295 Trier. ⓒ **0651/937100.** Fax 0651/37958. www.hotel-villa-huegel.de. 30 units. 132€– 156€ ($211–$250) double. Rates include buffet breakfast. AE, DC, MC, V. Free outdoor parking, 10€ ($16) in garage. Bus: 2 or 8. **Amenities:** Restaurant; bar; lounge; indoor heated pool; Jacuzzi; sauna; room service; laundry service; dry cleaning; nonsmoking rooms; rooms for those w/limited mobility. *In room:* TV, minibar, hair dryer, safe.

MODERATE

Hotel Kessler *(Value)*   The sunny Kessler is managed by an English-speaker who does everything he can to make your stay pleasant. Rooms are small but attractively maintained and furnished in a clean, modern style, all with neatly kept bathrooms containing tub/shower combos. The breakfast is very good.

Brückenstrasse 23 (next to the Karl-Marx-Haus), 54290 Trier. ⓒ **0651/978170.** Fax 0651/9781797. www.hotel-kessler-trier.de. 18 units. 72€–128€ ($115–$205) double; 120€–130€ ($192–$208) triple. Rates include buffet breakfast. No credit cards. Parking 4€ ($6.40) outside, 9€ ($12) in garage. Bus: 1, 2, 3, 4, 6, or 83. **Amenities:** Breakfast room; nonsmoking rooms. *In room:* TV, minibar, hair dryer.

Hotel Petrisberg   Petrisberg is beautifully situated at a point where a forest, a vineyard, and a private park meet. Each room has a view of the greenery outside. All units contain neat furnishings and bathrooms equipped with tub/shower combos. The ground-floor *Weinstube* is the gathering place for many locals, particularly on weekends.

Sickingenstrasse 11–13 (a 10-min. walk from the Altstadt), 54296 Trier. ⓒ **0651/4640.** Fax 0651/46450. www.hotel-petrisberg.de. 35 units. 90€–95€ ($144–$152) double; 135€–150€ ($216–$240) suite. Rates include buffet breakfast. MC, V. Free outdoor parking, 5€ ($8) in garage. Bus: 6. **Amenities:** Breakfast room; lounge; all nonsmoking rooms. *In room:* TV, Wi-Fi.

INEXPENSIVE

Becker's Hotel ⪪ For Mosel wine lovers, this estate in the Olewig, a suburb of Trier, is the place for both food and lodgings. In summer head here for an alfresco meal on the terrace. On-site are a trio of dining choices, including an expensive gourmet restaurant specializing in an international cuisine, an informal wine cellar, and another restaurant featuring a regional cuisine. Management arranges guided tours, wine tastings, and cellar visits to its own estate offerings.

You can also lodge here in beautifully kept and individually decorated bedrooms, most with light-wood furnishings. Several rooms open onto private balconies overlooking the vineyards.

Olewiger Strasse 206, 54295 Trier-Olewig. ⓒ **0651/938080.** Fax 0651/9380888. www.weinhaus-becker.de. 30 units. 70€–110€ ($112–$176) double; 105€–110€ ($168–$176) junior suite; 120€ ($192) suite. AE, MC, V. **Amenities:** 3 restaurants; bar; Internet access; room service; laundry service; nonsmoking rooms. *In room:* TV.

Hotel Monopol If you're seeking inexpensive lodging, try the four-story Monopol. It's a completely updated, century-old hotel with a cooperative staff. Its rooms are both good size and well maintained, although the decor is completely sterile. Rooms with shower or tub also contain some nice touches, such as extra bed linen, comfortable chairs, a writing desk, and toiletries in the bathroom.

Bahnhofsplatz 7 (across from the Hauptbahnhof), 54292 Trier. ⓒ **0651/714090.** Fax 0651/7140910. www.hotel-monopol-trier.de. 35 units, 24 with shower or tub. 60€–68€ ($96–$109) double without shower or tub; 78€–95€ ($125–$152) double with shower or tub. Rates include buffet breakfast. MC, V. Bus: 1, 2, or 3. **Amenities:** Breakfast room. *In room:* TV.

WHERE TO DINE

Pfeffermühle ⪪⪪ FRENCH This is clearly the best restaurant in Trier. Siegberg and Angelika Walde use fresh ingredients and maintain a bright, well-decorated dining room. The restaurant occupies two pale-pink-and-white dining rooms, elegant and restrained, of a historic 19th-century house whose windows overlook the Mosel. From a freshly made gooseliver terrine appetizer to the petit fours for dessert, the nouvelle French cuisine here is terrific. Try the assorted fresh fish with homemade noodles as your main course. The list of Mosel wines is extensive. In summer, guests can enjoy their meals on a terrace.

Zurlaubener Ufer 76, Zurlauben. ⓒ **0651/26133.** Reservations required. Main courses 22€–28€ ($35–$45); fixed-price menus 32€–68€ ($51–$109). MC, V. Tues–Sat noon–2pm; Mon–Sat 6:30–9:30pm. Bus: 5.

Schlemmereule ⪪ GERMAN/CONTINENTAL At a location opposite the Dom, culinary whiz Peter Schmalen has brought some excitement to bored taste buds in the city. First, the setting is romantic—in the Palais Walderdorff complex that dates from the 1800s. In summer, try for a table in the courtyard. One specialty is plain old spaghetti, given a sublime twist with fresh truffles. A delectable pikeperch steams under a golden-brown potato crust. Finish off with the town's best crème brûlée. Schmalen proudly boasts one of the town's finest wine lists, with some marvelous Mosel vintages.

Palais Walderdorff, Domfreihof 1B. ⓒ **0651/73616.** Reservations required. Main courses 18€–24€ ($29–$38). AE, DC, MC, V. Wed–Mon noon–2:30pm and 6–11pm.

Weinstube Kesselstatt ⪪ GERMAN The wine cellar prides itself on stocking only Rieslings produced in nearby vineyards—an excellent selection. Anyone interested in sampling the region's legendary wines can head down to the cellar here. You get not only wine but platters of traditional German food. In summer a shady terrace fills up quickly. Inside you dine at old wooden tables resting under exposed beams. Menu items are made with fresh ingredients and changed with the seasons. Try such dishes as slices of duck breast in an herb vinaigrette or else filet of turbot with vegetables, even pork medallions in a pepper sauce. The *Stube* lies in the baroque landmark, Palais Kesselstatt, which was the residence of the counts of Kesselstatt.

Liebfrauenstrasse 10. ℂ 0651/41178. Reservations recommended. Main courses 12€–16€ ($19–$26); wine 6€–9€ ($9.60–$14) per glass. AE, MC, V. Daily 10am–midnight. Bus: 1.

Zum Domstein *(Finds* RHINELAND   Charming Zum Domstein overlooks the flower stands and the fountain in Trier's central plaza. Ask for one of the wine tastings, which will get you three glasses of wine (from the Mosel, the Ruwer, or the Saar) starting at 9€ ($14), depending on the vintages selected. In addition, about a dozen local and international wines are sold by the glass, while hundreds more, available by the bottle, are stored in the cellars.

The food here is as tempting as the wine; a typically savory offering is a platter of filet of trout in a Riesling sauce or knuckle of lamb with vegetables. All the dishes are redolent of old-fashioned flavors; it is said that some were even served by the Romans, who preferred them with rich sauces. In winter, you'll want to find a spot near the huge tiled stove.

This restaurant is constructed above one of the oldest cellars in town, the **Römischer Weinkeller** (Roman wine cellar), originally built around A.D. 326. Original Roman artifacts, many connected with food and cooking, decorate the room. Dishes here are prepared according to recipes attributed to Marcus Gavius Apicius, said to have been the foremost chef at the court of Emperor Tiberius.

Hauptmarkt 5. ℂ 0651/74490. Reservations recommended. Main courses lunch 8€–15€ ($13–$24), dinner 13€–20€ ($21–$32); fixed-price menu in the Roman wine cellar 20€–40€ ($32–$64). MC, V. Daily 11:30am–2pm and 6–9:30pm. Bus: 1, 2, or 12.

EXPLORING TRIER

Every day May to October, the tourist office (see above) conducts a 2-hour **walking tour** of the town. Tours are conducted in German at 10:30am and 2:30pm. Tours in English are conducted at 1:30pm only on Saturday. The cost is 7€ ($11) per adult, 3.50€ ($5.60) for children 6 to 14.

VISITING THE ROMAN RUINS

When the last Roman prefect departed from Trier in about A.D. 400, he left behind a vast collection of monuments from centuries of Roman domination. **Porta Nigra (Black Gate)** *(*** (ℂ 0651/75424) is the best-preserved Roman structure in Germany, the only survivor of the great wall that once surrounded Trier. The huge sandstone blocks, assembled without mortar, were held together with iron clamps—the marks can still be seen. From outside the gate, the structure appeared to be simply two arched entrances between rounded towers leading directly into the town, but intruders soon discovered that the arches opened into an inner courtyard where they were at the mercy of the town's defenders. During the Middle Ages, the Greek hermit Simeon, later canonized, chose the east tower as his retreat. After his death, the archbishop turned the gate into a huge double church. When Napoleon came this way, however, he ordered all the architectural changes to be removed and the original Roman core restored. Porta Nigra is open daily April to September 9am to 6pm, October and

---

Moments **Trailing Bacchus into the Underground**

Since medieval times, Trier has served as a warehouse and distribution center for thousands of liters of wine fermented in its underground cellars. At least 40 of these cellars lie beneath the streets of the city and surrounding suburbs and hamlets. The oldest and most venerable of these is owned by **Vereinigte Hospitien,** Krahnen Ufer Strasse 19 (© **0651/9451210**), an organization that's also involved in running a network of local hospitals and hospices. Tours include tastes of some of the vintages and cost 8.50€ ($14) per person. Be warned that if it's inconvenient for the staff to receive you, they'll be quick to tell you. The local tourist office will usually help you arrange a tour of either of these cellars or of others belonging to local competitors.

March 9am to 5pm, and November to February 9am to 4pm. Admission is 2.10€ ($3.40) for adults and 1€ ($1.60) for children. A family pass is 5.10€ ($8.20).

The Imperial Palace district, stretching along the site of the former medieval wall of the city, begins with the Roman building known today as the **Basilica,** Basilikaplatz (© **0651/72468**). Although much of the structure has been demolished, the huge hall that remains—believed to be the throne room—gives some idea of the grandeur of the original palace. The two tiers of windows are arranged within high-rising arches in which fragments of the original wall paintings can be seen. Five large heating chambers outside the walls sent warm air through the hollow floor, in the unique method of Roman central heating. Today the Basilica serves as the main Protestant church in the city. It's open April to October Monday to Saturday 10am to 6pm and Sunday noon to 6pm; November to March hours are Tuesday to Saturday 11am to noon and 3 to 4pm, and Sunday noon to 1pm. Admission is free.

Next to the Basilica stands the 17th-century **Kurfürstliches Palais (Electoral Palace;** © **0651/9494202**), built in the German Renaissance style as a residence for the archbishop-electors, the town's governors. The palace cannot be entered because its interior is used for city offices, but the adjoining **Palastgarten (Palace Gardens)** 𝄐, full of ponds, flowers, and rococo statues, are always open and free.

Kaiserthermen (Imperial Baths) 𝄐𝄐 (© **0651/44262**), at the south end of Palastgarten, were erected in the early 4th century by Constantine I. Of the huge complex, only the ruins of the hot baths remain. These were among the largest in the Roman Empire, and although never completed, they were used in connection with the Imperial Palace. They're open daily April to September 9am to 6pm, October and March 9am to 5pm, and November to February 9am to 4pm. Admission is 2.10€ ($3.40) for adults and 1€ ($1.60) for children.

The **Amphitheater,** Amphitheaterplatz (© **0651/73010**), is the oldest Roman construction in Trier, dating from A.D. 100. The stone seats, arranged in three circles separated by broad promenades, held at least 20,000 people. The ruins are open daily April to September 9am to 6pm, October and March 9am to 5pm, and November to February 9am to 4pm. Admission is 2.10€ ($3.40) adults, 1€ ($1.60) children. A family pass is 5.10€ ($8.20).

A **collective ticket,** which grants admission to the amphitheater, the two sets of Roman baths, and the Porta Nigra, costs 6.20€ ($9.90) for adults and 2.50€ ($4) for students and children 17 and under. It is available from the tourist office.

Der Trierer Dom (Trier Cathedral) ⟨★⟩ From the outside, this cathedral, with its rough-hewn stonework, looks more like a fortress than a church. It's the third church to stand on the site of the former 4th-century palace of the Empress Helena, mother of Constantine. It was begun in 1035 in Romanesque style, but later Gothic and baroque additions have only helped give the ecclesiastical architecture a timeless unity. The interior combines baroque decoration with Gothic vaulting and archways. On the south aisle is a magnificent tympanum depicting Christ between the Virgin and St. Peter. Die Schatzkammer (Treasury Museum) contains many important works of art, including the 10th-century St. Andrew's Altar, an unusual portable altar made of wood and covered with gold and ivory.

Domfreihof (north of the Palace Gardens and Basilica). 𝄞 0651/9790790. Cathedral free; Treasury 1.50€ ($2.40) adults, .50€ (80¢) children 11 and under. Cathedral Apr–Oct daily 6:30am–6pm; Nov–Mar daily 6:30am–5:30pm. Treasury Apr–Oct Mon–Sat 10am–5pm; Nov–Mar Mon–Sat 10am–noon and 2–4:30pm.

Karl-Marx-Haus This old burgher's house is where Karl Marx (1818–83) was born and where he lived until he finished school in 1835. The museum has exhibits on Marx's personal history, volumes of poetry, original letters, and photographs with personal dedications. There's also a collection of rare first editions and international editions of his works, as well as exhibits on the development of socialism in the 19th century. In the vicinity of the museum is a study center, **Studienzentrum Karl-Marx-Haus,** Johannesstrasse 28 (same phone), for research on Marx and Engels.

Brückenstrasse 10. 𝄞 0651/970680. Admission 3€ ($4.80) adults, 2€ ($3.20) children. Apr–Oct daily 10am–6pm; Nov–Mar Mon 2–5pm, Tues–Sun 10am–1pm and 2–5pm. Bus: 1, 2, 3, or 4.

Liebfrauenkirche ⟨★⟩ Set to reopen in 2010, this parish church, separated from the cathedral by a narrow passageway, is more pleasing aesthetically than its older neighbor. Begun in 1235, it was among the first German examples of Gothic architecture. The ground plan is in the shape of a Greek cross, creating a circular effect with all points equidistant from the central high altar. The structure is supported by 12 circular columns, rather than the typical open buttresses. The interior is bathed in sunlight, which streams through the high transoms. Although its restoration after the war changed some of the effect of the central construction, it's still unique among German churches.

Some of the church's more important works of art are now in the **Bischöfliches Museum,** Windstrasse 8 (𝄞 0651/7105255). The sepulcher of Bishop Karl von Metternich, who represented the archbishopric during the Thirty Years' War, is among the most interesting items. Admission is 3.50€ ($5.60) for adults and 2€ ($3.20) for children.

Liebfrauenstrasse 2. 𝄞 0651/9790790. Free admission. Apr–Oct daily 7:30am–6pm; Nov–Mar daily 7:30am–5:30pm. Bischöfliches Museum: Apr–Oct Mon–Sat 9am–5pm, Sun 1–5pm; Nov–Mar Tues–Sat 9am–5pm, Sun 1–5pm.

Rheinisches Landesmuseum ⟨★★⟩ This is one of the outstanding museums of Roman antiquities north of the Alps. Numerous reliefs from funerary monuments show daily life in Roman times. The museum's most popular exhibit is the *Mosel Ship,* a sculpture of a wine-bearing vessel crowning a big burial monument of the 3rd century A.D. Also on display are many mosaics and frescoes, ceramics, glassware, a 2,700-year-old Egyptian casket complete with mummy, an outstanding numismatic collection, and prehistoric and medieval art and sculpture.

Weimarer Allee 1 (between the Imperial Baths and the Basilica, at the edge of the Palace Gardens). © **0651/97740.** Admission 3€ ($4.80) adults, 2€ ($3.20) children. Mon–Fri 9:30am–5pm; Sat–Sun 10:30am–5pm. Closed Mon Nov–Apr. Bus: 2, 6, 16, 26, or 30.

BOAT TOURS

Trier owes much of its majesty to the river that nurtured its medieval commerce. You can take a day cruise for a waterside view of its historic banks. Easter to October, boats depart Tuesday to Sunday at 9am from the Zurlauben (city docks) for a 4-hour trip along the river to **Bernkastel** (see "Bernkastel-Kues," earlier in this chapter), passing vineyards, wine hamlets, historic churches, and semi-ruined fortresses en route. Participants spend 2 hours exploring Bernkastel before returning on the same boat to Trier, arriving back at 7:30pm. The cost is 26€ ($42) per person.

If you don't want to spend so much time on the river, you can take a shorter, hourlong excursion to the nearby historic hamlet of **Pfalzel.** Boats depart from Trier's docks Easter to October daily at 11am, 12:30pm, 2pm, 3:15pm, and 4:30pm. Round-trip is 10€ ($16). You can prolong your excursion with a walk along the riverbanks in Pfalzel or return on the next boat, almost immediately after your arrival.

For information on either of these excursions, contact the tourist office (see "Visitor Information," earlier in this section) or the boat operator **Gebrüder Kolb** (© **0651/ 26666** in Trier).

TRIER AFTER DARK

The cathedral hosts a series of free **organ recitals** in May, June, August, and September. Contact the tourist office (see "Visitor Information," earlier in this section) for schedules.

TUFA (© **0651/7182410**) presents theater, established touring bands, and the occasional dance party. Across from the Dom (cathedral) stands **Walderdorff,** Domfreihof (© **0651/9944412**), a cafe by day, but an action-packed bar and dance club at night. The club runs late (10pm–4am) and only on Thursday to Saturday, with the dancing not launched until 12:30am. The cafe and bar are open Sunday to Thursday from 9:30am to 1am, Friday and Saturday until 2am. A cover is sometimes imposed at the dance club, but the actual fee varies depending on the evening. Sometimes live bands are brought in. A club with a beer garden, **Exhaus,** Zurmainer Strasse 114 (© **0651/25191**), has both dancing and bands, usually Wednesday to Saturday. Days vary, but the hours are 8pm to 2am. Call to see what's scheduled. Cover is 8€ to 15€ ($13–$24).

The aptly named **Irish Pub,** Jakobstrasse 10 (© **0651/49539**), serves toasted sandwiches, along with Guinness and Harp. Many evenings you'll find an Irish, English, or German band entertaining a rowdy drinking crowd.

The area's nightlife hot spot is **Riverside,** a complex of bars and restaurants, about 1.5km (1 mile) north of the town center.

17

The Fairy-Tale Road

The area between Frankfurt and Hamburg is Germany's most neglected tourist destination, yet it holds many discoveries. Some of Germany's best-preserved medieval towns, as well as some major spas, lie in the flatlands and rolling hills of Lower Saxony and North Hesse. The character of the area ranges widely, from the bustle of the port of Bremen to the isolation of the Lüneburg Heath.

You'll also find the beautiful Harz Mountains, perhaps the country's last stronghold of paganism, still a land of legends and fanciful names. It is said that the last bear was killed in the Harz in 1705, the last lynx in 1817, but wildcats, badgers, deer, and foxes remain, as well as many limestone caves. The beech trees that grow in the Harz range have unusual size and great beauty, and walnut trees abound.

The highlight of this area is a drive along the **Fairy-Tale Road** ✶✶✶, stretching for 595km (369 miles) from the town of Hanau in the south to Bremen in the north. For an abbreviated form of this relatively long tour, see "Suggested Itineraries" in chapter 4.

As you travel this winding route, thoughts of your childhood memories will live again, as you encounter such characters as Sleeping Beauty, Rumpelstiltskin, and the Pied Piper. The dark forests and countryside inspired the Brothers Grimm and their fairy tales, which are read to children all over the world today.

Train service is available to the larger cities and towns, but it's best to rent a car and explore the region at random, scurrying down some country road when you spot Little Red Riding Hood along some mysterious lane.

Although the Fairy-Tale Road tour ends in Bremen, some of the most fascinating cities of Lower Saxony and the Harz Mountains are yet to be explored if you have the time. These include the ancient cities of Lüneburg, Celle, Goslar, and Göttingen.

1 Hanau

20km (13 miles) E of Frankfurt, 89km (55 miles) SW of Fulda

The Fairy-Tale Road begins in the gateway town of Hanau, where the Brothers Grimm were born. Now virtually a far eastern suburb of Frankfurt, it is not a pretty town but its association with the Grimm Brothers leads to a never-ending stream of visitors.

ESSENTIALS

GETTING THERE **By Train & Bus** From the main rail station at Frankfurt, take the S8 or S9 train to the Hanau Hauptbahnhof, the trip taking only 30 minutes, a one-way ticket costing 6€ ($9.60). The fare includes a bus ride from the train station to the Marktplatz.

By Car   Motorists from Frankfurt can head east along autoroute 66 into Hanau.

VISITOR INFORMATION   The **Tourist Information Centre** sits behind the Rathaus (town hall) at Am Markt 14 (© **06181/295950;** www.hanau.de), open Monday to Thursday 9:30am to 6pm, Friday 8:30am to 1pm, and Saturday 9am to noon.

WHERE TO STAY & DINE

Best Western Premier Hotel Villa Stokkum ℛ   The premier place for food and lodgings lies 4km (2½ miles) southwest of the center. Overlooking the River Main Valley, this is a Mediterranean style hotel, rated four stars by the government. Rooms are furnished comfortably, but not lavishly, with modern pieces, soundproof windows, and marble bathrooms. Each unit comes with a bedside table and desk. The on-site restaurant, Bella Gusta, serves a savory Mediterranean and regional cuisine, with meals costing 25€ to 35€ ($40–$56).

Steinheimer Vorstadt 70, 63456 Hanau-Steinheim. © 06181/6640. Fax 06181/661580. www.wenckscherhof.de. 135 units. 128€–185€ ($205–$296) double. AE, DC, MC, V. Parking 10€ ($16). **Amenities:** Restaurant; bar; Internet access; room service; laundry service; dry cleaning. *In room:* TV, minibar, safe, hair dryer.

EXPLORING HANAU

At the Markplatz (the central square) you encounter **Nationaldenkmal Brüder Grimm,** a memorial erected in 1898 to the famous brothers. More Grimm memorabilia is found at **Schloss Philippsruhe & Schlosspark** at Philippsruher Allee 45 (© **06181/20209;** www.museen-hanau.de), open Tuesday to Sunday 10 am to 4pm, charging 2.50€ ($4) for adults and 1.50€ ($2.40) for children. A short ride on bus no. 10 delivers you to the castle. The baroque castle, with its extensive park and orangery, was built on the banks of the Main River at the beginning of the 18th century. Today it houses the Hanau Historical Museum with splendid rooms, including some devotees to relics of the Grimm Brothers. The attraction's Paper Toy Theatre Museum is a delight for children, presenting paper toy shows for them.

Also opening onto Markplatz at no. 14 is the **Rathaus,** dating from the 1700s. Every day at 10am, noon, 4pm, and 6pm, it honors another celebrated native son, the composer, Paul Hindemith (1895–1963), by presenting a concert of one of his canons.

The **Altes Rathaus** or Old Town Hall stands at Alstädter Markt 6 (© **06181/256556;** www.museen-hanau.de), open Tuesday to Sunday 10am to noon and 2 to 5pm, charging an admission of 2.50€ ($4) for adults or 1.50€ ($2.40) for children. It was the town hall from 1537 to 1900, but today is home to the Deutches Goldschmiedehaus (German Goldsmiths' House). This museum celebrates Hanau's history beginning in the latter 18th century when it became one of the German centers for goldsmiths. The museum has a permanent collection of silver and gold artifacts and also hosts changing exhibitions.

2 Gelnhausen

35km (21 miles) NE of Frankfurt, 20km (12 miles) NE of Hanau

More attractive than Hanau, Gelnhausen makes a better choice for an overnight stop along the Fairy-Tale Road. Lying in the Kinzig Valley in eastern Hesse, it is situated about midway between Frankfurt and Fulda (see section 4).

Gelnhausen once stood on the old trading route, the Via Regia, between Frankfurt and Leipzig. For that reason in 1170 the Emperor Friedrich I (Barbarossa) combined three older villages to create this town. The town thrived until the Thirty Years' War

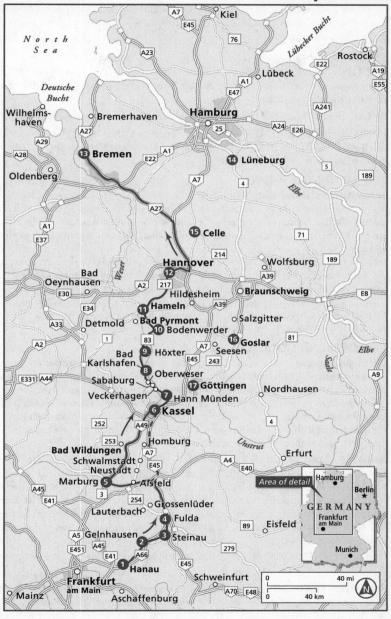

*North
Sea*

*Deutsche
Bucht*

Lübecker Bucht

Kiel

A7

E45

76

A23

Rostock

Lübeck

E22

A19

E55

A1

E47

A241

Wilhelms-
haven

Bremerhaven

Hamburg

A27

25

A24

E26

A29

A28

13 Bremen

E22

A1

14 Lüneburg

5

189

Oldenberg

A27

A7

4

Elbe

A1

E37

15 Celle

214

71

Weser

Bad
Oeynhausen

Hannover

Wolfsburg

189

12

A39

E8

E30

A2

217

E34

11 Hameln

Hildesheim

Braunschweig

A39

Detmold

Bad Pyrmont

Salzgitter

A33

10 Bodenwerder

Elbe

A2

83

16 Goslar

81

1

9 Höxter

Seesen

A7

Bad
Karlshafen

E45

243

Saale

A9

E331 A44

8

Oberweser

17 Göttingen

Sababurg

Veckerhagen

7

Nordhausen

Hann Münden

6 Kassel

Unstrut

252

A49

Homburg

4

Erfurt

253

A7

Bad Wildungen

Schwalmstadt

E45

Neustadt

A4

E40

5 Marburg

Alsfeld

A45

3

254

A41

Lauterbach

Grossenlüder

89

Eisfeld

A5

Gelnhausen

4 Fulda

E451

2

3 Steinau

A45

E41

1 Hanau

A66

279

E45

Schweinfurt

**Frankfurt
am Main**

Schweinfurt

Mainz

Aschaffenburg

A70 E48

Area of detail

Hamburg

Berlin ★

GERMANY

Frankfurt
am Main

Munich

0   40 mi

0   40 km

(1618–48), which ruined it. In the latter 19th century, it came back. Germans claim that one of Gelnhausen's native sons, Philipp Reis (1834–1874), was the "co-inventor" of the telephone.

ESSENTIALS

GETTING THERE **By Train** Trains leave Frankfurt's Hauptbahnhof for Gelnhausen every 30 minutes during the day. Most of these trains are direct, but some require a transfer at Hanau.

By Car From Hanau (see above), follow the autobahn (A66) into Gelnhausen.

VISITOR INFORMATION The local **Tourist Office** is at Obermarkt 24 (✆ **06051/830300**), open Monday to Friday 8am to 4:30pm, Saturday 9am to 4:30pm, and Sunday 2 to 4:30pm.

WHERE TO STAY & DINE

Romantisches Hotel Burg Mühle ✦ The best place for food and lodgings in town takes its name, *Mühle,* meaning mill, from its former role as both the mill and sawmill for Red Beard's castle nearby. Bedrooms show a little wear and tear but they are well maintained and comfortable, also affordable. Most rooms are quite spacious, and some of them open onto private balconies. The hotel is primarily known for its restaurant, where full meals cost from 25€ to 40€ ($40–$64). In the restaurant, the old water wheel of the former mill still turns, as diners enjoy well-prepared regional cuisine, including a wide variety of German beers including the original Budweiser.

Burgstrasse 2, 63571 Gelnhausen. ✆ 06051/82050. Fax 06051/820554. www.burgmuehle.de. 40 units. 98€–108€ ($157–$173) double. Rates include breakfast. DC, MC, V. **Amenities:** Restaurant; bar; spa; public Internet; room service; laundry service; nonsmoking rooms. *In room:* TV, minibar, fridge.

EXPLORING GELNHAUSEN

You might begin your tour at the **Untermarkt (lower market square).** Even though it's called that, it is the highest point in town and is dominated by the towers of **Marienkirche (St. Mary's Church).** You can enter through the south door (usually) daily from 9am to 5pm. Built in the Rhineland Romanesque style, it is known for its *Chorraum* ✦✦ or chancel, one of the masterpieces of 13th-century decorative architecture. The church was built between 1170 and 1250. In its present form, it was finally completed in 1467. Other attractions include:

Barbarossaburg (Imperial Palace) Now in ruins, the castle was built by "Red Beard" Barbarossa at the end of the 12th century, and the German Imperial Diet met here in 1180. Although only a fraction of its original grandeur, it is the best preserved imperial palace remaining from the Hohenstaufen period in Germany. The living quarters of the emperor, a fine example of Romanesque architecture, can still be seen. The castle lies on an island in the Kinzig River, and you can walk beneath the ruined ramparts along the water.

Burgstrasse 14. ✆ 06051/3805. Admission 2€ ($3.20). Mar–Oct Tues–Sun 10am–5pm; Nov–Dec Tues–Sun 10am–4pm.

Hexenturm Tower Built around 1420, this is one of the guard towers remaining from the city's once-fortified walls. Crowned by a pointed spire, it was named "witches" tower because women suspected of witchcraft were locked up here before facing burning at the stake or drowning (their hands and feet were bound, and they were thrown into the river). A collection of instruments of torture from the Middle Ages can be viewed inside. *Note:* The tower is only accessible via the weekly tour.

Am Fretzenstein. ⓒ 06051/830300. Tour 2€ ($3.20). Tours Sun 2:30pm. May–Oct.

3 Steinau an der Strasse

30km (18 miles) NE of Gelhhausen, 65km (40 miles) NE of Frankfurt

A major stop along the Fairy-Tale Road, this little town was the childhood home of the Brothers Grimm, sons of a local magistrate. The town grew up in the 1200s, and many of its antique half-timbered houses, which open onto cobblestone streets, are here to greet you today.

A former mayor once informed us—after a few beers—that if we went walking in the surrounding forests, you were sure to come upon not only Little Red Hiding Hood and Snow White, but also Hansel and Gretel. Steinau still follows its medieval layout with its castle dominating the town and its surrounding walls.

ESSENTIALS

GETTING THERE   By Train   From Frankfurt's Hauptbahnhof, trains arrive in Steinau at the rate of every 75 to 90 minutes during the day after stopping at such small towns as Hanau and Gelnhausen. From Steinau, the same train continues to our next destinations—Fulda and Kassel.

By Car   From our last stopover at Gelnhausen, continue northeast along the A66 into Steinau.

VISITOR INFORMATION   The **Tourist Information Office** is at 70 Brüder-Grimm-Strasse (ⓒ **06663/96310**), open Monday to Friday 8am to 4:30pm and Saturday 9am to 4:30pm.

WHERE TO STAY & DINE

Brathähnchenfarm ⓡ *(Finds)*   Your best bet lies outside of the center and is reached by climbing up a steep hill. You're greeted by a friendly staff who welcomes you into the well-maintained and comfortably furnished bedrooms. The rooms may be a little on the small side, but they are well equipped and open onto views of the neighboring mountains.

Most guests show up to sample the restaurant's cuisine, which features specialties that are thrown on the grill and cooked to perfection. The name of the hotel/restaurant, Brathähnchenfarm, means "roast chicken farm," and that just happens to be the specialty of the chef. Diners drive for miles around to feast on it. Of course, you can order many other mains, ranging from spare ribs on the grill to pork knuckle. We like to finish off with the baked apple flambé. The restaurant doesn't serve on Mondays.

Im Ohl 1, 36396 Steinau an der Strasse. ⓒ **06663/228.** Fax 06663/1579. www.brathaehnchenfarm.de. 14 units. 65€ ($104) double. Rates include breakfast. AE, MC, V (hotel only). Closed mid-Dec to mid-Feb. **Amenities:** Restaurant; bar; room service; laundry service. *In room:* TV.

EXPLORING STEINAU

Brüder Grimm Haus & Museum Steinau   The Grimm Brothers lived in this house from 1791 to 1796. Today, the half-timbered house, along with its adjoining courtyard, has been attractively restored and is filled with memorabilia of the story-telling brothers, including picture books. Many old household objects and agricultural equipment are also displayed.

Adjacent to the house, a museum displays memorabilia of Steinau—it's like an "attic" of the town, with old inn signs, an antique coach, and other artifacts.

80 Brüder-Grimm-Strasse. ℂ **06663/7605**. Admission 2€ ($3.20) for either the house or museum, 1.50€ ($2.40) for children; combination ticket to both 4€ ($6.40) adults, 3€ ($4.80) children. Daily Jan 2–Dec 23 11am–5pm.

Schloss Steinau ℛ   Towering over the town, the castle, with its towers and turrets, does indeed look like something out of a fairy tale by the Brothers Grimm. The original castle was constructed in the Middle Ages, but the present building is Renaissance (1528–55), and was the country residence of the Counts of Hanau. The complex is shaped like an irregular pentagon, with four wings, four pavilions, and two gatehouses. The foundation walls can still be seen today, and the castle is surrounded by a deep moat.

On-site is the **Grimm Museum,** with mementos of the Grimm family, including the family Bible and spoons with which they ate their porridge. There's also an exhibition of marionettes from the Steinauer Marionettentheater installed in the former stables. Performances are held here most weekends at 3pm, tickets costing 6.50€ ($10). For more information call ℂ **06663/245** or visit www.die-holzkoeppe.de.

The castle doesn't have an official address but you don't need it. It's clearly evident.

ℂ **06663/6843**. www.steinau.de/en/inhalt/Schloss_Frame.html. Admission 3.50€ ($5.60) adults, 2.50€ ($4) children. Mar–Oct Tues–Thurs and Sat–Sun 10am–5pm; Nov–Dec 12 Tues–Thurs and Sat–Sun 10am–4pm.

4 Fulda

100km (62 miles) NE of Frankfurt, 32km (20 miles) NE of Steinau an der Strasse

The economic center of East Hesse, the Episcopal city of Fulda dates from 744. It is visited chiefly today because of its baroque core, with a cathedral and a palace.

In the Christian world, it is forever linked to St. Boniface, the "Apostle of Germany." This English missionary was sent here by Pope Gregory II in the 700s to preach the gospel to the "pagan" Germans. He was murdered in 754 and his body brought back to Fulda, where a cult formed around his tomb (see Dom, below).

Much of the extensive building activities that began in Fulda in the early 18th century remain to delight visitors today. With some justification, Fulda is called the "City of Baroque."

ESSENTIALS

GETTING THERE   By Train   Trains from Frankfurt's Hauptbahnhof arrive daily about every 75 or 90 minutes. Trip time is about 1 hour and 15 minutes.

By Car   From Steinau an der Strasse, our last stopover, continue northeast along A66 into Fulda.

VISITOR INFORMATION   The **Fulda Tourist Information Office** is at Bonifatiusplatz 1, Palais Buttlar (ℂ **0661/0021814**), open Monday to Friday 8:30am to 6pm, Saturday 9:30am to 4pm, and Sunday 10am to 2pm.

WHERE TO STAY & DINE

Maritim Hotel am Schloss Garten ℛ   This is one of the most luxurious stopovers along the Fairy-Tale Road, one of the nuggets of the Maritim chain of first-class hotels. Its rooms overlook Fulda Palace Park, where visitors can take a leisurely stroll. The midsize guest rooms, completely modernized and filled with comfortable, tasteful furnishings, are in a contemporary wing opening into a central atrium. Part of the hotel, including a spacious breakfast room, is in a beautiful Orangery dating from the 1700s and completely restored. In the cellar you can enjoy good regional cooking under medieval vaulted arches in the Dianakeller Restaurant, where complete meals range in price from 26€ to 40€ ($42–$64).

Pauluspromenade 2, 36037 Fulda. (✆) 0661/2820. Fax 0661/282-499. www.maritim.de. 112 units. 155€–208€ ($248–$333) double; 390€ ($624) suite. AE, DC, MC, V. **Amenities:** Restaurant; bar; pool; room service; laundry service. *In room:* TV, Wi-Fi, minibar, hair dryer, safe.

Romantik Hotel Goldener Karpfen (★★   For the lover of the baroque who wants a more romantic hotel than the Maritim, this centuries-old inn is a viable option. It's much smaller than the Maritim, with less facilities, but it is more glamorous for those who love antiques. Its baroque facade was from the mid-18th century but was vastly altered at the beginning of the 20th century, though many architectural adornments remain. The bedrooms are modernized, exceedingly comfortable, beautifully furnished, and inviting. This hotel is another good choice for dining. In fact, we prefer the cuisine at its first-class restaurant to the other hotel restaurants in the area, with its Persian rugs and elegant furnishings and meals ranging in price from 28€ to 50€ ($45–$80).

Simpliziusbrunnen 1, 36037 Fulda. (✆) 0661/868800. Fax 0661/0100. www.hotel-goldener-karpfen.de 50 units. 130€–250€ ($208–$400) double; 280€–450€ ($448–$720) suite. AE, DC, MC, V. **Amenities:** Restaurant; bar; room service; laundry service; nonsmoking rooms. *In room:* TV, Wi-Fi, minibar, hair dryer, safe.

EXPLORING FULDA

Dom (Cathedral) (★   The object of a pilgrimage from the devout who flock here to see the tomb of St. Boniface, the cathedral was built in the Italian baroque style by Johann Dientzenhofer between 1704 and 1712. It is the best known baroque building in Fulda, with the tomb of the saint lying in the Bonifatiusgruft, a crypt beneath the high altar. A funerary monument in an alabaster bas-relief from the 1700s represents the saint.

Organ matinees are held in the cathedral every Saturday in May, June, September, and October. The Dom's tall twin spires dominate the Old Town. On-site is the Dommuseum containing liturgical robes, sacred vessels, and a collection of reliquaries from Boniface. You can even see such relics as the sword and the book with which he tried to hold off his murderers.

Eduard Schick Platz 1–3. (✆) 0661/87207. Admission to cathedral free, museum 2.10€ ($3.40). Cathedral Apr–Oct daily 6am–6pm; Nov–Mar daily 6am–5pm. Museum Apr–Oct Tues–Sat 10am–5:30pm, Sun 12:30–5:30pm; Nov, Dec, and mid-Feb to Mar Tues–Sat 10am–12:30pm and 1:30–4pm, Sun 12:30-4pm.

Stadtschloss (City Palace)   This is the most spectacular baroque building in Fulda, the former resident of the prince-bishops. You can visit the large Banquering Hall and the famous **Hall of Mirrors** (★★, even the restored 18th-century princely apartments, as well as several classically designed exhibitions rooms from the 19th century. A stunning collection of Fulda and Thuringian porcelain is also on display.

Schlosstrasse 1. (✆) 0661/102-1813. Admission 3€ ($4.80). Sat–Thurs 10am–6pm; Fri 2–6pm.

Vonderau Museum   Housed in a former Jesuit seminary, the town's major museum offers a trio of permanent exhibitions, including a history of Fulda from prehistoric times until the present. You'll see everything from ancient burial sites to the famous Fulda Mobil, a small car built in Fulda and prized by collectors. Paintings and sculptures are exhibited in one gallery, and there is also a natural history department with life-size dioramas depicting local flora and fauna. The planetarium seats only 35 visitors, so reservations are needed for performances Thursday at 7pm, Friday at 5 and 8pm, Saturday at 3 and 8pm, and Sunday at 10:30am and 3pm.

Jesuitenplatz 2. ℂ **0661/928-350.** Admission 3.50€ ($5.60) to planetarium, 3€ ($4.80) to museum. Tues–Sun 10am–5pm.

5 Marburg ★★

60km (35 miles) NW of Fulda, 93km (58 miles) SW of Kassel

From Fulda you can head directly north into the little city of Kassel, or else you can detour west slightly to one of the most rewarding towns along the Fairy-Tale Road.

Once a great pilgrimage center, Marburg forms the heart of a triangle of Cologne, Frankfurt, and Kassel. Pilgrims came to venerate the relics of St. Elizabeth (1207–31) of Hungary. Known doing her short life for her generous deeds to others, Elizabeth was canonized in 1235, and the site of her tomb in the Gothic church built for her made Marburg a major center of pilgrimage for Christians.

Today, the town, lying on a rocky outcrop, consists of half-timbered houses rising along the hill upward from the Lahn River and crowned by a castle.

A free elevator on Pilgrimstein (site of the tourist office) will deliver you from the bottom of town at the river to the peak of the Old Town to avoid a steep climb.

ESSENTIALS

GETTING THERE **By Train** Trains from Frankfurt's Hauptbahnof depart at hourly intervals throughout the day, and then travel directly, with stops but without transfers, to Marburg, a trip that takes about an hour. There are also direct trains, several per day, from Kassel to Marburg, a trip that takes abut an hour with no transfers needed.

By Car From Fulda (our last stopover) follow the B254 northwest to the village of Alsfeld, 34km (21 miles), where you might want to stop for a bite to eat and a tour of its narrow streets and half-timbered houses. You can follow route B62 west into Marburg.

VISITOR INFORMATION The **Marburg Tourist Office** is at Pilgrimstein 26 (ℂ **06421/99120**), open Monday to Friday 9am to 6pm, Saturday 10am to 2pm.

WHERE TO STAY & DINE

At some point during your day stop in for drinks at the **Café Vetter,** Reitgasse 4 (ℂ **06421/25888**), which has the most panoramic vistas of Old Marburg from its outdoor terrace. For four generations, members of the same family have been welcoming the world to their famous old cafe, which now features Internet access. On weekends, piano music fills the air.

Best Western Marburg Hotel Am Schlossberg ★ This longtime favorite stands near the river at a point where the elevator rises to the Old Town. Its developers weren't afraid to use color, employing fire-engine red, Halloween orange, sunflower yellow, and a fruity apricot. Bedrooms are midsize and attractively and comfortably furnished. In the Tartagua Restaurant, with its open-air terrace and beer cellar, regional meals range in price from 25€ to 35€ ($40–$56). Am Schlossberg serves the best breakfast buffet in town.

Pilgrimstein 29, 35037 Marburg. ℂ **06421/9180.** Fax 06421/918444. www.schlossberg-marburg.de. 146 units. 122€ ($195) double; 142€–160€ ($227–$256) suite. AE, DC, MC, V. Parking 10€ ($16). **Amenities:** Restaurant; bar; fitness center; room service; laundry service; nonsmoking rooms. *In room:* TV, Wi-Fi, fridge, hair dryer.

> **Fun Fact Stack 'Em Up**
>
> As amazing as it sounds, some of Marburg's houses can be reached only through a skylight, as some of them are stacked one on top of another. That means that in some cases a house will have a back door five floors above the front door.

Vila Vita Hotel Rosenpark ★★   Such an elegant luxury hotel in such a small town comes as a delightful surprise. Close to the center, the hotel stands in the meadows of the Lahn River, with one of the best spas along the Fairy-Tale Road. Its dramatic pavilion, with its glass dome, shelters the finest restaurants and bars in the city. Bedrooms are good size, each beautifully furnished and comfortably appointed, so much so you'll think you're at a resort hotel. The creative cuisine served in a trio of restaurants is the finest in the area, especially at the gourmet restaurant, Bel Etage. More affordable food is served at the Rosenkavalier, with traditional regional recipes a feature in the most rustic Zirbelstube.

Rosenstrasse 18, 35037 Marburg. © **06421/60050.** Fax 06421/6006-100. http://vilavitahotels.com. 233€–328€ ($373–$525) double; 390€–662€ ($624–$1,059) suite. AE, DC, MC, V. Parking 15€ ($24). **Amenities:** 3 restaurants; 3 bars; spa; room service; laundry service. *In room:* A/C, TV, Wi-Fi, minibar, hair dryer, safe.

EXPLORING MARBURG

The most beautiful illustrations in the Grimm fairy tales were done in Marburg—the Brothers Grimm studied here at the university from 1802 to 1805, and Jacob once remarked of the town, "I think there are more steps in the streets than in the houses." Today there are more than 100 pubs, many quaint and rustic, catering to the student population.

Most of the restaurants, bars, and student cafes center around the **Markplatz** or Obermarkt, with some of the best preserved houses, especially no. 14 and no. 21, dating from the mid–16th century. The oldest preserved house, which is still inhabited, dates from 1323 and stands at no. 18 on the square.

Students gather to catch up on the latest gossip around a fountain dedicated to St. George. Also opening onto the Markplatz is the 16th-century Gothic **Rathaus,** known for its mechanical cock crowing the hours from its gable. Allow at least 2 hours for a walking tour of the Old Town, highlighted by a visit to the following buildings:

Elisabethkirche ★★   Constructed from 1235 to 1283, this remarkable church is the first truly Gothic church to be built in Germany. The landmark structure is graced with two 80m (262-ft.) towers housing 700-year-old bells. The town's most beloved daughter, St. Elizabeth, is entombed here. A Hungarian princess, she was betrothed at 4 to marry (at 12) Ludwig IV of Thuringia. He lost his life in the Crusades, and she gave up all her wealth to share with the poor, dying of exhaustion at the age of 24.

In the sacristy is the 13th-century reliquary containing the saint's bones and other artifacts. Her shrine is a masterpiece in gold completed by craftsmen from the Rhineland in 1250. Religious art, statues, and frescoes fill the cathedral, making it a virtual ecclesiastical museum.

Elisabethstrasse 3. © **06421/65497.** www.elisabethkirche-mr.de Admission 2€ ($3.20) for St. Elizabeth's Shrine. Apr–Sept daily 9am–6pm; Oct daily 9am–5pm; Nov–Mar daily 10am–4pm.

Phillips University of Marburg   It is not exactly a tourist attraction, although its life dominates the town today. From St. Elisabeth's church follow Steinweg, Neustadt, Wettergasse, and Reitgasse to reach the university.

The main part of the university was founded in 1527 by Landgrave Philipp of Hesse, becoming the first German Protestant university. Except for a church from the 14th century, most of its buildings are from the latter 19th century, including the largest university library in western Germany. A professor here from 1892 to 1917, Emil von Behring, won the Nobel Prize in 1901 for discovering a vaccine for diphtheria.

On Pilgrimstein you can take an elevator from below to the highest peak in Marburg, where the **Marburg Schloss** stands in Schlosspark, with panoramic views in all directions. Luther and Zwingli debated in this schloss in 1429, and today the castle is part of the university buildings.

6 Kassel

100km (62 miles) NE of Marburg

The city of Kassel is the capital of the Fairy-Tale Road and the Brothers Grimm lived here as teenagers (from 1805–1830 it was the hometown of their mother). They worked as librarians at the court of Napoléon's youngest brother, Jerome Bonaparte, who was the King of Westphalia. The brothers were greatly inspired by the storyteller Dorothea Viehmann (see Autobahnrastätte Knallhütte, below).

Much of Kassel's 1,000-year-old history went down in ruins in World War II, and rebuilding was haphazard, with little regard for its rich architectural past. But from the rubble rose a city of both cultural and industrial significance, its grace note being its series of parks and gardens that take the curse off many modern buildings. Kassel was designed with many traffic-free promenades and pedestrian tunnels. Some two-thirds of Kassel consists of "green lungs" in the form of parks, tree-lined streets, and woodlands.

The town was first mentioned in A.D. 913 as Chassala or Chassela. In medieval times it was spelled "Castle" and was for a time a stronghold of the Franconian kings.

This former seat of the Landgraves is known for its grottoes, Wilhelmshöhe Park, its waterfalls, and Schloss (Castle), all of which are documented below.

Kassel sits on the banks of the Fulda River in a heavily wooded part of Germany between the Meissner-Kaufungen and the Habischswald natural parks on government-protected land.

ESSENTIALS

GETTING THERE   By Train   Trains arrive from Frankfurt's Hauptbahnhof every 75 to 90 minutes during the day (trip time: 1½ hr.). Trains stop at such places as Steinau and Fulda. Once at Kassel, train routes become fragmented, fanning out in many directions across Lower Saxony.

By Car   From Marburg (our last stopover), follow route A49 northeast into Kassel. The A44 (to Dortmund) and the A7 (Fulda to Hannover) autobahns cross in Kassel.

VISITOR INFORMATION   For information, **Kassel Tourist Office GmbH** is at Obere Königstrasse 15 (© **0561/7077707**), open Monday to Friday 9am to 6pm, Saturday 9am to 2pm. Here you can purchase the **Kassel Card,** sold only to two travelers at a time and costing 10€ ($16) for 24 hours or 13€ ($21) for a 72-hour period. The card grants free transport on the city's trams and buses, discounted admission to its museums and attractions, and even discounts at some shops. It also grants free participation in tourist office walking tours and discounts on bus tours which normally cost 13€ ($21) but only 5€ ($8) with the card.

SPECIAL EVENTS   Documenta 👁👁👁 is a famous art fair that has taken place every 5 years in Kassel since 1955, with musical and dramatic presentations at the Freericianum in Friedrichsplatz 18, 34117 Kassel (© 0561/707270; www.documenta.de). The festival has been hailed in the press as the erudite heavyweight of global art exhibitions. Originally its goal was to show the world that Nazi-era nationalism was passé in Germany. Art lovers, some 650,000 of them, pour into the city for the festival, with celebrity attendees ranging from David Bowie to Queen Beatrix of the Netherlands.

SHOPPING   The main street for shopping is the traffic-free **Königstrasse,** in the center of the city. It's lined with many specialty shops and department stores along with cafes with outdoor terraces in summer. Check out the **Königsgalerie** at Obere Königstrasse 39, a glass-roof atrium filled with boutiques, taverns, cafes, and restaurants.

WHERE TO STAY

Ramada Hotel Kassel City Centre 👁   This leading hotel in the town center rises 14 floors, and while it's not an architectural masterpiece, it offers the most comfortable and best-furnished rooms. It also has the most amenities of all its competitors. Bedrooms are midsize to spacious, and the hotel is geared both to the business traveler and the visitor intent on discovering Kassel. Its recreation area on the top floor is the best in Kassel, with a fitness center, solarium, and steam bath. Its drinking and dining facilities are also first class, with a market-fresh cuisine.

Baumbachstrasse 2, 34119 Kassel. © 0561/78100. Fax 0561/7810100. www.ramada.com. 169 units. 120€–138€ ($192–$221) double; from 178€ ($285) suite. AE, DC, MC, V. Parking 7€ ($11). **Amenities:** Restaurant; bistro; bar; fitness club; business center; laundry service; dry cleaning; nonsmoking rooms; rooms for those w/limited mobility. *In room:* A/C, TV, Wi-Fi, minibar, fridge (in some rooms), hair dryer, iron.

Residenz Domus   This longtime favorite near the Hauptbahnhof (train station) was erected in 1905 as the first reinforced concrete building in Kassel and was once the headquarters of a local trading house. Its red clinker facade was strong enough to withstand the bombs of World War II. Over the years the four-story hotel has been much altered and improved to stay abreast of the changing times. Today it has a light, airy decor and modern furnishings and amenities. Many rooms and bathrooms are extremely spacious.

Erzbergerstrasse 1–5, 34117 Kassel. © 0561/703330. Fax 0561/70333498. www.hotel-domus-kassel.de. 55 units. 91€–130€ ($146–$208) double. Rates include breakfast. AE, DC, MC, V. Parking 6€ ($9.60). **Amenities:** Breakfast room; room service; laundry service. *In room:* TV, minibar, hair dryer.

Schlosshotel Bad Wilhelmshöhe 👁👁   This hotel is misnamed. It's not an old castle at all, but a completely modern building constructed directly across the street from the palace. As early as 1767 an inn here was receiving guests, and German troops were once billeted here after World War I. However, Allied bombings leveled the hotel in World War II, and it was rebuilt in 1955. Today, it has large, individually furnished bedrooms, some with balconies overlooking the sprawling castle park and its buildings. Quality materials such as hardwood floors in the bedrooms and green marble in the bathrooms add a touch of elegance.

Schloss 8, 34131 Kasssel. © 0561/38880. Fax 0561/3088428. www.schlosshotel-kassel.de. 101 units. 86€–132€ ($138–$211) double; 145€–175€ ($232–$280) junior suite. AE, DC, MC, V. Free parking. **Amenities:** Restaurant; bar; room service; laundry service; dry cleaning; nonsmoking rooms. *In room:* TV, hair dryer.

WHERE TO DINE

Autobahnrastätte Knallhütte GERMAN   Dating from 1752, this brewery-cum-tavern was the home of Dorothea Viehmann, the famous storyteller and the main source of many of the fairy tales later published by the Brothers Grimm, including "Hansel and Gretel," "Little Red Riding Hood," and "Rumpelstiltskin." Today the old road that runs by the inn is now Autobahn A49 between the Baunatal Mitte and Baunatal Nord exits. The local brew is still served here, alongside regional specialties including Biersuppe. Expect old-fashioned German dishes such as tender veal and roast pork with dumplings and cabbage. Schnitzels fill the platters and herring is always a feature, as is rumpsteak with fried potatoes.

Knallhütterstrasse 1, Baunatal-Rengershausen. Ⓒ **0561/492076.** www.knallhuette.de. Reservations not needed. Main courses 9.90€–15€ ($16–$24). MC, V. Daily 11am–midnight.

EXPLORING KASSEL

Brüder Grimm Museum   The surrounding Waldeck Region and Reinhards Forest, as well as Kassel itself, were responsible for the birth of many legends and tales about witches, sleeping princesses, strange beasts, and magic spells. These tall tales had a profound influence on the Brothers Grimm as teenagers. Their lives and creative output are documented in this museum of their memorabilia, containing letters, portraits, and mementos of the famous brothers, including a collection of their fairy tales from the first copy printed up until today. You'll also see art, including drawings, by the third brother, Ludwig Emil Grimm. The exhibition rooms are located in the baroque-style Palais Bellevue, which was originally designed as an observatory for Hesse's Landgrave Karl in 1714.

Brüder Grimm Platz. Ⓒ **0561/103235.** www.grimms.de. Admission 1.50€ ($2.40). Thurs–Tues 10am–5pm; Wed 10am–8pm.

Wilhelmshöhe 𝕬𝕬   This is the chief attraction of Kassel, and you will want to spend a minimum of 3 hours taking in all its attractions. (Sometimes visitors, mainly German, spend all day exploring the park alone.) **Wilhelmshöhe Park** 𝕬𝕬, Europe's largest hill park, sprawls across 350 hectares (865 acres) at the western edge of the city, a magnificent garden with 800 species of trees dating from 1701 when it was laid out in the baroque style.

The crowning achievement is the **Statue of Hercules** at the highest point of the park. This giant is a copy of a statue originally created in 1717, and it's mounted atop an eight-sided "Oktogon." You can climb the stairs of the statue's castlelike base for one of the **greatest panoramas** 𝕬𝕬𝕬 in the area. Try to time your visit for a Wednesday or Sunday afternoon at 2:30pm from mid-May to September, when water gushes down a series of cascades from a fountain below the statue. The total height of the monument is 72m (236 ft.).

Also in the park stands **Löwenburg**, a faux castle from 1800, which was constructed at the height of the sentimental romanticism period. The castle, called the Lion Fortress in English, contains a collection of medieval armor and weapons along with tapestries and antique furniture.

The **Schloss** itself, completed in 1803, is in the neoclassical style. Built on a wooded slope where a monastery once stood, it was the summer residence of the landgraves and the electors of Hessen-Kassel. For 7 years, it was the residence of Napoléon's brother, Jerome, during the Napoleonic era, and it also became the summer palace of Kaiser Wilhelm II. Napoléon III was imprisoned here from 1870 to 1871.

The state apartments are lavishly furnished with antiques, including the *Kassel Apollo*, a statue from the 2nd century A.D.

The main reason to visit is to see the **Old Masters Gallery** 𝔊𝔊𝔊, a treasure trove of art collected by the landgraves. The collection includes 11 Rembrandts, including a trio of self-portraits of the artist. Other highlights include Dürer's *Portrait of Elizabeth Tucher* and landscapes by Jan Brueghel. The Italian School is represented by works by Titian and Tintoretto, with the Spanish School featuring paintings by Murillo and Ribera. There are also eight paintings by Rubens and seven by Frans Hals.

The city arranges summer concerts in the park.

Schlosspark 3. © 0561/312456. Admission 2€ ($3.20). Mar–Oct Tues–Sun 10am–5pm; Nov–Feb Tues–Sun 10am–3pm.

AFTER DARK

Friedrich-Ebert-Strasse is the center of dance clubs and bars, but more sophisticated nightlife centers around the **Kassel Casino,** Maurerstrasse 11 (© **0561/930850**), costing 1€ ($1.60) to enter. It is entered through the Kurfürsten Galerie, and it features roulette and card games, plus the latest slot machines. The casino is open daily Monday to Saturday 9am to 3am, Sunday noon to 3am.

A SIDE TRIP FROM KASSEL: BAD WILDUNGEN

If you'd like to take a short break for a little R&R, you can drive down to one of the oldest and most historic spas of Germany, a short distance from Kassel, for a recuperative break from all those fairy tales.

Lying 43km (27 miles) south of Kassel, Bad Wildungen is more than 700 years old. Its healing mineral springs have long attracted northern Europeans to the rolling hills and deep forests of the Waldeck region, southwest of Kassel. Thousands of annual visitors come here seeking treatment for kidney and gallbladder disorders or simply for rest and relaxation and the numerous cultural activities.

ESSENTIALS

GETTING THERE   By Train   There's frequent service on the Kassel-Fritzlar line from Kassel. For information, call © **01805/996633** (11861 in Germany; www. bahn.de). The nearest airport is at Frankfurt am Main, about 150km (100 miles) away.

By Bus   Bus service in the region is provided by **B.K.W. GmbH** (© **05621/802810** for information).

By Car   From Kassel, take Route 49 southwest, then go west on Route 253.

VISITOR INFORMATION   For information, contact the **Kur-und Verkeehrsverein,** Bad Wildungen (© **05621/9656715;** www.badwildungen.de), open Monday to Friday 8:30am to 4:30pm and Saturday 9am to noon.

WHERE TO STAY

Göbel's Hotel Quellenhof   This white-sided hotel has a mansard roof and Art Nouveau gables dating from the year of its construction in 1873. Rooms are international in decor and carefully outfitted. All come equipped with neatly kept bathrooms containing tub/shower combos.

Brunnenallee 54 (across the street from the Kurpark), 35437 Bad Wildungen. © 05621/8070. Fax 05621/807500. www.goebels-quellenhof.de. 109 units. 122€–136€ ($195–$218) double; 142€ ($227) suite. AE, DC, MC, V. Parking 6€ ($9.60). **Amenities:** 2 restaurants; bar; casino; fitness center; whirlpool; sauna; solarium; room service; massage; laundry service; dry cleaning; nonsmoking rooms. *In room:* TV, minibar, hair dryer, safe.

Maritim Badehotel ☞ The Maritim Badehotel is located in the center of the town's clinical and cultural activities. No hotel in Bad Wildungen comes close to this one for comfort, style, amenities, and facilities. This place evokes the grandeur of another era. Large and rambling, it branches out in two great wings from the circular domed entrance. The renovated rooms are large, comfortable, sunlit, and airy, all with views of the Waldeck woodlands and spa gardens. All are equipped with neatly kept bathrooms containing tub/shower combos.

Dr.-Marc-Strasse 4 (at the entrance to the gardens, in the Kurpark), 34537 Bad Wildungen. ℂ 05621/7999. Fax 05621/ 799798. www.maritim.de. 245 units. 135€–168€ ($216–$269) double; 195€–320€ ($312–$512) suite. Rates include buffet breakfast. AE, DC, MC, V. Parking 10€ ($16). **Amenities:** Restaurant; bar; lounge; indoor heated pool; sauna; solarium; room service; massage; babysitting; laundry service; dry cleaning; nonsmoking rooms; rooms for those w/limited mobility. *In room:* TV, Wi-Fi, minibar, hair dryer.

WHERE TO DINE

The hotel dining rooms enjoy a culinary monopoly in Bad Wildungen; there is no major independent restaurant.

Park Restaurant INTERNATIONAL   Stylish, airy, and international, this is the showcase restaurant of the Hotel Quellenhof (see above). Though it's a top place to dine, its prices are affordable. The immaculately clean interior is outfitted with lots of green plants. The staff is alert and well trained. Menu items include well-prepared salads, roasted meats, pastas, pastries, and such traditional German dishes as sauerbraten and *Rostbraten* (roast beef).

In the Hotel Quellenhof, Brunnenallee 54. ℂ 05621/8070. Reservations recommended. Main courses 12€–26€ ($19–$42). AE, DC, MC, V. Daily 7–10am, noon–2pm, and 6–10pm.

EXPLORING BAD WILDUNGEN

Rising above the Altstadt is the massive tower of the 14th-century **Stadtkirche** (ℂ 05621/4011), the most impressive (and oldest) structure in the town, with interesting Hallenkirch architecture. It was restored in 1995. The highlight of the church is its remarkable *Niederwildungen Altarpiece,* one of the best examples of early German painting. Painted in 1403 by Master Konrad von Soest, the wing-paneled altarpiece contains a large, dramatic scene of the crucifixion, flanked by six smaller scenes from the life of Christ. The work shows a French influence in the use of delicate colors and figures, made even more vivid by the use of actual gold. The church is open daily 10:30am to noon and 2 to 5pm.

The **spa gardens** augment the town's natural wooded surroundings with carefully planted flowers from all parts of the world, as well as with several attractive buildings, including two band shells where outdoor concerts are frequently given. The grounds are dotted with lawn chairs. The modern horseshoe-shaped arcade houses the George-Viktor Spring, plus several exclusive shops and a small auditorium.

SHOPPING   Bad Wildungen's shops carry fashion suitable for Germany's most sophisticated cities. Shops line either side of the Brunnenallee. One of the most appealing is **Manhenke,** Brunnenstrasse 52 (ℂ 05621/960253), which sells clothes and accessories for both men and women.

BAD WILDUNGEN AFTER DARK

The tourist office keeps a list of special events, which are staged almost every week. Concerts and theater usually take place in the **Neues Kurhaus** in the town center. For tickets, call ℂ 05621/704773.

Spielbank, Brunnenallee 54 (℃ **05621/960056**), located in the Hotel Quellenhof (see above), is the resort's only casino. Minor league as Germany's casinos go, it's open daily 2:30pm to midnight, with an entrance fee of 2.50€ ($4). Bring your passport (you must be 18 or older to enter and gamble). Men must wear sports jackets.

Nighttime diversions in Bad Wildungen revolve around the **Brunnenallee** and its extension, the **Brunnenstrasse,** in the form of lively bars and cafes that stay open until around 2am. Some of the best include the **Warsteiner Treff,** Brunnenstrasse 66 (℃ **05621/74172**).

7 Hann. Münden ⟨★

150km (93m) S of Hannover, 24km (15 m) NE of Kassel

This little gem of a town with the odd name (once known as Hannoversch Münden), is filled with some 700 half-timbered houses. Parts of it look like a movie set. It lies at the confluence of the Werra and Fulda rivers, which join to form the Wester River.

Many of its houses are 6 centuries old. The poet Alexander von Humboldt claimed that the town is one of the seven most beautifully situated in the world.

The little city's fortified towers and remains of its old wall speak of its importance in the Middle Ages.

ESSENTIALS

GETTING THERE   By Train   Trains arrive from Kassel throughout the day, taking 16 minutes, and from Göttingen, taking 36 minutes. There are also major rail links with Hannover (trip time: 1½ hr.) and Frankfurt (trip time: 2¼ hr.).

By Car   From Kassel (see above) follow Autobahn E45 northeast until you see the turnoff to Hann. Münden.

VISITOR INFORMATION   The **Tourist Information Office** is at the Rathaus on Lotzestrasse (℃ **05541/75313**), open May to October Monday to Friday 8am to 5:30pm, Saturday 10am to 3pm, and Sunday 11am to 3pm; and November to April Monday to Thursday 9am–4pm and Friday 9am–1pm.

SPECIAL EVENTS   In summer the town celebrates its connection with the notorious quack, Dr. Johann Andreas Eisenbart (1663–1727). The Doctor Eisenbart Theatre Company, founded in 1957, stages a play about the man who "could make the blind walk and the lame see."

On one Sunday in May and June and every Sunday in July and August at 11:15am, plays are staged in front of the historic Rathaus, with tickets costing 4€ ($6.40) for adults or 1.50€ ($2.40) for ages 4 to 12. For information on these plays, contact the tourist office above.

The doctor became the subject of a ribald drinking song that immortalized him. In the song he performs such feats as shooting out an aching tooth with a gun. There's a statue of the quack in front of his former home at 79 Langestrasse.

WHERE TO STAY

Alte Rathausschanke   In the historic town center, this is the most atmospheric place to stay. It often hosts bikers following the routes through the Weser Valley. Its bedrooms are just above the hostel level but are comfortable and individually furnished. Since many young people on a budget patronize the hotel, the staff provides a washing machine and dryer for them. A generous breakfast buffet is included every morning.

Ziegelstrasse 12, 34346 Hann. Münden. ℂ **05541/75313.** Fax 05541/75404. 10 units. 60€ ($96) double. No credit cards. **Amenities:** Breakfast room; bike storage; nonsmoking rooms. *In room:* TV, Wi-Fi, beverage maker.

WHERE TO DINE

Ratsbrauhaus GERMAN   The Rathaus of Münden, dating from 1605, is a fine example of the Weser Renaissance style with its gabled peaks. Its cellar is no less an architectural curiosity, with much of its original decor intact. You get good hearty fare here, including such dishes as venison pâté as an appetizer, followed by veal chops with a mustard sauce and, on occasion, breast of goose with red cranberries or a tender rack of lamb. Seafood such as oysters and lobsters are also featured.

Markplatz 3. ℂ **05541/957107.** Reservations not needed. Main courses 8€–18€ ($13–$29). MC, V. Tues–Fri 6–10:30pm; Sat 11am–2pm and 6–10:30pm; Sun 11am–2pm.

EXPLORING HANN. MÜNDEN

Allow at least 1½ to 2 hours to walk around the central core of the old town, taking in (or photographing) all those half-timbered buildings.

St. Blaise's Church   This is the one church of general interest to visitors, as it dates from the end of the 13th century. The chancel, the southern lateral apse, and the eastern bay were constructed at this time. The rest of the church was finished at various times, including the vaulting of the tower chamber in 1519 and the landmark tower itself in 1584. That tower is adorned with a lantern cupola. In the nave is the tomb of William of Brunswick, who died in 1503.

Kirchplatz. ℂ **05541/75313** (tourist office). Free admission. Summer only, daily 11am–4pm.

EXCURSION TO SABABURG

For your next stopover, head north from Hann. Münden on B80. At the village of Veckerhagen follow the signposts left into Sababurg, which lies 100 km (62 miles) south of Hannover, 60 km (36 miles) west of Göttingen, and 38 km (24 miles) north of Kassel. After driving through the luxuriant Forest of Reinhard, one of the largest in Germany, you come up to **Sababurg Castle,** a distance of 24 km (15 miles) from Hann. Münden. The castle has been turned into a hotel (see below).

This castle is where Sleeping Beauty, in the fairy tale by the Brothers Grimm, slept for a century. The castle has had a long and turbulent history since it was built in 1334 by the archbishop of Mainz. It eventually fell into ruins, but in 1490 Count Wilhelm I constructed a hunting lodge on the site. Troops plundered the castle during the Thirty Years' War, and Friedrich II turned the castle back into a hunting lodge in 1765, but that, too, was allowed to deteriorate until its present restoration. In the castle courtyard, where briar roses bloom, you can almost expect to see the handsome prince preparing to awaken Sleeping Beauty with a kiss.

Surrounding the castle is **Tierpark Sababurg** 🐾, Sababurgstrasse (ℂ **05671/8001-2251**), one of the oldest wildlife refuges in Europe, home to such animals as the bison and reindeer as well as a vast array of waterfowl. The surrounding acres of ancient oaks and beech trees added to the fairy-tale atmosphere of the area. Charging 4.50€ ($7.20) admission, the park is open daily as follows: April to September 8am to 7pm, October 9am to 6pm, November to February 10am to 4pm, and March 9am to 5pm.

WHERE TO STAY

Dornröschenschloss Sababurg 🐾   In a section of Sleeping Beauty's castle a luxury hotel and restaurant has been constructed. Bedrooms are furnished in a period style, and, in spite of the medieval atmosphere, modern amenities have been installed.

Rooms are beautifully furnished in modern or traditional and carry various themes, including a dedication to a unicorn. For the most panoramic units, ask for one of the tower rooms. Some of the bedrooms are found in a wing dating from 1572. Afternoon tea is served on the courtyard terrace, overlooking ancient trees. A formal restaurant serving an international cuisine opens onto views of the park.

Im Reinshardswald, 34369 Hofgeismar. © **05671/8080.** Fax 05671/808200. www.sababurg.de. 17 units. 155€–195€ ($248–$312) double; 220€ ($352) tower room. AE, DC, MC, V. **Amenities:** Restaurant; bar; room service; babysitting; laundry service. *In room:* TV, hair dryer.

8 Bad Karlshafen

37km (23 miles) N of Kassel, 15km (9.3 miles) S of Höxter, 42km (26 miles) N of Hann. Münden

This is a spa town built in the baroque style in 1699 by the Huguenots and lying at the confluence of the Diemel and Weser rivers. Its baroque buildings rise grandly in stark white.

Americans are fascinated to learn that German troops embarked from here to join the English forces in the American War of Independence. Barges took these troops down the Weser to Bremen, where they shipped out to try to prevent the United States from declaring its independence.

Its major building is the **Rathaus** at Hafenplatz 8 (now the center for tourist information; see below).

ESSENTIALS

GETTING THERE   By Train   From Frankfurt, there's a train every hour that goes to Göttingen, a traveling distance of 2 hours. From Göttingen, there are about 10 trains a day to Bad Karlshafen, a travel time of around 60 minutes. From Höxter, there are direct trains departing every 2 hours for Bad Karlshafen, a travel distance of about 37 minutes each way.

By Car   After leaving our last stopover at Sababurg, head east to rejoin Route 80, following it northwest into Bad Karlshafen.

VISITOR INFORMATION   The Tourist Office is at the Rathaus at Hafenplatz 8 (© **05672/999920**), open May to October daily 9am to 7:30pm, and November to April Monday to Friday 9am to noon and 2 to 4pm.

WHERE TO STAY & DINE

Heissischer Hof ⋆   In the center of town this hotel is your best bet for both food and good rooms. Its restaurant with its umbrella-shaded terrace is its main attraction, with meals costing 20€ to 38€ ($32–$61). The cuisine is market fresh, the recipes international, including some hearty regional fare as well. Bedrooms are beautifully furnished and well maintained, many filled with spa devotees.

Carlstrasse 13–15, 34385 Bad Karlshafen. © **05672/1059.** Fax 05672/2515. www.hess-hof.de. 17 units. 136€ ($218) double. AE, DC, MC, V. **Amenities:** Restaurant; bar; indoor pool; fitness center; room service; laundry service. *In room:* TV, minibar, hair dryer.

EXPLORING BAD KARLSHAFEN

Bad Karlshafen is famed today as a health resort centering around its huge spa facility, **Kristall Weserbergland-Therme,** at Kurpromenade 1 (© **05672/92110**), open Sunday to Thursday 9am to 10pm, and Friday and Saturday 9am to 11pm. Entrance to the spa, including a sauna bath, costs 19€ ($30).

In the environs, **Porzellanmanufaktur Fürstenberg** lies in Schloss Fürstenberg, Meinbrexener Strasse in the town of Fürstenburg (© **05271/4010;** www.fuerstenberg-porzellan.com), 8km (5 miles) south of Höxter, our next destination. You can visit it after leaving Bad Karlshafen, heading to Höxter.

This baroque castle rising over the Weser River is the second-oldest porcelain manufacturer in the country. Its trademark is a blue F under the glaze, and its porcelain has been highly prized by collectors ever since 1753.

Although the porcelain is sold at many outlets, there is nothing quite like buying it at its home base, where shipping can be arranged. If you call in advance the day before, you can arrange for a tour of the factory. On-site is a sales shop selling the porcelain, along with a museum tracing the factory's history, and even a cafe for lunch.

Entrance to the museum costs 4€ ($6.40), and it's open April to October Tuesday to Sunday 10am to 5pm, November to March Saturday and Sunday 10am to 5pm. The on-site shop is open only April to November Tuesday to Sunday 10am to 5pm.

9 Höxter

24km (14 miles) N of Bad Karlshafen, 70km (44 miles) S of Hannover

On the left bank of the Weser River, the walled town of Höxter merits at least an hour of your time as you explore its historic core.

GETTING THERE **By Train** Direct trains run back and forth between Bad Karlshafen and Höxter every 2 hours during the day (trip time: 37 min.).

By Car From Bad Karlshafen, follow the signs out of town to Route 83, which you take north into Höxter.

VISITOR INFORMATION The **Touristik- und Kulturinformation** is in the Historisches Rathaus, Weserstrasse 11 (© **05271/19433;** www.hoexter.de), open Monday to Friday 9am to 6pm, Saturday 10am to 4pm.

WHERE TO STAY & DINE

Ringhotel Niedersachsen 👍 One of the better members of the Ring chain, this venerated hotel is the best place to stay in the area. It's known for its thermal baths and for its spacious garden. The bedrooms are the finest in the area, 15 of them containing a balcony opening onto views. Rooms are equipped with up-to-date amenities and even suggest a touch of luxury. This antique Höxter building has kept abreast of the times. The restaurant, popular with locals and visitors alike, has a garden terrace. The chefs specialize in fresh river fish and other regional dishes, with meals averaging around 28€ ($45).

Grubestrasse 3–7, 37671 Höxter. © 05271/688444. www.hotelniedersachsen.de. 80 units. 140€ ($224) double; 198€ ($317) junior suite. AE, DC, MC, V. Parking 6.50€ ($11). **Amenities:** 2 restaurants; bar; indoor pool; spa; Internet access; room service; laundry service; dry cleaning. *In room:* TV, minibar, safe.

EXPLORING HÖXTER

The **Dechanei (Deanery)** standing in the Markt (the market square) in the center of town dates from 1561, and the **Rathaus,** also on the square, from 1613. This municipal building is a classic example of the Weser Renaissance style, a trio of half-timbered structures with a crooked old tower that looks like something from a Brothers Grimm fairy tale.

Höxter, among other towns, lays claim for the inspiration of the tale of "Hansel and Gretel." On the first Saturday of each month from May to September the town presents the drama. Ask at the tourist office (see above) for more details.

After visiting the marketplace, you can walk down **Westerbachstrasse** to discover many more half-timbered houses dating from the Middle Ages. Another church to visit is **St. Kilian's** at An der Kiliankirche, dating from the 11th century. Its treasures include a 15th-century aisle and an early-16th-century Crucifixion group of sculpture. Its pulpit was built in 1597 and is an outstanding piece of Renaissance craftsmanship, decorated with motifs in alabaster.

From the center of town, take Corveyer Allée for 3 km (2 miles) to **Reichsabtei Corvey (the Imperial Abbey of Corvey)** in the village of Corvey (© **05271/694010**). Schloss Corvey (its other name) stands on a hillside overlooking the Weser River and was one of the oldest Benedictine abbeys in Germany. It was planned by Charlemagne himself but constructed by his son, Ludwig the Pious, in 822. In the 9th and 10th centuries, the abbey was one of the major cultural centers of north Germany.

During the Thirty Years' War, most of Corvey Abbey was destroyed, the only section remaining being the west facade of the church with its two spires. The abbey was rebuilt around 1730 in its present form, together with the church, monastery, and farm buildings. Guided tours take you through the library and imperial halls, and on the second floor is an exhibition of folkloric objects and prehistoric relics. In May and June a music festival is held in the great hall, the Kaisersaal. Admission to the castle is 4.20€ ($6.70), or .60€ ($1) to the abbey church. It's open April to October daily 9am to 6pm.

You can have lunch at the on-site **Schlossrestaurant** (© **05271/83230**) under centuries-old linden trees, enjoying regional specialties.

10 Bodenwerder

25km (16 miles) S of Hameln; 34km (21 miles) N of Höxter, 70km (43 miles) S of Hannover

This is the hometown of Lügenbaron (the lying baron) von Münchhausen (1720–97). This spinner of tall tales was the biggest liar in the history of Germany—unless you want to get political and include Hitler in that competition.

The Münchhausen name has gone down in literary history. His narrative about his travels and campaigns in Russia increased his renown and was translated into many languages. The actual author was Rudolph Erich Raspe, who became acquainted with Von Münchhausen upon his retirement in 1760 from Russian service against the Turks. The baron was widely known for his exploits, including a claim that he rode a cannonball toward the enemy stronghold. Reconsidering as he neared his target, he jumped onto a cannonball shot by the enemy and rode it safely back to his troops.

From May to October during the first Sunday of every month, the **Münchhausenplay** is performed in front of the Rathaus. Locals re-enact scenes from Münchhausen's colorful, if distorted, life.

ESSENTIALS

GETTING THERE   By Train   From Hannover's Hauptbahnhof, trains depart every hour for Hameln, a travel distance of 1 hour and 5 minutes. At Hameln, in front of its railway station, bus no. 520 continues on, at hourly intervals, to Bodenwerder, a travel time of 50 minutes.

By Car   From Höxter, continue north along Route 83 into Bodenwerder.

VISITOR INFORMATION   The **Tourist Information** is at Münchhausenplatz 3 (② **05533/40541**), open Monday to Friday 9am to 12:30pm and 2 to 5pm, and Saturday 10am to 12:30pm.

WHERE TO STAY & DINE

Goldener Anker   This half-timbered old favorite, under the direction of the Schoppe family, dates from 1837 but has been modernized. The Weser River, where boats tie up, virtually runs by its front door. In summer the action overflows onto a biergarten fronting the river. Most people come here for food and drink in the tavern, and it attracts both visitors and locals. The menu features an array of regional specialties, including the best steaks in town. Meals begin at 20€ ($31) per person. Bedrooms listed as standard are cozy and comfortably furnished; those rated deluxe are roomier with better plumbing fixtures.

Brückenstrasse 5, 37619 Bodenwerder. ② **05533/400730.** Fax 05533/400733. www.bodenwerder-hotel.de. 16 units. 50€ ($80) double. MC, V. **Amenities:** Restaurant; beer garden; bar; room service; laundry service; free bikes; nonsmoking rooms. *In room:* TV.

Parkhotel Deutsches Haus 🅰   Next door to the former home of Baron von Münchhausen (now the city hall) stands this half-timbered hotel that is the most inviting and comfortable in town. A country aura is evoked by its oak paneling and old wooden beams. The bedrooms have been modernized and are attractively furnished. The hotel stands on its own landscaped grounds, which appear even larger since they lie next to the city park. Meals cost 28€ ($45) and in summer are served on a terrace near the Weser River. In honor of the baron, the house dish is named *Kugeln* or "cannonballs" (turkey, pork, and fresh vegetables).

Münchhausenplatz 4, 37619 Bodenwerder. ② **05533/3925.** Fax 05533/4113. www.hotel-deutsches-haus-boden werder.de. 42 units. 83€–99€ ($133–$158) double. AE, MC, V. **Amenities:** 2 restaurants; bar; summer terrace; room service; laundry service; nonsmoking rooms. *In room:* TV, Wi-Fi, minibar, hair dryer.

EXPLORING BODENWERDER

Münchhausen-Erinnerungszimmer   This memorial room devoted to the great liar was the family home of the Von Münchhausen family. Today it is the Rathaus, and it's filled with mementos of this storyteller, including that cannonball he allegedly rode. You can trace some of his "adventures" in the museum—but don't believe a word of it. The fountain in front evokes a tale he told about his horse. He became suspicious when he noticed that the horse had an insatiable thirst, then he discovered that the horse had been cut in two parts. No sooner did it drink water, the liquid ran out the rear of the half horse into the fountain.

Münchhausenplatz 1. ② **05533/409147.** Admission 2€ ($3.20). Apr–Oct daily 10am–noon and 2–5pm.

11 Hameln 🄰

45km (28 miles) SW of Hannover, 48km (30 miles) W of Hildesheim

Hameln (Hamelin in English) has many interesting buildings and a history dating from the 11th century, but its main claim to fame is the Pied Piper folk tale, immortalized by the Brothers Grimm, Goethe, and Robert Browning, among others. According to legend, in 1284 the town was infested by rats. Soon after, a piper appeared and offered, for a fee, to lure the vermin into the Weser River. The rat catcher successfully performed the service, but the stingy denizens of Hameln refused to pay, claiming that he was a sorcerer. So the piper reappeared the next Sunday and played a tune that lured the town's children, except one lame boy, into a mysterious door in a hill. The children and the Pied Piper were never heard from again.

There is some historical basis for the story. It appears that, several centuries ago, for some unknown reason, the children of Hameln did indeed leave the town. The story of the Pied Piper is retold every summer Sunday at noon in a special performance at the **Hochzeitshaus (Wedding House)** on Osterstrasse. In the town shops, you can buy rat figures made of almost every conceivable material, including candy.

ESSENTIALS

GETTING THERE   By Plane   The nearest major airport is Hannover-Langen-hagen, 55km (34 miles) away.

By Train   The **Hameln Bahnhof** lies on the Hannover-Hameln-Altenbeken line, with frequent connections. Depending on the train, trip time from Hannover ranges from 45 to 55 minutes. For information, call ℭ **01805/996633** (11861 in Germany; www.bahn.de).

By Bus   Local and regional bus service to nearby towns and Hannover is available from **Grossraum-Verkehr Hannover** (ℭ **01803/19449;** www.gvh.de). Buses stop in front of the Hauptbahnhof.

By Car   It takes 3 hours to reach Hameln from Frankfurt and 6 to 7 hours from Munich. From Frankfurt, head northeast along the A5 Autobahn, then north on the A7, and finally west on A27. From Munich, take the A9 Autobahn north to Nürn-berg, the A3 west to Würzburg, then the A7 north toward Hannover, and finally take the A27 west to Hameln.

VISITOR INFORMATION   Contact the **Hameln Marketing und Tourismus GmbH,** Deisterallee 1 (ℭ **05151/957823;** www.hameln.de), open May to September Mon-day to Friday 9am to 6:30pm, Saturday 9:30am to 4pm, and Sunday 9:30am to 1pm; October to March Monday to Friday 9am to 6pm and Saturday 9:30am to 1pm; and April Monday to Friday 9am to 6:30pm, and Saturday 9:30am to 4pm.

WHERE TO STAY

Hotel zur Börse   This balconied hotel within the walls of the Altstadt can be iden-tified by the four peaks of its modern roofline. The interior is refreshingly uncluttered. Rooms are spacious and well maintained with bathrooms equipped with tub/shower combos.

Osterstrasse 41A, 31785 Hameln. ℭ **05151/7080.** Fax 05151/25485. www.hotel-zur-boerse.de. 31 units. 89€ ($142) double. Rates include buffet breakfast. AE, DC, MC, V. Parking 6.50€ ($10). Bus: 1 or 2. **Amenities:** Restau-rant; bar; lounge; room service; nonsmoking rooms. In room: TV, minibar, hair dryer, safe, trouser press.

Komfort-Hotel Garni Christinenhof   The gabled windows of this half-timbered, 300-year-old building overlook a cobble-stoned street in the middle of the Altstadt. Despite the antique facade, much of the hotel's interior is streamlined and modern, with many conveniences. All units contain neatly kept bathrooms with tub/shower combinations. Rooms are small yet well furnished.

Alte Markstrasse 18, 31785 Hameln. ℭ **05151/95080.** Fax 05151/43611. www.christinenhof-hameln.de. 30 units. 100€–120€ ($160–$192) double. Rates include buffet breakfast. MC, V. Free parking. Closed Dec 20–Jan 6. **Ameni-ties:** Breakfast room; lounge; indoor heated pool; sauna; laundry service; dry cleaning. In room: TV, minibar, hair dryer.

Mercure Hotel Hameln   This hotel stands in a park with lots of trees but is within walking distance of the heart of the Altstadt, at the northern edge of the Burgergarten. It rises like a modern collection of building blocks, with oversize glass walls. Rooms are standard and functional, and all contain bathrooms with tub/shower combos.

164er Ring 3, 31785 Hameln. ℭ 05151/7920. Fax 05151/792191. www.mercure.com. 105 units. 166€–270€ ($266–$432) double. AE, DC, MC, V. Parking 8€ ($13). Bus: 1 or 2. **Amenities:** Restaurant; bar; indoor heated pool; health club; sauna; solarium; room service; massage; babysitting; laundry service; dry cleaning; nonsmoking rooms; 1 room for those w/limited mobility. *In room:* TV, Wi-Fi, minibar, hair dryer.

WHERE TO DINE

Rattenfängerhaus GERMAN   The "Rat-Catcher's House" dates from 1603. A meal here is practically like eating in a museum. The place is a little too touristy and crowded for some tastes, but it's an enduring favorite nonetheless. You can order traditional German dishes, including various kinds of schnitzels, roasted goose, or filets of salmon with hollandaise sauce.

Osterstrasse 28. ℭ 05151/3888. Reservations recommended. Main courses 6€–21€ ($9.60–$34); fixed-price menu 23€ ($37). AE, DC, MC, V. Daily 11am–3pm and 6–11pm. Bus: 1 or 2.

EXPLORING HAMELN

Hameln's most interesting building is the **Gothic Münster,** at the end of Bäckerstrasse, overlooking the Weser River. Other attractions include the **Rattenfängerhaus** (see above), with frescoes illustrating the Pied Piper legend, and the **Hochzeitshaus (Wedding House)** on Osterstrasse, with its three attractive gables. The finest houses in the town are built in what is known as Weser-Renaissance style. You can admire these nicely sculpted late-16th-century houses as you stroll along the pedestrians-only streets. One of the best examples of the Weser-Renaissance style, which can be enjoyed by looking at its facade, is **Dempterscheshaus,** built in 1607. This house, at Pferdemarkt, standing in the middle of town, has protruding bay windows. This patrician building is also characterized by fine chiseled stones and decorations of ornaments and coats-of-arms.

SHOPPING   There are lots of opportunities to buy folkloric art objects here. One of the best bets for souvenir and gift hunting, **Renner,** Am Markt 6 (ℭ 05151/94420), has some genuinely charming objects. You might also want to go window shopping along the town's best shopping streets, the **Osterstrasse** and the **Bäckerstrasse.**

NIGHTLIFE   The town's **Weserbergland Festhalle,** Rathausplatz (ℭ 05151/916220), hosts an array of concerts, opera and ballet performances, and theatrical productions. Call the theater or the visitor information center (see above) for upcoming events and ticket information. Tickets are 9.50€ to 22€ ($15–$35).

12 Hannover

122km (76 miles) SE of Bremen, 151km (94 miles) S of Hamburg, 288km (179 miles) W of Berlin

This modest little city south of Hamburg still basks in the glow of Expo 2000, when more foreigners visited than ever before. It remains one of Germany's hubs of industry, transportation, and commerce, and its annual industrial trade fair is still the largest such fair in the world, attracting producers and buyers from around the globe.

Even with a big-money investment in its inner city, Hannover is hardly a city of grace and beauty. Although it has certain idyllic sections, including one of the finest baroque gardens in the world; a 2.5km (1½-mile) man-made lake, the Maschsee; and the encircling Eilenriede Forest, Hannover is a mere shadow of its former self. The royal court checked out in the early 19th century, heading for greener fields and greater power in London.

ESSENTIALS

GETTING THERE   By Plane   Hannover is served by **Hannover-Langenhagen International Airport,** 10km (6 miles) north of the city center. Many international airlines fly here. Flying time between Hannover and Munich is 1 hour, 10 minutes; between Frankfurt and Hannover, 50 minutes. For flight information, call ℂ **01803/ 19449** or visit www.hannover-airport.de. Catch the S-Bahn to the Hauptbahnhof. The cost is 2.70€ ($4.30) each way. Service is 5am to midnight, every 30 minutes.

By Train   Hannover lies at the junction of an important network of rail lines linking Scandinavia to Italy and Paris to Moscow. Some 500 trains per day pass through, with frequent connections to major German and European cities. Nineteen trains arrive daily from Berlin (trip time: 1 hr., 35 min.), 40 trains from Frankfurt (trip time: 2 hr., 21 min., or 3 hr., depending on the train), and 40 trains from Hamburg (trip time: 1 hr. 11 min., to 1½ hr.). For information call ℂ **01805/996633** (11861 in Germany; www.bahn.de).

By Bus   Long-distance bus service to major German cities is offered by **Deutsche Touring GmbH,** Hamburger Allee 19, opposite the Hauptbahnhof (ℂ **0511/329419**).

By Car   Access is via the A1 Autobahn north or south and from the A2 east and west.

VISITOR INFORMATION   Contact **Hannover Tourist Information,** located at Ernst-August-Platz 2 (ℂ **0511/12345111;** www.hannover.de). Here you can reserve hotel rooms (ask about special weekend packages), book sightseeing tours, obtain general information about the city, and purchase tickets for local events as well as for trains, trams, and buses. The office is open Monday to Friday 9am to 6pm and Saturday 9am to 2pm.

GETTING AROUND   The local public-transport system includes commuter trains, an extensive underground network, trams, and buses operated by several companies. Service is frequent and extensive. For information and schedules, contact **Grossraum-Verkehr Hannover** (ℂ **0511/16683000;** www.gvh.de).

WHERE TO STAY

Crowne Plaza ☆   This is one of the most imaginatively designed hotels in Hannover, with a lot more charm and atmosphere than other leading contenders. It sits on a quiet street in the central business district. Inside you'll find illuminated Plexiglas columns and sweeping expanses of russet-colored marble. The hotel serves an affluent clientele, often including visiting celebrities. Rooms are spacious and elegantly furnished, all with immaculately kept bathrooms with tub/shower combos.

Hinuberstrasse 6, 30175 Hannover. ℂ **0511/34950.** Fax 0511/3495123. www.ichotelsgroup.com. 201 units. 184€–201€ ($294–$322) double; from 250€ ($400) suite. Rates include buffet breakfast. AE, DC, MC, V. Parking 19€ ($30). Tram: 16. **Amenities:** 2 restaurants; bar; fitness center; spa; sauna; solarium; business center; room service; babysitting; laundry service; dry cleaning; nonsmoking rooms; 1 room for those w/limited mobility. *In room:* A/C, TV, Wi-Fi, minibar, coffeemaker, hair dryer, iron, safe.

Hotel Königshof am Funkturm ☆   Both the skylights and the modernized crenellations on this hotel's mansard roof make it look like an updated feudal fortress. The hotel was built in 1984 above a glass-and-steel shopping arcade in the town center.

Each plushly carpeted room has a couch that converts to a bed and a bathroom with a tub/shower combination. Only breakfast is served at the hotel, but there's an Italian restaurant across the street.

Friesenstrasse 65, 30161 Hannover. © 0511/33980. Fax 0511/3398111. www.koenigshof-hannover.de. 91 units. 76€–281€ ($122–$450) double; 102€–338€ ($163–$541) suite. Rates include buffet breakfast. AE, DC, MC, V. Parking 7.50€ ($12). Bus: 20 or 39. **Amenities:** Restaurant; breakfast room; bar; lounge; nonsmoking rooms. *In room:* TV, Wi-Fi, minibar, trouser press.

Kastens Hotel Luisenhof 👫👫 This is the leading hotel in town. Its stately glass-and-stone facade is just minutes from the Hauptbahnhof in the city center. A series of modernizations have enhanced comfort while maintaining conservative good taste. The carefully renovated rooms are spacious, stylishly furnished, and impeccably kept, all with bathrooms containing tub/shower combinations.

Luisenstrasse 1–3 (near the Hauptbahnhof), 30159 Hannover. © 0511/30440. Fax 0511/3044807. www.kastens-luisenhof.de. 145 units. 157€–427€ ($251–$683) double; 270€–970€ ($432–$1,552) suite. Children 11 and under stay free in parent's room. Rates include buffet breakfast. AE, DC, MC, V. Parking 10€ ($16). Tram: 16. **Amenities:** Restaurant; bar; fitness room; sauna; steam room; room service; laundry service; dry cleaning; nonsmoking rooms; rooms for those w/limited mobility. *In room:* A/C (in some), TV, minibar, hair dryer, safe.

Loccumer Hof 🎯*Value* Situated near the train station, this is one of Hannover's best deals, a good, clean, and decent choice. The utilitarian rooms and bathrooms are small, with tub/shower combinations. Service and frills are minimal, but the beds are comfortable and the hotel is well maintained. The hotel has added six deluxe doubles and two suites, each more spacious and better equipped than the standard doubles.

Kurt-Schumacher-Strasse 14–16 (near the Hauptbahnhof), 30159 Hannover. © 0511/12640. Fax 0511/131192. www.loccumerhof.com. 95 units. 117€–520€ ($187–$832) double; 102€–590€ ($163–$944) deluxe double; 118€–640€ ($189–$1,024) suite. Higher rates during trade fairs. Rates include buffet breakfast. AE, DC, MC, V. Parking 7€ ($11). Tram: 16. **Amenities:** Restaurant; bar; lounge; nonsmoking rooms; rooms for those w/limited mobility. *In room:* TV, Wi-Fi, minibar, hair dryer.

WHERE TO DINE
EXPENSIVE

Basil 👫👫 ECLECTIC The hippest restaurant in Hannover draws a chic clientele to a dining room known for its modern cuisine, fresh ingredients, and alert waitstaff. The setting is a riding hall built in 1867 for the Royal Prussian military. Guests dine in an antique atmosphere under a vaulted ceiling. We prefer a table in the delightful garden where we've spotted Hannover's most famous son, former Chancellor Gerhard Schröder, dining. Like Clichy (see below), where the food is only slightly better, Basil changes each menu at least every 3 weeks, and it's always based on what's fresh and flavorful at the market. Recipes range from the coasts of the Mediterranean to Asia. We recently arrived in spring to enjoy a *Spargel* (asparagus menu). Had it been autumn, game dishes would have been featured. The accent of the menu is always on fish, as exemplified by the likes of sea bream in a zesty lime sauce with spring onions, or perhaps moist and tender trout stuffed with fresh spinach.

Dragonerstrasse 30A. © 0511/622636. Reservations required. Main courses 16€–23€ ($26–$37); fixed-price menus 23€–36€ ($37–$58). AE, MC, V. Mon–Sat 6:30pm–2am. U-Bahn: U1 or U2 to Dragonerstrasse.

Clichy Restaurant 👫👫 CONTINENTAL/MEDITERRANEAN This haven of refined cuisine doesn't get the press that Landhaus Ammann enjoys, but it is the most consistently reliable dining choice in the city. For more than 2 decades, its guiding light, Ekkehard Reimann, has coddled his guests with fine cuisine backed up by a well-stocked cellar. A Hannover food critic recently wrote, "For the inexperienced gourmet, a visit here is unforgettable." We'd include experienced gourmets in that appraisal as well. Specials rely on the day's shopping, as Chef Reimann believes in using the best seasonal ingredients available. Year after year, his cooking lives up to a superb standard, and his dishes are marked by intense flavors and precise techniques.

Weissekreuzstrasse 31. ℂ 0511/312447. Reservations required. Main courses 22€–30€ ($35–$48). AE, MC. Mon–Fri noon–2:30pm; daily 6–11pm. Tram: 3 or 7.

Wichmann 𝒢 GERMAN/FRENCH   This family-owned, white-walled, shuttered inn, with its slate walks and carefully tended flower beds, is worth the trip. The garden serves as a pleasant setting for dining in the summer months. The place is an oasis of comfort. Cooking is German gutbürgerlich—wholesome and hearty. Try specialties such as fish terrine, rack of lamb, homemade noodles, and wine and cheese from all over Germany. The place lies 4km (2.4 miles) south of central Hannover in the satellite town of Hannover-Döhren. *Note:* The owners don't speak English.

Hildesheimer Strasse 230, at Hannover-Döhren. ℂ 0511/831671. Reservations required. Main courses 21€–33€ ($34–$53); fixed-price lunch 30€ ($48), dinner 65€ ($104). AE, MC, V. Daily noon–3pm and 6–11pm. Tram: 1 or 8.

MODERATE

Altdeutsche Bierstube GERMAN   With a decor that has changed little since its original construction around 1860, this old-fashioned *Bierstube* remains stable and solid, despite the monumental changes that have transformed the society around it. The unpretentious food is hearty, wholesome, and filling, with the regular fare augmented by seasonal specialties. Favorites include pork knuckles with sauerkraut, filet of beef, and mixed grills. Most dishes are priced at the lower end of the scale.

Köbelingerstrasse 1. ℂ 0511/344921. Reservations required. Main courses 10€–23€ ($16–$37); fixed-price menus 20€–22€ ($32–$35). AE, DC, MC, V. Mon–Fri 11:30am–3pm; Mon–Sat 6pm–1am. Closed holidays. U-Bahn: Lister Platz.

Steuerndieb *(Finds* INTERNATIONAL   In 1329, a stone-sided tower was erected about 1.5km (1 mile) east of central Hannover to guard the lumber produced in Eilenriede Forest. The tower's name, Steuerndieb, translates from the archaic German as "Stop, thieves!" Around 1850 a rustic restaurant was built on the site, and it has been known ever since for hearty and flavorful food. Many of the specialties are cooked over an open fire, and the restaurant offers a locally inspired menu that, unlike those of many other restaurants, features game year-round. Two popular dishes are venison with red cabbage, dumplings, and black-cherry sauce; and rabbit with black-pepper sauce and red cabbage.

The establishment also has a modern wing containing seven simple, white-walled rooms, each with a private bathroom, TV, telephone, and view overlooking the forest. Doubles cost 80€ ($128), including a buffet breakfast.

Steuerndieb 1. ℂ 0511/909960. Reservations not required. Main courses 14€–22€ ($22–$35); fixed-price menus 33€–55€ ($53–$88). AE, DC, MC, V. Mon–Sat 11am–3pm and 6–11pm; Sun 11am–3pm. Tram: 3 or 7.

INEXPENSIVE

Brauhaus Ernst August HANNOVERIAN   This is a beer lover's Valhalla, established both as a brewery and a restaurant 2 decades ago. It specializes in only one kind of brew, a Pils, with no preservatives added, priced at 3.20€ ($5.10) for a half-liter. At the on-site gift shop you can buy all sorts of items related to beer, including mugs and the evocative beer bottles with porcelain stoppers, which invading GIs in 1945 named "snap daddies." Old-fashioned Hannoverian specialties are featured, and everything is tasty and filling, including a goulash that's a meal in itself and a rich cream of potato soup. *Wursts* are the most popular items, although steaks, schnitzels, spare ribs, and chicken cutlets are also available. In spring, asparagus dishes dominate the menu. It's customary to precede your beer drinking or eating with a bolting shot of *Brauerschluck* (Brewer's Gulp), a lethal schnapps brewed on-site.

Schmiedstrasse 13. 𝄪 0511/365950. Reservations not required. Main courses 8€–18€ ($13–$29); snacks and Wursts 1.80€–8.50€ ($2.90–$14). V. Beer Sun–Thurs 8am–3am, Fri–Sat 8am–5am; warm food daily 11:30am–11pm.

EXPLORING HANNOVER

Marktkirche (Market Church), the Gothic brick basilica on Marktplatz, is one of Hannover's oldest structures, built in the mid–14th century. **Altes Rathaus (Old Town Hall),** facing the square, dates from 1425. It was badly damaged in the war but has been restored and now houses the civic archives.

Herrenhäuser Garten (Royal Gardens of Herrenhäusen) 𝄐𝄐 No matter where you go in Hannover, you won't be far from a park or garden. But make sure you don't miss this one, the only surviving example of Dutch/Low German early baroque–style gardening. Designers from France, the Netherlands, England, and Italy, as well as Germany, worked together to create this masterpiece of living art. **Grosse Garten,** from 1666, is the largest garden, consisting of a rectangle surrounded by a moat. Within the maze of walks and trees are examples of French baroque, rococo, and Low German rose and flower gardens. The Grosse Garten also contains one of the highest fountains in Europe, shooting jets of water 72m (236 ft.) into the air, and the world's only existing baroque hedge-theater (1692), where plays by Shakespeare, Molière, and Brecht are still performed, along with ballets and jazz concerts. The smaller 17th-century **Berggarten,** across Herrenhäuser Strasse from the Grosse Garten, is a botanical garden with houses containing rare orchids and other tropical flowers.

Herrenhäuser Strasse 4. 𝄪 0511/16844543. Admission 4€ ($6.40) adults, free for children 13 and under. Apr–Sept daily 8am–7pm; Oct–Mar daily 8am–4:30pm. Waterworks display May–Sept Mon–Fri 11am–noon and 3–5pm; Sat–Sun and holidays 11am–noon and 2–5pm. U-Bahn: Herrenhäuser Gärten.

Niedersächsisches Landesmuseum Hannover (Lower Saxony State Museum) 𝄐 *Kids* The Landesmuseum is one of the most important regional museums in Germany. There are exhibits on northern European biology and geology, ethno-medicine and ethno-botany, and on the history of Lower Saxony from the Paleolithic Age up to the Middle Ages. The aquarium shows a world of exotic fish, amphibians, and reptiles. In the Kindermuseum, children can learn about prehistoric times with activities like grinding corn or working stone tools.

The museum's art gallery contains treasures spanning 7 centuries. A highlight is Meister Bertram von Minden's *Passion Altar* (1390–1400). You'll also see paintings by Rembrandt, Van Dyck, and Rubens (his *Madonna*), as well as the *Four Times of Day* series by Caspar David Friedrich.

Willy-Brandt-Allee (near the Maschpark). 𝄪 0511/9807686. www.nlmh.de. Admission 4€ ($6.40) adults, 3€ ($4.80) students and children. Tues–Wed and Fri–Sun 10am–5pm; Thurs 10am–7pm. Tram: 1, 2, 4, 5, 6, 8, 11, 16, or 18. Bus: 131,132, or 267.

Rathaus The "new" Rathaus is a large structure, built between 1901 and 1913. An inclined elevator—the only one in Europe other than the elevator at the Eiffel Tower—takes visitors up to the 10m (33-ft.) dome. The building is attractive because of its location in the Maschpark, by a small lake. It's just a short distance from the extensive artificial Maschsee, frequented by Hannoverians for its beach, boats, and restaurants.

Trammplatz 2. © **0511/1680.** Elevator ride to dome 3€ ($4.80) adults, 2€ ($3.20) students and children. Apr–Oct Mon–Fri 9:30am–6:30pm; Sat–Sun 10am–6:30pm. Closed Nov–Mar. U-Bahn: Markthalle. Tram: 3, 7, or 9. Bus: 120.

Sprengel Museum ☆☆ Although this museum of modern art, one of the best in Germany, has been around since 1979, it is gaining increasing renown for its two dozen annual exhibitions, now among the most cutting edge in Europe. These temporary shows stand side by side with the museum's permanent collection, which includes some of the greatest names in modern art—Picasso, of course, but also Paul Klee, Max Ernst, Max Beckman, and the like. The museum is named for Dr. Bernhard Sprengel, who started the original collection with its array of French modern and expressionism.

Over the years the museum has expanded to include some of the most significant artists of the 20th century, and it also created one of the best departments of photography in Germany. In 1993, it acquired the Kurt Schwitters archives. He was a native son of Hannover and one of the leading Dadaists; in fact, the square on which the museum sits was named after him.

Kurt-Schwitters-Platz 2. © **0511/16843875.** www.sprengel-museum.de. Admission 7€ ($11) adults, 4€ ($6.40) students, free for ages 11 and under. Tues 10am–8pm; Wed–Sun 10am–6pm.

SHOPPING

The oldest and largest flea market in Germany, the **Flohmarkt,** sprawls across Am Hohen Ufer (U-Bahn: Markthalle) every Saturday from 7am to 4pm. Stalls are set up along the banks of the Leine River. The city is hardly confined to flea markets, however. Hannover is one of the most fashion-conscious cities of the country, sometimes called "the Milan of Germany." It is the home of stylish clothing, and Hannoverians are among the most fashionably dressed Germans.

Your first destination may be the glassed-over **Galerie Luise,** a multilevel shopping mall at the corner of Luisenstrasse and Rathenaustrasse (bus: 120), with upscale shops for clothing and home furnishings. **Terner,** Luisenstrasse 9 (© **0511/363931;** tram: 5) has designer-inspired clothing for men, women, and children.

HANNOVER AFTER DARK

Hannover Vorschau, a monthly newspaper devoted exclusively to the city's nightlife and cultural venues, is available at news kiosks and in the city's hotels.

THE PERFORMING ARTS The **Nieder Sächsische Stadtstheater Hannover GmbH,** Opernplatz 1 (© **0511/99991111;** U-Bahn: Kröpcke), built between 1845 and 1852, is the region's leading venue for ballet, concerts, and opera. Depending on the performance, tickets cost from 15€ to 60€ ($24–$96) each. Less formal, with popular as well as classical offerings, is the **N. D. R. Symphoniker,** Rudolf Benigsen Ufer 22 (© **0511/9880;** bus: 2 or 6), an ugly postwar building whose charm derives from what goes on inside. You can hear poetry readings, jazz and rock-'n'-roll concerts, and chamber orchestras. Tickets cost 15€ to 35€ ($24–$56).

BARS Many of Hannover's most appealing bars are Irish pubs. The biggest and best of the lot is **MacGowan's Irish Pub,** Bruderstrasse 4 (© **0511/14589;** U-Bahn: Steintor or Hauptbahnhof). It's open daily 5pm to 2am, and serves Guinness and Murphy's on tap, along with sandwiches, fish and chips, and Irish stew. When Irish music bands are booked, a cover ranging from 8€ to 10€ ($13–$16) is imposed.

DANCE CLUBS   The best place for mainstream dance is **Osho Disco,** Raschplatz 7L (© **0511/342217;** U-Bahn: Hauptbahnhof), a longtime survivor of the club scene. It plays funk, house, and other dance music. It's open 10pm to "whenever" Wednesday to Sunday. Cover is 2.50€ to 8€ ($4–$13). One of its leading competitors is **Palo Palo,** Raschplatz 8A (© **0511/331073;** U-Bahn: Hauptbahnhof), where house, funk, blues, reggae, and Motown play every night 9:30pm until dawn, for a cover of 5€ to 8€ ($8–$13).

LIVE MUSIC   An alternative venue, **Café Glocksee,** Glockseestrasse 35 (© **0511/ 1614712;** tram: 10), stages hard-core, punk, and techno shows. Thursday concerts start at 9pm. On Friday and Saturday, it's disco mania 11pm to 7am and again on Wednesday 6pm to 2am. The cover charge ranges from 3€ to 13€ ($4.80–$21).

GAY CLUBS   **Schwul Sau,** Schaufeldstrasse 30A (© **0511/7000525;** tram: 6), hosts discos, theater performances, and private parties, attended by a crowd of gay and straight arts-conscious patrons. It's open Tuesday, Wednesday, and Friday 8pm to 3am, Saturday 9pm to at least 7am, and Sunday 3pm to 2am. Cover is 8€ to 10€ ($13–$16) for parties or theater events, and 5€ ($8) for dancing. There's no cover Tuesday, Wednesday, or Sunday. A hip and happening dance spot, **Men's Factory,** Engelbosteler Damm 7 (© **0511/702487;** tram: 6), is open on Friday for a mixed dance night and Saturday for gay dance night. On Friday, the cover is 9.50€ ($15); Saturday, it's 8€ ($13).

A CASINO   The **Spielbank,** Österstrasse 40 (© **0511/980660;** U-Bahn: Kröpcke), has an impressive roster of blackjack, roulette, and slot machines. It's set within a modern building, with none of the Belle Epoque trappings or decorations you might have hoped for, and contains both a bar and a restaurant. Men are required to wear jackets and ties, and women are requested to dress appropriately. The casino is open daily 3pm to 3am. Admission costs 2.50€ ($4), and you must show your passport to enter (you must be 18 or older to enter and gamble).

13 Bremen ★/★

119km (74 miles) SW of Hamburg, 122km (76 miles) NW of Hannover

Bremen, Germany's oldest coastal city, is second only to Hamburg among German ports. As soon as you arrive at "this ancient town by the gray river," you see how closely Bremen is tied to the sea. The sights and smells of coffee, cacao, tropical fruit, lumber, and tobacco give the city an international flavor.

Bremen grew from a little fishing settlement on a sandy slope of a river. It was already a significant port when it was made an Episcopal see in 787. In the 11th century, under the progressive influence of Archbishop Adalbert, Bremen became known as the "Rome of the North." During the Middle Ages, it was one of the strongest members of the Hanseatic League, and in 1646 it became a free imperial city. It remains one of Europe's most important ports.

ESSENTIALS
GETTING THERE   **By Plane**   The **Bremen Flughafen** (© **0421/55950;** www.airport-bremen.de) lies only 3km (2 miles) southeast of the city center (take S-Bahn 5). It is used mainly as a commuter airport for flights within Germany.

Bremen

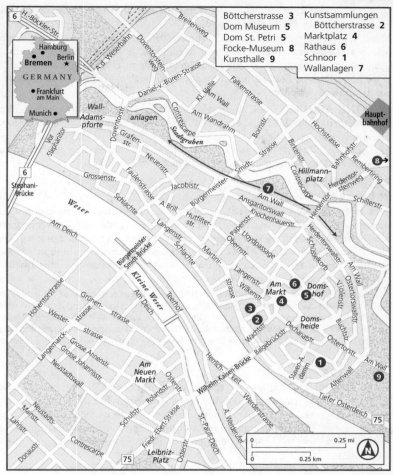

Böttcherstrasse **3**	Kunstsammlungen
Dom Museum **5**	Böttcherstrasse **2**
Dom St. Petri **5**	Marktplatz **4**
Focke-Museum **8**	Rathaus **6**
Kunsthalle **9**	Schnoor **1**
	Wallanlagen **7**

By Train Bremen has excellent rail connections with leading German cities. Its **Hauptbahnhof** lies on major rail lines, including Hamburg-Bremen-Osnabrück-Münster and Hannover-Bremen-Bremerhaven. Thirty trains arrive daily from Hamburg (trip time: 1 hr.), 35 trains from Hannover (trip time: 1 hr.), 13 trains from Berlin (trip time: 5 hr.), and 50 trains from Frankfurt (trip time: 4 hr. 15 min.). For information call © **01805/996633** (11861 in Germany; www.bahn.de).

By Bus Rail travel to Bremen is far more efficient, but the city does have some bus links to other towns. Call © **0421/5596333** for information. The bus station is in front of the railway station.

By Car Access by car is via the A7 Autobahn east and west and the A27 north and south.

VISITOR INFORMATION   Contact the **Bremer Touristik Zentrale GmbH,** Findorffstrasse 105 (© **01805/101030;** call is .14€ (20¢) per minute). Hours are Monday to Friday 9am to 6pm and Saturday 9am to 1pm. There's also a second branch at **Liebfrauenkircher Hof,** near Marktplatz. It is open Monday to Friday 10am to 6:30pm, Saturday and Sunday 10am to 4:30pm. There is yet another branch at the **Main Railway Station,** open Monday to Friday 9am to 7pm and Saturday and Sunday 9:30am to 6pm.

GETTING AROUND   For information about public transportation within Bremen, call © **01805/826826.** The cost is .12€ (19¢) per minute. A single ticket, good for one trip on the city's network of buses and trams, costs 2.15€ ($3.50) to most destinations. For 5.70€ ($9.10), two adults and up to five children may ride all day on the network. The meter on local taxis begins at 2.30€ ($3.70).

WHERE TO STAY
VERY EXPENSIVE
Park Hotel Bremen 🏅🏅🏅   This hotel is the most outstanding and charming in Bremen. It occupies an enviable site, in a park whose meandering lakes, exotic trees, and zoo are the pride of the city. It's also just a short ride from the center of town. The hotel's terra-cotta dome and evenly proportioned side wings were rebuilt in 1955 to emulate a turn-of-the-20th-century pleasure pavilion. Rooms are generally spacious and well appointed, with large windows overlooking the park.

Im Burgerpark, 28209 Bremen. © **0421/34080.** Fax 0421/3408602. www.park-hotel-bremen.de. 177 units. 255€–315€ ($408–$504) double; from 345€ ($552) junior suite; from 645€ ($1,032) suite. Rates include buffet breakfast. AE, DC, MC, V. Free parking in front of the hotel; 20€ ($32) in the garage. Tram: 5 or 6. Bus: 26. **Amenities:** 2 restaurants; bar; outdoor pool; fitness room; spa; Jacuzzi; sauna; free bicycles; salon; room service; babysitting; laundry service; dry cleaning; nonsmoking rooms; rooms for those w/limited mobility. *In room:* A/C (in some), TV, Wi-Fi, minibar, hair dryer, safe.

EXPENSIVE
Hilton Bremen 🏅🏅   At long last the city of Bremen has a Hilton. Even so, it's not as glamorous or as luxurious as the Park Hotel (see above), but the local Hilton is a modernized, tasteful bastion of comfort, ideal for both the commercial traveler and the vacationer. The Hilton stands on the historic Böttcherstrasse, near the Weser River, a block from the shopping district and within an easy walk of many of the major sights.

Bedrooms are spacious and decorated in cool, soothing pastels. Furnishings are in a stylish modern setting with tiled bathrooms with tub/shower combos, and accommodations range from standard to deluxe, with the junior suites being among the best units in town, complete with a separate working and seating area.

Böttcherstrasse 2, 28195 Bremen. © **0421/36960.** Fax 0421/3696960. www.hilton.com. 235 units. 155€–190€ ($248–$304) double; 225€–270€ ($360–$432) junior suite. AE, DC, MC, V. Parking 18€ ($29). Tram: 1, 2, or 3. **Amenities:** 2 restaurants; bar; indoor heated pool; gym; jogging track; sauna; business center; room service; babysitting; laundry service; dry cleaning; nonsmoking rooms; rooms for those w/limited mobility. *In room:* A/C, TV, Wi-Fi, minibar, hair dryer, safe.

Hotel Mercure Columbus   Mercure Columbus offers attractive and tasteful rooms, all with private bathrooms containing tub/shower combinations. An elegant recent renovation has set a higher standard for this hotel, putting it on the same footing as Munte am Stadtwald or Hotel zur Post (see both below).

Bahnhofsplatz 5–7, 28195 Bremen. ℂ **0421/30120.** Fax 0421/3012123. www.mercurehotel.de. 148 units. 99€–138€ ($158–$221) double; from 119€ ($190) suite. Rates include buffet breakfast. AE, DC, MC, V. Parking 12€ ($19). Tram: 1, 5, 6, or 10. **Amenities:** Restaurant; breakfast room; bar; lounge; fitness center; sauna; solarium; car rental; room service; massage; babysitting; laundry service; dry cleaning; nonsmoking rooms; 1 room for those w/limited mobility. *In room:* TV, Wi-Fi (in some), minibar, hair dryer.

MODERATE

Best Western Wellness Hotel zur Post ⟨R⟩   Hotel zur Post offers top-notch facilities and comfort, as well as Bremen's leading restaurant. Rooms are first-rate and slightly larger than average. All units contain tidily kept bathrooms with tub/shower combinations. Its proximity to the Hauptbahnhof makes it an ideal choice for train passengers.

Bahnhofsplatz 11, 28195 Bremen. ℂ **800/780-7234** in the U.S. and Canada, or 0421/30590. Fax 0421/3059591. www.bestwestern.com. 177 units. 128€–175€ ($205–$280) double; from 330€ ($528) suite. AE, DC, MC, V. Parking 12€ ($19). Tram: 1, 5, 6, or 10. **Amenities:** 3 restaurants; 2 bars; indoor heated pool; fitness center; spa; Jacuzzi; sauna; solarium; salon; room service; babysitting; laundry service; dry cleaning; nonsmoking rooms; 1 room for those w/limited mobility. *In room:* TV, dataport, minibar, coffeemaker, hair dryer, iron, safe.

Hotel Munte am Stadtwald ⟨R⟩ *Value*   You'll think you're in the country at this brick hotel because it fronts directly on one of Bremen's biggest parks. The handsome rooms range from medium to spacious; all contain neatly kept bathrooms with tub/shower combinations. The public rooms are inviting and comfortable, often filled with greenery to make them more homelike. The hotel is bright and friendly, with a helpful staff. For such a reasonably priced hotel, the swimming pool, sauna, steam bath, and solarium come as added luxuries.

Parkallee 299 (in the Burgerpark, about 2.5km/1½ miles from the center), 28213 Bremen. ℂ **0421/22020.** Fax 0421/2202609. www.hotel-munte.de. 134 units. 122€–170€ ($195–$272) double; 180€–246€ ($288–$394) suite. Rates include buffet breakfast. AE, DC, MC, V. Free outdoor parking; 8€ ($13) in garage. Bus: 22 or 23. **Amenities:** 2 restaurants; bar; lounge; indoor heated pool; sauna; solarium; steam room; room service; laundry service; dry cleaning; nonsmoking rooms. *In room:* TV, minibar, hair dryer.

Residence   Residence advertises itself as an Art Deco hotel. The elegant public areas have high ceilings with polished crisscrossed timbers and chandeliers. Rooms are comfortably furnished but small, all equipped with bathrooms containing tub/shower combinations.

Hohenlohestrasse 42, 28209 Bremen. ℂ **0421/348710.** Fax 0421/342322. www.hotelresidence.de. 30 units. 90€–145€ ($144–$232) double. Rates include buffet breakfast. AE, DC, MC, V. Free outdoor parking, 9€ ($14) in garage. Tram: 4, 5, 6, or 10. **Amenities:** Breakfast room; bar; sauna; solarium; room service; laundry service; dry cleaning; nonsmoking rooms. *In room:* TV, Wi-Fi, minibar, hair dryer.

INEXPENSIVE

Best Western Hotel Schaper-Siedenburg   Near the train station, this hotel is short on style but big on comfort and maintenance—all at an affordable price. It's in a commercial section of town with a lot of noise and traffic, but rooms on the inner side of the atrium are fairly peaceful. Rooms are in a rather minimalist style with modern furniture and small tiled bathrooms with showers or tubs. The marketplace and the historic sections of the Altstadt (old town) are an easy walk away.

Bahnhofstrasse 8, 28195 Bremen. ℂ **800/780-7234** in the U.S. and Canada, or 0421/30870. Fax 0421/308788. www.schaper-siedenburg.de. 88 units. 95€–120€ ($152–$192) double; 120€–140€ ($192–$224) apt. Rates include breakfast. AE, DC, MC, V. Parking 10€ ($16). **Amenities:** Restaurant; breakfast room; room service; laundry service; dry cleaning; nonsmoking rooms; 1 room for those w/limited mobility. *In room:* TV, minibar, coffeemaker, hair dryer, safe.

Hotel Buthman *Finds* This is an old but restored Bürger house on a tranquil side street within an easy walk of both the rail station and the Altstadt. For nearly half a century, the helpful Buthman family has operated this inn. Many frugally minded locals from the countryside, in Bremen on business or holiday, guard this as a cherished address kind to their pocketbooks. The rooms are cozy and midsize, each with traditional furnishings and a small bathroom with shower. We prefer no. 5 on the upper floor, with its high-ceilinged comfort and its snugness away from the bustle of the city.

Löningstrasse 29, 28195 Bremen. © **0421/326397.** Fax 0421/3398816. www.hotel-buthmann.de. 10 units. 75€–100€ ($120–$160) double. AE, DC, MC, V. Parking 6€ ($9.60). Bus: any to Town Center. **Amenities:** Breakfast room. *In room:* TV.

WHERE TO DINE

As a seaport, Bremen has developed its own style of cooking, concentrating much of its effort, naturally, on seafood from Scandinavia and the North Sea.

VERY EXPENSIVE

L'Orchidée im Bremer Ratskeller ★★★ FRENCH/MODERN GERMAN Year after year, this restaurant continues its run as Bremen's best and most lauded. It's run by the previously recommended Hotel zur Post, but enjoys a location at a different address in the old Bremer Rathaus. Veteran chefs watch over a well-trained kitchen crew, and the service is sophisticated and skillful. The dishes are simply delicious. Try the terrine of smoked eel and shrimp followed either by filet of turbot with lobster or breast of pigeon in a red-wine sauce. The desserts are made fresh daily, and the wine list is extensive.

Am Markt. © **0421/3347927.** Reservations required. Main courses 32€–38€ ($51–$61); fixed-price dinners 74€–95€ ($118–$152). AE, MC, V. Tues–Sat 6:30–10pm. Closed 2 weeks at Easter and in July and Aug. Tram: 1, 5, 6, or 10.

EXPENSIVE

Grashoff's Bistro ★★ *Finds* INTERNATIONAL This restaurant is well managed, charming, and concerned with quality and ambience. Its only real flaw is that the bistro caters to mobs of office workers and shoppers at lunchtime; dinner is a quieter affair. You'll get a distinct sense of the arts here and a few memories of Paris, thanks to dozens of framed pictures hung edge to edge across the cream-colored, bistro-inspired walls. Menu items include a succulent version of spaghetti with lobster; flank steak in a pepper sauce; an oft-changing roster of fresh fish; and desserts such as crème brûlée, fresh pastries, and tarts.

Contrescarpe 80. © **0421/14749.** Reservations recommended. Main courses 21€–26€ ($34–$42). AE, DC, MC, V. Mon–Fri noon–7:30pm; Sat noon–4pm. Tram: 4, 6, or 8.

Meierei im Burgerpark ★ CONTINENTAL This lovely restaurant, in the center of a city park, is managed by the Park Hotel (see above). Locals often combine a meal here with a promenade in the park. The restaurant occupies what was originally a local aristocrat's summerhouse, sheathed in lacy gingerbread and ringed with ornate verandas. It contains an assortment of dining rooms furnished in Hanseatic style. Typical, and very good, dishes include fresh fish, consommé with scallops and saffron, fried breast of duck filled with herbs, sautéed squab with forest mushroom risotto, and medallions of monkfish with orange butter–and–basil sauce.

Im Burgerpark. © **0421/3408619.** Reservations required. Main courses lunch 18€–21€ ($29–$34), dinner 22€–25€ ($35–$40); fixed-price lunch 22€–26€ ($35–$42). AE, DC, MC, V. Tues–Sun noon–2:30pm and 6–10pm. Tram: 8.

MODERATE

Ratskeller ✪ GERMAN/INTERNATIONAL This Ratskeller is one of Germany's most celebrated—and certainly one of the best. It's traditional for friends to gather in the evening over a good bottle of Mosel or Rhine wine (no beer is served). Appetizers include an assortment of smoked fish as well as creamy fish soup flavored with saffron; main courses often include fried pikeperch in a basil sauce and chicken ragout Bremen style (in a crayfish sauce with calves' sweetbreads and tongues, mushrooms, sausages, and a vegetable risotto). The outstanding wine list is one of the longest lists of German vintages in the world. Some of the decorative kegs have contained wine for nearly 200 years. There's also a less formal bistro, with a limited list of less expensive traditional dishes that include corned beef hash and simple platters of fresh fish.

Am Markt (in the Rathaus). ✆ 0421/321676. Reservations recommended. Restaurant main courses 17€–24€ ($27–$38); bistro main courses 10€–15€ ($16–$24). AE, DC, MC, V. Restaurant daily noon–2:30pm and 7–10:30pm; bistro daily 11am–midnight. Tram: 1, 3, 5, 24, or 25.

INEXPENSIVE

Alte Gilde GERMAN Alte Gilde is located in one of the most ornately decorated houses in Bremen. In spite of the new building surrounding it, the 17th-century structure, with its gilt gargoyles and sea serpents, clings tenaciously to the past. The restaurant is in the vaulted cellar. The chef prepares many fresh fish dishes, along with such specialties as braised calves' livers, breast of chicken with a curry-flavored cream sauce, and pan-fried filet of pork with mushrooms. An especially good dish is rump steak Provençale with paprika, onions, tomatoes, and fresh mushrooms.

Ansgaritorstrasse 24 (entrance on Obernstrasse). ✆ 0421/171712. Reservations recommended. Main courses 8€–16€ ($13–$26); set menus 19€–30€ ($30–$48). AE, DC, MC, V. Mon–Sat 8am–11pm. Tram: 2 or 3. Bus: 25, 26, or 27.

EXPLORING BREMEN
ORGANIZED TOURS

Bremen has both bus and walking tours of its historic sites. **Bus tours,** conducted in both German and English, depart from the Hauptbahnhof Tuesday to Sunday at 10:30am. They cost 17€ ($27) for adults and 11€ ($18) for children 11 and under. **Walking tours** depart every day at 2pm, last 2 hours, and cost 6.50€ ($10). From April 14 to October 6, there is an additional walking tour conducted on Saturday at 11am. The combination of a morning bus tour with an afternoon walking tour offers a broadly comprehensive overview of Bremen. Tickets should be reserved in advance, then picked up at the tourist office (see "Visitor Information," above).

The city also sponsors **boat trips** around the harbor. They depart from the jetty in front of the Martinikirche every day March to October. You can reach the jetty from Marktplatz by walking southwest along Böttcherstrasse for about 3 minutes. Tours depart at 11:45am, 1:30, and 3:15pm. The cost is 9€ ($14) for adults and 5€ ($8) for children 13 and under. For more information, call the tourist office (see above) or **Hal Över** (✆ 0421/338989).

THE TOP ATTRACTIONS

The main sights center on **Marktplatz** ✪✪, the "parlor" of Bremen life for more than 1,000 years. The 9m (30-ft.) statue (ca. 1404) of the city's protector, Roland, bears the "sword of justice" and a shield decorated with an imperial eagle. Local legend has it that as long as the statue stands in Marktplatz, Bremen will survive as a free city. During

World War II, when this area was hard hit by Allied bombs, extensive measures were taken to protect the statue.

Across the square from the Rathaus stands an example of a happy merger of Gothic and Renaissance architecture, the **Schötting,** a 16th-century guild hall used by the chamber of commerce. Somewhat in contrast to these ancient masterpieces is the **Haus der Bürgerschaft,** home of Bremen's Parliament. The 1966 structure was scaled down to fit in with its surroundings. Even though it's a maze of glass, concrete, and steel, it doesn't look entirely out of place.

Dom St. Petri (St. Peter's Cathedral) ★★

St. Peter's, set back from the square, towers majestically over all other buildings in the Altstadt. Originally designed in 1043 as the archbishop's church, it was rebuilt in the 13th, 16th, and 19th centuries. There's a 12th-century bronze baptismal font in one of the Romanesque crypts. In the Bleikeller (Lead Cellar), there's a bizarre collection of mummified corpses of workers who fell from the roof during the construction. Their bodies were discovered in 1695.

You can also visit the **Dom Museum** (✆ **0421/3650475**), which displays artifacts found during the large-scale restoration of the Dom, including medieval tombs and 15th-century wall paintings. Other exhibits include the remains of an early Romanesque building and a collection of historic altar implements.

Sandstrasse 10–12. ✆ **0421/365040.** www.stpetridom.de. Cathedral free; museum and tower 3€ ($4.80) adults, 1.70€ ($2.70) students, seniors, and children; lead cellar 1.40€ ($2.30) adults, 1€ ($1.60) children. Cathedral year-round Mon–Fri 10am–5pm; Sat 10am–2pm; Sun 2–5pm. Museum May–Oct Mon–Fri 10am–5pm, Sat 10am–1:30pm, Sun 2–5pm; Nov–Apr Mon–Fri 11am–4pm, Sat 10am–noon, Sun 2–5pm. Lead cellar and tower May–Oct Mon–Fri 10am–5pm, Sat 10am–noon (cellar Sun 10am–noon); closed Nov–Apr and holidays. Museum, cellar, and tower closed May 1, Oct 3, Dec 24–25 and 31, Good Friday. Bus: 24, 25, N3, or 56. Tram: 2, 3, 4, 5, 68, or N1.

Focke-Museum ★

This is one of the best regional museums in this area of Germany, and we particularly applaud the user-friendly way in which the various exhibitions are displayed. The glory days of Bremen as a maritime power in the Middle Ages and through the Renaissance era are evoked in the main gallery. For safekeeping, and because they were deteriorating in the weather, the original statues carved for the facade of the Rathaus are on display here, along with ecclesiastical art, secular art, and various objets d'art, much of it retrieved from town houses of the long-departed Bremen aristocracy. Lots of portraits of fat merchants also attest to the former prosperity of Bremen. In addition, you can wander back into history to the days of the conquering Romans. Although the Roman collection is the richest, there are artifacts from prehistoric times along with Saxon antiquities. Americans may be particularly interested in documents showing the massive transport of German emigrants to the U.S. on the steamers operated by the Norddeutscher Lloyd Shipline. In the park on the museum grounds is a typical thatched farmhouse once common to Lower Saxony.

Schwachhauser Heerstrasse 240. ✆ **0421/6996000.** www.focke-museum.de. Admission 4€ ($6.40) adults, 2€ ($3.20) children 6–18, free for children 5 and under. Tues 10am–9pm; Wed–Sun 10am–5pm. S. Bahn: Focke Museum. Tram: 4 or 5.

Kunsthalle ★

This art gallery has long been celebrated for its 19th- and 20th-century French and German art, including paintings by such masters as Rubens, Rembrandt, Tiepolo, Delacroix, Courbet, and Picasso.

In the summer of 2001, the museum made world headlines with the stunning announcement that a treasure trove of art, which had hung here for a century until its disappearance in 1945, had been returned. The story of the return sounds like a movie plot. The rare paintings, worth millions, included works by Rembrandt and Dürer, and had been stashed in a castle for safekeeping by Nazi soldiers. Soviet troops uncovered the works and handed them over to the KGB. In time they were shipped to the Baku Museum in Azerbaijan from which they were eventually stolen. The art later turned up in New York when a Japanese businessman and an Azerbaijani wrestler were arrested in a Brooklyn apartment where the stolen art was stashed.

The star of the purloined works is Dürer's drawing, *The Women's Bathhouse*, showing a voluptuous scene of six nude women. There's also a Rembrandt drawing, *Woman Standing with Raised Hands.*

All the stolen works can be seen on display on Tuesday. On any other day, you must call ahead for an appointment. However, even without these works, the Kunsthalle is worth a 2-hour visit.

Der Kunstverein in Bremen, Am Wall 207. (© 0421/329080. www.kunsthalle-bremen.de. Admission 5€ ($8) adults, 2.50€ ($4) students and children, 8€ ($13) family ticket. Tues 10am–6pm; Wed–Sun 10am–5pm. Bus: 1, 4, or 6. Tram: 2 or 3.

Rathaus 🎯 The 560-year-old Rathaus has seen several periods of transformation. Outside, at the west end, is one of the more recent additions: a sculpture of Bremen's visitors from the land of Grimm—the Bremen town musicians. The donkey, dog, cat, and cock are stacked, pyramid style, in a constant pose for ever-present cameras. The original Gothic foundations of the Rathaus remain basically unchanged, but the upper section reflects the 17th-century Weser-Renaissance style in the facade; the tall windows alternate with relief statues of Charlemagne and the electors of the Holy Roman Empire. The upper hall, part of the original structure, contains a beautifully carved early-17th-century oak staircase. A mural of *The Judgment of Solomon* (1537) reminds us that the hall was originally a council chamber and courtroom. Below the lower hall lies the historic Ratskeller (see above).

Marktplatz. (© 0421/3610. Admission 5€ ($8) adults, free for children 11 and under. For tours, inquire at the tourist office (see "Visitor Information," earlier in this section). Tours generally begin Mon–Sat at 11am, noon, 3, and 4pm, and Sun 11am and noon. Tram: 1, 2, 3, or 5. Bus: 30, 31, or 34.

MORE SIGHTS

One of Bremen's biggest attractions, **Böttcherstrasse** 🎯 (© 0421/338820; www.boettcherstrasse.de; tram: 4), running from Marktplatz to the Weser River, is a brick-paved reproduction of a medieval alley, complete with shops, restaurants, a museum, and galleries. The street was designed to present a picture of Bremen life, past and present. It was the brainchild of a wealthy Bremen merchant, Ludwig Roselius, and was dedicated in 1926 and rebuilt after World War II. Try to visit around noon, 3, or 6pm, when the Meissen bells strung between two gables set up a chorus of chimes for a full 15 minutes. Besides fine handicraft and pottery shops, the street also contains buildings of historical significance.

Kunstsammlungen Böttcherstrasse 🎯, Böttcherstrasse 6–10 (© 0421/3365077; tram: 4), consists of two adjoining buildings. The **Roselius House** is a 16th-century merchant's home with a collection of medieval objets d'art and furniture. Next door, the **Paula-Becker-Modersohn House** (© 0421/3365066) is dedicated to Bremen's outstanding painter (1876–1907) and contains many of her best works, including paintings, drawings, and prints. The two upper floors house works of the sculptor, painter, and architect Bernhard Hoetger (1874–1949). The museum is open Tuesday to Sunday 11am to 6pm. Admission is 5€ ($8) for adults and 3€ ($4.80) for children ages 7 to 16.

> ### *Moments* Rampart Promenade
>
> This walk, which the Germans call **Wallanlagen** ☘ (tram: 4, 5, or 6), is a peaceful green park where the ramparts protecting this Hanseatic city used to stand. Its gardens divide the Altstadt from the newer extensions of the city. The park is just a few short blocks from Marktplatz, along the canal (once Bremen's crown-shaped moat). Its major attraction is a still-functioning ancient windmill.

Schnoor (tram: 4, 5, or 6), the old quarter of Bremen, has undergone restoration. The cottages of this east-end district, once homes of simple fishermen, have been rented to artists and artisans in an effort to revive many old arts and crafts. Sightseers visit not only for the atmosphere but also for the unusual restaurants, shops, and art galleries.

SHOPPING

Bremen has thrived on business and commerce since it was founded. Today, you'll find lots of shopping options along two streets, **Obernstrasse** and **Sögestrasse,** as well as dozens of boutique-inspired gift shops in the **Schnoor.** The city's cutest stuffed teddy bears, available in all sizes and degrees of fuzziness, are sold at **Bärenhaus,** Stavendamm 9 (© **0421/3378419;** tram: 4, 5, or 6), for prices that begin at 14€ ($18) for your garden-variety bear and can go much, much higher. Next door is **Rapunzel,** Schnoor 17 (© **0421/326403**), an emporium for gift items, as well as T-shirts, souvenirs, books, and marionettes modeled after figures from the Brothers Grimm.

The best shop for women's fashions is **Roland Kleidung,** Sögestrasse 18–20 (© **0421/4788570;** tram: 4, 5, or 6), although the town's largest department store, **Karstadt,** Obernstrasse 1 (© **0421/30710;** tram: 4, 5, or 6), also stocks an impressive selection of less expensive garments. Antiques, including some brass fixtures salvaged from old ships, are sold at **Antikitäten B&M,** Fedelhörn 19 (© **0421/328282;** tram: 10).

Leder-Koopman, Georgstrasse 56 (© **0471/302829;** tram: 4, 5, or 6), has been making quality wallets, belts, bags, and other leather products for 100 years. Visit their shop to admire a level of craftsmanship that has become a rare commodity, and chances are you won't leave empty-handed. Bargain hunters swarm over the city's riverfront **flea markets.** The Weserflohmarkt is held at the Schlactel and Weser promenade every Saturday 10am to 4pm.

BREMEN AFTER DARK

Bremen nightlife offers a full range of activities. Many pubs and clubs, including those geared toward the gay community, are located in the **Ostertorsteinweg** district (tram: 10).

THE PERFORMING ARTS   Classical concerts, opera, and dance performances by visiting companies are held in the **Theater am Goetheplatz** complex, Am Goetheplatz 1–3 (© **0421/36530;** tram: 2 or 3). Call for a list of scheduled performers, ticket prices, and available seating. One of its stages, Schauspielhaus (© **0421/36530**), houses a theatrical company that occasionally performs in English. Tickets are 12€ to 27€ ($19–$43) during the September-to-June season. Opera and other musical performances are scheduled in the **Musiktheater,** Am Goetheplatz (© **0421/36530;**

tram: 2 or 3), where tickets are 12€ to 35€ ($19–$56). Experimental theater and modern dance can be found in the **Concordia,** Schwachhauser Heerstrasse 3 (© **0421/ 9868966;** tram: 1 or 4; bus: 25), where a seat costs 14€ to 25€ ($22–$40). To attend productions of the Bremen Shakespeare Company, head for the **Theater am Leibnitz-platz,** Friedrich-Ebert-Strasse at Leibnitzplatz (© **0421/500333;** tram: 6), where tickets are 11€ to 17€ ($18–$27).

BARS   An early-evening bar, **Achim's Beck Haus,** Carl-Ronning-Strasse 1 (© **0421/ 15555;** www.beckshaus.de; tram: 4, 5, or 6), is a gathering place for drinks and simple pub fare. It's open Monday to Thursday 10am to 11:30pm, Friday 10am to 1am, and Saturday 10am to 1:30am. An art-scene hangout with a large street-front terrace and a sometimes-rowdy clientele, **Litfass,** Ostertorsteinweg 22 (© **0421/703292;** tram: 2 or 3), has the longest bar in town. It serves breakfast, snacks, coffee, and beer. It's open Sunday to Thursday 10am to 2am, Friday and Saturday 10am to 4am.

A CASINO   Bremen's centrally located casino, **Casino Bremen,** Boettcher Strasse 3 (© **0421/329000;** www.westspiel.de; tram: 4, 6, or 8), contains roulette and blackjack tables. Admission is 2.50€ ($4), and a passport is required (you must be 18 years old to enter and gamble), as are jackets and ties for men. The casino is open daily 3pm to 3am.

DANCE CLUBS   One of Bremen's clubs-of-the-minute is **Stubu Club,** Rembertiring 21 (© **0421/326398**). Open only Thursday to Saturday from 9:30pm to 3am, it offers high-energy dance music on its street level and a somewhat calmer, more contemplative ambience upstairs. Expect doses of house, punk rock, and garage music, and clients ranging in age from 23 to 50. The cover charge runs from 4€ to 6€ ($6.40–$9.60). In winter, **Modernes,** Neustadtswall 28 (© **0421/505553;** tram: 1, 4, 5, 6 or 8), is a movie house during the week, with dancing and live music on the weekend. The rest of the year, bands usually play from 7 to 11pm; afterwards, it's a dance club. The cover charge is 8€ ($13) when there's just dancing; when there's live music, it's 15€ to 26€ ($24–$42). Twice monthly, there's a free show.

GAY CLUBS   Much of the gay nightlife in and around Bremen is diverted into the clubs of nearby Hamburg, but there are still a few good spots. A gay and lesbian bar of note, mostly for men, is **Rat und Tat,** Theodor-Körner-Strasse 1 (© **0421/700007;** tram: 10).

LIVE MUSIC   For music in a bar setting, check out the band lineup at **Aladdin's,** Hannoverschestrasse 11 (© **0421/435150;** bus: 40), which also houses a two-room dance club and a bar with rock-'n'-roll memorabilia. It's open Wednesday to Saturday 10pm to 7am; cover is 7€ to 12€ ($11–$19). **Moments,** Vordem Stein Tor 64 (© **0421/7926633;** tram: 2, 3, or 10), hosts live rhythm and blues as well as jazz for a crowd of loyal regulars. Cover is 5€ to 8.50€ ($8–$14). The place functions as a dance club on some nights; cover is then 7.50€ ($12). Moments is open Tuesday to Sunday from 8pm until dawn.

VARIETY   Popular with children and adults, the ambitious puppet theater **Theatrium,** Wüste Stätte 11 (© **0421/326813;** tram: 2 or 3), produces entertaining interpretations of books, plays, and movies, ranging from classical works to Woody Allen. Tickets cost 7.50€ ($12) for adults, 5€ ($8) for children. In the same building, **Theater im Schnoor** (© **0421/326054**) presents cabaret and underground theater productions. Tickets are 16€ to 22€ ($26–$35).

The German Emigration Center in Bremerhaven

In 2005, the first emigration museum opened in Europe, appropriately sited at Bremerhaven, where seven million people departed to the New World between 1830 and 1974. These various periods of mass exodus were not just to the United States but to Canada as well as South America and Australia. The **Deutsches Auswandererhaus (German Emigration Center)** lies at Columbusstrasse 65 (℗ **0471/902200;** www.dah-bremerhaven.de). Since its opening, many emigrants, or their descendants, have come here seeking their roots. One of the most moving exhibits is of mannequins depicting emigrants as they gathered to board the ship that will carry them into "the unknown." Motives for immigration included poverty, adventure, ambition, family quarrels, and, later, escape from the Nazis. Old photos reveal how the people lived in a self-contained village awaiting passage across the seas. Perhaps the most evocative of the exhibits are the old and battered suitcases in which the emigrants stuffed the few items they were taking from the Old World to the New. Admission is 11€ ($17) for adults, 6€ ($9.60) for children 4 to 14. Bremerhaven is a 50-minute drive north of Bremen. Hours are March to October daily 10am to 6pm, November to February daily 10am to 5pm.

---

14 Lüneburg ⫷★⫸★

124km (77 miles) NE of Hannover, 132km (82 miles) E of Bremen, 55km (34 miles) SE of Hamburg

Motorists driving south from Scandinavia through the Baltic port of Lübeck often find themselves on the Old Salt Road leading to the Hanseatic city of Lüneburg. This was the route over which the "white gold" of Lüneburg's salt mines was transported to the Scandinavian countries during the Middle Ages. Because of its heavy salt deposits, Lüneburg became a spa, which it still is today. In the **Kurpark** is a bathing house where visitors can take brine mud baths. In the **spa gardens,** there are indoor swimming pools, sauna baths, and tennis courts.

Lüneburg is also the ideal starting point for excursions into the **Lüneburg Heath,** especially beautiful in late summer when the heather is in bloom.

ESSENTIALS

GETTING THERE   By Train   The **Lüneburg Bahnhof** (℗ **01805/996633,** 11861 in Germany; www.bahn.de) lies on two major rail lines, the Hamburg-Hannover line and the Lüneburg-Lübeck-Kiel-Flensburg line, with frequent connections.

By Bus   Long-distance bus service into Lüneburg is provided by **KVG GmbH** (℗ **04131/405303**). The bus station is in front of the railway station.

By Car   Access is via Route 4 from Hamburg.

VISITOR INFORMATION   Lüneburg Tourist Information is in the Rathaus, Am Markt 1 (℗ **04131/2076620;** www.lueneburg.de). It's open Monday to Friday 9am to 6pm, Saturday and Sunday 9am to 4pm (closed Sat–Sun Dec–Feb).

WHERE TO STAY

Bremer Hof   The logo of this hotel is an illustration of the animal musicians of Bremen, who, with their noise, frightened away robbers. The facade looks like something out of the 16th century. Rooms are modern and sunny, but a bit small. All units have

The Lüneburg Heath 🐾

The Lüneburger Heide (Lüneburg Heath) is one of the major attractions of northern Germany. The heath covers nearly 775 sq. km (300 sq. miles) and includes many beautiful spots. The sandy soil is mainly covered with brush and heather, although there are a few oak and beech forests in the northern valleys. Toward late summer, the flowering heath turns from green to purple; August and September are the most beautiful months. The best way to approach the heath is via the old town of Lüneburg, the area's transportation hub.

You'll find dramatic, windswept, and bleakly evocative scenery in the **Naturschützpark Lüneburger Heide** 🐾🐾, a 260-sq.-km (101-sq.-mile) sanctuary for plants and wildlife. Its highest point is the Wilsederberg, a low-lying peak only 168m (551 ft.) above sea level, accessible via a network of footpaths from the hamlet of Wilsede. This reserve, in the center of the heath, is a peaceful, pastoral scene of shepherds, sheep, and undulating hills. Strict laws enforce the maintenance of the thatch-roofed houses and rural atmosphere. One of the park's most charming hamlets is Undeloh, which has a good hotel, the Heiderose, Gästehaus Heideschmiede, Wilseder Strasse 29 (© **04189/311**), renting doubles for 92€ to 98€ ($147–$157), including breakfast. Also, a number of villages—listed on only the most detailed of maps—post *Zimmer frei* (room for rent) signs. These accommodations may be on a heath farm or even a horse farm.

For information, contact Fremdenverkehrsverbund Lüneburger Heide e.V., Barkhausenstrasse 35, Lüneburg (© **04131/73730**), the park's administrative headquarters, which can furnish maps and information on horseback riding and cycling; it's open Monday to Friday 8am to 6pm. To reach the park from Lüneburg, drive 35km (22 miles) west, following the signs to Salzhausen. After you cross the bridge over the A7 Autobahn, follow the brown-and-white signs to the park. The tourist office (see above) compiles a list every summer of places where you can rent a bike.

bathrooms, some with showers and some with tub/shower combinations. A 400-year-old wine cellar is open on weekends.

Lünestrasse 12–13 (a 2-min. walk from Marktplatz), 21335 Lüneburg. © **04131/2240**. Fax 04131/224224. www.bremer-hof.de. 53 units. 93€–135€ ($149–$216) double. Rates include buffet breakfast. AE, DC, MC, V. Parking 5€ ($8). Bus: 3. **Amenities:** Restaurant; lounge; room service; laundry service; dry cleaning; nonsmoking rooms. *In room:* TV, hair dryer.

Hotel Bargenturm   This three-story hotel at the edge of Lüneburg's historic center is one of the most modern in town. Its concrete walls and large expanses of glass make no concessions to the antique architecture of other parts of the city. Rooms are decorated with a no-nonsense, comfortable modernity. All contain neatly kept bathrooms with tub/shower combinations. The staff is multilingual and efficient.

St. Lambertiplatz, 21335 Lüneburg. © **04131/7290**. Fax 04131/729499. www.hotel-bargenturm.de. 40 units. 119€–129€ ($190–$206) double; 149€–159€ ($238–$254) junior suite. DC, MC, V. Parking 7.50€ ($12). **Amenities:** Restaurant; bar; sauna; spa; room service; nonsmoking rooms. *In room:* TV, Wi-Fi, minibar, hair dryer.

Hotel Berggström ✦✦✦ One of the best hotels in northern Germany, this charming pocket of posh lies on the river. Instead of checking in, you may want to move in. Our favorite spot here is the terrace opening onto a view of the Märchentürm (fairy-tale tower), enjoying light Mediterranean dishes from the on-site Marina Café. Later you can retreat to the Piano Bar for entertainment and drinks. The hotel is convenient to all the attractions of town and lies only a 5-minute walk from the rail station.

Each of the spacious and well-furnished bedrooms comes with a state-of-the-art bathroom with both tub and shower. Furnishings are in a tasteful modern style with a range of antique reproductions.

Bei der lüner Mühle, 21335 Lüneburg. ✆ 04131/3080. Fax 04131/308499. www.bergstroem.de. 125 units. 136€–183€ ($218–$293) double; 213€ ($341) junior suite; 243€ ($389) suite. Children 15 and under sleep free in parent's room. AE, V. Parking 9€ ($14). **Amenities:** Restaurant; 2 bars; beer garden; indoor heated pool; gym; sauna; solarium; room service; laundry service; dry cleaning; nonsmoking rooms. *In room:* A/C, TV, Wi-Fi (in some), minibar, safe.

WHERE TO DINE

Ratskeller GERMAN/CONTINENTAL The Ratskeller serves satisfying but unspectacular meals in a town not known for its restaurants. The varied menu includes game and regional specialties, according to the season. You can always count on good home-style cooking in a pleasant setting, backed up by a fine wine list. Parts of the decor date from 1328.

Am Markt 1 (on the market sq.). ✆ 04131/31757. Reservations recommended. Main courses 8€–20€ ($13–$32). AE, MC, V. Thurs–Tues 11am–10pm. Closed Jan 6–20. Bus: 3.

Zum Heidkrug ✦✦✦ CONTINENTAL Set within a stone-sided antique building (ca. 1470) in Lüneburg's historic core, this is the best-recommended and most sought-after dining option in town. Within a contemporary dining room with vaguely medieval touches, you'll order from the most creative menu in town. Items are sumptuous and change frequently, according to the inspiration of owner/chef Michael Röhm. Expect dishes that include, for example, a medley of cheeses from small farms along the north coast of Germany; strips of roasted suckling pig with wild mushrooms; grilled monkfish with tahini and grilled zucchini with curried soup; or roasted saddle of lamb with tomatoes, white garlic crust, onion jam, and gnocchi. The restaurant maintains seven comfortably appointed bedrooms upstairs, each priced at 88€ to 110€ ($141–$176) for two occupants, with breakfast included.

Am Berge 5. ✆ 04131/24160. www.zumheidkrug.de. Reservations required. Main courses 22€–25€ ($35–$40); fixed-price menus 42€–91€ ($67–$146). AE, MC, V. Wed–Sat noon–2pm and 6–9:30pm.

EXPLORING LÜNEBURG

Although the buildings in this 1,000-year-old city are largely from its most prosperous period, the 15th and 16th centuries, a total of 7 centuries of architecture are represented. The **Rathaus** ✦✦, Am Markt 1, reached along Auf der Meere, is a perfect example of several trends in architecture and design. You enter through a Gothic doorway into a Renaissance hall. The Great Council Room is the building's most outstanding feature, with sculptures and bas-reliefs by Albert von Soest (1566–84). Daily guided tours are conducted all year at 10am, 11:30am, 1pm, 2:30pm, and 3:30pm. The cost is 3.50€ ($5.60) for adults and 2.50€ ($4) for students and children. For information, call ✆ 04131/309230.

To understand Lüneburg's role as "the Salt City," visit the **Deutsches Salzmuseum,** Sülfmeisterstrasse 1 (✆ 04131/45065). Inside, a series of exhibits explore life in the Middle Ages and the role of salt in the region's economy and culture. Admission is 5€

($8) for adults, 4€ ($6.40) for students and children, and 16€ ($26) for a family ticket. The museum is open May to September Monday to Friday 9am to 5pm, Saturday and Sunday 10am to 5pm; daily hours off season are 10am to 5pm. Tours are Monday to Friday 11am, 12:30pm, and 3pm, and Saturday and Sunday 11:30am and 3pm.

SHOPPING
The heath area is known for its craftspeople. Some of the best local arts and crafts are on sale at the tourist office (see above). The town's largest department store is **Karstadt,** Grosse Bäckerstrasse 31 (℃ **04131/3040**). The main shopping streets are **Bäckerstrasse** and **Grapengiesserstrasse,** both lying in pedestrian zones.

LÜNEBURG AFTER DARK
Students make this a rowdier place with a later nightlife than most other small towns. Bars are located along the river on **Am Stintmarkt.** The most popular place for drinking and dancing is **Garage,** Auf der Hude 72 (℃ **04131/35879**). DJs play varied styles of popular music on Friday and Saturday from 10pm to around 4am. It has a cover charge ranging from 6€ to 10€ ($9.60–$16).

Another important nightlife area is the **Schroederstrasse,** which is lined chock-ablock with bars and *Nacht-cafés* (night cafes) some of which provide live music. Locals like to duck in and out of as many bars as possible along this street during the course of an evening.

15 Celle ⭐⭐

45km (28 miles) NE of Hannover, 111km (69 miles) SE of Bremen, 117km (73 miles) S of Hamburg

The well-preserved town of Celle stands at the edge of a silent expanse of moorland, looking like something out of a picture book. Its ancient half-timbered houses were untouched by the war. Look for the wooden beams on the facades of the houses, which are often engraved with biblical quotations. Most of the houses date from the 16th and 17th centuries—the oldest was built in 1526—but they're in such good condition that they could have been constructed in the 1900s.

ESSENTIALS
GETTING THERE   By Train   Celle Hauptbahnhof is on the Hamburg-Hannover rail line, with frequent connections to major German cities. Forty trains arrive daily from Hannover (trip time: 20–30 min.), and the same number pull in from Hamburg (trip time: 1 hr., 10 min., to 1½ hr.). For information call ℃ **01805/996633** (11861 in Germany; www.bahn.de).

By Car   Access by car is via the A7 Autobahn north and south, or Route 214.

VISITOR INFORMATION   Contact the **Verkehrsverein,** Markt 14–16 (℃ **05141/1212;** www.region-celle.de), open October to April Monday to Friday 9 to 5pm, Saturday 10am to 1pm; May to September Monday to Friday 9am to 6pm, Saturday 10am to 4pm, and Sunday 11am to 2pm.

WHERE TO STAY
Fürstenhof Celle ⭐⭐   This hotel, quite sophisticated for such a provincial town, is by far the best in Celle. It's a small-scale 17th-century manor house flanked by timbered wings. A towering chestnut tree shades the brick courtyard in front of the salmon-colored mansion. We prefer the comfort and style of the older rooms in the

main house to the more modern rooms in an annex beyond the rear courtyard. Rooms range from medium to spacious, and all are equipped with bathrooms containing tub/shower combos.

Hannoverschestrasse 55, 29221 Celle (at the edge of town). ℂ **05141/2010.** Fax 05141/201120. www.fuerstenhof. de. 73 units. 185€–255€ ($296–$408) double; 250€–340€ ($400–$544) suite. AE, DC, MC, V. Parking 19€ ($30). Bus: 3, 5, or 10. **Amenities:** 3 restaurants; bar; indoor heated pool; sauna; salon; room service; massage; babysitting; laundry service; dry cleaning; nonsmoking rooms; rooms for those w/limited mobility. *In room:* TV, Wi-Fi (in some), minibar, hair dryer, safe.

Hotel Celler Hof ✪ *(Value* Celler Hof stands on the street where jousting tournaments were once held. The old-world 1890 architecture of the hotel and its neighboring timbered houses renders the interior furnishings incongruously modern, though they are quite pleasing. Rooms, ranging from medium to spacious, have neatly kept bathrooms with tub/shower combinations. Many have a view of the castle. No dinner is served.

Stechbahn 11, 29221 Celle. ℂ **05141/911960.** Fax 05141/9119644. www.cellerhof.de. 47 units. 105€ ($168) double. Rates include buffet breakfast. AE, DC, MC, V. Parking 13€ ($21). Bus: 3, 5, or 10. **Amenities:** Breakfast room; bar; lounge; fitness room; steam room; babysitting; laundry service; dry cleaning; nonsmoking rooms. *In room:* TV, Wi-Fi, minibar, hair dryer, iron.

Hotel Schifferkrug This is an old-time favorite. The brick-and-timber walls of this comfortable hotel have witnessed more than 3 centuries of innkeeping. The small-to medium-size rooms have lace curtains and eiderdowns. All units have neatly kept bathrooms containing tub/shower combos.

Speicherstrasse 9, 29221 Celle. ℂ **05141/374776.** Fax 05141/3747788. www.schifferkrug-celle.de. 12 units. 80€–120€ ($128–$192) double. AE, MC, V. Rates include buffet breakfast. Free parking. Bus: 3, 5, or 10. **Amenities:** Restaurant; bar; laundry service; dry cleaning. *In room:* TV, Wi-Fi (in some).

WHERE TO DINE

Historischer Ratskeller ✪ GERMAN Historischer Ratskeller is plusher than the typical beer hall and has better food. It occupies a historic site within the 14th-century walls of the town hall. Attentive waiters are constantly passing by, carrying silver platters heaped with spicy, flavorful German dishes, such as a carpaccio of salmon and sole flavored with fresh lemon and black pepper, or an especially good filet of pork tenderloin with fresh asparagus and other vegetables. Another specialty is a tender Argentinian roast beef with fresh mushrooms and grilled tomatoes.

Markt 14. ℂ **05141/29099.** Reservations recommended. Main courses 10€–20€ ($16–$32); fixed-price menus 20€–29€ ($32–$46). AE, MC, V. Mon–Sat 11:30am–2:30pm and 5:30pm–midnight; Sun 11:30am–2:30pm. Bus: 3, 5, or 10.

Restaurant Endtenfang ✪✪✪ FRENCH/GERMAN Celle's most prestigious and stylish restaurant occupies an appealingly old-fashioned dining room on the street level of the Fürstenhof Celle (see above). Service is efficient, helpful, and friendly. The menu focuses on game dishes, including two succulent versions of duck. (The word *Endtenfang*, from an old regional dialect, means "the hunting reserve for duck shooting.") Traditional accompaniments include a pepper-cream sauce, cabbage roulade, a potato-and-pear gratin, and fresh mushrooms, along with slices of red apples. Other main courses include halibut sautéed with fresh coriander and veal liver cooked with baby onions. The small dumplings that accompany many dishes are light and feathery.

In the Fürstenhof Celle, Hannoverschestrasse 55. ℂ **05141/2010.** Reservations recommended. Main courses 22€–48€ ($35–$77). AE, DC, MC, V. Tues–Sat noon–2pm and 6:30–10pm.

Ringhotel Celler Tor GERMAN/INTERNATIONAL   The Celler Tor is a cliché of German charm, with its gabled red-tile roof and banks of geraniums. When local residents want to celebrate a special occasion, they head here, knowing they can get a great selection of gutbürgerlich fare—that is, food fondly remembered from childhood. In season, that means wild game, such as ragout of stag with mushrooms. But the chefs also excel in preparing more modern dishes, including medallions of anglerfish in an herby crust with a paprika mousse and wild rice. Another tasty dish is the filet of roast salmon with an orange-butter sauce. We'd also recommend the pork steak with fresh mushrooms in a cream sauce, or the medallions of veal with shrimp and a lime-laced pepper sauce.

The Celler Tor also rents 73 good rooms. A double costs 142€ to 162€ ($227–$259), including buffet breakfast; eight suites are also available, at 182€ ($291) each. Facilities include two indoor heated pools, a workout room, a sauna, a solarium, and massage facilities.

Scheuener Strasse 2 (about 3km/2 miles outside town). © 05141/5900. Fax 05141/590490. www.celler-tor.de. Reservations recommended. Main courses 16€–24€ ($26–$38); fixed-price menus 32€–42€ ($51–$67). AE, DC, MC, V. Daily noon–3pm and 6–10pm. Bus: 8.

EXPLORING CELLE

Bomann Museum   For a picture of 16th- to 20th-century everyday life in Celle and the surrounding countryside, visit this fine regional museum. Included is a complete 16th-century farmhouse, as well as rooms from old cottages, period costumes, and Hannoverian uniforms from 1803 to 1866. In the portrait gallery of the Brunswick-Lüneburg dukes, you can see pictures of the electors, later kings of England and Hannover.

Schlossplatz 7. © 05141/12372. www.bomann-museum.de. Admission 5€ ($8) adults, 3€ ($4.80) children, 8€ ($13) family ticket. Tues–Sun 10am–5pm. Bus: 2, 3, or 4.

Herzogschloss   One of the landmarks of the town, the Herzogschloss is a square Renaissance castle, with a tower at each corner, surrounded by a moat. It once was the palace of the dukes of Brunswick and Lüneburg. The palace's bizarre 16th-century chapel was designed by Martin de Vos, with galleries and elaborate ornamentation. The pride of the castle, and of the town, is its baroque theater, the oldest still in regular use today—it dates from 1674. Call the tourist office (see "Visitor Information," above) to arrange for a tour given by an English-speaking guide.

West of the Altstadt. © 05141/12373. Admission 5€ ($8) adults, 3€ ($4.80) children. Tours Apr–Oct Tues–Sun on the hour from noon–4pm; Nov–Mar Tues–Sun 11am and 3pm. Bus: 2, 3, or 4.

16 Goslar ✮✮

90km (56 miles) SE of Hannover, 43km (27 miles) S of Braunschweig, 60km (37 miles) SE of Hildesheim

In spite of Goslar's growth, the old portion of the town looks just as it did hundreds of years ago. This ancient Hanseatic and imperial town at the foot of the Harz Mountains owed its early prosperity to the Harz silver mines, which were worked as early as 968. The 600-year-old streets are still in use today, as are the carved, half-timbered houses.

For hikers and other outdoor enthusiasts, Goslar is a good starting point for day trips and excursions into the **Harz Mountains** ✮✮, where some of the area's best ski resorts and several spas are found. Bus tours into the Harz Mountains can be booked at the tourist office (see below).

The legends and folklore associated with the Harz Mountains are perhaps more intriguing than the mountains themselves. Walpurgis Eve (the famous Witches' Sabbath) is still celebrated each year on the night of April 30. The mountain on which the witches supposedly danced in olden times was the **Brocken,** whose granite top has been flattened by erosion. The area around the Brocken is now a national park.

ESSENTIALS
GETTING THERE   By Plane   The nearest major airport is in Hannover.

By Train   The **Goslar Bahnhof** is on the Hannover-Hildesheim-Goslar-Bad Harzburg rail line, with frequent connections. It takes about 1½ hours to get to Goslar from Hannover. For information, call ✆ **01805/996633** (11861 in Germany; www.bahn.de).

By Bus   Long-distance bus service to Goslar is available through **Reisebüro Bokelmann,** Marktkirchhof 1 (✆ **05321/381990**). Regional bus service to all parts of the city and nearby towns is offered by **Regionalbus Braunschweig GmbH,** Hildesheimer Strasse 53 (✆ **05321/34310;** www.rbb-bus.de).

By Car   Access is via the A7 Autobahn north and south; exit at either Seesen or Rüden.

VISITOR INFORMATION   Contact the **Kur- und Fremdenverkehrs-Gesellschaft,** Markt 7 (✆ **05321/78060**), open November to April Monday to Friday 9:15am to 5pm and Saturday 9:30am to 2pm; and May to October Monday to Friday 9:15am to 6pm, Saturday 9:30am to 4pm, and Sunday 9:30am to 2pm.

WHERE TO STAY
Goldene Krone *(Value)*   This 300-year-old village inn has enjoyed a long history of providing a good and decent shelter for some of the most illustrious visitors to Goslar. Under new management, which took over in the late spring of 2007, the tradition continues. If you enjoy local color, this is a real find. Rooms are small and simple but homelike and clean, with bathrooms containing tub/shower combos; they're a great value for the price.

Breitestrasse 46 (near the Breites Tor), 38640 Goslar. ✆ 05321/34490. Fax 05321/344950. www.goldene-krone-goslar.de. 17 units. 85€–120€ ($136–$192) double. Rates include buffet breakfast. AE, DC, MC, V. Free parking. Bus: A or B. **Amenities:** Bar/lounge; laundry service; dry cleaning. *In room:* TV, hair dryer.

Hotel Der Achtermann *(★)*   This hotel is a bustling but somewhat dowdy government-rated three-star hotel whose extras rival those of four-star hotels nearby. Just after World War II, one of the round-sided 500-year-old watchtowers in the city's wraparound fortifications was enlarged with a white-sided extension, thereby creating an intriguing but rather cumbersome-looking amalgam of old and new architecture. Rooms are well furnished and comfortable, except for a few that are a bit too small (most, however, are spacious).

Rosentorstrasse 20, 38640 Goslar. ✆ 05321/70000. Fax 05321/7000999. www.der-achtermann.de. 152 units. 99€–149€ ($158–$238) double. Rates include buffet breakfast. AE, DC, MC, V. **Amenities:** Restaurant; breakfast room; bar; lounge; indoor heated pool; exercise room; spa; Jacuzzi; sauna; solarium; room service; massage; laundry service; dry cleaning; nonsmoking rooms; 1 room for those w/limited mobility. *In room:* TV, Wi-Fi, minibar, hair dryer.

Kaiserworth *(★★)*   The Kaiserworth is a big, old-fashioned hotel, right in the heart of town. The building dates from 1494 and is itself a sightseeing attraction. The exterior is Gothic, with an arched arcade across the front, topped by a turreted oriel window facing Marktplatz. The large rooms are designed for comfort; the corner rooms are big enough to be suites. All rooms contain tub/shower combos. Room nos. 102, 106, 110, 202, and 206 have the best views of the nearby Glockenspiel performance outside.

Markt 3, 38640 Goslar. ⓒ 05321/7090. Fax 05321/709345. www.kaiserworth.de. 66 units. 122€–182€ ($195–$291) double; 207€ ($331) suite. Rates include buffet breakfast. AE, DC, MC, V. Parking 8€ ($13). Bus: A or B. **Amenities:** Restaurant; bar; room service; laundry service; dry cleaning; nonsmoking rooms. *In room:* TV, hair dryer.

WHERE TO DINE

Die Worth ⚔ NORTH GERMAN   This is the most rustic and also the most attractive dining room in Goslar. The restaurant is in a Gothic stone crypt with vaulted ceiling and arches, stained-glass windows, wrought-iron lanterns, and trestle tables. The food is good and the portions are hearty, although all the recipes are very familiar. In season, roast game is featured with wild mushrooms, mashed apples, and berries. Rump steak is always an excellent choice, as is the more unusual *Harzer Blaubeer Schmandschnitzel*, a local recipe that combines pork schnitzel with blueberry-flavored cream sauce.

In the Kaiserworth, Markt 3. ⓒ 05321/7090. www.kaiserworth.de. Main courses 13€–28€ ($21–$45). AE, DC, MC, V. Daily breakfast 6–11am, lunch 11:30am–2pm, coffee and cake 2:30–5pm, dinner 5:30–11pm. Bus: A or B.

EXPLORING GOSLAR

To explore this 1,000-year-old town, park your car, put on a pair of comfortable shoes, and set out on foot through the **Altstadt** ⚔⚔⚔, which has more than 1,000 half-timbered buildings from the 15th to the 18th centuries. The impressive **Rathaus** ⚔ was built in 1450. The portico, with Gothic cross-vaulting, opening on to the Marktplatz, was used by merchants for centuries. Above this is the citizens' meeting hall and the councilmen's meeting chamber, lavishly decorated in the early 1300s with a cycle of 55 paintings depicting biblical and heathen iconography and believed to incorporate the zinc miners returning home from the Rammelsberg mines.

Marktplatz ⚔, in front of the Rathaus, was for a long time the town's hub of activity. In the center of the large square is a 13th-century fountain with two bronze basins and the German imperial eagle at the top. Many visitors think seeing the **Glockenspiel** perform is the highlight of their visit. Every day at noon, 3pm, and 6pm (there's a smaller version of the spectacle at 9am), a procession of mechanized miners, representing the silver trade of long ago, traipses out of the innards of the clock tower.

The churches of Goslar provide a look into the architectural history of the area. Many of the oldest—five had already been built by 1200—have been expanded and altered from their original Romanesque style to their current Gothic appearance. The Romanesque **Marktkirche,** just behind the Rathaus, has 700-year-old stained-glass windows and a 16th-century bronze baptismal font. From Marktplatz, take Rosentorstrasse north to reach the 11th-century **Jakobikirche,** later transformed into a Gothic masterpiece, complete with baroque altars. The church contains a *Pietà* by Hans Witten (1520). Farther down the street, the **Neuwerkkirche,** in a garden, has retained its purely Romanesque basilica, and its well-preserved sanctuary contains a richly decorated choir and stucco reliefs. It was originally constructed as a Cistercian convent in the late 1100s.

The 12th-century **Frankenberg Kirche,** on Bergstrasse, was completely remodeled in the 1700s. Over the elaborate baroque pulpit and altars hangs the intricately carved Nun's Choir Gallery, bedecked with gilded saints and symbols.

Finds Into the Depths of an Ancient Mine

Just outside Goslar, about 1.5km (1 mile) south of the town center (follow the signs), you can explore an ancient mine. As early as the 3rd century A.D., lead, zinc, copper, silver, tin, and a little gold were being mined here. The **Weltkulturerbe Rammelsberg,** Bergtal 19 (© 05321/7500; www.rammelsberg.de), conducts guided tours at hourly intervals, on foot or on a small underground train. The museum is open daily 9am to 6pm (closed Dec 24 and 31). Walking tours cost 11€ ($18) for adults and 6.50€ ($10) for children. Prices include a ride on the underground train. For more information, call either the museum or the tourist office in Goslar (© 05321/78060).

One of the reminders that Goslar was once a free imperial and Hanseatic city is the **Breites Tor (Broad Gate),** a three-towered town gate with walls up to 4m (13 ft.) thick. From here, you can follow the old town fortifications to the **Kaiserpfalz,** Kaiserbleek 6 (© **05321/3119693**), a Romanesque palace that was the ruling seat of the emperors in the 11th and 12th centuries. You can view the 19th-century murals that cover its walls and visit the Ulrichskapelle, where the heart of Heinrich III was placed inside a large sarcophagus. The site is open April to October daily 10am to 5pm, and November to March daily 10am to 4pm. Admission is 4.50€ ($7.20) for adults and 2.50€ ($4) for children.

For a quick overview of Goslar's history, visit the **Goslarer Museum,** at the corner of Abzuchstrasse and Königstrasse 1 (© **05321/43394**), which has displays of the architecture of the early town and several relics of the past. The museum also contains a large geological collection from the Harz Mountains. It's open April to October Tuesday to Sunday 10am to 5pm, and November to March Tuesday to Sunday 10am to 4pm. Admission is 3€ ($4.80) for adults and 1.50€ ($2.40) for children.

17 Göttingen

132km (82 miles) S of Hannover, 47km (29 miles) NE of Kassel, 109km (68 miles) SW of Braunschweig

Heinrich Heine described the Gothic town of Göttingen as "famed for its sausages and university." The latter is one of the oldest and most respected in Germany and, in time, Göttingen became the most popular university town in Europe. The university was established in 1737 by George II, king of England and elector of Hannover.

Medieval romanticism and lively student life make Göttingen worth a day's visit. By making a slight detour, you can explore the town before dipping into the fairy-tale country of the upper Weser Valley. Göttingen is halfway between Bonn and Berlin.

ESSENTIALS

GETTING THERE   By Train   Göttingen has frequent daily rail connections from Munich (trip time: 6 hr.), Frankfurt (2½ hr.), and Hannover (1 hr.). It lies on the major Kassel-Bebra-Göttingen-Hannover line, with frequent connections in all directions. For information, call © **01805/996633** (11861 in Germany; www.bahn.de).

By Bus   Regional bus service to other parts of Lower Saxony is offered by **Regionalbus Braunschweig GmbH** (© **0551/19449;** www.rbb-bus.de).

By Car   Access is via the A7 Autobahn, which runs north to Hannover and Hamburg.

VISITOR INFORMATION Contact **Tourist-Information,** Altes Rathaus, Markt 9 ((C) **0551/499800;** www.goettingen.de), open November to March Monday to Friday 9:30am to 6pm, Saturday 10am to 6pm; April to October hours are Monday to Friday 9:30am to 6pm, Saturday 10am to 6pm, and Sunday 10am to 4pm.

GETTING AROUND A network of buses runs throughout the city daily from 6am to around 10:30pm. Their main junction point is at the corner of the Judenstrasse and Friedrichstrasse, at the edge of the Altstadt. Fare is 1.80€ ($2.90), with a four-ticket package priced at 5.90€ ($9.50). The tourist office (see above) sells a **Go Card** allowing free transfer on all municipal buses and reduced admission to a few tourist sights, costing 5€ ($8) for 1 day or 12€ ($19) for 3 days.

WHERE TO STAY

Central Hotel *(Finds* Although this quiet hotel on a pedestrian walkway is centrally located, its best feature is the imaginative care the designers have used to decorate the rooms. For example, one is flamboyantly wallpapered and curtained in vivid yellow-and-white tones, and another appears to be covered in pink silk. Each unit comes with a small, tiled bathroom with shower.

Judenstrasse 12 (near the university), 37073 Göttingen. (C) **0551/57157.** Fax 0551/57105. www.hotel-central.com. 32 units. 80€–150€ ($128–$240) double; from 150€ ($240) suite. Rates include buffet breakfast. AE, DC, MC, V. Parking 8€ ($13). Bus: 4, 8, 10, 11, or 14. **Amenities:** Breakfast room; lounge; indoor heated pool; Jacuzzi; nonsmoking rooms. *In room:* TV (in some rooms).

Eden-Hotel *(* The centrally located Eden-Hotel is the best choice in town after Gebhards (see below). The comfortable rooms have more amenities than most in this price range, and the private bathrooms come with tubs or showers. Both business travelers and vacationers appreciate the health club and the pool. Even if you're not a guest you may want to check out the on-site Italian restaurant **La Locanda,** with main courses costing 8€ to 25€ ($13–$40). In addition, top-rate German and international dishes are served at **Pampel-Muse,** where main courses range from 10€ to 25€ ($16–$40).

Reinhauser Landstrasse 22A, 37083 Göttingen (near the new Rathaus). (C) **0551/507200.** Fax 0551/5072111. www.eden-hotel.de. 100 units. 94€–228€ ($150–$365) double; 107€–268€ ($171–$429) triple. Rates include buffet breakfast. AE, DC, MC, V. Free parking. Bus: 4, 8, or 10. **Amenities:** 2 restaurants; indoor heated pool; sauna; solarium; room service; babysitting; laundry service; dry cleaning; nonsmoking rooms. *In room:* TV, Wi-Fi, minibar, hair dryer, trouser press, safe.

Romantik Hotel Gebhards *(** Gebhards is the best hotel in town. It's housed in a grand building that evokes a Tuscan villa, with a modern balconied annex built onto the back. The renovated interior offers high-ceilinged public areas and a pleasant bar. Rooms are well designed and furnished. The cheapest double has a toilet and shower; the most expensive is an apartment with a complete private bathroom with a tub/shower combo.

Goethe-Allee 22–23 (in front of the Bahnhof), 37073 Göttingen. (C) **0551/49680.** Fax 0551/4968110. www.gebhards hotel.de. 61 units. 135€–180€ ($216–$288) double; 210€–250€ ($336–$400) suite. Rates include buffet breakfast. AE, DC, MC, V. Free parking. Bus: 4, 8, 10, 11, or 14. **Amenities:** Restaurant; bar; Jacuzzi; sauna; room service; laundry service; dry cleaning; nonsmoking rooms. *In room:* TV, minibar, hair dryer.

WHERE TO DINE

Ratskeller *(* NORTH GERMAN This 600-year-old restaurant lies in the historic cellar of the Altes Rathaus. This is the best place to eat in town (faint praise, as Göttingen is not known for its restaurants) and the menu is varied and extensive. The chef is known for his *Tafelspitz* (boiled beef). Other specialties include *Alte Platte des Deutsch Landwirt* (Old German Farmer's Plate, consisting of chicken breast and pork steak with fried potatoes and roast onions) or fresh trout *au bleu* with parsley potatoes.

Markt 9. © 0551/56433. Reservations recommended. Main courses 11€–18€ ($18–$29). AE, DC, MC, V. Daily 11:30am–midnight. Closed Christmas Eve. Bus: 4, 8, 10, 11, or 14.

Zum Schwarzen Bären NORTH GERMAN   This fine restaurant is housed in a black-and-white timbered building (ca. 1500) that still has the original stained-glass leaded windows. Inside, the ambience is tavern style, with a ceramic stove in the corner and dining rooms with intimate booths. The innkeeper recommends (and we agree) the brook trout from the Harz Mountains or *Bärenpfanne* (various filets with *Spätzle*).

Kurzestrasse 12. © 0551/58284. Reservations required. Main courses 12€–24€ ($19–$38); set lunch 12€–15€ ($19–$24), dinner 15€–25€ ($24–$40). AE, MC, V. Tues–Sun noon–2pm; daily 6–10pm. Bus: 4, 8, 10, 11, or 14.

EXPLORING GÖTTINGEN

In the center of Göttingen, you can wander down narrow streets, looking at wide-eaved, half-timbered houses. Many of the facades are carved and painted, and some bear marble plaques noting the famous people who lived inside, such as the more than 40 Nobel Prize winners who temporarily made their home here.

Altes Rathaus (bus: 4, 8, 10, 11, or 14) was originally built for trade purposes around 1270, but it wasn't completed until 1443. Its highlights are the open arcade, the Gothic heating system, and the Great Hall, in which the people of Göttingen once received princes and dignitaries, held courts of law, and gave feasts. **Marktplatz,** in front of the Town Hall, is the most interesting section of Göttingen. Here, since 1910, stands the "most-kissed girl in the world," the smiling statue of the **Ganseliesel** on the market fountain. By tradition, every student who attains a degree must plant a kiss on the lips of the little goose-girl.

Stadtisches Museum, Ritterplan 7–8 (© 0551/4002845; bus: 3, 8, or 9), chronicles the history and culture of southern Lower Saxony. The most interesting exhibits are in the Göttingen history wing on the second floor. Surprisingly, the museum takes an uncompromising look at the town's Nazi past—most German towns tend to downplay it. Everything is here, from *Hitlerjugend* memorabilia to pages ripped from the local Nazi-run newspaper. The museum is open Tuesday to Friday 10am to 5pm and Saturday and Sunday 11am to 5pm. Admission is 2€ ($3.20) for adults and 1€ ($1.60) for children.

SHOPPING

The commercial heart of town is **Wenderstrasse** and **Grönestrasse,** both of which are pedestrian malls during most of the shopping day. Here, you'll find an appealing roster of cafes and delicatessens selling sausages and cakes, as well as purveyors of the German-style good life. If you want souvenirs, the local tourist office (see above) sells T-shirts, cigarette lighters, beer mugs, and posters. Antiques are found at **Bohm,** Barfusserstrasse 12 (© 0551/4886988). For the works of local and international painters and sculptors, try **Galerie Apex,** Burgstrasse 46 (© 0551/46886).

GÖTTINGEN AFTER DARK

Pick up a copy of *Universitätsstadt Göttingen Informationsheft* for a complete rundown of entertainment listings.

THE PERFORMING ARTS   The local symphony orchestra and boys choir are very active, and an annual Handel music festival is held in late May or early June.

Information on schedules, venues, and tickets is available by calling ℂ **0551/56700** or by contacting the tourist office (above). Tickets are 12€ to 133€ ($19–$213).

For 100 years, the **Deutsches Theater,** Theaterplatz 11 (ℂ **0551/49690**), has been staging classical and contemporary drama. Its counterpart, the **Junges Theater,** Hospitalstrasse 6 (ℂ **0551/495015**), has produced experimental works for 40 years. Performances of both are held Tuesday to Sunday, with tickets costing 10€ to 15€ ($16–$24) for adults and 7.50€ to 11€ ($12–$18) for students. The box office is open Monday to Saturday 11am to 1pm and 6 to 8:30pm.

BARS   Ratskeller (see above) has already been recommended as the place to dine in this university center. Its beer cellar is also the most evocative spot to have a beer, or many beers if you like to drink as the locals do in this 600-year-old establishment. More half-liters are consumed here than at any other place in town. As you lift a mug, imagine that you're standing in the footsteps of previous patrons such as Otto von Bismarck, the Brothers Grimm (they were former faculty members at the university), or, more ominously, Werner Heisenberg, head of the German A-bomb project. One of the more offbeat social centers is **KAZ (Kommunikations Aktions-Zentrum),** Hospitalstrasse 6 (ℂ **0551/53062**), where everyone from seniors to anarchists meet for drinks in one of the two on-premises pubs. One also serves traditional German cuisine; the other offers sandwiches. Within the complex, political forums, local discussion groups, and cultural associations meet regularly. Opening hours change with the seasons and the scheduling of volunteers and group discussion leaders, but in most cases, the center is open Monday to Thursday noon to 2am, Friday noon to 4am, and Saturday 11am to 1am.

LIVE MUSIC   Performance jazz is featured 1 night a week (exact night varies—call for details) at the excellent **Blue Note,** Wilhelmsplatz 3 (ℂ **0551/46907**); on other nights, musicians explore blues, salsa, African, reggae, and other Caribbean styles. It's open Sunday to Thursday 10pm to 2am, Friday and Saturday to 3am. Cover for most bands is 8€ to 16€ ($13–$26); regular cover is usually 2.50€ ($4). Popular with locals and students, **Irish Pub,** Mühlenstrasse 4 (ℂ **0551/45664**), hosts live music every night of the week, from local rockers to visiting Irish folk bands. The pub serves Guinness, Kilkenny, and hard cider. There's never a cover, and it's open nightly 5pm to 2am.

STUDENT TAVERNS   A visit to Göttingen is traditionally capped by going to one of the student taverns, such as the cramped but convivial **ADe,** Prinzenstrasse 16 (ℂ **0551/56545**), open daily 6pm to 1am; or **Irish Pub** (see above).

18

Hamburg

Hamburg has many faces. A walk down the neon-lit Reeperbahn at night will revive old memories of "Sin City Europe." A ride around Alster Lake in the city center will reveal the elegance of its finest parks and buildings. And a stroll along one of Hamburg's many canals explains why this city has been called the "Venice of the North." Contrasts are evident wherever you look in Hamburg. Amid the steel-and-glass structures of the modern city is the old baroque Hauptkirche St. Michaelis. A Sunday-morning visit to the Altona fish market will give you a good look at early shoppers mingling with late-night partiers.

Hamburg has had to be flexible to recover from the many disasters of its 1,200-year history. This North Sea port was almost totally destroyed during World War II. But out of the rubble of the old, the industrious Hamburgers rebuilt a larger and more beautiful city, with huge parks, impressive buildings, and important cultural institutions. Today, Hamburg is the greenest city in Europe, with nearly 50% of its surface area marked with water, woodlands, farmland, and some 1,400 parks and gardens. Green is, in fact, the city's official color.

Hamburg, Germany's second-most populated city (after Berlin), lies on the Elbe River, 109km (68 miles) from the North Sea, 285km (177 miles) northwest of Berlin, 119km (74 miles) northeast of Bremen, and 150km (93 miles) north of Hannover.

1 Orientation

ARRIVING

BY PLANE The **Airport Hamburg-Fuhlsbüttel,** Paul-Baumer-Platz 1–3 (© **040/ 50750;** www.ham.airport.de), is 8km (5 miles) north of the city center. It's served by many scheduled airlines and charter companies, with regular flights to major German airports and many European and intercontinental destinations. **Lufthansa** (© **01803/ 803803;** www.lufthansa.com) offers flights to Hamburg from most major German cities, and many national carriers fly into Hamburg, including Air France from Paris and British Airways from London. United Airlines, Delta, and Lufthansa offer direct flights from the United States. For flight information in Hamburg, call © **040/50750.**

An ultramodern terminal and passenger pier at the airport has a roof shaped like an enormous aircraft wing. This terminal contains an array of shops and boutiques—even a branch of Harrods of London—as well as restaurants and other establishments.

The Hamburger Verkehrsverbund (HVV) **Air Express bus no. 110** runs every 10 minutes, linking the airport with the city's rapid-transit rail network (both U-Bahn and S-Bahn). A bus departs for the airport from the Hauptbahnhof every 15 minutes 5:40am to 11pm daily. Airport buses heading for the Hauptbahnhof leave daily 5am to 9:20pm. The one-way fare is 3€ ($4.80) for adults and 1.50€ ($2.40) for children

11 and under. A taxi from the airport to the city costs about 25€ ($40), with a trip time of about 25 minutes, depending on traffic.

BY TRAIN   There are two major rail stations, the centrally located **Hamburg Hauptbahnhof,** Hachmannplatz 10 (© **040/39183046**), and **Hamburg-Altona** (© **040/39182387**), in the western part of the city. Most trains arrive at the Hauptbahnhof, although trains from the north of Germany, including Westerland and Schleswig, pull into Altona. The two stations are connected by train and S-Bahn. Hamburg has frequent train connections with all major German cities, as well as frequent continental connections. From Berlin, 15 trains arrive daily (trip time: 2½ hr.), 37 from Bremen (trip time: 54 min. to 1 hr., 16 min.), and 33 from Hannover (trip time: 1½ hr.). For information, call © **01805/996633** (11861 in Germany; www.bahn.de).

BY BUS   Because of Hamburg's location astride most of the rail lines of north Germany, the majority of passengers arrive by train. But if the bus appeals to you, call **Central Omnibus** (© **040/247576**). From their headquarters across from the railway station, they'll supply information on fares and schedules for the buses that funnel passengers in from other cities. Information about short-haul buses from surrounding towns and villages is available from **Hamburger Verkehrsverbund** (© **040/19449**).

BY CAR   The A1 Autobahn reaches Hamburg from the south and west, the A7 from the north and south, the A23 from the northwest, and the A24 from the east. Road signs and directions to Hamburg are frequently posted.

VISITOR INFORMATION

For visitors to Hamburg, information is offered at several centers. **Tourist-Information,** Hauptbahnhof, Kirchenallee exit (© **040/30051300**), is open Monday to Saturday 8am to 9pm, Sunday 10am to 6pm (phone inquiries are accepted daily 8am–8pm). **Port Information,** St. Pauli Landungsbrücken (© **040/30051300**), is open April to October daily 8am to 6pm, and November to March daily 10am to 6 pm. There is another tourist office at the airport, at terminals 1 and 2 (arrivals area), open daily 6am to 11pm. For tourist information in Hamburg contact the visitor information hot line at © **040/30051300** or see www.hamburg-tourism.de.

CITY LAYOUT

Hamburg is a showplace of modern architecture; historic structures stand side by side with towering steel-and-glass buildings. The 12 sq. km (4½ sq. miles) of parks and gardens are a vital part of the city, as are the 57 sq. km (22 sq. miles) of rivers and lakes. The city is not compact and can't be easily covered on foot. Many sections of interest are far apart; you'll have to depend on public transportation or taxis.

The **Alster** is the perfect starting point for a pleasurable exploration of Hamburg. This lake, rimmed by the city's most significant buildings, sparkles with the white sails of small boats and ripples with the movement of motor launches. The lake is divided by the Lombard and John F. Kennedy bridges into the **Binnenalster (Inner Alster)** and the larger **Aussenalster (Outer Alster).** The Binnenalster is flanked on the south and the west by the **Jungfernstieg,** one of Europe's best-known streets and Hamburg's most vital artery and shopping district. For landlubbers, the best view of the Alster is from this "maiden's path."

From the Hauptbahnhof, on the eastern fringe of the heart of town in the vicinity of the Binnenalster, two major shopping streets fan out in a southwesterly direction, toward St. Petri Church and the Rathaus. They are **Spitalerstrasse** (reserved for pedestrians) and

Mönckebergstrasse, paralleling it to the south. These streets contain some of the city's finest stores. Stay on Mönckebergstrasse to reach **Rathausmarkt,** which is dominated by the Rathaus, a Renaissance-style city hall palace.

The center of Hamburg offers fine opportunities for walking; for example, the eastern shoreline of the Binnenalster opens onto **Ballindamm,** which contains many elegant stores. At the foot of this lake is the Jungfernstieg, already mentioned, and along its western shoreline is yet another main artery, the Neuer Jungfernstieg. At the intersection of the Jungfernstieg and Neuer Jungfernstieg is one of the more fascinating streets in Hamburg, the **Colonnaden,** a colonnade of shops and cafes. In this neighborhood stands the **Hamburgische Staatsoper,** the famous modern opera house.

A "city within a city" is growing up in the former docklands that extend 3km (2 miles) along the Elbe River. Known as HafenCity, this emerging borough is expected to double the population of central Hamburg with a concert hall, bars, slick office buildings, and hundreds of waterfront apartments. Still in transition and still a construction site, HafenCity can be toured daily at 3pm. Tours leave from Am Sandtorkai 30 (② **040/ 369-01799**).

NEIGHBORHOODS IN BRIEF

Central Hamburg This is Hamburg's commercial and shopping district, seat of many of its finest hotels and restaurants. The district centers on Binnenalster and the Rathaus (City Hall). Boat rides on the Alster lakes are a major attraction. Many historic buildings that withstood World War II are here, including St. Petri, the oldest surviving structure.

The Harbor The Port of Hamburg is the world's fifth-largest harbor, stretching for nearly 40km (25 miles) along the Elbe River. More than 1,500 ships from all over the world call each month. Since 1189, this has been one of the busiest centers for trade on the Continent, making Hamburg one of Germany's wealthiest cities.

St. Pauli This is Hamburg's nightlife center, with lots of erotica. The district is split by its famous street, the Reeperbahn, neon-lit and dazzling, offering all sorts of nighttime pleasures—cafes, sex shows, bars, dance clubs, and music halls.

Altona Formerly a city in its own right, this western district is now integrated into greater Hamburg. It was once populated mainly by Jews and Portuguese. Today it's the scene of Hamburg's famous Fischmarkt, which takes place at dawn every Sunday.

Pöseldorf Northwest of Aussenalster, this is a tree-filled residential district, with many villas dating from the 1800s. A large number of exemplary Jugendstil buildings can still be seen here. The district is mostly occupied by upwardly mobile professionals, including a lot of media stars.

GETTING AROUND

A word to the wise: Park your car and use public transportation in this busy city. Practically all public transportation services in the Hamburg area—the **U-Bahn** (subway), **S-Bahn** (city rail), **A-Bahn** (commuter rail), **buses,** and **harbor ferries**—are run by **Hamburger Verkehrsverbund (HVV),** Steinstrasse 12. For information, call ② **040/ 19449.** Tickets are sold at Automats and railroad ticket counters.

> ## *Value* **Have Card, Will Travel**
>
> The Hamburg Card offers unlimited travel on all public transport in Hamburg, as well as admission to 11 Hamburg museums and a 30% discount on city tours, guided tours of the port, and lake cruises. A 1-day card goes for 8€ ($13) for individuals (for one adult and up to three children 14 years old and under) or 12€ ($19) for families. A 3-day card costs 18€ ($29) for individuals and 30€ ($48) for families. You can get these cards at some hotels, major U-Bahn stations, and the tourist office, or call ℂ 040/30051300.

BY PUBLIC TRANSPORTATION   Hamburg's **U-Bahn,** one of the best in Germany, serves the entire central area and connects with the **S-Bahn** surface trains in the suburbs. This network is the fastest means of getting around, but buses provide a good alternative. The advantage of surface travel, of course, is that you get to see more of the city. For information, call ℂ **040/19449.**

Fares for both U-Bahn and the bus are 1.60€ to 8.50€ ($2.60–$14), depending on the distance. You buy your ticket from the driver or from vending machines at stops and stations. If you plan to make a day of it, you can purchase a **day ticket** (known as an All-Day Ticket) for unlimited use of public transportation services for 6€ ($9.60).

BY TAXI   Taxis are available at all hours; call ℂ **040/211211** or 040/666666. Taxi meters begin at 2.40€ ($3.90) and charge 1.70€ ($2.70) per kilometer after that.

FAST FACTS: Hamburg

American Express The Amex office in Hamburg is at Weiderstrasse 134 (ℂ **040/ 180094030;** U-Bahn: Saarlandstrasse) and is open Monday to Friday 9:30am to 8pm and Saturday 9:30am to 3pm.

Business Hours Most **banks** are open Monday to Friday 8:30am to 12:30pm and 1:30 to 3:30pm (many until 5:30pm Thurs). Most **businesses** and **stores** are open Monday to Friday 9am to 6pm and Saturday 9am to 2pm (to 4 or 6pm on the first Sat of the month).

Car Rentals We don't recommend that you rent a car for touring Hamburg, but an automobile is ideal for the environs. Rentals are available at **Avis,** Gleis 12 in the Hauptbahnhof (ℂ **040/3287-3800;** U-Bahn: Hauptbahnhof), or at **Hertz,** Kirchenallee 34–36 (ℂ **040/2801201;** U-Bahn: Hauptbahnhof).

Consulates Consulate General of the U.S., Alsterufer 27–28 (ℂ **040/41171100);** British Consulate-General, Harvestehuder Weg 8A (ℂ **040/4480320);** Canadian Consulate, Ballindamm 35 (ℂ **040/4600270).**

Currency Exchange The most convenient place for recent arrivals to exchange currency is the **ReiseBank** at the Hauptbahnhof (ℂ **040/323483),** which is open daily 7:30am to 10pm. The same bank maintains a branch at the Altona Station (ℂ **040/3903770),** open Monday to Friday 7:30am to 8pm, and Saturday 9am to 2pm and 2:45 to 5pm. There's also a branch in Terminal 2 of Hamburg's airport (ℂ **040/50753374),** open daily 8am to 9pm.

Doctor or Dentist Ask at the British or American consulates, or go to **Allgemeines Krankenhaus Sankt Georg**, Lohmühlenstrasse 5, 20099 Hamburg (© **040/1818850**; U-Bahn: Lohmühlenstrasse), where you'll find an English-speaking staff.

Drugstores Pharmacies that stock foreign drugs include **Internationale Apotheke**, Ballindamm 37 (© **040/335333**; U-Bahn: Jungfernstieg), open Monday to Friday 8am to 7pm. **Roth's Alte Englische Apotheke**, Jungfernstieg 48 (© **040/343906**; U-Bahn: Jungfernstieg), is open Monday to Friday 8:30am to 8pm and Saturday 9am to 6pm.

Emergencies Dial © **110** for the police; for an ambulance, an emergency doctor or dentist, or the fire brigade, dial © **112**; and © **01805/101112** for the **German Automobile Association (ADAC)**.

Post Office The post office at the Hauptbahnhof, Hachmannplatz 13, is convenient. You can make long-distance calls here far cheaper than at your hotel. Telegrams, telexes, and faxes can also be sent. It's open Monday to Friday 8am to 8pm, Saturday 8am to 6pm, and Sunday 10am to 4pm. A branch office located at the airport is open Monday to Friday 6:30am to 9pm, Saturday 8am to 6pm, and Sunday 10am to 6pm. For information on either post office call © **01802/3333**.

Safety Hamburg, like all big cities of the world, has its share of crime. The major crimes that tourists encounter are pickpocketing and purse/camera snatching. Most robberies occur in the big tourist areas, such as the Reeperbahn and the area around the Hauptbahnhof, which can be dangerous at night, but much less so than in Frankfurt or Munich.

Toilets See "Fast Facts: Germany" in the appendix. There are several decent public facilities in the center of Hamburg.

Transit Information For U-Bahn and S-Bahn rail information, call the Hauptbahnhof, Hachmannplatz 10 (© **01805/996633**, 11861 in Germany).

2 Where to Stay

Hamburg is an expensive city with an abundance of first-class hotels but a limited number of budget accommodations, especially in the center of the city. During a busy convention period, you may have trouble finding a room. A department within **Hamburg's Tourismus Centrale (Tourist Information Office)**, in the Hauptbahnhof, at Kirchenallee in the Wandelhalle (© **040/30051300**; fax 040/30051333), can book accommodations. Rooms from more than 200 hotels in all price categories are available. There's a fee of 4€ ($6.40) per reservation. You can use this agency on a last-minute basis, but no more than 7 days in advance of the time you'll need the room. Hotel-booking desks can also be found at the airport in Arrival Hall A.

NEAR THE HAUPTBAHNHOF
VERY EXPENSIVE
Kempinski Hotel Atlantic 𝕬𝕬𝕬 This sumptuous hotel, the Kempinski chain's flagship, is one of the two great hotels of the north. It's in a central location filled with trees and imposing villas and was one of the few buildings in the neighborhood to

escape the bombs of World War II. Michael Jackson, Prince, and Madonna cast their votes for this hotel, but we still think Raffles Vier Jahreszeiten (see below) is number one. Many of the high-ceilinged, spacious bedrooms open onto lakeside views. All have lots of extras, including windows that open (as opposed to being permanently sealed), deluxe toilet articles, bathroom scales, and maid and butler service around the clock.

An der Alster 72–79 (near the Aussenalster), 20099 Hamburg. (C) 800/426-3135 in the U.S. or 040/28880. Fax 040/ 247129. www.kempinski.atlantic.de. 252 units. 225€–550€ ($360–$880) double; from 515€ ($824) suite. AE, DC, MC, V. Parking 32€ ($51). U-Bahn: Hauptbahnhof. **Amenities:** 2 restaurants; bar; indoor heated pool; 2 fitness rooms; spa; sauna; solarium; concierge; room service; massage; babysitting; laundry service; dry cleaning; nonsmoking rooms. *In room:* TV, Wi-Fi, minibar, hair dryer, safe.

Le Royal Meridien Hamburg 🏨🏨🏨

Opening in the heart of Hamburg on Lake Aussenalster, the city's latest government-rated five-star hotel features what it calls "Art + Tech" bedrooms spread over nine floors. These rooms, designed by London-based Yvonne Golds, feature such attractions as the signature Le Meridien giant bed, 42-inch flat plasma-screen TVs, high-speed Internet access, and separate power showers with assorted massage nozzles among other endearments such as handcrafted etched-glass headboards. Using a neutral backdrop, color is used dramatically either in painted wall panels or soft furnishings. Furniture is designed using a minimal palette of materials such as pale maple or stained steel and glass (clear, frosted, or etched). The majority of the bedrooms and six two-story suites offer sweeping views of the lake, and the top-floor restaurant and bar enjoys one of Hamburg's best panoramic views from a hotel. The cuisine is the creation of Michel Rostang, the two-star Michelin chef fabled in France. At all times, 600 original pieces of art, the work of 50 Hamburg artists, are on exhibit.

An der Alster 52–56, 20099 Hamburg. (C) 040/21000. Fax 040/2100-1111. www.lemeridien.com. 284 units. 229€–299€ ($366–$478) double; from 419€ ($670) suite. AE, DC, MC, V. Parking 20€ ($32). S-Bahn/U-Bahn: Hauptbahnhof. **Amenities:** Restaurant; 2 bars; indoor heated pool; fitness center; sauna; steam room; solarium; business services; room service; laundry service; dry cleaning; nonsmoking rooms; rooms for those w/limited mobility. *In room:* A/C, TV, Wi-Fi, minibar, beverage maker, hair dryer, iron, safe.

Park Hyatt Hamburg 🏨🏨 (Kids)

Hyatt took the Levantehaus, a traditional 1912 warehouse, and transformed it into one of Hamburg's best government-rated five-star hotels. In the heart of Hamburg, close to the rail station, the Hyatt occupies the top seven floors of the building, which means rooms with views. Rooms are somewhat minimalist but nonetheless tastefully and comfortably appointed. Even the standard units are large, each with a contemporary bathroom with a tub/shower combination and lots of gadgets. The suites at the Hyatt feature such additional facilities as whirlpools and saunas. A special feature is Club Olympus with its mammoth pool, gym and aerobic studio, and massages and beauty treatments.

At Apples Restaurant, Mediterranean dishes are creatively prepared in an open kitchen in front of guests.

Bugenhagenstrasse 8–10, Neustadt 20095 Hamburg. (C) 040/33321234. Fax 040/33321235. www.hamburg.park. hyatt.com. 252 units. 205€–410€ ($328–$656) double; from 445€ ($712) suite. Children 11 and under stay free in parent's room. AE, DC, MC, V. Parking 15€ ($24). U-Bahn: Hauptbahnhof. **Amenities:** 2 restaurants; bar; indoor heated pool; fitness center; spa; Jacuzzi; whirlpool; sauna; solarium; children's programs; business center; salon; room service; babysitting; laundry service; dry cleaning; nonsmoking rooms; rooms for those w/limited mobility. *In room:* A/C, TV, Wi-Fi, minibar, coffeemaker, hair dryer, safe.

EXPENSIVE

Aussen Alster 🏨

Small and exclusive, and on a quiet residential street, Aussen Alster attracts actors, advertising directors, executives, writers, and artists. Its stylish,

Where to Stay & Dine in Hamburg

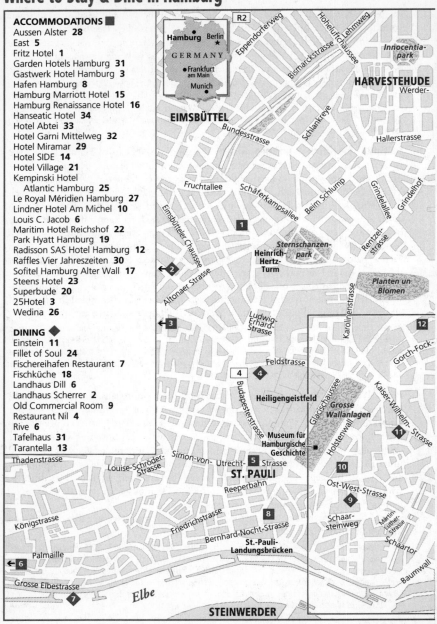

ACCOMMODATIONS ■
Aussen Alster **28**
East **5**
Fritz Hotel **1**
Garden Hotels Hamburg **31**
Gastwerk Hotel Hamburg **3**
Hafen Hamburg **8**
Hamburg Marriott Hotel **15**
Hamburg Renaissance Hotel **16**
Hanseatic Hotel **34**
Hotel Abtei **33**
Hotel Garni Mittelweg **32**
Hotel Miramar **29**
Hotel SIDE **14**
Hotel Village **21**
Kempinski Hotel
    Atlantic Hamburg **25**
Le Royal Méridien Hamburg **27**
Lindner Hotel Am Michel **10**
Louis C. Jacob **6**
Maritim Hotel Reichshof **22**
Park Hyatt Hamburg **19**
Radisson SAS Hotel Hamburg **12**
Raffles Vier Jahreszeiten **30**
Sofitel Hamburg Alter Wall **17**
Steens Hotel **23**
Superbude **20**
25Hotel **3**
Wedina **26**

DINING ◆
Einstein **11**
Fillet of Soul **24**
Fischereihafen Restaurant **7**
Fischküche **18**
Landhaus Dill **6**
Landhaus Scherrer **2**
Old Commercial Room **9**
Restaurant Nil **4**
Rive **6**
Tafelhaus **31**
Tarantella **13**

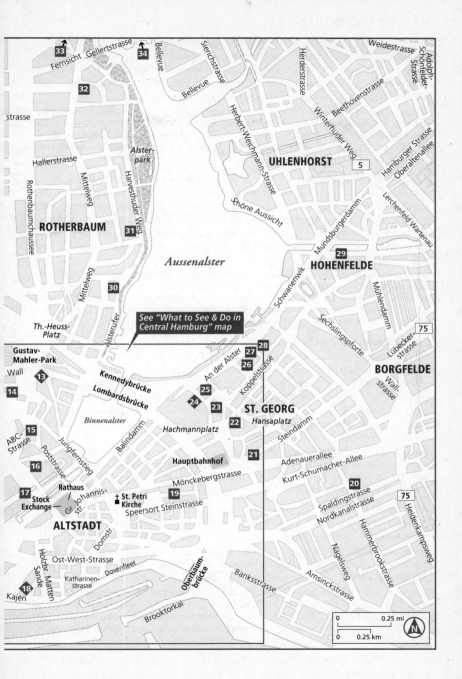

ultramodern interior was designed by one of Germany's most famous interior design-ers, Burkardt Stoelck, who along with his partner, Hamburg film producer Klaus Fed-dermann, manages the place with panache. Rooms are small to medium size, white-walled, angular, and consciously simple. Everything is designed for style and comfort, from the luxurious beds to the immaculate bathrooms.

Schmilinskystrasse 11 (a 5-min. walk from the rail station and a 3-min. walk from the Alster), 20099 Hamburg. ℂ 040/241557. Fax 040/2803231. www.aussen-alster.de. 27 units. 145€–175€ ($232–$280) double. Rates include buffet breakfast. AE, DC, MC, V. Closed Dec 22–29. Parking 14€ ($22). U-Bahn: Hauptbahnhof. **Amenities:** Restau-rant; bar; sauna; solarium; room service; laundry service; dry cleaning; nonsmoking rooms. *In room:* TV, Wi-Fi, hair dryer.

Maritim Hotel Reichshof ⍟

When this long-venerated hotel was built in 1910, it was the largest hotel in Europe. In World War II, it lost most of its upper floors, but the landmark Art Nouveau lobby remained intact. The Reichshof is a favorite with business travelers, so more than half its rooms are classified as singles. The comfort-able rooms are medium to spacious and have double-glazing; those on the top floor feature views of the city. Bathrooms are small but have up-to-date plumbing and tub/shower combos.

Kirchenallee 34–36 (across from the Hauptbahnhof), 20099 Hamburg. ℂ 040/248330. Fax 040/24833888. www. maritim.de. 305 units. 136€–196€ ($218–$314) double; 210€–310€ ($336–$496) suite. Rates include buffet break-fast. AE, DC, MC, V. Parking 15€ ($24). U-Bahn: Hauptbahnhof. **Amenities:** 2 restaurants; bar; lounge; indoor heated pool; sauna; solarium; room service; babysitting; laundry service; dry cleaning; nonsmoking rooms; 1 room for those w/limited mobility. *In room:* TV, Wi-Fi, minibar, hair dryer, safe.

Sofitel Hamburg Alter Wall ⍟⍟

Between the harbor and the Hamburg city hall, this deluxe hotel opens onto the Alster Canal, with views from its front windows. For both the business traveler and the vacationer, it is a good choice for supreme comfort, with such features as king-size beds and large marble bathrooms, along with plush lux-uries such as bathrobes. The Mediterranean cuisine in its Ticino restaurant lures hun-dreds of nonguests. Rooms come in various configurations depending on your needs and your purse. The Hanseatic facade in the 1800s sheltered Postsparkassenamt, the Hamburg mail service customer's bank.

Alter Wall 40, Alstadt, 20457 Hamburg. ℂ 040/369500. Fax 040/36950100. www.dorint.com. 257 units. 229€–313€ ($366–$501) double; from 373€ ($597) suite. AE, DC, MC, V. U-Bahn: Rödingsmarkt. Parking 22€ ($35). **Amenities:** Restaurant; bar; indoor pool; gym; room service; laundry service; dry cleaning; nonsmoking rooms. *In room:* A/C, TV, Wi-Fi, hair dryer, minibar, safe.

MODERATE

Steens Hotel 〈Value 〈Kids

Despite its classy location, a short walk from the much more expensive Atlantic Hotel, this century-old house charges reasonable rates. Rooms are carefully maintained but short on style. Each has a private shower; all but two have a private toilet. Breakfast is the only meal served. This simple but clean and safe hotel is a great option for families on a budget.

Holzdamm 43 (near the Alster), 20099 Hamburg. ℂ 040/244642. Fax 040/2803593. www.steens-hotel.com. 11 units, 2 without bathroom. 85€ ($136) double without bathroom; 190€ ($304) double with bathroom. Rates include continental breakfast. AE, MC, V. Parking 10€ ($16). U-Bahn: Hauptbahnhof. **Amenities:** Breakfast room; lounge; squash court; fitness center; sauna; solarium; bicycle rental; massage; babysitting; nonsmoking rooms. *In room:* TV, minibar, hair dryer.

Wedina

This converted 18th-century town house is a quiet retreat. Most rooms open onto a small, informal Tuscan-style garden. All are tastefully styled and range from small to medium, each with a firm bed and a tidy bathroom with a tub/shower combo. The hotel is owned and run by an English-speaking family. *Be warned:* This hotel has no elevator. If you lodge on the third floor, be prepared to carry luggage up 55 steps.

Gurlittstrasse 23 (near the lake, a 5-min. walk from the Hauptbahnhof), 20099 Hamburg. © **040/2808900.** Fax 040/2803894. www.wedina.de. 59 units. 108€–170€ ($173–$272) double. Rates include buffet breakfast. AE, DC, MC, V. Bus: 6. **Amenities:** Breakfast room; bar; lounge. *In room:* TV, hair dryer.

INEXPENSIVE
Hotel Village   Originally built a century ago, this hotel was a brothel for many years. Rising five turquoise-colored stories above a busy neighborhood near the central railway station, the hotel retains some of its now artfully seamy overtones, including public areas outfitted with touches of toreador scarlet and black, an elegantly paneled breakfast room, and a number of bedrooms with naughty-looking ceiling mirrors and/or racy baldachins. Each room has a different color scheme: for example, gold-toned brocade wallpaper or bright magenta.

Steindamm 4, Altstadt 20099 Hamburg. © **040/806490.** Fax 040/48064949. www.hotel-village.de. 20 units, 16 with bathroom and 4 with shared bathroom. 65€ ($104) double without bathroom; 85€–100€ ($136–$160) double with bathroom. Rates include continental breakfast. AE, MC, V. Parking nearby 10€ ($16). U-Bahn: Hauptbahnhof. *In room:* TV.

IN ST. PAULI
MODERATE
Lindner Hotel Am Michel ⊛⊛   Built in a typical Hanseatic style, with a red-brick facade, this government-rated four-star hotel is centrally located, offering elegantly furnished rooms and suites. Equipped with state-of-the-art technology, the streamlined, midsize bedrooms are soundproof with lots of little extras, including multimedia entertainment. Guests receive a free pass to the health club on the seventh floor.

Neanderstrasse 20, 20459 Hamburg. © **040/403070670.** Fax 040/40307067-777. www.lindner.de. 259 units. 127€–169€ ($203–$270) double; from 199€ ($318) suite. AE, DC, MC, V. U-Bahn: St. Pauli. **Amenities:** 2 restaurants; bar; health club; room service; laundry service; dry cleaning; nonsmoking rooms; rooms for those w/limited mobility. *In room:* A/C, TV, Wi-Fi, hair dryer, minibar, safe.

INEXPENSIVE
Fritzhotel ⊛ *(Finds*   In the St. Pauli district, close to the nightlife center of Hamburg, this small hotel is part of an old apartment block. Rather minimalist in decor, it is a house of personality, taste, and comfort. The better rooms open onto private balconies, and each is individually decorated in a modern style, with a tiled bathroom with shower kept sparkling clean. Those seeking more tranquillity should ask for one of the rooms overlooking the tree-studded courtyard. The district in which the hotel lies has been gentrified and contains the studios of many artists who live and work nearby. The little hotel does not serve breakfast, but there are many cafes in the neighborhood.

Schanzenstrasse 101–103, 20357 Hamburg. © **040/82222830.** Fax 040/822228322. www.fritzhotel.com. 17 units. 90€ ($144) double; 125€ ($200) suite. AE, MC, V. U-Bahn: Sternschanze. **Amenities:** Nonsmoking rooms. *In room:* TV, minibar.

IN ST. GEORG
Superbude *(Value*   Visitors looking for the budget deal of Hamburg can book into this small hotel and hostel, lying in the St. Georg district, not far from the Alster River and the city center. Simplicity itself prevails at this government-rated two-star hotel, but so does cleanliness and comfort. The living is basic, and so is the price. The two- or four-bed units are set up with individual color schemes. With four people sharing

a four-bed room, the cost is only 16€ ($26) per person, a remarkable bargain for Hamburg.

Spaldingstrasse 152, 20097 Hamburg. © 040/3808780. Fax 040/380878-100. www.superbude.de. 64 units. 59€–133€ ($94–$213) double. 16€ ($26) per person in 4-bed room. U-Bahn: Berliner Tor. **Amenities:** Breakfast room. *In room:* No phone.

IN BINNENALSTER & NEUSTADT
VERY EXPENSIVE

Raffles Vier Jahreszeiten ★★★   This warm, mellow hotel is the finest in Germany and one of the best in the world. It was founded in 1897 by Friedrich Haerlin, but today it's run by a Japanese company. Its position is ideal, right on the Binnenalster. Built in the baronial style, it evokes the grand Edwardian hotels. Antiques are used profusely throughout. Despite the large size, personal service is a hallmark. Although no two rooms are alike, they are all beautiful, with period furnishings, Oriental rugs, and all the modern luxuries, including bedside controls, double-glazing on the windows, and bathrooms containing tub/shower combos. This is a hotel for connoisseurs.

Neuer Jungfernstieg 9–14 (on the Binnenalster), 20354 Hamburg. © 800/223-6800 in the U.S. and Canada, or 040/34943151. Fax 040/34942606. www.hvj.de. 157 units. 300€–385€ ($480–$616) double; from 475€ ($760) suite. AE, DC, MC, V. Parking 25€ ($40). U-Bahn: Hauptbahnhof. **Amenities:** 3 restaurants; 2 bars; cafe; coffee shop; health club; sauna; solarium; room service; massage; babysitting; laundry service; dry cleaning; nonsmoking rooms; rooms for those w/limited mobility. *In room:* TV, Wi-Fi, minibar, hair dryer, safe.

EXPENSIVE

Hamburg Marriott Hotel ★   This traditionally styled hotel is one of the finest in Hamburg. It was built on the site of the old Gänsemarkt, where geese were sold in the Middle Ages. The hotel is also near the Hanse Viertel shopping complex. The fashionable surrounding area is filled with boutiques, wine bars, shops, and restaurants. Rooms range from small to large. The lower price listed in the range below is for standard rooms, the higher for studios. Lavish suites are also available.

ABC Strasse 52, 20354 Hamburg. © 800/228-9290 in the U.S. or 040/35050. Fax 040/35051777. www.marriott-hotels.com. 277 units. 179€–269€ ($286–$430) double; from 339€ ($542) suite. AE, DC, MC, V. Parking 26€ ($42). U-Bahn: Gänsemarkt. **Amenities:** Restaurant; bar; indoor heated pool; fitness center; spa; whirlpool; sauna; car rental; business center; room service; babysitting; laundry service; dry cleaning; nonsmoking rooms; rooms for those w/limited mobility. *In room:* A/C, TV, minibar, hair dryer, iron, safe.

Hamburg Renaissance Hotel ★★   Occupying a 19th-century building, this nine-story hotel offers 20th-century comforts. From the sunken, antiques-furnished lobby to the carpeted bar area, you'll be welcomed by the staff and serenaded by a resident pianist. Rooms range from well-appointed doubles to sumptuously upholstered suites. Most are quite spacious, with paired queen-size, king-size, or twin beds, plus large bathrooms with robes, make-up mirrors, phones, and tub/shower combos. The hotel was constructed behind the facade of a historic building, and the entire complex was designed with connections to the Hanse Viertel Galerie Passage, Europe's longest shopping arcade.

Grosse Bleichen, Hanse-Viertel, 20354 Hamburg. © 800/228-9290 in the U.S. and Canada, or 040/349180. Fax 040/34918919. www.renaissancehotels.com. 205 units. 189€–229€ ($302–$366) double; from 269€ ($430) suite. AE, DC, MC, V. Parking 25€ ($40). U-Bahn: Jungfernstieg. **Amenities:** Restaurant; bar; indoor heated pool; fitness center; sauna; room service; massage; babysitting; laundry; dry cleaning; nonsmoking rooms; rooms for those w/limited mobility. *In room:* A/C, TV, Wi-Fi, minibar, hair dryer, iron, trouser press, safe.

Hotel SIDE ★★   Angular, offbeat, and postmodern, this hotel, which opened in 2001, is a favorite destination of journalists and fashionistas. It rises 11 stone- and glass-sheathed floors above the street, with an additional four stories underground. Rooms are built around a central atrium, in a dramatic cream, white, and brown color scheme that was created by Matteo Thun, the well-known Milan designer. (He even designed the hotel ashtrays.) The top two stories are reserved for suites, all encased in an architectural "box" that seems to float over the structure below. On the eighth floor guests can enjoy a terrace that opens onto panoramic views of Hamburg. Bedrooms are efficiently organized with secret closets and storage space, and each contains deep upholsteries of a tasteful modern design, along with luxurious bathrooms with tub/shower combinations. Each suite has a kitchenette, coffeemaker, and two washbasins.

49 Drehbahn, 20354 Hamburg. © 040/309990. Fax 040/30999399. www.side-hamburg.de. 178 units. 225€–300€ ($360–$480) double; 380€–680€ ($608–$1,088) suite. AE, DC, MC, V. Parking 18€ ($29). U-Bahn: Gänsemarkt or Stephansplatz. **Amenities:** Restaurant; bar; indoor heated pool; health club/exercise room; Jacuzzi; sauna; solarium; steam room; room service; babysitting; laundry service; dry cleaning; nonsmoking rooms; rooms for those w/limited mobility. *In room:* A/C, TV, Wi-Fi, minibar, hair dryer, safe.

Radisson SAS Hotel Hamburg *(Kids)*   This 27-story high-rise hotel is of real architectural interest. It looks like a collection of narrow black lines banded together vertically. Although it's very professionally run and has many winning features, we'd rank it after the Marriott. The medium-size rooms are beautifully appointed, many with paneled walls. Ten floors are reserved for nonsmokers. Children particularly enjoy this hotel—it lies within sight of the botanical gardens and has a large breakfast buffet.

Marseillerstrasse 2 (in the Planten und Blomen Park), 20355 Hamburg. © 040/35020. Fax 040/35023530. www. radisson.com/hamburgde. 560 units. 115€–200€ ($184–$320) double; 175€–195€ ($280–$312) business-class double; from 375€ ($600) suite. AE, DC, MC, V. Parking 14€ ($22). Bus: 102. **Amenities:** 3 restaurants; cafe; 3 bars; nightclub; indoor heated pool; fitness center; 2 saunas; solarium; room service; massage; babysitting; laundry service; dry cleaning; nonsmoking rooms; rooms for those w/limited mobility. *In room:* A/C, TV, Wi-Fi, minibar, beverage maker (in some), hair dryer, trouser press, safe.

MODERATE

Hafen Hamburg *(★)*   This Hamburg landmark, constructed in the Wilhelmian style, offers panoramic views of the river and the harbor traffic. It attracts the commercial traveler who's not on an expense account. The functionally furnished rooms are unusually spacious. If they're within your budget, book the more expensive harbor-view rooms. Each comes with a well-equipped private bathroom with a tub/shower combo.

Seewartenstrasse 9, 20459 Hamburg. © 040/311130. Fax 040/3111370601. www.hotel-hamburg.de. 355 units. 100€–200€ ($160–$320) double. AE, DC, MC, V. Parking 10€ ($16). U-Bahn: Landungsbrücken. **Amenities:** Restaurant; 3 bars; fitness center nearby; sauna; laundry service; dry cleaning; nonsmoking rooms; rooms for those w/limited mobility. *In room:* TV, minibar, hair dryer, safe.

IN THE REEPERBAHN

East *(★★) (Finds)*   This sophisticated hotel originated in the early 20th century as a brick-fronted, industrial-looking iron foundry. A team of designers transformed it, achieving a radical, postmodern feel with a high-tech design motif. Whiffs of the Industrial Age are artfully preserved, even celebrated. The tasteful bedrooms fall into five categories, ranging from "Small" to "XX-Large." In all, this is the first swanky retreat ever to open in the funky red-light district.

Everything is minimalist, with "rainfall" shower heads, luxe toiletries, stained-glass windows, and undulating columns. In summer, local guests lounge on the rattan chaise longues in the open-air courtyard or take to the rooftop terrace.

Simon-von-Utrecht Strasse 31, 20359 Hamburg. ✆ **040/309930**. Fax 040/303200. www.east-hotel.de. 78 units. 155€–425€ ($248–$680) double. AE, DC, MC, V. Parking 20€ ($32). U-Bahn: St. Pauli. **Amenities:** Restaurant; bar; gym; sauna; room service; massage; babysitting; laundry service; dry cleaning; nonsmoking rooms; rooms for those w/limited mobility. *In room:* A/C, TV, Wi-Fi (in most), minibar, hair dryer, safe.

IN HARVESTEHUDE

Garden Hotels Hamburg 🐸 *Kids* *Finds*   This hotel dates from 1791, and over the years it has entertained many luminaries, including King Christian VIII of Denmark in 1824. The location, however, isn't for everyone. It stands in the Hamburg-Harvestehude district on the western sector of the Outer Alster Lake, about a mile from the historic heart of town and some 10km (6 miles) from the airport. This feature makes it attractive to families with kids, since boating on the lake is available. Families also appreciate the helpfulness of the friendly staff and the hotel pool. Modern art and well-chosen antiques add to the sophisticated comfort of the rooms. Most are generously sized, and the luxurious bathrooms have tub/shower combos.

Magdalenenstrasse 60 (1.5km/1 mile from the center), 20148 Hamburg. ✆ **040/414040**. Fax 040/4140420. www.garden-hotels.de. 60 units. 155€–195€ ($248–$312) double; 230€–280€ ($368–$448) suite. AE, DC, MC, V. Parking 15€ ($24). U-Bahn: Hallerstrasse. **Amenities:** Breakfast room; bar; room service; babysitting; laundry service; dry cleaning; nonsmoking rooms. *In room:* TV, Wi-Fi (in some), minibar, kitchenette (in some), hair dryer, safe, trouser press.

Hotel Abtei 🐸🐸 *Finds*   This discovery is 2km (1¼ mile) north of the center of Harvestehude, a highly desirable if somewhat out-of-the-way address for a little hotel. Small scale and charming, this bijou-style hotel was a posh private home in the 1890s and then fell into disrepair in the early 1970s, when it became a shelter for the indigent. Today, it's a plush, smart hotel with decor and ambience that recall an English country house. Rooms are cushy, conservative, and rich looking, in tones of green, red, and yellow. Antiques, including pieces of mahogany and cherrywood, are scattered about, and a trio of suites have their own private conservatories.

Abteistrasse 14, Harvestehude, 20149 Hamburg. ✆ **040/442905**. Fax 040/449820. www.abtei-hotel.de. 11 units. 190€–250€ ($304–$400) double; 250€–300€ ($400–$480) suite. AE, MC, V. U-Bahn: Klosterstern. **Amenities:** Room service; babysitting; laundry service; dry cleaning. *In room:* TV, minibar, safe.

Hotel Garni Mittelweg 🐸 *Finds*   A real discovery, this stylishly decorated family hotel lies in the upscale Pöseldorf, within an easy stroll of the Aussenalster. The place is imbued with a country charm. Once the town house of a wealthy merchant and his family in the 19th century, the hotel has now been tastefully converted to receive guests, with modern amenities added. Bedrooms are attractively furnished and comfortable.

Mittelweg 59, Hamburg 20149. ✆ **040/4141010**. Fax 040/41410120. www.hotel-mittelweg.de. 39 units. 105€–150€ ($168–$240) double. AE, MC, V. Parking 10€ ($16). S-Bahn: Dammtor. **Amenities:** Breakfast room; room service; babysitting; nonsmoking rooms. *In room:* TV, minibar, hair dryer, safe.

IN WINTERHUDE

Hanseatic Hotel 🐸🐸 *Finds*   This hotel, on the banks of the Alster River, close to the Winterhude Market, is the smallest and most delightful place to stay in Hamburg. In summer, a little flower garden blooms in the front. The town house, painted a soothing white, was built around 1930. The interior evokes an English gentlemen's club, complete with prints of horses, chintz upholstery, and leather-bound books. Rooms, ranging from small to medium, are furnished in a one-of-a-kind manner, containing many antiques. All units are equipped with tidily kept bathrooms containing tub/shower combinations. Breakfast is the only meal served, but there's a bistro next door and other restaurants in the vicinity.

Sierichstrasse 150, 22299 Hamburg-Winterhude. © **040/485772.** Fax 040/485773. www.hanseatic-hamburg.de. 14 units. 170€–225€ ($272–$360) double. Rates include continental breakfast. MC, V. U-Bahn: Hudtwalckerstrasse. Ferry: Alster. **Amenities:** Bar; lounge; babysitting; nonsmoking rooms. *In room:* TV, minibar, hair dryer.

IN NIENSTEDTEN

Louis C. Jacob ★★★   Lying outside the city center along the Elbe, this tranquil deluxe hotel compares to the Vier Jahreszeiten and Kempinski Hotel Atlantic (see above). In summer, you can sit out under linden trees 2 centuries old and enjoy views of the river traffic. Built in 1791 as a guesthouse, it has been brought up to modernity after a major overhaul. The owners believe in spectacular luxury and coddling their guests. The hotel owns one of the biggest private art collections in the north of Germany. The medium to spacious rooms are elegantly appointed and decorated, with walk-in closets and state-of-the-art bathrooms, each with deluxe toiletries and a tub/shower combo.

Elbchaussee 401, 22609 Hamburg. © **040/82255405.** Fax 040/82255444. www.hotel-jacob.de. 85 units. 255€–485€ ($408–$776) double; from 345€ ($552) suite. AE, DC, MC, V. Parking 20€ ($32). 13km (8 miles) west via Elbchaussee. **Amenities:** 2 restaurants; bar; lounge; room service; babysitting; laundry service; dry cleaning; nonsmoking rooms. *In room:* A/C, TV, Wi-Fi, minibar, coffeemaker, hair dryer, safe.

IN UHLENHORST

Hotel Miramar ★ *Finds*   One of the most hospitable couples in Hamburg welcomes visitors to their hotel outside the central area (but still convenient to public transportation). The establishment is a bit modest, but most comfortable and well maintained— plus infinitely affordable. The hotel lies in a safe neighborhood only a block from the nearest subway station. Across the street is one of Hamburg's colorful canals. The hotel is in a restored Jugendstil (Art Nouveau) house constructed in 1904. Most of the well-furnished bedrooms are on the ground floor, those in the rear opening onto a forested area. The breakfast buffet is one of the most elaborate we've encountered in Hamburg.

Armgartstrasse 20, 22087 Hamburg-Uhlenhorst. © **040/2209395.** Fax 040/2273418. www.hotelmiramar.de. 12 units. 110€ ($176) double. AE, DC, MC, V. Rates include buffet breakfast. Free parking on street. U-Bahn: Uhlandstrasse. **Amenities:** Breakfast room; babysitting; laundry service; dry cleaning. *In room:* TV, no phone (in some).

IN BAHRENFELD

Gastwerk Hotel Hamburg ★★ *Finds*   In one of the most stunning rescues of a decaying industrial building in Hamburg, an old public gasworks has been recycled and given new life as a modern boutique hotel. Developers preserved as much of the industrial structure—they call it "culture"—as was possible when they converted it into a comfortable hotel with a mixture of contemporary and traditional design and all the amenities you'd expect from a high-end hotel. Bedrooms range from luxurious suites—one designed by Sir Terence Conran—to classic loft spaces with exposed brick walls and mahogany furnishings. All the rooms, both public and private, are imbued with a light, intimate feeling. Bedrooms are midsize to spacious, and are inviting and beautifully maintained each with a balcony.

Forum Altes Gastwerk, Daimlerstrasse 67, 22761 Hamburg. © **040/890620.** Fax 040/8906220. www.gastwerk-hotel. de. 141 units. 136€–182€ ($218–$291) double; 192€–373€ ($307–$597) suite. AE, DC, MC, V. Free parking. U-Bahn: Bahrenfeld. **Amenities:** Restaurant; bar; health club; sauna; steam room; babysitting; laundry service; dry cleaning; nonsmoking rooms; rooms for those w/limited mobility. *In room:* A/C, TV, Wi-Fi, minibar, hair dryer.

25Hotel *ℱ Finds* In the western business district, this new designer hotel lies 1km (½ mile) from the Altona Station and the River Elbe. Young designers individually created the bedrooms, which come in three sizes: small, medium, and large. There is a certain chic charm here if you like minimalism. The manager claims that the hotel was created to "meet the demands of creative metropolitan nomads." The lobby and restaurant, the latter serving excellent food, flow into each other.

Paul-Dessau-Strasse 2, 22761 Hamburg. ℭ **040/855-07-0.** Fax 040/855-55-07. www.25hours-hotel.com. 89 units. 125€–155€ ($200–$248) double. Rates include continental breakfast. AE, DC, V. Free parking. S-Bahn: Bahrenfeld. **Amenities:** Restaurant; 2 bars; babysitting; laundry service. *In room:* A/C, TV, beverage maker, hair dryer.

3 Where to Dine

Hamburg life is married to the sea, and that includes the cuisine: lobster from Helgoland; shrimp from Büsum; turbot, plaice, and sole from the North Sea; and huge quantities of fresh oysters. Of course, there's also the traditional meat dish, *Stubenküchen* (hamburger steak), and the favorite sailor's dish, *Labskaus,* made with beer, onions, cured meat, potatoes, herring, and pickles. *Aalsuppe* (eel soup) is the best known of all Hamburg's typical dishes. To locate the restaurants in this section, see the "Where to Stay & Dine in Hamburg" map on p. 628.

NEAR THE HAUPTBAHNHOF

Fillet of Soul *ℱ* INTERNATIONAL Its name implies a role as a jazz club, but that's not the case with this cozy, postmodern dining room that's positioned on the ground floor of the wing of the Deichtorhallen that's devoted to the photography exhibits. Here, within a minimalist setting that includes walls painted in a vibrant tone of red, but softened with lots of exposed wood, you'll find a restaurant favored by local residents who seek it out as an entity unto itself, with little or no intention of ever actually visiting the museum that contains it. The place does a somewhat languid business as a morning and midafternoon cafe, but its real heart and soul is devoted to its role as a restaurant. The kitchen changes its menu according to the seasons and the availability of fresh ingredients, but regular menu items are likely to include pink-roasted breast of goose with saffron-flavored rice and Thai basil; pan-fried zanderfish with bacon-studded sauerkraut and parsley sauce; and, for lighter appetites, spinach salads accented with grilled strips of salmon. Raspberry-flavored tiramisu makes for a tempting dessert.

In the Deichtorhallen Museum, Deichtorstrasse 2. ℭ **040/7070-5800.** Reservations recommended. Lunch main courses 9€–12€ ($14–$19); dinner main courses 18€–24€ ($29–$38). Cafe and bar Tues–Sun 11am–midnight. Restaurant Tues–Sun noon–3pm and 6–10pm. No credit cards. U-Bahn: Steinstrasse.

IN BINNENALSTER & NEUSTADT

Eisenstein INTERNATIONAL The food here is representative of the wide range of cultures that Hamburgers have been exposed to, thanks to the city's role as a great port. The menu lists specialties from Thailand, Japan (including sushi and sashimi), southern France, and Italy, as well as traditional and very fresh versions of the North German cuisine that Hamburg excels in—particularly fresh Atlantic fish prepared virtually any way you want. The setting is a solid-looking, much-restored factory and former warehouse with soaring, russet-colored brick walls that envelop diners in a cozy womb against the sometimes gray weather outside. The clientele is artsy, hip, and stylish; the staff is cooperative; and the food is surprisingly flavorful, considering its diversity.

Friedensallee 9. © **040/3904606.** Reservations recommended. Main courses 19€–23€ ($30–$36); fixed-price dinners 30€–34€ ($48–$54). No credit cards. Daily 11am–11pm. U-Bahn: Altona Bahnhof.

Fischküche ☆ SEAFOOD   Breezy and unpretentious, this restaurant prides itself on specializing exclusively in fish. It's in a modern building, with a dining room brightly outfitted in bold colors and extravagant chandeliers. Menu items include a changing array of reasonably priced seafood brought in fresh daily. Choices vary with the day's catch but might include several different preparations of clear or creamy lobster soup, marinated crabmeat salad, flounder with spaghetti and tandoori sauce, codfish with potatoes and mustard sauce, and filet of monkfish with king prawns, vegetables, and balsamic rice. It's hardly haute cuisine, but locals flock here for the robust specialties and no-nonsense service.

Kajen 12 (a 1-min. walk from the Elbe). © **040/365631.** Reservations recommended. Main courses 16€–28€ ($26–$45); fixed-price menus 36€–38€ ($58–$61). AE, DC, MC, V. Mon–Fri noon–3pm and 6–10:30pm; Sat 6–11pm. U-Bahn: Rödingsmarkt.

Tarantella ☆ GERMAN/INTERNATIONAL   *Fashionistas*, models, and the media elite, as well as the David Beckhams of Hamburg, flock to this restaurant in the Casino Esplanade. The open-to-view kitchen hides no secrets of the chefs as they concoct such sublime plates as lobsters plucked from a tank or such grandmotherly dishes as crispy suckling pig with creamy sauerkraut. Begin with such imaginative appetizers as octopus carpaccio with arugula pesto and a sorbet, or sautéed foie gras with kumquats. Among the more delightful main courses are a braised saddle of venison on lentils or a saddle of veal with fried asparagus. Monkfish comes with fried baby calamari and a wild garlic risotto studded with almonds.

Stephansplatz 10. © **040/65067790.** Reservations required. 15€–27€ ($24–$43). AE, MC, V. Sun–Wed 11:30am–midnight; Thurs–Sat 11:30am–1am. U-Bahn: Stephansplatz.

IN ALTONA
EXPENSIVE
Fischereihafen Restaurant ☆☆ SEAFOOD   Fischereihafen, established some 4 decades ago, is the best seafood restaurant in town if you prefer true local fare to the internationally oriented cuisine of other restaurants. Every day, the staff buys only the freshest fish and shellfish at the Hamburg auction hall. The menu changes daily, depending on what seafood is available. The second floor is said to be full of "fish and VIPs"—the latter have included the likes of Helmut Kohl and Tina Turner. Appetizers include filet of sole and lobster or a plate of fresh oysters; the house special is turbot with salmon mousse dotted with truffles. A favorite local main course is a plate of giant shrimp with exotic fruits in a curry-cream sauce. Picture windows open onto a view of the Elbe.

Grosse Elbstrasse 143 (a 10-min. taxi ride from the wharf area of Landungsbrücken). © **040/381816.** Reservations required. Main courses 18€–42€ ($28–$67); "Hamburg menu" 39€ ($62). AE, DC, MC, V. Sun–Thurs 11:30am–10pm; Fri–Sat 11:30am–10:30pm. S-Bahn: Königstrasse.

Landhaus Scherrer ☆☆☆ CONTINENTAL   Once a brewery, the Landhaus is now a citadel of gastronomy on the Elbe at Altona. It has gained a reputation for impeccable service and imaginatively prepared cuisine. The chef's superbly precise, inventive cookery combines northern German and international flavors with stunning results. A special dish for two is crispy whole north German duck with seasoned vegetables and au gratin potatoes. An unusual variation might be roast goose with rhubarb in cassis sauce. Other specialties include stuffed oxtail with savoy cabbage and a burgundy sauce; boiled filet of cod with a mustard sauce; and filets of sole with chanterelle mushrooms and a chive sauce.

Elbchaussee 130. © 040/8801325. Reservations required. Main courses 28€–39€ ($45–$62); fixed-price menus 89€–109€ ($142–$174). AE, DC, MC, V. Mon–Sat noon–3:30pm and 6:30–10:30pm. Bus: 135.

MODERATE

Landhaus Dill 🀄🀄 CONTINENTAL   This restaurant is imbued with a country charm, its windows opening onto views of the River Elbe. Although it's close to the street, the terrace is an ideal place to enjoy a warm Hamburg night. The young chefs are completely at ease with their recipes, which, for diversity, cross borders from Germany to Austria, with significant inspiration from western France. Nothing beats the lobster salad that the maitre d' prepares at your table. After that celestial beginning, you can go on to sample saddle of lamb in a rosemary sauce or filet of turbot under a sesame nut crust with a mushroom sauce.

Elbchaussee 94. © 040/3905077. Reservations required. Main courses 18€–27€ ($29–$43); set-price menus 25€–50€ ($40–$80). AE, DC, MC, V. Tues–Sun noon–3pm and 5:30–10:30pm. U-Bahn: Altona.

IN ST. PAULI

Old Commercial Room *Finds* NORTHERN GERMAN   This restaurant, founded in 1643, is so tied into Hamburg maritime life that many residents consider it the premier sailors' stopover. It's the best place in town for *Labskaus* (sailor's hash); if you order it, you're given a numbered certificate proclaiming you a genuine *Labskaus* eater. You can also order many other traditional north German dishes. The restaurant's name, along with that of the street, speaks of the historic mercantile links between Hamburg and England.

Englische Planke 10 (at the foot of St. Michaelis). © 040/366319. Reservations required. Main courses 14€–38€ ($22–$61); fixed-price menus 28€–65€ ($45–$104). AE, DC, MC, V. Daily noon–midnight. Closed Dec 24. U-Bahn: St. Pauli.

Restaurant Nil INTERNATIONAL   Even though the name of this restaurant refers to Egypt's River Nile, don't imagine a decor influenced either by the desert or the Arab world. What you get is upscale French bistro, replete with mirrors, oiled mahogany, and polished brass. The name refers to the bounty provided by the Nile, as interpreted by north German tastes, and the cooking is superb. Clients tend to be in publishing and the arts; many are cultural movers and shakers who have adopted this place as a favorite hangout. Dishes include a carpaccio of beef with a black-olive marinade and shiitake mushrooms; saltimbocca of ham and calves' livers prepared with artichoke hearts; braised leg of turkey stuffed with sautéed leeks and served with noodles in an orange-flavored whiskey sauce; and beef bourguignon with braised shallots, mushrooms, and mashed potatoes.

Neuer Pferdemarkt 5. © 040/4397823. Reservations recommended. Main courses 13€–22€ ($21–$35); fixed-price menus 35€–59€ ($56–$94). No credit cards. Daily 6pm–midnight. U-Bahn: Feldstrasse.

IN ALTONA

Rive 🀄 *Finds* SEAFOOD   This riverside restaurant near the ferry terminal on the Elbe River specializes in some of the best and freshest fish dishes in the city. You get not only a panoramic view of the water, with container ships going by, but delectable seafood such as lobster and clams. Its harborside oyster bar is reason enough to make the journey. Other than shellfish, specialties include herring with a choice of three sauces and pan-fried fish with mustard sauce. Outdoor tables are placed on a water-front terrace that's heated in spring and fall.

Van-der-Smissen-Strasse 1, Altona. © 040/3805919. Reservations recommended. Main courses 17€–24€ ($27–$38); fixed-price lunch 19€ ($30), dinner 49€ ($78). AE. Daily noon–midnight. U-Bahn: Altona.

IN BAHRENFELD

Tafelhaus ✪✪ MEDITERRANEAN A favorite of visiting celebrities, Tafelhaus lies in one of the less attractive industrial neighborhoods. But once you get inside, you're treated to a fresh and varied medley of Mediterranean dishes, some with a hint of Asia as well. The Saarbrücken-born chef, Christian Rach, is a whiz in the kitchen, concocting such delights as curried-apple soup or an herby risotto with tiger shrimp. One of the most imaginative dishes we've sampled here is veal shank with a bed of avocado mousse and mango salsa. For dessert, a real change-of-pace flavor is provided by the curd cheese torte with a fresh rhubarb sauce. The decor is modern, a single artfully designed room outfitted in tones of soft red and ochre. The restaurant overlooks a garden, where in summer tables are set out.

Neumühlen 17. © 040/892760. Reservations required. Main courses 22€–40€ ($35–$64); fixed-price 3-course lunch 40€ ($63); fixed-price dinners 59€–71€ ($94–$114). AE, DC, MC, V. Mon–Fri noon–4pm and 7pm–midnight; Sat 7pm–midnight. Closed 2 weeks in Jan, 3 weeks in July. U-Bahn: Bahrenfeld.

4 Exploring Hamburg

Before you tour the city, you can get a sweeping view of Hamburg from the tower of the finest baroque church in northern Germany, **Hauptkirche St. Michaelis** ✪, Michaeliskirchplatz, Krayenkamp 4C (© **040/37678100;** U-Bahn: Rödingsmarkt or St. Pauli). Take the elevator or climb the 449 steps to enjoy the sweeping view from the top of the hammered-copper tower. The crypt is one of the largest in Europe and contains the tombs of such famous citizens as composer Carl Philipp Emanuel Bach and the church's builder, Ernst Georg Sonnin. Hours are daily May to October 9am to 7:30pm, and November to April 10am to 5:30pm. Entrance to the church is free, but to use the stairs or elevator costs 2.50€ ($4) for adults, 1.25€ ($2) for children. A combination ticket for the tower and crypt costs 3€ ($4.80) for adults, 2€ ($3.20) for children.

The **Altstadt** actually has little old architecture left, but there are a few sights among the canals that run through this section from the Alster to the Elbe. The largest of the old buildings is the **Rathaus,** Rathausplatz (© **040/428310;** U-Bahn: Rathausmarkt), which is modern in comparison to many of Germany's town halls. This Renaissance-style structure was built in the late 19th century on a foundation of 3,780 pinewood piles. It has a sumptuous 647-room interior and can be visited on guided tours costing 2€ ($3.20). Tours in English are given hourly Monday to Friday 10am to 3pm, and Saturday and Sunday 10am to 1pm (there are no tours during official functions). The Rathaus's 49m (161-ft.) clock tower overlooks Rathausmarkt and the **Alster Fleet,** the city's largest canal.

A few blocks away is the 12th-century **St. Petri Kirche,** Speersort 10 (© **040/3257400;** U-Bahn: Rathausmarkt). The lion-head knocker on the main door is the oldest piece of art in Hamburg, dating from 1342. The church is open Monday to Friday 10am to 6pm, Saturday 10am to 5pm, and Sunday 9am to 9pm.

The nearby 14th-century Gothic **St. Jacobi Kirche,** Jakobikirchhof 22, with an entrance on Steinstrasse (© **040/3037370;** U-Bahn: Mönckebergstrasse), was damaged in World War II but has been restored. It contains several medieval altars, pictures, and sculptures, as well as one of the largest baroque organs in the world (Arp-Schnitger, ca.

1693). The church is open Monday to Saturday 10am to 5pm. Guided tours in English can be arranged.

A **monument to the Beatles** is being constructed here in the city where the Fab Four launched their international career 45 years ago. Radio station Oldie 95, the sponsor, raised $625,000 for the steel monument, which is being built on the corner of the St. Pauli district where the Beatles sang "Love Me Do" in 1962. The monument will also honor early Beatle Stuart Sutcliffe, who died in Hamburg in 1962.

THE TOP ATTRACTIONS

Carl Hagenbeck's Tierpark *kids* Hamburg's zoo, one of Europe's best, was founded in 1848 and today is home to about 2,500 animals belonging to 360 species. The unfenced paddocks and beautifully landscaped park are world famous. There are sea lion shows, rides on elephants and camels, a train ride through "fairyland," and a spacious children's playground. In 2007 a tropical aquarium opened, which makes Hagenbeck competitive with the more famous aquarium in Berlin. A restaurant serves well-prepared fixed-price menus at 15€ to 18€ ($24–$29), 11:30am to closing time.

Hagenbeckallee at Steilingen (in the northwest suburbs). (C) **040/5300330**. www.hagenbeck.de. Admission 15€ ($24) adults, 10€ ($16) ages 4–16, free for children 2 and under; 45€ ($72) family ticket. Parking 2.50€ ($4). Mar–Oct daily 9am–5pm (closes later in nice weather); Nov–Feb daily 9am–4:30pm. U-Bahn: Hagenbeck's Tierpark.

Kunsthalle This is northern Germany's leading art museum, which reopened in the spring of 2006 after extensive renovations and much improved lighting. Be sure to see the outstanding **altarpiece** painted for the St. Petri Church in 1379 by Master Bertram, Hamburg's first painter known by name and a leading 14th-century German master. The 24 scenes on the wing panels depict the biblical story of humankind from creation to the flight into Egypt. Note the panel showing the creation of the animals, in which a primitive Christ-like figure is surrounded by animals. As a sardonic note, one little fox is chewing the neck of the lamb next to it. The museum also contains works by Master Francke, a Dominican monk. The altar of St. Thomas à Becket (ca. 1424) is the first known work to depict Becket's murder in Canterbury cathedral.

The collection also includes the distinctive visions of Philipp Otto Runge and Carl David Friedrich; German Impressionists Max Liebermann and Lovis Corinth; and 20th-century artists Munch, Andy Warhol, Joseph Beuys, Picasso, Kirchner, Otto Dix, Beckmann, Kandinsky, and Paul Klee. In addition, the museum has an entire wing devoted to contemporary art.

Glockengiesser Wall. (C) **040/428131200**. www.hamburger-kunsthalle.de. Admission 8.50€ ($14) adults, 5€ ($8) children 4–12, free for children 3 and under, 14€ ($22) family ticket. Tues–Sun 10am–6pm (Thurs until 9pm). U-Bahn: Hauptbahnhof.

NEARBY ATTRACTIONS

Every ship that passes the landscaped peninsula at **Willkomm-Höft (Welcome Point)** is welcomed in its own language, as well as in German, from sunrise to sunset (8am–8pm in summer). The ships' national anthems are played as a salute. The station was founded in the late spring of 1952, at the point where a sailor first catches sight of the soaring cranes and slipways of the Port of Hamburg. As a vessel comes in, you'll see the Hamburg flag on a 40m (131-ft.) mast lowered in salute. The ship replies by dipping its flag. More than 50 arriving ships, and as many departing ones, pass Willkomm-Höft each day.

The point can be reached by car from Hamburg via the Elbchaussee or Ostdorfer Landstrasse to Wedel in half an hour. You can also go to Wedel by S-Bahn; a bus will

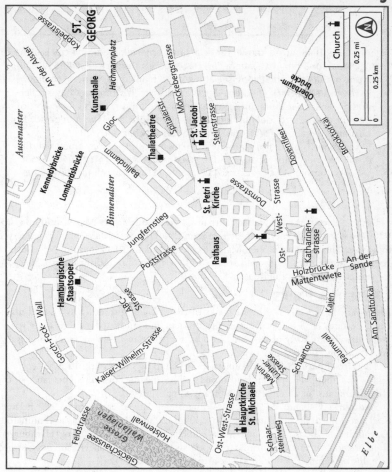

take you from the station to the point, or you can enjoy the 15-minute walk. In the summer, you can take a HADAG riverboat, leaving from St. Pauli Landungsbrücken, an hour's ferry ride.

In Wedel, you can have lunch at **Schulauer Fährhaus,** Parnastrasse 29 (℗ **04103/ 92000;** S-Bahn: Wedel), attractively situated on the wide lower Elbe. The sons of Otto Friedrich Behnke, who founded Willkomm-Höft, run the restaurant. It has large enclosed and open verandas, as well a spacious tea garden. Guests are welcomed for breakfast, lunch, tea, or dinner. Fish dishes are a specialty, and the restaurant's bakery turns out a tempting array of goodies. Children, especially, will delight in watching the ships go by as they eat. Main courses run 10€ to 17€ ($16–$27). It's open daily 9am to 11pm. No credit cards are accepted.

(Kids) Family-Friendly Activities

Although Hamburg is known for its X-rated entertainment, the city is actually ideal for a family vacation. **Carl Hagenbeck's Tierpark** (© **040/5300330**) is one of Europe's great zoos (see above), and many other parks in Hamburg have amusements for children—for example, the **Wallringpark** has a roller-skating rink. Boat tours of the Alster and more lengthy tours of the Port of Hamburg will also delight kids. **Willkomm-Höft** and the **Buddelschiff-Museum** (see above for details) are also fun for children.

Language is often not a problem for children, so they may enjoy the children's theater, **Theater für Kinder,** Max-Brauer-Allee 76 (© **040/382538; U-Bahn: Altona**). All tickets cost 11€ to 20€ ($18–$32); call for show times.

In the cellars of the Schulauer Fährhaus is the **Buddelschiff-Museum** (© **04103/ 920016;** www.buddel.de), where more than 200 little vessels are carefully preserved in bottles. The museum is open March to October, daily 10am to 6pm; November to February, hours are Saturday and Sunday only 10am to 6pm. Admission is 2.50€ ($4) for adults and free for children.

GARDENS & PARKS

Alsterpark lies on the northwest banks of Alster Lake, spread across 72 well-manicured hectares (178 acres). Beautiful shade trees and cultivated gardens greet you at every turn. From many places, you'll also have a panoramic view of the Hamburg skyline. Enter on Harvestehuderweg.

The **Hirschpark** (S-Bahn: Blankensee) is Hamburg's deer park. Its main entrance is at Mühlenberg. The park is landscaped and has a game enclosure. You can visit the Hirschparkhaus for an old-fashioned tea with pastries.

Stadtpark (U-Bahn: Borgweg, in Winterhude), spread across some 182 hectares (450 acres) north of the center, has some 30km (20 miles) of footpaths and numerous recreational facilities. These include a planetarium, sunbathing areas (Hamburgers often prefer their sun sans attire), and open-air pools. Music concerts are often staged here during summer. For your safety, avoid this place after dark.

Finally, **Wallringpark** (U-Bahn: Stephansplatz) is a quartet of beautifully maintained parks and gardens, including the flower garden Planten und Blomen, the Alter Botanischer Garten, and the Grosse and Kleine (big and little) Wallanlagen parks, with many recreational facilities. A miniature railway connects all four. The entire complex is a popular leisure park, with a roller-skating rink, playgrounds, greenhouses filled with tropical plants, restaurants, and an ice-skating rink in winter. A particular highlight is the illuminated-fountain concert, with classical or pop music, at the onset of darkness—June to August 10pm, earlier as the summer wanes. The largest Japanese garden in Europe is in **Planten und Blomen.** Here, rock gardens, flowering plants, miniature trees, and winding pathways attract garden enthusiasts.

BOAT TOURS

You can tour Hamburg by water, on both the Inner and the Outer Alster, experiencing all the charm of the Alsterpark, the villas, and the sailing boats set against the panorama of towers and church spires. **ATG-Alster-Touristik,** Am Anleger Jungfern-stieg (℃ **040/3574240;** www.alstertouristik.de), has daily departures about every 30 minutes from 10am to 6pm, with trips lasting 50 minutes. November to March, tours depart daily at 10:30am, noon, 1:30, and 3pm. The ships leave from the Jungfernstieg quayside (U-Bahn: Jungfernstieg). Cassettes with a description of the tour in English and a brochure in four languages (including English) are available from the captain. Trips cost 10€ ($16) for adults and 5€ ($8) for children 15 and under.

HADAG Seetouristik und Fährdienst AG, Bei den St. Pauli, Fischmarkt 28 (℃ **040/3117070;** www.hadag.de), also conducts tours through the watery channels of Hamburg, in a comfortable heated pleasure boat. Tours are conducted in both German and English. They depart at hourly intervals every day April to October 9am to 6pm, and from November to March 10:30am to 3:30pm. Boats leave from the Landungsbrücken, Pier 3. The fare is 10€ ($16) for adults, 5€ ($8) for children 13 and under, and 20€ ($32) for a family ticket.

5 Sports & Outdoor Pursuits

BOATING

A paddle on the Aussenalster (Outer Alster Lake) can be one of the most relaxing and charming warm-weather activities in Hamburg. **H. Pieper** (℃ **040/247578**) and **Alfred Seebeck** (℃ **040/247652**) rent rowboats, paddleboats, and one-occupant sailing dinghies; prices begin at 12€ to 18€ ($19–$29) per hour. Each of these boat-rental outfits is open only April to late September, daily 10am to 8pm.

GOLF

Hamburg has many golf clubs, including **Hamburger Golf-Club Falkenstein,** In de Bargen 59 (℃ **040/812177**). Greens fees range from 45€ to 55€ ($72–$88) for 18 holes.

JOGGING

Our favorite route, either for long walks or jogging, is the pedestrian walkway that circumnavigates the Alster lakes. The total perimeter of the larger of the two lakes measures about 6km (4 miles); that of the more congested Binnenalster is about 1.5km (1 mile). The public parks flanking the northwestern edge of the inner city are also suitable.

SPECTATOR SPORTS

For information about soccer matches and other spectator events, contact the **Hamburger Sportbund (Hamburg Sports Association),** Schäferkampsallee 1, 20357 Hamburg (℃ **040/419080**).

SWIMMING

The rivers and lakes in Hamburg are being cleaned up, and there are many swimming pools. Two of the most popular are the **Alster-Schwimmhalle,** Ifflandstrasse 21 (℃ **040/223012;** U-Bahn: Lohmühlenstrasse), and the **Holthusenbad,** Goernestrasse 21 (℃ **040/474754;** U-Bahn: Eppendorfer Baum). The latter has the advantage of artificial waves, thermal baths, and steam baths. Both pools charge 9€ ($14) per day.

TENNIS

Not surprisingly, the country that gave the world Steffi Graf and Boris Becker has no lack of tennis facilities. For names and addresses of tennis facilities, as well as information about upcoming tournaments, contact the **Deutscher Tennis Bund,** Hallerstrasse 89 (© **040/411780**).

Hamburg is also the home of the **Hamburg Tennis Masters Series,** one of the nine Masters Series events that rank just below the Grand Slams. Previously known as the "German Open," it is also a major warm-up for the famous French Open, the only Grand Slam event to be played on clay. The Hamburg tournament is also played on clay (usually in May).

6 Shopping

Hamburg is a city of merchants. In general, stores are open Monday to Friday 9am to 6:30pm (some until 8pm Thurs) and on Saturday 9am to 2pm (until 4 or 6pm on *langer Samstag,* the first Sat of the month). Unfortunately, the best shops are not concentrated in one location. Two of the oldest and most prestigious shopping streets, **Grosse Bleichen** and **Neuer Wall,** run parallel to the canals, connected transversely by Jungfernstieg and Ufer Strasse on the Binnenalster. Less expensive shopping streets are Spitalstrasse and Mönckebergstrasse.

Hamburg has nine major shopping malls. The glass-roofed **Hanse Viertel Galerie Passage** is some 200m (660 ft.) long. There's a scattering of upscale cafes here and even a stand-up seafood bar where glasses of beer or *Sekt* (sparkling wine) are served at tiny tables.

Mönckebergstrasse (U-Bahn: Hauptbahnhof), a street connecting the main station with the Rathaus, is the city's traditional shopping district. Here you'll find big department stores such as **Karstadt,** Mönckebergstrasse 16 (© **040/30940**), part of a chain that carries many of the same brands and items as the other leading department stores, all competitively priced. The store is open Monday to Friday 9am to 8pm and Saturday 9am to 4pm. A thrifty alternative, **Kaufhof,** Mönckebergstrasse 3 (© **040/ 333070**), carries less expensive items than the surrounding department stores and also offers better deals on merchandise markdowns. Bargain hunters combing the store are apt to be successful. Hours are Monday to Saturday 9:30am to 8pm. More fashionable and upscale than any of the three mentioned above is **Alsterhaus,** Jungfernstieg 16–20 (© **040/359010**), which some New Yorkers have compared favorably to Bloomingdale's (same hours as Karstadt).

If you walk down Bergstrasse to the second part of the city center, you pass along **Jungfernstieg,** with tourist boats of the Alster Fleet on the right and a teeming shopping street on the other side. About a block farther along, you come to the **Hamburger Hof,** the elegant entrance to one of the most attractive chains of shopping galleries in Europe. At the end of Jungfernstieg, you can cross Gänsemarkt to **Gänsemarkt Passage,** another shopping gallery, with stores on three levels.

An upmarket and youthfully fashionable shopping area is in **Eppendorf** (U-Bahn: Eppendorfer Baum), Hamburg's oldest village, first mentioned in written history in 1140. Many prosperous and avant-garde Hamburgers live in the stately area's 19th-century homes and apartments. The shopping district, from Klosterstern to Eppendorfer Markt, has exclusive boutiques selling fashions from Paris, Milan, and New York; colorful shops with odds and ends for your home; antiques shops; and places where you can not only make purchases but watch goldsmiths, hat makers, potters, and weavers at work.

The Hamburg **Fischmarkt (fish market),** between Hexenberg and Grosse Elbstrasse (U-Bahn: Landungsbrücken), is held every Sunday from 5am in summer or

7am otherwise. Flowers, fruit, vegetables, plants, and pets are also for sale at this traditional market, in existence since 1703. It sometimes seems that the fish are just an afterthought nowadays. The nearby taverns are open to serve Fischmarkt visitors and vendors.

Jil Sander, Neuer Wall 43 (© **040/37518704;** S-Bahn: Dammtor), is the best place to go for chic women's styling. Jil Sander burst upon Europe's fashion scene from her native city of Hamburg and has taken special efforts to make this three-floor store the flagship of her increasingly successful operation. Part of the success of her designs derives from their wearability—they are appropriate for the office, the boardroom, or cocktail hour. Another popular choice for women's fashions is **Escada Boutique,** Neuer Wall 32 (© **040/363296;** U-Bahn: Hauptbahnhof), owned by the German design company of the same name. This store carries the firm's complete collection of women's sports, evening, business, and knitwear, plus accessories that include hats, bags, gloves, and shoes. A less expensive division of Escada, **Laurel Boutique,** Neuer Wall 41 (© **040/3743270;** U-Bahn: Hauptbahnhof), appeals to an active, younger clientele with alternative takes on casual day and elegant evening wear.

For high-fashion men's clothing, go to **Thomas-i-Punkt,** Gänsemarkt 24 (© **040/342009;** U-Bahn: Hauptbahnhof), where you'll find suits, jackets, shirts, shoes, and belts carrying the exclusive Omen label. Ties, handkerchiefs, and other accessories are also available. Shoes, well made and fashionably styled, are sold to both men and women at **Schuhhaus Prange,** Jungfernstieg 38 (© **040/343151;** U-Bahn: Jungfernstieg).

One of the city's leading hairdressers, for both men and women, is **Marlies Müller** Königsbergerstrasse 6 (© **040/6403829;** S-Bahn: Dammtor). Besides hair styling and beauty treatments, a large perfume and cosmetic selection is also offered here.

Brahmfeld & Gutruf, Jungfernstieg 12 (© **040/346103;** U-Bahn: Jungfernstieg), is one of Germany's oldest jewelers, founded in 1743.

A store with a nautical nature, **Binikowski,** Lokstedter Weg 68 (© **040/462852;** U-Bahn: Eppendorfer Baum), established in 1955, is the place to find a *Buddelschiff* (ship in a bottle), as well as ship models and clocks. **Captain's Cabin,** Bei Dim St. Pauli Landungsbrücken 3 (© **040/316373;** S-Bahn: Landungsbrücken), stocks ship models, telescopes, barometers, figureheads, lamps, nautical clothing for the whole family, prints, posters, and more.

7 Hamburg After Dark

To find out what's happening in Hamburg, pick up a copy of *Hamburger Vorschau* for 2€ ($3.20). Published once a month, it's available at various tourist offices, most hotels, and most newsstands.

THE PERFORMING ARTS

Hamburgische Staatsoper (Hamburg State Opera) ★★★   This modern opera house was built after the bombings of World War II. Its acoustics and technical facilities are among the most advanced in the world. The venue is the home of the **Hamburg State Opera** and the **Hamburg Ballet,** the latter directed by Californian John Neumeier. Ticket office Grosstheaterstrasse 34. © **040/356868.** Tickets 10€–90€ ($16–$144). U-Bahn: Stephansplatz. S-Bahn: Dammtor.

Musikhalle ★★   This survivor of Germany's romantic age lies a few steps away from the Staatsoper, with which it shares some facilities and staff members. The building was painstakingly restored after World War II. It hosts concerts by the **Hamburg**

Tips Ticket-Buying Tips

Tickets to sporting events, including soccer matches, are best acquired through the **Hamburger Sportbund (Hamburg Sports Association)**, Schäferkampsallee 1, 20357 Hamburg (✆ **040/419080**). **Theater-Kasse Reckewell**, Einkaufcentrum shopping mall on Osterfer Landstrasse 1 (✆ **040/801013**), can arrange virtually everything else. A third option, for cultural (not necessarily sporting) events, is to contact Hamburg's **Tourismus Centrale (Tourist Information Office)**, in the "Wendelhalle" of the city's main railway station (✆ **040/30051300**).

Symphony, the **Hamburg Philharmonic**, the **NDR Symphony,** and the renowned **Monteverdi-Chor,** known for its interpretations of baroque and Renaissance music. Touring orchestras also perform here. For tickets, call either the number listed below or the number listed for the Staatsoper (see above). Johannes-Brahms-Platz. ✆ 040/357666. www.laeiszhalle.de. Tickets up to 38€ ($61). U-Bahn: Stephansplatz. S-Bahn: Dammtor.

THEATER   Hamburg is blessed with more than 40 theaters, but for most of these, a good knowledge of German is necessary. An exception, the **English Theatre of Hamburg,** Lerchenfeld 14 (✆ 040/2277089; www.englishtheatre.de; U-Bahn: Mundsburg), is the only English-speaking theater in the northern part of Germany. Tickets are 13€ to 32€ ($21–$51). Performances are Monday to Saturday at 7:30pm; a matinee is presented on Tuesday and Friday at 11am.

If you understand German, try the **Deutsches Schauspielhaus** ⚘, Kirchenallee 39 (✆ 040/248713; U-Bahn: Hauptbahnhof). It's one of the outstanding theaters in the German-speaking world, performing both classics and modern plays.

Other theaters are the cutting-edge **Thaliatheater,** Alstertor (✆ 040/328140; U-Bahn: Jungfernstieg), and the **Kammerspiele,** Hartungstrasse 9–11 (✆ 040/44123660; U-Bahn: Hallerstrasse). Both stage a wide range of plays as well as musical shows. A new production usually opens every month. Tickets at these theaters range from 10€ to 45€ ($16–$72). Small ensemble performances such as *Evening with Marlene Dietrich* are the specialty of the **Schmidt Theater,** Spielbudenplatz 24 (✆ 040/3177880; S-Bahn: Reeperbahn). Its companion, **Schmidts Tivoli,** Spielbudenplatz 27–28 (same phone), hosts musicals and other popular performances. Tickets are 9€ to 46€ ($14–$74). All of these are closed on Monday.

Two of Hamburg's busiest theaters are the **Neue Flora Theater,** Stresemannstrasse 159A (✆ 01805/4444; U-Bahn: Altona), and the **Operettenhaus,** Spielbudenplatz 1 (same phone; S-Bahn: Reeperbahn), which have enjoyed an unprecedented success with German-language versions of U.S. and British musicals. The cost of seeing shows is 32€ to 126€ ($51–$202), depending on your seat and the night you attend.

THE BAR SCENE

Bar Hamburg ⚘   This is one of the chicest bars in north Germany, attracting the likes of Bryan Adams or Mick Jagger if they're in town, plus Hamburg's most beautiful models (of either sex), artists, media types, and interior designers. It lies between the elegant Kempinski Hotel Atlantic and the red-light district near the train station. Decorated with "chocolate-ice-cream-colored" leather sofas and plastic wood, it is said to have sparked "a power lounge revolution" among bars. From 7pm nightly until "indecently late," patrons sip drinks and dig into tasty snacks. Some of the best DJs in Hamburg keep you entertained with jazz, house, and lounge music. Rautenbergstrasse 6–8. © 040/28054880. U-Bahn: Hauptbahnhof.

Neo This bustling singles bar attracts a roiling mass of single or at least permissively semi-attached people, many of them rather good looking, who congregate within a venue that combines aspects of a cafe with a cocktail bar and restaurant. The decor is minimalist and modern, centered on a very large rectangular bar area in its center. Large windows flood the place with light during the day, and furniture is painted in ultra-neon tones of pink, green, and blue. The specialty here, other than mating games, is cocktails, prepared by a staff of mixologists, at least one of whom always seems to be shaking up a container of martinis. Other choices include caipirinhas; a Prince of Wales (made with *Sekt*, Cointreau, and fresh oranges); and a Swimming Pool (with vodka, Blue Curaçao, and several kinds of rum). If you get hungry, know in advance that the menu consists mostly of small dishes that are meant to be combined with other small dishes into something resembling a two-fisted meal. Perfect for the mannequins and photo-models who favor this place might be a diet-conscious California Body Shaper, made with turkey breast, pineapple slices, and cheese. 11 Martinistrasse, in Eppendorf. © 040/4677-9936. Small platters 6.90€–14€ ($11–$22); cocktails 7€–9€ ($11–$14). Mon–Thurs 9am–1am; Fri–Sat 9am–2am; Sun 9am–midnight. S-Bahn: Kellinghusenstrasse.

Schwenders This is one of Hamburg's most venerated wine houses. The place today often attracts some 400 or more patrons to its Belle Epoque setting, filled with nooks and crannies, even though there's room for only 200 to sit down. Musical entertainment might be anything from a Viennese operetta to cabaret, sometimes performed by local (often amateur or temporarily out-of-work) musicians. Deli cold cuts and excellent cheese will do if you want something to eat with your drinks. Live classical music is played October to March. The bar is open Monday to Thursday 11am to midnight, Friday to Sunday 11am to 3am. Grossneumarkt 1. © 040/345423. U-Bahn: Rödingsmarkt.

Shamrock The oldest Irish pub in Hamburg, the Shamrock has been in business for nearly 2 decades. It's a popular hangout for students and a transient English-speaking crowd that comes to soak up the Guinness, Kilkenny, Harp, and hard cider on tap. Every Tuesday night, the pub hosts quiz night. It's open Sunday to Thursday 1pm to 2am and Friday and Saturday 5pm to 4am. Feldstrasse 40. © 040/43277275. U-Bahn: Altona.

THE CLUB & MUSIC SCENE
JAZZ
Cotton Club ★★ The legendary Cotton Club is the oldest (some 36 years) and best established of the Hamburg jazz clubs. Jazz and Dixieland bands come here from throughout Europe and the United States. Hours are Friday and Saturday 8pm to 1am and Monday to Thursday 8pm to midnight; September to April, it's also open Sunday 11pm to 3am. Alter Steinweg 10. © 040/343878. Cover 6.50€–12€ ($10–$19). S-Bahn: Stadthausbrücke.

ROCK
Club Grosse Freiheit (Grosse Freiheit 36) ★★ This club, now world-famous, is where the Beatles performed in their earliest days. Today, it's a free-for-all venue whose acts change almost nightly and whose guests in the recent past have included Prince and Willie Nelson. Even the civic and municipal authorities of Hamburg view it as one of their preeminent cultural treasures. For recorded information about upcoming acts, call © 040/31777811. Grosse Freiheit 36. © 040/3177780. Cover 4€–20€ ($6.40–$32). S-Bahn: Reeperbahn.

Moments **The Reeperbahn: A Walk on the Wild Side**

Commercialized sex flourishes in many towns, but hardworking, entrepreneurial Hamburg has succeeded better than almost anywhere else at transforming it into a tourist attraction. The place where it all hangs out is the **St. Pauli district** (U-Bahn: St. Pauli; S-Bahn: Reeperbahn), just east of the center. St. Pauli's midsection—the "genital zone," as it's sometimes called—is the **Reeperbahn,** a half-mile thoroughfare whose name literally translates as "rope street," referring to the massive amounts of hempen rope produced here during the 18th and 19th centuries for ships in Germany's biggest harbor.

In the 19th century, most forms of entertainment, including theaters, were banned from the city's more respectable medieval core. As one resident of the district remarked, "Bourgeois Protestants don't know how to have fun." Consequently, this neighborhood near the great port developed entertainment options of its own, and sailors from around the world were safely channeled into a neighborhood where their recreational activities were out of sight (and out of mind) of the city's sober business establishment. Hamburg's first theater opened on the Reeperbahn in 1842. By the 1860s, the question, "Whatch'a doing, sailor?" became the unofficial motto of an army of prostitutes who set up shop (with the legal sanction of municipal authorities) in the district.

The city's official line is that the Reeperbahn is Hamburg's second-greatest attraction and asset (the first is the port itself). The authorities see their policies as a rare instance of civic and moral enlightenment unparalleled in any other city, except for Amsterdam's more sanitized sex scene. They make frequent references to their requirement that every officially sanctioned working girl submit to a medical examination every 2 weeks—and pay income tax on her profits. Hamburg's most talked-about police station, **Davidwache,** at the corner of the Davidstrasse and the Reeperbahn, provides highly visible and omnipresent police protection.

What are the rules of the game and what should you do to survive such an "in-your-face" neighborhood? Throw your sense of scheduling to the wind and take a nap on the day of your visit. Mornings in St. Pauli are burned-out, unenthusiastic times, when virtually everyone is recovering from the bacchanals of the night before. Midafternoons perk up a bit. But regardless of the fogs that roll in from the Baltic and the damp chill that's an inseparable part of the Hamburg experience, by 8pm the district's bars and theaters (legitimate and otherwise) are roaring away. Between midnight and 5am, you'll find thousands of women and men in drag, strutting

Fabrik   This cultural center is similar in style to the Markthalle (see below). Originally it was an old ammunition depot (ca. 1830), until it burned down; later, it was reconstructed in the same style. Open 8pm to midnight (later Sat and Sun), Fabrik is a nightclub beloved by those who survived the 1970s more or less intact. It offers a

their stuff along the turf. German enterprise has honored these women (and their reputation for a good time) by naming one of Hamburg's native beers in their honor—the famous "St. Pauli Girl."

There's a distinct pecking order among the working girls, based on the neighborhood, or street, where they're headquartered. The most exclusive and expensive area is **Herbertstrasse,** where plate-glass windows allow the women to display their charms to window shoppers. By city ordinance, this street is only open to men over the age of 18. Less expensive rents can be found on the streets near Herbertstrasse: Gunterstrasse, Erichstrasse, Friedrichstrasse, Davidstrasse, and Gerhardstrasse. Lots of the women here are from the Eastern Bloc, and lately there's been a distressing trend for run-away teenagers to join their ranks. Cross-dressers and transsexuals ply their trade here, too.

If it's erotic theater you're looking for, you'll have to move a few blocks away to **Grosse Freiheit,** a street whose name appropriately translates as "Great Freedom." Any act of sexual expression, with every conceivable per-mutation, except those that involve animals (bestiality is one of the few things expressly forbidden), is shown in these theaters. Be it joyful, be it dis-gusting, it's all here, often performed by artists whose barely concealed boredom sometimes permeates the setting in a way that elsewhere would be embarrassing, but here seems merely surreal.

You aren't likely to be solicited at a performance—municipal regulations forbid prostitution, or overt solicitation, inside erotic theaters. But there's nothing to prevent a member of the audience from suddenly deciding to be a performer—it's been known to happen, if rarely. And there's nothing that prevents performers setting up an off-premises rendezvous. In any event, caveat emptor.

Off-the-record theaters include **Safari,** Grosse Freiheit 24 (© **040/313233;** S-Bahn: Reeperbahn), where you're likely to find the press agent for the city of Hamburg entertaining foreign travel writers. Expect to pay a fixed price of around 23€ ($37) for one beer.

The district also contains the **Erotic Art Museum,** Bernhard 69 (© **040/ 317840;** www.eroticartmuseum.de). This institution is privately owned and funded, and closed to anyone 15 and under. It manages to present its dis-plays in a way that's both academic and titillating, and it has a street-level gift shop featuring erotic books. Admission is 8€ ($13) adults, 5€ ($8) stu-dents. It's open Sunday to Thursday noon to 10pm and Friday and Saturday noon to midnight.

mixed program likely to feature African bands, jazz, and blues. Barnerstrasse 36 (5 min. from Bahnhof Altona). © **040/391070.** Cover 10€–35€ ($16–$56). U-Bahn: Altona.

Logo   Because of its position near Hamburg's university, this club attracts lots of col-lege students, although many *Big Chill* survivors in their 40s and 50s gravitate here as well. It's a small, informal place that often features rock bands. Sometimes well-known singers appear in concert. It's open daily 8pm (live music begins at 9pm) to 2 or 3am. Audiences often sit on the floor. Grindelallee 5. (✆ **040/362622**. Cover 5€–19€ ($8–$30). S-Bahn: Dammtor.

Markthalle ✿   This is one of the most visible live-music venues in Hamburg, with a special emphasis on up-and-coming British groups and sometimes heavy metal and high-volume electronics. The building functioned early in the 20th century as a covered marketplace. Inside is an amphitheater with a stage and a large area for standing or sitting on notoriously uncomfortable benches. Performances usually begin at 9pm, with the ticket office opening about an hour before. Klosterwall 11. (✆ **040/339491**. Cover 11€–28€ ($18–$45). S-Bahn: Hauptbahnhof; U-Bahn: Steinstrasse.

DRAG SHOWS

Pulverfass   The best-known drag show in town, Pulverfass is usually featured on the "Hamburg by Night" tours, which are escorted bus tours that take travelers to a few nightclubs. This place is not for the timid. Female impersonators from all over Europe appear, and you might find the shows downright vulgar, especially if you know German. There are shows nightly (for which you need reservations) at 8:30 and 11:30pm, and also at 2:30am Friday and Saturday. Within the same building, with a view of the stage, there's a restaurant, **Teatro-Café,** which is open daily 5pm to 3am, and serves French- and German-inspired fixed-price menus for 39€ to 44€ ($62–$70) each. Reeperbahn 147. (✆ **040/249791**. Cover 15€–24€ ($24–$38). U-Bahn: Steindamm.

DANCE CLUBS

Golden Cut ✿   Set at the junction of three historic neighborhoods (St. Georg, the Innenstadt, and the Altstadt), this is a well-known and likable restaurant that expands after 10:30pm on weekends into a high-powered dance club. The restaurant and its club are separated by what management calls "a chill-out lounge." After you've chilled out for a while, you might want to move deeper into an environment of black-lacquered tables, wood paneling, cream-colored walls, a ceiling that's swathed in fabric as a means of keeping the noise from reverberating, and a color scheme of pale green and copper. Menu items in the restaurant are international and well prepared, deriving from Japan (sushi and Kobe beef), Thailand (curries and dishes laced with lemon grass), and continental Europe (filet steak layered Rossini-style, with foie gras; medallions of monkfish in butter-flavored parsley sauce). Main courses in the restaurant cost from 18€ to 25€ ($29–$40). The club is open Friday to Sunday, plus the first Thursday of every month from 10pm to 5am; the restaurant is open Tuesday to Saturday noon to 5pm and 6pm to 1am. Ages for clients of the club average around 23 to 25 for women and around 32 to 35 for men. Holzdamm 61. (✆ **040/8510-3532**. U-Bahn: Hauptbahnhof.

Molotow   This is the place to dance to funk—George Clinton and Bootsy Collins have been elevated to god status here. Say you've seen Parliament-Funkadelic, and you may make lifelong friends. Opening hours may vary, but usually it opens Wednesday and Sunday at 8pm, Thursday to Saturday at 11pm; closing time depends on the energy of the dancers. Spielbudenplatz 5. (✆ **040/310845**. Cover 3€–15€ ($4.80–$24). S-Bahn: Reeperbahn.

Top of the Town   This eagle's nest attracts a relatively youthful crowd, many of whom show up to dance, drink, and talk. A DJ spins out danceable tunes. This club isn't nearly as wild and crazy as those within less restrictive parts of town, such as the

Reeperbahn. Nonetheless, it can be fun, and there's a gorgeous Hamburg panorama spread out in front of you. It's open Monday to Saturday 9:30pm to around 4am. On the 26th floor of the Radisson SAS Hotel Hamburg, Marseiller Strasse 2. ℭ **040/35024300.** Cover 5€ ($8) Fri–Sat only; no cover for guests of the hotel. Bus: 102.

GAY CLUBS

Hamburg, like Berlin, is one of the major gay havens of Europe, with a particularly dense concentration of gay boutiques and cafes along the Lange Reihe in St. Pauli. A little journal, *Dorn Rosa,* distributed at most gay and lesbian bars, lists (in German) the clubs, restaurants, bars, and events that cater to a gay, lesbian, and bisexual clientele.

Café Gnosa   More than any other eatery in Hamburg, this comes the closest to fulfilling the need for an official "gay restaurant." Set near the railway station, it's open daily 10am to 1am. Platters of food range from 6€ to 25€ ($9.60–$40) and feature all-day breakfasts, steaks, fish, salads, and all kinds of coffee and drinks. Café Gnosa's bar is one of the most frequented gay bars in the area of the Hauptbahnhof and is quite cruisy. Lange Reihe 93. ℭ **040/243034.** U-Bahn: Hauptbahnhof.

Pit Club-Saloon/Tom's Bar   This is the best-established and most popular gay men's bar in Hamburg, known to virtually every gay male in town. Begin your night in the street-level dance club, work your way up to a watering hole one floor above, and end your evening in the cellar, where leather is optional but encouraged. Women, if they come here at all (which is rare), usually remain in the street-level club. At least one part of this place is open every night 10pm until dawn; every Wednesday to Sunday, additional sections open for greater space. Pulverteich 17. ℭ **040/25328943.** Cover 4€ ($6.40) for cellar leather bar; 6€ ($9.60) for street-level dance club and first-floor "jeans bar." U-Bahn: Hauptbahnhof.

A CASINO

Spielbank Hamburg   This casino offers roulette, blackjack, and poker, played according to international rules. You can also enjoy a drink at the bar, taking in the panoramic view over the roofs and lakes of Hamburg. The minimum stake for roulette is 2€ ($3.20), for blackjack 5€ ($8). Men should wear jackets and ties. Everyone needs a passport to get in (you must be 18 or over to enter and gamble). The casino is open daily 3pm to 3am. Stephansplatz 10. ℭ **040/4501760.** U-Bahn: Stephansplatz.

19

Schleswig-Holstein

In this region, you can walk along the dunes and hear the roaring sea break fiercely on the rocks, or you can lie on a tranquil beach while tiny waves lap at your feet. Sound inconsistent? Not in Schleswig-Holstein, Germany's northernmost province, which borders both the turbulent, chilly North Sea and the smooth, gentle Baltic. Between these two bodies of water are rolling groves and meadows, lakes and ponds, and little fishing villages with thatched cottages. Fashionable seaside resorts dot both shorelines

and nearby islands. Even in the coldest weather you can swim in heated seawater at the resorts of Westerland and Helgoland. In Kiel, you can wander around the harbor or explore Schleswig with its Viking memories.

Hamburg is the ideal gateway to the region, and it is easily traversed without a car. Where the trains end, local buses take you the rest of the way, linking small towns and villages. Should you decide to rent a car, bear in mind that roads are overcrowded in July and August.

1 Lübeck ★★★

92km (57 miles) SE of Kiel, 66km (41 miles) NE of Hamburg

Lübeck is a city of high-gabled houses, massive gates, strong towers, and towering steeples. It was made a free imperial city in 1226, and was the capital of the Hanseatic League, which controlled trade along the Baltic as far as Russia.

The Hanseatic merchants decorated their churches with art treasures and gilded their spires to show off their wealth. Many of these survivors of history stand side by side with postwar housing developments, and the neon lights of the business district shine on the streets and narrow passageways of bygone days.

Lübeck has had several famous sons. As a young man, Willy Brandt, who later became West German chancellor and won the Nobel Peace Prize, opposed the Nazis so vehemently that he had to flee on a boat to Norway. Thomas Mann's 1902 novel *Buddenbrooks,* set here, catapulted the 27-year-old author to international fame. In 1929, he won the Nobel Prize for literature.

ESSENTIALS

GETTING THERE By Train The **Lübeck Hauptbahnhof** lies on major rail lines linking Denmark and Hamburg, and on the Hamburg-Lüneburg-Lübeck-Kiel-Flensburg and Lübeck-Rostock-Stralsund lines, with frequent connections. From Hamburg, 32 trains arrive daily (trip time: 48 min.), 23 from Berlin (trip time: 3–4 hr.). For information, call © **01805/996633.**

By Bus Long-distance bus service to and from such cities as Berlin, Kiel, and Flensburg is provided by **Autokraft GmbH** (© **0431/6660**).

By Ferry Ferryboat service from the region around Lübeck to Denmark lies astride the main railway lines between Hamburg and Copenhagen, and is therefore among the busiest in Europe. Service is offered by **ScandLines** (*℟* **0381/5435850;** www. scandlines.de), with boats leaving every 30 minutes, 24 hours a day, every day of the year. The port on the German side is in Puttgarden; the one on the Danish side is in Rødby, a 2-hour train ride from Copenhagen. The trip takes about 45 minutes. Railway cars, trucks, and conventional automobiles are all taken on board. Round-trip transport for a car with up to four passengers averages 120€ ($192), with slight variations depending on the season.

TT Line operates between the German port of Travemünde and the Swedish port of Trelleborg. Call *℟* **04502/80181** for bookings and departure times. And for transport by boat between Lübeck and the faraway Baltic port of Helsinki, **Finnlines** (*℟* **0451/ 15070**) provides daily service, usually favored by vacationers during mid-summer.

By Car Access to Lübeck is via the A1 Autobahn north and south.

VISITOR INFORMATION For tourist information, contact the **Lübeck-Informations-Zentrum,** Holstentorplatz 1–5 (*℟* **01805/882233**), January to May and October to November Monday to Friday 9:30am to 6pm and Saturday 10am to 3pm; June to September Monday to Friday 9:30am to 7pm, Saturday 10am to 3pm, and

Sunday 10am to 2pm; and December Monday to Friday 9:30am to 6pm and Saturday 10am to 3pm.

GETTING AROUND   The Altstadt and the attractions outlined below can be reached by taking bus no. 1, 5, 11, or 21. Fare is 2.10€ ($3.40).

SPECIAL EVENTS   Lübeck is the center of the **Schleswig-Holstein Music Festival** (© **0451/389570;** www.shmf.de), with performances during July and August every year. At the **Christmas market,** vendors from northwestern Germany sell their wares—many of them handmade items from toys to pottery—during the 3 weeks before Christmas on the Rathausplatz.

WHERE TO STAY
EXPENSIVE
Radisson SAS Senator Hotel Lübeck 𝕲𝕲   This well-designed and -run hotel is the best in town. Although the bulk of its clients are businesspeople, it has equal appeal to other visitors. The soundproof and medium-size rooms are well kept and attractively furnished. The sleekly maintained bathrooms come with a basket of toiletries and tub/shower combos.

Willy-Brandt-Allee 6 (on the banks of the river, connected to the Altstadt by pedestrian bridge), 23554 Lübeck. © **800/333-3333** in the U.S. or 0451/1420. Fax 0451/1422222. www.lubeck.radissonsas.com. 224 units. 125€–195€ ($200–$312) double; from 350€ ($560) suite. AE, DC, MC, V. Parking 13€ ($21). Bus: 12. **Amenities:** 2 restaurants; 2 bars; indoor heated pool; sauna; solarium; steam room; car-rental desk; room service; massage; babysitting; laundry service; dry cleaning; nonsmoking rooms; rooms for those w/limited mobility. *In room:* A/C, TV, Wi-Fi, beverage maker (in some), minibar, hair dryer.

MODERATE
Kaiserhof 𝕲 *Value*   The Kaiserhof, frankly, could probably demand a higher price for its rooms, as it ranks up near the top with the Radisson (see above). Built as it is from two former patrician town houses outside the city center on a tree-lined boulevard, this hotel has a fashionable yet homelike environment. Rooms come in various shapes and sizes and are individually furnished. Some overflow guests stay in a more sterile but still quite comfortable annex. Bathrooms are compact and have tub/shower combos.

Kronsforder Allee 11–13, 23560 Lübeck. © **0451/703301.** Fax 0451/795083. www.kaiserhof-luebeck.de. 60 units. 135€ ($216) double; 215€ ($344) suite. Rates include buffet breakfast. AE, DC, MC, V. Free outdoor parking. Bus: 2, 7, 10, 16, or 32. **Amenities:** Restaurant; breakfast room; bar; lounge; indoor heated pool; sauna; solarium; room service; laundry service; dry cleaning; nonsmoking rooms; rooms for those w/limited mobility. *In room:* TV, minibar, hair dryer, safe.

Ringhotel Jensen *Value*   The Jensen is one of Lübeck's best moderately priced hotels, a good value if your expectations aren't too high. The small to medium rooms are modestly furnished in traditional German style. Some have fine views of the Hanseatic architecture across the canal. The buffet breakfast is served in a delightful room with picture windows overlooking the canal.

An der Obertrave 4–5 (near the Holstentor), 23552 Lübeck. © **0451/702490.** Fax 0451/73386. www.ringhotel-jensen.de. 42 units. 85€–108€ ($136–$173) double; 179€ ($286) suite. Children 11 and under stay free in parent's room. Rates include buffet breakfast. AE, DC, MC, V. Parking 7€ ($11) nearby. Bus: 1, 3, or 11. **Amenities:** Restaurant; room service; laundry service; all nonsmoking rooms. *In room:* TV, Wi-Fi, minibar, hair dryer.

Scandic Hotel 𝕲   This first-class hotel is close to the ferry docks and, as a result, attracts many Scandinavians as well as businesspeople. The medium-size rooms are well maintained. Half are nonsmoking, and some accommodate people with allergies. All units have bathrooms with tub/shower combos.

Travemünder Allee 3 (near the Burgtor entrance of the Old Town), 23568 Lübeck. ℂ **0451/37060.** Fax 0451/ 3706666. www.scandic-hotels.com. 158 units. 92€–193€ ($147–$309) double; 220€–350€ ($352–$560) suite. AE, DC, MC, V. Free outdoor parking; 12€ ($19) in garage. Bus: 12. **Amenities:** Restaurant; bar; indoor heated pool; fitness room; sauna; room service; babysitting; laundry service; dry cleaning; nonsmoking rooms; 1 room for those w/limited mobility. *In room:* A/C, TV, Wi-Fi, minibar, beverage maker (in some), hair dryer, trouser press.

INEXPENSIVE

Hotel Excelsior   This is a good, functional hotel and not a lot more. It's in a symmetrical baroque building with splendid proportions and a modernized interior. It's especially convenient if you're traveling to Lübeck by rail. Rooms are small to medium and have a shower or tub.

Hansestrasse 3 (near Lindenplatz, opposite the central bus station and next to the train station), 23558 Lübeck. ℂ **0451/88090.** Fax 0451/880999. www.hotel-excelsior-luebeck.de. 61 units. 85€–120€ ($136–$192) double; 130€–180€ ($208–$288) suite. Rates include buffet breakfast. AE, DC, MC, V. Free outdoor parking; 6€ ($9.60) underground. Bus: 11 or 12. **Amenities:** Dining room; lounge; nonsmoking rooms. *In room:* TV, minibar (in most), hair dryer.

Zur alten Stadtmauer 🛇 ⓥ*alue*   In the heart of Old Town, this historic hotel is a safe, snug, and inexpensive nest for the night. Its front rooms open onto a view of St. Marien Kirche. Personalized service and a homelike atmosphere make this an intriguing choice. Rooms are spread across two floors, each modestly but nicely decorated, and all but a few singles come with private bathrooms with showers and toilets. The large buffet breakfast will fortify you for the day.

An der Mauer 57, 23552 Lübeck. ℂ **0451/73702.** Fax 0451/73239. www.hotelstadtmauer.de. 24 units. 70€–100€ ($112–$160) double. Rates include breakfast. AE, DC, MC, V. Parking 5€ ($8). **Amenities:** Breakfast room; babysitting; laundry service; nonsmoking rooms. *In room:* TV.

WHERE TO DINE

Haus der Schiffergesellschaft 🛇 NORTHERN GERMAN   Entering this restaurant, with ship models and other nautical memorabilia, is like going inside a museum of Hanseatic architecture. The restaurant was once patronized exclusively by sailors. Today, good food (and lots of it) is served on scrubbed-oak plank tables with high-backed wooden booths carved with the coats of arms of Baltic merchants. Often, you must share a table. One of the most expensive items is an elaborate sole meunière with salad. Many regional dishes are featured, such as baked black pudding with slices of apple and lamb's lettuce. Try the roast rack of lamb with rosemary sauce, green beans, and homemade noodles. You may want to have a drink in the cocktail bar of the historic Gotteskeller (Tues–Sat 5pm–4am).

Breitestrasse 2. ℂ **0451/76776.** Reservations required. Main courses 12€–19€ ($19–$30). MC, V. Daily 10am–midnight. Bus: 1 or 2.

Historischer Weinkeller 🛇🛇 INTERNATIONAL   This first-class restaurant and 12th-century wine cellar, in the basement of Holy Ghost Hospital, is the third-best dining spot in town, topped only by the Wullenwever, which has better (and more expensive) food, and Das Schabbelhaus, which has a more refined atmosphere (see both below). You may begin with North Sea shrimp served with a quail egg and caviar or assorted fish in aspic. For a main dish, try venison cutlet in garlic butter with fried potatoes, Atlantic sole with buttery potatoes, or Barbary duck with a sauce flavored with cranberries and balsamic vinegar. A few meat dishes are also featured.

Heiligen-Geist-Hospital, Koberg 8. ✆ 0451/76234. Reservations recommended. Main courses 13€–25€ ($21–$40). AE, MC, V. Daily noon–midnight. Bus: 1 or 3.

Roberto Rossi in Das Schabbelhaus ★★ MEDITERRANEAN   A classic example of Hanseatic architecture on a medieval street, the Schabbelhaus is encased in two patrician buildings from the 16th and 17th centuries. In the restaurant, ceiling-high studio windows overlook the small gardens. The more tradition-minded were shocked when one of the most historically evocative German restaurants was transformed into an upscale venue for artfully prepared Italian food. Today you can sample such delights as spinach salad with strips of goosemeat and a sweet-and-sour walnut sauce, followed by veal steak under an apple and celery crust. Another delectable dish is the asparagus salad with Parma ham with a tartare of red beets. You might also sample such dishes as medallions of seawolf with a zucchini purée and black-olive sauce or else braised octopus with a watercress marinade. We're also fond of the turbot in a lemon grass sauce.

Mengstrasse 48–52. ✆ 0451/72011. Reservations recommended. Main courses 18€–33€ ($28–$53); fixed-price lunch 25€ ($39), dinner 39€ ($62). AE, MC, V. Mon–Sat noon–2:30pm and 6–11pm. Bus: 5, 7, 11, 12, 14, or 16.

Wullenwever ★★★ FRENCH/CONTINENTAL   Roy Petermann, in his elegant 16th-century house, has established himself as one of the finest chefs in northern Germany. Scion of a distinguished culinary family, he has brought a refined and imaginative cuisine to Lübeck. Chandeliers and oil paintings enhance the ambience and, in summer, tables overflow onto a flower-filled courtyard. Using only the best and freshest produce, his dishes have subtle depths of flavor and texture. Game is featured in the autumn, and seafood is always available.

Beckergrube 71. ✆ 0451/704333. Reservations required, as far in advance as possible. Main courses 26€–38€ ($42–$61); fixed-price menus 50€–85€ ($80–$136). AE, MC, V. Tues–Sat 7–11pm. Closed 2 weeks in Mar and Oct. Bus: 12.

Zimmermann's Lübecker Hanse ★ FRENCH/REGIONAL   This is one of Lübeck's most praised restaurants. It has an authentically weathered exterior and dark paneling inside. French food, regional meals, and lots of seafood are offered. You may want to try the *plats du jour;* they are invariably fresh and well prepared. Fresh fish from the Baltic is another good choice. In season, wild game is featured.

Kolk 3–7. ✆ 0451/78054. Reservations recommended. Main courses 14€–28€ ($22–$44). AE, DC, MC, V. Mon–Fri 11:30am–2:30pm and 6pm–midnight. Closed Jan 1–14. Bus: 1, 3, or 11.

EXPLORING LÜBECK

Lübeck's **Altstadt** ★★★ is surrounded by the Trave River and connecting canals, giving it an islandlike appearance. It suffered heavily during World War II, when about one-fifth of the city was leveled. Damaged buildings have been restored or reconstructed, and Lübeck still offers a wealth of historic attractions.

Just across the west bridge from the Altstadt, the **Holstentor (Holsten Gate)** ★★ is the first monument to greet visitors emerging from the Bahnhof. Once the main town entrance, it was built in the 15th century as much to awe visitors with the power and prestige of Lübeck as to defend it against intruders. To the outside world, the towers look simple and defiant, rather like part of a great palace. But on the city side, they contain a wealth of decoration, with windows, arcades, and rich terra-cotta friezes. Within the gate is the **Museum Holstentor** (✆ 0451/1224129), housing a model of Lübeck as it appeared in the mid–15th century. Hours are Tuesday to Friday 10am to

4pm, Saturday and Sunday 11am to 5pm. Admission is 5€ ($8) for adults and 1€ ($1.60) for children 17 and under.

Der Salzspeicher (Salt Lofts), viewed from the riverside, near the Holstentor, are among Lübeck's most attractive sights. In the 16th century, these buildings stored the salt from Lüneburg before it was shipped to Scandinavia. Each of the six buildings is different, reflecting trends in Renaissance gabled architecture.

The **Rathaus** ⊕, Rathausplatz (© **0451/1221005**), traces its origins from 1230. It has been rebuilt several times, but remains of the original structure are in the vaulting and Romanesque pillars in the cellar and the Gothic south wall. The towering walls have been made with open-air medallions to relieve the pressure on the Gothic-arcaded ground floor and foundations. Tours are Monday to Friday at 11am, noon, and 3pm, costing 3€ ($4.80) for adults and 1.50€ ($2.40) for children.

Marienkirche (St. Mary's Church; no phone), across Marktplatz from the Rathaus, is the most exceptional church in Lübeck, possibly in northern Germany. Built on the highest point in the Altstadt, it has flying buttresses and towering windows that leave the rest of the city's rooftops at its feet. Some of its greatest art treasures were bombed and destroyed in 1942, but after the fire was put out, earlier painted decorations on the walls and clerestory were discovered. The bells fell in a World War II air raid and became embedded in the floor of the church, where they remain to this day. Organ concerts take place during the summer months, carrying on the tradition established by St. Mary's best-known organist and composer, Dietrich Buxtehude (1668–1707).

Buddenbrookhaus, Mengstrasse 4 (© **0451/1224192**), near Marienkirche, is the house where author Thomas Mann's grandparents lived. It's a big, solid stone structure with a gabled roof and a recessed doorway. Above a leaded-glass fan over the heavy double doors is the date 1758. This is the house Mann (1875–1955) described as the home of the family in *Buddenbrooks*. The museum also highlights Thomas's brother, Heinrich Mann (1871–1950), author of *Professor Unrat,* the inspiration for the movie *The Blue Angel.* The house is open daily 10am to 5pm; admission is 5€ ($8) for adults, 2.60€ ($4.20) for students, 9€ ($14) for a family ticket, and free for children 13 and under.

In addition to Thomas Mann, Lübeck was also the home of Germany's most prominent living writer, Günter Grass (born in 1927). He is still known all over the world for his most famous novel, *The Tin Drum,* published in 1959. Grass won the Nobel Prize for literature in 1999. The museum at the **Günter Grass-Haus,** Glockengiesserstrasse 21 (© **0451/1224190**), explores the author's "double gifts" in literature, sculpture, graphics, and music—or, in the words of the curator, "we are a crossroads forum where literature and the visual arts meet." Exhibits include manuscripts of Grass—with bold corrections—and even the machines on which he wrote, going from an old-fashioned Olivetti typewriter to computer. In the courtyard garden, you'll get a rare look at some of his sculptures. Admission is 5€ ($8). It is open April to December daily 10am to 6pm, January to March daily 11am to 5pm.

It's said that within an area of 5 sq. km (2 sq. miles) around the Marktplatz stand 1,000 medieval houses. Nearby is **Petersgrube,** the finest street in Lübeck, lined with restored houses. A walk through the old streets of Lübeck reveals a continuing use of brick (the city insisted on this after fires in the 13th c.). The effect is one of unity among all the houses, churches, shops, and guildhalls.

Haus der Schiffergesellschaft (Seamen's Guild House) ⊕, on Breitestrasse, is one of the last of the elaborate guild houses of Hanseatic Lübeck, built in 1535 in Renaissance style, with stepped gables and high-Gothic blind windows. It's worth seeing just for the medieval furnishings and the beamed ceilings in the main hall, now a restaurant (p. 655).

Museen Behnhaus/Drägerhaus, Königstrasse 9–11, north of Glockengiesser Strasse (© 0451/1224148; www.die-luebecker-museen.de), was formed from two patrician houses. Like many such houses in the town, they are tall and narrow, constructed that way to avoid heavy taxes based on frontage. The museum displays mostly German Impressionists and paintings from around 1900. There is an outstanding collection of German Romantic and "Nazarene" paintings and drawings, especially by Johann Friedrich Overbeck and his school. The Behnhaus has a permanent exhibition of contemporary paintings, including Schumacher, Schultze, Rainer, Antes, and Kirkeby, along with such 20th-century artists as Kirchner, Beckmann, Lehmbruck, and Barlach. Both houses are open April to September Tuesday to Sunday 10am to 5pm; October to March hours are Tuesday to Friday 10am to 4pm, and Saturday and Sunday 11am to 5pm. Admission is 5€ ($8) for adults, 2€ ($3.20) for students, 1€ ($1.60) for children 6 to 18, and free for children 5 and under.

You can take an excursion boat around **Lübeck Harbor,** departing from Trave Landing, right in front of the Jensen hotel. In season, departures are every half-hour daily, 10am to 6pm.

SHOPPING

Lübeck is a center for antiques stores. One of the best is **Antiquitäten Bannow Günther,** Fleischhauerstrasse 87 (© 0451/77338), carrying antique silver, crystal, porcelain, books, pewter, and English, Danish, and German furniture; any article can be shipped to your home. And if you're looking for souvenirs that celebrate Lübeck's rich maritime traditions, head for the town's best handicrafts shop, **Kunsthaus Lübeck,** Königstrasse 20 (© 0451/75700), where tin, pewter, glass sculpting, pottery, and antique books will help you remember your visit. **Breitestrasse,** a pedestrian walkway throughout most of the day, is the main shopping street in town. Much of Lübeck's Altstadt is banned to cars, which makes for a pleasant afternoon of wandering.

J. G. Niederegger, Breitestrasse 89 (© 0451/53010), sells that "sweetest of all sweetmeats," famous Lübeck marzipan. It's been across from the main entrance to the Rathaus since 1806. On the ground floor, you can buy treats to take away, or you can go upstairs to a pleasant cafe, where you can order dessert and the best brewed coffee in Lübeck. Ask for their pastry specialty, a nut torte resting under a huge slab of fresh marzipan. You'll pay around 30€ ($48) per kilo (about 15€/$24 per lb.) for marzipan. The shop is open 9am to 6pm daily. MasterCard and Visa are accepted.

LÜBECK AFTER DARK

Two newsletters, *Piste* and *Szene Journal,* free at most hotels, have news of local happenings.

Lübeck is known for its organ concerts; about two a week are presented in various churches during summer. The tourist office (see "Visitor Information," earlier in this chapter) has complete details, or check with **Musik und Kongresshallen Lübeck,** Willy-Brandt-Allee 10 (© 0451/79040), about the many concert and theater opportunities in town. The most important theater venue is **Theater Combinale,** Huxstrasse 115 (© 0451/78817; bus: 11). Its plays range from experimental to classic. Most performances are on Friday and Saturday from August to June. Tickets are 10€ to 21€ ($16–$34) for adults and 7.50€ to 15€ ($12–$24) for students and children 16 and under.

Finnegan, Mengstrasse 42 (ⓒ **0451/71110;** bus: 12), won an award in 1996 and 1999 from Guinness as the best Irish pub in northern Germany. Naturally, Guinness is on tap, as well as Kilkenny, and five or six whiskeys. On Wednesday, Thursday, and Saturday, bands play rock and Irish music from 8pm to midnight. The pub is open Tuesday to Saturday 7pm to 4am.

2 Kiel (★

88km (55 miles) SE of the Danish border at Flensburg, 97km (60 miles) N of Hamburg, 92km (57 miles) NW of Lübeck

A natural harbor at the end of a 15km (10-mile) extension of the Baltic Sea made Kiel a center for commerce with northern European countries. The opening of the Kiel Canal in 1895 connected the Baltic with the North Sea and western trade.

It celebrated its 750th anniversary in 1992, but streets and buildings do little to suggest that Kiel was ever anything other than a modern city. Almost all its buildings were destroyed during World War II, and the town was rebuilt with broad streets, spacious squares, and green parks. Nearby resorts make this a vacation spot as well.

ESSENTIALS

GETTING THERE   If you wish to fly to Kiel, check locally—it may not be possible. At press time, the airport had shut down with no date of reopening announced.

By Train   The **Kiel Hauptbahnhof** is on two major rail lines, the Neumünster-Hamburg and the Flensburg-Kiel-Lübeck-Lüneburg lines, with frequent connections. From Hamburg, there are 40 trains daily (trip time: 1 hr., 10 min.). For information, call ⓒ **01805/996633.**

By Bus   Long-distance bus service to Berlin and Flensburg, as well as local and regional service, is provided by **Autokraft GmbH,** in Kiel (ⓒ **0431/6660**). Buses pull into the Bahnhofplatz. The tourist office (see below) will provide you with schedules.

By Ferry   Service between Kiel and Oslo, Norway, is provided by **Color Line GmbH,** in Kiel (ⓒ **0431/73000**). **Stena Line,** in Kiel (ⓒ **0431/9090**), offers service between Kiel and Gothenburg (Göteborg), Sweden.

By Car   To reach Kiel from Hamburg, head north along the A7 Autobahn; from Lübeck, take Route 76 west.

VISITOR INFORMATION   Contact **Tourist Information Kiel,** Andreas-Gayk-Strasse 31 (ⓒ **0180/5656700**). It's open year-round Monday to Friday 9am to 6pm, and from May to September, also Saturday 10am to 2pm.

GETTING AROUND   Most attractions in Kiel center around the harbor, reached by bus no. 41 or 42. Fare is 2.10€ ($3.40).

SPECIAL EVENTS   **Kieler Woche (Kiel Week),** held each June, celebrates the port's close ties to the sea. This week of special events, held for more than 100 years, includes a spectacular regatta in which more than 1,500 yachts race on the water of the Kieler Förde. In 1936 and 1972, the Olympic yacht races were held on the waters at Schilksee. For information, call the **Kieler Wochenbüro** at ⓒ **0431/901905,** or check out www.kieler-woche.de.

WHERE TO STAY

Hotel Kieler Yacht Club (★ (Finds   This yacht club offers unusually fine guest facilities. It's in an old classical building, standing back from the harbor, with an adjoining contemporary motel annex. Rooms are comfortable but unexciting. For style, we prefer those in the main building. All units have neatly arranged bathrooms with tub/shower combinations.

Hindenburgufer 70, 24105 Kiel. © 0431/88130. Fax 0431/8813444. www.hotel-kyc.de. 57 units. 146€–190€ ($234–$304) double; 190€–213€ ($304–$341) suite. Rates include buffet breakfast. AE, DC, MC, V. Free outdoor parking; 10€ ($13) in garage. Bus: 41. **Amenities:** Restaurant; bar; room service; laundry service; dry cleaning; nonsmoking rooms; rooms for those w/limited mobility. *In room:* TV, Wi-Fi, minibar, hair dryer.

Hotel Wiking   The Wiking, in the center of town, has well-furnished rooms for reasonable prices. The dark facade is ornamented with balconies painted a vividly contrasting white. Rooms are a bit small but are well maintained, each equipped with a comfortable bed, plus a compact bathroom with shower stalls.

Schützenwall 1–3, 24114 Kiel. ©/fax 0431/661090. www.hotel-wiking.com. 42 units. 86€–92€ ($138–$147) double. Rates include continental breakfast. AE, DC, MC, V. Free parking. Bus: 51 or 91. **Amenities:** Breakfast room; bar; lounge; sauna; solarium. *In room:* TV, hair dryer.

Steigenberger Conti-Hansa 𝒢𝒢   Conti-Hansa, located between the edge of the harbor and a well-groomed city park, is Kiel's premier hotel. It's well maintained, modern, and solidly comfortable. The medium-size rooms are outfitted in streamlined contemporary furniture; most look out over the harbor or the park. All have bathrooms with tub/shower combos.

Schlossgarten 7, 24103 Kiel. © 800/223-5652 in the U.S. and Canada, or 0431/51150. Fax 0431/5115444. www.kiel.steigenberger.de. 165 units. 139€–179€ ($222–$286) double; 189€–403€ ($302–$645) suite. Rates include buffet breakfast. AE, DC, MC, V. Parking 18€ ($29). Bus: 22, 32, 33, or 62. **Amenities:** 2 restaurants; bar; fitness center; sauna; solarium; room service; laundry service; dry cleaning; nonsmoking rooms; rooms for those w/limited mobility. *In room:* TV, Wi-Fi, minibar, hair dryer, trouser press.

WHERE TO DINE

Kieler Yacht Club CONTINENTAL   The food here is solid and reliable, though not dazzling. The main attraction, naturally, is seafood. Try the filet of haddock with mustard sauce and potatoes. Other chef's specialties are saddle of venison with savoy cabbage, roasted lamb in wine sauce with herbs, and an assortment of meal-size salads. The bar, a local hangout, attracts the yachting set.

Hindenburgufer 70. © 0431/8813442. Reservations recommended. Main courses 11€–29€ ($18–$46). AE, DC, MC, V. Daily noon–midnight. Bus: 41 or 51.

Quam 𝒢 *Finds* INTERNATIONAL   Charming and cosmopolitan, with an eclectic cuisine that draws on the culinary traditions of Europe and Asia, this restaurant fills three rooms of a stone-fronted building in the historic core of Kiel, a few steps from the waterfront. You'll pass through a pleasant, flower-studded garden to reach the interior, where a maximum of only 65 diners at a time dine within a warm and cozy ocher- and russet-colored decor. Menu items are flavorful and imaginative—a world's tour of flavor. The best examples include carpaccio of rump steak with pesto-flavored beans; sashimi of salmon with soy-flavored dressing; marinated and grilled young hen with seasonal vegetables; duckling with braised shallots and wine sauce; oven-baked dorado studded with herbs, served with mushroom-flavored butter sauce; and a pungent version of slow-cooked tandoori chicken.

Düppelstrasse 60. © 0431/85195. Reservations recommended. Main courses 18€–21€ ($29–$34); set menu 32€ ($51). AE, MC, V. Mon–Sat 6–11pm. Bus: 62.

Restaurant im Schloss 𝒢 CONTINENTAL   The most elegant formal restaurant in Kiel offers superb cuisine, service, and wine. The Schloss, a stone building (ca.

1965) overlooking the harbor, looks like a museum set in a park. If you reserve, you can get a window table that opens onto the water. The cuisine has a creative and light-hearted style, using the freshest of produce and exquisite versions of lamb. Many fish dishes are from the north German seas. Try, for example, terrine of salmon and zander in cream sauce, followed by filet of lamb breast brushed with white breadcrumbs and baked with fresh herbs.

Wall 74. (C) 0431/91155. Reservations required. Main courses 18€–26€ ($29–$42). AE, DC, MC, V. Tues–Fri 11am–3pm; Tues–Sun 6–9:30pm. Bus: 1.

Restaurant Jakob CONTINENTAL   Set in the lobby of one of Kiel's most comfortable hotels, this restaurant boasts a plush, modern decor and views over the harbor. You may begin with a crepe filled with Jacob mussels served on red lentils, or a soup—perhaps lobster soup with cognac. Main dishes range from the mundane (strips of turkey breast in a curry-and-yogurt sauce) to the sublime (saddle of boar with a juniper-berry sauce). Try the filet of pork medallions on a peppery savoy cabbage with a shallot sauce, or filet of lamb with green beans and fresh mushrooms. Dessert may be a slice of apricot cake with ice cream.

In the Steigenberger Conti-Hansa, Schlossgarten 7. (C) 0431/5115407. Reservations recommended. Main courses 18€–24€ ($29–$38). AE, DC, MC, V. Mon–Sat 11:30am–2:30pm and 6–10:30pm; Sun 6–10:30pm. Bus: 1 or 12.

EXPLORING THE HARBOR & BEYOND

For the best overall look at the city and harbor, go to the Rathaus's 107m (350-ft.), **century-old tower,** much of which was restored after the devastating bombs of World War II. May to September, guided tours (in English and German) are offered Wednesday at 2pm for 11€ ($18) per person. For a closer view over the harbor, take a stroll along the **Hindenburgufer (Hindenburg Embankment)** 𝕽, which stretches for 3km (2 miles) along the west side of the fjord, opposite the shipyards. Perches along this embankment are especially favored by spectators during regattas. Call tourist information for additional details.

If you'd like to go to the beach, take a short steamer trip to one of the nearby Baltic towns, such as Laboe, about 15km (10 miles) to the north. Besides the beach, the town's main attraction is the restored World War II submarine **U-Boot 995,** Strandstrasse 92, Kiel-Laboe ((C) 04343/42700; bus: 100 from the Kiel Hauptbahnhof). April to October, you can tour it every day 9:30am to 7pm (to 5pm Nov–Mar). Admission is 2.50€ ($4) adults, 1.80€ ($2.90) students and children ages 6 to 17.

The open-air **Schleswig-Holsteinisches Freilichtmuseum** 𝕽𝕽, Alte Hamburger Landstrasse ((C) 0431/659660; www.freilichtmuseum-sh.de; bus: 501 or 502), is in Molfsee, 6km (4 miles) south of Kiel. Farms and rustic country homes, dating from the 16th to the 19th centuries, have been assembled here. Craftspeople operate shops while working animals perform their tasks. A half-timbered inn serves tasty lunches. The site is open April to October daily 9am to 5pm, November to March Sundays and holidays 11am to 4pm. Admission is 6€ ($9.60) for adults, 4€ ($6.40) students and children, free for children 5 and under, and 13€ ($21) for a family ticket.

KIEL AFTER DARK

Take a stroll after dark through the salt air and fog of this seafaring city, admiring the Hanseatic architecture and the ever-present sense of gloomy nostalgia. Along the way, you can stop at any of the small bars of the Altstadt. One of the most visible old-fashioned nightlife options in Kiel is **Kieler Bräuerei,** Alter Markt 9 ((C) 0431/906290), which brews and serves, on-site, a medium-dark beer that locals compare to the better-known Düsseldorfer. Most clients come just for the beer, which starts at about 3€ ($4.80) for approximately a pint, but if you're hungry, head for the self-service cafeteria, also on-site, for heaping platters of sauerkraut, sausage, salads, and prepared meats (try the pig on a spit, rotating behind glass for your viewing pleasure), sold by the kilo. Expect to pay around 4€ to 12€ ($6.40–$19) for a platter.

Hemingway, Alter Markt (© **0431/96812**), named in honor of Papa, is the hippest bar in town, drawing a chic young crowd nightly.

3 Schleswig /★

48km (30 miles) NW of Kiel, 34km (21 miles) S of Flensburg

This one-time Viking stronghold on the Schlei (an arm of the Baltic) is Schleswig-Holstein's oldest town, with 1,200 years of history. Everything is steeped in legend, even the seagulls. According to tradition, the birds nesting on Seagull Island in the middle of the Schlei are fellow conspirators of Duke Abel, who in 1250 murdered his brother, King Eric. The crime was discovered when the king's body washed ashore. The duke went mad, eventually died, and was impaled and buried in the Tiergarten. His followers became seagulls, doomed to nest forever on Seagull Island.

ESSENTIALS

GETTING THERE   By Train   The **Schleswig Bahnhof** is on the Flensburg-Neumünster-Hamburg and Westerland-Hamburg rail lines, with frequent connections. Trains from Hamburg arrive daily (trip time: 2 hr., 20 min.). For information, call © **01805/996633.**

By Bus   Long-distance bus service to and from Hamburg, Flensburg, and Kiel is provided by **Autokraft GmbH** in Kiel (© **0431/6660**).

By Car   Access by car is via the A7 Autobahn north or south.

VISITOR INFORMATION   For information, contact **Tourist-Information,** Plessenstrasse 7 (© **04621/850056;** www.schleswig.de). Hours are May to September Monday to Friday 9:30am to 5:30pm, Saturday 9:30am to 12:30pm; October to April Monday to Thursday 10am to 4pm, and Friday 10am to 1pm.

GETTING AROUND   Buses fan out from Königstrasse and Plessenstrasse, in the town center. Fare is 2.10€ ($3.40). Buses operate every day 6am to 9pm.

WHERE TO STAY

Hotel Waldschlösschen ★   This elegant country hotel, finer than any of the in-town properties, is equipped with every convenience to make your stay comfortable. Rooms range from small to medium, each with a compact bathroom with tub/shower combination. Outside, there's a rock garden, a gabled house, an elongated annex, and lots of trees.

Kolonnenweg 152 (1.5km/1 mile southwest of town), 24837 Schleswig-Pulverholz. © **04621/3830.** Fax 04621/383105. www.hotel-schleswig.com. 115 units. 125€–145€ ($200–$232) double; 220€ ($352) suite. Rates include buffet breakfast. AE, DC, MC, V. Free parking. Bus: 1, 2, 3, or 4. **Amenities:** Restaurant; bar; indoor heated pool; whirlpool; sauna; solarium; room service; babysitting; laundry service; dry cleaning; nonsmoking rooms; rooms for those w/limited mobility; bowling alley. *In room:* TV, Wi-Fi, minibar, hair dryer, safe.

Ringhotel Strandhalle Schleswig *Value*   Established a century ago, with frequent renovations, the Strandhalle may not be as good as the Waldschlösschen, but it has many winning features, especially for those who'd like to stay within Schleswig and absorb the atmosphere of this ancient town. Actually, this hotel is more of a holiday resort—right on the water, with its own rowboats available. The owners maintain an informal atmosphere. Rooms are small but neatly kept, each with a somewhat cramped bathroom with shower stall. Nonetheless, the hotel is good value for the area. Ask for a room opening on the water, with a view of the yacht harbor.

Strandweg 2, 24837 Schleswig. © **04621/9090.** Fax 04621/909100. www.hotel-strandhalle.de. 25 units. 103€–127€ ($165–$203) double. Rates include buffet breakfast. AE, DC, MC, V. Parking 9€ ($14). Bus: 1, 2, 3, 4, or 5. **Amenities:** Restaurant; breakfast room; lounge; indoor heated pool; bike rental; table tennis. *In room:* TV, minibar, hair dryer, safe.

WHERE TO DINE

Stadt Flensburg GERMAN   Set in an architecturally distinguished town house dating from the late 17th century, this is a small-scale and cozy restaurant that's a short walk from the Schloss Gottorf. Designed with a simple decor that seats only 60 diners at a time, it's outfitted in tones of brown and beige, with wood paneling, a sense of sudsy beeriness, and an aura of old-fashioned protocol. Menu items include lots of fresh fish, including a well-flavored version of zander (pikeperch) with herbs, butter sauce, salad, and roasted potatoes; a succulent version of roasted lamb; steaks; and roast duck and, when it's available, goose, served with red cabbage and potatoes in a style that many locals remember from their childhoods. It's the kind of cuisine that's marvelously accompanied by beer, available on tap in both light and dark versions.

Lollfuss 102. © **04621/23984.** Reservations recommended. Main courses 12€–16€ ($19–$26). AE, DC, MC, V. Thurs–Tues noon–3pm and 6–11pm. Bus: 1 or 2.

EXPLORING SCHLESWIG

Dom St. Petri (St. Peter's Cathedral) &   The jewel of Schleswig is St. Peter's Cathedral, a brick Romanesque-Gothic Hallenkirche (hall church) begun in the 12th century. Its towering spire makes the rest of the Altstadt seem like so many dollhouses by comparison. Inside is the outstanding 16th-century *Bordesholm Altarpiece,* a powerful work carved in oak by Hans Bruggeman for the convent at Bordesholm. Its elaborately carved Gothic panels contain nearly 400 figures. The cathedral and cloisters also possess art treasures, including the *Blue Madonna* by J. Ovens and 13th-century frescoes.

Süderdomstrasse 1. © **04621/963054.** Free admission. May–Sept Mon–Sat 9am–5pm, Sun 1:30–5pm; Oct–Apr Mon–Sat 10am–4pm, Sun 1:30–4pm. Bus: 1, 2, 3, 4, or 5.

Schloss Gottorf   A dam and a bridge connect this castle, located on a small island, with the town. As you walk around the harbor, the panorama of the Altstadt and the widening bay opens up behind you. The castle is the largest in Schleswig-Holstein. The foundations date from the original 13th-century ducal palace; the present structure was built mainly in the 16th and 17th centuries and has been reconditioned since 1948 to house two museums.

   Archäologisches Landesmuseum (Provincial Museum of Archaeology) & (© **04621/8130**) has a most remarkable exhibit (in a separate building): the **Nydam Boat** &&&, a 4th-century ship found in the Nydam marshes in 1863. In the same room are artifacts and weapons discovered with the ship and Viking corpses preserved in the moor, all adding up to one of the major archaeological finds in northern Germany.

   Schleswig-Holstein Staatsmuseum (Schleswig-Holstein State Museum) & (© **04621/8130**), also housed in the castle, contains an exceptional collection of fine and applied art from medieval times to the 20th century, including painting, sculpture, furniture, textiles, and weapons. Outstanding are the late-Gothic King's Hall, the 17th-century ducal living rooms with rich stucco ceilings, and the Renaissance chapel with a private pew for the ducal family, decorated with intricate and elaborate carvings and inlays. Two buildings east of the castle house collections of contemporary art, including outstanding works of German expressionism and modern sculpture, plus the ethnological collection of implements and tools used by farmers, artisans, and fishermen.

On a small island in the Burgsee, a bay at the west end of the Schlei. ℂ **04621/8130.** Admission (including both museums) 6€ ($9.60) adults, 3€ ($4.80) children, 13€ ($21) family ticket, free for children 5 and under. Apr–Oct daily 10am–6pm; Nov–Mar Tues–Fri 10am–4pm, Sat–Sun 10am–5pm. Bus: 1, 2, 3, or 4.

Wikinger Museum Haithabu   Haithabu was one of the most prominent settlements of northern Europe during the Viking era. This Viking museum, opened in 1985, contains the finds of archaeological excavations of the Viking-age town of Haithabu. Exhibits cover all aspects of daily life. There's even a Viking long ship. In summer, you can reach this site via a scenic 20-minute boat ride. Departures are from Stadthafen, the town quay in Schleswig, south of the cathedral. After you dock, it's a 10-minute walk to the museum. In winter, you'll have to walk 3km (2 miles) from the rail station.

Durchwahl, 2.5km (1½ miles) from Schleswig. ℂ **04621/8130.** Admission 4€ ($6.40) adults, 2.50€ ($4) children, 9€ ($14) family ticket, free for children 5 and under. Mar 10–Oct daily 10am–6pm; Nov–Mar 9 Tues–Sun 10am–5pm.

SCHLESWIG AFTER DARK

If you're looking for action, head for **Lollfuss,** running parallel to the Schlei between Schloss Gottorf and a north-side residential area. Many places here are cafes during the day and bars at night. The best and most popular pub of the lot is **Patio,** Lollfuss 3 (ℂ **04621/29999;** bus: 1 or 2), an intimate two-story structure that usually stays open until midnight or 1am (considered very late in this small town). It also has Schleswig's most popular outdoor terrace. If you get hungry, you'll find pastas, salads, pizzas, and steaks for 4.50€ to 16€ ($7.20–$26).

4 The Island of Sylt ⓐⓐ

20km (13 miles) W of the Danish border, 193km (120 miles) NW of Hamburg

The long, narrow island of Sylt (pronounced *Zoolt*) and its capital, Westerland, form the northernmost point of Germany. Sylt lies in the North Sea off the coasts of Denmark and Schleswig-Holstein, the largest island of the Frisian archipelago, which stretches from Denmark to the Netherlands. The "Watt" is the name given to the coast facing the mainland.

People come to breathe the iodine-rich air and enjoy the rain-soaked North Sea climate that Germans call *Reizklima.* Sylt is the most exclusive resort in Germany, and its hotel prices reflect that status. Sylt also has a sizable gay and lesbian population and is often called "The Fire Island of Europe." In the 1960s, Sylt became famous for "the rich and the naked," when the entire island was reportedly an ongoing bacchanalian frenzy. It's quieted down since then. Temperatures in midsummer are usually in the low 70s (low to mid-20s Celsius), but rain can come at any minute, and winds on the beach are a constant, giving rise to the Sylt "mink," or yellow oilskin, which chic visitors wear to protect themselves from the elements.

The spa here has facilities for the treatment of everything from heart disease to skin irritations. The basic therapy is sunshine, pure air, and seawater, but in recent years, mud baths have also become a method of treatment. Some of the more remote sections of the dunes have been turned into nudist beaches for purists in the art of sunshine therapy. In addition to bathing, there are facilities in and around Westerland for horseback riding, surfing, golf, and tennis, as well as theater and concerts.

ESSENTIALS

GETTING THERE   By Plane   The nearest international airport is at Hamburg (see chapter 18). From there you can fly to the regional **Sylt Airport** (✆ 04651/ 920612). There's also regularly scheduled air service from Berlin and Düsseldorf.

By Train   The only link between the mainland and the island of Sylt is the railroad causeway running from the mainland town of Niebüll. If you wish to bring your car to the island, you'll have to load it on the train at Niebüll for the slow ride (see "By Car," below). No advance booking is necessary—you just arrive and take your chances. Passengers are carried free.

Westerland Bahnhof lies on the Westerland-Hamburg and the Westerland-Lübeck lines, with frequent connections. Seventeen trains arrive from Hamburg daily (trip time: 2 hr., 40 min., to 3 hr., 20 min., depending on the train). For information, call ✆ **01805/996633.**

By Car-Ferry   An alternative way of reaching Sylt is to take a car-ferry between the Danish port of Havneby, on the island of Rømo (easily accessible via highway from Germany), and the German port of List, at the northern tip of Sylt. There are at least a dozen daily crossings between those points in summer, with a much-reduced schedule in winter. Reservations for your car are possible. Round-trip passage for a car with a driver and up to three passengers costs 85€ ($136). For information, call the **Rømo-Sylt Line** (✆ **0180/3103030**).

By Bus   The few buses that pull into Sylt are forced to ride the flatcars on the rail line across the Hindenburg Causeway for the final stretch of their journey. Many passengers prefer to get off in Niebüll and transfer onto one of the passenger trains that make the frequent crossings to Westerland from other parts of Germany and Europe. Rail fare between Niebüll and Westerland costs 22€ ($35) per person, round-trip. The ride takes between 30 and 45 minutes each way.

By Car   Construction of a conventional bridge from Schleswig-Holstein to Sylt has never really been feasible. Therefore, cars headed to Sylt are loaded onto flatcars at the mainland railway junction of Niebüll and hauled out across the Hindenburg Damm (Hindenburg Causeway) to the railway station of Westerland. Drivers must stay in their cars, with the doors closed, eventually arriving at Westerland 30 to 40 minutes later. For information on these and all other (conventional) trains between the German mainland and Sylt, call the **Deutsche Bahn** information service in Westerland at ✆ **01805/996633.** Trains depart at 30-minute intervals daily 5am to midnight. No reservations are accepted for hauling your car across. Round-trip transport for most cars costs 85€ ($136). Access to Niebüll is possible via the A7 Autobahn north or south.

VISITOR INFORMATION   For information, contact the **Sylt Tourismus Zentrale,** Keitumer Landstrasse 10B (✆ 04651/6026). It's open May to October daily 9am to 5pm, and November to April Monday to Saturday 9am to 4pm.

WHERE TO STAY

Hotel Clausen   This four-story building has long been a local favorite. Today, its congenial English-speaking owners occupy the upper (fourth) floor. On the building's

A Disappearing Playground

Scientists warn that the western coast of Sylt is one of the most fragile ecosystems in Germany and may one day be reclaimed by the sea. The entire island is little more than a strip, only 550m (1,800 ft.) wide at its narrowest point, that's composed mostly of sand and very little rock. As such, it presents little resistance to the onslaught of erosion and deterioration. The sand dunes, warmed by the Gulf Stream, are forever shifting, and the winds sweeping in from the North Sea can move them by as much as 3.5m (12 ft.) in only a year. Although the winter months in general, and storms at any time of the year, are highly destructive, it's during strong south winds that most erosion takes place, and on some mornings after violent storms, huge amounts of sand migrate from the beachfront out into the North Sea.

In the 1970s, a series of *Tetrapoden* (four-legged concrete structures that look like giant jacks) were built on the sands of Westerland and Hornum beaches, in an unsuccessful attempt to hold back erosion. (They were later judged useless, and their construction discontinued.)

Today, everyone's favorite solution is one of the simplest: Whenever funds are allocated by the municipal budget, you'll see one or more barges moored offshore, pumping sand from deepwater sites back onto beaches of Sylt. Severe penalties exist for anyone removing salt grasses and scrub from the beachfronts, as do strict regulations against building new houses on fragile land.

If there is an air of desperation about the Germans who love and frolic in this North Sea playground, it is because they know it won't be here forever.

lower stories is a series of small but tidily maintained rooms, each fitted with a quality mattress on a good bed. Bathrooms are also small and have shower stalls. Breakfast is the only meal served, but many restaurants are nearby.

Friedrichstrasse 20 (in Westerland's pedestrian zone, a 3-min. walk from the beach), 25980 Westerland/Sylt. ℂ 04651/92290. Fax 04651/28007. www.hotel-clausen-sylt.de. 20 units. 90€–160€ ($144–$256) double; 125€–165€ ($200–$264) suite. Rates include buffet breakfast. MC, V. Parking 5€ ($8). Closed Jan 7–21. **Amenities:** Breakfast room; lounge; room service. *In room:* TV, hair dryer, safe.

Hotel Miramar 🟢 This hotel, on a bluff above the beach, has the second-best accommodations in Westerland, just below Stadt Hamburg (see below). Surrounded by an arched veranda, its public areas are graced with large arched windows with views of the sea. An octagonal light, left over from the building's 1903 construction, illuminates the salon from above. The high-ceilinged rooms are quite comfortable and each comes with a luxurious bed and a bathroom equipped with a tub/shower combo.

Friedrichstrasse 43, 25980 Westerland/Sylt. ℂ **04651/8550.** Fax 04651/855222. www.hotel-miramar.de. 67 units. 190€–395€ ($304–$632) double; 280€–780€ ($448–$1,248) suite. Rates include buffet breakfast. AE, DC, MC, V. Parking 12€ ($19). **Amenities:** Restaurant; bar; indoor heated pool; health club; 2 saunas; room service; massage; babysitting; laundry service; dry cleaning; rooms for those w/limited mobility. *In room:* TV, Wi-Fi, minibar, hair dryer, safe.

Hotel Wünschmann This hotel is in the heart of the tourist belt of Westerland, yet only minutes from the sand dunes. Rooms are in a complex of modern buildings (with

more than two dozen boutiques), but the hotel's interior exudes old-world tranquillity. The midsize bedrooms are individually decorated so you won't feel you're staying in a peas-in-a-pod motel. Each is cheerful and inviting, with comfortable furnishings and medium-size bathrooms with tub/shower combinations.

Andreas-Dirks-Strasse 4, 25980 Westerland. ⓒ **04651/5025.** Fax 04651/5028. www.hotel-wuenschmann.de. 35 units. 115€–255€ ($184–$408) double; 242€–321€ ($387–$514) suite. Rates include continental breakfast. AE, V. Parking 10€ ($16). Closed mid-Nov to mid-Dec. **Amenities:** Dining room; lounge; sauna; room service; laundry service; dry cleaning. *In room:* TV, hair dryer, safe.

Stadt Hamburg ✦✦✦ This is the best hotel on the island, though it looks more like a well-appointed country home than a hotel. Built in the 1880s as a grand Belle Epoque summer hotel, it was enlarged in 1991 with the construction of an elegant annex, in which the hotel's suites and its more expensive rooms are housed today. Less expensive rooms, and the restaurant, still lie within the hotel's original core. The gleaming white entrance is reached through a white picket fence, and its rear windows overlook a well-kept lawn. Each spacious room is individually furnished, with homey touches. Mattresses and linens are the island's finest, and the bathrooms are state of the art.

Strandstrasse 2 (next to the casino), 25980 Westerland/Sylt. ⓒ **04651/8580.** Fax 04651/858220. www.hotel stadthamburg.com. 72 units. 145€–310€ ($232–$496) double; 315€–520€ ($504–$832) suite. AE, MC, V. Parking 12€ ($19). **Amenities:** 2 restaurants; lounge; indoor heated pool; fitness center; spa; sauna; room service; massage; babysitting; laundry service; dry cleaning. *In room:* TV, Wi-Fi, hair dryer, safe.

WHERE TO DINE

Alte Friesenstube *Finds* NORTHERN GERMAN/FRISIAN This restaurant is refreshingly down to earth amid the pretentiousness of Sylt. Its thatched building was constructed in 1648. The menus are written on the wall in a German dialect, but someone will assist you in deciphering the offerings, which include regional pork, fish, and beef dishes. Especially popular is duck with orange sauce and *Panfische* (a local saltwater fish) with roasted potatoes and mustard sauce. No one puts on airs, and the kitchen sticks to the robust fare the islanders have been eating for decades.

Gaadt 4, Westerland. ⓒ **04651/1228.** Reservations required. Main courses 17€–28€ ($27–$44). No credit cards. Tues–Sun 6–10:30pm. Closed Jan.

Hardy auf Sylt FRENCH This round, thatched restaurant offers a nostalgic interior featuring furniture dating from about 1890. Finely worked columns, old oil portraits, beautiful glass lamps, and skillfully wrought candlesticks combine to create a relaxed, intimate feeling. The menu is adjusted seasonally. There's a fine selection of French and German wines.

Norderstrasse 65, Westerland. ⓒ **04651/22775.** Reservations required. Main courses 16€–23€ ($26–$36). No credit cards. Tues–Sun 6pm–midnight. Closed Jan 15–Feb 15 and Nov 30–Dec 20.

Jörg Müller ✦✦✦ CONTINENTAL/FRENCH This is Sylt's most elegant restaurant. Its brick building is almost a landmark in itself, thanks to its thatched roof, steep gables, and Frisian architecture. Menu items change with the seasons and feature a blend of contemporary Continental cuisine with imaginative variations of French recipes, which may include lobster salad with herb-flavored vinaigrette sauce, sliced and braised gooseliver with segments of glazed apples, or roast salt-marsh lamb flavored with herbs and served with ratatouille-flavored cream sauce. You can also enjoy local oysters with compote of red shallots and champagne sauce or halibut baked in fennel.

Süderstrasse 8 (a 5-min. walk from the center of Westerland). ℭ **04651/27789**. Reservations required. Main courses 28€–42€ ($45–$67); fixed-price menus 90€–118€ ($144–$189). AE, DC, MC, V. Tues–Sun 6–10pm. Closed Nov 25–Dec 18.

Restaurant Stadt Hamburg ⭐⭐ GERMAN/INTERNATIONAL   Top-rate cuisine is offered here in an attractive, luxurious setting of dark colors and hardwood paneling. The menu is so wide ranging it may be hard to make up your mind. A great way to begin is with the smooth cream of lobster soup. Many seafood specialties are featured, such as pan-fried fresh North Sea sole and turbot medallions in saffron sauce with zucchini. Another good dish is the rack of lamb (raised on the salty grasslands of the island). For dessert, try homemade *rote Grütze*—berries and cherries topped with vanilla ice cream.

Strandstrasse 2, Westerland. ℭ **04651/8580**. Reservations recommended. Main courses 19€–30€ ($30–$48); fixed-price dinner 41€–80€ ($66–$128). AE, MC, V. Daily 6–10pm. Bus: Centrale Omnibus Bahnhof.

Web Christel (Value NORTHERN GERMAN   Favored by local residents for its reasonable prices and cozy ambience, this restaurant occupies a century-old Frisian house in the center of Westerland, opposite its more glamorous (and more expensive) rival, Jörg Müller (see above). Menu items include a wide selection of fish, such as classic versions of turbot in an herb-butter-mustard sauce and sole prepared in the meunière style or grilled and served with hollandaise sauce. Roast duck with two different sauces is also available. A signature dish is fettuccini with lobster and fresh vegetables. The staff is warm and polite.

Süderstrasse 11 (opposite Jörg Müller), Westerland. ℭ **04651/22900**. Reservations recommended. Main courses 16€–32€ ($26–$51); fixed-price menus 27€–40€ ($43–$64). No credit cards. Thurs–Tues 5–11pm.

SHOPPING

Few other holiday destinations in Germany are as frenetic about clothing as Sylt. Garments are removed and put on again with abandon on this island with fickle weather and an extremely clothes-conscious population. You'll find impressive inventories of expensively casual clothing on Sylt—items that are artfully simple, easy to don, easy to doff, and easy to look at. The island's best shopping streets are the **Friedrichstrasse,** in Westerland, and the **Strönwai,** in Kampen, both lined with boutiques associated with the great names of European fashion.

SYLT AFTER DARK

Disco Pony, Strönwai, in Kampen (ℭ **04651/42182**), where both indoor and outdoor bar areas encompass views of the sea and the scrub-covered coastline that flanks it, mostly attracts a clientele under 40. There's no cover charge.

Also in Kampen is Disco Pony's major competitor **Club Rotes Kliff,** Alte Dorfstrasse (ℭ **04651/43400**), distinguished by its hip but not necessarily young crowd. There's no cover charge.

Appendix:
Fast Facts, Toll-Free Numbers & Websites

1 Fast Facts: Germany

ATM NETWORKS/CASHPOINTS See "Money & Costs," p. 53.

BUSINESS HOURS Most **banks** are open Monday to Friday 8:30am to 1pm and 2:30 to 4pm (Thurs to 5:30pm). Money exchanges at airports and border-crossing points are generally open daily from 6am to 10pm. Exchanges at border railroad stations are kept open for arrivals of all international trains. Most **businesses** are open Monday to Friday from 9am to 5pm and on Saturday from 9am to 1pm. Store hours can vary from town to town, but **shops** are generally open Monday to Friday 9 or 10am to 6 or 6:30pm (Thurs to 8:30pm). Saturday hours are generally from 9am to 1 or 2pm, except on the first Saturday of the month, when stores may remain open until 4pm.

CAR RENTALS See "Toll-Free Numbers & Websites," p. 673.

DRINKING LAWS As in many European countries, drinking laws are flexible, enforced only if a problem develops. Officially, you must be 18 to consume any kind of alcoholic beverage. Bars and cafes rarely request proof of age. Drinking while driving, however, is treated as a very serious offense.

DRIVING RULES See "Getting There and Getting Around," p. 47.

DRUG LAWS Penalties for illegal drug possession in Germany are severe. You could go to jail or be deported immediately.

DRUGSTORES Pharmaceuticals are sold at an *Apotheke*. For cosmetics, go to a *Drogerie*. German pharmacies take turns staying open nights, on Sundays, and on holidays, and each *Apotheke* posts a list of those that are open off hours.

ELECTRICITY In most places, the electricity is 220 volts AC (50 cycles). You need a transformer and a plug that fits the German socket for your U.S. appliances. Many leading hotels will supply these.

EMBASSIES & CONSULATES The following embassies and consulates are in Berlin. The embassy of the **United States** is at Pariser Platz 2 (② 030/2385-174; U-Bahn: Zoologischer Garden), open Monday to Friday 8:30am to 3pm. The **U.K. Embassy** is at Wilhelmstrasse 70 (② 030/204570; U-Bahn: Anhalter Bahnhof), open Monday to Friday 8am to 4:30pm. The **Australian Embassy** is at Wallstrasse 76–79 (② 030/8800880; U-Bahn: Spittel-markt), open Monday to Thursday 8:30am to 5pm and Friday 8:30am to 4:15pm. The **Canadian Embassy** is at Leipziger Platz 17 (② 030/203120; U-Bahn: Potsdamer Place), open Monday to Friday 9am to noon. The **Irish Embassy** is at Friedrichstrasse 200 (② 030/220720; U-Bahn: Uhlandstrasse), open Monday to Friday 9:30am to noon and 2:30 to 3:45pm. The **New Zealand Embassy** is at Friedrichstrasse 60 (② 030/206210; U-Bahn: Friedrichstrasse), open Monday to Friday 9am to 1pm and 2 to 5:30pm.

EMERGENCIES   Throughout Germany the emergency number for **police** is ℭ **110;** for fire or to call an ambulance, dial ℭ **112.**

GASOLINE (PETROL)   Gasoline or petrol is widely available throughout Germany, and service stations appear frequently along the autobahns. The least expensive gasoline is at stations marked SB-TANKEN (self-service), but remember that gasoline is much more expensive than in the U.S. Of course, gasoline prices throughout the world, including Germany, are currently changing weekly.

HOLIDAYS   Public holidays are January 1 (New Year's Day), Easter (Good Friday and Easter Monday), May 1 (Labor Day), Ascension Day (10 days before Pentecost/Whitsunday, the seventh Sun after Easter), Whitmonday (day after Pentecost/Whitsunday), October 3 (Day of German Unity), November 17 (Day of Prayer and Repentance), and December 25 and 26 (Christmas). In addition, the following holidays are observed in some German states: January 6 (Epiphany), Corpus Christi (10 days after Pentecost), August 15 (Assumption), and November 1 (All Saints' Day).

INSURANCE   Since Germany is far from home for most of us, and a number of things could go wrong—lost luggage, trip cancellation, or a medical emergency—consider some of the following options.

Medical Insurance   For travel overseas, most U.S. health plans (including Medicare and Medicaid) do not provide coverage, and the ones that do often require you to pay for services up front and reimburse you only after you return home.

As a safety net, you may want to buy travel medical insurance, particularly if you're traveling to a remote or high-risk area where emergency evacuation might be necessary. If you require additional medical insurance, try **MEDEX Assistance** (ℭ 410/453-6300; www.medexassist.com) or **Travel Assistance International** (ℭ 800/821-2828; www.travelassistance.com; for general information on services, call the company's **Worldwide Assistance Services, Inc.** at ℭ 800/777-8710).

Canadians should check with their provincial health plan offices or call **Health Canada** (ℭ 866/225-0709; www.hc-sc.gc.ca) to find out the extent of their coverage and what documentation and receipts they must take home in case they are treated overseas.

Travelers from the U.K. should carry their European Health Insurance Card (EHIC), which replaced the E111 form as proof of entitlement to free/reduced cost medical treatment abroad (ℭ 0845/606-2030; www.ehic.org.uk). Note, however, that the EHIC only covers "necessary medical treatment," and for repatriation costs, lost money, baggage, or cancellation, travel insurance from a reputable company should always be sought (www.travelinsuranceweb.com).

Travel Insurance   The cost of travel insurance varies widely, depending on the destination, the cost and length of your trip, your age and health, and the type of trip you're taking, but expect to pay between 5% and 8% of the vacation itself. You can get estimates from various providers through **InsureMyTrip.com** (ℭ 800/487-4722). Enter your trip cost and dates, your age, and other information, for prices from more than a dozen companies.

U.K. citizens and their families who make more than one trip abroad per year may find an annual travel insurance policy works out cheaper. Check **www.moneysupermarket.com** (ℭ 0845/345-5708), which compares prices across a wide range of providers for single- and multi-trip policies.

Most big travel agents offer their own insurance and will probably try to sell you their package when you book a holiday. Think before you sign. **Britain's Consumers' Association** recommends that you insist on seeing the policy and reading the fine print before buying travel insurance. **The Association of British Insurers** (℅ 020/7600-3333; www.abi. org.uk) gives advice by phone and publishes "Holiday Insurance," a free guide to policy provisions and prices. You might also shop around for better deals: Try **Columbus Direct** (℅ 0870/033-9988; www.columbusdirect.net).

Trip Cancellation Insurance Trip-cancellation insurance will help retrieve your money if you have to back out of a trip or depart early, or if your travel supplier goes bankrupt. Trip cancellation traditionally covers such events as sickness, natural disasters, and State Department advisories. The latest news in trip-cancellation insurance is the availability of **expanded hurricane coverage** and the **"any-reason"** cancellation coverage—which costs more but covers cancellations made for any reason. You won't get back 100% of your prepaid trip cost, but you'll be refunded a substantial portion. **Travel-Safe** (℅ 888/885-7233; www.travel safe.com) offers both types of coverage. Expedia also offers any-reason cancellation coverage for its air-hotel packages. For details, contact one of the following recommended insurers: **Access America** (℅ 866/807-3982; www.accessamerica. com), **Travel Guard International** (℅ 800/826-4919; www.travelguard. com), **Travel Insured International** (℅ 800/243-3174; www.travelinsured. com), and **Travelex Insurance Services** (℅ 888/457-4602; www.travelex-insurance.com).

LANGUAGE German, of course, is the official language, but English is widely understood. Germans start learning English in grade school. Chances are you won't need to invest in the Berlitz book for German.

LOST & FOUND Be sure to tell all of your credit card companies the minute you discover your wallet has been lost or stolen. Your credit card company or insurer also may require that you file a police report and provide a report number or record of the loss. Most credit card companies have an emergency toll-free number to call if your card is lost or stolen; they may be able to wire you a cash advance immediately or deliver an emergency credit card in a day or two. Visa's emergency number, outside the U.S., is ℅ 410/581-3836; in Germany it's 0800/811-8440; or you can call collect. American Express cardholders should call collect ℅ 336/393-1111. MasterCard holders should call collect ℅ 314/542-7111.

Identity theft and fraud are potential complications of losing your wallet, especially if you've lost your driver's license along with your cash and credit cards. Notify the major credit-reporting bureaus immediately; placing a fraud alert on your records may protect you against liability for criminal activity. The three major U.S. credit-reporting agencies are **Equifax** (℅ 800/766-0008; www.equifax. com), **Experian** (℅ 888/397-3742; www. experian.com), and **TransUnion** (℅ 800/ 680-7289; www.transunion.com). Finally, if you've lost all forms of photo ID, call your airline and explain; they might allow you to board the plane if you have a copy of your passport or birth certificate and a copy of the police report you've filed. If you need emergency cash over the weekend when all banks and American Express offices are closed, you can have money wired to you via **Western Union** (℅ 800/325-6000; www.westernunion. com).

MAIL General delivery—mark it POSTE RESTANTE—can be used in any major town or city in Germany. You can pick up your mail upon presentation of a valid identity card or passport. Street mailboxes are painted yellow. It costs 1.70€ ($2.70) for the first 5g (about ⅕ oz.) to send an airmail letter to the United States or Canada, and 1€ ($1.60) for postcards. All letters to the U.K. cost .70€ ($1.10).

MEASUREMENTS   See the chart on the inside back cover of this book for details on converting metric measurements to nonmetric equivalents.

PASSPORTS   Allow plenty of time before your trip to apply for a passport; processing normally takes 3 weeks but can take longer during busy periods (especially spring). And keep in mind that if you need a passport in a hurry, you'll pay a higher processing fee.

For Residents of Australia: You can pick up an application from your local post office or any branch of Passports Australia, but you must schedule an interview at the passport office to present your application materials. Call the **Australian Passport Information Service** at ℂ **131-232,** or visit the government website at www. passports.gov.au.

For Residents of Canada: Passport applications are available at travel agencies throughout Canada or from the central **Passport Office,** Department of Foreign Affairs and International Trade, Ottawa, ON K1A 0G3 (ℂ **800/567-6868;** www. ppt.gc.ca).

For Residents of Ireland: You can apply for a 10-year passport at the **Passport Office,** Setanta Centre, Molesworth Street, Dublin 2 (ℂ **01/671-1633;** www. dfa.ie). Those under age 18 and over 65 must apply for a 3-year passport. You can also apply at 1A South Mall, Cork (ℂ **021/494-4700**) or at most main post offices.

For Residents of New Zealand: You can pick up a passport application at any New Zealand Passports Office or download it

from their website. Contact the **Passports Office** at ℂ **0800/225-050** in New Zealand or 04/474-8100, or log on to **www.passports.govt.nz.**

For Residents of the United Kingdom: To pick up an application for a standard 10-year passport (5-year passport for children age 15 and under), visit your nearest passport office, major post office, or travel agency, or contact the **United Kingdom Passport Service** at ℂ **0870/ 521-0410** (www.ukpa.gov.uk).

For Residents of the United States: Whether you're applying in person or by mail, you can download passport applications from the U.S. Department of State website at **http://travel.state.gov.** To find your regional passport office, either check the U.S. Department of State website or call the **National Passport Information Center** toll-free number (ℂ **877/487-2778**) for automated information.

POLICE   Throughout the country, dial ℂ 110 for emergencies.

SMOKING   Check before lighting up in public places. Several German states have introduced, or plan to introduce, partial bans on smoking in restaurants and bars.

TAXES   As a member of the European Union, Germany imposes a tax on most goods and services known as a **value-added tax (VAT)** or, in German, *Mehrwertsteuer.* Nearly everything is taxed at 16%, including vital necessities such as gas and luxury items such as jewelry. Food and books are taxed at 7%. VAT is included in the prices of restaurants and hotels. Goods for sale, such as cameras, also have the 16% tax already factored into the price. Stores that display a tax-free sticker will issue you a **Tax-Free Shopping Check** at the time of purchase. When leaving the country, have your check stamped by the German Customs Service as your proof of legal export. You can then get a cash refund at one of the Tax-Free Shopping Service offices in the major airports and many train stations, even at some of the bigger ferry terminals. Otherwise, you must send the checks to Tax-Free Shopping Service, Mengstrasse 19, 23552 Lübeck, Germany. If you want the payment to be credited to your bankcard or your bank account, mention this. There is no airport departure tax.

TELEPHONES   Refer to "Staying Connected" on p. 67.

TIME   Germany operates on Central European time (CET), which means that the country is 6 hours ahead of Eastern Standard Time (EST) in the United States and 1 hour ahead of Greenwich Mean Time (GMT). Summer daylight saving time begins in Germany in April and ends in September—there's a slight difference in the dates from year to year—so there may be a period in early spring and in the fall when there's a 7-hour difference between EST and CET.

TIPPING   If a restaurant bill says *Bedienung,* that means a service charge has already been added, so just round up to the nearest euro. If not, add 10% to 15%. Bellhops get 1€ ($1.60) per bag, as does the doorperson at your hotel, restaurant, or nightclub. Room-cleaning staffs get small tips in Germany, as do concierges who perform some special favors. Tip hairdressers or barbers 5% to 10%.

TOILETS   Use the word *Toilette* (pronounced twah-*leh*-tah). Women's toilets are usually marked with an F for *Frauen,* and men's toilets with an H for *Herren.* Germany, frankly, doesn't have enough public toilets, except in transportation centers. The locals have to rely on bars, cafes, or restaurants—and using them isn't always appreciated if you're not a paying customer.

2 Toll-Free Numbers & Websites

MAJOR U.S. AIRLINES
(*flies internationally as well)

American Airlines*
℡ 800/433-7300 (in U.S. and Canada)
℡ 020/7365-0777 (in U.K.)
www.aa.com

Continental Airlines*
℡ 800/523-3273 (in U.S. and Canada)
℡ 084/5607-6760 (in U.K.)
www.continental.com

Delta Air Lines*
℡ 800/221-1212 (in U.S. and Canada)
℡ 084/5600-0950 (in U.K.)
www.delta.com

Northwest Airlines
℡ 800/225-2525 (in U.S. and Canada)
℡ 870/0507-4074 (in U.K.)
www.flynaa.com

United Airlines*
℡ 800/864-8331 (in U.S. and Canada)
℡ 084/5844-4777 in U.K.
www.united.com

US Airways*
℡ 800/428-4322 (in U.S. and Canada)
℡ 084/5600-3300 (in U.K.)
www.usairways.com

MAJOR INTERNATIONAL AIRLINES

Aeroméxico
℡ 800/237-6639 (in U.S.)
℡ 020/7801-6234 (in U.K., information only)
www.aeromexico.com

Air France
℡ 800/237-2747 (in U.S.)
℡ 800/375-8723 (in U.S. and Canada)
℡ 087/0142-4343 (in U.K.)
www.airfrance.com

Air India
℡ 212/407-1371 (in U.S.)
℡ 91 22 2279 6666 (in India)
℡ 020/8745-1000 (in U.K.)
www.airindia.com

Alitalia
© 800/223-5730 (in U.S.)
© 800/361-8336 (in Canada)
© 087/0608-6003 (in U.K.)
www.alitalia.com

American Airlines
© 800/433-7300 (in U.S. and Canada)
© 020/7365-0777 (in U.K.)
www.aa.com

British Airways
© 800/247-9297 (in U.S. and Canada)
© 087/0850-9850 (in U.K.)
www.british-airways.com

China Airlines
© 800/227-5118 (in U.S.)
© 022/715-1212 (in Taiwan)
www.china-airlines.com

Continental Airlines
© 800/523-3273 (in U.S. and Canada)
© 084/5607-6760 (in U.K.)
www.continental.com

Delta Air Lines
© 800/221-1212 (in U.S. and Canada)
© 084/5600-0950 (in U.K.)
www.delta.com

EgyptAir
© 212/581-5600 (in U.S.)
© 020/7734-2343 (in U.K.)
© 09/007-0000 (in Egypt)
www.egyptair.com

El Al Airlines
© 972/3977-1111 (outside Israel)
© *2250 (from any phone in Israel)
www.elal.co.il

Emirates Airlines
© 800/777-3999 (in U.S.)
© 087/0243-2222 (in U.K.)
www.emirates.com

Finnair
© 800/950-5000 (in U.S. and Canada)
© 087/0241-4411 (in U.K.)
www.finnair.com

Iberia Airlines
© 800/722-4642 (in U.S. and Canada)
© 087/0609-0500 (in U.K.)
www.iberia.com

Japan Airlines
© 012/025-5931 (international)
www.jal.co.jp

Korean Air
© 800/438-5000 (in U.S. and Canada)
© 0800/413-000 (in U.K.)
www.koreanair.com

Lufthansa
© 800/399-5838 (in U.S.)
© 800/563-5954 (in Canada)
© 087/0837-7747 (in U.K.)
www.lufthansa.com

Olympic Airlines
© 800/223-1226 (in U.S.)
© 514/878-9691 (in Canada)
© 087/0606-0460 (in U.K.)
www.olympicairlines.com

Swiss Air
© 877/359-7947 (in U.S. and Canada)
© 084/5601-0956 (in U.K.)
www.swiss.com

Turkish Airlines
© 90 212 444 0 849
www.thy.com

United Airlines*
© 800/864-8331 (in U.S. and Canada)
© 084/5844-4777 (in U.K.)
www.united.com

US Airways*
© 800/428-4322 (in U.S. and Canada)
© 084/5600-3300 (in U.K.)
www.usairways.com

Virgin Atlantic Airways
© 800/821-5438 (in U.S. and Canada)
© 087/0574-7747 (in U.K.)
www.virgin-atlantic.com

BUDGET AIRLINES
Air Berlin
© 087/1500-0737 (in U.K.)
© 018/0573-7800 (in Germany)
© 180/573-7800 (all others)
www.airberlin.com

Ryanair
© 1 353 1 249 7700 (in U.S.)
© 081/830-3030 (in Ireland)
© 087/1246-0000 (in U.K.)
www.ryanair.com

CAR-RENTAL AGENCIES

Auto Europe
© 888/223-5555 (in U.S. and Canada)
© 0800/2235-5555 (in U.K.)
www.autoeurope.com

Avis
© 800/331-1212 (in U.S. and Canada)
© 084/4581-8181 (in U.K.)
www.avis.com

Budget
© 800/527-0700 (in U.S.)
© 087/0156-5656 (in U.K.)
© 800/268-8900 (in Canada)
www.budget.com

Hertz
© 800/645-3131 (in U.S. and Canada)
© 800/654-3001 (for international
reservations)
www.hertz.com

Kemwel (KHA)
© 877/820-0668
www.kemwel.com

National
© 800/CAR-RENT (800/227-7368)
www.nationalcar.com

Thrifty
© 800/847-4389 (in U.S. and Canada)
© 918/669-2168 (international)
www.thrifty.com

MAJOR HOTEL & MOTEL CHAINS

Best Western International
© 800/780-7234 (in U.S. and Canada)
© 0800/393-130 (in U.K.)
www.bestwestern.com

Four Seasons
© 800/819-5053 (in U.S. and Canada)
© 0800/6488-6488 (in U.K.)
www.fourseasons.com

Hilton Hotels
© 800/HILTONS (800/445-8667)
(in U.S. and Canada)
© 087/0590-9090 (in U.K.)
www.hilton.com

Holiday Inn
© 800/315-2621 (in U.S. and Canada)
© 0800/405-060 (in U.K.)
www.holidayinn.com

Hyatt
© 888/591-1234 (in U.S. and Canada)
© 084/5888-1234 (in U.K.)
www.hyatt.com

InterContinental Hotels & Resorts
© 800/424-6835 (in U.S. and Canada)
© 0800/1800-1800 (in U.K.)
www.ichotelsgroup.com

Marriott
© 877/236-2427 (in U.S. and Canada)
© 0800/221-222 (in U.K.)
www.marriott.com

Radisson Hotels & Resorts
© 888/201-1718 (in U.S. and Canada)
© 0800/374-411 (in U.K.)
www.radisson.com

Ramada Worldwide
© 888/2-RAMADA (888/272-6232)
(in U.S. and Canada)
© 080/8100-0783 (in U.K.)
www.ramada.com

Sheraton Hotels & Resorts
© 800/325-3535 (in U.S.)
© 800/543-4300 (in Canada)
© 0800/3253-5353 (in U.K.)
www.starwoodhotels.com/sheraton

Westin Hotels & Resorts
© 800/937-8461 (in U.S. and Canada)
© 0800/3259-5959 (in U.K.)
www.starwoodhotels.com/westin

Index

INDEX 679

Frommer's® Complete Travel Guides

Frommer's® Day by Day Guides

Pauline Frommer's Guides: See More. Spend Less.

ROMMER'S® PORTABLE GUIDES

Acapulco, Ixtapa & Zihuatanejo
Amsterdam
Aruba, Bonaire & Curacao
Australia's Great Barrier Reef
Bahamas
Big Island of Hawaii
Boston
California Wine Country
Cancún
Cayman Islands
Charleston
Chicago
Dominican Republic

Florence
Las Vegas
Las Vegas for Non-Gamblers
London
Maui
Nantucket & Martha's Vineyard
New Orleans
New York City
Paris
Portland
Puerto Rico
Puerto Vallarta, Manzanillo & Guadalajara

Rio de Janeiro
San Diego
San Francisco
Savannah
St. Martin, Sint Maarten, Anguila & St. Bart's
Turks & Caicos
Vancouver
Venice
Virgin Islands
Washington, D.C.
Whistler

FROMMER'S® CRUISE GUIDES

Alaska Cruises & Ports of Call

Cruises & Ports of Call

European Cruises & Ports of Call

FROMMER'S® NATIONAL PARK GUIDES

Algonquin Provincial Park
Banff & Jasper
Grand Canyon

National Parks of the American West
Rocky Mountain
Yellowstone & Grand Teton

Yosemite and Sequoia & Kings Canyon
Zion & Bryce Canyon

FROMMER'S® WITH KIDS GUIDES

Chicago
Hawaii
Las Vegas
London

National Parks
New York City
San Francisco

Toronto
Walt Disney World® & Orlando
Washington, D.C.

FROMMER'S® PHRASEFINDER DICTIONARY GUIDES

Chinese
French

German
Italian

Japanese
Spanish

SUZY GERSHMAN'S BORN TO SHOP GUIDES

France
Hong Kong, Shanghai & Beijing
Italy

London
New York
Paris

San Francisco
Where to Buy the Best of Everything.

FROMMER'S® BEST-LOVED DRIVING TOURS

Britain
California
France
Germany

Ireland
Italy
New England
Northern Italy

Scotland
Spain
Tuscany & Umbria

THE UNOFFICIAL GUIDES®

Adventure Travel in Alaska
Beyond Disney
California with Kids
Central Italy
Chicago
Cruises
Disneyland®
England
Hawaii

Ireland
Las Vegas
London
Maui
Mexico's Best Beach Resorts
Mini Mickey
New Orleans
New York City
Paris

San Francisco
South Florida including Miami & the Keys
Walt Disney World®
Walt Disney World® for Grown-ups
Walt Disney World® with Kids
Washington, D.C.

SPECIAL-INTEREST TITLES

Athens Past & Present
Best Places to Raise Your Family
Cities Ranked & Rated
500 Places to Take Your Kids Before They Grow Up
Frommer's Best Day Trips from London
Frommer's Best RV & Tent Campgrounds in the U.S.A.

Frommer's Exploring America by RV
Frommer's NYC Free & Dirt Cheap
Frommer's Road Atlas Europe
Frommer's Road Atlas Ireland
Retirement Places Rated